NAICS Desk Reference

THE NORTH AMERICAN INDUSTRY
CLASSIFICATION SYSTEM
DESK REFERENCE

Based entirely on the *North American Industry Classification System* (NAICS) developed by the governments of the United States of America, Canada, and Mexico. Replaces the *Standard Industrial Classification* (SIC) coding system last updated in 1987. Developed by the staff of JIST Works, Inc.

JIST Publishing

NAICS Desk Reference
The North American Industry Classification System Desk Reference

© 2000 by JIST Works, Inc.

Published by JIST Works, Inc.
8902 Otis Avenue
Indianapolis, IN 46216-1033

Phone: 1-800-648-5478   Fax: 1-800-JIST-FAX   E-mail: editorial@jist.com

Visit us at www.JIST.com! Please visit our Web site for information and online ordering of our many books, videos, and other materials.

Volume Orders: This book may be purchased in large quantities at special discount for distribution to staff accountants and others. Please contact our sales department for details at 1-800-648-5478.

Related books: JIST publishes a variety of books on careers, occupational information, business, and other topics. Those most closely related to the subject of this book include:

* *North American Industry Classification System* – This is a complete reprint of the 1247-page book developed by the U.S. Office of Management and Budget.

* *Career Guide to Industries* – This is a reprint of a publication titled *Career Guide to Industries* originally published by the U. S. Bureau of Labor Statistics.

Printed in the United States of America   3 2280 00717 4972

Library of Congress Cataloging-in-Publication Data

NAICS desk reference : (The North American Industry Classification System desk reference).
    p. cm.
  ISBN 1-56370-694-6
    1. Industries--North America--Classification. 2. Commercial products--North America--Classification. I. Title: North American Industry Classification System desk reference. II. JIST Works, Inc.

HF1041.5.N35 2000
338'.02'0127--dc21   00-023827

ISBN 1-56370-694-6

About This Book

If you need to provide an industry code to a government or business document, this is the book you need. It presents the new North American Industry Classification System (NAICS) that replaces the older Standard Industrial Classification (SIC) system.

If you are an accountant, banker, attorney, job placement specialist, or other professional who used to need SIC codes, you need the information in this book. All Federal documents requiring an industry designation—such as tax and financial reporting forms—now require the use of NAICS codes.

Unfortunately, until the release of this book, there has been only one printed reference for NAICS codes—a 1247-page book published by the U.S. government. While that book is comprehensive, it is too large and complex to use on a regular basis for the many people who simply need to determine the correct NAICS code to use on a form.

We think this new book will provide most people with what they need: quick access to the correct NAICS industry code. We tried to make it easy to use, and this book is considerably less expensive than the larger book published by the government.

Quick Tips on Using This Book

We created this book to be easy to use. While we encourage you to read the introduction for obscure details, you can start using the book simply by looking at the Table of Contents. It includes brief comments on how to use each of the major sections of the book. This is followed by a listing of the NAICS industry sectors and subsectors, which will give you an overview of the NAICS structure. Here are some additional tips to get you off to a quick start in using this book:

- **If you know the old SIC code number:** If you already have the old SIC code, use the SIC-to-NAICS Crosswalk that begins on page 257 to find the new NAICS code and industry name.

- **If you have the old SIC industry name:** You can find the new NAICS industry name and code number by looking in the alphabetic index at the end of this book. It will show you where to find the new NAICS industry name and code number.

- **If you don't know either the old SIC industry name or code number:** No problem. Just look up the name of the industry in the alphabetic index. This index cross-references an industry by more than one of its common names, so you are likely to find it even if you are not using the "official" NAICS or SIC industry name. If you are not even sure of the industry name, you can use the NAICS Industries Within Groups of Related Industries section to help you select an industry name and code that most closely matches what you are seeking.

We hope you find the *NAICS Desk Reference* indispensable the more you use it. If you have any comments or suggestions, we would like to hear from you. Please e-mail us at editorial@jist.com.

Table of Contents

NAICS Industry Sectors and Subsectors

NAICS has 20 major industry "sectors" and 96 more specific "subsectors" that are presented below, along with the page numbers where you can find their descriptions. Sectors use a two-digit number with related subsectors using those two numbers, plus a third digit. This table will help you understand how NAICS industries are organized. For a more detailed table, refer to the "NAICS Industries Within Groups of Related Industries" beginning on page xvii. It presents the NAICS sectors and subsectors plus 311 more specific industry groupings and the 1,170 specific industry titles and codes.

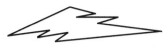

Introduction

Statistics Canada, Mexico's Instituto Nacional de Estadística, Geografía e Informática (INEGI), and the Economic Classification Policy Committee (ECPC) of the United States, acting on behalf of the Office of Management and Budget, have created a common classification system to replace the existing classification of each country, the Standard Industrial Classification (1980) of Canada, the Mexican Classification of Activities and Products (1994), and the Standard Industrial Classification (1987) of the United States.

The North American Industry Classification System (NAICS) is unique among industry classifications in that it is constructed within a single conceptual framework. Economic units that have similar production processes are classified in the same industry, and the lines drawn between industries demarcate, to the extent practicable, differences in production processes. This supply-based, or production-oriented, economic concept was adopted for NAICS because an industry classification system is a framework for collecting and publishing information on both inputs and outputs, for statistical uses that require that inputs and outputs be used together and be classified consistently. Examples of such uses include measuring productivity, unit labor costs, and the capital intensity of production, estimating employment-output relationships, constructing input-output tables, and other uses that imply the analysis of production relationships in the economy. The classification concept for NAICS will produce data that facilitate such analyses.

In the design of NAICS, attention was given to developing production-oriented classifications for (a) new and emerging industries, (b) service industries in general, and (c) industries engaged in the production of advanced technologies. These special emphases are embodied in the particular features of NAICS,

discussed below. These same areas of special emphasis account for many of the differences between the structure of NAICS and the structures of industry classification systems in use elsewhere. NAICS provides enhanced industry comparability among the three NAFTA trading partners, while also increasing compatibility with the two-digit level of the International Standard Industrial Classification (ISIC Rev.3) of the United Nations.

NAICS divides the economy into twenty sectors. Industries within these sectors are grouped according to the production criterion. Though the goods/services distinction is not explicitly reflected in the structure of NAICS, five sectors are largely goods-producing and fifteen are entirely services-producing industries.

A new feature of NAICS is the creation of an Information sector that groups industries that primarily create and disseminate a product subject to copyright. The NAICS Information sector brings together those activities that transform information into a commodity that is produced and distributed, and activities that provide the means for distributing those products, other than through traditional wholesale-retail distribution channels. A few of the new and important industries in this sector include: software publishing; database and directory publishing; satellite telecommunications; paging, cellular and other wireless telecommunications; and on-line information and other information services. Also included in the Information sector are newspaper, book, and periodical publishing (formerly included in manufacturing); motion picture and sound recording industries; libraries; and other information services. Another feature of NAICS is a sector for Professional, Scientific and Technical Services, which comprises establishments engaged in activities where human capital is the major input. The industries within this sector are each defined by the expertise and training of the service provider. The sector includes such industries as offices of lawyers; engineering services; architectural services; advertising agencies; and interior design services. Thirty-five NAICS industries comprise this sector, many of which are now recognized for the first time. A new sector for Arts, Entertainment and Recreation greatly expands the number of industries providing services in these three areas.

Another new sector, Health Care and Social Assistance, recognizes the merging of the boundaries of health care and social assistance. The industries in this new sector are arranged in an order that reflects the range and extent of health care and social assistance provided. Some new industries are family planning centers, outpatient mental health and substance abuse centers, and continuing into community care facilities for the elderly.

In the Manufacturing sector, an important new subsector, Computer and Electronic Product Manufacturing, brings together industries producing electronic products and their components. The manufacture of computers, communications equipment, and semiconductors, for example, are grouped into the same subsector because of the inherent technological similarities of their production processes, and the likelihood that these technologies will continue to converge in the future. An important change is that reproduction of packaged software is placed in this sector, rather than in the services sector, because the reproduction of packaged software is a manufacturing process, and the product moves through the wholesale and retail distribution systems like any other manufactured product. NAICS acknowledges the importance of these electronic industries, their rapid growth over the past several years and the likelihood that these industries will, in the future, become even more important in the economies of the three North American countries.

This NAICS structure reflects the levels at which data comparability was agreed upon by the three statistical agencies. The boundaries of all the sectors of NAICS have been delineated. In most sectors, NAICS provides for compatibility at the industry (five-digit) level. However, for real estate; utilities; finance and insurance; and for three of the four subsectors in other services (except public administration), three-country compatibility will occur either at the industry group (four-digit) or subsector (three-digit) levels. For these sectors,

differences in the economies of the three countries prevent full compatibility at the NAICS industry level. For retail trade, wholesale trade, construction, and public administration, the three countries' statistical agencies have agreed, at this time, only on the boundaries of the sector (two-digit level). Below the agreed-upon level of compatibility, each country may add additional detailed industries, as necessary to meet national needs, provided that this additional detail aggregates to the NAICS level.

Background

In 1937, the Central Statistical Board established an Interdepartmental Committee on Industrial Classification "to develop a plan of classification of various types of statistical data by industries and to promote the general adoption of such classification as the standard classification of the Federal Government." The List of Industries for manufacturing was first available in 1938, with the List of Industries for nonmanufacturing following in 1939. These Lists of Industries became the first Standard Industrial Classification (SIC) for the United States.

The SIC was developed for use in the classification of establishments by type of activity in which they are primarily engaged; for purposes of facilitating the collection, tabulation, presentation, and analysis of data relating to establishments; and for promoting uniformity and comparability in the presentation of statistical data collected by various agencies of the United States Government, State agencies, trade associations, and private research organizations. The SIC covered the entire field of economic activities by defining industries in accordance with the composition and structure of the economy.

Since the inception of the SIC in the 1930s, the system has been periodically revised to reflect the economy's changing industrial composition and organization. The last revision of the SIC was in 1987.

Rapid changes in both the U.S. and world economies brought the SIC under increasing criticism. In 1991, an International Conference on the Classification of Economic Activities was convened in Williamsburg, Virginia, to provide a forum for responding to such criticism and to explore new approaches to classifying economic activity. In July 1992, the Office of Management and Budget (OMB) established the Economic

Classification Policy Committee (ECPC) and charged it with a "fresh slate" examination of economic classifications for statistical purposes. The ECPC prepared a number of issue papers regarding classification, consulted with outside users, and ultimately joined with Mexico's Instituto Nacional de Estadística, Geografía e Informática (INEGI) and Statistics Canada to develop the North American Industry Classification System (NAICS), which replaces the 1987 U.S. SIC and the classification systems of Canada (1980 SIC) and Mexico (1994 Mexican Classification of Activities and Products [CMAP]).

Purpose of NAICS

NAICS is an industry classification system that groups establishments into industries based on the activities in which they are primarily engaged. It is a comprehensive system covering the entire field of economic activities, producing and nonproducing. There are 20 sectors in NAICS and 1,170 industries in NAICS United States.

NAICS was developed by Mexico's INEGI, Statistics Canada, and the U.S. ECPC (the latter acting on behalf of OMB) to provide common industry definitions for Canada, Mexico, and the United States that will facilitate economic analyses of the economies of the three North American countries. The statistical agencies in the three countries produce information on inputs and outputs, industrial performance, productivity, unit labor costs, and employment. NAICS, which is based on a production-oriented concept, ensures maximum usefulness of industrial statistics for these and similar purposes.

NAICS United States will be used by U.S. statistical agencies to: facilitate the collection, tabulation, presentation, and analysis of data relating to establishments, and to provide uniformity and comparability in the presentation of statistical data describing the U.S. economy. NAICS United States is designed for statistical purposes. Although the classification also may be used for various administrative, regulatory and taxation purposes, the requirements of government agencies that use it for nonstatistical purposes played no role in its development.

Development of NAICS

The U.S. ECPC established by OMB in 1992 was chaired by the Bureau of Economic Analysis, U.S. Department of Commerce, with representatives from the Bureau of the Census, U.S. Department of Commerce, and the Bureau of Labor Statistics, U.S. Department of Labor. The ECPC was asked to examine economic classifications for statistical purposes and to determine the desirability of developing a new industry classification system for the United States based on a single economic concept. On March 31, 1993, OMB published a **Federal Register Notice** (58FR16990-17004) announcing the intention to revise the SIC for 1997, the establishment of the ECPC, and the process for revising the SIC.

The ECPC established seven subcommittees composed of senior economists, statisticians, and classification specialists representing 20 of the Federal agencies that use the SIC for statistical programs. Those subcommittees, which were Agriculture, Forestry, and Fishing; Manufacturing and Mining; Construction; Distribution Networks (retail trade, wholesale trade, and transportation, communications, and utilities); Finance, Insurance, and Real Estate; Business and Personal Services; and Health, Social Assistance, and Public Administration, were responsible for developing the proposed structure of NAICS in cooperation with representatives from INEGI and Statistics Canada. The ECPC also established the U.S. Coordinating Committee that was responsible for coordinating the work of the U.S. subcommittees and the work with INEGI and Statistics Canada.

In July 1994, the OMB announced plans to develop a new industry classification system in cooperation with Mexico's INEGI and Statistics Canada. The new system—NAICS—replaces the current U.S. SIC. The concepts of the new system and the principles upon which NAICS was to be developed were announced in a July 26, 1994 **Federal Register** (59FR38092-38096) notice and were as follows:

1. NAICS will be erected on a production-oriented or supply-based conceptual framework. This means that producing units that use identical or similar production processes will be grouped together in NAICS.

2. The system will give special attention to developing production-oriented classifications for (a) new and emerging industries, (b) service industries in general, and (c) industries engaged in the production of advanced technologies.

3. Time series continuity will be maintained to the extent possible. However, changes in the economy and proposals from data users must be considered. In addition, adjustments will be required for sectors where the United States, Canada, and Mexico have incompatible industry classification definitions in order to produce a common industry system for all three North American countries.

4. The system will strive for compatibility with the two-digit level of the International Standard Industrial Classification of All Economic Activities (ISIC, Rev. 3) of the United Nations.

The structure of NAICS was developed in a series of meetings among the three countries. Public proposals for individual industries from all three countries were considered for acceptance if the proposed industry was based on the production-oriented concept of the system. In the United States, public comments also were solicited as groups of subsectors of NAICS were completed and agreed upon by the three countries. The ECPC published the proposed industries for those subsectors in a series of five successive **Federal Register** notices, in 1995 and 1996, asking for comments from interested data users.

Conceptual Framework

NAICS is erected on a production-oriented or supply-based conceptual framework in that establishments are grouped into industries according to similarity in the processes used to produce goods or services. A production-oriented industry classification system ensures that statistical agencies in the three countries can produce information on inputs and outputs, industrial performance, productivity, unit labor costs, employment, and other statistics and structural changes occurring in each of the three economies.

When an industry is defined on a production-oriented concept, producing units within the industry's boundaries share a basic production process; they use closely similar technology. In the language of economics, producing units within an industry share the same production functions; producing units in different industries have different production functions. The boundaries between industries thus demarcate, in principle, differences in production processes and production technologies.

The reasoning behind the three countries' decision to base NAICS on a production-oriented concept is summarized as follows: An industry is a grouping of economic activities. Though it inevitably groups the products of the economic activities that are included in the industry definition, it is not solely a grouping of products; put another way, an industry groups producing units. Accordingly, an industry classification system provides a framework for collecting data on inputs and outputs together.

The uses of economic data that require that data on inputs and outputs be used together and be collected on the same basis, include production analyses, productivity measurement, and studying input usage and input intensities. The North American statistical agencies developed NAICS using a production-oriented concept as the framework for two reasons: an industry classification system groups producing units, not products or services; and groupings of producing units permit the collection of data on inputs and outputs on a comparable basis, which is required for production-oriented analysis, but do not facilitate a comprehensive collection of data on the total output of any particular product or service, which is required for market-oriented analysis. Thus, the efficient organizing concept of an industry classification system is production-oriented rather than market-oriented.

Structure of NAICS

The structure of NAICS is hierarchical, much like that of the 1987 SIC. The first two digits of the structure designate the NAICS sectors that represent general categories of economic activities. NAICS classifies all economic activities into 20 sectors. The NAICS sectors, their two-digit codes, and the distinguishing activities of each are:

11 Agriculture, Forestry, Fishing and Hunting—Activities of this sector are growing crops, raising animals, harvesting timber, and harvesting fish and other animals from farms, ranches, or the animals' natural habitats.

21 Mining—Activities of this sector are extracting naturally occurring mineral solids, such as coal and ore; liquid minerals, such as crude petroleum; and gases, such as natural gas; and beneficiating (e.g., crushing, screening, washing, and flotation) and other

preparation at the mine site, or as part of mining activity.

22 Utilities–Activities of this sector are generating, transmitting, and/or distributing electricity, gas, steam, and water and removing sewage through a permanent infrastructure of lines, mains, and pipe.

23 Construction–Activities of this sector are erecting buildings and other structures (including additions); heavy construction other than buildings; and alterations, reconstruction, installation, and maintenance and repairs.

31-33 Manufacturing–Activities of this sector are the mechanical, physical, or chemical transformation of material, substances, or components into new products.

41-43 Wholesale Trade–Activities of this sector are selling or arranging for the purchase or sale of goods for resale; capital or durable nonconsumer goods; and raw and intermediate materials and supplies used in production, and providing services incidental to the sale of the merchandise.

44-46 Retail Trade–Activities of this sector are retailing merchandise generally in small quantities to the general public and providing services incidental to the sale of the merchandise.

48-49 Transportation and Warehousing–Activities of this sector are providing transportation of passengers and cargo, warehousing and storing goods, scenic and sightseeing transportation, and supporting these activities.

51 Information–Activities of this sector are distributing information and cultural products, providing the means to transmit or distribute these products as data or communications, and processing data.

52 Finance and Insurance–Activities of this sector involve the creation, liquidation, or change in ownership of financial assets (financial transactions) and/or facilitating financial transactions.

53 Real Estate and Rental and Leasing–Activities of this sector are renting, leasing, or otherwise allowing the use of tangible or intangible assets (except copyrighted works), and providing related services.

54 Professional, Scientific, and Technical Services–Activities of this sector are performing professional, scientific, and technical services for the operations of other organizations.

55 Management of Companies and Enterprises–Activities of this sector are the holding of securities of companies and enterprises, for the purpose of owning controlling interest or influencing their management decision, or administering, overseeing, and managing other establishments of the same company or enterprise and normally undertaking the strategic or organizational planning and decision making of the company or enterprise.

56 Administrative and Support and Waste Management and Remediation Services–Activities of this sector are performing routine support activities for the day-to-day operations of other organizations.

61 Educational Services–Activities of this sector are providing instruction and training in a wide variety of subjects.

62 Health Care and Social Assistance–Activities of this sector are providing health care and social assistance for individuals.

71 Arts, Entertainment, and Recreation–Activities of this sector are operating or providing services to meet varied cultural, entertainment, and recreational interests of their patrons.

72 Accommodation and Food Services–Activities of this sector are providing customers with lodging and/or preparing meals, snacks, and beverages for immediate consumption.

81 Other Services (except Public Administration)–Activities of this sector are providing services not elsewhere specified, including repairs, religious activities, grantmaking, advocacy, laundry, personal care, death care, and other personal services.

91-93 Public Administration–Activities of this sector are administration, management, and oversight of public programs by Federal, State, and local governments.

NAICS uses a six-digit coding system to identify particular industries and their placement in this hierarchical structure of the classification system. The first two digits of the code designate the sector, the third designates the subsector, the fourth digit designates the industry group, the fifth digit designates the NAICS industry, and the sixth digit designates the national industry. A zero as the sixth digit generally indicates that the NAICS industry and the U.S. industry are the same.

The subsectors, industry groups, and NAICS industries, in accord with the conceptual principle of NAICS, are production-oriented combinations of establishments. However, the production distinctions become more narrowly defined as one moves down the hierarchy.

NAICS agreements permit each country to designate detailed industries, below the level of a NAICS industry, to meet national needs. The United States has such industry detail in many places in the new classification system to recognize large, important U.S. industries that cannot be recognized in the other countries because of size, specialization, or organization of the industry.

Typically the level at which comparable data will be available for Canada, Mexico, and the United States is the five-digit NAICS industry; for some sectors (or subsectors or industry groups) however, the three countries agreed upon the boundaries at a higher level of detail rather than the detailed industry structure (five-digit). Agreement was reached at the sector level for construction; wholesale trade; retail trade; and public administration and at the subsector level for finance; personal and laundry services; religious, grantmaking, civic, and professional and similar organizations; and waste management and remediation services. For insurance and real estate, the three countries agreed on comparability at the industry group level.

Differences in the economies of the three countries or time constraints necessitated these modifications. For each of these sectors, except wholesale trade and public administration, Canada and the United States have agreed upon an industry structure and hierarchy to ensure comparability of statistics between those two countries. Canada and the United States also have established the same national detail (six-digit) industries where possible, adopting the same codes to describe comparable industries. For this reason, the numbers of the U.S. industries may not be consecutive.

In a few cases, it was necessary for the United States to use all of the numbers available to establish its six-digit detail so that the same six-digit codes do not

represent comparable industries in the U.S. and Canada. In Appendix A, a "CAN" notation in the first column indicates comparability between the two countries. In Part I, Titles and Descriptions, a superscript or "CAN" at the end of an industry title indicates the same thing. A blank in the first column or no superscript indicates comparability among the three countries.

NAICS with U.S. detail will be known as NAICS United States (denoted by "US" in Appendix A and a superscript "US" at the end of the title in Part I) while Canada and Mexico will produce six-digit detail and will publish that detail as NAICS Canada and NAICS (SCIAN in Spanish) Mexico.

Definition of an Establishment

NAICS is a classification system for establishments. The establishment as a statistical unit is defined as the smallest operating entity for which records provide information on the cost of resources—materials, labor, and capital—employed to produce the units of output. The output may be sold to other establishments and receipts or sales recorded, or the output may be provided without explicit charge, that is, the good or service may be "sold" within the company itself.

The establishment, in NAICS United States, is generally a single physical location, where business is conducted or where services or industrial operations are performed (for example, a factory, mill, store, hotel, movie theater, mine, farm, airline terminal, sales office, warehouse, or central administrative office). There are cases where records identify distinct and separate economic activities performed at a single physical location (e.g., shops in a hotel). These retailing activities, operated out of the same physical location as the hotel, are identified as separate establishments and classified in retail trade while the hotel is classified in accommodations. In such cases, each activity is treated as a separate establishment provided: (1) no one industry description in the classification includes such combined activities; (2) separate reports can be prepared on the number of employees, their wages and salaries, sales or receipts, and expenses; and (3) employment and output are significant for both activities.

Exceptions to the single location exist for physically dispersed operations, such as construction, transportation, and communication. For these activities the individual sites, projects, fields, networks, lines, or systems of such dispersed activities are not normally considered to be establishments. The establishment is represented by those relatively permanent main or branch offices, terminals, stations, and so forth, that are either (1) directly responsible for supervising such activities, or (2) the base from which personnel operate to carry out these activities.

Although an establishment may be identical with the enterprise (company), the two terms should not be confused. An enterprise (company) may consist of more than one establishment. Such multiunit enterprises may have establishments in more than one industry in NAICS. If such enterprises have a separate establishment primarily engaged in providing headquarters services, these establishments are classified in NAICS Sector 55, Management of Companies and Enterprises.

Although all establishments have output, they may or may not have receipts. In large enterprises it is not unusual for establishments to exist that solely serve other establishments of the same enterprise (auxiliary establishments). In such cases, these units often do not collect receipts from the establishments they serve. This type of support (captive) activity is found throughout the economy and involves goods producing activities as well as services.

In the 1987 SIC, auxiliary service establishments, defined as establishments primarily engaged in performing management or support services for other establishments of the same enterprise, were classified to industries based on the industry classification of the establishments they serviced—not the primary activity. However, captive goods producing establishments, defined as operating establishments, were classified based on what they did, not whom they served. This traditional treatment of auxiliary units implied that captive services producing establishments should be treated differently from captive goods producing units.

NAICS changes this traditional classification of auxiliary establishments. NAICS is based on the economic principle that establishments should be grouped together based on their production processes and does not distinguish between captive services and goods establishments. Those units that carry out support

activities for the enterprise to which they belong are classified, to the extent feasible, according to the NAICS code related to their own activity and, if possible, to that of the enterprise they support. This means that warehouses that provide storage facilities for their own enterprise will be classified as a warehouse and not as an automobile assembly plant (if that is the primary unit they serve).

Determining an Establishment's Industry Classification

An establishment is classified to an industry when its primary activity meets the definition for that industry. Because establishments may perform more than one activity, it is necessary to determine procedures for identifying the primary activity of the establishment.

In most cases, if an establishment is engaged in more than one activity, the industry code is assigned based on the establishment's principal product or group of products produced or distributed, or services rendered. Ideally, the principal product or service should be determined by its relative share of current production costs and capital investment at the establishment. In practice, however, it is often necessary to use other variables such as revenue, shipments, or employment as proxies for measuring significance.

There are two types of combined activities that are given special attention in NAICS. They are vertical integration and joint production. These combined activities have an economic basis and occur in both goods-producing and services-producing sectors. In some cases, there are efficiencies to be gained from combining certain activities in the same establishment. Some of these combinations occur so commonly or frequently that their combination can be treated as a third activity in its own right and explicitly classified in a specific industry.

One approach to classifying these activities would be to use the primary activity rule, that is, whichever activity is largest. However, the fundamental principle of NAICS is that establishments that employ the same production process should be classified in the same industry. If the premise that the combined activities correspond to a distinct third activity is accepted, then using the primary activity rule would place establishments performing the same combination of activities in different industries, thereby violating the production principle of NAICS. A second reason for NAICS recognizing combined activities is to improve the stability of establishment classification, both over time and among the various agencies that implement the classification. An establishment should remain classified in the same industry unless its production process changes, and different agencies should code the same establishment or type of establishment in the same way. A consistent treatment of establishments with combined activities is more likely if they are classified to a single industry.

Vertical integration involves consecutive stages of fabrication or production processes in which the output of one step is the input of the next. In general, establishments will be classified based on the final process in a vertically integrated production environment, unless specifically identified as classified in another industry. For example, paper may be produced either by establishments that first produce pulp and then consume that pulp to produce paper or by those establishments producing paper from purchased pulp. NAICS specifically specifies that both of these types of paper-producing processes should be classified in 32212, Paper Mills, the industry, or the final step in paper manufacturing, rather than in NAICS 32211, Pulp Mills. In other cases, NAICS specifies that vertically integrated establishments be classified in the industry representing the first stage of the manufacturing process. For example, steel mills that make steel and also perform other activities such as producing steel castings are classified in NAICS 33111, Iron and Steel Mills and Ferroalloy Manufacturing, the first stage of the manufacturing process.

The joint production of goods or services represents the second type of combined activities. For example, automobile dealers both sell and repair autos; automotive parts dealers may both sell parts and repair automobiles; and musical instrument stores may both sell and rent instruments. In the manufacturing sector, establishments may make two different products such as women's dresses and women's suits, activities that are classified in two different NAICS United States detailed industries. In general, receipts/sales and revenue data are used as a proxy to determine primary activity for these establishments. The assumption is that the activity generating the most receipts is also the activity using the most resources and most in-

dicative of the production process. In some cases, however, these combined activities have been assigned to a specific NAICS industry. Most of these activities involve either the sale and repair of goods or the sale and rental of goods in the same establishment. For example, establishments that both sell automobile parts and repair automobiles are classified in NAICS 44131, Automotive Parts and Accessories Stores, and those music stores that both sell and rent musical instruments are classified in NAICS 45114, Musical Instrument and Supplies Stores. In other cases, specific industries have been identified for these combined activities, such as 44711, Gasoline Stations with Convenience Stores. Classification rules related to the agreement to permit individual country detail at the six-digit level for NAICS sometimes results in less comparable NAICS industries at the five-digit level and above. For example in NAICS, the assignment of the industry code is at the most detailed level of the classification (the six-digit U.S. detail code), except for agriculture. That is, if the value of an establishment's production consists of 30 percent from computers, 30 percent from computer storage devices, and 40 percent from semiconductors and related devices, it will be classified in U.S. detail industry 334413, Semiconductor and Related Device Manufacturing, that will be aggregated to NAICS 33441, Semiconductor and Other Electronic Component Manufacturing, the level at which comparable information is shown for all three countries. If the classification for the above example were at the five-digit NAICS level, that establishment would be classified in NAICS 33411, Computer and Peripheral Equipment Manufacturing. There would then be more comparable information at the NAICS level, but it would be impossible to classify this establishment to a U.S. detail six-digit industry. In agriculture, however, NAICS coding will be at the five-digit NAICS level. This is possible because of the identification in NAICS of combination farms. Therefore, the above situation does not occur.

Comparison of NAICS to the International Standard Industrial Classification (ISIC)

Recognizing the need for international comparability of economic statistics, the United Nations (UN) first adopted an International Standard Industrial Classification (ISIC) system in 1948. Revisions to the ISIC structure and codes were adopted by the UN's Statistical Commission in 1958, 1968, and 1989.

Similar to NAICS, ISIC was designed primarily to provide classifications for grouping establishments (rather than enterprises or firms), and the primary focus for the ISIC classification system is the kind of activity in which establishments or other statistical entities are engaged. The main criteria employed in delineating divisions and groups (the two- and three-digit categories, respectively) of ISIC are: (a) the character of the goods and services produced; (b) the uses to which the goods and services are put; and (c) the inputs, the process, and the technology of production. The third classification criterion of the ISIC is the conceptual foundation of NAICS, and thus, NAICS is aligned more closely with ISIC than was the 1987 SIC system. However, there are differences between the NAICS and ISIC classification schemes. Most important, perhaps, is the single (production process) conceptual framework of NAICS. As noted elsewhere, this is unique among industry classifications. Distinctions also were made during ISIC's development with regard to (1) select characteristics of goods and services produced; (2) the range of kinds of activity frequently carried out under the same ownership or control; (3) differences between enterprises in scale, organization of activities, capital requirements, and finance; and (4) the pattern of categories at various levels of classification in national classifications.

The ISIC groups economic activity into 17 broad Sections, 60 Divisions, 159 Groups, and 292 Classes. In the coding system, Sections are distinguished by the letters A through Q and the Divisions, Groups, and Classes are identified as the two-digit, three-digit, and four-digit groupings, respectively. NAICS United States groups economic activity into 20 sectors, 96 subsectors, 311 industry groups, 459 NAICS industries (for which there is comparability among all three countries), and 1,170 U.S. industries corresponding to the two-digit, three-digit, four-digit, and five-digit levels in the coding system. In some cases, the NAICS U.S. industry codes include a sixth-digit to identify an economic type unique to the United States, but within the general NAICS structure.

In the development of NAICS industries, the statistical agencies of the three countries strove to create industries that did not cross ISIC two-digit boundaries. A detailed concordance among NAICS United States and ISIC, Revision 3 will be conducted and the results of that concordance published on the NAICS Internet web site (http://www.census.gov/naics).

International Standard Industrial Classification of all Economic Activities, Statistical Papers, Series M., No. 4, Department of International Economic and Social Affairs, Statistical Office, United Nations, New York, 1958, *International Standard Industrial Classification of All Economic Activities,* Statistical Papers, Series M., No. 4, Rev. 2, Department of International Economic and Social Affairs, Statistical Office, United Nations, New York, 1968. *International Standard Industrial Classification of All Economic Activities,* Statistical Papers, Series M., No. 4., Rev. 3, Department of International Economic and Social Affairs, Statistical Office, United Nations, New York, 1990.

Key to the Country Identifier in Subsectors

Industries specific to one country or another are shown with the following designations.

US–United States industry only.
CAN–United States and Canadian industries are comparable.
When neither US nor CAN appears, Canadian, Mexican, and United States industries are comparable.

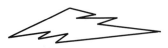

NAICS United States Structure

Sector	Name	Sub-sectors	Industry groups	NAICS 5-digit industries	U.S. 6-digit industries	Total industries	New industries
11	Agriculture, Forestry, Fishing and Hunting	5	19	42	32	64	20
21	Mining	3	5	10	28	29	–
22	Utilities	1	3	6	6	10	6
23	Construction	3	14	28	–	28	3
31–33	Manufacturing	21	84	184	408	474	79
42	Wholesale Trade	2	18	69	–	69	–
44–45	Retail Trade	12	27	61	18	72	17
48–49	Transportation and Warehousing	11	29	42	25	57	28
51	Information	4	9	28	12	34	20
52	Finance and Insurance	5	11	32	15	42	23
53	Real Estate and Rental and Leasing	3	8	19	9	24	15
54	Professional, Scientific, and Technical Services	1	9	35	17	47	28
55	Management of Companies and Enterprises	1	1	1	3	3	1
56	Administrative and Support and Waste Management and Remediation Services	2	11	29	23	43	29
61	Educational Services	1	7	12	7	17	12
62	Health Care and Social Assistance	4	18	30	16	39	27
71	Arts, Entertainment, and Recreation	3	9	23	3	25	19
72	Accommodation and Food Service	2	7	11	7	15	10
81	Other Services (except Public Administration)	3	14	30	30	49	19
92	Public Administration	8	8	29	–	29	2
	Total	**96**	**311**	**721**	**659**	**1170**	**358**

NAICS Industries Within Groups of Related Industries

This section lists all 1,170 NAICS industries organized into related groups. While additional details on the NAICS coding system is in the introduction to this book, we thought a quick overview would be helpful here.

NAICS organizes industries into increasingly specific groups and subgroups of related industries. It also uses a six-digit coding system that is logical once you understand how it works. The first two digits of the code designate the major industry sector, the third digit designates the sub-sector, the fourth digit designates the industry group, the fifth digit designates the NAICS industry, and the sixth digit designates the national industry, if present. A zero as the sixth digit generally indicates that the NAICS industry and the U.S. industry are the same. Here are a few more comments on this system. We'll provide an example of this numbering system in just a moment.

Major Industry Sector: There are 20 major NAICS industry sectors. These are presented in the large bold letters in the table that follows. The first one is "Agriculture, Forestry, Fishing, and Hunting," which you will see at the beginning of the table. Each Industry Sector is given a two-digit code number, with the Agriculture, Forestry, Fishing, and Hunting sector having a NAICS two-digit code of 11.

Subsectors: Each NAICS industry sector is divided into "subsectors" of more specialized industry groupings. There are 96 subsectors, with the Agriculture, Forestry, Fishing, and Hunting sector having five of them, including Crop Production; Animal Production; Forestry and Logging; Fishing, Hunting and Trapping; and Agriculture and Support Activities. Each NAICS subsector uses the first two digits of its industry sector plus a third digit. For example, the Animal Production subsector has a NAICS code of 112, with the first two digits referring to its sector code of 11.

Industry Groups: Industry subsectors are further divided into 311 more specific "Industry Groups." The NAICS code for each of these industry groups uses the first three digits of its related subsector plus a fourth digit. For example, the Animal Production industry subsector is further divided into industry groups including Cattle Ranching and Farming (1121), Hog and Pig Farming (1122), Poultry and Egg Production (1123) and others.

Specific NAICS Industry Title and Number: Finally, the 1,170 specific NAICS industry names are arranged within the NAICS Industry Groups. Specific industry titles use the first four digits of its industry group plus a fifth and, sometimes, a sixth digit. Continuing our example, the Poultry and Egg Farming industry group includes the specific industry titles of Chicken and Egg Production (11231); Broilers and Other Meat Type Chicken Production (11232); Turkey Production (11233); Poultry Hatcheries (11234); and Other Poultry Production (11239). Unless you are looking for a NAICS code for duck producers, this is more than most of us care to know. But, as our example illustrates, you will have to dig down to the specific industry title in order to know, precisely, what NAICS code to assign to your duck producer. A good table, but not perfect.

There will be times when the list that follows will not give you a definitive NAICS code to use without referring to the "Titles and Descriptions of NAICS Industries" section of this book. There you will find descriptions that should clarify things for you, should you not be sure. You can also often quickly find the correct NAICS industry name and code number by looking for it in the alphabetic index at the end of this book.

Code	Short Title	Code	Short Title

11 AGRICULTURE, FORESTRY, FISHING AND HUNTING

111 Crop Production

1111 Oilseed and Grain Farming
- 11111 Soybean Farming
- 11112 Oilseed (except Soybean) Farming
- 11113 Dry Pea and Bean Farming
- 11114 Wheat Farming
- 11115 Corn Farming
- 11116 Rice Farming
- 11119 Other Grain Farming
- 111191 Oilseed and Grain Combination Farming
- 111199 All Other Grain Farming

1112 Vegetable and Melon Farming
- 11121 Vegetable and Melon Farming
- 111211 Potato Farming
- 111219 Other Vegetable (except Potato) and Melon Farming

1113 Fruit and Tree Nut Farming
- 11131 Orange Groves
- 11132 Citrus (except Orange) Groves
- 11133 Noncitrus Fruit and Tree Nut Farming
- 111331 Apple Orchards
- 111332 Grape Vineyards
- 111333 Strawberry Farming
- 111334 Berry (except Strawberry) Farming
- 111335 Tree Nut Farming
- 111336 Fruit and Tree Nut Combination Farming
- 111339 Other Noncitrus Fruit Farming

1114 Greenhouse, Nursery, and Floriculture Production
- 11141 Food Crops Grown Under Cover
- 111411 Mushroom Production
- 111419 Other Food Crops Grown Under Cover
- 11142 Nursery and Floriculture Production
- 111421 Nursery and Tree Production
- 111422 Floriculture Production

1119 Other Crop Farming
- 11191 Tobacco Farming
- 11192 Cotton Farming
- 11193 Sugarcane Farming
- 11194 Hay Farming
- 11199 All Other Crop Farming
- 111991 Sugar Beet Farming
- 111992 Peanut Farming
- 111998 All Other Miscellaneous Crop Farming

112 Animal Production

1121 Cattle Ranching and Farming
- 11211 Beef Cattle Ranching and Farming, including Feedlots
- 112111 Beef Cattle Ranching and Farming
- 112112 Cattle Feedlots
- 11212 Dairy Cattle and Milk Production
- 11213 Dual Purpose Cattle Ranching and Farming

1122 Hog and Pig Farming
- 11221 Hog and Pig Farming

1123 Poultry and Egg Production
- 11231 Chicken Egg Production
- 11232 Broilers and Other Meat Type Chicken Production
- 11233 Turkey Production
- 11234 Poultry Hatcheries
- 11239 Other Poultry Production

1124 Sheep and Goat Farming
- 11241 Sheep Farming
- 11242 Goat Farming

1125 Animal Aquaculture
- 11251 Animal Aquaculture
- 112511 Finfish Farming and Fish Hatcheries
- 112512 Shellfish Farming
- 112519 Other Animal Aquaculture

1129 Other Animal Production
- 11291 Apiculture
- 11292 Horse and Other Equine Production
- 11293 Fur-Bearing Animal and Rabbit Production
- 11299 All Other Animal Production

113 Forestry and Logging

1131 Timber Tract Operations
- 11311 Timber Tract Operations

1132 Forest Nurseries and Gathering of Forest Products
- 11321 Forest Nurseries and Gathering of Forest Products

1133 Logging
- 11331 Logging

Code	Short Title	Code	Short Title

114 Fishing, Hunting and Trapping

1141 Fishing
    11411   Fishing
    114111   Finfish Fishing
    114112   Shellfish Fishing
    114119   Other Marine Fishing
1142 Hunting and Trapping
    11421   Hunting and Trapping

115 Support Activities for Agriculture and Forestry

1151 Support Activities for Crop Production
    11511   Support Activities for Crop Production
    115111   Cotton Ginning
    115112   Soil Preparation, Planting, and Cultivating
    115113   Crop Harvesting, Primarily by Machine
    115114   Postharvest Crop Activities (except Cotton Ginning)
    115115   Farm Labor Contractors and Crew Leaders
    115116   Farm Management Services
1152 Support Activities for Animal Production
    11521   Support Activities for Animal Production
1153 Support Activities for Forestry
    11531   Support Activities for Forestry

21 MINING

211 Oil and Gas Extraction

2111 Oil and Gas Extraction
    21111   Oil and Gas Extraction
    211111   Crude Petroleum and Natural Gas Extraction
    211112   Natural Gas Liquid Extraction

212 Mining (except Oil and Gas)

2121 Coal Mining
    21211   Coal Mining
    212111   Bituminous Coal and Lignite Surface Mining
    212112   Bituminous Coal Underground Mining
    212113   Anthracite Mining
2122 Metal Ore Mining
    21221   Iron Ore Mining

21222   Gold Ore and Silver Ore Mining
212221   Gold Ore Mining
212222   Silver Ore Mining
21223   Copper, Nickel, Lead, and Zinc Mining
212231   Lead Ore and Zinc Ore Mining
212234   Copper Ore and Nickel Ore Mining
21229   Other Metal Ore Mining
212291   Uranium-Radium-Vanadium Ore Mining
212299   All Other Metal Ore Mining
2123 Nonmetallic Mineral Mining and Quarrying
    21231   Stone Mining and Quarrying
    212311   Dimension Stone Mining and Quarrying
    212312   Crushed and Broken Limestone Mining and Quarrying
    212313   Crushed and Broken Granite Mining and Quarrying
    212319   Other Crushed and Broken Stone Mining and Quarrying
    21232   Sand, Gravel, Clay, and Ceramic and Refractory Minerals Mining and Quarrying
    212321   Construction Sand and Gravel Mining
    212322   Industrial Sand Mining
    212324   Kaolin and Ball Clay Mining
    212325   Clay and Ceramic and Refractory Minerals Mining
    21239   Other Nonmetallic Mineral Mining and Quarrying
    212391   Potash, Soda, and Borate Mineral Mining
    212392   Phosphate Rock Mining
    212393   Other Chemical and Fertilizer Mineral Mining
    212399   All Other Nonmetallic Mineral Mining

213 Support Activities for Mining

2131 Support Activities for Mining
    21311   Support Activities for Mining
    213111   Drilling Oil and Gas Wells
    213112   Support Activities for Oil and Gas Operations
    213113   Support Activities for Coal Mining
    213114   Support Activities for Metal Mining
    213115   Support Activities for Nonmetallic Minerals (except Fuels)

Code	Short Title	Code	Short Title

Code	Short Title	Code	Short Title

Code	Short Title

Code	Short Title

Code	Short Title
322212	Folding Paperboard Box Manufacturing
322213	Setup Paperboard Box Manufacturing
322214	Fiber Can, Tube, Drum, and Similar Products Manufacturing
322215	Nonfolding Sanitary Food Container Manufacturing
32222	Paper Bag and Coated and Treated Paper Manufacturing
322221	Coated and Laminated Packaging Paper and Plastics Film Manufacturing
322222	Coated and Laminated Paper Manufacturing
322223	Plastics, Foil, and Coated Paper Bag Manufacturing
322224	Uncoated Paper and Multiwall Bag Manufacturing
322225	Laminated Aluminum Foil Manufacturing for Flexible Packaging Uses
322226	Surface-Coated Paperboard Manufacturing
32223	Stationery Product Manufacturing
322231	Die-Cut Paper and Paperboard Office Supplies Manufacturing
322232	Envelope Manufacturing
322233	Stationery, Tablet, and Related Product Manufacturing
32229	Other Converted Paper Product Manufacturing
322291	Sanitary Paper Product Manufacturing
322299	All Other Converted Paper Product Manufacturing

323 Printing and Related Support Activities

Code	Short Title
3231	Printing and Related Support Activities
32311	Printing
323110	Commercial Lithographic Printing
323111	Commercial Gravure Printing
323112	Commercial Flexographic Printing
323113	Commercial Screen Printing
323114	Quick Printing
323115	Digital Printing
323116	Manifold Business Forms Printing
323117	Books Printing

Code	Short Title
323118	Blankbook, Looseleaf Binders, and Devices Manufacturing
323119	Other Commercial Printing
32312	Support Activities for Printing
323121	Tradebinding and Related Work
323122	Prepress Services

324 Petroleum and Coal Products Manufacturing

Code	Short Title
3241	Petroleum and Coal Products Manufacturing
32411	Petroleum Refineries
32412	Asphalt Paving, Roofing, and Saturated Materials Manufacturing
324121	Asphalt Paving Mixture and Block Manufacturing
324122	Asphalt Shingle and Coating Materials Manufacturing
32419	Other Petroleum and Coal Products Manufacturing
324191	Petroleum Lubricating Oil and Grease Manufacturing
324199	All Other Petroleum and Coal Products Manufacturing

325 Chemical Manufacturing

Code	Short Title
3251	Basic Chemical Manufacturing
32511	Petrochemical Manufacturing
32512	Industrial Gas Manufacturing
32513	Synthetic Dye and Pigment Manufacturing
325131	Inorganic Dye and Pigment Manufacturing
325132	Synthetic Organic Dye and Pigment Manufacturing
32518	Other Basic Inorganic Chemical Manufacturing
325181	Alkalies and Chlorine Manufacturing
325182	Carbon Black Manufacturing
325188	All Other Basic Inorganic Chemical Manufacturing
32519	Other Basic Organic Chemical Manufacturing
325191	Gum and Wood Chemical Manufacturing
325192	Cyclic Crude and Intermediate Manufacturing
325193	Ethyl Alcohol Manufacturing

326 Plastics and Rubber Products Manufacturing

Code	Short Title

Code		Short Title	Code		Short Title

Code	Short Title
33142	Copper Rolling, Drawing, Extruding, and Alloying
331421	Copper Rolling, Drawing, and Extruding
331422	Copper Wire (except Mechanical) Drawing
331423	Secondary Smelting, Refining, and Alloying of Copper
33149	Nonferrous Metal (except Copper and Aluminum) Rolling, Drawing, Extruding, and Alloying
331491	Nonferrous Metal (except Copper and Aluminum) Rolling, Drawing, and Extruding
331492	Secondary Smelting, Refining, and Alloying of Nonferrous Metal (except Copper and Aluminum)

3315 Foundries

Code	Short Title
33151	Ferrous Metal Foundries
331511	Iron Foundries
331512	Steel Investment Foundries
331513	Steel Foundries (except Investment)
33152	Nonferrous Metal Foundries
331521	Aluminum Die-Casting Foundries
331522	Nonferrous (except Aluminum) Die-Casting Foundries
331524	Aluminum Foundries (except Die-Casting)
331525	Copper Foundries (except Die-Casting)
331528	Other Nonferrous Foundries (except Die-Casting)

332 Fabricated Metal Product Manufacturing

3321 Forging and Stamping

Code	Short Title
33211	Forging and Stamping
332111	Iron and Steel Forging
332112	Nonferrous Forging
332114	Custom Roll Forming
332115	Crown and Closure Manufacturing
332116	Metal Stamping
332117	Powder Metallurgy Part Manufacturing

3322 Cutlery and Handtool Manufacturing

Code	Short Title
33221	Cutlery and Handtool Manufacturing
332211	Cutlery and Flatware (except Precious) Manufacturing
332212	Hand and Edge Tool Manufacturing
332213	Saw Blade and Handsaw Manufacturing

Code	Short Title
332214	Kitchen Utensil, Pot, and Pan Manufacturing

3323 Architectural and Structural Metals Manufacturing

Code	Short Title
33231	Plate Work and Fabricated Structural Product Manufacturing
332311	Prefabricated Metal Building and Component Manufacturing
332312	Fabricated Structural Metal Manufacturing
332313	Plate Work Manufacturing
33232	Ornamental and Architectural Metal Products Manufacturing
332321	Metal Window and Door Manufacturing
332322	Sheet Metal Work Manufacturing
332323	Ornamental and Architectural Metal Work Manufacturing

3324 Boiler, Tank, and Shipping Container Manufacturing

Code	Short Title
33241	Power Boiler and Heat Exchanger Manufacturing
33242	Metal Tank (Heavy Gauge) Manufacturing
33243	Metal Can, Box, and Other Metal Container (Light Gauge) Manufacturing
332431	Metal Can Manufacturing
332439	Other Metal Container Manufacturing

3325 Hardware Manufacturing

Code	Short Title
33251	Hardware Manufacturing

3326 Spring and Wire Product Manufacturing

Code	Short Title
33261	Spring and Wire Product Manufacturing
332611	Spring (Heavy Gauge) Manufacturing
332612	Spring (Light Gauge) Manufacturing
332618	Other Fabricated Wire Product Manufacturing

3327 Machine Shops; Turned Product; and Screw, Nut, and Bolt Manufacturing

Code	Short Title
33271	Machine Shops
33272	Turned Product and Screw, Nut, and Bolt Manufacturing
332721	Precision Turned Product Manufacturing
332722	Bolt, Nut, Screw, Rivet, and Washer Manufacturing

3328 Coating, Engraving, Heat Treating, and Allied Activities

Code	Short Title
33281	Coating, Engraving, Heat Treating, and Allied Activities

Code	Short Title	Code	Short Title

Code	Short Title
332811	Metal Heat Treating
332812	Metal Coating, Engraving (except Jewelry and Silverware), and Allied Services to Manufacturers
332813	Electroplating, Plating, Polishing, Anodizing, and Coloring
3329	Other Fabricated Metal Product Manufacturing
33291	Metal Valve Manufacturing
332911	Industrial Valve Manufacturing
332912	Fluid Power Valve and Hose Fitting Manufacturing
332913	Plumbing Fixture Fitting and Trim Manufacturing
332919	Other Metal Valve and Pipe Fitting Manufacturing
33299	All Other Fabricated Metal Product Manufacturing
332991	Ball and Roller Bearing Manufacturing
332992	Small Arms Ammunition Manufacturing
332993	Ammunition (except Small Arms) Manufacturing
332994	Small Arms Manufacturing
332995	Other Ordnance and Accessories Manufacturing
332996	Fabricated Pipe and Pipe Fitting Manufacturing
332997	Industrial Pattern Manufacturing
332998	Enameled Iron and Metal Sanitary Ware Manufacturing
332999	All Other Miscellaneous Fabricated Metal Product Manufacturing

333 Machinery Manufacturing

Code	Short Title
3331	Agriculture, Construction, and Mining Machinery Manufacturing
33311	Agricultural Implement Manufacturing
333111	Farm Machinery and Equipment Manufacturing
333112	Lawn and Garden Tractor and Home Lawn and Garden Equipment Manufacturing
33312	Construction Machinery Manufacturing
33313	Mining and Oil and Gas Field Machinery Manufacturing

Code	Short Title
333131	Mining Machinery and Equipment Manufacturing
333132	Oil and Gas Field Machinery and Equipment Manufacturing
3332	Industrial Machinery Manufacturing
33321	Sawmill and Woodworking Machinery Manufacturing
33322	Plastics and Rubber Industry Machinery Manufacturing
33329	Other Industrial Machinery Manufacturing
333291	Paper Industry Machinery Manufacturing
333292	Textile Machinery Manufacturing
333293	Printing Machinery and Equipment Manufacturing
333294	Food Product Machinery Manufacturing
333295	Semiconductor Machinery Manufacturing
333298	All Other Industrial Machinery Manufacturing
3333	Commercial and Service Industry Machinery Manufacturing
33331	Commercial and Service Industry Machinery Manufacturing
333311	Automatic Vending Machine Manufacturing
333312	Commercial Laundry, Drycleaning, and Pressing Machine Manufacturing
333313	Office Machinery Manufacturing
333314	Optical Instrument and Lens Manufacturing
333315	Photographic and Photocopying Equipment Manufacturing
333319	Other Commercial and Service Industry Machinery Manufacturing
3334	Ventilation, Heating, Air-Conditioning, and Commercial Refrigeration Equipment Manufacturing
33341	Ventilation, Heating, Air-Conditioning, and Commercial Refrigeration Equipment Manufacturing
333411	Air Purification Equipment Manufacturing
333412	Industrial and Commercial Fan and Blower Manufacturing
333414	Heating Equipment (except Warm Air Furnaces) Manufacturing

Code	Short Title	Code	Short Title

Code	Short Title
333415	Air-Conditioning and Warm Air Heating Equipment and Commercial and Industrial Refrigeration Equipment Manufacturing
3335	Metalworking Machinery Manufacturing
33351	Metalworking Machinery Manufacturing
333511	Industrial Mold Manufacturing
333512	Machine Tool (Metal Cutting Types) Manufacturing
333513	Machine Tool (Metal Forming Types) Manufacturing
333514	Special Die and Tool, Die Set, Jig, and Fixture Manufacturing
333515	Cutting Tool and Machine Tool Accessory Manufacturing
333516	Rolling Mill Machinery and Equipment Manufacturing
333518	Other Metalworking Machinery Manufacturing
3336	Engine, Turbine, and Power Transmission Equipment Manufacturing
33361	Engine, Turbine, and Power Transmission Equipment Manufacturing
333611	Turbine and Turbine Generator Set Units Manufacturing
333612	Speed Changer, Industrial High-Speed Drive, and Gear Manufacturing
333613	Mechanical Power Transmission Equipment Manufacturing
333618	Other Engine Equipment Manufacturing
3339	Other General Purpose Machinery Manufacturing
33391	Pump and Compressor Manufacturing
333911	Pump and Pumping Equipment Manufacturing
333912	Air and Gas Compressor Manufacturing
333913	Measuring and Dispensing Pump Manufacturing
33392	Material Handling Equipment Manufacturing
333921	Elevator and Moving Stairway Manufacturing
333922	Conveyor and Conveying Equipment Manufacturing
333923	Overhead Traveling Crane, Hoist, and Monorail System Manufacturing

Code	Short Title
333924	Industrial Truck, Tractor, Trailer, and Stacker Machinery Manufacturing
33399	All Other General Purpose Machinery Manufacturing
333991	Power-Driven Handtool Manufacturing
333992	Welding and Soldering Equipment Manufacturing
333993	Packaging Machinery Manufacturing
333994	Industrial Process Furnace and Oven Manufacturing
333995	Fluid Power Cylinder and Actuator Manufacturing
333996	Fluid Power Pump and Motor Manufacturing
333997	Scale and Balance (except Laboratory) Manufacturing
333999	All Other Miscellaneous General Purpose Machinery Manufacturing

334 Computer and Electronic Product Manufacturing

Code	Short Title
3341	Computer and Peripheral Equipment Manufacturing
33411	Computer and Peripheral Equipment Manufacturing
334111	Electronic Computer Manufacturing
334112	Computer Storage Device Manufacturing
334113	Computer Terminal Manufacturing
334119	Other Computer Peripheral Equipment Manufacturing
3342	Communications Equipment Manufacturing
33421	Telephone Apparatus Manufacturing
33422	Radio and Television Broadcasting and Wireless Communications Equipment Manufacturing
33429	Other Communications Equipment Manufacturing
3343	Audio and Video Equipment Manufacturing
33431	Audio and Video Equipment Manufacturing
3344	Semiconductor and Other Electronic Component Manufacturing
33441	Semiconductor and Other Electronic Component Manufacturing
334411	Electron Tube Manufacturing
334412	Bare Printed Circuit Board Manufacturing

Code	Short Title
334413	Semiconductor and Related Device Manufacturing
334414	Electronic Capacitor Manufacturing
334415	Electronic Resistor Manufacturing
334416	Electronic Coil, Transformer, and Other Inductor Manufacturing
334417	Electronic Connector Manufacturing
334418	Printed Circuit Assembly (Electronic Assembly) Manufacturing
334419	Other Electronic Component Manufacturing
3345	Navigational, Measuring, Electromedical, and Control Instruments Manufacturing
33451	Navigational, Measuring, Electromedical, and Control Instruments Manufacturing
334510	Electromedical and Electrotherapeutic Apparatus Manufacturing
334511	Search, Detection, Navigation, Guidance, Aeronautical, and Nautical System and Instrument Manufacturing
334512	Automatic Environmental Control Manufacturing for Residential, Commercial, and Appliance Use
334513	Instruments and Related Products Manufacturing for Measuring, Displaying, and Controlling Industrial Process Variables
334514	Totalizing Fluid Meter and Counting Device Manufacturing
334515	Instrument Manufacturing for Measuring and Testing Electricity and Electrical Signals
334516	Analytical Laboratory Instrument Manufacturing
334517	Irradiation Apparatus Manufacturing
334518	Watch, Clock, and Part Manufacturing
334519	Other Measuring and Controlling Device Manufacturing
3346	Manufacturing and Reproducing Magnetic and Optical Media
33461	Manufacturing and Reproducing Magnetic and Optical Media
334611	Software Reproducing

Code	Short Title
334612	Prerecorded Compact Disc (except Software), Tape, and Record Reproducing
334613	Magnetic and Optical Recording Media Manufacturing

335 Electrical Equipment, Appliance, and Component Manufacturing

Code	Short Title
3351	Electric Lighting Equipment Manufacturing
33511	Electric Lamp Bulb and Part Manufacturing
33512	Lighting Fixture Manufacturing
335121	Residential Electric Lighting Fixture Manufacturing
335122	Commercial, Industrial, and Institutional Electric Lighting Fixture Manufacturing
335129	Other Lighting Equipment Manufacturing
3352	Household Appliance Manufacturing
33521	Small Electrical Appliance Manufacturing
335211	Electric Housewares and Household Fan Manufacturing
335212	Household Vacuum Cleaner Manufacturing
33522	Major Appliance Manufacturing
335221	Household Cooking Appliance Manufacturing
335222	Household Refrigerator and Home Freezer Manufacturing
335224	Household Laundry Equipment Manufacturing
335228	Other Major Household Appliance Manufacturing
3353	Electrical Equipment Manufacturing
33531	Electrical Equipment Manufacturing
335311	Power, Distribution, and Specialty Transformer Manufacturing
335312	Motor and Generator Manufacturing
335313	Switchgear and Switchboard Apparatus Manufacturing
335314	Relay and Industrial Control Manufacturing
3359	Other Electrical Equipment and Component Manufacturing
33591	Battery Manufacturing
335911	Storage Battery Manufacturing
335912	Primary Battery Manufacturing
33592	Communication and Energy Wire and Cable Manufacturing

Code		Short Title
	335921	Fiber Optic Cable Manufacturing
	335929	Other Communication and Energy Wire Manufacturing
	33593	Wiring Device Manufacturing
	335931	Current-Carrying Wiring Device Manufacturing
	335932	Noncurrent-Carrying Wiring Device Manufacturing
	33599	All Other Electrical Equipment and Component Manufacturing
	335991	Carbon and Graphite Product Manufacturing
	335999	All Other Miscellaneous Electrical Equipment and Component Manufacturing

336 Transportation Equipment Manufacturing

3361		Motor Vehicle Manufacturing
	33611	Automobile and Light Duty Motor Vehicle Manufacturing
	336111	Automobile Manufacturing
	336112	Light Truck and Utility Vehicle Manufacturing
	33612	Heavy Duty Truck Manufacturing
3362		Motor Vehicle Body and Trailer Manufacturing
	33621	Motor Vehicle Body and Trailer Manufacturing
	336211	Motor Vehicle Body Manufacturing
	336212	Truck Trailer Manufacturing
	336213	Motor Home Manufacturing
	336214	Travel Trailer and Camper Manufacturing
3363		Motor Vehicle Parts Manufacturing
	33631	Motor Vehicle Gasoline Engine and Engine Parts Manufacturing
	336311	Carburetor, Piston, Piston Ring, and Valve Manufacturing
	336312	Gasoline Engine and Engine Parts Manufacturing
	33632	Motor Vehicle Electrical and Electronic Equipment Manufacturing
	336321	Vehicular Lighting Equipment Manufacturing
	336322	Other Motor Vehicle Electrical and Electronic Equipment Manufacturing

Code		Short Title
	33633	Motor Vehicle Steering and Suspension Components (except Spring) Manufacturing
	33634	Motor Vehicle Brake System Manufacturing
	33635	Motor Vehicle Transmission and Power Train Parts Manufacturing
	33636	Motor Vehicle Seating and Interior Trim Manufacturing
	33637	Motor Vehicle Metal Stamping
	33639	Other Motor Vehicle Parts Manufacturing
	336391	Motor Vehicle Air-Conditioning Manufacturing
	336399	All Other Motor Vehicle Parts Manufacturing
3364		Aerospace Product and Parts Manufacturing
	33641	Aerospace Product and Parts Manufacturing
	336411	Aircraft Manufacturing
	336412	Aircraft Engine and Engine Parts Manufacturing
	336413	Other Aircraft Parts and Auxiliary Equipment Manufacturing
	336414	Guided Missile and Space Vehicle Manufacturing
	336415	Guided Missile and Space Vehicle Propulsion Unit and Propulsion Unit Parts Manufacturing
	336419	Other Guided Missile and Space Vehicle Parts and Auxiliary Equipment Manufacturing
3365		Railroad Rolling Stock Manufacturing
	33651	Railroad Rolling Stock Manufacturing
3366		Ship and Boat Building
	33661	Ship and Boat Building
	336611	Ship Building and Repairing
	336612	Boat Building
3369		Other Transportation Equipment Manufacturing
	33699	Other Transportation Equipment Manufacturing
	336991	Motorcycle, Bicycle, and Parts Manufacturing
	336992	Military Armored Vehicle, Tank, and Tank Component Manufacturing

Code	Short Title

Code	Short Title		Code	Short Title

422   Wholesale Trade, Nondurable Goods

Code	Short Title
42233	Women's, Children's, and Infants' Clothing and Accessories Wholesalers
42234	Footwear Wholesalers

4224 Grocery and Related Product Wholesalers
- 42241 General Line Grocery Wholesalers
- 42242 Packaged Frozen Food Wholesalers
- 42243 Dairy Product (except Dried or Canned) Wholesalers
- 42244 Poultry and Poultry Product Wholesalers
- 42245 Confectionery Wholesalers
- 42246 Fish and Seafood Wholesalers
- 42247 Meat and Meat Product Wholesalers
- 42248 Fresh Fruit and Vegetable Wholesalers
- 42249 Other Grocery and Related Products Wholesalers

4225 Farm Product Raw Material Wholesalers
- 42251 Grain and Field Bean Wholesalers
- 42252 Livestock Wholesalers
- 42259 Other Farm Product Raw Material Wholesalers

4226 Chemical and Allied Products Wholesalers
- 42261 Plastics Materials and Basic Forms and Shapes Wholesalers
- 42269 Other Chemical and Allied Products Wholesalers

4227 Petroleum and Petroleum Products Wholesalers
- 42271 Petroleum Bulk Stations and Terminals
- 42272 Petroleum and Petroleum Products Wholesalers (except Bulk Stations and Terminals)

4228 Beer, Wine, and Distilled Alcoholic Beverage Wholesalers
- 42281 Beer and Ale Wholesalers
- 42282 Wine and Distilled Alcoholic Beverage Wholesalers

4229 Miscellaneous Nondurable Goods Wholesalers
- 42291 Farm Supplies Wholesalers
- 42292 Book, Periodical, and Newspaper Wholesalers
- 42293 Flower, Nursery Stock, and Florists' Supplies Wholesalers
- 42294 Tobacco and Tobacco Product Wholesalers
- 42295 Paint, Varnish, and Supplies Wholesalers

Code	Short Title
42299	Other Miscellaneous Nondurable Goods Wholesalers

44–45 RETAIL TRADE

441 Motor Vehicle and Parts Dealers

4411 Automobile Dealers
- 44111 New Car Dealers
- 44112 Used Car Dealers

4412 Other Motor Vehicle Dealers
- 44121 Recreational Vehicle Dealers
- 44122 Motorcycle, Boat, and Other Motor Vehicle Dealers
- 441221 Motorcycle Dealers
- 441222 Boat Dealers
- 441229 All Other Motor Vehicle Dealers

4413 Automotive Parts, Accessories, and Tire Stores
- 44131 Automotive Parts and Accessories Stores
- 44132 Tire Dealers

442 Furniture and Home Furnishings Stores

4421 Furniture Stores
- 44211 Furniture Stores

4422 Home Furnishings Stores
- 44221 Floor Covering Stores
- 44229 Other Home Furnishings Stores
- 442291 Window Treatment Stores
- 442299 All Other Home Furnishings Stores

443 Electronics and Appliance Stores

4431 Electronics and Appliance Stores
- 44311 Appliance, Television, and Other Electronics Stores
- 443111 Household Appliance Stores
- 443112 Radio, Television, and Other Electronics Stores
- 44312 Computer and Software Stores
- 44313 Camera and Photographic Supplies Stores

444 Building Material and Garden Equipment and Supplies Dealers

4441 Building Material and Supplies Dealers
- 44411 Home Centers
- 44412 Paint and Wallpaper Stores

Code	Short Title		Code	Short Title

Code	Short Title
44413	Hardware Stores
44419	Other Building Material Dealers
4442	Lawn and Garden Equipment and Supplies Stores
44421	Outdoor Power Equipment Stores
44422	Nursery and Garden Centers

445 Food and Beverage Stores

Code	Short Title
4451	Grocery Stores
44511	Supermarkets and Other Grocery (except Convenience) Stores
44512	Convenience Stores
4452	Specialty Food Stores
44521	Meat Markets
44522	Fish and Seafood Markets
44523	Fruit and Vegetable Markets
44529	Other Specialty Food Stores
445291	Baked Goods Stores
445292	Confectionery and Nut Stores
445299	All Other Specialty Food Stores
4453	Beer, Wine, and Liquor Stores
44531	Beer, Wine, and Liquor Stores

446 Health and Personal Care Stores

Code	Short Title
4461	Health and Personal Care Stores
44611	Pharmacies and Drug Stores
44612	Cosmetics, Beauty Supplies, and Perfume Stores
44613	Optical Goods Stores
44619	Other Health and Personal Care Stores
446191	Food (Health) Supplement Stores
446199	All Other Health and Personal Care Stores

447 Gasoline Stations

Code	Short Title
4471	Gasoline Stations
44711	Gasoline Stations with Convenience Stores
44719	Other Gasoline Stations

448 Clothing and Clothing Accessories Stores

Code	Short Title
4481	Clothing Stores
44811	Men's Clothing Stores
44812	Women's Clothing Stores
44813	Children's and Infants' Clothing Stores
44814	Family Clothing Stores
44815	Clothing Accessories Stores
44819	Other Clothing Stores
4482	Shoe Stores
44821	Shoe Stores
4483	Jewelry, Luggage, and Leather Goods Stores
44831	Jewelry Stores
44832	Luggage and Leather Goods Stores

451 Sporting Goods, Hobby, Book, and Music Stores

Code	Short Title
4511	Sporting Goods, Hobby, and Musical Instrument Stores
45111	Sporting Goods Stores
45112	Hobby, Toy, and Game Stores
45113	Sewing, Needlework, and Piece Goods Stores
45114	Musical Instrument and Supplies Stores
4512	Book, Periodical, and Music Stores
45121	Book Stores and News Dealers
451211	Book Stores
451212	News Dealers and Newsstands
45122	Prerecorded Tape, Compact Disc, and Record Stores

452 General Merchandise Stores

Code	Short Title
4521	Department Stores
45211	Department Stores
4529	Other General Merchandise Stores
45291	Warehouse Clubs and Superstores
45299	All Other General Merchandise Stores

453 Miscellaneous Store Retailers

Code	Short Title
4531	Florists
45311	Florists
4532	Office Supplies, Stationery, and Gift Stores
45321	Office Supplies and Stationery Stores
45322	Gift, Novelty, and Souvenir Stores
4533	Used Merchandise Stores
45331	Used Merchandise Stores
4539	Other Miscellaneous Store Retailers
45391	Pet and Pet Supplies Stores
45392	Art Dealers
45393	Manufactured (Mobile) Home Dealers
45399	All Other Miscellaneous Store Retailers

Code	Short Title	Code	Short Title

Code	Short Title		Code	Short Title

Code	Short Title
4859	Other Transit and Ground Passenger Transportation
48599	Other Transit and Ground Passenger Transportation
485991	Special Needs Transportation
485999	All Other Transit and Ground Passenger Transportation

486 Pipeline Transportation

4861	Pipeline Transportation of Crude Oil
48611	Pipeline Transportation of Crude Oil
4862	Pipeline Transportation of Natural Gas
48621	Pipeline Transportation of Natural Gas
4869	Other Pipeline Transportation
48691	Pipeline Transportation of Refined Petroleum Products
48699	All Other Pipeline Transportation

487 Scenic and Sightseeing Transportation

4871	Scenic and Sightseeing Transportation, Land
48711	Scenic and Sightseeing Transportation, Land
4872	Scenic and Sightseeing Transportation, Water
48721	Scenic and Sightseeing Transportation, Water
4879	Scenic and Sightseeing Transportation, Other
48799	Scenic and Sightseeing Transportation, Other

488 Support Activities for Transportation

4881	Support Activities for Air Transportation
48811	Airport Operations
488111	Air Traffic Control
488119	Other Airport Operations
48819	Other Support Activities for Air Transportation
4882	Support Activities for Rail Transportation
48821	Support Activities for Rail Transportation
4883	Support Activities for Water Transportation
48831	Port and Harbor Operations
48832	Marine Cargo Handling
48833	Navigational Services to Shipping
48839	Other Support Activities for Water Transportation

4884	Support Activities for Road Transportation
48841	Motor Vehicle Towing
48849	Other Support Activities for Road Transportation
4885	Freight Transportation Arrangement
48851	Freight Transportation Arrangement
4889	Other Support Activities for Transportation
48899	Other Support Activities for Transportation
488991	Packing and Crating
488999	All Other Support Activities for Transportation

491 Postal Service

4911	Postal Service
49111	Postal Service

492 Couriers and Messengers

4921	Couriers
49211	Couriers
4922	Local Messengers and Local Delivery
49221	Local Messengers and Local Delivery

493 Warehousing and Storage

4931	Warehousing and Storage
49311	General Warehousing and Storage
49312	Refrigerated Warehousing and Storage
49313	Farm Product Warehousing and Storage
49319	Other Warehousing and Storage

51 INFORMATION

511 Publishing Industries

5111	Newspaper, Periodical, Book, and Database Publishers
51111	Newspaper Publishers
51112	Periodical Publishers
51113	Book Publishers
51114	Database and Directory Publishers
51119	Other Publishers
511191	Greeting Card Publishers
511199	All Other Publishers
5112	Software Publishers
51121	Software Publishers

Code	Short Title
52314	Commodity Contracts Brokerage
5232	Securities and Commodity Exchanges
52321	Securities and Commodity Exchanges
5239	Other Financial Investment Activities
52391	Miscellaneous Intermediation
52392	Portfolio Management
52393	Investment Advice
52399	All Other Financial Investment Activities
523991	Trust, Fiduciary, and Custody Activities
523999	Miscellaneous Financial Investment Activities

524 Insurance Carriers and Related Activities

5241	Insurance Carriers
52411	Direct Life, Health, and Medical Insurance Carriers
524113	Direct Life Insurance Carriers
524114	Direct Health and Medical Insurance Carriers
52412	Direct Insurance (except Life, Health, and Medical) Carriers
524126	Direct Property and Casualty Insurance Carriers
524127	Direct Title Insurance Carriers
524128	Other Direct Insurance (except Life, Health, and Medical) Carriers
52413	Reinsurance Carriers
5242	Agencies, Brokerages, and Other Insurance Related Activities
52421	Insurance Agencies and Brokerages
52429	Other Insurance Related Activities
524291	Claims Adjusting
524292	Third Party Administration of Insurance and Pension Funds
524298	All Other Insurance Related Activities

525 Funds, Trusts, and Other Financial Vehicles

5251	Insurance and Employee Benefit Funds
52511	Pension Funds
52512	Health and Welfare Funds
52519	Other Insurance Funds
5259	Other Investment Pools and Funds

Code	Short Title
52591	Open-End Investment Funds
52592	Trusts, Estates, and Agency Accounts
52593	Real Estate Investment Trusts
52599	Other Financial Vehicles

53 REAL ESTATE AND RENTAL AND LEASING

531 Real Estate

5311	Lessors of Real Estate
53111	Lessors of Residential Buildings and Dwellings
53112	Lessors of Nonresidential Buildings (except Miniwarehouses)
53113	Lessors of Miniwarehouses and Self-Storage Units
53119	Lessors of Other Real Estate Property
5312	Offices of Real Estate Agents and Brokers
53121	Offices of Real Estate Agents and Brokers
5313	Activities Related to Real Estate
53131	Real Estate Property Managers
531311	Residential Property Managers
531312	Nonresidential Property Managers
53132	Offices of Real Estate Appraisers
53139	Other Activities Related to Real Estate

532 Rental and Leasing Services

5321	Automotive Equipment Rental and Leasing
53211	Passenger Car Rental and Leasing
532111	Passenger Car Rental
532112	Passenger Car Leasing
53212	Truck, Utility Trailer, and RV (Recreational Vehicle) Rental and Leasing
5322	Consumer Goods Rental
53221	Consumer Electronics and Appliances Rental
53222	Formal Wear and Costume Rental
53223	Video Tape and Disc Rental
53229	Other Consumer Goods Rental
532291	Home Health Equipment Rental
532292	Recreational Goods Rental
532299	All Other Consumer Goods Rental
5323	General Rental Centers
53231	General Rental Centers

Code	Short Title	Code	Short Title

5324 Commercial and Industrial Machinery and Equipment Rental and Leasing

    53241 Construction, Transportation, Mining, and Forestry Machinery and Equipment Rental and Leasing

    532411 Commercial Air, Rail, and Water Transportation Equipment Rental and Leasing

    532412 Construction, Mining, and Forestry Machinery and Equipment Rental and Leasing

    53242 Office Machinery and Equipment Rental and Leasing

    53249 Other Commercial and Industrial Machinery and Equipment Rental and Leasing

533 Lessors of Nonfinancial Intangible Assets (except Copyrighted Works)

5331 Lessors of Nonfinancial Intangible Assets (except Copyrighted Works)

    53311 Lessors of Nonfinancial Intangible Assets (except Copyrighted Works)

54 PROFESSIONAL, SCIENTIFIC, AND TECHNICAL SERVICES

541 Professional, Scientific, and Technical Services

5411 Legal Services

    54111 Offices of Lawyers

    54112 Offices of Notaries

    54119 Other Legal Services

    541191 Title Abstract and Settlement Offices

    541199 All Other Legal Services

5412 Accounting, Tax Preparation, Bookkeeping, and Payroll Services

    54121 Accounting, Tax Preparation, Bookkeeping, and Payroll Services

    541211 Offices of Certified Public Accountants

    541213 Tax Preparation Services

    541214 Payroll Services

    541219 Other Accounting Services

5413 Architectural, Engineering, and Related Services

    54131 Architectural Services

    54132 Landscape Architectural Services

54133 Engineering Services

54134 Drafting Services

54135 Building Inspection Services

54136 Geophysical Surveying and Mapping Services

54137 Surveying and Mapping (except Geophysical) Services

54138 Testing Laboratories

5414 Specialized Design Services

    54141 Interior Design Services

    54142 Industrial Design Services

    54143 Graphic Design Services

    54149 Other Specialized Design Services

5415 Computer Systems Design and Related Services

    54151 Computer Systems Design and Related Services

    541511 Custom Computer Programming Services

    541512 Computer Systems Design Services

    541513 Computer Facilities Management Services

    541519 Other Computer Related Services

5416 Management, Scientific, and Technical Consulting Services

    54161 Management Consulting Services

    541611 Administrative Management and General Management Consulting Services

    541612 Human Resources and Executive Search Consulting Services

    541613 Marketing Consulting Services

    541614 Process, Physical Distribution, and Logistics Consulting Services

    541618 Other Management Consulting Services

    54162 Environmental Consulting Services

    54169 Other Scientific and Technical Consulting Services

5417 Scientific Research and Development Services

    54171 Research and Development in the Physical, Engineering, and Life Sciences

    54172 Research and Development in the Social Sciences and Humanities

5418 Advertising and Related Services

    54181 Advertising Agencies

    54182 Public Relations Agencies

    54183 Media Buying Agencies

    54184 Media Representatives

    54185 Display Advertising

Code	Short Title	Code	Short Title

55 MANAGEMENT OF COMPANIES AND ENTERPRISES

551 Management of Companies and Enterprises

56 ADMINISTRATIVE AND SUPPORT AND WASTE MANAGEMENT AND REMEDIATION SERVICES

561 Administrative and Support Services

562 Waste Management and Remediation Services

Code	Short Title	Code	Short Title

Code	Short Title
62151	Medical and Diagnostic Laboratories
621511	Medical Laboratories
621512	Diagnostic Imaging Centers
6216	Home Health Care Services
62161	Home Health Care Services
6219	Other Ambulatory Health Care Services
62191	Ambulance Services
62199	All Other Ambulatory Health Care Services
621991	Blood and Organ Banks
621999	All Other Miscellaneous Ambulatory Health Care Services

622 Hospitals

Code	Short Title
6221	General Medical and Surgical Hospitals
62211	General Medical and Surgical Hospitals
6222	Psychiatric and Substance Abuse Hospitals
62221	Psychiatric and Substance Abuse Hospitals
6223	Specialty (except Psychiatric and Substance Abuse) Hospitals
62231	Specialty (except Psychiatric and Substance Abuse) Hospitals

623 Nursing and Residential Care Facilities

Code	Short Title
6231	Nursing Care Facilities
62311	Nursing Care Facilities
6232	Residential Mental Retardation, Mental Health and Substance Abuse Facilities
62321	Residential Mental Retardation Facilities
62322	Residential Mental Health and Substance Abuse Facilities
6233	Community Care Facilities for the Elderly
62331	Community Care Facilities for the Elderly
623311	Continuing Care Retirement Communities
623312	Homes for the Elderly
6239	Other Residential Care Facilities
62399	Other Residential Care Facilities

624 Social Assistance

Code	Short Title
6241	Individual and Family Services
62411	Child and Youth Services
62412	Services for the Elderly and Persons with Disabilities
62419	Other Individual and Family Services
6242	Community Food and Housing, and Emergency and Other Relief Services
62421	Community Food Services
62422	Community Housing Services
624221	Temporary Shelters
624229	Other Community Housing Services
62423	Emergency and Other Relief Services
6243	Vocational Rehabilitation Services
62431	Vocational Rehabilitation Services
6244	Child Day Care Services
62441	Child Day Care Services

71 ARTS, ENTERTAINMENT, AND RECREATION

711 Performing Arts, Spectator Sports, and Related Industries

Code	Short Title
7111	Performing Arts Companies
71111	Theater Companies and Dinner Theaters
71112	Dance Companies
71113	Musical Groups and Artists
71119	Other Performing Arts Companies
7112	Spectator Sports
71121	Spectator Sports
711211	Sports Teams and Clubs
711212	Racetracks
711219	Other Spectator Sports
7113	Promoters of Performing Arts, Sports, and Similar Events
71131	Promoters of Performing Arts, Sports, and Similar Events with Facilities
71132	Promoters of Performing Arts, Sports, and Similar Events without Facilities
7114	Agents and Managers for Artists, Athletes, Entertainers, and Other Public Figures
71141	Agents and Managers for Artists, Athletes, Entertainers, and Other Public Figures
7115	Independent Artists, Writers, and Performers
71151	Independent Artists, Writers, and Performers

712 Museums, Historical Sites, and Similar Institutions

Code	Short Title
7121	Museums, Historical Sites, and Similar Institutions
71211	Museums

Code	Short Title
71212	Historical Sites
71213	Zoos and Botanical Gardens
71219	Nature Parks and Other Similar Institutions

713 Amusement, Gambling, and Recreation Industries

7131	Amusement Parks and Arcades
71311	Amusement and Theme Parks
71312	Amusement Arcades
7132	Gambling Industries
71321	Casinos (except Casino Hotels)
71329	Other Gambling Industries
7139	Other Amusement and Recreation Industries
71391	Golf Courses and Country Clubs
71392	Skiing Facilities
71393	Marinas
71394	Fitness and Recreational Sports Centers
71395	Bowling Centers
71399	All Other Amusement and Recreation Industries

72 ACCOMMODATION AND FOOD SERVICES

721 Accommodation

7211	Traveler Accommodation
72111	Hotels (except Casino Hotels) and Motels
72112	Casino Hotels
72119	Other Traveler Accommodation
721191	Bed-and-Breakfast Inns
721199	All Other Traveler Accommodation
7212	RV (Recreational Vehicle) Parks and Recreational Camps
72121	RV (Recreational Vehicle) Parks and Recreational Camps
721211	RV (Recreational Vehicle) Parks and Campgrounds
721214	Recreational and Vacation Camps (except Campgrounds)
7213	Rooming and Boarding Houses
72131	Rooming and Boarding Houses

722 Food Services and Drinking Places

7221	Full-Service Restaurants

Code	Short Title
72211	Full-Service Restaurants
7222	Limited-Service Eating Places
72221	Limited-Service Eating Places
722211	Limited-Service Restaurants
722212	Cafeterias
722213	Snack and Nonalcoholic Beverage Bars
7223	Special Food Services
72231	Food Service Contractors
72232	Caterers
72233	Mobile Food Services
7224	Drinking Places (Alcoholic Beverages)
72241	Drinking Places (Alcoholic Beverages)

81 OTHER SERVICES (EXCEPT PUBLIC ADMINISTRATION)

811 Repair and Maintenance

8111	Automotive Repair and Maintenance
81111	Automotive Mechanical and Electrical Repair and Maintenance
811111	General Automotive Repair
811112	Automotive Exhaust System Repair
811113	Automotive Transmission Repair
811118	Other Automotive Mechanical and Electrical Repair and Maintenance
81112	Automotive Body, Paint, Interior, and Glass Repair
811121	Automotive Body, Paint, and Interior Repair and Maintenance
811122	Automotive Glass Replacement Shops
81119	Other Automotive Repair and Maintenance
811191	Automotive Oil Change and Lubrication Shops
811192	Car Washes
811198	All Other Automotive Repair and Maintenance
8112	Electronic and Precision Equipment Repair and Maintenance
81121	Electronic and Precision Equipment Repair and Maintenance
811211	Consumer Electronics Repair and Maintenance
811212	Computer and Office Machine Repair and Maintenance

Code	Short Title		Code	Short Title

Code	Short Title
92112	Legislative Bodies
92113	Public Finance Activities
92114	Executive and Legislative Offices, Combined
92115	American Indian and Alaska Native Tribal Governments
92119	Other General Government Support

922 Justice, Public Order, and Safety Activities

Code	Short Title
9221	Justice, Public Order, and Safety Activities
92211	Courts
92212	Police Protection
92213	Legal Counsel and Prosecution
92214	Correctional Institutions
92215	Parole Offices and Probation Offices
92216	Fire Protection
92219	Other Justice, Public Order, and Safety Activities

923 Administration of Human Resource Programs

Code	Short Title
9231	Administration of Human Resource Programs
92311	Administration of Education Programs
92312	Administration of Public Health Programs
92313	Administration of Human Resource Programs (except Education, Public Health, and Veterans' Affairs Programs)
92314	Administration of Veterans' Affairs

924 Administration of Environmental Quality Programs

Code	Short Title
9241	Administration of Environmental Quality Programs
92411	Administration of Air and Water Resource and Solid Waste Management Programs

Code	Short Title
92412	Administration of Conservation Programs

925 Administration of Housing Programs, Urban Planning, and Community Development

Code	Short Title
9251	Administration of Housing Programs, Urban Planning, and Community Development
92511	Administration of Housing Programs
92512	Administration of Urban Planning and Community and Rural Development

926 Administration of Economic Programs

Code	Short Title
9261	Administration of Economic Programs
92611	Administration of General Economic Programs
92612	Regulation and Administration of Transportation Programs
92613	Regulation and Administration of Communications, Electric, Gas, and Other Utilities
92614	Regulation of Agricultural Marketing and Commodities
92615	Regulation, Licensing, and Inspection of Miscellaneous Commercial Sectors

927 Space Research and Technology

Code	Short Title
9271	Space Research and Technology
92711	Space Research and Technology

928 National Security and International Affairs

Code	Short Title
9281	National Security and International Affairs
92811	National Security
92812	International Affairs

Sector 11: Agriculture, Forestry, Fishing and Hunting

Overview of this Sector as a Whole

The Agriculture, Forestry, Fishing and Hunting sector comprises establishments primarily engaged in growing crops, raising animals, harvesting timber, and harvesting fish and other animals from a farm, ranch, or their natural habitats.

The establishments in this sector are often described as farms, ranches, dairies, greenhouses, nurseries, orchards, or hatcheries. A farm may consist of a single tract of land or a number of separate tracts that may be held under different tenures. For example, one tract may be owned by the farm operator and another rented. It may be operated by the operator alone or with the assistance of members of the household or hired employees, or it may be operated by a partnership, corporation, or other type of organization. When a landowner has one or more tenants, renters, croppers, or managers, the land operated by each is considered a farm. The sector distinguishes two basic activities: agricultural production and agricultural support activities. Agricultural production includes establishments performing the complete farm or ranch operation, such as farm owner-operators, tenant farm operators, and sharecroppers. Agricultural support activities include establishments that perform one or more activities associated with farm operation, such as soil preparation, planting, harvesting, and management, on a contract or fee basis.

Excluded from the Agriculture, Forestry, Fishing and Hunting sector are establishments primarily engaged in agricultural research and establishments primarily engaged in administering programs for regulating and conserving land, mineral, wildlife, and forest use. These establishments are classified in Industry 54171, Research and Development in the Physical, Engineering, and Life Sciences; and Industry 92412, Administration of Conservation Programs, respectively.

111 Crop Production

Industries in the Crop Production subsector grow crops mainly for food and fiber. The subsector comprises establishments, such as farms, orchards, groves, greenhouses, and nurseries, primarily engaged in growing crops, plants, vines, or trees and their seeds. The industries in this subsector are grouped by similarity of production activity, including biological and physiological characteristics and economic requirements, the length of growing season, degree of crop rotation, extent of input specialization, labor requirements, and capital demands. The production process is typically completed when the raw product or commodity grown reaches the "farm gate" for market, that is, at the point of first sale or price determination. Establishments are classified to the crop production subsector when crop production (i.e., value of crops for market) accounts for one-half or more of the establishment's total agricultural production. Within the subsector, establishments are classified to a specific industry when a product or industry family of products (i.e., oilseed and grain farming, vegetable and melon farming, fruit and tree nut farming) account for one-half or more of the establishment's agricultural production. Establishments with one-half or more crop production with no one product or family of products of an industry accounting for one-half of the establishment's agricultural production are treated as general combination crop farming and are classified in Industry 11199, All Other Crop Farming.

Industries in the Crop Production subsector include establishments that own, operate, and manage and those that operate and manage. Those that manage only are classified in Subsector 115, Support Activities for Agriculture and Forestry.

1111 Oilseed and Grain Farming

This industry group comprises establishments primarily engaged in (1) growing oilseed and/or grain crops and/or (2) producing oilseed and grain seeds. These crops have an annual life cycle and are typically grown in open fields.

111110 Soybean Farming

This industry comprises establishments primarily engaged in growing soybeans and/or producing soybean seeds.

Growing soybeans in combination with grain(s) with the soybeans or grain(s) not accounting for one-half of the establishment's agricultural production (value of crops for market) 111191

111120 Oilseed (except Soybean) Farming

This industry comprises establishments primarily engaged in growing fibrous oilseed producing plants and/or producing oilseed seeds, such as sunflower, safflower, flax, rape, canola, and sesame.

111130 Dry Pea and Bean Farming

This industry comprises establishments primarily engaged in growing dried peas, beans, and/or lentils.

Growing fresh green beans and peas 111219

111140 Wheat Farming

This industry comprises establishments primarily engaged in growing wheat and/or producing wheat seeds.

Growing wheat in combination with oilseed(s) with the wheat or oilseed(s) not accounting for one-half of the establishment's agricultural production (value of crops for market) 111191

111150 Corn Farming

This industry comprises establishments primarily engaged in growing corn (except sweet corn) and/or producing corn seeds.

111160 Rice Farming

This industry comprises establishments primarily engaged in growing rice (except wild rice) and/or producing rice seeds.

11119 Other Grain Farming

This industry comprises establishments primarily engaged in (1) growing grain(s) and/or producing grain seeds (except wheat, corn, and rice) or (2) growing a combination of grain(s) and oilseed(s) with no one grain (or family of grains) or oilseed (or family of oilseeds) accounting for one-half of the establishment's agriculture production (value of crops for market). Combination grain(s) and oilseed(s) establishments may produce oilseed(s) and grain(s) seeds and/or grow oilseed(s) and grain(s).

111191 Oilseed and Grain Combination Farming[US]

This U.S. industry comprises establishments engaged in growing a combination of oilseed(s) and grain(s) with no one oilseed (or family of oilseeds) or grain (or family of grains) accounting for one-half of the establishment's agricultural production (value of crops for market). These establishments may produce oilseed(s) and grain(s) seeds and/or grow oilseed(s) and grain(s).

Growing one grain (or family of grains) or oilseed (or family of oilseeds) accounting for one-half of the establishment's agriculture production (value of crops for market) 1111

111199 All Other Grain Farming[US]

This U.S. industry comprises establishments primarily engaged in growing grains and/or producing grain(s) seeds (except wheat, corn, rice, and oilseed(s) and grain(s) combinations).

1112 Vegetable and Melon Farming

This industry group comprises establishments primarily engaged in growing root and tuber crops (except sugar beets and peanuts) or edible plants and/or producing root and tuber or edible plant seeds. The crops included in this group have an annual growth cycle and are grown in open fields. Climate and cultural practices limit producing areas but often permit the growing of a combination of crops in a year.

11121 Vegetable and Melon Farming

This industry comprises establishments primarily engaged in one or more of the following: (1) growing vegetable and/or melon crops; (2) producing vegetable and melon seeds; and (3) growing vegetable and/or melon bedding plants.

111211 Potato Farming^{CAN}

This U.S. industry comprises establishments primarily engaged in growing potatoes and/or producing seed potatoes (except sweet potatoes).

111219 Other Vegetable (except Potato) and Melon Farming^{CAN}

This U.S. industry comprises establishments primarily engaged in one or more of the following: (1) growing melons and/or vegetables (except potatoes; dry peas; dry beans; field, silage, or seed corn; and sugar beets); (2) producing vegetable and/or melon seeds; and (3) growing vegetable and/or melon bedding plants.

Growing potatoes 111211
Growing sugar beets 111991
Growing vegetables and melons under glass or protective cover 111419
Growing dry peas and beans 111130
Growing corn (except sweet corn) 111150
Canning, pickling, and/or drying (artificially) vegetables 31142
Growing fruit on trees and other fruit-bearing plants (except melons) 1113

1113 Fruit and Tree Nut Farming

This industry group comprises establishments primarily engaged in growing fruit and/or tree nut crops. The crops included in this industry group are generally not grown from seeds and have a perennial life cycle.

111310 Orange Groves

This industry comprises establishments primarily engaged in growing oranges.

111320 Citrus (except Orange) Groves

This industry comprises establishments primarily engaged in growing citrus fruits (except oranges).

Growing oranges 111310

11133 Noncitrus Fruit and Tree Nut Farming

This industry comprises establishments primarily engaged in one or more of the following: (1) growing noncitrus fruits (e.g., apples, grapes, berries, peaches); (2) growing tree nuts (e.g., pecans, almonds, pistachios); or (3) growing a combination of fruit(s) and tree nut(s) with no one fruit (or family of fruit) or family of tree nuts accounting for one-half of the establishment's agriculture production (value of crops for market).

111331 Apple Orchards^{US}

This U.S. industry comprises establishments primarily engaged in growing apples.

Growing apples in combination with tree nut(s) with the apples or family of tree nuts not accounting for one-half of the establishment's agriculture production (i.e., value of crops for market) 111336

111332 Grape Vineyards^{US}

This U.S. industry comprises establishments primarily engaged in growing grapes and/or growing grapes to sun dry into raisins.

111333 Strawberry Farming^{US}

This U.S. industry comprises establishments primarily engaged in growing strawberries.

Growing strawberries in combination with tree nut(s) with the strawberries or family of tree nuts not accounting for one-half of the establishment's agriculture production (i.e., value of crops for market) 111336

111334 Berry (except Strawberry) Farming^{US}

This U.S. industry comprises establishments primarily engaged in growing berries.

111335 Tree Nut Farming^{US}

This U.S. industry comprises establishments primarily engaged in growing tree nuts.

111336 Fruit and Tree Nut Combination Farming^{US}

This U.S. industry comprises establishments primarily engaged in growing a combination of fruit[s] and tree nut[s] with no one fruit (or family of fruit) or family of tree nuts accounting for one-half of the establishment's agriculture production (i.e., value of crops for market).

Growing fruit(s) or the family of tree nut(s) accounting for one-half of the establishment's agriculture production (i.e., value of crops for market) 1113

111339 Other Noncitrus Fruit Farming^{US}

This U.S. industry comprises establishments primarily engaged in growing noncitrus fruits (except apples, grapes, berries, and fruit[s] and tree nut[s] combinations).

1114 Greenhouse, Nursery, and Floriculture Production

This industry group comprises establishments primarily engaged in growing crops of any kind under cover and/or growing nursery stock and flowers. "Under cover" is generally defined as greenhouses, cold frames, cloth houses, and lath houses. The crops grown are removed at various stages of maturity and have annual and perennial life cycles. The nursery stock includes short rotation woody crops that have growth cycles of 10 years or less.

11141 Food Crops Grown Under Cover

This industry comprises establishments primarily engaged in growing food crops (e.g., fruits, melons, tomatoes) under glass or protective cover.

Growing vegetable and melon bedding plants 11121

111411 Mushroom Production^{CAN}

This U.S. industry comprises establishments primarily engaged in growing mushrooms under cover in mines underground, or in other controlled environments.

111419 Other Food Crops Grown Under Cover^{CAN}

This U.S. industry comprises establishments primarily engaged in growing food crops (except mushrooms) under glass or protective cover.

Growing mushrooms under cover 111411

11142 Nursery and Floriculture Production

This industry comprises establishments primarily engaged in (1) growing nursery and floriculture products (e.g., nursery stock, shrubbery, cut flowers, flower seeds, foliage plants) under cover or in open fields and/or (2) growing short rotation woody trees with a growing and harvesting cycle of 10 years or less for pulp or tree stock (e.g., cut Christmas trees, cottonwoods).

111421 Nursery and Tree Production^{CAN}

This U.S. industry comprises establishments primarily engaged in (1) growing nursery products, nursery stock, shrubbery, bulbs, fruit stock, sod, and so forth, under cover or in open fields and/or (2) growing short rotation woody trees with a growth and harvest cycle of 10 years or less for pulp or tree stock.

111422 Floriculture Production^{CAN}

This U.S. industry comprises establishments primarily engaged in growing and/or producing floriculture products (e.g., cut flowers and roses, cut cultivated greens, potted flowering and foliage plants, and flower seeds) under cover and in open fields.

Retailing floriculture products primarily purchased from others 444220

1119 Other Crop Farming

This industry group comprises establishments primarily engaged in (1) growing crops (except oilseed and/or grain; vegetable and/or melon; fruit and tree nut; and greenhouse, nursery, and/or floriculture products). These establishments grow crops, such as tobacco, cotton, sugarcane, hay, sugar beets, peanuts, agave, herbs and spices, and hay and grass seeds; or (2) growing a combination of crops (except a combination of oilseed[s] and grain[s] and a combination of fruit[s] and tree nut[s]).

111910 Tobacco Farming

This industry comprises establishments primarily engaged in growing tobacco.

111920 Cotton Farming

This industry comprises establishments primarily engaged in growing cotton.

Ginning cotton **115111**

111930 Sugarcane Farming

This industry comprises establishments primarily engaged in growing sugarcane.

111940 Hay Farming

This industry comprises establishments primarily engaged in growing hay, alfalfa, clover, and/or mixed hay.

11199 All Other Crop Farming

This industry comprises establishments primarily engaged in (1) growing crops (except oilseeds and/or grains; vegetables and/or melons; fruits and/or tree nuts; greenhouse, nursery and/or floriculture products; tobacco; cotton; sugarcane; or hay) or (2) growing a combination of crops (except a combination of oilseed[s] and grain[s]; and a combination of fruit[s]

and tree nut[s]) with no one crop or family of crops accounting for one-half of the establishment's agricultural production (i.e., value of crops for market).

111991 Sugar Beet Farming[US]

This U.S. industry comprises establishments primarily engaged in growing sugar beets.

Growing beets (except sugar beets) **111219**

111992 Peanut Farming[US]

This U.S. industry comprises establishments primarily engaged in growing peanuts.

111998 All Other Miscellaneous Crop Farming[US]

This U.S. industry comprises establishments primarily engaged in one of the following: (1) growing crops (except oilseeds and/or grains; vegetables and/or melons; fruits and/or tree nuts; greenhouse, nursery and/or floriculture products; tobacco; cotton; sugarcane; hay; sugar beets; peanuts); (2) growing a combination of crops (except a combination of oilseed[s] and grain[s]; and a combination of fruit[s] and tree nut[s]) with no one crop or family of crop(s) accounting for one-half of the establishment's agricultural production (i.e., value of crops for market); or (3) gathering tea or maple sap.

112 Animal Production

Industries in the Animal Production subsector raise or fatten animals for the sale of animals or animal products. The subsector comprises establishments, such as ranches, farms, and feedlots primarily engaged in keeping, grazing, breeding, or feeding animals. These animals are kept for the products they produce or for eventual sale. The animals are generally raised in various environments, from total confinement or captivity to feeding on an open range pasture. The industries in this subsector are grouped by important factors, such as suitable grazing or pasture land, specialized buildings, type of equipment, and the amount and types of labor required.

Establishments are classified to the Animal Production subsector when animal production (i.e., value of animals for market) accounts for one-half or more of the establishment's total agricultural production. Establishments with one-half or more animal production with no one animal product or family of animal products of an industry accounting for one-half of the establishment's agricultural production are treated as combination animal farming classified to Industry 11299, All Other Animal Production.

1121 Cattle Ranching and Farming

This industry group comprises establishments primarily engaged in raising cattle, milking dairy cattle, or feeding cattle for fattening.

11211 Beef Cattle Ranching and Farming, including Feedlots

This industry comprises establishments primarily engaged in raising cattle (including cattle for dairy herd replacements), or feeding cattle for fattening.

112111 Beef Cattle Ranching and Farming^{US}

This U.S. industry comprises establishments primarily engaged in raising cattle (including cattle for dairy herd replacements).

Milking dairy cattle **112120**

112112 Cattle Feedlots^{US}

This U.S. industry comprises establishments primarily engaged in feeding cattle for fattening.

Operating stockyards for transportation and not buying, selling, or auctioning livestock **488999**

112120 Dairy Cattle and Milk Production

This industry comprises establishments primarily engaged in milking dairy cattle.

112130 Dual-Purpose Cattle Ranching and Farming

This industry comprises establishments primarily engaged in raising cattle for both milking and meat production.

1122 Hog and Pig Farming

112210 Hog and Pig Farming

This industry comprises establishments primarily engaged in raising hogs and pigs. These establishments may include farming activities, such as breeding, farrowing, and the raising of weanling pigs, feeder pigs, or market size hogs.

Operating stockyards for transportation and not buying, selling, or auctioning livestock **488999**

1123 Poultry and Egg Production

This industry group comprises establishments primarily engaged in breeding, hatching, and raising poultry for meat or egg production.

112310 Chicken Egg Production

This industry comprises establishments primarily engaged in raising chickens for egg production. The eggs produced may be for use as table eggs or hatching eggs.

Raising chickens for the production of meat **112320**

112320 Broilers and Other Meat Type Chicken Production

This industry comprises establishments primarily engaged in raising broilers, fryers, roasters, and other meat type chickens.

Raising chickens for egg production **112310**

112330 Turkey Production

This industry comprises establishments primarily engaged in raising turkeys for meat or egg production.

112340 Poultry Hatcheries

This industry comprises establishments primarily engaged in hatching poultry of any kind.

112390 Other Poultry Production

This industry comprises establishments primarily engaged in raising poultry (except chickens for meat or egg production and turkeys).

1124 Sheep and Goat Farming

This industry group comprises establishments primarily engaged in raising sheep, lambs, and goats, or feeding lambs for fattening.

112410 Sheep Farming

This industry comprises establishments primarily engaged in raising sheep and lambs, or feeding lambs for fattening. The sheep or lambs may be raised for sale or wool production.

Operating stockyards for transportation and not buying, selling, or auctioning livestock **488999**

112420 Goat Farming

This industry comprises establishments primarily engaged in raising goats.

1125 Animal Aquaculture

11251 Animal Aquaculture

This industry comprises establishments primarily engaged in the farm raising of finfish, shellfish, or any other kind of animal aquaculture. These establishments use some form of intervention in the rearing process to enhance production, such as holding in captivity, regular stocking, feeding, and protecting from predators.

The catching or taking of fish and other aquatic animals from their natural habitat **11411**

112511 Finfish Farming and Fish Hatcheries[US]

This U.S. industry comprises establishments primarily engaged in (1) farm raising finfish (e.g., catfish, trout, goldfish, tropical fish, minnows) and/or (2) hatching fish of any kind.

The catching or taking of finfish from their natural habitat **114111**

112512 Shellfish Farming[US]

This U.S. industry comprises establishments primarily engaged in farm raising shellfish (e.g., crayfish, shrimp, oysters, clams, mollusks).

The catching or taking of shellfish from their natural habitat **114112**

112519 Other Animal Aquaculture[US]

This U.S. industry comprises establishments primarily engaged in farm raising animal aquaculture (except finfish and shellfish). Alligator, frog, or turtle production is included in this industry.

1129 Other Animal Production

This industry group comprises establishments prima-rily engaged in raising animals and insects (except cattle, hogs and pigs, poultry, sheep and goats, animal aquaculture) for sale or product production. These establishments are primarily engaged in raising one of the following: bees, horses and other equines, rabbits and other fur-bearing animals, and so forth, and producing products, such as honey and other bee products. Establishments primarily engaged in raising a combination of animals with no one animal or family of animals accounting for one-half of the establishment's agricultural production (i.e., value of animals for market) are included in this industry group.

112910 Apiculture

This industry comprises establishments primarily engaged in raising bees. These establishments may collect and gather honey; and/or sell queen bees, packages of bees, royal jelly, bees' wax, propolis, venom, and/or other bee products.

112920 Horses and Other Equine Production

This industry comprises establishments primarily engaged in raising horses, mules, donkeys, and other equines.

112930 Fur-Bearing Animal and Rabbit Production

This industry comprises establishments primarily engaged in raising fur-bearing animals including rabbits. These animals may be raised for sale or for their pelt production.

The trapping or hunting of wild fur-bearing animals **114210**

112990 All Other Animal Production

This industry comprises establishments primarily engaged in: (1) raising animals (except cattle, hogs and pigs, poultry, sheep and goats, animal aquaculture, apiculture, horses and other equines; and fur-bearing animals including rabbits) or (2) raising a combination of animals, with no one animal or family of animals accounting for one-half of the establishment's agricultural production (i.e., value of animals for market) are included in this industry.

113 Forestry and Logging

Industries in the Forestry and Logging subsector grow and harvest timber on a long production cycle (i.e., of 10 years or more). Long production cycles use different production processes than short production cycles, which require more horticultural interventions prior to harvest, resulting in processes more similar to those found in the Crop Production subsector. Consequently, Christmas tree production and other production involving production cycles of less than 10 years, are classified in the Crop Production subsector.

Industries in this subsector specialize in different stages of the production cycle. Reforestation requires production of seedlings in specialized nurseries. Timber production requires natural forest or suitable areas of land that are available for a long duration. The maturation time for timber depends upon the species of tree, the climatic conditions of the region, and the intended purpose of the timber. The harvesting of timber (except when done on an extremely small scale) requires specialized machinery unique to the industry. Establishments gathering forest products, such as gums, barks, balsam needles, rhizomes, fibers, Spanish moss, and ginseng and truffles, are also included in this subsector.

1131 Timber Tract Operations

113110 Timber Tract Operations

This industry comprises establishments primarily engaged in the operation of timber tracts for the purpose of selling standing timber.

1132 Forest Nurseries and Gathering of Forest Products

113210 Forest Nurseries and Gathering of Forest Products

This industry comprises establishments primarily engaged in (1) growing trees for reforestation and/or (2) gathering forest products, such as gums, barks, balsam needles, rhizomes, fibers, Spanish moss, ginseng, and truffles.

1133 Logging

113310 Logging

This industry comprises establishments primarily engaged in one or more of the following: (1) cutting timber; (2) cutting and transporting timber; and (3) producing wood chips in the field.

Trucking timber **484220**

114 Fishing, Hunting and Trapping

Industries in the Fishing, Hunting, and Trapping subsector harvest fish and other wild animals from their natural habitats and are dependent upon a continued supply of the natural resource. The harvesting of fish is the predominant economic activity of this subsector and it usually requires specialized vessels that, by the nature of their size, configuration and equipment, are not suitable for any other type of production, such as transportation.

Hunting and trapping activities utilize a wide variety of production processes and are classified in the same subsector as fishing because the availability of resources and the constraints imposed, such as conservation requirements and proper habitat maintenance, are similar.

1141 Fishing

11411 Fishing

This industry comprises establishments primarily engaged in the commercial catching or taking of finfish, shellfish, or miscellaneous marine products from a natural habitat, such as the catching of bluefish, eels, salmon, tuna, clams, crabs, lobsters, mussels, oysters, shrimp, frogs, sea urchins, and turtles.

114111 Finfish Fishing[US]

This U.S. industry comprises establishments primarily engaged in the commercial catching or taking of finfish (e.g., bluefish, salmon, trout, tuna) from their natural habitat.

114112 Shellfish Fishing[US]

This U.S. industry comprises establishments prima-rily engaged in the commercial catching or taking of shellfish (e.g., clams, crabs, lobsters, mussels, oysters, sea urchins, shrimp) from their natural habitat.

Farm raising shellfish 112512

114119 Other Marine Fishing[US]

This U.S. industry comprises establishments primarily engaged in the commercial catching or taking of marine animals (except finfish and shellfish).

1142 Hunting and Trapping

114210 Hunting and Trapping

This industry comprises establishments primarily engaged in one or more of the following: (1) commercial hunting and trapping; (2) operating commercial game preserves, such as game retreats; and (3) operating hunting preserves.

115 Support Activities for Agriculture and Forestry

Industries in the Support Activities for Agriculture and Forestry subsector provide support services that are an essential part of agricultural and forestry production. These support activities may be performed by the agriculture or forestry producing establishment or conducted independently as an alternative source of inputs required for the production process for a given crop, animal, or forestry industry. Establishments that primarily perform these activities independent of the agriculture or forestry producing establishment are in this subsector.

1151 Support Activities for Crop Production

11511 Support Activities for Crop Production

This industry comprises establishments primarily engaged in providing support activities for growing crops.

115111 Cotton Ginning[US]

This U.S. industry comprises establishments prima-rily engaged in ginning cotton.

115112 Soil Preparation, Planting, and Cultivating[US]

This U.S. industry comprises establishments prima-rily engaged in performing a soil preparation activity or crop production service, such as plowing, fertilizing, seed bed preparation, planting, cultivating, and crop protecting services.

115113 Crop Harvesting, Primarily by Machine[US]

This U.S. industry comprises establishments prima-rily engaged in mechanical harvesting, picking, and combining of crops, and related activities. The machinery used is provided by the servicing establishment.

115114 Postharvest Crop Activities (except Cotton Ginning)[US]

This U.S. industry comprises establishments prima-rily engaged in performing services on crops, subsequent to their harvest, with the intent of preparing them for market or further processing. These establishments provide postharvest activities, such as crop cleaning, sun drying, shelling, fumigating, curing, sorting, grading, packing, and cooling.

115115 Farm Labor Contractors and Crew Leaders[US]

This U.S. industry comprises establishments primarily engaged in supplying labor for agricultural production or harvesting.

115116 Farm Management Services[US]

This U.S. industry comprises establishments primarily engaged in providing farm management services on a contract or fee basis usually to citrus groves, orchards, or vineyards. These establishments always provide management and may arrange or contract for the partial or the complete operations of the farm establishment(s) it manages. Operational activities may include cultivating, harvesting, and/or other specialized agricultural support activities.

1152 Support Activities for Animal Production

115210 Support Activities for Animal Production

This industry comprises establishments primarily engaged in performing support activities related to raising livestock (e.g., cattle, goats, hogs, horses, poultry, sheep). These establishments may perform one or more of the following: (1) breeding services for animals, including companion animals (e.g., cats, dogs, pet birds); (2) pedigree record services; (3) boarding horses; (4) dairy herd improvement activities; (5) livestock spraying; and (6) sheep dipping and shearing.

1153 Support Activities for Forestry

115310 Support Activities for Forestry

This industry comprises establishments primarily engaged in performing particular support activities related to timber production, wood technology, forestry economics and marketing, and forest protection. These establishments may provide support activities for forestry, such as estimating timber, forest firefighting, forest pest control, and consulting on wood attributes and reforestation.

Public administration and conservation of forest lands **924120**

SECTOR 21:   MINING

OVERVIEW OF THIS SECTOR AS A WHOLE

The Mining sector comprises establishments that extract naturally occurring mineral solids, such as coal and ores; liquid minerals, such as crude petroleum; and gases, such as natural gas. The term mining is used in the broad sense to include quarrying, well operations, beneficiating (e.g., crushing, screening, washing, and flotation), and other preparation customarily performed at the mine site, or as a part of mining activity.

The Mining sector distinguishes two basic activities: mine operation and mining support activities. Mine operation includes establishments operating mines, quarries, or oil and gas wells on their own account or for others on a contract or fee basis. Mining support activities include establishments that perform exploration (except geophysical surveying) and/or other mining services on a contract or fee basis.

Establishments in the Mining sector are grouped and classified according to the natural resource mined or to be mined. Industries include establishments that develop the mine site, extract the

---

211

natural resources, and /or those that beneficiate (i.e., prepare) the mineral mined. Beneficiation is the process whereby the extracted material is reduced to particles that can be separated into mineral and waste, the former suitable for further processing or direct use. The operations that take place in beneficiation are primarily mechanical, such as grinding, washing, magnetic separation, and centrifugal separation. In contrast, manufacturing operations primarily use chemical and electro-chemical processes, such as electrolysis and distillation. However some treatments, such as heat treatments, take place in both the beneficiation and the manufacturing (i.e., smelting/refining) stages. The range of preparation activities varies by mineral and the purity of any given ore deposit. While some minerals, such as petroleum and natural gas, require little or no preparation, others are washed and screened, while yet others, such as gold and silver, can be transformed into bullion before leaving the mine site.

Mining, beneficiating, and manufacturing activities often occur in a single location. Separate receipts will be collected for these activities whenever possible. When receipts cannot be broken out between mining and manufacturing, establishments that mine or quarry nonmetallic minerals, beneficiate the nonmetallic minerals into more finished manufactured products are classified based on the primary activity of the establishment. A mine that manufactures a small amount of finished products will be classified in Sector 21, Mining. An establishment that mines whose primary output is a more finished manufactured product will be classified in Sector 31-33, Manufacturing.

211 Oil and Gas Extraction

Industries in the Oil and Gas Extraction subsector operate and/or develop oil and gas field properties. Such activities may include exploration for crude petroleum and natural gas; drilling, completing, and equipping wells; operating separators, emulsion breakers, desilting equipment, and field gathering lines for crude petroleum; and all other activities in the preparation of oil and gas up to the point of shipment from the producing property. This subsector includes the production of crude petroleum, the mining and extraction of oil from oil shale and oil sands, and the production of natural gas and recovery of hydrocarbon liquids.

Establishments in this subsector include those that operate oil and gas wells on their own account or for others on a contract or fee basis. Establishments primarily engaged in providing support services, on a fee or contract basis, required for the drilling or operation of oil and gas wells (except geophysical surveying and mapping) are classified in Subsector 213, Support Activities for Mining.

2IIII Oil and Gas Extraction

This industry comprises establishments primarily engaged in operating and/or developing oil and gas field properties and establishments primarily engaged in recovering liquid hydrocarbons from oil and gas field gases. Such activities may include exploration for crude petroleum and natural gas; drilling, completing, and equipping wells; operation of separators, emulsion breakers, desilting equipment, and field gathering lines for crude petroleum; and all other activi-ties in the preparation of oil and gas up to the point of shipment from the producing property. This industry includes the production of crude petroleum, the mining and extraction of oil from oil shale and oil sands, the production of natural gas and the recovery of hydrocarbon liquids from oil and gas field gases. Establishments in this industry operate oil and gas wells on their own account or for others on a contract or fee basis.

Performing oil field services for operators on a contract or fee basis **2I3II**

Manufacturing acyclic and cyclic aromatic hydrocarbons from refined
   petroleum or liquid hydrocarbons **32511**
Refining crude petroleum into refined petroleum and liquid hydrocarbons
   32411
Recovering helium from natural gas **32512**

211111 Crude Petroleum and Natural Gas Extraction[US]

This U.S. industry comprises establishments primarily engaged in (1) the exploration, development and/or the production of petroleum or natural gas from wells in which the hydrocarbons will initially flow or can be produced using normal pumping techniques, or (2) the production of crude petroleum from surface shales or tar sands or from reservoirs in which the hydrocarbons are semisolids. Establishments in this industry operate oil and gas wells on their own account or for others on a contract or fee basis.

Performing oil field services for operators on a contract or fee basis **21311**
Refining crude petroleum into refined petroleum and liquid hydrocarbons
   324110
Recovering helium from natural gas **325120**

211112 Natural Gas Liquid Extraction[US]

This U.S. industry comprises establishments primarily engaged in the recovery of liquid hydrocarbons from oil and gas field gases. Establishments primarily engaged in sulfur recovery from natural gas are included in this industry.

Manufacturing acyclic and cyclic aromatic hydrocarbons from refined
   petroleum or converting refined petroleum into liquid hydrocarbons
   (petrochemicals) and/or recovering liquid hydrocarbons **325110**
Refining crude petroleum into refined petroleum and liquid hydrocarbons
   324110
Recovering helium from natural gas **325120**

212 Mining (except Oil and Gas)

Industries in the Mining (except Oil and Gas) subsector primarily engage in mining, mine site development, and beneficiating (i.e, preparing) metallic minerals and nonmetallic minerals, including coal. The term "mining" is used in the broad sense to include ore extraction, quarrying, and beneficiating (e.g., crushing, screening, washing, sizing, concentrating, and flotation), customarily done at the mine site.

Beneficiation is the process whereby the extracted material is reduced to particles that can be separated into mineral and waste, the former suitable for further processing or direct use. The operations that take place in beneficiation are primarily mechanical, such as grinding, washing, magnetic separation, centrifugal separation, and so on. In contrast, manufacturing operations primarily use chemical and electrochemical processes, such as electrolysis, distillation, and so on. However some treatments, such as heat treatments, take place in both stages: the beneficiation and the manufacturing (i.e., smelting/refining) stages. The range of preparation activities varies by mineral and the purity of any given ore deposit. While some minerals, such as petroleum and natural gas, require little or no preparation, others are washed and screened, while yet others, such as gold and silver, can be transformed into bullion before leaving the mine site. Establishments in the Mining (except Oil and Gas) subsector include those that have complete responsibility for operating mines and quarries (except oil and gas wells) and those that operate mines and quarries (except oil and gas wells) for others on a contract or fee basis. Establishments primarily engaged in providing support services, on a contract or fee basis, required for the mining and quarrying of minerals are classified in Subsector 213, Support Activities for Mining.

21211 Coal Mining

This industry comprises establishments primarily engaged in one or more of the following: (1) mining bituminous coal, anthracite, and lignite by underground mining, auger mining, strip mining, culm bank mining, and other surface mining; (2) developing coal mine sites; and (3) beneficiating (i.e, preparing) coal (e.g., cleaning, washing, screening, and sizing coal).

Manufacturing code oven products in coke oven establishments **32419**
Manufacturing coal products in steel mills **33111**

212111 Bituminous Coal and Lignite Surface Mining[US]

This U.S. industry comprises establishments primarily engaged in one or more of the following: (1) surface mining or development of bituminous coal and lignite; (2) developing bituminous coal and lignite surface mine sites; and (3) beneficiating bituminous coal (e.g., cleaning, washing, screening, and sizing coal) whether mined on surface or underground.

Manufacturing coke oven products in coke oven establishments **324199**
Underground mining of bituminous coal **212112**
Mining and/or beneficiating anthracite coal **212113**

212112 Bituminous Coal Underground Mining[US]

This U.S. industry comprises establishments primarily engaged in one or more of the following: (1) the underground mining of bituminous coal; (2) developing bituminous coal underground mine sites; and (3) the underground mining and beneficiating bituminous coal (e.g, cleaning, washing, screening, and sizing coal).

Manufacturing coke oven products in coke oven establishments **324199**
Surface mining and/or beneficiating of bituminous coal or lignite **212111**
Mining and/or beneficiating anthracite coal **212113**

212113 Anthracite Mining[US]

This U.S. industry comprises establishments primarily engaged in one or more of the following: (1) mining anthracite coal; (2) developing anthracite coal mining sites; and (3) beneficiating anthracite coal (e.g., cleaning, washing, screening, and sizing coal).

Manufacturing coke oven products in coke oven establishments **324199**
Surface mining and/or beneficiating bituminous coal or lignite **212111**
Underground mining of bituminous coal **212112**

2122 Metal Ore Mining

This industry group comprises establishments primarily engaged in developing mine sites or mining metallic minerals, and establishments primarily engaged in ore dressing and beneficiating (i.e., preparing) operations, such as crushing, grinding, washing, drying, sintering, concentrating, calcining, and leaching. Beneficiating may be performed at mills operated in conjunction with the mines served or at mills, such as custom mills, operated separately.

212210 Iron Ore Mining

This industry comprises establishments primarily engaged in (1) developing mine sites, mining, and/or beneficiating (i.e., preparing) iron ores and manganiferous ores valued chiefly for their iron content and/or (2) producing sinter iron ore (except iron ore produced in iron and steel mills) and other iron ore agglomerates.

Manufacturing pig iron ore **331111**

21222 Gold Ore and Silver Ore Mining

This industry comprises establishments primarily engaged in developing the mine site, mining, and/or beneficiating (i.e., preparing) ores valued chiefly for their gold and or silver content. Establishments primarily engaged in the transformation of the gold and silver into bullion or dore bar in combination with mining activities are included in this industry.

Manufacturing gold or silver bullion or dore bar without mining **33141**

212221 Gold Ore Mining[US]

This U.S. industry comprises establishments primarily engaged in developing the mine site, mining, and/ or beneficiating (i.e., preparing) ores valued chiefly for their gold content. Establishments primarily engaged in transformation of the gold into bullion or dore bar in combination with mining activities are included in this industry.

Manufacturing gold bullion or dore bar without mining **331419**

212222 Silver Ore Mining[US]

This U.S. industry comprises establishments primarily engaged in developing the mine site, mining, and/ or beneficiating (i.e, preparing) ores valued chiefly for their silver content. Establishments primarily engaged in transformation of the silver into bullion or dore bar in combination with mining activities are included in this industry.

Manufacturing silver bullion or dore bar without mining **331419**

21223 Copper, Nickel, Lead, and Zinc Mining

This industry comprises establishments primarily engaged in developing the mine site, mining, and/or beneficiating (i.e., preparing) ores valued chiefly for their copper, nickel, lead, or zinc content. Beneficiating includes the transformation of ores into concentrates.

212

Refining copper concentrates **33141**
Developing the mine site, mining, and/or beneficiating iron and
   manganiferous ores valued for their iron content **21221**

212231 Lead Ore and Zinc Ore Mining^{CAN}

This U.S. industry comprises establishments primarily engaged in developing the mine site, mining, and/
or beneficiating (i.e., preparing) lead ores, zinc ores,
or lead-zinc ores.

212234 Copper Ore and Nickel Ore Mining^{US}

This U.S. industry comprises establishments primarily engaged in (1) developing the mine site, mining,
and/or beneficiating (i.e, preparing) copper and/or
nickel ores, and (2) recovering copper concentrates
by the precipitation, leaching, or electrowinning of
copper ore.

Refining copper concentrates are **331411**

21229 Other Metal Ore Mining

This industry comprises establishments primarily
engaged in developing the mine site, mining, and/or
beneficiating (i.e., preparing) metal ores (except iron
and manganiferous ores valued for their iron content,
gold ore, silver ore, copper, nickel, lead, and zinc ore).

Developing the mine site, mining, and/or beneficiating iron and
   manganiferous ores valued chiefly for their iron content **21221**
Developing the mine site, mining, and/or beneficiating ores valued chiefly for
   their gold or silver content **21222**
Developing the mine site, mining, and/or beneficiating ores valued chiefly for
   their copper, nickel, lead, or zinc content **21223**
Enriching uranium **32518**

212291 Uranium-Radium-Vanadium Ore Mining^{US}

This U.S. industry comprises establishments primarily engaged in developing the mine site, mining, and/
or beneficiating (i.e., preparing) uranium-radium-
vanadium ores.

Enriching uranium **325188**

212299 All Other Metal Ore Mining^{US}

This U.S. industry comprises establishments primarily engaged in developing the mine site, mining, and/
or beneficiating (i.e., preparing) metal ores (except
iron and manganiferous ores valued for their iron
content, gold ore, silver ore, copper, nickel, lead, zinc,
and uranium-radium-vanadium ore).

Developing the mine site, mining, and/or beneficiating iron and
   manganiferous ores valued for their iron content **212210**
Developing the mine site, mining, and/or beneficiating ores valued chiefly for
   their gold or silver content **21222**
Developing the mine site, mining, and/or beneficiating ores valued chiefly for
   their copper, nickel, lead, or zinc content **21223**
Developing the mine site, mining, and/or beneficiating uranium-radium-
   vanadium ores **212291**

2123 Nonmetallic Mineral Mining and Quarrying

This industry group comprises establishments primarily engaged in developing mine sites, or in mining
or quarrying nonmetallic minerals (except fuels). Also
included are certain well and brine operations, and
preparation plants primarily engaged in beneficiating (e.g., crushing, grinding, washing, and concentrating) nonmetallic minerals.

Beneficiation is the process whereby the extracted
material is reduced to particles that can be separated
into mineral and waste, the former suitable for further processing or direct use. The operations that take
place in beneficiation are primarily mechanical, such
as grinding, washing, magnetic separation, and centrifugal separation. In contrast, manufacturing operations primarily use chemical and electrochemical
processes, such as electrolysis and distillation. However some treatments, such as heat treatments, take
place in both the beneficiation and the manufacturing (i.e., smelting/refining) stages. The range of preparation activities varies by mineral and the purity of
any given ore deposit. While some minerals, such as
petroleum and natural gas, require little or no preparation, others are washed and screened, while yet
others, such as gold and silver, can be transformed
into bullion before leaving the mine site.

21231 Stone Mining and Quarrying

This industry comprises (1) establishments primarily
engaged in developing the mine site, mining or quarrying dimension stone (i.e., rough blocks and/or slabs
of stone), or mining and quarrying crushed and broken stone and/or (2) preparation plants primarily
engaged in benefici-ating stone (e.g., crushing, grinding, washing, screening, pulverizing, and sizing).

Producing lime **32741**
Quarrying and dressing dimension stone **32799**

212311 Dimension Stone Mining and Quarrying^{US}

This U.S. industry comprises establishments primarily engaged in developing the mine site and/or mining or quarrying dimension stone (i.e., rough blocks and/or slabs of stone).

Dressing dimension stone and manufacturing stone products **327991**

212312 Crushed and Broken Limestone Mining and Quarrying^{US}

This U.S. industry comprises (1) establishments primarily engaged in developing the mine site, mining or quarrying crushed and broken limestone (including related rocks, such as dolomite, cement rock, marl, travertine, and calcareous tufa), and (2) preparation plants primarily engaged in beneficiating limestone (e.g., grinding or pulverizing).

Producing lime **327410**
Mining or quarrying bituminous limestone **212319**

212313 Crushed and Broken Granite Mining and Quarrying^{US}

This U.S. industry comprises (1) establishments primarily engaged in developing the mine site, and/or mining or quarrying crushed and broken granite (including related rocks, such as gneiss, syenite, and diorite) and (2) preparation plants primarily engaged in beneficiating granite (e.g. grinding or pulverizing).

212319 Other Crushed and Broken Stone Mining and Quarrying^{US}

This U.S. industry comprises (1) establishments primarily engaged in developing the mine site and/or mining or quarrying crushed and broken stone (except limestone and granite), (2) preparation plants primarily engaged in beneficiating (e.g., grinding and pulverizing) stone (except limestone and granite), and (3) establishments primarily engaged in mining or quarrying bituminous limestone and bituminous sandstone.

Mining or quarrying crushed and broken limestone **212312**
Mining or quarrying crushed and broken granite **212313**

21232 Sand, Gravel, Clay, and Ceramic and Refractory Minerals Mining and Quarrying

This industry comprises (1) establishments primarily

engaged in developing the mine site and/or mining, quarrying, dredging for sand and gravel, or mining clay, (e.g., china clay, paper clay and slip clay) and (2) preparation plants primarily engaged in beneficiating (e.g., washing, screening, and grinding) sand and gravel, clay, and ceramic and refractory minerals.

Calcining, dead burning, or otherwise processing (i.e., beyond basic preparation) clay or refractory minerals **32799**
Shaping, molding, baking, burning, or hardening nonclay ceramics, clay and nonclay refractories, and structural clay products **32712**
Shaping, molding, glazing, and firing pottery, ceramics, and plumbing fixtures **32711**

212321 Construction Sand and Gravel Mining^{US}

This U.S. industry comprises establishments primarily engaged in one or more of the following: (1) operating commercial grade (i.e., construction) sand and gravel pits; (2) dredging for commercial grade sand and gravel; and (3) washing, screening, or otherwise preparing commercial grade sand and gravel.

Mining industrial grade sand **212322**

212322 Industrial Sand Mining^{US}

This U.S. industry comprises establishments primarily engaged in one or more of the following: (1) operating industrial grade sand pits; (2) dredging for industrial grade sand; and (3) washing, screening, or otherwise preparing industrial grade sand.

Mining commercial (i.e., construction) grade gravel **212321**

212324 Kaolin and Ball Clay Mining^{US}

This U.S. industry comprises (1) establishments primarily engaged in developing the mine site and/or mining kaolin or ball clay (e.g., china clay, paper clay, and slip clay) and (2) establishments primarily engaged in beneficiating (i.e., preparing) kaolin or ball clay.

Calcining, dead burning, or otherwise processing (i.e., beyond basic preparation) kaolin and ball clay **327992**

212325 Clay and Ceramic and Refractory Minerals Mining^{US}

This U.S. industry comprises establishments primarily engaged in one or more of the following: (1) mining clay (except kaolin and ball), ceramic, or refractory minerals; (2) developing the mine site for clay, ceramic, or refractory minerals; and (3) beneficiating (i.e., preparing) clay (except kaolin and ball), ceramic, or refractory minerals.

Shaping, molding, baking, burning, or hardening clay and nonclay refractories, and structural clay products **32712**
Developing the mine site, mining, and/or beneficiating kaolin or ball clay **212324**
Shaping, molding, glazing, and firing pottery, ceramics, and plumbing fixtures **32711**

21239 Other Nonmetallic Mineral Mining and Quarrying

This industry comprises establishments primarily engaged in developing the mine site, mining, and/or milling or otherwise beneficiating (i.e., preparing) nonmetallic minerals (except coal, stone, sand, gravel, clay, ceramic, and refractory minerals).

Mining or quarrying dimension stone **21231**
Mining or quarrying sand, gravel, clay and ceramic and refractory minerals **21232**
Calcining, dead burning, or otherwise processing (i.e., beyond basic preparation) minerals, such as talc, mica, feldspar, barite, and soapstone **32799**
Manufacturing boron compounds and potassium salts **32518**
Manufacturing table salt **31194**
Manufacturing salt (except table salt) **32599**
Manufacturing phosphoric acid, superphosphates, or other phosphatic fertilizer materials **32531**

212391 Potash, Soda, and Borate Mineral Mining[US]

This U.S. industry comprises establishments primarily engaged in developing the mine site, mining and/or milling, or otherwise beneficiating (i.e., preparing) natural potassium, sodium, or boron compounds. Drylake brine operations are included in this industry, as well as establishments engaged in producing the specified minerals from underground and open pit mines.

Manufacturing boron compounds and potassium salts **325188**
Manufacturing sodium carbonate **325181**
Manufacturing table salt **311942**

212392 Phosphate Rock Mining[US]

This U.S. industry comprises establishments primarily engaged in developing the mine site, mining, milling, and/or drying or otherwise beneficiating (i.e., preparing) phosphate rock.

Manufacturing phosphoric acid, superphosphates, or other phosphatic fertilizer materials **325312**

212393 Other Chemical and Fertilizer Mineral Mining[US]

This U.S. industry comprises establishments primarily engaged in developing the mine site, mining, milling, and/or drying or otherwise beneficiating (i.e., preparing) chemical or fertilizer mineral raw materials (except potash, soda, boron, and phosphate rock).

Mining and/or milling or otherwise beneficiating natural potassium, sodium, or boron compounds **212391**
Manufacturing industrial salt **325998**
Mining, milling, drying, and/or sintering or otherwise beneficiating phosphate rock **212392**
Manufacturing table salt **311942**

212399 All Other Nonmetallic Mineral Mining[US]

This U.S. industry comprises establishments primarily engaged in developing the mine site, mining and/or milling or otherwise beneficiating (i.e., preparing) nonmetallic minerals (except stone, sand, gravel, clay, ceramic, refractory minerals, chemical and fertilizer minerals).

Mining or quarrying dimension stone **21231**
Mining, quarrying, or beneficiating sand, gravel, clay, and ceramic and refractory minerals **21232**
Mining, quarrying or beneficiating natural potash, soda, and borate **212391**
Mining and/or milling or otherwise beneficiating phosphate rock **212392**

213 Support Activities for Mining

Industries in the Support Activities for Mining subsector group establishments primarily providing support services, on a fee or contract basis, required for the mining and quarrying of minerals and for the extraction of oil and gas. Establishments performing exploration (except geophysical surveying and mapping) for minerals, on a contract or fee basis, are included in this subsector. Exploration includes traditional prospecting methods, such as taking core samples and making geological observations at prospective sites.

The activities performed on a fee or contract basis by establishments in the Support Activities for Mining subsector are also often performed in-house by mining operators. These activities include: taking core samples, making geological observations at prospective sites, and such oil and gas operations as spudding in, drilling in, redrilling, directional drilling, excavating slush pits and cellars; grading and building foundations at well locations; well surveying; running, cutting, and pulling casings, tubes and rods; cementing wells; shooting wells; perforating well casings; acidizing and chemically treating wells; and cleaning out, bailing, and swabbing wells.

213

21311 Support Activities for Mining

This industry comprises establishments primarily engaged in providing support services, on a fee or contract basis, required for the mining and quarrying of minerals and for the extraction of oil and gas. Drilling, taking core samples, and making geological observations at prospective sites (except geophysical surveying and mapping) for minerals, on a fee or contract basis, is included in this industry.

Performing geophysical surveying services for minerals (i.e., coal, metal ores, oil and gas, and nonmetallic minerals) on a contract or fee basis **54136**
Mining, quarrying, and/or beneficiating on a contract or fee basis **212**
Operating oil and gas field properties on a contract or fee basis **211**

213111 Drilling Oil and Gas Wells^{CAN}

This U.S. industry comprises establishments primarily engaged in drilling oil and gas wells for others on a contract or fee basis. This industry includes contractors that specialize in spudding in, drilling in, redrilling, and directional drilling.

Performing exploration (except geophysical surveying and mapping) services for oil and gas on a contract or fee basis **213112**
Performing geophysical surveying and mapping services for oil and gas on a contract or fee basis **541360**

213112 Support Activities for Oil and Gas Operations^{US}

This U.S. industry comprises establishments primarily engaged in performing oil and gas field services (except contract drilling) for others, on a contract or fee basis. Services included are exploration (except geophysical surveying and mapping); excavating slush pits and cellars; grading and building foundations at well locations; well surveying; running, cutting, and pulling casings, tubes, and rods; cementing wells; shooting wells; perforating well casings; acidizing and chemically treating wells; and cleaning out, bailing, and swabbing wells.

Contract drilling for oil and gas **213111**
Operating oil and gas field properties on a contract or fee basis **211**

Performing geophysical surveying and mapping services for oil and gas on a contract or fee basis **541360**

213113 Support Activities for Coal Mining^{US}

This U.S. industry comprises establishments primarily engaged in providing support services, on a fee or contract basis, required for coal mining. Exploration for coal is included in this industry. Exploration includes traditional prospecting methods, such as taking core samples and making geological observations at prospective sites.

Performing geophysical surveying services for coal on a contract or fee basis **541360**
Operating coal mines or quarries on a contract or fee basis **2121**

213114 Support Activities for Metal Mining^{US}

This U.S. industry comprises establishments primarily engaged in providing support services, on a fee or contract basis, required for the mining and quarrying of metallic minerals and for the extraction of metal ores. Exploration for minerals is included in this industry. Exploration (except geophysical surveying and mapping services) includes traditional prospecting methods, such as taking core samples and making geological observations at prospective sites.

Performing geophysical surveying services for metallic minerals on a contract or fee basis **541360**
Operating metallic mineral mines or quarries on a contract or fee basis **2122**

213115 Support Activities for Nonmetallic Minerals (except Fuels)^{US}

This U.S. industry comprises establishments primarily engaged in providing support services, on a fee or contract basis, required for the mining and quarrying of nonmetallic minerals and for the extraction of nonmetallic minerals. Exploration for minerals is included in this industry. Exploration (except geophysical surveying and mapping services) includes traditional prospecting methods, such as taking core samples and making geological observations at prospective sites.

Performing geophysical survey services for nonmetallic minerals on a contract or fee basis **541360**

Operating nonmetallic mineral mines or quarries on a contract or fee basis **2123**

SECTOR 22:   UTILITIES

OVERVIEW OF THIS SECTOR AS A WHOLE

The Utilities sector comprises establishments engaged in the provision of the following utility services: electric power, natural gas, steam supply, water supply, and sewage removal. Within this sector, the specific activities associated with the utility services provided vary by utility: electric power includes generation, transmission, and distribution; natural gas includes distribution; steam supply includes provision and/or distribution; water supply includes treatment and distribution; and sewage removal includes collection, treatment, and disposal of waste through sewer systems and sewage treatment facilities.

Excluded from this sector are establishments primarily engaged in waste management services classified in Subsector 562, Waste Management and Remediation Services. These establishments also collect, treat, and dispose of waste materials; however, they do not use sewer systems or sewage treatment facilities.

---

221 Utilities

Industries in the Utilities subsector provide electric power, natural gas, steam supply, water supply, and sewage removal through a permanent infrastructure of lines, mains, and pipes. Establishments are grouped together based on the utility service provided and the particular system or facilities required to perform the service.

2211 Electric Power Generation, Transmission and Distribution^{CAN}

This industry group comprises establishments primarily engaged in generating, transmitting, and/or distributing electric power. Establishments in this industry group may perform one or more of the following activities: (1) operate generation facilities that produce electric energy; (2) operate transmission systems that convey the electricity from the generation facility to the distribution system; and (3) operate distribution systems that convey electric power received from the generation facility or the transmission system to the final consumer.

22111 Electric Power Generation^{CAN}

This industry comprises establishments primarily

engaged in operating electric power generation facilities. These facilities convert other forms of energy, such as water power (i.e., hydroelectric), fossil fuels, nuclear power, and solar power, into electrical energy. The establishments in this industry produce electric energy and provide electricity to transmission systems or to electric power distribution systems.

Operating trash incinerators that also generate electricity **56221**

221111 Hydroelectric Power Generation^{CAN}

This U.S. industry comprises establishments primarily engaged in operating hydroelectric power generation facilities. These facilities use water power to drive a turbine and produce electric energy. The electric energy produced in these establishments is provided to electric power transmission systems or to electric power distribution systems.

221112 Fossil Fuel Electric Power Generation[CAN]

This U.S. industry comprises establishments primarily engaged in operating fossil fuel powered electric power generation facilities. These facilities use fossil fuels, such as coal, oil, or gas, in internal combustion or combustion turbine conventional steam process to produce electric energy. The electric energy produced in these establishments is provided to electric power transmission systems or to electric power distribution systems.

221113 Nuclear Electric Power Generation[CAN]

This U.S. industry comprises establishments primarily engaged in operating nuclear electric power generation facilities. These facilities use nuclear power to produce electric energy. The electric energy produced in these establishments is provided to electric power transmission systems or to electric power distribution systems.

221119 Other Electric Power Generation[CAN]

This U.S. industry comprises establishments primarily engaged in operating electric power generation facilities (except hydroelectric, fossil fuel, nuclear). These facilities convert other forms of energy, such as solar, wind, or tidal power, into electrical energy. The electric energy produced in these establishments is provided to electric power transmission systems or to electric power distribution systems.

Operating trash disposal incinerators that also generate electricity **562213**
Operating hydroelectric power generation facilities **221111**
Operating fossil fuel powered electric power generation facilities **221112**
Operating nuclear electric power generation facilities **221113**

22112 Electric Power Transmission, Control, and Distribution[CAN]

This industry comprises establishments primarily engaged in operating electric power transmission systems, controlling (i.e., regulating voltages) the transmission of electricity, and/or distributing electricity. The transmission system includes lines and transformer stations. These establishments arrange, facilitate, or coordinate the transmission of electricity from the generating source to the distribution centers, other electric utilities, or final consumers. The distribution system consists of lines, poles, meters, and wiring that deliver the electricity to final consumers.

Generating electric energy **22111**

221121 Electric Bulk Power Transmission and Control[CAN]

This U.S. industry comprises establishments primarily engaged in operating electric power transmission systems and/or controlling (i.e., regulatory voltage) the transmission of electricity from the generating source to distribution centers or other electric utilities. The transmission system includes lines and transformer stations.

Generating electric energy **22111**
Distributing electricity to final consumers **221122**

221122 Electric Power Distribution[CAN]

This U.S. industry comprises electric power establishments primarily engaged in (1) operating electric power distribution systems (i.e., consisting of lines, poles, meters, and wiring) or (2) operating as electric power brokers or agents that arrange the sale of electricity via power distribution systems operated by others.

Generating electric energy **22111**
Transmitting electricity between generating sources or distribution centers **221121**

221210 Natural Gas Distribution[CAN]

This industry comprises: (1) establishments primarily engaged in operating gas distribution systems (e.g., mains, meters); (2) establishments known as gas marketers that buy gas from the well and sell it to a distribution system; (3) establishments known as gas brokers or agents that arrange the sale of gas over gas distribution systems operated by others; and (4) establishments primarily engaged in transmitting and distributing gas to final consumers.

Pipeline transportation of natural gas from process plants to local distribution systems **486210**
Retailing liquefied petroleum (LP) gas via direct selling **454312**

221310 Water Supply and Irrigation Systems[CAN]

This industry comprises establishments primarily engaged in operating water treatment plants and/or operating water supply systems. The water supply system may include pumping stations, aqueducts, and/or distribution mains. The water may be used for drinking, irrigation, or other uses.

221

221320 Sewage Treatment Facilities[CAN]

This industry comprises establishments primarily engaged in operating sewer systems or sewage treatment facilities that collect, treat, and dispose of waste.

Operating waste treatment or disposal facilities (except sewer systems or sewage treatment facilities) **56221**

Pumping (i.e., cleaning) septic tanks and cesspools **562991**
Cleaning and rodding sewers and catch basins **562998**

221330 Steam and Air-Conditioning Supply[CAN]

This industry comprises establishments primarily engaged in providing steam, heated air, or cooled air. The steam distribution may be through mains.

SECTOR 23: CONSTRUCTION

OVERVIEW OF THIS SECTOR AS A WHOLE

The Construction sector comprises establishments primarily engaged in the construction of buildings and other structures, heavy construction (except buildings), additions, alterations, reconstruction, installation, and maintenance and repairs. Establishments engaged in demolition or wrecking of buildings and other structures, clearing of building sites, and sale of materials from demolished structures are also included. This sector also includes those establishments engaged in blasting, test drilling, landfill, leveling, earthmoving, excavating, land drainage, and other land preparation. The industries within this sector have been defined on the basis of their unique production processes. As with all industries, the production processes are distinguished by their use of specialized human resources and specialized physical capital. Construction activities are generally administered or managed at a relatively fixed place of business, but the actual construction work is performed at one or more different project sites. This sector is divided into three subsectors of construction activities: (1) building construction and land subdivision and land development; (2) heavy construction (except buildings), such as highways, power plants, and pipelines; and (3) construction activity by special trade contractors. Establishments classified in Subsector 233, Building, Developing, and General Contracting and Subsector 234, Heavy Construction, usually assume responsibility for an entire construction project, and may subcontract some or all of the actual construction work. Operative builders who build on their own account for sale, and land subdividers and land developers, who engage in subdividing real property into lots for sale, are included in Subsector 233, Building, Developing, and General Contracting. (Special trade contractors are included in Subsector 234, Heavy Construction, if they are engaged in activities primarily relating to heavy construction, such as grading for highways.) Establishments included in these subsectors operate as general contractors, design-builders, engineer-constructors, joint-venture contractors, and turnkey construction contractors. Establishments identified as construction management firms are also included. Establishments classified in Subsector 235, Special Trade Contractors, are primarily engaged in specialized construction activities, such as plumbing, painting, and electrical work, and work for builders and general contractors under subcontract or directly for project owners. Establishments engaged in demolition or wrecking of buildings and other structures, dismantling of machinery, excavating, shoring and underpinning, anchored earth retention activities, foundation drilling, and grading for buildings are also included in this subsector.

"Force account" construction is construction work performed by an establishment primarily engaged in some business other than construction, for its own account and use, and by employees of the establishment. This activity is not included in this industry sector unless the construction work performed is the primary activity of a separate establishment of the enterprise. The installation of prefabricated building equipment and materials, such as elevators and revolving doors, is classified in the Construction sector. Installation work incidental to sales by employees of a manufacturing or retail establishment is classified as an activity of those establishments.

233 Building, Developing, and General Contracting[US]

Industries in the Building, Developing, and General Contracting subsector comprises establishments primarily responsible for the entire construction (i.e., new work, additions, alterations, and repair) of building projects. Builders, developers, and general contractors, as well as land subdividers and land developers are included in this subsector. Establishments identified as construction management firms for building projects are also included. The construction work may be for others and performed by custom builders, general contractors, design builders, engineer-constructors, joint-venture contractors, and turnkey contractors, or may be on their own account for sale and performed by speculative or operative builders.

233110 Land Subdivision and Land Development[US]

This industry comprises establishments primarily engaged in subdividing real property into lots and/or developing building lots for sale.

Constructing buildings on lots they subdivide or develop **2332** or **2333**

233210 Single Family Housing Construction[US]

This industry comprises establishments primarily responsible for the entire construction (i.e., new work, additions, alterations, and repairs) of single family residential housing units (e.g., single family detached houses, town houses, or row houses where each housing unit is separated by a ground-to-roof wall and where no housing units are constructed above or below). This industry includes establishments responsible for additions and alterations to mobile homes and on-site assembly of modular and prefabricated houses. Establishments identified as single family construction management firms are also included in this industry. Establishments in this industry may perform work for others or on their own account for sale as speculative or operative builders. Kinds of establishments include single family housing custom builders, general contractors, design builders, engineer-constructors, joint-venture contractors, and turnkey contractors.

Performing mobile home site setup and tie-down work **235990**
Performing specialized construction work on single family housing units generally on a subcontract basis **235**

233220 Multifamily Housing Construction[US]

This industry comprises establishments primarily responsible for the entire construction (i.e., new work, additions, alterations, and repairs) of multifamily residential housing units (e.g., highrise, garden, and town house apartments where each unit is not separated by a ground-to-roof wall). The units may be constructed for sale as condominiums or cooperatives, or for rental as apartments. Establishments identified as multifamily construction management firms are also included in this industry. Establishments in this industry may perform work for others or on their own account for sale as speculative or operative builders. Kinds of establishments include multifamily housing general contractors, design builders, engineer-constructors, joint-venture contractors, and turnkey contractors.

Performing specialized construction work on multifamily housing units generally on a subcontract basis **235**
Developing, constructing, and operating residential buildings on their own account for investment purposes **531110**

2333 Nonresidential Building Construction[US]

233310 Manufacturing and Industrial Building Construction[US]

This industry comprises establishments primarily responsible for the entire construction (i.e., new work, additions, alterations, and repairs) of manufacturing and industrial buildings (e.g., plants, mills, factories). Establishments identified as manufacturing and industrial building construction management firms are also included in this industry. Kinds of establishments include manufacturing and industrial building general contractors, design builders, engineer-constructors, joint-venture contractors, and turnkey contractors.

Constructing commercial and institutional buildings **233320**
Constructing heavy, nonbuilding industrial structures **234930**

Performing specialized construction work on manufacturing and industrial buildings generally on a subcontract basis **235**

233320 Commercial and Institutional Building Construction[US]

This industry comprises establishments primarily responsible for the entire construction (i.e., new work, additions, alterations, and repairs) of commercial and institutional buildings (e.g., stores, schools, hospitals office buildings, public warehouses). Establishments identified as commercial and institutional building construction management firms are also included in this industry. Kinds of establishments include commercial and institutional building general contractors, design builders, engineer-constructors, joint-venture contractors, and turnkey contractors.

Performing specialized construction work on commercial and institutional buildings generally on a subcontract basis **235**
Constructing manufacturing and industrial buildings **233310**

234 Heavy Construction[US]

Industries in the Heavy Construction subsector group establishments that engage in the construction of heavy engineering and industrial projects (except buildings), for example, highways, power plants, and pipelines. The construction work performed may include new work, reconstruction, or repairs. Establishments identified as heavy construction management firms are also included. Establishments in this subsector usually assume responsibility for entire nonbuilding projects but may subcontract some or all of the actual construction work. Special trade contractors are included in this group if they are engaged in activities primarily related to heavy construction, for example, grading for highways. Kinds of establishments include heavy construction general contractors, design builders, engineer-constructors, and joint-venture contractors.

2341 Highway, Street, Bridge, and Tunnel Construction[US]

234110 Highway and Street Construction[US]

This industry comprises: (1) establishments primarily responsible for the entire construction (i.e., new work, reconstruction, or repairs) of highways (except elevated), streets, roads, or airport runways; (2) establishments identified as highway and street construction management firms; and (3) establishments identified as special trade contractors engaged in performing subcontract work primarily related to highway and street construction (e.g., grading for highways, installing guardrails, public sidewalk construc-

tion). Establishments in this industry may subcontract some or all of the actual construction work. Kinds of establishments include highway and street general contractors, design builders, engineer-constructors, and joint-venture contractors.

Constructing elevated highways **234120**
Constructing private driveways and private sidewalks **235710**
Traffic lane painting **235210**

234120 Bridge and Tunnel Construction[US]

This industry comprises: (1) establishments primarily responsible for the entire construction (i.e., new work, reconstruction, or repairs) of bridges, viaducts, elevated highways, and tunnels; (2) establishments identified as bridge and tunnel construction management firms; and (3) establishments identified as special trade contractors primarily engaged in performing subcontract work related to bridge and tunnel construction. Establishments in this industry may subcontract some or all of the actual construction work. Kinds of establishments include bridge and tunnel general contractors, design builders, engineer-constructors, and joint-venture contractors.

Entire subway construction projects as general contractors, design-builders, engineer-constructors, or joint-venture contractors **234990**
Bridge painting **235210**

2349 Other Heavy Construction[US]

This industry group comprises establishments primarily engaged in heavy nonbuilding construction (except highway, street, bridge, and tunnel construction).

234910 Water, Sewer, and Pipeline Construction[US]

This industry comprises: (1) establishments primarily responsible for the entire construction (i.e., new work, reconstruction, rehabilitation, or repairs) of water mains, sewers, drains, gas mains, natural gas pumping stations, and gas and oil pipelines; (2) establishments identified as water, sewer, and pipeline construction management firms; and (3) establishments identified as special trade contractors engaged in activities primarily related to water, sewer, and pipeline construction. Establishments in this industry may subcontract some or all of the actual construction work. Kinds of establishments include water, sewer, and pipeline general contractors, design builders, engineer-constructors, and joint-venture contractors.

Construction of water and sewer treatment plants **234990**

234920 Power and Communication Transmission Line Construction[US]

This industry comprises: (1) establishments primarily responsible for the entire construction (i.e., new work, reconstruction, or repairs) of electric power and communication transmission lines and towers, radio and television transmitting/receiving towers, cable laying, and cable television lines; (2) establishments identified as power and communication transmission line construction management firms; and (3) estab-

lishments identified as special trade contractors engaged inactivities primarily related to power and communication transmission line construction. Establishments in this industry may subcontract some or all of the actual construction work. Kinds of establishments include power and communication transmission line general contractors, design builders, engineer-constructors, and joint-venture contractors.

Performing electrical work within buildings **235310**
Installation and maintenance of power and communication transmission
   lines performed by broadcasting and telecommunications companies
   513

234930 Industrial Nonbuilding Structure Construction[US]

This industry comprises: (1) establishments primarily responsible for the entire construction (i.e., new work, reconstruction, or repairs) of heavy industrial nonbuilding structures, such as chemical complexes or facilities, cement plants, petroleum refineries, industrial incinerators, ovens, kilns, power plants (except hydroelectric plants), and nuclear reactor containment structures; (2) establishments identified as industrial nonbuilding construction management firms; and (3) establishments identified as special trade contractors engaged in activities primarily related to industrial nonbuilding construction. Establishments in this industry may subcontract some or all of the actual construction work. Kinds of establishments include industrial nonbuilding general contractors, design builders, engineer-constructors, and joint-venture contractors.

Constructing manufacturing and industrial buildings **233310**
Constructing hydroelectric plants **234990**

234990 All Other Heavy Construction[US]

This industry comprises: (1) establishments primarily responsible for the entire construction (i.e., new work, reconstruction, or repairs) of heavy nonbuilding construction projects (except highway, street, bridge, tunnel, water lines, sewer lines, pipelines, power and communication transmission lines, and industrial nonbuilding structures); (2) establishments identified as all other heavy construction management firms; (3) establishments primarily engaged in construction equipment rental with an operator; and (4) establishments identified as special trade contractors engaged in activities related primarily to all other heavy con-

234

struction. Typical projects constructed by establishments in this industry include athletic fields, dams, dikes, docks, drainage projects, golf courses, harbors, parks, reservoirs, canals, sewage treatment plants, water treatment plants, hydroelectric plants, subways, and other mass transit projects. Establishments in this industry may subcontract some or all of the actual construction work. Kinds of establishments include heavy construction general contractors, design build-ers, engineer-constructors, and joint-venture contractors.

Constructing highways (except elevated) and streets **234110**
Constructing bridges via ducts, elevated highways, and tunnels **234120**
Constructing water mains, sewers, and pipelines **234910**
Constructing communication transmission lines **234920**
Constructing industrial nonbuilding structures **234930**
Heavy equipment rental without an operator **532412**

235 Special Trade Contractors[US]

Industries in the Special Trade Contractors subsector engage in specialized construction activities, such as plumbing, painting, and electrical work. Those establishments that engage in activities primarily related to heavy construction, such as grading for highways, are classified in Subsector 234, Heavy Construction. The activities of this subsector may be subcontracted from builders or general contractors or it may be performed directly for project owners. The construction work performed may include new work, additions, alterations, or maintenance and repairs. Special trade contractors usually perform most of their work at the job site, although they may have shops where they perform prefabrication and other work.

235110 Plumbing, Heating, and Air-Conditioning Contractors[US]

This industry comprises establishments primarily engaged in one or more of the following: (1) installing plumbing, heating, and air-conditioning equipment; (2) servicing plumbing, heating, and air-conditioning equipment; and (3) the combined activity of selling and installing plumbing, heating, and air-conditioning equipment. The plumbing, heating, and air-conditioning work performed includes new work, additions, alterations, and maintenance and repairs. The activities performed by these establishments range from duct fabrication and installation at the site to installation of refrigeration equipment, installation of sprinkler systems, and installation of environmental controls.

235210 Painting and Wall Covering Contractors[US]

This industry comprises establishments primarily engaged in interior or exterior painting and interior wall covering. The painting and wall covering work performed includes new work, additions, alterations, and maintenance and repairs. Activities performed by these establishments range from bridge, ship, and traffic lane painting to paint and wall covering removal.

Roof painting **235610**
Installing wood paneling **235510**

235310 Electrical Contractors[US]

This industry comprises establishments primarily engaged in one or more of the following: (1) performing electrical work at the site (e.g., installing wiring); (2) servicing electrical equipment at the site; and (3) the combined activity of selling and installing electrical equipment. The electrical work performed includes new work, additions, alterations, and maintenance and repairs.

Constructing power and communication transmission lines **234920**
Installing burglar and fire alarms **561621**

2354 Masonry, Drywall, Insulation, and Tile Contractors[US]

235410 Masonry and Stone Contractors[US]

This industry comprises establishments primarily engaged in masonry work, stone setting, and other stone work. The masonry work, stone setting, and other stone work performed includes new work, additions, alterations, and maintenance and repairs. Activities performed by establishments in this industry range from the construction of foundations made of block, stone, or brick to glass block laying; exterior marble, granite and slate work; and tuck pointing.

Installing concrete parking areas, foundations, retaining walls, and private driveways and walks **235710**

235420 Drywall, Plastering, Acoustical, and Insulation Contractors[US]

This industry comprises establishments primarily engaged in drywall, plaster work, acoustical, and building insulation work. The drywall, plaster work, acoustical, and insulation work performed includes new work, additions, alterations, and maintenance and repairs. Plaster work includes applying plain or ornamental plaster, including installation of lathing to receive plaster.

Insulating pipes and boilers **235990**

235430 Tile, Marble, Terrazzo, and Mosaic Contractors[US]

This industry comprises establishments primarily engaged in (1) setting and installing ceramic tile, marble (interior only), terrazzo, and mosaic and/or (2) mixing marble particles and cement to make terrazzo at the job site. The tile, marble, terrazzo, and mosaic work performed includes new work, additions, alterations, and maintenance and repairs.

Manufacturing precast terrazzo products **327390**
Exterior marble work **235410**

2355 Carpentry and Floor Contractors[US]

235510 Carpentry Contractors[US]

This industry comprises establishments primarily engaged in framing, carpentry, and finishing work. The carpentry work performed includes new work, additions, alterations, and maintenance and repairs. Activities performed by establishments in this industry range from the installation of doors and windows to paneling, steel framing work, and ship joinery.

Building custom kitchen cabinets in a shop **337110**

235520 Floor Laying and Other Floor Contractors[US]

This industry comprises establishments primarily engaged in the installation of resilient floor tile, carpeting, linoleum, and wood or resilient flooring. The floor laying and other floor work performed includes new work, additions, alterations, and maintenance and repairs.

Installing stone or ceramic floor tile **235430**
Laying concrete flooring **235710**
Selling and installing carpet and other flooring products as retail establishments **44–45**

235610 Roofing, Siding, and Sheet Metal Contractors[US]

This industry comprises establishments primarily engaged in the installation of roofing, siding, sheet metal work, and roof drainage-related work, such as downspouts and gutters. Activities performed by these establishments also include treating roofs (i.e., by spraying, painting, or coating), copper smithing, tin smithing, installing skylights, installing metal ceilings, flashing, duct work, and capping. The roofing, siding, and sheet metal work performed includes new work, additions, alterations, and maintenance and repairs.

235710 Concrete Contractors[US]

This industry comprises establishments primarily engaged in the use of concrete and asphalt to produce parking areas, building foundations, structures, and retaining walls, and in the use of all materials to produce patios, private driveways, and private walks. Activities performed by these establishments include grout and shotcrete work. The concrete work performed includes new work, additions, alterations, and maintenance and repairs.

Constructing or paving streets, highways, and public sidewalks **234110**
Constructing swimming pools **235990**

235810 Water Well Drilling Contractors[US]

This industry comprises establishments primarily engaged in drilling, tapping, and capping of water wells, and geothermal drilling. The water well drilling work performed includes new work, servicing, and maintenance and repairs.

Drilling oil and gas field water intake wells **21311**

2359 Other Special Trade Contractors[US]

This industry group comprises establishments primarily engaged in specialized construction activities (except plumbing, painting, electrical, masonry, drywall, insulation, tile, carpentry, flooring work, roofing, siding, sheet metal, concrete, and water well drilling).

235910 Structural Steel Erection Contractors[US]

This industry comprises establishments primarily engaged in one or more of the following: (1) erecting metal, structural steel, and similar products of prestressed or precast concrete to produce structural elements, building exteriors, and elevator fronts; (2) setting rods, bars, rebar, mesh, and cages, to reinforce poured-in-place concrete; and (3) erecting cooling towers and metal storage tanks. The structural steel erection work performed includes new work, additions, alterations, reconstruction, and maintenance and repairs.

Structural work for nonbuilding projects 234

235920 Glass and Glazing Contractors[US]

This industry comprises establishments primarily engaged in installing glass (i.e., glazing work) and/or tinting glass. The glass work performed includes new work, additions, alterations, and maintenance and repairs.

Replacement, repair, and/or tinting of automotive glass 811122

235930 Excavation Contractors[US]

This industry comprises establishments primarily engaged in preparing land for building construction. Activities performed by these establishments are drilling shafts, foundation digging, foundation drilling, and grading. The excavation work performed includes new work, additions, alterations, and repairs.

Concrete work 235710
Trenching, earthmoving and land clearing not related to building construction 234
Earth retention or shoring 235990

235940 Wrecking and Demolition Contractors[US]

This industry comprises establishments primarily engaged in the wrecking and demolition of buildings and other structures, including underground tank removal and the dismantling of steel oil tanks, except those for hazardous materials. The establishments engaged in wrecking and demolition work may or may not sell materials derived from demolishing operations.

Demolition of tanks in oil fields 213112
Environmental remediation work, such as the removal of underground steel tanks for hazardous materials 562910

235950 Building Equipment and Other Machinery Installation Contractors[US]

This industry comprises establishments primarily engaged in one or more of the following: (1) the installation or dismantling of building equipment, machinery or other industrial equipment (except plumbing, heating, air conditioning or electrical equipment); (2) machine rigging; and (3) millwriting. Types of equipment installed include automated and revolving doors, conveyor systems, dumbwaiters, dust collecting equipment, elevators, small incinerators, pneumatic tubes systems, and built-in vacuum cleaning systems. The building equipment and other machinery installation work performed includes new work, additions, alterations, and maintenance and repairs.

Installing plumbing, heating, or air-conditioning equipment 235110
Installing electrical equipment 235310
Constructing of industrial incinerator, furnace, and oven structures 234930
Manufacturing of industrial equipment with incidental installation 31–33

235990 All Other Special Trade Contractors[US]

This industry comprises establishments primarily engaged in specialized construction work, (except plumbing, painting, electrical, masonry, drywall, insulation, tile, carpentry, flooring, roofing, siding, sheet metal work, concrete work, glass and glazing, structural steel erection, excavation, wrecking and demolition, and building equipment installation work). Activities undertaken by these establishments include constructing swimming pools and fences, house moving, waterproofing, dewatering, dampproofing, fireproofing, and sandblasting; installing antennas, artificial turf, awnings, countertops, fire escapes, forms for poured concrete, gasoline pumps, lightning conductors, ornamental metal, shoring systems, and signs (on buildings); and specialized activities, such as bathtub refinishing, coating and glazing of concrete surfaces, gas leakage detection, insulation of pipes and boilers, mobile home site setup and tie-down, posthole digging, radon remediation, scaffolding work, and on-site welding. The other special trade work performed includes new work, additions, alterations, and maintenance and repairs.

Installing plumbing, heating, and air-conditioning equipment **235110**
Painting and interior wall covering **235210**
Installing electrical equipment **235310**

Masonry work, drywall work, insulation work, and tile work **2354**
Carpentry work **235510**
Installing flooring **235520**
Installing roofing, siding, and sheet metal **235610**
The use of concrete and asphalt in their work **235710**
Erecting structural steel **235910**
Installing or tinting glass **235920**
Preparing land for building construction **235930**

311

SECTOR 31-33: MANUFACTURING

OVERVIEW OF THIS SECTOR AS A WHOLE

The Manufacturing sector comprises establishments engaged in the mechanical, physical, or chemical transformation of materials, substances, or components into new products. The assembling of component parts of manufactured products is considered manufacturing, except in cases where the activity is appropriately classified in Sector 23, Construction. Establishments in the Manufacturing sector are often described as plants, factories, or mills and characteristically use power-driven machines and materials-handling equipment. However, establishments that transform materials or substances into new products by hand or in the worker's home and those engaged in selling to the general public products made on the same premises from which they are sold, such as bakeries, candy stores, and custom tailors, may also be included in this sector. Manufacturing establishments may process materials or may contract with other establishments to process their materials for them. Both types of establishments are included in manufacturing. The materials, substances, or components transformed by manufacturing establishments are raw materials that are products of agriculture, forestry, fishing, mining, or quarrying as well as products of other manufacturing establishments. The materials used may be purchased directly from producers, obtained through customary trade channels, or secured without recourse to the market by transferring the product from one establishment to another, under the same ownership. The new product of a manufacturing establishment may be finished in the sense that it is ready for utilization or consumption, or it may be semifinished to become an input for an establishment engaged in further manufacturing. For example, the product of the alumina refinery is the input used in the primary production of aluminum; primary aluminum is the input to an aluminum wire drawing plant; and aluminum wire is the input for a fabricated wire product manufacturing establishment.

The subsectors in the Manufacturing sector generally reflect distinct production processes related to material inputs, production equipment, and employee skills. In the machinery area, where assembling is a key activity, parts and accessories for manufactured products are classified in the industry of the finished manufactured item when they are made for separate sale. For example, a replacement refrigerator door would be classified with refrigerators and an attachment for a piece of metal working machinery would be classified with metal working machinery. However, components, input from other manufacturing establishments, are classified based on the production function of the component manufacturer. For example, electronic components are classified in Subsector 334, Computer and Electronic Product Manufacturing and stampings are classified in Subsector 332, Fabricated Metal Product Manufacturing.

Manufacturing establishments often perform one or more activities that are classified outside the Manufacturing sector of NAICS. For instance, almost all manufacturing has some captive research and development or administrative operations, such as accounting, payroll, or management. These captive services are treated the same as captive manufacturing activities. When the services are provided by separate establishments, they are classified to the NAICS sector where such services are primary, not in manufacturing.

The boundaries of manufacturing and the other sectors of the classification system can be somewhat blurry. The establishments in the manufacturing sector are engaged in the transformation of materials into new products. Their output is a new product. However, the definition of what constitutes a new product can be somewhat subjective. As clarification, the following activities are considered manufacturing in NAICS:

Milk bottling and pasteurizing; Water bottling and processing; Fresh fish packaging (oyster shucking, fish filleting); Apparel jobbing (assigning of materials to contract factories or shops for fabrication or other contract operations) as well as contracting on materials owned by others; Printing and related activities; Ready-mixed concrete production; Leather converting; Grinding of lenses to prescription; Wood preserving; Electroplating, plating, metal heat treating, and polishing for the trade; Lapidary work for the trade; Fabricating signs and advertising displays; Rebuilding or remanufacturing machinery (i.e., automotive parts) Ship repair and renovation; Machine shops; and Tire retreading.

Conversely, there are activities that are sometimes considered manufacturing, but which for NAICS are classified in another sector (i.e., not classified as manufacturing). They include: 1. Logging, classified in Sector 11, Agriculture, Forestry, Fishing and Hunting is considered a harvesting operation; 2. The beneficiating of ores and other minerals, classified in Sector 21, Mining, is considered part of the activity of mining; 3. The construction of structures and fabricating operations performed at the site of construction by contractors, is classified in Sector 23, Construction; 4. Establishments engaged in breaking of bulk and redistribution in smaller lots, including packaging, repackaging, or bottling products, such as liquors or chemicals; the customized assembly of computers; sorting of scrap; mixing paints to customer order; and cutting metals to customer order, classified in Sector 42, Wholesale Trade or Sector 44-45, Retail Trade, produce a modified version of the same product, not a new product; and 5. Publishing and the combined activity of publishing and printing, classified in Sector 51, Information, perform the transformation of information into a product where as the value of the product to the consumer lies in the information content, not in the format in which it is distributed (i.e., the book or software diskette).

311 Food Manufacturing

Industries in the Food Manufacturing subsector transform livestock and agricultural products into products for intermediate or final consumption. The industry groups are distinguished by the raw materials (generally of animal or vegetable origin) processed into food products. The food products manufactured in these establishments are typically sold to wholesalers or retailers for distribution to consumers, but establishments primarily engaged in retailing bakery and candy products made on the premises not for immediate consumption are included. Manufacturing beverages are classified in Subsector 312, Beverage and Tobacco Product Manufacturing.

31111 Animal Food Manufacturing

This industry comprises establishments primarily engaged in manufacturing food and feed for animals from ingredients, such as grains, oilseed mill products, and meat products.

Slaughtering animals for feed **31161**
Manufacturing vitamins and minerals for animals **32541**

311111 Dog and Cat Food Manufacturing^{CAN}

This U.S. industry comprises establishments primarily engaged in manufacturing dog and cat food from ingredients, such as grains, oilseed mill products, and meat products.

Manufacturing food for animals (except dog and cat) **311119**
Slaughtering animals for feed **31161**
Manufacturing vitamins and minerals for dogs and cats **32541**

311119 Other Animal Food Manufacturing^{CAN}

This U.S. industry comprises establishments primarily engaged in manufacturing animal food (except dog and cat) from ingredients, such as grains, oilseed mill products, and meat products.

Manufacturing dog and cat foods **311111**
Slaughtering animals for feed **31161**
Manufacturing vitamins and minerals for animals **32541**

3112 Grain and Oilseed Milling

31121 Flour Milling and Malt Manufacturing

This industry comprises establishments primarily engaged in one or more of the following: (1) milling flour or meal from grains or vegetables; (2) preparing flour mixes or doughs from flour milled in the same establishment; (3) milling, cleaning, and polishing rice; and (4) manufacturing malt from barley, rye, or other grains.

Preparing breakfast cereals from flour milled in the same establishment **31123**
Crushing soybeans or wet milling corn and vegetables **31122**
Manufacturing prepared flour mixes or doughs from flour ground elsewhere **31182**
Brewing malt beverages **31212**
Mixing purchased dried and dehydrated ingredients with purchased rice **31199**
Drying and/or dehydrating ingredients and packaging them with purchased rice **31142**
Manufacturing malt extract and syrups **31194**

311211 Flour Milling^{CAN}

This U.S. industry comprises establishments primarily engaged in (1) milling flour or meal from grains (except rice) or vegetables and/or (2) milling flour and preparing flour mixes or doughs.

Preparing breakfast cereals from flour milled in the same establishment **311230**
Manufacturing prepared flour mixes or doughs from flour ground elsewhere **311822**
Milling rice or cleaning and polishing rice **311212**
Wet milling corn and vegetables **311221**
Crushing soybean and extracting soybean oil **311222**

311

311212 Rice Milling^{US}

This U.S. industry comprises establishments primarily engaged in one of the following: (1) milling rice; (2) cleaning and polishing rice; or (3) milling, cleaning, and polishing rice. The establishments in this industry may package the rice they mill with other ingredients.

Drying and/or dehydrating ingredients and packaging them with purchased rice **311423**
Mixing purchased dried and/or dehydrated ingredients with purchased rice **311999**

311213 Malt Manufacturing^{US}

This U.S. industry comprises establishments primarily engaged in manufacturing malt from barley, rye, or other grains.

Brewing malt beverages **312120**
Manufacturing malt extract and syrups **311942**

31122 Starch and Vegetable Fats and Oils Manufacturing

This industry comprises establishments primarily engaged in one or more of the following: (1) wet milling corn and vegetables; (2) crushing oilseeds and tree nuts; (3) refining and/or blending vegetable oils; (4) manufacturing shortening and margarine; and (5) blending purchased animal fats with vegetable fats.

Manufacturing table syrups from corn syrup and starch base dessert powders **31199**
Reducing maple sap to maple syrup **11199**
Milling flour or meal from grains and vegetables **31121**
Wet milling corn to produce nonpotable ethyl alcohol **32519**
Rendering or refining animal fats and oils **31161**
Manufacturing laundry starches **32561**

311221 Wet Corn Milling^{CAN}

This U.S. industry comprises establishments primarily engaged in wet milling corn and other vegetables (except to make ethyl alcohol). Examples of products made in these establishments are corn sweeteners, such as glucose, dextrose, and fructose; corn oil; and starches (except laundry).

Refining and/or blending corn oil from purchased oils **311225**
Manufacturing sweetening syrups from corn syrup and starch base dessert powders **311999**
Reducing maple sap to maple syrup **111998**
Milling corn **311211**
Wet milling corn to produce nonpotable ethyl alcohol **325193**
Manufacturing laundry starches **325612**

311222 Soybean Processing^{US}

This U.S. industry comprises establishments engaged in crushing soybeans. Examples of products produced in these establishments are soybean oil, soybean cake and meal, and soybean protein isolates and concentrates.

Refining and/or blending soybean oil from purchased oil **311225**
Wet milling corn and other vegetables **311221**
Crushing oilseeds (except soybeans) and tree nuts **311223**

311223 Other Oilseed Processing^{US}

This U.S. industry comprises establishments engaged in crushing oilseeds (except soybeans) and tree nuts, such as cottonseeds, linseeds, peanuts, and sunflower seeds.

Wet milling corn and other vegetables **311221**
Crushing soybeans **311222**
Refining and/or blending vegetable, oilseed, and tree nut oils from purchased oils **311225**

311225 Fats and Oils Refining and Blending^{CAN}

This U.S. industry comprises establishments primarily engaged in one or more of the following: (1) manufacturing shortening and margarine from purchased fats and oils; (2) refining and/or blending vegetable, oilseed, and tree nut oils from purchased oils; and (3) blending purchased animal fats with purchased vegetable fats.

Refining and/or blending soybean oil in soybean crushing mills **311222**
Refining and/or blending corn oil made by wet corn milling **311221**
Refining and/or blending oilseeds (except soybeans) and tree nuts in crushing mills **311223**

Rendering or refining animal fats and oils **31161**

311230 Breakfast Cereal Manufacturing

This industry comprises establishments primarily engaged in manufacturing breakfast cereal foods.

Manufacturing nonchocolate-coated granola bars and other types of breakfast bars **311340**
Manufacturing chocolate-coated granola bars from purchased chocolate **311330**
Manufacturing chocolate-coated granola bars from cacao beans **311320**
Manufacturing coffee substitutes from grain **311920**

3113 Sugar and Confectionery Product Manufacturing

This industry group comprises (1) establishments that process agricultural inputs, such as sugarcane, beet, and cacao, to give rise to a new product (sugar or chocolate) and (2) those that begin with sugar and chocolate and process these further.

31131 Sugar Manufacturing

This industry comprises establishments primarily engaged in manufacturing raw sugar, liquid sugar, and refined sugar from sugarcane, raw cane sugar and sugarbeets.

Manufacturing corn sweeteners by wet milling corn **31122**
Manufacturing table syrups from corn syrup and starch base dessert powders **31199**
Reducing maple sap to maple syrup **11199**
Manufacturing synthetic sweeteners (i.e., sweetening agents), such as saccharin and sugar substitutes (i.e., synthetic sweetener blended with other ingredients), **325**

311311 Sugarcane Mills^{US}

This U.S. industry comprises establishments primarily engaged in processing sugarcane.

Manufacturing refined cane sugar from raw cane sugar **311312**
Manufacturing beet sugar **311313**
Manufacturing corn sweetener by wet milling corn **311221**
Manufacturing table syrups from corn syrup **311999**
Manufacturing synthetic sweeteners (i.e., sweetening agents), such as saccharin and sugar substitutes (i.e., synthetic sweetener blended with other ingredients), **325**

311312 Cane Sugar Refining^{US}

This U.S. industry comprises establishments prima-

rily engaged in refining cane sugar from raw cane sugar.

Processing and refining sugarcane **311311**
Manufacturing beet sugar **311313**
Manufacturing corn sweetener by wet milling corn **311221**
Reducing maple sap to maple syrup **111998**
Manufacturing table syrups from corn syrup **311999**
Manufacturing synthetic sweeteners (i.e., sweetening agents), such as
saccharin and sugar substitutes (i.e., synthetic sweetener blended with
other ingredients), **325**

311313 Beet Sugar Manufacturing[US]

This U.S. industry comprises establishments primarily engaged in manufacturing refined beet sugar from sugarbeets.

Manufacturing raw cane sugar and/or refined cane sugar from sugarcane
311311
Manufacturing refined cane sugar from raw cane sugar **311312**
Manufacturing corn sweeteners by wet milling corn **311221**
Manufacturing table syrups from corn syrup **311999**
Reducing maple sap to maple syrup **111998**
Manufacturing synthetic sweeteners (i.e., sweetening agents), such as
saccharin and sugar substitutes (i.e., synthetic sweetener blended with
other ingredients), **325**

311320 Chocolate and Confectionery Manufacturing from Cacao Beans

This industry comprises establishments primarily engaged in shelling, roasting, and grinding cacao beans and making chocolate cacao products and chocolate confectioneries.

Manufacturing, not for immediate consumption, chocolate confectioneries
from chocolate made elsewhere **311330**
Manufacturing, not for immediate consumption, nonchocolate candies
311340
Preparing and selling confectioneries for immediate consumption **722213**
Retailing confectioneries not for immediate consumption made elsewhere
445292

311330 Confectionery Manufacturing from Purchased Chocolate

This industry comprises establishments primarily engaged in manufacturing chocolate confectioneries from chocolate produced elsewhere. Included in this industry are establishments primarily engaged in retailing chocolate confectionery products not for immediate consumption made on the premises from chocolate made elsewhere.

Manufacturing chocolate confectioneries from cacao beans **311320**
Manufacturing nonchocolate confectioneries **311340**
Retailing confectioneries not for immediate consumption made elsewhere
445292
Preparing and selling confectioneries for immediate consumption **722213**

311340 Nonchocolate Confectionery Manufacturing

This industry comprises establishments primarily engaged in manufacturing nonchocolate confectioneries. Included in this industry are establishments primary engaged in retailing nonchocolate confectionery products not for immediate consumption made on the premises.

Manufacturing chocolate confectioneries from cacao beans **311320**
Manufacturing chocolate confectioneries from chocolate made elsewhere
311330
Retailing confectioneries not for immediate consumption made elsewhere
445292
Preparing and selling confectioneries for immediate consumption **722213**
Roasting, salting, drying, cooking, or canning nuts and seeds **311911**

3114 Fruit and Vegetable Preserving and Specialty Food Manufacturing

This industry group includes (1) establishments that freeze food and (2) those that use preservation processes, such as pickling, canning, and dehydrating. Both types begin their production process with inputs of vegetable or animal origin.

31141 Frozen Food Manufacturing

This industry comprises establishments primarily engaged in manufacturing frozen fruit, frozen juices, frozen vegetables, and frozen specialty foods (except seafood), such as frozen dinners, entrees, and side dishes; frozen pizza; frozen whipped toppings; and frozen waffles, pancakes, and french toast.

Manufacturing frozen dairy specialties **31152**
Manufacturing frozen bakery products **31181**
Manufacturing frozen seafood products **31171**
Manufacturing frozen meat products **31161**

311411 Frozen Fruit, Juice, and Vegetable Manufacturing[US]

This U.S. industry comprises establishments primarily engaged in manufacturing frozen fruits; frozen vegetables; and frozen fruit juices, ades, drinks, cocktail mixes and concentrates.

Manufacturing frozen specialty foods **311412**

311

311412 Frozen Specialty Food Manufacturing^{US}

This U.S. industry comprises establishments primarily engaged in manufacturing frozen specialty foods (except seafood), such as frozen dinners, entrees, and side dishes; frozen pizza; frozen whipped topping; and frozen waffles, pancakes, and french toast.

Manufacturing frozen dairy specialties **311520**
Manufacturing frozen bakery products **311813**
Manufacturing frozen fruits, frozen fruit juices, and frozen vegetables **311411**
Manufacturing frozen meat products **31161**
Manufacturing frozen seafood products **311712**

31142 Fruit and Vegetable Canning, Pickling, and Drying

This industry comprises establishments primarily engaged in manufacturing canned, pickled, and dried fruits, vegetables, and specialty foods. Establishments in this industry may package the dried or dehydrated ingredients they make with other purchased ingredients. Examples of products made by these establishments are canned juices; canned baby foods; canned soups (except seafood); canned dry beans; canned tomato-based sauces, such as catsup, salsa, chili, spaghetti, barbeque, and tomato paste, pickles, relishes, jams and jellies, dried soup mixes and bullions, and sauerkraut.

Manufacturing canned dairy products **31151**
Manufacturing canned seafood soups and seafood products **31171**
Manufacturing canned meat products **31161**
Milling rice and packaging it with other ingredients or manufacturing vegetable flours and meals **31121**
Manufacturing dry pasta and packaging it with other ingredients **31182**
Mixing purchased dried and/or dehydrated potatoes, rice, and pasta and packaging them with other purchased ingredients; mixing purchased dried and/or dehydrated ingredients for soup mixes and bouillon; and manufacturing canned puddings **31199**
Manufacturing dry salad dressing and dry sauce mixes **31194**
Manufacturing canned fruit and vegetable drinks, cocktails, and ades **31211**

311421 Fruit and Vegetable Canning^{US}

This U.S. industry comprises establishments primarily engaged in manufacturing canned, pickled, and brined fruits and vegetables. Examples of products made in these establishments are canned juices; canned jams and jellies; canned tomato-based sauces, such as catsup, salsa, chili, spaghetti, barbeque, and tomato paste; pickles, relishes, and sauerkraut.

Manufacturing canned baby foods, canned soups (except seafood), and canned specialty foods (except seafood) **311422**

Manufacturing canned seafood soups and canned seafood products **311711**
Manufacturing canned meat products **31161**
Manufacturing canned fruit and canned vegetable drinks, "ades,' and cocktails **312111**

311422 Specialty Canning^{US}

This U.S. industry comprises establishments primarily engaged in manufacturing canned specialty foods. Examples of products made in these establishments are canned baby food, canned baked beans, canned soups (except seafood), canned spaghetti, and other canned nationality foods.

Manufacturing canned dairy products **311514**
Manufacturing canned fruits, canned vegetables, and canned juices **311421**
Manufacturing canned seafood soups and canned seafood products **311711**
Manufacturing canned meat products **31161**
Manufacturing canned puddings **311999**

311423 Dried and Dehydrated Food Manufacturing^{US}

This U.S. industry comprises establishments primarily engaged in (1) drying (including freeze-dried) and/or dehydrating fruits, vegetables, and soup mixes and bouillon and/or (2) drying and/or dehydrating ingredients and packaging them with other purchased ingredients, such as rice and dry pasta.

Milling rice and packaging it with other ingredients **311212**
Manufacturing dry pasta and packaging it with other ingredients **311823**
Manufacturing vegetable flours and meals **311211**
Mixing purchased dried and/or dehydrated potatoes, rice, and dry pasta, and packaging them with other purchased ingredients, and mixing purchased dried and/or dehydrated ingredients for soup mixes and bouillon **311999**
Manufacturing dry salad dressing and dry sauce mixes **311942**

3115 Dairy Product Manufacturing

This industry group comprises establishments that manufacture dairy products from raw milk, processed milk, and dairy substitutes.

31151 Dairy Product (except Frozen) Manufacturing

This industry comprises establishments primarily engaged in one or more of the following: (1) manufacturing dairy products (except frozen) from raw milk and/or processed milk products; (2) manufacturing dairy substitutes (except frozen) from soybeans and other nondairy substances; and (3) manufacturing dry, condensed, concentrated, and evaporated dairy and dairy substitute products.

Manufacturing cheese-based salad dressings **31194**
Manufacturing margarine or margarine-butter blends **31122**
Manufacturing frozen whipped toppings **31141**
Manufacturing ice cream, frozen yogurt, and other frozen dairy desserts
     31152

311511 Fluid Milk Manufacturing^{CAN}

This U.S. industry comprises establishments primarily engaged in (1) manufacturing processed milk products, such as pasteurized milk or cream and sour cream and/or (2) manufacturing fluid milk dairy substitutes from soybeans and other nondairy substances.

Manufacturing dry mix whipped toppings, canned milk, and ultra high
     temperature milk **311514**
Manufacturing frozen whipped toppings **311412**
Manufacturing ice cream and frozen yogurt and other frozen desserts
     311520

311512 Creamery Butter Manufacturing^{US}

This U.S. industry comprises establishments primarily engaged in manufacturing creamery butter from milk and/or processed milk products.

Manufacturing margarine or margarine-butter blends **311225**

311513 Cheese Manufacturing^{US}

This U.S. industry comprises establishments primarily engaged in (1) manufacturing cheese products (except cottage cheese) from raw milk and/or processed milk products and/or (2) manufacturing cheese substitutes from soybean and other nondairy substances.

Manufacturing cheese-based salad dressings **311941**
Manufacturing cottage cheese **311511**

311514 Dry, Condensed, and Evaporated Dairy Product Manufacturing^{US}

This U.S. industry comprises establishments primarily engaged in manufacturing dry, condensed, and evaporated milk and dairy substitute products.

Manufacturing fluid milk products **311511**
Manufacturing creamery butter **311512**
Manufacturing cheese products **311513**

311520 Ice Cream and Frozen Dessert Manufacturing

This industry comprises establishments primarily engaged in manufacturing ice cream, frozen yogurts, frozen ices, sherbets, frozen tofu, and other frozen desserts (except bakery products).

Manufacturing frozen bakery products **311813**
Manufacturing ice cream and ice milk mixes **311514**

31161 Animal Slaughtering and Processing

This industry comprises establishments primarily engaged in one or more of the following: (1) slaughtering animals; (2) preparing processed meats and meat byproducts; and (3) rendering and/or refining animal fat, bones, and meat scraps. This industry includes establishments primarily engaged in assembly cutting and packing of meats (i.e., boxed meats) from purchased carcasses.

Manufacturing canned meat for baby food **31142**
Manufacturing meat-based animal feeds from carcasses **31111**
Blending purchased animal fats with vegetable fats **31122**
Manufacturing canned and frozen specialty foods containing meat, such as
     nationality foods (e.g., enchiladas, pizza, egg rolls) and frozen dinners
     3114
Drying, freezing, or breaking eggs **31199**
Cutting meat (except box meat) **42247**

311611 Animal (except Poultry) Slaughtering^{CAN}

This U.S. industry comprises establishments primarily engaged in slaughtering animals (except poultry and small game). Establishments that slaughter and prepare meats are included in this industry.

Processing meat and meat byproducts (except poultry and small game) from
     purchased meats **311612**
Slaughtering and/or processing poultry and small game **311615**
Rendering lard and other animal fats and oils, animal fat, bones, and meat
     scraps **3116133**
Manufacturing canned and frozen specialty foods containing meat, such as
     nationality foods (e.g., enchiladas, egg rolls, pizza) and frozen dinners
     3114

311612 Meat Processed from Carcasses^{US}

This U.S. industry comprises establishments primarily engaged in processing or preserving meat and meat byproducts (except poultry and small game) from purchased meats. This industry includes establishments primarily engaged in assembly cutting and packing of meats (i.e., boxed meats) from purchased meats.

Slaughtering animals (except poultry and small game) **311611**
Slaughtering poultry and small game **311615**

Rendering animal fat, bones, and meat scraps **311613**
Manufacturing canned meats for baby food **311422**
Manufacturing meat-based animal feeds from carcasses **31111**
Manufacturing canned and frozen specialty foods containing meat, such as nationality foods (e.g., enchiladas, egg rolls, pizza) and frozen dinners **3114**
Cutting meat (except boxed meat) **422470**

311613 Rendering and Meat Byproduct Processing[US]

This U.S. industry comprises establishments primarily engaged in rendering animal fat, bones, and meat scraps.

Blending purchased animal fats with vegetable fats **311225**

311615 Poultry Processing[CAN]

This U.S. industry comprises establishments primarily engaged in (1) slaughtering poultry and small game and/or (2) preparing processed poultry and small game meat and meat byproducts.

Slaughtering animals (except poultry and small game) and/or preparing meats **311611**
Preparing meat and meat byproducts (except poultry and small game) from purchased meats **311612**
Rendering animal fat, bones, and meat scraps **311613**
Canning poultry and small game for baby food **311422**
Producing meat-based animal feeds from carcasses **31111**
Manufacturing canned and frozen meat products, such as nationality foods (e.g., enchiladas, egg rolls, pizza) and frozen dinners **3114**
Drying, freezing, and breaking eggs **311999**

31171 Seafood Product Preparation and Packaging

This industry comprises establishments primarily engaged in one or more of the following: (1) canning seafood (including soup); (2) smoking, salting, and drying seafoods; (3) eviscerating fresh fish by removing heads, fins, scales, bones, and entrails; (4) shucking and packing fresh shellfish; (5) processing marine fats and oils; and (6) freezing seafood. Establishments known as "floating factory ships" that are engaged in the gathering and processing of seafood into canned seafood products are included in this industry.

311711 Seafood Canning[US]

This U.S. industry comprises establishments primarily engaged in (1) canning seafood (including soup) and marine fats and oils and/or (2) smoking, salting, and drying seafoods. Establishments known as "floating factory ships" that are engaged in the gathering

and processing of seafood into canned seafood products are included in this industry.

Preparing fresh and frozen seafood and marine fats and oils **311712**

311712 Fresh and Frozen Seafood Processing[US]

This U.S. industry comprises establishments primarily engaged in one or more of the following: (1) eviscerating fresh fish by removing heads, fins, scales, bones, and entrails; (2) shucking and packing fresh shellfish; (3) manufacturing frozen seafood; and (4) processing fresh and frozen marine fats and oils.

Canning and curing seafood **311711**

3118 Bakeries and Tortilla Manufacturing

31181 Bread and Bakery Product Manufacturing

This industry comprises establishments primarily engaged in manufacturing fresh and frozen bread and other bakery products.

Manufacturing cookies and crackers **31182**
Preparing and selling bakery products (e.g., cookies, pretzels) for immediate consumption **72221**
Retailing bakery products not for immediate consumption made elsewhere **44529**
Manufacturing pretzels (except soft) **31191**

311811 Retail Bakeries[CAN]

This U.S. industry comprises establishments primarily engaged in retailing bread and other bakery products not for immediate consumption made on the premises from flour, not from prepared dough.

Retailing bakery products not for immediate consumption made elsewhere **445291**
Preparing and selling bakery products (e.g.,cookies, pretzels) for immediate consumption **722213**
Manufacturing fresh or frozen breads and other fresh bakery (except cookies and crackers) products **311812**
Manufacturing cookies and crackers **311821**

311812 Commercial Bakeries[US]

This U.S. industry comprises establishments primarily engaged in manufacturing fresh and frozen bread and bread-type rolls and other fresh bakery (except cookies and crackers) products.

Retailing bread and other bakery products not for immediate consumption made on the premises from flour, not from prepared dough **311811**

Manufacturing frozen bakery products (except bread) **311813**
Preparing and selling bakery products (e.g., cookies, pretzels) for immediate
consumption **722213**
Retailing bakery products not for immediate consumption made elsewhere
445291
Manufacturing cookies and crackers **311821**
Manufacturing pretzels (except soft) **311919**

311813 Frozen Cakes, Pies, and Other Pastries Manufacturing[US]

This U.S. industry comprises establishments primarily engaged in manufacturing frozen bakery products (except bread), such as cakes, pies, and doughnuts.

Manufacturing frozen breads **311812**
Retailing bakery products not for immediate consumption made on the
premises from flour, not from prepared dough **311811**
Preparing and selling bakery products (e.g., cookies, pretzels) for immediate
consumption **722213**
Manufacturing cookies and crackers **311821**
Retailing bakery products not for immediate consumption made elsewhere
445291

31182 Cookie, Cracker, and Pasta Manufacturing

This industry comprises establishments primarily engaged in one of the following: (1) manufacturing cookies and crackers; (2) preparing flour and dough mixes and dough from flour ground elsewhere; and (3) manufacturing dry pasta. The establishments in this industry may package the dry pasta they manufacture with other ingredients.

Preparing and selling bakery products (eg., cookies, pretzels) for immediate
consumption **72221**
Retailing bakery products not for immediate consumption made elsewhere
44529
Manufacturing bakery products (e.g., bread, cookies, pies) **31181**
Milling flour and preparing flour mixes or doughs **31121**
Manufacturing canned pasta specialties **31142**
Manufacturing fresh pasta **31199**
Manufacturing pretzels (except soft) **31191**
Mixing purchased dried and/or dehydrated ingredients with purchased dry
pasta **31199**
Drying and/or dehydrating ingredients and packaging them with purchased
dry pasta **31142**

311821 Cookie and Cracker Manufacturing[CAN]

This U.S. industry comprises establishments primarily engaged in manufacturing cookies, crackers, and other products, such as ice cream cones.

Preparing and selling bakery products (e.g., cookies, pretzels) for immediate
consumption **722213**
Retailing bakery products not for immediate consumption made elsewhere
445291
Manufacturing bakery products (e.g., breads, cookies, pies) **31181**
Manufacturing pretzels (except soft) **311919**

311822 Flour Mixes and Dough Manufacturing from Purchased Flour[CAN]

This U.S. industry comprises establishments primarily engaged in manufacturing prepared flour mixes or dough mixes from flour ground elsewhere.

Milling flour and preparing flour mixes or doughs **311211**

311823 Dry Pasta Manufacturing[CAN]

This U.S. industry comprises establishments primarily engaged in manufacturing dry pasta. The establishments in this industry may package the dry pasta they manufacture with other ingredients.

Manufacturing fresh pasta **311991**
Manufacturing pasta specialties **3114**
Mixing purchased dried and/or dehydrated ingredients with purchased dry
pasta **311999**
Drying and/or dehydrating ingredients packaged with purchased dry pasta
311423

311830 Tortilla Manufacturing

This industry comprises establishments primarily engaged in manufacturing tortillas.

Manufacturing canned nationality foods using tortillas **311422**
Manufacturing frozen nationality foods using tortillas **311412**
Manufacturing tortilla chips **311919**

3119 Other Food Manufacturing

This industry group comprises establishments primarily engaged in manufacturing food (except animal food; grain and oilseed milling; sugar and confectionery products; preserved fruit, vegetable, and specialty foods; dairy products; meat products; seafood products; and bakeries and tortillas). The industry group includes industries with different productive processes, such as snack food manufacturing; coffee and tea manufacturing; concentrate, syrup, condiment, and spice manufacturing; and, in general, an entire range of other miscellaneous food product manufacturing.

31191 Snack Food Manufacturing

This industry comprises establishments primarily engaged in one or more of the following: (1) salting, roasting, drying, cooking, or canning nuts; (2) processing grains or seeds into snacks; (3) manufacturing peanut butter; and (4) manufacturing potato chips, corn chips, popped popcorn, pretzels (except soft), pork rinds, and similar snacks.

Manufacturing crackers **31182**
Manufacturing unpopped popcorn **31199**
Manufacturing chocolate or candy-coated nuts and candy-covered popcorn **3113**
Manufacturing soft pretzels **31181**

311911 Roasted Nuts and Peanut Butter Manufacturing^{CAN}

This U.S. industry comprises establishments primarily engaged in one or more of the following: (1) salting, roasting, drying, cooking, or canning nuts; (2) processing grains or seeds into snacks; and (3) manufacturing peanut butter.

Manufacturing chocolate or candy-coated nuts and candy-covered popcorn **3113**

311919 Other Snack Food Manufacturing^{CAN}

This U.S. industry comprises establishments primarily engaged in manufacturing snack foods (except roasted nuts and peanut butter).

Manufacturing cookies and crackers **311821**
Manufacturing candy covered popcorn and nonchocolate granola bars **311340**
Salting, roasting, drying, cooking, or canning nuts and seeds **311911**
Manufacturing unpopped popcorn **311999**
Manufacturing soft pretzels **311812**

311920 Coffee and Tea Manufacturing

This industry comprises establishments primarily engaged in one or more of the following: (1) roasting coffee; (2) manufacturing coffee and tea concentrates (including instant and freeze-dried); (3) blending tea; (4) manufacturing herbal tea; and (5) manufacturing coffee extracts, flavorings, and syrups.

Bottling and canning ice tea **312111**

311930 Flavoring Syrup and Concentrate Manufacturing

This industry comprises establishments primarily engaged in manufacturing flavoring syrup drink concentrates and related products for soda fountain use or for the manufacture of soft drinks.

Manufacturing chocolate syrup **311320**
Manufacturing flavoring extracts (except coffee and meat) and natural food colorings **311942**
Manufacturing coffee extracts **311920**
Manufacturing meat extracts **31161**
Manufacturing powdered drink mixes (except coffee, tea, chocolate, or milk-based) and table syrup from corn syrup **311999**
Reducing maple sap to maple syrup **111998**
Manufacturing natural nonfood colorings **325199**

31194 Seasoning and Dressing Manufacturing

This industry comprises establishments primarily engaged in one or more of the following: (1) manufacturing dressings and sauces, such as mayonnaise, salad dressing, vinegar, mustard, horseradish, soy sauce, tarter sauce, Worcestershire sauce, and other prepared sauces (except tomato-based and gravies); (2) manufacturing spices, table salt, seasoning, and flavoring extracts (except coffee and meat), and natural food colorings; and (3) manufacturing dry mix food preparations, such as salad dressing mixes, gravy and sauce mixes, frosting mixes, and other dry mix preparations.

Manufacturing catsup and other tomato-based sauces **31142**
Mixing purchased dried and/or dehydrated potato, rice, and pasta and packaging them with other purchased ingredients, and manufacturing prepared frosting **31199**
Drying and/or dehydrating ingredients for dry soup mixes and bouillon **31142**
Mixing purchased dried and/or dehydrated ingredients for dry soup mixes and bouillon **31199**
Manufacturing industrial salts **32599**
Manufacturing flavoring syrups (except coffee) **31193**
Manufacturing synthetic food colorings **32513**
Manufacturing natural organic colorings for nonfood uses **32519**
Manufacturing coffee extracts **31192**
Manufacturing gravies **31199**

311941 Mayonnaise, Dressing, and Other Prepared Sauce Manufacturing^{US}

This U.S. industry comprises establishments primarily engaged in manufacturing mayonnaise, salad dressing, vinegar, mustard, horseradish, soy sauce, tarter sauce, Worcestershire sauce, and other prepared sauces (except tomato-based and gravy).

Manufacturing catsup and similar tomato-based sauces **311421**

Manufacturing dry salad dressing and dry sauce mixes **311942**
Manufacturing gravies **311999**

311942 Spice and Extract Manufacturing[US]

This U.S. industry comprises establishments primarily engaged in (1) manufacturing spices, table salt, seasonings, flavoring extracts (except coffee and meat), and natural food colorings and/or (2) manufacturing dry mix food preparations, such as salad dressing mixes, gravy and sauce mixes, frosting mixes, and other dry mix preparations.

Manufacturing catsup and other tomato-based sauces **311421**
Manufacturing mayonnaise, dressings, and prepared nontomato-based sauces **311941,**
Manufacturing industrial salts **325998**
Drying and/or dehydrating ingredients for dry soup mixes and bouillon **311423**
Mixing purchased dried and/or dehydrated ingredients for dry soup mixes and bouillon **311999**
Manufacturing flavoring syrups **311930**
Manufacturing dried and dehydrated potato, rice, or dry pasta packaged with other ingredients, and prepared frostings **311999**
Manufacturing coffee extracts **311920**
Manufacturing meat extracts **31161**
Manufacturing synthetic food colorings **325132**
Manufacturing natural organic colorings for nonfood uses **325199**

31199 All Other Food Manufacturing

This industry comprises establishments primarily engaged in manufacturing food (except animal food; grain and oilseed milling; sugar and confectionery products; preserved fruits, vegetables, and specialties; dairy products; meat products; seafood products; bakeries and tortillas; snack foods; coffee and tea; flavoring syrups and concentrates; seasonings; and dressings). Included in this industry are establishments primarily engaged in mixing purchased dried and/or dehydrated ingredients including those mixing purchased dried and/or dehydrated ingredients for soup mixes and bouillon.

Manufacturing animal foods **3111**
Milling grain and oilseed **3112**
Manufacturing sugar and confectionery products **3113**
Preserving fruit, vegetables, and specialty foods **3114**
Manufacturing dairy products **3115**
Manufacturing meat products **3116**
Manufacturing seafood products **3117**
Manufacturing bakery and tortilla products **3118**

Manufacturing snack foods **31191**
Manufacturing coffee and tea **31192**
Manufacturing flavoring syrups and concentrates **31193**
Manufacturing seasonings and dressings **31194**
Milling rice and packaging it with other ingredients **311121**
Manufacturing dry pasta and packaging it with other ingredients **311823**
Drying and/or dehydrating ingredients and packaging them with other purchased ingredients **31142**

311991 Perishable Prepared Food Manufacturing[US]

This U.S. industry comprises establishments primarily engaged in manufacturing perishable prepared foods, such as salads, sandwiches, prepared meals, fresh pizza, fresh pasta, and peeled or cut vegetables.

311999 All Other Miscellaneous Food Manufacturing[US]

This U.S. industry comprises establishments primarily engaged in manufacturing food (except animal food; grain and oilseed milling; sugar and confectionery products; preserved fruits, vegetables, and specialties; dairy products; meat products; seafood products; bakeries and tortillas; snack foods; coffee and tea; flavoring syrups and concentrates; seasonings and dressings; and perishable prepared food). Included in this industry are establishments primarily engaged in mixing purchased dried and/or dehydrated ingredients including those mixing purchased dried and/or dehydrated ingredients for soup mixes and bouillon.

Manufacturing animal foods **3111**
Milling grain and oilseed **3112**
Manufacturing sugar and confectionery products **3113**
Preserving fruit, vegetable, and specialty foods **3114**
Manufacturing dairy products **3115**
Manufacturing meat products **3116**
Manufacturing seafood products **3117**
Manufacturing bakery and tortilla products **3118**
Manufacturing snack foods **31191**
Manufacturing coffee and tea **31192**
Manufacturing flavoring syrups and concentrates **31193**
Manufacturing seasonings and dressings **31194**
Manufacturing perishable prepared foods **311991**
Milling rice and packaging it with other ingredients **311212**
Manufacturing dry pasta and packaging it with ingredients **311823**
Drying and/or dehydrating ingredients and packaging them with other purchased ingredients **311423**

312 Beverage and Tobacco Product Manufacturing

Industries in the Beverage and Tobacco Product Manufacturing subsector manufacture beverages and tobacco products. The industry group, Beverage Manufacturing, includes three types of establishments: (1) those that manufacture nonalcoholic beverages; (2) those that manufacture alcoholic beverages through the fermentation process; and (3) those that produce distilled alcoholic beverages. Ice manufacturing, while not a beverage, is included with nonalcoholic beverage manufacturing because it uses the same production process as water purification. In the case of activities related to the manufacture of beverages, the structure follows the defined productive processes. Brandy, a distilled beverage, was not placed under distillery product manufacturing, but rather under the NAICS class for winery product manufacturing since the productive process used in the manufacturing of alcoholic grape-based beverages produces both wines (fermented beverage) and brandies (distilled beverage). The industry group, Tobacco Manufacturing, includes two types of establishments: (1) those engaged in redrying and stemming tobacco and (2) those that manufacture tobacco products, such as cigarettes and cigars.

3121 Beverage Manufacturing

31211 Soft Drink and Ice Manufacturing

This industry comprises establishments primarily engaged in one or more of the following: (1) manufacturing soft drinks; (2) manufacturing ice; and (3) purifying and bottling water.

Canning fruit and vegetable juices **31142**
Manufacturing soft drink bases **31193**
Manufacturing nonalcoholic cider **31199**
Manufacturing dry ice **32512**
Manufacturing milk-based drinks **31151**
Manufacturing nonalcoholic beers **31212**
Manufacturing nonalcoholic wines **31213**
Bottling purchased purified water **42249**

312111 Soft Drink Manufacturing[US]

This U.S. industry comprises establishments primarily engaged in manufacturing soft drinks and artificially carbonated waters.

Canning fruit and vegetable juices **311421**
Manufacturing fruit syrups for flavoring **31193**
Manufacturing nonalcoholic cider **311999**
Purifying and bottling water (except artificially carbonated and flavored water) **312112**
Manufacturing nonalcoholic beers **312120**
Manufacturing nonalcoholic wines **312130**

312112 Bottled Water Manufacturing[US]

This U.S. industry comprises establishments primarily engaged in purifying and bottling water (includ-

ing naturally carbonated).

Manufacturing artificially carbonated waters **312111**
Bottling purchased purified water **422490**

312113 Ice Manufacturing[US]

This U.S. industry comprises establishments primarily engaged in manufacturing ice.

Manufacturing dry ice **325120**

312120 Breweries

This industry comprises establishments primarily engaged in brewing beer, ale, malt liquors, and non-alcoholic beer.

Bottling purchased malt beverages **422810**
Manufacturing malt **311213**

312130 Wineries

This industry comprises establishments primarily engaged in one or more of the following: (1) growing grapes and manufacturing wine and brandies; (2) manufacturing wine and brandies from grapes and other fruits grown elsewhere; and (3) blending wines and brandies.

Bottling wines made elsewhere are classified in Industry **422820**

312140 Distilleries

This industry comprises establishments primarily engaged in one or more of the following: (1) distilling potable liquors (except brandies); (2) distilling and blending liquors; and (3) blending and mixing liquors and other ingredients.

Manufacturing nonpotable ethyl alcohol **325193**
Bottling liquors made elsewhere **422820**
Manufacturing brandies **312130**

3122 Tobacco Manufacturing

312210 Tobacco Stemming and Redrying

This industry comprises establishments primarily engaged in the stemming and redrying of tobacco.

Reconstituting tobacco **312229**
Selling leaf tobacco as merchant wholesalers, agents, or brokers, and that also engage in stemming tobacco **422940**

31222 Tobacco Product Manufacturing

This industry comprises establishments primarily

engaged in manufacturing cigarettes, cigars, smoking and chewing tobacco, and reconstituted tobacco.

Stemming and redrying tobacco **31221**

312221 Cigarette Manufacturing[US]

This U.S. industry comprises establishments primarily engaged in manufacturing cigarettes.

Manufacturing cigars, smoking tobacco, chewing tobacco, and reconstituted tobacco **312229**

312229 Other Tobacco Product Manufacturing[US]

This U.S. industry comprises establishments primarily engaged in manufacturing tobacco products (except cigarettes).

Manufacturing cigarettes **312221**
Stemming and redrying tobacco **312210**

---

313 Textile Mills

Industries in the Textile Mills subsector group establishments that transform a basic fiber (natural or synthetic) into a product, such as yarn or fabric, that is further manufactured into usable items, such as apparel, sheets towels, and textile bags for individual or industrial consumption. The further manufacturing may be performed in the same establishment and classified in this subsector, or it may be performed at a separate establishment and be classified elsewhere in manufacturing. The main processes in this subsector include preparation and spinning of fiber, knitting or weaving of fabric, and the finishing of the textile. The NAICS structure follows and captures this process flow. Major industries in this flow, such as preparation of fibers, weaving of fabric, knitting of fabric, and fiber and fabric finishing, are uniquely identified. Texturizing, throwing, twisting, and winding of yarn contains aspects of both fiber preparation and fiber finishing and is classified with preparation of fibers rather than with finishing of fiber.

NAICS separates the manufacturing of primary textiles and the manufacturing of textile products (except apparel) when the textile product is produced from purchased primary textiles, such as fabric. The manufacturing of textile products (except apparel) from purchased fabric is classified in Subsector 314, Textile Product Mills, and apparel from purchased fabric is classified in Subsector 315, Apparel Manufacturing. Excluded from this subsector are establishments that weave or knit fabric and make garments. These establishments are included in Subsector 315, Apparel Manufacturing.

31311 Fiber, Yarn, and Thread Mills

This industry comprises establishments primarily engaged in one or more of the following: (1) spinning yarn; (2) manufacturing thread of any fiber; (3) texturizing, throwing, twisting, and winding pur-

chased yarn or manmade fiber filaments; and (4) producing hemp yarn and further processing into rope or bags.

Manufacturing artificial and synthetic fibers and filaments and texturizing these filaments **32522**

313111 Yarn Spinning Mills[US]

This U.S. industry comprises establishments primarily engaged in spinning yarn from any fiber and/or producing hemp yarn and further processing into rope or bags.

313112 Yarn Texturizing, Throwing, and Twisting Mills[US]

This U.S. industry comprises establishments primarily engaged in texturizing, throwing, twisting, spooling, or winding purchased yarns or manmade fiber filaments.

Manufacturing artificial and synthetic fiber and filament and texturizing these fibers and filaments **32522**

313113 Thread Mills[US]

This U.S. industry comprises establishments primarily engaged in manufacturing thread (e.g., sewing, hand-knitting, crochet) of all fibers.

3132 Fabric Mills

313210 Broadwoven Fabric Mills

This industry comprises establishments primarily engaged in weaving broadwoven fabrics and felts (except tire fabrics and rugs). Establishments in this industry may weave only, weave and finish, or weave, finish, and further fabricate fabric products.

Weaving widths specifically constructed for cutting to narrow widths **313221**
Weaving or tufting carpet and rugs **314110**
Making tire cord and fabrics **31499**

31322 Narrow Fabric Mills and Schiffli Machine Embroidery

This industry comprises establishments primarily engaged in one or more of the following: (1) weaving or braiding narrow fabrics; (2) manufacturing Schiffli machine embroideries; and (3) making fabric-covered elastic yarn and thread.

313221 Narrow Fabric Mills[US]

This U.S. industry comprises establishments primarily engaged in (1) weaving or braiding narrow fabrics in their final form or initially made in wider widths that are specially constructed for narrower widths and/or (2) making fabric-covered elastic yarn and thread. Establishments in this industry may weave only; weave and finish; or weave, finish, and further fabricate fabric products.

313222 Schiffli Machine Embroidery[US]

This U.S. industry comprises establishments primarily engaged in manufacturing Schiffli machine embroideries.

313230 Nonwoven Fabric Mills

This industry comprises establishments primarily engaged in manufacturing nonwoven fabrics and felts. Processes used include bonding and/or interlocking fibers by mechanical, chemical, thermal, or solvent means, or by combinations thereof.

31324 Knit Fabric Mills

This industry comprises establishments primarily engaged in one of the following: (1) knitting weft (i.e., circular) and warp (i.e., flat) fabric; (2) knitting and finishing weft and warp fabric; (3) manufacturing lace; or (4) manufacturing, dyeing, and finishing lace and lace goods. Establishments in this industry may knit only; knit and finish; or knit, finish, and further fabricate fabric products (except apparel).

Knitting apparel **3151**

313241 Weft Knit Fabric Mills[US]

This U.S. industry comprises establishments primarily engaged in knitting weft (i.e., circular) fabric or knitting and finishing weft fabric. Establishments in this industry may knit only; knit and finish; or knit, finish, and further fabricate fabric products (except apparel).

Knitting apparel **3151**

313249 Other Knit Fabric and Lace Mills[US]

This U.S. industry comprises establishments primarily engaged in one of the following: (1) knitting warp (i.e., flat) fabric; (2) knitting and finishing warp fabric; (3) manufacturing lace; or (4) manufacturing, dyeing, or finishing lace and lace goods. Establishments in this industry may knit only; knit and finish;

or knit, finish, and further fabricate fabric products (except apparel).

Knitting apparel **3151**

3133 Textile and Fabric Finishing and Fabric Coating Mills

31331 Textile and Fabric Finishing Mills

This industry comprises (1) establishments primarily engaged in finishing of textiles, fabrics, and apparel, and (2) establishments of converters who buy fabric goods in the grey, have them finished on contract, and sell at wholesale. Finishing operations include: bleaching, dyeing, printing (e.g., roller, screen, flock, plisse), stonewashing, and other mechanical finishing, such as preshrinking, shrinking, sponging, calendering, mercerizing, and napping; as well as cleaning, scouring, and the preparation of natural fibers and raw stock.

Coating or impregnating fabrics **31332**
Knitting or knitting and finishing fabric **31324**
Manufacturing and finishing apparel **315**
Weaving and finishing fabrics **3132**
Manufacturing and finishing rugs and carpets **31411**
Printing on apparel **32311**

313311 Broadwoven Fabric Finishing Mills[US]

This U.S. industry comprises (1) establishments primarily engaged in finishing broadwoven fabrics and (2) establishments of converters who buy broadwoven fabrics in the grey, have them finished on contract, and sell at wholesale. Finishing operations include bleaching, dyeing, printing (roller, screen, flock,

plisse), and other mechanical finishing, such as preshrinking, shrinking, sponging, calendering, mercerizing and napping.

Coating or impregnating fabrics **313320**
Weaving and finishing broadwoven fabrics **313210**

313312 Textile and Fabric Finishing (except Broadwoven Fabric) Mills[US]

This U.S. industry comprises (1) establishments primarily engaged in dyeing, bleaching, printing, and other finishing of textiles, apparel, and fabrics (except broadwoven) and (2) establishments of converters who buy fabrics (except broadwoven) in the grey, have them finished on contract, and sell at wholesale. Finishing operations include bleaching, dyeing, printing (e.g., roller, screen, flock, plisse), stonewashing, and other mechanical finishing, such as preshrinking, shrinking, sponging, calendering, mercerizing and napping; as well as cleaning, scouring, and the preparation of natural fibers and raw stock.

Knitting and finishing fabric **31324**
Finishing broadwoven fabric **313311**
Weaving and finishing narrow woven fabric **313221**
Manufacturing and finishing apparel **315**
Coating or impregnating fabrics **313320**
Printing on apparel **32311**

313320 Fabric Coating Mills

This industry comprises establishments primarily engaged in coating, laminating, varnishing, waxing, and rubberizing textiles and apparel.

Dyeing and finishing textiles **31331**

314

---

314 Textile Product Mills

Industries in the Textile Product Mills subsector group establishments that made textile products (except apparel). With a few exceptions, processes used in these industries are generally cut and sew (i.e., purchasing fabric and cutting and sewing to make nonapparel textile products, such as sheets and towels).

3141 Textile Furnishings Mills

314110 Carpet and Rug Mills

This industry comprises establishments primarily engaged in (1) manufacturing woven, tufted, and other

carpets and rugs, such as art squares, floor mattings, needlepunch carpeting, and door mats and mattings, from textile materials or from twisted paper, grasses, reeds, sisal, jute, or rags and/or (2) finishing carpets and rugs.

31412 Curtain and Linen Mills

This industry comprises establishments primarily engaged in manufacturing household textile products, such as curtains, draperies, linens, bedspreads, sheets, tablecloths, towels, and shower curtains, from purchased materials.

Weaving fabrics **31321**
Manufacturing lace curtains on lace machines **31324**
Manufacturing textile blanket, wardrobe, and laundry bags **31491**
Manufacturing mops **33999**

314121 Curtain and Drapery Mills[US]

This U.S. industry comprises establishments primarily engaged in manufacturing window curtains and draperies from purchased fabrics or sheet goods. The curtains and draperies may be made on a stock or custom basis for sale to individual retail customers.

Manufacturing lace curtains on lace machines **313249**

314129 Other Household Textile Product Mills[US]

This U.S. industry comprises establishments primarily engaged in manufacturing household textile products (except window curtains and draperies), such as bedspreads, sheets, tablecloths, towels, and shower curtains, from purchased materials.

Weaving fabrics **313210**
Manufacturing blanket, laundry, and wardrobe bags **314911**
Manufacturing mops **339994**
Manufacturing window curtains and draperies **314121**

3149 Other Textile Product Mills

This industry group comprises establishments primarily engaged in making textile products, (except carpets and rugs, curtains and draperies, and other household textile products) from purchased materials.

31491 Textile Bag and Canvas Mills

This industry comprises establishments primarily engaged in manufacturing textile bags, awnings, tents, and related products from purchased textile fabrics.

Manufacturing plastic bags **32611**
Manufacturing canvas blinds and shades **33792**
Manufacturing luggage **31699**
Manufacturing women's handbags and purses of leather or other material (except precious metal) **31699**

314911 Textile Bag Mills[US]

This U.S. industry comprises establishments primarily engaged in manufacturing bags from purchased textile fabrics or yarns.

Manufacturing plastics bags **326111**
Manufacturing luggage **316991**
Manufacturing women's handbags and purses of leather or other material, except precious metal **316992**

314912 Canvas and Related Product Mills[US]

This U.S. industry comprises establishments primarily engaged in manufacturing canvas and canvas-like products, such as awnings, sails, tarpaulins, and tents, from purchased fabrics.

Manufacturing canvas blinds and shades **337920**
Manufacturing canvas bags **314911**

31499 All Other Textile Product Mills

This industry comprises establishments primarily engaged in manufacturing nonapparel textile products (except carpet, rugs, curtains, linens, bags, and canvas products) from purchased materials.

Manufacturing yarns and thread **31311**
Manufacturing carpets and rugs **31411**
Manufacturing apparel **315**
Manufacturing curtains and linens **31412**
Manufacturing textile bags and canvas products **31491**

314991 Rope, Cordage, and Twine Mills[US]

This U.S. industry comprises establishments primarily engaged in manufacturing rope, cable, cordage, twine, and related products from all materials (e.g., abaca, sisal, henequen, hemp, cotton, paper, jute, flax, manmade fibers including glass).

Manufacturing yarns and filaments **313111**

314992 Tire Cord and Tire Fabric Mills[US]

This U.S. industry comprises establishments primarily engaged in manufacturing cord and fabric of polyester, rayon, cotton, glass, steel, or other materials for use in reinforcing rubber tires, industrial belting, and similar uses.

314999 All Other Miscellaneous Textile Product Mills[US]

This U.S. industry comprises establishments primarily engaged in manufacturing textile products (except carpets and rugs; curtains and linens; textile bags and canvas products; rope, cordage, and twine; and tire cords and tire fabrics) from purchased materials.

Manufacturing yarns and thread **31311**

Manufacturing carpets and rugs **314110**
Manufacturing curtains and linens **31412**
Manufacturing textile bags and canvas products **31491**
Manufacturing tire cords and tire fabrics **314992**

315 Apparel Manufacturing

Industries in the Apparel Manufacturing subsector group establishments with two distinct manufacturing processes: (1) cut and sew (i.e., purchasing fabric and cutting and sewing to make a garment) and (2) the manufacture of garments in establishments that first knit fabric and then cut and sew the fabric into a garment. The Apparel Manufacturing subsector includes a diverse range of establishments manufacturing full lines of ready-to-wear apparel and custom apparel: apparel contractors, performing cutting or sewing operations on materials owned by others; jobbers performing entrepreneurial functions involved in apparel manufacture; and tailors, manufacturing custom garments for individual clients are all included. Knitting, when done alone, is classified in the Textile Mills subsector, but when knitting is combined with the production of complete garments, the activity is classified in Apparel Manufacturing.

3151 Apparel Knitting Mills

This industry group comprises establishments primarily engaged in knitting apparel or knitting fabric and then manufacturing apparel. This industry group includes jobbers performing entrepreneurial functions involved in knitting apparel and accessories. Knitting fabric, without manufacturing apparel, is classified in Subsector 313, Textile Mills.

31511 Hosiery and Sock Mills

This industry comprises establishments primarily engaged in knitting or knitting and finishing hosiery and socks.

Manufacturing orthopedic hosiery **33911**
Manufacturing slipper socks from purchased socks **31621**
Finishing apparel products only **31331**

315111 Sheer Hosiery Mills[US]

This U.S. industry comprises establishments primarily engaged in knitting or knitting and finishing women's, misses', and girls' full-length and knee-length sheer hosiery (except socks).

Knitting or knitting and finishing socks **315119**
Finishing apparel products only **313312**
Manufacturing orthopedic hosiery **339113**

315119 Other Hosiery and Sock Mills[US]

This U.S. industry comprises establishments primarily engaged in knitting or knitting and finishing hosiery (except women's, misses', and girls' sheer hosiery).

Knitting or knitting and finishing women's, misses', and girls' full-length
    and knee-length sheer hosiery **315111**
Manufacturing orthopedic hosiery **339113**
Finishing apparel products only **313312**
Manufacturing slipper socks from purchased socks **316212**

31519 Other Apparel Knitting Mills

This industry comprises establishments primarily engaged in one of the following: (1) knitting underwear, outerwear, and/or nightwear; (2) knitting fabric and manufacturing underwear, outerwear, and/or nightwear; or (3) knitting, manufacturing, and finishing knit underwear, outerwear, and/or nightwear.

Manufacturing outerwear, underwear, and nightwear from purchased fabric
    3152
Finishing apparel products only **31331**

315191 Outerwear Knitting Mills[US]

This U.S. industry comprises establishments primarily engaged in one or more of the following: (1) knitting outerwear; (2) knitting fabric and manufacturing outerwear; and (3) knitting, manufacturing, and finishing knit outerwear. Examples of products made in knit outerwear mills are shirts, shorts, sweat suits, sweaters, gloves, and pants.

Manufacturing outerwear from purchased fabric **3152**
Finishing apparel products only **313312**
Knitting underwear and nightwear, knitting fabric and manufacturing underwear and nightwear, or knitting, manufacturing, and finishing knit underwear and nightwear **315192**

315192 Underwear and Nightwear Knitting Mills[US]

This U.S. industry comprises establishments primarily engaged in one of the following: (1) knitting underwear and nightwear; (2) knitting fabric and manufacturing underwear and nightwear; or (3) knitting, manufacturing, and finishing knit underwear and nightwear. Examples of products produced in underwear and nightwear knitting mills are briefs, underwear T-shirts, pajamas, nightshirts, foundation garments, and panties.

Manufacturing underwear and nightwear from purchased fabric **3152**
Finishing apparel products only **313312**

3152 Cut and Sew Apparel Manufacturing

This industry group comprises establishments primarily engaged in manufacturing cut and sew apparel from woven fabric or purchased knit fabric. Included in this industry group is a diverse range of establishments manufacturing full lines of ready-to-wear apparel and custom apparel: apparel contractors, performing cutting or sewing operations on materials owned by others; jobbers performing entrepreneurial functions involved in apparel manufacture; and tailors, manufacturing custom garments for individual clients. Establishments weaving or knitting fabric, without manufacturing apparel, are classified in Subsector 313, Textile Mills.

31521 Cut and Sew Apparel Contractors[CAN]

This industry comprises establishments commonly referred to as contractors primarily engaged in (1) cutting materials owned by others for apparel and accessories and/or (2) sewing materials owned by others for apparel and accessories.

Manufacturing men's and boys' apparel from purchased fabric **31522**
Manufacturing women's and girls' apparel from purchased fabric **31523**
Manufacturing infants' apparel and all other cut and sew apparel from purchased fabric **31529**
Manufacturing apparel accessories from purchased fabric **31599**

315211 Men's and Boys' Cut and Sew Apparel Contractors[US]

This U.S. industry comprises establishments commonly referred to as contractors primarily engaged in (1) cutting materials owned by others for men's and boys' apparel and/or (2) sewing materials owned by others for men's and boys' apparel.

Manufacturing men's and boys' apparel from purchased fabric **31522**
Manufacturing infants' apparel from purchased fabric **315291**
Manufacturing men's and boys' apparel accessories from purchased fabric **31599**

315212 Women's, Girls', and Infants' Cut and Sew Apparel Contractors[US]

This U.S. industry comprises establishments commonly referred to as contractors primarily engaged in (1) cutting materials owned by others for women's, girls', and infants' apparel and accessories and/or (2) sewing materials owned by others for women's, girls', and infants' apparel and accessories.

Manufacturing women's and girls' apparel from purchased fabric **31523**
Manufacturing infants' apparel from purchased fabric **315291**
Manufacturing women's, girls', and infants' apparel accessories from purchased fabric **31599**

31522 Men's and Boys' Cut and Sew Apparel Manufacturing[CAN]

This industry comprises establishments primarily engaged in manufacturing men's and boys' cut and sew apparel from purchased fabric. Men's and boys' clothing jobbers, who perform entrepreneurial functions involved in apparel manufacture, including buying raw materials, designing and preparing samples, arranging for apparel to be made from their materials, and marketing finished apparel, are included.

Cutting and/or sewing materials owned by others for men's and boys' apparel **31521**
Knitting men's and boys' apparel or knitting fabric and manufacturing men's and boys' apparel **3151**
Manufacturing fur or leather apparel and team athletic uniforms **31529**

315221 Men's and Boys' Cut and Sew Underwear and Nightwear Manufacturing[CAN]

This U.S. industry comprises establishments primarily engaged in manufacturing men's and boys' underwear and nightwear from purchased fabric. Men's and boys' underwear and nightwear jobbers, who perform entrepreneurial functions involved in apparel manufacture, including buying raw materials, designing and preparing samples, arranging for apparel to be made from their materials, and marketing finished apparel, are included. Examples of products made by these establishments are briefs, bathrobes, underwear T-shirts and shorts, nightshirts, and pajamas.

Knitting men's and boys' underwear and nightwear and/or knitting and manufacturing men's and boys' underwear and nightwear **315192**
Cutting and/or sewing materials owned by others for men's and boys' underwear and nightwear **315211**

315222 Men's and Boys' Cut and Sew Suit, Coat, and Overcoat Manufacturing[CAN]

This U.S. industry comprises establishments primarily engaged in manufacturing men's and boys' suits, overcoats, sport coats, tuxedoes, dress uniforms, and other tailored apparel (except fur and leather) from purchased fabric. Men's and boys' suit, coat, and overcoat jobbers, who perform entrepreneurial functions involved in apparel manufacture, including buying raw materials, designing and preparing samples, arranging for apparel to be made from their materials, and marketing finished apparel, are included.

Manufacturing men's and boys' nontailored coats and jackets such as down coats and windbreakers made from purchased fabric **315228**
Manufacturing fur and leather apparel **315292**
Manufacturing men's and boys' washable service apparel from purchased fabric **315225**
Manufacturing men's and boys' team athletic uniforms from purchased fabric **315299**
Cutting and/or sewing materials owned by others for men's and boys' suits, coats, and overcoats **315211**

315223 Men's and Boys' Cut and Sew Shirt (except Work Shirt) Manufacturing[US]

This U.S. industry comprises establishments primarily engaged in manufacturing men's and boys' outerwear shirts from purchased fabric. Men's and boys' shirt (except work shirt) jobbers, who perform entrepreneurial functions involved in apparel manufacture, including buying raw materials, designing and preparing samples, arranging for apparel to be made from their materials, and marketing finished apparel, are included. Unisex outerwear shirts, such as T-shirts and sweatshirts that are sized without specific reference to gender (i.e., adult S, M, L, XL) are included in this industry.

Manufacturing men's and boys' work shirts from purchased fabric **315225**
Manufacturing men's and boys' underwear T-shirts and underwear tank tops from purchased fabric **315221**
Cutting and/or sewing materials owned by others for men's and boys' shirts **315211**
Knitting men's and boys' outerwear shirts or knitting fabric and manufacturing men's and boys' outerwear shirts **315191**

315224 Men's and Boys' Cut and Sew Trouser, Slack, and Jean Manufacturing[US]

This U.S. industry comprises establishments primarily engaged in manufacturing men's and boys' jeans, dungarees, and other separate trousers and slacks (except work pants) from purchased fabric. Men's and boys' trouser, slack, and jean jobbers, who perform entrepreneurial functions involved in apparel manufacture, including buying raw materials, designing and preparing samples, arranging for apparel to be made from their materials, and marketing finished apparel, are included.

Manufacturing men's and boys' work pants from purchased fabric **315225**
Manufacturing fur and leather apparel **315292**
Manufacturing men's and boys' sweatpants and shorts from purchased fabric **315228**
Cutting and/or sewing materials owned by others for men's and boys' separate trousers, slacks, and jeans **315211**

315225 Men's and Boys' Cut and Sew Work Clothing Manufacturing[US]

This U.S. industry comprises establishments primarily engaged in manufacturing men's and boys' work shirts, work pants (excluding jeans and dungarees), other work clothing, and washable service apparel from purchased fabric. Men's and boys' work clothing jobbers, who perform entrepreneurial functions involved in apparel manufacture, including buying raw materials, designing and preparing samples, arranging for apparel to be made from their materials, and marketing finished apparel, are included. Examples of products made by these establishments are washable service apparel, laboratory coats, work shirts, work pants (except jeans and dungarees), and hospital apparel.

Manufacturing men's and boys' separate trousers, slacks, and pants, including jeans and dungarees from purchased fabric **315224**
Cutting and/or sewing materials owned by others for men's and boys' work clothing **315211**

315

315228 Men's and Boys' Cut and Sew Other Outerwear Manufacturing[US]

This U.S. industry comprises establishments primarily engaged in manufacturing men's and boys' cut and sew outerwear from purchased fabric (except underwear, nightwear, shirts, suits, overcoats and tailored coats, separate trousers and slacks, and work clothing). Men's and boys' other outerwear jobbers, who perform entrepreneurial functions involved in apparel manufacture, including buying raw materials, designing and preparing samples, arranging for apparel to be made from their materials, and marketing finished apparel, are included. Unisex sweatpants and similar garments that are sized without specific reference to gender (i.e., adult S, M, L, XL) are also included in this industry. Examples of products made by these establishments are athletic clothing (except athletic uniforms), bathing suits, down coats, outerwear shorts, windbreakers and jackets, and jogging suits.

Manufacturing men's and boys' athletic uniforms from purchased fabric **315299**

Manufacturing leather and fur apparel **315292**

Knitting men's and boys' apparel or knitting fabric and manufacturing men's and boys' apparel **3151**

Cutting and/or sewing materials owned by others for men's and boys' apparel **315211**

Manufacturing men's and boys' underwear and nightwear from purchased fabric **315221**

Manufacturing men's and boys' tailored suits, coats, and overcoats from purchased fabric **315222**

Manufacturing men's and boys' outerwear shirts (except work shirts) from purchased fabric **315223**

Manufacturing men's and boys' separate pants, trousers, and slacks from purchased fabric **315224**

Manufacturing men's and boys' work clothing from purchased fabric **315225**

31523 Women's and Girls' Cut and Sew Apparel Manufacturing[CAN]

This industry comprises establishments primarily engaged in manufacturing women's and girls' apparel from purchased fabric. Women's and girls' clothing jobbers, who perform entrepreneurial functions involved in apparel manufacture, including buying raw materials, designing and preparing samples, arranging for apparel to be made from their materials, and marketing finished apparel, are included.

Knitting women's and girls' apparel or knitting fabric and manufacturing women's and girls' apparel **3151**

Manufacturing unisex outerwear garments, such as T-shirts, sweatshirts, and sweatpants that are sized without reference to specific gender (i.e., adult S, M, L, XL), **31522**

Cutting and/or sewing materials owned by others for women's and girls' apparel **31521**

Manufacturing fur or leather apparel and team athletic uniforms **31529**

315231 Women's and Girls' Cut and Sew Lingerie, Loungewear, and Nightwear Manufacturing[CAN]

This U.S. industry comprises establishments primarily engaged in manufacturing women's and girls' bras, girdles, and other underwear; lingerie; loungewear; and nightwear from purchased fabric. Women's and girls' lingerie, loungewear, and nightwear jobbers, who perform entrepreneurial functions involved in apparel manufacture, including buying raw materials, designing and preparing samples, arranging for apparel to be made from their materials, and marketing finished apparel, are included. Examples of products made by these establishments are bathrobes, foundation garments, nightgowns, pajamas, panties, and slips.

Knitting women's and girls' underwear, nightwear, and lingerie or knitting fabric and manufacturing women's and girls' underwear, nightwear, and lingerie **315192**

Cutting and/or sewing materials owned by others for women's and girls' underwear, nightwear, and lingerie **315212**

315232 Women's and Girls' Cut and Sew Blouse and Shirt Manufacturing[CAN]

This U.S. industry comprises establishments primarily engaged in manufacturing women's and girls' blouses and shirts from purchased fabric. Women's and girls' blouse and shirt jobbers, who perform entrepreneurial functions involved in apparel manufacture, including buying raw materials, designing and preparing samples, arranging for apparel to be made from their materials, and marketing finished apparel, are included.

Knitting women's and girls' blouses, shirts, and tops or knitting fabric and manufacturing women's and girls' blouses, shirts, and tops **315191**

Manufacturing unisex outerwear shirts, such as T-shirts and sweatshirts that are sized without specific reference to gender (i.e., adult S, M, L, XL), **315223**

Cutting and/or sewing materials owned by others for women's and girls' shirts and blouses **315212**

315233 Women's and Girls' Cut and Sew Dress Manufacturing[CAN]

This U.S. industry comprises establishments prima-

rily engaged in manufacturing women's and girls' dresses from purchased fabric. Women's and girls' dress jobbers, who perform entrepreneurial functions involved in apparel manufacture, including buying raw materials, designing and preparing samples, arranging for apparel to be made from their materials, and marketing finished apparel, are included.

Knitting women's and girls' dresses or knitting fabric and manufacturing women's and girls' dresses **315191**

Cutting and/or sewing materials owned by others for women's and girls' dresses **315212**

315234 Women's and Girls' Cut and Sew Suit, Coat, Tailored Jacket, and Skirt Manufacturing[CAN]

This U.S. industry comprises establishments primarily engaged in manufacturing women's and girls' suits, pantsuits, skirts, tailored jackets, vests, raincoats, and other tailored coats, (except fur and leather coats) from purchased fabric. Women's and girls' suit, coat, tailored jacket, and skirt jobbers, who perform entrepreneurial functions involved in apparel manufacture, including buying raw materials, designing and preparing samples, arranging for apparel to be made from their materials, and marketing finished apparel, are included.

Manufacturing women's and girls' team athletic uniforms from purchased fabric **315299**

Manufacturing women's and girls' separate slacks, jeans, pants, and nontailored coats and jackets, such as down coats and windbreakers from purchased fabric, **315239**

Manufacturing fur and leather apparel **315292**

Knitting women's and girls' tailored skirts, suits, vests, and coats or knitting fabric and manufacturing women's and girls' tailored skirts, suits, vests, and coats **315191**

Cutting and/or sewing materials owned by others for women's and girls' suits, coats, tailored jackets, and skirts **315212**

315239 Women's and Girls' Cut and Sew Other Outerwear Manufacturing[CAN]

This U.S. industry comprises establishments primarily engaged in manufacturing women's and girls' cut and sew apparel from purchased fabric (except underwear, lingerie, nightwear, blouses, shirts, dresses, suits, tailored coats, tailored jackets, and skirts). Women's and girls' other outerwear clothing jobbers, who perform entrepreneurial functions involved in apparel manufacture, including buying raw materials, designing and preparing samples, arranging for apparel to be made from their materials, and market-

ing finished apparel, are included. Examples of products made by these establishments are bathing suits, down coats, sweaters, jogging suits, outerwear pants and shorts, and windbreakers.

Manufacturing women's and girls' team athletic uniforms from purchased fabric **315299**

Knitting women's and girls' apparel or knitting fabric and manufacturing women's and girls' apparel **315191**

Manufacturing women's and girls' fur and leather apparel **315292**

Cutting and/or sewing materials owned by others for women's and girls' apparel **315212**

Manufacturing women's and girls' lingerie, loungewear, and nightwear from purchased fabric **315231**

Manufacturing women's and girls' blouses and outerwear shirts from purchased fabric **315232**

Manufacturing unisex sweatpants and similar outerwear garments that are sized without specific reference to gender (i.e., adult S, M, L, XL) **315228**

Manufacturing women's and girls' dresses from purchased fabric **315233**

Manufacturing women's and girls' suits, skirts, and tailored coats and jackets from purchased fabric **315234**

31529 Other Cut and Sew Apparel Manufacturing[CAN]

This industry comprises establishments primarily engaged in manufacturing cut and sew apparel from purchased fabric (except men's, boys', women's, and girls' apparel). This industry includes establishments manufacturing apparel, such as fur apparel, leather apparel, infants' apparel, costumes, and clerical vestments.

Manufacturing men's and boys' apparel from purchased fabric **31522**

Manufacturing women's and girls' apparel from purchased fabric **31523**

Knitting apparel or knitting fabric and manufacturing apparel **3151**

Cutting and/or sewing materials owned by others for apparel **31521**

Manufacturing fur and leather mittens and gloves **31599**

Dyeing and dressing furs **31611**

315291 Infants' Cut and Sew Apparel Manufacturing[CAN]

This U.S. industry comprises establishments primarily engaged in manufacturing infants' dresses, blouses, shirts, and all other infants' wear from purchased fabric. Infants' clothing jobbers, who perform entrepreneurial functions involved in apparel manufacture, including buying raw materials, designing and preparing samples, arranging for apparel to be made from their materials, and marketing finished apparel, are included. For the purposes of classification, the term "infants' apparel" includes apparel for young children of an age not exceeding 24 months.

315

Knitting infants' apparel or knitting fabric and manufacturing infants' apparel **315191**

Cutting and/or sewing materials owned by others for infants' apparel **315212**

315292 Fur and Leather Apparel Manufacturing[CAN]

This U.S. industry comprises establishments primarily engaged in manufacturing cut and sew fur and leather apparel, and sheep-lined clothing. Fur and leather apparel jobbers, who perform entrepreneurial functions involved in apparel manufacture, including buying raw materials, designing and preparing samples, arranging for apparel to be made from their materials, and marketing finished apparel, are included.

Cutting and/or sewing materials owned by others for apparel **31521**

Dyeing and dressing furs **316110**

Manufacturing fur and leather mittens and gloves **315992**

315299 All Other Cut and Sew Apparel Manufacturing[CAN]

This U.S. industry comprises establishments primarily engaged in manufacturing cut and sew apparel form purchased fabric (except cut and sew apparel contractors; men's and boys' cut and sew underwear, nightwear, suits, coats, shirts, trousers, work clothing, and other outerwear; women's and girls' lingerie, blouses, shirts, dresses, suits, coats, and other outerwear; infants' apparel; and fur and leather apparel). Clothing jobbers for these products, who perform entrepreneurial functions involved in apparel manufacture, including buying raw materials, designing and preparing samples, arranging for apparel to be made from their materials, and marketing finished apparel, are included. Examples of products made by these establishments are team athletic uniforms, band uniforms, academic caps and gowns, clerical vestments, and costumes.

Cutting and/or sewing materials owned by others for apparel **31521**

Knitting apparel or knitting fabric and manufacturing apparel **3151**

Manufacturing men's and boys' underwear and nightwear from purchased fabric **315221**

Manufacturing men's and boys' suits, coats, and overcoats from purchased fabric **315222**

Manufacturing men's and boys' shirts (except work shirts) from purchased fabric **315223**

Manufacturing men's and boys' pants, slacks, trousers, and jeans from purchased fabric **315224**

Manufacturing men's and boys' work clothing from purchased fabric **315225**

Manufacturing other men's and boys' outerwear from purchased fabric **315228**

Manufacturing women's and girls' lingerie and nightwear from purchased fabric **315231**

Manufacturing women's and girls' blouses and shirts from purchased fabric **315232**

Manufacturing women's and girls' dresses from purchased fabric **315233**

Manufacturing women's and girls' suits, tailored coats and jackets, and skirts from purchased fabric **315234**

Manufacturing other women's and girls' outerwear from purchased fabric **315239**

Manufacturing infants' apparel from purchased fabric **315291**

Manufacturing fur and leather apparel **315292**

3159 Apparel Accessories and Other Apparel Manufacturing

This industry group comprises establishments primarily engaged in manufacturing apparel accessories and other apparel (except apparel knitting mills, apparel contractors, men's and boys' cut and sew apparel, women's and girls' cut and sew apparel, infants' cut and sew apparel, fur and leather apparel, and all other cut and sew apparel). This industry group includes jobbers performing entrepreneurial functions involved in manufacturing apparel accessories.

31599 Apparel Accessories and Other Apparel Manufacturing

This industry comprises establishments primarily engaged in manufacturing apparel and accessories (except apparel knitting mills, cut and sew apparel contractors, men's and boys' cut and sew apparel, women's and girls' cut and sew apparel, and other cut and sew apparel). Jobbers, who perform entrepreneurial functions involved in apparel accessories manufacture, including buying raw materials, designing and preparing samples, arranging for apparel accessories to be made from their materials, and marketing finished apparel accessories, are included. Examples of products made by these establishments are belts, caps, gloves (except medical, sporting, safety), hats, and neckties.

Cutting and/or sewing materials owned by others for apparel accessories **31521**

Manufacturing paper hats and caps **32229**

Manufacturing plastics or rubber hats and caps (except bathing caps) **326**

Manufacturing athletic gloves, such as boxing gloves, baseball gloves, golf gloves, batting gloves, and racquetball gloves, **33992**

Manufacturing metal fabric, metal mesh, or rubber gloves **33911**

Knitting apparel, mittens, gloves, hats, and caps or knitting fabric and manufacturing apparel, mittens, gloves, hats, and caps **3151**

Cutting and/or sewing materials owned by others for apparel **31521**

Manufacturing men's and boys' underwear and outerwear from purchased fabric **31522**

Manufacturing women's and girls' underwear and outerwear from purchased fabric **31523**

Manufacturing other apparel from purchased fabric and manufacturing fur and leather apparel, hats, and caps **31529**

315991 Hat, Cap, and Millinery Manufacturing[US]

This U.S. industry comprises establishments primarily engaged in manufacturing cut and sew hats, caps, millinery, and hat bodies form purchased fabric. Jobbers, who perform entrepreneurial functions involved in hat, cap, and millinery manufacture, including buying raw materials, designing and preparing samples, arranging for hats, caps, and millinery to be made from their materials, and marketing finished hats, caps, and millinery, are included.

Cutting and/or sewing materials owned by others for hats, caps, and millinery **31521**

Manufacturing paper hats and caps **322299**

Manufacturing plastics or rubber hats and caps (except bathing caps) **326**

Manufacturing fur and leather hats and caps **315292**

315992 Glove and Mitten Manufacturing[US]

This U.S. industry comprises establishments primarily engaged in manufacturing cut and sew gloves (except rubber, metal, and athletic gloves) and mittens from purchased fabric, fur, leather, or from combinations of fabric, fur, or leather. Jobbers, who perform entrepreneurial functions involved in glove and mitten manufacture, including buying raw materials, designing and preparing samples, arranging for gloves and mittens to be made from their materials, and marketing finished gloves and mittens, are included.

Cutting and/or sewing materials owned by others for gloves and mittens **31521**

Knitting mittens and gloves or knitting fabric and manufacturing mittens and gloves **315191**

Manufacturing athletic gloves, such as boxing gloves, baseball gloves, golf gloves, batting gloves, and racquetball gloves **339920**

Manufacturing metal fabric, metal mesh, or rubber gloves **339113**

315993 Men's and Boys' Neckwear Manufacturing[US]

This U.S. industry comprises establishments primarily engaged in manufacturing men's and boys' cut and sew neckties, scarves, and mufflers from purchased fabric, leather, or from combinations of leather and fabric. Men's and boys' neckwear jobbers, who perform entrepreneurial functions involved in neckwear manufacture, including buying raw materials, designing and preparing samples, arranging for neckwear to be made from their materials, and marketing finished neckwear, are included.

Cutting and/or sewing materials owned by others for men's and boys' neckwear **315211**

315999 Other Apparel Accessories and Other Apparel Manufacturing[US]

This U.S. industry comprises establishments primarily engaged in manufacturing apparel and apparel accessories (except apparel knitting mills; cut and sew apparel contractors; cut and sew apparel; hats and caps; mittens and gloves; and men's and boys' neckwear). Jobbers for these products, who perform entrepreneurial functions involved in other apparel and accessory manufacture, including buying raw materials, designing and preparing samples, arranging for other apparel and accessories to be made from their materials, and marketing finished other apparel and accessories, are included. Examples of products made by these establishments are apparel trimmings and findings, belts, women's scarves, suspenders, and waterproof outerwear.

Knitting apparel or knitting fabric and manufacturing apparel **3151**

Cutting and/or sewing materials owned by others for apparel **31521**

Manufacturing men's and boys' cut and sew underwear and outerwear from purchased fabric **31522**

Manufacturing women's and girls' cut and sew underwear and outerwear from purchased fabric **31523**

Manufacturing infants' cut and sew apparel from purchased fabric **315291**

Manufacturing fur and leather apparel **315292**

Manufacturing hats, caps, and millinery **315991**

Manufacturing gloves and mittens **315992**

Manufacturing men's and boys' neckwear **315993**

316 Leather and Allied Product Manufacturing

Establishments in the Leather and Allied Product Manufacturing subsector transform hides into leather by tanning or curing and fabricating the leather into products for final consumption. It also includes the manufacture of similar products from other materials, including products (except apparel) made from "leather substitutes," such as rubber, plastics, or textiles. Rubber footwear, textile luggage, and plastics purses or wallets are examples of "leather substitute" products included in this group. The products made from leather substitutes are included in this subsector because they are made in similar ways leather products are made (e.g., luggage). They are made in the same establishments, so it is not practical to separate them. The inclusion of leather making in this subsector is partly because leather tanning is a relatively small industry that has few close neighbors as a production process, partly because leather is an input to some of the other products classified in this subsector and partly for historical reasons.

316110 Leather and Hide Tanning and Finishing

This industry comprises establishments primarily engaged in one or more of the following: (1) tanning, currying, and finishing hides and skins; (2) having others process hides and skins on a contract basis; and (3) dyeing or dressing furs.

31621 Footwear Manufacturing

This industry comprises establishments primarily engaged in manufacturing footwear (except orthopedic extension footwear).

Manufacturing orthopedic extension footwear **33911**

316211 Rubber and Plastics Footwear Manufacturing^{US}

This U.S. industry comprises establishments primarily engaged in manufacturing rubber and plastics footwear with vulcanized rubber or plastics soles, molded or cemented to rubber, plastics, or fabric uppers, and rubber and plastics protective footwear.

Manufacturing house slippers with fabric uppers and rubber or plastics soles **316212**
Manufacturing men's footwear (except athletic) with leather or vinyl uppers, regardless of sole material **316213**
Manufacturing women's footwear (except athletic) with leather or vinyl uppers, regardless of sole material **316214**
Manufacturing youths' children's and infants' footwear and athletic footwear with leather or vinyl uppers, regardless of sole material **316219**

316212 House Slipper Manufacturing^{US}

This U.S. industry comprises establishments primarily engaged in manufacturing house slippers and slipper socks, regardless of material.

316213 Men's Footwear (except Athletic) Manufacturing^{US}

This U.S. industry comprises establishments prima-

rily engaged in manufacturing men's footwear designed primarily for dress, street, and work. This industry includes men's shoes with rubber or plastics soles and leather or vinyl uppers.

Manufacturing men's footwear with fabric uppers and rubber or plastics soles **316211**
Manufacturing orthopedic extension footwear **339113**
Manufacturing men's leather or vinyl upper athletic footwear and youths' and boys' footwear **316219**

316214 Women's Footwear (except Athletic) Manufacturing^{US}

This U.S. industry comprises establishments primarily engaged in manufacturing women's footwear designed for dress, street, and work. This industry includes women's shoes with rubber or plastics soles and leather or vinyl uppers.

Manufacturing women's footwear with fabric uppers and rubber or plastics soles and rubber or plastics sandals **316211**
Manufacturing orthopedic extension footwear **339113**
Manufacturing women's leather or vinyl upper athletic footwear and youths' and girls' footwear **316219**

316219 Other Footwear Manufacturing^{US}

This U.S. industry comprises establishments primarily engaged in manufacturing other footwear (except rubber and plastics footwear); house slippers; men's footwear (except athletic); and women's footwear (except athletic)).

Manufacturing rubber and plastics footwear with fabric uppers **316211**
Manufacturing house slippers **316212**
Manufacturing men's footwear (except athletic) **316213**
Manufacturing orthopedic extension footwear **339113**
Manufacturing women's footwear (except athletic) **316214**

31699 Other Leather and Allied Product Manufacturing

This industry comprises establishments primarily

engaged in manufacturing leather products (except footwear and apparel) from purchased leather or leather substitutes (e.g., fabric, plastics).

Manufacturing leather apparel **31529**
Manufacturing leather gloves, mittens, belts, and apparel accessories **31599**
Manufacturing footwear **31621**
Manufacturing small articles made of metal carried on or about the person made of metal **33991**
Manufacturing leather gaskets **33999**

316991 Luggage Manufacturing[US]

This U.S. industry comprises establishments primarily engaged in manufacturing luggage of any material.

316992 Women's Handbag and Purse Manufacturing[US]

This U.S. industry comprises establishments primarily engaged in manufacturing women's handbags and purses of any material (except precious metal).

Manufacturing precious metal handbags and purses **339911**

316993 Personal Leather Good (except Women's Handbag and Purse) Manufacturing[US]

This U.S. industry comprises establishments prima-

rily engaged in manufacturing personal leather goods (i.e., small articles of any material [except metal] normally carried on or about the person or in a handbag). Examples of personal leather goods made by these establishments are billfolds, coin purses, key cases, toilet kits, and watchbands (except metal).

Manufacturing personal goods of precious metal **339911**
Manufacturing personal goods of metal (except precious) **339914**

316999 All Other Leather Good Manufacturing[US]

This U.S. industry comprises establishments primarily engaged in manufacturing leather goods (except footwear, luggage, handbags, purses, and personal leather goods).

Manufacturing leather gloves or mittens **315992**
Manufacturing leather apparel belts **315999**
Manufacturing footwear **31621**
Manufacturing luggage of any material **316991**
Manufacturing handbags and purses **316992**
Manufacturing personal leather goods, such as wallets and key cases, of all materials (except metal) **316993**
Manufacturing leather apparel **315292**
Manufacturing leather gaskets **339991**

321

321 Wood Product Manufacturing

Industries in the Wood Product Manufacturing subsector manufacture wood products, such as lumber, plywood, veneers, wood containers, wood flooring, wood trusses, manufactured homes (i.e., mobile home), and prefabricated wood buildings. The production processes of the Wood Product Manufacturing subsector include sawing, planing, shaping, laminating, and assembling of wood products starting from logs that are cut into bolts, or lumber that then may be further cut, or shaped by lathes or other shaping tools. The lumber or other transformed wood shapes may also be subsequently planed or smoothed, and assembled into finished products, such as wood containers.

The Wood Product Manufacturing subsector includes establishments that make wood products from logs and bolts that are sawed and shaped, and establishments that purchase sawed lumber and make wood products. With the exception of sawmills and wood preservation establishments, the establishments are grouped into industries mainly based on the specific products manufactured.

3211 Sawmills and Wood Preservation

This industry group comprises establishments whose primary production process begins with logs or bolts that are transformed into boards, dimension lumber, beams, timbers, poles, ties, shingles, shakes, siding,

and wood chips. Establishments that cut and treat round wood and/or treat wood products made in other establishments to prevent rotting by impregnation with creosote or other chemical compounds are also included in this industry group.

32III Sawmills and Wood Preservation

This industry comprises establishments primarily engaged in one or more of the following: (1) sawing dimension lumber, boards, beams, timber, poles, ties, shingles, shakes, siding, and wood chips from logs or bolts; (2) sawing round wood poles, pilings, and posts and treating them with preservatives; and (3) treating wood sawed, planed, or shaped in other establishments with creosote or other preservatives to prevent decay and to protect against fire and insects. Sawmills may plane the rough lumber that they make with a planing machine to achieve smoothness and uniformity of size.

Operating portable chipper mills in the field 11331
Manufacturing wood products (except round wood poles, pilings, and posts) and treating them with preservatives 321
Manufacturing veneer from logs and bolts or manufacturing engineered lumber and structural members other than solid wood 32121
Planing purchased lumber or manufacturing cut stock or dimension stock (i.e., shapes) from logs or bolts 32191

32III3 Sawmills[US]

This U.S. industry comprises establishments primarily engaged in sawing dimension lumber, boards, beams, timbers, poles, ties, shingles, shakes, siding, and wood chips from logs or bolts. Sawmills may plane the rough lumber that they make with a planing machine to achieve smoothness and uniformity of size.

Planing purchased lumber or manufacturing cut stock or dimension stock (i.e., shapes) from logs or bolts 32191
Manufacturing veneer from logs or bolts 32121
Operating portable chipper mills in the field 113310

32III4 Wood Preservation[CAN]

This U.S. industry comprises establishments primarily engaged in (1) treating wood sawed, planed, or shaped in other establishments with creosote or other preservatives, such as chromated copper arsenate, to prevent decay and to protect against fire and insects and/or (2) sawing round wood poles, pilings, and posts and treating them with preservatives.

Manufacturing wood products (except round wood poles, pilings, and posts) and treating them with preservatives 321

32I2I Veneer, Plywood, and Engineered Wood Product Manufacturing

This industry comprises establishments primarily engaged in one or more of the following: (1) manufacturing veneer and/or plywood; (2) manufacturing engineered wood members; and (3) manufacturing reconstituted wood products. This industry includes manufacturing plywood from veneer made in the same establishment or from veneer made in other establishments, and manufacturing plywood faced with nonwood materials, such as plastics or metal.

Manufacturing veneer and further processing that veneer into wood containers or wood container parts in the same establishment 32192
Manufacturing prefabricated wood buildings or wood sections, and panels for buildings 32199
Manufacturing solid wood structural members, such as dimension lumber and timber from logs or bolts in sawmills 32III

32I2II Hardwood Veneer and Plywood Manufacturing[CAN]

This U.S. industry comprises establishments primarily engaged in manufacturing hardwood veneer and/or hardwood plywood.

Manufacturing veneer and further processing that veneer into wood containers or wood container parts 321920
Manufacturing softwood veneer and softwood plywood 321212
Manufacturing reconstituted wood sheets and boards 321219

32I2I2 Softwood Veneer and Plywood Manufacturing[CAN]

This U.S. industry comprises establishments primarily engaged in manufacturing softwood veneer and/or softwood plywood.

Manufacturing veneer and further processing that veneer into wood containers or wood container parts 321920
Manufacturing hardwood veneer and hardwood plywood 321211
Manufacturing reconstituted wood sheets and boards 321219

32I2I3 Engineered Wood Member (except Truss) Manufacturing[US]

This U.S. industry comprises establishments primarily engaged in manufacturing fabricated or laminated wood arches and/or other fabricated or laminated wood structural members.

Manufacturing prefabricated wood buildings, or wood sections, and panels for buildings 321992
Manufacturing wood trusses 321214
Manufacturing solid wood structural members, such as dimension lumber and timber from logs or bolts, 321113

32I2I4 Truss Manufacturing[US]

This U.S. industry comprises establishments prima-

rily engaged in manufacturing laminated or fabricated wood roof and floor trusses.

Manufacturing wood I-joists **321213**

321219 Reconstituted Wood Product Manufacturing^{US}

This U.S. industry comprises establishments primarily engaged in manufacturing reconstituted wood sheets and boards.

Manufacturing softwood plywood **321212**
Manufacturing hardwood plywood **321211**

3219 Other Wood Product Manufacturing

This industry group comprises establishments primarily engaged in manufacturing wood products (except establishments operating sawmills and wood preservation facilities; and establishments manufacturing veneer, plywood, or engineered wood products).

32191 Millwork

This industry comprises establishments primarily engaged in manufacturing hardwood and softwood cut stock and dimension stock (i.e., shapes); wood windows and wood doors; and other millwork including wood flooring. Dimension stock or cut stock is defined as lumber and worked wood products cut or shaped to specialized sizes. These establishments generally use woodworking machinery, such as jointers, planers, lathes, and routers to shape wood.

Manufacturing dimension lumber, boards, beams, timbers, poles, ties, shingles, shakes, siding, and wood chips from logs and bolts **32111**
Fabricating millwork at the construction site **23**
Manufacturing wood furniture frames and finished wood furniture parts **33721**

321911 Wood Window and Door Manufacturing^{CAN}

This U.S. industry comprises establishments primarily engaged in manufacturing window and door units, sash, window and door frames, and doors from wood or wood clad with metal or plastics.

Fabricating wood windows or wood doors at the construction site **23**

321912 Cut Stock, Resawing Lumber, and Planing^{US}

This U.S. industry comprises establishments primarily engaged in one or more of the following: (1) manu-

facturing dimension lumber from purchased lumber; (2) manufacturing dimension stock (i.e., shapes) or cut stock; (3) resawing the output of sawmills; and (4) planing purchased lumber. These establishments generally use woodworking machinery, such as jointers, planers, lathes, and routers to shape wood.

Manufacturing dimension lumber, boards, beams, timbers, poles, ties, shingles, shakes, siding, and wood chips from logs or bolts **321113**
Manufacturing wood stairwork, wood molding, wood trim, and other millwork **321918**
Manufacturing wood furniture frames and finished wood furniture parts **337215**

321918 Other Millwork (including Flooring)^{US}

This U.S. industry comprises establishments primarily engaged in manufacturing millwork (except wood windows, wood doors, and cut stock).

Manufacturing wood windows and doors **321911**
Manufacturing cut stock, resawing lumber, and/or planing purchased lumber **321912**

321920 Wood Container and Pallet Manufacturing

This industry comprises establishments primarily engaged in manufacturing wood pallets, wood box shook, wood boxes, other wood containers, and wood parts for pallets and containers.

Manufacturing wood burial caskets **339995**

32199 All Other Wood Product Manufacturing

This industry comprises establishments primarily engaged in manufacturing wood products (except establishments operating sawmills and wood preservation facilities; and establishments manufacturing veneer, plywood, engineered wood products, millwork, wood containers, or pallets).

Operating sawmills or preserving wood **32111**
Manufacturing veneer, plywood, and engineered wood products **32121**
Manufacturing millwork **32191**
Manufacturing wood containers, pallets, and wood container parts **32192**
Manufacturing travel trailers with self-contained facilities for storage of water and waste **33621**
Fabricating of wood buildings or wood sections and panels for buildings at the construction site **23**

321991 Manufactured Home (Mobile Home) Manufacturing^{CAN}

This U.S. industry comprises establishments primarily engaged in making manufactured homes (i.e., mobile homes) and nonresidential mobile buildings. Manufactured homes are designed to accept permanent water, sewer, and utility connections and although equipped with wheels, they are not intended for regular highway movement.

Manufacturing prefabricated wood buildings not equipped with wheels **321992**

Manufacturing travel trailers with self-contained facilities for storage of water and waste **336214**

321992 Prefabricated Wood Building Manufacturing^CAN

This U.S. industry comprises establishments primarily engaged in manufacturing prefabricated wood buildings and wood sections and panels for prefabricated wood buildings.

Fabricating wood buildings or wood sections and panels for buildings at the construction site **23**

Making manufactured homes (i.e., mobile homes) **321991**

321999 All Other Miscellaneous Wood Product Manufacturing^CAN

This U.S. industry comprises establishments primarily engaged in manufacturing wood products (except establishments operating sawmills and preservation facilities; establishments manufacturing veneer, engineered wood products, millwork, wood containers, pallets, and wood container parts; and establishments making manufactured homes [i.e., mobile homes] and prefabricated buildings and components).

Operating sawmills and preserving wood **32111**

Manufacturing veneer and engineered wood products **32121**

Manufacturing millwork **32191**

Manufacturing boxes, box shook, wood containers, pallets, and wood parts for containers **321920**

Making manufactured homes (i.e., mobile homes) **321991**

Manufacturing prefabricated wood buildings or wood sections and panels for buildings **321992**

322 Paper Manufacturing

Industries in the Paper Manufacturing subsector make pulp, paper, or converted paper products. The manufacturing of these products is grouped together because they constitute a series of vertically connected processes. More than one is often carried out in a single establishment. There are essentially three activities. The manufacturing of pulp involves separating the cellulose fibers from other impurities in wood or used paper. The manufacturing of paper involves matting these fibers into a sheet. Converted paper products are made from paper and other materials by various cutting and shaping techniques and includes coating and laminating activities. The Paper Manufacturing subsector is subdivided into two industry groups, the first for the manufacturing of pulp and paper and the second for the manufacturing of converted paper products. Paper making is treated as the core activity of the subsector. Therefore, any establishment that makes paper (including paperboard), either alone or in combination with pulp manufacturing or paper converting, is classified as a paper or paperboard mill. Establishments that make pulp without making paper are classified as pulp mills. Pulp mills, paper mills and paperboard mills comprise the first industry group.

Establishments that make products from purchased paper and other materials make up the second industry group, Converted Paper Product Manufacturing. This general activity is then subdivided based, for the most part, on process distinctions. Paperboard container manufacturing uses corrugating, cutting, and shaping machinery to form paperboard into containers. Paper bag and coated and treated paper manufacturing establishments cut and coat paper and foil. Stationery product manufacturing establishments make a variety of paper products used for writing, filing, and similar applications. Other converted paper product manufacturing includes, in particular, the conversion of sanitary paper stock into such things as tissue paper and disposable diapers. An important process used in the Paper Bag and Coated and Treated Paper Manufacturing industry is lamination, often combined with coating. Lamination and coating makes a composite material with improved properties of strength, impermeability, and so on. The laminated materials may be paper, metal foil, or plastics film. While paper is often one of the components, it is not always. Lamination of plastics film to plastics film is classified in the NAICS Subsector 326, Plastics and Rubber Products Manufacturing, because establishments that do this often first make the film.

The same situation holds with respect to bags. The manufacturing of bags from plastics only, whether or not laminated, is classified in Subsector 326, Plastics and Rubber Products Manufacturing, but all other bag manufacturing is classified in this subsector. Excluded from this subsector are photosensitive papers. These papers are chemically treated and are classified in Industry 32599, All Other Chemical Product and Preparation Manufacturing.

3221 Pulp, Paper, and Paperboard Mills

This industry group comprises establishments primarily engaged in manufacturing pulp, paper, or paperboard.

322110 Pulp Mills

This industry comprises establishments primarily engaged in manufacturing pulp without manufacturing paper or paperboard. The pulp is made by separating the cellulose fibers from the other impurities in wood or other materials, such as used or recycled rags, linters, scrap paper, and straw.

Manufacturing both pulp and paper **32212**
Manufacturing both pulp and paperboard **322130**

32212 Paper Mills

This industry comprises establishments primarily engaged in manufacturing paper from pulp. These establishments may manufacture or purchase pulp. In addition, the establishments may convert the paper they make. The activity of making paper classifies an establishment into this industry regardless of the output.

Manufacturing pulp without manufacturing paper **32211**
Manufacturing paperboard **32213**
Converting paper without manufacturing paper **3222**
Manufacturing photographic sensitized paper **32599**

322121 Paper (except Newsprint) Mills[CAN]

This U.S. industry comprises establishments primarily engaged in manufacturing paper (except newsprint and uncoated groundwood paper) from pulp. These establishments may manufacture or purchase pulp. In addition, the establishments may also convert the paper they make.

Manufacturing newsprint and uncoated groundwood paper **322122**
Converting paper without manufacturing paper **3222**

Manufacturing paperboard **322130**
Manufacturing pulp without manufacturing paper **322110**
Manufacturing photographic sensitized paper from purchased paper
   325992

322122 Newsprint Mills[CAN]

This U.S. industry comprises establishments primarily engaged in manufacturing newsprint and uncoated groundwood paper from pulp. These establishments may manufacture or purchase pulp. In addition, the establishments may also convert the paper they make.

Manufacturing paper (except newsprint and uncoated groundwood) **322121**
Converting paper without manufacturing paper **3222**
Manufacturing paperboard **322130**
Manufacturing pulp without manufacturing paper **322110**

322130 Paperboard Mills

This industry comprises establishments primarily engaged in manufacturing paperboard from pulp. These establishments may manufacture or purchase pulp. In addition, the establishments may also convert the paperboard they make.

Manufacturing pulp without manufacturing paperboard **322110**
Converting paperboard without manufacturing paperboard **3222**
Manufacturing insulation board and other reconstituted wood fiberboard
   321219

3222 Converted Paper Product Manufacturing

This industry group comprises establishments primarily engaged in converting paper or paperboard without manufacturing paper or paperboard.

32221 Paperboard Container Manufacturing

This industry comprises establishments primarily engaged in converting paperboard into containers without manufacturing paperboard. These establishments use corrugating, cutting, and shaping machinery to form paperboard into containers. Products made by these establishments include boxes; corrugated sheets, pads, and pallets; paper dishes; and fiber drums and reels.

Manufacturing similar items of plastics materials **3261**
Manufacturing paperboard and converting paperboard into containers **32213**
Manufacturing egg cartons, food trays, and other food containers from molded pulp **32229**
Manufacturing paper and converting paper into containers **32212**
Manufacturing paper bags without manufacturing paper **32222**

322211 Corrugated and Solid Fiber Box Manufacturing^{CAN}

This U.S. industry comprises establishments primarily engaged in laminating purchased paper or paperboard into corrugated or solid fiber boxes and related products, such as pads, partitions, pallets, and corrugated paper without manufacturing paperboard. These boxes are generally used for shipping.

Manufacturing setup paperboard boxes (except corrugated or laminated solid fiber boxes) **322213**
Manufacturing folding paperboard boxes (except corrugated or laminated solid fiber boxes) **322212**
Manufacturing paperboard and converting paperboard into boxes **322130**

322212 Folding Paperboard Box Manufacturing^{CAN}

This U.S. industry comprises establishments primarily engaged in converting paperboard (except corrugated) into folding paperboard boxes without manufacturing paper and paperboard.

Manufacturing setup paperboard boxes (except corrugated) **322213**
Manufacturing corrugated and solid fiber boxes **322211**
Manufacturing paperboard and converting paperboard into containers **322130**
Manufacturing paper and converting paper into containers **32212**
Manufacturing milk cartons **322215**
Manufacturing paper bags **32222**

322213 Setup Paperboard Box Manufacturing^{CAN}

This U.S. industry comprises establishments primarily engaged in converting paperboard into setup paperboard boxes (i.e., rigid-sided boxes not shipped flat) without manufacturing paperboard.

Manufacturing folding paperboard boxes (except corrugated) **322212**
Manufacturing corrugated and solid fiber boxes **322211**
Manufacturing paperboard and converting paperboard into containers **322130**

322214 Fiber Can, Tube, Drum, and Similar Products Manufacturing^{US}

This U.S. industry comprises establishments primarily engaged in converting paperboard into fiber cans, tubes, drums, and similar products without manufacturing paperboard.

Manufacturing paperboard and converting paperboard into containers **322130**

322215 Nonfolding Sanitary Food Container Manufacturing^{US}

This U.S. industry comprises establishments primarily engaged in converting sanitary foodboard into food containers (except folding).

Manufacturing sanitary food containers of solely plastics materials **3261**
Manufacturing egg cartons, food trays, and other food containers from molded pulp **322299**
Manufacturing folding sanitary cartons **322212**

32222 Paper Bag and Coated and Treated Paper Manufacturing

This industry comprises establishments primarily engaged in one or more of the following: (1) cutting and coating paper and paperboard; (2) cutting and laminating paper and paperboard and other flexible materials (except plastics film to plastics film); (3) manufacturing bags or multiwall bags or sacks of paper, metal foil, coated paper, or laminates or coated combinations of paper and foil with plastics film; (4) manufacturing laminated aluminum and other converted metal foils from purchased foils; and (5) surface coating paper or paperboard.

Manufacturing paper from pulp **32212**
Manufacturing photographic sensitized paper **32599**
Manufacturing textile bags **31491**
Manufacturing single and multiwall plastics bags or plastics laminated bags **32611**
Making aluminum and aluminum foil **33131**
Cutting purchased aluminum foil into smaller lengths and widths **33299**

322221 Coated and Laminated Packaging Paper and Plastics Film Manufacturing^{US}

This U.S. industry comprises establishments primarily engaged in performing one or more of the following activities associated with the manufacturing of packaging materials: (1) cutting and coating paper; and (2) cutting and laminating paper with other flexible materials (except plastics to plastics or foil to paper laminates). The products made in this industry are made from purchased sheet materials and may be printed in the same establishment.

Manufacturing coated or laminated paper for nonpackaging purposes **322222**
Manufacturing unsupported plastics film **326113**
Manufacturing laminated aluminum foil for flexible packaging uses **322225**
Making aluminum and aluminum foil **33131**
Cutting purchased aluminum foil into smaller lengths and widths **332999**
Manufacturing paper from pulp **32212**

322222 Coated and Laminated Paper Manufacturing[US]

This U.S. industry comprises establishments primarily engaged in performing one or more of the following activities associated with making products designed for purposes other than packaging: (1) cutting and coating paper; (2) cutting and laminating paper and other flexible materials (except plastics film to plastics film); and (3) manufacturing converted aluminum and other metal foils for nonpackaging uses from purchased foils. The products made in this industry are made from purchased sheet materials and may be printed in the same establishment.

Manufacturing coated and laminated paper for packaging uses **322221**
Manufacturing photographic sensitized paper **325992**
Making aluminum and aluminum foil **33131**
Cutting purchased aluminum foil into smaller lengths and widths **332999**
Manufacturing laminated aluminum foil for flexible packaging uses **322225**

322223 Plastics, Foil, and Coated Paper Bag Manufacturing[US]

This U.S. industry comprises establishments primarily engaged in manufacturing bags of coated paper, of metal foil, or of laminated or coated combinations of plastics, foil, and paper, whether or not printed.

Manufacturing uncoated paper bags and multiwall bags and sacks **322224**
Manufacturing textile bags **314911**
Manufacturing single and multiwall plastics bags **326111**

322224 Uncoated Paper and Multiwall Bag Manufacturing[US]

This U.S. industry comprises establishments primarily engaged in manufacturing uncoated paper bags or multiwall bags and sacks.

Manufacturing single wall and multiwall bags from plastics unsupported film **326111**

Manufacturing bags of coated paper, of metal foil, or of laminated or coated combinations of plastics, foil, and paper bags **322223**
Manufacturing textile bags **314911**

322225 Laminated Aluminum Foil Manufacturing for Flexible Packaging Uses[US]

This U.S. industry comprises establishments primarily engaged in laminating aluminum and other metal foil into products with flexible packaging uses or gift wrap and other packaging wrap applications.

Manufacturing plain aluminum foil **331315**
Manufacturing laminated aluminum bags and liners **322223**
Manufacturing converted aluminum and other metal foils for nonpackaging uses from purchased foils **322222**
Manufacturing cookware, dinnerware, and other semirigid metal containers **332999**

322226 Surface-Coated Paperboard Manufacturing[US]

This U.S. industry comprises establishments primarily engaged in laminating, lining, or surface coating purchased paperboard to make other paperboard products.

32223 Stationery Product Manufacturing

This industry comprises establishments primarily engaged in converting paper or paperboard into products used for writing, filing, art work, and similar applications.

Manufacturing die-cut paper and paperboard products other than office supplies **322299**

322231 Die-Cut Paper and Paperboard Office Supplies Manufacturing[US]

This U.S. industry comprises establishments primarily engaged in converting paper rollstock or paperboard into die-cut paper or paperboard office supplies. For the purpose of this industry, office supplies are defined as office products, such as filing folders, index cards, rolls for adding machines, file separators and dividers, tabulating cards, and other paper and paperboard office supplies.

Manufacturing die-cut paper and paperboard products (except office supplies) **322299**
Manufacturing paper and paperboard products used for writing and similar applications (e.g., looseleaf fillers, notebooks, pads, stationery, tablets) **322233**

322232 Envelope Manufacturing^{US}

This U.S. industry comprises establishments primarily engaged in manufacturing envelopes for mailing or stationery of any material including combinations.

Manufacturing stationery **322233**

322233 Stationery, Tablet, and Related Product Manufacturing^{US}

This U.S. industry comprises establishments primarily engaged in converting paper and paperboard into products used for writing and similar applications (e.g., looseleaf fillers, notebooks, pads, stationery, tablets).

Manufacturing envelopes **322232**
Manufacturing die-cut paper and paperboard office supplies **322231**

32229 Other Converted Paper Product Manufacturing

This industry comprises establishments primarily engaged in (1) converting paper and paperboard into products (except containers, bags, coated and treated paper and paperboard, and stationery products), or (2) converting pulp into pulp products, such as disposable diapers, or molded pulp egg cartons, food trays, and dishes. Processes used include laminating or lining purchased paper or paperboard.

Manufacturing pulp from wood or from other materials **32211**
Manufacturing paper from pulp or making pulp and manufacturing paper **32212**
Manufacturing paperboard from pulp or making pulp and manufacturing paperboard **32213**

Manufacturing paperboard containers **32221**
Manufacturing bags of coated, laminated, or uncoated paper, of metal foil, or combinations thereof **32222**
Manufacturing stationery and other related office supplies **32223**

322291 Sanitary Paper Product Manufacturing^{CAN}

This U.S. industry comprises establishments primarily engaged in converting purchased sanitary paper stock or wadding into sanitary paper products, such as facial tissues and handkerchiefs, table napkins, toilet paper, towels, disposable diapers, sanitary napkins, and tampons.

322299 All Other Converted Paper Product Manufacturing^{CAN}

This U.S. industry comprises establishments primarily engaged in converting paper or paperboard into products (except containers, bags, coated and treated paper, stationery products, and sanitary paper products) or converting pulp into pulp products, such as egg cartons, food trays, and other food containers from molded pulp.

Manufacturing pulp from wood or from other materials **322110**
Manufacturing paper from pulp or making pulp and manufacturing paper **32212**
Manufacturing paperboard from pulp or making pulp and manufacturing paperboard **322130**
Manufacturing paperboard containers **32221**
Manufacturing bags of coated, laminated, or uncoated paper, of metal foil, or combinations thereof **32222**
Manufacturing stationery and other related office supplies **32223**

323 Printing and Related Support Activities

Industries in the Printing and Related Support Activities subsector print products, such as newspapers, books, periodicals, business forms, greeting cards, and other materials, and perform support activities, such as bookbinding, platemaking services, and data imaging. The support activities included here are an integral part of the printing industry, and a product (a printing plate, a bound book, or a computer disk or file) that is an integral part of the printing industry is almost always provided by these operations.

Processes used in printing include a variety of methods used to transfer an image from a plate, screen, or computer file to some medium, such as paper, plastics, metal, textile articles, or wood. The most prominent of these methods is to transfer the image from a plate or screen to the medium (lithographic, gravure, screen, and flexographic printing). A rapidly growing new technology uses a computer file to directly "drive" the printing mechanism to create the image and new electrostatic and other types of equipment (digital or nonimpact printing).

In contrast to many other classification systems that locate publishing of printed materials in manufacturing, NAICS classifies the publishing of printed products in Subsector 511, Publishing Industries. Though printing and publishing are often carried out by the same enterprise (a newspaper, for example), it is less and less the case that these distinct activities are carried out in the same establishment. When publishing and printing are done in the same establishment, the establishment is classified in Sector 51, Information, in the appropriate NAICS industry even if the receipts for printing exceed those for publishing.

This subsector includes printing on clothing because the production process for that activity is printing, not clothing manufacturing. For instance, the printing of T-shirts is included in this subsector. In contrast, printing on fabric (or grey goods) is not included. This activity is part of the process of finishing the fabric and is included in the NAICS Textile Mills subsector in Industry 31331, Textile and Fabric Finishing Mills.

323

3231 Printing and Related Support Activities

32311 Printing

This industry comprises establishments primarily engaged in printing on apparel and textile products, paper, metal, glass, plastics, and other materials, except fabric (grey goods). The printing processes employed include, but are not limited to, lithographic, gravure, screen, flexographic, digital, and letterpress. Establishments in this industry do not manufacture the stock that they print but may perform postprinting activities, such as bending, cutting, or laminating the materials they print, and mailing.

Providing photocopying service on nondigital photocopy equipment without performing traditional printing activities **56143**
Printing on grey goods **31331**
Printing and publishing, known as publishers, **511**
Performing prepress or postpress services without performing traditional printing activities **32312**

323110 Commercial Lithographic Printing[US]

This U.S. industry comprises establishments primarily engaged in lithographic (i.e., offset) printing without publishing (except books, grey goods, and manifold business forms). This industry includes establishments engaged in lithographic printing on purchased stock materials, such as stationery, letterhead, invitations, labels, and similar items, on a job order basis.

Quick printing **323114**
Printing on grey goods **31331**
Printing books and pamphlets **323117**
Printing manifold business forms including checkbooks **323116**
Manufacturing printed stationery, invitations, labels, and similar items **322**
Printing and publishing, known as publishers, **511**

323111 Commercial Gravure Printing[US]

This U.S. industry comprises establishments primarily engaged in gravure printing without publishing (except books, grey goods, and manifold business forms). This industry includes establishments engaged in gravure printing on purchased stock materials, such as stationery, letterhead, invitations, labels, and similar items, on a job order basis.

Printing on grey goods **31331**
Printing books and pamphlets **323117**
Printing manifold business forms including checkbooks **323116**
Manufacturing printed stationery, invitations, labels, and similar items **322**
Printing and publishing, known as publishers, **511**

323112 Commercial Flexographic Printing[US]

This U.S. industry comprises establishments primarily engaged in flexographic printing without publishing (except books, grey goods, and manifold business forms). This industry includes establishments engaged in flexographic printing on purchased stock materials, such as stationery, invitations, labels, and similar items, on a job order basis.

Printing on grey goods **31331**
Printing books and pamphlets **323117**
Printing manifold business forms including checkbooks **323116**
Manufacturing printed stationery, invitations, labels, and similar items **322**
Printing and publishing, known as publishers, **511**

323113 Commercial Screen Printing[CAN]

This U.S. industry comprises establishments primarily engaged in screen printing without publishing (except books, grey goods, and manifold business forms). This industry includes establishments engaged in screen printing on purchased stock materials, such as stationery, invitations, labels, and similar items, on a job order basis. Establishments primarily engaged in printing on apparel and textile products, such as T-shirts, caps, jackets, towels, and napkins, are included in this industry.

Printing on grey goods **31331**
Printing books and pamphlets **323117**
Printing manifold business forms including checkbooks **323116**
Manufacturing printed stationery, invitations, labels, and similar items **322**
Printing and publishing, known as publishers, **511**

323114 Quick Printing^{CAN}

This U.S. industry comprises establishments primarily engaged in traditional printing activities, such as short-run offset printing or prepress services, in combination with providing document photocopying service. Prepress services include receiving documents in electronic format and directly duplicating from the electronic file and formatting, colorizing, and otherwise modifying the original document to improve presentation. These establishments, known as quick printers, generally provide short-run printing and copying with fast turnaround times.

Providing photocopying service on nondigital photocopy equipment without performing traditional printing activities **561439**
Printing on lithographic equipment known as commercial lithographic printers **323110**
Digital printing on graphical material **323115**

323115 Digital Printing^{CAN}

This U.S. industry comprises establishments primarily engaged in printing graphical materials using digital printing equipment. Establishments known as digital printers typically provide sophisticated prepress services including using scanners to input images and computers to manipulate and format the graphic images prior to printing.

323116 Manifold Business Forms Printing^{CAN}

This U.S. industry comprises establishments primarily engaged in printing special forms, including checkbooks, for use in the operation of a business. The forms may be in single and multiple sets, including carbonized, interleaved with carbon, or otherwise processed for multiple reproduction.

Manufacturing single layered continuous computer paper and similar products **322231**

323117 Books Printing^{US}

This U.S. industry comprises establishments primarily engaged in printing or printing and binding books and pamphlets without publishing.

Printing and publishing, known as book publishers, **511**
Binding books without printing in the same establishment **323121**

323118 Blankbook, Looseleaf Binders, and Devices Manufacturing^{US}

This U.S. industry comprises establishments primarily engaged in manufacturing blankbooks, looseleaf devices, and binders. Establishments in this industry may print or print and bind.

Checkbook printing **323116**
Binding books without printing in the same establishment **323121**

323119 Other Commercial Printing^{US}

This U.S. industry comprises establishments primarily engaged in commercial printing (except lithographic, gravure, screen, or flexographic printing) without publishing (except books, grey goods, and manifold business forms). Printing processes included in this industry are letterpress printing and engraving printing. This industry includes establishments engaged in commercial printing on purchased stock materials, such as stationery, invitations, labels, and similar items, on a job order basis.

Lithographic, gravure, screen, or flexographic printing on purchased stock materials (except books, grey goods, and manifold business forms) **32311**
Printing on grey goods **31331**
Quick printing **323114**
Digital printing on graphical materials **323115**
Printing books and pamphlets **323117**
Printing manifold business forms including checkbooks **323116**
Manufacturing printed stationery, invitations, labels, and similar items **322**
Printing and publishing, known as book publishers, **511**

32312 Support Activities for Printing

This industry comprises establishments primarily engaged in performing prepress (e.g., platemaking, typesetting) and postpress services (e.g., book binding) in support of printing activities.

Engraving of the type done on metal **33281**
Manufacturing photosensitive plates for printing **32599**
Manufacturing blank plates for printing **33329**
Printing books or printing and binding books **32311**

323121 Tradebinding and Related Work[US]

This U.S. industry comprises establishments primarily engaged in one or more of the following: (1) tradebinding; (2) sample mounting; and (3) postpress services (e.g., book or paper bronzing, diecutting, edging, embossing, folding, gilding, gluing, indexing).

Printing books or printing and binding books **323117**

323122 Prepress Services[US]

This U.S. industry comprises (1) establishments primarily engaged in prepress services, such as imagesetting or typesetting, for printers and (2) establishments primarily engaged in preparing film or plates for printing purposes.

Engraving of the type done on metal **332812**
Manufacturing blank plates (except photosensitive plates) for printing **333293**
Manufacturing photosensitive plates for printing **325992**

324

324 Petroleum and Coal Products Manufacturing

The Petroleum and Coal Products Manufacturing subsector is based on the transformation of crude petroleum and coal into usable products. The dominant process is petroleum refining that involves the separation of crude petroleum into component products through such techniques as cracking and distillation.

In addition, this subsector includes establishments that primarily further process refined petroleum and coal products and produce products, such as asphalt coatings and petroleum lubricating oils. However, establishments that manufacture petrochemicals from refined petroleum are classified in Industry 32511, Petrochemical Manufacturing.

3241 Petroleum and Coal Products Manufacturing

324110 Petroleum Refineries

This industry comprises establishments primarily engaged in refining crude petroleum into refined petroleum. Petroleum refining involves one or more of the following activities: (1) fractionation; (2) straight distillation of crude oil; and (3) cracking.

Manufacturing asphalt paving, roofing, and saturated materials from refined petroleum **32412**
Manufacturing paper mats and felts and saturating them with asphalt or tar into rolls and sheets **322121**
Blending or compounding refined petroleum to make lubricating oils and greases and/or re-refining used petroleum lubricating oils **324191**
Manufacturing synthetic lubricating oils and greases **325998**
Recovering natural gasoline and/or liquid hydrocarbons from oil and gas field gases **21111**
Manufacturing acyclic and cyclic aromatic hydrocarbons (i.e., petrochemicals) from refined petroleum or liquid hydrocarbons **325110**
Manufacturing cyclic and acyclic chemicals (except petrochemicals) **32519**
Manufacturing coke oven products in steel mills **331111**
Manufacturing coke oven products in coke oven establishments **324199**

324112 Asphalt Paving, Roofing, and Saturated Materials Manufacturing

This industry comprises establishments primarily engaged in (1) manufacturing asphalt and tar paving mixtures and blocks and roofing cements and coatings from purchased asphaltic materials and/or (2) saturating purchased mats and felts with asphalt or tar from purchased asphaltic materials.

Refining crude petroleum and manufacturing asphalt and tar paving, roofing, and saturated materials **324110**
Manufacturing paper mats and felts and saturating them with asphalt or tar **32212**

324121 Asphalt Paving Mixture and Block Manufacturing[CAN]

This U.S. industry comprises establishments primarily engaged in manufacturing asphalt and tar paving mixtures and blocks from purchased asphaltic materials.

Refining crude petroleum and manufacturing asphalt and tar paving mixtures and blocks **324110**

324122 Asphalt Shingle and Coating Materials Manufacturing^{CAN}

This U.S. industry comprises establishments primarily engaged in (1) saturating purchased mats and felts with asphalt or tar from purchased asphaltic materials and (2) manufacturing asphalt and tar and roofing cements and coatings from purchased asphaltic materials.

Refining crude petroleum and saturating purchased mats and felts with asphalt or tar into rolls and sheets and/or refining crude petroleum and manufacturing asphalt and tar roofing cements and coatings **324110**
Manufacturing paper mats and felts and saturating them with asphalt or tar into rolls and sheets **322121**

32419 Other Petroleum and Coal Products Manufacturing

This industry comprises establishments primarily engaged in manufacturing petroleum products (except asphalt paving, roofing and saturated materials) from refined petroleum or coal products made in coke ovens not integrated with a steel mill.

Manufacturing petroleum products by refining crude petroleum **32411**
Manufacturing asphalt and tar paving, roofing, and saturated materials from refined petroleum **32412**
Manufacturing coke oven products in steel mills **33111**
Manufacturing acyclic and cyclic aromatic hydrocarbons (i.e., petrochemicals) from refined petroleum or liquid hydrocarbons **32511**
Manufacturing cyclic and acyclic organic chemicals (except petrochemicals) **32519**
Manufacturing synthetic lubricating oils and greases **32599**

324191 Petroleum Lubricating Oil and Grease Manufacturing^{US}

This U.S. industry comprises establishments primarily engaged in blending or compounding refined petroleum to make lubricating oils and greases and/or re-refining used petroleum lubricating oils.

Refining crude petroleum and manufacturing lubricating oils and greases **324110**
Manufacturing synthetic lubricating oils and greases **325998**

324199 All Other Petroleum and Coal Products Manufacturing^{US}

This U.S. industry comprises establishments primarily engaged in manufacturing petroleum products (except asphalt paving, roofing, and saturated materials and lubricating oils and greases) from refined petroleum and coal products made in coke ovens not integrated with a steel mill.

Manufacturing petroleum products by refining crude petroleum **324110**
Manufacturing asphalt paving and roofing materials from refined petroleum **32412**
Blending and compounding petroleum lubricating oils and greases and/or re-refining used petroleum lubrication oils and greases **324191**
Manufacturing coke oven products in steel mills **331111**
Manufacturing acyclic and cyclic aromatic hydrocarbons (i.e., petrochemicals) from refined petroleum or liquid hydrocarbons **325110**
Manufacturing cyclic and acyclic organic chemicals (except petrochemicals) **32519**

325 Chemical Manufacturing

The Chemical Manufacturing subsector is based on the transformation of organic and inorganic raw materials by a chemical process and the formulation of products. This subsector distinguishes the production of basic chemicals that comprise the first industry group from the production of intermediate and end products produced by further processing of basic chemicals that make up the remaining industry groups.

This subsector does not include all industries transforming raw materials by a chemical process. It is common for some chemical processing to occur during mining operations. These beneficiating operations, such as copper concentrating, are classified in Sector 21, Mining. Furthermore, the refining of crude petroleum is included in Subsector 324, Petroleum and Coal Products Manufacturing. In addition, the manufacturing of aluminum oxide is included in Subsector 331, Primary Metal Manufacturing; and beverage distilleries are classified in Subsector 312, Beverage and Tobacco Product Manufacturing. As in the case of these two activities, the grouping of industries into subsectors may take into account the association of the activities performed with other activities in the subsector.

325l Basic Chemical Manufacturing

This industry group comprises establishments primarily engaged in manufacturing chemicals using basic processes, such as thermal cracking and distillation. Chemicals manufactured in this industry group are usually separate chemical elements or separate chemically-defined compounds.

325110 Petrochemical Manufacturing

This industry comprises establishments primarily engaged in (1) manufacturing acyclic (i.e., aliphatic) hydrocarbons such as ethylene, propylene, and butylene made from refined petroleum or liquid hydrocarbon and/or (2) manufacturing cyclic aromatic hydrocarbons such as benzene, toluene, styrene, xylene, ethyl benzene, and cumene made from refined petroleum or liquid hydrocarbons.

Manufacturing petrochemicals by refining crude petroleum 324110
Manufacturing acetylene 325120
Manufacturing basic organic chemicals (except petrochemicals) 325190
Recovering liquid hydrocarbons from oil and gas field gases 211110

325120 Industrial Gas Manufacturing

This industry comprises establishments primarily engaged in manufacturing industrial organic and inorganic gases in compressed, liquid, and solid forms.

Manufacturing chlorine gas 325181
Manufacturing ethane and butane gases made from refined petroleum or liquid hydrocarbons 325110

325l3 Synthetic Dye and Pigment Manufacturing

This industry comprises establishments primarily engaged in manufacturing synthetic organic and inorganic dyes and pigments, such as lakes and toners (except electrostatic and photographic).

Manufacturing wood byproducts used as dying materials 32519
Manufacturing carbon, bone, and lamp black 32518
Manufacturing electrostatic and photographic toners 32599
Manufacturing natural food colorings 31193
Manufacturing natural organic colorings for nonfood uses 32519

325l3l Inorganic Dye and Pigment Manufacturing[US]

This U.S. industry comprises establishments primarily engaged in manufacturing inorganic dyes and pigments.

Manufacturing wood byproducts used as dyeing materials 325191

Manufacturing organic synthetic dyes and pigments 325132
Manufacturing carbon, bone, and lamp black 325182
Manufacturing natural food colorings 311930

325132 Synthetic Organic Dye and Pigment Manufacturing[US]

This U.S. industry comprises establishments primarily engaged in manufacturing synthetic organic dyes and pigments, such as lakes and toners (except electrostatic and photographic).

Manufacturing wood byproducts used as dyeing materials 325191
Manufacturing inorganic dyes and pigments 325131
Manufacturing electrostatic and photographic toners 325992
Manufacturing natural food colorings 311930
Manufacturing natural organic colorings for nonfood uses (except wood byproducts) 325199

325l8 Other Basic Inorganic Chemical Manufacturing

This industry comprises establishments primarily engaged in manufacturing basic inorganic chemicals (except industrial gases and synthetic dyes and pigments).

Manufacturing inorganic dyes and pigments 32513
Manufacturing household bleaches 32561
Mining and/or beneficiating alkalies 21239
Manufacturing chlorine preparations (e.g., for swimming pools) 32599
Manufacturing nitrogenous and phosphoric fertilizers and fertilizer materials 32531
Manufacturing aluminum oxide (alumina) 33131
Manufacturing inorganic insecticidal, herbicidal, fungicidal and pesticidal preparations 32532
Manufacturing photographic chemicals 32599

325l8l Alkalies and Chlorine Manufacturing[CAN]

This U.S. industry comprises establishments primarily engaged in manufacturing chlorine, sodium hydroxide (i.e., caustic soda), and other alkalies often using an electrolysis process.

Mining and beneficiating alkalies 212391
Manufacturing chlorine preparations (e.g., for swimming pools) 325998
Manufacturing industrial bleaches 325188
Manufacturing household bleaches 325611

325l82 Carbon Black Manufacturing[US]

This U.S. industry comprises establishments primarily engaged in manufacturing carbon black, bone black, and lamp black.

Manufacturing pigments 32513

325

325188 All Other Basic Inorganic Chemical Manufacturing[US]

This U.S. industry comprises establishments primarily engaged in manufacturing basic inorganic chemicals (except industrial gases, inorganic dyes and pigments, alkalies and chlorine, and carbon black).

Manufacturing industrial gases **325120**
Manufacturing inorganic dyes and pigments **325131**
Manufacturing alkalies and chlorine **325181**
Manufacturing carbon black **325182**
Manufacturing household bleaches **325612**
Manufacturing nitrogenous and phosphoric fertilizers and fertilizer material **32531**
Manufacturing aluminum oxide (i.e., alumina) **331311**
Manufacturing inorganic insecticidal, herbicidal, fungicidal, and pesticidal preparations **325320**
Manufacturing photographic chemicals **325992**

32519 Other Basic Organic Chemical Manufacturing

This industry comprises establishments primarily engaged in manufacturing basic organic chemicals (except petrochemicals, industrial gases, and synthetic dyes and pigments).

Manufacturing petrochemicals from refined petroleum or liquid hydrocarbons **32511**
Manufacturing petrochemicals by refining crude petroleum **32411**
Manufacturing organic industrial gases **32512**
Manufacturing synthetic organic dyes and pigments **32513**
Manufacturing natural glycerin **32561**
Manufacturing activated charcoal **32599**
Manufacturing organic insecticidal, herbicidal, fungicidal, and pesticidal preparations **32532**
Manufacturing elastomers **32521**
Manufacturing urea **32531**
Manufacturing coal tar crudes in integrated steel mills with coke ovens **33111**
Manufacturing coal tar crudes in coke ovens not intergrated with steel mills and fuel briquettes from refined petroleum **32419**
Manufacturing natural food colorings **31194**

325191 Gum and Wood Chemical Manufacturing[US]

This U.S. industry comprises establishments primarily engaged in (1) distilling wood or gum into products, such as tall oil and wood distillates, and (2) manufacturing wood or gum chemicals, such as naval stores, natural tanning materials, charcoal briquettes, and charcoal (except activated).

Manufacturing activated charcoal **325998**
Manufacturing fuel briquettes from refined petroleum **324199**

325192 Cyclic Crude and Intermediate Manufacturing[US]

This U.S. industry comprises establishments primarily engaged in (1) distilling coal tars and/or (2) manufacturing cyclic crudes or, cyclic intermediates (i.e., hydrocarbons, except aromatic petrochemicals) from refined petroleum or natural gas.

Manufacturing cyclic chemicals (except aromatic and intermediates) **325199**
Manufacturing aromatic petrochemicals from refined petroleum or natural gas **325110**
Manufacturing aromatic petrochemicals by refining crude petroleum **324110**
Distilling wood products **325191**
Manufacturing coal tar crudes in steel mills with coke ovens **331111**
Manufacturing coal tar crudes in coke oven establishments and fuel briquettes from refined petroleum **324199**

325193 Ethyl Alcohol Manufacturing[US]

This U.S. industry comprises establishments primarily engaged in manufacturing nonpotable ethyl alcohol.

Distilling liquors (except brandy) **312140**
Manufacturing brandies **312130**

325199 All Other Basic Organic Chemical Manufacturing[US]

This U.S. industry comprises establishments primarily engaged in manufacturing basic organic chemical products (except aromatic petrochemicals, industrial gases, synthetic organic dyes and pigments, gum and wood chemicals, cyclic crudes and intermediates, and ethyl alcohol).

Manufacturing aromatic petrochemicals from refined petroleum or natural gas **325110**
Manufacturing aromatic petrochemicals by refining crude petroleum **324110**
Manufacturing organic industrial gases **325120**
Manufacturing synthetic organic dyes and pigments **325132**
Manufacturing ethyl alcohol **325193**
Manufacturing organic insecticidal, herbicidal, fungicidal, and pesticidal preparations **325320**
Manufacturing elastomers **325210**
Manufacturing urea **325311**
Manufacturing natural glycerin **325611**
Manufacturing natural food colorings **311942**

3252 Resin, Synthetic Rubber, and Artificial Synthetic Fibers and Filaments Manufacturing

32521 Resin and Synthetic Rubber Manufacturing

This industry comprises establishments primarily engaged in one or more of the following: (1) manufacturing synthetic resins, plastics materials, and nonvulcanizable elastomers and mixing and blending resins on a custom basis; (2) manufacturing noncustomized synthetic resins; and (3) manufacturing synthetic rubber.

Manufacturing plastics resins and converting resins into plastics products **3261**
Processing natural, synthetic, or reclaimed rubber into intermediate or final products **3262**
Custom compounding resins made elsewhere **32599**
Manufacturing resin adhesives **32552**

325211 Plastics Material and Resin Manufacturing[US]

This U.S. industry comprises establishments primarily engaged in (1) manufacturing resins, plastics materials, and nonvulcanizable thermoplastic elastomers and mixing and blending resins on a custom basis and/or (2) manufacturing noncustomized synthetic resins.

Manufacturing plastics resins and converting the resins into plastics products **3261**
Custom compounding resins made elsewhere **325991**
Manufacturing plastics adhesives **325520**

325212 Synthetic Rubber Manufacturing[US]

This U.S. industry consists of establishments primarily engaged in manufacturing synthetic rubber.

Processing natural, synthetic, or reclaimed rubber into intermediate or final products (except adhesives) **3262**
Manufacturing rubber adhesives **325520**

32522 Artificial and Synthetic Fibers and Filaments Manufacturing[CAN]

This industry comprises establishments primarily engaged in (1) manufacturing cellulosic (i.e., rayon and acetate) and noncellulosic (i.e., nylon, polyolefin, and polyester) fibers and filaments in the form of monofilament, filament yarn, staple, or tow or (2) manufacturing and texturing cellulosic and noncellulosic fibers and filaments.

Texturizing cellulosic and noncellulosic fiber and filament made elsewhere **31311**
Manufacturing textile glass fibers **32721**

325221 Cellulosic Organic Fiber Manufacturing[US]

This U.S. industry comprises establishments primarily engaged in (1) manufacturing cellulosic (i.e., rayon and acetate) fibers and filaments in the form of monofilament, filament yarn, staple, or tow or (2) manufacturing and texturizing cellulosic fibers and filaments.

Texturizing cellulosic fibers and filaments made elsewhere **313112**
Manufacturing noncellulosic fibers and filaments **325222**

325222 Noncellulosic Organic Fiber Manufacturing[US]

This U.S. industry consists of establishments primarily engaged in (1) manufacturing noncellulosic (i.e., nylon, polyolefin, and polyester) fibers and filaments in the form of monofilament, filament yarn, staple, or tow or (2) manufacturing and texturizing noncellulosic fibers and filaments.

Texturizing noncellulosic fibers **313112**
Manufacturing cellulose fibers **325221**
Manufacturing textile glass fibers **327212**

3253 Pesticide, Fertilizer, and Other Agricultural Chemical Manufacturing

32531 Fertilizer Manufacturing

This industry comprises establishments primarily engaged in one or more of the following: (1) manufacturing nitrogenous or phosphatic fertilizer materials; (2) manufacturing fertilizers from sewage or animal waste; (3) manufacturing nitrogenous or phosphatic materials and mixing with other ingredients into fertilizers; and (4) mixing ingredients made elsewhere into fertilizers.

325311 Nitrogenous Fertilizer Manufacturing[CAN]

This U.S. industry comprises establishments primarily engaged in one or more of the following: (1) manufacturing nitrogenous fertilizer materials and mixing ingredients into fertilizers; (2) manufacturing fertilizers from sewage or animal waste; and (3) manufacturing nitrogenous materials and mixing them into fertilizers.

Mixing ingredients made elsewhere into nitrogenous fertilizers **325314**

325312 Phosphatic Fertilizer Manufacturing[US]

This U.S. industry comprises establishments primarily engaged in (1) manufacturing phosphatic fertilizer materials or (2) manufacturing phosphatic materials and mixing them into fertilizers.

Mixing ingredients made elsewhere into phosphatic fertilizers **325314**

325314 Fertilizer (Mixing Only) Manufacturing[CAN]

This U.S. industry comprises establishments primarily engaged in mixing ingredients made elsewhere into fertilizers.

Manufacturing nitrogenous fertilizer materials or fertilizer materials from sewage or animal waste and mixing these ingredients into nitrogenous fertilizers **325311**

Manufacturing phosphatic fertilizer materials and mixing ingredients into fertilizers **325312**

325320 Pesticide and Other Agricultural Chemical Manufacturing

This industry comprises establishments primarily engaged in the formulation and preparation of agricultural and household pest control chemicals (except fertilizers).

Manufacturing basic chemicals requiring further processing before use as agriculture chemicals **3251**

Manufacturing fertilizers **325310**

Manufacturing agricultural lime products **327410**

32541 Pharmaceutical and Medicine Manufacturing

This industry comprises establishments primarily engaged in one or more of the following: (1) manufacturing biological and medicinal products; (2) processing (i.e., grading, grinding, and milling) botanical drugs and herbs; (3) isolating active medicinal principals from botanical drugs and herbs; and (4) manufacturing pharmaceutical products intended for internal and external consumption in such forms as ampoules, tablets, capsules, vials, ointments, powders, solutions, and suspensions.

325411 Medicinal and Botanical Manufacturing[US]

This U.S. industry comprises establishments primarily engaged in (1) manufacturing uncompounded medicinal chemicals and their derivatives (i.e., generally for use by pharmaceutical preparation manufacturers) and/or (2) grading, grinding, and milling uncompounded botanicals.

Manufacturing packaged compounded medicinals and botanicals **325412**

Manufacturing vaccines, toxoids, blood fractions, and culture media of plant or animal origin (except for diagnostic use) **325414**

325412 Pharmaceutical Preparation Manufacturing[US]

This U.S. industry comprises establishments primarily engaged in manufacturing in-vivo diagnostic substances and pharmaceutical preparations (except biological) intended for internal and external consumption in dose forms, such as ampoules, tablets, capsules, vials, ointments, powders, solutions, and suspensions.

Manufacturing uncompounded medicinal chemicals and their derivatives **325411**

Manufacturing in-vitro diagnostic substances **325413**

Manufacturing vaccines, toxoids, blood fractions, and culture media of plant or animal origin (except for diagnostic use) **325414**

325413 In-Vitro Diagnostic Substance Manufacturing[US]

This U.S. industry comprises establishments primarily engaged in manufacturing in-vitro (i.e., not taken internally) diagnostic substances, such as chemical, biological, or radioactive substances. The substances are used for diagnostic tests that are performed in test tubes, petri dishes, machines, and other diagnostic test-type devices.

Manufacturing in-vivo diagnostic substances **325412**

325414 Biological Product (except Diagnostic) Manufacturing[CAN]

This U.S. industry comprises establishments primarily engaged in manufacturing vaccines, toxoids, blood fractions, and culture media of plant or animal origin (except diagnostic).

Manufacturing in-vitro diagnostic substances **325413**

Manufacturing pharmaceutical preparations (except biological and in-vivo diagnostic substances) **325412**

3255 Paint, Coating, and Adhesive Manufacturing

325510 Paint and Coating Manufacturing

This industry comprises establishments primarily engaged in (1) mixing pigments, solvents, and binders into paints and other coatings, such as stains, varnishes, lacquers, enamels, shellacs, and water repellant coatings for concrete and masonry, and/or (2) manufacturing allied paint products, such as putties, paint and varnish removers, paint brush cleaners, and frit.

Manufacturing creosote **32519**
Manufacturing caulking compounds and sealants **325520**
Manufacturing artists' paints **339942**
Manufacturing turpentine **325191**

325520 Adhesive Manufacturing

This industry comprises establishments primarily engaged in manufacturing adhesives, glues, and caulking compounds.

Manufacturing asphalt and tar roofing cements from purchased asphaltic materials **324122**
Manufacturing gypsum based caulking compounds **327420**

3256 Soap, Cleaning Compound, and Toilet Preparation Manufacturing

32561 Soap and Cleaning Compound Manufacturing

This industry comprises establishments primarily engaged in manufacturing and packaging soap and other cleaning compounds, surface active agents, and textile and leather finishing agents used to reduce tension or speed the drying process.

Manufacturing synthetic glycerin **32519**
Manufacturing industrial bleaches **32518**
Manufacturing shampoos and shaving preparations **32562**

325611 Soap and Other Detergent Manufacturing[US]

This U.S. industry comprises establishments primarily engaged in manufacturing and packaging soaps and other detergents, such as laundry detergents; dishwashing detergents; toothpaste gels, and tooth powders; and natural glycerin.

Manufacturing synthetic glycerin **325199**
Manufacturing shampoos and shaving preparations **325620**

325612 Polish and Other Sanitation Good Manufacturing[US]

This U.S. industry comprises establishments primarily engaged in manufacturing and packaging polishes and specialty cleaning preparations.

Manufacturing chlorine dioxide (i.e., industrial bleaching agent) **325188**

325613 Surface Active Agent Manufacturing[US]

This U.S. industry comprises establishments primarily engaged in (1) manufacturing bulk surface active agents for use as wetting agents, emulsifiers, and penetrants, and/or (2) manufacturing textiles and leather finishing agents used to reduce tension or speed the drying process.

325620 Toilet Preparation Manufacturing

This industry comprises establishments primarily engaged in preparing, blending, compounding, and packaging toilet preparations, such as perfumes, shaving preparations, hair preparations, face creams, lotions (including sunscreens), and other cosmetic preparations.

Manufacturing toothpaste **325611**

3259 Other Chemical Product and Preparation Manufacturing

This industry group comprises establishments primarily engaged in manufacturing chemical products (except basic chemicals; resins, synthetic rubber, cellulosic and noncellulosic fibers and filaments; pesticides, fertilizers, and other agricultural chemicals; pharmaceuticals and medicines; paints, coatings, and adhesives; soaps and cleaning compounds; and toilet preparations).

325910 Printing Ink Manufacturing

This industry comprises establishments primarily engaged in manufacturing printing and inkjet inks and inkjet cartridges.

Recycling inkjet cartridges **811212**
Manufacturing writing, drawing, and stamping ink **325998**
Manufacturing toners and toner cartridges for photocopiers, fax machines, computer printers and similar office machines **325992**
Manufacturing inkjet cartridges **334119**

325920 Explosives Manufacturing

This industry comprises establishments primarily engaged in manufacturing explosives.

Manufacturing ammunition, ammunition detonators, and percussion caps **332992**
Manufacturing pyrotechnics **325998**

32599 All Other Chemical Product and Preparation Manufacturing

This industry comprises establishments primarily engaged in manufacturing chemical products (except basic chemicals, resins, and synthetic rubber; cellulosic and noncellulosic fibers and filaments; pesticides, fertilizers, and other agricultural chemicals; pharmaceuticals and medicines; paints, coatings, and adhesives; and soaps, cleaning compounds, and toilet preparations; printing inks; and explosives).

Manufacturing basic chemicals **3251**
Manufacturing resins, synthetic rubber, and artificial synthetic fibers and filaments **3252**
Manufacturing pesticides, fertilizers, and other agricultural chemicals **3253**
Manufacturing pharmaceuticals and medicine including medicinal vegetable gelatin (i.e., agar-agar) **3254**
Manufacturing paints, coatings, and adhesives **3255**
Manufacturing soaps and cleaning compounds **3256**
Manufacturing printing and inkjet inks **32591**
Manufacturing explosives **32592**
Manufacturing photographic toner cartridges **33331**
Manufacturing computer printer toner cartridges **33411**
Manufacturing facsimile toner cartridges **33429**
Manufacturing photographic paper stock (i.e., unsensitized) and paper mats, mounts, easels, and folders for photographic use **322**
Manufacturing dessert gelatins **31199**
Manufacturing medicinal gelatins **32541**

325991 Custom Compounding of Purchased Resins^{CAN}

This industry comprises establishments primarily engaged in (1) custom mixing and blending plastics resins made elsewhere or (2) reformulating plastics resins from recycled plastics products.

Manufacturing synthetic resins and custom mixing and blending resins **325211**

325992 Photographic Film, Paper, Plate, and Chemical Manufacturing^{US}

This U.S. industry comprises establishments primarily engaged in manufacturing sensitized film, sensitized paper, sensitized cloth, sensitized plates, toners (i.e., for photocopiers, laser printers, and similar electrostatic printing devices), toner cartridges, and photographic chemicals.

Manufacturing photographic paper stock (i.e., unsensitized) and paper mats, mounts, easels, and folders for photographic use **322**

325998 All Other Miscellaneous Chemical Product and Preparation Manufacturing^{US}

This U.S. industry comprises establishments primarily engaged in manufacturing chemical products (except basic chemicals, resins, synthetic rubber; cellulosic and noncellulosic fiber and filaments; pesticides, fertilizers, and other agricultural chemicals; pharmaceuticals and medicines; paints, coatings and adhesives; soap, cleaning compounds, and toilet preparations; printing inks; explosives; custom compounding of purchased resins; and photographic films, papers, plates, and chemicals).

Manufacturing basic chemicals **3251**
Manufacturing resins, synthetic rubber, and artificial synthetic fibers and filaments **3252**
Manufacturing pesticides, fertilizers, and other agricultural chemicals **3253**
Manufacturing pharmaceuticals and medicines including medicinal vegetable gelatin (i.e., agar-agar) **3254**
Manufacturing paints, coatings, and adhesives **3255**
Manufacturing soaps and cleaning compounds **3256**
Manufacturing printing and inkjet inks **325910**
Manufacturing explosives **325920**
Custom compounding purchased plastics resins **325991**
Manufacturing photographic films, papers, plates, and chemicals **325992**
Manufacturing dessert gelatin **311999**

326 Plastics and Rubber Products Manufacturing

Industries in the Plastics and Rubber Products Manufacturing subsector make goods by processing plastics materials and raw rubber. The core technology employed by establishments in this subsector is that of plastics or rubber product production. Plastics and rubber are combined in the same subsector because plastics are increasingly being used as a substitute for rubber; however the subsector is generally restricted to the production of products made of just one material, either solely plastics or rubber.

Many manufacturing activities use plastics or rubber, for example the manufacture of footwear, or furniture. Typically, the production process of these products involves more than one material. In these cases, technologies that allow disparate materials to be formed and combined are of central importance in describing the manufacturing activity. In NAICS, such activities (the footwear and furniture manufacturing) are not classified in the Plastics and Rubber Products Manufacturing subsector because the core technologies for these activities are diverse and involve multiple materials.

Within the Plastics and Rubber Products Manufacturing subsector, a distinction is made between plastics and rubber products at the industry group level, although it is not a rigid distinction, as can be seen from the definition of Industry 32622, Rubber and Plastics Hose and Belting Manufacturing. As materials technology progresses, plastics are increasingly being used as a substitute for rubber; and eventually, the distinction may disappear as a basis for establishment classification. In keeping with the core technology focus of plastics, lamination of plastics film to plastics film as well as the production of bags from plastics only is classified in this subsector. Lamination and bag production involving plastics and materials other than plastics are classified in the NAICS Subsector 322, Paper Manufacturing.

326

3261 Plastics Product Manufacturing

This industry group comprises establishments primarily engaged in processing new or spent (i.e., recycled) plastics resins into intermediate or final products, using such processes as compression molding; extrusion molding; injection molding; blow molding; and casting. Within most of these industries, the production process is such that a wide variety of products can be made.

32611 Unsupported Plastics Film, Sheet, and Bag Manufacturing

This industry comprises establishments primarily engaged in (1) converting plastics resins into unsupported plastics film and sheet and/or (2) forming, coating or laminating plastics film and sheet into plastics bags.

Laminating plastics sheet (except for packaging) **32613**
Manufacturing plastics blister and bubble packaging **32619**
Coating or laminating combinations of plastics, foils and paper (except plastics film to plastics film) into film, sheet or bags **32222**

326111 Unsupported Plastics Bag Manufacturing[CAN]

This U.S. industry comprises establishments primarily engaged in (1) converting plastics resins into plastics bags or (2) forming, coating or laminating plastics film and sheet into single wall or multiwall plastics bags. Establishments in this industry may print on the bags they manufacture.

Manufacturing laminated or coated combinations of plastics, foils and paper (except plastics film to plastics film) materials into single wall bags **322223**
Manufacturing laminated or coated combinations of plastics, foils and paper (except plastics film to plastics film) into multiwalled bags **322224**

326112 Unsupported Plastics Packaging Film and Sheet Manufacturing[US]

This U.S. industry comprises establishments primarily engaged in converting plastics resins into plastics packaging (flexible) film and packaging sheet.

Converting plastics resins into plastics film and unlaminated sheet (except packaging) **326113**
Laminating or coating packaging combinations of plastics, foils and paper (except plastics film to plastics film) film and sheet **322221**
Laminating or coating combinations of plastics, foils, and paper (except plastics film to plastics film) nonpackaging film and sheet **322222**
Laminating plastics sheet (except for packaging) **326130**
Manufacturing plastics bags **326111**

326113 Unsupported Plastics Film and Sheet (except Packaging) Manufacturing[US]

This U.S. industry comprises establishments primarily engaged in converting plastics resins into plastics film and unlaminated sheet (except packaging).

Converting plastics resins into plastics packaging film and unlaminated packaging sheet **326112**
Laminating plastics sheet (except for packaging) **326130**
Laminating or coating a combination of plastics, foils, and paper (except plastics film to plastics film) nonpackaging film and sheet **322222**
Manufacturing plastics bags **326111**

32612 Plastics Pipe, Pipe Fitting, and Unsupported Profile Shape Manufacturing

This industry comprises establishments primarily engaged in manufacturing plastics pipes and pipe fittings, and plastics profile shapes such as rod, tube, and sausage casings.

Manufacturing plastics hose **32622**
Manufacturing noncurrent carrying plastics conduit **33593**
Manufacturing plastics plumbing fixtures **32619**
Manufacturing plastics film, plastics unlaminated sheet, and plastics bags **32611**

326121 Unsupported Plastics Profile Shapes Manufacturing^CAN

This U.S. industry comprises establishments primarily engaged in converting plastics resins into nonrigid plastics profile shapes (except film, sheet and bags), such as rod, tube, and sausage casings.

Manufacturing plastics film, plastics unlaminated sheet, and plastics bags **32611**
Manufacturing plastics hoses **326220**

326122 Plastics Pipe and Pipe Fitting Manufacturing^CAN

This U.S. industry comprises establishments primarily engaged in converting plastics resins into rigid plastics pipes and pipe fittings.

Manufacturing plastics hose **326220**
Manufacturing noncurrent-carrying plastics conduit **335932**
Manufacturing plastics plumbing fixtures **326191**

326130 Laminated Plastics Plate, Sheet, and Shape Manufacturing

This industry comprises establishments primarily engaged in laminating plastics profile shapes such as plate, sheet (except packaging), and rod. The lamination process generally involves bonding or impregnating profiles with plastics resins and compressing them under heat.

Manufacturing plastics film, plastics unlaminated sheet, and plastics bags **32611**
Coating or laminating nonplastics film, sheet, or bags with plastics **32222**
Manufacturing plastics bags **326111**

326140 Polystyrene Foam Product Manufacturing

This industry comprises establishments primarily engaged in manufacturing polystyrene foam products.

Manufacturing plastics foam products (except polystyrene) **326150**

326150 Urethane and Other Foam Product (except Polystyrene) Manufacturing

This industry comprises establishments primarily engaged in manufacturing plastics foam products (except polystyrene).

Manufacturing polystyrene foam products **326140**

326160 Plastics Bottle Manufacturing

This industry comprises establishments primarily engaged in manufacturing plastics bottles.

Manufacturing plastics containers (except bottles) **326199**

32619 Other Plastics Product Manufacturing

This industry comprises establishments primarily engaged in manufacturing resilient floor covering and other plastics products (except film, sheet, bags, profile shapes, pipes, pipe fittings, laminates, foam products, and bottles).

Manufacturing plastics film, plastics unlaminated sheet, and plastics bags **32611**
Manufacturing plastics pipes, pipe fittings and plastics profile shapes (except films, sheet, bags) **32612**
Laminating plastics profile shapes, such as plate, sheet and rod, **32613**
Manufacturing polystyrene foam products **32614**
Manufacturing foam products (except polystyrene) **32615**
Manufacturing plastics bottles **32616**
Manufacturing plastics furniture parts **33721**
Assembling plastics components into plumbing fixture fittings, such as faucets, **33291**
Manufacturing rubber floor mats and rubber treads **32629**

326191 Plastics Plumbing Fixture Manufacturing^CAN

This U.S. industry comprises establishments primarily engaged in manufacturing plastics or fiberglass plumbing fixtures. Examples of products made by these establishments are plastics or fiberglass bathtubs, hot tubs, portable toilets, and shower stalls.

Assembling plastics components into plumbing fixture fittings, such as faucets, **332913**
Manufacturing plastics pipe and pipe fittings **326122**

326192 Resilient Floor Covering Manufacturing^CAN

This U.S. industry comprises establishments primarily engaged in manufacturing resilient floor coverings for permanent installation.

Manufacturing rubber floor mats and rubber treads **326299**

326199 All Other Plastics Product Manufacturing[US]

This U.S. industry comprises establishments primarily engaged in manufacturing plastics products (except film, sheet, bags, profile shapes, pipes, pipe fittings, laminates, foam products, bottles, plumbing fixtures, and resilient floor coverings).

Manufacturing plastics film, plastics unlaminated sheet, and plastics bags **32611**
Manufacturing plastics pipes, pipe fittings, and plastics profile shapes (except film, sheet, bags) **32612**
Manufacturing plastic pipes and pipe fittings **326122**
Laminating plastics profile shapes, such as plate, sheet, and rod, **326130**
Manufacturing polystyrene foam products **326140**
Manufacturing foam (except polystyrene) products **326150**
Manufacturing plastics bottles **326160**
Manufacturing plastics furniture parts and components **337215**
Manufacturing plastics plumbing fixtures **326191**
Manufacturing resilient floor coverings **326192**
Assembling plastics components into plumbing fixtures fittings, such as faucets, **332913**

3262 Rubber Product Manufacturing

This industry group comprises establishments primarily engaged in processing natural, and synthetic or reclaimed rubber materials into intermediate or final products using processes such as vulcanizing, cementing, molding, extruding, and lathe-cutting.

32621 Tire Manufacturing

This industry comprises establishments primarily engaged in manufacturing tires and inner tubes from natural and synthetic rubber and retreading or rebuilding tires.

Repairing tires, such as plugging, **81119**
Retailing tires **44132**

326211 Tire Manufacturing (except Retreading)[US]

This U.S. industry comprises establishments primarily engaged in manufacturing tires and inner tubes from natural and synthetic rubber.

Retreading or rebuilding tires **326212**

326212 Tire Retreading[US]

This U.S. industry comprises establishments primarily engaged in retreading, or rebuilding tires.

Repairing tires, such as pluggings **811198**

Retailing tires **441320**
Manufacturing tires and inner tubes from natural and synthetic rubber **326211**

326220 Rubber and Plastics Hoses and Belting Manufacturing

This industry comprises establishments primarily engaged in manufacturing rubber hose and/or plastics (reinforced) hose and belting from natural and synthetic rubber and/or plastics resins. Establishments manufacturing garden hoses from purchased hose are included in this industry.

Manufacturing rubber tubing **326299**
Manufacturing plastics tubing **326121**
Manufacturing fluid power hose assemblies **332912**

32629 Other Rubber Product Manufacturing

This industry comprises establishments primarily engaged in manufacturing rubber products (except tires, hoses, and belting) from natural and synthetic rubber.

Manufacturing rubber hoses and belting **32622**
Rubberizing fabric **31332**
Manufacturing rubber gaskets, packing and sealing devices **33999**
Manufacturing rubber gloves **33911**
Manufacturing rubber clothing accessories (e.g., bathing caps) **31599**
Manufacturing rubber toys **33993**

326291 Rubber Product Manufacturing for Mechanical Use[US]

This U.S. industry comprises establishments primarily engaged in molding, extruding or lathe-cutting rubber to manufacture rubber goods (except tubing) for mechanical applications. Products of this industry are generally parts for motor vehicles, machinery, and equipment.

Manufacturing rubber tubing from natural and synthetic rubber and manufacturing rubber products for mechanical applications using a process other than molding, extruding or lathe-cutting **326299**

326299 All Other Rubber Product Manufacturing[US]

This U.S. industry comprises establishments primarily engaged in manufacturing rubber products (except tires; hoses and belting; and molded, extruded, and lathe-cut rubber goods for mechanical applications) from natural and synthetic rubber.

Manufacturing tires and inner tubes and tire rebuilding **32621**
Manufacturing rubber hoses and belting **326220**
Molding, extruding, and lathe-cutting rubber to manufacture rubber goods (except tubing) for mechanical applications **326291**
Rubberizing fabrics **313320**

Manufacturing rubber gaskets, packing and sealing devices **339991**
Manufacturing rubber toys **33993**
Manufacturing rubber gloves **339113**
Manufacturing rubber clothing accessories (e.g., bathing caps) **315999**

327 Nonmetallic Mineral Product Manufacturing

The Nonmetallic Mineral Product Manufacturing subsector transforms mined or quarried nonmetallic minerals, such as sand, gravel, stone, clay, and refractory materials, into products for intermediate or final consumption. Processes used include grinding, mixing, cutting, shaping, and honing. Heat often is used in the process and chemicals are frequently mixed to change the composition, purity, and chemical properties for the intended product. For example, glass is produced by heating silica sand to the melting point (sometimes combined with cullet or recycled glass) and then drawn, floated, or blow molded to the desired shape or thickness. Refractory materials are heated and then formed into bricks or other shapes for use in industrial applications. The Nonmetallic Mineral Product Manufacturing subsector includes establishments that manufacture products, such as bricks, refractories, ceramic products, and glass and glass products, such as plate glass and containers. Also included are cement and concrete products, lime, gypsum and other nonmetallic mineral products including abrasive products, ceramic plumbing fixtures, statuary, cut stone products, and mineral wool. The products are used in a wide range of activities from construction and heavy and light manufacturing to articles for personal use. Mining, beneficiating, and manufacturing activities often occur in a single location. Separate receipts will be collected for these activities whenever possible. When receipts cannot be broken out between mining and manufacturing, establishments that mine or quarry nonmetallic minerals, beneficiate the nonmetallic minerals and further process the nonmetallic minerals into a more finished manufactured product are classified based on the primary activity of the establishment. A mine that manufactures a small amount of finished products will be classified in Sector 21, Mining. An establishment that mines whose primary output is a more-finished manufactured product will be classified in the Manufacturing Sector.

Excluded from the Nonmetallic Mineral Product Manufacturing subsector are establishments that primarily beneficiate mined nonmetallic minerals. Beneficiation is the process whereby the extracted material is reduced to particles that can be separated into mineral and waste, the former suitable for further processing or direct use. Beneficiation establishments are included in Sector 21, Mining.

3271 Clay Product and Refractory Manufacturing

32711 Pottery, Ceramics, and Plumbing Fixture Manufacturing

This industry comprises establishments primarily engaged in shaping, molding, glazing, and firing pottery, ceramics, and plumbing fixtures made entirely or partly of clay or other ceramic materials.

Manufacturing ferrite microwave devices and electronic components **334**
Manufacturing enameled iron and steel plumbing fixtures **33299**

Manufacturing metal bathroom accessories **332**
Manufacturing plastic bathroom accessories, cultured marble, and other plastic plumbing fixtures **32619**
Manufacturing clay building materials, such as ceramic tile, bricks, and clay roofing tiles, and refractories **32712**

327111 Vitreous China Plumbing Fixture and China and Earthenware Bathroom Accessories Manufacturing[US]

This U.S. industry comprises establishments primarily engaged in manufacturing vitreous china plumbing fixtures and china and earthenware bathroom accessories, such as faucet handles, towel bars, and soap dishes.

Manufacturing enameled iron and steel plumbing fixtures **332998**
Manufacturing metal bathroom accessories **332**
Manufacturing plastic bathroom accessories **326199**
Manufacturing cultured marble and other plastic plumbing fixtures **326191**
Manufacturing china and earthenware products (except bathroom fixtures and accessories) **327112**

327112 Vitreous China, Fine Earthenware, and Other Pottery Product Manufacturing[US]

This U.S. industry comprises establishments primarily engaged in manufacturing table and kitchen articles, art and ornamental items, and similar vitreous china, fine earthenware, stoneware, coarse earthenware, and pottery products.

Manufacturing vitreous china plumbing fixtures **327111**
Manufacturing porcelain and ceramic electrical products, such as insulators, **327113**
Manufacturing clay building materials, such as ceramic tile, bricks, and clay roofing tiles, and refractories, **32712**

327113 Porcelain Electrical Supply Manufacturing[US]

This U.S. industry comprises establishments primarily engaged in manufacturing porcelain electrical insulators, molded porcelain parts for electrical devices, ferrite or ceramic magnets, and electronic and electrical supplies from nonmetallic minerals, such as clay and ceramic materials.

Manufacturing ferrite microwave devices and electronic components **334**

32712 Clay Building Material and Refractories Manufacturing

This industry comprises establishments primarily engaged in shaping, molding, baking, burning, or hardening clay refractories, nonclay refractories, ceramic tile, structural clay tile, brick, and other structural clay building materials.

Manufacturing glass blocks **32721**
Manufacturing concrete brick and block **32733**
Manufacturing resilient flooring **32619**

327121 Brick and Structural Clay Tile Manufacturing[US]

This U.S. industry comprises establishments primarily engaged in manufacturing brick and structural clay tiles.

327122 Ceramic Wall and Floor Tile Manufacturing[US]

This U.S. industry comprises establishments primarily engaged in manufacturing ceramic wall and floor tiles.

Manufacturing structural clay tiles **327121**
Manufacturing clay drain tiles **327123**
Manufacturing resilient flooring and asphalt floor tiles **326192**

327123 Other Structural Clay Product Manufacturing[US]

This U.S. industry comprises establishments primarily engaged in manufacturing clay sewer pipe, drain tile, flue lining tile, architectural terra-cotta, and other structural clay products.

Manufacturing bricks and structural clay tiles **327121**
Manufacturing ceramic floor and wall tiles **327122**
Manufacturing clay refractories **327124**
Manufacturing nonclay refractories **327125**

327124 Clay Refractory Manufacturing[US]

This U.S. industry comprises establishments primarily engaged in manufacturing clay refractory, mortar, brick, block, tile, and fabricated clay refractories, such as melting pots. A refractory is a material that will retain its shape and chemical identity when subjected to high temperatures and is used in applications that require extreme resistance to heat, such as furnace linings.

Manufacturing nonclay refractories **327125**

327125 Nonclay Refractory Manufacturing[US]

This U.S. industry comprises establishments primarily engaged in manufacturing nonclay refractory, mortar, brick, block, tile, and fabricated nonclay refractories such as graphite, magnesite, silica, or alumina crucibles. A refractory is a material that will retain its shape and chemical identity when subjected to high temperatures and is used in applications that require extreme resistance to heat, such as furnace linings.

Manufacturing clay refractories **327124**

32721 Glass and Glass Product Manufacturing

This industry comprises establishments primarily engaged in manufacturing glass and/or glass products. Establishments in this industry may manufacture glass and/or glass products by melting silica sand or cullet, or purchasing glass.

Manufacturing glass wool (i.e., fiberglass) insulation products **32799**
Manufacturing optical lenses (except ophthalmic), such as magnifying, photographic, and projection lenses, **33331**
Grinding ophthalmic (i.e., eyeglass) lenses for the trade **33911**
Manufacturing fiber optic cable from purchased fiber optic strand **33592**

327211 Flat Glass Manufacturing[US]

This U.S. industry comprises establishments primarily engaged in (1) manufacturing flat glass by melting silica sand or cullet or (2) manufacturing both flat glass and laminated glass by melting silica sand or cullet.

Manufacturing laminated glass from purchased flat glass **327215**

327212 Other Pressed and Blown Glass and Glassware Manufacturing[US]

This U.S. industry comprises establishments primarily engaged in manufacturing glass by melting silica sand or cullet and making pressed, blown, or shaped glass or glassware (except glass packaging containers).

Manufacturing flat glass **327211**
Manufacturing glass packaging containers in glassmaking operations **327213**
Manufacturing glass wool (i.e., fiberglass) insulation **327993**
Manufacturing glassware from purchased glass **327215**
Manufacturing fiber optic cable **335921**

327213 Glass Container Manufacturing[US]

This U.S. industry comprises establishments primarily engaged in manufacturing glass packaging containers.

327215 Glass Product Manufacturing Made of Purchased Glass[CAN]

This U.S. industry comprises establishments primarily engaged in remelting, pressing, blowing, or shaping purchased glass.

Manufacturing optical lenses (except ophthalmic), such as magnifying, photographic and projection lenses, **333314**

3273 Cement and Concrete Product Manufacturing

327310 Cement Manufacturing

This industry comprises establishments primarily engaged in manufacturing portland, natural, masonry, pozzalanic, and other hydraulic cements. Cement manufacturing establishments may calcine earths or mine, quarry, manufacture, or purchase lime.

Mining or quarrying limestone **212312**
Manufacturing lime **327410**
Manufacturing ready-mix concrete **327320**
Manufacturing dry mix concrete **327999**

327320 Ready-Mix Concrete Manufacturing

This industry comprises establishments, such as batch plants or mix plants, primarily engaged in manufacturing concrete delivered to a purchaser in a plastic and unhardened state. Ready-mix concrete manufacturing establishments may mine, quarry, or purchase sand and gravel.

Operating sand or gravel pits **212321**
Manufacturing dry mix concrete **327999**

32733 Concrete Pipe, Brick, and Block Manufacturing

This industry comprises establishments primarily engaged in manufacturing concrete pipe, brick, and block.

Manufacturing concrete products (except brick, block, and pipe) **32739**

327331 Concrete Block and Brick Manufacturing[US]

This U.S. industry comprises establishments primarily engaged in manufacturing concrete block and brick.

327332 Concrete Pipe Manufacturing[US]

This U.S. industry comprises establishments primarily engaged in manufacturing concrete pipe.

327390 Other Concrete Product Manufacturing

This industry comprises establishments primarily engaged in manufacturing concrete products (except block, brick, and pipe).

Manufacturing concrete brick and block **327331**
Manufacturing concrete pipe **327332**

3274 Lime and Gypsum Product Manufacturing

327410 Lime Manufacturing

This industry comprises establishments primarily engaged in manufacturing lime from calcitic limestone, dolomitic limestone, or other calcareous materials, such as coral, chalk, and shells. Lime manufacturing establishments may mine, quarry, collect, or purchase the sources of calcium carbonate.

Manufacturing dolomite refractories **327125**

327420 Gypsum Product Manufacturing

This industry comprises establishments primarily engaged in manufacturing gypsum products such as wallboard, plaster, plasterboard, molding, ornamental moldings, statuary, and architectural plaster work. Gypsum product manufacturing establishments may mine, quarry, or purchase gypsum.

Operating gypsum mines or quarries **212399**

3279 Other Nonmetallic Mineral Product Manufacturing

The Other Nonmetallic Mineral Product Manufacturing industry group comprises establishments manufacturing nonmetallic mineral products (except clay products, refractory products, glass products, cement and concrete products, lime, and gypsum products).

327910 Abrasive Product Manufacturing

This industry comprises establishments primarily engaged in manufacturing abrasive grinding wheels of natural or synthetic materials, abrasive-coated products, and other abrasive products.

Manufacturing plastic scouring pads **326199**
Manufacturing metallic scouring sponges and soap impregnated scouring pads **332999**

32799 All Other Nonmetallic Mineral Product Manufacturing

This industry comprises establishments primarily engaged in manufacturing nonmetallic mineral prod-

ucts (except pottery, ceramics, and plumbing fixtures; clay building materials and refractories; glass and glass products; cement; ready-mix concrete; concrete products; lime; gypsum products; and abrasive products).

Manufacturing pottery, ceramics, and plumbing fixtures **32711**
Mining or quarrying stone, earth, or other nonmetallic minerals **2123**
Buying and selling semifinished monuments and tombstones with no work
    other than polishing, lettering, or shaping to custom order **42**
Manufacturing clay building materials and refractories **32712**
Manufacturing glass and glass products **32721**
Manufacturing cement **32731**
Mixing and delivering ready-mix concrete **32732**
Manufacturing concrete pipe, brick, and block **32733**
Manufacturing concrete products (except pipe, brick, and block) **32739**
Manufacturing lime **32741**
Manufacturing gypsum products **32742**
Manufacturing abrasive products **32791**
Manufacturing metallic scouring pads and steel wool **33299**

327991 Cut Stone and Stone Product Manufacturing[US]

This U.S. industry comprises establishments primarily engaged in cutting, shaping, and finishing granite, marble, limestone, slate, and other stone for building and miscellaneous uses. Stone product manufacturing establishments may mine, quarry, or purchase stone.

Mining or quarrying stone **2123**
Buying and selling semifinished monuments and tombstones with no work
    other than polishing, lettering, or shaping to custom order **42**

327992 Ground or Treated Mineral and Earth Manufacturing[US]

This U.S. industry comprises establishments primarily engaged in calcining, dead burning, or otherwise processing beyond beneficiation, clays, ceramic and refractory minerals, barite, and miscellaneous nonmetallic minerals.

Crushing, grinding, pulverizing, washing, screening, sizing, or otherwise
    beneficiating mined clays, ceramics and refractory, and other
    miscellaneous nonmetallic minerals **2123**

327993 Mineral Wool Manufacturing[US]

This U.S. industry comprises establishments primarily engaged in manufacturing mineral wool and mineral wool (i.e. fiberglass) insulation products made of such siliceous materials as rock, slag, and glass or combinations thereof.

Manufacturing metallic scouring pads and steel wool **332999**

327

327999 All Other Miscellaneous Nonmetallic Mineral Product Manufacturing[US]

This U.S. industry comprises establishments primarily engaged in manufacturing nonmetallic mineral products (except pottery, ceramics, and plumbing fixtures; clay building materials and refractories; glass and glass products; cement; ready-mix concrete; concrete products; lime; gypsum products; abrasive products; cut stone and stone products; ground and treated minerals and earth; and mineral wool).

Manufacturing pottery, ceramics, and plumbing fixtures **32711**

Manufacturing clay building materials and refractories **32712**
Manufacturing glass and glass products **32721**
Manufacturing cement **327310**
Mixing and delivering ready-mix concrete **327320**
Manufacturing concrete pipe, brick, and block **32733**
Manufacturing concrete products (except pipe, brick, and block) **327390**
Manufacturing lime **327410**
Manufacturing gypsum products **327420**
Manufacturing abrasives and abrasive products **327910**
Manufacturing cut stone and stone products **327991**
Manufacturing ground and treated minerals and earth (i.e., not at the mine site) **327992**
Manufacturing mineral wool and fiberglass insulation products **327993**

331 Primary Metal Manufacturing

Industries in the Primary Metal Manufacturing subsector smelt and/or refine ferrous and nonferrous metals from ore, pig or scrap, using electrometallurgical and other process metallurgical techniques. Establishments in this subsector also manufacture metal alloys and superalloys by introducing other chemical elements to pure metals. The output of smelting and refining, usually in ingot form, is used in rolling, drawing, and extruding operations to make sheet, strip, bar, rod, or wire, and in molten form to make castings and other basic metal products. Primary manufacturing of ferrous and nonferrous metals begins with ore or concentrate as the primary input. Establishments manufacturing primary metals from ore and/or concentrate remain classified in the primary smelting, primary refining, or iron and steel mill, industries regardless of the form of their output. Establishments primarily engaged in secondary smelting and/or secondary refining recover ferrous and nonferrous metals from scrap and/or dross. The output of the secondary smelting and/or secondary refining industries is limited to shapes, such as ingot or billet, that will be further processed. Recovery of metals from scrap often occurs in establishments that are primarily engaged in activities, such as rolling, drawing, extruding, or similar processes. Excluded from the Primary Metal Manufacturing subsector are establishments primarily engaged in manufacturing ferrous and nonferrous forgings (except ferrous forgings made in steel mills) and stampings. Although forging, stamping, and casting are all methods used to make metal shapes, forging and stamping do not use molten metals and are included in Subsector 332, Fabricated Metal Product Manufacturing.

33111 Iron and Steel Mills and Ferroalloy Manufacturing

This industry comprises establishments primarily engaged in one or more of the following: (1) direct reduction of iron ore; (2) manufacturing pig iron in molten or solid form; (3) converting pig iron into steel; (4) manufacturing ferroalloys; (5) making steel; (6) making steel and manufacturing shapes (e.g., bar, plate, rod, sheet, strip, wire); and (7) making steel and forming pipe and tube.

Manufacturing nonferrous superalloys, such as cobalt or nickel-based superalloys, **33149**

Operating coke ovens **32419**

331111 Iron and Steel Mills[US]

This U.S. industry comprises establishments primarily engaged in one or more of the following: (1) direct reduction of iron ore; (2) manufacturing pig iron in molten or solid form; (3) converting pig iron into steel; (4) making steel; (5) making steel and manufacturing shapes (e.g., bar, plate, rod, sheet, strip, wire); and (6) making steel and forming tube and pipe.

Operating coke ovens **324199**

331112 Electrometallurgical Ferroalloy Product Manufacturing[US]

This U.S. industry comprises establishments primarily engaged in manufacturing electrometallurgical ferroalloys. Ferroalloys add critical elements, such as silicon and manganese for carbon steel and chromium, vanadium, tungsten, titanium, and molybdenum for low- and high-alloy metals. Ferroalloys include iron-rich alloys and more pure forms of elements added during the steel manufacturing process that alter or improve the characteristics of the metal being made.

Manufacturing electrometallurgical steel and iron-based superalloys **331111**
Manufacturing nonferrous superalloys, such as cobalt or nickel-based superalloys, **331492**

3312 Steel Product Manufacturing from Purchased Steel

This industry group comprises establishments primarily engaged in manufacturing iron and steel tube and pipe, drawing steel wire, and rolling or drawing shapes from purchased iron or steel.

331210 Iron and Steel Pipe and Tube Manufacturing from Purchased Steel

This industry comprises establishments primarily engaged in manufacturing welded, riveted, or seamless pipe and tube from purchased iron or steel.

Making steel and further processing the steel into steel pipe and tube **331111**

33122 Rolling and Drawing of Purchased Steel

This industry comprises establishments primarily engaged in rolling and/or drawing steel shapes, such as plate, sheet, strip, rod, and bar, from purchased steel.

Making steel and rolling and/or drawing steel **33111**
Manufacturing wire products from purchased wire **33261**

331221 Rolled Steel Shape Manufacturing[CAN]

This U.S. industry comprises establishments primarily engaged in rolling or drawing shapes (except wire), such as plate, sheet, strip, rod, and bar, from purchased steel.

Making steel and rolling or drawing steel shapes **331111**
Drawing wire from purchased steel **331222**

331222 Steel Wire Drawing[CAN]

This U.S. industry comprises establishments primarily engaged in drawing wire from purchased steel.

Making steel and drawing steel wire **331111**
Manufacturing wire products, such as nails, spikes, and paper clips, from purchased steel wire **33261**

33131 Alumina and Aluminum Production and Processing

This industry comprises establishments primarily engaged in one or more of the following: (1) refining alumina; (2) making (i.e., the primary production) aluminum from alumina; (3) recovering aluminum from scrap or dross; (4) alloying purchased aluminum; and (5) manufacturing aluminum primary forms (e.g., bar, foil, pipe, plate, rod, sheet, tube, wire).

Manufacturing aluminum oxide abrasives and refractories **327**
Operating facilities where co-mingled recyclable materials, such as paper, plastics, used beverage cans, and metals are sorted into distinct categories without also smelting or refining **56292**

331311 Alumina Refining[US]

This U.S. industry comprises establishments primarily engaged in refining alumina (i.e., aluminum oxide) generally from bauxite.

Manufacturing aluminum oxide abrasives and refractories **327**
Making aluminum from alumina **331312**

331312 Primary Aluminum Production[US]

This U.S. industry comprises establishments primarily engaged in (1) making aluminum from alumina and/or (2) making aluminum from alumina and rolling, drawing, extruding, or casting the aluminum they make into primary forms (e.g., bar, billet, ingot, plate, rod, sheet, strip). Establishments in this industry may make primary aluminum or aluminum-based alloys from alumina.

Refining alumina **331311**
Recovering aluminum from scrap or alloying purchased aluminum **331314**

331

331314 Secondary Smelting and Alloying of Aluminum[US]

This U.S. industry comprises establishments primarily engaged in (1) recovering aluminum and aluminum alloys from scrap and/or dross (i.e., secondary smelting) and making billet or ingot (except by rolling) and/or (2) manufacturing alloys, powder, paste, or flake from purchased aluminum.

Making aluminum and/or aluminum alloys from alumina **331312**
Refining alumina **331311**
Manufacturing aluminum sheet, plate, and foil from purchased aluminum or by recovering aluminum from scrap and flat rolling or continuous casting **331315**
Manufacturing aluminum extruded products from purchased aluminum or by recovering aluminum from scrap and extruding **331316**
Manufacturing rolled ingot, billet from purchased aluminum or by recovering aluminum from scrap and rolling or drawing **331319**
Sorting and breaking up scrap metal without also smelting or refining **421930**
Operating facilities where co-mingled recyclable materials, such as paper, plastics, used beverage cans, and metals, are sorted into distinct categories without also smelting or refining **562920**

331315 Aluminum Sheet, Plate, and Foil Manufacturing[US]

This U.S. industry comprises establishments primarily engaged in (1) flat rolling or continuous casting sheet, plate, foil and welded tube from purchased aluminum and/or (2) recovering aluminum from scrap and flat rolling or continuous casting sheet, plate, foil, and welded tube in integrated mills.

Making aluminum from alumina and flat rolling or continuous casting aluminum sheet, plate, foil, and welded tube **331312**

331316 Aluminum Extruded Product Manufacturing[US]

This U.S. industry comprises establishments primarily engaged in (1) extruding aluminum bar, pipe, and tube blooms or extruding or drawing tube from purchased aluminum; and/or (2) recovering aluminum from scrap and extruding bar, pipe, and tube blooms or drawing tube in integrated mills.

Making aluminum from alumina and extruding aluminum bar, pipe, tube or tube blooms **331312**

331319 Other Aluminum Rolling and Drawing[US]

This U.S. comprises establishments primarily engaged

in (1) rolling, drawing, or extruding shapes (except flat rolled sheet, plate, foil, and welded tube; extruded rod, bar, pipe, and tube blooms; and drawn or extruded tube) from purchased aluminum and/or (2) recovering aluminum from scrap and rolling, drawing or extruding shapes (except flat rolled sheet, plate, foil, and welded tube; extruded rod, bar, pipe, and tube blooms; and drawn or extruded tube) in integrated mills.

Flat rolling sheet, plate, foil, and welded tube from either purchased aluminum or by recovering aluminum from scrap and flat rolling or continuous casting **331315**
Extruding rod, bar, pipe, tube and tube blooms or drawing tube from purchased aluminum or by recovering aluminum from scrap and extruding **331316**
Making aluminum from alumina and making aluminum shapes **331312**

3314 Nonferrous Metal (except Aluminum) Production and Processing

33141 Nonferrous Metal (except Aluminum) Smelting and Refining

This industry comprises establishments primarily engaged in (1) smelting ores into nonferrous metals and/or (2) the primary refining of nonferrous metals (except aluminum) using electrolytic or other processes.

Making aluminum from alumina or recovery of aluminum from scrap **33131**
Recovering copper or copper alloys from scrap or dross and/or alloying, rolling, drawing, and extruding purchased copper **33142**
Recovering nonferrous metals (except copper and aluminum) from scrap and/or alloying, rolling, drawing, and extruding purchased nonferrous metals (except copper and aluminum) **33149**
Mining and making copper and other nonferrous concentrates (including gold and silver bullion) using processes, such as solvent extraction or electrowinning, **2122**
Sorting and breaking up scrap metal without also smelting or refining **42**
Operating facilities where co-mingled recyclable materials, such as paper, plastics, used beverage cans, and metals, are sorted into distinct categories without also smelting or refining **56292**

331411 Primary Smelting and Refining of Copper[US]

This U.S. industry comprises establishments primarily engaged in (1) smelting copper ore and/or (2) the primary refining of copper by electrolytic methods or other processes. Establishments in this industry make primary copper and copper-based alloys, such as brass and bronze, from ore or concentrates.

Recovering copper or copper alloys from scrap and making primary forms; and/or alloying purchased copper **331423**

Mining and making copper concentrates by processes, such as solvent extraction or electrowinning, **212234**

Drawing copper wire (except mechanical) from purchased copper or recovering copper from scrap and drawing wire (except mechanical) **331422**

Rolling, drawing, or extruding copper shapes (except communication and energy wire) from purchased copper or recovering copper from scrap and rolling, drawing, and extruding copper shapes **331421**

331419 Primary Smelting and Refining of Nonferrous Metal (except Copper and Aluminum)[US]

This U.S. industry comprises establishments primarily engaged in (1) making (i.e., the primary production) nonferrous metals by smelting ore and/or (2) the primary refining of nonferrous metals by electrolytic methods or other processes.

Recovering nonferrous metals (except copper and aluminum) from scrap and making primary forms and/or alloying purchased nonferrous metals (except copper and aluminum) **331492**

Making aluminum from alumina **331312**

Primary smelting and primary refining of copper **331411**

Mining and making copper and other nonferrous concentrates (including gold and silver bullion), by processes, such as solvent extraction or electrowinning, **2122**

Rolling, drawing, and/or extruding nonferrous metal shapes (except copper and aluminum) from purchased nonferrous metals (except copper and aluminum) or by recovering nonferrous metals (except copper and aluminum) and rolling, drawing, or extruding **331491**

33142 Copper Rolling, Drawing, Extruding, and Alloying

This industry comprises establishments primarily engaged in one or more of the following: (1) recovering copper or copper alloys from scraps; (2) alloying purchased copper; (3) rolling, drawing, or extruding shapes, (e.g., bar, plate, sheet, strip, tube, and wire) from purchased copper; and (4) recovering copper or copper alloys from scrap and rolling drawing, or extruding shapes (e.g., bar, plate, sheet, strip, tube, and wire).

Smelting copper ore, primary copper refining, and/or rolling, drawing or extruding primary copper made in the same establishment **33141**

Manufacturing wire products from purchased wire **33261**

Insulating purchased copper wire **33592**

Sorting and breaking up scrap metal without also smelting or refining **42**

Operating facilities where co-mingled recyclable materials, such as paper, plastics, used beverage cans, and metals, are sorted into distinct categories without also smelting or refining **56292**

Die-casting purchased copper **33152**

Recovering nonferrous metals (except copper and aluminum) from scrap, and/or rolling, drawing, extruding, or alloying purchased nonferrous metals (except copper and aluminum) **33149**

331421 Copper Rolling, Drawing, and Extruding[US]

This U.S. industry comprises establishments primarily engaged in (1) rolling, drawing, and/or extruding shapes—for example, bar, plate, sheet, strip, tube (except bare or insulated copper communication or energy wire—from purchased copper; and/or (2) recovering copper from scrap and rolling, drawing, and/or extruding shapes—for example, bar, plate, sheet, strip, tube (except bare or insulated copper communication or energy wire in integrated mills.)

Recovering copper or copper alloys from scrap and making primary forms and/or alloying purchased copper **331423**

Drawing copper wire (except mechanical) from purchased copper or recovering copper from scrap and drawing copper wire (except mechanical) **331422**

Die-casting purchased copper **331522**

Making primary copper and rolling, drawing, and/or extruding copper shapes (e.g., bar, plate, rod, sheet, strip) **331411**

Rolling, drawing, or extruding shapes from purchased nonferrous metal (except copper and aluminum) or recovering nonferrous metals from scrap and rolling, drawing or extruding **331491**

331422 Copper Wire (except Mechanical) Drawing[US]

This U.S. industry comprises establishments primarily engaged in drawing or drawing and insulating communication and energy wire and cable from purchased copper or in integrated secondary smelting and wire drawing plants.

Manufacturing copper mechanical wire from purchased copper or by recovering copper from scrap and drawing or extruding **331421**

Insulating purchased copper wire **335929**

Manufacturing wire products from purchased copper wire **33261**

331

331423 Secondary Smelting, Refining, and Alloying of Copper[US]

This U.S. industry comprises establishments primarily engaged in (1) recovering copper and copper alloys from scrap and/or (2) alloying purchased copper. Establishments in this industry make primary forms, such as ingot, wire bar, cake, and slab from copper or copper alloys, such as brass and bronze.

Sorting and breaking up scrap metal without also smelting or refining **421930**

Operating facilities where co-mingled recyclable materials, such as paper, plastics, used beverage cans, and metals, are sorted into distinct categories without also smelting or refining **562920**

Smelting copper ore and/or the primary refining of copper **331411**

Recovering copper and copper alloys from scrap and rolling, drawing, or extruding shapes **331421**

Recovering copper and copper alloys from scrap and drawing wire (except mechanical) **331422**

Recovering nonferrous metals (except copper, aluminum) from scrap and making primary forms and/or alloying purchased nonferrous metals (except copper and aluminum) **331492**

33149 Nonferrous Metal (except Copper and Aluminum) Rolling, Drawing, Extruding, and Alloying

This industry comprises establishments primarily engaged in one or more of the following: (1) recovering nonferrous metals (except copper and aluminum) and nonferrous metal alloys from scrap; (2) alloying purchased nonferrous metals (except copper and aluminum); (3) rolling, drawing, and extruding shapes from purchased nonferrous metals (except copper and aluminum); and (4) recovering nonferrous metals from scrap (except copper and aluminum) and rolling, drawing, or extruding shapes in integrated facilities.

Rolling, drawing, and/or extruding aluminum or secondary smelting and alloying of aluminum **33131**

Recovering copper and copper alloys from scrap, alloying purchased copper, rolling, drawing, or extruding shapes from purchased copper, and recovering copper or copper alloys from scrap and rolling, drawing, or extruding shapes in integrated mills **33142**

Insulating purchased nonferrous wire **33592**

Making primary nonferrous metals and rolling, drawing, or extruding nonferrous metal shapes **33141**

Manufacturing products from purchased wire **33261**

Sorting and breaking up scrap metal without also smelting or refining **42**

Operating facilities where co-mingled recyclable materials, such as paper, plastics, used beverage cans, and metals, are sorted into distinct categories without also smelting or refining **56292**

331491 Nonferrous Metal (except Copper and Aluminum) Rolling, Drawing, and Extruding[US]

This U.S. industry comprises establishments primarily engaged in (1) rolling, drawing, or extruding shapes (e.g., bar, plate, sheet, strip, tube) from purchased nonferrous metals) and/or (2) recovering nonferrous metals from scrap and rolling, drawing, and/or extruding shapes (e.g., bar, plate, sheet, strip, tube) in integrated mills.

Rolling, drawing, and/or extruding shapes from purchased copper or recovering copper from scrap and rolling, drawing, or extruding shapes **331421**

Recovering nonferrous metals (except copper and aluminum) from scrap and making primary forms and/or alloying purchased nonferrous metals **331492**

Rolling, drawing, and/or extruding aluminum **33131**

Making primary nonferrous metals and rolling, drawing, or extruding nonferrous metal shapes **331419**

Insulating purchased nonferrous wire **335929**

331492 Secondary Smelting, Refining, and Alloying of Nonferrous Metal (except Copper and Aluminum)[US]

This U.S. industry comprises establishments primarily engaged in (1) alloying purchased nonferrous metals and/or (2) recovering nonferrous metals from scrap. Establishments in this industry make primary forms (e.g., bar, billet, bloom, cake, ingot, slab, slug, wire) using smelting or refining processes.

Recovering aluminum and aluminum alloys from scrap and/or alloying purchased aluminum **331314**

Sorting and breaking up scrap metal without also smelting or refining **421930**

Recovering nonferrous metals from scrap and rolling, drawing, or extruding shapes in integrated facilities **331491**

Operating facilities where co-mingled recyclable materials, such as paper, plastics, used beverage cans, and metals, are sorted into distinct categories without also smelting or refining **562920**

Recovering copper and copper alloys from scrap and making primary forms; and/or alloying purchased copper **331423**

3315 Foundries

This industry group comprises establishments primarily engaged in pouring molten metal into molds or dies to form castings. Establishments making castings and further manufacturing, such as machining or assembling, a specific manufactured product are classified in the industry of the finished product. Foundries may perform operations, such as cleaning and deburring, on the castings they manufacture. More involved processes, such as tapping, threading, milling, or machining to tight tolerances, that transform castings into more finished products are classified elsewhere in the manufacturing sector based on the product being made. Establishments in this industry group make castings from purchased metals or in integrated secondary smelting and casting facilities. When the production of primary metals is combined with making castings, the establishment is classified in 331 with the primary metal being made.

33151 Ferrous Metal Foundries

This industry comprises establishments primarily engaged in pouring molten iron and steel into molds of a desired shape to made castings. Establishments in this industry purchase iron and steel made in other establishments.

331511 Iron Foundries^{CAN}

This U.S. industry comprises establishments primarily engaged in pouring molten pig iron or iron alloys into molds to manufacture castings, (e.g., cast iron man-hole covers, cast iron pipe, cast iron skillets). Establishments in this industry purchase iron made in other establishments.

331512 Steel Investment Foundries^{US}

This U.S. industry comprises establishments primarily engaged in manufacturing steel investment castings. Investment molds are formed by covering a wax shape with a refractory slurry. After the refractory slurry hardens, the wax is melted, leaving a seamless mold. Investment molds provide highly detailed, consistent castings. Establishments in this industry purchase steel made in other establishments.

Manufacturing steel castings (except steel investment castings) **331513**

331513 Steel Foundries (except Investment)^{US}

This U.S. industry comprises establishments primarily engaged in manufacturing steel castings (except steel investment castings). Establishments in this industry purchase steel made in other establishments.

Manufacturing steel investment castings **331512**

33152 Nonferrous Metal Foundries

This industry comprises establishments primarily engaged in pouring and/or introducing molten nonferrous metal, under high pressure, into metal molds or dies to manufacture castings. Establishments in this industry purchase nonferrous metals made in other establishments.

Manufacturing iron or steel castings **33151**

331521 Aluminum Die-Casting Foundries^{US}

This U.S. industry comprises establishments primarily engaged in introducing molten aluminum, under high pressure, into molds or dies to make aluminum die-castings. Establishments in this industry purchase aluminum made in other establishments.

Pouring molten aluminum into molds to manufacture aluminum castings **331524**

331522 Nonferrous (except Aluminum) Die-Casting Foundries^{US}

This U.S. industry comprises establishments primarily engaged in introducing molten nonferrous metal (except aluminum), under high pressure, into molds to make nonferrous metal die-castings. Establishments in this industry purchase nonferrous metals made in other establishments.

Manufacturing aluminum die-castings **331521**
Pouring molten aluminum into molds to manufacture aluminum castings **331524**
Pouring molten copper into molds to manufacture copper castings **331525**
Pouring molten nonferrous metal (except copper and aluminum) into molds to manufacture nonferrous (except copper and aluminum) castings **331528**

331524 Aluminum Foundries (except Die-Casting)[US]

This U.S. industry comprises establishments primarily engaged in pouring molten aluminum into molds to manufacture aluminum castings. Establishments in this industry purchase aluminum made in other establishments.

Manufacturing aluminum die-castings **331521**

331525 Copper Foundries (except Die-Casting)[US]

This U.S. industry comprises establishments primarily engaged in pouring molten copper into molds to manufacture copper castings. Establishments in this industry purchase copper made in other establishments.

Manufacturing copper die-castings **331522**

331528 Other Nonferrous Foundries (except Die-Casting)[US]

This U.S. industry comprises establishments primarily engaged in pouring molten nonferrous metals (except aluminum and copper) into molds to manufacture nonferrous castings (except aluminum die-castings, nonferrous (except aluminum) die-castings, aluminum castings, and copper castings). Establishments in this industry purchase nonferrous metals, such as nickel, lead, and zinc, made in other establishments.

Manufacturing aluminum die-castings **331521**
Manufacturing nonferrous (except aluminum) die-castings **331522**
Pouring molten aluminum into molds to manufacture aluminum castings **331524**
Manufacturing copper castings **331525**

332 Fabricated Metal Product Manufacturing

Industries in the Fabricated Metal Product Manufacturing subsector transform metal into intermediate or end products, other than machinery, computers and electronics, and metal furniture or treating metals and metal formed products fabricated elsewhere. Important fabricated metal processes are forging, stamping, bending, forming, and machining, used to shape individual pieces of metal; and other processes, such as welding and assembling, used to join separate parts together. Establishments in this subsector may use one of these processes or a combination of these processes.

The NAICS structure for this subsector distinguishes the forging and stamping processes in a single industry. The remaining industries, in the subsector, group establishments based on similar combinations of processes used to make products.

The manufacturing performed in the Fabricated Metal Product Manufacturing subsector begins with manufactured metal shapes. The establishments in this sector further fabricate the purchased metal shapes into a product. For instance, the Spring and Wire Product Manufacturing industry starts with wire and fabricates such items.

Within manufacturing there are other establishments that make the same products made by this subsector; only these establishments begin production further back in the production process. These establishments have a more integrated operation. For instance, one establishment may manufacture steel, draw it into wire, and make wire products in the same establishment. Such operations are classified in the Primary Metal Manufacturing subsector.

33211 Forging and Stamping

This industry comprises establishments primarily engaged in one or more of the following: (1) manufacturing forgings from purchased metals; (2) manufacturing metal custom roll forming products; (3) manufacturing metal stamped and spun products (except automotive, cans, coins); and (4) manufacturing powder metallurgy products. Establishments making metal forgings, metal stampings, and metal spun products and further manufacturing (e.g., machining, assembling) a specific manufactured product are classified in the industry of the finished product. Metal forging, metal stamping, and metal spun products establishments may perform surface finishing operations, such as cleaning and deburring, on the products they manufacture.

Manufacturing metal forgings in integrated primary metal establishments **331**

Stamping automotive stampings **33637**

Manufacturing and installing rolled formed seamless gutters at construction sites **23561**

Stamping coins **33991**

332111 Iron and Steel Forging[US]

This U.S. industry comprises establishments primarily engaged in manufacturing iron and steel forgings from purchased iron and steel by hammering mill shapes. Establishments making iron and steel forgings and further manufacturing (e.g., machining, assembling) a specific manufactured product are classified in the industry of the finished product. Iron and steel forging establishments may perform surface finishing operations, such as cleaning and deburring, on the forgings they manufacture.

Manufacturing iron and steel forgings in integrated iron and steel mills **331111**

Manufacturing nonferrous forgings **332112**

332112 Nonferrous Forging[US]

This U.S. industry comprises establishments primarily engaged in manufacturing nonferrous forgings from purchased nonferrous metals by hammering mill shapes. Establishments making nonferrous forgings and further manufacturing (e.g., machining, assembling) a specific manufactured product are classified in the industry of the finished product. Nonferrous forging establishments may perform surface finishing operations, such as cleaning and deburring, on the forgings they manufacture.

Manufacturing iron and steel forgings **332111**

Manufacturing nonferrous forgings in integrated primary or secondary nonferrous metal production facilities **331**

332114 Custom Roll Forming[US]

This U.S. industry comprises establishments primarily engaged in custom roll forming metal products by use of rotary motion of rolls with various contours to bend or shape the products.

Manufacturing and installing rolled formed seamless gutters at construction sites **235610**

332115 Crown and Closure Manufacturing[US]

This U.S. industry comprises establishments primarily engaged in stamping metal crowns and closures, such as bottle caps and home canning lids and rings.

332116 Metal Stamping[US]

This U.S. industry comprises establishments primarily engaged in manufacturing unfinished metal stampings and spinning unfinished metal products (except crowns, cans, closures, automotive, and coins). Establishments making metal stampings and metal spun products and further manufacturing (e.g., machining, assembling) a specific product are classified in the industry of the finished product. Metal stamping and metal spun products establishments may perform surface finishing operations, such as cleaning and deburring, on the products they manufacture.

Stamping automotive stampings **336370**

Stamping metal crowns and closures **332115**

Manufacturing metal cans **332431**

Stamping coins **339911**

332117 Powder Metallurgy Part Manufacturing[US]

This U.S. industry comprises establishments primarily engaged in manufacturing powder metallurgy products by compacting them in a shaped die and sintering. Establishments in this industry generally make a wide range of parts on a job or order basis.

33221 Cutlery and Handtool Manufacturing

This industry comprises establishments primarily engaged in one or more of the following: (1) manufacturing nonprecious and precious plated metal cutlery and flatware; (2) manufacturing nonpowered hand and edge tools, (3) manufacturing nonpowered handsaws; (4) manufacturing saw blades, all types (including those for sawing machines); and (5) manufacturing metal kitchen utensils (except cutting-type) and pots and pans (except those manufactured by casting [e.g., cast iron skillets] or stamped without further fabrication).

Manufacturing precious (except precious plated) metal cutlery and flatware **33991**

Manufacturing electric razors and hair clippers for use on humans **33521**

Manufacturing power hedge shears and trimmers and electric hair clippers for use on animals **33311**

Manufacturing metal cutting dies, attachments, and accessories for machine tools **3335I**

Manufacturing handheld power-driven handtools **33399**

Manufacturing finished cast iron kitchen utensils (i.e., cast iron skillets) and castings for kitchen utensils, pots, and pans **3315**

3322II Cutlery and Flatware (except Precious) Manufacturing^{US}

This U.S. industry comprises establishments primarily engaged in manufacturing nonprecious and precious plated metal cutlery and flatware.

Manufacturing precious (except precious plated) metal cutlery and flatware **339912**

Manufacturing electric razors and hair clippers for use on humans and housewares **33521I**

Manufacturing power hedge shears and trimmers and electric hair clippers for animal use **333112**

Manufacturing nonelectric hair clippers for use on animals **332212**

332212 Hand and Edge Tool Manufacturing^{US}

This industry comprises establishments primarily engaged in manufacturing nonpowered hand and edge tools (except saws).

Manufacturing saw blades and handsaws **332213**

Manufacturing metal cutting dies, attachments, and accessories for machine tools **3335I**

Manufacturing handheld power-driven handtools **333991**

Manufacturing electric razors and hair clippers for use on humans **335211**

Manufacturing electric hair clippers for use on animals **333111**

Manufacturing nonelectric household-type scissors and shears **332211**

332213 Saw Blade and Handsaw Manufacturing^{US}

This U.S. industry comprises establishments primarily engaged in (1) manufacturing nonpowered hand-

saws and/or (2) manufacturing saw blades, all types (including those for power sawing machines).

Manufacturing handheld powered saws **333991**

332214 Kitchen Utensil, Pot, and Pan Manufacturing^{US}

This U.S. industry comprises establishments primarily engaged in manufacturing metal kitchen utensils (except cutting-type), pots, and pans (except those manufactured by casting [e.g., cast iron skillets] or stamped without further fabrication).

Manufacturing finished cast metal kitchen utensils or castings for kitchen utensils **3315**

Manufacturing stampings for kitchen utensils, pots, and pans **332116**

Manufacturing metal cutting-type kitchen utensils **332211**

3323 Architectural and Structural Metals Manufacturing

33231 Plate Work and Fabricated Structural Product Manufacturing

This industry comprises establishments primarily engaged in manufacturing one or more of the following: (1) prefabricated metal buildings, panels and sections; (2) structural metal products; and (3) metal plate work products.

Making manufactured homes (i.e., mobile homes) and prefabricated wood buildings **32199**

Constructing buildings, bridges, and other heavy construction projects on site **23**

Building ships, boats and barges **33661**

Manufacturing power boilers and heat exchangers **33241**

Manufacturing heavy gauge tanks **33242**

Manufacturing metal plate cooling towers **33341**

Manufacturing metal windows, doors and studs **33232**

33231I Prefabricated Metal Building and Component Manufacturing^{CAN}

This U.S. industry comprises establishments primarily engaged in manufacturing prefabricated metal buildings, panels and sections.

Making manufactured homes (i.e., mobile homes) and prefabricated wood buildings **32199**

Constructing prefabricated buildings on site **233**
Manufacturing metal windows and doors **332321**

332312 Fabricated Structural Metal Manufacturing[US]

This U.S. industry comprises establishments primarily engaged in fabricating structural metal products, such as concrete reinforcing bars and fabricated bar joists.

Manufacturing metal windows and doors **332321**
Manufacturing metal studs **332322**
Constructing buildings, bridges and other heavy construction projects on site **23**
Building ships, boats and barges **33661**
Prefabricating metal buildings, panels and sections **332311**

332313 Plate Work Manufacturing[US]

This industry comprises establishments primarily engaged in manufacturing fabricated metal plate work by cutting, punching, bending, shaping, and welding purchased metal plate.

Manufacturing power boilers and heat exchangers **332410**
Manufacturing heavy gauge tanks **332420**
Manufacturing metal plate cooling towers **333415**

33232 Ornamental and Architectural Metal Products Manufacturing

This industry comprises establishments primarily engaged in manufacturing one or more of the following: (1) metal framed windows (i.e., typically using purchased glass) and metal doors; (2) sheet metal work; and (3) ornamental and architectural metal products.

Manufacturing metal covered (i.e., clad) wood windows and doors **32191**
Manufacturing bins, cans, vats, and light tanks of sheet metal **33243**
Manufacturing prefabricated metal buildings, panels, and sections **33231**
Fabricating sheet metal work on site **23**
Manufacturing metal stampings (except automotive, coins) and custom roll forming products **33211**
Manufacturing automotive stampings **33637**
Stamping coins **33991**

332321 Metal Window and Door Manufacturing[CAN]

This U.S. industry comprises establishments primarily engaged in manufacturing metal framed windows (i.e., typically using purchased glass) and metal doors.

Examples of products made by these establishments are metal doorframes; metal framed window and door screens; metal molding and trim (except automotive); and metal curtain walls.

Manufacturing wood or metal covered (i.e., clad) wood framed windows and doors **321911**
Manufacturing metal automotive molding and trim **336370**

332322 Sheet Metal Work Manufacturing[US]

This U.S. industry comprises establishments primarily engaged in manufacturing sheet metal work (except stampings).

Manufacturing sheet metal bins, vats and light tanks of sheet metal **332439**
Manufacturing metal cans, lids, and ends **332431**
Fabricating sheet metal work on site **23**
Manufacturing metal stampings (except automotive, coins) and custom roll forming products **33211**
Manufacturing automotive stampings **336370**
Stamping coins **339911**

332323 Ornamental and Architectural Metal Work Manufacturing[US]

This U.S. industry comprises establishments primarily engaged in manufacturing ornamental and architectural metal work, such as staircases, metal open steel flooring, fire escapes, railings, and scaffolding.

Manufacturing prefabricated metal buildings, panels, and sections **332311**

3324 Boiler, Tank, and Shipping Container Manufacturing

332410 Power Boiler and Heat Exchanger Manufacturing

This industry comprises establishments primarily engaged in manufacturing power boilers and heat exchangers. Establishments in this industry may perform installation in addition to manufacturing power boilers and heat exchangers.

Manufacturing heavy gauge metal tanks **332420**
Manufacturing stream or hot water low pressure heating boilers **333414**
Installing power boilers and heat exchanges without manufacturing **235110**

332420 Metal Tank (Heavy Gauge) Manufacturing

This industry comprises establishments primarily engaged in cutting, forming, and joining heavy gauge metal to manufacture tanks, vessels, and other containers.

Manufacturing power boilers **332410**
Manufacturing light gauge metal containers **33243**
Installing heavy gauge metal tanks without manufacturing **23**

33243 Metal Can, Box, and Other Metal Container (Light Gauge) Manufacturing

This industry comprises establishments primarily engaged in forming light gauge metal containers.

Manufacturing foil containers **33299**
Reconditioning barrels and drums **81131**
Manufacturing heavy gauge metal containers **33242**

332431 Metal Can Manufacturing^{CAN}

This U.S. industry comprises establishments primarily engaged in manufacturing metal cans, lids, and ends.

Manufacturing foil containers **332999**
Manufacturing light gauge metal containers (except cans) **332439**

332439 Other Metal Container Manufacturing^{CAN}

This U.S. industry comprises establishments primarily engaged in manufacturing metal (light gauge) containers (except cans).

Manufacturing foil containers **332999**
Manufacturing metal cans **332431**
Reconditioning barrels and drums **811310**
Manufacturing heavy gauge metal containers **332420**

332510 Hardware Manufacturing

This industry comprises establishments primarily engaged in manufacturing metal hardware, such as metal hinges, metal handles, keys, and locks (except coin-operated, time locks).

Manufacturing bolts, nuts, screws, rivets, washers, hose clamps, and turn
　buckles **332722**
Manufacturing nails and spikes from wire drawn elsewhere **332618**
Manufacturing metal furniture parts (except hardware) **337215**
Drawing wire and manufacturing nails and spikes **331**

Manufacturing pole line and transmission hardware **335932**
Manufacturing coin-operated locking mechanisms **333311**
Manufacturing time locks **334518**
Manufacturing fireplace fixtures and equipment, traps, handcuffs and leg
　irons, ladder jacks, and other like metal products **332999**
Manufacturing fire hose nozzles and couplings **332919**
Manufacturing luggage and utility racks **336399**

33261 Spring and Wire Product Manufacturing

This industry comprises establishments primarily engaged in (1) manufacturing steel springs by forming, such as cutting, bending, and heat winding metal rod or strip stock and/or (2) manufacturing wire springs and fabricated wire products from wire drawn elsewhere (except watch and clock springs).

Manufacturing watch and clock springs from purchased wire **33451**
Drawing wire and manufacturing wire products **331**
Manufacturing nonferrous insulated wire from wire drawn elsewhere **33592**

332611 Spring (Heavy Gauge) Manufacturing^{CAN}

This U.S. industry comprises establishments primarily engaged in manufacturing heavy gauge springs by forming, such as cutting, bending, and heat winding rod or strip stock.

Manufacturing light gauge springs from purchased wire or strip **332612**
Drawing wire and manufacturing wire spring **331**

332612 Spring (Light Gauge) Manufacturing^{US}

This U.S. industry comprises establishments primarily engaged in manufacturing light gauge springs from purchased wire or strip.

Manufacturing watch and clock springs **334518**
Manufacturing heavy gauge springs **332611**
Drawing wire and manufacturing wire spring **331**

332618 Other Fabricated Wire Product Manufacturing^{US}

This industry comprises establishments primarily engaged in manufacturing fabricated wire products (except springs) made from purchased wire.

Drawing wire and manufacturing wire products **331**
Manufacturing heavy gauge springs **332611**
Manufacturing light gauge springs from purchased wire or strip **332612**
Insulating nonferrous wire from wire drawn elsewhere **33592**

3327 Machine Shops; Turned Product; and Screw, Nut, and Bolt Manufacturing

332710 Machine Shops

This industry comprises establishments known as machine shops primarily engaged in machining metal parts on a job or order basis. Generally machine shop jobs are low volume using machine tools, such as lathes (including computer numerically controlled); automatic screw machines; and machines for boring, grinding, and milling.

Repairing industrial machinery and equipment **81131**

33272 Turned Product and Screw, Nut, and Bolt Manufacturing

This industry comprises establishments primarily engaged in (1) machining precision turned products or (2) manufacturing metal bolts, nuts, screws, rivets, and other industrial fasteners. Included in this industry are establishments primarily engaged manufacturing parts for machinery and equipment on a customized basis.

Manufacturing plastics fasteners **32619**

332721 Precision Turned Product Manufacturing[US]

This U.S. industry comprises establishments known as precision turned manufacturers primarily engaged in machining precision products of all materials on a job or order basis. Generally precision turned product jobs are large volume using machines, such as automatic screw machines, rotary transfer machines, computer numerically controlled (CNC) lathes, or turning centers.

Manufacturing metal bolts, nuts, screws, rivets, washers, and other industrial fasteners on machines, such as headers, threaders, and nut forming machines, **332722**

332722 Bolt, Nut, Screw, Rivet, and Washer Manufacturing[US]

This U.S. industry comprises establishments primarily engaged in manufacturing metal bolts, nuts, screws, rivets, and washers, and other industrial fasteners using machines, such as headers, threaders, and nut forming machines.

Manufacturing precision turned products **332721**
Plastics fasteners **326199**

33281 Coating, Engraving, Heat Treating, and Allied Activities

This industry comprises establishments primarily engaged in one or more of the following: (1) heat treating metals and metal products; (2) enameling, lacquering, varnishing metals and metal products; (3) hot dip galvanizing metals and metal products; (4) engraving, chasing, or etching metals and metal products (except jewelry; personal goods carried on or about the person, such as compacts and cigarette cases; precious metal products [except precious plated flatware and other plated ware]; and printing plates); (5) powder coating metals and metal products; (6) electroplating, plating, anodizing, coloring, and finishing metals and metal products; and (7) providing other metal surfacing services for the trade. Establishments in this industry coat engravings and heat treat metals and metal formed products fabricated elsewhere.

Engraving, chasing or etching jewelry, metal personal goods, or precious (except precious plated) metal flatware and other plated ware **33991**
Engraving, chasing or etching printing plates **32312**

332811 Metal Heat Treating[US]

This U.S. industry comprises establishments primarily engaged in heat treating, such as annealing, tempering, and brazing, metals and metal products for the trade. Establishments primarily engaged in both fabricating and heat treating metal products are classified in the Manufacturing sector according to the product made.

332812 Metal Coating, Engraving (except Jewelry and Silverware), and Allied Services to Manufacturers[US]

This U.S. industry comprises establishments primarily engaged in one or more of the following: (1) enameling, lacquering, and varnishing metals and metal products; (2) hot dip galvanizing metals and metal products; (3) engraving, chasing, or etching metals and metal products (except jewelry; personal goods carried on or about the person, such as compacts and cigarette cases; precious metal products (except precious plated flatware and other plated ware); and printing plates); (4) powder coating metals and metal products; and (5) providing other metal surfacing services for the trade.

Engraving, chasing or etching jewelry, metal personal goods, or precious metal products (except precious plated metal flatware and other plated ware) **33991**

Engraving, chasing or etching printing plates **323122**

332813 Electroplating, Plating, Polishing, Anodizing, and Coloring^{US}

This U.S. industry comprises establishments primarily engaged in electroplating, plating, anodizing, coloring, buffing, polishing, cleaning, and sandblasting metals and metal products for the trade. Establishments primarily engaged in both fabricating and electroplating, plating, polishing, anodizing, and coloring products are classified in the Manufacturing sector according to the product made.

3329 Other Fabricated Metal Product Manufacturing

This industry group comprises establishments primarily engaged in manufacturing fabricated metal products (except forgings and stampings, cutlery and handtools, architectural and structural metals, boilers, tanks, shipping containers, hardware, spring and wire products, machine shop products, turned products, screws, and nuts and bolts).

33291 Metal Valve Manufacturing

This industry comprises establishments primarily engaged in manufacturing one or more of the following metal valves: (1) industrial valves; (2) fluid power valves and hose fittings; (3) plumbing fixture fittings and trim; and (4) other metal valves and pipe fittings.

Manufacturing fluid power cylinder and pumps **33399**

Manufacturing intake and exhaust valves for internal combustion engines **33631**

Manufacturing metal shower rods and metal couplings from purchased metal pipe **33299**

Manufacturing plastics aerosol spray nozzles **32619**

Casting iron pipe fittings and couplings without machining **33151**

Manufacturing plastics pipe fittings and couplings **32612**

332911 Industrial Valve Manufacturing^{US}

This U.S. industry comprises establishments primarily engaged in manufacturing industrial valves and valves for water works and municipal water systems.

Manufacturing fluid power valves **332912**

Manufacturing plumbing and heating valves **332919**

332912 Fluid Power Valve and Hose Fitting Manufacturing^{US}

This U.S. industry comprises establishments primarily engaged in manufacturing fluid power valves and hose fittings.

Manufacturing fluid power cylinders **333995**

Manufacturing fluid power pumps **333996**

Manufacturing intake and exhaust valves for internal combustion engines **336311**

Manufacturing industrial-type valves **332911**

Manufacturing plumbing and heating valves **332919**

332913 Plumbing Fixture Fitting and Trim Manufacturing^{US}

This U.S. industry comprises establishments primarily engaged in manufacturing metal and plastics plumbing fixture fittings and trim, such as faucets, flush valves, and shower heads.

Manufacturing metal shower rods **332999**

Manufacturing fire hose nozzles, lawn hose nozzles, water traps, and couplings **332919**

332919 Other Metal Valve and Pipe Fitting Manufacturing^{US}

This U.S. industry comprises establishments primarily engaged in manufacturing metal valves (except industrial valves, fluid power valves, fluid power hose fittings, and plumbing fixture fittings and trim).

Manufacturing fluid power valves and hose fittings **332912**

Manufacturing industrial valves **332911**
Manufacturing plastics aerosol spray nozzles **326199**
Casting iron pipe fittings and couplings without machining **331511**
Manufacturing metal couplings from purchased metal pipe **332996**
Manufacturing plastics pipe fittings and couplings **326122**

33299 All Other Fabricated Metal Product Manufacturing

This industry comprises establishments primarily engaged in manufacturing fabricated metal products (except forgings and stampings, cutlery and handtools, architectural and structural metal products, boilers, tanks, shipping containers, hardware, spring and wire products, machine shop products, turned products, screws, nuts and bolts, and metal valves).

Manufacturing forging and stamping and powder metallurgy parts **332II**
Manufacturing cutlery and handtools **332211**
Manufacturing architectural and structural metals **3323**
Manufacturing boilers, tanks, and shipping containers **3324**
Manufacturing hardware and safe and vault locks **33251**
Manufacturing spring and wire products **33261**
Manufacturing machine shop products, turned products, screws, and nuts and bolts **3327**
Coating, engraving, heat treating and allied activities **33281**
Manufacturing plain bearings **33361**
Manufacturing military tanks **33699**
Manufacturing guided missiles **33641**
Manufacturing cast iron pipe and fittings **33151**
Manufacturing pipe system fittings (except cast iron couplings and couplings made from purchased pipe) and metal aerosol spray nozzles **33291**
Manufacturing welded and seamless steel pipes from purchased steel **33121**
Manufacturing plastics plumbing fixtures and plastics portable chemical toilets **32619**
Manufacturing vitreous and semivitreous pottery sanitary ware **327II**
Manufacturing blasting caps, detonating caps, and safety fuses **32592**
Manufacturing fireworks **32599**
Manufacturing metal furniture frames **33721**
Manufacturing nonprecious metal trophies **33991**
Manufacturing metal mechanically refrigerated drinking fountains **33341**
Manufacturing metal foil bags **32222**
Manufacturing aluminum foil **33131**
Manufacturing metal foil (except aluminum) **3314**
Manufacturing metal burial vaults **33999**

332991 Ball and Roller Bearing Manufacturing[CAN]

This U.S. industry comprises establishments prima-

rily engaged in manufacturing ball and roller bearings of all materials.

Manufacturing plain bearings **333613**

332992 Small Arms Ammunition Manufacturing[US]

This U.S. industry comprises establishments primarily engaged in manufacturing small arms ammunition.

Manufacturing ammunition (except small arms) **332993**
Manufacturing blasting and detonating caps and safety fuses **325920**
Manufacturing fireworks **325998**

332993 Ammunition (except Small Arms) Manufacturing[US]

This U.S. industry comprises establishments primarily engaged in manufacturing ammunition (except small arms). Examples of products made by these establishments are bombs, depth charges, rockets (except guided missiles), grenades, mines, and torpedoes.

Manufacturing small arms ammunition **332992**
Manufacturing blasting and detonating caps and safety fuses **325920**
Manufacturing fireworks **325998**
Manufacturing guided missiles **336414**

332994 Small Arms Manufacturing[US]

This U.S. industry comprises establishments primarily engaged in manufacturing small firearms that are carried and fired by the individual.

Manufacturing firearms (except small) **332995**

332995 Other Ordnance and Accessories Manufacturing[US]

This U.S. industry comprises establishments primarily engaged in manufacturing ordnance (except small arms) and accessories.

Manufacturing small arms **332994**
Manufacturing military tanks **336992**
Manufacturing guided missiles **336414**

332996 Fabricated Pipe and Pipe Fitting Manufacturing[US]

This U.S. industry comprises establishments prima-

rily engaged in fabricating (such as cutting, threading and bending) metal pipes and pipefittings made from purchased metal pipe.

Manufacturing cast iron pipe and fittings **331511**
Manufacturing pipe system fittings (except cast iron couplings) **332919**
Manufacturing welded and seamless steel pipes from purchased steel **331210**

332997 Industrial Pattern Manufacturing[US]

This U.S. industry comprises establishments primarily engaged in manufacturing industrial patterns.

332998 Enameled Iron and Metal Sanitary Ware Manufacturing[US]

This U.S. industry comprises establishments primarily engaged in manufacturing enameled iron and metal sanitary ware.

Manufacturing plastics plumbing fixtures **326191**
Manufacturing vitreous and semivitreous pottery sanitary ware **327111**
Manufacturing plastics portable chemical toilets **326199**
Manufacturing metal mechanically refrigerated drinking fountains **333415**

332999 All Other Miscellaneous Fabricated Metal Product Manufacturing[US]

This U.S. industry comprises establishments primarily engaged in manufacturing fabricated metal products (except forgings and stampings, cutlery and handtools, architectural and structural metals, boilers, tanks, shipping containers, hardware, spring and wire products, machine shop products, turned prod-

ucts, screws, nuts and bolts, metal valves, ball and roller bearings, ammunition, small arms and other ordnances, fabricated pipes and pipe fittings, industrial patterns, and enameled iron and metal sanitary ware).

Manufacturing forgings and stampings **33211**
Manufacturing cutlery and handtools **33221**
Manufacturing architectural and structural metals **3323**
Manufacturing boilers, tanks, and shipping containers **3324**
Manufacturing hardware and safe and vault locks **332510**
Manufacturing spring and wire products **33261**
Manufacturing machine shop products, turned products, screws, and nut and bolt **3327**
Coating, engraving, heat treating and allied activities **33281**
Manufacturing ball and roller bearings **332991**
Manufacturing small arms ammunition **332992**
Manufacturing ammunition (except small arms) **332993**
Manufacturing small firearms that are carried and fired by the individual **332994**
Manufacturing ordnances (except small) and accessories **332995**
Manufacturing metal pipes and pipe fittings from metal pipe produced elsewhere **332996**
Manufacturing cast iron pipe and fittings **331511**
Manufacturing welded and seamless steel pipes from purchased steel **331210**
Manufacturing metal furniture frames **337215**
Manufacturing powder metallurgy parts **332117**
Manufacturing metal boxes **332439**
Manufacturing metal nozzles, hose couplings, and aerosol valves **332919**
Manufacturing nonprecious metal trophies **339914**
Manufacturing metal foil bags **322223**
Manufacturing aluminum foil **33131**
Manufacturing metal foil (except aluminum) **3314**
Manufacturing metal burial vaults **339995**

333 Machinery Manufacturing

Industries in the Machinery Manufacturing subsector create end products that apply mechanical force, for example, the application of gears and levers, to perform work. Some important processes for the manufacture of machinery are forging, stamping, bending, forming, and machining that are used to shape individual pieces of metal. Processes, such as welding and assembling are used to join separate parts together. Although these processes are similar to those used in metal fabricating establishments, machinery manufacturing is different because it typically employs multiple metal forming processes in manufacturing the various parts of the machine. Moreover, complex assembly operations are an inherent part of the production process.

In general, design considerations are very important in machinery production. Establishments specialize in making machinery designed for particular applications. Thus, design is considered to be part of the production process for the purpose of implementing NAICS. The NAICS structure reflects this by defining industries and industry groups that make machinery for different applications. A broad distinction exists between machinery that is generally used in a variety of industrial applications (i.e., general purpose machinery) and machinery that is designed to be used in a particular industry (i.e., special purpose machinery). Three industry groups consist of special purpose machinery–Agricultural, Construction, and Mining Machinery Manufacturing; Industrial Machinery Manufacturing; and Commercial and Service Machinery Manufacturing. The other industry groups make general-purpose machinery: Ventilation, Heating, Air Conditioning, and Commercial Refrigeration Equipment Manufacturing; Metalworking Machinery Manufacturing; Engine, Turbine, and Power Transmission Equipment Manufacturing; and Other General Purpose Machinery Manufacturing.

3331 Agriculture, Construction, and Mining Machinery Manufacturing

33311 Agricultural Implement Manufacturing

This industry comprises establishments primarily engaged in manufacturing farm machinery and equipment, powered mowing equipment and other powered home lawn and garden equipment.

Manufacturing agricultural handtools and nonpowered lawnmowers **33221**
Manufacturing farm conveyors **33392**
Manufacturing forestry machinery and equipment such as brush, limb and log chippers; log splitters; and equipment **33312**

333111 Farm Machinery and Equipment Manufacturing[US]

This U.S. industry comprises establishments primarily engaged in manufacturing agricultural and farm machinery and equipment, and other turf and grounds care equipment, including planting, harvesting, and grass mowing equipment (except lawn and garden-type).

Manufacturing farm conveyors **333922**
Manufacturing tractors and lawnmowers for home lawn and garden care **333112**
Manufacturing construction-type tractors **333120**

333112 Lawn and Garden Tractor and Home Lawn and Garden Equipment Manufacturing[US]

This U.S. industry comprises establishments primarily engaged in manufacturing powered lawnmowers, lawn and garden tractors, and other home lawn and garden equipment, such as tillers, shredders, and yard vacuums and blowers.

Manufacturing commercial mowing and other turf and grounds care equipment **333111**
Manufacturing nonpowered lawn and garden shears, edgers, pruners, and lawnmowers **33221**

333120 Construction Machinery Manufacturing

This industry comprises establishments primarily engaged in manufacturing construction machinery, surface mining machinery, and logging equipment.

Manufacturing drilling and underground mining machinery and equipment **33313**
Manufacturing industrial plant overhead traveling cranes, hoists, truck-type cranes and hoists, winches, aerial work platforms, and automotive wrecker hoists **33392**
Manufacturing rail layers, ballast distributors and other railroad track-laying equipment **336510**

33313 Mining and Oil and Gas Field Machinery Manufacturing

This industry comprises establishments primarily engaged in manufacturing oil and gas field and underground mining machinery and equipment.

Manufacturing offshore oil and gas well drilling and production floating platforms **33661**
Manufacturing surface mining machinery and equipment **33312**
Manufacturing coal and ore conveyors **33392**
Manufacturing underground mining locomotives **33651**
Manufacturing pumps and pumping equipment **33391**

333131 Mining Machinery and Equipment Manufacturing[US]

This U.S. industry comprises establishments primarily engaged in (1) manufacturing under-ground mining machinery and equipment, such as coal breakers, mining cars, core drills, coal cutters, rock drills and

(2) manufacturing mineral beneficiating machinery and equipment used in surface or underground mines.

Manufacturing surface mining machinery and equipment **333120**
Manufacturing well-drilling machinery **333132**
Manufacturing coal and ore conveyors **333922**
Manufacturing underground mining locomotives **336510**

333132 Oil and Gas Field Machinery and Equipment Manufacturing^{US}

This U.S. industry comprises establishments primarily engaged in (1) manufacturing oil and gas field machinery and equipment, such as oil and gas field drilling machinery and equipment; oil and gas field production machinery and equipment; and oil and gas field derricks and (2) manufacturing water well drilling machinery.

Manufacturing offshore oil and gas well drilling and production floating platforms **336611**
Manufacturing underground mining drills **333131**
Manufacturing pumps and pumping equipment **333911**

3332 Industrial Machinery Manufacturing

333210 Sawmill and Woodworking Machinery Manufacturing

This industry comprises establishments primarily engaged in manufacturing sawmill and wood-working machinery (except handheld), such as circular and band sawing equipment, planing machinery, and sanding machinery.

Manufacturing planes, axes, drawknives, and handsaws **33221**
Manufacturing power-driven handtools **333991**

333220 Plastics and Rubber Machinery Manufacturing

This industry comprises establishments primarily engaged in manufacturing plastics and rubber products making machinery, such as plastics compression, extrusion and injection molding machinery and equipment, and tire building and recapping machinery and equipment.

Manufacturing industrial metal molds for plastics and rubber products making machinery **333511**

33329 Other Industrial Machinery Manufacturing

This industry comprises establishments primarily engaged in manufacturing industrial machinery (except agricultural and farm-type, construction, mining, sawmill and woodworking, and plastics and rubber products making machinery).

Manufacturing agricultural and farm-type, construction, and mining machinery **3331**
Manufacturing sawmill and woodworking machinery **33321**
Manufacturing plastics and rubber products making machinery **33322**
Manufacturing food and beverage packaging machinery **33399**
Manufacturing commercial and industrial refrigeration and freezer equipment **33341**
Manufacturing commercial-type cooking and food warming equipment, automotive maintenance equipment (except mechanics' handtools) and photocopiers **33331**
Manufacturing mechanics' handtools **33221**

333291 Paper Machinery Manufacturing^{CAN}

This U.S. industry comprises establishments primarily engaged in manufacturing paper industry machinery for making paper and paper products, such as pulp making machinery, paper and paperboard making machinery, and paper and paperboard converting machinery.

Manufacturing printing machinery **333293**

333292 Textile Machinery Manufacturing^{US}

This U.S. industry comprises establishments primarily engaged in manufacturing textile machinery for making thread, yarn, and fiber.

Manufacturing sewing machines **333298**

333293 Printing Machinery and Equipment Manufacturing^{US}

This U.S. industry comprises establishments primarily engaged in manufacturing printing and bookbinding machinery and equipment, such as printing presses, typesetting machinery, and bindery machinery.

Manufacturing textile printing machinery **333292**
Manufacturing photocopiers **333315**

333294 Food Product Machinery Manufacturing[US]

This U.S. industry comprises establishments primarily engaged in manufacturing food and beverage manufacturing-type machinery and equipment, such as dairy product plant machinery and equipment (e.g., homogenizers, pasteurizers, ice cream freezers), bakery machinery and equipment (e.g., dough mixers, bake ovens, pastry rolling machines), meat and poultry processing and preparation machinery, and other commercial food products machinery (e.g., slicers, choppers, and mixers).

Manufacturing food and beverage packaging machinery **333993**
Manufacturing commercial and industrial refrigeration and freezer equipment **333415**
Manufacturing commercial-type cooking and food warming equipment **333319**

333295 Semiconductor Machinery Manufacturing[US]

This U.S. industry comprises establishments primarily engaged in manufacturing wafer processing equipment, semiconductor assembly and packaging equipment, and other semiconductor making machinery.

Manufacturing printed circuit board manufacturing machinery **333298**
Manufacturing semiconductor testing instruments **334515**

333298 All Other Industrial Machinery Manufacturing[US]

This U.S. industry comprises establishments primarily engaged in manufacturing industrial machinery (except agricultural and farm-type, construction and mining machinery, sawmill and woodworking machinery, plastics and rubber making machinery, paper and paperboard making machinery, textile machinery, printing machinery and equipment, food manufacturing-type machinery, and semiconductor making machinery).

Manufacturing agricultural and farm-type, construction, and mining machinery **3331**
Manufacturing sawmill and woodworking machinery **333210**
Manufacturing plastics and rubber products making machinery **333220**
Manufacturing paper and paperboard making machinery **333291**
Manufacturing textile machinery **333292**
Manufacturing printing and bookbinding machinery and equipment **333293**

Manufacturing food and beverage manufacturing-type machinery **333294**
Manufacturing semiconductor making machinery **333295**
Manufacturing automotive maintenance equipment (except mechanics' handtools) **333319**
Manufacturing mechanics' handtools **332212**

3333 Commercial and Service Machinery Manufacturing

33331 Commercial and Service Machinery Manufacturing

This industry comprises establishments primarily engaged in manufacturing commercial and service machinery, such as automatic vending machinery, commercial laundry and dry-cleaning machinery, office machinery, photographic and photocopying machinery, optical instruments and machinery, automotive maintenance equipment (except mechanic's handtools), industrial vacuum cleaners, and commercial-type cooking equipment.

Manufacturing household-type appliances **3352**
Manufacturing computer and peripheral equipment (including point-of-sale terminals and funds transfer devices [ATMs]) **33411**
Manufacturing facsimile equipment **33421**
Manufacturing timeclocks, timestamps, and electron and proton microscopes **33451**
Manufacturing pencil sharpeners and staplers **33994**
Manufacturing sensitized film, paper, cloth, and plates, and prepared photographic chemicals **32599**
Manufacturing ophthalmic focus lenses **33911**
Manufacturing television, video, and digital cameras **334**
Manufacturing coin-operated arcade games **33999**
Manufacturing mechanics' handtools **33221**
Manufacturing molded plastics lens blanks **32619**
Manufacturing molded glass lens blanks **32721**

333311 Automatic Vending Machine Manufacturing[US]

This U.S. industry comprises establishments primarily engaged in (1) manufacturing coin, token, currency or magnetic card operated vending machines and/or (2) manufacturing coin operated mechanism for machines, such as vending machines, lockers, and laundry machines.

Manufacturing coin-operated arcade games **339999**

333312 Commercial Laundry, Drycleaning, and Pressing Machine Manufacturing[US]

This U.S. industry comprises establishments primarily engaged in manufacturing commercial and industrial laundry and drycleaning equipment and pressing machines.

Manufacturing household-type laundry equipment **335224**

333313 Office Machinery Manufacturing[US]

This U.S. industry comprises establishments primarily engaged in manufacturing office machinery (except computers and photocopying equipment), such as mailhandling machinery and equipment, calculators, typewriters, and dedicated word processing equipment.

Manufacturing computers and peripheral (including point-of-sale terminals and automatic teller machines [ATMs]) equipment **3341I**
Manufacturing photocopy equipment **333315**
Manufacturing facsimile equipment **334210**
Manufacturing timeclocks and timestamps **334518**
Manufacturing pencil sharpeners, staplers, staple removers, hand paper punches, cutters, trimmers, and other hand office equipment **339942**

333314 Optical Instrument and Lens Manufacturing[US]

This U.S. industry comprises establishments primarily engaged in one or more of the following: (1) manufacturing optical instruments and lens, such as binoculars, microscopes (except electron, proton), telescopes, prisms, and lenses (except ophthalmic); (2) coating or polishing lenses (except ophthalmic); and (3) mounting lenses (except ophthalmic).

Manufacturing ophthalmic focus lenses **339115**
Manufacturing electron and proton microscopes **334516**
Manufacturing molded plastics lens blanks **326199**
Manufacturing molded glass lens blanks **327212**

333315 Photographic and Photocopying Equipment Manufacturing[US]

This U.S. industry comprises establishments primarily engaged in manufacturing photographic and photocopying equipment, such as cameras (except television, video, digital projectors, film developing equipment, photocopying equipment, and microfilm equipment).

Manufacturing sensitized film, paper, cloth, and plates, and prepared photographic chemicals **325992**
Manufacturing photographic lenses **333314**
Manufacturing television, video, and digital cameras **334**

333319 Other Commercial and Service Machinery Manufacturing[US]

This U.S. industry comprises establishments primarily engaged in manufacturing commercial and service industry equipment (except automatic vending machines, commercial laundry, drycleaning and pressing machines, office machinery, optical instruments and lenses, and photographic and photocopying equipment).

Manufacturing automatic vending machines **333311**
Manufacturing commercial laundry drycleaning and pressing machines **333312**
Manufacturing office machinery **333313**
Manufacturing optical instruments and lenses **333314**
Manufacturing photographic and photocopying equipment **333315**
Manufacturing household-type appliances **3352**
Manufacturing mechanics' handtools **332212**

3334 Ventilation, Heating, Air-Conditioning, and Commercial Refrigeration Equipment Manufacturing

3334I Ventilation, Heating, Air-Conditioning, and Commercial Refrigeration Equipment Manufacturing

This industry comprises establishments primarily engaged in manufacturing ventilating, heating, air-conditioning, and commercial and industrial refrigeration and freezer equipment.

Manufacturing household-type fans (except attic), portable electric space heaters, humidifiers, dehumidifiers, and air purification equipment **33521**
Manufacturing household-type appliances, such as cooking stoves, ranges, refrigerators, and freezers **33522**
Manufacturing commercial-type cooking equipment **33329**
Manufacturing industrial, power, and marine boilers **33241**
Manufacturing industrial process furnaces and ovens **33399**
Manufacturing motor vehicle air-conditioning systems and compressors **33639**

333411 Air Purification Equipment Manufacturing[US]

This U.S. industry comprises establishments primarily engaged in manufacturing stationary air purification equipment, such as industrial dust and fume collection equipment, electrostatic precipitation equipment, warm air furnace filters, air washers, and other dust collection equipment.

Manufacturing air-conditioning units (except motor vehicle) **333415**
Manufacturing motor vehicle air-conditioning systems and compressors **336391**
Manufacturing household-type fans (except attic) and portable air purification equipment **335211**
Manufacturing industrial and commercial blowers, industrial and commercial exhaust and ventilating fans, and attic fans **333412**

333412 Industrial and Commercial Fan and Blower Manufacturing[US]

This U.S. industry comprises establishments primarily engaged in manufacturing attic fans and industrial and commercial fans and blowers, such as commercial exhaust fans and commercial ventilating fans.

Manufacturing air-conditioning units (except motor vehicle) **333415**
Manufacturing motor vehicle air-conditioning systems and compressors **336391**
Manufacturing household-type fans (except attic) and portable air purification equipment **335211**
Manufacturing stationary air purification equipment **333411**

333414 Heating Equipment (except Warm Air Furnaces) Manufacturing[US]

This U.S. industry comprises establishments primarily engaged in manufacturing heating equipment (except electric and warm air furnaces), such as heating boilers, heating stoves, floor and wall furnaces, and wall and baseboard heating units.

Manufacturing warm air furnaces **333415**
Manufacturing electric space heaters **335211**
Manufacturing household-type cooking stoves and ranges **335221**
Manufacturing industrial, power, and marine boilers **332410**
Manufacturing industrial process furnaces and ovens **333994**
Manufacturing commercial-type cooking equipment **333319**

333415 Air-Conditioning and Warm Air Heating Equipment and Commercial and Industrial Refrigeration Equipment Manufacturing[US]

This U.S. industry comprises establishments primarily engaged in (1) manufacturing air-conditioning (except motor vehicle) and warm air furnace equipment and/or (2) manufacturing commercial and industrial refrigeration and freezer equipment.

Manufacturing motor vehicle air-conditioning systems and compressors **336391**
Manufacturing household-type refrigerators and freezers **335222**
Manufacturing portable electric space heaters, humidifiers, and dehumidifiers **335211**
Manufacturing heating boilers, heating stoves, floor and wall mount furnaces, and electric wall and baseboard heating units **333414**
Manufacturing furnace air filters **333411**

3335 Metalworking Machinery Manufacturing

33351 Metalworking Machinery Manufacturing

This industry comprises establishments primarily engaged in manufacturing metalworking machinery, such as metal cutting and metal forming machine tools; cutting tools; and accessories for metalworking machinery; special dies, tools, jigs, and fixtures; industrial molds; rolling mill machinery; assembly machinery; coil handling, conversion, or straightening equipment; and wire drawing and fabricating machines.

Manufacturing handtools (except power-driven), cutting dies (except metal cutting), sawblades, and handsaws **33221**
Manufacturing casting molds for heavy steel ingots **33151**
Manufacturing power-driven handtools and welding and soldering equipment **33399**

333511 Industrial Mold Manufacturing[CAN]

This U.S. industry comprises establishments primarily engaged in manufacturing industrial molds for casting metals or forming other materials, such as plastics, glass, or rubber.

Manufacturing casting molds for steel ingots **331511**

333512 Machine Tool (Metal Cutting Types) Manufacturing[US]

This U.S. industry comprises establishments primarily engaged in manufacturing metal cutting machine tools (except handtools).

Manufacturing welding and soldering equipment **333992**
Manufacturing metal-forming machine tools **333513**
Manufacturing power-driven metal cutting handtools **333991**
Manufacturing accessories and attachments for metal cutting machine tools **333515**

333513 Machine Tool (Metal Forming Types) Manufacturing[US]

This U.S. industry comprises establishments primarily engaged in manufacturing metal forming machine tools (except handtools), such as punching, sheering, bending, forming, pressing, forging, and die-casting machines.

Manufacturing welding and soldering equipment **333992**
Manufacturing metal-cutting machine tools **333512**
Manufacturing power-driven handtools **333991**
Manufacturing rolling mill machinery and equipment **333516**
Manufacturing accessories and attachments for metal forming machine tools **333515**

333514 Special Die and Tool, Die Set, Jig, and Fixture Manufacturing[US]

This U.S. industry comprises establishments, known as tool and die shops, primarily engaged in manufacturing special tools and fixtures, such as cutting dies and jigs.

Manufacturing molds for die-casting and foundry casting; and metal molds for plaster working, rubber working, plastics working, and glass working machinery **333511**
Manufacturing molds for heavy steel ingots **331511**
Manufacturing cutting dies for materials other than metal **332212**

333515 Cutting Tool and Machine Tool Accessory Manufacturing[US]

This U.S. industry comprises establishments primarily engaged in manufacturing accessories and attachments for metal cutting and metal forming machine tools.

Manufacturing accessories and attachments for cutting and forming machines (except metal cutting, metal forming machinery) **332212**
Manufacturing saw blades and handsaws **332213**

333516 Rolling Mill Machinery and Equipment Manufacturing[US]

This U.S. industry comprises establishments primarily engaged in manufacturing rolling mill machinery and equipment for metal production.

333518 Other Metalworking Machinery Manufacturing[US]

This U.S. industry comprises establishments primarily engaged in manufacturing metal working machinery (except industrial molds; metal cutting machine tools; metal forming machine tools; special dies and tools, die sets, jigs, and fixtures; cutting tools and machine tool accessories; and rolling mill machinery and equipment).

Manufacturing industrial molds **333511**
Manufacturing metal cutting machinery **333512**
Manufacturing metal forming machinery **333513**
Manufacturing special dies and tools, die sets, jigs, and fixtures **333514**
Manufacturing cutting tools and machine tool accessories **333515**
Manufacturing rolling mill machinery **333516**

3336 Engine, Turbine, and Power Transmission Equipment Manufacturing

33361 Engine, Turbine, and Power Transmission Equipment Manufacturing

This industry comprises establishments primarily engaged in manufacturing turbines, power transmission equipment, and internal combustion engines (except automotive gasoline and aircraft).

Manufacturing motor vehicle power transmission equipment **33635**
Manufacturing aircraft engines and aircraft power transmission equipment **33641**
Manufacturing ball and roller bearings **33299**
Manufacturing automotive engines (except diesel) **33631**
Manufacturing electric power transmission, electric power distribution equipment, generators, or prime mover generator sets (except turbines) **33531**

333611 Turbine and Turbine Generator Set Units Manufacturing[CAN]

This U.S. industry comprises establishments primarily engaged in manufacturing turbines (except aircraft); and complete turbine generator set units, such as steam, hydraulic, gas, and wind.

Manufacturing aircraft turbines **336412**
Manufacturing generators or prime mover generator sets (except turbines) **335312**

333612 Speed Changer, Industrial High-Speed Drive, and Gear Manufacturing[US]

This U.S. industry comprises establishments primarily engaged in manufacturing gears, speed changers, and industrial high-speed drives (except hydrostatic).

Manufacturing motor vehicle power transmission equipment **336350**
Manufacturing aircraft power transmission equipment **336413**
Manufacturing industrial hydrostatic transmissions **333613**

333613 Mechanical Power Transmission Equipment Manufacturing[US]

This U.S. industry comprises establishments primarily engaged in manufacturing mechanical power transmission equipment (except motor vehicle and aircraft), such as plain bearings, brakes and clutches (except motor vehicle and electromagnetic industrial control), couplings, joints, and drive chains.

Manufacturing motor vehicle power transmission equipment **336350**
Manufacturing aircraft power transmission equipment **336413**
Manufacturing ball and roller bearings **332991**
Manufacturing gears, speed changers, and industrial high-speed drives (except hydrostatic) **333612**

333618 Other Engine Equipment Manufacturing[US]

This U.S. industry comprises establishments primarily engaged in manufacturing internal combustion engines (except automotive gasoline and aircraft).

Manufacturing gasoline motor vehicle engines and motor vehicle transmissions **3363**
Manufacturing gasoline aircraft engines and aircraft transmissions **33641**
Manufacturing turbine and turbine generator sets units **333611**
Manufacturing speed changers and industrial high-speed drivers and gears **333612**
Manufacturing mechanical power transmission equipment (except motor vehicle and aircraft) **333613**

3339 Other General Purpose Machinery Manufacturing

33391 Pump and Compressor Manufacturing

This industry comprises establishments primarily engaged in manufacturing pumps and compressors, such as general purpose air and gas compressors, nonagricultural spraying and dusting equipment, general purpose pumps and pumping equipment (except fluid power pumps and motors), and measuring and dispensing pumps.

Manufacturing fluid power pumps and motors and handheld pneumatic spray guns **33399**
Manufacturing agricultural spraying and dusting equipment **33311**
Manufacturing laboratory vacuum pumps **33911**
Manufacturing pumps and air-conditioning systems and compressors for motor vehicles **3363**
Manufacturing air-conditioning systems and compressors (except motor vehicle) **33341**

333911 Pump and Pumping Equipment Manufacturing[US]

This U.S. industry comprises establishments primarily engaged in manufacturing general purpose pumps and pumping equipment (except fluid power pumps and motors), such as reciprocating pumps, turbine pumps, centrifugal pumps, rotary pumps, diaphragm pumps, domestic water system pumps, oil well and oil field pumps and sump pumps.

Manufacturing fluid power pumps and motors **333996**
Manufacturing measuring and dispensing pumps **333913**
Manufacturing vacuum pumps (except laboratory) **333912**
Manufacturing laboratory vacuum pumps **339111**
Manufacturing fluid pumps for motor vehicles, such as oil pumps, water pumps, and power steering pumps, **3363**

333912 Air and Gas Compressor Manufacturing[US]

This U.S. industry comprises establishments primarily engaged in manufacturing general purpose air and gas compressors, such as reciprocating compressors, centrifugal compressors, vacuum pumps (except laboratory), and nonagricultural spraying and dusting compressors and spray gun units.

333

Manufacturing refrigeration and air-conditioning (except motor vehicle) systems and compressors **333415**

Manufacturing motor vehicle air-conditioning systems and compressors **336391**

Manufacturing fluid power pumps and motors **333996**

Manufacturing agricultural spraying and dusting equipment **333111**

Manufacturing laboratory vacuum pumps **339111**

Manufacturing handheld pneumatic spray guns **333991**

333913 Measuring and Dispensing Pump Manufacturing^{US}

This U.S. industry comprises establishments primarily engaged in manufacturing measuring and dispensing pumps, such as gasoline pumps and lubricating oil measuring and dispensing pumps.

Manufacturing pumps and pumping equipment for general industrial use **333911**

33392 Material Handling Equipment Manufacturing

This industry comprises establishments primarily engaged in manufacturing material handling equipment, such as elevators and moving stairs; conveyors and conveying equipment; overhead traveling cranes, hoists, and monorail systems; and industrial trucks, tractors, trailers, and stacker machinery.

Manufacturing motor vehicle-type trailers **33621**

Manufacturing farm-type tractors **33311**

Manufacturing construction-type tractors and cranes **33312**

Manufacturing power transmission pulleys **33361**

333921 Elevator and Moving Stairway Manufacturing^{US}

This U.S. industry comprises establishments primarily engaged in manufacturing elevators and moving stairways.

Manufacturing commercial conveyor systems and equipment **333922**

333922 Conveyor and Conveying Equipment Manufacturing^{US}

This U.S. industry comprises establishments primarily engaged in manufacturing conveyors and conveying equipment, such as gravity conveyors, trolley conveyors, tow conveyors, pneumatic tube conveyors, carousel conveyors, farm conveyors, and belt conveyors.

Manufacturing passenger or freight elevators, dumbwaiters, and moving stairways **333921**

Manufacturing overhead traveling cranes and monorail systems **333923**

333923 Overhead Traveling Crane, Hoist, and Monorail System Manufacturing^{US}

This U.S. industry comprises establishments primarily engaged in manufacturing overhead traveling cranes, hoists, and monorail systems.

Manufacturing construction-type cranes **333120**

Manufacturing aircraft loading hoists **333924**

Manufacturing power transmission pulleys **333613**

333924 Industrial Truck, Tractor, Trailer, and Stacker Machinery Manufacturing^{US}

This U.S. industry comprises establishments primarily engaged in manufacturing industrial trucks, tractors, trailers, and stackers (i.e., truck-type) such as forklifts, pallet loaders and unloaders, and portable loading docks.

Manufacturing motor vehicle-type trailers **336212**

Manufacturing farm-type tractors **333111**

Manufacturing construction-type tractors **333120**

33399 All Other General Purpose Machinery Manufacturing

This industry comprises establishments primarily engaged in manufacturing general purpose machinery (except ventilation, heating, air-conditioning, and commercial refrigeration equipment; metal working machinery; engines, turbines, and power transmission equipment; pumps and compressors; and material handling equipment).

Manufacturing ventilating, heating, air-conditioning (except motor vehicle), commercial refrigeration, and furnace filters **33341**

Manufacturing metalworking machinery **3335**

Manufacturing engine, turbine and power transmission equipment **3336**

Manufacturing pumps and compressors **33391**

Manufacturing material handling equipment **33392**

Manufacturing motor vehicle air-conditioning systems and compressors, engine filters, and pumps **3363**

Manufacturing laboratory scales, balances, ovens, and furnaces **39911**

Manufacturing metal cutting and metal forming machinery **33351**

Manufacturing power driven heavy construction and mining hand operated tools, such as tampers and augers, **33312** and **33313**

Manufacturing bakery ovens and industrial kilns, such as cement, wood, and chemical, **33329**

Manufacturing mechanical jacks, handheld soldering irons, countersink bits, drill bits, router bits, milling cutters, and other machine tools for woodcutting **33221**

Manufacturing carnival amusement park equipment, automotive maintenance equipment, and coin-operated vending machines **33331**

Manufacturing transformers for arc-welding **33531**

333991 Power-Driven Handtool Manufacturing[US]

This U.S. industry comprises establishments primarily engaged in manufacturing power-driven (e.g., battery, corded, pneumatic) handtools, such as drills, screwguns, circular saws, chain saws, staplers, and nailers.

Manufacturing metal cutting-type and metal forming-type machines (including home workshop) **33351**

Manufacturing countersink bits, drill bits, router bits, milling cutters, and other machine tools for woodcutting **332212**

Manufacturing power-driven heavy construction or mining hand operated tools, such as tampers, jackhammers, and augers, **333120** and **333130**

Manufacturing powered home lawn and garden equipment **333112**

333992 Welding and Soldering Equipment Manufacturing[US]

This U.S. industry comprises establishments primarily engaged in manufacturing welding and soldering equipment and accessories (except transformers), such as arc, resistance, gas, plasma, laser, electron beam, and ultrasonic welding equipment; welding electrodes; coated or cored welding wire; and soldering equipment (except handheld).

Manufacturing handheld soldering irons **332212**

Manufacturing transformers for arc-welding **335311**

333993 Packaging Machinery Manufacturing[US]

This U.S. industry comprises establishments primarily engaged in manufacturing packaging machinery, such as wrapping, bottling, canning, and labeling machinery.

333994 Industrial Process Furnace and Oven Manufacturing[US]

This U.S. comprises establishments primarily engaged in manufacturing industrial process furnaces, ovens,

induction and dielectric heating equipment, and kilns (except cement, chemical, wood).

Manufacturing bakery ovens **333294**

Manufacturing cement, wood, and chemical kilns **333298**

Manufacturing cremating ovens **333999**

Manufacturing laboratory furnaces and ovens **339111**

333995 Fluid Power Cylinder and Actuator Manufacturing[US]

This U.S. industry comprises establishments primarily engaged in manufacturing fluid power (i.e., hydraulic and pneumatic) cylinders and actuators.

333996 Fluid Power Pump and Motor Manufacturing[US]

This U.S. industry comprises establishments primarily engaged in manufacturing fluid power (i.e., hydraulic and pneumatic) pumps and motors.

Manufacturing fluid pumps for motor vehicles, such as oil pumps, water pumps, and power steering pumps **3363**

Manufacturing general purpose pumps (except fluid power) **333911**

Manufacturing air compressors **333912**

333997 Scale and Balance (except Laboratory) Manufacturing[US]

This U.S. industry comprises establishments primarily engaged in manufacturing scales and balances (except laboratory).

Manufacturing laboratory scales and balances **339111**

333999 All Other Miscellaneous General Purpose Machinery Manufacturing[US]

This U.S. industry comprises establishments primarily engaged in manufacturing general purpose machinery (except ventilating, heating, air-conditioning, and commercial refrigeration equipment; metal working machinery; engines, turbines, and power transmission equipment; pumps and compressors; material handling equipment; power-driven handtools; welding and soldering equipment; packaging machinery; industrial process furnaces and ovens; fluid power cylinders and actuators; fluid power pumps and motors; and scales and balances).

Manufacturing ventilating, heating, air-conditioning (except motor vehicle), and commercial refrigeration **33341**

Manufacturing motor vehicle air-conditioning systems and compressors **336391**

Manufacturing metalworking machinery **3335**

Manufacturing engine, turbine, and power transmission equipment **3336**

Manufacturing pumps and compressors **33391**

Manufacturing material handling equipment **33392**

Manufacturing power-driven handtools **333991**

Manufacturing welding and soldering equipment (except handheld soldering irons) **333992**

Manufacturing packaging machinery **333993**

Manufacturing bakery ovens and cement, wood, and chemical kilns **333298**

Manufacturing industrial process furnaces and ovens (except bakery) **333994**

Manufacturing fluid power cylinders and actuators **333995**

Manufacturing fluid power pumps and motors **333996**

Manufacturing scales and balances (except laboratory) **333997**

Manufacturing carnival and amusement park equipment, automotive maintenance equipment and coin-operated vending machines **33331**

Manufacturing motor vehicle engine filters and pumps **3363**

Manufacturing mechanical jacks **332212**

334 Computer and Electronic Product Manufacturing

Industries in the Computer and Electronic Product Manufacturing subsector group establishments that manufacture computers, computer peripherals, communications equipment, and similar electronic products, and establishments that manufacture components for such products. The Computer and Electronic Product Manufacturing industries have been combined in the hierarchy of NAICS because of the economic significance they have attained. Their rapid growth suggests that they will become even more important to the economies of all three North American countries in the future, and in addition their manufacturing processes are fundamentally different from the manufacturing processes of other machinery and equipment. The design and use of integrated circuits and the application of highly specialized miniaturization technologies are common elements in the production technologies of the computer and electronic subsector. Convergence of technology motivates this NAICS subsector. Digitalization of sound recording, for example, causes both the medium (the compact disc) and the equipment to resemble the technologies for recording, storing, transmitting, and manipulating data. Communications technology and equipment have been converging with computer technology. When technologically-related components are in the same sector, it makes it easier to adjust the classification for future changes, without needing to redefine its basic structure. The creation of the Computer and Electronic Product Manufacturing subsector will assist in delineating new and emerging industries because the activities that will serve as the probable sources of new industries, such as computer manufacturing and communications equipment manufacturing, or computers and audio equipment are brought together. As new activities emerge, they are less likely therefore, to cross the subsector boundaries of the classification.

33411 Computer and Peripheral Equipment Manufacturing

This industry comprises establishments primarily engaged in manufacturing and/or assembling electronic computers, such as mainframes, personal computers, workstations, laptops, and computer servers; and computer peripheral equipment, such as storage devices, printers, monitors, input/output devices and terminals. Computers can be analog, digital, or hybrid. Digital computers, the most common type, are devices that do all of the following: (1) store the processing program or programs and the data immediately necessary for the execution of the program; (2) can be freely programmed in accordance with the requirements of the user; (3) perform arithmetical computations specified by the user; and (4) execute, without human intervention, a processing program that requires the computer to modify its execution by logical decision during the processing run. Analog computers are capable of simulating mathematical models and comprise at least analog, control, and programming elements.

Manufacturing digital telecommunications switches, local area network and wide area network communications equipment, such as bridges, routers, and gateways, **33421**

Manufacturing blank magnetic and optical recording media **33461**

Manufacturing external audio speakers for computer use **33431**

Manufacturing internal loaded printed circuit board devices, such as sound, video, controller, and network interface cards; internal and external computer modems; and semiconductor storage devices, **33441**

334111 Electronic Computer Manufacturing^{US}

This U.S. industry comprises establishments primarily engaged in manufacturing and/or assembling electronic computers, such as mainframes, personal computers, workstations, laptops, and computer servers. Computers can be analog, digital, or hybrid. Digital computers, the most common type, are devices that do all of the following: (1) store the processing program or programs and the data immediately necessary for the execution of the program; (2) can be freely programmed in accordance with the requirements of the user; (3) perform arithmetical computations specified by the user; and (4) execute, without human intervention, a processing program that requires the computer to modify its execution by logical decision during the processing run. Analog computers are capable of simulating mathematical models and contain at least analog, control, and programming elements. The manufacture of computers includes the assembly or integration of processors, coprocessors, memory, storage, and input/output devices into a user-programmable final product.

Manufacturing digital telecommunications switches, local area network and wide area network communication equipment, such as bridges, routers, and gateways, **334210**

Manufacturing blank magnetic and optical recording media **334613**

Manufacturing internal, loaded, printed circuit board devices, such as sound, video, controller, and network interface cards; internal and external computer modems; and solid state storage devices for computers, **33441**

334112 Computer Storage Device Manufacturing^{US}

This U.S. industry comprises establishments primarily engaged in manufacturing computer storage devices that allow the storage and retrieval of data from a phase change, magnetic, optical, or magnetic/optical media. Examples of products made by these estab-

lishments are CD-ROM drives, floppy disk drives, hard disk drives, and tape storage and backup units.

Manufacturing blank magnetic and optical recording media **334613**

Manufacturing semiconductor storage devices, such as memory chips, **334413**

Manufacturing drive controller cards, internal or external to the storage device **334418**

334113 Computer Terminal Manufacturing^{US}

This U.S. industry comprises establishments primarily engaged in manufacturing computer terminals. Computer terminals are input/output devices that connect with a central computer for processing.

Manufacturing point-of-sale terminals, funds transfer, automatic teller machines, and monitors **334119**

Manufacturing internal loaded printed circuit board devices, such as sound, video, controller, and network interface cards for computer terminals, **334418**

334119 Other Computer Peripheral Equipment Manufacturing^{US}

This U.S. industry comprises establishments primarily engaged in manufacturing computer peripheral equipment (except storage devices and computer terminals).

Manufacturing local area network and wide area network communications equipment, such as bridges, routers, and gateways, **334210**

Manufacturing computer storage devices **334112**

Manufacturing computer terminals **334113**

Manufacturing external audio speakers for computer use **334310**

Manufacturing internal, loaded, printed circuit board devices, such as sound, video, controller, and network interface cards; and internal and external computer modems used as computer peripherals, **334418**

3342 Communications Equipment Manufacturing

334210 Telephone Apparatus Manufacturing

This industry comprises establishments primarily engaged in manufacturing wire telephone and data communications equipment. These products may be standalone or board-level components of a larger system. Examples of products made by these establishments are central office switching equipment, cordless telephones (except cellular), PBX equipment, telephones, telephone answering machines, and data communications equipment, such as bridges, routers, and gateways.

Manufacturing internal and external computer modems, fax/modems and electronic components used in telephone apparatus **3344I**
Manufacturing cellular telephones **334220**

334220 Radio and Television Broadcasting and Wireless Communications Equipment Manufacturing

This industry comprises establishments primarily engaged in manufacturing radio and television broadcast and wireless communications equipment. Examples of products made by these establishments are: transmitting and receiving antennas, cable television equipment, GPS equipment, pagers, cellular phones, mobile communications equipment, and radio and television studio and broadcasting equipment.

Manufacturing household-type audio and video equipment, such as televisions and radio sets, **334310**
Manufacturing wired and nonwired intercommunications equipment (i.e., intercoms) **334290**

334290 Other Communications Equipment Manufacturing

This industry comprises establishments primarily engaged in manufacturing communications equipment (except telephone apparatus, and radio and television broadcast, and wireless communications equipment).

Manufacturing telephone apparatus **334210**
Manufacturing radio and television broadcast and wireless communication equipment **334220**
Manufacturing automobile audio and related equipment **334310**

334310 Audio and Video Equipment Manufacturing

This industry comprises establishments primarily engaged in manufacturing electronic audio and video equipment for home entertainment, motor vehicle, public address and musical instrument amplifications. Examples of products made by these establishments are video cassette recorders, televisions, stereo equipment, speaker systems, household-type video cameras,

jukeboxes, and amplifiers for musical instruments and public address systems.

Manufacturing telephone answering machines **334210**
Manufacturing photographic (i.e., still and motion picture) equipment **333315**
Manufacturing phonograph needles and cartridges **3344I**
Manufacturing auto theft alarms **334290**
Manufacturing mobile radios, such as citizens band and FM transceivers for household or motor vehicle uses; studio and broadcast video cameras; and cable decoders and satellite television equipment, **334220**

3344I Semiconductor and Other Electronic Component Manufacturing

This industry comprises establishments primarily engaged in manufacturing semiconductors and other components for electronic applications. Examples of products made by these establishments are capacitors, resistors, microprocessors, bare and loaded printed circuit boards, electron tubes, electronic connectors, and computer modems.

Manufacturing X-ray tubes **33451**
Manufacturing glass blanks for electron tubes **3272I**
Manufacturing telephone system components or modules **3342I**
Manufacturing communications antennas **33422**
Manufacturing coils, switches, transformers, connectors, capacitors, rheostats, and similar devices for electrical applications **335**

3344II Electron Tube Manufacturing[US]

This U.S. industry comprises establishments primarily engaged in manufacturing electron tubes and parts (except glass blanks). Examples of products made by these establishments are cathode ray tubes (i.e., picture tubes), klystron tubes, magnetron tubes, and traveling wave tubes.

Manufacturing X-ray tubes **334517**
Manufacturing glass blanks for electron tubes **3272I**

334412 Bare Printed Circuit Board Manufacturing[US]

This U.S. industry comprises establishments primarily engaged in manufacturing bare (i.e., rigid or flexible) printed circuit boards without mounted electronic components. These establishments print, perforate, plate, screen, etch, or photoprint interconnecting pathways for electric current on laminates.

Loading components onto printed circuit boards, or whose output is loaded
    printed circuit boards **334418**
Manufacturing printed circuit laminates **334419**

334413 Semiconductor and Related Device Manufacturing^{US}

This U.S. industry comprises establishments primarily engaged in manufacturing semiconductors and
related solid state devices. Examples of products made
by these establishments are integrated circuits,
memory chips, microprocessors, diodes, transistors,
solar cells and other optoelectronic devices.

334414 Electronic Capacitor Manufacturing^{US}

This U.S. industry comprises establishments primarily engaged in manufacturing electronic fixed and
variable capacitors and condensers.

Manufacturing electrical capacitors for power generation and distribution,
    heavy industrial equipment, induction heating and melting, and similar
    industrial applications **335999**

334415 Electronic Resistor Manufacturing^{US}

This U.S. industry comprises establishments primarily engaged in manufacturing electronic resistors, such
as fixed and variable resistors, resistor networks, ther-
mistors, and varistors.

Manufacturing electronic rheostats **334419**

334416 Electronic Coil, Transformer, and Other Inductor Manufacturing^{US}

This U.S. industry comprises establishments primarily engaged in manufacturing electronic inductors,
such as coils and transformers.

Manufacturing electrical transformers used in the generation, storage,
    transmission, transformation, distribution, and utilization of electrical
    energy **335311**

334417 Electronic Connector Manufacturing^{US}

This U.S. industry comprises establishments primarily engaged in manufacturing electronic connectors,
such as coaxial, cylindrical, rack and panel, pin and
sleeve, printed circuit and fiber optic.

Manufacturing electrical connectors, such as plugs, bus bars, twist on wire
    connectors and terminals, **335931**

334418 Printed Circuit Assembly (Electronic Assembly) Manufacturing^{US}

This U.S. industry comprises establishments primarily engaged in loading components onto printed circuit boards or who manufacture and ship loaded
printed circuit boards. Also known as printed circuit
assemblies, electronics assemblies, or modules, these
products are printed circuit boards that have some or
all of the semiconductor and electronic components
inserted or mounted and are inputs to a wide variety
of electronic systems and devices.

Manufacturing printed circuit laminates **334419**
Manufacturing bare printed circuit boards **334412**
Manufacturing telephone system components or modules **334210**

334419 Other Electronic Component Manufacturing^{US}

This U.S. industry comprises establishments primarily engaged in manufacturing electronic components
(except electron tubes; bare printed circuit boards;
semiconductors and related devices; electronic capacitors; electronic resistors; coils, transformers and other
inductors; connectors; and loaded printed circuit
boards).

Manufacturing electron tubes **334411**
Manufacturing bare printed circuit boards **334412**
Manufacturing semiconductors and related devices **334413**
Manufacturing electronic capacitors **334414**
Manufacturing electronic resistors **334415**
Manufacturing electronic inductors **334416**
Manufacturing electronic connectors **334417**
Loading components onto printed circuit boards or whose output is loaded
    printed circuit boards **334418**
Manufacturing communications antennas **334220**

3345 Navigational, Measuring, Electromedical, and Control Instruments Manufacturing

33451 Navigational, Measuring, Electromedical, and Control Instruments, Manufacturing

This industry comprises establishments primarily
engaged in manufacturing navigational, measuring,
electromedical, and control instruments. Examples of

products made by these establishments are aeronautical instruments, appliance regulators and controls (except switches), laboratory analytical instruments, navigation and guidance systems, and physical properties testing equipment.

Manufacturing global positioning system (GPS) equipment **33422**
Manufacturing motor control switches and relays (including timing relays) **33531**
Manufacturing switches for appliances **33593**
Manufacturing optical instruments **33331**
Manufacturing equipment for measuring and testing communications signals **3342**
Manufacturing glass watch and clock crystals **32721**
Manufacturing plastics watch and clock crystals **32619**
Manufacturing medical thermometers and other nonelectrical medical apparatus **3391**

334510 Electromedical and Electrotherapeutic Apparatus Manufacturing[US]

This U.S. industry comprises establishments primarily engaged in manufacturing electromedical and electrotherapeutic apparatus, such as magnetic resonance imaging equipment, medical ultrasound equipment, pacemakers, hearing aids, electrocardiographs, and electromedical endoscopic equipment.

Manufacturing medical irradiation apparatus **334517**
Manufacturing nonelectrical medical and therapeutic apparatus **3391**

334511 Search, Detection, Navigation, Guidance, Aeronautical, and Nautical System and Instrument Manufacturing[US]

This U.S. industry comprises establishments primarily engaged in manufacturing search, detection, navigation, guidance, aeronautical, and nautical systems and instruments. Examples of products made by these establishments are aircraft instruments (except engine), flight recorders, navigational instruments and systems, radar systems and equipment, and sonar systems and equipment.

Manufacturing global positioning system (GPS) equipment **334220**
Manufacturing aircraft engine instruments and meteorological systems and equipment **334519**

334512 Automatic Environmental Control Manufacturing for Residential, Commercial, and Appliance Use[US]

This U.S. industry comprises establishments primarily engaged in manufacturing automatic controls and regulators for applications, such as heating, air-conditioning, refrigeration and appliances.

Manufacturing industrial process controls **334513**
Manufacturing motor control switches and relays **335314**
Manufacturing switches for appliances **335931**
Manufacturing appliance timers **334518**

334513 Instruments and Related Products Manufacturing for Measuring, Displaying, and Controlling Industrial Process Variables[US]

This U.S. industry comprises establishments primarily engaged in manufacturing instruments and related devices for measuring, displaying, indicating, recording, transmitting, and controlling industrial process variables. These instruments measure, display or control (monitor, analyze, and so forth) industrial process variables, such as temperature, humidity, pressure, vacuum, combustion, flow, level, viscosity, density, acidity, concentration, and rotation.

Manufacturing instruments for measuring or testing of electricity and electrical signals **334515**
Manufacturing medical thermometers **339112**
Manufacturing glass hydrometers and thermometers for other nonmedical uses **334519**
Manufacturing instruments and instrumentation systems for laboratory analysis of samples **334516**
Manufacturing optical alignment and display instruments, optical comparators, and optical test and inspection equipment **333314**

334514 Totalizing Fluid Meter and Counting Device Manufacturing[US]

This U.S. industry comprises establishments primarily engaged in manufacturing totalizing (i.e., registering) fluid meters and counting devices. Examples of products made by these establishments are gas consumption meters, water consumption meters, parking meters, taxi meters, motor vehicle gauges, and fare collection equipment.

Manufacturing integrating meters and counters for measuring the characteristics of electricity and electrical signals **334515**

Manufacturing instruments and devices that measure, display, or control (i.e., monitor or analyze) related industrial process variables **334513**

334515 Instrument Manufacturing for Measuring and Testing Electricity and Electrical Signals[US]

This U.S. industry comprises establishments primarily engaged in manufacturing instruments for measuring and testing the characteristics of electricity and electrical signals. Examples of products made by these establishments are circuit and continuity testers, volt meters, ohm meters, wattmeters, multimeters, and semiconductor test equipment.

Manufacturing electronic monitoring, evaluating, and other electronic support equipment for navigational, radar, and sonar systems **334511**

Manufacturing equipment for measuring and testing communications signals **3342**

334516 Analytical Laboratory Instrument Manufacturing[US]

This U.S. industry comprises establishments primarily engaged in manufacturing instruments and instrumentation systems for laboratory analysis of the chemical or physical composition or concentration of samples of solid, fluid, gaseous, or composite material.

Manufacturing instruments for monitoring and analyzing continuous samples from medical patients **334510**

Manufacturing instruments and related devices that measure, display, or control (i.e., monitor or analyze) industrial process variables **334513**

334517 Irradiation Apparatus Manufacturing[US]

This U.S. industry comprises establishments primarily engaged in manufacturing irradiation apparatus and tubes for applications, such as medical diagnostic, medical therapeutic, industrial, research, and scientific evaluation. Irradiation can take the form of beta-rays, gamma-rays, X-rays, or other ionizing radiation.

334518 Watch, Clock, and Part Manufacturing[US]

This U.S. industry comprises establishments primarily engaged in manufacturing and/or assembling: clocks; watches; timing mechanisms for clockwork operated devices; time clocks; time and date recording devices; and clock and watch parts (except crystals), such as springs, jewels, and modules.

Manufacturing glass watch and clock crystals **32721**

Manufacturing plastics watch and clock crystals **326199**

Manufacturing timing relays **335314**

334519 Other Measuring and Controlling Device Manufacturing[US]

This U.S. industry comprises establishments primarily engaged in manufacturing measuring and controlling devices (except search, detection, navigation, guidance, aeronautical, and nautical instruments and systems; automatic environmental controls for residential, commercial, and appliance use; instruments for measurement, display, and control of industrial process variables; totalizing fluid meters and counting devices; instruments for measuring and testing electricity and electrical signals; analytical laboratory instruments; watches, clocks, and parts; irradiation equipment; and electromedical and electrotherapeutic apparatus).

Manufacturing medical thermometers **339112**

Manufacturing search, detection, navigation, guidance, aeronautical, and nautical systems and instruments **334511**

Manufacturing automatic controls and regulators for applications, such as heating, air-conditioning, refrigeration and appliances, **334512**

Manufacturing instruments and related devices that measure, display, or control (i.e., monitor or analyze) industrial process variables **334513**

Manufacturing totalizing (i.e., registering) fluid meters and counting devices, including motor vehicle gauges **334514**

Manufacturing instruments for measuring and testing the characteristics of electricity and electrical signals **334515**

Manufacturing instruments for laboratory analysis of the physical composition or concentration of samples of solid, fluid, gaseous, or composite materials **334516**

Manufacturing and/or assembling watches, clocks, or parts **334518**

Manufacturing X-ray apparatus, tubes, or related irradiation apparatus **334517**

Manufacturing electromedical and electrotherapeutic apparatus **334510**

334

3346 Manufacturing and Reproducing Magnetic and Optical Media

33461 Manufacturing and Reproducing Magnetic and Optical Media

This industry comprises establishments primarily engaged in (1) manufacturing optical and magnetic media, such as blank audio tape, blank video tape, and blank diskettes and/or (2) mass duplicating (i.e., making copies) audio, video, software, and other data on magnetic, optical, and similar media.

Designing, developing, and publishing prepackaged software **51121**
Audio, motion picture and/or video production and/or distribution **512**

334611 Software Reproducing^{US}

This U.S. industry comprises establishments primarily engaged in mass reproducing computer software. These establishments do not generally develop any software, they mass reproduce data and programs on magnetic media, such as diskettes, tapes, or cartridges. Establishments in this industry mass reproduce products, such as CD-ROMs and game cartridges.

Designing, developing, and publishing prepackaged software **511210**

334612 Prerecorded Compact Disc (except Software), Tape, and Record Reproducing^{US}

This U.S. industry comprises establishments primarily engaged in mass reproducing audio and video material on magnetic or optical media. Examples of products mass reproduced by these establishments are audio compact discs, prerecorded audio and video cassettes, and laser discs.

Designing, developing, and publishing prepackaged software **511210**
Audio, motion picture and/or video production and/or distribution **512**
Manufacturing blank audio and video tape, blank diskettes, and blank optical discs **334613**

334613 Magnetic and Optical Recording Media Manufacturing^{US}

This U.S. industry comprises establishments primarily engaged in manufacturing magnetic and optical recording media, such as blank magnetic tape, blank diskettes, blank optical discs, hard drive media, and blank magnetic tape cassettes.

Mass reproducing computer software **334611**
Mass reproducing audio and video material **334612**

335 Electrical Equipment, Appliance, and Component Manufacturing

Industries in the Electrical Equipment, Appliance, and Component Manufacturing subsector manufacture products that generate, distribute and use electrical power. Electric Lighting Equipment Manufacturing establishments produce electric lamp bulbs, lighting fixtures, and parts. Household Appliance Manufacturing establishments make both small and major electrical appliances and parts. Electrical Equipment Manufacturing establishments make goods, such as electric motors, generators, transformers, and switchgear apparatus. Other Electrical Equipment and Component Manufacturing establishments make devices for storing electrical power (e.g., batteries), for transmitting electricity (e.g., insulated wire), and wiring devices (e.g., electrical outlets, fuse boxes, and light switches).

3351 Electric Lighting Equipment Manufacturing

335110 Electric Lamp Bulb and Part Manufacturing

This industry comprises establishments primarily engaged in manufacturing electric light bulbs and tubes, and parts and components (except glass blanks for electric light bulbs).

Manufacturing glass blanks for electric light bulbs **327212**
Manufacturing vehicular lighting fixtures **336321**
Manufacturing light emitting diodes (LEDs) **334413**
Manufacturing other lighting fixtures (except vehicular) **33512**

33512 Lighting Fixture Manufacturing

This industry comprises establishments primarily engaged in manufacturing electric lighting fixtures (except vehicular), nonelectric lighting equipment, lamp shades (except glass and plastics) and lighting fixture components (except current-carrying wiring devices).

Manufacturing vehicular lighting fixtures **33632**
Manufacturing electric light bulbs, tubes, and parts **33511**
Manufacturing current-carrying wiring devices for lighting fixtures **33593**
Manufacturing ceiling fans or bath fans with integrated lighting fixtures **33521**
Manufacturing plastics lamp shades **32619**
Manufacturing glassware and glass parts for lighting fixtures **32721**
Manufacturing signaling devices that incorporate electric light bulbs, such as traffic and railway signals, **33429**

335121 Residential Electric Lighting Fixture Manufacturing[US]

This U.S. industry comprises establishments primarily engaged in manufacturing fixed or portable residential electric lighting fixtures and lamp shades of metal, paper, or textiles. Residential electric lighting fixtures include those for use both inside and outside the residence.

Manufacturing glassware for residential lighting fixtures **32721**
Manufacturing plastics lamp shades **326199**
Manufacturing electric light bulbs, tubes, and parts **335110**
Manufacturing ceiling fans or bath fans with integrated lighting fixtures **335211**
Manufacturing current-carrying wiring devices for lighting fixtures **335931**
Manufacturing other lighting fixtures, such as street lights, flashlights, and nonelectric lighting fixtures, **335129**

335122 Commercial, Industrial, and Institutional Electric Lighting Fixture Manufacturing[US]

This U.S. industry comprises establishments primarily engaged in manufacturing commercial, industrial, and institutional electric lighting fixtures.

Manufacturing glassware for commercial, industrial, and institutional electric lighting fixtures **32721**
Manufacturing residential electric lighting fixtures **335121**
Manufacturing current-carrying wiring devices for lighting fixtures **335931**
Manufacturing other lighting fixtures, such as street lights, flashlights, and nonelectric lighting equipment, **335129**

335129 Other Lighting Equipment Manufacturing[US]

This U.S. industry comprises establishments primarily engaged in manufacturing electric lighting fixtures (except residential, commercial, industrial, institutional, and vehicular electric lighting fixtures) and nonelectric lighting equipment.

Manufacturing glassware for lighting fixtures **32721**
Manufacturing electric light bulbs, tubes, and parts **335110**
Manufacturing current-carrying wiring devices for lighting fixtures **335931**
Manufacturing commercial, industrial, and institutional electric lighting fixtures **335122**
Manufacturing vehicular lighting fixtures **336321**
Manufacturing signaling devices that incorporate electric light bulbs, such as traffic and railway signals, **334290**

335

3352 Household Appliance Manufacturing

33521 Small Electrical Appliance Manufacturing

This industry comprises establishments primarily engaged in manufacturing small electric appliances and electric housewares, household-type fans, household-type vacuum cleaners, and other electric household-type floor care machines.

Manufacturing room air-conditioners, attic fans, wall and baseboard heating units for permanent installation, and commercial ventilation and exhaust fans **33341**
Manufacturing commercial, industrial, and institutional vacuum cleaners, and mechanical carpet sweepers **33331**
Manufacturing major household-type appliances, such as washing machines, dryers, stoves, and hot water heaters, **33522**
Installing central vacuum cleaning systems **23**

335211 Electric Housewares and Household Fan Manufacturing[US]

This U.S. industry comprises establishments primarily engaged in manufacturing small electric appliances and electric housewares for heating, cooking, and other purposes, and electric household-type fans (except attic fans).

Manufacturing attic fans **333412**
Manufacturing wall and baseboard heating units for permanent installation **333414**
Manufacturing room air-conditioners **333415**
Manufacturing microwave and convection ovens **335221**

335212 Household Vacuum Cleaner Manufacturing[US]

This U.S. industry comprises establishments primarily engaged in manufacturing electric vacuum cleaners, electric floor waxing machines, and other electric floor care machines typically for household use.

Manufacturing electric vacuum cleaners for commercial, industrial, and
    institutional uses, and mechanical carpet sweepers **333319**
Installing central vacuum cleaning systems **235950**

33522 Major Appliance Manufacturing

This industry comprises establishments primarily engaged in manufacturing household-type cooking appliances, household-type laundry equipment, household-type refrigerators, upright and chest freezers, and other electrical and nonelectrical major household-type appliances, such as dishwashers, water heaters, and garbage disposal units.

Manufacturing small electric appliances and electric housewares, such as hot
    plates, griddles, toasters, and electric irons, **33521**
Manufacturing commercial and industrial refrigerators and freezers **33341**
Manufacturing commercial-type cooking equipment and commercial-type
    laundry, dry-cleaning, and pressing equipment **33331**
Manufacturing household-type sewing machines **33329**

335221 Household Cooking Appliance Manufacturing[US]

This U.S. industry comprises establishments primarily engaged in manufacturing household-type electric and nonelectric cooking equipment (except small electric appliances and electric housewares).

Manufacturing small electric appliances and electric housewares used for
    cooking, such as electric skillets, electric hot plates, electric griddles,
    toasters, and percolators, **335211**
Manufacturing commercial-type cooking equipment **333319**

335222 Household Refrigerator and Home Freezer Manufacturing[US]

This U.S. industry comprises establishments primarily engaged in manufacturing household-type refrigerators and upright and chest freezers.

Manufacturing commercial and industrial refrigeration equipment, such as
    refrigerators and freezers, **333415**

335224 Household Laundry Equipment Manufacturing[US]

This U.S. industry comprises establishments primarily engaged in manufacturing household-type laundry equipment.

Manufacturing portable electric irons **335211**
Manufacturing commercial-type laundry and drycleaning equipment
    333312

335228 Other Major Household Appliance Manufacturing[US]

This U.S. industry comprises establishments primarily engaged in manufacturing electric and nonelectric major household-type appliances (except cooking equipment, refrigerators, upright and chest freezers, and household-type laundry equipment).

Manufacturing household-type cooking equipment **335221**
Manufacturing household-type sewing machines **333298**
Manufacturing household-type refrigerators and upright and chest freezers
    335222
Manufacturing small electric appliances **335211**

3353 Electrical Equipment Manufacturing

33531 Electrical Equipment Manufacturing

This industry comprises establishments primarily engaged in manufacturing power, distribution, and specialty transformers; electric motors, generators, and motor generator sets; switchgear and switchboard apparatus; relays; and industrial controls.

Manufacturing turbine generator set units and electric outboard motors
    33361
Manufacturing electronic component-type transformers and switches **33441**
Manufacturing environmental controls and industrial process control
    instruments **33451**
Manufacturing switches for electrical circuits, such as pushbutton and snap
    switches, **33593**
Manufacturing complete for welding and soldering equipment **33399**
Manufacturing starting motors and generators for internal combustion
    engines **33632**

335311 Power, Distribution, and Specialty Transformer Manufacturing[CAN]

This U.S. industry comprises establishments prima-

rily engaged in manufacturing power, distribution, and specialty transformers (except electronic components). Industrial-type and consumer-type transformers in this industry vary (e.g., step up or step down) voltage but do not convert alternating to direct or direct to alternating current.

Manufacturing electronic component-type transformers **334416**

335312 Motor and Generator Manufacturing[CAN]

This U.S. industry comprises establishments primarily engaged in manufacturing electric motors (except internal combustion engine starting motors), power generators (except battery charging alternators for internal combustion engines), and motor generator sets (except turbine generator set units). This industry includes establishments rewinding armatures on a factory basis.

Manufacturing electric outboard motors **333618**
Manufacturing gas, steam, or hydraulic turbine generator set units **333611**
Rewinding armatures, not on a factory basis, **811310**
Manufacturing complete welding and soldering equipment **333992**

335313 Switchgear and Switchboard Apparatus Manufacturing[US]

This U.S. industry comprises establishments primarily engaged in manufacturing switchgear and switchboard apparatus.

Manufacturing relays **335314**
Manufacturing switches for electronic applications **334419**
Manufacturing snap, pushbutton, and similar switches for electrical circuits **335931**

335314 Relay and Industrial Control Manufacturing[US]

This U.S. industry comprises establishments primarily engaged in manufacturing relays, motor starters and controllers, and other industrial controls and control accessories.

Manufacturing environmental and appliance control equipment **334512**
Manufacturing instruments for controlling industrial process variables **334513**

3359 Other Electrical Equipment and Component Manufacturing

This industry group comprises establishments manu-facturing electrical equipment and components (except electric lighting equipment, household-type appliances, transformers, switchgear, relays, motors, and generators).

33591 Battery Manufacturing

This industry comprises establishments primarily engaged in manufacturing primary and storage batteries.

335911 Storage Battery Manufacturing[US]

This U.S. industry comprises establishments primarily engaged in manufacturing storage batteries.

Manufacturing primary batteries **335912**

335912 Primary Battery Manufacturing[US]

This U.S. industry comprises establishments primarily engaged in manufacturing wet or dry primary batteries.

Manufacturing storage batteries **335911**

33592 Communication and Energy Wire and Cable Manufacturing

This industry comprises establishments insulating fiber-optic cable, and manufacturing insulated non-ferrous wire and cable from nonferrous wire drawn in other establishments.

Drawing nonferrous wire **331**
Manufacturing cable sets consisting of insulated wire and various connectors for electronic applications **33441**
Manufacturing extension cords, appliance cords, and similar electrical cord sets from purchased, insulated wire or cable **33599**
Manufacturing unsheathed fiber-optic materials **32721**

335921 Fiber Optic Cable Manufacturing[US]

This U.S. industry comprises establishments primarily engaged in manufacturing insulated fiber-optic cable from purchased fiber-optic strand.

Manufacturing unsheathed fiber-optic materials **32721**
Manufacturing insulated nonferrous wire and cable from purchased wire **335929**

335

335929 Other Communication and Energy Wire Manufacturing[US]

This U.S. industry comprises establishments primarily engaged in manufacturing insulated wire and cable of nonferrous metals from purchased wire.

Manufacturing cable sets consisting of insulated wire and various connectors for electronic applications **334419**

Manufacturing extension cords, appliance cords, and similar electrical cord sets from purchased insulated wire **335999**

Drawing and insulating copper wire in the same establishment **331422**

Drawing nonferrous wire (except copper and aluminum) **331491**

33593 Wiring Device Manufacturing

This industry comprises establishments primarily engaged in manufacturing current-carrying wiring devices and noncurrent-carrying wiring devices for wiring electrical circuits.

Manufacturing ceramic and glass insulators **327**

Manufacturing electronic component-type connectors, sockets, and switches **33441**

335931 Current-Carrying Wiring Device Manufacturing[US]

This U.S. industry comprises establishments primarily engaged in manufacturing current-carrying wiring devices.

Manufacturing electronic component-type connectors **334417**

Manufacturing noncurrent-carrying wiring devices **335932**

Manufacturing electronic component-type sockets and switches **334419**

335932 Noncurrent-Carrying Wiring Device Manufacturing[US]

This U.S. industry comprises establishments primarily engaged in manufacturing noncurrent-carrying wiring devices.

Manufacturing porcelain and ceramic insulators **327113**

Manufacturing current-carrying wiring devices **335931**

Manufacturing glass insulators **32721**

33599 All Other Electrical Equipment and Component Manufacturing

This industry comprises establishments primarily engaged in manufacturing electrical equipment (except electric lighting equipment, household-type appliances, transformers, motors, generators, switchgear, relays, industrial controls, batteries, communication and energy wire and cable, and wiring devices).

Manufacturing lighting equipment **3351**

Manufacturing household-type appliances **3352**

Manufacturing transformers, motors, generators, switchgear, relays, and industrial controls **33531**

Manufacturing batteries **33591**

Manufacturing communication and energy wire **33592**

Manufacturing current-carrying and noncurrent-carrying wiring devices **33593**

Manufacturing carbon or graphite gaskets **33999**

Manufacturing electronic component-type rectifiers, voltage regulating integrated circuits, power converting integrated circuits, electronic capacitors, electronic resistors, and similar devices **33441**

335991 Carbon and Graphite Product Manufacturing[US]

This U.S. industry comprises establishments primarily engaged in manufacturing carbon, graphite, and metal-graphite brushes and brush stock; carbon or graphite electrodes for thermal and electrolytic uses; carbon and graphite fibers; and other carbon, graphite, and metal-graphite products.

Manufacturing carbon or graphite gaskets **339991**

335999 All Other Miscellaneous Electrical Equipment and Component Manufacturing[US]

This U.S. industry comprises establishments primarily engaged in manufacturing industrial and commercial electric apparatus and other equipment (except lighting equipment, household appliances, transformers, motors, generators, switchgear, relays, industrial controls, batteries, communication and energy wire and cable, wiring devices, and carbon and graphite products). This industry includes power converters (i.e., AC to DC and DC to AC), power supplies, surge suppressors, and similar equipment for industrial-type and consumer-type equipment.

Manufacturing lighting equipment **3351**

Manufacturing household-type appliances **3352**

Manufacturing transformers, motors, generators, switchgear, relays, and industrial controls **33531**

Manufacturing primary and storage batteries **33591**

Manufacturing communication and energy wire and cable from purchased wire **33592**

Manufacturing current-carrying and noncurrent-carrying wiring devices **33593**

Manufacturing electronic component-type rectifiers (except semiconductor) **334419**

Manufacturing semiconductor rectifiers, voltage regulating integrated circuits, power converting integrated circuits, and similar semiconductor devices **334413**

Manufacturing electronic component-type capacitors and condensers **334414**

Manufacturing carbon and graphite products **335991**

---

336 Transportation Equipment Manufacturing

336

Industries in the Transportation Equipment Manufacturing subsector produce equipment for transporting people and goods. Transportation equipment is a type of machinery. An entire subsector is devoted to this activity because of the significance of its economic size in all three North American countries.

Establishments in this subsector utilize production processes similar to those of other machinery manufacturing establishments, bending, forming, welding, machining, and assembling metal or plastic parts into components and finished products. However, the assembly of components and subassemblies and their further assembly into finished vehicles tends to be a more common production process in this subsector than in the Machinery Manufacturing subsector. NAICS has industry groups for the manufacture of equipment for each mode of transport—road, rail, air, and water. Parts for motor vehicles warrant a separate industry group because of their importance and because parts manufacture requires less assembly, and the establishments that manufacture only parts are not as vertically integrated as those that make complete vehicles. Land use motor vehicle equipment not designed for highway operation (e.g., agricultural equipment, construction equipment, and materials handling equipment) is classified in the appropriate NAICS subsector based on the type and use of the equipment.

3361 Motor Vehicle Manufacturing

33611 Automobile and Light Duty Motor Vehicle Manufacturing

This industry comprises establishments primarily engaged in (1) manufacturing complete automobile and light duty motor vehicles (i.e., body and chassis or unibody) or (2) manufacturing chassis only.

Manufacturing car, truck, and bus bodies and assembling vehicles on a purchased chassis and manufacturing kit cars for highway use **33621**

336111 Automobile Manufacturing[US]

This U.S. industry comprises establishments primarily engaged in (1) manufacturing complete automobiles (i.e., body and chassis or unibody) or (2) manufacturing automobile chassis only.

Manufacturing car bodies and assembling vehicles on a purchased chassis and manufacturing kit cars for highway use **336211**

336112 Light Truck and Utility Vehicle Manufacturing[US]

This U.S. industry comprises establishments primarily engaged in (1) manufacturing complete light trucks and utility vehicles (i.e., body and chassis) or (2) manufacturing light truck and utility vehicle chassis only. Vehicles made include light duty vans, pickup trucks, minivans, and sport utility vehicles.

Manufacturing truck and bus bodies and assembling vehicles on a purchased chassis **336211**

336120 Heavy Duty Truck Manufacturing

This industry comprises establishments primarily engaged in (1) manufacturing heavy duty truck chassis and assembling complete heavy duty trucks, buses, heavy duty motor homes, and other special purpose heavy duty motor vehicles for highway use or (2) manufacturing heavy duty truck chassis only.

Manufacturing truck and bus bodies and assembling vehicles on a purchased chassis **336211**

Manufacturing motor homes on purchased chassis **336213**

Manufacturing vans, minivans, and light trucks **336112**

Manufacturing military armored vehicles **336992**

Manufacturing off highway construction equipment **333120**

3362 Motor Vehicle Body and Trailer Manufacturing

33621 Motor Vehicle Body and Trailer Manufacturing

This industry comprises establishments primarily engaged in (1) manufacturing motor vehicle bodies and cabs or (2) manufacturing truck, automobile and utility trailers, truck trailer chassis, detachable trailer bodies and detachable trailer chassis. The products made may be sold separately or may be assembled on purchased chassis and sold as complete vehicles. Motor homes are units where the motor and the living quarters are contained in the same integrated unit, while travel trailers are designed to be towed by a motor unit, such as an automobile or a light truck.

Making manufactured homes (i.e., mobile homes) **32199**

Customizing automotive vehicle and trailer interiors (i.e. van conversions) on an individual basis **81112**

Manufacturing light duty motor home chassis and assembling complete motor homes **33611**

Manufacturing heavy duty truck chassis and assembling heavy duty trucks, buses, motor homes, and other special purpose heavy duty motor vehicles for highway use **33612**

336211 Motor Vehicle Body Manufacturing[CAN]

This U.S. industry comprises establishments primarily engaged in manufacturing truck and bus bodies and cabs and automobile bodies. The products made may be sold separately or may be assembled on purchased chassis and sold as complete vehicles.

Manufacturing heavy duty chassis and assembling heavy duty trucks, buses, motor homes, and other special purpose heavy duty motor vehicles for highway use **336120**

336212 Truck Trailer Manufacturing[CAN]

This U.S. industry comprises establishments primarily engaged in manufacturing truck trailers, truck trailer chassis, cargo container chassis, detachable trailer bodies, and detachable trailer chassis for sale separately.

Manufacturing utility trailers, light-truck trailers, and travel trailers **336214**

336213 Motor Home Manufacturing[US]

This U.S. industry comprises establishments primarily engaged in (1) manufacturing motor homes on purchased chassis and/or (2) manufacturing conversion vans on an assembly line basis. Motor homes are units where the motor and the living quarters are integrated in the same unit.

Manufacturing light duty motor homes chassis and assembling complete motor homes **336112**

Customizing automotive vehicle and trailer interiors (i.e. van conversions) on an individual basis **811121**

Producing manufactured homes (i.e., mobile homes) **321991**

336214 Travel Trailer and Camper Manufacturing[US]

This U.S. industry comprises establishments primarily engaged in one or more of the following: (1) manufacturing travel trailers and campers designed to attach to motor vehicles; (2) manufacturing pickup coaches (i.e., campers) and caps (i.e., covers) for mounting on pickup trucks; and (3) manufacturing automobile, utility and light-truck trailers. Travel trailers do not have their own motor but are designed to be towed by a motor unit, such as an automobile or a light truck.

Making manufactured homes (i.e., mobile homes) designed to accept permanent water, sewer, and utility connections and equipped with wheels, but not intended for regular highway use, **321991**

3363 Motor Vehicle Parts Manufacturing

33631 Motor Vehicle Gasoline Engine and Engine Parts Manufacturing

This industry comprises establishments primarily engaged in manufacturing and/or rebuilding motor vehicle gasoline engines, and engine parts, whether or not for vehicular use.

Manufacturing wiring harnesses and other vehicular electrical and electronic equipment **33632**

Manufacturing transmission and power train equipment **33635**
Manufacturing radiators **33639**
Manufacturing steering and suspension components **33633**
Manufacturing parts for machine repair and equipment parts (except electric) on a job or shop basis **33271**
Manufacturing rubber and plastic belts and hoses without fittings **32622**
Manufacturing stationary and diesel engines **33361**

336311 Carburetor, Piston, Piston Ring, and Valve Manufacturing^{US}

This U.S. industry comprises establishments primarily engaged in manufacturing and/or rebuilding carburetors, pistons, piston rings, and engine intake and exhaust valves.

Manufacturing parts for machine repair and equipment parts (except electric) on a job or shop basis **332710**

336312 Gasoline Engine and Engine Parts Manufacturing^{US}

This U.S. industry comprises establishments primarily engaged in manufacturing and/or rebuilding gasoline motor vehicle engines and gasoline motor vehicle engine parts, excluding carburetors, pistons, piston rings, and valves.

Manufacturing wiring harnesses and other vehicular electrical and electronic equipment **336322**
Manufacturing transmission and power train equipment **336350**
Manufacturing radiators **336399**
Manufacturing steering and suspension components **336330**
Manufacturing rubber and plastic belts and hoses without fittings **326220**
Manufacturing stationary and diesel engines **333618**

33632 Motor Vehicle Electrical and Electronic Equipment Manufacturing

This industry comprises establishments primarily engaged in (1) manufacturing vehicular lighting and/or (2) manufacturing and/or rebuilding motor vehicle electrical and electronic equipment. The products made can be used for all types of transportation equipment (i.e., aircraft, automobiles, trains, ships).

Manufacturing automotive lamps **33511**
Manufacturing batteries **33591**
Manufacturing electric motors for motor vehicles (including electric vehicles) **33531**

Manufacturing railway traffic control signals and passenger car alarms **33429**
Manufacturing car stereos **33431**

336321 Vehicular Lighting Equipment Manufacturing^{US}

This U.S. industry comprises establishments primarily engaged in manufacturing vehicular lighting fixtures.

Manufacturing automotive lamps (i.e., bulbs) **335110**

336322 Other Motor Vehicle Electrical and Electronic Equipment Manufacturing^{US}

This U.S. industry comprises establishments primarily engaged in manufacturing and/or rebuilding electrical and electronic equipment for motor vehicles and internal combustion engines.

Manufacturing vehicular lighting equipment **336321**
Manufacturing automotive lamps **335110**
Manufacturing batteries **335911**
Manufacturing electric motors for electric vehicles **335312**
Manufacturing railway traffic control signals and passenger car alarms **334290**
Manufacturing car stereos **334310**

336330 Motor Vehicle Steering and Suspension Components (except Spring) Manufacturing

This industry comprises establishments primarily engaged in manufacturing and/or rebuilding motor vehicle steering mechanisms and suspension components (except springs).

Manufacturing springs **33261**

336340 Motor Vehicle Brake System Manufacturing

This industry comprises establishments primarily engaged in manufacturing and/or rebuilding motor vehicle brake systems and related components.

Manufacturing rubber and plastics belts and hoses without fittings **326220**

336350 Motor Vehicle Transmission and Power Train Parts Manufacturing

This industry comprises establishments primarily engaged in manufacturing and/or rebuilding motor vehicle transmission and power train parts.

336360 Motor Vehicle Seating and Interior Trim Manufacturing

This industry comprises establishments primarily engaged in manufacturing motor vehicle seating, seats, seat frames, seat belts, and interior trimmings.

Manufacturing convertible tops for vehicles and those manufacturing air bags **336399**

336370 Motor Vehicle Metal Stamping

This industry comprises establishments primarily engaged in manufacturing motor vehicle stampings, such as fenders, tops, body parts, trim, and molding.

Manufacturing stampings (except motor vehicle) **332116**

33639 Other Motor Vehicle Parts Manufacturing

This industry comprises establishments primarily engaged in manufacturing and/or rebuilding motor vehicle parts and accessories (except motor vehicle gasoline engines and engine parts, motor vehicle electrical and electronic equipment, motor vehicle steering and suspension components, motor vehicle brake systems, motor vehicle transmission and power train parts, motor vehicle seating and interior trim, and motor vehicle stampings).

Manufacturing motor vehicle gasoline engines and engine parts **33631**
Manufacturing motor vehicle electrical and electronic equipment **33632**
Manufacturing motor vehicle steering and suspension components **33633**
Manufacturing motor vehicle brake systems **33634**
Manufacturing motor vehicle transmission and power train parts **33635**
Manufacturing motor vehicle seating and interior trim **33636**
Manufacturing motor vehicle stampings **33637**
Manufacturing air-conditioning systems and compressors (except motor vehicle air-conditioning systems) **33341**

336391 Motor Vehicle Air-Conditioning Manufacturing[US]

This U.S. industry comprises establishments primarily engaged in manufacturing air-conditioning systems and compressors for motor vehicles, such as automobiles, trucks, buses, aircraft, farm machinery, construction machinery, and other related vehicles.

Manufacturing air-conditioning systems and compressors (except motor vehicle air-conditioning systems) **333415**

336399 All Other Motor Vehicle Parts Manufacturing[US]

This U.S. industry comprises establishments primarily engaged in manufacturing and/or rebuilding motor vehicle parts and accessories (except motor vehicle gasoline engines and engine parts, motor vehicle electrical and electronic equipment, motor vehicle steering and suspension components, motor vehicle brake systems, motor vehicle transmission and power train parts, motor vehicle seating and interior trim, motor vehicle stampings, and motor vehicle air-conditioning systems and compressors).

Manufacturing motor vehicle gasoline engines and engine parts **33631**
Manufacturing motor vehicle electrical and electronic equipment **33632**
Manufacturing motor vehicle steering and suspension components **336330**
Manufacturing motor vehicle brake systems **336340**
Manufacturing motor vehicle transmission and power train parts **336350**
Manufacturing motor vehicle seating and interior trim **336360**
Manufacturing motor vehicle stampings **336370**
Manufacturing motor vehicle air-conditioning systems and compressors **336391**

3364 Aerospace Product and Parts Manufacturing

33641 Aerospace Product and Parts Manufacturing

This industry comprises establishments primarily engaged in one or more of the following: (1) manufacturing complete aircraft, missiles, or space vehicles; (2) manufacturing aerospace engines, propulsion units, auxiliary equipment or parts; (3) developing and making prototypes of aerospace products; (4) aircraft conversion (i.e., major modifications to systems); and (5) complete aircraft or propulsion systems overhaul and rebuilding (i.e., periodic restoration of aircraft to original design specifications).

Manufacturing space satellites **33422**
Repair of aircraft or aircraft engines (except overhauling, conversion, and rebuilding) **48819**
Aerospace research and development (except prototype production) **54171**
Manufacturing aircraft engine intake and exhaust valves, pistons, or engine filters **33631**
Manufacturing of aircraft seating **33636**
Manufacturing aeronautical, navigational, and guidance systems and instruments **33451**

Manufacturing aircraft engine electrical (aeronautical electrical) equipment or aircraft lighting fixtures **33632**
Manufacturing of aircraft fluid power subassemblies **33291**

336411 Aircraft Manufacturing^{US}

This U.S. industry comprises establishments primarily engaged in one or more of the following: (1) manufacturing or assembling complete aircraft; (2) developing and making aircraft prototypes; (3) aircraft conversion (i.e., major modifications to systems); and (4) complete aircraft overhaul and rebuilding (i.e., periodic restoration of aircraft to original design specifications).

Manufacturing guided missiles and space vehicles **336414**
Repair of aircraft (except overhauling, conversion, and rebuilding) **488190**
Aircraft research and development (except prototype production) **541710**

336412 Aircraft Engine and Engine Parts Manufacturing^{US}

This U.S. industry comprises establishments primarily engaged in one or more of the following: (1) manufacturing aircraft engines and engine parts; (2) developing and making prototypes of aircraft engines and engine parts; (3) aircraft propulsion system conversion (i.e., major modifications to systems); and (4) aircraft propulsion systems overhaul and rebuilding (i.e., periodic restoration of aircraft propulsion system to original design specifications).

Manufacturing guided missile and space vehicle propulsion units and parts **336415**
Manufacturing aircraft intake and exhaust valves and pistons **336311**
Manufacturing aircraft internal combustion engine filters **336312**
Repair of aircraft engines (except overhauling, conversion, and rebuilding) **488190**
Research and development establishments primarily engaged in aircraft engine and engine parts R&D (except prototype production) **541710**
Manufacturing aeronautical instruments **334511**

336413 Other Aircraft Parts and Auxiliary Equipment Manufacturing^{US}

This U.S. industry comprises establishment primarily engaged in (1) manufacturing aircraft parts or auxiliary equipment (except engines and aircraft fluid power subassemblies) and/or (2) developing and making prototypes of aircraft parts and auxiliary

equipment. Auxiliary equipment includes such items as crop dusting apparatus, armament racks, inflight refueling equipment, and external fuel tanks.

Manufacturing aircraft engines and engine parts **336412**
Manufacturing aeronautical instruments **334511**
Manufacturing aircraft lighting fixtures **336321**
Manufacturing aircraft engine electrical (aeronautical electrical) equipment **336322**
Manufacturing guided missile and space vehicle parts and auxiliary equipment **336419**
Manufacturing of aircraft fluid power subassemblies **332912**
Manufacturing of aircraft seating **336360**
Research and development establishments primarily engaged in aircraft parts and auxiliary equipment R&D (except prototype production) **541710**

336414 Guided Missile and Space Vehicle Manufacturing^{US}

This U.S. industry comprises establishments primarily engaged in (1) manufacturing complete guided missiles and space vehicles and/or (2) developing and making prototypes of guided missile or space vehicles.

Manufacturing space satellites **334220**
Guided missile and space vehicle research and development (except prototype production) **541710**

336415 Guided Missile and Space Vehicle Propulsion Unit and Propulsion Unit Parts Manufacturing^{US}

This U.S. industry comprises establishments primarily engaged in (1) manufacturing guided missile and/or space vehicle propulsion units and propulsion unit parts and/or (2) developing and making prototypes of guided missile and space vehicle propulsion units and propulsion unit parts.

Guided missile and space propulsion unit and propulsion unit parts research and development (except prototype production) **541710**

336419 Other Guided Missile and Space Vehicle Parts and Auxiliary Equipment Manufacturing^{US}

This U.S. comprises establishments primarily engaged in (1) manufacturing guided missile and space vehicle parts and auxiliary equipment (except guided missile and space vehicle propulsion units and propulsion unit parts) and/or (2) developing and making prototypes of guided missile and space vehicle parts and auxiliary equipment.

336

Manufacturing navigational and guidance systems **334511**

Manufacturing guided missile and space vehicle propulsion units and propulsion unit parts **336415**

Guided missile and space vehicle parts and auxiliary equipment research and development (except prototype production) **541710**

3365 Railroad Rolling Stock Manufacturing

336510 Railroad Rolling Stock Manufacturing

This industry comprises establishments primarily engaged in one or more of the following: (1) manufacturing and/or rebuilding locomotives, locomotive frames and parts; (2) manufacturing railroad, street, and rapid transit cars and car equipment for operation on rails for freight and passenger service; and (3) manufacturing rail layers, ballast distributors, rail tamping equipment and other railway track maintenance equipment.

Manufacturing mining rail cars **333131**

Manufacturing locomotive fuel lubricating or cooling medium pumps **333911**

Repairing railroad and transit cars **488210**

Repairing railroad cars and locomotive engines, but not owned by railroad or local transit companies, **811310**

3366 Ship and Boat Building

33661 Ship and Boat Building

This industry comprises establishments primarily engaged in operating shipyards or boat yards (i.e., ship or boat manufacturing facilities). Shipyards are fixed facilities with drydocks and fabrication equipment capable of building a ship, defined as watercraft typically suitable or intended for other than personal or recreational use. Boats are defined as watercraft typically suitable or intended for personal use. Activities of shipyards include the construction of ships, their repair, conversion and alteration, the production of prefabricated ship and barge sections, and specialized services, such as ship scaling.

Manufacturing rubber boats **32629**

Manufacturing nonrigid (i.e., inflatable) plastics boats **32619**

Ship repairs performed in floating drydocks **48839**

336611 Ship Building and Repairing^{CAN}

This U.S. industry comprises establishments primarily engaged in operating a shipyard. Shipyards are fixed facilities with drydocks and fabrication equipment capable of building a ship, defined as watercraft typically suitable or intended for other than personal or recreational use. Activities of shipyards include the construction of ships, their repair, conversion and alteration, the production of prefabricated ship and barge sections, and specialized services, such as ship scaling.

Ship repairs performed in floating drydocks **488390**

336612 Boat Building^{CAN}

This U.S. industry comprises establishments primarily engaged in building boats. Boats are defined as watercraft not built in shipyards and typically of the type suitable or intended for personal use.

Ship building or ship repairs performed in a shipyard **336611**

Manufacturing rubber boats and life rafts **326299**

Manufacturing nonrigid (i.e., inflatable) plastics boats **326199**

3369 Other Transportation Equipment Manufacturing

This industry group comprises establishments primarily engaged in manufacturing transportation equipment (except motor vehicles and parts, aerospace products and parts, railroad rolling stock, ship building, and boat manufacturing).

33699 Other Transportation Equipment Manufacturing

This industry comprises establishments primarily engaged in manufacturing motorcycles, bicycles, metal tricycles, complete military armored vehicles, tanks, self-propelled weapons, vehicles pulled by draft animals, and other transportation equipment (except motor vehicles, boats, ships, railroad rolling stock, and aerospace products), including parts thereof.

Manufacturing ships and boats **33661**

Manufacturing aerospace products and parts **33641**

Manufacturing motor vehicle parts **3363**

Manufacturing children's vehicles (except bicycles and metal tricycles) **33993**

Manufacturing railroad rolling stock **33651**

Manufacturing motor vehicles **3361**

336991 Motorcycle, Bicycle, and Parts Manufacturing[US]

This U.S. industry comprises establishments primarily engaged in manufacturing motorcycles, bicycles, tricycles, and similar equipment, and parts.

Manufacturing children's vehicles (except bicycles and metal tricycles) **339932**

Manufacturing golf carts and other similar personnel carriers **336999**

336992 Military Armored Vehicle, Tank, and Tank Component Manufacturing[US]

This U.S. industry comprises establishments primarily engaged in manufacturing complete military armored vehicles, combat tanks, specialized components

for combat tanks, and self-propelled weapons.

Manufacturing nonarmored military universal carriers **336112**

336999 All Other Transportation Equipment Manufacturing[US]

This U.S. industry comprises establishments primarily engaged in manufacturing transportation equipment (except motor vehicles, motor vehicle parts, boats, ships, railroad rolling stock, aerospace products, motorcycles, bicycles, armored vehicles and tanks).

Manufacturing motorcycles, bicycles and parts **336991**

Manufacturing military armored vehicles, tanks, and tank components **336992**

Manufacturing ships and boats **33661**

Manufacturing aerospace products and parts **33641**

Manufacturing motor vehicle parts **3363**

Manufacturing railroad rolling stock **336510**

Manufacturing motor vehicles **3361**

337

337 Furniture and Related Product Manufacturing

Industries in the Furniture and Related Product Manufacturing subsector make furniture and related articles, such as mattresses, window blinds, cabinets, and fixtures. The processes used in the manufacture of furniture include the cutting, bending, molding, laminating, and assembly of such materials as wood, metal, glass, plastics, and rattan. However, the production process for furniture is not solely bending metal, cutting and shaping wood, or extruding and molding plastics. Design and fashion trends play an important part in the production of furniture. The integrated design of the article for both esthetic and functional qualities is also a major part of the process of manufacturing furniture. Design services may be performed by the furniture establishment's work force or may be purchased from industrial designers.

Furniture may be made of any material, but the most common ones used in North America are metal and wood. Furniture manufacturing establishments may specialize in making articles primarily from one material. Some of the equipment required to make a wooden table, for example, is different from that used to make a metal one. However, furniture is usually made from several materials. A wooden table might have metal brackets, and a wooden chair a fabric or plastics seat. Therefore, in NAICS, furniture initially is classified based on the type of furniture (application for which it is designed) rather than the material used. For example, an upholstered sofa is treated as household furniture, although it may also be used in hotels or offices. When classifying furniture according to the component material from which it is made, furniture made from more than one material is classified based on the material used in the frame, or if there is no frame, the predominant component material. Upholstered household furniture (excluding kitchen and dining room chairs with upholstered seats) is classified without regard to the frame material. Kitchen or dining room chairs with upholstered seats are classified according to the frame material.

Furniture may be made on a stock or custom basis and may be shipped assembled or unassembled (i.e., knockdown). The manufacture of furniture parts and frames is included in this subsector.

Some of the processes used in furniture manufacturing are similar to processes that are used in other segments of manufacturing. For example, cutting and assembly occurs in the production of wood trusses that are classified in Subsector 321, Wood Product Manufacturing. However, the multiple processes that distinguish wood furniture manufacturing from wood product manufacturing warrant inclusion of wooden furniture manufacturing in the Furniture and Related Product Manufacturing subsector. Metal furniture manufacturing uses techniques that are also employed in the manufacturing of roll-formed products classified in Subsector 332, Fabricated Metal Product Manufacturing. The molding process for plastics furniture is similar to the molding of other plastics products. However, plastics furniture producing establishments tend to specialize in furniture.

NAICS attempts to keep furniture manufacturing together, but there are two notable exceptions: seating for transportation equipment and laboratory and hospital furniture. These exceptions are related to that fact that some of the aspects of the production process for these products, primarily the design, are highly integrated with that of other manufactured goods, namely motor vehicles and health equipment.

337I Household and Institutional Furniture and Kitchen Cabinet Manufacturing

This industry group comprises establishments manufacturing household-type furniture, such as living room, kitchen and bedroom furniture and institutional (i.e., public building) furniture, such as furniture for schools, theaters, and churches.

337110 Wood Kitchen Cabinet and Countertop Manufacturing

This industry comprises establishments primarily engaged in manufacturing wood or plastics laminated on wood kitchen cabinets, bathroom vanities, and countertops (except freestanding). The cabinets and counters may be made on a stock or custom basis.

Manufacturing metal kitchen and bathroom cabinets (except freestanding) **337124**
Manufacturing plastics countertops **326199**
Manufacturing stone countertops **327991**
Manufacturing wood or plastics laminated on wood countertops (except kitchen and bathroom) **337215**

33712 Household and Institutional Furniture Manufacturing

This industry comprises establishments primarily

engaged in manufacturing household-type and public building furniture (i.e., library, school, theater, and church furniture). The furniture may be made on a stock or custom basis and may be assembled or unassembled (i.e., knockdown).

Manufacturing laboratory and hospital furniture **33911**
Manufacturing wood or plastics laminated on wood kitchen cabinets, bathroom vanities, and countertops (except freestanding) **33711**
Manufacturing office-type furniture and/or office or store fixtures **33721**
Repairing or refinishing furniture **81142**

337121 Upholstered Household Furniture Manufacturing^{CAN}

This U.S. industry comprises establishments primarily engaged in manufacturing upholstered household-type furniture. The furniture may be made on a stock or custom basis.

Reupholstering furniture or upholstering frames to individual order **811420**
Wood kitchen and dining room chairs with upholstered seats or backs **337122**
Metal kitchen and dining room chairs with upholstered seats or backs **337124**
Kitchen and dining room chairs (except wood and metal) with upholstered seats or backs **337125**

337122 Nonupholstered Wood Household Furniture Manufacturing[US]

This U.S. industry comprises establishments primarily engaged in manufacturing nonupholstered wood household-type furniture and freestanding cabinets (except television, radio, and sewing machine cabinets). The furniture may be made on a stock or custom basis and may be assembled or unassembled (i.e., knockdown).

Manufacturing reed, rattan, plastics and similar furniture **337125**
Manufacturing wood or plastics laminated on wood kitchen cabinets, bathroom vanities, and countertops (except freestanding) **337110**
Manufacturing wood television, stereo, loudspeaker, and sewing machine cabinets (i.e., housings) **337129**
Repairing or refinishing furniture **811420**

337124 Metal Household Furniture Manufacturing[US]

This U.S. industry comprises establishments primarily engaged in manufacturing metal household-type furniture and freestanding cabinets. The furniture may be made on a stock or custom basis and may be assembled or unassembled (i.e., knockdown).

Manufacturing metal laboratory and hospital furniture including beds **33911**

337125 Household Furniture (except Wood and Metal) Manufacturing[US]

This U.S. industry comprises establishments primarily engaged in manufacturing household-type furniture of materials other than wood or metal, such as plastics, reed, rattan, wicker, and fiberglass. The furniture may be made on a stock or custom basis and may be assembled or unassembled (i.e., knockdown).

Manufacturing concrete, ceramic, or stone furniture **327**
Manufacturing upholstered household-type furniture **337121**
Manufacturing metal household-type furniture **337124**
Manufacturing nonupholstered wood household-type furniture **337122**

337127 Institutional Furniture Manufacturing[CAN]

This U.S. industry comprises establishments primarily engaged in manufacturing institutional-type furniture (e.g., library, school, theater, and church furniture). The furniture may be made on a stock or custom basis and may be assembled or unassembled (i.e., knockdown).

Manufacturing laboratory and hospital furniture **33911**
Manufacturing wood kitchen cabinets, wood bathroom vanities, and countertops designed for permanent installation **337110**
Manufacturing office-type furniture and/or office or store fixtures **33721**
Repairing or refinishing furniture **811420**

337129 Wood Television, Radio, and Sewing Machine Cabinet Manufacturing[US]

This industry comprises establishments primarily engaged in manufacturing wood cabinets used as housings by television, stereo, loudspeaker, and sewing machine manufacturers.

Manufacturing plastics housings used by television, stereo, loudspeaker, and sewing machine manufacturers **326199**
Manufacturing metal housings used by television, stereo, loudspeaker, and sewing machine manufacturers **332322**
Manufacturing freestanding wood household-type cabinets (e.g., entertainment centers, stands) for consumer electronics **337122**
Manufacturing freestanding metal household-type cabinets (e.g., entertainment centers, stands) for consumer electronics **337124**
Manufacturing freestanding household-type cabinets (e.g., entertainment centers, stands) (except wood and metal) for consumer electronics **337125**

3372 Office Furniture (including Fixtures) Manufacturing

33721 Office Furniture (including Fixtures) Manufacturing

This industry comprises establishments primarily engaged in manufacturing office furniture and/or office and store fixtures. The furniture may be made on a stock or custom basis and may be assembled or unassembled (i.e., knockdown).

Manufacturing millwork on a factory basis **32191**
Manufacturing household-type and institutional-type furniture **33712**
Manufacturing refrigerated cabinets, showcases, and display cases **33341**
Manufacturing metal safes and vaults **33299**

337211 Wood Office Furniture Manufacturing[US]

This U.S. industry comprises establishments primarily engaged in manufacturing wood office-type furniture. The furniture may be made on a stock or custom basis and may be assembled or unassembled (i.e., knockdown).

337

337212 Custom Architectural Woodwork and Millwork Manufacturing[US]

This U.S. industry comprises establishments primarily engaged in manufacturing custom designed interiors consisting of architectural woodwork and fixtures utilizing wood, wood products, and plastics laminates. All of the industry output is made to individual order on a job shop basis and requires skilled craftsmen as a labor input. A job might include custom manufacturing of display fixtures, gondolas, wall shelving units, entrance and window architectural detail, sales and reception counters, wall paneling, and matching furniture.

Manufacturing millwork on a factory basis **321918**
Manufacturing wood office-type furniture on a stock or custom basis **337211**
Manufacturing wood office-type furniture and store fixtures on a stock basis **337215**

337214 Office Furniture (except Wood) Manufacturing[CAN]

This U.S. industry comprises establishments primarily engaged in manufacturing nonwood office-type furniture. The furniture may be made on a stock or custom basis and may be assembled or unassembled (i.e., knockdown).

337215 Showcase, Partition, Shelving, and Locker Manufacturing[CAN]

This U.S. industry comprises establishments primarily engaged in manufacturing wood and nonwood office and store fixtures, shelving, lockers, frames, partitions, and related fabricated products of wood and nonwood materials, including plastics laminated fixture tops. The products are made on a stock basis and may be assembled or unassembled (i.e., knockdown). Establishments exclusively making furniture parts (e.g., frames) are included in this industry.

Manufacturing refrigerated cabinets, showcases, and display cases **333415**
Manufacturing metal safes and vaults **332999**
Manufacturing wood or plastics laminated kitchen and bathroom countertops **337110**

3379 Other Furniture Related Product Manufacturing

This industry group comprises establishments manufacturing furniture related products, such as mattresses, blinds, and shades.

337910 Mattress Manufacturing

This industry comprises establishments primarily engaged in manufacturing innerspring, box spring, and noninnerspring mattresses, including mattresses for waterbeds.

Manufacturing individual wire springs **33261**
Manufacturing inflatable mattresses **326**

337920 Blind and Shade Manufacturing

This industry comprises establishments primarily engaged in manufacturing one or more of the following: venetian blinds, other window blinds, shades; curtain and drapery rods, poles; and/or curtain and drapery fixtures. The blinds and shades may be made on a stock or custom basis and may be made of any material.

Manufacturing canvas awnings **314912**
Manufacturing curtains and draperies **314121**

339 Miscellaneous Manufacturing

Industries in the Miscellaneous Manufacturing subsector make a wide range of products that cannot readily be classified in specific NAICS subsectors in manufacturing. Processes used by these establishments vary significantly, both among and within industries. For example, a variety of manufacturing processes are used in manufacturing sporting and athletic goods that include products, such as tennis racquets and golf balls. The processes for these products differ from each other, and the processes differ significantly from the fabrication processes used in making dolls or toys, the melting and shaping of precious metals to make jewelry, and the bending, forming, and assembly used in making medical products.

The industries in this subsector are defined by what is made rather than how it is made. Although individual establishments might be appropriately classified elsewhere in the NAICS structure, for historical continuity, these product-based industries were maintained. In most cases, no one process or material predominates for an industry.

Establishments in this subsector manufacture products as diverse as medical equipment and supplies, jewelry, sporting goods, toys, and office supplies.

3391 Medical Equipment and Supplies Manufacturing

33911 Medical Equipment and Supplies Manufacturing

This industry comprises establishments primarily engaged in manufacturing medical equipment and supplies. Examples of products made by these establishments are laboratory apparatus and furniture, surgical and medical instruments, surgical appliances and supplies, dental equipment and supplies, orthodontic goods, dentures, and orthodontic appliances.

Manufacturing laboratory instruments, X-ray apparatus, electromedical apparatus (including electronic hearing aids), and thermometers (except medical) **33451**
Manufacturing molded glass lens blanks **32721**
Manufacturing molded plastics lens blanks **32619**
Retailing and grinding prescription eyeglasses **44613**
Manufacturing sporting goods helmets and protective equipment **33992**

339111 Laboratory Apparatus and Furniture Manufacturing[US]

This U.S. industry comprises establishments primarily engaged in manufacturing laboratory apparatus and laboratory and hospital furniture (except dental). Examples of products made by these establishments are hospital beds, operating room tables, laboratory balances and scales, furnaces, ovens, centrifuges, cabinets, cases, benches, tables, and stools.

Manufacturing dental laboratory apparatus and furniture **339114**
Manufacturing laboratory instruments **334516**

339112 Surgical and Medical Instrument Manufacturing[US]

This U.S. industry comprises establishments primarily engaged in manufacturing medical, surgical, ophthalmic, and veterinary instruments and apparatus

(except electrotherapeutic, electromedical and irradiation apparatus). Examples of products made by these establishments are syringes, hypodermic needles, anesthesia apparatus, blood transfusion equipment, catheters, surgical clamps, and medical thermometers.

Manufacturing electromedical and electrotherapeutic apparatus **334510**
Manufacturing surgical and orthopedic appliances **339113**
Manufacturing dental equipment, dental supplies, dental laboratory apparatus, and dental laboratory furniture **339114**
Manufacturing laboratory apparatus and laboratory and hospital furniture (except dental) **339111**
Manufacturing thermometers (except medical) **334519**

339113 Surgical Appliance and Supplies Manufacturing[US]

This U.S. industry comprises establishments primarily engaged in manufacturing surgical appliances and supplies. Examples of products made by these establishments are orthopedic devices, prosthetic appliances, surgical dressings, crutches, surgical sutures, and personal industrial safety devices (except protective eyeware).

Manufacturing dental equipment, dental supplies, dental laboratory apparatus, and dental laboratory furniture **339114**
Manufacturing laboratory apparatus and laboratory and hospital furniture (except dental) **339111**
Manufacturing electronic hearing aids **334510**
Manufacturing industrial protective eyeware **339115**
Manufacturing sporting goods helmets and protective equipment **339920**

339114 Dental Equipment and Supplies Manufacturing[US]

This U.S. industry comprises establishments primarily engaged in manufacturing dental equipment and supplies used by dental laboratories and offices of dentists, such as dental chairs, dental instrument delivery systems, dental hand instruments, and dental impression material.

Manufacturing dentures, crowns, bridges, and orthodontic appliances customized for individual application **339116**

Manufacturing laboratory apparatus and laboratory and hospital furniture (except dental) **339111**

339115 Ophthalmic Goods Manufacturing[US]

This U.S. industry comprises establishments primarily engaged in manufacturing ophthalmic goods. Examples of products made by these establishments are prescription eyeglasses (except manufactured in a retail setting), contact lenses, sunglasses, eyeglass frames, and reading glasses made to standard powers.

Manufacturing molded glass lens blanks **327212**

Manufacturing molded plastics lens blanks **326199**

Retailing and grinding prescription eyeglasses **446130**

339116 Dental Laboratories[US]

This U.S. industry comprises establishments primarily engaged in manufacturing dentures, crowns, bridges, and orthodontic appliances customized for individual application.

Manufacturing dental equipment and supplies **339114**

3399 Other Miscellaneous Manufacturing

33991 Jewelry and Silverware Manufacturing

This industry comprises establishments primarily engaged in one or more of the following: (1) manufacturing, engraving, chasing, or etching jewelry; (2) manufacturing metal personal goods (i.e., small articles carried on or about the person, such as compacts or cigarette cases); (3) manufacturing, engraving, chasing, or etching precious metal solid, precious metal clad, or pewter cutlery and flatware; (4) manufacturing, engraving, chasing, or etching personal metal goods (i.e., small articles carried on or about the person, such as compacts or cigarette cases); (5) stamping coins; (6) manufacturing unassembled jewelry parts and stock shop products, such as sheet, wire, and tubing; (7) cutting, slabbing, tumbling, carving, engraving, polishing, or faceting precious or semiprecious stones and gems; (8) recutting, repolishing, and setting gem stones; and (9) drilling, sawing, and peeling cultured and costume pearls.

Manufacturing nonprecious and precious plated metal cutlery and flatware **33221**

Manufacturing nonprecious plated ware (except cutlery, flatware) **33299**

Engraving, chasing, or etching nonprecious and precious plated metal flatware and other plated ware and plated jewelry **33281**

Manufacturing synthetic stones or gem stones **32799**

Manufacturing personal goods (except metal) carried on or about the person, such as compacts and cigarette cases, **31699**

339911 Jewelry (except Costume) Manufacturing[US]

This U.S. industry comprises establishments primarily engaged in one or more of the following: (1) manufacturing, engraving, chasing, or etching precious metal solid or precious metal clad jewelry; (2) manufacturing, engraving, chasing, or etching personal goods (i.e., small articles carried on or about the person, such as compacts or cigarette cases) made of precious solid or clad metal; and (3) stamping coins.

Manufacturing, engraving, chasing, or etching costume jewelry and nonprecious metal personal goods **339914**

Manufacturing jewelers' materials or performing lapidary work **339913**

Plating jewelry **332813**

339912 Silverware and Hollowware Manufacturing[US]

This U.S. industry comprises establishments primarily engaged in manufacturing, engraving, chasing, or etching precious metal solid, precious metal clad, or pewter flatware and other plated ware.

Manufacturing nonprecious and precious plated metal cutlery and flatware **332211**

Manufacturing nonprecious metal plated ware (except cutlery and flatware) **332999**

Engraving, chasing, or etching nonprecious and precious plated metal cutlery, flatware and other plated ware **332812**

Manufacturing, engraving, chasing, or etching precious (except precious plated) metal jewelry and personal goods **339911**

339913 Jewelers' Material and Lapidary Work Manufacturing[US]

This U.S. industry comprises establishments primarily engaged in one or more of the following: (1) manufacturing unassembled jewelry parts and stock shop products, such as sheet, wire, and tubing; (2) cutting, slabbing, tumbling, carving, engraving, polishing or faceting precious or semiprecious stones and gems; (3) recutting, repolishing, and setting gem stones; and (4) drilling, sawing, and peeling cultured pearls.

Manufacturing synthetic stones **327999**
Manufacturing costume pearls **339914**

339914 Costume Jewelry and Novelty Manufacturing[US]

This U.S. industry comprises establishments primarily engaged in (1) manufacturing, engraving, chasing, and etching costume jewelry; and/or (2) manufacturing, engraving, chasing, or etching nonprecious metal personal goods (i.e., small articles carried on or about the person, such as compacts or cigarette cases). This industry includes establishments primarily engaged in manufacturing precious plated jewelry and precious plated personal goods.

Manufacturing, engraving, chasing, or etching precious (except precious plated) metal jewelry and novelties **339911**
Manufacturing personal goods (except metal) carried on or about the person, such as compacts and cigarette cases, **316993**
Manufacturing synthetic stones **327999**

339920 Sporting and Athletic Goods Manufacturing

This industry comprises establishments primarily engaged in manufacturing sporting and athletic goods (except apparel and footwear).

Manufacturing athletic apparel **315**
Manufacturing athletic footwear **316219**
Manufacturing small arms and small arms ammunition **33299**

33993 Doll, Toy, and Game Manufacturing

This industry comprises establishments primarily engaged in manufacturing dolls, toys, and games, such as complete dolls, doll parts, doll clothes, action figures, toys, games (including electronic), hobby kits, and children's vehicles (except metal bicycles and tricycles).

Manufacturing bicycles and metal tricycles **33699**
Manufacturing sporting and athletic goods **33992**
Manufacturing coin-operated game machines **33999**
Manufacturing electronic video game cartridges and reproducing video game software **33461**

339931 Doll and Stuffed Toy Manufacturing[US]

This U.S. industry comprises establishments prima-

rily engaged in manufacturing complete dolls, doll parts, and doll clothes, action figures, and stuffed toys.

Manufacturing toys (except stuffed) **339932**

339932 Game, Toy, and Children's Vehicle Manufacturing[US]

This U.S. industry comprises establishments primarily engaged in manufacturing games (including electronic), toys, and children's vehicles (except bicycles and metal tricycles).

Manufacturing dolls and stuffed toys **339931**
Manufacturing metal tricycles and bicycles **336991**
Manufacturing sporting and athletic goods **339920**
Manufacturing coin-operated game machines **339999**
Mass reproducing electronic video game cartridges **334611**

33994 Office Supplies (except Paper) Manufacturing

This industry comprises establishments primarily engaged in manufacturing office supplies. Examples of products made by these establishments are pens, pencils, felt tip markers, crayons, chalk, pencil sharpeners, staplers, hand operated stamps, modeling clay, and inked ribbons.

Manufacturing writing, drawing, and india inks **32599**
Manufacturing drafting tables and boards **33712**
Manufacturing rubber erasers **32629**
Manufacturing paper office supplies **322**
Manufacturing manifold business forms, blankbooks, and looseleaf binders **32311**
Manufacturing inkjet cartridges **32591**

339941 Pen and Mechanical Pencil Manufacturing[US]

This U.S. industry comprises establishments primarily engaged in manufacturing pens, ballpoint pen refills and cartridges, mechanical pencils, and felt tipped markers.

Manufacturing nonmechanical pencils and pencil leads **339942**
Manufacturing writing, drawing, and india inks **325998**
Manufacturing rubber erasers **326299**

339942 Lead Pencil and Art Good Manufacturing[US]

This U.S. industry comprises establishments primarily engaged in manufacturing nonmechanical pencils, and art goods. Examples of products made by

339

these establishments are pencil leads, crayons, chalk, framed blackboards, pencil sharpeners, staplers, artists' palettes and paints, and modeling clay.

Manufacturing mechanical pencils **339941**
Manufacturing writing, drawing, and india inks **325998**
Manufacturing rubber erasers **326299**
Manufacturing paper office supplies **322**
Printing manifold business forms and manufacturing blankbooks and looseleaf binders and devices **32311**
Manufacturing drafting tables and boards **337127**

339943 Marking Device Manufacturing[US]

This U.S. industry comprises establishments primarily engaged in manufacturing marking devices, such as hand operated stamps, embossing stamps, stamp pads, and stencils.

Manufacturing felt tipped markers **339941**

339944 Carbon Paper and Inked Ribbon Manufacturing[US]

This U.S. industry comprises establishments primarily engaged in manufacturing carbon paper and inked ribbons.

Manufacturing inkjet cartridges **325910**

339950 Sign Manufacturing

This industry comprises establishments primarily engaged in manufacturing signs and related displays of all materials (except printing paper and paperboard signs, notices, displays).

Printing advertising specialties or printing paper and paperboard signs, notices, and displays **32311**
Manufacturing die-cut paperboard displays **322299**
Sign lettering and painting **541890**

33999 All Other Miscellaneous Manufacturing

This industry comprises establishments primarily engaged in miscellaneous manufacturing (except medical equipment and supplies, jewelry and flatware, sporting and athletic goods, dolls, toys, games, office supplies [except paper], and signs).

Manufacturing medical equipment and supplies **3391**
Manufacturing jewelry and flatware **33991**

Manufacturing sporting and athletic goods **33992**
Manufacturing dolls, toys, and games **33993**
Manufacturing office supplies (except paper) **39994**
Manufacturing signs **33995**
Manufacturing concrete burial vaults **32739**
Manufacturing Christmas tree glass ornaments and glass lamp shades **32721**
Manufacturing Christmas tree lighting sets **33512**
Manufacturing beauty and barber chairs **33712**
Manufacturing burnt wood articles **32199**
Dressing and bleaching furs **31611**
Manufacturing paper, textile, and metal lamp shades **33512**
Manufacturing plastics lamp shades **32619**
Manufacturing matches **32599**
Manufacturing metal products, such as metal combs and hair curlers, **33299**
Manufacturing plastics products, such as plastics combs and hair curlers, **32619**
Manufacturing electric hair clippers for use on humans **33521**

339991 Gasket, Packing, and Sealing Device Manufacturing[US]

This industry comprises establishments primarily engaged in manufacturing gaskets, packing, and sealing devices of all materials.

339992 Musical Instrument Manufacturing[US]

This U.S. industry comprises establishments primarily engaged in manufacturing musical instruments (except toys).

Manufacturing toy musical instruments **339932**

339993 Fastener, Button, Needle, and Pin Manufacturing[US]

This U.S. industry comprises establishments primarily engaged in manufacturing fasteners, buttons, needles, pins, and buckles (except precious metals or precious and semiprecious stones and gems).

Manufacturing buttons, pins, and buckles made of precious metals or precious and semiprecious stones and gems **339911**
Manufacturing hypodermic and suture needles **339112**
Manufacturing phonograph and styli needles **334419**

339994 Broom, Brush, and Mop Manufacturing[US]

This U.S. industry comprises establishments prima-

rily engaged in manufacturing brooms, mops, and brushes.

339995 Burial Casket Manufacturing[US]

This U.S. industry comprises establishments primarily engaged in manufacturing burial caskets, cases, and vaults (except concrete).

Manufacturing concrete burial vaults **327390**

339999 All Other Miscellaneous Manufacturing[US]

This U.S. industry comprises establishments primarily engaged in miscellaneous manufacturing (except medical equipment and supplies, jewelry and flatware, sporting and athletic goods, dolls, toys, games, office supplies [except paper], musical instruments, fasteners, buttons, needles, pins, brooms, brushes, mops, and burial caskets).

Manufacturing medical equipment and supplies **3391**
Manufacturing jewelry and flatware **33991**
Manufacturing sporting and athletic goods **339920**

Manufacturing dolls, toys, and games **33993**
Manufacturing office supplies (except paper) **39994**
Manufacturing signs **33995**
Manufacturing gasket, packing, and sealing devices **339991**
Manufacturing musical instruments **339992**
Manufacturing fasteners, buttons, needles, and pins **339993**
Manufacturing brooms, brushes, and mops **339994**
Manufacturing burial caskets **339995**
Manufacturing Christmas tree glass ornaments and glass lamp shades **327215**
Manufacturing Christmas tree lighting sets **335129**
Manufacturing beauty and barber chairs **337127**
Manufacturing burnt wood articles **321999**
Dressing and bleaching furs **316110**
Manufacturing paper, textile, and metal lamp shades **335121**
Manufacturing plastics lamp shades **326199**
Manufacturing matches **325998**
Manufacturing metal products, such as metal combs and hair curlers, **332999**
Manufacturing plastics products, such as plastics combs and hair curlers, **326199**
Manufacturing electric hair clippers for use on humans **335211**

421

SECTOR 42: WHOLESALE TRADE

OVERVIEW OF THIS SECTOR AS A WHOLE

The Wholesale Trade sector comprises establishments engaged in wholesaling merchandise, generally without transformation, and rendering services incidental to the sale of merchandise. The wholesaling process is an intermediate step in the distribution of merchandise. Wholesalers are organized to sell or arrange the purchase or sale of (a) goods for resale (i.e., goods sold to other wholesalers or retailers), (b) capital or durable nonconsumer goods, and (c) raw and intermediate materials and supplies used in production.

Wholesalers sell merchandise to other businesses and normally operate from a warehouse or office. These warehouses and offices are characterized by having little or no display of merchandise. In addition, neither the design nor the location of the premises is intended to solicit walk-in traffic. Wholesalers do not normally use advertising directed to the general public. Customers are generally reached initially via telephone, in-person marketing, or by specialized advertising that may include Internet and other electronic means. Follow-up orders are either vendor-initiated or client-initiated, generally based on previous sales, and typically exhibit strong ties between sellers and buyers. In fact, transactions are often conducted between wholesalers and clients that have long-standing business relationships.

This sector comprises two main types of wholesalers: those that sell goods on their own account and those that arrange sales and purchases for others for a commission or fee.

(1) Establishments that sell goods on their own account are known as wholesale merchants, distributors, jobbers, drop shippers, import/export merchants, and sales branches. These establishments typically maintain their own warehouse, where they receive and handle goods for their customers. Goods are generally sold without transformation, but may include integral functions, such as sorting, packaging, labeling, and other marketing services.

(2) Establishments arranging for the purchase or sale of goods owned by others or purchasing goods on a commission basis are known as agents and brokers, commission merchants, import/export agents and brokers, auction companies, and manufacturers' representatives. These establishments operate from offices and generally do not own or handle the goods they sell. Some wholesale establishments may be connected with a single manufacturer and promote and sell the particular manufacturers' products to a wide range of other wholesalers or retailers. Other wholesalers may be connected to a retail chain or a limited number of retail chains and only provide a variety of products needed by that particular retail operation(s). These wholesalers may obtain the products from a wide range of manufacturers. Still other wholesalers may not take title to the goods, but act as agents and brokers for a commission.

Although, in general, wholesaling normally denotes sales in large volumes, durable nonconsumer goods may be sold in single units. Sales of capital or durable nonconsumer goods used in the production of goods and services, such as farm machinery, medium and heavy duty trucks, and industrial machinery, are always included in wholesale trade.

421 Wholesale Trade, Durable Goods[US]

Industries in the Wholesale Trade, Durable Goods subsector sell or arrange the purchase or sale of capital or durable goods to other businesses. Durable goods are new or used items generally with a normal life expectancy of three years or more. Durable goods wholesale trade establishments are engaged in wholesaling products, such as motor vehicles, furniture, construction materials, machinery and equipment (including household-type appliances), metals and minerals (except petroleum), sporting goods, toys and hobby goods, recyclable materials, and parts. The detailed industries within the subsector are organized in the classification structure based on the products sold. Within an industry, the types of establishments may vary, including wholesale merchants and/or agents and brokers.

4211 Motor Vehicle and Motor Vehicle Parts and Supplies Wholesalers[US]

This industry group comprises establishments primarily engaged in wholesaling automobiles and other motor vehicles, motor vehicle supplies, tires, and new and used parts.

421110 Automobile and Other Motor Vehicle Wholesalers[US]

This industry comprises establishments primarily engaged in wholesaling new and used passenger automobiles, trucks, trailers, and other motor vehicles, such as motorcycles, motor homes, and snowmobiles.

421120 Motor Vehicle Supplies and New Parts Wholesalers[US]

This industry comprises establishments primarily engaged in wholesaling motor vehicle supplies, accessories, tools, and equipment; and new motor vehicle parts (except new tires and tubes).

Wholesaling new and/or used tires and tubes **421130**
Wholesaling automotive chemicals (except lubricating oils and greases)
   422690
Wholesaling lubricating oils and greases **422720**

421130 Tire and Tube Wholesalers[US]

This industry comprises establishments primarily engaged in wholesaling new and/or used tires and tubes for passenger and commercial vehicles.

421140 Motor Vehicle Parts (Used) Wholesalers[US]

This industry comprises establishments primarily engaged in wholesaling used motor vehicle parts (except used tires and tubes) and establishments primarily engaged in dismantling motor vehicles for the purpose of selling the parts.

Dismantling motor vehicles for the purpose of selling scrap **421930**

4212 Furniture and Home Furnishing Wholesalers[US]

421210 Furniture Wholesalers[US]

This industry comprises establishments primarily engaged in wholesaling furniture (except hospital beds, medical furniture, and drafting tables).

Wholesaling partitions, shelving, lockers, and store fixtures **421440**
Wholesaling hospital beds and medical furniture **421450**
Wholesaling drafting tables **421490**

421220 Home Furnishing Wholesalers[US]

This industry comprises establishments primarily engaged in wholesaling home furnishings and/or housewares.

Wholesaling electrical household-type goods **421620**

4213 Lumber and Other Construction Materials Wholesalers[US]

421310 Lumber, Plywood, Millwork, and Wood Panel Wholesalers[US]

This industry comprises establishments primarily

engaged in wholesaling lumber; plywood; reconstituted wood fiber products; wood fencing; doors and windows and their frames (all materials); wood roofing and siding; and/or other wood or metal millwork.

Wholesaling timber and timber products, such as railroad ties, logs, firewood, and pulpwood, **421990**

421320 Brick, Stone, and Related Construction Material Wholesalers[US]

This industry comprises establishments primarily engaged in wholesaling stone, cement, lime, construction sand, and gravel; brick; asphalt and concrete mixtures; and/or concrete, stone, and structural clay products.

Wholesaling refractory brick and other refractory products **421840**

421330 Roofing, Siding, and Insulation Material Wholesalers[US]

This industry comprises establishments primarily engaged in wholesaling nonwood roofing and nonwood siding and insulation materials.

Wholesaling wood roofing and wood siding **421310**

421390 Other Construction Material Wholesalers[US]

This industry comprises (1) establishments primarily engaged in wholesaling manufactured homes (i.e., mobile homes) and/or prefabricated buildings and (2) establishments primarily engaged in wholesaling construction materials (except lumber, plywood, millwood, wood panel, brick, stone, roofing, siding, and insulation material).

Wholesaling products of the primary metals industries **421510**
Wholesaling lumber; plywood; reconstituted wood fiber products; wood fencing; doors, windows, and their frames; wood roofing and wood siding; and other wood or metal millwork **421310**
Wholesaling stone, cement, lime, construction sand and gravel; brick; asphalt and concrete mixtures (except ready-mix concrete); and/or concrete, stone, and structural clay products **421320**
Wholesaling nonwood roofing and nonwood siding and insulation materials **421330**

4214 Professional and Commercial Equipment and Supplies Wholesalers[US]

This industry group comprises establishments primarily engaged in wholesaling photographic equipment and supplies; office, computer, and computer peripheral equipment; and medical, dental, hospital, ophthalmic, and other commercial and professional equipment and supplies.

421410 Photographic Equipment and Supplies Wholesalers[US]

This industry comprises establishments primarily engaged in wholesaling photographic equipment and supplies (except office equipment).

Wholesaling household-type video cameras **421620**

421420 Office Equipment Wholesalers[US]

This industry comprises establishments primarily engaged in wholesaling office machines and related equipment (except computers and computer peripheral equipment).

Wholesaling office furniture **421210**
Wholesaling computers and computer peripheral equipment **421430**

421430 Computer and Computer Peripheral Equipment and Software Wholesalers[US]

This industry comprises establishments primarily engaged in wholesaling computers, computer peripheral equipment, loaded computer boards, and/or computer software.

Wholesaling modems and other electronic communications equipment **421690**

421440 Other Commercial Equipment Wholesalers[US]

This industry comprises establishments primarily engaged in wholesaling commercial and related machines and equipment (except photographic equipment and supplies; office equipment; and computers and computer peripheral equipment and software) generally used in restaurants and stores.

Wholesaling photographic equipment and supplies **421410**

Wholesaling office machines and related equipment **421420**
Wholesaling computers, computer peripheral equipment, and computer software **421430**
Wholesaling laboratory scales and balances **421490**

421450 Medical, Dental, and Hospital Equipment and Supplies Wholesalers[US]

This industry comprises establishments primarily engaged in wholesaling medical professional equipment, instruments, and supplies (except ophthalmic equipment, instruments and goods used by ophthalmologists, optometrists, and opticians).

Wholesaling professional equipment, instruments and/or goods sold, prescribed, or used by ophthalmologists, optometrists, and opticians **421460**

421460 Ophthalmic Goods Wholesalers[US]

This industry comprises establishments primarily engaged in wholesaling professional equipment, instruments, and/or goods sold, prescribed, or used by ophthalmologists, optometrists, and opticians.

421490 Other Professional Equipment and Supplies Wholesalers[US]

This industry comprises establishments primarily engaged in wholesaling professional equipment and supplies (except ophthalmic goods and medical, dental, and hospital equipment and supplies).

Wholesaling medical professional equipment, instruments, and supplies used by medical and dental practitioners (except ophthalmic equipment, instruments, and goods used by ophthalmologists, optometrists, and opticians) and medical facilities **421450**
Wholesaling silverware and plated flatware **421940**
Wholesaling books **422920**

4215 Metal and Mineral (except Petroleum) Wholesalers[US]

421510 Metal Service Centers and Offices[US]

This industry comprises establishments primarily engaged in wholesaling products of the primary metals industries. Service centers maintain inventory and may perform functions, such as sawing, shearing, bending, leveling, cleaning, or edging, on a custom basis as part of sales transactions. Sales offices are usually affiliated or owned by a particular manufacturer and take orders but have no inventory.

Wholesaling gold, silver, and platinum **421940**
Wholesaling automotive, industrial, and other recyclable metal scrap **421930**

421520 Coal and Other Mineral and Ore Wholesalers^{US}

This industry comprises establishments primarily engaged in wholesaling coal, coke, metal ores, and/or nonmetallic minerals (except precious and semiprecious stones and minerals used in construction, such as sand and gravel).

Wholesaling nonmetallic minerals used in construction, such as sand and gravel, **421320**
Wholesaling crude petroleum **4227**

4216 Electrical Goods Wholesalers^{US}

421610 Electrical Apparatus and Equipment, Wiring Supplies, and Construction Material Wholesalers^{US}

This industry comprises establishments primarily engaged in wholesaling electrical construction materials; wiring supplies; electric light fixtures; light bulbs; and/or electrical power equipment for the generation, transmission, distribution, or control of electric energy.

421620 Electrical Appliance, Television, and Radio Set Wholesalers^{US}

This industry comprises establishments primarily engaged in wholesaling household-type electrical appliances, room air-conditioners, gas clothes dryers, and/or household-type audio or video equipment.

Wholesaling nonhousehold-type video cameras **421410**

421690 Other Electronic Parts and Equipment Wholesalers^{US}

This industry comprises establishments primarily engaged in wholesaling electronic parts and equip-

ment (except electrical apparatus and equipment, wiring supplies and construction material; and electrical appliances, television and radio sets).

Wholesaling household-type electrical appliances, televisions, and radio sets **421620**
Wholesaling computers, computer peripheral equipment, and loaded computer boards **421430**

4217 Hardware, and Plumbing and Heating Equipment and Supplies Wholesalers^{US}

421710 Hardware Wholesalers^{US}

This industry comprises establishments primarily engaged in wholesaling hardware, knives, or handtools.

Wholesaling nails, noninsulated wire, and screening **421510**
Wholesaling motor vehicle handtools and equipment **421120**
Wholesaling machinists' precision handtools **421830**

421720 Plumbing and Heating Equipment and Supplies (Hydronics) Wholesalers^{US}

This industry comprises establishments primarily engaged in wholesaling plumbing equipment, hydronic heating equipment, household-type gas appliances (except gas clothes dryers), and/or supplies.

Selling and installing plumbing, heating and air conditioning equipment **235110**
Wholesaling warm air heating and air-conditioning equipment **421730**

421730 Warm Air Heating and Air-Conditioning Equipment and Supplies Wholesalers^{US}

This industry comprises establishments primarily engaged in wholesaling warm air heating and air-conditioning equipment and supplies.

Wholesaling household-type electrical appliances and room air-conditioners **421620**
Wholesaling hydronic heating equipment **421720**

421740 Refrigeration Equipment and Supplies Wholesalers^{US}

This industry comprises establishments primarily engaged in wholesaling refrigeration equipment (except household-type refrigerators, freezers, and air-conditioners).

Wholesaling household-type refrigerators, freezers, and room air-conditioners **421620**

4218 Machinery, Equipment, and Supplies Wholesalers[US]

This industry group comprises establishments primarily engaged in wholesaling construction, mining, farm, garden, industrial, service establishment, and transportation machinery, equipment, and supplies.

421810 Construction and Mining (except Oil Well) Machinery and Equipment Wholesalers[US]

This industry comprises establishments primarily engaged in wholesaling specialized machinery, equipment, and related parts generally used in construction, mining (except oil well) and logging activities.

Wholesaling oil well machinery and equipment **421830**

421820 Farm and Garden Machinery and Equipment Wholesalers[US]

This industry comprises establishments primarily engaged in wholesaling specialized machinery, equipment, and related parts generally used in agricultural, farm, and lawn and garden activities.

421830 Industrial Machinery and Equipment Wholesalers[US]

This industry comprises establishments primarily engaged in wholesaling specialized machinery, equipment, and related parts generally used in manufacturing, oil well, and warehousing activities.

Wholesaling specialized machinery, equipment, and related parts generally used in construction, mining (except oil well), and logging activities **421810**

421840 Industrial Supplies Wholesalers[US]

This industry comprises establishments primarily engaged in wholesaling supplies used in machinery and equipment generally used in manufacturing, oil well, and warehousing activities.

Wholesaling hydraulic and pneumatic (fluid-power) pumps, motors, pistons, and valves **421830**

421850 Service Establishment Equipment and Supplies Wholesalers[US]

This industry comprises establishments primarily engaged in wholesaling specialized equipment and supplies of the type used by service establishments (except specialized equipment and supplies used in offices, stores, hotels, restaurants, schools, health and medical facilities, photographic facilities, as well as specialized equipment used in transportation and construction activities).

Wholesaling janitorial and automotive chemicals **422690**

421860 Transportation Equipment and Supplies (except Motor Vehicle) Wholesalers[US]

This industry comprises establishments primarily engaged in wholesaling transportation equipment and supplies (except marine pleasure craft and motor vehicles).

Wholesaling motor vehicles and motor vehicle parts **4211**

4219 Miscellaneous Durable Goods Wholesalers[US]

This industry group comprises establishments primarily engaged in wholesaling sporting, recreational, toy, hobby, and jewelry goods and supplies, and precious stones and metals.

421910 Sporting and Recreational Goods and Supplies Wholesalers[US]

This industry comprises establishments primarily engaged in wholesaling sporting goods and accessories; billiard and pool supplies; sporting firearms and ammunition; and/or marine pleasure craft, equipment, and supplies.

Wholesaling motor vehicles and trailers **421110**
Wholesaling motorized passenger golf carts **421860**
Wholesaling athletic apparel **4223**

421920 Toy and Hobby Goods and Supplies Wholesalers[US]

This industry comprises establishments primarily engaged in wholesaling games, toys, fire-works, playing cards, hobby goods and supplies, and/or related goods.

421930 Recyclable Material Wholesalers[US]

This industry comprises establishments primarily engaged in wholesaling scrap from automotive, industrial, and other recyclable materials. Included in this industry are auto wreckers primarily engaged in dismantling motor vehicles for the purpose of wholesaling scrap.

Dismantling motor vehicles for the purpose of selling used parts **421140**

421940 Jewelry, Watch, Precious Stone, and Precious Metal Wholesalers[US]

This industry comprises establishments primarily engaged in wholesaling jewelry, precious and semi-precious stones, precious metals and metal flatware, costume jewelry, watches, clocks, silverware, and/or jewelers' findings.

Wholesaling precious metal ores or concentrates **421520**

421990 Other Miscellaneous Durable Goods Wholesalers[US]

This industry comprises establishments primarily engaged in wholesaling durable goods (except motor vehicle and motor vehicle parts and supplies; furniture and home furnishings; lumber and other construction materials; professional and commercial equipment and supplies; metals and minerals (except petroleum); electrical goods; hardware, and plumbing and heating equipment and supplies; machinery, equipment and supplies; sporting and recreational goods and supplies; toy and hobby goods and supplies; recyclable materials; and jewelry, watches, precious stones and precious metals).

Wholesaling automobiles and other motor vehicles, motor vehicle supplies, tires, and new and used parts **4211**
Wholesaling furniture and home furnishings **4212**
Wholesaling lumber, plywood, millwork, wood panels, brick, stone, roofing, siding, and other nonelectrical construction materials **4213**
Wholesaling photographic; office; computer and computer peripheral; medical, dental, hospital, ophthalmic; and other commercial and professional equipment and supplies **4214**
Wholesaling coal and other minerals and ores and semifinished metal products **4215**
Wholesaling electrical goods **4216**
Wholesaling hardware, and plumbing, heating, air conditioning, and refrigeration equipment and supplies **4217**
Wholesaling construction, mining, farm, garden, industrial, service establishment, and transportation machinery, equipment and supplies **4218**
Wholesaling sporting goods and accessories; billiard and pool supplies; sporting firearms and ammunition; and/or marine pleasure craft, equipment, and supplies **421910**
Wholesaling toys, fireworks, playing cards, hobby goods and supplies and/or related goods **421920**
Wholesaling automotive, industrial, and other recyclable materials **421930**

422 Wholesale Trade, Nondurable Goods[US]

Industries in the Wholesale Trade, Nondurable Goods subsector sell or arrange the purchase or sale of nondurable goods to other businesses. Nondurable goods are items generally with a normal life expectancy of less than three years. Nondurable goods wholesale trade establishments are engaged in wholesaling products, such as paper and paper products, chemicals and chemical products, drugs, textiles and textile products, apparel, footwear, groceries, farm products, petroleum and petroleum products, alcoholic beverages, books, magazines, newspapers, flowers and nursery stock, and tobacco products.

The detailed industries within the subsector are organized in the classification structure based on the products sold. Within an industry, the types of establishments may vary, including wholesale merchants and/or agents and brokers.

4221 Paper and Paper Product Wholesalers[US]

422110 Printing and Writing Paper Wholesalers[US]
This industry comprises establishments primarily engaged in wholesaling bulk printing and/or writing paper generally on rolls for further processing.

Wholesaling stationery **422120**

422120 Stationery and Office Supplies Wholesalers[US]

This industry comprises establishments primarily

engaged in wholesaling stationery, office supplies and/or gift wrap.

Wholesaling bulk printing and/or writing paper **422110**

422130 Industrial and Personal Service Paper Wholesalers^{US}

This industry comprises establishments primarily engaged in wholesaling wrapping and other coarse paper, paperboard, converted paper (except stationery and office supplies), and/or related disposable plastics products.

Stationery, office supplies, and/or gift wrap **422120**

4222 Drugs and Druggists' Sundries Wholesalers^{US}

422210 Drugs and Druggists' Sundries Wholesalers^{US}

This industry comprises establishments primarily engaged in wholesaling biological and medical products; botanical drugs and herbs; and pharmaceutical products intended for internal and external consumption in such forms as ampoules, tablets, capsules, vials, ointments, powders, solutions, and suspensions.

Wholesaling surgical, dental, and hospital equipment **421450**

4223 Apparel, Piece Goods, and Notions Wholesalers^{US}

422310 Piece Goods, Notions, and Other Dry Goods Wholesalers^{US}

This industry comprises establishments primarily engaged in wholesaling piece goods, fabrics, yarns, thread and other notions, and/or hair accessories.

Converters who buy fabric goods in the grey, have them finished on a contract basis, and sell at wholesale **31331**

422320 Men's and Boys' Clothing and Furnishings Wholesalers^{US}

This industry comprises establishments primarily engaged in wholesaling men's and/or boys' clothing and furnishings.

Wholesaling unisex clothing and men's fur clothing **422330**

422330 Women's, Children's, and Infants' Clothing and Accessories Wholesalers^{US}

This industry comprises establishments primarily engaged in wholesaling (1) women's, children's, infants', and/or unisex clothing and accessories and/or (2) fur clothing.

422340 Footwear Wholesalers^{US}

This industry comprises establishments primarily engaged in wholesaling footwear (including athletic) of leather, rubber, and other materials.

4224 Grocery and Related Product Wholesalers^{US}

422410 General Line Grocery Wholesalers^{US}

This industry comprises establishments primarily engaged in wholesaling a general line (wide range) of groceries.

422420 Packaged Frozen Food Wholesalers^{US}

This industry comprises establishments primarily engaged in wholesaling packaged frozen foods (except dairy products).

Wholesaling frozen dairy products **422430**

422430 Dairy Product (except Dried or Canned) Wholesalers^{US}

This industry comprises establishments primarily engaged in wholesaling dairy products (except dried or canned).

Wholesaling dried or canned dairy products and dairy substitutes **422490**

422440 Poultry and Poultry Product Wholesalers^{US}

This industry comprises establishments primarily engaged in wholesaling poultry and/or poultry products (except canned and packaged frozen).

Wholesaling packaged frozen poultry **422420**
Wholesaling canned poultry **422490**

422450 Confectionery Wholesalers^{US}

This industry comprises establishments primarily engaged in wholesaling confectioneries; salted or roasted nuts; popcorn; potato, corn, and similar chips; and/or fountain fruits and syrups.

Wholesaling frozen pretzels **422420**

422460 Fish and Seafood Wholesalers[US]

This industry comprises establishments primarily engaged in wholesaling fish and seafood (except canned or packaged frozen).

Wholesaling packaged frozen fish and seafood **422420**
Wholesaling canned fish and seafood **422490**

422470 Meat and Meat Product Wholesalers[US]

This industry comprises establishments primarily engaged in wholesaling meats and meat products (except canned and packaged frozen) and/or lard.

Wholesaling packaged frozen meats **422420**
Wholesaling canned meats **422490**

422480 Fresh Fruit and Vegetable Wholesalers[US]

This industry comprises establishments primarily engaged in wholesaling fresh fruits and vegetables.

422490 Other Grocery and Related Products Wholesalers[US]

This industry comprises establishments primarily engaged in wholesaling groceries and related products (except a general line of groceries; packaged frozen food; dairy products [except dried and canned]; poultry products [except canned]; confectioneries; fish and seafood [except canned]; meat products [except canned]; and fresh fruits and vegetables). Included in this industry are establishments primarily engaged in bottling and wholesaling spring and mineral waters processed by others.

Wholesaling grains, field beans, livestock, and other farm product raw materials **4225**
Wholesaling beer, wine, and distilled alcoholic beverages **4228**
Bottling soft drinks **31211**
Wholesaling a general line of groceries **422410**
Wholesaling packaged frozen foods (except dairy) **422420**
Wholesaling dairy products **422430**
Wholesaling poultry and poultry products (except canned and packaged frozen) **422440**
Wholesaling confectioneries; salted or roasted nuts; popcorn; potato, corn, and similar chips; and/or fountain fruits and syrups **422450**
Wholesaling fish and seafoods (except canned and packaged frozen) **422460**

Wholesaling meats (except canned and packaged frozen) **422470**
Wholesaling fresh fruits and vegetables **422480**

4225 Farm Product Raw Material Wholesalers[US]

This industry group comprises establishments primarily engaged in wholesaling agricultural products (except raw milk, live poultry, and fresh fruit and vegetables), such as grains, field beans, livestock, and other farm product raw materials (excluding seeds).

422510 Grain and Field Bean Wholesalers[US]

This industry comprises establishments primarily engaged in wholesaling grains, such as corn, wheat, oats, barley, and unpolished rice; dry beans; and soybeans and other inedible beans. Included in this industry are establishments primarily engaged in operating country or terminal grain elevators primarily for the purpose of wholesaling.

Wholesaling field and garden seeds **422910**

422520 Livestock Wholesalers[US]

This industry comprises establishments primarily engaged in wholesaling livestock (except horses and mules).

Wholesaling horses and mules **422590**

422590 Other Farm Product Raw Material Wholesalers[US]

This industry comprises establishments primarily engaged in wholesaling farm products (except grain and field beans, livestock, raw milk, live poultry, and fresh fruits and vegetables).

Wholesaling raw milk **422430**
Wholesaling live poultry (except chicks) **422440**
Wholesaling grain, dry beans, and soybeans and other inedible beans **422510**
Wholesaling livestock (except horses and mules), such as cattle, hogs, sheep, and goats, **422520**

4226 Chemical and Allied Products Wholesalers[US]

This industry group comprises establishments primarily engaged in wholesaling chemicals; plastics materials and basic forms and shapes; and allied products.

422

422610 Plastics Materials and Basic Forms and Shapes Wholesalers[US]

This industry comprises establishments primarily engaged in wholesaling plastics materials and resins, and unsupported plastics film, sheet, sheeting, rod, tube, and other basic forms and shapes.

422690 Other Chemical and Allied Products Wholesalers[US]

This industry comprises establishments primarily engaged in wholesaling chemicals and allied products (except agricultural and medicinal chemicals, paints and varnishes, fireworks, and plastics materials and basic forms and shapes).

Wholesaling ammunition **4219**
Wholesaling biological and medical products; botanical drugs and herbs; and pharmaceutical products intended for internal and external consumption in such forms as ampoules, tablets, capsules, vials, ointments, powders, solutions, and suspensions **422210**
Wholesaling farm supplies, such as animal feeds, fertilizers, agricultural chemicals, pesticides, seeds and plant bulbs, **422910**
Wholesaling paints, and varnishes and similar coatings, pigments, wallpaper, and supplies, such as paint brushes and rollers, **422950**
Wholesaling lubricating oils and greases **422720**
Wholesaling fireworks **421920**

4227 Petroleum and Petroleum Products Wholesalers[US]

422710 Petroleum Bulk Stations and Terminals[US]

This industry comprises establishments with bulk liquid storage facilities primarily engaged in wholesaling crude petroleum and petroleum products, including liquefied petroleum gas.

Bulk storage of petroleum **493190**

422720 Petroleum and Petroleum Products Wholesalers (except Bulk Stations and Terminals)[US]

This industry comprises establishments primarily engaged in wholesaling petroleum and petroleum products (except from bulk liquid storage facilities).

Wholesaling crude petroleum and petroleum products from bulk liquid storage facilities **422710**

4228 Beer, Wine, and Distilled Alcoholic Beverage Wholesalers[US]

422810 Beer and Ale Wholesalers[US]

This industry comprises establishments primarily engaged in wholesaling beer, ale, porter, and other fermented malt beverages.

422820 Wine and Distilled Alcoholic Beverage Wholesalers[US]

This industry comprises establishments primarily engaged in wholesaling wine, distilled alcoholic beverages, and/or neutral spirits and ethyl alcohol used in blended wines and distilled liquors.

4229 Miscellaneous Nondurable Goods Wholesalers[US]

This industry group comprises establishments primarily engaged in wholesaling nondurable goods, such as farm supplies; books, periodicals and newspapers; flowers; nursery stock; paints; varnishes; tobacco and tobacco products; and other miscellaneous nondurable goods, such as cut Christmas trees and pet supplies.

422910 Farm Supplies Wholesalers[US]

This industry comprises establishments primarily engaged in wholesaling farm supplies, such as animal feeds, fertilizers, agricultural chemicals, pesticides, plant seeds, and plant bulbs.

Wholesaling pet food **422490**
Wholesaling grains **422510**
Wholesaling pet supplies **422990**

422920 Book, Periodical, and Newspaper Wholesalers[US]

This industry comprises establishments primarily engaged in wholesaling books, periodicals, and newspapers.

422930 Flower, Nursery Stock, and Florists' Supplies Wholesalers[US]

This industry comprises establishments primarily engaged in wholesaling flowers, florists' supplies, and/or nursery stock (except seeds and plant bulbs).

Wholesaling cut Christmas trees **422990**

422940 Tobacco and Tobacco Product Wholesalers[US]

This industry comprises establishments primarily engaged in wholesaling tobacco products, such as cigarettes, snuff, cigars, and pipe tobacco.

Wholesaling leaf tobacco **422590**

422950 Paint, Varnish, and Supplies Wholesalers[US]

This industry comprises establishments primarily engaged in wholesaling paints, varnishes, and similar coatings; pigments; wallpaper; and supplies, such as paint brushes and rollers.

Wholesaling artists' paints **422990**

422990 Other Miscellaneous Nondurable Goods Wholesalers[US]

This industry comprises establishments primarily engaged in wholesaling nondurable goods (except printing and writing paper; stationery and office supplies; industrial and personal service paper; drugs and druggists' sundries; apparel, piece goods, and notions; grocery and related products; farm product raw materials; chemical and allied products; petroleum and petroleum products; beer, wine, and distilled alcoholic beverages; farm supplies; books, periodicals and newspapers; flower, nursery stock and florists' supplies; tobacco and tobacco products; and paint, varnishes, wallpaper, and supplies).

Wholesaling advertising specialties **541870**
Wholesaling farm supplies **422910**
Wholesaling books, periodicals, and newspapers **422920**
Wholesaling flowers, nursery stock, and florists' supplies **422930**
Wholesaling tobacco and its products **422940**
Wholesaling paints, varnishes, and similar coatings; pigments; wallpaper; and supplies **422950**
Wholesaling bulk printing and/or writing paper **422110**
Wholesaling stationery, office supplies, and/or gift wrap **422120**
Wholesaling wrapping and other coarse paper, paperboard, converted paper (except stationery and office supplies), and related disposable plastics products **422130**
Wholesaling biological and medical products; botanical drugs and herbs; and pharmaceutical products intended for internal and external consumption **422210**
Wholesaling clothing and accessories, footwear, piece goods, yard goods, notions, and/or hair accessories **4223**
Wholesaling meat, poultry, seafood, confectioneries, fruits and vegetables; and other groceries **4224**
Wholesaling grains, field beans, livestock, and other farm product raw materials **4225**
Wholesaling chemicals; plastics materials and basic forms and shapes; and allied products **4226**
Wholesaling petroleum and petroleum products **4227**
Wholesaling beer, ale, wine, and distilled alcoholic beverages **4228**
Wholesaling pet foods **422490**

441

Sector 44-45: Retail Trade

Overview of this Sector as a Whole

The Retail Trade sector comprises establishments engaged in retailing merchandise, generally without transformation, and rendering services incidental to the sale of merchandise. The retailing process is the final step in the distribution of merchandise; retailers are, therefore, organized to sell merchandise in small quantities to the general public. This sector comprises two main types of retailers: store and nonstore retailers.

Store retailers operate fixed point-of-sale locations, located and designed to attract a high volume of walk-in customers. In general, retail stores have extensive displays of merchandise and use mass-media advertising to attract customers. They typically sell merchandise to the general public for personal or household consumption, but some also serve business and institutional clients. These include establishments, such as office supply stores, computer and software stores, building materials dealers, plumbing supply stores, and electrical supply stores. Catalog showrooms, gasoline services stations, automotive dealers, and mobile home dealers are treated as store retailers.

In addition to retailing merchandise, some types of store retailers are also engaged in the provision of after-sales services, such as repair and installation. For example, new automobile dealers, electronic and appliance stores, and musical instrument and supply stores often provide repair services. As a general rule, establishments engaged in retailing merchandise and providing after-sales services are classified in this sector.

The first eleven subsectors of retail trade are store retailers. The establishments are grouped into industries and industry groups typically based on one or more of the following criteria:

(a) The merchandise line or lines carried by the store; for example, specialty stores are distinguished from general-line stores.

(b) The usual trade designation of the establishments. This criterion applies in cases where a store type is well recognized by the industry and the public, but difficult to define strictly in terms of commodity lines carried; for example, pharmacies, hardware stores, and department stores.

(c) Capital requirements in terms of display equipment; for example, food stores have equipment requirements not found in other retail industries.

(d) Human resource requirements in terms of expertise; for example, the staff of an automobile dealer requires knowledge in financing, registering, and licensing issues that are not necessary in other retail industries.

Nonstore retailers, like store retailers, are organized to serve the general public, but their retailing methods differ. The establishments of this subsector reach customers and market merchandise with methods, such as the broadcasting of "infomercials," the broadcasting and publishing of direct-response advertising, the publishing of paper and electronic catalogs, door-to-door solicitation, in-home demonstration, selling from portable stalls (street vendors, except food), and distribution through vending machines. Establishments engaged in the direct sale (nonstore) of products, such as home heating oil dealers and home delivery newspaper routes.

The buying of goods for resale is a characteristic of retail trade establishments that particularly distinguishes them from establishments in the agriculture, manufacturing, and construction industries. For example, farms that sell their products at or from the point of production are not classified in retail, but rather in agriculture. Similarly, establishments that both manufacture and sell their products to the general public are not classified in retail, but rather in manufacturing. However, establishments that engage in processing activities incidental to retailing are classified in retail. This includes establishments, such as optical goods stores that do in-store grinding of lenses, and meat and seafood markets.

Wholesalers also engage in the buying of goods for resale, but they are not usually organized to serve the general public. They typically operate from a warehouse or office and neither the design nor the location of these premises is intended to solicit a high volume of walk-in traffic. Wholesalers supply institutional, industrial, wholesale, and retail clients; their operations are, therefore, generally organized to purchase, sell, and deliver merchandise in larger quantities. However, dealers of durable nonconsumer goods, such as farm machinery and heavy duty trucks, are included in wholesale trade even if they often sell these products in single units.

441 Motor Vehicle and Parts Dealers^{CAN}

Industries in the Motor Vehicle and Parts Dealers subsector retail motor vehicle and parts merchandise from fixed point-of-sale locations. Establishments in this subsector typically operate from a showroom and/or an open lot where the vehicles are on display. The display of vehicles and the related parts require little by way of display equipment. The personnel generally include both the sales and sales support staff familiar with the requirements for registering and financing a vehicle as well as a staff of parts experts and mechanics trained to provide repair and maintenance services for the vehicles. Specific industries have been included in this subsector to identify the type of vehicle being retailed.

Sales of capital or durable nonconsumer goods, such as medium and heavy-duty trucks, are always included in wholesale trade. These goods are virtually never sold through retail methods.

4411 Automobile Dealers ^{CAN}

This industry group comprises establishments primarily engaged in retailing new and used automobiles and light trucks, such as sport utility vehicles, and passenger and cargo vans.

441110 New Car Dealers ^{CAN}

This industry comprises establishments primarily engaged in retailing new automobiles and light trucks, such as sport utility vehicles, and passenger and cargo vans, or retailing these new vehicles in combination with activities, such as repair services, retailing used cars, and selling replacement parts and accessories.

Retailing used automobiles and light trucks without retailing new
    automobiles and light trucks **441120**
Providing automotive repair services without retailing new automotive
    vehicles **8111**

441120 Used Car Dealers ^{CAN}

This industry comprises establishments primarily engaged in retailing used automobiles and light trucks, such as sport utility vehicles, and passenger and cargo vans.

Retailing new automobiles and light trucks **441110**

4412 Other Motor Vehicle Dealers ^{CAN}

This industry group comprises establishments primarily engaged in retailing new and used vehicles (except automobiles, light trucks, such as sport utility vehicles, and passenger and cargo vans).

441210 Recreational Vehicle Dealers ^{CAN}

441

This industry comprises establishments primarily engaged in retailing new and/or used recreational vehicles commonly referred to as RVs or retailing these new vehicles in combination with activities, such as repair services and selling replacement parts and accessories.

Retailing new or used boat trailers and utility trailers **44122**
Retailing manufactured homes (i.e., mobile homes), parts, and equipment
    453930

44122 Motorcycle, Boat, and Other Motor Vehicle Dealers ^{CAN}

This industry comprises establishments primarily engaged in retailing new and used motor-cycles, boats, and other vehicles (except automobiles, light trucks, and recreational vehicles), or retailing these new vehicles in combination with activities, such as repair services and selling replacement parts and accessories.

Retailing new nonmotorized bicycles, surfboards, or wind sail boards **45111**
Retailing used nonmotorized bicycles, surfboards, or wind sail boards **45331**
Retailing new or used automobiles and light trucks **4411**
Retailing new or used recreational vehicles, such as travel trailers, **44121**
Retailing fuel and marine supplies at a marina **71393**

441221 Motorcycle Dealers^{US}

This U.S. industry comprises establishments primarily engaged in retailing new and/or used motorcycles, motor scooters, motor bikes, mopeds, off-road all-terrain vehicles, and personal watercraft, or retailing these new vehicles in combination with repair services and selling replacement parts and accessories.

Providing motorcycle repair services without retailing new motorcycles **811490**
Retailing new nonmotorized bicycles **451110**
Retailing used nonmotorized bicycles **453310**
Retailing new or used boats **441222**

441222 Boat Dealers^{US}

This U.S. industry comprises establishments primarily engaged in (1) retailing new and/or used boats or retailing new boats in combination with activities, such as repair services and selling replacement parts and accessories, and/or (2) retailing new and/or used outboard motors, boat trailers, marine supplies, parts, and accessories.

Retailing new surfboards or wind sail boards **451110**
Retailing used surfboards or wind sail boards **453310**
Providing boat repair services without retailing new boats **811490**
Retailing new or used personal watercraft **441221**
Operating docking and/or storage facilities for pleasure craft owners **713930**

441229 All Other Motor Vehicle Dealers^{US}

This U.S. industry comprises establishments primarily engaged in retailing new and/or used utility trailers and vehicles (except automobiles, light trucks, recreational vehicles, motorcycles, boats, motor scooters, motorbikes, off-road all-terrain vehicles, and personal watercraft) or retailing these new vehicles in combination with activities, such as repair services and selling replacement parts and accessories.

Retailing new automobiles and light trucks **441110**
Retailing used automobiles and light trucks **441120**
Retailing new or used recreational vehicles, such as travel trailers, **441210**

Retailing new or used motorcycles, motor scooters, motorbikes, off-road all-terrain vehicles, and personal watercraft **441221**
Retailing new or used boats, outboard motors, boat trailers, and marine supplies **441222**

4413 Automotive Parts, Accessories, and Tire Stores^{CAN}

441310 Automotive Parts and Accessories Stores^{CAN}

This industry comprises one or more of the following: (1) establishments known as automotive supply stores primarily engaged in retailing new, used, and/or rebuilt automotive parts and accessories; (2) automotive supply stores that are primarily engaged in both retailing automotive parts and accessories and repairing automobiles; and (3) establishments primarily engaged in retailing and installing automotive accessories.

Retailing automotive parts and accessories via electronic home shopping, mail-order, or direct sale **454**
Retailing new or used tires **441320**
Repairing and replacing automotive parts, such as transmissions, mufflers, brake linings, and glass (except establishments known as automotive supply stores), **81111**

441320 Tire Dealers^{CAN}

This industry comprises establishments primarily engaged in retailing new and/or used tires and tubes or retailing new tires in combination with automotive repair services.

Retailing tires via electronic home shopping, mail-order, or direct sale **454**
Providing automotive repair services without retailing new tires **811198**

442 Furniture and Home Furnishings Stores^{CAN}

Industries in the Furniture and Home Furnishings Stores subsector retail new furniture and home furnishings merchandise from fixed point-of-sale locations. Establishments in this subsector usually operate from showrooms and have substantial areas for the presentation of their products. Many offer interior decorating services in addition to the sale of products.

4421 Furniture Stores^{CAN}

442110 Furniture Stores^{CAN}

This industry comprises establishments primarily engaged in retailing new furniture, such as household furniture (e.g., baby furniture box springs and mattresses) and outdoor furniture; office furniture (except those sold in combination with office supplies and equipment); and/or furniture sold in combination with major appliances, home electronics, home furnishings, and/or floor covering.

Retailing furniture via electronic home shopping, mail-order, or direct sale **454**

Retailing used furniture **453310**

Retailing custom furniture made on premises **337**

Retailing new office furniture and a range of new office equipment and supplies **453210**

4422 Home Furnishings Stores^{CAN}

This industry group comprises establishments primarily engaged in retailing new home furnishings (except furniture).

442210 Floor Covering Stores^{CAN}

This industry comprises establishments primarily engaged in retailing new floor coverings, such as rugs and carpets, vinyl floor coverings, and floor tile (except ceramic or wood only); or retailing new floor coverings in combination with installation and repair services.

Retailing floor coverings via electronic home shopping, mail-order, or direct sale **454**

Installing floor coverings without retailing new floor coverings **235520**

Retailing ceramic floor tile or wood floor coverings only **444190**

Retailing used rugs and carpets **453310**

44229 Other Home Furnishings Stores^{CAN}

This industry comprises establishments primarily engaged in retailing new home furnishings (except furniture and floor coverings).

Retailing home furnishings via electronic home shopping, mail-order, or direct sale **454**

Retailing custom curtains and draperies made on premises **31412**

Retailing new mirrored glass, lighting fixtures, and new ceramic floor tile or wood floor coverings only **44419**

Retailing new furniture **44211**

Retailing new floor coverings (except ceramic or wood only) **44221**

Retailing used home furnishings **45331**

442291 Window Treatment Stores^{CAN}

This U.S. industry comprises establishments primarily engaged in retailing new window treatments, such as curtains, drapes, blinds, and shades.

Retailing window treatments via electronic home shopping, mail-order, or direct sale **454**

Retailing custom curtains and draperies made on premises **314121**

442299 All Other Home Furnishings Stores^{US}

This U.S. industry comprises establishments primarily engaged in retailing new home furnishings (except floor coverings, furniture, and window treatments).

Selling home furnishings via electronic home shopping, mail-order, or direct sale **454**

Retailing new mirrored glass lighting fixtures **444190**

Retailing new furniture **442110**

Retailing new floor coverings **442210**

Retailing new window treatments **442291**

Retailing used home furnishings **453310**

443

443 Electronics and Appliance Stores^{CAN}

Industries in the Electronics and Appliance Stores subsector retail new electronics and appliance merchandise from point-of-sale locations. Establishments in this subsector often operate from locations that have special provisions for floor displays requiring special electrical capacity to accommodate the proper demonstration of the products. The staff includes sales personnel knowledgeable in the characteristics and warranties of the line of goods retailed and may also include trained repair persons to handle the maintenance and repair of the electronic equipment and appliances. The classifications within this subsector are made principally on the type of product and knowledge required to operate each type of store.

4431 Electronics and Appliance Stores^{CAN}

This industry group comprises establishments primarily engaged in retailing the following new products: household-type appliances, cameras, computers, and other electronic goods.

44311 Appliance, Television, and Other Electronics Stores^{CAN}

This industry comprises establishments primarily engaged in retailing one of the following: (1) retailing an array of new household-type appliances and consumer-type electronic products, such as radios, televisions, and computers; (2) specializing in retailing a single line of new consumer-type electronic products (except computers); and (3) retailing these new products in combination with repair services.

Retailing new electronic products via electronic home shopping, mail-order, or direct sale **454**

Retailing new computers, computer peripherals, and prepackaged computer software without retailing other consumer-type electronic products or office equipment, office furniture, and office supplies; or retailing these products in combination with repair services **44312**

Retailing new computers, computer peripherals, and prepackaged software in combination with retailing new office equipment, office furniture, and office supplies **45321**

Retailing new sewing machines in combination with selling new sewing supplies, fabrics, patterns, yarns, and other needlework accessories **45113**

Retailing new electronic toys **45112**

Providing television or other electronic products repair services without retailing new televisions or electronic products **81121**

Providing appliance repair services without retailing new appliances **81141**

Retailing used appliance and electronic products **45331**

Retailing new still and motion picture cameras **44313**

Retailing automotive electronic sound systems **44131**

443111 Household Appliance Stores[US]

This U.S. industry comprises establishments known as appliance stores primarily engaged in retailing an array of new household appliances, such as refrigerators, dishwashers, ovens, irons, coffeemakers, hair dryers, electric razors, room air-conditioners, microwave ovens, sewing machines, and vacuum cleaners, or retailing new appliances in combination with appliance repair services.

Retailing household appliances via electronic home shopping, mail-order, or direct sale **454**

Retailing new sewing machines in combination with selling new sewing supplies, fabrics, patterns, yarns, and other needlework accessories **451130**

Providing appliance repair services without retailing new appliances **811412**

Retailing used appliances **453310**

443112 Radio, Television, and Other Electronics Stores[US]

This U.S. industry comprises: (1) establishments known as consumer electronics stores primarily engaged in retailing a general line of new consumer-type electronic products; (2) establishments specializing in retailing a single line of consumer-

type electronic products (except computers); or (3) establishments primarily engaged in retailing these new electronic products in combination with repair services.

Retailing electronic goods via electronic home shopping, mail-order, or direct sale **454**

Retailing automotive electronic sound systems **441310**

Retailing new computers, computer peripherals, and prepackaged computer software without retailing other consumer-type electronic products or office equipment, office furniture and office supplies; or retailing these new computer products in combination with repair services **443120**

Retailing new computers, computer peripherals, and prepackaged software in combination with retailing new office equipment, office furniture, and office supplies **453210**

Retailing new still and motion picture cameras **443130**

Providing television or other electronic equipment repair services without retailing new televisions or electronic products **81121**

Retailing new electronic toys **451120**

Retailing used electronics **453310**

443120 Computer and Software Stores[CAN]

This industry comprises establishments primarily engaged in retailing new computers, computer peripherals, and prepackaged computer software without retailing other consumer-type electronic products or office equipment, office furniture and office supplies; or retailing these new products in combination with repair and support services.

Retailing computers and software via electronic home shopping, mail-order, or direct sale **454**

Retailing new electronic toys, such as video games and handheld electronic games, **451120**

Providing computer repair services without retailing new computers **811212**

Retailing new computers, computer peripherals, and prepackaged software in combination with retailing new office equipment, office furniture, and office supplies **453210**

Retailing a general line of new electronic products or specializing in retailing a single line of consumer-type electronic products (except computers) **443112**

Retailing used computers, computer software, video games, and handheld electronic games **453310**

443130 Camera and Photographic Supplies Stores[CAN]

This industry comprises establishments primarily engaged in either retailing new cameras, photographic equipment, and photographic supplies or retailing new cameras and photographic equipment in combination with activities, such as repair services and film developing.

Retailing camera and photographic supplies via electronic home shopping, mail-order, or direct sale **454**

Retailing new video cameras **443112**

One-hour film developing without retailing a range of new photographic equipment and supplies **812922**

Providing repair services for photographic equipment without retailing new photographic equipment **811211**

Developing film and/or producing photographic prints, slides, and enlargements (except one-hour photofinishing labs) **812921**

Retailing used cameras and photographic equipment **453310**

---

444 Building Material and Garden Equipment and Supplies Dealers^{CAN}

Industries in the Building Material and Garden Equipment and Supplies Dealers subsector retail new building material and garden equipment and supplies merchandise from fixed point-of-sale locations. Establishments in this subsector have display equipment designed to handle lumber and related products and garden equipment and supplies that may be kept either indoors or outdoors under covered areas. The staff is usually knowledgeable in the use of the specific products being retailed in the construction, repair, and maintenance of the home and associated grounds.

444

4441 Building Material and Supplies Dealers^{CAN}

This industry group comprises establishments primarily engaged in retailing new building materials and supplies.

444110 Home Centers^{CAN}

This industry comprises establishments known as home centers primarily engaged in retailing a general line of new home repair and improvement materials and supplies, such as lumber, plumbing goods, electrical goods, tools, housewares, hardware, and lawn and garden supplies, with no one merchandise line predominating. The merchandise lines are normally arranged in separate departments.

444120 Paint and Wallpaper Stores^{CAN}

This industry comprises establishments known as paint and wallpaper stores primarily engaged in retailing paint, wallpaper, and related supplies.

444130 Hardware Stores^{CAN}

This industry comprises establishments known as hardware stores primarily engaged in retailing a general line of new hardware items, such as tools and builders' hardware.

Retailing hardware items via electronic home shopping, mail order, or direct sale **454**

Retailing a general line of home repair and improvement materials and supplies known as home centers **444110**

Retailing used hardware items **453310**

444190 Other Building Material Dealers^{CAN}

This industry comprises establishments (except those known as home centers, paint and wallpaper stores, and hardware stores) primarily engaged in retailing specialized lines of new building materials, such as lumber, fencing, glass, doors, plumbing fixtures and supplies, electrical supplies, prefabricated buildings and kits, and kitchen and bath cabinets and countertops to be installed.

Retailing building materials via electronic home shopping, mail-order, or direct sale **454**

Retailing used building materials **453310**

Providing carpentry/installation services for products **235510**

Installing plumbing fixtures and supplies **235110**

Installing electrical supplies, such as lighting fixtures and ceiling fans, **235310**

Making custom furniture (e.g. kitchen cabinets) **337**

Retailing a general line of new hardware items, known as hardware stores, **444130**

Retailing paint and wallpaper, known as paint and wallpaper stores, **444120**

Retailing a general line of home repair and improvement materials and supplies, known as home centers, **444110**

4442 Lawn and Garden Equipment and Supplies Stores^{CAN}

This industry group comprises establishments primarily engaged in retailing new lawn and garden equipment and supplies.

444210 Outdoor Power Equipment Stores^{CAN}

This industry comprises establishments primarily engaged in retailing new outdoor power equipment or retailing new outdoor power equipment in combination with activities, such as repair services and selling replacement parts.

Retailing outdoor power equipment via electronic home shopping, mail-order, or direct sale **454**

Providing outdoor power equipment repair services without retailing new outdoor power equipment **811411**

Retailing used outdoor power equipment **453310**

444220 Nursery and Garden Centers^{CAN}

This industry comprises establishments primarily engaged in retailing nursery and garden products, such as trees, shrubs, plants, seeds, bulbs, and sod, that are predominantly grown elsewhere. These establishments may sell a limited amount of a product they grow themselves.

Retailing nursery and garden products via electronic home shopping, mail-order, or direct sale **454**

Providing landscaping services **561730**

Growing and retailing nursery stock **111421**

445 Food and Beverage Stores^{CAN}

Industries in the Food and Beverage Stores subsector usually retail food and beverage merchandise from fixed point-of-sale locations. Establishments in this subsector have special equipment (e.g., freezers, refrigerated display cases, refrigerators) for displaying food and beverage goods. They have staff trained in the processing of food products to guarantee the proper storage and sanitary conditions required by regulatory authority.

4451 Grocery Stores^{CAN}

This industry group comprises establishments primarily engaged in retailing a general line of food products.

445110 Supermarkets and Other Grocery (except Convenience) Stores^{CAN}

This industry comprises establishments generally known as supermarkets and grocery stores primarily engaged in retailing a general line of food, such as canned and frozen foods; fresh fruits and vegetables; and fresh and prepared meats, fish, and poultry. Included in this industry are delicatessen-type establishments primarily engaged in retailing a general line of food.

Retailing automotive fuels in combination with a convenience store or food mart **447110**

Retailing a limited line of goods, known as convenience stores or food marts (except those with fuel pumps), **445120**

Retailing frozen food and freezer plans via direct sales to residential customers **454390**

Providing food services in delicatessen-type establishments **722211**

Retailing fresh meat in delicatessen-type establishments **445210**

445120 Convenience Stores^{CAN}

This industry comprises establishments known as convenience stores or food marts (except those with fuel pumps) primarily engaged in retailing a limited line of goods that generally includes milk, bread, soda, and snacks.

Retailing a general line of food, known as supermarkets and grocery stores, **445110**

Retailing automotive fuels in combination with a convenience store or food mart **447110**

4452 Specialty Food Stores^{CAN}

This industry group comprises establishments primarily engaged in retailing specialized lines of food.

445210 Meat Markets^{CAN}

This industry comprises establishments primarily engaged in retailing fresh, frozen, or cured meats and poultry. Delicatessen-type establishments primarily engaged in retailing fresh meat are included in this industry.

Retailing meat and poultry via electronic home shopping, mail-order, or direct sale **454**

Retailing a general line of food, known as supermarkets and grocery stores, **445110**

Providing food services in delicatessen-type establishments **722211**

445220 Fish and Seafood Markets^{CAN}

This industry comprises establishments primarily engaged in retailing fresh, frozen, or cured fish and seafood products.

Retailing fish and seafood products via electronic home shopping, mail-order, or direct sale **454**

445230 Fruit and Vegetable Markets^{CAN}

This industry comprises establishments primarily engaged in retailing fresh fruits and vegetables.

Retailing fruits and vegetables via electronic home shopping, mail-order, or direct sale **454**

Growing and selling vegetables and/or fruits at roadside stands **111**

44529 Other Specialty Food Stores^{CAN}

This industry comprises establishments primarily engaged in retailing specialty foods (except meat, fish, seafood, and fruits and vegetables) not for immediate consumption and not made on premises.

Retailing specialty foods via electronic home shopping, mail-order, or direct sale **454**

Retailing baked goods made on the premises, but not for immediate consumption **31181**

Retailing fresh, frozen, or cured meats and poultry **44521**

Retailing fresh, frozen, or cured fish and seafood products **44522**

Retailing fresh fruits and vegetables **44523**

Retailing candy and confectionery products not for immediate consumption and not made on premises **3113**

Selling snack foods (e.g., doughnuts, bagels, ice cream, popcorn) for immediate consumption **722**

445291 Baked Goods Stores^{CAN}

This U.S. industry comprises establishments primarily engaged in retailing baked goods not for immediate consumption and not made on the premises.

Retailing baked goods via electronic home shopping, mail-order, or direct sale **454**

Selling snack foods (e.g., doughnuts, bagels, ice cream, popcorn) for immediate consumption **722213**

Retailing baked goods made on the premises but not for immediate consumption **311811**

445292 Confectionery and Nut Stores^{CAN}

This U.S. industry comprises establishments primarily engaged in retailing candy and other confections, nuts, and popcorn not for immediate consumption and not made on the premises.

Retailing confectionery goods and nuts via electronic home shopping, mail-order, or direct sale **454**

Retailing confectionery goods and nuts made on premises and not packaged for immediate consumption **3113**

Selling snack foods (e.g., doughnuts, bagels, ice cream, popcorn) for immediate consumption **722213**

Retailing baked goods made on the premises but not for immediate consumption **311811**

445299 All Other Specialty Food Stores^{CAN}

This U.S. industry comprises establishments primarily engaged in retailing miscellaneous specialty foods (except meat, fish, seafood, fruit and vegetables, confections, nuts, popcorn, and baked goods) not for immediate consumption and not made on the premises.

Retailing specialty foods via electronic home shopping, mail-order, or direct sale **454**

Selling snack foods (e.g., doughnuts, bagels, ice cream, popcorn) for immediate consumption **722213**

Retailing fresh, frozen, or cured meats and poultry **445210**

Retailing fresh, frozen, or cured fish and seafood products **445220**

Retailing fresh fruits and vegetables **445230**

Retailing candy and other confections, nuts, and popcorn not for immediate consumption and not made on the premises **445292**

Retailing baked goods not for immediate consumption and not made on the premises **445291**

4453 Beer, Wine, and Liquor Stores^{CAN}

445310 Beer, Wine, and Liquor Stores^{CAN}

This industry comprises establishments primarily engaged in retailing packaged alcoholic beverages, such as ale, beer, wine, and liquor.

Retailing packaged liquor in combination with providing prepared drinks for immediate consumption on the premises **722410**

445

446 Health and Personal Care Stores^{CAN}

Industries in the Health and Personal Care Stores subsector retail health and personal care merchandise from fixed point-of-sale locations. Establishments in this subsector are characterized principally by the products they retail, and some health and personal care stores may have specialized staff trained in dealing with the products. Staff may include pharmacists, opticians, and other professionals engaged in retailing, advising customers, and/or fitting the product sold to the customer's needs.

4461 Health and Personal Care Stores^{CAN}

This industry group comprises establishments primarily engaged in retailing health and personal care products.

446110 Pharmacies and Drug Stores^{CAN}

This industry comprises establishments known as pharmacies and drug stores engaged in retailing prescription or nonprescription drugs and medicines.

Retailing food supplement products, such as vitamins, nutrition supplements, and body enhancing supplements, **446191**
Retailing prescription and nonprescription drugs via electronic home shopping, mail-order, or direct sale **454**

446120 Cosmetics, Beauty Supplies, and Perfume Stores^{CAN}

This industry comprises establishments known as a cosmetic or perfume stores or beauty supply shops primarily engaged in retailing cosmetics, perfumes, toiletries, and personal grooming products.

Providing beauty parlor services **812112**
Retailing perfumes, cosmetics, and beauty supplies via electronic home shopping, mail-order, or direct sale **454**

446130 Optical Goods Stores^{CAN}

This industry comprises establishments primarily engaged in one or more of the following: (1) retailing and fitting prescription eyeglasses and contact lenses; (2) retailing prescription eyeglasses in combination with the grinding of lenses to order on the premises; and (3) selling nonprescription eyeglasses.

Grinding lenses without retailing lenses **339115**
The private or group practice of optometry, even though glasses and contact lenses are sold at these establishments **621320**
Retailing eyeglasses and contact lenses via mail-order **454110**

44619 Other Health and Personal Care Stores^{CAN}

This industry comprises establishments primarily engaged in retailing health and personal care items (except drugs, medicines, optical goods, perfumes, cosmetics, and beauty supplies).

Retailing health and personal care items via electronic home shopping, mail-order, or direct sale **454**
Retailing orthopedic shoes **44821**
Retailing orthopedic and prosthetic appliances that are made on premises **33911**
Retailing prescription and nonprescription drugs and medicines **44611**
Retailing eyeglasses and contact lenses **44613**
Retailing perfumes, cosmetics, and beauty supplies **44612**
Retailing naturally organic foods, such as fruits and vegetables, dairy products, and cereals and grains, **445**

446191 Food (Health) Supplement Stores^{CAN}

This U.S. industry comprises establishments primarily engaged in retailing food supplement products, such as vitamins, nutrition supplements, and body enhancing supplements.

Retailing food supplement products via electronic home shopping, mail-order, or direct sale **454**
Retailing prescription and nonprescription drugs and medicines **446110**
Retailing naturally organic foods, such as fruits and vegetables, dairy products, and cereals and grains, **445**

446199 All Other Health and Personal Care Stores^{CAN}

This U.S. industry comprises establishments primarily engaged in retailing specialized lines of health and personal care merchandise (except drugs, medicines, optical goods, cosmetics, beauty supplies, perfume, and food supplement products).

Retailing specialized health and personal care merchandise via electronic home shopping, mail-order, or direct sale **454**
Retailing food supplement products **446191**
Retailing prescription or nonprescription drugs and medicines **446110**

Retailing eyeglasses and contact lenses **446130**
Retailing perfumes, cosmetics, and beauty supplies **446120**

Retailing orthopedic shoes **448210**
Retailing orthopedic and prosthetic appliances that are made on premises
   339113

447 Gasoline Stations^{CAN}

Industries in the Gasoline Stations subsector group establishments retailing automotive fuels (e.g., gasoline, diesel fuel, gasohol) and automotive oils and retailing these products in combination with convenience store items. These establishments have specialized equipment for the storage and dispensing of automotive fuels.

4471 Gasoline Stations^{CAN}

447110 Gasoline Stations with Convenience Stores^{CAN}

This industry comprises establishments engaged in retailing automotive fuels (e.g., diesel fuel, gasohol, gasoline) in combination with convenience store or food mart items. These establishments can either be in a convenience store (i.e., food mart) setting or a gasoline station setting. These establishments may also provide automotive repair services.

Retailing automotive fuels without a convenience store **447190**
Retailing a limited line of goods, known as convenience stores or food marts
   (except those with fuel pumps), **445120**

447190 Other Gasoline Stations^{CAN}

This industry comprises establishments known as gasoline stations (except those with convenience stores) primarily engaged in one of the following: (1) retailing automotive fuels (e.g., diesel fuel, gasohol, gasoline) or (2) retailing these fuels in combination with activities, such as repair services, selling automotive oils, replacement parts, and accessories, and/or with restaurants.

Repairing motor vehicles without retailing automotive fuels **81111**
Retailing automotive fuels in combination with a convenience store or food
   mart **447110**

448 Clothing and Clothing Accessories Stores^{CAN}

Industries in the Clothing and Clothing Accessories Stores subsector retailing new clothing and clothing accessories merchandise from fixed point-of-sale locations. Establishments in this subsector have similar display equipment and staff that is knowledgeable regarding fashion trends and the proper match of styles, colors, and combinations of clothing and accessories to the characteristics and tastes of the customer.

4481 Clothing Stores^{CAN}

This industry group comprises establishments primarily engaged in retailing new clothing.

448110 Men's Clothing Stores^{CAN}

This industry comprises establishments primarily engaged in retailing a general line of new men's and boys' clothing. These establishments may provide basic alterations, such as hemming, taking in or letting out seams, or lengthening or shortening sleeves.

Retailing men's and boys' clothing via electronic home shopping, mail-order,
   or direct sale **454**
Retailing custom men's clothing made on the premises **3152**
Retailing new men's and boys' accessories **448150**
Retailing specialized new apparel, such as raincoats, leather coats, fur
   apparel, and swimwear, **448190**
Retailing new clothing for all genders and age groups **448140**
Retailing secondhand clothes **453310**
Providing clothing alterations and repair **811490**

448120 Women's Clothing Stores^{CAN}

This industry comprises establishments primarily

engaged in retailing a general line of new women's, misses' and juniors' clothing, including maternity wear. These establishments may provide basic alterations, such as hemming, taking in or letting out seams, or lengthening or shortening sleeves.

Retailing women's clothing via electronic home shopping, mail-order, or direct sale **454**

Retailing custom women's clothing made on premises **3152**

Retailing new women's accessories **448150**

Retailing new clothing for all genders and age groups **448140**

Retailing specialized new apparel, such as bridal gowns, raincoats, leather coats, fur apparel, and swimwear, **448190**

Retailing secondhand clothes **453310**

Providing clothing alterations and repair **811490**

448130 Children's and Infants' Clothing Stores[CAN]

This industry comprises establishments primarily engaged in retailing a general line of new children's and infants' clothing. These establishments may provide basic alterations, such as hemming, taking in or letting out seams, or lengthening or shortening sleeves.

Retailing children's and infants' clothing via electronic home shopping, mail-order, or direct sale **454**

Retailing new children's and infants' accessories **448150**

Retailing new clothing for all genders or age groups **448140**

Retailing secondhand clothes **453310**

Providing clothing alterations and repair **811490**

448140 Family Clothing Stores[CAN]

This industry comprises establishments primarily engaged in retailing a general line of new clothing for men, women, and children, without specializing in sales for an individual gender or age group. These establishments may provide basic alterations, such as hemming, taking in or letting out seams, or lengthening or shortening sleeves.

Retailing clothing for all genders via electronic home shopping, mail-order, or direct sale **454**

Retailing new men's and boys' clothing **448110**

Retailing new children's and infants' clothing **448130**

Retailing new women's, misses', and juniors' clothing **448120**

Retailing specialized new apparel, such as raincoats, bridal gowns, leather coats, fur apparel, and swimwear, **448190**

Retailing secondhand clothes **453310**

Providing clothing alterations and repair **811490**

448150 Clothing Accessories Stores[CAN]

This industry comprises establishments primarily

engaged in retailing single or combination lines of new clothing accessories, such as hats and caps, costume jewelry, gloves, handbags, ties, wigs, toupees, and belts.

Retailing specialized lines of clothing via electronic home shopping, mail-order, or direct sale **454**

Retailing precious jewelry and watches **448310**

Retailing used clothing accessories **453310**

Retailing luggage, briefcases, trunks, or these products in combination with a general line of leather items (except leather apparel), known as luggage and leather goods stores, **448320**

Retailing leather apparel **448190**

448190 Other Clothing Stores[CAN]

This industry comprises establishments primarily engaged in retailing specialized lines of new clothing (except general lines of men's, women's, children's, infants', and family clothing). These establishments may provide basic alterations, such as hemming, taking in or letting out seams, or lengthening or shortening sleeves.

Retailing specialized apparel via electronic home shopping, mail-order, or direct sale **454**

Retailing custom apparel and accessories made on the premises **315**

Retailing new women's, misses', and juniors' clothing, including maternity wear **448120**

Retailing new men's and boys' clothing **448110**

Retailing new children's and infants' clothing **448130**

Retailing new clothing for all genders or age groups **448140**

Retailing athletic uniforms **451110**

Retailing secondhand clothes **453310**

Retailing luggage, briefcases, trunks, or these products in combination with a general line of leather items (except leather apparel), known as luggage and leather good stores, **448320**

Providing clothing alterations and repair **811490**

4482 Shoe Stores[CAN]

448210 Shoe Stores[CAN]

This industry comprises establishments primarily engaged in retailing all types of new footwear (except hosiery and specialty sports footwear, such as golf shoes, bowling shoes, and spiked shoes). Establishments primarily engaged in retailing new tennis shoes or sneakers are included in this industry.

Retailing footwear via electronic home shopping, mail-order, or direct sale **454**

Retailing hosiery **448190**
Retailing new specialty sports footwear (e.g., bowling shoes, golf shoes, spiked shoes) **451110**
Retailing used footwear **453310**

4483 Jewelry, Luggage, and Leather Goods Stores^{CAN}

This industry group comprises establishments primarily engaged in retailing new jewelry (except costume jewelry); new silver and plated silverware; new watches and clocks; and new luggage with or without a general line of new leather goods and accessories, such as hats, gloves, handbags, ties, and belts.

448310 Jewelry Stores^{CAN}

This industry comprises establishments primarily engaged in retailing one or more of the following items: (1) new jewelry (except costume jewelry); (2) new sterling and plated silverware; and (3) new watches and clocks. Also included are establishments retailing these new products in combination with lapidary work and/or repair services.

Retailing new costume jewelry **448150**
Retailing jewelry via electronic home shopping, mail-order, or direct sale **454**
Retailing antiques or used jewelry, silverware, and watches and clocks **453310**
Providing jewelry or watch and clock repair without retailing new jewelry or watches and clocks **811490**
Cutting and setting gem stones **339913**

448320 Luggage and Leather Goods Stores^{CAN}

This industry comprises establishments known as luggage and leather goods stores primarily engaged in retailing new luggage, briefcases, trunks, or these new products in combination with a general line of leather items (except leather apparel), such as belts, gloves, and handbags.

Retailing luggage and leather goods via electronic home shopping, mail-order, or direct sale **454**
Retailing used luggage and leather goods **453310**
Retailing single or combination lines of new clothing accessories (e.g., gloves, handbags, or leather belts) **448150**
Retailing new leather coats **448190**

451 Sporting Goods, Hobby, Book, and Music Stores^{CAN}

Industries in the Sporting Goods, Hobby, Book, and Music Stores subsector are engaged in retailing and providing expertise on use of sporting equipment or other specific leisure activities, such as needlework and musical instruments. Book stores are also included in this subsector.

4511 Sporting Goods, Hobby, and Musical Instrument Stores^{CAN}

This industry group comprises establishments primarily engaged in retailing new sporting goods, games and toys, and musical instruments.

451110 Sporting Goods Stores^{CAN}

This industry comprises establishments primarily engaged in retailing new sporting goods, such as bicycles and bicycle parts; camping equipment; exercise and fitness equipment; athletic uniforms; specialty sports footwear; and sporting goods, equipment, and accessories.

Retailing sporting goods via electronic home shopping, mail order, or direct sale **454**

Retailing new or used campers (pickup coaches) and camping trailers **441210**
Retailing new or used snowmobiles, motorized bicycles, and motorized golf carts **44122**
Retailing new shoes (except specialty sports footwear, such as golf shoes, bowling shoes, and spiked shoes) **448210**
Repairing or servicing sporting goods, without retailing new sporting goods **811490**
Retailing used sporting goods and used bicycles **453310**

451120 Hobby, Toy, and Game Stores^{CAN}

This industry comprises establishments primarily engaged in retailing new toys, games, and hobby and craft supplies (except needlecraft).

Retailing toys, games, and hobby and craft supplies via electronic home shopping, mail-order, or direct sale **454**

Retailing artists' supplies or collectors' items, such as coins, stamps, autographs, and cards **453998**

Retailing new computer software (e.g., game software) **443120**

Retailing used toys, games, and hobby supplies **453310**

Retailing new sewing supplies, fabrics, and needlework accessories **451130**

451130 Sewing, Needlework, and Piece Goods Stores^{CAN}

This industry comprises establishments primarily engaged in retailing new sewing supplies, fabrics, patterns, yarns, and other needlework accessories or retailing these products in combination with selling new sewing machines.

Retailing sewing supplies via electronic home shopping, mail-order, or direct sale **454**

Retailing new sewing machines only and in combination with retailing other new appliances **443111**

Retailing used sewing, needlework, and piece goods **453310**

451140 Musical Instrument and Supplies Stores^{CAN}

This industry comprises establishments primarily engaged in retailing new musical instruments, sheet music, and related supplies; or retailing these new products in combination with musical instrument repair, rental, or music instruction.

Retailing musical instruments, sheet music, and related supplies via electronic home shopping, mail-order, or direct sale **454**

Retailing new musical recordings **451220**

Retailing used musical instruments, sheet music, and related supplies **453310**

4512 Book, Periodical, and Music Stores^{CAN}

This industry group comprises establishments primarily engaged in retailing new books, newspapers, magazines, and prerecorded audio and video media.

45121 Book Stores and News Dealers^{CAN}

This industry comprises establishments primarily engaged in retailing new books, newspapers, magazines, and other periodicals.

Retailing newspapers, magazines, and other periodicals via electronic home shopping, mail-order, or direct sale **454**

Home delivery of newspapers **45439**

Retailing used books, newspapers, magazines, and other periodicals **45331**

451211 Book Stores^{US}

This U.S. industry comprises establishments primarily engaged in retailing new books.

Retailing books via electronic home shopping, mail-order, or direct sale **454**

Retailing used books **453310**

451212 News Dealers and Newsstands^{US}

This U.S. industry comprises establishments primarily engaged in retailing current newspapers, magazines, and other periodicals.

Home delivery of newspapers **454390**

Retailing newspapers and periodicals by mail-order **454110**

Retailing used newspapers, magazines, and other periodicals **453310**

451220 Prerecorded Tape, Compact Disc, and Record Stores^{CAN}

This industry comprises establishments primarily engaged in retailing new prerecorded audio and video tapes, compact discs (CDs), and phonograph records.

Retailing new computer software **443120**

Retailing prerecorded tapes, compact discs, and records by mail-order **454110**

Retailing used phonograph records and prerecorded audio and video tapes and discs **453310**

Retailing new audio sound equipment (except automotive) **443112**

452 General Merchandise Stores^{CAN}

Industries in the General Merchandise Stores subsector retail new general merchandise from fixed point-of-sale locations. Establishments in this subsector are unique in that they have the equipment and staff capable of retailing a large variety of goods from a single location. This includes a variety of display equipment and staff trained to provide information on many lines of products.

4521 Department Stores^{CAN}

452110 Department Stores^{CAN}

This industry comprises establishments known as department stores primarily engaged in retailing a wide range of the following new products with no one merchandise line predominating: apparel, furniture, appliances and home furnishings; and selected additional items, such as paint, hardware, toiletries, cosmetics, photographic equipment, jewelry, toys, and sporting goods. Merchandise lines are normally arranged in separate departments.

Retailing prepackaged grocery items in combination with general lines of merchandise with no one merchandise line predominating **452910**
Retailing general lines of merchandise via electronic home shopping, mail-order, or direct sale **454**
Retailing used merchandise **453310**

4529 Other General Merchandise Stores^{CAN}

This industry group comprises establishments primarily engaged in retailing new goods in general merchandise stores (except department stores).

452910 Warehouse Clubs and Superstores^{CAN}

This industry comprises establishments known as warehouse clubs, superstores or supercenters primarily engaged in retailing a general line of groceries in combination with general lines of new merchandise, such as apparel, furniture, and appliances.

Retailing general lines of merchandise via electronic home shopping, mail-order, or direct sale **454**
Retailing a general line of food, generally known as supermarkets and grocery stores, **445110**
Retailing general lines of new merchandise with little grocery item sales **452990**
Retailing new merchandise in department stores **452110**
Retailing used merchandise **453310**

452990 All Other General Merchandise Stores^{CAN}

This industry comprises establishments primarily engaged in retailing new goods in general merchandise stores (except department stores, warehouse clubs, superstores, and supercenters). These establishments retail a general line of new merchandise, such as apparel, automotive parts, dry goods, hardware, groceries, housewares or home furnishings, and other lines in limited amounts, with none of the lines predominating.

Retailing general lines of merchandise via electronic home shopping, mail-order, or direct sale **454**
Retailing automotive parts **441310**
Retailing merchandise in department stores **452110**
Retailing merchandise in warehouse clubs, superstores, or supercenters **452910**
Retailing merchandise in catalogue showrooms of mail-order houses **454110**
Retailing a general line of new hardware items, known as hardware stores, **444130**
Retailing a general line of new home repair and improvement materials and supplies, known as home centers, **444110**
Retailing used merchandise **453310**

453

453 Miscellaneous Store Retailers^{CAN}

Industries in the Miscellaneous Store Retailers subsector retail merchandise from fixed point-of-sale locations (except new or used motor vehicles and parts; new furniture and house furnishings; new appliances and electronic products; new building materials; and garden equipment and supplies; food and beverages; health and personal care goods; gasoline; new clothing and accessories; and new sporting goods, hobby goods, books, and music). Establishments in this subsector include stores with unique characteristics like florists, used merchandise stores, and pet and pet supply stores as well as other store retailers.

4531 Florists^{CAN}

453110 Florists^{CAN}

This industry comprises establishments known as florists primarily engaged in retailing cut flowers, floral arrangements, and potted plants purchased from others. These establishments usually prepare the arrangements they sell.

Retailing flowers or nursery stock grown on premises **11142**

Retailing trees, shrubs, plants, seeds, bulbs, and sod grown elsewhere **444220**

Retailing flowers via electronic home shopping, mail-order, or direct sale **454**

4532 Office Supplies, Stationery, and Gift Stores^{CAN}

453210 Office Supplies and Stationery Stores^{CAN}

This industry comprises establishments primarily engaged in one or more of the following: (1) retailing new stationery, school supplies, and office supplies; (2) selling a combination of new office equipment, furniture, and supplies; and (3) selling new office equipment, furniture, and supplies in combination with selling new computers.

Retailing stationery, school supplies, and office supplies via electronic shopping, mail-order, or direct sale **454**

Retailing greeting cards **453220**

Retailing new typewriters **443112**

Retailing new computers without retailing other consumer-type electronic products or office equipment, furniture, and supplies **443120**

Printing business forms **32311**

Retailing new office furniture **442110**

Retailing used office supplies **453310**

453220 Gift, Novelty, and Souvenir Stores^{CAN}

This industry comprises establishments primarily engaged in retailing new gifts, novelty merchandise, souvenirs, greeting cards, seasonal and holiday decorations, and curios.

Retailing gifts and novelties via electronic home shopping, mail-order, or direct sale **454**

Retailing stationery **453210**

Retailing used curios and novelties **453310**

4533 Used Merchandise Stores^{CAN}

453310 Used Merchandise Stores^{CAN}

This industry comprises establishments primarily engaged in retailing used merchandise, antiques, and secondhand goods (except motor vehicles, such as automobiles, RVs, motorcycles, and boats; motor vehicle parts; tires; and mobile homes).

Retailing used merchandise via electronic home shopping, mail-order, or direct sale **454**

Operating pawnshops **522298**

Retailing used automobiles **441120**

Retailing used automobile parts (except tires and tubes) **441310**

Retailing used tires **441320**

Retailing used mobile homes **453930**

Retailing used motorcycles **441221**

Retailing used recreational vehicles **441210**

Retailing used boats **441222**

Retailing used aircraft, snowmobiles, and utility trailers **441229**

Retailing a general line of used merchandise on an auction basis (not for others) **453998**

4539 Other Miscellaneous Store Retailers^{CAN}

This industry group comprises establishments primarily engaged in retailing new miscellaneous specialty store merchandise (except motor vehicle and parts dealers; furniture and home furnishings stores; consumer-type electronics and appliance stores; building material and garden equipment and supplies dealers; food and beverage stores; health and personal care stores; gasoline stations; clothing and clothing accessories stores; sporting goods, hobby, book, and music stores; general merchandise stores; florists; office supplies, stationery, and gift stores; and used merchandise stores).

453910 Pet and Pet Supplies Stores^{CAN}

This industry comprises establishments primarily engaged in retailing pets, pet foods, and pet supplies.

Retailing pets, pet foods, and pet supplies via electronic home shopping, mail-order, or direct sale **454**

Providing pet grooming and boarding services **812910**

Providing veterinary services **541940**

453920 Art Dealers^{CAN}

This industry comprises establishments primarily engaged in retailing original and limited edition art works. Included in this industry are establishments primarily engaged in displaying works of art for retail sale in art galleries.

Retailing original and limited edition art works via electronic home shopping, mail-order, or direct sale **454**

Retailing art reproductions (except limited editions) **442299**
Retailing artists' supplies **453998**
Displaying works of art not for retail sale in art galleries **712110**

453930 Manufactured (Mobile) Home Dealers^{CAN}

This industry comprises establishments primarily engaged in retailing new and/or used manufactured homes (i.e., mobile homes), parts, and equipment.

Retailing new or used motor homes, campers, and travel trailers **441210**
Retailing prefabricated buildings and kits without construction **444190**

45399 All Other Miscellaneous Store Retailers^{CAN}

This industry comprises establishments primarily engaged in retailing specialized lines of merchandise (except motor vehicle and parts dealers; furniture and home furnishings stores; electronic and appliance stores; building material and garden equipment and supplies dealers; food and beverage stores; health and personal care stores; gasoline stations; clothing and clothing accessories stores; sporting goods, hobby, book, and music stores; general merchandise stores; florists; office supplies, stationery and gift stores; used merchandise stores; pet and pet supplies; art dealers; and manufactured home (i.e., mobile home) dealers). This industry also includes establishments primarily engaged in retailing a general line of new and used merchandise on an auction basis.

Retailing merchandise via electronic home shopping, mail-order, or direct sale **454**
Auctioning on the location of others as independent auctioneers **56199**
Retailing pets and pet supplies **45391**
Retailing original and limited edition art works **45392**
Retailing manufactured homes (i.e., mobile homes) **45393**
Retailing new books **45121**
Retailing new jewelry (except costume jewelry) **44831**
Retailing new costume jewelry **44815**
Retailing used merchandise (except automobiles, RVs, mobile homes, motorcycles, boats, motor vehicle parts, and tires) **453310**

453991 Tobacco Stores^{US}

This U.S. industry comprises establishments primarily engaged in retailing cigarettes, cigars, tobacco, pipes, and other smokers' supplies.

Retailing tobacco products and supplies via electronic home shopping, mail-order, or direct sale **454**

453998 All Other Miscellaneous Store Retailers (except Tobacco Stores)^{US}

This U.S. industry comprises establishments primarily engaged in retailing specialized lines of merchandise (except motor vehicle and parts dealers; furniture and home furnishings stores; electronic and appliance stores; building material and garden equipment and supplies dealers; food and beverage stores; health and personal care stores; gasoline stations; clothing and clothing accessories stores; sporting goods, hobby, book and music stores; general merchandise stores; florists; office supplies, stationery and gift stores; used merchandise stores; pet and pet supplies stores; art dealers; manufactured home (i.e., mobile homes) dealers; and tobacco stores). This industry also includes establishments primarily engaged in retailing a general line of new and used merchandise on an auction basis.

Retailing specialized lines of merchandise via electronic home shopping, mail-order, of direct sale **454**
Auctioning (i.e., on the location of others as independent auctioneers) **561990**
Retailing pets and pet supplies **453910**
Retailing original and limited edition art works **453920**
Retailing manufactured homes (i.e., mobile homes) **453930**
Retailing cigarettes, cigars, tobacco, pipes, and other smokers' supplies **453991**
Retailing antiques **453310**
Retailing new books **451211**
Retailing new jewelry (except costume jewelry) **448310**
Retailing new costume jewelry **448150**

454

454 Nonstore Retailers^{CAN}

Industries in the Nonstore Retailers subsector retail merchandise using methods, such as the broadcasting of infomercials, the broadcasting and publishing of direct-response advertising, the publishing of paper and electronic catalogues, door-to-door solicitation, in-home demonstration, selling from portable stalls and distribution through vending machines. Establishments in this subsector include mail-order houses, vending machine operators, home delivery sales, door-to-door sales, party plan sales, electronic shopping, and sales through portable stalls (e.g., street vendors, except food). Establishments engaged in the direct sale (i.e., nonstore) of products, such as home heating oil dealers, newspaper delivery are included in this subsector.

4541 Electronic Shopping and Mail-Order Houses[CAN]

454110 Electronic Shopping and Mail-Order Houses[CAN]

This industry comprises establishments primarily engaged in retailing all types of merchandise by means of mail or by electronic media, such as interactive television or computer. Included in this industry are establishments primarily engaged in retailing from catalogue showrooms of mail-order houses.

Providing telemarketing (e.g., telephone marketing) services for others **561422**

4542 Vending Machine Operators[CAN]

454210 Vending Machine Operators[CAN]

This industry comprises establishments primarily engaged in retailing merchandise through vending machines that they service.

Selling insurance policies through vending machines **524**
Supplying and servicing coin-operated photobooths, restrooms, and lockers **812990**
Supplying and servicing coin-operated amusement and gambling devices in places of business operated by others **713**

4543 Direct Selling Establishments[CAN]

This industry group comprises establishments primarily engaged in nonstore retailing (except electronic, mail-order, or vending machine sales). These establishments typically go to the customers' location rather than the customer coming to them (e.g., door-to-door sales, home parties). Examples of establishments in this industry are home delivery newspaper routes; home delivery of heating oil, liquefied petroleum (LP) gas, and other fuels; locker meat provisioners; frozen food and freezer plan providers; coffee break services providers; and bottled water or water softener services.

45431 Fuel Dealers[CAN]

This industry comprises establishments primarily engaged in retailing heating oil, liquefied petroleum (LP) gas, and other fuels via direct selling.

Providing oil burner repair services **81141**
Installing oil burners **23511**

454311 Heating Oil Dealers[US]

This U.S. industry comprises establishments primarily engaged in retailing heating oil via direct selling.

Providing oil burner repair services **811411**
Installing oil burners **235110**

454312 Liquefied Petroleum Gas (Bottled Gas) Dealers[US]

This U.S. industry comprises establishments primarily engaged in retailing liquefied petroleum (LP) gas via direct selling.

454319 Other Fuel Dealers[US]

This U.S. industry comprises establishments primarily engaged in retailing fuels (except liquefied petroleum gas and heating oil) via direct selling.

454390 Other Direct Selling Establishments[CAN]

This industry comprises establishments primarily engaged in retailing merchandise (except food for immediate consumption and fuel) via direct sale to the customer by means, such as in-house sales (i.e., party plan merchandising), truck or wagon sales, and portable stalls (i.e., street vendors).

Preparing and selling meals and snacks for immediate consumption from motorized vehicles or nonmotorized carts catering a route **722330**
Retailing heating oil via direct sale **454311**
Retailing liquefied petroleum (LP) gas via direct sale **454312**
Retailing other fuels, such as coal or wood, via direct sale **454319**

Sector 48-49: Transportation and Warehousing

Overview of this Sector as a Whole

The Transportation and Warehousing sector includes industries providing transportation of passengers and cargo, warehousing and storage for goods, scenic and sightseeing transportation, and support activities related to modes of transportation. Establishments in these industries use transportation equipment or transportation related facilities as a productive asset. The type of equipment depends on the mode of transportation. The modes of transportation are air, rail, water, road, and pipeline.

The Transportation and Warehousing sector distinguishes three basic types of activities: subsectors for each mode of transportation, a subsector for warehousing and storage, and a subsector for establishments providing support activities for transportation. In addition, there are subsectors for establishments that provide passenger transportation for scenic and sightseeing purposes, postal services, and courier services.

A separate subsector for support activities is established in the sector because, first, support activities for transportation are inherently multimodal, such as freight transportation arrangement, or have multimodal aspects. Secondly, there are production process similarities among the support activity industries.

One of the support activities identified in the support activity subsector is the routine repair and maintenance of transportation equipment (e.g., aircraft at an airport, railroad rolling stock at a railroad terminal, or ships at a harbor or port facility). Such establishments do not perform complete overhauling or rebuilding of transportation equipment (i.e., periodic restoration of transportation equipment to original design specifications) or transportation equipment conversion (i.e., major modification to systems). An establishment that primarily performs factory (or shipyard) overhauls, rebuilding, or conversions of aircraft, railroad rolling stock, or a ship is classified in Subsector 336, Transportation Equipment Manufacturing according to the type of equipment. Many of the establishments in this sector often operate on networks, with physical facilities, labor forces, and equipment spread over an extensive geographic area. Warehousing establishments in this sector are distinguished from merchant wholesaling in that the warehouse establishments do not sell the goods.

Excluded from this sector are establishments primarily engaged in providing travel agent services that support transportation and other establishments, such as hotels, businesses, and government agencies. These establishments are classified in Sector 56, Administrative and Support, Waste Management, and Remediation Services. Also, establishments primarily engaged in providing rental and leasing of transportation equipment without operator are classified in Subsector 532, Rental and Leasing Services.

481

---

481 Air Transportation

Industries in the Air Transportation subsector provide air transportation of passengers and/or cargo using aircraft, such as airplanes and helicopters. The subsector distinguishes scheduled from nonscheduled air transportation. Scheduled air carriers fly regular routes on regular schedules and operate even if flights are only partially loaded. Nonscheduled carriers often operate during nonpeak time slots at busy airports. These establishments have more flexibility with respect to choice of airport, hours of operation, load factors, and similar operational characteristics. Nonscheduled carriers provide chartered air transportation of passengers, cargo, or specialty flying services. Specialty flying services establishments use general purpose aircraft to provide a variety of specialized flying services.

Scenic and sightseeing air transportation and air courier services are not included in this subsector but are included in Subsector 487, Scenic and Sightseeing Transportation and in Subsector 492, Couriers and Messengers. Although these activities may use aircraft, they are different from the activities included in air transportation. Air sightseeing does not usually involve place-to-place transportation; the passenger's flight (e.g., balloon ride, aerial sightseeing) typically starts and ends at the same location. Courier services (individual package or cargo delivery) includes more than air transportation; road transportation is usually required to deliver the cargo to the intended recipient.

4811 Scheduled Air Transportation

48111 Scheduled Air Transportation

This industry comprises establishments primarily engaged in providing air transportation of passengers and/or cargo over regular routes and on regular schedules. Establishments in this industry operate flights even if partially loaded. Establishments primarily engaged in providing scheduled air transportation of mail on a contract basis are included in this industry.

Providing air courier services **49211**
Providing air transportation of passengers, cargo, or specialty flying services with no regular routes and regular schedules **48121**
Providing helicopter rides for scenic and sightseeing transportation **48799**

481111 Scheduled Passenger Air Transportation[US]

This U.S. industry comprises establishments primarily engaged in providing air transportation of passengers or passengers and freight over regular routes and on regular schedules. Establishments in this industry operate flights even if partially loaded. Scheduled air passenger carriers including commuter and helicopter carriers (except scenic and sightseeing) are included in this industry.

Providing air transportation of passengers or passengers and cargo with no regular routes and regular schedules **481211**
Providing helicopter rides for scenic and sightseeing transportation **487990**
Providing air transportation of cargo (without transporting passengers) over regular routes and on regular schedules **481112**

481112 Scheduled Freight Air Transportation[US]

This U.S. industry comprises establishments primarily engaged in providing air transportation of cargo without transporting passengers over regular routes and on regular schedules. Establishments in this industry operate flights even if partially loaded. Establishments primarily engaged in providing scheduled air transportation of mail on a contract basis are included in this industry.

Providing air courier services **492110**
Providing air transportation of cargo with no regular routes and regular schedules **481212**
Providing air transportation of passengers or passengers and cargo over regular routes and on regular schedules **481112**

4812 Nonscheduled Air Transportation

48121 Nonscheduled Air Transportation

This industry comprises establishments primarily engaged in (1) providing air transportation of passengers and/or cargo with no regular routes and regular schedules or (2) providing specialty flying services with no regular routes and regular schedules using general purpose aircraft. These establishments have more flexibility with respect to choice of airports, hours of operation, load factors, and similar operational characteristics.

Crop dusting using specialized aircraft 11511

Fighting forest fires using specialized water bombers 11531

Providing air transportation of passengers and/or cargo over regular routes and on regular schedules 48111

Providing specialized air sightseeing services 48799

Aerial gathering of geophysical data 54136

Providing aerial and/or other surveying and mapping services 54137

Providing air ambulance services using specialized equipment 62191

Operating specialized flying schools, including all training for commercial pilots 61151

Operating recreation aviation clubs 71399

Operating advocacy aviation clubs 81331

Providing air courier services 49211

481211 Nonscheduled Chartered Passenger Air Transportation[US]

This U.S. industry comprises establishments primarily engaged in providing air transportation of passengers or passengers and cargo with no regular routes and regular schedules.

Providing specialty air transportation or flying services with no regular routes and regular schedules using general purpose aircraft 481219

Providing specialized air sightseeing services 487990

Providing air transportation of passengers or passengers and cargo over regular routes and on regular schedules 481111

Providing air transportation of cargo (without transporting passengers) with no regular routes and schedules 481212

481212 Nonscheduled Chartered Freight Air Transportation[US]

This U.S. industry comprises establishments prima-

rily engaged in providing air transportation of cargo without transporting passengers with no regular routes and regular schedules.

Providing specialty air transportation or flying services with no regular routes and regular schedules using general purpose aircraft 481219

Providing air courier services 492110

Providing air transportation of cargo without transporting passengers over regular routes and on regular schedules 481112

Providing air transportation of cargo and passengers with no regular routes and schedules 481211

481219 Other Nonscheduled Air Transportation[US]

This U.S. industry comprises establishments primarily engaged in providing air transportation with no regular routes and regular schedules (except nonscheduled chartered passenger and/or cargo air transportation). These establishments provide a variety of specialty air transportation or flying services based on individual customer needs using general purpose aircraft.

Providing air transportation of passengers or passengers and cargo with no regular routes and regular schedules 481211

Providing air transportation of cargo without transporting passengers with no regular routes and regular schedules 481212

Crop dusting using specialized aircraft 115112

Fighting forest fires using specialized water bombers 115310

Providing specialized air sightseeing services 487990

Operating specialized flying schools, including all training for commercial pilots 611512

Providing specialized air ambulance services using specialized equipment 621999

Operating recreation aviation clubs 713990

Operating advocacy aviation clubs 813319

Aerial gathering of geophysical data for surveying and mapping 541360

Providing aerial and/or other surveying and mapping services 541370

482

---

482 Rail Transportation

Industries in the Rail Transportation subsector provide rail transportation of passengers and/or cargo using railroad rolling stock. The railroads in this subsector primarily either operate on networks, with physical facilities, labor force, and equipment spread over an extensive geographic area, or operate over a short distance on a local rail line.

Scenic and sightseeing rail transportation and street railroads, commuter rail, and rapid transit are not included in this subsector but are included in Subsector 487, Scenic and Sightseeing Transportation, and Subsector 485, Transit and Ground Passenger Transportation, respectively.

Although these activities use railroad rolling stock, they are different from the activities included in rail transportation. Sightseeing and scenic railroads do not usually involve place-to-place transportation; the passenger's trip typically starts and ends at the same location. Commuter railroads operate in a manner more consistent with local and urban transit and are often part of integrated transit systems.

482I Rail Transportation

482II Rail Transportation

This industry comprises establishments primarily engaged in operating railroads (except street railroads, commuter rail, urban rapid transit, and scenic and sightseeing trains). Line-haul railroads and short line railroads are included in this industry.

Operating street railroads, commuter rail, and urban rapid transit systems **485I**
Operating scenic and sightseeing trains **487II**
Operating switching and terminal facilities as separate establishments **4882I**

482III Line-Haul Railroads[US]

This U.S. industry comprises establishments known as line-haul railroads primarily engaged in operating railroads for the transport of passengers and/or cargo over a long distance within a rail network. These establishments provide for the intercity movement of trains between the terminals and stations on main and branch lines of a line-haul rail network (except for local switching services).

Operating switching and terminal facilities as separate establishments **488210**
Operating railroads over a short distance on local rail lines **482112**
Operating commuter rail systems **485112**

482112 Short Line Railroads[CAN]

This U.S. industry comprises establishments known as short line railroads primarily engaged in operating railroads for the transport of cargo over a short distance on local rail lines not part of a rail network.

Operating street railroads, commuter rail, and urban rapid transit systems **485I**
Operating scenic and sightseeing trains **487110**
Operating switching and terminal facilities as separate establishments **488210**
Operating railroads for the transport of passengers and/or cargo over a long distance **482III**

483 Water Transportation

Industries in the Water Transportation subsector provide water transportation of passengers and cargo using watercraft, such as ships, barges, and boats.

The subsector is composed of two industry groups: (1) one for deep sea, coastal, and Great Lakes; and (2) one for inland water transportation. This split typically reflects the difference in equipment used.

Scenic and sightseeing water transportation services are not included in this subsector but are included in Subsector 487, Scenic and Sightseeing Transportation. Although these activities use watercraft, they are different from the activities included in water transportation. Water sightseeing does not usually involve place-to-place transportation; the passenger's trip starts and ends at the same location.

4831 Deep Sea, Coastal, and Great Lakes Water Transportation

48311 Deep Sea, Coastal, and Great Lakes Water Transportation

This industry comprises establishments primarily engaged in providing deep sea, coastal, Great Lakes, and St. Lawrence Seaway water transportation. Marine transportation establishments using the facilities of the St. Lawrence Seaway Authority Commission are considered to be using the Great Lakes Water Transportation System.

Providing inland water transportation on lakes, rivers, or intracoastal waterways (except on the Great Lakes System) **48321**
Providing scenic and sightseeing water transportation, such as harbor cruises, **48721**
Operating floating casinos (i.e., gambling cruises, riverboat gambling casinos) **71321**

483111 Deep Sea Freight Transportation^US

This U.S. industry comprises establishments primarily engaged in providing deep sea transportation of cargo to or from foreign ports.

Providing deep sea transportation of cargo to and from domestic ports **483113**

483112 Deep Sea Passenger Transportation^US

This U.S. industry comprises establishments primarily engaged in providing deep sea transportation of passengers to or from foreign ports.

Providing deep sea transportation of passengers to and from domestic ports **483114**
Operating floating casinos (i.e., gambling cruises) **713210**

483113 Coastal and Great Lakes Freight Transportation^US

This U.S. industry comprises establishments primarily engaged in providing water transporta-tion of cargo in coastal waters, on the Great Lakes System, or deep seas between ports of the United States, Puerto Rico, and United States island possessions or protectorates. Marine transportation establishments using the facilities of the St. Lawrence Seaway Authority Commission are considered to be using the Great Lakes Water Transportation System. Establishments primarily engaged in providing coastal and/or Great Lakes

barge transportation services are included in this industry.

Providing deep sea transportation of cargo to or from foreign ports **483111**
Providing inland water transportation of cargo on lakes, rivers, or intracoastal waterways (except on the Great Lakes System) **483211**

483114 Coastal and Great Lakes Passenger Transportation^US

This U.S. industry comprises establishments primarily engaged in providing water transportation of passengers in coastal waters, the Great Lakes System, or deep seas between ports of the United States, Puerto Rico, and United States island possessions and protectorates. Marine transportation establishments using the facilities of the St. Lawrence Seaway Authority Commission are considered to be using the Great Lakes Water Transportation System.

Providing inland water transportation of passengers on lakes, rivers or intracoastal waterways (except on the Great Lakes System) **483212**
Providing scenic and sightseeing water transportation, such as harbor cruises, **487210**
Operating floating casinos (i.e., gambling cruises) **713210**

483

4832 Inland Water Transportation

48321 Inland Water Transportation

This industry comprises establishments primarily engaged in providing inland water transportation of passengers and/or cargo on lakes, rivers, or intracoastal waterways (except on the Great Lakes System).

Providing water transportation in deep sea, coastal, or on the Great Lakes System **4831**
Providing scenic and sightseeing water transportation, such as harbor cruises, **48721**
Operating floating casinos (i.e., gambling cruises, riverboat gambling casinos) **71321**

483211 Inland Water Freight Transportation^US

This U.S. industry comprises establishments primarily engaged in providing inland water transportation of cargo on lakes, rivers, or intracoastal waterways (except on the Great Lakes System).

Providing deep sea transportation of cargo to and from foreign ports **483111**
Providing water transportation of cargo in coastal waters or on the Great Lakes System **483113**

483212 Inland Water Passenger Transportation[US]

This U.S. industry comprises establishments primarily engaged in providing inland water transportation of passengers on lakes, rivers, or intracoastal waterways (except on the Great Lakes System).

Providing deep sea transportation of passengers to and from foreign ports **483112**

Operating cruise ships or ferries in coastal waters or on the Great Lakes System **483114**

Providing scenic and sightseeing water transportation, such as harbor cruises, **487210**

484 Truck Transportation

Industries in the Truck Transportation subsector provide over-the-road transportation of cargo using motor vehicles, such as trucks and tractor trailers. The subsector is subdivided into general freight trucking and specialized freight trucking. This distinction reflects differences in equipment used, type of load carried, scheduling, terminal, and other networking services. General freight transportation establishments handle a wide variety of general commodities, generally palletized, and transported in a container or van trailer. Specialized freight transportation is the transportation of cargo that, because of size, weight, shape, or other inherent characteristics require specialized equipment for transportation.

Each of these industry groups is further subdivided based on distance traveled. Local trucking establishments primarily carry goods within a single metropolitan area and its adjacent nonurban areas. Long distance trucking establishments carry goods between metropolitan areas. The Specialized Freight Trucking industry group includes a separate industry for Used Household and Office Goods Moving. The household and office goods movers are separated because of the substantial network of establishments that has developed to deal with local and long-distance moving and the associated storage. In this area, the same establishment provides both local and long-distance services, while other specialized freight establishments generally limit their services to either local or long-distance hauling.

4841 General Freight Trucking

This industry group comprises establishments primarily engaged in providing general freight trucking. General freight establishments handle a wide variety of commodities, generally palletized, and transported in a container or van trailer. The establishments of this industry group provide a combination of the following network activities: local pickup, local sorting and terminal operations, line-haul, destination sorting and terminal operations, and local delivery.

484110 General Freight Trucking, Local

This industry comprises establishments primarily engaged in providing local general freight trucking. General freight establishments handle a wide variety of commodities, generally palletized and transported in a container or van trailer. Local general freight trucking establishments usually provide trucking within a metropolitan area that may cross state lines. Generally the trips are same-day return.

Operating independent trucking terminals **488490**

Providing general freight long-distance trucking including all North American international travel **48412**

48412 General Freight Trucking, Long-Distance

This industry comprises establishments primarily engaged in providing long-distance general freight trucking. General freight establishments handle a wide variety of commodities, generally palletized and transported in a container or van trailer. Long-distance general freight trucking establishments usually provide trucking between metropolitan areas that may cross North American country borders. Included in this industry are establishments operating as truckload (TL) or less than truckload (LTL) carriers.

Providing courier services **49211**

Providing warehousing services of general freight **49311**

Providing specialized freight trucking **4842**

Operating independent trucking terminals **48849**

Providing local general freight trucking services **48411**

484121 General Freight Trucking, Long-Distance, Truckload[CAN]

This U.S. industry comprises establishments primarily engaged in providing long-distance general freight truckload (TL) trucking. These long-distance general freight truckload carrier establishments provide full truck movement of freight from origin to destination. The shipment of freight on a truck is characterized as a full single load not combined with other shipments.

Providing general freight long-distance, less than truckload trucking
    484122
Providing specialized freight trucking **4842**
Operating independent trucking terminals **488490**
Providing local general freight trucking services **484110**

484122 General Freight Trucking, Long-Distance, Less Than Truckload[CAN]

This U.S. industry comprises establishments primarily engaged in providing long-distance, general freight, less than truckload (LTL) trucking. LTL carriage is characterized as multiple shipments combined onto a single truck for multiple deliveries within a network. These establishments are generally characterized by the following network activities: local pickup, local sorting and terminal operations, line-haul, destination sorting and terminal operations, and local delivery.

Providing courier services **492110**
Providing warehousing services of general freight **493110**
Providing specialized freight trucking **4842**
Operating independent trucking terminals **488490**
Providing general freight long-distance truckload trucking **484121**
Providing local general freight trucking services **484110**

4842 Specialized Freight Trucking

This industry group comprises establishments primarily engaged in providing local or long-distance specialized freight trucking. The establishments of this industry are primarily engaged in the transportation of freight that, because of size, weight, shape, or other inherent characteristics, requires specialized equipment, such as flatbeds, tankers, or refrigerated trailers. This industry includes the transportation of used household, institutional, and commercial furniture and equipment.

484210 Used Household and Office Goods Moving

This industry comprises establishments primarily engaged in providing local or long-distance trucking of used household, used institutional, or used commercial furniture and equipment. Incidental packing and storage activities are often provided by these establishments.

484220 Specialized Freight (except Used Goods) Trucking, Local

This industry comprises establishments primarily engaged in providing local, specialized trucking. Local trucking establishments provide trucking within a metropolitan area that may cross state lines. Generally the trips are same-day return.

Providing long-distance specialized freight (except used goods) trucking including all North American international travel **48423**
Providing local general freight trucking **484110**
Providing trucking of used household and office goods **484210**
Providing waste collection **5621**

484230 Specialized Freight (except Used Goods) Trucking, Long-Distance

This industry comprises establishments primarily engaged in providing long-distance specialized trucking. These establishments provide trucking between metropolitan areas that may cross North American country borders.

Providing local specialized freight trucking (except used goods) **484220**
Providing long-distance general freight trucking including all North American international travel **48412**
Providing trucking of used household and office goods **484210**

485 Transit and Ground Passenger Transportation

Industries in the Transit and Ground Passenger Transportation subsector include a variety of passenger transportation activities, such as urban transit systems; chartered bus, school bus, and interurban bus transportation; and taxis. These activities are distinguished based primarily on such production process factors as vehicle types, routes, and schedules. In this subsector, the principal splits identify scheduled transportation as separate from nonscheduled transportation. The scheduled transportation industry groups are Urban Transit Systems, Interurban and Rural Bus Transportation, and School and Employee Bus Transportation. The nonscheduled industry groups are the Charter Bus Industry and Taxi and Limousine Service. The Other Transit and Ground Passenger Transportation Industry group includes both scheduled and nonscheduled transportation.

Scenic and sightseeing ground transportation services are not included in this subsector but are included in Subsector 487, Scenic and Sightseeing Transportation. Sightseeing does not usually involve place-to-place transportation; the passenger's trip starts and ends at the same location.

4851 Urban Transit Systems

48511 Urban Transit Systems

This industry comprises establishments primarily engaged in operating local and suburban passenger transit systems over regular routes and on regular schedules within a metropolitan area and its adjacent nonurban areas. Such transportation systems involve the use of one or more modes of transport including light rail, commuter rail, subways, streetcars, as well as buses and other motor vehicles.

Providing scenic and sightseeing transportation **48711**
Providing support services to transit and ground transportation **4884**
Providing interurban and rural bus transportation **48521**

485111 Mixed Mode Transit Systems[US]

This U.S. industry comprises establishments primarily engaged in operating local and suburban ground passenger transit systems using more than one mode of transport over regular routes and on regular schedules within a metropolitan area and its adjacent nonurban areas.

Providing support services to transit and ground passenger transportation **4884**

485112 Commuter Rail Systems[US]

This U.S. industry comprises establishments primarily engaged in operating local and suburban commuter rail systems over regular routes and on a regular schedule within a metropolitan area and its adjacent nonurban areas. Commuter rail is usually characterized by reduced fares, multiple ride, and commutation tickets and mostly used by passengers during the morning and evening peak periods.

Operating local and suburban mass passenger transit systems using both commuter rail and another mode of transport **485111**

Operating a subway system **485119**
Providing scenic and sightseeing transportation on land **487110**

485113 Bus and Other Motor Vehicle Transit Systems[US]

This U.S. industry comprises establishments primarily engaged in operating local and suburban passenger transportation systems using buses or other motor vehicles over regular routes and on regular schedules within a metropolitan area and its adjacent nonurban areas.

Operating local and suburban passenger transportation systems using both a bus or other motor vehicle and another mode of transport **485111**
Providing interurban and rural bus transportation **485210**
Providing scenic and sightseeing transportation using buses or other motor vehicles **487110**

485119 Other Urban Transit Systems[US]

This U.S. industry comprises establishments primarily engaged in operating local and suburban ground passenger transit systems (except mixed mode transit systems, commuter rail systems, and buses and other motor vehicles) over regular routes and on regular schedules within a metropolitan area and its adjacent nonurban areas.

Operating local and suburban ground passenger transit systems using more than one mode of transport **485111**
Providing local and suburban passenger transportation using commuter rail systems **485112**
Operating local and suburban bus transit systems **485113**

4852 Interurban and Rural Bus Transportation

485210 Interurban and Rural Bus Transportation

This industry comprises establishments primarily

engaged in providing bus passenger transportation over regular routes and on regular schedules, principally outside a single metropolitan area and its adjacent nonurban areas.

Providing scenic and sightseeing transportation using buses **487110**
Providing buses for charter **485510**
Operating local and suburban bus transit systems **485113**
Operating independent bus terminals **488490**

4853 Taxi and Limousine Service

485310 Taxi Service

This industry comprises establishments primarily engaged in providing passenger transportation by automobile or van, not operated over regular routes and on regular schedules. Establishments of taxicab owner/operator, taxicab fleet operators, or taxicab organizations are included in this industry.

Providing special needs transportation services (except to and from school or work) for the infirm, elderly, or handicapped **485991**
Providing limousine services **485320**
Providing scheduled shuttle services between hotels, airports, or other destination points **485999**

485320 Limousine Service

This industry comprises establishments primarily engaged in providing an array of specialty and luxury passenger transportation services via limousine or luxury sedans generally on a reserved basis. These establishments do not operate over regular routes and on regular schedules.

Providing taxi services **485310**
Providing scheduled shuttle services between hotels, airports, or other destination points **485999**

4854 School and Employee Bus Transportation

485410 School and Employee Bus Transportation

This industry comprises establishments primarily engaged in providing buses and other motor vehicles to transport pupils to and from school or employees to and from work.

Operating local and suburban bus transit systems **485113**
Providing interurban and rural bus transportation **485210**
Providing buses for charter **485510**

4855 Charter Bus Industry

485510 Charter Bus Industry

This industry comprises establishments primarily engaged in providing buses for charter. These establishments provide bus services to meet customers' road transportation needs and generally do not operate over fixed routes and on regular schedules.

Providing scenic and local sightseeing transportation using buses **487110**
Providing interurban and rural bus transportation **485210**

4859 Other Transit and Ground Passenger Transportation

48599 Other Transit and Ground Passenger Transportation

This industry comprises establishments primarily engaged in providing other transit and ground passenger transportation (except urban transit systems, interurban and rural bus transportation, taxi services, school and employee bus transportation, charter bus services, and limousine services (except shuttle services)). Shuttle services (except employee bus) and special needs transportation services are included in this industry. Shuttle services establishments generally travel within a metropolitan area and its adjacent nonurban areas on regular routes, on regular schedules and provide services between hotels, airports, or other destination points. Special needs transportation establishments provide passenger transportation to the infirm, elderly, or handicapped. These establishments may use specially equipped vehicles to provide passenger transportation.

Providing school or employee bus transportation for the infirm, elderly, or handicapped **48541**
Providing ambulance services for emergency and medical purposes **62191**
Operating urban transit systems **4851**
Providing interurban and rural bus transportation **48521**
Providing taxi services and/or limousine services (except shuttle services) **4853**
Providing buses for charter **48551**

485991 Special Needs Transportation[US]

This U.S. industry comprises establishments primarily engaged in providing special needs transportation (except to and from school or work) to the infirm, elderly, or handicapped. These establishments may use specially equipped vehicles to provide passenger transportation.

Providing school or employee bus transportation for the infirm, elderly, or handicapped **485410**
Providing ambulance services for emergency and medical purposes **62191**

485999 All Other Transit and Ground Passenger Transportation[US]

This U.S. industry comprises establishments primarily engaged in providing ground passenger transportation (except urban transit systems; interurban and rural bus transportation, taxi and/or limousine services (except shuttle services), school and employee bus transportation, charter bus services, and special needs transportation). Establishments primarily engaged in operating shuttle services and vanpools are included in this industry. Shuttle services establishments generally provide travel on regular routes and on regular schedules between hotels, airports, or other destination points.

Providing urban transit systems **4851**
Providing interurban and rural bus transportation **485210**
Providing taxi and/or limousine services (except shuttle services) **4853**
Providing school and employee bus transportation (including for the infirm, elderly, or handicapped) **485410**
Providing buses for charter **485510**
Providing special needs transportation (except to and from school or work) for the infirm, elderly, or handicapped **485991**
Providing ambulance services for emergency and medical purposes **621910**

---

486 Pipeline Transportation

Industries in the Pipeline Transportation subsector use transmission pipelines to transport products, such as crude oil, natural gas, refined petroleum products, and slurry. Industries are identified based on the products transported (i.e., pipeline transportation of crude oil, natural gas, refined petroleum products, and other products).

The Pipeline Transportation of Natural Gas industry includes the storage of natural gas because the storage is usually done by the pipeline establishment and because a pipeline is inherently a network in which all the nodes are interdependent.

4861 Pipeline Transportation of Crude Oil

486110 Pipeline Transportation of Crude Oil

This industry comprises establishments primarily engaged in the pipeline transportation of crude oil.

Providing the pipeline transportation of natural gas **486210**
Providing the pipeline transportation of refined petroleum products **486910**

4862 Pipeline Transportation of Natural Gas

486210 Pipeline Transportation of Natural Gas

This industry comprises establishments primarily engaged in the pipeline transportation of natural gas from processing plants to local distribution systems.

Providing natural gas to the end consumer **221210**

4869 Other Pipeline Transportation

This industry group comprises establishments primarily engaged in the pipeline transportation of products (except crude oil and natural gas).

486910 Pipeline Transportation of Refined Petroleum Products

This industry comprises establishments primarily engaged in the pipeline transportation of refined petroleum products.

486990 All Other Pipeline Transportation

This industry comprises establishments primarily engaged in the pipeline transportation of products except crude oil, natural gas, and refined petroleum products.

Providing pipeline transportation of crude oil **486110**
Providing pipeline transportation of natural gas **486210**
Providing pipeline transportation of refined petroleum products **486910**
Providing pipeline transportation of water **221310**

487 Scenic and Sightseeing Transportation

Industries in the Scenic and Sightseeing Transportation subsector utilize transportation equipment to provide recreation and entertainment. These activities have a production process distinct from passenger transportation carried out for the purpose of other types of for-hire transportation. This process does not emphasize efficient transportation; in fact, such activities often use obsolete vehicles, such as steam trains, to provide some extra ambience. The activity is local in nature, usually involving a same-day return to the point of departure. The Scenic and Sightseeing Transportation subsector is separated into three industries based on the mode: land, water, and other.

Activities that are recreational in nature and involve participation by the customer, such as white-water rafting, are generally excluded from this subsector, unless they impose an impact on part of the transportation system. Charter boat fishing, for example, is included in the Scenic and Sightseeing Transportation, Water industry.

4871 Scenic and Sightseeing Transportation, Land

487110 Scenic and Sightseeing Transportation, Land

This industry comprises establishments primarily engaged in providing scenic and sightseeing transportation on land, such as sightseeing buses and trolleys, steam train excursions, and horse-drawn sightseeing rides. The services provided are usually local and involve same-day return to place of origin.

Operating aerial trams or aerial cable cars **487990**
Providing sporting services, such as pack trains, **713990**
Providing intercity and rural bus transportation **485210**
Providing buses for charter **485510**
Operating local and suburban passenger transit systems **48511**
Providing passenger travel arrangements and tours **5615**

4872 Scenic and Sightseeing Transportation, Water

487210 Scenic and Sightseeing Transportation, Water

This industry comprises establishments primarily engaged in providing scenic and sightseeing transportation on water. The services provided are usually local and involve same-day return to place of origin.

Providing recreation services, such as fishing guides, white-water rafting, parasailing, and water skiing **713990**
Providing water taxi services **48321**
Providing water transportation of passengers **483**
Operating floating casinos (i.e., gambling cruises or riverboat casinos) **713210**
Providing boat rental without operators **532292**

4879 Scenic and Sightseeing Transportation, Other

487990 Scenic and Sightseeing Transportation, Other

This industry comprises establishments primarily engaged in providing scenic and sightseeing transportation (except on land and water). The services provided are usually local and involve same-day return to place of departure.

Providing recreational activities, such as hang gliding, **713990**
Providing scheduled or nonscheduled air transportation of passengers or specialty flying services **481**

488 Support Activities for Transportation

Industries in the Support Activities for Transportation subsector provide services that support transportation. These services may be provided to transportation carrier establishments or to the general public. This subsector includes a wide array of establishments, including air traffic control services, marine cargo handling, and motor vehicle towing.

The Support Activities for Transportation subsector includes services to transportation but is separated by type of mode serviced. The Support Activities for Rail Transportation industry includes services to the rail industry (e.g., railroad switching and terminal establishments). Ship repair and maintenance not done in a shipyard are included in Other Support Activities for Water Transportation. An example would be a floating drydock services in a harbor. Excluded from this subsector are establishments primarily engaged in providing factory conversion and overhaul of transportation equipment, which are classified in Subsector 336, Transportation Equipment Manufacturing. Also, establishments primarily engaged in providing rental and leasing of transportation equipment without operator are classified in Subsector 532, Rental and Leasing Services.

4881 Support Activities for Air Transportation

This industry group comprises establishments primarily engaged in providing services to the air transportation industry. These services include airport operation, servicing, repairing (except factory conversion and overhaul of aircraft), maintaining and storing aircraft, and ferrying aircraft.

48811 Airport Operations

This industry comprises establishments primarily engaged in (1) operating international, national, or civil airports or public flying field or (2) supporting airport operations (except special food services contractors), such as rental of hangar space, air traffic control services, baggage handling services, and cargo handling services.

Providing factory conversion, overhaul, and rebuilding of aircraft **33641**
Wholesaling fuel at airports **42272**
Providing airport janitorial services **56172**
Providing food services at airports on a contractual arrangement (i.e., food service contractors) **72231**

488111 Air Traffic Control[CAN]

This U.S. industry comprises establishments primarily engaged in providing air traffic control services to regulate the flow of air traffic.

488119 Other Airport Operations[CAN]

This U.S. industry comprises establishments primarily engaged in (1) operating international, national, or civil airports, or public flying field or (2) supporting airport operations, such as rental of hangar space, and providing baggage handling and/or cargo handling services.

Providing air traffic control services **488111**
Providing factory conversion, overhaul, and rebuilding of aircraft **33641**
Wholesaling fuel at airports **422720**
Providing airport janitorial services **561720**
Providing food services at airports on a contractual arrangement **722310**

488190 Other Support Activities for Air Transportation

This industry comprises establishments primarily engaged in providing specialized services for air transportation (except air traffic control and other airport operations).

Wholesaling fuel at airports **422720**
Providing aircraft janitorial services **561720**
Providing air traffic control services **488111**
Providing airport operations (except air traffic control) **488119**
Providing factory conversion, overhaul, and rebuilding of aircraft **33641**
Providing food services to airlines on a contractual arrangement **722310**

4882 Support Activities for Rail Transportation

488210 Support Activities for Rail Transportation

This industry comprises establishments primarily engaged in providing specialized services for railroad transportation including servicing, routine repairing (except factory conversion, overhaul or rebuilding of rolling stock), and maintaining rail cars; loading and unloading rail cars; and operating independent terminals.

Providing railroad car rental **532411**
Factory conversion, overhaul, or rebuilding of railroad rolling stock **336510**
Providing rail car janitorial services **561720**
Providing dredging services **234990**

4883 Support Activities for Water Transportation

488310 Port and Harbor Operations

This industry comprises establishments primarily engaged in operating ports, harbors (including docking and pier facilities), or canals.

Providing stevedoring and other marine cargo handling services **488320**
Providing navigational services to shipping **488330**
Operating docking and/or storage facilities and commonly known as marinas **713930**

488320 Marine Cargo Handling

This industry comprises establishments primarily engaged in providing stevedoring and other marine cargo handling services (except warehousing).

Preparing freight for transportation **488991**
Operating general merchandise, refrigerated, or other warehousing and storage facilities **493**
Operating docking and pier facilities **488310**

488330 Navigational Services to Shipping

This industry comprises establishments primarily engaged in providing navigational services to shipping. Marine salvage establishments are included in this industry.

Providing water transportation of barges (except coastal or Great Lake barge transportation services) **483211**
Providing coastal and/or Great Lakes barge transportation services **483113**

488390 Other Support Activities for Water Transportation

This industry comprises establishments primarily engaged in providing services to water transportation (except port and harbor operations; marine cargo handling services; and navigational services to shipping).

Ship painting **235210**
Providing ship janitorial services **561720**
Operating port, harbor, or canal facilities **488310**
Providing stevedoring and other marine cargo handling services **488320**
Providing navigational services to shipping **488330**
Providing ship overhauling or repairs in a shipyard **336611**

4884 Support Activities for Road Transportation

488410 Motor Vehicle Towing

This industry comprises establishments primarily engaged in towing light or heavy motor vehicles, both local and long distance. These establishments may provide incidental services, such as storage and emergency road repair services.

Operating gasoline stations **4471**
Providing automotive repair and maintenance **8111**
Both retailing automotive parts and accessories, and repairing automobiles and known as automotive supply stores—are classified Industry **441310**

488490 Other Support Activities for Road Transportation

This industry comprises establishments primarily engaged in providing services (except motor vehicle towing) to road network users.

Providing automotive repair and maintenance **8111**
Providing towing services to motor vehicles **488410**
Providing a network for busing in combination with providing terminal services **485210**
Providing a network for trucking in combination with providing terminal services **484**

4885 Freight Transportation Arrangement

488510 Freight Transportation Arrangement

This industry comprises establishments primarily engaged in arranging transportation of freight between shippers and carriers. These establishments are usually known as freight forwarders, marine shipping agents, or customs brokers and offer a combination of services spanning transportation modes.

Tariff and freight rate consulting services **541614**

4889 Other Support Activities for Transportation

48899 Other Support Activities for Transportation

This industry comprises establishments primarily engaged in providing support activities to transpor-

488

tation (except for air transportation; rail transportation; water transportation; road transportation; and freight transportation arrangement).

Providing support activities for air transportation **4881**
Providing support activities for rail transportation **4882**
Providing support activities for water transportation **4883**
Providing support activities for road transportation **4884**
Arranging transportation of freight between shippers and carriers **48851**
Providing tariff and freight rate consulting services **54161**
Operating stockyards for fattening livestock **112**
Providing packaging and labeling services **56191**

488991 Packing and Crating[US]

This U.S. industry comprises establishments primarily engaged in packing, crating, and otherwise preparing goods for transportation.

Providing packaging and labeling services **561910**

488999 All Other Support Activities for Transportation[US]

This U.S. industry comprises establishments primarily engaged in providing support activities to transportation (except for air transportation; rail transportation; water transportation; road transportation; freight transportation arrangement; and packing and crating).

Operating stockyards for fattening livestock **112**
Providing tariff and freight rate consulting services **541614**
Providing packing and crating services for transportation **488991**
Providing support activities for air transportation **4881**
Providing support activities for rail transportation **488210**
Providing support activities for water transportation **4883**
Providing support activities for road transportation **4884**
Arranging transportation of freight between shippers and carriers **488510**

491 Postal Service

The Postal Service subsector includes the activities of the National Post Office and its subcontractors in delivering letters and small parcels, normally without pick-up at the senders' location. These articles can be described as those that can be handled by one person without using special equipment. This allows the collection, pick-up, and delivery operations to be done with limited labor costs and minimal equipment. Sorting and transportation activities, where necessary, are generally mechanized. The restriction to small parcels distinguishes these establishments from those in the transportation industries.

The traditional activity of the National Postal Service is described in this subsector. Subcontractors include rural Post Offices on contract to the Postal Service.

Bulk transportation of mail on contract to the Postal Service is not included here, because it is usually done by transportation establishments that carry other customers' cargo as well.

4911 Postal Service

491110 Postal Service

This industry comprises establishments primarily engaged in operating the National Postal Service. Establishments primarily engaged in performing one or more postal service, such as sorting, routing, and/or delivery, on a contract basis (except the bulk transportation of mail) are included in this industry.

Providing bulk transportation of mail on a contract basis to and from postal service establishments **4841**
Providing courier services **492110**
Providing mailbox services along with other business services **561431**
Providing local messenger and delivery services **492210**

492 Couriers and Messengers

Industries in the Couriers and Messengers subsector provide intercity and/or local delivery of parcels. These articles can be described as those that may be handled by one person without using special equipment. This allows the collection, pick-up, and delivery operations to be done with limited labor costs and minimal equipment. Sorting and transportation activities, where necessary, are generally mechanized. The restriction to small parcels partly distinguishes these establishments from those in the transportation industries. The complete network of courier services establishments also distinguishes these transportation services from local messenger and delivery establishments in this subsector. This includes the establishments that perform intercity transportation as well as establishments that, under contract to them, perform local pick-up and delivery. Messengers, which usually deliver within a metropolitan or single urban area, may use bicycle, foot, small truck, or van.

4921 Couriers

492110 Couriers

This industry comprises establishments primarily engaged in providing air, surface, or combined courier delivery services of parcels generally between metropolitan areas or urban centers. The establishments of this industry form a network including courier local pick-up and delivery to serve their customers' needs.

Providing messenger and delivery services within a metropolitan area or within an urban center **492210**
Providing the truck transportation of palletized general freight **4841**

4922 Local Messengers and Local Delivery

492210 Local Messengers and Local Delivery

This industry comprises establishments primarily engaged in providing local messenger and delivery services of small items within a single metropolitan or within an urban center. These establishments generally provide point-to-point pickup and delivery and do not operate as part of an intercity courier network.

Providing local letter and parcel delivery services as part of an intercity courier network **492110**
Operating the National Postal Service or providing postal services on a contract basis (except the bulk transportation of mail) **491110**
Providing the bulk transportation of mail on a contract basis to and from Postal Service establishments **4841**

493

493 Warehousing and Storage

Industries in the Warehousing and Storage subsector are primarily engaged in operating warehousing and storage facilities for general merchandise, refrigerated goods, and other warehouse products. These establishments provide facilities to store goods. They do not sell the goods they handle. These establishments take responsibility for storing the goods and keeping them secure. They may also provide a range of services, often referred to as logistics services, related to the distribution of goods. Logistics services can include labeling, breaking bulk, inventory control and management, light assembly, order entry and fulfillment, packaging, pick and pack, price marking and ticketing, and transportation arrangement. However, establishments in this industry group always provide warehousing or storage services in addition to any logistic services. Furthermore, the warehousing or storage of goods must be more than incidental to the performance of services, such as price marking.

Bonded warehousing and storage services and warehouses located in free trade zones are included in the industries of this subsector.

4931 Warehousing and Storage

493110 General Warehousing and Storage

This industry comprises establishments primarily engaged in operating merchandise warehousing and storage facilities. These establishments generally handle goods in containers, such as boxes, barrels, and/or drums, using equipment, such as forklifts, pallets, and racks. They are not specialized in handling bulk products of any particular type, size, or quantity of goods or products.

Renting or leasing space for self storage **531130**
Selling in combination with handling and/or distributing goods to other wholesale or retail establishments **42**

493120 Refrigerated Warehousing and Storage

This industry comprises establishments primarily engaged in operating refrigerated warehousing and storage facilities. Establishments primarily engaged in the storage of furs for the trade are included in this industry. The services provided by these establishments include blast freezing, tempering, and modified atmosphere storage services.

Storing furs (except for the trade) and garments **812320**

493130 Farm Product Warehousing and Storage

This industry comprises establishments primarily engaged in operating bulk farm product warehousing and storage facilities (except refrigerated). Grain elevators primarily engaged in storage are included in this industry.

Operating refrigerated warehousing and storage facilities **493120**
Storing grains and field beans (i.e., grain elevators) as an incidental activity to sales **42251**

493190 Other Warehousing and Storage

This industry comprises establishments primarily engaged in operating warehousing and storage facilities (except general merchandise, refrigerated, and farm product warehousing and storage).

Renting or leasing space for self storage **531130**
Storing hazardous materials for treatment and disposal **562211**
Operating general warehousing and storage facilities **493110**
Operating refrigerated warehousing and storage facilities **493120**
Operating farm product warehousing and storage facilities **493130**

SECTOR 51: INFORMATION

OVERVIEW OF THIS SECTOR AS A WHOLE

The Information sector comprises establishments engaged in the following processes: (a) producing and distributing information and cultural products, (b) providing the means to transmit or distribute these products as well as data or communications, and (c) processing data. The main components of this sector are the publishing industries, including software publishing, the motion picture and sound recording industries, the broadcasting and telecommunications industries, and the information services and data processing industries. The expressions "information age" and "global information economy" are used with considerable frequency today. The general idea of an "information economy" includes both the notion of industries primarily producing, procesing, and distributing information, as well as the idea that every industry is using available information and information technology to reorganize and make themselves more productive.

For the purpose of developing NAICS, it is the transformation of information into a commodity that is produced and distributed by a number of growing industries that is at issue. The information sector groups three types of establishments: (1) those engaged in producing and distributing information and cultural products; (2) those that provide the means to transmit or distribute these products as well as data or communications; and (3) those that process data. Cultural products are those that directly express attitudes, opinions, ideas, values, and artistic creativity; provide entertainment; or offer information and analysis concerning the past and present. Included in this definition are popular, mass-produced, products as well as cultural products that normally have a more limited audience, such as poetry books, literary magazines, or classical records. These activities were formerly classified throughout the existing national classifications. Traditional publishing is in manufacturing; broadcasting in communications; software production in business services; film production in amusement services; and so forth. The unique characteristics of information and cultural products, and of the processes involved in their production and distribution, distinguish the Information sector from the goods-producing and service-producing sectors. Some of these characteristics are:

1. Unlike traditional goods, an "information or cultural product," such as a newspaper on-line or television program, does not necessarily have tangible qualities, nor is it necessarily associated with a particular form. A movie can be shown at a movie theater, on a television broadcast, through video-on-demand or rented at a local video store. A sound recording can be aired on radio, embedded in multimedia products, or sold at a record store.

2. Unlike traditional services, the delivery of these products does not require direct contact between the supplier and the consumer.

3. The value of these products to the consumer lies in their informational, educational, cultural, or entertainment content, not in the format in which they are distributed. Most of these products are protected from unlawful reproduction by copyright laws.

4. The intangible property aspect of information and cultural products makes the processes involved in their production and distribution very different from goods and services. Only those possessing the rights to these works are authorized to reproduce, alter, improve, and distribute them. Acquiring and using these rights often involves significant costs. In addition, technology is revolutionizing the distribution of these products. It is possible to distribute them in a physical form, via broadcast, or on-line.

5. Distributors of information and cultural products can easily add value to the products they distribute. For instance, broadcasters add advertising not contained in the original product. This capacity means that unlike traditional distributors, they derive revenue not from sale of the distributed product to the final consumer, but from those who pay for the privilege of adding information to the original product. Similarly, a database publisher can acquire the rights to thousands of previously published newspaper and periodical articles and add new value by providing search and software and organizing the information in a way that facilitates research and retrieval. These products often command a much higher price than the original information.

The distribution modes for information commodities may either eliminate the necessity for traditional manufacture, or reverse the conventional order of manufacture-distribute: A newspaper distributed on-line, for example, can be printed locally or by the final consumer. Similarly, it is anticipated that packaged software, which today is mainly bought through the traditional retail channels, will soon be available mainly on-line. The NAICS Information sector is designed to make such economic changes transparent as they occur, or to facilitate designing surveys that will monitor the new phenomena and provide data to analyze the changes. Many of the industries in the NAICS Information sector are engaged in producing products protected by copyright law, or in distributing them (other than distribution by traditional wholesale and retail methods). Examples are traditional publishing industries, software and database publishing industries, and film and sound industries. Broadcasting and telecommunications industries and information providers and processors are also included in the Information sector, because their technologies are so closely linked to other industries in the Information sector.

511 Publishing Industries

Industries in the Publishing Industries subsector group establishments engaged in the publishing of newspapers, magazines, other periodicals, and books, as well as database and software publishing. In general, these establishments, which are known as publishers, issue copies of works for which they usually possess copyright. Works may be in one or more formats including traditional print form, CD-ROM, or on-line. Publishers may publish works originally created by others for which they have obtained the rights and/or works that they have created in-house. Software publishing is included here because the activity, creation of a copyrighted product and bringing it to market, is equivalent to the creation process for other types of intellectual products. In NAICS, publishing, the reporting, writing, editing, and other processes that are required to create an edition of a newspaper, is treated as a major economic activity in its own right, rather than as a subsidiary activity to a manufacturing activity, printing. Thus, publishing is classified in the Information sector; whereas, printing remains in the NAICS Manufacturing sector. In part, the NAICS classification reflects the fact that publishing increasingly takes place in establishments that are physically separate from the associated printing establishments. More crucially, the NAICS classification of book and newspaper publishing is intended to portray their roles in a modern economy, in which they do not resemble manufacturing activities. Music publishers are not included in the Publishing Industries subsector, but are included in the Motion Picture and Sound Recording Industries subsector. Reproduction of prepackaged software is treated in NAICS as a manufacturing activity; on-line distribution of software products is in the Information sector, and custom design of software to client specifications is included in the Professional, Scientific, and Technical Services sector. These distinctions arise because of the different ways that software is created, reproduced, and distributed. The Information sector does not include products, such as manifold business forms. Information is not the essential component of these items. Establishments producing these items are included in Subsector 323, Printing and Related Support Activities.

5III Newspaper, Periodical, Book, and Database Publishers

This industry group comprises establishments primarily engaged in publishing newspapers, magazines, other periodicals, books, databases, and other works, such as calendars, greeting cards, and maps. These works are characterized by the intellectual creativity required in their development and are usually protected by copyright. Publishers distribute or arrange for the distribution of these works.

Publishing establishments may create the works in-house, contract for, purchase, or compile works that were originally created by others. These works may be published in one or more formats, such as print and/or electronic form, including on-line. Establishments in this industry may print, reproduce, or offer direct access to the works themselves or may arrange with others to carry out such functions.

Establishments that both print and publish may fill excess capacity with commercial or job printing. However, the publishing activity is still considered to be the primary activity of these establishments.

5IIII0 Newspaper Publishers

This industry comprises establishments known as newspaper publishers. Establishments in this industry carry out operations necessary for producing and distributing newspapers, including gathering news; writing news columns, feature stories, and editorials; and selling and preparing advertisements. These establishments may publish newspapers in print or electronic form.

Printing newspapers without publishing **32311**
Supplying the news media with information, such as news, reports, and pictures, **5I4II0**
Selling advertising space **541840**

511120 Periodical Publishers

This industry comprises establishments known as magazine or periodical publishers. These establishments carry out the operations necessary for producing and distributing magazines and other periodicals, such as gathering, writing, and editing articles, and selling and preparing advertisements. These establishments may publish magazines and other periodicals in print or electronic form.

Printing periodicals without publishing **32311**
Publishing databases and directories **511140**
Selling advertising space **541840**

511130 Book Publishers

This industry comprises establishments known as book publishers. Establishments in this industry carry out design, editing, and marketing activities necessary for producing and distributing books. These establishments may publish books in print, electronic, or audio form.

Printing books without publishing **32311**
Music publishers **512230**
Direct sales activities without publishing **454390**

511140 Database and Directory Publishers

This industry comprises establishments primarily engaged in publishing compilations and collections of information or facts that are logically organized to facilitate their use. These collections may be published in print or electronic form. Electronic versions may be provided directly to customers by the establishment or offered through on-line services or third-party vendors.

Printing without publishing databases and directories **32311**
Publishing encyclopedias **511130**
Direct access to databases developed by others **514191**
Publishing computer software **511210**

511119 Other Publishers

This industry comprises establishments known as publishers (except newspaper, magazine, book, directory, database, and music publishers). These establishments may publish works in print or electronic form.

Newspaper publishers **51111**
Magazine and other periodical publishers **51112**
Book publishers **51113**
Directory and database publishing **51114**
Music publishers **51223**
Manufacturing manifold business forms **32311**

511191 Greeting Card Publishers[US]

This U.S. industry comprises establishments primarily engaged in publishing greeting cards.

Printing greeting cards without publishing **32311**

511199 All Other Publishers[US]

This U.S. industry comprises establishments generally known as publishers (except newspaper, magazine, book, directory, database, music, and greeting card publishers). These establishment may publish works in print or electronic form.

Newspaper publishers **511110**
Magazine or other periodical publishers **511120**
Book publishers **511130**
Directory and database publishing **511140**
Greeting card publishing **511191**
Music publishers **512230**
Manufacturing manifold business forms **323116**
Manufacturing day schedulers **323118**

511

5112 Software Publishers

511210 Software Publishers

This industry comprises establishments primarily engaged in computer software publishing or publishing and reproduction. Establishments in this industry carry out operations necessary for producing and distributing computer software, such as designing, providing documentation, assisting in installation, and providing support services to software purchasers. These establishments may design, develop, and publish, or publish only.

Reselling packaged software **42** or **44–45**
Designing software to meet the needs of specific users **541511**
Mass duplication of software **334611**

512 Motion Picture and Sound Recording Industries

Industries in the Motion Picture and Sound Recording Industries subsector group establishments involved in the production and distribution of motion pictures and sound recordings. While producers and distributors of motion pictures and sound recordings issue works for sale as traditional publishers do, the processes are sufficiently different to warrant placing establishments engaged in these activities in a separate subsector. Production is typically a complex process that involves several distinct types of establishments that are engaged in activities, such as contracting with performers, creating the film or sound content, and providing technical postproduction services. Film distribution is often to exhibitors, such as theaters and broadcasters, rather than through the wholesale and retail distribution chain. When the product is in a mass-produced form, NAICS treats production and distribution as the major economic activity as it does in the Publishing Industries subsector, rather than as a subsidiary activity to the manufacture of such products.

This subsector does not include establishments primarily engaged in the wholesale distribution of video cassettes and sound recordings, such as compact discs and audio tapes; these establishments are included in the Wholesale Trade sector. Reproduction of video cassettes and sound recordings that is carried out separately from establishments engaged in production and distribution is treated in NAICS as a manufacturing activity.

5121 Motion Picture and Video Industries

This industry group comprises establishments primarily engaged in the production and/or distribution of motion pictures, videos, television programs, or commercials; in the exhibition of motion pictures; or in the provision of postproduction and related services.

512110 Motion Picture and Video Production

This industry comprises establishments primarily engaged in producing, or producing and distributing motion pictures, videos, television programs, or television and video commercials.

Producing motion pictures and videos on contract as independent producers **711510**
Providing teleproduction and other postproduction services **512191**
Providing video taping of weddings, special events, and/or business inventories **54192**
Providing motion picture laboratory services **512199**
Providing mass duplication and packaging of video tapes **334612**
Acquiring distribution rights and distributing motion pictures and videos **512120**

512120 Motion Picture and Video Distribution

This industry comprises establishments primarily engaged in acquiring distribution rights and distributing film and video productions to motion picture theaters, television networks and stations, and exhibitors.

Producing and distributing motion pictures and videos **512110**
Wholesaling video cassette tapes and discs **421690**
Providing mass duplication and packaging of video tapes **334612**
Providing motion picture footage (via film libraries) to producers **512199**
Renting video tapes and discs to the general public **532230**
Selling video cassettes and discs to the general public **451220**

512113 Motion Picture and Video Exhibition

This industry comprises establishments primarily engaged in operating motion picture theaters and/or exhibiting motion pictures or videos at film festivals, and so forth.

512131 Motion Picture Theaters (except Drive-Ins)[US]

This U.S. industry comprises establishments primarily engaged in operating motion picture theaters (except drive-ins) and/or exhibiting motion pictures or videos at film festivals, and so forth.

512132 Drive-In Motion Picture Theaters[US]

This U.S. industry comprises establishments primarily engaged in operating drive-in motion picture theaters.

51219 Postproduction Services and Other Motion Picture and Video Industries

This industry comprises establishments primarily engaged in providing postproduction services and other services to the motion picture industry, including specialized motion picture or video postproduction services, such as editing, film/tape transfers, subtitling, credits, closed captioning, and computer-produced graphics, animation and special effects, as well as developing and processing motion picture film.

Mass duplicating video tapes and film **33461**
Providing audio services for film, television, and video productions **51224**
Renting wardrobes and costumes for motion picture production **53222**
Renting studio equipment **53249**
Casting actors and actresses with production companies **56131**

512191 Teleproduction and Other Postproduction Services[US]

This U.S. industry comprises establishments primarily engaged in providing specialized motion picture or video postproduction services, such as editing, film/tape transfers, subtitling, credits, closed captioning, and animation and special effects.

Mass duplicating video tapes and film **33461**
Developing and processing motion picture film **512199**
Providing audio services for film, television, and video productions **512240**
Acquiring distribution rights and distributing film and video productions to motion picture theaters, television networks and stations, and exhibitors **512120**

512199 Other Motion Picture and Video Industries[US]

This U.S. industry comprises establishments primarily engaged in providing motion picture and video services (except motion picture and video production, distribution, exhibition, and teleproduction and other postproduction services).

Renting wardrobes and costumes for motion picture production **532220**
Renting studio equipment **532490**
Casting actors and actresses with production companies **561310**
Motion picture and video production **512110**
Motion picture and video distribution **512120**
Teleproduction and other postproduction services **512191**
Motion picture and video exhibition **51213**

5122 Sound Recording Industries

This industry group comprises establishments primarily engaged in producing and distributing musical recordings, in publishing music, or in providing sound recording and related services.

512210 Record Production

This industry comprises establishments primarily engaged in record production (e.g., tapes, CDs). These establishments contract with artists and arrange and finance the production of original master recordings. Establishments in this industry hold the copyright to the master recording and derive most of their revenues from the sales, leasing, and licensing of master recordings. Establishments in this industry do not have their own duplication or distribution capabilities.

Releasing, promoting, and distributing recordings **512220**
Promoting and authorizing the use of musical works in various media **512230**
Mass duplication services **334612**
Wholesaling music recordings **421690**
Managing the careers of artists **711410**
Providing facilities and technical expertise for recording musical performances **512240**
Producing albums on contract as independent producers **711510**

512

512220 Integrated Record Production/Distribution

This industry comprises establishments primarily engaged in releasing, promoting, and distributing sound recordings. These establishments manufacture or arrange for the manufacture of recordings, such as audio tapes/cassettes and compact discs, and promote and distribute these products to wholesalers, retailers, or directly to the public. Establishments in this industry produce master recordings themselves, or obtain reproduction and distribution rights to master recordings produced by record production companies or other integrated record companies.

Contracting with musical artists, arranging for the production of master recordings, and marketing the reproduction rights **512210**
Providing facilities and technical expertise for recording musical performances **512240**
Mass duplication of recorded products **334612**
Wholesaling records, tapes, and compact discs without producing recordings **42**
Retailing records, tapes, and compact discs without producing recordings **44–45**

512230 Music Publishers

This industry comprises establishments primarily engaged in acquiring and registering copyrights for musical compositions in accordance with law and promoting and authorizing the use of these compositions in recordings, radio, television, motion pictures, live performances, print, or other media. Establishments in this industry represent the interests of the songwriter or other owners of musical compositions to produce revenues from the use of such works, generally through licensing agreements. These establishments may own the copyright or act as administrator of the music copyrights on behalf of copyright owners.

Independent songwriters who act as their own publishers **711510**

512240 Sound Recording Studios

This industry comprises establishments primarily engaged in providing the facilities and technical expertise for sound recording in a studio. Establishments in this industry may provide audio production or postproduction services for producing master recordings, and may provide audio services for film, television, and video productions.

Releasing, promoting, and distributing sound recordings **512220**
Providing mass duplication of recorded products **334612**
Contracting with musical artists, arranging for the production of master recordings, and marketing the reproduction rights **512210**

512290 Other Sound Recording Industries

This industry comprises establishments primarily engaged in providing sound recording services (except record production, distribution, music publishing, and sound recording in a studio). Establishments in this industry provide services, such as the audio recording of meetings and conferences.

Producing records, including contracting with musical artists, arranging and financing the production of master recordings, and marketing the reproduction rights **512210**
Releasing, promoting, and distributing sound recordings **512220**
Promoting and authorizing the use of musical works in various media **512230**
Providing facilities and expertise for recording musical performance **512240**
Providing mass duplication of recorded products **334612**
Organizing and promoting the presentation of performing arts productions **7113**

513 Broadcasting and Telecommunications

Industries in the Broadcasting and Telecommunications subsector include establishments providing point-to-point communications and the services related to that activity. The industry groups (Radio and Television Broadcasting, Cable Networks and Program Distribution, and Telecommunications) are based on differences in the methods of communication and in the nature of services provided. The Radio and Television Broadcasting industry group includes establishments that operate broadcasting studios and facilities for over the air or satellite delivery of radio and television programs of entertainment, news, talk, and the like. These establishments are often engaged in the production and purchase of programs and generating revenues from the sale of air time to advertisers and from donations, subsidies, and/or the sale of programs. The Cable Networks and Program Distribution industry group includes two types of establishments. Those in the Cable Networks industry operate studios and facilities for the broadcasting of programs that are typically narrowcast in nature (limited format, such as news, sports, education, and youth-oriented programming). The services of these establishments are typically sold on a subscription or fee basis. Delivery of the programs to customers is handled by other establishments in the Cable and Other Program Distribution industry that operate cable systems, direct-to-home satellite systems, or other similar systems. The Telecommunications industry group is primarily engaged in operating, maintaining, and/or providing access to facilities for the transmission of voice, data, text, sound, and full motion picture video between network termination points. A transmission facility may be based on a single technology or a combination of technologies. Establishments primarily engaged as independent contractors in the maintenance and installation of broadcasting and telecommunications systems are classified in Sector 23, Construction.

5131 Radio and Television Broadcasting

This industry group comprises establishments primarily engaged in operating broadcast studios and facilities for over-the-air or satellite delivery of radio and television programs. These establishments are often engaged in the production or purchase of programs or generate revenues from the sale of air time to advertisers, from donations and subsidies, or from the sale of programs.

51311 Radio Broadcasting

This industry comprises establishments primarily engaged in broadcasting audio signals. These establishments operate radio broadcasting studios and facilities for the transmission of aural programming by radio to the public, to affiliates, or to subscribers. The radio programs may include entertainment, news, talk shows, business data, or religious services.

Producing taped radio programming **51229**

513111 Radio Networks^{US}

This U.S. industry comprises establishments primarily engaged in assembling and transmitting aural programming to their affiliates or subscribers via over-the-air broadcasts, cable, or satellite. The programming covers a wide variety of material, such as news services, religious programming, weather, sports, or music.

Producing taped radio programming **512290**

513112 Radio Stations^{US}

This U.S. industry comprises establishments primarily engaged in broadcasting aural programs by radio to the public. Programming may originate in their own studios, from an affiliated network, or from external sources.

513120 Television Broadcasting

This industry comprises establishments primarily engaged in broadcasting images together with sound. These establishments operate television broadcasting studios and facilities for the programming and transmission of programs to the public. These establishments also produce or transmit visual programming to affiliated broadcast television stations, which in turn broadcast the programs to the public on a prede-termined schedule. Programming may originate in their own studios, from an affiliated network, or from external sources.

Producing taped television program materials **512110**
Furnishing cable and other pay television services **513220**
Producing and broadcasting television programs for cable and satellite television systems **513210**

5132 Cable Networks and Program Distribution

This industry group comprises establishments that primarily assemble program material and transmit television programs for cable and satellite systems, or that operate these systems.

513210 Cable Networks

This industry comprises establishments primarily engaged in operating studios and facilities for the broadcasting of programs on a subscription or fee basis. The broadcast programming is typically narrowcast in nature (e.g., limited format, such as news, sports, education, or youth-oriented). These establishments produce programming in their own facilities or acquire programming from external sources. The programming material is usually delivered to a third party, such as cable systems or direct-to-home satellite systems, for transmission to viewers.

Producing taped television program material **512110**
Producing and transmitting television programs to affiliated stations **513120**
Furnishing cable and other pay television services **513220**
Retailing merchandise by electronic media, such as television, **454110**

513220 Cable and Other Program Distribution

This industry comprises establishments primarily engaged as third-party distribution systems for broadcast programming. The establishments of this industry deliver visual, aural, or textual programming received from cable networks, local television stations, or radio networks to consumers via cable or direct-to-home satellite systems on a subscription or fee basis. These establishments do not generally originate programming material.

Producing and broadcasting television programs for cable and satellite television systems **513210**
Maintenance and installation of cable systems as independent contractors **23**

5I33 Telecommunications

This industry group comprises establishments primarily engaged in operating, maintaining or providing access to facilities for the transmission of voice, data, text, and full motion picture video between network termination points and telecommunications reselling. Transmission facilities may be based on a single technology or a combination of technologies.

5I33I0 Wired Telecommunications Carriers

This industry comprises establishments engaged in (1) operating and maintaining switching and transmission facilities to provide direct communications via landlines, microwave, or a combination of landlines and satellite linkups or (2) furnishing telegraph and other nonvocal communications using their own facilities.

Broadcasting scheduled television programs via cable or satellite facilities on a subscription or fee basis **513220**
Providing coin-operated pay telephones **812990**
Operating and maintaining wireless networks **51332**
Reselling telecommunications, without operating a network **513330**
Publishing telephone directories **5III40**
Maintaining and installing wired telecommunication systems as independent contractors **23**

5I332 Wireless Telecommunications Carriers (except Satellite)

This industry comprises establishments primarily engaged in operating and maintaining switching and transmission facilities that provide direct communications via airwaves. Included in this industry are establishments providing wireless telecommunications network services, such as cellular telephone or paging services.

Providing telephone answering services using pagers **56142**

5I3321 Paging[US]

This U.S. industry comprises establishments primarily engaged in operating paging networks. The establishments of this industry may also supply and maintain equipment used to receive signals.

Providing telephone answering services using pagers **561421**

5I3322 Cellular and Other Wireless Telecommunications[US]

This U.S. industry comprises establishments primarily engaged in operating cellular telecommunications and other wireless telecommunications networks (except paging).

Operating paging networks **513321**

5I3330 Telecommunications Resellers

This industry comprises establishments primarily engaged in purchasing access and network capacity from owners and operators of the networks and reselling wired and wireless telecommunications services to businesses and households. Establishments in this industry resell telecommunications; they do not operate and maintain telecommunications switching and transmission facilities.

Operating and maintaining wired telecommunications networks **513310**
Reselling satellite telecommunications services **513340**
Operating and maintaining wireless telecommunications **51332**

5I3340 Satellite Telecommunications

This industry comprises establishments primarily engaged in providing point-to-point telecommunications services to other establishments in the telecommunications and broadcasting industries by forwarding and receiving communications signals via a system of satellites or reselling satellite telecommunications.

Providing direct-to-home satellite television systems to individual households or consumers **513220**

5I3390 Other Telecommunications

This industry comprises establishments primarily engaged in (1) providing specialized telecommunications applications, such as satellite tracking, communications telemetry, and radar station operations or (2) providing satellite terminal stations and associated facilities operationally connected with one or more terrestrial communications systems and capable of transmitting telecommunications to or receiving telecommunications from satellite systems.

Providing satellite telecommunications **513340**
Providing custom design, programming, or facilities management services for integrated computer and telecommunications systems or operations **54I5I**

514 Information Services and Data Processing Services

Industries in the Information Services and Data Processing Services subsector group establishments providing information, storing information, providing access to information, and processing information. The main components of the subsector are news syndicates, libraries, archives, on-line information service providers, and data processors.

5141 Information Services

This industry group comprises establishments primarily engaged in providing information, storing information, and/or providing access to information.

514110 News Syndicates

This industry comprises establishments primarily engaged in supplying information, such as news reports, articles, pictures, and features, to the news media.

Independent writers and journalists (including photojournalists) **711510**

514120 Libraries and Archives

This industry comprises establishments primarily engaged in providing library or archive services. These establishments are engaged in maintaining collections of documents (e.g., books, journals, newspapers, and music) and facilitating the use of such documents (recorded information regardless of its physical form and characteristics) as are required to meet the informational, research, educational, or recreational needs of their user. These establishments may also acquire, research, store, preserve, and generally make accessible to the public historical documents, photographs, maps, audio material, audiovisual material, and other archival material of historical interest. All or portions of these collections may be accessible electronically.

Providing stock footage (via motion picture and video tape libraries) to the media, multimedia, and advertising industries **512199**
Distributing film and video productions to motion picture theaters, television networks and stations, and exhibitors **512120**

51419 Other Information Services

This industry comprises establishments primarily engaged in providing information services (except news syndicates, libraries, and archives). Included in

this industry are Internet service providers, on-line information access services, and telephone-based (i.e., toll call) information services. On-line information services establishments are engaged in the provision of direct access to computer-held information published by others via telecommunications networks. These establishments often provide electronic mail services, bulletin boards, browsers, and search routines.

Publishing or compiling and offer direct on-line access to information that they publish or compile **511**
Supplying information to the news media **514110**
Operating libraries and archives **514120**

514191 On-Line Information Services[CAN]

This U.S. industry comprises Internet access providers, Internet service providers, and similar establishments primarily engaged in providing direct access through telecommunications networks to computer-held information compiled or published by others.

Publishing or compiling information and offering direct on-line access to the information that they publish or compile **511**

514199 All Other Information Services[CAN]

This U.S. industry comprises establishments primarily engaged in providing information services (except news syndicates, libraries, archives, and on-line information access). Activities performed by establishments in this industry include telephone-based information recordings and information search services on a contract basis.

Publishing or compiling and offer direct on-line access to information that they publish or compile **511**
Supplying information to the news media **514110**
Operating libraries and archives **514120**
Providing on-line information services **514191**

514

5142 Data Processing Services

514210 Data Processing Services

This industry comprises establishments primarily engaged in providing electronic data processing services. These establishments may provide complete processing and preparation of reports from data supplied by customers; specialized services, such as automated data entry services; or may make data processing resources available to clients on an hourly or timesharing basis.

Providing text processing and desktop publishing services **561410**

Providing on-site management and operation of a client's data-processing facilities **541513**

Providing on-line access to information and services developed by others **514191**

Providing access to microcomputers and office equipment, as well as other office support services **56143**

Processing financial transactions, such as credit card transactions, **522320**

Providing payroll processing services using data processing techniques **541214**

SECTOR 52: FINANCE AND INSURANCE

OVERVIEW OF THIS SECTOR AS A WHOLE

The Finance and Insurance sector comprises establishments primarily engaged in financial transactions (transactions involving the creation, liquidation, or change in ownership of financial assets) and/or in facilitating financial transactions. Three principal types of activities are identified:

1. Raising funds by taking deposits and/or issuing securities and, in the process, incurring liabilities. Establishments engaged in this activity use raised funds to acquire financial assets by making loans and/or purchasing securities. Putting themselves at risk, they channel funds from lenders to borrowers and transform or repackage the funds with respect to maturity, scale and risk. This activity is known as financial intermediation.

2. Pooling of risk by underwriting insurance and annuities. Establishments engaged in this activity collect fees, insurance premiums, or annuity considerations; build up reserves; invest those reserves; and make contractual payments. Fees are based on the expected incidence of the insured risk and the expected return on investment.

3. Providing specialized services facilitating or supporting financial intermediation, insurance, and employee benefit programs.

In addition, monetary authorities charged with monetary control are included in this sector. The subsectors, industry groups, and industries within the NAICS Finance and Insurance sector are defined on the basis of their unique production processes. As with all industries, the production processes are distinguished by their use of specialized human resources and specialized physical capital. In addition, the way in which these establishments acquire and allocate financial capital, their source of funds, and the use of those funds provides a third basis for distinguishing characteristics of the production process. For instance, the production process in raising funds through deposit-taking is different from the process of raising funds in bond or money markets. The process of making loans to individuals also requires different production processes than does the creation of investment pools or the underwriting of securities. Most of the Finance and Insurance subsectors contain one or more industry groups of (1) intermediaries with similar patterns of raising and using funds and (2) establishments engaged in activities that facilitate, or are otherwise related to, that type of financial or insurance intermediation. Industries within this sector are defined in terms of activities for which a production process can be specified, and many of these activities are not exclusive to a particular type of financial institution. To deal with the varied activities taking place within existing financial institutions, the approach is to split these institutions into components performing specialized services. This requires defining the units engaged in providing those services and developing procedures that allow for their delineation. These units are the equivalents for finance and insurance of the establishments defined for other industries.

The output of many financial services, as well as the inputs and the processes by which they are combined, cannot be observed at a single location and can only be defined at a higher level of the organizational structure of the enterprise. Additionally, a number of independent activities that represent separate and distinct production processes may take place at a single location belonging to a multilocation financial firm. Activities are more likely to be homogeneous with respect to production characteristics than are locations, at least in financial services. The classification defines activities broadly enough that it can be used both by those classifying by location and by those employing a more top-down approach to the delineation of the establishment. Establishments engaged in activities that facilitate, or are otherwise related to, the various types of intermediation have been included in individual subsectors, rather than in a separate subsector dedicated to services alone because these services are performed by intermediaries as well as by specialist establishments and the extent to which the activity of the intermediaries can be separately identified is not clear.

The Finance and Insurance sector has been defined to encompass establishments primarily engaged in financial transactions; that is, transactions involving the creation, liquidation, or change in ownership of financial assets or in facilitating financial transactions. Financial industries are extensive users of electronic means for facilitating the verification of financial balances, authorizing transactions, transferring funds to and from transactors' accounts, notifying banks (or credit card issuers) of the individual transactions, and providing daily summaries. Since these transaction processing activities are integral to the production of finance and insurance services, establishments that principally provide a financial transaction processing service are classified to this sector, rather than to the data processing industry in the Information sector. Legal entities that hold portfolios of assets on behalf of others are significant and data on them are required for a variety of purposes. Thus for NAICS, these funds, trusts, and other financial vehicles are the fifth subsector of the Finance and Insurance sector. These entities earn interest, dividends, and other property income, but have little or no employment and no revenue from the sale of services. Separate establishments and employees devoted to the management of funds Group 5239, Other Financial Investment Activities.

521 Monetary Authorities—Central Bank

The Monetary Authorities—Central Bank subsector groups establishments that engage in performing central banking functions, such as issuing currency, managing the Nation's money supply and international reserves, holding deposits that represent the reserves of other banks and other central banks, and acting as fiscal agent for the central government.

521 Monetary Authorities—Central Bank

521110 Monetary Authorities—Central Bank[CAN]

This industry comprises establishments primarily engaged in performing central banking functions, such as issuing currency, managing the Nation's money supply and international reserves, holding deposits that represent the reserves of other banks and other central banks, and acting as fiscal agent for the central government.

Board of Governors of the Federal Reserve System **921130**

522 Credit Intermediation and Related Activities

Industries in the Credit Intermediation and Related Activities subsector group establishments that (1) lend funds raised from depositors; (2) lend funds raised from credit market borrowing; or (3) facilitate the lending of funds or issuance of credit by engaging in such activities as mortgage and loan brokerage, clearinghouse and reserve services, and check cashing services.

5221 Depository Credit Intermediation^{CAN}

This industry group comprises establishments primarily engaged in accepting deposits (or share deposits) and in lending funds from these deposits. Within this group, industries are defined on the basis of differences in the types of deposit liabilities assumed and in the nature of the credit extended.

522110 Commercial Banking^{CAN}

This industry comprises establishments primarily engaged in accepting demand and other deposits and making commercial, industrial, and consumer loans. Commercial banks and branches of foreign banks are included in this industry.

Credit card banking **522210**
Industrial banks and primarily engaged in accepting deposits **522190**
Depository institutions primarily engaged in trust activities **523991**

522120 Savings Institutions^{US}

This industry comprises establishments primarily engaged in accepting time deposits, making mortgage and real estate loans, and investing in high-grade securities. Savings and loan associations and savings banks are included in this industry.

Accepting demand and other deposits and making all types of loans **522110**

522130 Credit Unions^{CAN}

This industry comprises establishments primarily engaged in accepting members' share deposits in cooperatives that are organized to offer consumer loans to their members.

522190 Other Depository Credit Intermediation^{CAN}

This industry comprises establishments primarily engaged in accepting deposits and lending funds (except commercial banking, savings institutions, and credit unions). Establishments known as industrial

banks or Morris Plans and primarily engaged in accepting deposits, and private banks (i.e., unincorporated banks) are included in this industry.

Accepting demand and other deposits and making all types of loans **522110**
Accepting time deposits **522120**
Accepting members' share deposits in cooperatives **522130**
Industrial banks and Morris Plans, providing nondepository credit **52229**

5222 Nondepository Credit Intermediation^{CAN}

This industry group comprises establishments, both public (government-sponsored enterprises) and private, primarily engaged in extending credit or lending funds raised by credit market borrowing, such as issuing commercial paper or other debt instruments or by borrowing from other financial intermediaries. Within this group, industries are defined on the basis of the type of credit being extended.

522210 Credit Card Issuing^{CAN}

This industry comprises establishments primarily engaged in providing credit by issuing credit cards. Credit card issuance provides the funds required to purchase goods and services in return for payment of the full balance or payments on an installment basis. Credit card banks are included in this industry.

Issuing cards that contain a stored prepaid value are classified with the industry providing the service represented by the cards, such as transit fare cards, in Subsector 482, Rail Transportation, and long-distance telephone cards in Subsector 513, Broadcasting and Telecommunications, respectively.

522220 Sales Financing^{CAN}

This industry comprises establishments primarily engaged in sales financing or sales financing in combination with leasing. Sales financing establishments are primarily engaged in lending money for the purpose of providing collaterized goods through a contractual installment sales agreement, either directly from or through arrangements with dealers.

Not engaged in sales financing, but primarily engaged in providing leases for equipment and other assets **532**

52229 Other Nondepository Credit Intermediation^{CAN}

This industry comprises establishments primarily engaged in making cash loans or extending credit through credit instruments (except credit cards and sales finance agreements).

Providing credit sales by issuing credit cards **52221**
Providing leases for equipment and other assets without sales financing **532**
Accepting deposits and lending funds from these deposits **5221**
Arranging loans for others on a commission or fee basis **52231**
Guaranteeing international trade loans **52412**

522291 Consumer Lending^{CAN}

This U.S. industry comprises establishments primarily engaged in making unsecured cash loans to consumers.

Accepting deposits and lending funds from these deposits **5221**
Arranging loans for others on a commission or fee basis **522310**

522292 Real Estate Credit^{US}

This U.S. industry comprises establishments primarily engaged in lending funds with real estate as collateral.

Servicing loans **522390**
Arranging loans for others on a commission or fee basis **522310**
Accepting deposits and lending funds secured by real estate **5221**

522293 International Trade Financing^{US}

This U.S. industry comprises establishments primarily engaged in providing one or more of the following: (1) working capital funds to U.S. exporters; (2) lending funds to foreign buyers of U.S. goods; and (3) lending funds to domestic buyers of imported goods.

Guaranteeing international trade loans **524126**
Brokering international trade loans **522310**
Accepting deposits and lending funds from these deposits **5221**

522294 Secondary Market Financing^{US}

This U.S. industry comprises establishments primarily engaged in buying, pooling, and repackaging loans for sale to others on the secondary market.

522298 All Other Nondepository Credit Intermediation^{US}

This U.S. industry comprises establishments primarily engaged in providing nondepository credit (except credit card issuing, sales financing, consumer lending, real estate credit, international trade financing, and secondary market financing). Examples of types of lending in this industry are: short-term inventory credit, agricultural lending (except real estate and sales financing) and consumer cash lending secured by personal property.

Providing credit sales funding **522210**
Sales financing or sales financing in combination with leasing **522220**
Making unsecured cash loans to consumers **522291**
Lending funds with real estate as collateral **522292**
International trade financing **522293**
Buying, pooling, and repackaging loans for sale to others on the secondary market **522294**
Industrial banks or Morris Plans, engaged in accepting deposits **522190**

5223 Activities Related to Credit Intermediation^{CAN}

This industry group comprises establishments primarily engaged in facilitating credit intermediation by performing activities, such as arranging loans by bringing borrowers and lenders together and clearing checks and credit card transactions.

522310 Mortgage and Nonmortgage Loan Brokers^{CAN}

This industry comprises establishments primarily engaged in arranging loans by bringing borrowers and lenders together on a commission or fee basis.

Lending funds with real estate as collateral **522292**
Servicing loans **522390**

522320 Financial Transactions Processing, Reserve, and Clearinghouse Activities^{CAN}

This industry comprises establishments primarily engaged in providing one or more of the following: (1) financial transaction processing (except central banks); (2) reserve and liquidity services (except central banks); and (3) check or other financial instrument clearinghouse services (except central banks).

Nonfinancial data and electronic transaction processing **5142**
Check clearing and other financial transaction processing **521110**

522390 Other Activities Related to Credit Intermediation[CAN]

This industry comprises establishments primarily engaged in facilitating credit intermediation (except mortgage and loan brokerage; and financial transactions processing, reserve, and clearinghouse activities).

Arranging loans for others on a commission or fee basis **522310**

Providing financial transactions processing, reserve, and clearinghouse activities **522320**

Foreign currency exchange dealing **523130**

Providing escrow services (except real estate) **523991**

---

523 Securities, Commodity Contracts, and Other Financial Investments and Related Activities

Industries in the Securities, Commodity Contracts, and Other Financial Investments and Related Activities subsector group establishments that are primarily engaged in one of the following: (1) underwriting securities issues and/or making markets for securities and commodities; (2) acting as agents (i.e., brokers) between buyers and sellers of securities and commodities; (3) providing securities and commodity exchange services; and (4) providing other services, such as managing portfolios of assets; providing investment advice; and trust, fiduciary, and custody services.

5231 Securities and Commodity Contracts Intermediation and Brokerage

This industry group comprises establishments primarily engaged in putting capital at risk in the process of underwriting securities issues or in making markets for securities and commodities; and those acting as agents and/or brokers between buyers and sellers of securities and commodities, usually charging a commission.

523110 Investment Banking and Securities Dealing[CAN]

This industry comprises establishments primarily engaged in underwriting, originating, and/or maintaining markets for issues of securities. Investment bankers act as principals (i.e., investors who buy or sell on their own account) in firm commitment transactions or act as agents in best effort and standby commitments. This industry also includes establishments acting as principals in buying or selling securities generally on a spread basis, such as securities dealers or stock option dealers.

Acting as agents (i.e., brokers) in buying or selling securities on a commission or transaction fee basis **523120**

Investment clubs or individual investors primarily engaged in buying or selling financial contracts (e.g., securities) on their own account **523910**

523120 Securities Brokerage[CAN]

This industry comprises establishments primarily engaged in acting as agents (i.e., brokers) between buyers and sellers in buying or selling securities on a commission or transaction fee basis.

Investment banking and securities dealing (i.e., buying or selling securities on their own account) **523110**

523130 Commodity Contracts Dealing[CAN]

This U.S. industry comprises establishments primarily engaged in acting as principals (i.e., investors who buy or sell for their own account) in buying or selling spot or futures commodity contracts or options, such as precious metals, foreign currency, oil, or agricultural products, generally on a spread basis.

Acting as agents (i.e., brokers) in buying or selling spot or future commodity contracts on a commission or transaction fee basis **523140**

Buying and selling physical commodities for resale to other than the general public **421**

523140 Commodity Contracts Brokerage[CAN]

This industry comprises establishments primarily engaged in acting as agents (i.e., brokers) in buying or selling spot or future commodity contracts or options on a commission or transaction fee basis.

Acting as principals in buying or selling spot or futures commodity contracts generally on a spread basis **523130**

Buying and selling physical commodities for resale to other than the general public **421**

5232 Securities and Commodity Exchanges

523210 Securities and Commodity Exchanges

This industry comprises establishments primarily engaged in furnishing physical or electronic marketplaces for the purpose of facilitating the buying and selling of stocks, stock options, bonds, or commodity contracts.

Investment banking, and securities dealing, securities brokering commodity contracts dealing, or commodity contracts brokering **5231**

5239 Other Financial Investment Activities

This industry group comprises establishments primarily engaged in one of the following: (1) acting as principals in buying or selling financial contracts (except investment bankers, securities dealers, and commodity contracts dealers); (2) acting as agents (i.e., brokers) (except securities brokerages and commodity contracts brokerages) in buying or selling financial contracts; or (3) providing other investment services (except securities and commodity exchanges), such as portfolio management; investment advice; and trust, fiduciary, and custody services.

523910 Miscellaneous Intermediation^{CAN}

This industry comprises establishments primarily engaged in acting as principals (except investment bankers, securities dealers, and commodity contracts dealers) in buying or selling of financial contracts generally on a spread basis. Principals are investors that buy or sell for their own account.

Investment banking, securities dealing, securities brokering, commodity contracts dealing, or commodity contracts brokering **5231**

523920 Portfolio Management^{CAN}

This industry comprises establishments primarily engaged in managing the portfolio assets (i.e., funds) of others on a fee or commission basis. Establishments in this industry have the authority to make investment decisions, and they derive fees based on the size and/or overall performance of the portfolio.

Investment banking and securities dealing, commodity contracts dealing, or commodity contracts brokering **5231**

523930 Investment Advice^{CAN}

This industry comprises establishments primarily engaged in providing customized investment advice to clients on a fee basis, but do not have the authority to execute trades. Primary activities performed by establishments in this industry are providing financial planning advice and investment counseling to meet the goals and needs of specific clients. Establishments providing investment advice in conjunction with their primary activity, such as portfolio management, or the sale of stocks, bonds, annuities, and real estate, are classified according to their primary activity.

Publishers providing generalized investment information to subscribers **511**

52399 All Other Financial Investment Activities^{CAN}

This industry comprises establishments primarily engaged in acting as agents or brokers (except securities brokerages and commodity contracts brokerages) in buying and selling financial contracts providing financial investment activities (except securities and commodity exchanges, portfolio management, and investment advice).

Investment banking and securities dealing, securities brokering commodity contracts dealing, or commodity contracts brokering **5231**
Acting as principals (except investment bankers, securities dealers, and commodity contracts dealers) in buying or selling financial contracts (except securities or commodity contracts) **52391**
Furnishing physical or electronic marketplaces for the purpose of facilitating the buying and selling of securities and commodities **52321**
Managing the portfolio assets (i.e., funds) of others **52392**
Providing customized investment advice **52393**
Awarding grants from trust funds **81321**
Performing real estate escrow or real estate fiduciary activities **53139**
Financial transactions processing, reserve, and clearinghouse activities **52232**

523991 Trust, Fiduciary, and Custody Activities^{US}

This U.S. industry comprises establishments primarily engaged in providing trust, fiduciary, and custody services to others, as instructed, on a fee or contract basis, such as bank trust offices and escrow agencies (except real estate).

Managing the portfolio assets (i.e., funds) of others **523920**
Performing real estate escrow or real estate fiduciary activities **531390**
Awarding grants from trust funds **81321**

523

523999 Miscellaneous Financial Investment Activities[US]

This U.S. industry comprises establishments primarily engaged in acting as agents and/or brokers (except securities brokerages and commodity contracts brokerages) in buying or selling financial contracts and those providing financial investment services (except securities and commodity exchanges; portfolio management; investment advice; and trust, fiduciary, and custody services) on a fee or commission basis.

Investment banking and securities dealing, commodity contracts dealing, or commodity contracts brokering **5231**

Acting as principals (except investment bankers, securities dealers, and commodity contracts dealers) in buying or selling financial contracts **523910**

Furnishing physical or electrical marketplaces for the purpose of facilitating the buying and selling of securities and commodities **523210**

Managing the portfolio assets (i.e., funds) of others **523920**

Providing customized investment advice **523930**

Providing trust, fiduciary, and custody services to others **523991**

Financial transactions processing, reserve, and clearinghouse activities **522320**

---

524 Insurance Carriers and Related Activities

Industries in the Insurance Carriers and Related Activities subsector group establishments that are primarily engaged in one of the following (1) underwriting (assuming the risk, assigning premiums, and so forth) annuities and insurance policies or (2) facilitating such underwriting by selling insurance policies, and by providing other insurance and employee-benefit related services.

5241 Insurance Carriers

This industry group comprises establishments primarily engaged in underwriting (assuming the risk, assigning premiums, and so forth) annuities and insurance policies and investing premiums to build up a portfolio of financial assets to be used against future claims. Direct insurance carriers are establishments that are primarily engaged in initially underwriting and assuming the risk of annuities and insurance policies. Reinsurance carriers are establishments that are primarily engaged in assuming all or part of the risk associated with an existing insurance policy (or set of policies) originally underwritten by another insurance carrier.

Industries are defined in terms of the type of risk being insured against, such as death, loss of employment because of age or disability, and property damage. Contributions and premiums are set on the basis of actuarial calculations of probable payouts based on risk factors from experience tables and expected investment returns on reserves.

5241I Direct Life, Health, and Medical Insurance Carriers[CAN]

This industry comprises establishments primarily engaged in initially underwriting (i.e., assuming the risk and assigning premiums) annuities and life insurance policies, disability income insurance policies, accidental death and dismemberment insurance policies, and health and medical insurance policies.

Reinsuring life insurance policies **52413**

Legal entities (i.e., funds, plans, and/or programs) organized to provide insurance and employee benefits exclusively for the sponsor, firm, or its employees or members **5251**

HMO establishments providing health care services **62149**

524113 Direct Life Insurance Carriers[US]

This U.S. industry comprises establishments primarily engaged in initially underwriting (i.e., assuming the risk and assigning premiums) annuities and life insurance policies, disability income insurance policies, and accidental death and dismemberment insurance policies.

Reinsuring life insurance policies, disability income insurance policies, and accidental death and dismemberment insurance policies **524130**

Legal entities (i.e., funds, plans, and/or programs) organized to provide insurance and employee benefits exclusively for the sponsor, firm, or its employees or members **5251**

524114 Direct Health and Medical Insurance Carriers[US]

This U.S. industry comprises establishments primarily engaged in initially underwriting (i.e., assuming the risk and assigning premiums) health and medical insurance policies. Group hospitalization plans and HMO establishments (except those providing health care services) that provide health and medical insurance policies without providing health care services are included in this industry.

Provide both health care services and underwrite health and medical insurance **621491**

Reinsuring health insurance policies **524130**

Legal entities (i.e., funds, plans, and/or programs) organized to provide health- and welfare-related employee benefits exclusively for the sponsor's employees or members **525120**

52412 Direct Insurance (except Life, Health, and Medical) Carriers[CAN]

This industry comprises establishments primarily engaged in initially underwriting (i.e., assuming the risk and assigning premiums) various types of insurance policies (except life, disability income, accidental death and dismemberment, and health and medical insurance policies).

Reinsuring insurance policies **524130**

Legal entities (i.e., funds, plans, and/or programs) organized to provide insurance and employee benefits exclusively for the sponsor, firm, or its employees or members **5251**

Initially underwriting annuities and life insurance policies, disability income insurance policies, accidental death and dismemberment insurance policies, and health and medical insurance policies **52411**

524126 Direct Property and Casualty Insurance Carriers[US]

This U.S. industry comprises establishments primarily engaged in initially underwriting (i.e., assuming the risk and assigning premiums) insurance policies that protect policyholders against losses that may occur as a result of property damage or liability.

Reinsuring property and casualty insurance policies **524130**

524127 Direct Title Insurance Carriers[US]

This U.S. industry comprises establishments primarily engaged in initially underwriting (i.e., assuming the risk and assigning premiums) insurance policies to protect the owners of real estate or real estate creditors against loss sustained by reason of any title defect to real property.

Reinsuring title insurance policies **524130**

524128 Other Direct Insurance (except Life, Health, and Medical) Carriers[US]

This U.S. industry comprises establishments primarily engaged in initially underwriting (e.g., assuming the risk, assigning premiums) insurance policies (except life, disability income, accidental death and dismemberment, health and medical, property and casualty, and title insurance policies).

Reinsuring insurance policies **524130**

Initially underwriting annuities and life insurance policies, disability income insurance policies, and accidental death and dismemberment insurance policies **524113**

Initially underwriting health and medical insurance policies **524114**

Initially underwriting property and casualty insurance policies **524126**

Initially underwriting title insurance policies **524127**

524130 Reinsurance Carriers[CAN]

This industry comprises establishments primarily engaged in assuming all or part of the risk associated with existing insurance policies originally underwritten by other insurance carriers.

Initially underwriting annuities and life insurance policies, disability income insurance policies, accidental death and dismemberment insurance policies, and health and medical insurance policies **52411**

Initially underwriting various types of insurance policies (except life, disability income, accidental death and dismemberment, and health and medical insurance policies) **52412**

5242 Agencies, Brokerages, and Other Insurance Related Activities

This industry group comprises establishments primarily engaged in (1) acting as agents (i.e., brokers) in selling annuities and insurance policies or (2) providing other employee benefits and insurance related services, such as claims adjustment and third party administration.

524210 Insurance Agencies and Brokerages[CAN]

This industry comprises establishments primarily engaged in acting as agents (i.e., brokers) in selling annuities and insurance policies.

Underwriting annuities and insurance policies **5241**

52429 Other Insurance Related Activities[CAN]

This industry comprises establishments primarily engaged in providing services related to insurance (except insurance agencies and brokerages).

524

Managing the portfolio assets (i.e., funds) of others **52392**
Acting as agents (i.e., brokers) in selling annuities and insurance policies **52421**
Providing actuarial consulting services **54161**

524291 Claims Adjusting^{CAN}

This U.S. industry comprises establishments primarily engaged in investigating, appraising, and settling insurance claims.

524292 Third Party Administration of Insurance and Pension Funds^{US}

This U.S. industry comprises establishments primarily engaged in providing third party administration services of insurance and pension funds, such as claims processing and other administrative services

to insurance carriers, employee-benefit plans, and self-insurance funds.

Managing the portfolio assets (i.e., funds) of others **523920**
Providing actuarial consulting services **541612**

524298 All Other Insurance Related Activities^{US}

This U.S. industry comprises establishments primarily engaged in providing insurance services on a contract or fee basis (except insurance agencies and brokerages, claims adjusting, and third party administration). Insurance advisory services and insurance ratemaking services are included in this industry.

Providing actuarial consulting services **541612**
Acting as agents (i.e., brokers) in selling annuities and insurance policies **524210**
Insurance clailms adjusting **524291**
Third party administration services of insurance and pension funds **524292**

525 Funds, Trusts, and Other Financial Vehicles^{US}

Industries in the Funds, Trusts, and Other Financial Vehicles subsector are comprised of legal entities (i.e., funds, plans, and/or programs) organized to pool securities or other assets on behalf of shareholders or beneficiaries of employee benefit or other trust funds. The portfolios are customized to achieve specific investment characteristics, such as diversification, risk, rate of return, and price volatility. These entities earn interest, dividends, and other property income, but have little or no employment and no revenue from the sale of services.

525I Insurance and Employee Benefit Funds^{US}

This industry group comprises legal entities (i.e., funds, plans, and/or programs) organized to provide insurance and employee benefits exclusively for the sponsor, firm, or its employees or members.

525110 Pension Funds^{US}

This industry comprises legal entities (i.e., funds, plans, and/or programs) organized to provide retirement income benefits exclusively for the sponsor's employees or members.

Managing portfolios of pension funds **523920**
Initially underwriting annuities **524113**

525120 Health and Welfare Funds^{US}

This industry comprises legal entities (i.e., funds, plans, and/or programs) organized to provide medi-

cal, surgical, hospital, vacation, training, and other health- and welfare-related employee benefits exclusively for the sponsor's employees or members.

Managing portfolios of health and welfare funds **523920**
Third party claims administration of health and welfare plans **524292**

525190 Other Insurance Funds^{US}

This industry comprises legal entities (i.e., funds [except pension, and health- and welfare-related employee benefit funds]) organized to provide insurance exclusively for the sponsor, firm, or its employees or members. Self-insurance funds (except employee benefit funds) and workers' compensation insurance funds are included in this industry.

Legal entities (i.e., funds, plans, and/or programs) organized to provide retirement income benefits exclusively for the sponsor's employees or members **525110**
Legal entities (i.e., funds, plans, and/or programs) organized to provide health- and welfare-related employee benefits exclusively for the sponsor's employees or members **525120**

Managing portfolios of insurance funds **523920**

Third party claims administration of insurance, and other employee benefit funds **524292**

Providing insurance on a fee or contract basis **5241**

5259 Other Investment Pools and Funds[US]

This industry group comprises legal entities (i.e., investment pools and/or funds) organized to pool securities or other assets (except insurance and employee-benefit funds) on behalf of shareholders, unitholders, or beneficiaries.

525910 Open-End Investment Funds[US]

This industry comprises legal entities (i.e., open-end investment funds) organized to pool assets that consist of securities or other financial instruments. Shares in these pools are offered to the public in an initial offering with additional shares offered continuously and perpetually and redeemed at a specific price determined by the net asset value.

525920 Trusts, Estates, and Agency Accounts[US]

This industry comprises legal entities, trusts, estates, or agency accounts, administered on behalf of the beneficiaries under the terms of a trust agreement, will, or agency agreement.

Managing portfolios of trusts **523920**

Administering personal estates **523991**

525930 Real Estate Investment Trusts[US]

This industry comprises legal entities that are Real Estate Investment Trusts (REITs). Legal entities of mortgage-backed investment funds that are not REITs are classified elsewhere in the Funds, Trusts, and Other Financial Vehicles subsector based on the types of funds.

Legal entities of investments in real estate that are not REITs **5311**

525990 Other Financial Vehicles[US]

This industry comprises legal entities (i.e., funds [except insurance and employee benefit funds; open-end investment funds; trusts, estates, and agency accounts; and Real Estate Investment Trusts (REITs)]).

Legal entities (i.e., funds, plans, and programs) that provide insurance and employee benefits exclusively for the sponsor, firm, or its employees or members **5251**

Legal entities (i.e., open-end investment funds) organized to pool assets that consist of securities or other financial instruments, where the pools are offered to the public in an initial offering with additional shares offered continuously and perpetually at a specific price determined by the net asset value, **525910**

Legal entities (i.e., trusts, estates, or agency accounts) administered on behalf of the beneficiaries under the terms of a trust agreement, will, or agency agreement **525920**

Legal entities that are Real Estate Investment Trusts (REITs) **525930**

531

Sector 53: Real Estate and Rental Leasing

Overview of this Sector as a Whole

The Real Estate and Rental and Leasing sector comprises establishments primarily engaged in renting, leasing, or otherwise allowing the use of tangible or intangible assets, and establishments providing related services. The major portion of this sector comprises establishments that rent, lease, or otherwise allow the use of their own assets by others. The assets may be tangible, as is the case of real estate and equipment, or intangible, as is the case with patents and trademarks.

This sector also includes establishments primarily engaged in managing real estate for others, selling, renting and/or buying real estate for others, and appraising real estate. These activities are closely related to this sector's main activity, and it was felt that from a production basis they would best be included here. In addition, a substantial proportion of property management is self-performed by lessors.

The main components of this sector are the real estate lessors industries; equipment lessors industries (including motor vehicles, computers, and consumer goods); and lessors of nonfinancial intangible assets (except copyrighted works).

Excluded from this sector are real estate investment trusts (REITs) and establishments primarily engaged in renting or leasing equipment with operators. REITs are classified in Subsector 525, Funds, Trusts, and Other Financial Vehicles because they are considered investment vehicles. Establishments renting or leasing equipment with operators are classified in various subsectors of NAICS depending on the nature of the services provided (e.g, transportation, construction, agriculture). These activities are excluded from this sector because the client is paying for the expertise and knowledge of the equipment operator, in addition to the rental of the equipment. In many cases, such as, the rental of heavy construction equipment, the operator is essential to operate the equipment.

531 Real Estate

Industries in the Real Estate subsector group establishments that are primarily engaged in renting or leasing real estate to others; managing real estate for others; selling, buying, or renting real estate for others; and providing other real estate related services, such as appraisal services. Establishments primarily engaged in subdividing and developing unimproved real estate and constructing buildings for sale are classified in Subsector 233, Building, Developing, and General Contracting. Real Estate Investment Trusts (REITs) are classified in Subsector 525, Funds, Trusts, and Other Financial Vehicles because they are considered investment vehicles.

5311 Lessors of Real Estate

531110 Lessors of Residential Buildings and Dwellings[CAN]

This industry comprises establishments primarily engaged in acting as lessors of buildings used as residences or dwellings, such as single-family homes, apartment buildings, and town homes. Included in this industry are owner-lessors and establishments renting real estate and then acting as lessors in subleasing it to others. The establishments in this industry may manage the property themselves or have another establishment manage it for them.

Managing residential real estate for others **531311**

531120 Lessors of Nonresidential Buildings (except Miniwarehouses)[CAN]

This industry comprises establishments primarily engaged in acting as lessors of buildings (except

miniwarehouses and self-storage units) that are not used as residences or dwellings. Included in this industry are owner-lessors and establishments renting real estate and then acting as lessors in subleasing it to others. The establishments in this industry may manage the property themselves or have another establishment manage it for them.

Acting as lessors of buildings used as residences or dwellings **531110**
Renting or leasing space for self-storage **531130**
Managing nonresidential real estate for others **531312**
Managing and operating arenas, stadiums, theaters, or other related
  facilities and promoting and organizing performing arts productions,
  sports events, and similar events at those facilities **711310**
Operating public and contract general merchandise warehousing and storage
  facilities **493110**

531130 Lessors of Miniwarehouses and Self-Storage Units[CAN]

This industry comprises establishments primarily engaged in renting or leasing space for self-storage. These establishments provide secure space (i.e., rooms, compartments, lockers, containers, or outdoor space) where clients can store and retrieve their goods.

Operating public and contract general merchandise warehousing and storage facilities **493110**
Operating coin-operated lockers **812990**

531190 Lessors of Other Real Estate Property^{CAN}

This industry comprises establishments primarily engaged in acting as lessors of real estate (except buildings), such as manufactured home (i.e., mobile home) sites, vacant lots, and grazing land.

Acting as lessors of buildings used as residences or dwellings including manufactured (mobile) homes on-site **531110**
Acting as lessors of buildings (except miniwarehouses and self-storage units) that are not used as residences or dwellings **531120**
Renting or leasing space for self-storage **531130**

5312 Offices of Real Estate Agents and Brokers

531210 Offices of Real Estate Agents and Brokers

This industry comprises establishments primarily engaged in acting as agents and/or brokers in one or more of the following: (1) selling real estate for others; (2) buying real estate for others; and (3) renting real estate for others.

5313 Activities Related to Real Estate

This industry group comprises establishments primarily engaged in providing real estate services (except lessors of real estate and offices of real estate agents and brokers). Included in this industry group are establishments primarily engaged in activities, such as, managing real estate for others and appraising real estate.

53131 Real Estate Property Managers^{CAN}

This industry comprises establishments primarily engaged in managing real property for others. Management includes ensuring that various activities associated with the overall operation of the property are performed, such as collecting rents, and oversee-

ing other services (e.g., maintenance, security, trash removal.)

Acting as lessors of real estate **5311**
Formed on behalf of individual condominium owners or homeowners **81399**

531311 Residential Property Managers^{US}

This U.S. industry comprises establishments primarily engaged in managing residential real estate for others.

Managing nonresidential real estate for others **531312**
Acting as lessors of buildings used as residences or dwellings **531110**
Formed on behalf of individual residential condominium owners or homeowners **81399**

531312 Nonresidential Property Managers^{US}

This U.S. industry comprises establishments primarily engaged in managing nonresidential real estate for others.

Managing residential real estate for others **531311**
Acting as lessors of buildings (except miniwarehouses and self storage units) that are not used as residences or dwellings **531120**
Renting or leasing space for self-storage **531130**
Formed on behalf of individual nonresidential condominium owner **81399**

531320 Offices of Real Estate Appraisers^{CAN}

This industry comprises establishments primarily engaged in estimating the fair market value of real estate.

53139 Other Activities Related to Real Estate^{CAN}

531390 Other Activities Related to Real Estate^{CAN}

This industry comprises establishments primarily engaged in performing real estate related services (except lessors of real estate, offices of real estate agents and brokers, real estate property managers, and offices of real estate appraisers).

Acting as lessors of real estate **5311**
Selling, buying, and/or renting real estate for others **531210**
Managing real estate for others **53131**
Estimating fair market value of real estate **531320**
Researching public land records for ownership of titles and/or conveying real estate titles **541191**

531

532 Rental and Leasing Services

Industries in the Rental and Leasing Services subsector include establishments that provide a wide array of tangible goods, such as automobiles, computers, consumer goods, and industrial machinery and equipment, to customers in return for a periodic rental or lease payment. The subsector includes two main types of establishments: (1) those that are engaged in renting consumer goods and equipment and (2) those that are engaged in leasing machinery and equipment of the kind often used for business operations. The first type typically operates from a retail-like or store-front facility and maintains inventories of goods that are rented for short periods of time. The latter type typically does not operate from retail-like locations or maintain inventories, and offers longer term leases. These establishments work directly with clients to enable them to acquire the use of equipment on a lease basis, or they work with equipment vendors or dealers to support the marketing of equipment to their customers under lease arrangements. Equipment lessors generally structure lease contracts to meet the specialized needs of their clients and use their remarketing expertise to find other users for previously leased equipment. Establishments that provide operating and capital (i.e., finance) leases are included in this subsector. Establishments primarily engaged in leasing in combination with providing loans are classified in Sector 52, Finance and Insurance. Establishments primarily engaged in leasing real property are classified in Subsector 531, Real Estate. Those establishments primarily engaged in renting or leasing equipment with operators are classified in various subsectors of NAICS depending on the nature of the services provided (e.g., Transportation, Construction, Agriculture). These activities are excluded from this subsector since the client is paying for the expertise and knowledge of the equipment operator, in addition to the rental of the equipment. In many cases, such as the rental of heavy construction equipment, the operator is essential to operate the equipment. Likewise, since the provision of crop harvesting services includes both the equipment and operator, it is included in the agriculture subsector. The rental or leasing of copyrighted works is classified in Sector 51, Information, and the rental or leasing of assets, such as patents, trademarks, and/or licensing agreements is classified in Subsector 533, Lessors of Nonfinancial Intangible Assets (except Copyrighted Works).

5321 Automotive Equipment Rental and Leasing

This industry group comprises establishments primarily engaged in renting or leasing the following types of vehicles: passenger cars and trucks without drivers, and utility trailers. These establishments generally operate from a retail-like facility. Some establishments offer only short-term rental, others only longer term leases, and some provide both types of services.

53211 Passenger Car Rental and Leasing

This industry comprises establishments primarily engaged in renting or leasing passenger cars without drivers.

Renting or leasing passenger cars with drivers (e.g., limousines, hearses, taxis) **4853**

Retailing passenger cars through sales or lease arrangements **4411**
Leasing passenger cars in combination with providing loans to buyers of such vehicles **52**

532111 Passenger Car Rental^CAN

This U.S. industry comprises establishments primarily engaged in renting passenger cars without drivers, generally for short periods of time.

Leasing passenger cars without drivers, generally for long periods of time **532112**
Renting or leasing passenger cars with drivers (e.g., limousines, hearses, taxis) **4853**

532112 Passenger Car Leasing^CAN

This U.S. industry comprises establishments primarily engaged in leasing passenger cars without drivers, generally for long periods of time.

Renting passenger cars without drivers, generally for short periods of time **532111**

Renting or leasing passenger cars with drivers (e.g., limousines, hearses, taxis) **4853**

Retailing passenger cars through sales or lease arrangements **4411**

Leasing passenger cars in combination with providing loans to buyers of such vehicles **52**

532120 Truck, Utility Trailer, and RV (Recreational Vehicle) Rental and Leasing

This industry comprises establishments primarily engaged in renting or leasing, without drivers, one or more of the following: trucks, truck tractors or buses: semitrailers, utility trailers, or RVs (recreational vehicles).

Renting recreational goods, such as pleasure boats, canoes, motorcycles, mopeds, or bicycles, **53229**

Renting or leasing farm tractors, industrial equipment, and industrial trucks, such as forklifts and other materials handling equipment, **532490**

Renting or leasing mobile home sites **53119**

Retailing vehicles commonly referred to as RVs through sales or lease arrangements **44121**

Leasing trucks, utility trailers, and RVs in combination with providing loans to buyers of such vehicles **52**

5322 Consumer Goods Rental

This industry group comprises establishments primarily engaged in renting personal and household-type goods. Establishments classified in this industry group generally provide short-term rental although in some instances, the goods may be leased for longer periods of time. These establishments often operate from a retail-like or store-front facility.

532210 Consumer Electronics and Appliances Rental

This industry comprises establishments primarily engaged in renting consumer electronics equipment and appliances, such as televisions, stereos, and refrigerators. Included in this industry are appliance rental centers.

Renting or leasing computers **532420**

Renting a range of consumer, commercial, and industrial equipment, such as lawn and garden equipment, home repair tools, and party and banquet equipment, **532310**

532220 Formal Wear and Costume Rental

This industry comprises establishments primarily engaged in renting clothing, such as formal wear, costumes (e.g., theatrical), or other clothing (except laundered uniforms and work apparel).

Laundering and supplying uniforms and other work apparel **81233**

532230 Video Tape and Disc Rental

This industry comprises establishments primarily engaged in renting prerecorded video tapes and discs for home electronic equipment.

Theatrical distribution of motion pictures and videos **512**

Renting video recorders and players **532210**

Retailing prerecorded video tapes and discs **451220**

53229 Other Consumer Goods Rental

This industry comprises establishments primarily engaged in renting consumer goods (except consumer electronics and appliances, formal wear and costumes, and prerecorded video tapes).

Renting consumer electronics and appliances **53221**

Renting formal wear and costumes **53222**

Renting prerecorded video tapes **53223**

Renting a general line of products, such as lawn and garden equipment, home repair tools, and party and banquet equipment, **53231**

Renting medical equipment (except home health equipment), such as electromedical and electrotherapeutic apparatus, **53249**

Providing home health care services and home health equipment **62161**

Retailing and renting musical instruments **45114**

532291 Home Health Equipment Rental[US]

This U.S. industry comprises establishments primarily engaged in renting home-type health and invalid equipment, such as wheel chairs, hospital beds, oxygen tanks, walkers, and crutches.

Renting medical equipment (except home health equipment), such as electromedical and electrotherapeutic apparatus, **532490**

Providing home health care services and home health equipment **62161**

532292 Recreational Goods Rental[US]

This U.S. industry comprises establishments primarily engaged in renting recreational goods, such as bicycles, canoes, motorcycles, skis, sailboats, beach chairs, and beach umbrellas.

532299 All Other Consumer Goods Rental[US]

This U.S. industry comprises establishments primarily engaged in renting consumer goods and products (except consumer electronics and appliances; formal

532

wear and costumes; prerecorded video tapes and discs for home electronic equipment; home health furniture and equipment; and recreational goods). Included in this industry are furniture rental centers and party rental supply centers.

Renting consumer electronics and appliances **532210**
Renting formal wear and costumes **532220**
Renting video tapes **532230**
Renting home health furniture and equipment **532291**
Renting recreational goods **532292**
Retailing and renting musical instruments **451140**
Renting a range of consumer, commercial, and industrial equipment, such as lawn and garden equipment, home repair tools, and party and banquet equipment, **532310**

5323 General Rental Centers

532310 General Rental Centers

This industry comprises establishments primarily engaged in renting a range of consumer, commercial, and industrial equipment. Establishments in this industry typically operate from conveniently located facilities where they maintain inventories of goods and equipment that they rent for short periods of time. The type of equipment that establishments in this industry provide often includes, but is not limited to: audio-visual equipment, contractors and builders tools and equipment, home repair tools, lawn and garden equipment, moving equipment and supplies, and party and banquet equipment and supplies.

Renting trucks and trailers without drivers **532120**
Renting party and banquet equipment **53229**
Renting heavy construction equipment without operators **532412**
Renting specialized types of commercial and industrial equipment, such as garden tractors or public address systems, **532490**

5324 Commercial and Industrial Machinery and Equipment Rental and Leasing

This industry group comprises establishments primarily engaged in renting or leasing commercial-type and industrial-type machinery and equipment. The types of establishments included in this industry group are generally involved in providing capital or investment-type equipment that clients use in their business operations. These establishments typically cater to a business clientele and do not generally operate a retail-like or store-front facility.

5324I Construction, Transportation, Mining, and Forestry Machinery and Equipment Rental and Leasing

This industry comprises establishments primarily engaged in renting or leasing one or more of the following without operators: heavy construction, off-highway transportation, mining, and forestry machinery and equipment. Establishments in this industry may rent or lease products, such as aircraft, railroad cars, steamships, tugboats, bulldozers, earthmoving equipment, well-drilling machinery and equipment, or cranes.

Renting or leasing automobiles or trucks without operators **5321**
Renting or leasing air, rail, highway, and water transportation equipment with operators **48–49**
Renting or leasing heavy construction equipment with operators **23499**
Renting or leasing heavy equipment for mining with operators **21311**
Renting or leasing heavy equipment for forestry with operators **1153**
Leasing heavy equipment in combination with providing loans to buyers of such equipment **52**

532411 Commercial Air, Rail, and Water Transportation Equipment Rental and Leasing[US]

This U.S. industry comprises establishments primarily engaged in renting or leasing off-highway transportation equipment without operators, such as aircraft, railroad cars, steamships, or tugboats.

Renting or leasing air, rail, highway, and water transportation equipment with operators **48–49**
Renting pleasure boats **532292**
Renting or leasing automobiles or trucks without drivers **5321**

532412 Construction, Mining, and Forestry Machinery and Equipment Rental and Leasing[US]

This U.S. industry comprises establishments primarily engaged in renting or leasing heavy equipment without operators that may be used for construction, mining, or forestry, such as bulldozers, earthmoving equipment, well-drilling machinery and equipment, or cranes.

Renting or leasing heavy construction equipment with operators **23499**
Renting or leasing heavy equipment for mining with operators **21311**
Renting or leasing heavy equipment for forestry with operators **1153**
Leasing heavy equipment in combination with providing loans to buyers of such equipment **52**

or software installation services are included in this industry.

Providing custom computer programming services **541511**
Providing computer systems integration design services **541512**
Providing computer systems and/or data processing facilities management services **541513**

5416 Management, Scientific, and Technical Consulting Services

54161 Management Consulting Services

This industry comprises establishments primarily engaged in providing advice and assistance to businesses and other organizations on management issues, such as strategic and organizational planning; financial planning and budgeting; marketing objectives and policies; human resource policies, practices, and planning; production scheduling; and control planning.

Providing a range of day-to-day office administrative services, such as financial planning, billing and recordkeeping, personnel, and physical distribution and logistics, **56111**
Administering, overseeing, and managing other establishments of the company or enterprise (except government establishments) **55111**
Administering, overseeing, and managing governmental programs **92**
Professional and management development training **61143**
Listing employment vacancies and in selecting, referring, and placing applicants in employment **56131**
Developing and implementing public relations plans **54182**
Developing and conducting marketing research or public opinion polling **54191**
Planning and designing industrial processes and systems **54133**
Planning and designing computer systems **54151**
Providing financial investment advice services **52393**

541611 Administrative Management and General Management Consulting Services[CAN]

This U.S. industry comprises establishments primarily engaged in providing operating advice and assistance to businesses and other organizations on administrative management issues, such as financial planning and budgeting, equity and asset management, records management, office planning, strategic and organizational planning, site selection, new business startup, and business process improvement. This industry also includes establishments of general management consultants that provide a full range of administrative; human resource; marketing; process,

physical distribution, and logistics; or other management consulting services to clients.

Providing a range of day-to-day office administrative services, such as financial planning, billing and recordkeeping, personnel, and physical distribution and logistics, **561110**
Administering, overseeing, and managing other establishments of the company or enterprise (except government establishments) **551114**
Administering, overseeing, and managing governmental programs **92**
Providing investment advice **523930**

541612 Human Resources and Executive Search Consulting Services[CAN]

This U.S. industry comprises establishments primarily engaged in providing advice and assistance to businesses and other organizations in one or more of the following areas: (1) human resource and personnel policies, practices, and procedures; (2) employee benefits planning, communication, and administration; (3) compensation systems planning; (4) wage and salary administration; and (5) executive search and recruitment.

Professional and management development training **611430**
Listing employment vacancies and in selecting, referring, and placing applicants in employment **561310**

541613 Marketing Consulting Services[US]

This U.S. industry comprises establishments primarily engaged in providing operating advice and assistance to businesses and other organizations on marketing issues, such as developing marketing objectives and policies, sales forecasting, new product developing and pricing, licensing and franchise planning, and marketing planning and strategy.

Developing and implementing public relations plans **541820**
Developing and conducting marketing research or public opinion polling **541910**

541614 Process, Physical Distribution, and Logistics Consulting Services[US]

This U.S. industry comprises establishments primarily engaged in providing operating advice and assistance to businesses and other organizations in areas, such as: (1) manufacturing operations improvement; (2) productivity improvement; (3) production planning and control; (4) quality assurance and quality control; (5) inventory management; (6) distribution networks; (7) warehouse use, operations, and utilization; (8) transportation and shipment of goods

541

and materials; and (9) materials management and handling.

Planning and designing industrial processes and systems **541330**
Providing computer systems integration design services **541512**

541618 Other Management Consulting Services[US]

This U.S. industry comprises establishments primarily engaged in providing management consulting services (except administrative and general management consulting; human resources consulting; marketing consulting; or process, physical distribution, and logistics consulting). Establishments providing telecommunications or utilities management consulting services are included in this industry.

Providing administrative and general management consulting services
541611
Providing human resources and executive search consulting services **541612**
Providing marketing consulting services **541613**
Providing process, physical distribution, and logistics consulting services
541614

541620 Environmental Consulting Services

This industry comprises establishments primarily engaged in providing advice and assistance to businesses and other organizations on environmental issues, such as the control of environmental contamination from pollutants, toxic substances, and hazardous materials. These establishments identify problems (e.g., inspect buildings for hazardous materials), measure and evaluate risks, and recommend solutions. They employ a multidisciplined staff of scientists, engineers, and other technicians with expertise in areas, such as air and water quality, asbestos contamination, remediation, and environmental law. Establishments providing sanitation or site remediation consulting services are included in this industry.

Environmental remediation **562910**
Providing environmental engineering services **541330**

541690 Other Scientific and Technical Consulting Services

This industry comprises establishments primarily engaged in providing advice and assistance to businesses and other organizations on scientific and technical issues (except environmental).

Environmental consulting **541620**

5417 Scientific Research and Development Services

This industry group comprises establishments engaged in conducting original investigation undertaken on a systematic basis to gain new knowledge (research) and/or the application of research findings or other scientific knowledge for the creation of new or significantly improved products or processes (experimental development). The industries within this industry group are defined on the basis of the domain of research; that is, on the scientific expertise of the establishment.

541710 Research and Development in the Physical, Engineering, and Life Sciences

This industry comprises establishments primarily engaged in conducting research and experimental development in the physical, engineering, or life sciences, such as agriculture, electronics, environmental, biology, botany, biotechnology, computers, chemistry, food, fisheries, forests, geology, health, mathematics, medicine, oceanography, pharmacy, physics, veterinary, and other allied subjects.

Providing physical, chemical, or other analytical testing services (except medical or veterinary) **541380**
Providing medical laboratory testing for humans **621511**
Providing veterinary testing services **541940**

541720 Research and Development in the Social Sciences and Humanities

This industry comprises establishments primarily engaged in conducting research and analyses in cognitive development, sociology, psychology, language, behavior, economic, and other social science and humanities research.

Marketing research **541910**

5418 Advertising and Related Services

541810 Advertising Agencies

This industry comprises establishments primarily engaged in creating advertising campaigns and placing such advertising in periodicals, newspapers, radio and television, or other media. These establishments are organized to provide a full range of services (i.e., through in-house capabilities or subcontracting), including advice, creative services, account management, production of advertising material, media planning, and buying (i.e., placing advertising).

Purchasing advertising space from media outlets and reselling it directly to advertising agencies or individual companies **541830**
Conceptualizing and producing artwork or graphic designs without providing other advertising agency services **541430**
Creating direct mail advertising campaigns **541860**
Providing marketing consulting services **541613**
Selling media time or space for media owners as independent representatives **541840**

541820 Public Relations Agencies

This industry comprises establishments primarily engaged in designing and implementing public relations campaigns. These campaigns are designed to promote the interests and image of their clients. Establishments providing lobbying, political consulting, or public relations consulting are included in this industry.

541830 Media Buying Agencies

This industry comprises establishments primarily engaged in purchasing advertising time or space from media outlets and reselling it to advertising agencies or individual companies directly.

Selling time and space to advertisers for media owners as independent representatives **541840**
Creating advertising campaigns and placing such advertising in media **541810**

541840 Media Representatives

This industry comprises establishments of independent representatives primarily engaged in selling media time or space for media owners.

Purchasing advertising time or space from media outlets and reselling it directly to advertising agencies or individual companies **541830**
Creating advertising campaigns and placing such advertising in media **541810**

541850 Display Advertising

This industry comprises establishments primarily engaged in creating and designing public display advertising, campaign materials, such as printed, painted, or electronic displays, and/or placing such displays on indoor or outdoor billboards and panels, or on or within transit vehicles or facilities, shopping malls, retail (in-store) displays, and other display structures or sites.

Providing sign lettering and painting services **541890**
Printing paper on paperboard signs **32311**
Erecting display boards **23**
Manufacturing electrical, mechanical, or plate signs and point-of-sale advertising displays **339950**

541860 Direct Mail Advertising

This industry comprises establishments primarily engaged in (1) creating and designing advertising campaigns for the purpose of distributing advertising materials (e.g., coupons, flyers, samples) or specialties (e.g., key chains, magnets, pens with customized messages imprinted) by mail or other direct distribution; and/or (2) preparing advertising materials or specialties for mailing or other direct distribution. These establishments may also compile, maintain, sell, and rent mailing lists.

The direct distribution or delivery (e.g., door-to-door, windshield placement) of advertisements or samples **541870**
Distributing advertising specialties for clients who wish to use such materials for promotional purposes **541890**
Creating advertising campaigns and placing such advertising in media **541810**
Compiling and selling mailing lists without providing direct mail advertising services **511140**

541870 Advertising Material Distribution Services

541

This industry comprises establishments primarily engaged in the direct distribution or delivery of advertisements (e.g., circulars, coupons, handbills) or samples. Establishments in this industry use methods, such as delivering advertisements or samples door-to-door, placing flyers or coupons on car windshields in parking lots, or handing out samples in retail stores.

Creating and designing advertising campaigns for the purpose of distributing advertising materials or samples through the mail or by other direct distribution **541860**
Publishing newspapers or operating television stations or on-line information services **51**
Distributing advertising specialties (e.g., key chains, magnets, or pens with customized messages imprinted) to clients who wish to use such materials for promotional purposes **541890**

541890 Other Services Related to Advertising

This industry comprises establishments primarily engaged in providing advertising services (except advertising agency services, public relations agency services, media buying agency services, media representative services, display advertising services, direct mail advertising services, advertising material distribution services, and marketing consulting services).

Creating advertising campaigns and placing such advertising in newspapers, television, or other media **541810**

Designing and implementing public relations campaigns **541820**

Purchasing advertising time or space from media outlets and reselling it directly to advertising agencies or individual companies **541830**

Selling media time or space for media owners as independent representatives **541840**

Providing display advertising services (except aerial) **541850**

Providing direct distribution or delivery (e.g., door-to-door, windshield placement) of advertisements or samples **541870**

Providing direct mail advertising services **541860**

Publishing newspapers or operating television stations or on-line information services **51**

Providing marketing consulting services **541613**

5419 Other Professional, Scientific, and Technical Services

This industry group comprises establishments engaged in professional, scientific, and technical services (except legal services; accounting, tax preparation, bookkeeping, and related services; architectural, engineering, and related services; specialized design services; computer systems design and related services; management, scientific, and technical consulting services; scientific research and development services; and advertising and related services).

541910 Marketing Research and Public Opinion Polling

This industry comprises establishments primarily engaged in systematically gathering, recording, tabulating, and presenting marketing and public opinion data.

Providing research and analysis in economics, sociology, and related fields **541720**

Providing advice and counsel on marketing strategies **541613**

54192 Photographic Services

This industry comprises establishments primarily engaged in providing still, video, or digital photography services. These establishments may specialize in a particular field of photography, such as commercial

and industrial photography, portrait photography, and special events photography. Commercial or portrait photography studios are included in this industry.

Producing film and videotape for commercial exhibition or sale **51211**

Developing still photographs **81292**

Developing motion picture film **51219**

Taking, developing, and selling artistic, news or other types of photographs on a freelance basis, such as photojournalists, **71151**

Supplying and servicing automatic photography machines in places of business operated by others **81299**

541921 Photography Studios, Portrait[US]

This U.S. industry comprises establishments known as portrait studios primarily engaged in providing still, video, or digital portrait photography services.

Producing film and videotape for commercial exhibition or sale **512110**

Developing still photographs **81292**

Developing motion picture film **512199**

Taking, developing, and selling artistic, news or other types of photographs on a freelance basis, such as photojournalists, **711510**

Supplying and servicing automatic photography machines in places of business operated by others **812990**

541922 Commercial Photography[US]

This U.S. industry comprises establishments primarily engaged in providing commercial photography services, generally for advertising agencies, publishers, and other business and industrial users.

Producing film and videotape for commercial exhibition or sale **512110**

Developing still photographs **81292**

Developing motion picture film **512199**

Taking, developing, and selling artistic, news, or other types of photographs on a freelance basis, such as photojournalists, **711510**

Supplying and servicing coin-operated photography machines in places of business operated by others **812990**

541930 Translation and Interpretation Services

This industry comprises establishments primarily engaged in translating written material and interpreting speech from one language to another and establishments primarily engaged in providing sign language services.

Providing transcription services **561410**

Providing real-time (i.e., simultaneous) closed captioning services for live television performances, at meetings and conferences **561492**

Providing film or tape closed captioning services **512191**

Analyzing handwriting **541990**

541940 Veterinary Services

This industry comprises establishments of licensed veterinary practitioners primarily engaged in the practice of veterinary medicine, dentistry, or surgery for animals; and establishments primarily engaged in providing testing services for licensed veterinary practitioners.

Providing veterinary research and development services **541710**
Providing nonveterinary pet care services, such as boarding or grooming pets, **812910**
Providing animal breeding services or boarding horses **115210**
Transporting pets **485991**

541990 All Other Professional, Scientific, and Technical Services

This industry comprises establishments primarily engaged in the provision of professional, scientific, or technical services (except legal services; accounting, tax preparation, bookkeeping, and related services; architectural, engineering, and related services; specialized design services; computer systems design and related services; management, scientific, and technical consulting services; scientific research and development services; advertising and related services; market research and public opinion polling; photographic services; translation and interpretation services; and veterinary services).

Providing legal services **5411**
Providing accounting, tax preparation, bookkeeping, and payroll services **5412**
Providing architectural, engineering, and related services **5413**
Providing specialized design services **5414**
Providing computer systems design and related services **5415**
Providing management, scientific, and technical consulting services **5416**
Providing scientific research and development services **5417**
Providing advertising and related services **5418**
Providing marketing research and public opinion polling **541910**
Providing photographic services **54192**
Providing translation and interpretation services **541930**
Providing veterinary services **541940**
Providing real estate appraisal services **531320**

SECTOR 55: MANAGEMENT OF COMPANIES AND ENTERPRISES

OVERVIEW OF THIS SECTOR AS A WHOLE

The Management of Companies and Enterprises sector comprises (1) establishments that hold the securities of (or other equity interests in) companies and enterprises for the purpose of owning a controlling interest or influencing management decisions or (2) establishments (except government establishments) that administer, oversee, and manage establishments of the company or enterprise and that normally undertake the strategic or organizational planning and decisionmaking role of the company or enterprise. Establishments that administer, oversee, and manage may hold the securities of the company or enterprise.

Establishments in this sector perform essential activities that are often undertaken, in-house, by establishments in many sectors of the economy. By consolidating the performance of these activities of the enterprise at one establishment, economies of scale are achieved. Government establishments primarily engaged in administering, overseeing, and managing governmental programs are classified in Sector 92, Public Administration. Establishments primarily engaged in providing a range of day-to-day office administrative services, such as financial planning, billing and recordkeeping, personnel, and physical distribution and logistics are classified in Industry 56111, Office Administrative Services.

551

551 Management of Companies and Enterprises

Industries in the Management of Companies and Enterprises subsector include three main types of establishments: (1) those that hold the securities of (or other equity interests in) companies and enterprises; (2) those (except government establishments) that administer, oversee, and manage other establishments of the company or enterprise but do not hold the securities of these establishments; and (3) those that both administer, oversee, and manage other establishments of the company or enterprise and hold the securities of (or other equity interests in) these establishments. Those establishments that administer, oversee, and manage normally undertake the strategic or organizational planning and decisionmaking role of the company or enterprise.

5511 Management of Companies and Enterprises

55111 Management of Companies and Enterprises

This industry comprises (1) establishments primarily engaged in holding the securities of (or other equity interests in) companies and enterprises for the purpose of owning a controlling interest or influencing the management decisions or (2) establishments (except government establishments) that administer, oversee, and manage other establishments of the company or enterprise and that normally undertake the strategic or organizational planning and decisionmaking role of the company or enterprise. Establishments that administer, oversee, and manage may hold the securities of the company or enterprise.

Holding the securities of depository banks and operating these entities **5221**
Government establishments primarily engaged in administering, overseeing, and managing governmental programs **92**

55111 Offices of Bank Holding Companies[US]

This U.S. industry comprises legal entities known as bank holding companies primarily engaged in holding the securities of (or other equity interests in) companies and enterprises for the purpose of owning a controlling interest or influencing the management decisions of these firms. The holding companies in this industry do not administer, oversee, and manage other establishments of the company or enterprise whose securities they hold.

Holding the securities of (or other equity interests in) a company or enterprise and administering, overseeing, and managing establishments of the company or enterprise whose securities they hold **551114**
Holding the securities of depository banks and operating these entities **5221**

551112 Offices of Other Holding Companies[US]

This U.S. industry comprises legal entities known as holding companies (except bank holding) primarily engaged in holding the securities of (or other equity interests in) companies and enterprises for the purpose of owning a controlling interest or influencing the management decisions of these firms. The holding companies in this industry do not administer, oversee, and manage other establishments of the company or enterprise whose securities they hold.

Holding the securities of (or other equity interests in) depository banks for the purpose of owning a controlling interest or influencing the management decisions of these firms **551111**
Holding the securities of (or other equity interests in) a company or enterprise and administering, overseeing, and managing establishments of the company or enterprise whose securities they hold **551114**

551114 Corporate, Subsidiary, and Regional Managing Offices[CAN]

This U.S. industry comprises establishments (except government establishments) primarily engaged in administering, overseeing, and managing other establishments of the company or enterprise. These establishments normally undertake the strategic or organizational planning and decisionmaking role of the company or enterprise. Establishments in this industry may hold the securities of the company or enterprise.

Administering, overseeing, and managing governmental programs **92**
Legal entities known as bank holding companies that do not administer, oversee, and manage other establishments of the companies or enterprises whose securities they hold **551111**
Legal entities known as holding companies (except bank holding) that do not administer, oversee, and manage other establishments of the companies or enterprises whose securities they hold **551112**

SECTOR 56: ADMINISTRATIVE AND SUPPORT AND WASTE MANAGEMENT AND REMEDIATION SERVICES

OVERVIEW OF THIS SECTOR AS A WHOLE

The Administrative and Support and Waste Management and Remediation Services sector comprises establishments performing routine support activities for the day-to-day operations of other organizations. These essential activities are often undertaken in-house by establishments in many sectors of the economy. The establishments in this sector specialize in one or more of these support activities and provide these services to clients in a variety of industries and, in some cases, to households. Activities performed include: office administration, hiring and placing of personnel, document preparation and similar clerical services, solicitation, collection, security and surveillance services, cleaning, and waste disposal services.

The administrative and management activities performed by establishments in this sector are typically on a contract or fee basis. These activities may also be performed by establishments that are part of the company or enterprise. However, establishments involved in administering, overseeing, and managing other establishments of the company or enterprise, are classified in Sector 55, Management of Companies and Enterprises. These establishments normally undertake the strategic and organizational planning and decisionmaking role of the company or enterprise. Government establishments engaged in administering, overseeing, and managing governmental programs are classified in Sector 92, Public Administration.

561 Administrative and Support Services

Industries in the Administrative and Support Services subsector group establishments engaged in activities that support the day-to-day operations of other organizations. The processes employed in this sector (e.g., general management, personnel administration, clerical activities, cleaning activities) are often integral parts of the activities of establishments found in all sectors of the economy. The establishments classified in this subsector have specialized in one or more of these activities and can, therefore, provide services to clients in a variety of industries and, in some cases, to households. The individual industries of this subsector are defined on the basis of the particular process that they are engaged in and the particular services they provide. Many of the activities performed in this subsector are ongoing routine support functions that all businesses and organizations must do and that they have traditionally done for themselves. Recent trends, however, are to contract or purchase such services from businesses that specialize in such activities and can, therefore, provide the services more efficiently. The industries in this subsector cannot be viewed as strictly "support." The Travel Arrangement and Reservation Services industry group, includes travel agents, tour operators, and providers of other travel arrangement services, such as hotel and restaurant reservations and arranging the purchase of tickets, serves many types of clients, including individual consumers. This group was placed in this subsector because the services are often of the "support" nature (e.g., travel arrangement) and businesses and other organizations are increasingly the ones purchasing such services.

561

The administrative and management activities performed by establishments in this sector are typically on a contract or fee basis. These activities may also be performed by establishments that are part of the company or enterprise. However, establishments involved in administering, overseeing, and managing other establishments of the company or enterprise, are classified in Sector 55, Management of Companies and Enterprises. These establishments normally undertake the strategic and organizational planning and decisionmaking role of the company or enterprise. Government establishments engaged in administering, overseeing and managing governmental programs are classified in Sector 92, Public Administration.

5611 Office Administrative Services

561110 Office Administrative Services

This industry comprises establishments primarily engaged in providing a range of day-to-day office administrative services, such as financial planning; billing and recordkeeping; personnel; and physical distribution and logistics. These establishments do not provide operating staff to carry out the complete operations of a business.

Holding the securities or financial assets of companies and enterprises for the purpose of controlling them and influencing their management decisions **551111**
Administering, overseeing, and managing other establishments of the company or enterprise (except government establishments) **551114**
Administering, overseeing, and managing governmental programs **92**
Providing computer facilities management **541513**
Providing construction management **23**
Providing farm management **115116**
Managing real property for others **53131**
Providing food services management at institutional, governmental, commercial, or industrial locations **722310**
Providing management advice without day-to-day management **54161**

5612 Facilities Support Services

561210 Facilities Support Services

This industry comprises establishments primarily engaged in providing operating staff to perform a combination of support services within a client's facilities. Establishments in this industry typically provide a combination of services, such as janitorial; maintenance; trash disposal; guard and security; mail routing reception; laundry; and related services to support operations within facilities. These establishments provide operating staff to carry out these support activities; but, are not involved with or responsible for the core business or activities of the client. Establishments providing facilities (except computer and/or data processing) operation support services and establishments operating correctional facilities (i.e., jails) on a contract or fee basis are included in this industry.

Providing on-site management and operation of a client's computer systems and/or data processing facilities **541513**
Government correctional institutions **922140**

5613 Employment Services

561310 Employment Placement Agencies

This industry comprises establishments primarily engaged in listing employment vacancies and in referring or placing applicants for employment. The individuals referred or placed are not employees of the employment agencies.

Providing executive search consulting services **541612**
Supplying their own employees for limited periods of time to supplement the working force of a client's business **561320**
Providing human resources and human resource management services to clients **561330**
Representing models, entertainers, athletes, and other public figures in the capacity as their agent or manager **711410**

561320 Temporary Help Services

This industry comprises establishments primarily engaged in supplying workers to clients' businesses for limited periods of time to supplement the working force of the client. The individuals provided are employees of the temporary help service establishment. However, these establishments do not provide direct supervision of their employees at the clients' work sites.

Providing human resources and human resource management services to clients **561330**
Supplying farm labor **115115**
Providing operating staff to perform a combination of services to support operations within a client's facilities **561210**

Listing employment vacancies and in referring or placing applicants for employment **561310**

Representing models, entertainers, athletes, and other public figures in the capacity as their agent or manager **711410**

561330 Employee Leasing Services

This industry comprises establishments primarily engaged in providing human resources and human resource management services to staff client businesses. Establishments in this industry operate in a coemployment relationship with client businesses or organizations and are specialized in performing a wide range of human resource and personnel management duties, such as payroll accounting, payroll tax return preparation, benefits administration, recruiting, and managing labor relations. Employee leasing establishments typically acquire and lease back some or all of the employees of their clients and serve as the employer of the leased employees for payroll, benefits, and related purposes. Employee leasing establishments exercise varying degrees of decisionmaking relating to their human resource or personnel management role, but do not have management accountability for the work of their clients' operations with regard to strategic planning, output, or profitability. Professional employer organizations (PEO) and establishments providing labor or staff leasing services are included in this industry.

Supplying their own employees for limited periods of time to supplement the working force of a client's business **561320**

Listing employment vacancies and in referring or placing applicants for employment **561310**

5614 Business Support Services

This industry group comprises establishments engaged in performing activities that are ongoing routine, business support functions that businesses and organizations traditionally do for themselves.

561410 Document Preparation Services

This industry comprises establishments primarily engaged in one or more of the following: (1) letter or resume writing; (2) document editing or proofreading; (3) typing, word processing, or desktop publishing; and (4) stenographic (except court reporting or stenotype recording), transcription, and other secretarial services.

Providing verbatim reporting and steno recording of live legal proceedings and transcribing subsequent recorded materials **561492**

Performing prepress and postpress services in support of printing activities **32312**

Providing document translation services **541930**

Photocopying, duplicating, and other document copying services, with or without a range of other office support services (except printing) **561439**

Providing document copying services in combination with printing services, with or without a range of other office support services, and establishments known as quick or digital printers **32311**

56142 Telephone Call Centers

This industry comprises (1) establishments primarily engaged in answering telephone calls and relaying messages to clients and (2) establishments primarily engaged in providing telemarketing services on a contract or fee basis for others, such as promoting clients' products or services by telephone; taking orders for clients by telephone; and soliciting contributions or providing information for clients by telephone. Telemarketing establishments never own the product or provide the service that they are representing and generally can originate and/or receive calls for others.

Providing paging and beeper transmission services **51332**

Organizing and conducting fundraising campaigns on a contract or fee basis, that may include telephone solicitation services **56149**

Gathering, recording, tabulating, and presenting marketing and public opinion data, that may include telephone canvassing services **54191**

561421 Telephone Answering Services[US]

This U.S. industry comprises establishments primarily engaged in answering telephone calls and relaying messages to clients.

Providing paging or beeper transmission services **51332**

561422 Telemarketing Bureaus[US]

This U.S. industry comprises establishments primarily engaged in providing telemarketing services on a contract or fee basis for others, such as: (1) promoting clients' products or services by telephone, (2) taking orders for clients by telephone, and (3) soliciting contributions or providing information for clients by telephone. These establishments never own the product or provide the services they are representing and generally can originate and/or receive calls for others.

561

Organizing and conducting fundraising campaigns on a contract or fee basis, that may include telephone solicitation services **561499**

Gathering, recording, tabulating, and presenting marketing and public opinion data, that may include telephone canvassing services **541910**

56143 Business Service Centers

This industry comprises (1) establishments primarily engaged in providing mailbox rental and other postal and mailing services (except direct mail advertising); (2) establishments, generally known as copy centers or shops, primarily engaged in providing photocopying, duplicating, blueprinting, and other document copying services without also providing printing services (i.e., offset printing, quick printing, digital printing, prepress services); and (3) establishments that provide a range of office support services (except printing services), such as mailing services, document copying services, facsimile services, word processing services, on-site PC rental services, and office product sales.

Operating contract post offices **49111**
Delivering letters and parcels **492**
Providing voice mailbox services **56142**
Providing direct mail advertising services **54186**
Providing document copying services in combination with printing services, with or without a range of other office support services, and establishments known as quick or digital printers **32311**

561431 Private Mail Centers[US]

This U.S. industry comprises (1) establishments primarily engaged in providing mailbox rental and other postal and mailing (except direct mail advertising) services or (2) establishments engaged in providing these mailing services along with one or more other office support services, such as facsimile services, word processing services, on-site PC rental services, and office product sales.

Operating contract post offices **491110**
Delivering letters and parcels **492**
Providing voice mailbox services **561421**
Providing direct mail advertising services **541860**

561439 Other Business Service Centers (including Copy Shops)[US]

This U.S. industry comprises (1) establishments generally known as copy centers or shops primarily engaged in providing photocopying, duplicating, blueprinting, and other document copying services,

without also providing printing services (e.g., offset printing, quick printing, digital printing, prepress services) and (2) establishments (except private mail centers) engaged in providing a range of office support services (except printing services), such as document copying services, facsimile services, word processing services, on-site PC rental services, and office product sales.

Providing document copying services in combination with printing services, with or without a range of other office support services, and establishments known as quick or digital printers **32311**
Providing mailbox rental and other postal and mailing services with or without one or more other office support services (except printing) **561431**

561440 Collection Agencies

This industry comprises establishments primarily engaged in collecting payments for claims and remitting payments collected to their clients.

Repossessing tangible assets **561491**
Providing financing to others by factoring accounts receivables (i.e., assuming the risk of collection and credit losses) **522298**

561450 Credit Bureaus

This industry comprises establishments primarily engaged in compiling information, such as credit and employment histories on individuals and credit histories on businesses, and providing the information to financial institutions, retailers, and others who have a need to evaluate the credit worthiness of these persons and businesses.

56149 Other Business Support Services

This industry comprises establishments primarily engaged in providing business support services (except secretarial and other document preparation services; telephone answering or telemarketing services; private mail services or document copying services conducted as separate activities or in conjunction with other office support services; monetary debt collection services; and credit reporting services).

Providing secretarial and other document preparation services **56141**
Providing telephone answering or telemarketing services **56142**
Providing private mail services; document copying services (except printing services); and/or a range of office support services (except printing) **56143**

Providing document copying services in combination with printing services, with or without a range of other office support services, and establishments known as quick or digital printers **32311**
Providing monetary debt collection services **56144**
Providing credit reporting services **56145**
Providing film or tape captioning or subtitling services **51219**

561491 Repossession Services[US]

This U.S. industry comprises establishments primarily engaged in repossessing tangible assets (e.g., automobiles, boats, equipment, planes, furniture, appliances) for the creditor as a result of delinquent debts.

Providing monetary debt collection services **561440**

561492 Court Reporting and Stenotype Services[US]

This U.S. industry comprises establishments primarily engaged in providing verbatim reporting and stenotype recording of live legal proceedings and transcribing subsequent recorded materials.

Providing stenotype recording of correspondence, reports, and other documents or in providing document transcription services **561410**
Providing film or tape captioning or subtitling services **512191**

561499 All Other Business Support Services[US]

This U.S. industry comprises establishments primarily engaged in providing business support services (except secretarial and other document preparation services; telephone answering and telemarketing services; private mail services or document copying services conducted as separate activities or in conjunction with other office support services; monetary debt collection services; credit reporting services; repossession services; and court reporting and stenotype recording services).

Providing secretarial and other document preparation services **561410**
Providing telephone answering or telemarketing services **56142**
Providing private mail services, document copying services without printing services and/or a range of office support services **56143**
Providing document copying services in combination with printing services (with or without one or more other office support services) and establishments known as quick or digital printers **32311**
Providing monetary debt collection services **561440**
Providing credit reporting services **561450**
Providing repossession services **561491**
Providing court reporting and stenotype services **561492**

5615 Travel Arrangement and Reservation Services

561510 Travel Agencies

This industry comprises establishments primarily engaged in acting as agents in selling travel, tour, and accommodation services to the general public and commercial clients.

Arranging and assembling tours that they generally sell through travel agencies or on their own account **561520**
Providing guide services, such as archeological, museum, tourist, hunting, or fishing, **713990**
Providing reservation services (e.g., accommodations, entertainment events, travel) **561599**

561520 Tour Operators

This industry comprises establishments primarily engaged in arranging and assembling tours. The tours are sold through travel agencies or tour operators. Travel or wholesale tour operators are included in this industry.

Acting as agents in selling travel, tour, and accommodation services to the general public and commercial clients **561510**
Conducting scenic and sightseeing tours **487**
Providing guide services, such as archeological, museum, tourist, hunting, or fishing, **713990**

56159 Other Travel Arrangement and Reservation Services

This industry comprises establishments (except travel agencies and tour operators) primarily engaged in providing travel arrangement and reservation services.

Arranging the rental of vacation properties **53121**
Travel agencies **56151**
Tour operators **56152**
Automobile clubs (i.e., enthusiasts' clubs) (except road and travel services) **81341**
Organizing, promoting, and/or managing events, such as business and trade shows, conventions, conferences, and meetings (whether or not they manage and provide the staff to operate the facilities in which these events take place), **56192**

561591 Convention and Visitors Bureaus[US]

This U.S. industry comprises establishments primarily engaged in marketing and promoting communities and facilities to businesses and leisure travelers through a range of activities, such as assisting organi-

561

zations in locating meeting and convention sites; providing travel information on area attractions, lodging accommodations, restaurants; providing maps; and organizing group tours of local historical, recreational, and cultural attractions.

Organizing, promoting, and/or managing events, such as business and trade shows, conventions, conferences, and meetings (whether or not they manage and provide the staff to operate the facilities in which these events take place), **561920**

561599 All Other Travel Arrangement and Reservation Services^{US}

This U.S. industry comprises establishments (except travel agencies, tour operators, and convention and visitors bureaus) primarily engaged in providing travel arrangement and reservation services.

Arranging the rental of vacation properties **531210**
Travel agencies **561510**
Tour operators **561520**
Convention and visitors bureaus **561591**
Organizing, promoting, and/or managing events, such as business and trade shows, conventions, conferences, and meetings (whether or not they manage and provide the staff to operate the facilities in which these events take place), **561920**
Automobile clubs (i.e., enthusiasts' clubs) (except road and travel services) **813410**

5616 Investigation and Security Services

56161 Investigation, Guard, and Armored Car Services

This industry comprises establishments primarily engaged in providing one or more of the following: (1) investigation and detective services; (2) guard and patrol services; and (3) picking up and delivering money, receipts, or other valuable items with personnel and equipment to protect such properties while in transit.

Providing credit checks **56145**
Selling, installing, monitoring, and maintaining security systems and devices (e.g., burglar and fire alarm systems) **56162**

561611 Investigation Services^{CAN}

This U.S. industry comprises establishments primarily engaged in providing investigation and detective services.

Providing credit checks **561450**

561612 Security Guards and Patrol Services^{CAN}

This U.S. industry comprises establishments primarily engaged in providing guard and patrol services, such as bodyguard, guard dog, and parking security services.

Selling, installing, monitoring, and maintaining security systems and devices, such as burglar and fire alarms and locking devices, **56162**

561613 Armored Car Services^{CAN}

This U.S. industry comprises establishments primarily engaged in picking up and delivering money, receipts, or other valuable items. These establishments maintain personnel and equipment to protect such properties while in transit.

56162 Security Systems Services

This industry comprises establishments engaged in (1) selling security systems, such as burglar and fire alarms and locking devices, along with installation, repair, or monitoring services or (2) remote monitoring of electronic security alarm systems.

Selling security systems for buildings without installation, repair, or monitoring services **42**
Retailing motor vehicle security systems with or without installation or repair services **44131**
Providing key duplication services **81149**

561621 Security Systems Services (except Locksmiths)^{CAN}

This U.S. industry comprises establishments primarily engaged in (1) selling security alarm systems, such as burglar and fire alarms, along with installation, repair, or monitoring services or (2) remote monitoring of electronic security alarm systems.

Selling security alarm systems for buildings, without installation, repair, or monitoring services, **42**
Retailing motor vehicle security systems with or without installation or repair services **441310**

561622 Locksmiths^{CAN}

This U.S. industry comprises establishments primarily engaged in (1) selling mechanical or electronic locking devices, safes, and security vaults, along with installation, repair, rebuilding, or adjusting services or (2) installing, repairing, rebuilding, and adjusting mechanical or electronic locking devices, safes, and security vaults.

Selling security systems, such as locking devices, safes, and vaults, without installation or maintenance services **42**
Providing key duplication services **811490**

5617 Services to Buildings and Dwellings

561710 Exterminating and Pest Control Services

This industry comprises establishments primarily engaged in exterminating and controlling birds, mosquitoes, rodents, termites, and other insects and pests (except for crop production and forestry production). Establishments providing fumigation services are included in this industry.

Providing pest control for crop or forestry production **115**

561720 Janitorial Services

This industry comprises establishments primarily engaged in cleaning building interiors, interiors of transportation equipment (e.g., aircraft, rail cars, ships), and/or windows.

Cleaning building exteriors (except sandblasting and window cleaning) or chimneys **561790**
Sandblasting building exteriors **235990**

561730 Landscaping Services

This industry comprises (1) establishments primarily engaged in providing landscape care and maintenance services and/or installing trees, shrubs, plants, lawns, or gardens and (2) establishments primarily engaged in providing these services along with the design of landscape plans and/or the construction (i.e., installation) of walkways, retaining walls, decks, fences, ponds, and similar structures.

Installing artificial turf or in constructing (i.e., installing) walkways, retaining walls, decks, fences, ponds, or similar structures **23**
Planning and designing the development of land areas for projects, such as parks and other recreational areas; airports; highways; hospitals; schools; land subdivisions; and commercial, industrial, and residential areas (without also installing trees, shrubs, plants, lawns/gardens, walkways, retaining walls, decks, and similar items or structures), **541320**
Retailing landscaping materials and providing the installation and maintenance of these materials **444220**

561740 Carpet and Upholstery Cleaning Services

This industry comprises establishments primarily engaged in cleaning and dyeing used rugs, carpets, and upholstery.

Rug repair not associated with rug cleaning **811490**
Reupholstering and repairing furniture **811420**

561790 Other Services to Buildings and Dwellings

This industry comprises establishments primarily engaged in providing services to buildings and dwellings (except exterminating and pest control; janitorial; landscaping care and maintenance; and carpet and upholstery cleaning).

Providing exterminating and pest control services **561710**
Providing janitorial services **561720**
Providing landscaping care and maintenance **561730**
Providing carpet and upholstery cleaning services **561740**
Sandblasting building exteriors **235990**

5619 Other Support Services

This industry group comprises establishments primarily engaged in providing day-to-day business and other organizational support services (except office administrative services; facilities support services; employment services; business support services; travel arrangement and reservation services; security and investigation services; and services to buildings and dwellings).

561910 Packaging and Labeling Services

This industry comprises establishments primarily engaged in packaging client owned materials. The services may include labeling and/or imprinting the package.

Processing clients' owned materials into a different product, such as mixing water and concentrate to produce soft drinks, **31–33**
Providing aerosol packaging services **325998**
Providing packing and crating services incidental to transportation **488991**
Providing warehousing services, as well as packaging or other logistics services **4931**
Providing packing and crating services for agricultural products **115114**

561920 Convention and Trade Show Organizers

This industry comprises establishments primarily engaged in organizing, promoting, and/or managing events, such as business and trade shows, conventions, conferences, and meetings (whether or not they manage and provide the staff to operate the facilities in which these events take place).

561

Organizing, promoting, and/or managing live performing arts productions, sports events, and similar events, such as festivals (whether or not they manage and provide the staff to operate the facilities in which that these events take place), **7113**

561990 All Other Support Services

This industry comprises establishments primarily engaged in providing day-to-day business and other organizational support services (except office administrative services, facilities support services, employment services, business support services, travel arrangement and reservation services, security and investigation services, services to buildings and other

structures, packaging and labeling services, and convention and trade show organizing services).

Providing office administrative services **561110**
Providing facilities support services **561210**
Providing employment services **5613**
Providing business support services **5614**
Providing travel arrangement and reservation services **5615**
Providing security and investigation services **5616**
Providing services to buildings and other structures **5617**
Providing packaging and labeling services **561910**
Organizing, promoting, and/or managing conferences, conventions, and trade shows (whether or not they manage and provide the staff to operate the facilities in which these events take place) **561920**

---

562 Waste Management and Remediation Services

Industries in the Waste Management and Remediation Services subsector group establishments engaged in the collection, treatment, and disposal of waste materials. This includes establishments engaged in local hauling of waste materials; operating materials recovery facilities (i.e., those that sort recyclable materials from the trash stream); providing remediation services (i.e., those that provide for the cleanup of contaminated buildings, mine sites, soil, or ground water); and providing septic pumping and other miscellaneous waste management services. There are three industry groups within the subsector that separate these activities into waste collection, waste treatment and disposal, and remediation and other waste management.

Excluded from this subsector are establishments primarily engaged in collecting, treating, and disposing waste through sewer systems or sewage treatment facilities that are classified in Industry 22132, Sewage Treatment Facilities and establishments primarily engaged in long-distance hauling of waste materials that are classified in Industry 48423, Specialized Freight (except Used Goods) Trucking, Long-Distance. Also, there are some activities that appear to be related to waste management, but that are not included in this subsector. For example, establishments primarily engaged in providing waste management consulting services are classified in Industry 54162, Environmental Consulting Services.

5621 Waste Collection^{CAN}

56211 Waste Collection^{CAN}

This industry comprises establishments primarily engaged in (1) collecting and/or hauling hazardous waste, nonhazardous waste, and/or recyclable materials within a local area and/or (2) operating hazardous or nonhazardous waste transfer stations. Hazardous waste collection establishments may be responsible for the identification, treatment, packaging, and labeling of wastes for the purposes of transport.

Long-distance trucking of waste **48423**

Operating facilities for separating and sorting recyclable materials from nonhazardous waste streams (i.e., garbage) and/or for sorting co-mingled recyclable materials, such as paper, plastics, and metal cans, into distinct categories **56292**
Collecting and/or hauling in combination with disposal of waste materials **56221**

562111 Solid Waste Collection^{US}

This U.S. industry comprises establishments primarily engaged in one or more of the following: (1) collecting and/or hauling nonhazardous solid waste (i.e., garbage) within a local area; (2) operating nonhazardous solid waste transfer stations; and (3) collecting and/or hauling mixed recyclable materials within a local area.

Long-distance trucking of waste **484230**
Collecting and/or hauling in combination with disposal of nonhazardous
    waste materials **56221**
Collecting and/or hauling hazardous waste within a local area and/or
    operating hazardous waste transfer stations **562112**
Collecting and removing debris, such as brush or rubble, within a local area
    562119
Operating facilities for separating and sorting recyclable materials from
    nonhazardous waste streams (i.e., garbage) and/or for sorting co-
    mingled recyclable materials, such as paper, plastics, and metal cans,
    into distinct categories **562920**

562112 Hazardous Waste Collection[US]

This U.S. industry comprises establishments primarily engaged in collecting and/or hauling hazardous
waste within a local area and/or operating hazardous waste transfer stations. Hazardous waste collection establishments may be responsible for the
identification, treatment, packaging, and labeling of
wastes for the purposes of transport.

Long-distance trucking of waste **484230**
Collecting and/or hauling in combination with disposal of hazardous waste
    materials **56221**
Collecting and/or hauling nonhazardous solid waste (i.e., garbage) and/or
    recyclable materials within a local area and/or operating nonhazardous
    solid waste transfer stations **562111**
Collecting and removing debris, such as brush or rubble, within a local area
    562119

562119 Other Waste Collection[US]

This U.S. industry comprises establishments primarily engaged in collecting and/or hauling waste (except nonhazardous solid waste and hazardous waste)
within a local area. Establishments engaged in brush
or rubble removal services are included in this industry.

Long-distance trucking of waste **484230**
Collecting and/or hauling in combination with disposal of waste materials
    Group **5622**
Collecting and/or hauling nonhazardous solid waste (i.e., garbage) or mixed
    recyclable materials within a local area or operating nonhazardous solid
    waste transfer stations **562111**
Collecting and/or hauling hazardous waste within a local area or operating
    hazardous waste transfer stations **562112**
Operating facilities for separating and sorting recyclable materials from
    nonhazardous waste streams (i.e., garbage) and/or for sorting co-
    mingled recyclable materials, such as paper, plastics, and metal cans,
    into distinct categories **562920**

5622 Waste Treatment and Disposal[CAN]

56221 Waste Treatment and Disposal[CAN]

This industry comprises establishments primarily
engaged in (1) operating waste treatment or disposal
facilities (except sewer systems or sewage treatment
facilities) or (2) the combined activity of collecting
and/or hauling of waste materials within a local area
and operating waste treatment or disposal facilities.
Waste combusters or incinerators (including those that
may produce byproducts such as electricity), solid
waste landfills, and compost dumps are included in
this industry.

Collecting, treating, and disposing waste through sewer systems or sewage
    treatment facilities **22132**
Manufacturing compost **32531**

562211 Hazardous Waste Treatment and Disposal[US]

This U.S. industry comprises establishments primarily engaged in (1) operating treatment and/or disposal facilities for hazardous waste or (2) the
combined activity of collecting and/or hauling of hazardous waste materials within a local area and operating treatment or disposal facilities for hazardous
waste.

Operating landfills for the disposal of nonhazardous solid waste **562212**
Operating combustors and incinerators for the disposal of nonhazardous
    solid waste **562213**
Collecting, treating, and disposing waste through sewer systems or sewage
    treatment facilities **221320**
Operating nonhazardous waste treatment and disposal facilities (except
    landfills, combustors, incinerators, and sewer systems or sewage
    treatment facilities) **562219**

562212 Solid Waste Landfill[US]

This U.S. industry comprises establishments primarily engaged in (1) operating landfills for the disposal
of nonhazardous solid waste or (2) the combined activity of collecting and/or hauling nonhazardous waste
materials within a local area and operating landfills
for the disposal of nonhazardous solid waste.

Operating treatment and/or disposal facilities for hazardous waste **562211**
Operating combustors and incinerators for the disposal of nonhazardous
    solid waste **562213**
Collecting, treating, and disposing waste through sewer systems or sewage
    treatment facilities **221320**

562

Operating nonhazardous waste treatment and disposal facilities (except landfills, combustors, incinerators, and sewer systems or sewage treatment facilities) **562219**
Manufacturing compost **325314**

562213 Solid Waste Combustors and Incinerators[US]

This U.S. industry comprises establishments primarily engaged in operating combustors and incinerators for the disposal of nonhazardous solid waste. These establishments may produce byproducts, such as electricity and steam.

Operating treatment and/or disposal facilities for hazardous waste **562211**
Operating landfills for the disposal of nonhazardous solid waste **562212**
Collecting, treating, and disposing waste through sewer systems or sewage treatment facilities **221320**
Operating nonhazardous waste treatment and disposal facilities (except landfills, combustors, incinerators, and sewer systems or sewage treatment facilities) **562219**

562219 Other Nonhazardous Waste Treatment and Disposal[US]

This U.S. industry comprises establishments primarily engaged in (1) operating nonhazardous waste treatment and disposal facilities (except landfills, combustors, incinerators and sewer systems or sewage treatment facilities) or (2) the combined activity of collecting and/or hauling of nonhazardous waste materials within a local area and operating waste treatment or disposal facilities (except landfills, combustors, incinerators and sewer systems, or sewage treatment facilities). Compost dumps are included in this industry.

Operating landfills for the disposal of nonhazardous solid waste **562212**
Operating combustors and incinerators for the disposal of nonhazardous solid waste **562213**
Collecting, treating, and disposing waste through sewer systems or sewage treatment facilities **221320**
Manufacturing compost **325314**

5629 Remediation and Other Waste Management Services[CAN]

This industry group comprises establishments primarily engaged in remediation and other waste management services (except waste collection, waste treatment and disposal, and waste management consulting services).

562910 Remediation Services[CAN]

This industry comprises establishments primarily engaged in one or more of the following: (1) remediation and cleanup of contaminated buildings, mine sites, soil, or ground water; (2) integrated mine reclamation activities, including demolition, soil remediation, waste water treatment, hazardous material removal, contouring land, and revegetation; and (3) asbestos, lead paint, and other toxic material abatement.

Developing remedial action plans **541620**
Excavating soil **235930**
Building modifications to alleviate radon gas **23**
Collecting, treating, and disposing waste water through sewer systems or sewage treatment facilities **221320**

562920 Materials Recovery Facilities[CAN]

This industry comprises establishments primarily engaged in (1) operating facilities for separating and sorting recyclable materials from nonhazardous waste streams (i.e., garbage) and/or (2) operating facilities where co-mingled recyclable materials, such as paper, plastics, used beverage cans, and metals, are sorted into distinct categories.

Wholesaling automotive, industrial, and other recyclable materials **421930**

56299 All Other Waste Management Services[CAN]

This industry comprises establishments primarily engaged in waste management services (except waste collection, waste treatment and disposal, remediation, operation of materials recovery facilities, and waste management consulting services).

Collecting and/or hauling waste within a local area **56211**
Long-distance trucking of waste **48423**
Operating treatment or disposal facilities (except sewer systems or sewage treatment facilities) for wastes **56221**
Collecting, treating, and disposing waste through sewer systems or sewage treatment facilities **22132**
Remediation and cleanup of contaminated buildings, mine sites, soil, or ground water **56291**
Operating facilities for separating and sorting recyclable materials from nonhazardous waste streams (i.e., garbage) or where co-mingled recyclable materials, such as paper, plastics, and metal cans, are sorted into distinct categories **56292**
Installing septic tanks **23511**
Providing waste management consulting services, such as developing remedial action plans, **54162**

562991 Septic Tank and Related Services[US]

This U.S. industry comprises establishments primarily engaged in (1) pumping (i.e., cleaning) septic tanks and cesspools and/or (2) renting and/or servicing portable toilets.

Installing septic tanks **235110**
Cleaning and rodding sewers and catch basins **562998**

562998 All Other Miscellaneous Waste Management Services[US]

This U.S. industry comprises establishments primarily engaged in providing waste management services (except waste collection, waste treatment and disposal, remediation, operation of materials recovery facilities, septic tank pumping and related services, and waste management consulting services).

Collecting and/or hauling waste within a local area **56211**
Long-distance trucking of waste **484230**
Operating treatment or disposal facilities (except sewer systems or sewage treatment facilities) for wastes **56221**
Collecting, treating, and disposing waste through sewer systems or sewage treatment facilities **221320**
Remediation and cleanup of contaminated buildings, mine sites, soil, or ground water **562910**
Operating facilities for separating and sorting recyclable materials from nonhazardous waste streams (i.e., garbage) or for sorting co-mingled recyclable materials, such as paper, plastics, and metal cans, into distinct categories **562920**
Pumping (i.e., cleaning) cesspools, portable toilets, and septic tanks or renting portable toilets **562991**
Providing waste management consulting services, such as developing remedial action plans, **541620**

Sector 61: Educational Services

Overview of this Sector as a Whole

The Educational Services sector comprises establishments that provide instruction and training in a wide variety of subjects. This instruction and training is provided by specialized establishments, such as schools, colleges, universities, and training centers. These establishments may be privately owned and operated for profit or not for profit, or they may be publicly owned and operated. They may also offer food and accommodation services to their students. Educational services are usually delivered by teachers or instructors that explain, tell, demonstrate, supervise, and direct learning. Instruction is imparted in diverse settings, such as educational institutions, the workplace, or the home through correspondence, television, or other means. It can be adapted to the particular needs of the students, for example sign language can replace verbal language for teaching students with hearing impairments. All industries in the sector share this commonality of process, namely, labor inputs of instructors with the requisite subject matter expertise and teaching ability.

611

611 Educational Services

Industries in the Educational Services subsector provide instruction and training in a wide variety of subjects. The instruction and training is provided by specialized establishments, such as schools, colleges, universities, and training centers.

The subsector is structured according to level and type of educational services. Elementary and secondary schools, junior colleges and colleges, universities, and professional schools correspond to a recognized series of formal levels of education designated by diplomas, associate degrees (including equivalent certificates), and degrees. The remaining industry groupsare based more on the type of instruction or training offered and the levels are not always as formally defined. The establishments are often highly specialized, many offering instruction in a very limited subject matter, for example ski lessons or one specific computer software package. Within the sector, the level and types of training that are required of the instructors and teachers vary depending on the industry.

Establishments that manage schools and other educational establishments on a contractual basis are classified in this subsector if they both manage the operation and provide the operating staff. Such establishments are classified in the educational services subsector based on the type of facility managed and operated.

6III Elementary and Secondary Schools

6IIII0 Elementary and Secondary Schools^{CAN}

This industry comprises establishments primarily engaged in furnishing academic courses and associated course work that comprise a basic preparatory education. A basic preparatory education ordinarily constitutes kindergarten through 12th grade. This industry includes school boards and school districts.

Providing preschool or prekindergarten education 624410
Military academies, college level 61131

6II2 Junior Colleges

6II2I0 Junior Colleges

This industry comprises establishments primarily engaged in furnishing academic, or academic and technical, courses and granting associate degrees, certificates, or diplomas below the baccalaureate level. The requirement for admission to an associate or equivalent degree program is at least a high school diploma or equivalent general academic training.

6II3 Colleges, Universities, and Professional Schools

6II3I0 Colleges, Universities, and Professional Schools

This industry comprises establishments primarily engaged in furnishing academic courses and granting degrees at baccalaureate or graduate levels. The requirement for admission is at least a high school diploma or equivalent general academic training.

Furnishing academic, or academic and technical, courses and granting associate degrees, certificates, or diplomas below the baccalaureate level 6II2I0

6II4 Business Schools and Computer and Management Training

6II4I0 Business and Secretarial Schools

This industry comprises establishments primarily engaged in offering courses in office procedures and secretarial and stenographic skills and may offer courses in basic office skills, such as word processing. In addition, these establishments may offer such classes as office machine operation, reception, communications, and other skills designed for individuals pursuing a clerical or secretarial career.

Offering computer training (except computer repair) 611420
Offering academic degrees (e.g., baccalaureate, graduate level) in business education 611310
Offering training in the maintenance and repair of computers 611519

6II420 Computer Training

This industry comprises establishments primarily engaged in conducting computer training (except computer repair), such as computer programming, software packages, computerized business systems, computer electronics technology, computer operations, and local area network management. Instruction may be provided at the establishment's facilities or at an off-site location, including the client's own facilities.

Offering training in the maintenance and repair of computers 61151

6II430 Professional and Management Development Training

This industry comprises establishments primarily engaged in offering an array of short duration courses and seminars for management and professional development. Training for career development may be provided directly to individuals or through employers' training programs; and courses may be customized or modified to meet the special needs of customers. Instruction may be provided at the establishment's facilities or at an off-site location, including the client's own facilities.

Advising clients on human resource and training issues without providing the training **541612**

Offering academic degrees (e.g., baccalaureate, graduate level) **611310**

6115 Technical and Trade Schools

61151 Technical and Trade Schools

This industry comprises establishments primarily engaged in offering vocational and technical training in a variety of technical subjects and trades. The training often leads to job-specific certification.

Offering courses in office procedures and secretarial and stenographic skills **61141**

Offering computer training (except computer repair) **61142**

Offering professional and management development training **61143**

Specialty air transportation services that may also provide flight training **48121**

Offering registered nursing training **61121**

611511 Cosmetology and Barber Schools[US]

This U.S. industry comprises establishments primarily engaged in offering training in barbering, hair styling, or the cosmetic arts, such as makeup or skin care. These schools provide job-specific certification.

611512 Flight Training[US]

This U.S. industry comprises establishments primarily engaged in offering aviation and flight training. These establishments may offer vocational training, recreational training, or both.

Specialty air transportation services that may also provide flight training **481219**

611513 Apprenticeship Training[US]

This U.S. industry comprises establishments primarily engaged in offering apprenticeship training programs. These programs involve applied training as well as course work.

611519 Other Technical and Trade Schools[US]

This U.S. industry comprises establishments prima-

rily engaged in offering job or career vocational or technical courses (except cosmetology and barber training, aviation and flight training, and apprenticeship training). The curriculums offered by these schools are highly structured and specialized and lead to job-specific certification.

Offering courses in office procedures and secretarial and stenographic skills **611410**

Offering computer training (except computer repair) **611420**

Offering professional and management development training **611430**

Offering registered nursing training with academic degrees (e.g., associate baccalaureate) **611210**

Offering aviation and flight training **611512**

Offering cosmetology and barber training **611511**

Offering apprenticeship training programs **611513**

6116 Other Schools and Instruction

This industry group comprises establishments primarily engaged in offering or providing instruction (except academic schools, colleges, and universities; and business, computer, management, technical, or trade instruction).

611610 Fine Arts Schools

This industry comprises establishments primarily engaged in offering instruction in the arts, including dance, art, drama, and music.

Offering courses in commercial and graphic arts and commercial photography **611519**

611620 Sports and Recreation Instruction

This industry comprises establishments, such as camps and schools, primarily engaged in offering instruction in athletic activities to groups of individuals. Overnight and day sports instruction camps are included in this industry.

Overnight recreational camps that may offer some athletic instruction in addition to other activities **721214**

Sports and recreation establishments that also offer athletic instruction **71**

Independent (i.e., freelance) athletes engaged in providing sports instruction and participating in spectator sporting events **711219**

611630 Language Schools

This industry comprises establishments primarily engaged in offering foreign language instruction (including sign language). These establishments are designed to offer language instruction ranging from

611

conversational skills for personal enrichment to intensive training courses for career or educational opportunities.

Providing translation and interpretation services **541930**

61169 All Other Schools and Instruction

This industry comprises establishments primarily engaged in offering instruction (except business, computer, management, technical, trade, fine arts, athletic, and language instruction). Also excluded from this industry are academic schools, colleges, and universities.

Offering elementary and secondary school instruction **61111**
Offering junior college instruction **61121**
Offering college, university, and professional school instruction with academic degrees (e.g., baccalaureate, graduate) **61131**
Offering business, computer (except computer repair), and management training **6114**
Offering technical and trade school instruction (e.g., computer repair and maintenance) **61151**
Offering fine arts instruction **61161**
Offering sports and recreation instruction **61162**
Offering language instruction **61163**

611691 Exam Preparation and Tutoring[US]

This U.S. industry comprises establishments primarily engaged in offering preparation for standardized examinations and/or academic tutoring services.

611692 Automobile Driving Schools[US]

This U.S. industry comprises establishments primarily engaged in offering automobile driving instruction.

Offering truck and bus driving instruction **611519**

611699 All Other Miscellaneous Schools and Instruction[US]

This U.S. industry comprises establishments primarily engaged in offering instruction (except business, computer, management, technical, trade, fine arts, athletic, language instruction, tutoring, and automobile driving instruction). Also excluded from this industry are academic schools, colleges, and universities.

Offering elementary and secondary school instruction **611110**
Offering junior college instruction **611210**
Offering college, university, and professional school instruction with academic degrees (e.g., baccalaureate, graduate) **611310**
Offering business, computer (except computer repair), and management training **6114**
Offering technical and trade school instruction (e.g., computer repair and maintenance) **61151**
Offering fine arts instruction **611610**
Offering sports and recreation instruction **611620**
Offering language instruction **611630**
Offering exam preparation and tutoring services **611691**
Offering automobile driving instruction **611692**

6117 Educational Support Services

611710 Educational Support Services

This industry comprises establishments primarily engaged in providing noninstructional services that support educational processes or systems.

Providing job training for the unemployed, underemployed, physically disabled, and persons who have a job market disadvantage because of lack of education or job skills **624310**
Conducting research and analyses in cognitive development **541720**

SECTOR 62: HEALTH CARE AND SOCIAL ASSISTANCE

OVERVIEW OF THIS SECTOR AS A WHOLE

The Health Care and Social Assistance sector comprises establishments providing health care and social assistance for individuals. The sector includes both health care and social assistance because it is sometimes difficult to distinguish between the boundaries of these two activities. The industries in this sector are arranged on a continuum starting with those establishments providing medical care exclusively, continuing with those providing health care and social assistance, and finally finishing with those providing only social assistance. The services provided by establishments in this sector are delivered by trained professionals. All industries in the sector share this commonality of process, namely, labor inputs of health practitioners or social workers with the requisite expertise. Many of the industries in the sector are defined based on the educational degree held by the practitioners included in the industry.

Excluded from this sector are aerobic classes in Subsector 713, Amusement, Gambling and Recreation Industries and nonmedical diet and weight reducing centers in Subsector 812, Personal and Laundry Services. Although these can be viewed as health services, these services are not typically delivered by health practitioners.

621 Ambulatory Health Care Services

Industries in the Ambulatory Health Care Services subsector provide health care services directly or indirectly to ambulatory patients and do not usually provide inpatient services. Health practitioners in this subsector provide outpatient services, with the facilities and equipment not usually being the most significant part of the production process.

6211 Offices of Physicians

62111 Offices of Physicians

This industry comprises establishments of health practitioners having the degree of M.D. (Doctor of medicine) or D.O. (Doctor of osteopathy) primarily engaged in the independent practice of general or specialized medicine (e.g., anesthesiology, oncology, ophthalmology, psychiatry) or surgery. These practitioners operate private or group practices in their own offices (e.g., centers, clinics) or in the facilities of others, such as hospitals or HMO medical centers.

Medical centers primarily engaged in providing emergency medical care for accident or trauma victims and ambulatory surgical centers, providing surgery on an outpatient basis **62149**
Oral pathologists **62121**
Speech or voice pathologists **62134**

621111 Offices of Physicians (except Mental Health Specialists)[US]

This U.S. industry comprises establishments of health practitioners having the degree of M.D. (Doctor of medicine) or D.O. (Doctor of osteopathy) primarily engaged in the independent practice of general or specialized medicine (except psychiatry or psychoanalysis) or surgery. These practitioners operate private or group practices in their own offices (e.g., centers, clinics) or in the facilities of others, such as hospitals or HMO medical centers.

Physicians in the independent practice of psychiatry or psychoanalysis
    621112
Freestanding medical centers providing emergency medical care for accident or catastrophe victims, and freestanding ambulatory surgical centers providing surgery on an outpatient basis **621493**
Oral pathologists **621210**
Speech or voice pathologists **621340**

621112 Offices of Physicians, Mental Health Specialists[US]

This U.S. industry comprises establishments of health practitioners having the degree of M.D. (Doctor of medicine) or D.O. (Doctor of osteopathy) primarily engaged in the independent practice of psychiatry or psychoanalysis. These practitioners operate private or group practices in their own offices (e.g., centers, clinics) or in the facilities of others, such as hospitals or HMO medical centers.

621

6212 Offices of Dentists

621210 Offices of Dentists

This industry comprises establishments of health practitioners having the degree of D.M.D. (Doctor of dental medicine), D.D.S. (Doctor of dental surgery), or D.D.Sc. (Doctor of dental science) primarily engaged in the independent practice of general or specialized dentistry or dental surgery. These practitioners operate private or group practices in their own offices (e.g., centers, clinics) or in the facilities of others, such as hospitals or HMO medical centers. They can provide either comprehensive preventive, cosmetic, or emergency care, or specialize in a single field of dentistry.

Dental laboratories making dentures, artificial teeth, and orthodontic appliances to order for dentists **339116**
Dental hygienists cleaning teeth and gums or denturists taking impressions for and fitting dentures **621399**

6213 Offices of Other Health Practitioners

This industry group comprises establishments of independent health practitioners (except physicians and dentists).

621310 Offices of Chiropractors

This industry comprises establishments of health practitioners having the degree of D.C. (Doctor of chiropractic) primarily engaged in the independent practice of chiropractic. These practitioners provide diagnostic and therapeutic treatment of neuromusculoskeletal and related disorders through the manipulation and adjustment of the spinal column and extremities, and operate private or group practices in their own offices (e.g., centers, clinics) or in the facilities of others, such as hospitals or HMO medical centers.

621320 Offices of Optometrists

This industry comprises establishments of health practitioners having the degree of O.D. (Doctor of optometry) primarily engaged in the independent practice of optometry. These practitioners provide eye examinations to determine visual acuity or the presence of vision problems and to prescribe eyeglasses, contact lenses, and eye exercises. They operate private or group practices in their own offices (e.g., centers, clin-ics) or in the facilities of others, such as hospitals or HMO medical centers, and may also provide the same service as opticians, such as selling and fitting prescription eyeglasses and contact lenses.

Opticians selling and fitting prescription eyeglasses and contact lenses **446130**
Physicians in the independent practice of ophthalmology **621111**

621330 Offices of Mental Health Practitioners (except Physicians)

This industry comprises establishments of independent mental health practitioners (except physicians) primarily engaged in (1) the diagnosis and treatment of mental, emotional, and behavioral disorders and/or (2) the diagnosis and treatment of individual or group social dysfunction brought about by such causes as mental illness, alcohol and substance abuse, physical and emotional trauma, or stress. These practitioners operate private or group practices in their own offices (e.g., centers, clinics) or in the facilities of others, such as hospitals or HMO medical centers.

Psychiatrists, psychoanalysts, and psychotherapists having the degree of M.D. (Doctor of medicine) or D.O. (Doctor of osteopathy) **621112**

621340 Offices of Physical, Occupational and Speech Therapists, and Audiologists

This industry comprises establishments of independent health practitioners primarily engaged in one of the following: (1) administering medically prescribed physical therapy treatment for patients suffering from injuries or muscle, nerve, joint, and bone disease; (2) planning and administering educational, recreational, and social activities designed to help patients or individuals with disabilities, regain physical or mental functioning or to adapt to their disabilities; and (3) diagnosing and treating speech, language, or hearing problems. These practitioners operate private or group practices in their own offices (e.g., centers, clinics) or in the facilities of others, such as hospitals or HMO medical centers.

62139 Offices of All Other Health Practitioners

This industry comprises establishments of independent health practitioners (except physicians; dentists; chiropractors; optometrists; mental health specialists; physical, occupational, and speech therapists; and audiologists). These practitioners operate private or group practices in their own offices (e.g., centers, clinics) or in the facilities of others, such as hospitals or HMO medical centers.

The independent practice of medicine (i.e., physicians) **62III**
The independent practice of dentistry **62I2I**
The independent practice of chiropractic **62I3I**
The independent practice of optometry **62I32**
The independent practice of mental health (except physicians) **62I33**
The independent practice of physical, occupational, and speech therapy and audiology **62I34**

62I39I Offices of Podiatrists[US]

This U.S. industry comprises establishments of health practitioners having the degree of D.P. (Doctor of podiatry) primarily engaged in the independent practice of podiatry. These practitioners diagnose and treat diseases and deformities of the foot and operate private or group practices in their own offices (e.g., centers, clinics) or in the facilities of others, such as hospitals or HMO medical centers.

62I399 Offices of All Other Miscellaneous Health Practitioners[US]

This U.S. industry comprises establishments of independent health practitioners (except physicians; dentists; chiropractors; optometrists; mental health specialists; physical, occupational, and speech therapists; audiologists; and podiatrists). These practitioners operate private or group practices in their own offices (e.g., centers, clinics) or in the facilities of others, such as hospitals or HMO medical centers.

The independent practice of medicine (i.e., physicians) **62III**
The independent practice of dentistry **62I2I0**
The independent practice of chiropractic **62I3I0**
The independent practice of optometry **62I320**
The independent practice of mental health (except physicians) **62I330**
The independent practice of physical, occupational, and speech therapy, and audiology **62I340**
The independent practice of podiatry **62I39I**

62I4 Outpatient Care Centers

62I4I0 Family Planning Centers

This industry comprises establishments with medical staff primarily engaged in providing a range of family planning services on an outpatient basis, such as contraceptive services, genetic and prenatal counsel-

ing, voluntary sterilization, and therapeutic and medically indicated termination of pregnancy.

62I420 Outpatient Mental Health and Substance Abuse Centers

This industry comprises establishments with medical staff primarily engaged in providing outpatient services related to the diagnosis and treatment of mental health disorders and alcohol and other substance abuse. These establishments generally treat patients who do not require inpatient treatment. They may provide a counseling staff and information regarding a wide range of mental health and substance abuse issues and/or refer patients to more extensive treatment programs, if necessary.

Licensed hospitals in inpatient treatment of mental health and substance abuse illnesses with an emphasis on medical treatment and monitoring **62220**
Inpatient treatment of mental health and substance abuse illness with an emphasis on residential care and counseling rather than medical treatment **62320**

62I49 Other Outpatient Care Centers

This industry comprises establishments with medical staff primarily engaged in providing general or specialized outpatient care (except family planning centers and outpatient mental health and substance abuse centers). Centers or clinics of health practitioners with different degrees from more than one industry practicing within the same establishment (i.e., Doctor of medicine and Doctor of dental medicine) are included in this industry.

Physician walk-in centers **62III**
Centers and clinics of health practitioners from the same industry in the independent practice of their profession **62III**
Family planning centers **62I4I**
Outpatient mental health and substance abuse centers **62I42**
HMO establishments (except those providing health care services) underwriting health and medical insurance policies **524II**
Licensed hospitals that also perform ambulatory surgery and emergency room services **622**

62I49I HMO Medical Centers[US]

This U.S. industry comprises establishments with physicians and other medical staff primarily engaged in providing a range of outpatient medical services to the health maintenance organization (HMO) subscribers with a focus generally on primary care.

621

These establishments are owned by the HMO. Included in this industry are HMO establishments that both provide health care services and underwrite health and medical insurance policies.

Health practitioners or health practitioner groups contracting to provide their services to subscribers of prepaid health plans **62III, 621210,** and **6213**

HMO establishments (except those providing health care services) primarily engaged in underwriting and administering health and medical insurance policies **524114**

621492 Kidney Dialysis Centers^{US}

This U.S. industry comprises establishments with medical staff primarily engaged in providing outpatient kidney or renal dialysis services.

621493 Freestanding Ambulatory Surgical and Emergency Centers^{US}

This U.S. industry comprises establishments with physicians and other medical staff primarily engaged in (1) providing surgical services (e.g., orthoscopic and cataract surgery) on an outpatient basis or (2) providing emergency care services (e.g., setting broken bones, treating lacerations, or tending to patients suffering injuries as a result of accidents, trauma, or medical conditions necessitating immediate medical care) on an outpatient basis. Outpatient surgical establishments have specialized facilities, such as operating and recovery rooms, and specialized equipment, such as anesthetic or X-ray equipment.

Physician walk-in centers **62IIII**
Licensed hospitals that also perform ambulatory surgery and emergency room services **622**

621498 All Other Outpatient Care Centers^{US}

This U.S. industry comprises establishments with medical staff primarily engaged in providing general or specialized outpatient care (except family planning centers, outpatient mental health and substance abuse centers, HMO medical centers, kidney dialysis centers, and freestanding ambulatory surgical and emergency centers). Centers or clinics of health practitioners with different degrees from more than one industry practicing within the same establishment (i.e., Doctor of medicine and Doctor of dental medicine) are included in this industry.

Physician walk-in centers **62IIII**

Centers and clinics of health practitioners from the same industry in the independent practice of their profession **62IIII**
Family planning centers **621410**
Outpatient mental health and substance abuse centers **621420**
HMO medical centers **621491**
Dialysis centers **621492**
Freestanding ambulatory surgical and emergency centers **621493**

6215 Medical and Diagnostic Laboratories

62151 Medical and Diagnostic Laboratories

This industry comprises establishments known as medical and diagnostic laboratories primarily engaged in providing analytic or diagnostic services, including body fluid analysis and diagnostic imaging, generally to the medical profession or to the patient on referral from a health practitioner.

Dental, optical, and orthopedic laboratories providing the following activities to the medical profession, respectively: making dentures, artificial teeth, and orthodontic appliances to prescription; grinding of lenses to prescription; and making orthopedic or prosthetic appliances to prescription **33911**

621511 Medical Laboratories^{US}

This U.S. industry comprises establishments known as medical laboratories primarily engaged in providing analytic or diagnostic services, including body fluid analysis, generally to the medical profession or to the patient on referral from a health practitioner.

Dental laboratories making dentures, artificial teeth, and orthodontic appliances to prescription **339116**
Optical laboratories grinding of lenses to prescription **339115**
Orthopedic laboratories making orthopedic or prosthetic appliances to prescription **339113**

621512 Diagnostic Imaging Centers^{US}

This U.S. industry comprises establishments known as diagnostic imaging centers primarily engaged in producing images of the patient generally on referral from a health practitioner.

6216 Home Health Care Services

621610 Home Health Care Services

This industry comprises establishments primarily engaged in providing skilled nursing services in the home, along with a range of the following: personal care services; homemaker and companion services; physical therapy; medical social services; medications; medical equipment and supplies; counseling; 24-hour home care; occupation and vocational therapy; dietary and nutritional services; speech therapy; audiology; and high-tech care, such as intravenous therapy.

In-home health services provided by establishments of health practitioners and others primarily engaged in the independent practice of their profession **62111**
Renting or leasing products for home health care **532291**

6219 Other Ambulatory Health Care Services

This industry group comprises establishments primarily engaged in providing ambulatory health care services (except offices of physicians, dentists, and other health practitioners; outpatient care centers; medical laboratories and diagnostic imaging centers; and home health care providers).

621910 Ambulance Services

This industry comprises establishments primarily engaged in providing transportation of patients by ground or air, along with medical care. These services are often provided during a medical emergency but are not restricted to emergencies. The vehicles are equipped with lifesaving equipment operated by medically trained personnel.

Providing transportation of the disabled or elderly (without medical care) **485991**

62199 All Other Ambulatory Health Care Services

This industry comprises establishments primarily engaged in providing ambulatory health care services (except office physicians, dentists, and other health practitioners; outpatient care centers; medical and

diagnostic laboratories; home health care providers; and ambulances).

The independent practice of medicine **62111**
The independent practice of dentistry **62121**
The independent practice of health care (except offices of physicians and dentists) **6213**
Providing general or specialized outpatient care services **6214**
Providing home health care services **62161**
Transportation of patients by ground or air, along with medical care **62191**
Medical and diagnostic laboratories providing analytic or diagnostic services **62151**

621991 Blood and Organ Banks[US]

This U.S. industry comprises establishments primarily engaged in collecting, storing, and distributing blood and blood products and storing and distributing body organs.

621999 All Other Miscellaneous Ambulatory Health Care Services[US]

This U.S. industry comprises establishments primarily engaged in providing ambulatory health care services (except offices of physicians, dentists, and other health practitioners; outpatient care centers; medical and diagnostic laboratories; home health care providers; ambulances; and blood and organ banks).

The independent practice of medicine **62111**
The independent practice of dentistry **621210**
The independent practice of health care (except offices of physicians and dentists) **6213**
Providing general or specialized outpatient care services **6214**
Providing home health care services **621610**
The transportation of patients by ground or air, along with medical care **621910**
Medical and diagnostic laboratories providing analytic or diagnostic services **62151**
Blood and organ banks **621991**

622

622 Hospitals

Industries in the Hospitals subsector provide medical, diagnostic, and treatment services that include physician, nursing, and other health services to inpatients and the specialized accommodation services required by inpatients. Hospitals may also provide outpatient services as a secondary activity. Establishments in the Hospitals subsector provide inpatient health services, many of which can only be provided using the specialized facilities and equipment that form a significant and integral part of the production process.

6221 General Medical and Surgical Hospitals

622110 General Medical and Surgical Hospitals

This industry comprises establishments known and licensed as general medical and surgical hospitals primarily engaged in providing diagnostic and medical treatment (both surgical and nonsurgical) to inpatients with any of a wide variety of medical conditions. These establishments maintain inpatient beds and provide patients with food services that meet their nutritional requirements. These hospitals have an organized staff of physicians and other medical staff to provide patient care services. These establishments usually provide other services, such as outpatient services, anatomical pathology services, diagnostic X-ray services, clinical laboratory services, operating room services for a variety of procedures, and pharmacy services.

6222 Psychiatric and Substance Abuse Hospitals

622210 Psychiatric and Substance Abuse Hospitals

This industry comprises establishments known and licensed as psychiatric and substance abuse hospitals primarily engaged in providing diagnostic, medical treatment, and monitoring services for inpatients who suffer from mental illness or substance abuse disorders. The treatment often requires an extended stay in the hospital. These establishments maintain inpatient beds and provide patients with food services that meet their nutritional requirements. They have an organized staff of physicians and other medical staff to provide patient care services. Psychiatric, psychological, and social work services are available at the facility. These hospitals usually provide other services, such as outpatient services, clinical laboratory services, diagnostic X-ray services, and electroencephalograph services.

Providing treatment of mental health and substance abuse illnesses on an exclusively outpatient basis **621420**

Hospitals providing inpatient treatment of mental health and substance abuse illness with the emphasis on counseling rather than medical treatment **623220**

Hospitals providing residential care for persons diagnosed with mental retardation **623210**

6223 Specialty (except Psychiatric and Substance Abuse) Hospitals

622310 Specialty (except Psychiatric and Substance Abuse) Hospitals

This industry consists of establishments known and licensed as specialty hospitals primarily engaged in providing diagnostic and medical treatment to inpatients with a specific type of disease or medical condition (except psychiatric or substance abuse). Hospitals providing long-term care for the chronically ill and hospitals providing rehabilitation, restorative, and adjustive services to physically challenged or disabled people are included in this industry. These establishments maintain inpatient beds and provide patients with food services that meet their nutritional requirements. They have an organized staff of physicians and other medical staff to provide patient care services. These hospitals may provide other services, such as outpatient services, diagnostic X-ray services, clinical laboratory services, operating room services, physical therapy services, educational and vocational services, and psychological and social work services.

Licensed hospitals providing diagnostic and therapeutic inpatient services for a variety of medical conditions, both surgical and nonsurgical, **622110**

Licensed hospitals providing diagnostic and treatment services for inpatients with psychiatric or substance abuse illnesses **622210**

Hospitals providing inpatient nursing and rehabilitative services to persons requiring convalescence **623110**

Hospitals providing residential care of persons diagnosed with mental retardation **623210**

Hospitals providing inpatient treatment for mental health and substance abuse illnesses with the emphasis on counseling rather than medical treatment **623220**

623 Nursing and Residential Care Facilities

Industries in the Nursing and Residential Care Facilities subsector provide residential care combined with either nursing, supervisory, or other types of care as required by the residents. In this subsector, the facilities are a significant part of the production process and the care provided is a mix of health and social services with the health services being largely some level of nursing services.

6231 Nursing Care Facilities

623110 Nursing Care Facilities

This industry comprises establishments primarily engaged in providing inpatient nursing and rehabilitative services. The care is generally provided for an extended period of time to individuals requiring nursing care. These establishments have a permanent core staff of registered or licensed practical nurses who, along with other staff, provide nursing and continuous personal care services.

Assisted-living facilities with on-site nursing care facilities **623311**
Psychiatric convalescent homes **623220**

6232 Residential Mental Retardation, Mental Health and Substance Abuse Facilities

This industry group comprises establishments primarily engaged in providing residential care (but not licensed hospital care) to people with mental retardation, mental illness, or substance abuse problems.

623210 Residential Mental Retardation Facilities

This industry comprises establishments (e.g., group homes, hospitals, intermediate care facilities) primarily engaged in providing residential care services for persons diagnosed with mental retardation. These facilities may provide some health care, though the focus is room, board, protective supervision, and counseling.

Providing inpatient treatment of mental health and substance abuse illnesses with an emphasis on counseling rather than medical treatment **623220**
Providing treatment of mental health and substance abuse illnesses on an exclusively outpatient basis **621420**
Licensed hospitals providing inpatient treatment of mental health and substance abuse illnesses with an emphasis on medical treatment and monitoring **622210**

623220 Residential Mental Health and Substance Abuse Facilities

This industry comprises establishments primarily engaged in providing residential care and treatment for patients with mental health and substance abuse illnesses. These establishments provide room, board, supervision, and counseling services. Although medical services may be available at these establishments, they are incidental to the counseling, mental rehabilitation, and support services offered. These establishments generally provide a wide range of social services in addition to counseling.

Providing treatment of mental health and substance abuse illnesses on an exclusively outpatient basis **621420**
Providing residential care for persons diagnosed with mental retardation **623210**
Licensed hospitals providing inpatient treatment of mental health and substance abuse illnesses with an emphasis on medical treatment and monitoring **622210**

6233 Community Care Facilities for the Elderly

62331 Community Care Facilities for the Elderly

This industry comprises establishments primarily engaged in providing residential and personal care services for (1) the elderly and other persons who are unable to fully care for themselves and/or (2) the elderly and other persons who do not desire to live independently. The care typically includes room, board, supervision, and assistance in daily living, such as housekeeping services. In some instances these establishments provide skilled nursing care for residents in separate on-site facilities.

Providing inpatient nursing and rehabilitative services **62311**
Apartment or condominium complexes where people live independently in rented housing units **53111**

623

623311 Continuing Care Retirement Communities[US]

This U.S. industry comprises establishments primarily engaged in providing a range of residential and personal care services with on-site nursing care facilities for (1) the elderly and other persons who are unable to fully care for themselves and/or (2) the elderly and other persons who do not desire to live independently. Individuals live in a variety of residential settings with meals, housekeeping, social, leisure, and other services available to assist residents in daily living. Assisted-living facilities with on-site nursing care facilities are included in this industry.

Providing inpatient nursing and rehabilitative services **623110**
Assisted-living facilities without on-site nursing care facilities **623312**
Apartment or condominium complexes where people live independently in rented housing units **531110**

623312 Homes for the Elderly[US]

This U.S. industry comprises establishments primarily engaged in providing residential and personal care services (i.e., without on-site nursing care facilities) for (1) the elderly or other persons who are unable to fully care for themselves and/or (2) the elderly or other persons who do not desire to live independently. The care typically includes room, board, supervision, and assistance in daily living, such as housekeeping services.

Assisted-living facilities with on-site nursing care facilities **623311**
Homes for the elderly with nursing care or rest homes with nursing care **623110**
Apartment or condominium complexes where people live independently in rented or owned housing units **53111**

6239 Other Residential Care Facilities

This industry group comprises establishments of residential care facilities (except residential mental retardation, mental health, and substance abuse facilities and community care facilities for the elderly).

623990 Other Residential Care Facilities

This industry comprises establishments primarily engaged in providing residential care (except residential mental retardation facilities, residential health and substance abuse facilities, continuing care retirement communities, and homes for the elderly). These establishments also provide supervision and personal care services.

Residential mental retardation facilities **623210**
Continuing care retirement communities **623311**
Residential mental health and substance abuse facilities **623220**
Homes for the elderly without nursing care **623312**
Providing inpatient nursing and rehabilitative services **623110**
Providing temporary shelter **624221**
Correctional camps **922140**

624 Social Assistance

Industries in the Social Assistance subsector provide a wide variety of social assistance services directly to their clients. These services do not include residential or accommodation services, except on a short stay basis.

6241 Individual and Family Services

624110 Child and Youth Services

This industry comprises establishments primarily engaged in providing nonresidential social assistance services for children and youth. These establishments provide for the welfare of children in such areas as adoption and foster care, drug prevention, life skills training, and positive social development.

Youth recreational centers **713940**
Youth recreational sports teams and leagues **713990**
Scouting organizations **813410**
Providing day care services for children **624410**

624120 Services for the Elderly and Persons with Disabilities

This industry comprises establishments primarily engaged in providing nonresidential social assistance services to improve the quality of life for the elderly, persons diagnosed with mental retardation, or persons with disabilities. These establishments provide for the welfare of these of individuals in such areas as day care, nonmedical home care or homemaker services, social activities, group support, and companionship.

Providing job training for persons diagnosed with mental retardation or persons with disabilities **624310**

Providing residential care for the elderly, persons diagnosed with mental retardation, or persons with disabilities **633**
Providing in-home health care services **621**

624190 Other Individual and Family Services

This industry comprises establishments primarily engaged in providing nonresidential individual and family social assistance services (except those specifically directed toward children, the elderly, persons diagnosed with mental retardation, or persons with disabilities).

Providing clinical psychological and psychiatric social counseling services **621330**
Providing child and youth social assistance services (except day care) **624110**
Providing child day care services **624410**
Providing social assistance services for the elderly, persons diagnosed with mental retardation, and persons with disabilities **624120**
Community action advocacy **813319**
Providing in-home health care services **621**

6242 Community Food and Housing, and Emergency and Other Relief Services

624210 Community Food Services

This industry comprises establishments primarily engaged in the collection, preparation, and delivery of food for the needy. Establishments in this industry may also distribute clothing and blankets to the poor. These establishments may prepare and deliver meals to persons who by reason of age, disability, or illness are unable to prepare meals for themselves; collect and distribute salvageable or donated food; or prepare and provide meals at fixed or mobile locations. Food banks, meal delivery programs, and soup kitchens are included in this industry.

62422 Community Housing Services

This industry comprises establishments primarily engaged in providing one or more of the following community housing services: (1) short term emergency shelter for victims of domestic violence, sexual assault, or child abuse; (2) temporary residential shelter for the homeless, runaway youths, and patients and families caught in medical crises; (3) transitional housing for low-income individuals and families; (4) volunteer construction or repair of low cost housing,

in partnership with the homeowner who may assist in construction or repair work; and (5) repair of homes for elderly or disabled homeowners. These establishments may operate their own shelter; or may subsidize housing using existing homes, apartments, hotels, or motels; or may require a low-cost mortgage or work (sweat) equity.

Central offices of government housing programs **92511**

624221 Temporary Shelters[US]

This U.S. industry comprises establishments primarily engaged in providing (1) short term emergency shelter for victims of domestic violence, sexual assault, or child abuse and/or (2) temporary residential shelter for homeless individuals or families, runaway youth, and patients and families caught in medical crises. These establishments may operate their own shelters or may subsidize housing using existing homes, apartments, hotels, or motels.

Providing emergency shelter for victims of domestic or international disasters or conflicts **624230**

624229 Other Community Housing Services[US]

This U.S. industry comprises establishments primarily engaged in providing one or more of the following community housing services: (1) transitional housing to low-income individuals and families; (2) volunteer construction or repair of low-cost housing, in partnership with the homeowner who may assist in the construction or repair work; and (3) the repair of homes for elderly or disabled homeowners. These establishments may subsidize housing using existing homes, apartments, hotels, or motels or may require a low-cost mortgage or sweat equity. These establishments may also provide low-income families with furniture and household supplies.

Central offices of government housing programs **925110**

624230 Emergency and Other Relief Services

This industry comprises establishments primarily engaged in providing food, shelter, clothing, medical relief, resettlement, and counseling to victims of domestic or international disasters or conflicts (e.g., wars).

624

6243 Vocational Rehabilitation Services

624310 Vocational Rehabilitation Services

This industry comprises (1) establishments primarily engaged in providing vocational rehabilitation or habilitation services, such as job counseling, job training, and work experience, to unemployed and underemployed persons, persons with disabilities, and persons who have a job market disadvantage because of lack of education, job skill, or experience and (2) establishments primarily engaged in providing training and employment to persons with disabilities. Vocational rehabilitation job training facilities (except schools) and sheltered workshops (i.e., work experience centers) are included in this industry.

Schools (except high schools) primarily engaged in providing vocational training **61151**
Vocational high schools **611110**
Providing career and vocational counseling (except rehabilitative) **611710**

6244 Child Day Care Services

624410 Child Day Care Services

This industry comprises establishments primarily engaged in providing day care of infants or children. These establishments generally care for preschool children, but may care for older children when they are not in school and may also offer prekindergarten educational programs.

Offering kindergarten educational programs **611110**

SECTOR 71: ARTS, ENTERTAINMENT, AND RECREATION

OVERVIEW OF THIS SECTOR AS A WHOLE

The Arts, Entertainment, and Recreation sector includes a wide range of establishments that operate facilities or provide services to meet varied cultural, entertainment, and recreational interests of their patrons. This sector comprises (1) establishments that are involved in producing, promoting, or participating in live performances, events, or exhibits intended for public viewing; (2) establishments that preserve and exhibit objects and sites of historical, cultural, or educational interest; and (3) establishments that operate facilities or provide services that enable patrons to participate in recreational activities or pursue amusement, hobby, and leisure time interests. Some establishments that provide cultural, entertainment, or recreational facilities and services are classified in other sectors. Excluded from this sector are: (1) establishments that provide both accommodations and recreational facilities, such as hunting and fishing camps and resort and casino hotels are classified in Subsector 721, Accommodation; (2) restaurants and night clubs that provide live entertainment in addition to the sale of food and beverages are classified in Subsector 722, Food Services and Drinking Places; (3) motion picture theaters, libraries and archives, and publishers of newspapers, magazines, books, periodicals, and computer software are classified in Sector 51, Information; and (4) establishments using transportation equipment to provide recreational and entertainment services, such as those operating sightseeing buses, dinner cruises, or helicopter rides are classified in Subsector 487, Scenic and Sightseeing Transportation.

711 Performing Arts, Spectator Sports, and Related Industries

Industries in the Performing Arts, Spectator Sports, and Related Industries subsector group establishments that produce or organize and promote live presentations involving the performances of actors and actresses, singers, dancers, musical groups and artists, athletes, and other entertainers, including independent (i.e., freelance) entertainers and the establishments that manage their careers. The classification recognizes four basic processes: (1) producing (i.e., presenting) events; (2) organizing, managing, and/or promoting events; (3) managing and representing entertainers; and (4) providing the artistic, creative and technical skills necessary to the production of these live events. Also, this subsector contains four industries for performing arts companies. Each is defined on the basis of the particular skills of the entertainers involved in the presentations. The industry structure for this subsector makes a clear distinction between performing arts companies and performing artists (i.e., independent or freelance). Although not unique to arts and entertainment, freelancing is a particularly important phenomenon in this Performing Arts, Spectator Sports, and Related Industries subsector. Distinguishing this activity from the production activity is a meaningful process differentiation. This approach, however, is difficult to implement in the case of musical groups (i.e., companies) and artists, especially pop groups. These establishments tend to be more loosely organized and it can be difficult to distinguish companies from freelancers. For this reason, NAICS includes one industry that covers both musical groups and musical artists.

This subsector contains two industries for Industry Group 7113, Promoters of Performing Arts, Sports, and Similar Events, one for those that operate facilities and another for those that do not. This is because there are significant differences in cost structures between those promoters that manage and provide the staff to operate facilities and those that do not. In addition to promoters without facilities other industries in this subsector include establishments that may operate without permanent facilities. These types of establishments include: performing arts companies, musical groups and artists, spectator sports, and independent (i.e., freelance) artists, writers, and performers. Excluded from this subsector are nightclubs. Some nightclubs promote live entertainment on a regular basis and it can be argued that they could be classified in Industry Group 7113, Promoters of Performing Arts, Sports, and Similar Events with Facilities. However, since most of these establishments function as any other drinking place when they do not promote entertainment and because most of their revenue is derived from sale of food and beverages, they are classified in Subsector 722, Food Services and Drinking Places.

7111 Performing Arts Companies

This industry group comprises establishments primarily engaged in producing live presentations involving the performances of actors and actresses, singers, dancers, musical groups and artists, and other performing artists.

711110 Theater Companies and Dinner Theaters

This industry comprises (1) companies, groups, or theaters primarily engaged in producing the following live theatrical presentations: musicals; operas; plays; and comedy, improvisational, mime, and puppet shows and (2) establishments, commonly known as dinner theaters, engaged in producing live theatrical productions and in providing food and beverages for consumption on the premises. Theater groups or companies may or may not operate their own theater or other facility for staging their shows.

711

Providing food and beverages for consumption on the premises and that also present live nontheatrical entertainment, such as night clubs, **722**

Organizing, managing, and/or promoting performing arts productions without producing their own shows **7113**

Companies, groups, or theaters producing all types of live theatrical dance presentations **711120**

Freelance producers and performing artists (except musicians and vocalists) in theatrical activities independent of a company or group **711510**

Musicians and vocalists **711130**

711120 Dance Companies

This industry comprises companies, groups, or theaters primarily engaged in producing all types of live theatrical dance (e.g., ballet, contemporary dance, folk dance) presentations. Dance companies or groups may or may not operate their own theater or other facility for staging their shows.

Providing food and beverages for consumption on the premises and that also present live dance entertainment, such as exotic clubs, **722**

Organizing, promoting, and/or managing dance productions without producing their own shows **7113**

Freelance producers and dancers in theatrical activities independent of a company or group **711510**

711130 Musical Groups and Artists

This industry comprises (1) groups primarily engaged in producing live musical entertainment (except theatrical musical or opera productions) and (2) independent (i.e., freelance) artists primarily engaged in providing live musical entertainment. Musical groups and artists may perform in front of a live audience or in a studio, and may or may not operate their own facilities for staging their shows.

Organizing, promoting, and/or managing concerts and other musical performances without producing their own shows **7113**

Companies, groups, or theaters producing theatrical musicals and opera productions **711110**

Freelance producers (except musical groups and artists) in musical activities independent of a company or group **711510**

711190 Other Performing Arts Companies

This industry comprises companies or groups (except theater companies, dance companies, musical groups, and artists) primarily engaged in producing live theatrical presentations.

Providing food and beverages for consumption on the premises and that also present live nontheatrical entertainment, such as comedy clubs or nightclubs, **722**

Organizing, promoting, and/or managing ice skating shows, circuses, and other live performing arts presentations without producing their own shows **7113**

Theater companies and groups (except dance) or dinner theaters producing musicals; plays; operas; and comedy, improvisational, mime, and puppet shows **711110**

Dance companies or groups **711120**

Freelance producers and performing artists (except musicians and vocalists) **711510**

Musical groups and independent musicians and vocalists **711130**

7112 Spectator Sports

71121 Spectator Sports

This industry comprises (1) sports teams or clubs primarily participating in live sporting events before a paying audience; (2) establishments primarily engaged in operating racetracks; (3) independent athletes engaged in participating in live sporting or racing events before a paying audience; (4) owners of racing participants, such as cars, dogs, and horses, primarily engaged in entering them in racing events or other spectator sports events; and (5) establishments, such as sports trainers, primarily engaged in providing specialized services to support participants in sports events or competitions. The sports teams and clubs included in this industry may or may not operate their own arena, stadium, or other facility for presenting their games or other spectator sports events.

Promoting sporting events without participating in sporting events **7113**

Participating in sporting events for recreational purposes without playing before a paying audience, such as youth league baseball teams, **71399**

Amateur, semiprofessional, or professional athletic associations or leagues **81399**

Representing or managing the careers of sports figures **71141**

Independent athletes providing sports instruction without participating in sporting events before a paying audience **61162**

Independent athletes endorsing products or making speeches **71151**

Raising horses, mules, donkeys, and other equines **112920**

711211 Sports Teams and Clubs^{CAN}

This U.S. industry comprises professional or semiprofessional sports teams or clubs primarily engaged in participating in live sporting events, such as baseball, basketball, football, hockey, soccer, and jai alai games, before a paying audience. These establishments may or may not operate their own arena, stadium, or other facility for presenting these events.

Promoting sporting events without participating in sporting events **7113**

Participating in sporting events for recreational purposes without playing before a paying audience, such as youth league baseball teams, **713990**

Amateur, semiprofessional, or professional athletic associations or leagues **813990**

711212 Racetracks^{US}

This U.S. industry comprises establishments primarily engaged in operating racetracks. These establishments may also present and /or promote the events, such as auto, dog, and horse races, held in these facilities.

Owners of racing participants, such as cars, dogs, and horses, entering them in racing events; trainers of racing participants; and independent athletes, such as jockeys and race car drivers, participating in racing events **711219**

711219 Other Spectator Sports[US]

This U.S. industry comprises (1) independent athletes, such as professional or semiprofessional golfers, boxers, and race car drivers, primarily engaged in participating in live sporting or racing events before a paying audience; (2) owners of racing participants, such as cars, dogs, and horses, primarily engaged in entering them in racing events or other spectator sports events; and (3) establishments, such as sports trainers, primarily engaged in providing specialized services required to support participants in sports events or competitions.

Operating racetracks **711212**
Representing or managing the careers of sports figures **711410**
Independent athletes providing sports instruction without participating in sporting events before a paying audience **611620**
Independent athletes endorsing products or making speeches **711510**
Raising horses, mules, donkeys, and other equines **112920**

7113 Promoters of Performing Arts, Sports, and Similar Events

711310 Promoters of Performing Arts, Sports, and Similar Events with Facilities

This industry comprises establishments primarily engaged in (1) organizing, promoting, and/or managing live performing arts productions, sports events, and similar events, such as State fairs, county fairs, agricultural fairs, concerts, and festivals, held in facilities that they manage and operate and/or (2) managing and providing the staff to operate arenas, stadiums, theaters, or other related facilities for rent to other promoters.

Producing live performances and that may also promote the performances and/or operate the facilities where the performances take place **711**
Operating racetracks and that may also promote the events held in these facilities **711212**
Presenting sporting events and that may also promote these sporting events and/or operate the stadiums or arenas where the sporting events take place **711211**

Organizing, promoting, and/or managing conventions, conferences, and trade shows and that may also operate the facilities where these events take place **561920**
Organizing, promoting, and/or managing performing arts productions, sports events, and similar events in facilities managed and operated by others **711320**
Leasing stadiums, arenas, theaters, and other related facilities to others without operating the facilities **531120**

711320 Promoters of Performing Arts, Sports, and Similar Events without Facilities

This industry comprises promoters primarily engaged in organizing, promoting, and/or managing live performing arts productions, sports events, and similar events, such as state fairs, county fairs, agricultural fairs, concerts, and festivals, in facilities that are managed and operated by others. Theatrical (except motion picture) booking agencies are included in this industry.

Booking motion pictures or videos **512199**
Producing live performances and that may also promote the performances **711**
Operating racetracks and that may also promote the events held in these facilities **711212**
Presenting sporting events and that may also promote these events **711211**
Organizing, promoting, and/or managing conventions, conferences, and trade shows and that may also operate the facilities where these events take place **561920**
Organizing, promoting, and/or managing performing arts, sports, and similar events in facilities they manage or operate **711310**
Operating amateur, semiprofessional, or professional athletic associations or leagues **813990**

7114 Agents and Managers for Artists, Athletes, Entertainers, and Other Public Figures

711410 Agents and Managers for Artists, Athletes, Entertainers, and Other Public Figures

This industry comprises establishments of agents and managers primarily engaged in representing and/or managing creative and performing artists, sports figures, entertainers, and other public figures. The representation and management includes activities, such as representing clients in contract negotiations; managing or organizing client's financial affairs; and generally promoting the careers of their clients.

Supplying models to clients **561320**
Model registries recruiting and placing models for clients **561310**

711

7115 Independent Artists, Writers, and Performers

711510 Independent Artists, Writers, and Performers

This industry comprises independent (i.e., freelance) individuals primarily engaged in performing in artistic productions, in creating artistic and cultural works or productions, or in providing technical expertise necessary for these productions. This industry also includes athletes and other celebrities exclusively engaged in endorsing products and making speeches or public appearances for which they receive a fee.

Freelance musicians and vocalists **711130**
Independent commercial artists and graphic designers **541430**
Artisans and craftspersons **31–33**

712 Museums, Historical Sites, and Similar Institutions

Industries in the Museums, Historical Sites, and Similar Institutions subsector engage in the preservation and exhibition of objects, sites, and natural wonders of historical, cultural, and/ or educational value.

7121 Museums, Historical Sites, and Similar Institutions

712110 Museums

This industry comprises establishments primarily engaged in the preservation and exhibition of objects of historical, cultural, and/or educational value.

Commercial art galleries selling art objects **453920**

712120 Historical Sites

This industry comprises establishments primarily engaged in the preservation and exhibition of sites, buildings, forts, or communities that describe events or persons of particular historical interest. Archeo-logical sites, battlefields, historical ships, and pioneer villages are included in this industry.

712130 Zoos and Botanical Gardens

This industry comprises establishments primarily engaged in the preservation and exhibition of live plant and animal life displays.

712190 Nature Parks and Other Similar Institutions

This industry comprises establishments primarily engaged in the preservation and exhibition of natural areas or settings.

Operating commercial hunting or fishing preserves (e.g., game farms) **114210**

713 Amusement, Gambling, and Recreation Industries

Industries in the Amusement, Gambling, and Recreation Industries subsector (1) operate facilities where patrons can primarily engage in sports, recreation, amusement, or gambling activities and/or (2) provide other amusement and recreation services, such as supplying and servicing amusement devices in places of business operated by others; operating sports teams, clubs, or leagues engaged in playing games for recreational purposes; and guiding tours without using transportation equipment.

This subsector does not cover all establishments providing recreational services. Other sectors of NAICS also provide recreational services. Providers of recreational services are often engaged in processes classified in other sectors of NAICS. For example, operators of resorts and hunting and fishing camps provide both accommodation and recreational facilities and services. These establishments are classified in Subsector 721, Accommodation, partly to reflect the significant costs associated with the provision of accommodation services and partly to ensure consistency with international standards. Likewise, establishments using transportation equipment to provide recreational and entertainment services, such as those operating sightseeing buses, dinner cruises, or helicopter rides, are classified in Subsector 48-49, Transportation and Warehousing. The industry groups in this subsector highlight particular types of activities: amusement parks and arcades, gambling industries, and other amusement and recreation industries. The groups, however, are not all inclusive of the activity. The Gambling Industries industry group does not provide for full coverage of gambling activities. For example, casino hotels are classified in Subsector 721, Accommodation; and horse and dog racing tracks are classified in Industry Group 7112, Spectator Sports.

7131 Amusement Parks and Arcades

This industry group comprises establishments primarily engaged in operating amusement parks and amusement arcades and parlors.

713110 Amusement and Theme Parks

This industry comprises establishments, known as amusement or theme parks, primarily engaged in operating a variety of attractions, such as mechanical rides, water rides, games, shows, theme exhibits, refreshment stands, and picnic grounds. These establishments may lease space to others on a concession basis.

Operating mechanical or water rides on a concession basis in amusement parks, fairs, and carnivals or in operating a single attraction, such as a waterslide, **713990**

Operating refreshment stands on a concession basis **7222**

Supplying and servicing coin-operated amusement (except gambling) devices in other's facilities **713990**

Supplying and servicing coin-operated gambling devices (e.g., slot machines) in places of business operated by others **713290**

Organizing, promoting, and/or managing events, such as carnivals and fairs, with or without facilities **7113**

713120 Amusement Arcades

This industry comprises establishments primarily engaged in operating amusement (except gambling, billiard, or pool) arcades and parlors.

Supplying and servicing coin-operated amusement (except gambling) devices in places of business operated by others or in operating billiard or pool parlors **713990**

Operating bingo, off-track betting, or slot machine parlors or in supplying and servicing coin-operated gambling devices (e.g., slot machines or video gambling terminals) in places of business operated by others **713290**

Operating casinos (except casino hotels) **713210**

Operating casino hotels **721120**

7132 Gambling Industries

This industry group comprises establishments (except casino hotels) primarily engaged in operating gambling facilities, such as casinos, bingo halls, and video gaming terminals, or in the provision of gambling services, such as lotteries and off-track betting. Casino hotels are classified in Industry 72112.

713210 Casinos (except Casino Hotels)

This industry comprises establishments primarily engaged in operating gambling facilities that offer table wagering games along with other gambling activities, such as slot machines and sports betting. These establishments often provide food and beverage services. Included in this industry are floating casinos (i.e., gambling cruises, riverboat casinos).

Operating bingo, off-track betting, or slot machine parlors or in supplying and servicing coin-operated gambling devices, such as slot machines and video gaming terminals in places of business operated by others, **713290**

Operating casino hotels **721120**

713290 Other Gambling Industries

This industry comprises establishments primarily engaged in operating gambling facilities (except casinos or casino hotels) or providing gambling services.

Operating casinos **713210**

Operating casino hotels **721120**

Operating facilities with coin-operated nongambling amusement devices **713120**

Supplying and servicing coin-operated nongambling amusement devices in places of business operated by others **713990**

Operating racetracks or presenting live racing or sporting events **71121**

7139 Other Amusement and Recreation Industries

713910 Golf Courses and Country Clubs

This industry comprises (1) establishments primarily engaged in operating golf courses (except miniature)

713

and (2) establishments primarily engaged in operating golf courses, along with dining facilities and other recreational facilities that are known as country clubs. These establishments often provide food and beverage services, equipment rental services, and golf instruction services.

Operating driving ranges and miniature golf courses **713990**
Operating resorts where golf facilities are combined with accommodations **7211**

713920 Skiing Facilities

This industry comprises establishments engaged in (1) operating downhill, cross-country, or related skiing areas and/or (2) operating equipment, such as ski lifts and tows. These establishments often provide food and beverage services, equipment rental services, and ski instruction services. Four season resorts without accommodations are included in this industry.

Operating resorts where skiing facilities are combined with accommodations **7211**

713930 Marinas

This industry comprises establishments, commonly known as marinas, engaged in operating docking and/or storage facilities for pleasure craft owners, with or without one or more related activities, such as retailing fuel and marine supplies; and repairing, maintaining, or renting pleasure boats.

Renting pleasure boats **532292**
Repairing pleasure boats **811490**
Retailing marine supplies **441222**
Retailing fuel for boats **447190**

713940 Fitness and Recreational Sports Centers

This industry comprises establishments primarily engaged in operating fitness and recreational sports facilities featuring exercise and other active physical fitness conditioning or recreational sports activities, such as swimming, skating, or racquet sports.

Providing nonmedical services to assist clients in attaining or maintaining a desired weight **812191**
Operating health resorts and spas where recreational facilities are combined with accommodations **721110**
Recreational sports clubs (i.e., sports teams) not operating sports facilities **713990**

713950 Bowling Centers

This industry comprises establishments engaged in operating bowling centers. These establishments often provide food and beverage services.

713990 All Other Amusement and Recreation Industries

This industry comprises establishments (except amusement parks and arcades; gambling industries; golf courses and country clubs; skiing facilities; marinas; fitness and recreational sports centers; and bowling centers) primarily engaged in providing recreational and amusement services.

Operating amusement parks and arcades **7131**
Operating gambling facilities (except casino hotels) or providing gambling services **7132**
Operating casino hotels **721120**
Operating golf courses (except miniature) and country clubs **713910**
Operating skiing facilities without hotel accommodation **713920**
Operating resorts where recreational facilities are combined with lodging **7211**
Operating marinas **713930**
Operating fitness and recreational sports centers **713940**
Operating bowling centers **713950**
Operating instructional camps, such as sports camps, fine arts camps, and computer camps, **61**
Independent athletes participating in sporting events before a paying audience **711219**
Independent athletes providing sports instruction without participating in sporting events before a paying audience **611620**
Independent athletes endorsing products or making speeches **71151**
Providing scenic and sightseeing transportation **487**
Aviation clubs providing specialty air and flying services **481219**
Aviation clubs advocating social and political causes **813319**
Amateur, semiprofessional, or professional athletic associations or leagues **813990**

SECTOR 72: ACCOMMODATION AND FOOD SERVICES

OVERVIEW OF THIS SECTOR AS A WHOLE

The Accommodation and Food Services sector comprises establishments providing customers with lodging and/or preparing meals, snacks, and beverages for immediate consumption. The sector includes both accommodation and food services establishments because the two activities are often combined at the same establishment.

Excluded from this sector are civic and social organizations; amusement and recreation parks; theaters; and other recreation or entertainment facilities providing food and beverage services.

721 Accommodation

Industries in the Accommodation subsector provide lodging or short-term accommodations for travelers, vacationers, and others. There is a wide range of establishments in these industries. Some provide lodging only; while others provide meals, laundry, and recreational facilities, as well as lodging. Lodging establishments are classified in this subsector even if the provision of complementary services generates more revenue. The types of complementary services provided vary from establishment to establishment.

The subsector is organized into three industry groups: (1) traveler accommodation, (2) recreational accommodation, and (3) rooming and boarding houses. The Traveler Accommodation industry group includes establishments that primarily provide traditional types of lodging services. This group includes hotels, motels, and bed and breakfast inns. In addition to lodging, these establishments may provide a range of other services to their guests. The RV (Recreational Vehicle) Parks and Recreational Camps industry group includes establishments that operate lodging facilities primarily designed to accommodate outdoor enthusiasts. Included are travel trailer campsites, recreation vehicle parks, and outdoor adventure retreats. The Rooming and Boarding Houses industry group includes establishments providing temporary or longer-term accommodations that for the period of occupancy may serve as a principal residence. Board (i.e., meals) may be provided but is not essential.

Establishments that manage short-stay accommodation establishments (e.g., hotels and motels) on a contractual basis are classified in this subsector if they both manage the operation and provide the operating staff. Such establishments are classified based on the type of facility managed and operated.

7211 Traveler Accommodation

721110 Hotels (except Casino Hotels) and Motels

This industry comprises establishments primarily engaged in providing short-term lodging in facilities known as hotels, motor hotels, resort hotels, and motels. The establishments in this industry may offer services, such as food and beverage services, recreational services, conference rooms and convention services, laundry services, parking, and other services.

Providing short-term lodging with a casino on the premises **721120**
Providing short-term lodging in facilities known as bed-and-breakfast inns, youth hostels, housekeeping cabins and cottages, and tourist homes **72119**

721

721120 Casino Hotels

This industry comprises establishments primarily engaged in providing short-term lodging in hotel facilities with a casino on the premises. The casino on premises includes table wagering games and may include other gambling activities, such as slot machines and sports betting. These establishments generally offer a range of services and amenities, such as food and beverage services, entertainment, valet parking, swimming pools, and conference and convention facilities.

Providing short-term lodging in facilities known as hotels and motels that provide limited gambling activities, such as slot machines, without a casino on the premises **721110**
Operating as stand-alone casinos **713210**

721199 Other Traveler Accommodation

This industry comprises establishments primarily engaged in providing short-term lodging (except hotels, motels, and casino hotels).

Providing short-term lodging in facilities known as hotels without a casino on the premises **72111**
Providing short-term lodging in facilities known as hotels with a casino on the premises **72112**

721191 Bed-and-Breakfast Inns^{CAN}

This U.S. industry comprises establishments primarily engaged in providing short-term lodging in facilities known as bed-and-breakfast inns. These establishments provide short-term lodging in private homes or small buildings converted for this purpose. Bed-and-breakfast inns are characterized by a highly personalized service and inclusion of a full breakfast in a room rate.

721199 All Other Traveler Accommodation^{US}

This U.S. industry comprises establishments primarily engaged in providing short-term lodging (except hotels, motels, casino hotels, and bed-and-breakfast inns).

Providing short-term lodging in facilities known as hotels without a casino on the premises **721110**
Providing short-term lodging in facilities known as hotels with a casino on the premises **721120**
Providing short-term lodging in establishments known as bed-and-breakfast inns **721191**

7212 RV (Recreational Vehicle) Parks and Recreational Camps

72121 RV (Recreational Vehicle) Parks and Recreational Camps

This industry comprises establishments primarily engaged in operating recreational vehicle parks and campgrounds and recreational and vacation camps. These establishments cater to outdoor enthusiasts and are characterized by the type of accommodation and by the nature and the range of recreational facilities and activities provided to their clients.

Operating recreational facilities without accommodations **713**
Operating instructional camps, such as sports camps, fine arts camps, and computer camps, **61**
Operating children's day camps (except instructional) **71399**
Acting as lessors of residential mobile home sites (i.e., trailer parks) **53119**

721211 RV (Recreational Vehicle) Parks and Campgrounds^{CAN}

This U.S. industry comprises establishments primarily engaged in operating sites to accommodate campers and their equipment, including tents, tent trailers, travel trailers, and RVs (recreational vehicles). These establishments may provide access to facilities, such as washrooms, laundry rooms, recreation halls and playgrounds, stores, and snack bars.

Operating recreational facilities without accommodations **713**
Acting as lessors of residential mobile home sites (i.e., trailer parks) **531190**

721214 Recreational and Vacation Camps (except Campgrounds)^{US}

This U.S. industry comprises establishments primarily engaged in operating overnight recreational camps, such as children's camps, family vacation camps, hunting and fishing camps, and outdoor adventure retreats that offer trail riding, white-water rafting, hiking, and similar activities. These establishments provide accommodation facilities, such as cabins and fixed camp sites, and other amenities, such as food services, recreational facilities and equipment, and organized recreational activities.

Operating instructional camps, such as sports camps, fine arts camps, and computer camps, **61**
Operating children's day camps (except instructional) **713990**

7213 Rooming and Boarding Houses

721310 Rooming and Boarding Houses

This industry comprises establishments primarily engaged in operating rooming and boarding houses and similar facilities, such as fraternity houses, sorority houses, off-campus dormitories, residential clubs, and workers' camps. These establishments provide temporary or longer-term accommodations which, for the period of occupancy, may serve as a principal residence. These establishments also may provide complementary services, such as housekeeping, meals, and laundry services.

722 Food Services and Drinking Places

Industries in the Food Services and Drinking Places subsector prepare meals, snacks, and beverages to customer order for immediate on-premises and off-premises consumption. There is a wide range of establishments in these industries. Some provide food and drink only; while others provide various combinations of seating space, waiter/waitress services and incidental amenities, such as limited entertainment. The industries in the subsector are grouped based on the type and level of services provided. The industry groups are full-service restaurants; limited-service eating places; special food services, such as food service contractors, caterers, and mobile food services, and drinking places.

Food services and drink activities at hotels and motels; amusement parks, theaters, casinos, country clubs, and similar recreational facilities; and civic and social organizations are included in this subsector only if these services are provided by a separate establishment primarily engaged in providing food and beverage services.

Excluded from this subsector are establishments operating dinner cruises. These establishments are classified in Subsector 487, Scenic and Sightseeing Transportation because those establishments utilize transportation equipment to provide scenic recreational entertainment.

7221 Full-Service Restaurants

This industry group comprises establishments primarily engaged in providing food services to patrons who order and are served while seated (i.e., waiter/waitress service) and pay after eating. Establishments that provide these type of food services to patrons with any combination of other services, such as carryout services are classified in this industry.

722110 Full-Service Restaurants

This industry comprises establishments primarily engaged in providing food services to patrons who order and are served while seated (i.e. waiter/waitress service) and pay after eating. These establishments may provide this type of food services to patrons in combination with selling alcoholic beverages, providing takeout services, or presenting live nontheatrical entertainment.

Providing food services where patrons generally order or select items and pay before eating 722211

Selling a specialty snack or nonalcoholic beverage for consumption on or near the premises 722213
Preparing and serving alcoholic beverages known as bars, taverns, or nightclubs 722410
Presenting live theatrical productions and providing food and beverages for consumption on the premises 711110

7222 Limited-Service Eating Places

This industry group comprises establishments primarily engaged in providing food services where patrons generally order or select items and pay before eating. Most establishments do not have waiter/waitress service, but some provide limited service, such as cooking to order (i.e., per special request), bringing food to seated customers, or providing off-site delivery.

72221 Limited-Service Eating Places

This industry comprises establishments primarily engaged in (1) providing food services where patrons

722

generally order or select items and pay before eating or (2) selling a specialty snack or nonalcoholic beverage for consumption on or near the premises. Food and drink may be consumed on the premises, taken out, or delivered to customers' location. Some establishments in this industry may provide these food services (except snack and nonalcoholic beverage bars) in combination with selling alcoholic beverages.

Providing food services to patrons who order and are served while seated and pay after eating in combination with providing takeout service **72211**

Retailing confectionery goods and nuts not packaged for immediate consumption **44529**

Retailing baked goods (e.g., pretzels, doughnuts, cookies, and bagels) not baked on the premises and not for immediate consumption **44529**

Retailing baked goods (e.g., doughnuts and bagels) and providing food services to patrons who order and are served while seated and pay after eating **72211**

Selling snacks and nonalcoholic beverages from mobile vehicles **72233**

Preparing and serving alcoholic beverages, known as bars, taverns, or nightclubs, **72241**

722211 Limited-Service Restaurants[US]

This U.S. industry comprises establishments primarily engaged in providing food services (except snack and nonalcoholic beverage bars) where patrons generally order or select items and pay before eating. Food and drink may be consumed on premises, taken out, or delivered to customers' location. Some establishments in this industry may provide these food services in combination with selling alcoholic beverages.

Preparing and serving meals for immediate consumption using cafeteria-style serving equipment that are known as cafeterias **722212**

Providing food services to patrons who order and are served while seated and they pay after eating **722110**

Selling a specialty snack (e.g., ice cream, frozen yogurt, candy, cookies) or nonalcoholic beverages, for consumption on or near the premises **722213**

Retailing confectionery goods and nuts not packaged for immediate consumption **445292**

Retailing baked goods (e.g., pretzels, doughnuts, cookies, and bagels) not baked on the premises and not for immediate consumption **445291**

Preparing and serving alcoholic beverages known as bars, taverns, or nightclubs, **722410**

Selling baked goods, (e.g., doughnuts and bagels) and providing food services to patrons who order and are served while seated and pay after eating, **722110**

722212 Cafeterias[US]

This U.S. industry comprises establishments, known as cafeterias, primarily engaged in preparing and serving meals for immediate consumption using cafeteria-style serving equipment, such as steam tables, a refrigerated area, and self-service nonalcoholic beverage dispensing equipment. Patrons select from food and drink items on display in a continuous cafeteria line.

Providing food services to patrons who order and are served while seated and pay after eating **722110**

Providing food services where patrons generally order or select items and pay before eating **722211**

722213 Snack and Nonalcoholic Beverage Bars[US]

This U.S. industry comprises establishments primarily engaged in (1) preparing and/or serving a specialty snack, such as ice cream, frozen yogurt, cookies, or popcorn or (2) serving nonalcoholic beverages, such as coffee, juices, or sodas for consumption on or near the premises. These establishments may carry and sell a combination of snack, nonalcoholic beverage, and other related products (e.g., coffee beans, mugs, coffee makers) but generally promote and sell a unique snack or nonalcoholic beverage.

Selling one or more of the following food specialties: hamburgers, hot dogs, pizza, chicken, specialty cuisines **722211**

Preparing and serving snacks and nonalcoholic beverages from mobile vehicles **722330**

Retailing confectionery goods and nuts not packaged for immediate consumption **445292**

Retailing baked goods (e.g., pretzels, doughnuts, cookies, and bagels) not baked on the premises and not for immediate consumption, **445291**

Retailing baked goods (e.g., doughnuts and bagels) and providing food services to patrons who order and are served while seated and pay after eating **722110**

7223 Special Food Services

This industry group comprises establishments primarily engaged in providing one of the following food services: (1) at the customers' location; (2) a location designated by the customer; or (3) from motorized vehicles or nonmotorized carts.

722310 Food Service Contractors

This industry comprises establishments primarily engaged in providing food services at institutional, governmental, commercial, or industrial locations of others based on contractual arrangements with these types of organizations for a specified period of time. The establishments of this industry provide food services for the convenience of the contracting organization or the contracting organization's customers. The contractual arrangement of these establishments with contracting organizations may vary from type of facility operated (e.g., cafeteria, restaurant, fast-food eating place), revenue sharing, cost structure, to providing personnel. Management staff is always provided by the food services contractor.

Providing food services on a single-event basis **722320**
Supplying and servicing food vending machines **454210**

722320 Caterers

This industry comprises establishments primarily engaged in providing single event-based food services. These establishments generally have equipment and vehicles to transport meals and snacks to events and/ or prepare food at an off-premise site. Banquet halls with catering staff are included in this industry. Examples of events catered by establishments in this industry are graduation parties, wedding receptions, business or retirement luncheons, and trade shows.

Preparing and serving meals and snacks for immediate consumption from motorized vehicles or nonmotorized carts **722330**
Providing food services at institutional, governmental, commercial, or industrial locations of others or providing food services (e.g., airline contractors, industrial caterers) based on contractual arrangements for a specified period of time **722310**
Renting facilities without their own catering staff **531120**

722330 Mobile Food Services

This industry comprises establishments primarily engaged in preparing and serving meals and snacks for immediate consumption from motorized vehicles or nonmotorized carts. The establishment is the central location from which the caterer route is serviced, not each vehicle, or cart. Included in this industry

are establishments primarily engaged in providing food services from vehicles, such as hot dog cart, and ice cream truck.

Providing food services where patrons generally order or select items and pay before eating **722211**
Selling unprepared foods, such as vegetables, melons, and nuts or fruit from carts **454390**
Selling and promoting specialty snacks (e.g.. ice cream, frozen yogurt, cookies, popcorn) or nonalcoholic beverages in nonmobile facilities for consumption on or near the premises, **722213**
Selling food specialties, such as hamburgers, hot dogs, chicken, pizza, or specialty cuisines from nonmobile facilities, **722211**
Operating as street vendors (except food) **454390**

7224 Drinking Places (Alcoholic Beverages)

This industry group comprises establishments primarily engaged in preparing and serving alcoholic beverages for immediate consumption.

722410 Drinking Places (Alcoholic Beverages)

This industry comprises establishments known as bars, taverns, nightclubs or drinking places primarily engaged in preparing and serving alcoholic beverages for immediate consumption. These establishments may also provide limited food services.

Preparing and serving alcoholic beverages (i.e., not known as bars or taverns) and providing food services to patrons who order and are served while seated and pay after eating **722110**
Preparing and serving alcoholic beverages (i.e., known as bars or taverns) and providing food services to patrons who order and are served while seated and pay after eating **722211**
Operating a civic or social association with a bar for their members **81341**
Retailing packaged alcoholic beverages not for immediate consumption on the premises **445310**
Operating discotheques or dance clubs without selling alcoholic beverages **713990**

SECTOR 81: OTHER SERVICES (EXCEPT PUBLIC ADMINISTRATION)

OVERVIEW OF THIS SECTOR AS A WHOLE

The Other Services (except Public Administration) sector comprises establishments engaged in providing services not specifically provided for elsewhere in the classification system. Establishments in this sector are primarily engaged in activities, such as equipment and machinery repairing, promoting or administering religious activities, grantmaking, advocacy, and providing drycleaning and laundry services, personal care services, death care services, pet care services, photofinishing services, temporary parking services, and dating services.

Private households that engage in employing workers on or about the premises in activities primarily concerned with the operation of the household are included in this sector. Excluded from this sector are establishments primarily engaged in retailing new equipment and also performing repairs and general maintenance on equipment. These establishments are classified in Sector 44–45, Retail Trade.

811 Repair and Maintenance

Industries in the Repair and Maintenance subsector restore machinery, equipment, and other products to working order. These establishments also typically provide general or routine maintenance (i.e., servicing) on such products to ensure they work efficiently and to prevent breakdown and unnecessary repairs.

The NAICS structure for this subsector brings together most types of repair and maintenance establishments and categorizes them based on production processes (i.e., on the type of repair and maintenance activity performed, and the necessary skills, expertise, and processes that are found in different repair and maintenance establishments). This NAICS classification does not delineate between repair services provided to businesses versus those that serve households. Although some industries primarily serve either businesses or households, separation by class of customer is limited by the fact that many establishments serve both. Establishments repairing computers and consumer electronics products are two examples of such overlap.

The Repair and Maintenance subsector does not include all establishments that do repair and maintenance. For example, a substantial amount of repair is done by establishments that also manufacture machinery, equipment, and other goods. These establishments are included in the Manufacturing sector in NAICS. In addition, repair of transportation equipment is often provided by or based at transportation facilities, such as airports, seaports, and these activities are included in the Transportation and Warehousing sector. A particularly unique situation exists with repair of buildings. Plumbing, electrical installation and repair, painting and decorating, and other construction-related establishments are often involved in performing installation or other work on new construction as well as providing repair services on existing structures. While some specialize in repair, it is difficult to distinguish between the two types and all have been included in the Construction sector.

Excluded from this subsector are establishments primarily engaged in rebuilding or remanufacturing machinery and equipment. These are classified in Sector 31–33, Manufacturing. Also excluded are retail establishments that provide after-sale services and repair. These are classified in Sector 44–45, Retail Trade.

8III Automotive Repair and Maintenance

This industry group comprises establishments involved in providing repair and maintenance services for automotive vehicles, such as passenger cars, trucks, and vans, and all trailers. Establishments in this industry group employ mechanics with specialized technical skills to diagnose and repair the mechanical and electrical systems for automotive vehicles, repair automotive interiors, and paint or repair automotive exteriors.

81111 Automotive Mechanical and Electrical Repair and Maintenance

This industry comprises establishments primarily engaged in providing mechanical or electrical repair and maintenance services for automotive vehicles, such as passenger cars, trucks and vans, and all trailers. These establishments specialize in or may provide a wide range of these services.

Retailing automotive vehicles and automotive parts and accessories and also providing automotive repair services **441**
Retailing motor fuels and also providing automotive vehicle repair services **4471**
Changing motor oil and lubricating the chassis of automotive vehicles **81119**
Providing automotive vehicle air-conditioning repair **81119**
Motorcycle repair and maintenance services **81149**

811111 General Automotive Repair^{CAN}

This U.S. industry comprises establishments primarily engaged in providing (1) a wide range of mechanical and electrical repair and maintenance services for automotive vehicles, such as passenger cars, trucks, and vans, and all trailers or (2) engine repair and replacement.

Retailing new automotive parts and accessories and also providing automotive repair services **441310**
Changing motor oil and lubricating the chassis of automotive vehicles **811191**
Replacing and repairing automotive vehicle exhaust systems **811112**
Replacing and repairing automotive vehicle transmissions **811113**
Retailing motor fuels and also providing automotive vehicle repair services **4471**
Retailing automobiles and light trucks for highway use and also providing automotive repair services **4411**
Motorcycle repair and maintenance services **811490**

811112 Automotive Exhaust System Repair^{CAN}

This U.S. industry comprises establishments primarily engaged in replacing or repairing exhaust systems of automotive vehicles, such as passenger cars, trucks, and vans.

Motorcycle repair and maintenance services **811490**

811113 Automotive Transmission Repair^{US}

This U.S. industry comprises establishments primarily engaged in replacing or repairing transmissions of automotive vehicles, such as passenger cars, trucks, and vans.

Motorcycle repair and maintenance services **811490**

811118 Other Automotive Mechanical and Electrical Repair and Maintenance^{US}

This U.S. industry comprises establishments primarily engaged in providing specialized mechanical or electrical repair and maintenance services (except engine repair and replacement, exhaust systems repair, and transmission repair) for automotive vehicles, such as passenger cars, trucks, and vans, and all trailers.

Providing a wide range of mechanical and electrical automotive vehicle repair or specializing in engine repair or replacement **811111**
Replacing and repairing automotive vehicle exhaust systems **811112**
Replacing and repairing automotive vehicle transmissions **811113**
Providing automotive vehicle air-conditioning repair **811198**
Motorcycle repair and maintenance services **811490**

81112 Automotive Body, Paint, Interior, and Glass Repair

This industry comprises establishments primarily engaged in providing one or more of the following: (1) repairing or customizing automotive vehicles, such as passenger cars, trucks, and vans, and all trailer bodies and interiors; (2) painting automotive vehicle and trailer bodies; (3) replacing, repairing, and/or tinting automotive vehicle glass; and (4) customizing automobile, truck, and van interiors for the physically disabled or other customers with special requirements.

Manufacturing automotive vehicles and trailers or customizing these vehicles on an assembly-line basis **336**
Motorcycle repair and maintenance services **81149**

811121 Automotive Body, Paint, and Interior Repair and Maintenance^{CAN}

This U.S. industry comprises establishments primarily engaged in repairing or customizing automotive vehicles, such as passenger cars, trucks, and vans, and all trailer bodies and interiors; and/or painting automotive vehicles and trailer bodies.

Automotive glass replacement, repair and/or tinting **811122**
Manufacturing automotive vehicles and trailers or customizing these vehicles on an assembly-line basis **336**
Motorcycle repair and maintenance services **811490**

811122 Automotive Glass Replacement Shops^{CAN}

This U.S. industry comprises establishments primarily engaged in replacing, repairing, and/or tinting

       811

automotive vehicle, such as passenger car, truck, and van, glass.

Motorcycle repair and maintenance service **811490**

81119 Other Automotive Repair and Maintenance

This industry comprises establishments primarily engaged in providing automotive repair and maintenance services (except mechanical and electrical repair and maintenance; transmission repair; and body, paint, interior, and glass repair) for automotive vehicles, such as passenger cars, trucks, and vans, and all trailers.

Tire retreading or recapping **32621**
Automotive vehicle mechanical and electrical repair and maintenance **81111**
Automotive body, paint, interior, and glass repair **81112**
Motorcycle repair and maintenance services **81149**

811191 Automotive Oil Change and Lubrication Shops^{US}

This U.S. industry comprises establishments primarily engaged in changing motor oil and lubricating the chassis of automotive vehicles, such as passenger cars, trucks, and vans.

Motorcycle repair and maintenance services **811490**

811192 Car Washes^{CAN}

This U.S. industry comprises establishments primarily engaged in cleaning, washing, and/or waxing automotive vehicles, such as passenger cars, trucks, and vans, and trailers.

811198 All Other Automotive Repair and Maintenance^{US}

This U.S. industry comprises establishments primarily engaged in providing automotive repair and maintenance services (except mechanical and electrical repair and maintenance; body, paint, interior, and glass repair; motor oil change and lubrication; and car washing) for automotive vehicles, such as passenger cars, trucks, and vans, and all trailers.

Tire retreading or recapping **32621**
Providing a range of mechanical and electrical automotive vehicle repair or specializing in engine repair or replacement **811111**
Replacing and repairing automotive vehicle exhaust systems **811112**
Replacing and repairing automotive vehicle transmissions **811113**
Repairing or customizing automotive vehicle bodies and interiors **811121**

Replacing, repairing, and/or tinting automotive glass **811122**
Changing motor oil and lubricating the chassis of automotive vehicles **811191**
Cleaning, washing, and/or waxing automotive vehicles and trailers **811192**
Motorcycle repair and maintenance services **811490**
Retailing and installing audio equipment **441310**

8112 Electronic and Precision Equipment Repair and Maintenance

This industry group comprises establishments primarily engaged in repairing electronic equipment, such as computers and communications equipment, and highly specialized precision instruments. Establishments in this industry group typically have staff skilled in repairing items having complex, electronic components.

81121 Electronic and Precision Equipment Repair and Maintenance

This industry comprises establishments primarily engaged in repairing and maintaining one or more of the following: (1) consumer electronic equipment; (2) computers; (3) office machines; (4) communication equipment; and (5) other electronic and precision equipment and instruments, without retailing these products as new. Establishments in this industry repair items, such as microscopes, radar and sonar equipment, televisions, stereos, video recorders, computers, fax machines, photocopying machines, two-way radios and other communications equipment, scientific instruments, and medical equipment.

Installing or maintaining home security systems **56162**
Retailing new radios, televisions, and other consumer electronics and also providing repair services **44311**
Retailing new computers and computer peripherals and also providing repair services **44312**
Rewinding armatures and rebuilding electric motors on a factory basis **33531**

811211 Consumer Electronics Repair and Maintenance^{US}

This U.S. industry comprises establishments primarily engaged in repairing and maintaining consumer electronics, such as televisions, stereos, speakers, video recorders, CD players, radios, and cameras, without retailing new consumer electronics.

Repairing computers and peripheral equipment **811212**
Installing or maintaining home security systems **561621**
Retailing new radios, televisions, and other consumer electronics and also providing repair services **443112**
Repairing two-way radios **811213**

811212 Computer and Office Machine Repair and Maintenance[US]

This U.S. industry comprises establishments primarily engaged in repairing and maintaining computers and office machines without retailing new computers and office machines, such as photocopying machines; and computer terminals, storage devices, printers; and CD-ROM drives.

Retailing new computers and computer peripherals and also providing repair services **443120**

Repairing and servicing fax machines **811213**

811213 Communication Equipment Repair and Maintenance[US]

This U.S. industry comprises establishments primarily engaged in repairing and maintaining communications equipment without retailing new communication equipment, such as telephones, fax machines, communications transmission equipment, and two-way radios.

Retailing new telephones and also providing repair services **443112**

Repairing stereo and other consumer electronic equipment **811211**

811219 Other Electronic and Precision Equipment Repair and Maintenance[US]

This U.S. industry comprises establishments primarily engaged in repairing and maintaining (without retailing) electronic and precision equipment (except consumer electronics, computers and office machines, and communications equipment). Establishments in this industry repair and maintain equipment, such as medical diagnostic imaging equipment, measuring and surveying instruments, laboratory instruments, and radar and sonar equipment.

Rewinding armatures and rebuilding electric motors on a factory basis **335312**

Repairing stereo and other consumer electronic equipment **811211**

Repairing computers and office machines **811212**

Repairing communications equipment **811213**

8113 Commercial and Industrial Machinery and Equipment (except Automotive and Electronic) Repair and Maintenance

811310 Commercial and Industrial Machinery and Equipment (except Automotive and Electronic) Repair and Maintenance

This industry comprises establishments primarily engaged in the repair and maintenance of commercial and industrial machinery and equipment. Establishments in this industry either sharpen/install commercial and industrial machinery blades and saws or provide welding (e.g., automotive, general) repair services; or repair agricultural and other heavy and industrial machinery and equipment (e.g., forklifts and other materials handling equipment, machine tools, commercial refrigeration equipment, construction equipment, and mining machinery).

Automotive repair (except welding) and maintenance are **8111**

Repairing and maintaining electronic and precision equipment **81121**

Repairing and servicing aircraft **488190**

Converting, rebuilding, and overhauling aircraft **336410**

Repairing and servicing railroad cars and engines **488210**

Rebuilding or remanufacturing railroad engines and cars **336510**

Repairing and overhauling ships at floating dry docks **4883**

Repairing and overhauling ships at shipyards **33661**

Rewinding armatures or rebuilding electric motors on a factory basis **335312**

Repairing and maintaining home and garden equipment (e.g., sharpening or installing blades and saws) **81141**

8114 Personal and Household Goods Repair and Maintenance

81141 Home and Garden Equipment and Appliance Repair and Maintenance

This industry comprises establishments primarily engaged in repairing and servicing home and garden equipment and/or household-type appliances without retailing new equipment or appliances. Establishments in this industry repair and maintain items, such as lawnmowers, edgers, snow- and leaf-blowers, washing machines, clothes dryers, and refrigerators.

Retailing outdoor power equipment and also providing repair services **44421**

Retailing an array of new appliances and also providing repair services **44311**

Repairing, servicing, or installing central heating and air-conditioning equipment **23**

Repairing commercial refrigeration equipment **81131**

811411 Home and Garden Equipment Repair and Maintenance[CAN]

This U.S. industry comprises establishments primarily engaged in repairing and servicing home and

811

garden equipment without retailing new home and garden equipment, such as lawnmowers, handheld power tools, edgers, snow- and leaf-blowers, and trimmers.

Retailing new outdoor power equipment and also providing repair services
444210

811412 Appliance Repair and Maintenance[US]

This U.S. industry comprises establishments primarily engaged in repairing and servicing household appliances without retailing new appliances, such as refrigerators, stoves, washing machines, clothes dryers, and room air-conditioners.

Installing central heating and air-conditioning equipment **235110**
Repairing commercial refrigeration equipment **811310**
Retailing an array of new appliances and also providing repair services
443111

811420 Reupholstery and Furniture Repair

This industry comprises establishments primarily engaged in one or more of the following: (1) reupholstering furniture; (2) refinishing furniture; (3) repairing furniture; and (4) repairing and restoring furniture.

Automotive vehicle and trailer upholstery repair **811121**
The restoration of museum pieces **711510**

811430 Footwear and Leather Goods Repair

This industry comprises establishments primarily engaged in repairing footwear and/or repairing other leather or leather-like goods without retailing new footwear and leather or leather-like goods, such as handbags and briefcases.

Retailing new luggage and leather goods and also providing repair services
448320
Shining shoes **812990**
Repairing leather clothing **811490**

811490 Other Personal and Household Goods Repair and Maintenance

This industry comprises establishments primarily engaged in repairing and servicing personal or household-type goods without retailing new personal and household-type goods (except home and garden equipment, appliances, furniture, and footwear and leather goods). Establishments in this industry repair items, such as garments; watches; jewelry; musical instruments; bicycles and motorcycles; motorboats, canoes, sailboats, and other recreational boats.

Repairing home and garden equipment **811411**
Repairing appliances **811412**
Reupholstering and repairing furniture **811420**
Repairing footwear and leather goods **811430**
Operating marinas and providing a range of other services including boat
     cleaning and repair **713930**
Drycleaning garments **8123**

812 Personal and Laundry Services

Industries in the Personal and Laundry Services subsector group establishments that provide personal and laundry services to individuals, households, and businesses. Services performed include: personal care services; death care services; laundry and drycleaning services; and a wide range of other personal services, such as pet care (except veterinary) services, photofinishing services, temporary parking services, and dating services.

The Personal and Laundry Services subsector is by no means all-inclusive of the services that could be termed personal services (i.e., those provided to individuals rather than businesses). There are many other subsectors, as well as sectors, that provide services to persons. Establishments providing legal, accounting, tax preparation, architectural, portrait photography, and similar professional services are classified in Sector 54, Professional, Scientific, and Technical Services; those providing job placement, travel arrangement, home security, interior and exterior house cleaning, exterminating, lawn and garden care, and similar support services are classified in Sector 56, Administrative and Support, Waste Management and Remediation Services; those providing health and social services are classified in Sector 62, Health Care and Social Assistance; those providing amusement and recreation services are classified in Sector 71, Arts,

Entertainment and Recreation; those providing educational instruction are classified in Sector 61, Educational Services; those providing repair services are classified in Subsector 811, Repair and Maintenance; and those providing spiritual, civic, and advocacy services are classified in Subsector 813, Religious, Grantmaking, Civic, Professional, and Similar Organizations.

8121 Personal Care Services[CAN]

This industry group comprises establishments, such as barber and beauty shops, that provide appearance care services to individual consumers.

81211 Hair, Nail, and Skin Care Services[CAN]

This industry comprises establishments primarily engaged in one or more of the following: (1) providing hair care services; (2) providing nail care services; and (3) providing facials or applying makeup (except permanent makeup).

Offering training in barbering, hair styling, or the cosmetic arts **61151**
Providing massage, electrolysis (i.e., hair removal), permanent makeup, or tanning services **81219**
Providing medical skin care services (e.g., cosmetic surgery, dermatology) **62**

812111 Barber Shops[US]

This U.S. industry comprises establishments known as barber shops or men's hair stylist shops primarily engaged in cutting, trimming, and styling boys' and men's hair; and/or shaving and trimming men's beards.

Offering training in barbering **611511**
Providing hair care services (except establishments known as barber shops or men's hair stylists) **812112**

812112 Beauty Salons[US]

This U.S. industry comprises establishments (except those known as barber shops or men's hair stylist shops) primarily engaged in one or more of the following: (1) cutting, trimming, shampooing, weaving, coloring, waving, or styling hair; (2) providing facials; and (3) applying makeup (except permanent makeup).

Cutting, trimming, and styling men's and boys' hair (known as barber shops or men's hair stylist shops) **812111**
Offering training in hair styling or the cosmetic arts **611511**
Providing nail care services **812113**
Providing massage, electrolysis (i.e., hair removal), permanent makeup, or tanning services **812199**
Providing medical skin care services (e.g., cosmetic surgery, dermatology) **62**

812113 Nail Salons[US]

This U.S. industry comprises establishments primarily engaged in providing nail care services, such as manicures, pedicures, and nail extensions.

81219 Other Personal Care Services[CAN]

This industry comprises establishments primarily engaged in providing personal care services (except hair, nail, facial, or nonpermanent makeup services).

Providing hair, nail, facial, or nonpermanent makeup services **81211**
Operating physical fitness facilities **71394**
Operating health resorts and spas that provide lodging **72111**
Providing medical or surgical hair replacement or weight reduction **62**

812191 Diet and Weight Reducing Centers[US]

This U.S. industry comprises establishments primarily engaged in providing nonmedical services to assist clients in attaining or maintaining a desired weight. The sale of weight reduction products, such as food supplements, may be an integral component of the program. These services typically include individual or group counseling, menu and exercise planning, and weight and body measurement monitoring.

Operating physical fitness facilities **713940**
Operating health resorts and spas that provide lodging **721110**
Providing medical or surgical weight reduction **62**

812199 Other Personal Care Services[US]

This U.S. industry comprises establishments primarily engaged in providing personal care services (except hair, nail, facial, nonpermanent makeup, or nonmedical diet and weight reducing services).

Cutting, trimming, and styling men's and boys' hair (known as barber shops or men's hair stylist shops) **812111**
Providing hair, facial, or nonpermanent makeup services (except establishments known as barber shops or men's hair stylist shops) **812112**
Nail care services **812113**
Providing nonmedical diet and weight reducing services **812191**
Providing medical or surgical hair replacement or weight reduction services **62**

812

8122 Death Care Services^{CAN}

812210 Funeral Homes and Funeral Services^{CAN}

This industry comprises establishments primarily engaged in preparing the dead for burial or interment and conducting funerals (i.e., providing facilities for wakes, arranging transportation for the dead, selling caskets and related merchandise). Funeral homes combined with crematories are included in this industry.

Establishments (except funeral homes) primarily engaged in cremating the dead **812220**

812220 Cemeteries and Crematories^{CAN}

This industry comprises establishments primarily engaged in operating sites or structures reserved for the interment of human or animal remains and/or cremating the dead.

Crematories combined with funeral homes **812210**

8123 Drycleaning and Laundry Services^{CAN}

812310 Coin-Operated Laundries and Drycleaners^{CAN}

This industry comprises (1) establishments primarily engaged in operating facilities with coin-operated or similar self-service laundry and drycleaning equipment for customer use on the premises and (2) establishments primarily engaged in supplying and servicing coin-operated or similar self-service laundry and drycleaning equipment for customer use in places of business operated by others, such as apartments and dormitories.

812320 Drycleaning and Laundry Services (except Coin-Operated)^{CAN}

This industry comprises establishments primarily engaged in one or more of the following: (1) providing drycleaning services (except coin-operated); (2) providing laundering services (except linen and uniform supply or coin-operated); (3) providing dropoff and pickup sites for laundries and/or drycleaners; and (4) providing specialty cleaning services for specific types of garments and other textile items (except carpets and upholstery), such as fur, leather, or suede

garments; wedding gowns; hats; draperies; and pillows. These establishments may provide all, a combination of, or none of the cleaning services on the premises.

Supplying laundered linens and uniforms on a rental or contract basis **81233**

Operating coin-operated or similar self-service laundry or drycleaning facilities **812310**

Cleaning used carpets and upholstery **561740**

81233 Linen and Uniform Supply^{CAN}

This industry comprises establishments primarily engaged in supplying, on a rental or contract basis, laundered items, such as uniforms, gowns and coats, table linens, bed linens, towels, clean room apparel, and treated mops or shop towels.

812331 Linen Supply^{US}

This U.S. industry comprises establishments primarily engaged in supplying, on a rental or contract basis, laundered items, such as table and bed linens; towels; diapers; and uniforms, gowns, or coats of the type used by doctors, nurses, barbers, beauticians, and waitresses.

Supplying, on a rental or contract basis, laundered industrial work uniforms and related work clothing **812332**

812332 Industrial Launderers^{US}

This U.S. industry comprises establishments primarily engaged in supplying, on a rental or contract basis, laundered industrial work uniforms and related work clothing, such as protective apparel (flame and heat resistant) and clean room apparel; dust control items, such as treated mops, rugs, mats, dust tool covers, cloths, and shop or wiping towels.

Supplying, on a rental or contract basis, laundered uniforms, gowns or coats of the type used by doctors, nurses, barbers, beauticians, and waitresses **812331**

8129 Other Personal Services^{CAN}

The industry group comprises establishments primarily engaged in providing personal services (except personal care services, death care services, or drycleaning and laundry services).

812910 Pet Care (except Veterinary) Services^{CAN}

This industry comprises establishments primarily engaged in providing pet care services (except veterinary), such as boarding, grooming, sitting, and training pets.

Practicing veterinary medicine **541940**
Boarding horses **115210**
Transporting pets **485991**

81292 Photofinishing^{CAN}

This industry comprises establishments primarily engaged in developing film and/or making photographic slides, prints, and enlargements.

Processing motion picture film for the motion picture and television
 industries **51219**

812921 Photofinishing Laboratories (except One-Hour)^{CAN}

This U.S. industry comprises establishments (except those known as "one-hour" photofinishing labs) primarily engaged in developing film and/or making photographic slides, prints, and enlargements.

Processing motion picture film for the motion picture and television
 industries **512199**
 "One-hour" photofinishing labs **812922**

812922 One-Hour Photofinishing^{CAN}

This U.S. industry comprises establishments known as "one-hour" photofinishing labs primarily engaged in developing film and/or making photographic slides, prints, and enlargements on a short turnaround or while-you-wait basis.

Photofinishing laboratories (except those known as "one-hour"
 photofinishing labs) **812921**

812930 Parking Lots and Garages^{CAN}

This industry comprises establishments primarily engaged in providing parking space for motor vehicles, usually on an hourly, daily, or monthly basis and/or valet parking services.

Providing extended or dead storage of motor vehicles **493190**

812990 All Other Personal Services^{CAN}

This industry comprises establishments primarily engaged in providing personal services (except personal care services, death care services, drycleaning and laundry services, pet care services, photofinishing services, or parking space and/or valet parking services).

Providing personal care services **8121**
Providing death care services **8122**
Providing drycleaning and laundry services **8123**
Providing pet care (except veterinary) services **812910**
Practicing veterinary medicine **541940**
Providing photofinishing services **81292**
Providing parking space for motor vehicles and/or valet parking services
 812930

813 Religious, Grantmaking, Civic, Professional, and Similar Organizations

Industries in the Religious, Grantmaking, Civic, Professional, and Similar Organizations subsector group establishments that organize and promote religious activities; support various causes through grantmaking; advocate various social and political causes; and promote and defend the interests of their members.

The industry groups within the subsector are defined in terms of their activities, such as establishments that provide funding for specific causes or for a variety of charitable causes; establishments that advocate and actively promote causes and beliefs for the public good; and establishments that have an active membership structure to promote causes and represent the interests of their members. Establishments in this subsector may publish newsletters, books, and periodicals, for distribution to their membership.

813

8131 Religious Organizations^{CAN}

813110 Religious Organizations^{CAN}

This industry comprises (1) establishments primarily engaged in operating religious organizations, such as churches, religious temples, and monasteries and/or (2) establishments primarily engaged in administering an organized religion or promoting religious activities.

Schools, colleges, or universities operated by religious organizations **61**
Radio and television stations operated by religious organizations **513**
Publishing houses operated by religious organizations **511**
Health and social assistance for individuals **62**
Used merchandise stores operated by religious organizations **453310**

8132 Grantmaking and Giving Services^{CAN}

81321 Grantmaking and Giving Services^{CAN}

This industry comprises (1) establishment known as grantmaking foundations or charitable trusts and (2) establishments primarily engaged in raising funds for a wide range of social welfare activities, such as health, educational, scientific, and cultural activities.

Providing trust management services for others **52392**
Organizing and conducting fundraising campaigns on a contract or fee basis **56149**
Providing telemarketing services for others **56142**
Raising funds for political purposes **81394**
Advocating social causes or issues **81331**
Conducting health research **54171**

813211 Grantmaking Foundations^{US}

This U.S. industry comprises establishments known as grantmaking foundations or charitable trusts. Establishments in this industry award grants from trust funds based on a competitive selection process or the preferences of the foundation managers and grantors; or fund a single entity, such as a museum or university.

Providing trust management services for others **523920**

813212 Voluntary Health Organizations^{US}

This U.S. industry comprises establishments primarily engaged in raising funds for health related research, such as disease (e.g., heart, cancer, diabetes) prevention, health education, and patient services.

Raising funds for a wide range of social welfare activities, such as educational, scientific, cultural, and health, **813219**
Organizing and conducting fundraising campaigns on a contract or fee basis **561499**
Providing telemarketing services for others **561422**
Establishments known as grantmaking foundations or charitable trusts **813211**
Conducting health research **541710**

813219 Other Grantmaking and Giving Services^{US}

This U.S. industry comprises establishments (except voluntary health organizations) primarily engaged in raising funds for a wide range of social welfare activities, such as educational, scientific, cultural, and health.

Raising funds for health related research **813212**
Establishments known as grantmaking foundations or charitable trusts **813211**
Organizing and conducting fundraising campaigns on a contract or fee basis **561499**
Providing telemarketing services for others **561422**
Raising funds for political purposes **813940**
Advocating social causes or issues **81331**

8133 Social Advocacy Organizations^{CAN}

81331 Social Advocacy Organizations^{CAN}

This industry comprises establishments primarily engaged in promoting a particular cause or working for the realization of a specific social or political goal to benefit a broad or specific constituency. These organizations may solicit contributions and offer memberships to support these goals.

Promoting the civic and social interests of their members **81341**
Promoting the interests of the organized labor and union employees **81393**
Providing legal services for social advocacy organizations **5411**

813311 Human Rights Organizations^{US}

This U.S. industry comprises establishments primarily engaged in promoting causes associated with human rights either for a broad or specific constituency. Establishments in this industry address issues, such as protecting and promoting the broad constitutional rights and civil liberties of individuals and those suffering from neglect, abuse, or exploitation; promoting the interests of specific groups, such as children, women, senior citizens, or persons with disabilities; improving relations between racial, ethnic, and cultural groups; and promoting voter education and registration. These organizations may solicit contributions and offer memberships to support these causes.

Promoting the interests of organized labor and union employees **813930**
Providing legal services for human rights organizations **5411**

813312 Environment, Conservation and Wildlife Organizations[US]

This U.S. industry comprises establishments primarily engaged in promoting the preservation and protection of the environment and wildlife. Establishments in this industry address issues, such as clean air and water; global warming; conserving and developing natural resources, including land, plant, water, and energy resources; and protecting and preserving wildlife and endangered species. These organizations may solicit contributions and offer memberships to support these causes.

Providing legal services for environment, conservation, and wildlife
   organizations **5411**

813319 Other Social Advocacy Organizations[US]

This U.S. industry comprises establishments primarily engaged in social advocacy (except human rights and environmental protection, conservation, and wildlife preservation). Establishments in this industry address issues, such as peace and international understanding; community action (excluding civic organizations); or advancing social causes, such as firearms safety, drunk driving prevention, drug abuse awareness. These organizations may solicit contributions and offer memberships to support these causes.

Advocating human rights issues **813311**
Promoting the preservation and protection of the environment and wildlife
   813312
Promoting the civic and social interests of their members **813410**
Providing legal services for social advocacy organizations **5411**
Providing community action services, such as community action services
   agencies, **624190**

8134 Civic and Social Organizations[CAN]

813410 Civic and Social Organizations[CAN]

This industry comprises establishments primarily engaged in promoting the civic and social interests of their members. Establishments in this industry may operate bars and restaurants for their members.

Insurance offices operated by fraternal benefit organizations **524**
Operating residential fraternity and sorority houses **721310**
Providing travel arrangements and reservation services, such as automobile
   travel clubs or motor travel clubs **561599**

8139 Business, Professional, Labor, Political, and Similar Organizations[CAN]

This industry group comprises establishments primarily engaged in promoting the interests of their members (except religious organizations, social advocacy organizations, and civic and social organizations). Examples of establishments in this industry are business associations, professional organizations, labor unions, and political organizations.

813910 Business Associations[CAN]

This industry comprises establishments primarily engaged in promoting the business interests of their members. These establishments may conduct research on new products and services; develop market statistics; sponsor quality and certification standards; lobby public officials; or publish newsletters, books, or periodicals for distribution to their members.

Promoting the professional interests of their members and the profession as
   a whole **813920**
Promoting the interests of organized labor and union employees, such as
   trade unions, **813930**
Lobbying public officials (i.e., lobbyists) **541820**

813920 Professional Organizations[CAN]

This industry comprises establishments primarily engaged in promoting the professional interests of their members and the profession as a whole. These establishments may conduct research; develop statistics; sponsor quality and certification standards; lobby public officials; or publish newsletters, books, or periodicals, for distribution to their members.

Promoting the business interests of their members **813910**
Lobbying public officials (i.e., lobbyists) **541820**

813930 Labor Unions and Similar Labor Organizations[CAN]

This industry comprises establishments primarily engaged in promoting the interests of organized labor and union employees.

813

813940 Political Organizations[CAN]

This industry comprises establishments primarily engaged in promoting the interests of national, state, or local political parties or candidates. Included are political groups organized to raise funds for a political party or individual candidates.

Organizing and conducting fundraising campaigns on a contract or fee basis **561499**

Providing telemarketing services for others **561422**

813990 Other Similar Organizations (except Business, Professional, Labor, and Political Organizations)[CAN]

This industry comprises establishments (except religious organizations, social advocacy organizations, civic and social organizations, business associations, professional organizations, labor unions, and political organizations) primarily engaged in promoting the interest of their members.

Operating religious organizations, such as churches, religious temples, and monasteries, **813110**

Raising funds for a wide range of social welfare activities and establishments known as grantmaking foundations or charitable trusts **81321**

Advocating social causes or issues **81331**

Promoting the civic and social interests of their members **813410**

Promoting the business interests of their members **813910**

Promoting the professional interests of their members and the profession as a whole **813920**

Promoting the interests of organized labor and union employees **813930**

Promoting the interests of national, state, or local political parties or candidates **813940**

Providing recreational and amusement services, such as recreational or youth sports teams and leagues, **713990**

814 Private Households

Industries in the Private Households subsector include private households that engage in employing workers on or about the premises in activities primarily concerned with the operation of the household. These private households may employ individuals, such as cooks, maids, and butlers, and outside workers, such as gardeners, caretakers, and other maintenance workers.

8141 Private Households

814110 Private Households

This industry comprises private households primarily engaged in employing workers on or about the premises in activities primarily concerned with the operation of the household. These private households may employ individuals, such as cooks, maids, nannies, and butlers, and outside workers, such as gardeners, caretakers, and other maintenance workers.

SECTOR 92: PUBLIC ADMINISTRATION

OVERVIEW OF THIS SECTOR AS A WHOLE

The Public Administration sector consists of establishments of federal, state, and local government agencies that administer, oversee, and manage public programs and have executive, legislative, or judicial authority over other institutions within a given area. These agencies also set policy, create laws, adjudicate civil and criminal legal cases, provide for public safety and for national defense. In general, government establishments in the Public Administration sector oversee governmental programs and activities that are not performed by private establishments. Establishments in this sector typically are engaged in the organization and financing of the production of public goods and services, most of which are provided for free or at prices that are not economically significant.

Government establishments also engage in a wide range of productive activities covering not only public goods and services but also individual goods and services similar to those produced in sectors typically identified with private-sector establishments. In general, ownership is not a criterion for classification in NAICS. Therefore, government establishments engaged in the production of private-sector-like goods and services should be classified in the same industry as private-sector establishments engaged in similar activities.

As a practical matter, it is difficult to identify separate establishment detail for many government agencies. To the extent that separate establishment records are available, the administration of governmental programs is classified in Sector 92, Public Administration, while the operation of that same governmental program is classified elsewhere in NAICS based on the activities performed. For example, the governmental administrative authority for an airport is classified in Industry 92612, Regulation and Administration of Transportation Programs, while operating the airport is classified in Industry 48811, Airport Operations. When separate records are not available to distinguish between the administration of a governmental program and the operation of it, the establishment is classified in Sector 92, Public Administration. Examples of government-provided goods and services that are classified in sectors other than Public Administration include: schools, classified in Sector 61, Educational Services; hospitals, classified in Subsector 622, Hospitals; establishments operating transportation facilities, classified in Sector 48–49, Transportation and Warehousing; the operation of utilities, classified in Sector 22, Utilities; and the Government Printing Office, classified in Subsector 323, Printing and Related Support Activities.

921 Executive, Legislative, and Other General Government Support[US]

The Executive, Legislative, and Other General Government Support subsector groups offices of government executives, legislative bodies, public finance and general government support.

92II Executive, Legislative, and Other General Government Support[US]

92III0 Executive Offices[US]

This industry comprises government establishments serving as offices of chief executives and their advisory committees and commissions. This industry includes offices of the president, governors, and mayors, in addition to executive advisory commissions.

921120 Legislative Bodies[US]

This industry comprises government establishments serving as legislative bodies and their advisory committees and commissions. Included in this industry are legislative bodies, such as Congress, state legislatures, and advisory and study legislative commissions.

921130 Public Finance Activities[US]

This industry comprises government establishments primarily engaged in public finance, taxation, and monetary policy. Included are financial administration activities, such as monetary policy; tax administration and collection; custody and disbursement of funds; debt and investment administration; auditing activities; and government employee retirement trust fund administration.

Administering income maintenance programs **923130**
Regulating insurance and banking institutions **926150**
Performing central banking functions, such as issuing currency and acting as the fiscal agent for the central government **521110**

921140 Executive and Legislative Offices, Combined[US]

This industry comprises government establishments serving as councils and boards of commissioners or supervisors and such bodies where the chief executive (e.g., county executive or city mayor) is a mem-

921

ber of the legislative body (e.g., county or city council) itself.

Serving as offices of chief executives **921110**
Serving as legislative bodies **921120**

921150 American Indian and Alaska Native Tribal Governments[US]

This industry comprises American Indian and Alaska Native governing bodies. Establishments in this industry perform legislative, judicial, and administrative functions for their American Indian and Alaska Native lands. Included in this industry are American Indian and Alaska Native councils, courts, and law enforcement bodies.

Government establishments providing public administration of American Indian and Alaska Native affairs **923130**

921190 Other General Government Support[US]

This industry comprises government establishments primarily engaged in providing general support for government. Such support services include personnel services, election boards, and other general government support establishments that are not classified elsewhere in public administration.

Serving as offices of chief executives and their advisory committees and commissions **921110**
Serving as legislative bodies and their advisory committees and commissions **921120**
Providing administration of public finance, tax collection, and monetary policy programs **921130**
Serving as combined executive and legislative offices **921140**
Serving as American Indian or Alaska Native tribal leadership **921150**

922 Justice, Public Order, and Safety Activities[US]

The Justice, Public Order, and Safety Activities subsector groups government establishments engaged in the administration of justice, public order, and safety programs.

9221 Justice, Public Order, and Safety Activities[US]

922110 Courts[US]

This industry comprises civilian courts of law (except Indian tribal and Alaska Native courts). Included in this industry are civilian courts, courts of law, and sheriffs' offices conducting court functions only.

Operating military courts **928110**
Operating Indian tribal or Alaska Native courts **921150**

922120 Police Protection[US]

This industry comprises government establishments primarily engaged in criminal and civil law enforcement, police, traffic safety, and other activities related to the enforcement of the law and preservation of order. Combined police and fire departments are included in this industry.

Prosecution **922130**
Collection of law enforcement statistics **922190**
Providing police service for the military or National Guard **928110**
Providing police service for tribal governments **921150**
Enforcing immigration laws **928120**
Sheriffs' offices conducting court functions only **922110**

Private establishments providing security and investigation services **56161**

922130 Legal Counsel and Prosecution[US]

This industry comprises government establishments primarily engaged in providing legal counsel or prosecution services for the government.

Collecting criminal justice statistics **922190**

922140 Correctional Institutions[US]

This industry comprises government establishments primarily engaged in managing and operating correctional institutions. The facility is generally designed for the confinement, correction, and rehabilitation of adult and/or juvenile offenders sentenced by a court.

Operating half-way houses for ex-criminal offenders and delinquent youths **623990**
Managing or operating correctional facilities owned by others **561210**

922150 Parole Offices and Probation Offices[US]

This industry comprises government establishments primarily engaged in judicially administering probation offices, parole offices and boards, and pardon boards.

Providing probation, parole, and pardon activities as an integral part of a central administrative corrections' office **922140**

922160 Fire Protection[US]

This industry comprises government establishments primarily engaged in fire fighting and other related fire protection activities. Government establishments providing combined fire protection and ambulance or rescue services are classified in this industry.

Forest fire fighting **115310**
Providing combined police and fire protection services **922120**
Providing fire fighting services as a commercial activity **561990**
Providing ambulance services without fire protection service **621910**

922190 Other Justice, Public Order, and Safety Activities[US]

This industry comprises government establishments primarily engaged in public order and safety (except

courts, police protection, legal counsel and prosecution, correctional institutions, parole offices, probation offices, pardon boards, and fire protection). These establishments include the general administration of public order and safety programs. Government establishments responsible for the collection of statistics on public safety are included in this industry.

Serving as civilian courts of law (except Indian tribal and Alaska Native) **922110**
Criminal and civil law enforcement, police, traffic safety and similar activities related to the enforcement of law **922120**
Providing legal counsel to or prosecution services for their governments **922130**
The confinement, correction, and rehabilitation of adult and juvenile offenders sentenced by a court **922140**
Judicially administering probation offices, parole offices and boards, and pardon boards **922150**
Fire fighting and other related fire protection activities **922160**

---

923 Administration of Human Resource Programs[US]

The Administration of Human Resources Programs subsector groups government establishments primarily engaged in the administration of human resource programs.

9231 Administration of Human Resource Programs[US]

923110 Administration of Education Programs[US]

This industry comprises government establishments primarily engaged in the central coordination, planning, supervision, and administration of funds, policies, intergovernmental activities, statistical reports and data collection, and centralized programs for educational administration. Government scholarship programs are included in this industry.

Schools and local school boards **611**

923120 Administration of Public Health Programs[US]

This industry comprises government establishments primarily engaged in the planning, administration, and coordination of public health programs and services, including environmental health activities, mental health, categorical health programs, health statistics, and immunization services. Government es-

tablishments primarily engaged in conducting public health-related inspections are included in this industry.

Operating hospitals (i.e., government or military) **622**
Providing health care in a clinical setting (i.e., military or government clinics) **621**
Inspecting food, plants, animals, and other agriculture products **926140**

923130 Administration of Human Resource Programs (except Education, Public Health, and Veterans' Affairs Programs)[US]

This industry comprises government establishments primarily engaged in the planning, administration, and coordination of programs for public assistance, social work, and welfare activities. The administration of Social Security, disability insurance, Medicare, unemployment insurance, and workers' compensation programs are included in this industry.

Administering veterans' programs **923140**
Operating state employment job service offices **561310**
Operating programs for public assistance, social work, and welfare **624**

923

923140 Administration of Veterans' Affairs[US]

This industry comprises government establishments primarily engaged in the administration of programs of assistance, training, counseling, and other services to veterans and their dependents, heirs, or survivors. Included in this industry are Veterans' Affairs offices that maintain liaison and coordinate activities with other service organizations and governmental agencies.

Government establishments operating veterans' hospitals **622**
Providing veterans' insurance **524**
Operating civic and social organizations for veterans **813410**

924 Administration of Environmental Quality Programs[US]

The Administration of Environmental Quality Programs subsector groups government establishments primarily engaged in the administration of environmental quality.

9241 Administration of Environmental Quality Programs[US]

924110 Administration of Air and Water Resource and Solid Waste Management Programs[US]

This industry comprises government establishments primarily engaged in one or more of the following: (1) the administration, regulation, and enforcement of air and water resource programs; (2) the administration and regulation of solid waste management programs; (3) the administration and regulation of water and air pollution control and prevention programs; (4) the administration and regulation of flood control programs; (5) the administration and regulation of drainage development and water resource consumption programs; (6) the administration and regulation of toxic waste removal and cleanup programs; and (7) coordination of these activities at intergovernmental levels.

Operating water and irrigation systems **221310**
Administering sanitation districts **926130**
Operating sewage treatment facilities **221320**
Providing waste collection, treatment, disposal, and/or remediation **562**

924120 Administration of Conservation Programs[US]

This industry comprises government establishments primarily engaged in the administration, regulation, supervision and control of land use, including recreational areas; conservation and preservation of natural resources; erosion control; geological survey program administration; weather forecasting program administration; and the administration and protection of publicly and privately owned forest lands. Government establishments responsible for planning, management, regulation and conservation of game, fish, and wildlife populations, including wildlife management areas and field stations; and other administrative matters relating to the protection of fish, game, and wildlife are included in this industry.

Operating parks **712190**
Operating forest property **113**
Geophysical surveying and/or mapping **541360**
Surveying and/or mapping (except geophysical) **541370**
Weather forecasting **541990**
Operating fish and game preserves **712130**
Serving as urban planning commissions **925120**

925 Administration of Housing Programs, Urban Planning, and Community Development[US]

The Administration of Housing Programs, Urban Planning, and Community Development subsector groups government establishments primarily engaged in the administration of housing, urban planning, and community development.

925I Administration of Housing Programs, Urban Planning, and Community Development^US

925II0 Administration of Housing Programs^US

This industry comprises government establishments primarily engaged in the administration and planning of housing programs.

Operating government rental housing **53I**
Conducting building inspections and enforcing building codes and standards
9261S0

Buying, pooling, and repackaging mortgages or home loans for sale to others
on the secondary market **522294**

925120 Administration of Urban Planning and Community and Rural Development^US

This industry comprises government establishments primarily engaged in the administration and planning of the development of urban and rural areas. Included in this industry are government zoning boards and commissions.

926 Administration of Economic Programs^US

This subsector comprises government establishments primarily engaged in the administration of economic programs.

926I Administration of Economic Programs^US

926II0 Administration of General Economic Programs^US

This industry comprises government establishments primarily engaged in the administration, promotion and development of economic resources, including business, industry, and tourism. Included in this industry are government establishments responsible for the development of general statistical data and analyses and promotion of the general economic well-being of the governed area.

926120 Regulation and Administration of Transportation Programs^US

This industry comprises government establishments primarily engaged in the administration, regulation, licensing, planning, inspection, and investigation of transportation services and facilities. Included in this industry are government establishments responsible for motor vehicle and operator licensing, the Coast Guard (except the Coast Guard Academy), and parking authorities.

Operating airports, railroads, depots, ports, toll roads and bridges, and other
transportation facilities **48–49**
Operating parking lots and parking garages **8I2930**
Operating automobile safety inspection and emission testing facilities Group
8III

Building and/or maintaining roads and highways **2341I0**
Providing air traffic control services **4881I1**
Operating weigh stations **488490**

926130 Regulation and Administration of Communications, Electric, Gas, and Other Utilities^US

This industry comprises government establishments primarily engaged in the administration, regulation, licensing and inspection of utilities, such as communications, electric power (including fossil, nuclear, solar, water, and wind), gas and water supply, and sewerage.

Operating utilities **221**

926140 Regulation of Agricultural Marketing and Commodities^US

This industry comprises government establishments primarily engaged in the planning, administration, and coordination of agricultural programs for production, marketing, and utilization, including educational and promotional activities. Included in this industry are government establishments responsible for regulating and controlling the grading and inspection of food, plants, animals, and other agricultural products.

Administering programs for developing economic data about agricultural
and trade in agricultural products **926I10**
Administering programs for the conservation of natural resources **924I**
Administering food stamp programs **923130**

926

926150 Regulation, Licensing, and Inspection of Miscellaneous Commercial Sectors[US]

This industry comprises government establishments primarily engaged in the regulation, licensing, and inspection of commercial sectors, such as retail trade, professional occupations, manufacturing, mining, construction and services. Included in this industry are government establishments maintaining physical stan-

dards, regulating hazardous conditions not elsewhere classified, and enforcing alcoholic beverage control regulations.

Regulating, administering, and inspecting transportation services and facilities **926120**

Regulating, administering, and inspecting communications, electric, gas, and other utilities **926130**

---

927 Space Research and Technology[US]

This subsector group comprises government establishments that conduct space research.

9271 Space Research and Technology[US]

927110 Space Research and Technology[US]

This industry comprises government establishments primarily engaged in the administration and opera-

tions of space flights, space research, and space exploration. Included in this industry are government establishments operating space flight centers.

Private establishments providing space freight transportation **481212**
Manufacturing aerospace vehicles and parts **33641**
Manufacturing space satellites **334220**

---

928 National Security and International Affairs[US]

This subsector comprises government establishments primarily engaged in national security and international affairs.

9281 National Security and International Affairs[US]

928110 National Security[US]

This industry comprises government establishments of the Armed Forces, including the National Guard, primarily engaged in national security and related activities.

Operating military service academies **611310**

Regulating and administering water transportation, such as the U.S. Coast Guard and the Merchant Marine, **926120**

928120 International Affairs[US]

This industry comprises establishments of U.S. and foreign governments primarily engaged in international affairs and programs relating to other nations and peoples.

Private sector trade associations and councils **813910**
Government establishments administering international trade, such as trade commissions and councils **926110**

SIC-TO-NAICS CROSSWALK

The table that follows will be very useful if you have the old SIC code and simply need to find its related new NAICS industry code and title. That task will be simple in most instances: just look up the old SIC code in the left column and find the new NAICS code and industry title in the right column. In some cases, the old SIC industry is divided into more than one NAICS industry, but is often easy to select the NAICS industry that best relates.

(pt) – Where you see "pt" following the NAICS industry name, it means that the NAICS industry is "part of" the old SIC industry. For example, the SIC industry "Popcorn Farms" presents the new NAICS "Corn Farming (pt)" title as its replacement. In this instance, popcorn farming is "part of" the more general new NAICS industry title of corn farming.

NEC – You will also see "NEC" occasionally in this table. It is short for "Not Elsewhere Classified."

SIC Code	SIC Industry Title	NAICS Code	NAICS Industry Title
0111	Wheat	11114	Wheat Farming
0112	Rice	11116	Rice Farming
0115	Corn	11115	Corn Farming (pt)
0116	Soybeans	11111	Soybean Farming
0119	. Dry Pea and Bean Farms	11113	Dry Pea and Bean Farming
0119	. Oilseed, Except Soybean, Farms	11112	Oilseed (except Soybean) Farming
0119	. Popcorn Farms	11115	Corn Farming (pt)
0119	. Combination Oilseed and Grain Farms	111191	Oilseed and Grain Combination Farming
0119	. Other Farms	111199	All Other Grain Farming
0131	Cotton	11192	Cotton Farming
0132	Tobacco	11191	Tobacco Farming
0133	Sugarcane and Sugar Beets		
0133	. Sugar Beets	111991	Sugar Beet Farming
0133	. Sugarcane	11193	Sugarcane Farming
0134	Irish Potatoes	111211	Potato Farming
0139	Field Crops, Except Cash Grains, NEC		
0139	. Hay Farms	11194	Hay Farming
0139	. Peanut Farming	111992	Peanut Farming
0139	. Sweet Potatoes and Yam Farms	111219	Other Vegetable (except Potato) and Melon Farming (pt)
0139	. Other Field Crop Farms	111998	All Other Miscellaneous Crop Farming (pt)
0161	Vegetables and Melons	111219	Other Vegetable (except Potato) and Melon Farming (pt)
0171	Berry Crops		

SIC Code	SIC Industry Title	NAICS Code	NAICS Industry Title
0171	. Strawberry Farms	111333	Strawberry Farming
0171	. Other Berry Farms	111334	Berry (except Strawberry) Farming
0172	Grapes	111332	Grape Vineyards
0173	Tree Nuts	111335	Tree Nut Farming
0174	Citrus Fruits		
0174	. Orange Groves and Farms	11131	Orange Groves
0174	. Other Citrus Groves and Farms	11132	Citrus (except Orange) Groves
0175	Deciduous Tree Fruits		
0175	. Apple Orchards and Farms	111331	Apple Orchards
0175	. Other Farms	111339	Other Noncitrus Fruit Farming (pt)
0179	Fruits and Tree Nuts, NEC		
0179	. Combination Fruit and Tree Nut Farms	111336	Fruit and Tree Nut Combination Farming
0179	. Other Farms	111339	Other Noncitrus Fruit Farming (pt)
0181	Ornamental Floriculture and Nursery Products		
0181	. Floriculture Farming	111422	Floriculture Production
0181	. Nursery Farming	111421	Nursery and Tree Production (pt)
0182	Food Crops Grown Under Cover		
0182	. Mushrooms, Growing Of	111411	Mushroom Production
0182	. Other Food Crops Grown Under Cover	111419	Other Food Crops Grown Under Cover
0191	General Farms, Primarily Crop	111998	All Other Miscellaneous Crop Farming (pt)
02	Agricultural production- livestock		
0211	Beef Cattle Feedlots	112112	Cattle Feedlots
0212	Beef Cattle, Except Feedlots	112111	Beef Cattle Ranching and Farming (pt)
0213	Hogs	11221	Hog and Pig Farming
0214	Sheep and Goats		
0214	. Sheep Farms	11241	Sheep Farming
0214	. Goat Farms	11242	Goat Farming
0219	General Livestock, Except Dairy and Poultry	11299	All Other Animal Production (pt)
0241	Dairy Farms		
0241	. Dairy Heifer Replacement Farms	112111	Beef Cattle Ranching and Farming (pt)
0241	. Dairy Farms	11212	Dairy Cattle and Milk Production
0251	Broiler, Fryers, and Roaster Chickens	11232	Broilers and Other Meat-Type Chicken Production
0252	Chicken Eggs	11231	Chicken Egg Production
0253	Turkey and Turkey Eggs	11233	Turkey Production
0254	Poultry Hatcheries	11234	Poultry Hatcheries

SIC Code	SIC Industry Title	NAICS Code	NAICS Industry Title
0259	Poultry and Eggs, NEC	11239	Other Poultry Production
0271	Fur-Bearing Animals and Rabbits	11293	Fur-Bearing Animal and Rabbit Production
0272	Horses and Other Equines	11292	Horse and Other Equine Production
0273	Animal Aquaculture		
0273	. Finfish Farms	112511	Finfish Farming and Fish Hatcheries (pt)
0273	. Shellfish Farms	112512	Shellfish Farming (pt)
0273	. Other Animal Aquaculture	112519	Other Animal Aquaculture (pt)
0279	Animal Specialities, NEC		
0279	. Alligator and Frog Production	112519	Other Animal Aquaculture (pt)
0279	. Bee Farms	11291	Apiculture
0279	. Other	11299	All Other Animal Production (pt)
0291	General Farms, Primarily Livestock and Animal Specialties	11299	All Other Animal Production (pt)
07	Agricultural services		
0711	Soil Preparation Services	115112	Soil Preparation, Planting, and Cultivating (pt)
0721	Crop Planting, Cultivating, and Protecting	115112	Soil Preparation, Planting, and Cultivating (pt)
0722	Crop Harvesting, Primarily by Machine	115113	Crop Harvesting, Primarily By Machine
0723	Crop Preparation Services For Market, except Cotton Ginning		
0723	. Other	115114	Postharvest Crop Activities (except Cotton Ginning)
0723	. Custom Grain Grinding	311119	Other Animal Food Manufacturing (pt)
0724	Cotton Ginning	115111	Cotton Ginning
0741	Veterinary Services For Livestock	54194	Veterinary Services (pt)
0742	Veterinary Services for Animal Specialties	54194	Veterinary Services (pt)
0751	Livestock Services, Except Veterinary		
0751	. Custom Slaughtering	311611	Animal (except Poultry) Slaughtering (pt)
0751	. Other Livestock Service, Except Veterinary	11521	Support Activities for Animal Production (pt)
0752	Animal Specialty Services, Except Veterinary		
0752	. Horses & Equines Services & Animal Production Breeding	11521	Support Activities for Animal Production (pt)
0752	. Pet Care Services	81291	Pet Care (except Veterinary) Services
0761	Farm Labor Contractors and Crew Leaders	115115	Farm Labor Contractors and Crew Leaders
0762	Farm Management Services	115116	Farm Management Services
0781	Landscape Counseling and Planning		
0781	. Horticulture Consulting	54169	Other Scientific and Technical Consulting Services (pt)
0781	. Landscape Architectural Services	54132	Landscape Architectural Services (pt)
0782	Lawn and Garden Services	56173	Landscaping Services (pt)

SIC Code	SIC Industry Title	NAICS Code	NAICS Industry Title
0783	Ornamental Shrub and Tree Services	56173	Landscaping Services (pt)
08	Forestry		
0811	Timber Tracts		
0811	. Short Rotation Woody Crops	111421	Nursery and Tree Production (pt)
0811	. Long Term Timber Farming	11311	Timber Tract Operations
0831	Forest Nurseries and Gathering of Forest Products		
0831	. Maple Sap	111998	All Other Miscellaneous Crop Farming (pt)
0831	. Other Forest Products	11321	Forest Nurseries and Gathering of Forest Products
0851	Forestry Services	11531	Support Activities for Forestry
09	Fishing, hunting, and trapping		
0912	Finfish	114111	Finfish Fishing
0913	Shellfish	114112	Shellfish Fishing
0919	Miscellaneous Marine Products		
0919	. Except Plant Aquaculture	114119	Other Marine Fishing
0919	. Plant Aquaculture	111998	All Other Miscellaneous Crop Farming (pt)
0921	Fish Hatcheries and Preserves		
0921	. Finfish Hatcheries	112511	Finfish Farming and Fish Hatcheries (pt)
0921	. Shellfish Hatcheries	112512	Shellfish Farming (pt)
0971	Hunting and Trapping, and Game Propagation	11421	Hunting and Trapping
	Mining		
10	Metal mining		
1011	Iron Ores	21221	Iron Ore Mining
1021	Copper Ores	212234	Copper Ore and Nickel Ore Mining (pt)
1031	Lead and Zinc Ores	212231	Lead Ore and Zinc Ore Mining
1041	Gold Ores	212221	Gold Ore Mining
1044	Silver Ores	212222	Silver Ore Mining
1061	Ferroalloy Ores, Except Vanadium		
1061	. Nickel Ore Mining	212234	Copper Ore and Nickel Ore Mining (pt)
1061	. Other Ferroalloys (except nickel)	212299	Other Metal Ore Mining (pt)
1081	Metal Mining Services		
1081	. Metal Mining (except geophysical surveying)	213114	Support Activities for Metal Mining
1081	. Geophysical Surveying and Mapping	54136	Geophysical Surveying and Mapping Services (pt)
1094	Uranium-Radium-Vanadium Ores	212291	Uranium-Radium-Vanadium Ore Mining
1099	Miscellaneous Metal Ores, NEC	212299	Other Metal Ore Mining (pt)
12	Coal mining		

SIC Code	SIC Industry Title	NAICS Code	NAICS Industry Title
1221	Bituminous Coal and Lignite Surface Mining	212111	Bituminous Coal and Lignite Surface Mining
1222	Bituminous Coal Underground Mining	212112	Bituminous Coal Underground Mining
1231	Anthracite Mining	212113	Anthracite Mining
1241	Coal Mining Services	213113	Support Activities for Coal Mining
13	Oil and gas extraction		
1311	Crude Petroleum and Natural Gas	211111	Crude Petroleum and Natural Gas Extraction
1321	Natural Gas Liquids	211112	Natural Gas Liquid Extraction (pt)
1381	Drilling Oil and Gas Wells	213111	Drilling Oil and Gas Wells
1382	Oil and Gas Field Exploration Services		
1382	. Geophysical Mapping and Surveying	54136	Geophysical Surveying and Mapping Services (pt)
1382	. Other Oil and Gas Field Exploration Services	213112	Support Activities for Oil and Gas Field Operations (pt)
1389	Oil and Gas Field Services, NEC	213112	Support Activities for Oil and Gas Field Operations (pt)
14	Nonmetallic minerals, except fuels		
1411	Dimension Stone	212311	Dimension Stone Mining and Quarrying
1422	Crushed and Broken Limestone	212312	Crushed and Broken Limestone Mining and Quarrying
1423	Crushed and Broken Granite	212313	Crushed and Broken Granite Mining and Quarrying
1429	Crushed and Broken Stone, NEC	212319	Other Crushed and Broken Stone Mining and Quarrying (pt)
1442	Construction Sand and Gravel	212321	Construction Sand and Gravel Mining
1446	Industrial Sand	212322	Industrial Sand Mining
1455	Kaolin and Ball Clay	212324	Kaolin and Ball Clay Mining
1459	Clay, Ceramic, and Refractory Minerals, NEC	212325	Clay and Ceramic and Refractory Minerals Mining
1474	Potash, Soda, and Borate Minerals	212391	Potash, Soda, and Borate Mineral Mining
1475	Phosphate Rock	212392	Phosphate Rock Mining
1479	Chemical and Fertilizer Mineral Mining, NEC	212393	Other Chemical and Fertilizer Mineral Mining
1481	Nonmetallic Minerals Services Except Fuels		
1481	. Except Geophysical Mapping and Surveying	213115	Support Activities for Nonmetallic Minerals (except Fuels)
1481	. Geophysical Surveying and Mapping Services	54136	Geophysical Surveying and Mapping Services (pt)
1499	Miscellaneous Nonmetallic Minerals, Except Fuels		
1499	. Bituminous Limestone and Bituminous Sandstone	212319	Other Crushed and Broken Stone Mining or Quarrying (pt)
1499	. Except Bituminous Limestone and Bituminous Sandstone	212399	All Other Nonmetallic Mineral Mining (pt)
	Construction		
15	General building contractors		
1521	General Contractors-Single-Family Houses	23321	Single Family Housing Construction (pt)
1522	General Contractors-Residential Bldgs, Other Than Single-Family		

SIC Code	SIC Industry Title	NAICS Code	NAICS Industry Title
1522	. Hotel and Motel Construction	23332	Commercial and Institutional Building Construction (pt)
1522	. Except Hotel and Motel Construction	23322	Multifamily Housing Construction (pt)
1531	Operative Builders		
1531	. Single Family Housing	23321	Single Family Housing Construction (pt)
1531	. Multifamily Housing	23322	Multifamily Housing Construction (pt)
1531	. Manufacturing and Light Industrial Buildings	23331	Manufacturing and Industrial Building Construction (pt)
1531	. Commercial and Institutional Buildings	23332	Commercial and Institutional Building Construction (pt)
1541	General Contractors-Industrial Buildings and Warehouses		
1541	. Public Warehouse Construction	23332	Commercial and Institutional Building Construction (pt)
1541	. Except Public Warehouse Construction	23331	Manufacturing and Industrial Building Construction (pt)
1542	General Contractors-Nonresidential Buildings, Other than Industrial Buildings and Warehouses	23332	Commercial and Institutional Building Construction (pt)
16	Heavy construction contractors		
1611	Highway and Street Construction, Except Elevated Highways	23411	Highway and Street Construction (pt)
1622	Bridge, Tunnel, and Elevated Highway Construction	23412	Bridge and Tunnel Construction (pt)
1623	Water, Sewer, Pipeline, and Communications and Power Line Construction		
1623	. Water, Sewer and Pipelines	23491	Water, Sewer, and Pipeline Construction (pt)
1623	. Power and Communication Transmission Lines	23492	Power and Communication Transmission Line Construction (pt)
1629	Heavy Construction, NEC		
1629	. Industrial Nonbuilding Structures Construction	23493	Industrial Nonbuilding Structure Construction (pt)
1629	. Nonbuilding Structures Except Industrial Construction	23499	All Other Heavy Construction (pt)
17	Special trade contractors		
1711	Plumbing, Heating, and Air-Conditioning	23511	Plumbing, Heating, and Air-Conditioning Contractors (pt)
1721	Painting and Paper Hanging	23521	Painting and Wall Covering Contractors (pt)
1731	Electrical Work	23531	Electrical Contractors
1741	Masonry, Stone Setting, and Other Stone Work	23541	Masonry and Stone Contractors
1742	Plastering, Drywall, Acoustical, and Insulation Work	23542	Drywall, Plastering, Acoustical, and Insulation Contractors (pt)
1743	Terrazzo, Tile, Marble, and Mosaic Work		
1743	. Fresco Work	23542	Drywall, Plastering, Acoustical, and Insulation Contractors (pt)
1743	. Except Fresco Work	23543	Tile, Marble, Terrazzo, and Mosaic Contractors
1751	Carpentry Work	23551	Carpentry Contractors
1752	Floor Laying and Other Floor Work, NEC	23552	Floor Laying and Other Floor Contractors
1761	Roofing, Siding, and Sheet Metal Work	23561	Roofing, Siding, and Sheet Metal Contractors
1771	Concrete Work		

SIC Code	SIC Industry Title	NAICS Code	NAICS Industry Title
1771	. Stucco Construction	23542	Drywall, Plastering, Acoustical, and Insulation Contractors (pt)
1771	. Except Stucco Construction	23571	Concrete Contractors
1781	Water Well Drilling	23581	Water Well Drilling Contractors
1791	Structural Steel Erection	23591	Structural Steel Erection Contractors
1793	Glass and Glazing Work	23592	Glass and Glazing Contractors (pt)
1794	Excavation Work	23593	Excavation Contractors
1795	Wrecking and Demolition Work	23594	Wrecking and Demolition Contractors
1796	Installation or Erection of Building Equipment, NEC	23595	Building Equipment and Other Machinery Installation Contractors
1799	Special Trade Contractors, NEC		
1799	. Paint and Wallpaper Stripping and Removal Contractors	23521	Painting and Wall Covering Contractors (pt)
1799	. Tinted Glass Work	23592	Glass and Glazing Contractors (pt)
1799	. Asbestos Abatement and Lead Paint Removal Contractors	56291	Remediation Services (pt)
1799	. All Other Special Trade Contractors	23599	All Other Special Trade Contractors
	Manufacturing		
20	Food and kindred products		
2011	Meat Packing Plants	311611	Animal (except Poultry) Slaughtering (pt)
2013	Sausages and Other Prepared Meats		
2013	. Lard Made From Purchased Material	311613	Rendering and Meat Byproduct Processing (pt)
2013	. Except Lard Made From Purchased Material	311612	Meat Processed from Carcasses (pt)
2015	Poultry Slaughtering and Processing		
2015	. Poultry Processing	311615	Poultry Processing
2015	. Egg Processing	311999	All Other Miscellaneous Food Manufacturing (pt)
2021	Creamery Butter	311512	Creamery Butter Manufacturing
2022	Natural, Processed, and Imitation Cheese	311513	Cheese Manufacturing
2023	Dry, Condensed, and Evaporated Dairy Products	311514	Dry, Condensed, and Evaporated Dairy Product Manufacturing
2024	Ice Cream and Frozen Desserts	31152	Ice Cream and Frozen Dessert Manufacturing
2026	Fluid Milk		
2026	. Ultra-High Temperature	311514	Dry, Condensed, and Evaporated Dairy Product Manufacturing (pt)
2026	. Except Ultra-High Temperature	311511	Fluid Milk Manufacturing
2032	Canned Specialties		
2032	. Canned Specialties	311422	Specialty Canning
2032	. Canned Pudding	311999	All Other Miscellaneous Food Manufacturing (pt)
2033	Canned Fruits, Vegetables, Preserves, Jams, and Jellies	311421	Fruit and Vegetable Canning (pt)

SIC Code	SIC Industry Title	NAICS Code	NAICS Industry Title
2034	Dried and Dehydrated Fruits, Vegetables, and Soup Mixes		
2034	. Dried and Dehydrated Fruits and Vegetables	311423	Dried and Dehydrated Food Manufacturing (pt)
2034	. Soup Mixes Made from Purchased Dried and Dehydrated Vegetables	311999	All Other Miscellaneous Food Manufacturing (pt)
2034	. Vegetable Flours	311211	Flour Milling (pt)
2035	Pickled Fruits and Vegetables, Vegetable Sauces and Seasonings, and Salad Dressings		
2035	. Pickled Fruits and Vegetables	311421	Fruit and Vegetable Canning (pt)
2035	. Sauces and Salad Dressings	311941	Mayonnaise, Dressing, and Other Prepared Sauce Manufacturing (pt)
2037	Frozen Fruits, Fruit Juices, and Vegetables	311411	Frozen Fruit, Juice, and Vegetable Processing
2038	Frozen Specialties, NEC	311412	Frozen Specialty Food Manufacturing
2041	Flour and Other Grain Mill Products	311211	Flour Milling (pt)
2043	Cereal Breakfast Foods		
2043	. Coffee Substitute	31192	Coffee and Tea Manufacturing (pt)
2043	. Breakfast Cereal	31123	Breakfast Cereal Manufacturing
2044	Rice Milling	311212	Rice Milling
2045	Prepared Flour Mixes and Doughs	311822	Flour Mixes and Dough Manufacturing from Purchased Flour
2046	Wet Corn Milling	311221	Wet Corn Milling
2046	. Refining Purchased Oil	311225	Fats and Oils Refining and Blending (pt)
2046	. Except Refining Purchased Oil	311221	Wet Corn Milling
2047	Dog and Cat Food	311111	Dog and Cat Food Manufacturing
2048	Prepared Feed and Feed Ingredients for Animals and Fowls, Except Dogs and Cats		
2048	. Animal Slaughtering for Pet Food	311611	Animal (except Poultry) Slaughtering (pt)
2048	. Except Slaughtering Animals for Pet Food	311119	Other Animal Food Manufacturing (pt)
2051	Bread and Other Bakery Products, Except Cookies and Crackers	311812	Commercial Bakeries (pt)
2052	Cookies and Crackers		
2052	. Cookie and Cracker	311821	Cookie and Cracker Manufacturing
2052	. Pretzels, Except Soft	311919	Other Snack Food Manufacturing (pt)
2052	. Unleavened Bread and Soft Pretzels	311812	Commercial Bakeries (pt)
2053	Frozen Bakery Products, Except Bread	311813	Frozen Cakes, Pies, and Other Pastries Manufacturing
2061	Cane Sugar, Except Refining	311311	Sugarcane Mills
2062	Cane Sugar Refining	311312	Cane Sugar Refining
2063	Beet Sugar	311313	Beet Sugar Manufacturing
2064	Candy and Other Confectionery Products		

SIC Code	SIC Industry Title	NAICS Code	NAICS Industry Title
2064	. Chocolate Confectionery	31133	Confectionery Manufacturing from Purchased Chocolate (pt)
2064	. Nonchocolate Confectionery Manufacturing	31134	Nonchocolate Confectionery Manufacturing (pt)
2066	Chocolate and Cocoa Products		
2066	. Chocolate Products Made From Purchased Chocolate	31133	Confectionery Manufacturing From Purchased Chocolate (pt)
2066	. Chocolate and Confectionery Products Made From Cacao Beans	31132	Chocolate and Confectionery Manufacturing from Cacao Beans
2067	Chewing Gum	31134	Nonchocolate Confectionery Manufacturing (pt)
2068	Salted and Roasted Nuts and Seeds	311911	Roasted Nuts and Peanut Butter Manufacturing (pt)
2074	Cottonseed Oil Mills		
2074	. Cottonseed Processing	311223	Other Oilseed Processing (pt)
2074	. Processing Purchased Cottonseed Oil	311225	Fats and Oils Refining and Blending (pt)
2075	Soybean Oil Mills		
2075	. Soybean Processing	311222	Soybean Processing (pt)
2075	. Processing Purchased Soybean Oil	311225	Fats and Oils Refining and Blending (pt)
2076	Vegetable Oil Mills, Except Corn, Cottonseed, and Soybeans		
2076	. Vegetable Oilseed Processing, except Corn, Cottonseed, and Soybeans	311223	Other Oilseed Processing (pt)
2076	. Processing Purchased Vegetable Oils, except Corn, Cottonseed, and Soybeans	311225	Fats and Oils Refining and Blending (pt)
2077	Animal and Marine Fats and Oils		
2077	. Animal Fats and Oils	311613	Rendering and Meat Byproduct Processing
2077	. Canned Marine Fats and Oils	311711	Seafood Canning (pt)
2077	. Fresh and Frozen Marine Fats and Oils	311712	Fresh and Frozen Seafood Processing (pt)
2079	Shortening, Table Oils, Margarine, and Other Edible Fats and Oils, NEC		
2079	. Processing Fats and Oils from Purchased Fats and Oils	311225	Fats and Oils Refining and Blending (pt)
2079	. Processing Soybean Oil from Soybeans Crushed in the Same Establishment	311222	Soybean Processing (pt)
2079	. Processing Vegetable Oils, except Soybeans, from Oilseeds Crushed in the Same Establishment	311223	Other Oilseed Processing (pt)
2082	Malt Beverages		
2082	. Malt Extract	311942	Spice and Extract Manufacturing (pt)
2082	. Except Malt Extract	31212	Breweries
2083	Malt	311213	Malt Manufacturing
2084	Wines, Brandy, and Brandy Spirits	31213	Wineries (pt)
2085	Distilled and Blended Liquors		
2085	. Applejack	31213	Wineries (pt)

SIC Code	SIC Industry Title	NAICS Code	NAICS Industry Title
2085	. Except Applejack	31214	Distilleries
2086	Bottled and Canned Soft Drinks and Carbonated Waters		
2086	. Soft Drinks	312111	Soft Drink Manufacturing
2086	. Bottled Water	312112	Bottled Water Manufacturing (pt)
2087	Flavoring Extracts and Flavoring Syrups NEC		
2087	. Coffee Flavoring and Syrups	31192	Coffee and Tea Manufacturing (pt)
2087	. Flavoring Syrup and Concentrate, Except Coffee	31193	Flavoring Syrup and Concentrate Manufacturing
2087	. Flavoring Extracts, Except Coffee, and Natural Food Colorings	311942	Spice and Extract Manufacturing (pt)
2087	. Powdered Drink Mix	311999	All Other Miscellaneous Food Manufacturing (pt)
2091	Canned and Cured Fish and Seafood	311711	Seafood Canning (pt)
2092	Prepared Fresh or Frozen Fish and Seafoods	311712	Fresh and Frozen Seafood Processing (pt)
2095	Roasted Coffee	31192	Coffee and Tea Manufacturing (pt)
2096	Potato Chips, Corn Chips, and Similar Snacks	311919	Other Snack Food Manufacturing (pt)
2097	Manufactured Ice	312113	Ice Manufacturing
2098	Macaroni, Spaghetti, Vermicelli, and Noodles	311823	Dry Pasta Manufacturing (pt)
2099	Food Preparations, NEC		
2099	. Reducing Maple Sap to Maple Syrup	111998	All Other Miscellaneous Crop Farming (pt)
2099	. Marshmallow Creme	31134	Nonchocolate Confectionery Manufacturing (pt)
2099	. Peanut Butter	311911	Roasted Nuts and Peanut Butter Manufacturing (pt)
2099	. Potatoes, Dried and Packaged with Other Ingredients Made in Dehydration Plants, and Bouillon	311423	Dried and Dehydrated Food Manufacturing (pt)
2099	. Perishable Prepared Food	311991	Perishable Prepared Food Manufacturing
2099	. Rice, Uncooked and Packaged with Other Ingredients Made in Rice Mills	311212	Rice Milling (pt)
2099	. Tortillas	31183	Tortilla Manufacturing
2099	. Dry Pasta Packaged with Other Ingredients Made in Dry Pasta Plants	311823	Dry Pasta Manufacturing (pt)
2099	. Tea	31192	Coffee and Tea Manufacturing (pt)
2099	. Vinegar, Prepared Dips Except Dairy and Cider	311941	Mayonnaise, Dressing, and Other Prepared Sauce Manufacturing (pt)
2099	. Spices and Extracts	311942	Spice and Extract Manufacturing (pt)
2099	. Other	311999	All Other Miscellaneous Food Manufacturing (pt)
21	Tobacco manufactures		
2111	Cigarettes	312221	Cigarette Manufacturing
2121	Cigars	312229	Other Tobacco Product Manufacturing (pt)
2131	Chewing and Smoking Tobacco and Snuff	312229	Other Tobacco Product Manufacturing (pt)

SIC Code	SIC Industry Title	NAICS Code	NAICS Industry Title
2141	Tobacco Stemming and Redrying		
2141	. Reconstituted Tobacco	312229	Other Tobacco Product Manufacturing (pt)
2141	. Redrying and Stemming	31221	Tobacco Stemming and Redrying
22	Textile mill products		
2211	Broadwoven Fabric Mills, Cotton	31321	Broadwoven Fabric Mills (pt)
2221	Broadwoven Fabric Mills, Manmade Fiber and Silk	31321	Broadwoven Fabric Mills (pt)
2231	Broadwoven Fabric Mills, Wool (Including Dyeing and Finishing)		
2231	. Except Wool Finishing only	31321	Broadwoven Fabric Mills (pt)
2231	. Wool Broadwoven Fabric Finishing only	313311	Broadwoven Fabric Finishing Mills (pt)
2231	. Wool Finishing only, Except Broadwoven Fabric	313312	Textile and Fabric Finishing (except Broadwoven Fabric) Mills (pt)
2241	Narrow Fabric and Other Smallware Mills: Cotton, Wool, Silk, and Manmade Fiber	313221	Narrow Fabric Mills (pt)
2251	Women's Full-Length and Knee-Length Hosiery, Except Socks		
2251	. Dyeing and Finishing Only	313312	Textile and Fabric Finishing (except Broadwoven Fabric) Mills (pt)
2251	. Except Dyeing and Finishing Only	315111	Sheer Hosiery Mills (pt)
2252	Hosiery, NEC		
2252	. Dyeing and Finishing Only	313312	Textile and Fabric Finishing (except Broadwoven Fabric) Mills (pt)
2252	. Girls' Hosiery, Except Dyeing and Finishing Only	315111	Sheer Hosiery Mills (pt)
2252	. Socks, Except Dyeing and Finishing Only	315119	Other Hosiery and Sock Mills
2253	Knit Outerwear Mills		
2253	. Dyeing and Finishing Only	313312	Textile and Fabric Finishing (except Broadwoven Fabric) Mills (pt)
2253	. Bathrobes and Lounging Robes Made in Knitting Mills Except Dyeing and Finishing Only	315192	Underwear and Nightwear Knitting Mills (pt)
2253	. Except Dyeing and Finishing Only and Bathrobes and Lounging Robes	315191	Outerwear Knitting Mills (pt)
2254	Knit Underwear and Nightwear Mills		
2254	. Dyeing and Finishing Only	313312	Textile and Fabric Finishing (except Broadwoven Fabric) Mills (pt)
2254	. Except Dyeing and Finishing Only	315192	Underwear and Nightwear Knitting Mills (pt)
2257	Weft Knit Fabric Mills		
2257	. Except Finishing	313241	Weft Knit Fabric Mills (pt)
2257	. Finishing Only	313312	Textile and Fabric Finishing (except Broadwoven Fabric) Mills (pt)
2258	Lace and Warp Knit Fabric Mills		

SIC Code	SIC Industry Title	NAICS Code	NAICS Industry Title
2258	. Except Finishing	313249	Other Knit Fabric and Lace Mills (pt)
2258	. Finishing Only	313312	Textile and Fabric Finishing (except Broadwoven Fabric) Mills (pt)
2259	Knitting Mills, NEC		
2259	. Knit Gloves and Mittens	315191	Outerwear Knitting Mills (pt)
2259	. Girdles	315192	Underwear and Nightwear Knitting Mills (pt)
2259	. Finished Articles of Weft Knit Fabric	313241	Weft Knit Fabric Mills (pt)
2259	. Knit Gloves and Mittens, Dyeing and Finishing Only	313312	Textile and Fabric Finishing (except Broadwoven Fabric) Mills (pt)
2259	. Finished Articles of Warp Knit Fabric	313249	Other Knit Fabric and Lace Mills (pt)
2261	Finishers of Broadwoven Fabrics of Cotton	313311	Broadwoven Fabric Finishing Mills (pt)
2262	Finishers of Broadwoven Fabrics of Manmade Fiber and Silk	313311	Broadwoven Fabric Finishing Mills (pt)
2269	Finishers of Textiles, NEC	313312	Textile and Fabric Finishing (except Broadwoven Fabric) Mills (pt)
2273	Carpets and Rugs	31411	Carpet and Rug Mills
2281	Yarn Spinning Mills	313111	Yarn Spinning Mills (pt)
2282	Yarn Texturizing, Throwing, Twisting, and Winding Mills	313112	Yarn Texturing, Throwing, and Twisting Mills
2284	Thread Mills		
2284	. Except Finishing	313113	Thread Mills (pt)
2284	. Finishing	313312	Textile and Fabric Finishing (except Broadwoven Fabric) Mills (pt)
2295	Coated Fabrics, Not Rubberized	31332	Fabric Coating Mills (pt)
2296	Tire Cord and Fabrics	314992	Tire Cord and Tire Fabric Mills
2297	Nonwoven Fabrics	31323	Nonwoven Fabric Mills (pt)
2298	Cordage and Twine	314991	Rope, Cordage and Twine Mills
2299	Textile Goods, NEC		
2299	. Broadwoven Fabric of Jute, Linen, Hemp, and Ramie and Handwoven	31321	Broadwoven Fabric Mills (pt)
2299	. Nonwoven Felt	31323	Nonwoven Fabric Mills (pt)
2299	. Finishing Thread and Yarn of Flax, Hemp, Jute, Linen, and Ramie	313312	Textile and Fabric Finishing (except Broadwoven Fabrics) Mills (pt)
2299	. Narrow Woven Fabric of Jute, Linen, Hemp, and Ramie	313221	Narrow Fabric Mills (pt)
2299	. Thread of Hemp, Linen, and Ramie	313113	Thread Mills (pt)
2299	. Yarn of Flax, Hemp, Jute, and Ramie	313111	Yarn Spinning Mills (pt)
2299	. Recovery and Processing of Fibers and Waste	314999	All Other Miscellaneous Textile Product Mills (pt)
23	Apparel and other textile products		
2311	Men's and Boys' Suits, Coats, and Overcoats		

SIC Code	SIC Industry Title	NAICS Code	NAICS Industry Title
2311	. Contractors	315211	Men's and Boys' Cut and Sew Apparel Contractors (pt)
2311	. Except Contractors	315222	Men's and Boys' Cut and Sew Suit, Coat, and Overcoat Manufacturing (pt)
2321	Men's and Boys' Shirts, Except Work Shirts		
2321	. Contractors	315211	Men's and Boys' Cut and Sew Apparel Contractors (pt)
2321	. Except Contractors	315223	Men's and Boys' Cut and Sew Shirt, (except Work Shirt) Manufacturing (pt)
2322	Men's and Boys' Underwear and Nightwear		
2322	. Contractors	315211	Men's and Boys' Cut and Sew Apparel Contractors (pt)
2322	. Except Contractors	315221	Men's and Boys' Cut and Sew Underwear and Nightwear Manufacturing (pt)
2323	Men's and Boys' Neckwear		
2323	. Contractors	315211	Men's and Boys' Cut and Sew Apparel Contractors (pt)
2323	. Except Contractors	315993	Men's and Boys' Neckwear Manufacturing
2325	Men's and Boys' Trousers and Slacks		
2325	. Contractors	315211	Men's and Boys' Cut and Sew Apparel Contractors (pt)
2325	. Except Contractors	315224	Men's and Boys' Cut And Sew Trouser, Slack, And Jean Manufacturing (pt)
2326	Men's and Boys' Work Clothing		
2326	. Contractors	315211	Men's and Boys' Cut and Sew Apparel Contractors (pt)
2326	. Except Contractors	315225	Men's and Boys' Cut and Sew Work Clothing Manufacturing
2329	Men's and Boys' Clothing, NEC		
2329	. Contractors	315211	Men's and Boys' Cut and Sew Apparel Contractors (pt)
2329	. Except Contractors	315228	Men's and Boys' Cut and Sew Other Outerwear Manufacturing (pt)
2329	. Athletic Uniforms, Except Contractors	315299	All Other Cut and Sew Apparel Manufacturing (pt)
2331	Women's, Misses', and Juniors' Blouses and Shirts		
2331	. Contractors	315212	Women's, Girls', and Infants' Cut and Sew Apparel Contractors (pt)
2331	. Except Contractors	315232	Women's and Girls' Cut and Sew Blouse and Shirt Manufacturing (pt)
2335	Women's, Misses', and Juniors' Dresses		
2335	. Contractors	315212	Women's, Girls', and Infants' Cut and Sew Apparel Contractors (pt)
2335	. Except Contractors	315233	Women's and Girls' Cut and Sew Dress Manufacturing (pt)
2337	Women's, Misses' and Juniors' Suits, Skirts, and Coats		
2337	. Contractors	315212	Women's, Girls', and Infants' Cut and Sew Apparel Contractors (pt)

SIC Code	SIC Industry Title	NAICS Code	NAICS Industry Title
2337	. Except Contractors	315234	Women's and Girls' Cut and Sew Suit, Coat, Tailored Jacket, and Skirt Manufacturing (pt)
2339	Women's, Misses', and Juniors' Outerwear, NEC		
2339	. Scarves, Except Contractors	315999	Other Apparel Accessories and Other Apparel Manufacturing (pt)
2339	. Contractors	315212	Women's, Girls', and Infants' Cut and Sew Apparel Contractors (pt)
2339	. Athletic Uniforms, Except Contractors	315299	All Other Cut and Sew Apparel Manufacturing (pt)
2339	. All Other, Except Contractors	315239	Women's and Girls' Cut and Sew Other Outerwear Manufacturing (pt)
2341	Women's, Misses', Children's, and Infants' Underwear and Nightwear		
2341	. Women's, Girls' and Infants' Contractors	315212	Women's, Girls', and Infants' Cut and Sew Apparel Contractors (pt)
2341	. Boys' Contractors	315211	Men's and Boys' Cut and Sew Apparel Contractors (pt)
2341	. Women's and Girls', Except Contractors	315231	Women's and Girls' Cut and Sew Lingerie, Loungewear, and Nightwear Manufacturing (pt)
2341	. Boys', Except Contractors	315221	Men's and Boys' Cut and Sew Underwear and Nightwear Manufacturing (pt)
2341	. Infants', Except Contractors	315291	Infants' Cut and Sew Apparel Manufacturing (pt)
2342	Brassieres, Girdles, and Allied Garments		
2342	. Contractors	315212	Women's, Girls', and Infants' Cut and Sew Apparel Contractors (pt)
2342	. Except contractors	315231	Women's and Girls' Cut and Sew Lingerie, Loungewear, and Nightwear Manufacturing (pt)
2353	Hats, Caps, and Millinery		
2353	. Men's and Boys' Contractors	315211	Men's and Boys' Cut and Sew Apparel Contractors (pt)
2353	. Women's, Girls', and Infants' Contractors	315212	Women's, Girls', and Infants' Cut and Sew Apparel Contractors (pt)
2353	. Except Contractors	315991	Hat, Cap, and Millinery Manufacturing
2361	Girls', Children's, and Infants' Dresses, Blouses, and Shirts		
2361	. Infants' Dresses, Blouses, and Shirts, Except Contractors	315291	Infants' Cut and Sew Apparel Manufacturing (pt)
2361	. Boys' Shirts, Except Contractors	315223	Men's and Boys' Cut and Sew Shirt, (except Work Shirt) Manufacturing (pt)
2361	. Boys' Shirt Contractors	315211	Men's and Boys' Cut and Sew Apparel Contractors (pt)
2361	. Girls' Blouses and Shirts, Except Contractors	315232	Women's and Girls' Cut and Sew Blouse and Shirt Manufacturing (pt)
2361	. Girls' Dresses, Except Contractors	315233	Women's and Girls' Cut and Sew Dress Manufacturing (pt)
2361	. Girls' and Infants' Contractors	315212	Women's, Girls', and Infants' Cut and Sew Apparel Contractors (pt)

SIC Code	SIC Industry Title	NAICS Code	NAICS Industry Title
2369	Girls', Children's, and Infants' Outerwear, NEC		
2369	. Infants' Outerwear, NEC, Except Contractors	315291	Infants' Cut and Sew Apparel Manufacturing (pt)
2369	. Boys' Suits and Coats, Except Contractors	315222	Men's and Boys' Cut and Sew Suit, Coat, and Overcoat Manufacturing (pt)
2369	. Boys' Trousers and Slacks, Except Contractors	315224	Men's and Boys' Cut and Sew Trouser, Slack, and Jean Manufacturing (pt)
2369	. Boys' Outerwear, NEC, Except Contractors	315228	Men's and Boys' Cut and Sew Other Outerwear Manufacturing (pt)
2369	. Boys' Robes, Except Contractors	315221	Men's and Boys' Cut and Sew Underwear and Nightwear Manufacturing (pt)
2369	. Boys' Contractors	315211	Men's and Boys' Cut and Sew Apparel Contractors (pt)
2369	. Girls' Suits, Coats, Skirts, Etc., Except Contractors	315234	Women's and Girls' Cut and Sew Suit, Coat, Tailored Jacket, and Skirt Manufacturing (pt)
2369	. Girls' Outerwear, NEC, Except Contractors	315239	Women's and Girls' Cut and Sew Other Outerwear Manufacturing (pt)
2369	. Girls' Robes, Except Contractors	315231	Women's and Girls' Cut and Sew Lingerie, Loungewear, and Nightwear Manufacturing (pt)
2369	. Girls' Contractors	315212	Women's, Girls', and Infants' Cut and Sew Apparel Contractors (pt)
2371	Fur Goods		
2371	. Men's and Boys' Contractors	315211	Men's and Boys' Cut and Sew Apparel Contractors (pt)
2371	. Women's, Girls', and Infants' Contractors	315212	Women's, Girls', and Infants' Cut and Sew Apparel Contractors (pt)
2371	. Except Contractors	315292	Fur and Leather Apparel Manufacturing (pt)
2381	Dress and Work Gloves, Except Knit and All-Leather		
2381	. Men's and Boys' Contractors	315211	Men's and Boys' Cut and Sew Apparel Contractors (pt)
2381	. Women's, Girls', and Infants' Contractors	315212	Women's, Girls', and Infants' Cut and Sew Apparel Contractors (pt)
2381	. Except Contractors	315992	Glove and Mitten Manufacturing (pt)
2384	Robes and Dressing Gowns		
2384	. Women's Except Contractors	315231	Women's and Girls' Cut and Sew Lingerie, Loungewear, and Nightwear Manufacturing (pt)
2384	. Men's Except Contractors	315221	Men's and Boys' Cut and Sew Underwear and Nightwear Manufacturing (pt)
2384	. Men's and Boys' Contractors	315211	Men's and Boys' Cut and Sew Apparel Contractors (pt)
2384	. Women's and Girls' Contractors	315212	Women's, Girls', and Infants' Cut and Sew Apparel Contractors (pt)
2385	Waterproof Outerwear		
2385	. Men's and Boys' Water Resistant or Water Repellent Tailored Overcoats	315222	Men's and Boys' Cut and Sew Suit, Coat, and Overcoat Manufacturing (pt)

SIC Code	SIC Industry Title	NAICS Code	NAICS Industry Title
2385	. Women's and Girls' Water Resistant or Water Repellent Tailored Coats	315234	Women's and Girls' Cut and Sew Suit, Coat, Tailored Jacket, and Skirt Manufacturing (pt)
2385	. Men's and Boys' Water Resistant or Water Repellent Nontailored Outerwear, except Rubber and Plastics and Contractors	315228	Men's and Boys' Cut and Sew Other Outerwear Manufacturing (pt)
2385	. Women's and Girls' Water Resistant or Water Repellent Nontailored Outerwear, except Rubber and Plastics and Contractors	315239	Women's and Girls' Cut and Sew Other Outerwear Manufacturing (pt)
2385	. Infants' Waterproof Outerwear Except Contractors	315291	Infants' Cut and Sew Apparel Manufacturing (pt)
2385	. Waterproof Rubber and Plastics Outerwear, Except Contractors	315299	All Other Cut and Sew Apparel Manufacturing (pt)
2385	. Accessories such as Aprons, Bibs, and Miscellaneous Waterproof Items, Except Contractors	315999	Other Apparel Accessories and Other Apparel Manufacturing (pt)
2385	. Men's and Boys' Contractors	315211	Men's and Boys' Cut and Sew Apparel Contractors (pt)
2385	. Women's and Girls' Contractors	315212	Women's, Girls', and Infants' Cut and Sew Apparel Contractors (pt)
2386	Leather and Sheep-Lined Clothing		
2386	. Men's and Boys' Contractors	315211	Men's and Boys' Cut and Sew Apparel Contractors (pt)
2386	. Women's, Girls', and Infants' Contractors	315212	Women's, Girls', and Infants' Cut and Sew Apparel Contractors (pt)
2386	. Except Contractors	315292	Fur and Leather Apparel Manufacturing (pt)
2387	Apparel Belts		
2387	. Men's and Boys' Contractors	315211	Men's and Boys' Cut and Sew Apparel Contractors (pt)
2387	. Women's, Girls', and Infants' Contractors	315212	Women's, Girls', and Infants' Cut and Sew Apparel Contractors (pt)
2387	. Except Contractors	315999	Other Apparel Accessories and Other Apparel Manufacturing (pt)
2389	Apparel and Accessories, NEC		
2389	. Handkerchiefs, Arm bands, etc.	315999	Other Apparel Accessories and Other Apparel Manufacturing (pt)
2389	. Academic and Clerical Outerwear	315299	All Other Cut and Sew Apparel Manufacturing (pt)
2389	. Garters and Garter Belts	315231	Women's and Girls' Cut and Sew Lingerie, Loungewear, and Nightwear Manufacturing (pt)
2389	. Women's Contractors	315212	Women's, Girls', and Infants' Cut and Sew Apparel Contractors (pt)
2389	. Men's Contractors	315211	Men's and Boys' Cut and Sew Apparel Contractors (pt)
2391	Curtains and Draperies	314121	Curtain and Drapery Mills (pt)
2392	Housefurnishings, Except Curtains and Draperies		
2392	. Blanket, Laundry, and Garment Storage Bags	314911	Textile Bag Mills (pt)

SIC Code	SIC Industry Title	NAICS Code	NAICS Industry Title
2392	. Dust Rags	314999	All Other Miscellaneous Textile Product Mills (pt)
2392	. Mops, Floor and Dust	339994	Broom, Brush, and Mop Manufacturing (pt)
2392	. Other Housefurnishings	314129	Other Household Textile Product Mills (pt)
2393	Textile Bags	314911	Textile Bag Mills (pt)
2394	Canvas and Related Products	314912	Canvas and Related Product Mills (pt)
2395	Pleating, Decorative and Novelty Stitching, and Tucking for the Trade		
2395	. Pleating and Stitching, Except Apparel Contractors	314999	All Other Miscellaneous Textile Product Mills (pt)
2395	. Men's and Boys' Apparel Contractors	315211	Men's and Boys' Cut and Sew Apparel Contractors (pt)
2395	. Women's, Girls', and Infants' Apparel Contractors	315212	Women's, Girls', and Infants' Cut and Sew Apparel Contractors (pt)
2396	Automotive Trimmings, Apparel Findings, and Related Products		
2396	. Textile Automotive Trimmings	33636	Motor Vehicle Seating and Interior Trim Manufacturing (pt)
2396	. Apparel Findings and Trimmings	315999	Other Apparel Accessories and Other Apparel Manufacturing (pt)
2396	. Printing and Embossing on Fabric Articles	323113	Commercial Screen Printing (pt)
2396	. Other Apparel Products	314999	All Other Miscellaneous Textile Product Mills (pt)
2397	Schiffli Machine Embroideries	313222	Schiffli Machine Embroidery
2399	Fabricated Textile Products, NEC		
2399	. Seat Belts and Seat and Tire Covers	33636	Motor Vehicle Seating and Interior Trim Manufacturing (pt)
2399	. Apparel and Apparel Accessories	315999	Other Apparel Accessories and Other Apparel Manufacturing (pt)
2399	. Other Fabricated Textile Products	314999	All Other Miscellaneous Textile Product Mills (pt)
24	Lumber and wood products		
2411	Logging	11331	Logging
2421	Sawmills and Planing Mills, General		
2421	. Lumber Manufacturing from Purchased Lumber, Softwood Cut Stock, Wood Lath and Planing Mill Products	321912	Cut Stock, Resawing Lumber, and Planing (pt)
2421	. Sawmills	321113	Sawmills (pt)
2421	. Softwood Flooring	321918	Other Millwork (including Flooring) (pt)
2421	. Kiln Drying	321999	All Other Miscellaneous Wood Product Manufacturing (pt)
2426	Hardwood Dimension and Flooring Mills		
2426	. Hardwood Flooring	321918	Other Millwork (including Flooring) (pt)
2426	. Wood Furniture Frames	337215	Showcase, Partition, Shelving, and Locker Manufacturing (pt)
2426	. Hardwood Dimension Lumber Made From Logs and Bolts	321113	Sawmills (pt)
2426	. Other Hardwood Dimension Except Flooring	321912	Cut Stock, Resawing Lumber, and Planing (pt)

SIC Code	SIC Industry Title	NAICS Code	NAICS Industry Title
2429	Special Product Sawmills, NEC		
2429	. Shingle Mills, Shakes	321113	Sawmills (pt)
2429	. Stave Manufacturing from Purchased Lumber	321912	Cut Stock, Resawing Lumber, and Planing (pt)
2429	. Cooperage Stock	32192	Wood Container and Pallet Manufacturing (pt)
2429	. Excelsior and Cooperage Headings	321999	All Other Miscellaneous Wood Product Manufacturing (pt)
2431	Millwork		
2431	. Wood Windows and Doors	321911	Wood Window and Door Manufacturing
2431	. Except Wood Windows and Doors	321918	Other Millwork (including Flooring) (pt)
2434	Wood Kitchen Cabinets	33711	Wood Kitchen Cabinet and Countertop Manufacturing (pt)
2435	Hardwood Veneer and Plywood	321211	Hardwood Veneer and Plywood Manufacturing
2436	Softwood Veneer and Plywood	321212	Softwood Veneer and Plywood Manufacturing
2439	Structural Wood Members, NEC		
2439	. Trusses	321214	Truss Manufacturing
2439	. Except Trusses	321213	Engineered Wood Member (except Truss) Manufacturing
2441	Nailed and Lock Corner Wood Boxes and Shook	32192	Wood Container and Pallet Manufacturing (pt)
2448	Wood Pallets and Skids	32192	Wood Container and Pallet Manufacturing (pt)
2449	Wood Containers, NEC	32192	Wood Container and Pallet Manufacturing (pt)
2451	Mobile Homes	321991	Manufactured Home (Mobile Home) Manufacturing
2452	Prefabricated Wood Buildings and Components	321992	Prefabricated Wood Building Manufacturing
2491	Wood Preserving	321114	Wood Preservation
2493	Reconstituted Wood Products	321219	Reconstituted Wood Product Manufacturing
2499	Wood Products, NEC		
2499	. Mirror and Picture Frames	339999	All Other Miscellaneous Manufacturing (pt)
2499	. Wood Cooling Towers	333414	Heating Equipment (except Warm Air Furnace) Manufacturing (pt)
2499	. Wood Tubs and Vats, Jewelry, Cigar Boxes, and Baskets, Except Fruit, Fish, and Bait	32192	Wood Container and Pallet Manufacturing (pt)
2499	. Other Wood Products	321999	All Other Miscellaneous Wood Product Manufacturing (pt)
25	Furniture and fixtures		
2511	Wood Household Furniture, Except Upholstered		
2511	. Wood Box Spring Frames	337215	Showcase, Partition, Shelving, and Locker Manufacturing (pt)
2511	. Except Wood Box Spring Frames	337122	Wood Household Furniture (except Upholstered) Manufacturing (pt)
2512	Wood Household Furniture, Upholstered	337121	Upholstered Household Furniture Manufacturing (pt)
2514	Metal Household Furniture		
2514	. Except Upholstered and Metal Box Spring Frames	337124	Metal Household Furniture Manufacturing

SIC Code	SIC Industry Title	NAICS Code	NAICS Industry Title
2514	. Upholstered	337121	Upholstered Household Furniture Manufacturing (pt)
2514	. Metal Box Spring Frames	337215	Showcase, Partition, Shelving, and Locker Manufacturing (pt)
2515	Mattresses, Foundations, and Convertible Beds		
2515	. Mattresses and Foundations	33791	Mattress Manufacturing
2515	. Convertible Sofas	337121	Upholstered Household Furniture Manufacturing (pt)
2517	Wood Television, Radio, Phonograph and Sewing Machine Cabinets	337129	Wood Television, Radio, and Sewing Machine Cabinet Manufacturing
2519	Household Furniture, NEC	337125	Household Furniture (except Wood and Metal) Manufacturing
2521	Wood Office Furniture	337211	Wood Office Furniture Manufacturing
2522	Office Furniture, Except Wood	337214	Office Furniture (except Wood) Manufacturing
2531	Public Building and Related Furniture		
2531	. Seats for Motor Vehicles	33636	Motor Vehicle Seating and Interior Trim Manufacturing (pt)
2531	. Furniture Made for Public Buildings	337127	Institutional Furniture Manufacturing (pt)
2531	. Blackboards	339942	Lead Pencil and Art Good Manufacturing (pt)
2541	Wood Office and Store Fixtures, Partitions, Shelving, and Lockers		
2541	. Wood Lunchroom Tables and Chairs	337127	Institutional Furniture Manufacturing (pt)
2541	. Custom Architectural Woodwork, Millwork and Fixtures	337212	Custom Architectural Woodwork and Millwork Manufacturing
2541	. Except Countertops, Custom Architectural Woodwork, Millwork, and Fixtures	337215	Showcase, Partition, Shelving, and Locker Manufacturing (pt)
2542	Office and Store Fixtures, Partitions, Shelving, and Lockers, Except Wood		
2542	. Lunchroom Tables and Chairs (except wood)	337127	Institutional Furniture Manufacturing (pt)
2542	. Except Lunchroom Tables and Chairs (except wood)	337215	Showcase, Partition, Shelving, and Locker Manufacturing (pt)
2591	Drapery Hardware and Window Blinds and Shades	33792	Blind and Shade Manufacturing
2599	Furniture and Fixtures, NEC		
2599	. Hospital Beds	339111	Laboratory Apparatus and Furniture Manufacturing (pt)
2599	. Except Hospital Beds	337127	Institutional Furniture Manufacturing (pt)
26	Paper and allied products		
2611	Pulp Mills		
2611	. Pulp Producing Mills Only	32211	Pulp Mills
2611	. Pulp Mills Producing Paper	322121	Paper (except Newsprint) Mills (pt)
2611	. Pulp Mills Producing Newsprint	322122	Newsprint Mills (pt)
2611	. Pulp Mills Producing Paperboard	32213	Paperboard Mills (pt)

SIC Code	SIC Industry Title	NAICS Code	NAICS Industry Title
2621	Paper Mills		
2621	. Except Newsprint Mills	322121	Paper (except Newsprint) Mills (pt)
2621	. Newsprint Mills	322122	Newsprint Mills (pt)
2631	Paperboard Mills	32213	Paperboard Mills (pt)
2652	Setup Paperboard Boxes	322213	Setup Paperboard Box Manufacturing
2653	Corrugated and Solid Fiber Boxes	322211	Corrugated and Solid Fiber Box Manufacturing (pt)
2655	Fiber Cans, Tubes, Drums, and Similar Products	322214	Fiber Can, Tube, Drum, and Similar Products Manufacturing
2656	Sanitary Food Containers, Except Folding	322215	Nonfolding Sanitary Food Container Manufacturing
2657	Folding Paperboard Boxes, Including Sanitary	322212	Folding Paperboard Box Manufacturing
2671	Packaging Paper and Plastics Film, Coated and Laminated		
2671	. Single-Web Paper, Paper Multiweb Laminated Rolls and Sheets for Packaging Uses	322221	Coated and Laminated Packaging Paper and Plastics Film Manufacturing
2671	. Plastics Packaging Film and Sheet	326112	Unsupported Plastics Packaging Film and Sheet Manufacturing
2672	Coated and Laminated Paper, NEC	322222	Coated and Laminated Paper Manufacturing (pt)
2673	Plastics, Foil, and Coated Paper Bags		
2673	. Except All Plastics	322223	Plastics, Foil, and Coated Paper Bag Manufacturing
2673	. Plastics Bags	326111	Unsupported Plastics Bag Manufacturing
2674	Uncoated Paper and Multiwall Bags	322224	Uncoated Paper and Multiwall Bag Manufacturing
2675	Die-Cut Paper and Paperboard and Cardboard		
2675	. File Folders, Tabulating Cards, and Other Paper and Paperboard Office Supplies	322231	Die-Cut Paper and Paperboard Office Supplies Manufacturing (pt)
2675	. Pasted, Lined, Laminated, or Surface-Coated Paperboard	322226	Surface-Coated Paperboard Manufacturing
2675	. Die-Cut Paper and Paperboard Products, Except Office Supplies and Pasted, Lined, Laminated, or Surface-Coated Paperboard	322299	All Other Converted Paper Product Manufacturing (pt)
2676	Sanitary Paper Products	322291	Sanitary Paper Product Manufacturing (pt)
2677	Envelopes	322232	Envelope Manufacturing
2678	Stationery, Tablets, and Related Products	322233	Stationery, Tablet, and Related Product Manufacturing
2679	Converted Paper and Paperboard Products, NEC		
2679	. Corrugated Paper	322211	Corrugated and Solid Fiber Box Manufacturing (pt)
2679	. Wallpaper and Gift Wrap Paper	322222	Coated and Laminated Paper Manufacturing (pt)
2679	. Paper Supplies for Business Machines and Other Paper Office Supplies	322231	Die-Cut Paper and Paperboard Office Supplies Manufacturing (pt)
2679	. Other Converted Paper and Paperboard Products, such as Paper Filters, Crepe Paper, and Laminated and Tiled Wallboard	322299	All Other Converted Paper Product Manufacturing (pt)
27	Printing and publishing		

SIC Code	SIC Industry Title	NAICS Code	NAICS Industry Title
2711	Newspapers: Publishing, or Publishing and Printing	51111	Newspaper Publishers
2721	Periodicals: Publishing, or Publishing and Printing	51112	Periodical Publishers (pt)
2731	Books: Publishing, or Publishing and Printing		
2731	. Music Book Publishing	51223	Music Publishers (pt)
2731	. All Other Book Publishers	51113	Book Publishers
2732	Book Printing	323117	Books Printing
2741	Miscellaneous Publishing		
2741	. Database Publishing	51114	Database and Directory Publishers (pt)
2741	. Shopping News	51112	Periodical Publishers (pt)
2741	. Technical Manuals and Books	51113	Book Publishers (pt)
2741	. Sheet Music Publishers	51223	Music Publishers (pt)
2741	. Miscellaneous Publishing, Except Database, Shopping News, Technical Manuals and Books, and Sheet Music	511199	All Other Publishers
2752	Commercial Printing, Lithographic		
2752	. Quick Printing	323114	Quick Printing (pt)
2752	. Except Quick Printing	323110	Commercial Lithographic Printing (pt)
2754	Commercial Printing, Gravure	323111	Commercial Gravure Printing (pt)
2759	Commercial Printing, NEC		
2759	. Screen Printing	323113	Commercial Screen Printing (pt)
2759	. Flexographic Printing	323112	Commercial Flexographic Printing (pt)
2759	. Quick Printing	323114	Quick Printing (pt)
2759	. Digital Printing, except Quick Printing	323115	Digital Printing
2759	. Other Commercial Printing	323119	Other Commercial Printing (pt)
2761	Manifold Business Forms	323116	Manifold Business Forms Printing (pt)
2771	Greeting Cards		
2771	. Lithographic Printing of Greeting Cards	323110	Commercial Lithographic Printing (pt)
2771	. Gravure Printing of Greeting Cards	323111	Commercial Gravure Printing (pt)
2771	. Flexographic Printing of Greeting Cards	323112	Commercial Flexographic Printing (pt)
2771	. Screen Printing of Greeting Cards	323113	Commercial Screen Printing (pt)
2771	. Other Printing of Greeting Cards	323119	Other Commercial Printing (pt)
2771	. Publishing Greeting Cards	511191	Greeting Card Publishers
2782	Blankbooks, Loose-leaf Binders and Devices		
2782	. Printing of Checkbooks	323116	Manifold Business Forms Printing (pt)
2782	. Blankbooks, Loose-leaf Binders and Devices	323118	Blankbook, Looseleaf Binders, and Devices Manufacturing
2789	Bookbinding and Related Work	323121	Tradebinding and Related Work

SIC Code	SIC Industry Title	NAICS Code	NAICS Industry Title
2791	Typesetting	323122	Prepress Services (pt)
2796	Platemaking and Related Services	323122	Prepress Services (pt)
28	Chemicals and allied products		
2812	Alkalies and Chlorine	325181	Alkalies and Chlorine Manufacturing
2813	Industrial Gases	32512	Industrial Gas Manufacturing (pt)
2816	Inorganic Pigments		
2816	. Except Bone and Lamp Black	325131	Inorganic Dye and Pigment Manufacturing (pt)
2816	. Bone and Lamp Black	325182	Carbon Black Manufacturing (pt)
2819	Industrial Inorganic Chemicals, NEC		
2819	. Recovering Sulfur from Natural Gas	211112	Natural Gas Liquid Extraction (pt)
2819	. Activated Carbon and Charcoal	325998	All Other Miscellaneous Chemical Product and Preparation Manufacturing (pt)
2819	. Alumina	331311	Alumina Refining
2819	. Inorganic Dyes	325131	Inorganic Dye and Pigment Manufacturing (pt)
2819	. Other	325188	All Other Basic Inorganic Chemical Manufacturing (pt)
2821	Plastics Material and Synthetic Resins, and Nonvulcanizable Elastomers	325211	Plastics Material and Resin Manufacturing
2822	Synthetic Rubber	325212	Synthetic Rubber Manufacturing
2823	Cellulosic Manmade Fibers	325221	Cellulosic Organic Fiber Manufacturing
2824	Manmade Organic Fibers, Except Cellulosic	325222	Noncellulosic Organic Fiber Manufacturing
2833	Medicinal Chemicals and Botanical Products	325411	Medicinal and Botanical Manufacturing
2834	Pharmaceutical Preparations	325412	Pharmaceutical Preparation Manufacturing (pt)
2835	In Vitro and In Vivo Diagnostic Substances		
2835	. Except In Vitro Diagnostic	325412	Pharmaceutical Preparation Manufacturing (pt)
2835	. In Vitro Diagnostic Substances	325413	In-Vitro Diagnostic Substance Manufacturing
2836	Biological Products, Except Diagnostic Substances	325414	Biological Product (except Diagnostic) Manufacturing
2841	Soaps and Other Detergents, Except Speciality Cleaners	325611	Soap and Other Detergent Manufacturing (pt)
2842	Speciality Cleaning, Polishing, and Sanitary Preparations	325612	Polish and Other Sanitation Good Manufacturing
2843	Surface Active Agents, Finishing Agents, Sulfonated Oils, and Assistants	325613	Surface Active Agent Manufacturing
2844	Perfumes, Cosmetics, and Other Toilet Preparations		
2844	. Toilet Preparations, Except Toothpaste	32562	Toilet Preparation Manufacturing
2844	. Toothpaste	325611	Soap and Other Detergent Manufacturing (pt)
2851	Paints, Varnishes, Lacquers, Enamels, and Allied Products	32551	Paint and Coating Manufacturing (pt)
2861	Gum and Wood Chemicals	325191	Gum and Wood Chemical Manufacturing
2865	Cyclic Organic Crudes and Intermediates, and Organic Dyes and Pigments		

SIC Code	SIC Industry Title	NAICS Code	NAICS Industry Title
2865	. Aromatics	32511	Petrochemical Manufacturing (pt)
2865	. Organic Dyes and Pigments	325132	Synthetic Organic Dye and Pigment Manufacturing
2865	. Other	325192	Cyclic Crude and Intermediate Manufacturing
2869	Industrial Organic Chemicals, NEC		
2869	. Aliphatics	32511	Petrochemical Manufacturing (pt)
2869	. Carbon Bisulfide	325188	All Other Inorganic Chemical Manufacturing (pt)
2869	. Ethyl Alcohol	325193	Ethyl Alcohol Manufacturing
2869	. Fluorocarbon Gases	32512	Industrial Gas Manufacturing (pt)
2869	. Other	325199	All Other Basic Organic Chemical Manufacturing (pt)
2873	Nitrogenous Fertilizers	325311	Nitrogenous Fertilizer Manufacturing
2874	Phosphatic Fertilizers	325312	Phosphatic Fertilizer Manufacturing
2875	Fertilizers, Mixing Only	325314	Fertilizer (Mixing Only) Manufacturing
2879	Pesticides and Agricultural Chemicals, NEC	32532	Pesticide and Other Agricultural Chemical Manufacturing
2891	Adhesives and Sealants	32552	Adhesive Manufacturing
2892	Explosives	32592	Explosives Manufacturing
2893	Printing Ink	32591	Printing Ink Manufacturing
2895	Carbon Black	325182	Carbon Black Manufacturing (pt)
2899	Chemicals and Chemical Preparations, NEC		
2899	. Frit	32551	Paint and Coating Manufacturing (pt)
2899	. Table Salt	311942	Spice and Extract Manufacturing (pt)
2899	. Fatty Acids	325199	All Other Basic Organic Chemical Manufacturing (pt)
2899	. Other	325998	All Other Miscellaneous Chemical Product and Preparation Manufacturing (pt)
29	Petroleum and coal products		
2911	Petroleum Refining	32411	Petroleum Refineries
2951	Asphalt Paving Mixtures and Blocks	324121	Asphalt Paving Mixture and Block Manufacturing
2952	Asphalt Felts and Coatings	324122	Asphalt Shingle and Coating Materials Manufacturing
2992	Lubricating Oils and Greases	324191	Petroleum Lubricating Oil and Grease Manufacturing
2999	Products of Petroleum and Coal, NEC	324199	All Other Petroleum and Coal Products Manufacturing (pt)
30	Rubber and miscellaneous plastics products		
3011	Tires and Inner Tubes	326211	Tire Manufacturing (except Retreading)
3021	Rubber and Plastics Footwear	316211	Rubber and Plastics Footwear Manufacturing
3052	Rubber and Plastics Hose and Belting	32622	Rubber and Plastics Hoses and Belting Manufacturing
3053	Gaskets, Packing, and Sealing Devices	339991	Gasket, Packing, and Sealing Device Manufacturing
3061	Molded, Extruded, and Lathe-Cut Mechanical Rubber Goods	326291	Rubber Product Manufacturing for Mechanical Use

SIC Code	SIC Industry Title	NAICS Code	NAICS Industry Title
3069	Fabricated Rubber Products, NEC		
3069	. Rubberizing Fabric or Purchased Textile Products	31332	Fabric Coating Mills (pt)
3069	. Rubber Pants and Raincoats	315299	All Other Cut and Sew Apparel Manufacturing (pt)
3069	. Rubber Bibs, Aprons, and Bathing Caps	315999	Other Apparel Accessories and Other Apparel (pt)
3069	. Rubber Gloves and Life Jackets	339113	Surgical Appliance and Supplies Manufacturing (pt)
3069	. Rubber Wet Suits	33992	Sporting and Athletic Goods Manufacturing (pt)
3069	. Rubber Toys, Except Dolls	339932	Game, Toy, and Children's Vehicle Manufacturing (pt)
3069	. Rubber Resilient Floor Covering	326192	Resilient Floor Covering Manufacturing (pt)
3069	. Other	326299	All Other Rubber Product Manufacturing
3081	Unsupported Plastics Film and Sheet	326113	Unsupported Plastics Film and Sheet (except Packaging) Manufacturing
3082	Unsupported Plastics Profile Shapes	326121	Unsupported Plastics Profile Shape Manufacturing (pt)
3083	Laminated Plastics Plate, Sheet, and Profile Shapes	32613	Laminated Plastics Plate, Sheet, and Shape Manufacturing
3084	Plastics Pipe	326122	Plastics Pipe and Pipe Fitting Manufacturing (pt)
3085	Plastics Bottles	32616	Plastics Bottle Manufacturing
3086	Plastics Foam Products		
3086	. Urethane and Other Foam Products	32615	Urethane and Other Foam Product (except Polystyrene) Manufacturing
3086	. Polystyrene Foam Products	32614	Polystyrene Foam Product Manufacturing
3087	Custom Compounding of Purchased Plastics Resins	325991	Custom Compounding of Purchased Resin
3088	Plastics Plumbing Fixtures	326191	Plastics Plumbing Fixtures Manufacturing
3089	Plastics Products, NEC		
3089	. Pipe Fittings	326122	Plastics Pipe and Pipe Fitting Manufacturing (pt)
3089	. Plastics Sausage Casings	326121	Unsupported Plastics Profile Shape Manufacturing (pt)
3089	. Finished Plastics Furniture Parts	337215	Showcase, Partition, Shelving, and Locker Manufacturing (pt)
3089	. Other	326199	All Other Plastics Product Manufacturing (pt)
31	Leather and leather products		
3111	Leather Tanning and Finishing	31611	Leather and Hide Tanning and Finishing (pt)
3131	Boot and Shoe Cut Stock and Findings		
3131	. Wood Heels	321999	All Other Miscellaneous Wood Product Manufacturing (pt)
3131	. Metal Buckles	339993	Fastener, Button, Needle, and Pin Manufacturing (pt)
3131	. Except Wood Heels and Metal Buckles	316999	All Other Leather Good Manufacturing (pt)
3142	House Slippers	316212	House Slipper Manufacturing
3143	Men's Footwear, Except Athletic	316213	Men's Footwear (except Athletic) Manufacturing
3144	Women's Footwear, Except Athletic	316214	Women's Footwear (except Athletic) Manufacturing

SIC Code	SIC Industry Title	NAICS Code	NAICS Industry Title
3149	Footwear, Except Rubber, NEC	316219	Other Footwear Manufacturing
3151	Leather Gloves and Mittens		
3151	. Men's and Boys' Contractors	315211	Men's and Boys' Cut and Sew Apparel Contractors (pt)
3151	. Women's, Girls', and Infants' Contractors Contractors (pt)	315212	Women's, Girls', and Infants' Cut and Sew Apparel
3151	. Except Contractors	315992	Glove and Mitten Manufacturing (pt)
3161	Luggage	316991	Luggage Manufacturing
3171	Women's Handbags and Purses	316992	Women's Handbag and Purse Manufacturing
3172	Personal Leather Goods, Except Women's Handbags and Purses	316993	Personal Leather Good (except Women's Handbag and Purse) Manufacturing
3199	Leather Goods, NEC	316999	All Other Leather Good Manufacturing (pt)
32	Stone, clay, glass, and concrete products		
3211	Flat Glass	327211	Flat Glass Manufacturing
3221	Glass Containers	327213	Glass Container Manufacturing
3229	Pressed and Blown Glass and Glassware, NEC	327212	Other Pressed and Blown Glass and Glassware Manufacturing
3231	Glass Products, Made of Purchased Glass	327215	Glass Product Manufacturing Made of Purchased Glass
3241	Cement, Hydraulic	32731	Cement Manufacturing
3251	Brick and Structural Clay Tile		
3251	. Slumped Brick	327331	Concrete Block and Brick Manufacturing (pt)
3251	. Except Slump Brick	327121	Brick and Structural Clay Tile Manufacturing
3253	Ceramic Wall and Floor Tile	327122	Ceramic Wall and Floor Tile Manufacturing
3255	Clay Refractories	327124	Clay Refractory Manufacturing
3259	Structural Clay Products, NEC	327123	Other Structural Clay Product Manufacturing
3261	Vitreous China Plumbing Fixtures and China and Earthenware Fittings and Bathroom Accessories	327111	Vitreous China Plumbing Fixture and China and Earthenware Bathroom Accessories Manufacturing
3262	Vitreous China Table and Kitchen Articles	327112	Vitreous China, Fine Earthenware, and Other Pottery Product Manufacturing (pt)
3263	Fine Earthenware (Whiteware) Table and Kitchen Articles	327112	Vitreous China, Fine Earthenware, and Other Pottery Product Manufacturing (pt)
3264	Porcelain Electrical Supplies	327113	Porcelain Electrical Supply Manufacturing
3269	Pottery Products, NEC	327112	Vitreous China, Fine Earthenware, and Other Pottery Product Manufacturing (pt)
3271	Concrete Block and Brick	327331	Concrete Block and Brick Manufacturing
3272	Concrete Products, Except Block and Brick		
3272	. Dry Mixture Concrete	327999	All Other Miscellaneous Nonmetallic Mineral Product Manufacturing (pt)
3272	. Concrete Pipes	327332	Concrete Pipe Manufacturing

SIC Code	SIC Industry Title	NAICS Code	NAICS Industry Title
3272	. Other Concrete Products	32739	Other Concrete Product Manufacturing
3273	Ready-Mixed Concrete	32732	Ready-Mix Concrete Manufacturing
3274	Lime	32741	Lime Manufacturing
3275	Gypsum Products	32742	Gypsum Product Manufacturing (pt)
3281	Cut Stone and Stone Products	327991	Cut Stone and Stone Product Manufacturing
3291	Abrasive Products		
3291	. Steel Wool With or Without Soap	332999	All Other Miscellaneous Fabricated Metal Product Manufacturing (pt)
3291	. Abrasive Products (Except Steel Wool With or Without Soap)	32791	Abrasive Product Manufacturing
3292	Asbestos Products		
3292	. Asbestos Brake Linings and Pads	33634	Motor Vehicle Brake System Manufacturing (pt)
3292	. Other Asbestos Products	327999	All Other Miscellaneous Nonmetallic Mineral Product Manufacturing (pt)
3295	Minerals and Earths, Ground or Otherwise Treated		
3295	. Grinding, Washing, Separating, etc. of Minerals in SIC 1455	212324	Kaolin and Ball Clay Mining (pt)
3295	. Grinding, Washing, Separating, etc. of Minerals in SIC 1459	212325	Clay and Ceramic and Refractory Minerals Mining (pt)
3295	. Grinding, Washing, Separating, etc. of Minerals in SIC 1479	212393	Other Chemical and Fertilizer Mineral Mining (pt)
3295	. Grinding, Washing, Separating, etc. of Minerals in SIC 1499	212399	All Other Nonmetallic Mineral Mining (pt)
3295	. Except Grinding, Washing, Separating, etc.	327992	Ground or Treated Mineral and Earth Manufacturing
3296	Mineral Wool	327993	Mineral Wool Manufacturing
3297	Nonclay Refractories	327125	Nonclay Refractory Manufacturing
3299	Nonmetallic Mineral Products, NEC		
3299	. Clay Statuary	327112	Vitreous China, Fine Earthenware, and Other Pottery Product Manufacturing (pt)
3299	. Moldings, Ornamental and Architectural Plaster Work, and Gypsum Statuary	32742	Gypsum Product Manufacturing (pt)
3299	. Other Nonmetallic Mineral Products	327999	All Other Miscellaneous Nonmetallic Mineral Product Manufacturing (pt)
33	Primary metal industries		
3312	Steel Works, Blast Furnaces (Including Coke Ovens), and Rolling Mills		
3312	. Coke Ovens, Not Integrated With Steel Mills	324199	All Other Petroleum and Coal Products Manufacturing (pt)
3312	. Hot Rolling Purchased Steel	331221	Rolled Steel Shape Manufacturing (pt)
3312	. Except Coke Ovens Not Integrated with Steel Mills and Hot Rolling Purchased Steel	331111	Iron and Steel Mills (pt)
3313	Electrometallurgical Products, Except Steel	331112	Electrometallurgical Ferroalloy Product Manufacturing
3315	Steel Wiredrawing and Steel Nails and Spikes		

SIC Code	SIC Industry Title	NAICS Code	NAICS Industry Title
3315	. Steel Wire Drawing	331222	Steel Wire Drawing
3315	. Nails, Spikes, Paper Clips, and Wire, Not Made in Wire Drawing Plants	332618	Other Fabricated Wire Product Manufacturing (pt)
3316	Cold-Rolled Steel Sheet, Strip, and Bars	331221	Rolled Steel Shape Manufacturing (pt)
3317	Steel Pipe and Tubes	33121	Iron and Steel Pipe and Tube Manufacturing from Purchased Steel
3321	Gray and Ductile Iron Foundries	331511	Iron Foundries (pt)
3322	Malleable Iron Foundries	331511	Iron Foundries (pt)
3324	Steel Investment Foundries	331512	Steel Investment Foundries
3325	Steel Foundries, NEC	331513	Steel Foundries (except Investment)
3331	Primary Smelting and Refining of Copper	331411	Primary Smelting and Refining of Copper
3334	Primary Production of Aluminum	331312	Primary Aluminum Production
3339	Primary Smelting and Refining of Nonferrous Metals, Except Copper and Aluminum	331419	Primary Smelting and Refining of Nonferrous Metals (except Copper and Aluminum)
3341	Secondary Smelting and Refining of Nonferrous Metals		
3341	. Aluminum	331314	Secondary Smelting and Alloying of Aluminum (pt)
3341	. Copper	331423	Secondary Smelting, Refining, and Alloying of Copper (pt)
3341	. Except Aluminum and Copper	331492	Secondary Smelting, Refining, and Alloying of Nonferrous Metals (except Copper and Aluminum) (pt)
3351	Rolling, Drawing, and Extruding of Copper	331421	Copper Rolling, Drawing, and Extruding
3353	Aluminum Sheet, Plate, and Foil	331315	Aluminum Sheet, Plate, and Foil Manufacturing
3354	Aluminum Extruded Products	331316	Aluminum Extruded Product Manufacturing
3355	Aluminum Rolling and Drawing, NEC	331319	Other Aluminum Rolling and Drawing, (pt)
3356	Rolling, Drawing, and Extruding of Nonferrous Metals, Except Copper and Aluminum	331491	Nonferrous Metal (except Copper and Aluminum) Rolling, Drawing, and Extruding (pt)
3357	Drawing and Insulating of Nonferrous Wire		
3357	. Aluminum Wire Drawing	331319	Other Aluminum Rolling and Drawing (pt)
3357	. Copper Wire Drawing	331422	Copper Wire (except Mechanical) Drawing
3357	. Wire Drawing Except Copper or Aluminum	331491	Nonferrous Metal (except Copper and Aluminum) Rolling, Drawing, and Extruding (pt)
3357	. Fiber Optic Cable - Insulating Only	335921	Fiber Optic Cable Manufacturing
3357	. All Other	335929	Other Communication and Energy Wire Manufacturing
3363	Aluminum Die-Castings	331521	Aluminum Die-Casting Foundries
3364	Nonferrous Die-Castings, Except Aluminum	331522	Nonferrous (except Aluminum) Die-Casting Foundries
3365	Aluminum Foundries	331524	Aluminum Foundries (except Die-Casting)
3366	Copper Foundries	331525	Copper Foundries (except Die-Casting)
3369	Nonferrous Foundries, Except Aluminum and Copper	331528	Other Nonferrous Foundries (except Die-Casting)

SIC Code	SIC Industry Title	NAICS Code	NAICS Industry Title
3398	Metal Heat Treating	332811	Metal Heat Treating
3399	Primary Metal Products, NEC		
3399	. Aluminum Powder, Paste, Flakes, etc.	331314	Secondary Smelting and Alloying of Aluminum (pt)
3399	. Copper Powder, Flakes, Paste, etc.	331423	Secondary Smelting, Refining, and Alloying of Copper (pt)
3399	. Other Nonferrous Powder, Paste, Flakes, etc.	331492	Secondary Smelting, Refining, and Alloying of Nonferrous Metals (except Copper and Aluminum) (pt)
3399	. Making Ferrous Metal Powder, Paste, and Flake From Purchased Iron or Steel	331221	Rolled Steel Shape Manufacturing (pt)
3399	. Nonferrous Nails, Brads, Staples, etc.	332618	Other Fabricated Wire Product Manufacturing (pt)
3399	. Laminated Steel	332813	Electroplating, Plating, Polishing, Anodizing, and Coloring (pt)
34	Fabricated metal products		
3411	Metal Cans	332431	Metal Can Manufacturing
3412	Metal Shipping Barrels, Drums, Kegs, and Pails	332439	Other Metal Container Manufacturing (pt)
3421	Cutlery		
3421	. Except Tool-Type Shears	332211	Cutlery and Flatware (except Precious) Manufacturing (pt)
3421	. Tool-Type Shears	332212	Hand and Edge Tool Manufacturing (pt)
3423	Hand and Edge Tools, Except Machine Tools and Handsaws	332212	Hand and Edge Tool Manufacturing (pt)
3425	Saw Blades and Handsaws	332213	Saw Blade and Handsaw Manufacturing
3429	Hardware, NEC		
3429	. Fireplace Fixtures, Traps, Handcuffs and Leg Irons, Ladder Jacks, and Other Like Metal Products	332999	All Other Miscellaneous Fabricated Metal Products Manufacturing (pt)
3429	. Vacuum and Insulated Bottles, Jugs, and Chests	332439	Other Metal Container Manufacturing (pt)
3429	. Turnbuckles and Hose Clamps	332722	Bolt, Nut, Screw, Rivet, and Washer Manufacturing (pt)
3429	. Luggage and Utility Racks	336399	All Other Motor Vehicle Parts Manufacturing (pt)
3429	. Fire Hose Nozzles and Couplings	332919	Other Metal Valve and Pipe Fitting Manufacturing (pt)
3429	. Convertible Bed Sleeper Mechanisms and Chair Glides	337215	Showcase, Partition, Shelving, and Locker Manufacturing (pt)
3429	. Other Hardware	33251	Hardware Manufacturing (pt)
3431	Enameled Iron and Metal Sanitary Ware	332998	Enameled Iron and Metal Sanitary Ware Manufacturing
3432	Plumbing Fixture Fittings and Trim		
3432	. Plumbing Fixture Fittings and Trim, Except Metal Shower Rods and Lawn Hose Nozzles	332913	Plumbing Fixture Fitting and Trim Manufacturing
3432	. Lawn Hose Nozzles	332919	Other Metal Valve and Pipe Fitting Manufacturing (pt)
3432	. Metal Shower Rods	332999	All Other Miscellaneous Fabricated Metal Product Manufacturing (pt)
3433	Heating Equipment, Except Electric and Warm Air Furnaces	333414	Heating Equipment Manufacturing, (except Warm Air Furnaces) (pt)
3441	Fabricated Structural Metal	332312	Fabricated Structural Metal Manufacturing (pt)

SIC Code	SIC Industry Title	NAICS Code	NAICS Industry Title
3442	Metal Doors, Sash, Frames, Molding, and Trim Manufacturing	332321	Metal Window and Door Manufacturing (pt)
3443	Fabricated Plate Work (Boiler Shops)		
3443	. Fabricated Plate Work and Metal Weldments	332313	Plate Work Manufacturing
3443	. Power Boilers and Heat Exchanges	33241	Power Boiler and Heat Exchanger Manufacturing (pt)
3443	. Heavy Gauge Tanks	33242	Metal Tank (Heavy Gauge) Manufacturing
3443	. Metal Cooling Towers	333414	Heating Equipment (except Warm Air Furnaces) Manufacturing (pt)
3444	Sheet Metal Work		
3444	. Ducts, Flumes, Flooring. Siding, Dampers, etc.	332322	Sheet Metal Work Manufacturing
3444	. Metal Bins and Vats	332439	Other Metal Container Manufacturing (pt)
3444	. Cooling Towers	333414	Heating Equipment (except Warm Air Furnaces) Manufacturing (pt)
3446	Architectural and Ornamental Metal Work	332323	Ornamental and Architectural Metal Work Manufacturing (pt)
3448	Prefabricated Metal Buildings and Components	332311	Prefabricated Metal Building and Component Manufacturing
3449	Miscellaneous Structural Metal Work		
3449	. Custom Roll Forming	332114	Custom Roll Forming
3449	. Fabricated Bar Joists and Concrete Reinforcing Bars	332312	Fabricated Structural Metal Manufacturing (pt)
3449	. Curtain Wall	332321	Metal Window and Door Manufacturing (pt)
3449	. Metal Plaster Bases	332323	Ornamental and Architectural Metal Work Manufacturing (pt)
3451	Screw Machine Products	332721	Precision Turned Product Manufacturing
3452	Bolts, Nuts, Screws, Rivets, and Washers	332722	Bolt, Nut, Screw, Rivet, and Washer Manufacturing (pt)
3462	Iron and Steel Forgings	332111	Iron and Steel Forging
3463	Nonferrous Forgings	332112	Nonferrous Forging
3465	Automotive Stamping	33637	Motor Vehicle Metal Stamping
3466	Crowns and Closures	332115	Crown and Closure Manufacturing
3469	Metal Stamping, NEC		
3469	. Metal Stamping, NEC (Except Kitchen Utensils, Pots and Pans for Cooking, and Coins)	332116	Metal Stamping
3469	. Kitchen Utensils and Pots and Pans for Cooking	332214	Kitchen Utensil, Pot, and Pan Manufacturing
3471	Electroplating, Plating, Polishing, Anodizing, and Coloring	332813	Electroplating, Plating, Polishing, Anodizing, and Coloring (pt)
3479	Coating, Engraving, and Allied Services, NEC		
3479	. Jewelry Engraving and Etching, Costume Jewelry	339914	Costume Jewelry and Novelty Manufacturing (pt)
3479	. Jewelry Engraving and Etching, Precious Metal	339911	Jewelry (except Costume) Manufacturing (pt)
3479	. Silverware and Flatware Engraving and Etching	339912	Silverware and Holloware Manufacturing (pt)

SIC Code	SIC Industry Title	NAICS Code	NAICS Industry Title
3479	. Other Coating, Engraving and Allied Services	332812	Metal Coating, Engraving (except Jewelry and Silverware), and Allied Services to Manufacturers
3482	Small Arms Ammunition	332992	Small Arms Ammunition Manufacturing
3483	Ammunition, Except for Small Arms	332993	Ammunition (except Small Arms) Manufacturing
3484	Small Arms	332994	Small Arms Manufacturing (pt)
3489	Ordnance and Accessories, NEC	332995	Other Ordnance and Accessories Manufacturing
3491	Industrial Valves	332911	Industrial Valve Manufacturing
3492	Fluid Power Valves and Hose Fittings	332912	Fluid Power Valve and Hose Fitting Manufacturing (pt)
3493	Steel Springs, Except Wire	332611	Spring (Heavy Gauge) Manufacturing
3494	Valves and Pipe Fittings, NEC		
3494	. Except Metal Pipe Hangers and Supports	332919	Other Metal Valve and Pipe Fitting Manufacturing (pt)
3494	. Metal Pipe Hangers and Supports	332999	All Other Miscellaneous Fabricated Metal Product Manufacturing (pt)
3495	Wire Springs		
3495	. Wire Springs (Except Watch and Clock Springs)	332612	Spring (Light Gauge) Manufacturing
3495	. Watch and Clock Springs	334518	Watch, Clock, and Part Manufacturing (pt)
3496	Miscellaneous Fabricated Wire Products		
3496	. Grocery Carts	333924	Industrial Truck, Tractor, Trailer, and Stacker Machinery Manufacturing (pt)
3496	. Except Grocery Carts	332618	Other Fabricated Wire Product Manufacturing (pt)
3497	Metal Foil and Leaf		
3497	. Laminated Aluminum Foil Rolls/Sheets for Flexible Packaging Uses	322225	Laminated Aluminum Foil Manufacturing for Flexible Packaging Uses
3497	. Foil and Foil Containers	332999	All Other Miscellaneous Fabricated Metal Product Manufacturing (pt)
3498	Fabricated Pipe and Pipe Fittings	332996	Fabricated Pipe and Pipe Fitting Manufacturing
3499	Fabricated Metal Products, NEC		
3499	. Metal Furniture Frames	337215	Showcase, Partition, Shelving, and Locker Manufacturing (pt)
3499	. Metal Motor Vehicle Seat Frames	33636	Motor Vehicle Seating and Interior Trim Manufacturing (pt)
3499	. Powder Metallurgy	332117	Powder Metallurgy Part Manufacturing
3499	. Metal Boxes	332439	Other Metal Container Manufacturing (pt)
3499	. Safe and Vault Locks	33251	Hardware Manufacturing (pt)
3499	. Metal Aerosol Valves	332919	Other Metal Valve and Pipe Fitting Manufacturing (pt)
3499	. Other Metal Products	332999	All Other Miscellaneous Fabricated Metal Product Manufacturing (pt)
35	Industrial machinery and equipment		

SIC Code	SIC Industry Title	NAICS Code	NAICS Industry Title
3511	Steam, Gas, and Hydraulic Turbines, and Turbine Generator Set Units	333611	Turbine and Turbine Generator Set Unit Manufacturing
3519	Internal Combustion Engines, NEC		
3519	. Stationary Engine Radiators	336399	All Other Motor Vehicle Parts Manufacturing (pt)
3519	. Except Stationary Engine Radiators	333618	Other Engine Equipment Manufacturing (pt)
3523	Farm Machinery and Equipment		
3523	. Farm Machinery and Equipment (Except Corrals, Stalls, Holding Gates, Hand Hair Clippers for Animals, Farm Conveyors, and Elevators)	333111	Farm Machinery and Equipment Manufacturing
3523	. Corrals, Stalls, Holding Gates	332323	Ornamental and Architectural Metal Work Manufacturing (pt)
3523	. Hand Hair Clippers for Animals	332212	Hand and Edge Tool Manufacturing(pt)
3523	. Farm Conveyors and Farm Elevators, Stackers, and Bale Throwers	333922	Conveyor and Conveying Equipment Manufacturing (pt)
3524	Lawn and Garden Tractors and Home Lawn and Garden Equipment		
3524	. Lawn and Garden Tractors and Home Lawn and Garden Equipment (Except Nonpowered Lawnmowers)	333112	Lawn and Garden Tractor and Home Lawn and Garden Equipment Manufacturing
3524	. Nonpowered Lawnmowers	332212	Hand and Edge Tool Manufacturing (pt)
3531	Construction Machinery and Equipment		
3531	. Railway Track Maintenance Equipment	33651	Railroad Rolling Stock Manufacturing (pt)
3531	. Winches, Aerial Work Platforms, and Automotive Wrecker Hoists	333923	Overhead Traveling Crane, Hoist, and Monorail System Manufacturing (pt)
3531	. Other Construction Machinery and Equipment	33312	Construction Machinery Manufacturing
3532	Mining Machinery and Equipment, Except Oil and Gas Field Machinery and Equipment	333131	Mining Machinery and Equipment Manufacturing
3533	Oil and Gas Field Machinery and Equipment	333132	Oil and Gas Field Machinery and Equipment Manufacturing
3534	Elevators and Moving Stairways	333921	Elevator and Moving Stairway Manufacturing
3535	Conveyors and Conveying Equipment	333922	Conveyor and Conveying Equipment Manufacturing (pt)
3536	Overhead Traveling Cranes, Hoists, and Monorail Systems	333923	Overhead Traveling Crane, Hoist, and Monorail System Manufacturing (pt)
3537	Industrial Trucks, Tractors, Trailers, and Stackers		
3537	. Industrial Trucks, Tractors, Trailers, and Stackers (Except Metal Pallets and Air Cargo Containers)	333924	Industrial Truck, Tractor, Trailer, and Stacker Machinery Manufacturing
3537	. Metal Pallets	332999	All Other Miscellaneous Fabricated Metal Product Manufacturing (pt)
3537	. Metal Air Cargo Containers	332439	Other Metal Container Manufacturing (pt)
3541	Machine Tools, Metal Cutting Type	333512	Machine Tool (Metal Cutting Types) Manufacturing
3542	Machine Tools, Metal Forming Type	333513	Machine Tool (Metal Forming Types) Manufacturing

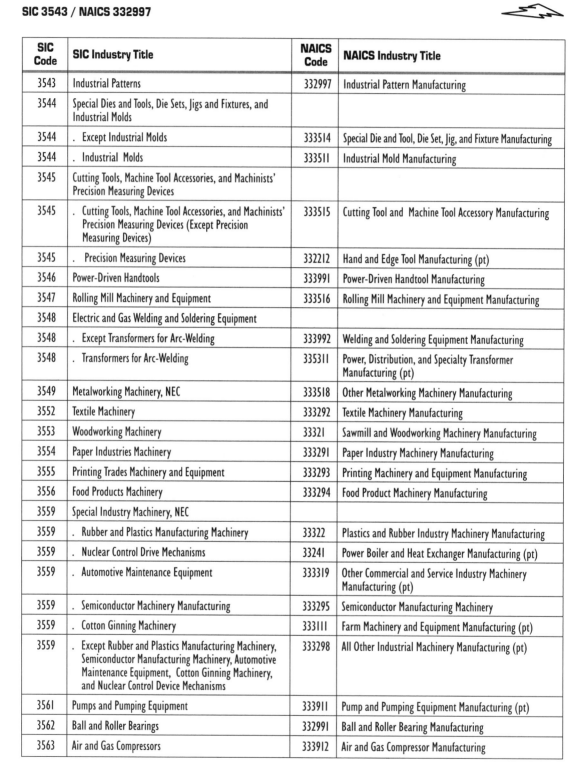

SIC Code	SIC Industry Title	NAICS Code	NAICS Industry Title
3543	Industrial Patterns	332997	Industrial Pattern Manufacturing
3544	Special Dies and Tools, Die Sets, Jigs and Fixtures, and Industrial Molds		
3544	. Except Industrial Molds	333514	Special Die and Tool, Die Set, Jig, and Fixture Manufacturing
3544	. Industrial Molds	333511	Industrial Mold Manufacturing
3545	Cutting Tools, Machine Tool Accessories, and Machinists' Precision Measuring Devices		
3545	. Cutting Tools, Machine Tool Accessories, and Machinists' Precision Measuring Devices (Except Precision Measuring Devices)	333515	Cutting Tool and Machine Tool Accessory Manufacturing
3545	. Precision Measuring Devices	332212	Hand and Edge Tool Manufacturing (pt)
3546	Power-Driven Handtools	333991	Power-Driven Handtool Manufacturing
3547	Rolling Mill Machinery and Equipment	333516	Rolling Mill Machinery and Equipment Manufacturing
3548	Electric and Gas Welding and Soldering Equipment		
3548	. Except Transformers for Arc-Welding	333992	Welding and Soldering Equipment Manufacturing
3548	. Transformers for Arc-Welding	335311	Power, Distribution, and Specialty Transformer Manufacturing (pt)
3549	Metalworking Machinery, NEC	333518	Other Metalworking Machinery Manufacturing
3552	Textile Machinery	333292	Textile Machinery Manufacturing
3553	Woodworking Machinery	33321	Sawmill and Woodworking Machinery Manufacturing
3554	Paper Industries Machinery	333291	Paper Industry Machinery Manufacturing
3555	Printing Trades Machinery and Equipment	333293	Printing Machinery and Equipment Manufacturing
3556	Food Products Machinery	333294	Food Product Machinery Manufacturing
3559	Special Industry Machinery, NEC		
3559	. Rubber and Plastics Manufacturing Machinery	33322	Plastics and Rubber Industry Machinery Manufacturing
3559	. Nuclear Control Drive Mechanisms	33241	Power Boiler and Heat Exchanger Manufacturing (pt)
3559	. Automotive Maintenance Equipment	333319	Other Commercial and Service Industry Machinery Manufacturing (pt)
3559	. Semiconductor Machinery Manufacturing	333295	Semiconductor Manufacturing Machinery
3559	. Cotton Ginning Machinery	333111	Farm Machinery and Equipment Manufacturing (pt)
3559	. Except Rubber and Plastics Manufacturing Machinery, Semiconductor Manufacturing Machinery, Automotive Maintenance Equipment, Cotton Ginning Machinery, and Nuclear Control Device Mechanisms	333298	All Other Industrial Machinery Manufacturing (pt)
3561	Pumps and Pumping Equipment	333911	Pump and Pumping Equipment Manufacturing (pt)
3562	Ball and Roller Bearings	332991	Ball and Roller Bearing Manufacturing
3563	Air and Gas Compressors	333912	Air and Gas Compressor Manufacturing

SIC Code	SIC Industry Title	NAICS Code	NAICS Industry Title
3564	Industrial and Commercial Fans and Blowers and Air Purification Equipment		
3564	. Air Purification Equipment	333411	Air Purification Equipment Manufacturing
3564	. Fans and Blowers	333412	Industrial and Commercial Fan and Blower Manufacturing
3565	Packaging Machinery	333993	Packaging Machinery Manufacturing
3566	Speed Changers, Industrial High-Speed Drives, and Gears	333612	Speed Changer, Industrial High-Speed Drive, and Gear Manufacturing
3567	Industrial Process Furnaces and Ovens	333994	Industrial Process Furnace and Oven Manufacturing
3568	Mechanical Power Transmission Equipment, NEC	333613	Mechanical Power Transmission Equipment Manufacturing
3569	General Industrial Machinery and Equipment, NEC		
3569	. Electric Swimming Pool Heaters	333414	Heating Equipment (except Warm Air Furnace) Manufacturing (pt)
3569	. Textile Fire Hose	314999	All Other Miscellaneous Textile Product Mills (pt)
3569	. Except Electric Swimming Pool Heaters and Textile Fire Hoses	333999	All Other Miscellaneous General Purpose Machinery Manufacturing (pt)
3571	Electronic Computers	334111	Electronic Computer Manufacturing
3572	Computer Storage Devices	334112	Computer Storage Device Manufacturing
3575	Computer Terminals	334113	Computer Terminal Manufacturing
3577	Computer Peripheral Equipment, NEC		
3577	. Plotter Controllers	334418	Printed Circuit Assembly (Electronic Assembly) Manufacturing (pt)
3577	. Magnetic Tape Cleaner	334613	Magnetic Optical Recording Media Manufacturing (pt)
3577	. Except Plotter Controllers and Magnetic Tape Cleaners	334119	Other Computer Peripheral Equipment Manufacturing (pt)
3578	Calculating and Accounting Machines, Except Electronic Computers		
3578	. Point of Sales Terminals and Fund Transfer Devices	334119	Other Computer Peripheral Equipment Manufacturing (pt)
3578	. Change Making Machines	333311	Automatic Vending Machine Manufacturing (pt)
3578	. Calculating and Accounting Machines, Except Point of Sales Terminals and Fund Transfer Devices, and Change Making Machines	333313	Office Machinery Manufacturing (pt)
3579	Office Machines, NEC		
3579	. Pencil Sharpeners, Staplers, and Other Office Equipment	339942	Lead Pencil and Art Good Manufacturing (pt)
3579	. Time Clocks and Other Time Recording Devices	334518	Watch, Clock, and Part Manufacturing (pt)
3579	. Other Office Machines	333313	Office Machinery Manufacturing (pt)
3581	Automatic Vending Machines	333311	Automatic Vending Machine Manufacturing
3582	Commercial Laundry, Drycleaning, and Pressing Machines	333312	Commercial Laundry, Drycleaning, and Pressing Machine Manufacturing

SIC Code	SIC Industry Title	NAICS Code	NAICS Industry Title
3585	Air-Conditioning and Warm Air Heating Equipment and Commercial and Industrial Refrigeration Equipment		
3585	. Motor Vehicle Air-Conditioning	336391	Motor Vehicle Air-Conditioning Manufacturing
3585	. Except Motor Vehicle Air-Conditioning	333415	Air-Conditioning and Warm Air Heating Equipment and Commercial Industrial Refrigeration Equipment Manufacturing
3586	Measuring and Dispensing Pumps	333913	Measuring and Dispensing Pump Manufacturing
3589	Service Industry Machinery, NEC	333319	Other Commercial and Service Industry Machinery Manufacturing (pt)
3592	Carburetors, Pistons, Piston Rings, and Valves	336311	Carburetor, Piston, Piston Ring, and Valve Manufacturing
3593	Fluid Power Cylinders and Actuators	333995	Fluid Power Cylinder and Actuator Manufacturing
3594	Fluid Power Pumps and Motors	333996	Fluid Power Pump and Motor Manufacturing
3596	Scales and Balances, Except Laboratory	333997	Scale and Balance (except Laboratory) Manufacturing
3599	Industrial and Commercial Machinery and Equipment, NEC		
3599	. Gasoline, Oil and Intake Filters for Internal Combustion Engines, Except Motor Vehicle	336399	All Other Motor Vehicle Part Manufacturing (pt)
3599	. Flexible Metal Hose	332999	All Other Miscellaneous Fabricated Metal Product Manufacturing (pt)
3599	. Carnival Amusement Park Equipment	333319	Other Commercial and Service Industry Machinery Manufacturing (pt)
3599	. Machine Shops	33271	Machine Shops
3599	. Other Industrial and Commercial Machinery and Equipment	333999	All Other Miscellaneous General Purpose Machinery Manufacturing (pt)
36	Electrical and Electronic Equipment		
3612	Power, Distribution, and Specialty Transformers	335311	Power, Distribution, and Specialty Transformer Manufacturing (pt)
3613	Switchgear and Switchboard Apparatus	335313	Switchgear and Switchboard Apparatus Manufacturing
3621	Motors and Generators	335312	Motor and Generator Manufacturing (pt)
3624	Carbon and Graphite Products	335991	Carbon and Graphite Product Manufacturing
3625	Relays and Industrial Controls	335314	Relay and Industrial Control Manufacturing
3629	Electrical Industrial Apparatus, NEC	335999	All Other Miscellaneous Electrical Equipment and Component Manufacturing (pt)
3631	Household Cooking Equipment	335221	Household Cooking Appliance Manufacturing
3632	Household Refrigerators and Home and Farm Freezers	335222	Household Refrigerator and Home Freezer Manufacturing
3633	Household Laundry Equipment	335224	Household Laundry Equipment Manufacturing
3634	Electric Housewares and Fans		
3634	. Except Wall and Baseboard Heating Units for Permanent Installation, and Electronic Cigarette Lighters	335211	Electric Housewares and Household Fan Manufacturing
3634	. Electronic Cigarette Lighters	339999	All Other Miscellaneous Manufacturing (pt)

SIC Code	SIC Industry Title	NAICS Code	NAICS Industry Title
3634	. Wall and Baseboard Heating Units For Permanent Installation	333414	Heating Equipment (except Warm Air Furnaces) Manufacturing (pt)
3635	Household Vacuum Cleaners	335212	Household Vacuum Cleaner Manufacturing (pt)
3639	Household Appliances, NEC		
3639	. Floor Waxing and Floor Polishing Machines	335212	Household Vacuum Cleaner Manufacturing (pt)
3639	. Household Sewing Machines	333298	All Other Industrial Machinery Manufacturing (pt)
3639	. Other Household Appliances	335228	Other Major Household Appliance Manufacturing
3641	Electric Lamp Bulbs and Tubes	33511	Electric Lamp Bulb and Part Manufacturing
3643	Current-Carrying Wiring Devices	335931	Current-Carrying Wiring Device Manufacturing
3644	Noncurrent-Carrying Wiring Devices		
3644	. Fish Wire, Electrical Wiring Tool	332212	Hand and Edge Tool Manufacturing (pt)
3644	. All Other Noncurrent-Carrying Wiring Devices	335932	Noncurrent-Carrying Wiring Device Manufacturing
3645	Residential Electric Lighting Fixtures	335121	Residential Electric Lighting Fixture Manufacturing (pt)
3646	Commercial, Industrial, and Institutional Electric Lighting Fixtures	335122	Commercial, Industrial, and Institutional Electric Lighting Fixture Manufacturing
3647	Vehicular Lighting Equipment	336321	Vehicular Lighting Equipment Manufacturing
3648	Lighting Equipment, NEC	335129	Other Lighting Equipment Manufacturing (pt)
3651	Household Audio and Video Equipment	33431	Audio and Video Equipment Manufacturing
3652	Phonograph Records and Prerecorded Audio Tapes and Disks		
3652	. Reproduction of Recording Media	334612	Prerecorded Compact Disc (Except Software), Tape, and Record Reproducing (pt)
3652	. Integrated Record Companies, Except Duplication Only	51222	Integrated Record Production/Distribution
3661	Telephone and Telegraph Apparatus		
3661	. Telephone and Telegraph Apparatus, Except Consumer External Modems	33421	Telephone Apparatus Manufacturing
3661	. Consumer External Modems	334418	Printed Circuit Assembly (Electronic Assembly) Manufacturing (pt)
3663	Radio and Television Broadcasting and Communications Equipment	33422	Radio and Television Broadcasting and Wireless Communications Equipment Manufacturing (pt)
3669	Communications Equipment, NEC	33429	Other Communications Equipment Manufacturing
3671	Electron Tubes	334411	Electron Tube Manufacturing
3672	Printed Circuit Boards	334412	Bare Printed Circuit Board Manufacturing
3674	Semiconductors and Related Devices	334413	Semiconductor and Related Device Manufacturing
3675	Electronic Capacitors	334414	Electronic Capacitor Manufacturing
3676	Electronic Resistors	334415	Electronic Resistor Manufacturing
3677	Electronic Coils, Transformers, and Other Inductors	334416	Electronic Coil, Transformer, and Other Inductor Manufacturing (pt)

SIC Code	SIC Industry Title	NAICS Code	NAICS Industry Title
3678	Electronic Connectors	334417	Electronic Connector Manufacturing
3679	Electronic Components, NEC		
3679	. Antennas	33422	Radio and Television Broadcasting and Wireless Communications Equipment Manufacturing (pt)
3679	. Radio Headphones	33431	Audio and Video Equipment Manufacturing (pt)
3679	. Printed Circuit/Electronics Assembly	334418	Printed Circuit Assembly (Electronic Assembly) Manufacturing (pt)
3679	. Other Electronic Components	334419	Other Electronic Component Manufacturing
3691	Storage Batteries	335911	Storage Battery Manufacturing
3692	Primary Batteries, Dry and Wet	335912	Primary Battery Manufacturing
3694	Electrical Equipment for Internal Combustion Engines	336322	Other Motor Vehicle Electrical and Electronic Equipment Manufacturing (pt)
3695	Magnetic and Optical Recording Media	334613	Magnetic and Optical Recording Media Manufacturing
3699	Electrical Machinery, Equipment, and Supplies, NEC		
3699	. Electronic Teaching Machines and Flight Simulators	333319	Other Commercial and Service Industry Machinery Manufacturing (pt)
3699	. Outboard Electric Motors	333618	Other Engine Equipment Manufacturing (pt)
3699	. Laser Welding and Soldering Equipment	333992	Welding and Soldering Equipment Manufacturing (pt)
3699	. Other Lasers		Classify According to Function
3699	. Christmas Tree Lighting Sets, Electric Insect Lamps, Electric Fireplace Logs, and Trouble Lights	335129	Other Lighting Equipment Manufacturing (pt)
3699	. Other Electrical Machinery, Equipment, and Supplies	335999	All Other Miscellaneous Electrical Equipment and Component Manufacturing (pt)
37	Transportation equipment		
3711	Motor Vehicles and Passenger Car Bodies		
3711	. Automobiles	336111	Automobile Manufacturing
3711	. Light Truck and Utility Vehicles	336112	Light Truck and Utility Vehicle Manufacturing
3711	. Heavy Duty Trucks	33612	Heavy Duty Truck Manufacturing
3711	. Kit Car and Other Passenger Car Bodies	336211	Motor Vehicle Body Manufacturing (pt)
3711	. Military Armored Vehicles	336992	Military Armored Vehicle, Tank, and Tank Component Manufacturing (pt)
3713	Truck and Bus Bodies	336211	Motor Vehicle Body Manufacturing (pt)
3714	Motor Vehicle Parts and Accessories		
3714	. Dump-Truck Lifting Mechanisms and Fifth Wheels	336211	Motor Vehicle Body Manufacturing (pt)
3714	. Gasoline Engines Including Rebuilt and Engine Parts Including Rebuilt for Motor Vehicles	336312	Gasoline Engine and Engine Parts Manufacturing

SIC Code	SIC Industry Title	NAICS Code	NAICS Industry Title
3714	. Wiring Harness Sets, Other than Ignition; Block Heaters and Battery Heaters; Instrument Board Assemblies; Permanent Defroster; Windshield Washer-Wiper Mechanisms; Cruise Control Mechanisms; and Other Electrical Equipment for Internal Combustion Engine	336322	Other Motor Vehicle Electrical and Electronic Equipment Manufacturing (pt)
3714	. Steering and Suspension Parts	33633	Motor Vehicle Steering and Suspension Components (except Spring) Manufacturing
3714	. Brake and Brake Systems, Including Assemblies	33634	Motor Vehicle Brake System Manufacturing (pt)
3714	. Transmissions and Power Train Parts, Including Rebuilding	33635	Motor Vehicle Transmission and Power Train Parts Manufacturing
3714	. Other Motor Vehicle Parts	336399	All Other Motor Vehicle Parts Manufacturing (pt)
3715	Truck Trailers	336212	Truck Trailer Manufacturing
3716	Motor Homes	336213	Motor Home Manufacturing
3721	Aircraft		
3721	. Research and Development	54171	Research and Development in the Physical, Engineering, and Life Sciences (pt)
3721	. Except Research and Development	336411	Aircraft Manufacturing
3724	Aircraft Engines and Engine Parts		
3724	. Except Research and Development	336412	Aircraft Engine and Engine Parts Manufacturing (pt)
3724	. Research and Development	54171	Research and Development in the Physical, Engineering, and Life Sciences (pt)
3728	Aircraft Parts and Auxiliary Equipment, NEC		
3728	. Fluid Power Aircraft Subassemblies	332912	Fluid Power Valve and Hose Fitting Manufacturing (pt)
3728	. Research and Development	54171	Research and Development in the Physical, Engineering, and Life Sciences (pt)
3728	. Target Drones	336411	Aircraft Engine and Engine Parts Manufacturing (pt)
3728	. Except Fluid Power Aircraft Subassemblies, Target Drones, and Research and Development	336413	Other Aircraft Parts and Auxiliary Equipment Manufacturing
3731	Ship Building and Repairing		
3731	. Floating Dry Docks Not Associated With Shipyards	48839	Other Support Activities for Water Transportation (pt)
3731	. Ship Building and Repairing Except Floating Dry Docks Not Associated With Shipyards	336611	Ship Building and Repairing
3732	Boat Building and Repairing		
3732	. Boat Repair	81149	Other Personal and Household Goods Repair and Maintenance (pt)
3732	. Boat Building	336612	Boat Building
3743	Railroad Equipment		
3743	. Locomotive Fuel Lubricating or Cooling Medium Pumps	333911	Pump and Pumping Equipment Manufacturing (pt)
3743	. Other Railroad Equipment	33651	Railroad Rolling Stock Manufacturing (pt)

SIC Code	SIC Industry Title	NAICS Code	NAICS Industry Title
3751	Motorcycles, Bicycles, and Parts	336991	Motorcycle, Bicycle, and Parts Manufacturing (pt)
3761	Guided Missiles and Space Vehicles		
3761	. Except Research and Development	336414	Guided Missile and Space Vehicle Manufacturing
3761	. Research and Development	54171	Research and Development in the Physical, Engineering, and Life Sciences (pt)
3764	Guided Missile and Space Vehicle Propulsion Units and Propulsion Unit Parts		Research and Development in the Physical, Engineering, and Life Sciences (pt)
3764	. Except Research and Development	336415	Guided Missile and Space Vehicle Propulsion Unit and Propulsion Unit Parts Manufacturing
3764	. Research and Development	54171	Research and Development in the Physical, Engineering, and Life Sciences (pt)
3769	Guided Missile Space Vehicle Parts and Auxiliary Equipment, NEC		
3769	. Except Research and Development	336419	Other Guided Missile and Space Vehicle Parts and Auxiliary Equipment Manufacturing
3769	. Research and Development	54171	Research and Development in the Physical, Engineering, and Life Sciences (pt)
3792	Travel Trailers and Campers	336214	Travel Trailer and Camper Manufacturing (pt)
3795	Tanks and Tank Components	336992	Military Armored Vehicle, Tank, and Tank Component Manufacturing (pt)
3799	Transportation Equipment, NEC		
3799	. Automobile, Boat, Utility and Light Truck Trailers	336214	Travel Trailer and Camper Manufacturing (pt)
3799	. Trailer Hitches	336399	All Other Motor Vehicle Parts Manufacturing (pt)
3799	. Wheelbarrows	333924	Industrial Truck, Tractor, Trailer, and Stacker Machinery Manufacturing (pt)
3799	. Other Transportation Equipment	336999	All Other Transportation Equipment Manufacturing
38	Instruments and related products		
3812	Search, Detection, Navigation, Guidance, Aeronautical, and Nautical Systems and Instruments	334511	Search, Detection, Navigation, Guidance, Aeronautical, and Nautical System and Instrument Manufacturing
3821	Laboratory Apparatus and Furniture	339111	Laboratory Apparatus and Furniture Manufacturing (pt)
3822	Automatic Controls for Regulating Residential and Commercial Environments and Appliances	334512	Automatic Environmental Control Manufacturing for Regulating Residential, Commercial, and Appliance Use
3823	Industrial Instruments for Measurement, Display, and Control of Process Variables; and Related Products	334513	Instruments and Related Product Manufacturing for Measuring Displaying, and Controlling Industrial Process Variables
3824	Totalizing Fluid Meters and Counting Devices	334514	Totalizing Fluid Meter and Counting Device Manufacturing (pt)
3825	Instruments for Measuring and Testing of Electricity and Electrical Signals		
3825	. Automotive Ammeters and Voltmeters	334514	Totalizing Fluid Meters and Counting Device Manufacturing (pt)

SIC Code	SIC Industry Title	NAICS Code	NAICS Industry Title
3825	. Except Automotive Ammeters and Voltmeters	334515	Instrument Manufacturing for Measuring and Testing Electricity and Electrical Signals
3826	Laboratory Analytical Instruments	334516	Analytical Laboratory Instrument Manufacturing
3827	Optical Instruments and Lenses	333314	Optical Instrument and Lens Manufacturing
3829	Measuring and Controlling Devices, NEC		
3829	. Motor Vehicle Gauges	334514	Totalizing Fluid Meter and Counting Device Manufacturing (pt)
3829	. Medical Thermometers	339112	Surgical and Medical Instrument Manufacturing (pt)
3829	. Electronic Chronometers	334518	Watch, Clock, and Part Manufacturing
3829	. Except Medical Thermometers, Electronic Chronometers, and Motor Vehicle Gauges	334519	Other Measuring and Controlling Device Manufacturing
3841	Surgical and Medical Instruments and Apparatus		
3841	. Tranquilizer Guns	332994	Small Arms Manufacturing (pt)
3841	. Operating Tables	339111	Laboratory Apparatus and Furniture Manufacturing (pt)
3841	. Except Tranquilizer Guns and Operating Tables	339112	Surgical and Medical Instrument Manufacturing (pt)
3842	Orthopedic, Prosthetic, and Surgical Appliances and Supplies		
3842	. Incontinent and Bed Pads	322291	Sanitary Paper Product Manufacturing (pt)
3842	. Orthopedic, Prosthetic, and Surgical Appliances and Supplies, except Electronic Hearing Aids	339113	Surgical Appliance and Supplies Manufacturing
3842	. Electronic Hearing Aids	334510	Electromedical and Electrotherapeutic Apparatus Manufacturing (pt)
3843	Dental Equipment and Supplies	339114	Dental Equipment and Supplies Manufacturing
3844	X-Ray Apparatus and Tubes and Related Irradiation Apparatus	334517	Irradiation Apparatus Manufacturing (pt)
3845	Electromedical and Electrotherapeutic Apparatus		
3845	. CT and CAT Scanners	334517	Irradiation Apparatus Manufacturing (pt)
3845	. Other Electromedical and Electrotherapeutic Apparatus	334510	Electromedical and Electrotherapeutic Apparatus Manufacturing (pt)
3851	Ophthalmic Goods		
3851	. Intra Ocular Lenses	339113	Surgical and Medical Instrument Manufacturing (pt)
3851	. Except Intra Ocular Lenses	339115	Ophthalmic Goods Manufacturing (pt)
3861	Photographic Equipment and Supplies		
3861	. Photographic Equipment and Supplies (Except Photographic Film, Paper, Plates and Chemicals)	333315	Photographic and Photocopying Equipment Manufacturing
3861	. Photographic Film, Paper, Plates and Chemicals	325992	Photographic Film, Paper, Plate, and Chemical Manufacturing
3873	Watches, Clocks, Clockwork Operated Devices and Parts	334518	Watch, Clock, and Part Manufacturing (pt)
39	Miscellaneous manufacturing industries		
3911	Jewelry, Precious Metal	339911	Jewelry (except Costume) Manufacturing (pt)

SIC Code	SIC Industry Title	NAICS Code	NAICS Industry Title
3914	Silverware, Plated Ware, and Stainless Steel Ware		
3914	. Cutlery and Flatware Nonprecious and Precious Plated	332211	Cutlery and Flatware (except Precious) Manufacturing (pt)
3914	. Precious Plated Holloware	332999	All Other Miscellaneous Fabricated Metal Product Manufacturing (pt)
3914	. Silverware, Plated Ware, and Stainless Steel Ware (Except Nonprecious and Precious Plated Metal Cutlery and Flatware)	339912	Silverware and Holloware Manufacturing (pt)
3915	Jewelers' Findings and Materials, and Lapidary Work		
3915	. Watch Jewels	334518	Watch, Clock, and Part Manufacturing (pt)
3915	. Except Watch Jewels	339913	Jewelers' Material and Lapidary Work Manufacturing
3931	Musical Instruments	339992	Musical Instrument Manufacturing
3942	Dolls and Stuffed Toys	339931	Doll and Stuffed Toy Manufacturing
3944	Games, Toys, and Children's Vehicles, Except Dolls and Bicycles		
3944	. Metal Tricycles	336991	Motorcycle, Bicycle, and Parts Manufacturing (pt)
3944	. Other Games, Toys, and Children's Vehicles	339932	Game, Toy, and Children's Vehicle Manufacturing
3949	Sporting and Athletic Goods, NEC	33992	Sporting and Athletic Good Manufacturing
3951	Pens, Mechanical Pencils, and Parts	339941	Pen and Mechanical Pencil Manufacturing
3952	Lead Pencils, Crayons, and Artist's Materials		
3952	. Drafting Tables and Boards	337127	Institutional Furniture Manufacturing (pt)
3952	. Drawing and India Ink	325998	All Other Miscellaneous Chemical and Preparation Manufacturing (pt)
3952	. Other	339942	Lead Pencil and Art Good Manufacturing (pt)
3953	Marking Devices	339943	Marking Device Manufacturing
3955	Carbon Paper and Inked Ribbons	339944	Carbon Paper and Inked Ribbon Manufacturing
3961	Costume Jewelry and Costume Novelties, Except Precious Metals	339914	Costume Jewelry and Novelty Manufacturing (pt)
3965	Fasteners, Buttons, Needles, and Pins	339993	Fastener, Button, Needle, and Pin Manufacturing (pt)
3991	Brooms and Brushes	339994	Broom, Brush, and Mop Manufacturing (pt)
3993	Signs and Advertising Specialties		
3993	. Signs	33995	Sign Manufacturing
3993	. Advertising Specialties		Classified According to the Product Produced
3995	Burial Caskets	339995	Burial Casket Manufacturing
3996	Linoleum, Asphalted-Felt-Base, and Other Hard Surface Floor Coverings, NEC	326192	Resilient Floor Covering Manufacturing (pt)
3999	Manufacturing Industries, NEC		
3999	. Beauty and Barber Chairs	337127	Institutional Furniture Manufacturing (pt)
3999	. Other Beauty and Barber Shop Equipment	333319	Other Commercial and Service Industry Machinery Manufacturing (pt)

SIC Code	SIC Industry Title	NAICS Code	NAICS Industry Title
3999	. Fur Dressing and Bleaching	31611	Leather and Hide Tanning and Finishing (pt)
3999	. Lamp Shades of Paper or Textile	335121	Residential Electric Lighting Fixture Manufacturing (pt)
3999	. Matches	325998	All Other Miscellaneous Chemical Product and Preparation Manufacturing (pt)
3999	. Metal Products, Such As Combs, Hair Curlers, etc.	332999	All Other Miscellaneous Fabricated Metal Product Manufacturing (pt)
3999	. Plastics Products, Such As Combs, Hair Curlers, etc.	326199	All Other Plastics Product Manufacturing (pt)
3999	. Electric Hair Clippers for Humans	335211	Electric Housewares and Household Fan Manufacturing (pt)
3999	. Tape Measures and Human Hair Clippers	332212	Hand and Edge Tool Manufacturing (pt)
3999	. Embroidery Kits	339932	Game, Toy, and Children's Vehicle Manufacturing (pt)
3999	. Other	339999	All Other Miscellaneous Manufacturing (pt)
	Transportation, Communications, and Utilities		
4011	Railroads, Line-haul Operating	482111	Line-Haul Railroads
4013	Railroad Switching and Terminal Establishments		
4013	. Beltline and Logging Railroads	482112	Short Line Railroads
4013	. Other	48821	Support Activities for Rail Transportation (pt)
41	Local and interurban passenger transit		
4111	Local and Suburban Transit		
4111	. Mixed Mode Transit Systems	485111	Mixed Mode Transit Systems
4111	. Commuter Rail Systems	485112	Commuter Rail Systems
4111	. Bus and Motor Vehicle Transit Systems	485113	Bus and Other Motor Vehicle Transit Systems
4111	. Other Urban Transit Systems	485119	Other Urban Transit Systems
4111	. Airport Limousine Transportation	485999	All Other Transit and Ground Passenger Transportation (pt)
4119	Local Passenger Transportation, NEC		
4119	. Ambulances	62191	Ambulance Service (pt)
4119	. Employee Transportation	48541	School and Employee Bus Transportation (pt)
4119	. Sightseeing Buses and Cable and Cog Railways, Except Scenic	48711	Scenic and Sightseeing Transportation, Land (pt)
4119	. Special Needs Transportation	485991	Special Needs Transportation
4119	. Hearse Rental with Driver and Carpool and Vanpool Operations	485999	All Other Transit and Ground Passenger Transportation (pt)
4119	. Automobile Rental with Driver and Limousine Rental with Driver	48532	Limousine Service
4121	Taxicabs	48531	Taxi Service (pt)
4131	Intercity and Rural Bus Transportation	48521	Interurban and Rural Bus Transportation
4141	Local Bus Charter Service	48551	Charter Bus Industry (pt)

SIC Code	SIC Industry Title	NAICS Code	NAICS Industry Title
4142	Bus Charter Service, Except Local	48551	Charter Bus Industry (pt)
4151	School Buses	48541	School and Employee Bus Transportation (pt)
4173	Terminal and Service Facilities for Motor Vehicle Passenger Transportation	48849	Other Support Activities for Road Transportation (pt)
42	Motor freight transportation and warehousing		
4212	Local Trucking Without Storage		
4212	. Solid Waste Collection Without Disposal	562111	Solid Waste Collection
4212	. Hazardous Waste Collection Without Disposal	562112	Hazardous Waste Collection
4212	. Other Waste Collection Without Disposal	562119	Other Waste Collection
4212	. Local General Freight Trucking Without Storage	48411	General Freight Trucking, Local (pt)
4212	. Household Goods Moving Without Storage	48421	Used Household and Office Goods Moving (pt)
4212	. Local Specialized Freight Trucking Without Storage	48422	Specialized Freight (except Used Goods) Trucking, Local (pt)
4213	Trucking, Except Local		
4213	. Long-distance Truckload General Freight Trucking	484121	General Freight Trucking, Long-Distance, Truckload
4213	. Long-distance Less Than Truckload General Freight Trucking	484122 Truckload	General Freight Trucking, Long-Distance, Less Than
4213	. Long-distance Household Goods Moving	48421	Used Household and Office Goods Moving (pt)
4213	. Long-distance Specialized Freight Trucking	48423	Specialized Freight (except Used Goods) Trucking, Long-Distance
4214	Local Trucking with Storage		
4214	. Local General Freight Trucking with Storage	48411	General Freight Trucking, Local (pt)
4214	. Local Household Goods Moving	48421	Used Household and Office Goods Moving (pt)
4214	. Local Specialized Freight Trucking with Storage	48422	Specialized Freight (except Used Goods) Trucking, Local (pt)
4215	Courier Services Except by Air		
4215	. Hub and Spoke Intercity Delivery	49211	Couriers (pt)
4215	. Local Delivery	49221	Local Messengers and Local Delivery
4221	Farm Product Warehousing and Storage	49313	Farm Product Warehousing and Storage
4222	Refrigerated Warehousing and Storage	49312	Refrigerated Warehousing and Storage (pt)
4225	General Warehousing and Storage		
4225	. General Warehousing and Storage	49311	General Warehousing and Storage (pt)
4225	. Miniwarehouses and Self-Storage Units	53113	Lessors of Miniwarehouses and Self Storage Units
4226	Special Warehousing and Storage, NEC		
4226	. Fur Storage	49312	Refrigerated Warehousing and Storage (pt)
4226	. General Warehousing in Foreign Trade Zones	49311	General Warehousing and Storage (pt)
4226	. Other	49319	Other Warehousing and Storage
4231	Terminal and Joint Terminal Maintenance Facilities for Motor Freight Transportation	48849	Other Support Activities for Road Transportation (pt)

SIC Code	SIC Industry Title	NAICS Code	NAICS Industry Title
43	U.S. Postal Service		
4311	United States Postal Service	49111	Postal Service (pt)
44	Water transportation		
4412	Deep Sea Foreign Transportation of Freight	483111	Deep Sea Freight Transportation
4424	Deep Sea Domestic Transportation of Freight	483113	Coastal and Great Lakes Freight Transportation (pt)
4432	Freight Transportation on the Great Lakes - St. Lawrence Seaway	483113	Coastal and Great Lakes Freight Transportation (pt)
4449	Water Transportation of Freight, NEC	483211	Inland Water Freight Transportation
4481	Deep Sea Transportation of Passengers, Except by Ferry		
4481	. Deep Sea Passenger Transportation	483112	Deep Sea Passenger Transportation
4481	. Coastal and Great Lakes Passenger Transportation	483114	Coastal and Great Lakes Passenger Transportation (pt)
4482	Ferries		
4482	. Coastal and Great Lakes Ferries	483114	Coastal and Great Lakes Passenger Transportation (pt)
4482	. Inland Water Ferries	483212	Inland Water Passenger Transportation (pt)
4489	Water Transportation of Passengers, NEC		
4489	. Water Taxis	483212	Inland Water Passenger Transportation (pt)
4489	. Airboats, Excursion Boats, and Sightseeing Boats	48721	Scenic and Sightseeing Transportation, Water (pt)
4491	Marine Cargo Handling		
4491	. Dock and Pier Operations	48831	Port and Harbor Operations (pt)
4491	. Except Dock and Pier Operations	48832	Marine Cargo Handling
4492	Towing and Tugboat Services	48833	Navigational Services to Shipping (pt)
4493	Marinas	71393	Marinas
4499	Water Transportation Services, NEC		
4499	. Boat and Ship Rental	532411	Commercial Air, Rail, and Water Transportation Equipment Rental and Leasing (pt)
4499	. Lighthouse and Canal Operations	48831	Port and Harbor Operations (pt)
4499	. Marine Salvage and Piloting Vessels In and Out of Harbors	48833	Navigational Services to Shipping (pt)
4499	. Other	48839	Other Support Activities for Water Transportation (pt)
45	Transportation by air		
4512	Air Transportation, Scheduled		
4512	. Scheduled Passenger Air Transportation	481111	Scheduled Passenger Air Transportation
4512	. Scheduled Freight Air Transportation	481112	Scheduled Freight Air Transportation
4513	Air Courier Services	49211	Couriers (pt)
4522	Air Transportation, Nonscheduled		
4522	. Air Ambulance	62191	Ambulance Services (pt)
4522	. Nonscheduled Charter Freight Air Transportation	481212	Nonscheduled Chartered Freight Air Transportation

SIC Code	SIC Industry Title	NAICS Code	NAICS Industry Title
4522	. Nonscheduled Charter Passenger Air Transportation	481211	Nonscheduled Chartered Passenger Air Transportation
4522	. Sightseeing Aircraft	48799	Scenic and Sightseeing Transportation , Other (pt)
4581	Airports, Flying Fields, and Airport Terminal Services		
4581	. Air Traffic Control	488111	Air Traffic Control (pt)
4581	. Airfreight Handling at Airports, Hangar Operations, Airport Terminal Services, Aircraft Storage, Airports, and Flying Fields	488119	Other Airport Operations (pt)
4581	. Aircraft Cleaning and Janitorial Services	56172	Janitorial Services (pt)
4581	. Aircraft Servicing and Repairing	48819	Other Support Activities for Air Transportation
46	Pipelines, except natural gas		
4612	Crude Petroleum Pipelines	48611	Pipeline Transportation of Crude Oil
4613	Refined Petroleum Pipelines	48691	Pipeline Transportation of Refined Petroleum Products
4619	Pipelines, NEC	48699	All Other Pipeline Transportation
47	Transportation services		
4724	Travel Agencies	56151	Travel Agencies
4725	Tour Operators	56152	Tour Operators
4729	Arrangement of Passenger Transportation, NEC		
4729	. Arrangement of Carpools and Vanpools	488999	All Other Support Activities for Transportation (pt)
4729	. Except Arrangement of Carpools and Vanpools	561599	All Other Travel Arrangement and Reservation Services (pt)
4731	Arrangement of Transportation of Freight and Cargo		
4731	. Freight Rate Auditors and Tariff Consultants	541614	Process, Physical Distribution, and Logistics Consulting Services (pt)
4731	. Except Freight Rate Auditors and Tariff Consultants	48851	Freight Transportation Arrangement
4741	Rental of Railroad Cars		
4741	. Rental of Railroad Cars	532411	Commercial Air, Rail, and Water Transportation Equipment Rental and Leasing (pt)
4741	. Grain Leveling in Railroad Cars, Grain Trimming for Railroad Equipment, Precooling of Fruits and Vegetables in Connection with Transportation, and Railroad Car Cleaning, Icing, Ventilating and Heating	48821	Support Activities for Rail Transportation (pt)
4783	Packing and Crating	488991	Packing and Crating
4785	Fixed Facilities and Inspection and Weighing Services for Motor Vehicle Transportation		
4785	. Marine Cargo Checkers	48839	Other Support Activities for Water Transportation (pt)
4785	. Except Marine Cargo Checkers	48849	Other Support Activities for Road Transportation (pt)
4789	Transportation Services, NEC		
4789	. Pipeline Terminals and Stockyards for Transportation	488999	All Other Support Activities for Transportation (pt)
4789	. Horse-drawn Cabs and Carriages	48711	Scenic and Sightseeing Transportation, Land (pt)

SIC Code	SIC Industry Title	NAICS Code	NAICS Industry Title
4789	. Dining Car Operations on a Fee or Contract Basis	72231	Food Service Contractors
4789	. Other	48821	Support Activities for Rail Transportation (pt)
48	Communications		
4812	Radiotelephone Communications		
4812	. Paging Carriers	513321	Paging
4812	. Cellular Carriers	513322	Cellular and Other Wireless Telecommunications (pt)
4812	. Paging and Cellular Resellers	51333	Telecommunications Resellers (pt)
4813	Telephone Communications, Except Radiotelephone		
4813	. Except Resellers	51331	Wired Telecommunications Carriers (pt)
4813	. Wired Resellers	51333	Telecommunications Resellers (pt)
4813	. Satellite Resellers	51334	Satellite Telecommunications (pt)
4822	Telegraph and Other Message Communications	51331	Wired Telecommunications Carriers (pt)
4832	Radio Broadcasting Stations		
4832	. Networks	513111	Radio Networks
4832	. Stations	513112	Radio Stations
4833	Television Broadcasting Stations	51312	Television Broadcasting
4841	Cable and Other Pay Television Services		
4841	. Cable Networks	51321	Cable Networks
4841	. Except Cable Networks	51322	Cable and Other Program Distribution
4899	Communications Services, NEC		
4899	. Taxi Cab Dispatch	48531	Taxi Service (pt)
4899	. Ship-to-Shore Broadcasting Communications	513322	Cellular and Other Wireless Telecommunications (pt)
4899	. Satellite Communications	51334	Satellite Telecommunications (pt)
4899	. Except Taxi Cab Dispatch Ship-to-Shore Communications and Satellite Communications	51339	Other Telecommunications
49	Electric, gas, and sanitary services		
4911	Electric Services		
4911	. Hydroelectric Power Generation	221111	Hydroelectric Power Generation (pt)
4911	. Electric Power Generation by Fossil Fuels	221112	Fossil Fuel Electric Power Generation (pt)
4911	. Electric Power Generation by Nuclear Fuels	221113	Nuclear Electric Power Generation (pt)
4911	. Other Electric Power Generation	221119	Other Electric Power Generation (pt)
4911	. Electric Power Transmission and Control	221121	Electric Bulk Power Transmission and Control (pt)
4911	. Electric Power Distribution	221122	Electric Power Distribution (pt)
4922	Natural Gas Transmission	48621	Pipeline Transportation of Natural Gas (pt)
4923	Natural Gas Transmission and Distribution		
4923	. Distribution	22121	Natural Gas Distribution (pt)

SIC Code	SIC Industry Title	NAICS Code	NAICS Industry Title
4923	. Transmission	48621	Pipeline Transportation of Natural Gas (pt)
4924	Natural Gas Distribution	22121	Natural Gas Distribution (pt)
4925	Mixed, Manufactured, or Liquefied Petroleum Gas Production and/or Distribution	22121	Natural Gas Distribution (pt)
4931	Electric and Other Services Combined		
4931	. Hydroelectric Power Generation When Combined with Other Services	221111	Hydroelectric Power Generation (pt)
4931	. Electric Power Generation by Fossil Fuels When Combined with Other Services	221112	Fossil Fuel Electric Power Generation (pt)
4931	. Electric Power Generation by Nuclear Fuels When Combined with Other Services	221113	Nuclear Electric Power Generation (pt)
4931	. Other Electric Power Generation When Combined with Other Services	221119	Other Electric Power Generation (pt)
4931	. Electric Power Transmission When Combined with Other Services	221121	Electric Bulk Power Transmission and Control (pt)
4931	. Electric Power Distribution When Combined with Other Services	221122	Electric Power Distribution (pt)
4931	. Natural Gas When Combined with Electric Services	22121	Natural Gas Distribution (pt)
4932	Gas and Other Services Combined	22121	Natural Gas Distribution (pt)
4939	Combination Utilities, NEC		
4939	. Hydroelectric Power Generation When Combined with Other Services	221111	Hydroelectric Power Generation (pt)
4939	. Electric Power Generation by Fossil Fuels When Combined with Other Services	221112	Fossil Fuel Electric Power Generation (pt)
4939	. Electric Power Generation by Nuclear Fuels When Combined with Other Services	221113	Nuclear Electric Power Generation (pt)
4939	. Other Power Generation When Combined with Other Services	221119	Other Electric Power Generation (pt)
4939	. Electric Power Transmission When Combined with Other Services	221121	Electric Bulk Power Transmission and Control (pt)
4939	. Electric Power Distribution When Combined with Other Services	221122	Electric Power Distribution (pt)
4939	. Natural Gas Distribution When Combined with Other Services	22121	Natural Gas Distribution (pt)
4941	Water Supply	22131	Water Supply and Irrigation Systems (pt)
4952	Sewerage Systems	22132	Sewage Treatment Facilities
4953	Refuse Systems		
4953	. Materials Recovery Facilities	56292	Materials Recovery Facilities
4953	. Hazardous Waste Treatment and Disposal	562211	Hazardous Waste Treatment and Disposal

SIC Code	SIC Industry Title	NAICS Code	NAICS Industry Title
4953	. Solid Waste Landfills	562212	Solid Waste Landfills
4953	. Solid Waste Combustors and Incinerators	562213	Solid Waste Combustors and Incinerators
4953	. Other Nonhazardous Waste Treatment and Disposal	562219	Other Nonhazardous Waste Treatment and Disposal
4959	Sanitary Services, NEC		
4959	. Vacuuming of Airport Runways	488119	Other Airport Operations (pt)
4959	. Remediation Services	56291	Remediation Services (pt)
4959	. Malaria Control and Mosquito Eradication	56171	Exterminating and Pest Control Services (pt)
4959	. Other	562998	All Other Miscellaneous Waste Management Services
4961	Steam and Air-Conditioning Supply	22133	Steam and Air-Conditioning Supply
4971	Irrigation Systems	22131	Water Supply and Irrigation Systems (pt)
	Wholesale Trade		
50	Wholesale trade—durable goods		
5012	Automobiles and Other Motor Vehicles	42111	Automobile and Other Motor Vehicle Wholesalers
5013	Motor Vehicle Supplies and New Parts		
5013	. Sold Via Retail Method	44131	Automotive Parts and Accessories Stores (pt)
5013	. Sold Via Wholesale Method	42112	Motor Vehicle Supplies and New Part Wholesalers
5014	Tires and Tubes		
5014	. Sold Via Retail Method	44132	Tire Dealers (pt) - Retail
5014	. Sold Via Wholesale Method	42113	Tire and Tube Wholesalers
5015	Motor Vehicle Parts, Used		
5015	. Sold Via Retail Method	44131	Automotive Parts and Accessories (pt)
5015	. Sold Via Wholesale Method	42114	Motor Vehicle Part (Used) Wholesalers
5021	Furniture		
5021	. Sold Via Retail Method	44211	Furniture Stores (pt)
5021	. Sold Via Wholesale Method	42121	Furniture Wholesalers
5023	Home Furnishings		
5023	. Sold Via Retail Method	44221	Floor Covering Stores (pt)
5023	. Sold Via Wholesale Method	42122	Home Furnishing Wholesalers
5031	Lumber, Plywood, Millwork, and Wood Panels	42131	Lumber, Plywood, Millwork, and Wood Panel Wholesalers
5032	Brick, Stone and Related Construction Materials		
5032	. Sold Via Retail Method	44419	Other Building Material Dealers (pt)
5032	. Sold Via Wholesale Method	42132	Brick, Stone and Related Construction Material Wholesalers
5033	Roofing, Siding, and Insulation Materials	42133	Roofing, Siding, and Insulation Material Wholesalers
5039	Construction Materials, NEC		

SIC Code	SIC Industry Title	NAICS Code	NAICS Industry Title
5039	. Sold Via Retail Method	44419	Other Building Material Dealers (pt)
5039	. Sold Via Wholesale Method	42139	Other Construction Material Wholesalers
5043	Photographic Equipment and Supplies	42141	Photographic Equipment and Supplies Wholesalers
5044	Office Equipment		
5044	. Sold Via Retail Method	45321	Office Supplies and Stationery Stores (pt)
5044	. Sold Via Wholesale Method	42142	Office Equipment Wholesalers
5045	Computers and Computer Peripheral Equipment and Software		
5045	. Sold Via Wholesale Method	42143	Computer and Computer Peripheral Equipment and Software Wholesalers
5045	. Sold Via Retail Method	44312	Computer and Software Stores (pt) - Retail
5046	Commercial Equipment, NEC	42144	Other Commercial Equipment Wholesalers
5047	Medical, Dental, and Hospital Equipment and Supplies		
5047	. Sold Via Wholesale Method	42145	Medical, Dental, and Hospital Equipment and Supplies Wholesalers
5047	. Sold Via Retail Method	446199	All Other Health and Personal Care Stores (pt) - Retail
5048	Ophthalmic Goods	42146	Ophthalmic Goods Wholesalers
5049	Professional Equipment and Supplies, NEC		
5049	. Sold Via Wholesale Method	42149	Other Professional Equipment and Supplies Wholesalers
5049	. Sold Via Retail Method	45321	Office Supplies and Stationery Stores (pt) - Retail
5051	Metals Service Centers and Offices	42151	Metals Service Centers and Offices
5052	Coal and Other Minerals and Ores	42152	Coal and Other Mineral and Ore Wholesalers
5063	Electrical Apparatus and Equipment Wiring Supplies, and Construction Materials		
5063	. Sold Via Retail Method	44419	Other Building Material Dealers (pt)
5063	. Sold Via Wholesale Method	42161	Electrical Apparatus and Equipment, Wiring Supplies, and Construction Material Wholesalers
5064	Electrical Appliances, Television and Radio Sets	42162	Electrical Appliance, Television, and Radio Set Wholesalers
5065	Electronic Parts and Equipment, NEC	42169	Other Electronic Parts and Equipment Wholesalers
5072	Hardware		
5072	. Sold Via Retail Method	44413	Hardware Stores (pt)
5072	. Sold Via Wholesale Method	42171	Hardware Wholesalers
5074	Plumbing and Heating Equipment and Supplies (Hydronics)		
5074	. Sold Via Retail Method	44419	Other Building Material Dealers (pt)
5074	. Sold Via Wholesale Method	42172	Plumbing and Heating Equipment and Supplies (Hydronics) Wholesalers
5075	Warm Air Heating and Air-Conditioning Equipment and Supplies	42173	Warm Air Heating and Air-Conditioning Equipment and Supplies Wholesalers

SIC Code	SIC Industry Title	NAICS Code	NAICS Industry Title
5078	Refrigeration Equipment and Supplies	42174	Refrigeration Equipment and Supplies Wholesalers
5082	Construction and Mining (Except Petroleum) Machinery and Equipment	42181	Construction and Mining (except Oil Well) Machinery and Equipment Wholesalers
5083	Farm and Garden Machinery and Equipment		
5083	. Sold Via Wholesale Method	42182	Farm and Garden Machinery and Equipment Wholesalers
5083	. Sold Via Retail Method	44421	Outdoor Power Equipment Stores (pt) - Retail
5084	Industrial Machinery and Equipment	42183	Industrial Machinery and Equipment Wholesalers (pt)
5085	Industrial Supplies		
5085	. Fluid Power Accessories	42183	Industrial Machinery and Equipment Wholesalers (pt)
5085	. Except Fluid Power Accessories	42184	Industrial Supplies Wholesalers
5087	Service Establishment Equipment and Supplies		
5087	. Sold Via Wholesale Method	42185	Service Establishment Equipment and Supplies Wholesalers
5087	. Sold Via Retail Method		
5087	. Beauty and Barber Shop Equipment and Supplies	44612	Cosmetics, Beauty Supplies, and Perfume Stores (pt)
5088	Transportation Equipment and Supplies, Except Motor Vehicles	42186	Transportation Equipment and Supplies (except Motor Vehicles) Wholesalers
5091	Sporting and Recreational Goods and Supplies	42191	Sporting and Recreational Goods and Supplies Wholesalers
5092	Toys and Hobby Goods and Supplies	42192	Toy and Hobby Goods and Supplies Wholesalers
5093	Scrap and Waste Materials	42193	Recyclable Material Wholesalers
5094	Jewelry, Watches, Precious Stones, and Precious Metals	42194	Jewelry, Watch , Precious Stone, and Precious Metal Wholesalers
5099	Durable Goods, NEC	42199	Other Miscellaneous Durable Goods Wholesalers (pt)
51	Wholesale trade—nondurable goods		
5111	Printing and Writing Paper	42211	Printing and Writing Paper Wholesalers
5112	Stationery and Office Supplies		
5112	. Sold Via Retail Method	45321	Office Supplies and Stationery Stores (pt)
5112	. Sold Via Wholesale Method	42212	Stationery and Office Supplies Wholesalers
5113	Industrial and Personal Service Paper	42213	Industrial and Personal Service Paper Wholesalers
5122	Drugs, Drug Proprietaries, and Druggists' Sundries	42221	Drugs and Druggists' Sundries Wholesalers
5131	Piece Goods, Notions, and Other Dry Goods		
5131	. Converters, Broadwoven Piece Good Fabric	313311	Broadwoven Fabric Finishing Mills (pt)
5131	. Converters, Except Broadwoven Fabric	313312	Textile and Fabric Finishing (except Broadwoven Fabric) Mills (pt)
5131	. Except Converters	42231	Piece Goods, Notions, and Other Dry Goods Wholesalers
5136	Men's and Boys' Clothing and Furnishings	42232	Men's and Boys' Clothing and Furnishings Wholesalers
5137	Women's, Children's, and Infants' Clothing and Accessories	42233	Women's, Children's, and Infants' Clothing and Accessories Wholesalers

SIC Code	SIC Industry Title	NAICS Code	NAICS Industry Title
5139	Footwear	42234	Footwear Wholesalers
5141	Groceries, General Line	42241	General Line Grocery Wholesalers
5142	Packaged Frozen Foods	42242	Packaged Frozen Food Wholesalers
5143	Dairy Products, Except Dried or Canned	42243	Dairy Products (except Dried or Canned) Wholesalers
5144	Poultry and Poultry Products	42244	Poultry and Poultry Product Wholesalers
5145	Confectionery	42245	Confectionery Wholesalers
5146	Fish and Seafoods	42246	Fish and Seafood Wholesalers
5147	Meats and Meat Products		
5147	. Boxed Beef	311612	Meat Processed from Carcasses (pt)
5147	. Except Boxed Beef	42247	Meat and Meat Product Wholesalers
5148	Fresh Fruits and Vegetables	42248	Fresh Fruit and Vegetable Wholesalers
5149	Groceries and Related Products, NEC		
5149	. Bottling Mineral or Spring Water	312112	Bottled Water Manufacturing (pt)
5149	. Except Bottling Mineral or Spring Water	42249	Other Grocery and Related Product Wholesalers
5153	Grain and Field Beans	42251	Grain and Field Bean Wholesalers
5154	Livestock	42252	Livestock Wholesalers
5159	Farm-Product Raw Materials, NEC	42259	Other Farm Product Raw Material Wholesalers
5162	Plastics Materials and Basic Forms and Shapes	42261	Plastics Materials and Basic Forms and Shapes Wholesalers
5169	Chemicals and Allied Products, NEC	42269	Other Chemical and Allied Products Wholesalers
5171	Petroleum Bulk Stations and Terminals		
5171	. Heating Oil Sold Via Retail Method	454311	Heating Oil Dealers (pt)
5171	. LP Gas Sold Via Retail Method	454312	Liquefied Petroleum Gas (Bottled Gas) Dealers (pt)
5171	. Sold Via Wholesale Method	42271	Petroleum Bulk Stations and Terminals
5172	Petroleum and Petroleum Products Wholesalers, Except Bulk Stations and Terminals	42272	Petroleum and Petroleum Products Wholesalers (except Bulk Stations and Terminals)
5181	Beer and Ale	42281	Beer and Ale Wholesalers
5182	Wine and Distilled Alcoholic Beverages	42282	Wine and Distilled Alcoholic Beverage Wholesalers
5191	Farm Supplies		
5191	. Lawn and Garden Supplies Sold Via Retail Method	44422	Nursery and Garden Centers (pt) - Retail
5191	. Except Lawn and Garden Supplies Sold Via Retail Method	42291	Farm Supplies Wholesalers
5192	Books, Periodicals, and Newspapers	42292	Book, Periodical, and Newspaper Wholesalers
5193	Flowers, Nursery Stock, and Florists' Supplies		
5193	. Sold Via Wholesale Method	42293	Flower, Nursery Stock, and Florists' Supplies Wholesalers
5193	. Sold Via Retail Method	44422	Nursery and Garden Centers (pt) - Retail
5194	Tobacco and Tobacco Products	42294	Tobacco and Tobacco Product Wholesalers
5198	Paint, Varnishes, and Supplies	42295	Paint, Varnish, and Supplies Wholesalers

SIC Code	SIC Industry Title	NAICS Code	NAICS Industry Title
5199	Nondurable Goods, NEC		
5199	. Advertising Specialties Goods Distributors	54189	Other Services Related to Advertising (pt)
5199	. Except Advertising Specialty	42299	Other Miscellaneous Nondurable Goods Wholesalers
	Retail Trade		
52	Building materials, hardware, garden supply, & mobile home		
5211	Lumber and Other Building Materials Dealers		
5211	. Home Centers	44411	Home Centers
5211	. Except Home Centers	44419	Other Building Material Dealers (pt)
5231	Paint, Glass, and Wallpaper Stores		
5231	. Paint and Wallpaper	44412	Paint and Wallpaper Stores (pt)
5231	. Glass Stores	44419	Other Building Material Dealers (pt)
5251	Hardware Stores	44413	Hardware Stores (pt)
5261	Retail Nurseries, Lawn and Garden Supply Stores		
5261	. Except Outdoor Power Equipment	44422	Nursery and Garden Centers (pt)
5261	. Outdoor Power Equipment Stores	44421	Outdoor Power Equipment Stores (pt)
5271	Mobile Home Dealers	45393	Manufactured (Mobile) Home Dealers
53	General merchandise stores		
5311	Department Stores	45211	Department Stores
5331	Variety Stores	45299	All Other General Merchandise Stores (pt)
5399	Miscellaneous General Merchandise Stores		
5399	. Warehouse Clubs and General Merchandise Combination Stores	45291	Warehouse Clubs and Superstores (pt)
5399	. All Other General Merchandise Stores	45299	All Other General Merchandise Stores (pt)
54	Food stores		
5411	Grocery Stores		
5411	. Convenience Stores with Gas	44711	Gasoline Stations with Convenience Stores (pt)
5411	. Supermarkets and Grocery Stores with Little General Merchandise	44511	Supermarkets and Other Grocery (except Convenience) Stores
5411	. Supermarkets and Grocery Stores with Substantial General Merchandise	45291	Warehouse Clubs and Superstores (pt)
5411	. Convenience Stores without Gas	44512	Convenience Stores
5421	Meat and Fish (Seafood) Markets, Including Freezer Provisioners		
5421	. Freezer Provisioners	45439	Other Direct Selling Establishments (pt)
5421	. Meat Markets	44521	Meat Markets (pt)
5421	. Fish and Seafood Markets	44522	Fish and Seafood Markets
5431	Fruit and Vegetable Markets	44523	Fruit and Vegetable Markets

SIC Code	SIC Industry Title	NAICS Code	NAICS Industry Title
5441	Candy, Nut, and Confectionery Stores		
5441	. Confectionery and Nut Stores	445292	Confectionery and Nut Stores
5441	. Chocolate Candy Stores, Preparing Candy on Premises	31133	Confectionery Manufacturing from Purchased Chocolate (pt)
5441	. Nonchocolate Candy Stores, Preparing Candy on Premises	31134	Nonchocolate Confectionery Manufacturing (pt)
5451	Dairy Products Stores	445299	All Other Specialty Food Stores (pt)
5461	Retail Bakeries		
5461	. Doughnut Shops, Pretzel Shops, Cookie Shops, Bagel Shops, and Other Such Shops that Make and Sell for Immediate Consumption	722213	Snack and Nonalcoholic Beverage Bars (pt)
5461	. Bakeries That Make and Sell at the Same Location	311811	Retail Bakeries
5461	. Sales Only of All Other Baked Goods	445291	Baked Goods Stores
5499	Miscellaneous Food Stores		
5499	. Poultry and Poultry Products	44521	Meat Markets (pt)
5499	. Food Supplement Stores	446191	Food (Health) Supplement Stores
5499	. All Other Miscellaneous Food Stores	445299	All Other Specialty Food Stores (pt)
55	Automotive dealers and gasoline service stations		
5511	Motor Vehicle Dealers (New and Used)	44111	New Car Dealers
5521	Motor Vehicle Dealers (Used Only)	44112	Used Car Dealers
5531	Auto and Home Supply Stores		
5531	. Tire Dealers	44132	Tire Dealers (pt)
5531	. Auto Supply Stores	44131	Automotive Parts and Accessories Stores (pt)
5531	. Other Auto and Home Supply Stores	45299	All Other General Merchandise (pt)
5541	Gasoline Service Stations		
5541	. With Convenience Store	44711	Gasoline Stations with Convenience Store (pt)
5541	. Except with Convenience Stores	44719	Other Gasoline Stations
5551	Boat Dealers	441222	Boat Dealers
5561	Recreational Vehicle Dealers	44121	Recreational Vehicle Dealers
5571	Motorcycle Dealers	441221	Motorcycle Dealers
5599	Automotive Dealers, NEC	441229	All Other Motor Vehicle Dealers
56	Apparel and accessory stores		
5611	Men's and Boys' Clothing and Accessory Stores		
5611	. Men's Clothing Stores	44811	Men's Clothing Stores
5611	. Men's Accessory Stores	44815	Clothing Accessories Stores (pt)
5621	Women's Clothing Stores	44812	Women's Clothing Stores
5632	Women's Accessory and Specialty Stores		
5632	. Specialty Stores	44819	Other Clothing Stores (pt)

SIC Code	SIC Industry Title	NAICS Code	NAICS Industry Title
5632	. Accessory Stores	44815	Clothing Accessories Stores (pt)
5641	Children's and Infants' Wear Stores	44813	Children's and Infants' Clothing Stores
5651	Family Clothing Stores	44814	Family Clothing Stores
5661	Shoe Stores	44821	Shoe Stores
5699	Miscellaneous Apparel and Accessory Stores		
5699	. Custom Tailors and Seamstresses	315	Included in Apparel Manufacturing Subsector Based on Type of Garment Produced
5699	. Miscellaneous Apparel	44819	Other Clothing Stores (pt)
5699	. Miscellaneous Accessories	44815	Clothing Accessories Stores (pt)
57	Furniture, home furnishings and equipment stores		
5712	Furniture Stores		
5712	. Custom Made Wood Nonupholstered Furniture, Except Cabinets and Upholstered	337122	Nonupholstered Wood Household Furniture Manufacturing (pt)
5712	. Custom Wood Cabinets	33711	Wood Kitchen Cabinet and Countertop Manufacturing (pt)
5712	. Upholstered Custom Made Furniture	337121	Upholstered Household Furniture Manufacturing (pt)
5712	. Except Custom Cabinet and Furniture Builders	44211	Furniture Stores (pt)
5713	Floor Covering Stores	44221	Floor Covering Stores (pt)
5714	Drapery, Curtain, and Upholstery Stores		
5714	. Drapery and Curtain Stores	442291	Window Treatment Stores (pt)
5714	. Upholstery Stores	45113	Sewing, Needlework and Piece Goods Stores (pt)
5714	. Custom Drapes	314121	Curtain and Drapery Mills (pt)
5714	. Custom Slipcovers	314129	Other Household Textile Product Mills (pt)
5719	Miscellaneous Homefurnishings Stores		
5719	. Blinds and Shades	442291	Window Treatment Stores (pt)
5719	. Pottery and Crafts Made and Sold on Site		Included in Manufacturing sector based on article produced
5719	. Except Blinds, Shades, and Pottery and Crafts Made and Sold on Site	442299	All Other Home Furnishings Stores (pt)
5722	Household Appliance Stores	443111	Household Appliance Stores
5731	Radio, Television, and Consumer Electronics Stores		
5731	. Except Auto Radio Stores	443112	Radio, Television, and Other Electronics Stores (pt)
5731	. Auto Radio Stores	44131	Automotive Parts and Accessories Stores (pt)
5734	Computer and Computer Software Stores	44312	Computer and Software Stores (pt)
5735	Record and Prerecorded Tape Stores	45122	Prerecorded Tape, Compact Disc, and Record Stores
5736	Musical Instrument Stores	45114	Musical Instrument and Supplies Stores
58	Eating and drinking places		
5812	Eating and Drinking Places		

SIC Code	SIC Industry Title	NAICS Code	NAICS Industry Title
5812	. Full Service Restaurants	72211	Full-Service Restaurants
5812	. Limited Service Restaurants	722211	Limited-Service Restaurants
5812	. Cafeterias	722212	Cafeterias
5812	. Snack and Nonalcoholic Beverage Bars	722213	Snack and Nonalcoholic Beverage Bars (pt)
5812	. Food Service Contractors	72231	Food Service Contractors
5812	. Caterers	72232	Caterers
5812	. Dinner Theaters	71111	Theater Companies and Dinner Theaters (pt)
5813	Drinking Places (Alcoholic Beverages)	72241	Drinking Places (Alcoholic Beverages)
59	Miscellaneous retail		
5912	Drug Stores and Proprietary Stores	44611	Pharmacies and Drug Stores
5921	Liquor Stores	44531	Beer, Wine, and Liquor Stores
5932	Used Merchandise Stores		
5932	. Pawnshops	522298	All Other Nondepository Credit Intermediation
5932	. Except pawn shops	45331	Used Merchandise Stores
5941	Sporting Goods Stores and Bicycle Shops	45111	Sporting Goods Stores
5942	Book Stores	451211	Book Stores
5943	Stationery Stores	45321	Office Supplies and Stationery Stores (pt)
5944	Jewelry Stores	44831	Jewelry Stores
5945	Hobby, Toy, and Game Shops	45112	Hobby, Toy, and Game Stores
5946	Camera and Photographic Supply Stores	44313	Camera and Photographic Supplies Stores
5947	Gift, Novelty, and Souvenir Shops	45322	Gift, Novelty, and Souvenir Stores
5948	Luggage and Leather Goods Stores	44832	Luggage and Leather Goods Stores
5949	Sewing, Needlework, and Piece Goods Stores	45113	Sewing, Needlework, and Piece Goods Stores (pt)
5961	Catalog and Mail-Order Houses	45411	Electronic Shopping and Mail-Order Houses
5962	Automatic Merchandising Machine Operator	45421	Vending Machine Operators
5963	Direct Selling Establishments		
5963	. Mobile Food Wagons	72233	Mobile Food Services
5963	. All Other Direct Selling Establishments	45439	Other Direct Selling Establishments (pt)
5983	Fuel Oil Dealers	454311	Heating Oil Dealers (pt)
5984	Liquefied Petroleum Gas (Bottled Gas) Dealers	454312	Liquefied Petroleum Gas (Bottled Gas) Dealers (pt)
5989	Fuel Dealers, NEC	454319	Other Fuel Dealers
5992	Florists	45311	Florists
5993	Tobacco Stores and Stands	453991	Tobacco Stores
5994	News Dealers and Newsstands	451212	News Dealers and Newsstands
5995	Optical Goods Stores		

SIC Code	SIC Industry Title	NAICS Code	NAICS Industry Title
5995	. Optical Stores Grinding Prescription Lenses, except 1-Hour Labs	339115	Ophthalmic Goods Manufacturing (pt)
5995	. Except Optical Laboratories Grinding Prescription Lenses	44613	Optical Goods Stores
5999	Miscellaneous Retail Stores, NEC		
5999	. Cosmetic Stores	44612	Cosmetics, Beauty Supplies, and Perfume Stores (pt)
5999	. Hearing Aid and Artificial Limb Stores	446199	All Other Health and Personal Care Stores (pt)
5999	. Pets and Pet Supply Stores	45391	Pet and Pet Supplies Stores
5999	. Art Dealers	45392	Art Dealers
5999	. Telephone and Typewriter Stores	443112	Radio, Television, and Other Electronics Stores (pt)
5999	. Other Miscellaneous Retail Stores	453998	All Other Miscellaneous Store Retailers (except Tobacco Stores) (pt)
	Finance, Insurance, and Real Estate		
60	Depository Institutions		
6011	Federal Reserve Banks	52111	Monetary Authorities-Central Banks
6019	Central Reserve Depository Institutions, NEC	522298	All Other Nondepository Credit Intermediation (pt)
6021	National Commercial Banks		
6021	. Commercial Banks	52211	Commercial Banking (pt)
6021	. Credit Card Issuing	52221	Credit Card Issuing (pt)
6022	State Commercial Banks		
6022	. Commercial Banks	52211	Commercial Banking (pt)
6022	. Credit Card Issuing	52221	Credit Card Issuing (pt)
6022	. Private and Industrial Banking	52219	Other Depository Intermediation
6029	Commercial Banks, NEC	52211	Commercial Banking (pt)
6035	Savings Institutions, Federally Chartered	52212	Savings Institutions (pt)
6036	Savings Institutions, Not Federally Chartered	52212	Savings Institutions (pt)
6061	Credit Unions, Federally Chartered	52213	Credit Unions (pt)
6062	Credit Unions, Not Federally Chartered	52213	Credit Unions (pt)
6081	Branches and Agencies of Foreign Banks		
6081	. International Trade Financing	522293	International Trade Financing (pt)
6081	. Branches of Foreign Banks	52211	Commercial Banking (pt)
6081	. Agencies of Foreign Banks, Except International Trade Financing	522298	All Other Nondepository Credit Intermediation (pt)
6082	Foreign Trade and International Banking Institutions		
6082	. International Trade Financing	522293	International Trade Financing (pt)
6082	. Foreign Trade and International Banking Institutions (except international trade financing)	522298	All Other Nondepository Credit Intermediation (pt)
6091	Nondeposit Trust Facilities	523991	Trust, Fiduciary, and Custody Activities (pt)

SIC Code	SIC Industry Title	NAICS Code	NAICS Industry Title
6099	Functions Related to Deposit Banking, NEC		
6099	. Clearinghouses and Electronic Funds Transfer	52232	Financial Transactions Processing, Reserve, and Clearinghouse Activities (pt)
6099	. Foreign Currency Exchange	52313	Commodity Contracts Dealing (pt)
6099	. Escrow and Fiduciary Agencies	523991	Trust, Fiduciary, and Custody Activities (pt)
6099	. Other	52239	Other Activities Related to Credit Intermediation (pt)
61	Nondepository credit institutions		
6111	Federal and Federally-Sponsored Credit Agencies		
6111	. Federal Land Banks	522292	Real Estate Credit (pt)
6111	. Trade Banks	522293	International Trade Financing (pt)
6111	. Secondary Market Financing	522294	Secondary Market Financing
6111	. Other	522298	All Other Nondepository Credit Intermediation (pt)
6141	Personal Credit Institutions		
6141	. Credit Card Issuing	52221	Credit Card Issuing (pt)
6141	. Installment Sales Financing	52222	Sales Financing (pt)
6141	. Industrial Nondeposit Banks	522298	All Other Nondepository Credit Intermediation (pt)
6141	. Other	522291	Consumer Lending
6153	Short-Term Business Credit Institutions, Except Agricultural		
6153	. Credit Card Issuing	52221	Credit Card Issuing (pt)
6153	. Business Sales Finance	52222	Sales Financing (pt)
6153	. Credit Card Service	52232	Financial Transactions Processing, Reserve, and Clearinghouse Activities (pt)
6153	. Other	52391	Miscellaneous Intermediation (pt)
6159	Miscellaneous Business Credit Institutions		
6159	. Finance Leasing Combined with Loan Making	522	Included in Credit Intermediation and Related Activities Subsector by Type of Credit
6159	. Finance Leasing Combined with Sales Financing	52222	Sales Financing (pt)
6159	. Farm Mortgage Companies	522292	Real Estate Credit (pt)
6159	. Finance Leasing Without Loan Making	532	Included in Rental and Leasing Services Subsector by Type of Equipment and Method of Operation
6159	. Trade Banks	522293	International Trade Financing (pt)
6159	. Secondary Market Financing	522294	Secondary Market Financing (pt)
6159	. All Other	522298	All Other Nondepository Credit Intermediation (pt)
6162	Mortgage Bankers and Loan Correspondents		
6162	. Mortgage Bankers and Originators	522292	Real Estate Credit
6162	. Mortgage Servicing	52239	Other Activities Related to Credit Intermediation (pt)

SIC Code	SIC Industry Title	NAICS Code	NAICS Industry Title
6163	Loan Brokers	52231	Mortgage and Nonmortgage Loan Brokers
62	Security, commodity brokers, and services		
6211	Security Brokers, Dealers, and Flotation Companies		
6211	. Security Dealers and Underwriters	52311	Investment Banking and Securities Dealing
6211	. Security Brokers	52312	Securities Brokerage
6211	. Oil and Gas Lease Brokers' Offices	523999	Miscellaneous Financial Investment Activities (pt)
6211	. Dealers and Brokers, Except Securities Commodities, and Oil and Gas Lease Brokers	52391	Miscellaneous Intermediation (pt)
6221	Commodity Contracts Brokers and Dealers		
6221	. Commodity Dealers	52313	Commodity Contracts Dealing (pt)
6221	. Commodity Brokers	52314	Commodity Contracts Brokerage
6231	Security and Commodity Exchanges	52321	Securities and Commodity Exchanges
6282	Investment Advice		
6282	. Portfolio Managers	52392	Portfolio Management (pt)
6282	. Other	52393	Investment Advice
6289	Services Allied With the Exchange of Securities or Commodities, NEC		
6289	. Securities Custodians	523991	Trust, Fiduciary, and Custody Activities (pt)
6289	. Other	523999	Miscellaneous Financial Investment Activities (pt)
63	Insurance carriers		
6311	Life Insurance		
6311	. Life Insurers, Direct	524113	Direct Life Insurance Carriers
6311	. Reinsurance Carriers, Life	52413	Reinsurance Carriers (pt)
6321	Accident and Health Insurance		
6321	. Disability Insurers, Direct	524113	Direct Life Insurance Carriers (pt)
6321	. Accident and Health Insurers, Direct	524114	Direct Health and Medical Insurance Carriers (pt)
6321	. Self Insurers	52519	Other Insurance Funds (pt)
6321	. Reinsurance Carriers, Accident and Health	52413	Reinsurance Carriers (pt)
6324	Hospital and Medical Service Plans		
6324	. Health and Medical Insurers, Direct	524114	Direct Health and Medical Insurance Carriers (pt)
6324	. Self Insurers	52519	Other Insurance Funds (pt)
6324	. Reinsurance Carriers, Health and Medical	52413	Reinsurance Carriers (pt)
6331	Fire, Marine, and Casualty Insurance		
6331	. Fire, Marine, and Casualty Insurers, Direct	524126	Direct Property and Casualty Insurance Carriers (pt)
6331	. Contact Lens Insurance	524128	Other Direct Insurance (except Life, Health, and Medical) Carriers (pt)

SIC Code	SIC Industry Title	NAICS Code	NAICS Industry Title
6331	. Self Insurers	52519	Other Insurance Funds (pt)
6331	. Reinsurance Carriers, Fire, Marine, and Casualty	52413	Reinsurance Carriers (pt)
6351	Surety Insurance		
6351	. Financial Responsibility Insurers, Direct	524126	Direct Property and Casualty Insurance Carriers (pt)
6351	. Reinsurance Carriers, Financial Responsibility	52413	Reinsurance Carriers (pt)
6361	Title Insurance		
6361	. Title Insurers, Direct	524127	Direct Title Insurance Carriers
6361	. Reinsurance Carriers, Title	52413	Reinsurance Carriers (pt)
6371	Pension, Health, and Welfare Funds		
6371	. Managers	52392	Portfolio Management (pt)
6371	. Administrators	524292	Third Party Administration of Insurance and Pension Funds (pt)
6371	. Pension Funds	52511	Pension Funds
6371	. Health and Welfare Funds	52512	Health and Welfare Funds
6371	. Profit Sharing Funds	52599	Other Financial Vehicles (pt)
6399	Insurance Carriers, NEC	524128	Other Direct Insurance (except Life, Health, and Medical) Carriers
64	Insurance agents, brokers, and service		
6411	Insurance Agents, Brokers, and Service		
6411	. Insurance Agents and Brokers	52421	Insurance Agencies and Brokerages
6411	. Claim Adjusters	524291	Claims Adjusting
6411	. Claim Processors	524292	Third Party Administrators of Insurance and Pension Funds (pt)
6411	. Other	524298	All Other Insurance Related Activities
65	Real estate		
6512	Operators of Nonresidential Buildings		
6512	. Stadium and Arena Owners	71131	Promoters of Performing Arts, Sports, and Similar Events with Facilities (pt)
6512	. Except Stadium and Arena Owners	53112	Lessors of Nonresidential Buildings (except Miniwarehouses)
6513	Operators of Apartment Buildings	53111	Lessors of Residential Buildings and Dwellings (pt)
6514	Operators of Dwellings Other Than Apartment Buildings	53111	Lessors of Residential Buildings and Dwellings (pt)
6515	Operators of Residential Mobile Home Sites	53119	Lessors of Other Real Estate Property(pt)
6517	Lessors of Railroad Property	53119	Lessors of Other Real Estate Property (pt)
6519	Lessors of Real Property, NEC	53119	Lessors of Other Real Estate Property (pt)
6531	Real Estate Agents and Managers		
6531	. Real Estate Agents and Brokers	53121	Offices of Real Estate Agents and Brokers

SIC Code	SIC Industry Title	NAICS Code	NAICS Industry Title
6531	. Condominium Associations	81399	Other Similar Organizations (except Business, Professional, Labor, and Political Organizations) (pt)
6531	. Residential Property Managers	531311	Residential Property Managers
6531	. Nonresidential Property Managers	531312	Nonresidential Property Managers
6531	. Real Estate Appraisers	53132	Offices of Real Estate Appraisers
6531	. Cemetery Management	81222	Cemeteries and Crematories (pt)
6531	. Other	53139	Other Activities Related to Real Estate
6541	Title Abstract Offices	541191	Title Abstract and Settlement Offices
6552	Land Subdividers and Developers, Except Cemeteries	23311	Land Subdivision and Land Development
6553	Cemetery Subdividers and Developers	81222	Cemeteries and Crematories (pt)
67	Holding and other investment offices		
6712	Offices of Bank Holding Companies	551111	Offices of Bank Holding Companies
6719	Offices of Holding Companies, NEC	551112	Offices of Other Holding Companies
6722	Management Investment Offices, Open-End	52591	Open-End Investment Funds
6726	Unit Investment Trusts, Face-Amount Certificate Offices, and Closed-End Management Investment Offices	52599	Other Financial Vehicles
6732	Education, Religious, and Charitable Trusts	813211	Grantmaking Foundations
6733	Trusts, Except Educational, Religious, and Charitable		
6733	. Managers	52392	Portfolio Management (pt)
6733	. Administrators of Private Estates	523991	Trust, Fiduciary, and Custody Services (pt)
6733	. Vacation Funds for Employees	52519	Other Insurance Funds (pt)
6733	. Personal Trusts, Estates, and Agency Accounts	52592	Trusts, Estates, and Agency Accounts
6792	Oil Royalty Traders		
6792	. Investing on Own Account	52391	Miscellaneous Intermediation (pt)
6792	. Oil Royalty Companies	53311	Lessors of Nonfinancial Intangible Assets (except Copyrighted Works) (pt)
6794	Patent Owners and Lessors	53311	Lessors of Nonfinancial Intangible Assets (except Copyrighted Works) (pt)
6798	Real Estate Investment Trusts	52593	Real Estate Investment Trusts
6799	Investors, NEC		
6799	. Venture Capital Companies, Investment Clubs, and Operators on Own Account	52391	Miscellaneous Intermediation (pt)
6799	. Commodity Contract Pool Operators	52392	Portfolio Management (pt)
6799	. Commodity Contract Trading Companies	52313	Commodity Contracts Dealing (pt)
	Service Industries		
70	Hotels, rooming houses, camps, and other lodging places		
7011	Hotels and Motels		

SIC Code	SIC Industry Title	NAICS Code	NAICS Industry Title
7011	. Hotels and Motels, except Casino Hotels	72111	Hotels (except Casino Hotels) and Motels (pt)
7011	. Casino Hotels	72112	Casino Hotels
7011	. Bed and Breakfast Inns	721191	Bed and Breakfast Inns
7011	. Other	721199	All Other Traveler Accommodation
7021	Rooming and Boarding Houses	72131	Rooming and Boarding Houses (pt)
7032	Sporting and Recreational Camps	721214	Recreational and Vacation Camps (except Campgrounds)
7033	Recreational Vehicle Parks and Campsites	721211	RV (Recreational Vehicle Parks) and Campgrounds
7041	Organization Hotels and Lodging Houses, on Membership Basis		
7041	. Organization Hotels	72111	Hotels (except Casino Hotels) and Motels (pt)
7041	. Other	72131	Rooming and Boarding Houses (pt)
72	Personal services		
7211	Power Laundries, Family and Commercial	81232	Drycleaning and Laundry Services (except Coin-Operated) (pt)
7212	Garment Pressing, and Agents for Laundries and Drycleaners	81232	Drycleaning and Laundry Services (except Coin-Operated) (pt)
7213	Linen Supply	812331	Linen Supply (pt)
7215	Coin-Operated Laundries and Drycleaning	81231	Coin-Operated Laundries and Drycleaners
7216	Drycleaning Plants, Except Rug Cleaning	81232	Drycleaning and Laundry Services (except Coin-Operated) (pt)
7217	Carpet and Upholstery Cleaning	56174	Carpet and Upholstery Cleaning Services
7218	Industrial Launderers	812332	Industrial Launderers
7219	Laundry and Garment Services, NEC		
7219	. Diaper Service	812331	Linen Supply (pt)
7219	. Clothing Alteration and Repair	81149	Other Personal and Household Goods Repair and Maintenance (pt)
7219	. Except Diaper Service and Clothing Alteration and Repair	81232	Drycleaning and Laundry Services (except Coin-Operated)
7221	Photographic Studios, Portrait	541921	Photographic Studios, Portrait
7231	Beauty Shops		
7231	. Beauty Shops and Salons	812112	Beauty Salons
7231	. Manicure and Pedicure Salons	812113	Nail Salons
7231	. Beauty and Cosmetology Schools	611511	Cosmetology and Barber Schools (pt)
7241	Barber Shops		
7241	. Barber Shops	812111	Barber Shops
7241	. Barber Colleges	611511	Cosmetology and Barber Schools (pt)
7251	Shoe Repair Shops and Shoeshine Parlors		
7251	. Shoe Repair Shops	81143	Footwear and Leather Goods Repair (pt)
7251	. Shoeshine Parlors	81299	All Other Personal Services (pt)

SIC Code	SIC Industry Title	NAICS Code	NAICS Industry Title
7261	Funeral Services and Crematories		
7261	. Crematories	81222	Cemeteries and Crematories (pt)
7261	. Funeral Homes and Funeral Services	81221	Funeral Homes
7291	Tax Return Preparation Services	541213	Tax Preparation Services
7299	Miscellaneous Personal Services, NEC		
7299	. Babysitting Bureaus	56131	Employment Placement Agencies (pt)
7299	. Diet and Weight Reducing Services	812191	Diet and Weight Reducing Centers
7299	. Valet Parking Services	81293	Parking Lots and Garages (pt)
7299	. Formal Wear and Costume Rental	53222	Formal Wear and Costume Rental (pt)
7299	. Personal Care Services	812199	Other Personal Care Services
7299	. All Other Miscellaneous Personal Services, NEC	81299	All Other Personal Services (pt)
73	Business services		
7311	Advertising Agencies	54181	Advertising Agencies
7312	Outdoor Advertising Services	54185	Display Advertising (pt)
7313	Radio, Television, and Publishers' Advertising Representatives	54184	Media Representatives
7319	Advertising, NEC		
7319	. Media Buying Services	54183	Media Buying Agencies
7319	. Display Advertising, Except Outdoor	54185	Display Advertising (pt)
7319	. Advertising Materials Distributor Services	54187	Advertising Material Distribution Services
7319	. Other	54189	Other Services Related to Advertising (pt)
7322	Adjustment and Collection Services	56144	Collection Agencies
7323	Credit Reporting Services	56145	Credit Bureaus
7331	Direct Mail Advertising Services		
7331	. Mailing List Compilers	51114	Database and Directory Publishers (pt)
7331	. Other	54186	Direct Mail Advertising
7334	Photocopying and Duplicating Services		
7334	. Instant Printing	323114	Quick Printing (pt)
7334	. Photocopying and Duplicating Services, Except Instant Printing	561439	Other Business Service Centers (including Copy Shops) (pt)
7335	Commercial Photography	541922	Commercial Photography (pt)
7336	Commercial Art and Graphic Design	54143	Graphic Design Services (pt)
7338	Secretarial and Court Reporting Services		
7338	. Secretarial Services	56141	Document Preparation Services
7338	. Court Reporting Services	561492	Court Reporting and Stenotype Services
7342	Disinfecting and Pest Control Services		

SIC Code	SIC Industry Title	NAICS Code	NAICS Industry Title
7342	. Disinfecting Services	56172	Janitorial Services (pt)
7342	. Exterminating and Pest Control Services	56171	Exterminating and Pest Control Services (pt)
7349	Building Cleaning and Maintenance Services, NEC		
7349	. Lighting Maintenance Services	56179	Other Services to Buildings and Dwellings (pt)
7349	. Except Lighting Maintenance Services	56172	Janitorial Services (pt)
7352	Medical Equipment Rental and Leasing		
7352	. Home Health Furniture and Equipment Rental and Leasing	532291	Home Health Equipment Rental
7352	. Medical Machinery Rental and Leasing	53249	Other Commercial and Industrial Machinery and Equipment Rental and Leasing (pt)
7353	Heavy Construction Equipment Rental and Leasing		
7353	. With Operator	23499	All Other Heavy Construction (pt)
7353	. Without Operator	532412	Construction, Mining, and Forestry Machinery and Equipment Rental and Leasing (pt)
7359	Equipment Rental and Leasing, NEC		
7359	. Consumer Electronics and Appliances Rental	53221	Consumer Electronics and Appliances Rental
7359	. General Rental Centers	53231	General Rental Centers
7359	. Residential Furniture, Party Supplies, and All Other Miscellaneous Consumer Goods Rental and Leasing	532299	All Other Consumer Goods Rental
7359	. Oilfield and Well Drilling Machinery and Equipment Rental and Leasing	532412	Construction, Mining, and Forestry Machinery and Equipment Rental and Leasing (pt)
7359	. Aircraft Rental and Leasing	532411	Commercial Air, Rail, and Water Transportation Equipment Rental and Leasing (pt)
7359	. Portable Toilet Rental	562991	Septic Tank and Related Services (pt)
7359	. Office Machinery and Equipment Rental and Leasing	53242	Office Machinery and Equipment Rental and Leasing (pt)
7359	. Industrial Trucks Rental and Leasing	53249	Other Commercial and Industrial Machinery and Equipment Rental and Leasing (pt)
7361	Employment Agencies		
7361	. Executive Placing Services	541612	Human Resources and Executive Search Consulting Services (pt)
7361	. Except Executive Placing Services	56131	Employment Placement Agencies (pt)
7363	Help Supply Services		
7363	. Temporary Help Supply	56132	Temporary Help Services
7363	. Employee Leasing Services	56133	Employee Leasing Services
7371	Computer Programming Services	541511	Custom Computer Programming Services
7372	Prepackaged Software		
7372	. Software Publishing	51121	Software Publishers
7372	. Reproduction of Software	334611	Software Reproducing

SIC Code	SIC Industry Title	NAICS Code	NAICS Industry Title
7373	Computer Integrated Systems Design	541512	Computer Systems Design Services (pt)
7374	Computer Processing and Data Preparation and Processing Services	51421	Data Processing Services
7375	Information Retrieval Services	514191	On-Line Information Services
7376	Computer Facilities Management Services	541513	Computer Facilities Management Services
7377	Computer Rental and Leasing	53242	Office Machinery and Equipment Rental and Leasing (pt)
7378	Computer Maintenance and Repair		
7378	. Retailing Computers From a Storefront and Repairing	44312	Computer and Software Stores (pt)
7378	. All Other Repair	811212	Computer and Office Machine Repair and Maintenance (pt)
7379	Computer Related Services, NEC		
7379	. Disk and Diskette Conversion and Recertification	51421	Data Processing Services (pt)
7379	. Computer Systems Consultants	541512	Computer Systems Design Services (pt)
7379	. Except Computer Systems Consultants and Disk and Diskette Conversion and Recertification	541519	Other Computer Related Services
7381	Detective, Guard, and Armored Car Services		
7381	. Detective Services	561611	Investigation Services
7381	. Guard Services	561612	Security Guards and Patrol Services
7381	. Armored Car Services	561613	Armored Car Services
7382	Security Systems Services	561621	Security Systems Services (except Locksmiths) (pt)
7383	News Syndicates		
7383	. Independent Correspondents	71151	Independent Artists, Writers, and Performers (pt)
7383	. Except Independent Correspondents	51411	News Syndicates
7384	Photofinishing Laboratories		
7384	. Photofinishing Laboratories (Except 1-Hour)	812921	Photofinishing Laboratories (except One-Hour)
7384	. One-Hour Photofinishing	812922	One-Hour Photo Finishing
7389	Business Services, NEC		
7389	. Sound Recording Studios	51224	Sound Recording Studios
7389	. Audio Taping Services	51229	Other Sound Recording Industries (pt)
7389	. Stock Photo Agencies and Press Clipping Services	514199	All Other Information Services (pt)
7389	. Process Services, Patent Agents, Notaries Public and Paralegal Services	541199	All Other Legal Services
7389	. Bail Bonding	81299	All Other Personal Services (pt)
7389	. Mapmaking Services	54137	Surveying and Mapping (except Geophysical) Services (pt)
7389	. Interior Design	54141	Interior Design Services
7389	. Industrial Design	54142	Industrial Design Services

SIC Code	SIC Industry Title	NAICS Code	NAICS Industry Title
7389	. Drafting Service	54134	Drafting Services
7389	. Fashion and Other Design Services	54149	Other Specialized Design Services
7389	. Sign Painting and Lettering Shops, Showcard Painting, Mannequin Decorating Services, and Other Advertising Related Business Services	54189	Other Services Related to Advertising (pt)
7389	. Translation and Interpretation Services	54193	Translation and Interpretation Services
7389	. Home and Building Inspection Services	54135	Building Inspection Services
7389	. Appraisers, Except Insurance and Real Estate, and Miscellaneous Professional, Scientific, and Technical Services	54199	All Other Professional, Scientific, and Technical Services
7389	. Microfilm Services	51421	Data Processing Services (pt)
7389	. Agents and Brokers for Authors and Artists and Speaker Bureaus	71141	Agents and Managers for Artists, Athletes, Entertainers, and Other Public Figures (pt)
7389	. Yacht Brokers	42186	Transportation Equipment and Supplies (except Motor Vehicle) Wholesalers
7389	. Telephone Answering Services	561421	Telephone Answering Services
7389	. Aerosol Packaging	325998	All Other Miscellaneous Chemical Product and Preparation Manufacturing (pt)
7389	. Telemarketing Bureaus and Telephone Soliciting Services	561422	Telemarketing Bureaus
7389	. Private Mail Centers and Mail Box Rental	561431	Private Mail Centers
7389	. Business Service Centers, Except Private Mail Centers and Mail Box Rental	561439	Other Business Service Centers (including Copy Shops)
7389	. Embroidery of Advertising on Shirts and Rug Binding for the Trade	314999	All Other Miscellaneous Textile Product Mills (pt)
7389	. Sponging Fabric for Tailors and Dressmakers	313311	Broadwoven Fabric Finishing Mills (pt)
7389	. Distribution of Telephone Directories on a Fee or Contract Basis	54187	Advertising Material Distribution Services
7389	. Post Office Contract Stations	49111	Postal Services (pt)
7389	. Apparel Pressing for the Trade	81232	Drycleaning and Laundry Services (except Coin-Operated)
7389	. Recovery and Repossession	561491	Repossession Services (pt)
7389	. Packaging and Labeling Services	56191	Packaging and Labeling Services
7389	. Swimming Pool Cleaning and Maintenance	56179	Other Services to Buildings and Dwellings (pt)
7389	. Hotel and Restaurant Reservation Services and Time Share Condominium Exchange	561599	All Other Travel Arrangement and Reservation Services (pt)
7389	. Convention and Trade Show Services	56192	Convention and Trade Show Organizers
7389	. Convention and Visitors Bureaus and Tourist Information Service	561591	Convention and Visitors Bureaus
7389	. Credit Card and Check Validation Services	52232	Financial Transactions, Processing, Reserve, and Clearinghouse Activities (pt)

SIC Code	SIC Industry Title	NAICS Code	NAICS Industry Title
7389	. Business Support Services, Except Telephone Answering, Telemarketing Bureaus, Private Mail Centers, and Repossession Services	561499	All Other Business Support Services
7389	. All Other Support Services	56199	All Other Support Services
75	Automotive repair, services, and parking		
7513	Truck Rental and Leasing, Without Drivers	53212	Truck, Utility Trailer, and RV (Recreational Vehicle) Rental and Leasing (pt)
7514	Passenger Car Rental	532111	Passenger Cars Rental
7515	Passenger Car Leasing	532112	Passenger Cars Leasing
7519	Utility Trailer and Recreational Vehicle Rental	53212	Truck, Utility Trailer and RV (Recreational Vehicles) Rental and Leasing (pt)
7521	Automobile Parking	81293	Parking Lots and Garages (pt)
7532	Top, Body, and Upholstery Repair Shops and Paint Shops	811121	Automotive Body, Paint, and Interior Repair and Maintenance
7533	Automotive Exhaust System Repair Shops	811112	Automotive Exhaust System Repair
7534	Tire Retreading and Repair Shops		
7534	. Retreading	326212	Tire Retreading
7534	. Repair	811198	All Other Automotive Repair and Maintenance (pt)
7536	Automotive Glass Replacement Shops	811122	Automotive Glass Replacement Shops (pt)
7537	Automotive Transmission Repair Shops	811113	Automotive Transmission Repair
7538	General Automotive Repair Shops	811111	General Automotive Repair
7539	Automotive Repair Shops, NEC	811118	Other Automotive Mechanical and Electrical Repair and Maintenance
7542	Carwashes	811192	Carwashes
7549	Automotive Services, Except Repair and Carwashes		
7549	. Automotive Window Tinting	811122	Automotive Glass Replacement Shops (pt)
7549	. Lubricating Services, Automotive	811191	Automotive Oil Change and Lubrication Shops
7549	. Towing	48841	Motor Vehicle Towing
7549	. Except Automotive Window Tinting, Lubricating Services, and Towing	811198	All Other Automotive Repair and Maintenance (pt)
76	Miscellaneous repair services		
7622	Radio and Television Repair Shops		
7622	. Retailing New Electronic Equipment from a Storefront and Repairing	443112	Radio, Television, and Other Electronics Stores (pt)
7622	. Other Stereo, TV, VCR, and Radio Repair	811211	Consumer Electronics Repair and Maintenance (pt)
7622	. Other Telecommunications Equipment Repair	811213	Communication Equipment Repair and Maintenance (pt)
7623	Refrigeration and Air-Conditioning Services and Repair Shops		

SIC Code	SIC Industry Title	NAICS Code	NAICS Industry Title
7623	. Retailing New Refrigerators from a Storefront and Repairing Refrigerators	443111	Household Appliance Stores (pt)
7623	. Commercial Refrigerator Equipment Repair	81131	Commercial and Industrial Machinery and Equipment (except Automotive and Electronic) Repair and Maintenance (pt)
7623	. Except Commercial and Retailing New Refrigerators from a Storefront and Repairing Refrigerators	811412	Appliance Repair and Maintenance (pt)
7629	Electrical and Electronic Repair Shops, NEC		
7629	. Retailing New Electrical and Electronic Appliances from a Storefront and Repairing	443111	Household Appliance Stores (pt)
7629	. Business and Office Machine Repair, Electrical	811212	Computer and Office Machine Repair and Maintenance (pt)
7629	. Telephone Set Repair	811213	Communication Equipment Repair and Maintenance (pt)
7629	. Electrical Measuring Instrument Repair and Calibration, Medical Equipment Repair, Electrical	811219	Other Electronic and Precision Equipment Repair and Maintenance (pt)
7629	. Appliance Repair, Electrical; Washing Machine Repair; Electric Razor Repair (except Retailing New Appliances from a Storefront and Repairing)	811412	Appliance Repair and Maintenance (pt)
7629	. Other Consumer Electronic Equipment Repair Except Computer, Radio, Television, Stereo, and VCR	811211	Consumer Electronics Repair and Maintenance (pt)
7631	Watch, Clock, and Jewelry Repair	81149	Other Personal and Household Goods Repair and Maintenance (pt)
7641	Reupholstery and Furniture Repair		
7641	. Antique Furniture Restoration	71151	Independent Artists, Writers, and Performers (pt)
7641	. Except Antique Furniture Restoration	81142	Reupholstery and Furniture Repair
7692	Welding Repair	81131	Commercial and Industrial Machinery and Equipment (except Automotive and Electronic) Repair and Maintenance (pt)
7694	Armature Rewinding Shops		
7694	. Repair	81131	Commercial and Industrial Machinery and Equipment (except Automotive and Electronic) Repair and Maintenance (pt)
7694	. Remanufacturing	335312	Motor and Generator Manufacturing (pt)
7699	Repair Shops and Related Services, NEC		
7699	. Boiler Cleaning	23511	Plumbing, Heating, and Air-Conditioning Contractors (pt)
7699	. Custom Picture Framing	442299	All Other Home Furnishings Stores (pt)
7699	. Locksmith Shops	561622	Locksmiths
7699	. Cesspool and Septic Tank Cleaning	562991	Septic Tank and Related Services (pt)
7699	. Furnace Ducts, Chimney, and Gutter Cleaning Services	56179	Other Services to Buildings and Dwellings (pt)
7699	. Sewer Cleaning and Rodding	562998	All Other Miscellaneous Waste Management Services (pt)
7699	. Ship Scaling	48839	Other Supporting Activities for Water Transportation (pt)

SIC Code	SIC Industry Title	NAICS Code	NAICS Industry Title
7699	. Other Non-Automotive Transportation Equipment and Industrial Machinery and Equipment	81131	Commercial and Industrial Machinery and Equipment (except Automotive and Electronic) Repair and Maintenance (pt)
7699	. Retailing New Bicycles from a Storefront and Repairing Bicycles	45111	Sporting Goods Stores (pt)
7699	. Farriers	11521	Support Activities for Animal Production (pt)
7699	. Camera Repair	811211	Consumer Electronics Repair and Maintenance (pt)
7699	. Typewriter Repair	811212	Computer and Office Machine Repair and Maintenance (pt)
7699	. Dental Instrument Repair, Laboratory Instrument Repair, Medical Equipment and Other Electronic and Precision Equipment Repair, Except Typewriters	811219	Other Electronic and Precision Equipment Repair and Maintenance (pt)
7699	. Lawnmower Repair Shops, Sharpening and Repairing Knives, Saws and Tools	811411	Home and Garden Equipment Repair and Maintenance
7699	. Taxidermists, and Antique Repair and Maintenance, Except Antique Car Restoration	71151	Independent Artists, Writers, and Performers
7699	. Gas Appliance Repair Service, Sewing Machine Repair, Stove Repair Shops, and Other Non-Electrical Appliances	811412	Appliance Repair and Maintenance (pt)
7699	. Leather Goods Repair Shops, Luggage Repair Shops, Pocketbook Repair Shops	81143	Footwear and Leather Goods Repair (pt)
7699	. Except Industrial, Electronic, Home and Garden, Appliance, Locksmith, and Leather Goods	81149	Other Personal and Household Goods Repair and Maintenance (pt)
78	Motion pictures		
7812	Motion Picture and Video Tape Production	51211	Motion Picture and Video Production
7819	Services Allied to Motion Picture Production		
7819	. Teleproduction and Post-Production Services	512191	Teleproduction and Other Post-Production Services
7819	. Casting Bureaus	56131	Employment Placement Agencies (pt)
7819	. Wardrobe Rental (Motion Pictures)	53222	Formal Wear and Costumes Rental (pt)
7819	. Rental of Motion Picture Equipment	53249	Other Commercial and Industrial Machinery and Equipment Rental and Leasing (pt)
7819	. Talent Payment Services	541214	Payroll Services (pt)
7819	. Film Directors and Related Motion Picture Production Services, Independent	71151	Independent Artists, Writers, and Performers (pt)
7819	. Reproduction of Video	334612	Prerecorded Compact Disc (Except Software), Tape, and Record Manufacturing (pt)
7819	. All Other Services	512199	Other Motion Picture and Video Industries (pt)
7822	Motion Picture and Video Tape Distribution		
7822	. Prerecorded Video Tapes (Wholesaling of)	42199	Other Miscellaneous Durable Goods Wholesalers (pt)
7822	. All Other	51212	Motion Picture and Video Distribution (pt)
7829	Services Allied to Motion Picture Distribution		

SIC Code	SIC Industry Title	NAICS Code	NAICS Industry Title
7829	. Booking Agencies	512199	Other Motion Picture and Video Industries (pt)
7829	. Film Archives	51412	Libraries and Archives (pt)
7829	. Commercial Distribution Film Libraries	51212	Motion Picture and Video Distribution (pt)
7832	Motion Picture Theaters, Except Drive-In	512131	Motion Picture Theaters, Except Drive-In
7833	Drive-In Motion Picture Theaters	512132	Drive-In Motion Picture Theaters
7841	Video Tape Rental	53223	Video Tapes and Disc Rental
79	Amusement and recreational services		
7911	Dance Studios, Schools, and Halls		
7911	. Dance Studios and Halls	71399	All Other Amusement and Recreation Industries (pt)
7911	. Dance Schools	61161	Fine Arts Schools (pt)
7922	Theatrical Producers (Except Motion Picture) and Miscellaneous Theatrical Services		
7922	. Casting Agencies	56131	Employment Placement Agencies (pt)
7922	. Theater and Opera Companies	71111	Theater Companies and Dinner Theaters (pt)
7922	. Theatrical Agents	71141	Agents and Managers for Artists, Athletes, Entertainers, and Other Public Figures (pt)
7922	. Theatrical Ticket Agencies	561599	All Other Travel Arrangement and Reservation Services (pt)
7922	. Costume Design, Theatrical	71151	Independent Artists, Writers, and Performers (pt)
7922	. Ballet and Dance Companies	71112	Dance Companies
7922	. Theater Operators	71131	Promoters of Performing Arts, Sports, and Similar Events with Facilities (pt)
7922	. Theatrical Promoters	71132	Promoters of Performing Arts, Sports, and Similar Events without Facilities (pt)
7922	. Producers of Radio Programs	51229	Other Sound Recording Industries (pt)
7922	. Theatrical Equipment Rental	53249	Other Commercial and Industrial Machinery and Equipment Rental and Leasing (pt)
7929	Bands, Orchestras, Actors, and Other Entertainers and Entertainment Groups		
7929	. Musical Groups and Artists, Orchestras	71113	Musical Groups and Artists
7929	. Actors and Actresses	71151	Independent Artists, Writers, and Performers (pt)
7929	. Except Musical Groups and Artists, Actors and Actresses	71119	Other Performing Arts Companies (pt)
7933	Bowling Centers	71395	Bowling Centers
7941	Professional Sports Clubs and Promoters		
7941	. Professional Sports Clubs	711211	Sports Teams and Clubs
7941	. Sports Agents	71141	Agents and Managers for Artists, Athletes, Entertainers, and Other Public Figures (pt)
7941	. Sports Promoters	71132	Promoters of Arts, Sports, and Similar Events without Facilities (pt)

SIC Code	SIC Industry Title	NAICS Code	NAICS Industry Title
7941	. Stadium Operators	71131	Promoters of Arts, Sports, and Similar Events with Facilities (pt)
7948	Racing, Including Track Operations		
7948	. Racetrack Operators	711212	Racetracks
7948	. Racing, except Track Operators	711219	Other Spectator Sports (pt)
7991	Physical Fitness Facilities	71394	Fitness and Recreational Sports Centers (pt)
7992	Public Golf Courses	71391	Golf Courses and Country Clubs (pt)
7993	Coin-Operated Amusement Devices		
7993	. Amusement Arcades	71312	Amusement Arcades
7993	. Gambling (Slot Machine) Operators	71329	Other Gambling Industries (pt)
7993	. Except Amusement Arcades and Slot Machine Operators	71399	All Other Amusement and Recreation Industries (pt)
7996	Amusement Parks	71311	Amusement and Theme Parks
7997	Membership Sports and Recreation Clubs		
7997	. Golf Clubs	71391	Golf Courses and Country Clubs (pt)
7997	. Recreation Clubs with Facilities	71394	Fitness and Recreational Sports Centers (pt)
7997	. Recreation Clubs Without Facilities	71399	All Other Amusement and Recreation Industries (pt)
7999	Amusement and Recreation Services, NEC		
7999	. Ticket Agencies	561599	All Other Travel Arrangement and Reservation Services (pt)
7999	. Aerial Tramways, Scenic and Amusement	48799	Scenic and Sightseeing Transportation, Other (pt)
7999	. Circus Companies and Traveling Carnival Shows	71119	Other Performing Arts Companies (pt)
7999	. Professional Athletes	711219	Other Spectator Sports (pt)
7999	. Skiing Facilities	71392	Skiing Facilities
7999	. Nonmembership Recreation Facilities	71394	Fitness and Recreational Sports Centers (pt)
7999	. Casinos, except Casino Hotels	71321	Casinos (except Casino Hotels)
7999	. Lottery, Bingo, Bookie and Other Gaming Operations	71329	Other Gambling Industries (pt)
7999	. Caverns and Miscellaneous Commercial Parks	71219	Nature Parks and Other Similar Institutions (pt)
7999	. Sports Instruction	61162	Sports and Recreation Instruction
7999	. Nonathletic Recreational Instruction	611699	All Other Miscellaneous Schools and Instruction (pt)
7999	. State Fairs, Agriculture Fairs, and County Fairs with Facilities	71131	Promoters of Performing Arts, Sports, and Similar Events with Facilities (pt)
7999	. State Fairs, Agriculture Fairs, and County Fairs without Facilities	71132	Promoters of Performing Arts, Sports, and Similar Events without Facilities (pt)
7999	. Sports Equipment Rental	532292	Recreational Goods Rental
7999	. Scenic Transport Operations, Land	48711	Scenic and Sightseeing Transportation, Land (pt)
7999	. Charter Fishing	48721	Scenic and Sightseeing Transportation, Water (pt)

SIC Code	SIC Industry Title	NAICS Code	NAICS Industry Title
7999	. Amusement and Recreation Services, NEC (except circuses, professional athletes, caverns and other commercial parks, skiing facilities, casinos and other gambling operations, amusement and recreation facilities, sports instruction, sports equipment	71399	All Other Amusement and Recreation Industries (pt)
80	Health services		
8011	Offices and Clinics of Doctors of Medicine		
8011	. Surgical and Emergency Centers	621493	Freestanding Ambulatory Surgical and Emergency Centers
8011	. HMO Medical Centers	621491	HMO Medical Centers
8011	. Offices of Physicians, Mental Health Specialists	621112	Offices of Physicians, Mental Health Specialists (pt)
8011	. Offices of Physicians Except Mental Health	621111	Offices of Physicians, (except Mental Health Specialists) (pt)
8021	Offices and Clinics of Dentists	62121	Offices of Dentists
8031	Offices and Clinics of Doctors of Osteopathy		
8031	. Offices of Doctors of Osteopathy, Except Mental Health	621111	Offices of Physicians (except Mental Health Specialists) (pt)
8031	. Offices of Doctors of Osteopathy, Mental Health Specialists	621112	Offices of Physicians, Mental Health Specialists (pt)
8041	Offices and Clinics of Chiropractors	62131	Offices of Chiropractors
8042	Offices and Clinics of Optometrists	62132	Offices of Optometrists
8043	Offices and Clinics of Podiatrists	621391	Offices of Podiatrists
8049	Offices and Clinics of Health Practitioners, NEC		
8049	. Mental Health Practitioners, Except Physicians	62133	Offices of Mental Health Practitioners (except Physicians)
8049	. Offices of Physical, Occupational, Recreational, and Speech Therapists and Audiologists	62134	Offices of Physical, Occupational, and Speech Therapists and Audiologists
8049	. Other Offices of Health Practitioners	621399	Offices of All Other Miscellaneous Health Practitioners
8051	Skilled Nursing Care Facilities		
8051	. Continuing Care Retirement Communities	623311	Continuing Care Retirement Communities (pt)
8051	. All Other Skilled Nursing Care Facilities	62311	Nursing Care Facilities (pt)
8052	Intermediate Care Facilities		
8052	. Continuing Care Retirement Communities	623311	Continuing Care Retirement Communities (pt)
8052	. Mental Retardation Facilities	62321	Residential Mental Retardation Facilities
8052	. Other Intermediate Care Facilities	62311	Nursing Care Facilities (pt)
8059	Nursing and Personal Care Facilities, NEC		
8059	. Continuing Care Retirement Communities	623311	Continuing Care Retirement Communities (pt)
8059	. Other Nursing and Personal Care Facilities	62311	Nursing Care Facilities (pt)
8062	General Medical and Surgical Hospitals	62211	General Medical and Surgical Hospitals (pt)
8063	Psychiatric Hospitals	62221	Psychiatric and Substance Abuse Hospitals (pt)
8069	Specialty Hospitals, Except Psychiatric		
8069	. Children's Hospitals	62211	General Medical and Surgical Hospitals (pt)

SIC Code	SIC Industry Title	NAICS Code	NAICS Industry Title
8069	. Substance Abuse Hospitals	62221	Psychiatric and Substance Abuse Hospitals (pt)
8069	. Other Specialty Hospitals	62231 Hospitals	Specialty (except Psychiatric and Substance Abuse)
8071	Medical Laboratories		
8071	. Diagnostic Imaging Centers	621512	Diagnostic Imaging Centers
8071	. Medical Laboratories, Except Diagnostic Imaging Centers	621511	Medical Laboratories
8072	Dental Laboratories	339116	Dental Laboratories
8082	Home Health Care Services	62161	Home Health Care Services
8092	Kidney Dialysis Centers	621492	Kidney Dialysis Centers
8093	Specialty Outpatient Facilities, NEC		
8093	. Family Planning Centers	62141	Family Planning Centers (pt)
8093	. Outpatient Mental Health Facilities	62142	Outpatient Mental Health and Substance Abuse Centers
8093	. Other Specialty Outpatient Facilities	621498	All Other Outpatient Care Facilities
8099	Health and Allied Services, NEC		
8099	. Blood and Organ Banks	621991	Blood and Organ Banks
8099	. Medical Artists	54143	Graphic Design Services (pt)
8099	. Medical Photography	541922	Commercial Photography (pt)
8099	. Childbirth Preparation Classes	62141	Family Planning Centers (pt)
8099	. Other Health and Allied Services	621999	All Other Miscellaneous Ambulatory Health Care Services
81	Legal services		
8111	Legal Services	54111	Offices of Lawyers
82	Educational services		
8211	Elementary and Secondary Schools	61111	Elementary and Secondary Schools
8221	Colleges, Universities, and Professional Schools	61131	Colleges, Universities, and Professional Schools
8222	Junior Colleges and Technical Institutes	61121	Junior Colleges
8231	Libraries	51412	Libraries and Archives
8243	Data Processing Schools		
8243	. Computer Repair Training	611519	Other Technical and Trade Schools (pt)
8243	. Except Computer Repair Training	61142	Computer Training
8244	Business and Secretarial Schools	61141	Business and Secretarial Schools
8249	Vocational Schools, NEC		
8249	. Vocational Apprenticeship Training	611513	Apprenticeship Training
8249	. Aviation Schools	611512	Flight Training (pt)
8249	. Other Technical and Trade Schools	611519	Other Technical and Trade Schools (pt)
8299	Schools and Educational Services, NEC		

SIC Code	SIC Industry Title	NAICS Code	NAICS Industry Title
8299	. Flying Instruction	611512	Flight Training (pt)
8299	. Automobile Driving Instruction	611692	Automobile Driving Schools
8299	. Curriculum Development, Educational	61171	Educational Support Services (pt)
8299	. Exam Preparation and Tutoring	611691	Exam Preparation and Tutoring
8299	. Art Drama and Music Schools	61161	Fine Arts Schools (pt)
8299	. Language Schools	61163	Language Schools
8299	. Professional and Management Development Training	61143	Professional and Management Development Training Schools
8299	. Cooking and Modeling Schools	611519	Other Technical and Trade Schools (pt)
8299	. All Other Schools and Educational Services, NEC	611699	All Other Miscellaneous Schools and Instruction
83	Social services		
8322	Individual and Family Social Services		
8322	. Child and Youth Services	62411	Child and Youth Services
8322	. Community Food Services	62421	Community Food Services
8322	. Community Housing Services, Except Temporary Shelters	624229	Other Community Housing Services
8322	. Emergency and Other Relief Services	62423	Emergency and Other Relief Services
8322	. Services for the Elderly and Persons with Disabilities	62412	Services for the Elderly and Persons with Disabilities
8322	. Temporary Shelter	624221	Temporary Shelters
8322	. Parole Offices and Probation Offices	92215	Parole Offices and Probation Offices
8322	. Other Individual and Family Services	62419	Other Individual and Family Services
8331	Job Training and Vocational Rehabilitation Services	62431	Vocational Rehabilitation Services
8351	Child Day Care Services	62441	Child Day Care Services (pt)
8361	Residential Care		
8361	. Homes for the Elderly	623312	Homes for the Elderly
8361	. Mental Health and Substance Abuse Facilities	62322	Residential Mental Health and Substance Abuse Facilities
8361	. Other Residential Care	62399	Other Residential Care Facilities
8399	Social Services, NEC		
8399	. Voluntary Health Organizations	813212	Voluntary Health Organizations
8399	. Grantmaking and Giving	813219	Other Grantmaking and Giving Services
8399	. Human Rights Organizations	813311	Human Rights Organizations
8399	. Environment, Conservation, and Wildlife Organizations	813312	Environment, Conservation, and Wildlife Organizations (pt)
8399	. All Other Social Advocacy Organizations	813319	Other Social Advocacy Organizations
84	Museums, art galleries, botanical & zoological gardens		
8412	Museums and Art Galleries		

SIC Code	SIC Industry Title	NAICS Code	NAICS Industry Title
8412	. Museums	71211	Museums
8412	. Historical and Heritage Sites	71212	Historical Sites
8422	Arboreta and Botanical or Zoological Gardens		
8422	. Botanical and Zoological Gardens	71213	Zoos and Botanical Gardens
8422	. Nature Parks and Reserves	71219	Nature Parks and Other Similar Institutions (pt)
86	Membership organizations		
8611	Business Associations	81391	Business Associations (pt)
8621	Professional Membership Organizations	81392	Professional Organizations
8631	Labor Unions and Similar Labor Organizations	81393	Labor Unions and Similar Labor Organizations
8641	Civic, Social, and Fraternal Associations		
8641	. Civic and Social Associations	81341	Civic and Social Organizations (except Business, Professional, Labor, and Political Organizations) (pt)
8641	. Homeowner and Condominium Associations	81399	Other Similar Organizations(pt)
8641	. American Indian and Alaska Native Tribal Governments	92115	American Indian and Alaska Native Tribal Governments
8651	Political Organizations	81394	Political Organizations
8661	Religious Organizations	81311	Religious Organizations
8699	Membership Organizations, NEC		
8699	. Except Humane Societies, Farm Business Organizations, Athletic Associations, and Travel Motor Clubs	81341	Civic and Social Organizations (pt)
8699	. Farm Business Organizations	81391	Business Associations (pt)
8699	. Humane Societies	813312	Environment, Conservation, and Wildlife Organizations (pt)
8699	. Travel Motor Clubs	561599	All Other Travel Arrangement and Reservation Services (pt)
8699	. Athletic Associations	81399	Other Similar Organizations (except Business, Professional, Labor, and Political Organizations) (pt)
87	Engineering and management services		
8711	Engineering Services	54133	Engineering Services (pt)
8712	Architectural Services	54131	Architectural Services
8713	Surveying Services		
8713	. Geophysical Surveying Services	54136	Geophysical Surveying and Mapping Services (pt)
8713	. Except Geophysical Surveying	54137	Surveying and Mapping (except Geophysical) Services (pt)
8721	Accounting, Auditing, and Bookkeeping Services		
8721	. Auditing Accountants	541211	Offices of Certified Public Accountants
8721	. Payroll Services	541214	Payroll Services (pt)
8721	. Other Accounting Services	541219	Other Accounting Services
8731	Commercial Physical and Biological Research	54171	Research and Development in the Physical, Engineering, and Life Sciences (pt)

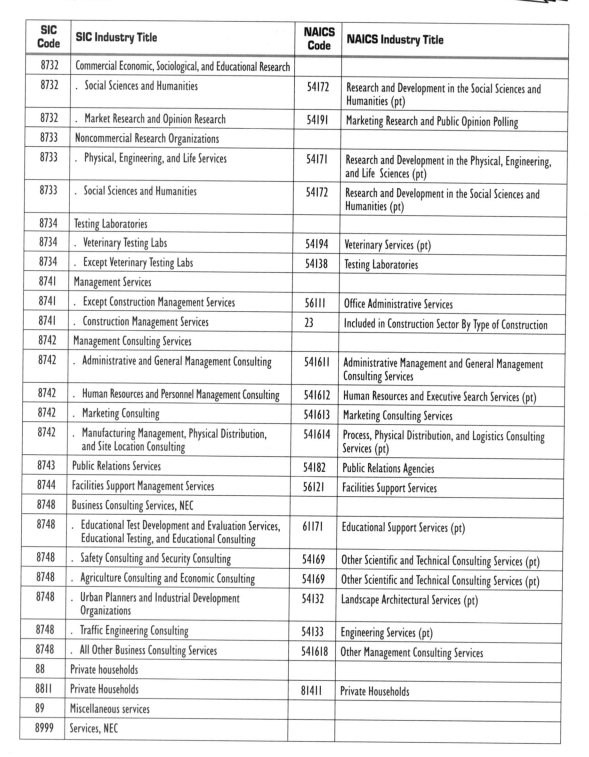

SIC Code	SIC Industry Title	NAICS Code	NAICS Industry Title
8732	Commercial Economic, Sociological, and Educational Research		
8732	. Social Sciences and Humanities	54172	Research and Development in the Social Sciences and Humanities (pt)
8732	. Market Research and Opinion Research	54191	Marketing Research and Public Opinion Polling
8733	Noncommercial Research Organizations		
8733	. Physical, Engineering, and Life Services	54171	Research and Development in the Physical, Engineering, and Life Sciences (pt)
8733	. Social Sciences and Humanities	54172	Research and Development in the Social Sciences and Humanities (pt)
8734	Testing Laboratories		
8734	. Veterinary Testing Labs	54194	Veterinary Services (pt)
8734	. Except Veterinary Testing Labs	54138	Testing Laboratories
8741	Management Services		
8741	. Except Construction Management Services	56111	Office Administrative Services
8741	. Construction Management Services	23	Included in Construction Sector By Type of Construction
8742	Management Consulting Services		
8742	. Administrative and General Management Consulting	541611	Administrative Management and General Management Consulting Services
8742	. Human Resources and Personnel Management Consulting	541612	Human Resources and Executive Search Services (pt)
8742	. Marketing Consulting	541613	Marketing Consulting Services
8742	. Manufacturing Management, Physical Distribution, and Site Location Consulting	541614	Process, Physical Distribution, and Logistics Consulting Services (pt)
8743	Public Relations Services	54182	Public Relations Agencies
8744	Facilities Support Management Services	56121	Facilities Support Services
8748	Business Consulting Services, NEC		
8748	. Educational Test Development and Evaluation Services, Educational Testing, and Educational Consulting	61171	Educational Support Services (pt)
8748	. Safety Consulting and Security Consulting	54169	Other Scientific and Technical Consulting Services (pt)
8748	. Agriculture Consulting and Economic Consulting	54169	Other Scientific and Technical Consulting Services (pt)
8748	. Urban Planners and Industrial Development Organizations	54132	Landscape Architectural Services (pt)
8748	. Traffic Engineering Consulting	54133	Engineering Services (pt)
8748	. All Other Business Consulting Services	541618	Other Management Consulting Services
88	Private households		
8811	Private Households	81411	Private Households
89	Miscellaneous services		
8999	Services, NEC		

SIC Code	SIC Industry Title	NAICS Code	NAICS Industry Title
8999	. Authors, Artists, and Related Technical Services, Independent	71151	Independent Artists, Writers, and Performers (pt)
8999	. Record Production	51221	Record Production
8999	. Scientific and Related Consulting Services	54169	Other Scientific and Technical Consulting Services (pt)
8999	. Music Publishing	51223	Music Publishers (pt)
8999	. Actuarial Consulting	541612	Human Resources and Executive Search Consulting Services (pt)
8999	. All Other Information Providers	514199	All Other Information Services (pt)
8999	. Environmental Consultants	54162	Environmental Consulting Services
	Public Administration		
91	Executive, legislative, and general government		
9111	Executive Offices	92111	Executive Offices
9121	Legislative Bodies	92112	Legislative Bodies
9131	Executive and Legislative Offices, Combined	92114	Executive and Legislative Offices, Combined
9199	General Government, NEC	92119	Other General Government Support
92	Justice, public order, and safety		
9211	Courts	92211	Courts
9221	Police Protection	92212	Police Protection
9222	Legal Counsel and Prosecution	92213	Legal Counsel and Prosecution
9223	Correctional Institutions	92214	Correctional Institutions
9224	Fire Protection	92216	Fire Protection
9229	Public Order and Safety, NEC	92219	Other Justice, Public Order, and Safety
93	Finance, taxation, and monetary policy		
9311	Public Finance, Taxation, and Monetary Policy	92113	Public Finance Activities
94	Administration of human resources		
9411	Administration of Educational Programs	92311	Administration of Education Programs
9431	Administration of Public Health Programs	92312	Administration of Public Health Programs
9441	Administration of Social, Human Resource and Income Maintenance Programs	92313	Administration of Human Resource Programs (except Education, Public Health, and Veterans' Affairs Programs)
9451	Administration of Veterans' Affairs, Except Health Insurance	92314	Administration of Veterans' Affairs
95	Environmental quality and housing		
9511	Air and Water Resource and Solid Waste Management	92411	Administration of Air and Water Resource and Solid Waste Management Programs
9512	Land, Mineral, Wildlife, and Forest Conservation	92412	Administration of Conservation Programs
9531	Administration of Housing Programs	92511	Administration of Housing Programs

SIC Code	SIC Industry Title	NAICS Code	NAICS Industry Title
9532	Administration of Urban Planning and Community and Rural Development	92512	Administration of Urban Planning and Community and Rural Development
96	Administration of economic programs		
9611	Administration of General Economic Programs	92611	Administration of General Economic Programs
9621	Regulation and Administration of Transportation Programs		
9621	. Air Traffic Control	488111	Air Traffic Control (pt)
9621	. Except Air Traffic Control	92612	Regulation and Administration of Transportation Programs
9631	Regulation and Administration of Communications, Electric, Gas, and Other Utilities	92613	Regulation and Administration of Communications, Electric, Gas, and Other Utilities
9641	Regulation of Agricultural Marketing and Commodities	92614	Regulation of Agricultural Marketing and Commodities
9651	Regulation, Licensing, and Inspection of Miscellaneous Commercial Sectors	92615	Regulation, Licensing, and Inspection of Miscellaneous Commercial Sectors
9661	Space Research and Technology	92711	Space Research and Technology
97	National security and international affairs		
9711	National Security	92811	National Security
9721	International Affairs	92812	International Affairs
9999	Nonclassifiable Establishments	99999	Unclassified Establishments

ALPHABETIC INDEX TO U.S. NAICS CODES AND TITLES

In some situations, this index can save you much frustration in finding the appropriate NAICS code number or industry title. Let's say, for example, that you are trying to identify the correct NAICS industry code for a marina (you know, where they sell, store, or work on boats). If you don't have its old SIC code, you could try to look it up in the "NAICS Industries Within Groups of Related Industries" section of this book. There, you may find it under a variety of possible categories. But you will probably waste time finding it, since it is under the rather obscure NAICS subgrouping titled "Amusement, Gambling & Recreation Industries" as NAICS code 71393, marinas. And you would have wasted even more time if you tried to look it up as a "boat sales and service" industry in the same place.

If you had used this index, on the other hand, you would have quickly found the word "marina" listed and would be on your merry way. Or, if you had tried to look it up in this index as "boat sales and service," you would have likely found it among the other entries beginning with the word "boat" as "Boating clubs with marinas"—again, saving lots of time.

So welcome to this useful index, hidden in the back of this book. If you ever use it successfully to save lots of time and aggravation, please consider sending the good editors at JIST a present or kind word, since we hardly ever hear nice things here about our many exciting and fascinating indexes.

U.S. NAICS Alphabetic Listing

Code	Description
513112	AM radio stations
334119	ATMs (automatic teller machines) manufacturing
311611	Abattoirs
621410	Abortion clinics
334519	Abrasion testing machines manufacturing
339114	Abrasive points, wheels, and disks, dental, manufacturing
327910	Abrasive products manufacturing
212322	Abrasive sand quarrying and/or beneficiating
212399	Abrasive stones (e.g., emery, grindstones, hones, pumice) mining and/or beneficiating
421840	Abrasives wholesaling
212399	Abrasives, natural, mining and/or beneficiating
322121	Absorbent paper stock manufacturing
332420	Absorbers, gas, manufacturing

Code	Description
334513	Absorption analyzers, industrial process type (e.g., infrared), manufacturing
234120	Abutment construction
611691	Academic tutoring services
611310	Academies, college or university
611110	Academies, elementary or secondary
611210	Academies, junior college
611310	Academies, military service (college)
611620	Academies, riding instruction
334511	Acceleration indicators and systems components, aerospace type, manufacturing
325199	Accelerators (i.e., basic synthetic chemical) manufacturing
334519	Accelerometers (except aerospace type) manufacturing
813319	Accident prevention associations
524130	Accidental and health reinsurance carriers

Code	Description
524113	Accidental death and dismemberment insurance carriers, direct
524113	Accidental death and dismemberment insurance underwriting, direct
339992	Accordions and parts manufacturing
561440	Account collection services
541219	Accountants' (except CPAs) offices
541219	Accountants' (except CPAs) private practices
541211	Accountants' (i.e., CPAs) offices, certified public
541211	Accountants' (i.e., CPAs) private practices, certified public
813920	Accountants' associations
541211	Accounting (i.e., CPAs) services, certified public
421420	Accounting machines wholesaling
541219	Accounting services (except CPAs)
332420	Accumulators, industrial pressure vessels, manufacturing
325211	Acetal resins manufacturing

Code	Description
325199	Acetaldehyde manufacturing
325221	Acetate fibers and filaments manufacturing
325191	Acetate of lime, natural, made by distillation of wood
313111	Acetate spun yarns made from purchased fiber
325199	Acetates, not specified elsewhere by process, manufacturing
325199	Acetic acid manufacturing
325199	Acetic anhydride manufacturing
325199	Acetin manufacturing
325191	Acetone, natural, manufacturing
325199	Acetone, synthetic, manufacturing
332420	Acetylene cylinders manufacturing
325120	Acetylene manufacturing
325411	Acetylsalicylic acid manufacturing
325132	Acid dyes, synthetic organic, manufacturing
325199	Acid esters, not specified elsewhere by process, manufacturing
324110	Acid oils made in petroleum refineries
562211	Acid waste disposal facilities
562211	Acid waste treatment facilities
334513	Acidity (i.e., pH) instruments, industrial process type, manufacturing
334516	Acidity (i.e., pH) measuring equipment, laboratory analysis-type, manufacturing
213112	Acidizing oil and gas field wells on a contract basis
311511	Acidophilus milk manufacturing
422690	Acids wholesaling
325199	Acids, organic, not specified elsewhere by process, manufacturing
111219	Acorn squash farming, field, bedding plant and seed production
541330	Acoustical engineering consulting services
235420	Acoustical paneling construction contractors
332323	Acoustical suspension systems, metal, manufacturing
541330	Acoustical system engineering design services

Code	Description
541380	Acoustics testing laboratories or services
325199	Acrolein manufacturing
325212	Acrylate rubber manufacturing
325212	Acrylate-butadiene rubber manufacturing
313112	Acrylic and modacrylic filament yarn throwing, twisting, texturizing, or winding purchased yarn
325222	Acrylic fibers and filaments manufacturing
326113	Acrylic film and unlaminated sheet (except packaging) manufacturing
325211	Acrylic resins manufacturing
325212	Acrylic rubber manufacturing
313111	Acrylic spun yarns made from purchased fiber
325222	Acrylonitrile fibers and filaments manufacturing
325199	Acrylonitrile manufacturing
325211	Acrylonitrile-butadiene-styrene (ABS) resins manufacturing
334519	Actinometers, meteorological, manufacturing
339931	Action figures manufacturing
325998	Activated carbon or charcoal manufacturing
624120	Activity centers for disabled persons, the elderly, and persons diagnosed with mental retardation
711510	Actors, independent
711510	Actresses, independent
541612	Actuarial consulting services
333995	Actuators, fluid power, manufacturing
621111	Acupuncturists' (MDs or DOs) offices (e.g., centers, clinics)
621399	Acupuncturists' (except MDs or DOs) offices (e.g., centers, clinics)
325110	Acyclic hydrocarbons (e.g., butene, ethylene, propene) (except acetylene) made from refined petroleum or liquid hydrocarbons
332993	Adapters, bombcluster, manufacturing
333313	Adding machines manufacturing

Code	Description
325998	Additive preparations for gasoline (e.g., antiknock preparations, detergents, gum inhibitors) manufacturing
561499	Address bar coding services
511140	Address list compilers
511140	Address list publishers
511140	Address list publishers and printing combined
511140	Address list publishing (i.e., establishments known as publishers)
323112	Address lists flexographic printing without publishing
323111	Address lists gravure printing without publishing
323110	Address lists lithographic (offset) printing without publishing
323119	Address lists printing (except flexographic, gravure, lithographic, screen) without publishing
323113	Address lists screen printing without publishing
421420	Addressing machines wholesaling
322222	Adhesive tape (except medical) made from purchased materials
339113	Adhesive tape, medical, manufacturing
325520	Adhesives (except asphalt, dental, gypsum base) manufacturing
422690	Adhesives and sealants wholesaling
325199	Adipic acid esters or amines manufacturing
325199	Adipic acid manufacturing
325199	Adiponitrile manufacturing
233320	Administration building construction
922110	Administrative courts
541611	Administrative management consulting services
561110	Administrative management services
523991	Administrators of private estates
327123	Adobe bricks manufacturing
624110	Adoption agencies
624110	Adoption services, child

Code	Description
325411	Adrenal derivatives, uncompounded, manufacturing
325412	Adrenal medicinal preparations manufacturing
611691	Adult literacy instruction
541810	Advertising agencies
541810	Advertising agency consulting services
541870	Advertising material (e.g., coupons, flyers, samples) direct distribution services
541860	Advertising material preparation services for mailing or other direct distribution
323110	Advertising materials (e.g., coupons, flyers) lithographic (offset) printing without publishing
541840	Advertising media representatives (i.e., independent of media owners)
511120	Advertising periodical publishers
511120	Advertising periodical publishers and printing combined
511120	Advertising periodical publishing (i.e., establishments known as publishers)
541850	Advertising services, indoor or outdoor display
541890	Advertising specialty (e.g., key-chain, magnet, pen) distribution services
541850	Advertising, aerial
921110	Advisory commissions, executive government
921120	Advisory commissions, legislative
487990	Aerial cable car, scenic and sightseeing, operation
333315	Aerial cameras manufacturing
115112	Aerial dusting or spraying (i.e., using specialized or dedicated aircraft)
541360	Aerial geophysical surveying services
541370	Aerial surveying (except geophysical) services
487990	Aerial tramway, scenic and sightseeing, operation

Code	Description
333923	Aerial work platforms manufacturing
713940	Aerobic dance and exercise centers
421860	Aeronautical equipment and supplies wholesaling
334511	Aeronautical systems and instruments manufacturing
325998	Aerosol can filling on a job order or contract basis
332431	Aerosol cans manufacturing
325998	Aerosol packaging services
332919	Aerosol valves manufacturing
325620	After-shave preparations manufacturing
332410	Aftercoolers (i.e., heat exchangers) manufacturing
325414	Agar culture media manufacturing
325411	Agar-agar grinding manufacturing
212399	Agate mining and/or beneficiating
111998	Agave farming
522293	Agencies of foreign banks (i.e., trade financing)
524210	Agencies, insurance
522310	Agencies, loan
531210	Agencies, real estate
531390	Agencies, real estate escrow
531390	Agents' offices, real estate escrow
711410	Agents, artists'
711410	Agents, authors'
711410	Agents, celebrities'
711410	Agents, entertainers'
812320	Agents, laundry and drycleaning
711410	Agents, modeling
711410	Agents, public figures'
531210	Agents, real estate
488510	Agents, shipping
711410	Agents, sports figures'
711410	Agents, talent
711410	Agents, theatrical talent
212210	Agglomerates, iron ore, beneficiating
333120	Aggregate spreaders manufacturing
325414	Aggressins (except in-vitro) manufacturing
551112	Agreement corporation (except international trade financing)

Code	Description
522293	Agreement corporations (i.e., international trade financing)
524126	Agricultural (i.e., crop, livestock) insurance carriers, direct
422910	Agricultural chemicals wholesaling
541690	Agricultural consulting services
926140	Agricultural cooperative extension program administration
522298	Agricultural credit institutions, making loans or extending credit (except real estate, sales financing)
711320	Agricultural fair managers without facilities
711320	Agricultural fair organizers without facilities
711320	Agricultural fair promoters without facilities
332212	Agricultural handtools (e.g., hay forks, hoes, rakes, spades), nonpowered, manufacturing
421820	Agricultural implements wholesaling
522298	Agricultural lending (except real estate, sales financing)
327410	Agricultural lime manufacturing
212312	Agricultural limestone mining and/or beneficiating
422910	Agricultural limestone wholesaling
532490	Agricultural machinery and equipment rental or leasing
811310	Agricultural machinery and equipment repair and maintenance services
421820	Agricultural machinery and equipment wholesaling
511120	Agricultural magazine and periodical publishers
511120	Agricultural magazine and periodical publishers and printing combined
511120	Agricultural magazine and periodical publishing (i.e., establishments known as publishers)
323112	Agricultural magazines and periodicals flexographic printing without publishing
323111	Agricultural magazines and periodicals gravure printing without publishing

Code	Description
323110	Agricultural magazines and periodicals lithographic (offset) printing without publishing
323119	Agricultural magazines and periodicals printing (except flexographic, gravure, lithographic, screen) without publishing
323113	Agricultural magazines and periodicals screen printing without publishing
926140	Agricultural marketing services government
926140	Agricultural pest and weed regulation, government
484220	Agricultural products trucking, local
531190	Agricultural property rental leasing
926140	Agriculture fair boards administration
115115	Agriculture production or harvesting crews
541710	Agriculture research and development laboratories or services
541690	Agrology consulting services
541690	Agronomy consulting services
624110	Aid to families with dependent children (AFDC)
928110	Air Force
621910	Air ambulance services
336399	Air bag assemblies manufacturing
336612	Air boat building
336340	Air brake systems and parts, automotive, truck, and bus, manufacturing
481212	Air cargo carriers (except air couriers), nonscheduled
481112	Air cargo carriers (except air couriers), scheduled
332439	Air cargo containers, metal, manufacturing
335313	Air circuit breakers manufacturing
481111	Air commuter carriers, scheduled
333912	Air compressors manufacturing
492110	Air courier services
332322	Air cowls, sheet metal, manufacturing
336399	Air filters, automotive, truck, and bus, manufacturing

Code	Description
334512	Air flow controllers (except valves), air-conditioning and refrigeration, manufacturing
313230	Air laid nonwoven fabrics manufacturing
481211	Air passenger carriers, nonscheduled
481111	Air passenger carriers, scheduled
421730	Air pollution control equipment and supplies wholesaling
335211	Air purification equipment, portable, manufacturing
333411	Air purification equipment, stationary, manufacturing
332420	Air receiver tanks, heavy gauge metal, manufacturing
333411	Air scrubbing systems manufacturing
711310	Air show managers with facilities
711320	Air show managers without facilities
711310	Air show organizers with facilities
711320	Air show organizers without facilities
711310	Air show promoters with facilities
711320	Air show promoters without facilities
235110	Air system balancing and testing contractors
481211	Air taxi services
334511	Air traffic control radar systems and equipment manufacturing
611519	Air traffic control schools
488111	Air traffic control services (except military)
928110	Air traffic control, military
333411	Air washers (i.e., air scrubbers) manufacturing
532210	Air-conditioner rental
811412	Air-conditioner, window, repair and maintenance services
336391	Air-conditioners, motor vehicle, manufacturing
421620	Air-conditioners, room, wholesaling
333415	Air-conditioners, unit (e.g., motor home, travel trailer, window), manufacturing
333415	Air-conditioning and warm air heating combination units manufacturing

Code	Description
333415	Air-conditioning compressors (except motor vehicle) manufacturing
333415	Air-conditioning condensers and condensing units manufacturing
333415	Air-conditioning equipment (except motor vehicle) manufacturing
421730	Air-conditioning equipment (except room units) wholesaling
235110	Air-conditioning installation contractors
221330	Air-conditioning supply
487210	Airboat (i.e., swamp buggy) operation
334511	Airborne navigational systems manufacturing
334220	Airborne radio communications equipment manufacturing
331491	Aircraft and automotive wire and cable (except aluminum, copper) made from purchased nonferrous metals (except aluminum copper) in wire drawing plants
331422	Aircraft and automotive wire or cable made from purchased copper in wire drawing plants
332995	Aircraft artillery manufacturing
336413	Aircraft assemblies, subassemblies, and parts (except engines) manufacturing
336413	Aircraft auxiliary parts (e.g., crop dusting, external fuel tanks, inflight refueling equipment) manufacturing
333999	Aircraft carrier catapults manufacturing
481219	Aircraft charter services (i.e., general purpose aircraft used for a variety of specialty air and flying services)
481211	Aircraft charter services, passenger
336413	Aircraft control surface assemblies manufacturing
336411	Aircraft conversions (i.e., major modifications to system)
441229	Aircraft dealers
336412	Aircraft engine and engine parts (except carburetors, pistons, piston rings, valves) manufacturing

Code	Description
333924	Aircraft engine cradles manufacturing
334519	Aircraft engine instruments manufacturing
336412	Aircraft engine overhauling
336412	Aircraft engine rebuilding
421860	Aircraft engines and parts wholesaling
421860	Aircraft equipment and supplies wholesaling
488190	Aircraft ferrying services
334511	Aircraft flight instruments (except engine instruments) manufacturing
336413	Aircraft fuselage wing tail and similar assemblies manufacturing
488119	Aircraft hangar rental
332510	Aircraft hardware, metal, manufacturing
488190	Aircraft inspection services
926120	Aircraft inspection, government
561720	Aircraft janitorial services
336321	Aircraft lighting fixtures manufacturing
333924	Aircraft loading hoists manufacturing
488190	Aircraft maintenance and repair services (except factory conversion, factory overhaul, factory rebuilding)
336411	Aircraft manufacturing
336411	Aircraft overhauling
488119	Aircraft parking service
336413	Aircraft propellers and parts manufacturing
336411	Aircraft rebuilding (i.e., restoration to original design specifications)
532411	Aircraft rental and leasing
336360	Aircraft seats manufacturing
488190	Aircraft testing services
314999	Aircraft tie down strap assemblies (except leather) manufacturing
326211	Aircraft tire manufacturing
336412	Aircraft turbines manufacturing
811420	Aircraft upholstery repair
421860	Aircraft wholesaling
333412	Aircurtains manufacturing

Code	Description
336413	Airframe assemblies (except for guided missiles) manufacturing
336419	Airframe assemblies for guided missiles manufacturing
334511	Airframe equipment instruments manufacturing
325612	Airfreshners manufacturing
722310	Airline food service contractors
561599	Airline reservation services
561599	Airline ticket offices
332313	Airlocks, fabricated metal plate work, manufacturing
481112	Airmail carriers, scheduled
532411	Airplane rental or leasing
488119	Airport baggage handling services
488119	Airport cargo handling services
531190	Airport leasing, not operating airport, rental or leasing
335311	Airport lighting transformers manufacturing
485999	Airport limousine services (i.e., shuttle)
488119	Airport operators (e.g., civil, international, national)
234110	Airport runway construction
488119	Airport runway maintenance services
485999	Airport shuttle services
488119	Airports, civil, operation and maintenance
334511	Airspeed instruments (aeronautical) manufacturing
212399	Alabaster mining and/or beneficiating
421610	Alarm apparatus, electric, wholesaling
334518	Alarm clocks manufacturing
561621	Alarm system monitoring services
334290	Alarm systems and equipment manufacturing
561621	Alarm systems sales combined with installation, maintenance, or monitoring services
323118	Albums (e.g., photo, scrap) manufacturing
422120	Albums, photo, wholesaling
422690	Alcohol, industrial, wholesaling

Code	Description
922120	Alcohol, tobacco, and firearms control
926150	Alcoholic beverage control boards
492210	Alcoholic beverage delivery service
722410	Alcoholic beverage drinking places
312140	Alcoholic beverages (except brandy) distilling
422810	Alcoholic beverages (except distilled spirits, wine) wholesaling
312130	Alcoholic beverages, brandy, distilling
422820	Alcoholic beverages, wine and distilled spirits wholesaling
624190	Alcoholism and drug addiction self-help organizations
624190	Alcoholism counseling (except medical treatment), nonresidential
623220	Alcoholism rehabilitation facilities (except licensed hospitals), residential
622210	Alcoholism rehabilitation hospitals
624190	Alcoholism self-help organizations
621420	Alcoholism treatment centers and clinics (except hospitals), outpatient
325199	Aldehydes manufacturing
312120	Ale brewing
422810	Ale wholesaling
111940	Alfalfa hay farming
311119	Alfalfa meal, dehydrated, manufacturing
311119	Alfalfa prepared as feed for animals
111998	Alfalfa seed farming
111419	Alfalfa sprout farming, grown under cover
422910	Alfalfa wholesaling
311119	Alfalfa, cubed, manufacturing
111998	Algae farming
325199	Alginates (e.g., calcium, potassium, sodium) manufacturing
325199	Alginic acid manufacturing
334519	Alidades, surveying, manufacturing
333319	Alignment equipment, motor vehicle, manufacturing
325110	Aliphatic (e.g., hydrocarbons) (except acetylene) made from refined petroleum or liquid hydrocarbons

Code	Description
324110	Aliphatic chemicals (i.e., acyclic) made in petroleum refineries
325181	Alkalies manufacturing
422690	Alkalies wholesaling
335912	Alkaline cell primary batteries manufacturing
335911	Alkaline cell storage batteries (i.e., nickel-cadmium, nickel-iron, silver oxide-zinc) manufacturing
335912	Alkaline manganese primary batteries manufacturing
325211	Alkyd resins manufacturing
324110	Alkylates made in petroleum refineries
421110	All terrain vehicles (ATVs) wholesaling
336999	All terrain vehicles (ATVs), wheeled or tracked, manufacturing
441221	All-terrain vehicle (ATV) dealers
325414	Allergenic extracts (except diagnostic substances) manufacturing
325414	Allergens manufacturing
621111	Allergists' offices (e.g., centers, clinics)
234110	Alley construction
112519	Alligator production, farm raising
331513	Alloy steel castings (except investment), unfinished, manufacturing
331314	Alloying purchased aluminum metals
331423	Alloying purchased copper
331423	Alloying purchased copper metals
331492	Alloying purchased nonferrous metals (except aluminum, copper)
325211	Allyl resins manufacturing
323121	Almanac binding without printing
511130	Almanac publishers
511130	Almanac publishers and printing combined
511130	Almanac publishing (i.e., establishments known as publishers)
323117	Almanacs printing and binding without publishing
323117	Almanacs printing without publishing
111335	Almond farming
115114	Almond hulling and shelling

Code	Description
311999	Almond pastes manufacturing
111998	Aloe farming
112990	Alpaca production
721110	Alpine skiing facilities with accommodations (i.e., ski resort)
713920	Alpine skiing facilities without accommodations
334515	Alternator and generator testers manufacturing
336322	Alternators and generators for internal combustion engines manufacturing
334511	Altimeters, aeronautical, manufacturing
212391	Alum, natural, mining and/or beneficiating
327125	Alumina fused refractories manufacturing
327113	Alumina porcelain insulators manufacturing
331311	Alumina refining
327125	Aluminous refractory cement manufacturing
331312	Aluminum alloys made from bauxite or alumina producing primary aluminum and manufacturing
331314	Aluminum alloys made from scrap or dross
331316	Aluminum bar made by extruding purchased aluminum
331316	Aluminum bar made in integrated secondary smelting and extruding mills
331314	Aluminum billet made from purchased aluminum
331314	Aluminum billet made in integrated secondary smelting and rolling mills
332431	Aluminum cans manufacturing
331524	Aluminum castings (except die-castings), unfinished, manufacturing
325188	Aluminum chloride manufacturing
332812	Aluminum coating of metal products for the trade
325188	Aluminum compounds, not specified elsewhere by process, manufacturing
331521	Aluminum die-casting foundries

Code	Description
331521	Aluminum die-castings, unfinished, manufacturing
331314	Aluminum extrusion ingot (i.e., billet), secondary
331314	Aluminum flakes made from purchased aluminum
331315	Aluminum foil made by flat rolling purchased aluminum
331315	Aluminum foil made in integrated secondary smelting and flat rolling mills
332112	Aluminum forgings made from purchased metals, unfinished
331524	Aluminum foundries (except die-casting)
332999	Aluminum freezer foil not made in rolling mills
325188	Aluminum hydroxide (i.e., alumina trihydrate) manufacturing
331312	Aluminum ingot and other primary aluminum production shapes made from bauxite or alumina
331314	Aluminum ingot made from purchased aluminum
331314	Aluminum ingot, secondary smelting of aluminum and manufacturing
331314	Aluminum ingot, secondary, manufacturing
332999	Aluminum ladders manufacturing
327910	Aluminum oxide (fused) abrasives manufacturing
331311	Aluminum oxide refining
331316	Aluminum pipe made by extruding purchased aluminum
331316	Aluminum pipe made in integrated secondary smelting and extruding mills
233310	Aluminum plant construction, general construction contractors
331315	Aluminum plate made by continuous casting purchased aluminum
331315	Aluminum plate made by flat rolling purchased aluminum
331315	Aluminum plate made in integrated secondary smelting and continuous casting mills
331315	Aluminum plate made in integrated secondary smelting and flat rolling mills

Code	Description
331312	Aluminum producing from alumina
331314	Aluminum recovering from scrap and making ingot and billet (except by rolling)
331316	Aluminum rod made by extruding purchased aluminum
331316	Aluminum rod made in integrated secondary smelting and extruding mills
331312	Aluminum shapes (e.g., bar, ingot, rod, sheet) made by producing primary aluminum and manufacturing
331315	Aluminum sheet made by flat rolling purchased aluminum
331315	Aluminum sheet made in integrated secondary smelting and flat rolling mills
331314	Aluminum smelting, secondary, and making ingot and billet (except by rolling)
325188	Aluminum sulfate manufacturing
331316	Aluminum tube blooms made by extruding purchased aluminum
331316	Aluminum tube blooms made in integrated secondary smelting and extruding mills
331316	Aluminum tube made by drawing or extruding purchased aluminum
331316	Aluminum tube made in integrated secondary smelting and drawing plants
331316	Aluminum tube made in integrated secondary smelting and extruding mills
331315	Aluminum welded tube made by flat rolling purchased aluminum
331315	Aluminum welded tube made in integrated secondary smelting and flat rolling mills
813410	Alumni associations
813410	Alumni clubs
325188	Alums (e.g., aluminum ammonium sulfate, aluminum potassium sulfate) manufacturing
212393	Alunite mining and/or beneficiating
333131	Amalgamators (i.e., metallurgical and mining machinery) manufacturing

Code	Description
339114	Amalgams, dental, manufacturing
111998	Amaranth farming
713990	Amateur sports teams, recreational
325920	Amatols manufacturing
212393	Amblygonite mining and/or beneficiating
922160	Ambulance and fire service combined
336213	Ambulance bodies manufacturing
621910	Ambulance services, air or ground
336211	Ambulances assembling on purchased chassis
421110	Ambulances wholesaling
621493	Ambulatory surgical centers and clinics, freestanding
921150	American Indian or Alaska Native tribal councils
921150	American Indian or Alaska Native tribal courts
921150	American Indian or Alaska Native, tribal chief's or chairman's office
212399	Amethyst mining and/or beneficiating
334516	Amino acid analyzers, laboratory-type, manufacturing
325211	Amino resins manufacturing
325211	Amino-aldehyde resins manufacturing
325192	Aminoanthraquinone manufacturing
325192	Aminoazobenzene manufacturing
325192	Aminoazotoluene manufacturing
325192	Aminophenol manufacturing
422690	Ammonia (except fertilizer material) wholesaling
325311	Ammonia, anhydrous and aqueous, manufacturing
422910	Ammonia, fertilizer material, wholesaling
325612	Ammonia, household-type, manufacturing
325188	Ammonium chloride manufacturing
325188	Ammonium compounds, not specified elsewhere by process, manufacturing

Code	Description
325188	Ammonium hydroxide manufacturing
325188	Ammonium molybdate manufacturing
325311	Ammonium nitrate manufacturing
325188	Ammonium perchlorate manufacturing
325312	Ammonium phosphates manufacturing
325311	Ammonium sulfate manufacturing
325188	Ammonium thiosulfate manufacturing
421990	Ammunition (except sporting) wholesaling
332993	Ammunition (i.e., more than 30 mm., more than 1.18 inch) manufacturing
332439	Ammunition boxes, metal, manufacturing
321920	Ammunition boxes, wood, manufacturing
332994	Ammunition carts (i.e., 30 mm or less, 1.18 inch or less) manufacturing
332995	Ammunition carts (i.e., more than 30 mm, more than 1.18 inch) manufacturing
332993	Ammunition loading and assembling plants
332992	Ammunition, small arms (i.e., 30 mm. or less, 1.18 inch or less), manufacturing
334515	Ampere-hour meters manufacturing
325411	Amphetamines, uncompounded, manufacturing
334310	Amplifiers (e.g., auto, home, musical instrument, public address) manufacturing
334220	Amplifiers, (e.g., RF power and IF), broadcast and studio equipment, manufacturing
335999	Amplifiers, magnetic, pulse, and maser, manufacturing
713120	Amusement arcades
233320	Amusement building construction
713990	Amusement device (except gambling) concession operators (i.e., supplying and servicing in others' facilities)

Code	Description
713120	Amusement device (except gambling) parlors, coin-operated
713120	Amusement devices (except gambling) operated in own facilities
339999	Amusement machines, coin-operated, manufacturing
421850	Amusement park equipment wholesaling
713110	Amusement parks (e.g., theme, water)
713990	Amusement ride concession operators (i.e., supplying and servicing in others' facilities)
325199	Amyl acetate manufacturing
325412	Analgesic preparations manufacturing
334111	Analog computers manufacturing
421490	Analytical instruments (e.g., chromatographic, photometers, spectrographs) wholesaling
334515	Analyzers for testing electrical characteristics manufacturing
334513	Analyzers, industrial process control type, manufacturing
235990	Anchored earth retention construction contractors
114111	Anchovy fishing
212325	Andalusite mining and/or beneficiating
332999	Andirons manufacturing
339112	Anesthesia apparatus manufacturing
621111	Anesthesiologists' offices (e.g., centers, clinics)
325412	Anesthetic preparations manufacturing
325411	Anesthetics, uncompounded, manufacturing
325412	Angiourographic diagnostic preparations manufacturing
333515	Angle rings (i.e., a machine tool accessory) manufacturing
332911	Angle valves, industrial-type, manufacturing
332999	Angle, irons metal, manufacturing
334511	Angle-of-attack instrumentation manufacturing
334511	Angle-of-yaw instrumentation manufacturing

Code	Description
112420	Angora goat farming
325311	Anhydrous ammonia manufacturing
311512	Anhydrous butterfat manufacturing
325222	Anidex fibers and filaments manufacturing
325192	Aniline manufacturing
112519	Animal aquaculture (except finfish, shellfish)
325182	Animal black manufacturing
813910	Animal breeders' associations
812220	Animal cemeteries
712130	Animal exhibits, live
311611	Animal fats (except poultry and small game) produced in slaughtering plants
311613	Animal fats rendering
311119	Animal feed mills (except dog and cat) manufacturing
311111	Animal feed mills, dog and cat, manufacturing
422910	Animal feeds (except pet food) wholesaling
311119	Animal feeds, prepared (except dog and cat), manufacturing
311111	Animal feeds, prepared, dog and cat, manufacturing
313112	Animal fiber yarn twisting or winding of purchased yarn
812910	Animal grooming services
422590	Animal hair wholesaling
541940	Animal hospitals
311613	Animal oil rendering
926140	Animal quarantine service, government
813312	Animal rights organizations
712130	Animal safari parks
115210	Animal semen banks
233320	Animal shelter/clinic construction
812910	Animal shelters
114210	Animal trapping, commercial
332999	Animal traps, metal (except wire), manufacturing
813312	Animal welfare associations or leagues
336999	Animal-drawn vehicles and parts manufacturing

Code	Description
711510	Animated cartoon artists, independent
512120	Animated cartoon distribution
512110	Animated cartoon production
512110	Animated cartoon production and distribution
325998	Anise oil manufacturing
315119	Anklets, sheer hosiery or socks, knitting or knitting and finishing
325191	Annato extract manufacturing
332811	Annealing metals for the trade
332420	Annealing vats manufacturing
711510	Announcers, independent radio and television
524113	Annuities underwriting
332991	Annular ball bearings manufacturing
334513	Annunciators, relay and solid-state types, industrial display, manufacturing
333298	Anodizing equipment manufacturing
332813	Anodizing metals and metal products for the trade
421620	Answering machines, telephone, wholesaling
561421	Answering services, telephone
325320	Ant poisons manufacturing
325412	Antacid preparations manufacturing
235990	Antenna installation construction contractors
421690	Antennas wholesaling
334220	Antennas, satellite, manufacturing
334220	Antennas, transmitting and receiving, manufacturing
325412	Anthelmintic preparations manufacturing
325192	Anthracene manufacturing
212113	Anthracite beneficiating (e.g., crushing, screening, washing, cleaning, sizing)
213113	Anthracite mine tunneling on a contract basis
212113	Anthracite mining and/or beneficiating
213113	Anthracite mining services on a contract basis

Code	Description
325132	Anthraquinone dyes manufacturing
332995	Antiaircraft artillery manufacturing
325412	Antibacterial preparations manufacturing
325412	Antibiotic preparations manufacturing
422210	Antibiotics wholesaling
325411	Antibiotics, uncompounded, manufacturing
325411	Anticholinergics, uncompounded, manufacturing
325411	Anticonvulsants, uncompounded, manufacturing
325412	Antidepressant preparations manufacturing
325411	Antidepressants, uncompounded, manufacturing
325998	Antifreeze preparations manufacturing
422690	Antifreeze wholesaling
325414	Antigens manufacturing
325412	Antihistamine preparations manufacturing
325131	Antimony based pigments manufacturing
212299	Antimony concentrates mining and/or beneficiating
212299	Antimony ores mining and/or beneficiating
325188	Antimony oxide (except pigments) manufacturing
331419	Antimony refining, primary
325412	Antineoplastic preparations manufacturing
325620	Antiperspirants, personal, manufacturing
813319	Antipoverty advocacy organizations
325412	Antipyretic preparations manufacturing
811121	Antique and classic automotive restoration
441120	Antique auto dealers
422920	Antique book wholesaling
811420	Antique furniture repair and restoration shops
421210	Antique furniture wholesaling
421220	Antique homefurnishing wholesaling

Code	Description
421220	Antique houseware wholesaling
421940	Antique jewelry wholesaling
453310	Antique shops
332913	Antiscald bath and shower valves manufacturing
325998	Antiscaling compounds manufacturing
325412	Antiseptic preparations manufacturing
422210	Antiseptics wholesaling
325414	Antiserums manufacturing
325412	Antispasmodic preparations manufacturing
332995	Antisubmarine projectors manufacturing
332995	Antitank rocket launchers manufacturing
325414	Antitoxins manufacturing
325414	Antivenoms manufacturing
531110	Apartment building rental or leasing
531110	Apartment hotel rental or leasing
531311	Apartment managers' offices
531110	Apartment rental or leasing
233220	Apartments (e.g., garden, high-rise) construction
212392	Apatite mining and/or beneficiating
212325	Aplite mining and/or beneficiating
446110	Apothecaries
331491	Apparatus wire and cord (except aluminum, copper) made from purchased nonferrous metals (except aluminum, copper) in wire drawing plants
331422	Apparatus wire or cord made from purchased copper in wire drawing plants
331319	Apparatus wire or cord made in aluminum wire drawing plants
448150	Apparel accessory stores
314999	Apparel fillings (e.g., cotton mill waste, kapok) manufacturing
315999	Apparel findings and trimmings cut and sewn from purchased fabric (except apparel contractors)
561910	Apparel folding and packaging services
812320	Apparel pressing services

Code	Description
448130	Apparel stores, children's and infants' clothing
448110	Apparel stores, men's and boys' clothing
453310	Apparel stores, used clothing
448120	Apparel stores, women's and girls' clothing
315211	Apparel trimmings and findings, men's and boys', cut and sew apparel contractors
315212	Apparel trimmings and findings, women's, girls', and infants', cut and sew apparel contractors
422310	Apparel trimmings wholesaling
313221	Apparel webbings manufacturing
315292	Apparel, fur (except apparel contractors), manufacturing
315211	Apparel, fur, men's and boys', cut and sew apparel contractors
315212	Apparel, fur, women's, girls', and infants', cut and sew apparel contractors
315211	Apparel, men's and boys', cut and sew apparel contractors
315212	Apparel, women's, girls', and infants', cut and sew contractors
111331	Apple orchards
312130	Applejack distilling
334512	Appliance controls manufacturing
335999	Appliance cords made from purchased insulated wire
332510	Appliance hardware, metal, manufacturing
334512	Appliance regulators (except switches) manufacturing
532210	Appliance rental
443111	Appliance stores, household-type
453310	Appliance stores, household-type, used
334518	Appliance timers manufacturing
811412	Appliance, household-type, repair and maintenance services without retailing new appliances
421720	Appliances, gas (except dryers, freezers, refrigerators), wholesaling
421620	Appliances, household-type (except gas ranges, gas water heaters), wholesaling

Code	Description
421450	Appliances, surgical, wholesaling
541511	Applications software programming services, custom computer
511210	Applications software, computer, packaged
321999	Applicators, wood, manufacturing
315211	Appliqueing on men's and boys' apparel
314999	Appliqueing on textile products (except apparel)
315212	Appliqueing on women's, girls', and infants' apparel
323118	Appointment books and refills manufacturing
541990	Appraisal (except real estate) services
531320	Appraisal services, real estate
531320	Appraisers' offices, real estate
611513	Apprenticeship training programs
111339	Apricot farming
812331	Apron supply services
316999	Aprons for textile machinery, leather, manufacturing
316999	Aprons, leather (e.g., blacksmith's, welder's), manufacturing
315999	Aprons, waterproof (e.g., plastics, rubberized fabric), rubberizing fabric and manufacturing aprons
315212	Aprons, waterproof (including plastics, rubberized fabric), woman's, girls', and infants', cut and sew apparel contractors
315999	Aprons, waterproof (including rubberized fabric, plastics), cut and sewn from purchased fabric (except apparel contractors)
315211	Aprons, waterproof (including rubberized fabric, plastics), men's and boys', cut and sew apparel contractors
315211	Aprons, work (except leather), men's and boys, cut and sew apparel contractors
315212	Aprons, work (except leather), women's, girls', and infants', cut and sew apparel contractors
315225	Aprons, work (except leather, waterproof), men's and boys', cut and sewn from purchased fabric (except apparel contractors)

Code	Description
315239	Aprons, work (except waterproof, leather), women's, misses', and girls', cut and sewn from purchased fabric (except apparel contractors)
332999	Aquarium accessories, metal, manufacturing
712130	Aquariums
327215	Aquariums made from purchased glass
234910	Aqueduct construction
541990	Arbitration and conciliation services (except by attorney, paralegal)
333513	Arbor presses, metalworking, manufacturing
712130	Arboreta
561730	Arborist services
333515	Arbors (i.e., a machine tool accessory) manufacturing
334510	Arc lamp units, electrotherapeutic (except infrared, ultraviolet), manufacturing
335129	Arc lighting fixtures (except electrotherapeutic), electric, manufacturing
333992	Arc welding equipment manufacturing
335311	Arc-welding transformers, separate solid-state, manufacturing
713120	Arcades, amusement
339113	Arch supports, orthopedic, manufacturing
541720	Archeological research and development services
712120	Archeological sites (i.e., public display)
339920	Archery equipment manufacturing
421910	Archery equipment wholesaling
713990	Archery ranges
321213	Arches, glue laminated or pre-engineered wood, manufacturing
421490	Architect's equipment and supplies wholesaling
541310	Architects' (except landscape) offices
541310	Architects' (except landscape) private practices
813920	Architects' associations

Code	Description
541320	Architects' offices, landscape
541320	Architects' private practices, landscape
541310	Architectural (except landscape) consultants' offices
541310	Architectural (except landscape) design services
541310	Architectural (except landscape) services
327331	Architectural block, concrete (e.g., fluted, ground face, screen, slump, split), manufacturing
325510	Architectural coatings (i.e., paint) manufacturing
332323	Architectural metalwork manufacturing
421390	Architectural metalwork wholesaling
327112	Architectural sculptures, clay, manufacturing
327991	Architectural sculptures, stone, manufacturing
541320	Architectural services, landscape
235610	Architectural sheet metal construction contractors
327123	Architectural terra cotta manufacturing
327390	Architectural wall panels, precast concrete, manufacturing
337212	Architectural woodwork and fixtures (i.e., custom designed interiors) manufacturing
514120	Archives
316211	Arctics, plastics or plastics soled fabric upper, manufacturing
316211	Arctics, rubber or rubber soled fabric, manufacturing
335129	Area and sports luminaries (e.g., stadium lighting fixtures), electric, manufacturing
711310	Arena operators
531120	Arena, no promotion of events, rental or leasing
212311	Argillite mining or quarrying
325120	Argon manufacturing
315999	Arm bands, elastic, cut and sewn from purchased fabric (except apparel contractors)

Code	Description
315211	Arm bands, elastic, men's and boys', cut and sew apparel contractors
315212	Arm bands, elastic, women's, girls', and infants', cut and sew apparel contractors
335314	Armature relays manufacturing
335312	Armature rewinding on a factory basis
811310	Armature rewinding services (except on an assembly line or factory basis)
335312	Armatures, industrial, manufacturing
928110	Armed forces
332993	Arming and fusing devices, missile, manufacturing
331111	Armor plate made in steel mills
331422	Armored cable made from purchased copper in wire drawing plants
331422	Armored cable, copper, made in integrated secondary smelting and drawing plants
561613	Armored car services
336992	Armored military vehicles and parts manufacturing
928110	Army
422690	Aromatic chemicals wholesaling
113210	Aromatic wood gathering
488999	Arrangement of car pools and vanpools
335931	Arrestors and coils, lighting, manufacturing
325320	Arsenate insecticides manufacturing
325188	Arsenates (except insecticides) manufacturing
325131	Arsenic based pigments manufacturing
325188	Arsenic compounds, not specified elsewhere by process, manufacturing
212393	Arsenic mineral mining and/or beneficiating
325320	Arsenite insecticides manufacturing
325188	Arsenites manufacturing
611610	Art (except commercial or graphic) instruction
453920	Art auctions
453920	Art dealers
712110	Art galleries (except retail)
453920	Art galleries retailing art
327420	Art goods (e.g., gypsum, plaster of paris) manufacturing
422990	Art goods wholesaling
712110	Art museums
315211	Art needlework contractors on men's and boys' apparel
315212	Art needlework contractors on women's, girls', and infants' apparel
314999	Art needlework on clothing for the trade
323111	Art print gravure printing without publishing
511199	Art print publishers
511199	Art print publishers and printing combined
511199	Art print publishing (i.e., establishment known as publishers)
323112	Art prints flexographic printing without publishing
323110	Art prints lithographic (offset) printing without publishing
323119	Art prints printing (except flexographic, gravure, lithographic, screen) without publishing
323113	Art prints screen printing without publishing
511199	Art publishers
511199	Art publishing (i.e., establishments known as publishers)
711510	Art restorers, independent
611610	Art schools (except academic), fine
611519	Art schools, commercial or graphic
541430	Art services, commercial
541430	Art services, graphic
541430	Art studios, commercial
453998	Art supply stores
621340	Art therapists' offices (e.g., centers, clinics)
111219	Artichoke farming, field, bedding plant and seed production
311421	Artichokes, canned, manufacturing
422990	Artificial Christmas trees wholesaling
339999	Artificial flower arrangements assembled from purchased components
422930	Artificial flowers wholesaling
334511	Artificial horizon instrumentation manufacturing
115210	Artificial insemination services for livestock
115210	Artificial insemination services for pets
339113	Artificial limbs manufacturing
235990	Artificial turf construction contractors
312111	Artificially carbonated waters manufacturing
332993	Artillery (i.e., more than 30 mm., more than 1.18 inch) manufacturing
339942	Artist's paint manufacturing
339942	Artist's supplies (except paper) manufacturing
711510	Artists (except commercial, musical), independent
711510	Artists (i.e., painters), independent
711410	Artists' agents or managers
422990	Artists' supplies wholesaling
541430	Artists, independent commercial
541430	Artists, independent graphic
541430	Artists, independent medical
926110	Arts and cultural program administration, government
711310	Arts event managers with facilities
711320	Arts event managers without facilities
711310	Arts event organizers with facilities
711320	Arts event organizers without facilities
711310	Arts event promoters with facilities
711320	Arts event promoters without facilities
711310	Arts festival managers with facilities
711320	Arts festival managers without facilities

Code	Description
711310	Arts festival organizers with facilities
711320	Arts festival organizers without facilities
711310	Arts festival promoters with facilities
711320	Arts festival promoters without facilities
562910	Asbestos abatement services
212399	Asbestos mining and/or beneficiating
562910	Asbestos removal contractors
325411	Ascorbic acid (i.e., vitamin C), uncompounded, manufacturing
315211	Ascots, men's and boys', cut and sew apparel contractors
315993	Ascots, men's and boys', cut and sewn from purchased fabric (except apparel contractors)
562111	Ash collection services
562111	Ash hauling, local
212399	Ash, volcanic, mining and/or beneficiating
327215	Ashtrays made from purchased glass
327212	Ashtrays, glass, made in glass making plants
327112	Ashtrays, pottery, manufacturing
111219	Asparagus farming, field, bedding plant and seed production
324110	Asphalt and asphaltic materials made in petroleum refineries
322121	Asphalt paper made in paper mills
234110	Asphalt paving (e.g., public sidewalks, roads, streets) contractors
324121	Asphalt paving blocks made from purchased asphaltic materials
324121	Asphalt paving mixtures made from purchased asphaltic materials
324110	Asphalt paving mixtures made in petroleum refineries
324121	Asphalt road compounds made from purchased asphaltic materials
212399	Asphalt rock mining and/or beneficiating

Code	Description
324122	Asphalt roofing cements made from purchased asphaltic materials
324122	Asphalt roofing coatings made from purchased asphaltic materials
333120	Asphalt roofing construction machinery manufacturing
421330	Asphalt roofing shingles wholesaling
324122	Asphalt saturated boards made from purchased asphaltic materials
324122	Asphalt saturated mats and felts made from purchased asphaltic materials and paper
235710	Asphalt seal coating construction contractors
324122	Asphalt shingles made from purchased asphaltic materials
235520	Asphalt tile construction contractors
212399	Asphalt, native, mining and/or beneficiating
235710	Asphalting of private driveways and parking areas construction contractors
541380	Assaying services
336213	Assembly line conversions of purchased vans and mini-vans
336312	Assembly line rebuilding of automotive and truck gasoline engines
336350	Assembly line rebuilding of automotive, truck, and bus transmissions
333518	Assembly machines manufacturing
233310	Assembly plant construction
336120	Assembly plants, heavy trucks, and buses on chassis of own manufacture
336112	Assembly plants, light trucks on chassis of own manufacture
336112	Assembly plants, mini-vans on chassis of own manufacture
336111	Assembly plants, passenger car, on chassis of own manufacture
336112	Assembly plants, sport utility vehicles on chassis of own manufacture
921130	Assessor's offices, tax
325613	Assistants, textile and leather finishing, manufacturing

Code	Description
623311	Assisted-living facilities with on-site nursing facilities
623312	Assisted-living facilities without on-site nursing care facilities
813311	Associations for retired persons, advocacy
325412	Astringent preparations manufacturing
812990	Astrology services
711219	Athletes, amateur, independent
711219	Athletes, independent (i.e., participating in live sports events)
813990	Athletic associations, regulatory
315228	Athletic clothing (except team athletic uniforms), men's, boys' and unisex (i.e., sized without regard to gender), cut and sewn from purchased fabric (except apparel contractors)
315239	Athletic clothing (except team athletic uniforms), women's, misses', and girls', cut and sewn from purchased fabric (except apparel contractors)
315191	Athletic clothing made in apparel knitting mills
315211	Athletic clothing, men's and boys', cut and sew apparel contractors
315212	Athletic clothing, women's, girls', and infants', cut and sew apparel contractors
713940	Athletic club facilities, physical fitness
713990	Athletic clubs (i.e., sports teams) not operating sports facilities, recreational
451110	Athletic equipment and supply stores (including uniforms)
234990	Athletic field construction
422340	Athletic footwear wholesaling
339920	Athletic goods (except ammunition, clothing, footwear, small arms) manufacturing
421910	Athletic goods (except apparel, footwear, nonspecialty) wholesaling
813990	Athletic leagues (i.e., regulating bodies)
448210	Athletic shoe (except bowling, golf, spiked) stores

Code	Description
316219	Athletic shoes (except rubber or plastics soled with fabric upper) manufacturing
316211	Athletic shoes, plastics or plastics soled fabric upper (except cleated), manufacturing
316211	Athletic shoes, rubber or rubber soled fabric uppers (except cleated), manufacturing
315119	Athletic socks, knitting or knitting and finishing
421910	Athletic uniforms wholesaling
315299	Athletic uniforms, team, cut and sewn from purchased fabric (except apparel contractors)
315211	Athletic uniforms, team, men's and boys', cut and sew apparel contractors
315212	Athletic uniforms, team, women's, girls', and infants, cut and sew apparel contractors
511199	Atlas publishers
511199	Atlas publishers and printing combined
511199	Atlas publishing (i.e., establishments known as publishers)
323112	Atlases flexographic printing without publishing
323111	Atlases gravure printing without publishing
323110	Atlases lithographic (offset) printing without publishing
323119	Atlases printing (except flexographic, gravure, lithographic, screen) without publishing
323113	Atlases screen printing without publishing
335999	Atom smashers (i.e., particle accelerators) manufacturing
339999	Atomizers (e.g., perfumes) manufacturing
325411	Atropine and derivatives manufacturing
316991	Attache cases, all materials, manufacturing
333112	Attachments, powered lawn and garden equipment, manufacturing
333412	Attic fans manufacturing

Code	Description
922130	Attorney generals' offices
541110	Attorneys' offices
541110	Attorneys' private practices
453998	Auction houses (general merchandise)
422590	Auction markets, horses and mules
422520	Auction markets, livestock (except horses, mules)
422590	Auction markets, tobacco
561990	Auctioneers, independent
421990	Audio and video tapes and disks, prerecorded, wholesaling
337129	Audio cabinets (i.e., housings), wood, manufacturing
443112	Audio equipment stores (except automotive)
421620	Audio equipment, household-type, wholesaling
512290	Audio recording of meetings or conferences
512240	Audio recording post-production services
532490	Audio visual equipment rental or leasing
334515	Audiofrequency oscillators manufacturing
334510	Audiological equipment, electromedical, manufacturing
621340	Audiologists' offices (e.g., centers, clinics)
334515	Audiometers (except medical) manufacturing
334613	Audiotape, blank, manufacturing
421690	Audiotapes, blank, wholesaling
541211	Auditing accountants' (i.e., CPAs) offices
541211	Auditing accountants' (i.e., CPAs) private practices
541211	Auditing services (i.e., CPA services), accounts
921190	Auditor's offices, government
233320	Auditorium construction
531120	Auditorium rental or leasing
541211	Auditors' (i.e., CPAs) offices, accounts
541211	Auditors' (i.e., CPAs) private practices, accounts

Code	Description
213113	Auger coal mining services on a contract basis
333120	Augers (except mining-type) manufacturing
333131	Augers, mining-type, manufacturing
332212	Augers, nonpowered, manufacturing
711410	Authors' agents or managers
711510	Authors, independent
421120	Auto body shop supplies wholesaling
721110	Auto courts, lodging
441310	Auto supply stores
339114	Autoclaves, dental, manufacturing
332420	Autoclaves, industrial-type, manufacturing
339111	Autoclaves, laboratory-type (except dental), manufacturing
336411	Autogiros manufacturing
235950	Automated and revolving door construction contractors
334510	Automated blood and body fluid analyzers (except laboratory) manufacturing
522320	Automated clearinghouses, bank or check (except central bank)
514210	Automated data processing services
332911	Automatic (i.e., controlling-type, regulating) valves, industrial-type, manufacturing
334516	Automatic chemical analyzers, laboratory-type, manufacturing
812310	Automatic laundries, coin-operated
454210	Automatic merchandising machine operators
333512	Automatic screw machines manufacturing
334119	Automatic teller machines (ATM) manufacturing
421420	Automatic teller machines (ATM) wholesaling
336350	Automatic transmissions, automotive, truck, and bus, manufacturing
421120	Automobile accessories (except tires, tubes) wholesaling
334220	Automobile antennas manufacturing
421110	Automobile auctions

Code	Description
336211	Automobile bodies, passenger car, manufacturing
484220	Automobile carrier trucking, local
484230	Automobile carrier trucking, long-distance
813410	Automobile clubs (except road and travel services)
561599	Automobile clubs, road and travel services
721110	Automobile courts, lodging
493190	Automobile dead storage
441110	Automobile dealers, new only or new and used
441120	Automobile dealers, used only
611692	Automobile driving schools
522220	Automobile finance leasing companies
522220	Automobile financing
421120	Automobile glass wholesaling
332510	Automobile hardware, metal, manufacturing
541420	Automobile industrial design services
524126	Automobile insurance carriers, direct
532112	Automobile leasing
333921	Automobile lifts (i.e., garage-type, service station) manufacturing
812930	Automobile parking garages or lots
441310	Automobile parts dealers
325612	Automobile polishes and cleaners manufacturing
541380	Automobile proving and testing grounds
711212	Automobile racetracks
611620	Automobile racing schools
711219	Automobile racing teams
334310	Automobile radio receivers manufacturing
532111	Automobile rental
485320	Automobile rental with driver (except shuttle service, taxis)
561491	Automobile repossession services
336360	Automobile seat covers manufacturing
332999	Automobile seat frames, metal, manufacturing

Code	Description
421120	Automobile service station equipment wholesaling
561920	Automobile show managers
561920	Automobile show organizers
561920	Automobile show promoters
332618	Automobile skid chains made from purchased wire
335911	Automobile storage batteries manufacturing
332611	Automobile suspension springs manufacturing
336212	Automobile transporter trailers, multi-car, manufacturing
336214	Automobile transporter trailers, single car, manufacturing
336360	Automobile trimmings, textile, manufacturing
333923	Automobile wrecker (i.e., tow truck) hoists manufacturing
336211	Automobile wrecker truck bodies manufacturing
336211	Automobile wreckers assembling on purchased chassis
336111	Automobiles assembling on chassis of own manufacture
421110	Automobiles wholesaling
339932	Automobiles, children's, manufacturing
421730	Automotive air-conditioners wholesaling
811198	Automotive air-conditioning repair shops
441310	Automotive audio equipment stores
811121	Automotive body shops
811118	Automotive brake repair shops
422690	Automotive chemicals (except lubrication greases, lubrication oils) wholesaling
811192	Automotive detailing services (i.e., cleaning, polishing)
334515	Automotive electrical engine diagnostic equipment manufacturing
811118	Automotive electrical repair shops
335931	Automotive electrical switches manufacturing
334519	Automotive emissions testing equipment manufacturing

Code	Description
811198	Automotive emissions testing services
811111	Automotive engine repair and replacement shops
811112	Automotive exhaust system repair and replacement shops
811118	Automotive front end alignment shops
811122	Automotive glass shops
336322	Automotive harness and ignition sets manufacturing
335110	Automotive light bulbs manufacturing
336321	Automotive lighting fixtures manufacturing
811191	Automotive oil change and lubrication shops
331319	Automotive or aircraft wire and cable made in aluminum wire drawing plants
811121	Automotive paint shops
441310	Automotive parts and supply stores
441310	Automotive parts dealers, used
421120	Automotive parts, new, wholesaling
811118	Automotive radiator repair shops
421620	Automotive radios wholesaling
811111	Automotive repair and replacement shops, general
811198	Automotive rustproofing and undercoating shops
334290	Automotive theft alarm systems manufacturing
441320	Automotive tire dealers
811198	Automotive tire repair (except retreading) shops
811113	Automotive transmission repair shops
811118	Automotive tune-up shops
811121	Automotive upholstery shops
811192	Automotive washing and polishing
336330	Automotive, truck and bus steering assemblies and parts manufacturing
336330	Automotive, truck and bus suspension assemblies and parts (except springs) manufacturing
339992	Autophones (organs with perforated music rolls) manufacturing

Code	Description
335311	Autotransformers for switchboards (except telephone switchboards) manufacturing
335311	Autotransformers manufacturing
712130	Aviaries
112990	Aviaries (i.e., raising birds for sale)
813319	Aviation advocacy organizations
481219	Aviation clubs providing a variety of air transportation activities to the general public
488119	Aviation clubs, primarily providing flying field services to the general public
713990	Aviation clubs, recreational
324110	Aviation fuels manufacturing
611512	Aviation schools
111339	Avocado farming
332212	Awls manufacturing
235990	Awning construction contractors
421390	Awnings (except canvas) wholesaling
314912	Awnings and canopies, outdoor, made from purchased fabrics
422990	Awnings, canvas, wholesaling
326199	Awnings, rigid plastics or fiberglass, manufacturing
332322	Awnings, sheet metal, manufacturing
332212	Axes manufacturing
336350	Axle bearings, automotive, truck, and bus, manufacturing
331111	Axles, rolled or forged, made in steel mills
111421	Azalea farming
325920	Azides explosive materials manufacturing
325132	Azine dyes manufacturing
325132	Azo dyes manufacturing
325192	Azobenzene manufacturing
332994	BB guns manufacturing
332992	BB shot manufacturing
448130	Baby clothing shops
422330	Baby clothing wholesaling
311422	Baby foods (including meats) canning
422490	Baby foods, canned, wholesaling
311514	Baby formula, fresh, processed, and bottled, manufacturing

Code	Description
421210	Baby furniture wholesaling
325620	Baby powder and baby oil manufacturing
333997	Baby scales manufacturing
812990	Baby shoe bronzing services
561310	Babysitting bureaus (i.e., registries)
624410	Babysitting services in provider's own home, child day care
624410	Babysitting services, child day care
332913	Backflow preventors, plumbing, manufacturing
112111	Backgrounding, cattle
333120	Backhoes manufacturing
311612	Bacon, slab and sliced, made from purchased carcasses
311611	Bacon, slab and sliced, produced in slaughtering plants
325414	Bacterial vaccines manufacturing
325414	Bacterins (i.e., bacterial vaccines) manufacturing
621511	Bacteriological laboratories, diagnostic
621511	Bacteriological laboratories, medical
541710	Bacteriological research and development laboratories or services
314999	Badges, fabric, manufacturing
332999	Badges, metal, manufacturing
326199	Badges, plastics, manufacturing
339920	Badminton equipment manufacturing
332313	Baffles, fabricated metal plate work, manufacturing
316110	Bag leather manufacturing
332993	Bag loading plants, ammunition, manufacturing
333993	Bag opening, filling, and closing machines manufacturing
722110	Bagel shops, full service
722213	Bagel shops, on premise baking and carryout service
311812	Bagels made in commercial bakeries
322223	Bags (except plastics only) made by laminating or coating combinations of purchased plastics, foil and paper

Code	Description
316991	Bags (i.e., luggage), all materials, manufacturing
313249	Bags and bagging fabric made in warp knitting mills
313241	Bags and bagging fabrics made in weft knitting mills
316991	Bags, athletic, manufacturing
322223	Bags, coated paper, made from purchased paper
322223	Bags, foil, made from purchased foil
339920	Bags, golf, manufacturing
313111	Bags, hemp, made from purchased fiber
322224	Bags, multiwall, made from purchased uncoated paper
422130	Bags, paper and disposable plastics, wholesaling
322224	Bags, paper, uncoated, made from purchased paper
314911	Bags, plastic, made from purchased woven plastics
326111	Bags, plastics film, single wall or multiwall, manufacturing
339920	Bags, punching, manufacturing
314911	Bags, rubberized fabric, manufacturing
314999	Bags, sleeping, manufacturing
314911	Bags, textile, made from purchased woven or knitted materials
422990	Bags, textile, wholesaling
322224	Bags, uncoated paper, made from purchased paper
812990	Bail bonding services
339920	Bait, artificial, fishing, manufacturing
421910	Bait, artificial, wholesaling
422990	Bait, live, wholesaling
112511	Baitfish production, farm raising
311422	Baked beans canning
311813	Baked goods (except bread, bread-type rolls), frozen, manufacturing
445210	Baked ham stores
311811	Bakeries with baking from flour on the premises, retailing not for immediate consumption
315211	Bakers' service apparel, washable, men's and boys', cut and sew apparel contractors

Code	Description
315225	Bakers' service apparel, washable, men's and boys', cut and sewn from purchased fabric (except apparel contractors)
315212	Bakers' service apparel, washable, women's, cut and sew apparel contractors
315239	Bakers' service apparel, washable, women's, misses', and girls, cut and sewn from purchased fabric (except apparel contractors)
333294	Bakery machinery and equipment manufacturing
421830	Bakery machinery and equipment wholesaling
333294	Bakery ovens manufacturing
422490	Bakery products (except frozen) wholesaling
311821	Bakery products, dry (e.g., biscuits, cookies, crackers), manufacturing
311812	Bakery products, fresh (i.e., bread, cakes, doughnuts, pastries), made in commercial bakeries
422420	Bakery products, frozen, wholesaling
445291	Bakery stores, retailing only (except immediate consumption)
311320	Baking chocolate made from cacao beans
311330	Baking chocolate made from purchased chocolate
311999	Baking powder manufacturing
333997	Balances (except laboratory-type) manufacturing
421440	Balances and scales (except laboratory) wholesaling
421490	Balances and scales, laboratory, wholesaling
339111	Balances and scales, laboratory-type, manufacturing
333319	Balancing equipment, motor vehicle, manufacturing
332323	Balcony railings, metal, manufacturing
333111	Bale throwers manufacturing
332618	Bale ties made from purchased wire
333111	Balers, farm-type (e.g., cotton, hay, straw), manufacturing

Code	Description
333999	Baling machinery (e.g., paper, scrap metal) manufacturing
332991	Ball bearings manufacturing
212324	Ball clay mining and/or beneficiating
333613	Ball joints (except aircraft, motor vehicle) manufacturing
339941	Ball point pens manufacturing
332911	Ball valves, industrial-type, manufacturing
335311	Ballasts (i.e., transformers) manufacturing
711120	Ballet companies
711510	Ballet dancers, independent
711120	Ballet productions, live theatrical
611610	Ballet schools (except academic)
316219	Ballet slippers manufacturing
453220	Balloon shops
812990	Balloon-o-gram services
326199	Balloons, plastics, manufacturing
326299	Balloons, rubber, manufacturing
713990	Ballrooms
339920	Balls, baseball, basketball, football, golf, tennis, pool, and bowling, manufacturing
339932	Balls, rubber (except athletic equipment), manufacturing
331111	Balls, steel, made in steel mills
113210	Balsam needles gathering
111339	Banana farming
115114	Banana ripening
315299	Band uniforms cut and sewn from purchased fabric (except apparel contractors)
315211	Band uniforms, men's and boys', cut and sew apparel contractors
315212	Band uniforms, women's, girls', and infants', cut and sew apparel contractors
339113	Bandages and dressings, surgical and orthopedic, manufacturing
422210	Bandages wholesaling
315212	Bandeaux, women's and girls', cut and sew apparel contractors
315231	Bandeaux, women's, misses', and girls', cut and sewn from purchased fabric (except apparel contractors)

Code	Description
711130	Bands
711130	Bands, dance
711130	Bands, musical
333210	Bandsaws, woodworking-type, manufacturing
339992	Banjos and parts manufacturing
334511	Bank and turn indicators and components (aeronautical instruments) manufacturing
233320	Bank building construction
531120	Bank building rental or leasing
332999	Bank chests, metal, manufacturing
332323	Bank fixtures, ornamental metal, manufacturing
522320	Bank clearinghouse associations
524128	Bank deposit insurance carriers, direct
551111	Bank holding companies (except managing)
523991	Bank trust offices
813910	Bankers' associations
926150	Banking regulatory agencies
611519	Banking schools (training in banking)
523110	Banking, investment
525920	Bankruptcy estates
521110	Banks, Federal Reserve
522110	Banks, commercial
522210	Banks, credit card
522190	Banks, private (i.e., unincorporated)
522120	Banks, savings
522293	Banks, trade (i.e., international trade financing)
314999	Banners made from purchased fabrics
332323	Bannisters, metal, manufacturing
531120	Banquet hall rental or leasing
722320	Banquet halls with catering staff
327991	Baptismal fonts, cut stone, manufacturing
813920	Bar associations
561499	Bar code imprinting services
331316	Bar made by extruding purchased aluminum
331319	Bar made by rolling purchased aluminum

Code	Description
333516	Bar mill machinery, metalworking, manufacturing
325611	Bar soaps manufacturing
331316	Bar, aluminum, made in integrated secondary smelting and extruding mills
331319	Bar, aluminum, made in integrated secondary smelting and rolling mills
331421	Bar, copper and copper alloy, made from purchased copper or in integrated secondary smelting and rolling, drawing or extruding plants
331491	Bar, nonferrous metals (except aluminum, copper), made from purchased metals in wire drawing plants or in integrated secondary smelting and rolling, drawing, or extruding plants
311421	Barbecue sauce manufacturing
335221	Barbecues, grills, and braziers manufacturing
331222	Barbed and twisted wire made in wire drawing plants
332618	Barbed wire made from purchased wire
611511	Barber colleges
421850	Barber shop equipment and supplies wholesaling
812111	Barber shops
332211	Barber's scissors, manufacturing
315211	Barbers' service apparel, washable, men's and boys', cut and sew apparel contractors
315225	Barbers' service apparel, washable, men's and boys', cut and sewn from purchased fabric (except apparel contractors)
325412	Barbiturate preparations manufacturing
325411	Barbiturates, uncompounded, manufacturing
325411	Barbituric acid manufacturing
336611	Barge building
532411	Barge rental or leasing
332312	Barge sections, prefabricated metal, manufacturing
483211	Barge transportation, canal

Code	Description
483113	Barge transportation, coastal or Great Lakes
212393	Barite mining and/or beneficiating
327992	Barite processing beyond beneficiation
325188	Barium compounds, not specified elsewhere by process, manufacturing
325188	Barium hydroxide manufacturing
325412	Barium in-vivo diagnostic substances manufacturing
212393	Barium ores mining and/or beneficiating
327992	Barium processing beyond beneficiation
113210	Bark gathering
111199	Barley farming, field and seed production
311119	Barley feed, chopped, crushed or ground, manufacturing
311211	Barley flour manufacturing
311213	Barley, malt, manufacturing
332323	Barn stanchions and standards manufacturing
334519	Barographs manufacturing
334519	Barometers manufacturing
332410	Barometric condensers manufacturing
233320	Barrack construction
321920	Barrel heading and staves manufacturing
332994	Barrels, gun (i.e., 30 mm. or less, 1.18 inch or less), manufacturing
332995	Barrels, gun (i.e., more than 30 mm., more than 1.18 inch), manufacturing
332439	Barrels, metal, manufacturing
421840	Barrels, new and reconditioned, wholesaling
321920	Barrels, wood, coopered, manufacturing
332999	Barricades, metal, manufacturing
541110	Barristers' offices
541110	Barristers' private practices
722410	Bars (i.e., drinking places), alcoholic beverage
331411	Bars made in primary copper smelting and refining mills

Code	Description
332312	Bars, concrete reinforcing, manufacturing
331111	Bars, iron, made in steel mills
421510	Bars, metal (except precious), wholesaling
331221	Bars, steel, made in cold rolling mills
331111	Bars, steel, made in steel mills
611519	Bartending schools
561990	Bartering services
325131	Barytes based pigments manufacturing
212393	Barytes mining and/or beneficiating
212319	Basalt crushed and broken stone mining and/or beneficiating
212311	Basalt mining or quarrying
561210	Base facilities operation support services
315211	Baseball caps (except plastics), men's and boys', cut and sew apparel contractors
315212	Baseball caps (except plastics), women's, girls', and infants', cut and sew apparel contractors
315991	Baseball caps cut and sewn from purchased fabric (except apparel contractors)
711211	Baseball clubs, professional or semiprofessional
713990	Baseball clubs, recreational
339920	Baseball equipment and supplies (except footwear, uniforms) manufacturing
421910	Baseball equipment and supplies wholesaling
611620	Baseball instruction, camps, or schools
711211	Baseball teams, professional or semiprofessional
315299	Baseball uniforms cut and sewn from purchased fabric (except apparel contractors)
315211	Baseball uniforms, men's and boys', cut and sew apparel contractors
315212	Baseball uniforms, women's and girls', cut and sew apparel contractors
421730	Baseboard heaters, electric, non-portable, wholesaling

Code	Description
333414	Baseboard heating equipment manufacturing
321918	Baseboards, floor, wood, manufacturing
332321	Baseboards, metal, manufacturing
711211	Basketball clubs, professional or semiprofessional
713990	Basketball clubs, recreational
339920	Basketball equipment and supplies (except footwear, uniforms) manufacturing
611620	Basketball instruction, camps, or schools
711211	Basketball teams, professional or semiprofessional
315299	Basketball uniforms cut and sewn from purchased fabric (except apparel contractors)
315211	Basketball uniforms, men's and boys', cut and sew apparel contractors
315212	Basketball uniforms, women's and girls', cut and sew apparel contractors
422990	Baskets wholesaling
331222	Baskets, iron or steel, made in wire drawing plants
332618	Baskets, metal, made from purchased wire
321920	Baskets, wood (e.g., round stave, veneer), manufacturing
337125	Bassinets, reed and rattan, manufacturing
339992	Bassoons manufacturing
212299	Bastnaesite mining and/or beneficiating
335211	Bath fans with integral lighting fixture, residential, manufacturing
335211	Bath fans, residential, manufacturing
314110	Bath mats and bath sets made in carpet mills
326299	Bath mats, rubber, manufacturing
325620	Bath salts manufacturing
442299	Bath shops
713990	Bathing beaches
315999	Bathing caps, rubber, manufacturing

Code	Description
315191	Bathing suits made in apparel knitting mills
315291	Bathing suits, infants', cut and sewn from purchased fabric (except apparel contractors)
315211	Bathing suits, men's and boys', cut and sew apparel contractors
315228	Bathing suits, men's and boys', cut and sewn from purchased fabric (except apparel contractors)
315212	Bathing suits, women's, girls', and infants', cut and sew apparel contractors
315239	Bathing suits, women's, misses', and girls', cut and sewn from purchased fabric (except apparel contractors)
315192	Bathrobes made in apparel knitting mills
315291	Bathrobes, infants', cut and sewn from purchased fabric (except apparel contractors)
315211	Bathrobes, men's and boys', cut and sew apparel contractors
315221	Bathrobes, men's and boys', cut and sewn from purchased fabric (except apparel contractors)
315212	Bathrobes, women's, girls', and infants', cut and sew apparel contractors
315231	Bathrobes, women's, misses', and girls', cut and sewn from purchased fabric (except apparel contractors)
421220	Bathroom accessories wholesaling
327111	Bathroom accessories, vitreous china and earthenware, manufacturing
326199	Bathroom and toilet accessories, plastics, manufacturing
332998	Bathroom fixtures manufacturing
333997	Bathroom scales manufacturing
337110	Bathroom vanities (except freestanding), stock or custom wood, manufacturing
812199	Baths, steam or turkish
235990	Bathtub refinishing construction contractors
332998	Bathtubs, metal, manufacturing
326191	Bathtubs, plastics, manufacturing

Code	Description
611620	Baton instruction
624221	Battered women's shelters
421610	Batteries (except automotive) wholesaling
421120	Batteries, automotive, wholesaling
335912	Batteries, primary, dry or wet, manufacturing
335911	Batteries, rechargeable, manufacturing
335911	Batteries, storage, manufacturing
311822	Batters, prepared, made from purchased flour
311211	Batters, prepared, made in flour mills
335999	Battery chargers, solid-state, manufacturing
334515	Battery testers, electrical, manufacturing
712120	Battlefields
314999	Batts and batting (except nonwoven fabrics) manufacturing
327125	Bauxite brick manufacturing
212299	Bauxite mining and/or beneficiating
325998	Bay oil manufacturing
454390	Bazaars (i.e., temporary stands)
532292	Beach chair rental
713990	Beach clubs, recreational
562998	Beach maintenance and cleaning services
316211	Beach sandals, plastics or plastics soled fabric upper, manufacturing
316211	Beach sandals, rubber or rubber soled fabric upper, manufacturing
532292	Beach umbrella rental
339999	Beach umbrellas manufacturing
713990	Beaches, bathing
315191	Beachwear made in apparel knitting mills
315291	Beachwear, infants', cut and sewn from purchased fabric (except apparel contractors)
315211	Beachwear, men's and boys', cut and sew apparel contractors
315228	Beachwear, men's and boys', cut and sewn from purchased fabric (except apparel contractors)
315212	Beachwear, women's, girls', and infants', cut and sew apparel contractors

Code	Description
315239	Beachwear, women's, misses', and girls', cut and sewn from purchased fabric (except apparel contractors)
333513	Beader machines, metalworking, manufacturing
314999	Beading on textile products (except apparel) for the trade
333292	Beaming machinery for yarn manufacturing
313112	Beaming yarn
321113	Beams, wood, made from logs or bolts
111219	Bean (except dry) farming, field and seed production
115114	Bean cleaning
111130	Bean farming, dry, field and seed production
111419	Bean sprout farming, grown under cover
311422	Beans, baked, canning
422510	Beans, dry, wholesaling
332212	Bearing pullers, handtools, manufacturing
336312	Bearings (e.g., camshaft, crankshaft, connecting rod), automotive and truck gasoline engine, manufacturing
421840	Bearings wholesaling
332991	Bearings, ball and roller, manufacturing
333613	Bearings, plain (except internal combustion engine), manufacturing
812112	Beautician services
611511	Beauty schools
812112	Beauty and barber shops, combined
711310	Beauty pageant managers with facilities
711320	Beauty pageant managers without facilities
711310	Beauty pageant organizers with facilities
711320	Beauty pageant organizers without facilities
711310	Beauty pageant promoters with facilities
711320	Beauty pageant promoters without facilities
421850	Beauty parlor equipment and supplies wholesaling

Code	Description
812112	Beauty parlors
422210	Beauty preparations wholesaling
812112	Beauty salons
812112	Beauty shops
422210	Beauty supplies wholesaling
446120	Beauty supply stores
721191	Bed and breakfast inns
337122	Bed frames, wood household-type, manufacturing
812331	Bed linen supply services
335211	Bedcoverings, electric, manufacturing
111422	Bedding plant growing (except vegetable and melon bedding plants)
315212	Bedjackets, women's, girls' and infants', cut and sew apparel contractors
315231	Bedjackets, women's, misses', juniors', and girls', cut and sewn from purchased fabric (except apparel contractors)
337122	Bedroom furniture (except upholstered), wood household-type, manufacturing
337122	Beds (except hospital), wood household-type, manufacturing
337124	Beds (including cabinet and folding), metal household-type (except hospital), manufacturing
339111	Beds, hospital, manufacturing
421450	Beds, hospital, wholesaling
337910	Beds, sleep-system ensembles (i.e., flotation, adjustable), manufacturing
337122	Beds, wood dormitory-type, manufacturing
337122	Beds, wood hotel-type, manufacturing
314129	Bedspreads and bed sets made from purchased fabrics
313249	Bedspreads and bed sets made in lace mills
313249	Bedspreads and bed sets made in warp knitting mills
313241	Bedspreads and bed sets made in weft knitting mills
112910	Bee production (i.e., apiculture)

Code	Description
311611	Beef carcasses, half carcasses, primal and sub-primal cuts, produced in slaughtering plants
112112	Beef cattle feedlots (except stockyards for transportation)
112111	Beef cattle ranching or farming
311611	Beef produced in slaughtering plants
311612	Beef stew made from purchased carcasses
311612	Beef, primal and sub-primal cuts, made from purchased carcasses
422910	Beekeeping supplies wholesaling
513321	Beeper (i.e., radio pager) communication carriers
327213	Beer bottles, glass, manufacturing
312120	Beer brewing
332431	Beer cans manufacturing
333415	Beer cooling and dispensing equipment manufacturing
332439	Beer kegs, light gauge metal, manufacturing
445310	Beer stores, packaged
422810	Beer wholesaling
325612	Beeswax polishes and waxes manufacturing
112910	Beeswax production
111219	Beet farming (except sugar beets), field, bedding plant and seed production
311313	Beet pulp, dried, manufacturing
311313	Beet sugar refining
541720	Behavioral research and development services
325412	Belladonna preparations manufacturing
332999	Bellows, hand, manufacturing
333999	Bellows, industrial type, manufacturing
339992	Bells (musical instruments) manufacturing
335999	Bells, electric, manufacturing
422310	Belt and buckle assembly kits wholesaling
333922	Belt conveyor systems manufacturing
316999	Belt laces, leather, manufacturing

Code	Description
316110	Belting butts, curried or rough, manufacturing
313221	Belting fabrics, narrow woven
316999	Belting for machinery, leather, manufacturing
316110	Belting leather, manufacturing
314999	Belting made from purchased fabrics
421840	Belting, industrial, wholesaling
326220	Belting, rubber (e.g., conveyor, elevator, transmission), manufacturing
482112	Beltline railroads
315999	Belts, apparel (e.g., fabric, leather, vinyl), cut and sewn from purchased fabric (except apparel contractors)
315211	Belts, apparel (e.g., fabric, leather, vinyl), men's and boys', cut and sew apparel contractors
315212	Belts, apparel (e.g., fabric, leather, vinyl), women's, girls', and infants', cut and sew apparel contractors
332618	Belts, conveyor, made from purchased wire
332618	Belts, drying, made from purchased wire
316999	Belts, leather safety, manufacturing
332994	Belts, machine gun (i.e., 30 mm. or less, 1.18 inch or less), manufacturing
332995	Belts, machine gun (i.e., more than 30 mm., more than 1.18 inch), manufacturing
315999	Belts, money, any material, cut and sewn from purchased fabric (except apparel contractors)
315211	Belts, money, any material, men's and boys', cut and sew apparel contractors
315212	Belts, money, any material, women's and girls', cut and sew apparel contractors
339111	Benches, laboratory-type, manufacturing
337127	Benches, park-type (except concrete, stone), manufacturing
337127	Benches, public building-type, manufacturing

Code	Description
337127	Benches, work, manufacturing
333513	Bending and forming machines, metalworking, manufacturing
332996	Bends, pipe, made from purchased metal pipe
541612	Benefit consulting services
111998	Bentgrass seed farming
212325	Bentonite mining and/or beneficiating
321999	Bentwood (steam bent) products (except furniture) manufacturing
325192	Benzaldehyde manufacturing
325320	Benzene hexachloride (BHC) insecticides manufacturing
325110	Benzene made from refined petroleum or liquid hydrocarbons
324110	Benzene made in petroleum refineries
325192	Benzoic acid manufacturing
311421	Berries, canned, manufacturing
422480	Berries, fresh, wholesaling
115113	Berries, machine harvesting
111334	Berry (except strawberry) farming
321920	Berry crates, wood, wirebound, manufacturing
321920	Berry cups, veneer and splint, manufacturing
333111	Berry harvesting machines manufacturing
212299	Beryl mining and/or beneficiating
327113	Beryllia porcelain insulators manufacturing
331528	Beryllium castings (except die-castings), unfinished manufacturing
212299	Beryllium concentrates beneficiating
331522	Beryllium die-castings, unfinished, manufacturing
212299	Beryllium ores mining and/or beneficiating
325188	Beryllium oxide manufacturing
331419	Beryllium refining, primary
334517	Beta-ray irradiation equipment manufacturing
335999	Betatrons manufacturing
813910	Better business bureaus

Code	Description
722213	Beverage (e.g., coffee, juice, soft drink) bars, nonalcoholic, fixed location
311930	Beverage bases manufacturing
422490	Beverage bases wholesaling
421830	Beverage bottling machinery wholesaling
422490	Beverage concentrates wholesaling
327213	Beverage containers, glass, manufacturing
421740	Beverage coolers, mechanical, wholesaling
311930	Beverage flavorings (except coffee based) manufacturing
722330	Beverage stands, nonalcoholic, mobile
311930	Beverage syrups (except coffee based) manufacturing
422810	Beverages, alcoholic (except distilled spirits, wine), wholesaling
312120	Beverages, beer, ale, and malt liquors, manufacturing
311514	Beverages, dietary, dairy and nondairy based
312111	Beverages, fruit and vegetable drinks, cocktails, and ades, manufacturing
311421	Beverages, fruit and vegetable juice, manufacturing
312140	Beverages, liquors (except brandies), manufacturing
311511	Beverages, milk based (except dietary), manufacturing
312112	Beverages, naturally carbonated bottled water, manufacturing
312111	Beverages, soft drink (including artificially carbonated waters), manufacturing
422820	Beverages, wine and distilled spirits, wholesaling
312130	Beverages, wines and brandies, manufacturing
314999	Bias bindings made from purchased fabrics
313221	Bias bindings, woven, manufacturing
611699	Bible schools (except degree granting)

Code	Description
813110	Bible societies
315999	Bibs and aprons, waterproof (e.g., plastics, rubber, similar materials), cut and sewn from purchased fabric (except apparel contractors)
315211	Bibs and aprons, waterproof (e.g., plastics, rubber, similar materials), men's and boys', cut and sew apparel contractors
315999	Bibs and aprons, waterproof (e.g., plastics, rubber, similar materials), rubberizing fabric and manufacturing bibs and aprons
315212	Bibs and aprons, waterproof (e.g., plastics, rubber, similar materials), women's, girls', and infants', cut and sew apparel contractors
315212	Bibs, waterproof, cut and sew apparel contractors
451110	Bicycle (except motorized) shops
453310	Bicycle (except motorized) shops, used
492210	Bicycle courier
333912	Bicycle pumps manufacturing
532292	Bicycle rental
811490	Bicycle repair and maintenance shops without retailing new bicycles
441221	Bicycle shops, motorized
421910	Bicycles (except motorized) wholesaling
336991	Bicycles and parts manufacturing
421110	Bicycles, motorized, wholesaling
327111	Bidets, vitreous china, manufacturing
561440	Bill collection services
541850	Billboard display advertising services
339950	Billboards manufacturing
333516	Billet mill machinery, metalworking, manufacturing
331111	Billets, steel, made in steel mills
316993	Billfolds, all materials, manufacturing
339920	Billiard equipment and supplies manufacturing
421910	Billiard equipment and supplies wholesaling

Code	Description
713990	Billiard parlors
713990	Billiard rooms
541219	Billing services
322130	Binder's board manufacturing
422120	Binders, looseleaf, wholesaling
333293	Bindery machinery manufacturing
314999	Binding carpets and rugs for the trade
333313	Binding equipment (i.e., plastics or tape binding), office-type, manufacturing
422310	Binding, textile, wholesaling
314999	Bindings, bias, made from purchased fabrics
313221	Bindings, narrow woven, manufacturing
713290	Bingo halls
713290	Bingo parlors
316991	Binocular cases manufacturing
333314	Binoculars manufacturing
421460	Binoculars wholesaling
332313	Bins, fabricated metal plate work, manufacturing
332439	Bins, metal, manufacturing
421390	Bins, storage, wholesaling
621498	Biofeedback centers and clinics, outpatient
339113	Biohazard protective clothing and accessories manufacturing
541380	Biological (except medical, veterinary) testing laboratories or services
541690	Biological consulting services
621511	Biological laboratories, diagnostic
422210	Biologicals and allied products wholesaling
541710	Biology research and development laboratories or services
541710	Biotechnology research and development laboratories or services
311119	Bird feed, prepared, manufacturing
112990	Bird production (e.g., canaries, love birds, parakeets, parrots)

Code	Description
561710	Bird proofing services
712190	Bird sanctuaries
621410	Birth control clinics
326299	Birth control devices (i.e., diaphragms, prophylactics) manufacturing
325412	Birth control pills manufacturing
311812	Biscuits, bread-type, made in commercial bakeries
331419	Bismuth refining, primary
112990	Bison production
333515	Bits and knives for metalworking lathes, planers, and shapers manufacturing
333515	Bits, drill, metalworking, manufacturing
332212	Bits, edge tool, woodworking, manufacturing
333120	Bits, rock drill, construction and surface mining-type, manufacturing
333132	Bits, rock drill, oil and gas field-type, manufacturing
333131	Bits, rock drill, underground mining-type, manufacturing
212399	Bitumens, native, mining and/or beneficiating
212111	Bituminous coal and lignite surface mine site development for own account
212111	Bituminous coal cleaning plants
212111	Bituminous coal crushing
213113	Bituminous coal mining services on a contract basis
212111	Bituminous coal or lignite beneficiating (e.g., cleaning, crushing, screening, washing)
213113	Bituminous coal or lignite surface mine site development on a contract basis
212111	Bituminous coal screening plants
212111	Bituminous coal stripping (except on a contract, fee, or other basis)
213113	Bituminous coal stripping service on a contract basis
212111	Bituminous coal surface mining and/or beneficiating
212112	Bituminous coal underground mine site development for own account

Code	Description
212112	Bituminous coal underground mining or mining and beneficiating
212111	Bituminous coal washeries
212319	Bituminous limestone mining and/or beneficiating
213113	Bituminous or lignite auger mining service on a contract basis
212319	Bituminous sandstone mining and/or beneficiating
325131	Black pigments (except carbon black, bone black, lamp black) manufacturing
421510	Black plate wholesaling
111334	Blackberry farming
421490	Blackboards wholesaling
339942	Blackboards, framed, manufacturing
327991	Blackboards, unframed, slate, manufacturing
331111	Blackplate made in steel mills
316999	Blacksmith's aprons, leather, manufacturing
311312	Blackstrap invert made from purchased raw cane sugar
311311	Blackstrap molasses made in sugarcane mill
235710	Blacktop, private driveways and parking areas, construction contractors
811310	Blade sharpening, commercial and industrial machinery and equipment
421710	Blades (e.g., knife, saw) wholesaling
333120	Blades for graders, scrapers, bulldozers, and snowplows manufacturing
332211	Blades, knife and razor, manufacturing
422210	Blades, razor, wholesaling
332213	Blades, saw, all types, manufacturing
325131	Blanc fixe (i.e., barium sulfate, precipitated) manufacturing
332992	Blank cartridges (i.e., 30 mm. or less, 1.18 inch or less) manufacturing
334613	Blank tapes, audio and video, manufacturing

Code	Description
421690	Blank tapes, audio and video, wholesaling
323118	Blankbooks and refills manufacturing
422120	Blankbooks wholesaling
314911	Blanket bags manufacturing
314129	Blankets (except electric) made from purchased fabrics or felts
421220	Blankets (except electric) wholesaling
313210	Blankets and bedspreads made in broadwoven fabric mills
335211	Blankets, electric, manufacturing
421620	Blankets, electric, wholesaling
313230	Blankets, nonwoven fabric, manufacturing
327212	Blanks for electric light bulbs, glass, made in glass making plants
333515	Blanks, cutting tool, manufacturing
327215	Blanks, ophthalmic lens and optical glass, made from purchased glass
327212	Blanks, ophthalmic lens and optical glass, made in glass making plants
321912	Blanks, wood (e.g., bowling pins, handles, textile machinery accessories), manufacturing
311411	Blast freezing on a contract basis
327992	Blast furnace slag processing
331111	Blast furnaces
212322	Blast sand quarrying and/or beneficiating
234990	Blasting (except building demolition)
325920	Blasting accessories (e.g., caps, fuses, ignitors, squibbs) manufacturing
325920	Blasting powders manufacturing
213113	Blasting services, coal mining, on a contract basis
213114	Blasting services, metal mining, on a contract basis
213115	Blasting services, nonmetallic minerals mining (except fuels) on a contract basis
337127	Bleacher seating manufacturing
422690	Bleaches wholesaling
325612	Bleaches, formulated for household use, manufacturing

Code	Description
325188	Bleaching agents, inorganic, manufacturing
325199	Bleaching agents, organic, manufacturing
313311	Bleaching broadwoven fabrics
212325	Bleaching clay mining and/or beneficiating
333292	Bleaching machinery for textiles manufacturing
313312	Bleaching textile products, apparel, and fabrics (except broadwoven)
212231	Blende (zinc) mining and/or beneficiating
311211	Blended flour made in flour mills
335211	Blenders, household-type electric, manufacturing
325620	Blending and compounding perfume bases
311119	Blending animal feed
312130	Blending brandy
312140	Blending distilled beverages (except brandy)
312130	Blending wines
336411	Blimps (i.e., aircraft) manufacturing
337920	Blinds (e.g., mini, venetian, vertical), all materials, manufacturing
421220	Blinds and shades, window, wholesaling
331411	Blister copper manufacturing
561910	Blister packaging services
333923	Block and tackle manufacturing
312113	Block ice manufacturing
324121	Blocks, asphalt paving, made from purchased asphaltic materials
327331	Blocks, concrete and cinder, manufacturing
327124	Blocks, fire clay, manufacturing
327212	Blocks, glass, made in glass making plants
321999	Blocks, tackle, wood, manufacturing
321999	Blocks, tailors' pressing wood, manufacturing
621511	Blood analysis laboratories
334516	Blood bank process equipment manufacturing

Code	Description
621991	Blood banks
325413	Blood derivative in-vitro diagnostic substances manufacturing
325414	Blood derivatives manufacturing
422210	Blood derivatives wholesaling
621991	Blood donor stations
325414	Blood fractions manufacturing
325413	Blood glucose test kits manufacturing
422210	Blood plasma wholesaling
339112	Blood pressure apparatus manufacturing
621999	Blood pressure screening facilities
621999	Blood pressure screening services
812990	Blood pressure testing machine concession operators, coin-operated
339111	Blood testing apparatus, laboratory-type, manufacturing
339112	Blood transfusion equipment manufacturing
333516	Blooming and slabbing mill machinery, metalworking, manufacturing
331111	Blooms, steel, made in steel mills
315191	Blouses made in apparel knitting mills
315291	Blouses, infants', manufacturing
315212	Blouses, women's, girls', and infants', cut and sew apparel contractors
315232	Blouses, women's, misses', and girls', cut and sewn from purchased fabric (except apparel contractors)
335211	Blow dryers, household-type electric, manufacturing
333220	Blow molding machinery for plastics manufacturing
332212	Blow torches manufacturing
333412	Blower filter units manufacturing
333111	Blowers, forage, manufacturing
421830	Blowers, industrial, wholesaling
333112	Blowers, leaf, manufacturing
221210	Blue gas, carbureted, production and distribution
111334	Blueberry farming
114111	Bluefish fishing
111998	Bluegrass-Kentucky seed farming

Code	Description
541340	Blueprint drafting services
333315	Blueprint equipment manufacturing
421420	Blueprinting equipment wholesaling
561439	Blueprinting services
212311	Bluestone mining or quarrying
325620	Blushes, face, manufacturing
921130	Board of Governors, Federal Reserve
321219	Board, bagasse, manufacturing
327420	Board, gypsum, manufacturing
321219	Board, particle, manufacturing
115210	Boarding horses
721310	Boarding houses
611110	Boarding schools, elementary or secondary
812910	Boarding services, pet
921120	Boards of supervisors, county and local
813910	Boards of trade
324122	Boards, asphalt saturated, made from purchased asphaltic materials
321999	Boards, bulletin, wood and cork, manufacturing
321999	Boards, wood (e.g., clip, ironing, meat, pastry), manufacturing
321113	Boards, wood, made from logs or bolts
321912	Boards, wood, resawing purchased lumber
336321	Boat and ship lighting fixtures manufacturing
441222	Boat dealers, new and used
541330	Boat engineering design services
484220	Boat hauling, truck, local
484230	Boat hauling, truck, long-distance
333923	Boat lifts manufacturing
532411	Boat rental (except pleasure)
532411	Boat rental or leasing, commercial
532292	Boat rental, pleasure
332312	Boat sections, prefabricated metal, manufacturing
441222	Boat trailer dealers
336212	Boat transporter trailers, multi-unit, manufacturing
336214	Boat transporter trailers, single-unit, manufacturing
336612	Boat yards (i.e., boat manufacturing facilities)

Code	Description
487210	Boat, fishing charter, operation
811490	Boat, pleasure, repair and maintenance services without retailing new boats
713930	Boating clubs with marinas
713990	Boating clubs without marinas
421860	Boats (except pleasure) wholesaling
336612	Boats (i.e., suitable or intended for personal use) manufacturing
326199	Boats, inflatable plastics, manufacturing
421910	Boats, pleasure (e.g., canoes, motorboats, sailboats), wholesaling
321912	Bobbin blocks and blanks, wood, manufacturing
322214	Bobbins, fiber, made from purchased paperboard
333292	Bobbins, textile machinery, manufacturing
339920	Bobsleds manufacturing
812320	Bobtailers, laundry and drycleaning
713990	Boccie ball courts
421110	Bodies, motor vehicle, wholesaling
713940	Body building studios, physical fitness
561612	Body guard services
811121	Body shops, automotive
315191	Body stockings made in apparel knitting mills
315212	Body stockings, women's, girls', and infants', cut and sew apparel contractors
315239	Body stockings, women's, misses', and girls', cut and sewn from purchased fabric (except apparel contractors)
332995	Bofors guns manufacturing
332410	Boiler casings manufacturing
235110	Boiler chipping, scaling, cleaning
235110	Boiler cleaning
235110	Boiler contractors
334513	Boiler controls, industrial, power, and marine-type, manufacturing
332919	Boiler couplings and drains, plumbing and heating-type, manufacturing
332911	Boiler gauge cocks, industrial-type, manufacturing

Code	Description
811310	Boiler repair and maintenance shops (except manufacturing)
331210	Boiler tubes, wrought, made from purchased iron
421720	Boilers (e.g., heating, hot water, power, steam) wholesaling
333414	Boilers, heating, manufacturing
332410	Boilers, power, manufacturing
311612	Bologna made from purchased carcasses
332722	Bolts, metal, manufacturing
326199	Bolts, nuts, and rivets, plastics, manufacturing
333924	Bomb lifts manufacturing
332993	Bomb loading and assembling plants
332993	Bombcluster adapters manufacturing
332993	Bombs manufacturing
523120	Bond brokerages
523110	Bond dealing (i.e., acting as a principal in dealing securities to investors)
322233	Bond paper made from purchased paper
322121	Bond paper made in paper mills
493190	Bonded warehousing (except farm products, general merchandise, refrigerated)
493130	Bonded warehousing, farm products (except refrigerated)
493110	Bonded warehousing, general merchandise
493120	Bonded warehousing, refrigerated
313230	Bonded-fiber fabrics manufacturing
332812	Bonderizing metal and metal products for the trade
524126	Bonding, fidelity or surety insurance, direct
812990	Bondsperson services
325182	Bone black manufacturing
327112	Bone china manufacturing
339112	Bone drills manufacturing
311119	Bone meal prepared as feed for animals and fowls
339999	Bone novelties manufacturing
339112	Bone plates and screws manufacturing

Code	Description
339112	Bone rongeurs manufacturing
311613	Bones, fat, rendering
323121	Book binding shops
323121	Book binding without printing
454110	Book clubs, not publishing, mail-order
813410	Book discussion clubs
332999	Book ends, metal, manufacturing
322222	Book paper made by coating purchased paper
322222	Book paper, coated, made from purchased paper
322121	Book paper, coated, made in paper mills
511130	Book publishers (e.g., hardback, paperback, tape)
511130	Book publishers and printing combined
511130	Book publishers publishing all formats
511130	Book publishers, university press
511130	Book publishing (i.e., establishments known as publishers)
451211	Book stores
453310	Book stores, used
316110	Bookbinder's leather manufacturing
333293	Bookbinding machines manufacturing
323121	Bookbinding without printing
337125	Bookcases (except wood and metal), household-type, manufacturing
337214	Bookcases (except wood), office-type, manufacturing
337124	Bookcases, metal household-type, manufacturing
337122	Bookcases, wood household-type, manufacturing
337211	Bookcases, wood office-type, manufacturing
713290	Bookies
512199	Booking agencies, motion picture
512199	Booking agencies, motion picture or video productions
711320	Booking agencies, theatrical (except motion picture)
541219	Bookkeepers' offices

Code	Description
541219	Bookkeepers' private practices
421420	Bookkeeping machines wholesaling
541219	Bookkeeping services
713290	Bookmakers
514120	Bookmobiles
323117	Books printing and binding without publishing
323117	Books printing without publishing
422920	Books wholesaling
422120	Books, sales or receipt, wholesaling
323116	Books, sales, manifold, printing
339920	Boomerangs manufacturing
813410	Booster clubs
486990	Booster pumping station (except natural gas, petroleum)
486110	Booster pumping station, crude oil transportation
486210	Booster pumping station, natural gas transportation
486910	Booster pumping station, refined petroleum products transportation
332993	Boosters and bursters, artillery, manufacturing
335311	Boosters, feeder voltage (i.e., electrical transformers), manufacturing
421850	Boot and shoe cut stock and findings wholesaling
316999	Boot and shoe cut stock and findings, leather, manufacturing
321999	Boot and shoe lasts, all materials, manufacturing
623990	Boot camps for delinquent youth
333298	Boot making and repairing machinery manufacturing
812990	Bootblack parlors
422340	Boots (e.g., hiking, western, work) wholesaling
316219	Boots, dress and casual (except plastics, rubber), children's and infants', manufacturing
316213	Boots, dress and casual (except plastics, rubber), men's, manufacturing
316214	Boots, dress and casual (except plastics, rubber), women's, manufacturing

Code	Description
316219	Boots, hiking (except rubber, plastics), children's and infants', manufacturing
316213	Boots, hiking (except rubber, plastics), men's, manufacturing
316214	Boots, hiking (except rubber, plastics), women's, manufacturing
316211	Boots, plastics or plastics soled fabric upper, manufacturing
316211	Boots, rubber or rubber soled fabric upper, manufacturing
212391	Borate, natural, mining and/or beneficiating
325188	Borax (i.e., sodium borate) manufacturing
212391	Borax, crude, ground or pulverized, mining and/or beneficiating
325320	Bordeaux mixture insecticides manufacturing
325188	Boric acid manufacturing
235930	Boring contractors, building construction
333512	Boring machines, metalworking, manufacturing
213114	Boring test holes for metal mining on a contract basis
213115	Boring test holes for nonmetallic minerals mining (except fuels) on a contract basis
333512	Boring, drilling, and milling machine combinations, metalworking, manufacturing
212391	Boron compounds prepared at beneficiating plants
325188	Boron compounds, not specified elsewhere by process, manufacturing
212391	Boron mineral mining and/or beneficiating
325188	Borosilicate manufacturing
325412	Botanical extract preparations (except in-vitro diagnostics) manufacturing
712130	Botanical gardens
325320	Botanical insecticides manufacturing
422210	Botanicals wholesaling
541710	Botany research and development laboratories or services

Code	Description
326199	Bottle caps and lids, plastics, manufacturing
332115	Bottle caps and tops, metal, stamping
321999	Bottle corks manufacturing
321999	Bottle covers, willow, rattan, and reed, manufacturing
561990	Bottle exchanges
335211	Bottle warmers, household-type electric, manufacturing
333993	Bottle washers, packaging machinery, manufacturing
454312	Bottled gas dealers, direct selling
422490	Bottled water (except water treating) wholesaling
454390	Bottled water providers, direct selling
421840	Bottles (except waste) wholesaling
327213	Bottles (i.e., bottling, canning, packaging), glass, manufacturing
326160	Bottles, plastics, manufacturing
332439	Bottles, vacuum, manufacturing
421930	Bottles, waste, wholesaling
312111	Bottling flavored water
333993	Bottling machinery (e.g., capping, filling, labeling, sterilizing, washing) manufacturing
421830	Bottling machinery and equipment wholesaling
335121	Boudoir lamp fixtures manufacturing
311422	Bouillon canning
311423	Bouillon made in dehydration plants
212319	Boulder crushed and broken mining and/or beneficiating
324199	Boulets (i.e., fuel bricks) made from refined petroleum
422590	Bovine semen wholesaling
315211	Bow ties, men's and boys', cut and sew apparel contractors
315993	Bow ties, men's and boys', cut and sewn from purchased fabric (except apparel contractors)
235990	Bowling alley installation and service construction contractors
713950	Bowling alleys
337127	Bowling center furniture manufacturing

Code	Description
713950	Bowling centers
421910	Bowling equipment and supplies wholesaling
451110	Bowling equipment and supply stores
611620	Bowling instruction
713990	Bowling leagues or teams, recreational
321912	Bowling pin blanks manufacturing
339920	Bowling pin machines, automatic, manufacturing
326199	Bowls and bowl covers, plastics, manufacturing
321999	Bowls, wood, turned and shaped, manufacturing
314999	Bows made from purchased fabrics
339920	Bows, archery, manufacturing
316999	Bows, shoe, leather, manufacturing
321920	Box cleats, wood, manufacturing
321920	Box lumber manufacturing
311991	Box lunches (for sale off premises) manufacturing
321920	Box shook manufacturing
337910	Box springs, assembled, made from purchased spring
316999	Box toes (i.e., shoe cut stock), leather, manufacturing
311612	Boxed beef made from purchased carcasses
311611	Boxed beef produced in slaughtering plants
311612	Boxed meat produced from purchased carcasses
311611	Boxed meats produced in slaughtering plants
711219	Boxers, independent professional
421840	Boxes and crates, industrial (except disposable plastics, paperboard, waste), wholesaling
321920	Boxes, cigar, wood and part wood, manufacturing
322211	Boxes, corrugated and solid fiber, made from purchased paper or paperboard
335932	Boxes, electrical wiring (e.g., junction, outlet, switch), manufacturing

Code	Description
322212	Boxes, folding (except corrugated), made from purchased paperboard
316991	Boxes, hat (except paper or paperboard), manufacturing
321920	Boxes, jewelry, wood or part wood, manufacturing
316999	Boxes, leather, manufacturing
332439	Boxes, light gauge metal, manufacturing
422130	Boxes, paperboard and disposable plastics, wholesaling
322215	Boxes, sanitary food (except folding), made from purchased paper or paperboard
322213	Boxes, setup (i.e., not shipped flat), made from purchased paperboard
322211	Boxes, shipping, laminated paper and paperboard, made from purchased paperboard
336211	Boxes, truck (e.g., cargo, dump, utility, van), assembled on purchased chassis
421930	Boxes, waste, wholesaling
321920	Boxes, wood, manufacturing
321920	Boxes, wood, plain or fabric covered, nailed or lock corner, manufacturing
711211	Boxing clubs, professional or semiprofessional
713990	Boxing clubs, recreational
339920	Boxing equipment manufacturing
711310	Boxing event managers with facilities
711320	Boxing event managers without facilities
711310	Boxing event organizers with facilities
711320	Boxing event organizers without facilities
711310	Boxing event promoters with facilities
711320	Boxing event promoters without facilities
337215	Boxspring frames manufacturing
813410	Boy guiding organizations
623990	Boys' and girls' residential facilities (e.g., homes, ranches, villages)
721214	Boys' camps (except day, instructional)

Code	Description
611620	Boys' camps, sports instruction
611620	Boys' camps, sports instructor
713990	Boys' day camps (except instructional)
315119	Boys' socks manufacturing
111334	Boysenberry farming
315212	Bra-slips, women's and girls', cut and sew apparel contractors
315231	Bra-slips, women's, misses', and juniors', cut and sewn from purchased fabric (except apparel contractors)
339911	Bracelets, precious metal, manufacturing
115112	Bracing of orchard trees and vines
332510	Brackets (i.e., builder's hardware-type), metal, manufacturing
332618	Brackets made from purchased wire
321918	Brackets, wood, manufacturing
421710	Brads wholesaling
331222	Brads, iron or steel, wire or cut, made in wire drawing plants
332618	Brads, metal, made from purchased wire
333292	Braiding machinery for textiles manufacturing
313221	Braiding narrow fabrics
336340	Brake and brake parts, automotive, truck, and bus, manufacturing
336340	Brake caliper assemblies, automotive, truck, and bus, manufacturing
336340	Brake cylinders, master and wheel, automotive, truck, and bus, manufacturing
336340	Brake discs (rotor), automotive, truck, and bus, manufacturing
336340	Brake drums, automotive, truck, and bus, manufacturing
325998	Brake fluid, synthetic, manufacturing
324191	Brake fluids, petroleum, made from refined petroleum
336340	Brake hose assemblies manufacturing
336340	Brake lining, automotive, truck, and bus, manufacturing
336340	Brake pads and shoes, automotive, truck, and bus, manufacturing

Code	Description
811118	Brake repair shops, automotive
333319	Brake service equipment (except mechanic's hand tools), motor vehicle, manufacturing
333613	Brakes and clutches (except electromagnetic industrial controls, motor vehicle) manufacturing
335314	Brakes and clutches, electromagnetic, manufacturing
336510	Brakes and parts for railroad rolling stock manufacturing
335314	Brakes, electromagnetic, manufacturing
333513	Brakes, press, metalworking, manufacturing
311212	Bran and other residues of milling rice
522110	Branches of foreign banks
521110	Branches, Federal Reserve Bank
533110	Brand name licensing
115210	Branding
339943	Branding irons (i.e., marking irons) manufacturing
422820	Brandy and brandy spirits wholesaling
312130	Brandy distilling
331522	Brass die-castings, unfinished, manufacturing
331525	Brass foundries (except die-casting)
421720	Brass goods, plumbers', wholesaling
325612	Brass polishes manufacturing
331421	Brass products, rolling, drawing, or extruding, made from purchased copper or in integrated secondary smelting and rolling, drawing or extruding plants
315212	Brassieres cut and sew apparel contractors
315231	Brassieres cut and sewn from purchased fabric (except apparel contractors)
332323	Brasswork, ornamental, manufacturing
335221	Braziers, barbecue, manufacturing
111335	Brazil nut farming
325191	Brazilwood extract manufacturing
332811	Brazing (i.e., hardening) metals and metal products for the trade

Code	Description
311822	Bread and bread-type roll mixes made from purchased flour
311812	Bread and bread-type rolls made in commercial bakeries
311999	Bread crumbs not made in bakeries
335211	Bread machines, household-type electric, manufacturing
333294	Bread slicing machinery manufacturing
333993	Bread wrapping machines manufacturing
212113	Breakers, anthracite mining and/or beneficiating
333131	Breakers, coal, manufacturing
332919	Breakers, vacuum, plumbing, manufacturing
311340	Breakfast bars, nonchocolate covered, manufacturing
311230	Breakfast cereals manufacturing
422490	Breakfast cereals wholesaling
234990	Breakwater construction
332313	Breechings, fabricated metal plate work, manufacturing
112990	Breeding of pets (e.g., birds, cats, dogs)
115210	Breeding, animal, services
312120	Breweries
311211	Brewers' and distillers' flakes and grits, corn, manufacturing
311213	Brewers' malt manufacturing
325191	Brewers' pitch made by distillation of wood
311212	Brewers' rice manufacturing
422490	Brewers' yeast wholesaling
333294	Brewery machinery manufacturing
235410	Bricklaying construction contractors
421320	Bricks (except refractory) wholesaling
327121	Bricks (i.e., common, face, glazed, hollow, vitrified), clay, manufacturing
327123	Bricks, adobe, manufacturing
327124	Bricks, clay refractory, manufacturing
327331	Bricks, concrete, manufacturing
327215	Bricks, glass, made from purchased glass

Code	Description
327212	Bricks, glass, made in glass making plants
327125	Bricks, nonclay refractory, manufacturing
315233	Bridal dresses or gowns, custom made
315233	Bridal dresses or gowns, women's, misses', and girls', cut and sewn from purchased fabric (except apparel contractors)
315212	Bridal dresses or gowns, women's, misses', and juniors', apparel contractors
448190	Bridal gown shops (except custom)
532220	Bridal wear rental
333999	Bridge and gate lifting machinery manufacturing
611699	Bridge and other card game instruction
321114	Bridge and trestle parts, wood, treating
234120	Bridge and tunnel construction management firms
713990	Bridge clubs, recreational
234120	Bridge construction
234120	Bridge decking construction
235210	Bridge painting construction contractors
332312	Bridge sections, prefabricated metal, manufacturing
488490	Bridge, tunnel, and highway operations
339116	Bridges, custom made in dental laboratories
334515	Bridges, electrical (e.g., Kelvin, megohm, vacuum tube, Wheatstone), manufacturing
316110	Bridle leather manufacturing
234990	Bridle path construction
316991	Briefcases, all materials, manufacturing
315291	Briefs, infants', cut and sewn from purchased fabric (except apparel contractors)
315192	Briefs, underwear, made in apparel knitting mills
315211	Briefs, underwear, men's and boys', cut and sew apparel contractors

Code	Description
315221	Briefs, underwear, men's and boys', cut and sewn from purchased fabric (except apparel contractors)
315231	Briefs, underwear, women's, misses', and girls', cut and sewn from purchased fabric (except apparel contractors)
315212	Briefs, women's, girls', and infants', cut and sew apparel contractors
212393	Brimstone mining and/or beneficiating
311421	Brining of fruits and vegetables
212210	Briquets, iron, mining and/or beneficiating
324199	Briquettes, petroleum, made from refined petroleum
422590	Bristles wholesaling
322130	Bristols board stock manufacturing
322121	Bristols paper stock manufacturing
333515	Broaches (i.e., a machine tool accessory) manufacturing
333512	Broaching machines, metalworking, manufacturing
334220	Broadcast equipment (including studio), for radio and television, manufacturing
541910	Broadcast media rating services
421690	Broadcasting equipment wholesaling
513111	Broadcasting networks, radio
513120	Broadcasting networks, television
611519	Broadcasting schools
513112	Broadcasting stations, radio
513120	Broadcasting stations, television
513112	Broadcasting studio, radio station
711110	Broadway theaters
313210	Broadwoven fabrics (except rugs, tire fabrics) weaving
313311	Broadwoven fabrics finishing
313210	Brocades weaving
111219	Broccoli farming, field, bedding plant and seed production
112320	Broiler chicken production
523140	Brokerages, commodity contracts
524210	Brokerages, insurance
522310	Brokerages, loan
522310	Brokerages, mortgage

Code	Description
531210	Brokerages, real estate
523120	Brokerages, securities
524210	Brokers' offices, insurance
522310	Brokers' offices, loan
522310	Brokers' offices, mortgage
531210	Brokers' offices, real estate
325188	Bromine manufacturing
325199	Bromochloromethane manufacturing
339112	Bronchoscopes (except electromedical) manufacturing
334510	Bronchoscopes, electromedical, manufacturing
331522	Bronze die-castings, unfinished, manufacturing
331525	Bronze foundries (except die-casting)
325910	Bronze printing inks manufacturing
331421	Bronze products, rolling, drawing, or extruding, made from purchased copper or in integrated secondary smelting and rolling, drawing or extruding plants
111199	Broomcorn farming
422590	Broomcorn wholesaling
421220	Brooms and brushes, household-type, wholesaling
339994	Brooms, hand and machine, manufacturing
311422	Broth (except seafood) canning
311313	Brown beet sugar refining
212111	Brown coal mining and/or beneficiating
212210	Brown ore mining and/or beneficiating
311313	Brown sugar made from beet sugar
311312	Brown sugar made from purchased raw cane sugar
311311	Brown sugar made in sugarcane mill
325411	Brucine manufacturing
212325	Brucite mining and/or beneficiating
335991	Brush blocks, carbon or molded graphite, manufacturing
321912	Brush blocks, wood, turned and shaped
234990	Brush clearing or cutting

Code	Description
562119	Brush collection services
562119	Brush hauling, local
562119	Brush removal services
335991	Brushes and brush stock contacts, electric, carbon and graphite, manufacturing
339942	Brushes, artists', manufacturing
339994	Brushes, household-type and industrial, manufacturing
339994	Brushes, paint (except artists'), manufacturing
326299	Brushes, rubber, manufacturing
333512	Brushing machines, metalworking, manufacturing
335991	Brushplates, carbon or graphite, manufacturing
111219	Brussel sprout farming, field, bedding plant and seed production
325620	Bubble bath preparations manufacturing
326199	Bubble packaging materials, plastics, manufacturing
333120	Bucket and scarifier teeth manufacturing
333922	Buckets, elevator or conveyor, manufacturing
333120	Buckets, excavating (e.g., clamshell, concrete, drag scraper, dragline, shovel), manufacturing
321920	Buckets, wood, coopered, manufacturing
339993	Buckles and buckle parts (including shoe) manufacturing
111199	Buckwheat farming
311211	Buckwheat flour manufacturing
921130	Budget agencies, government
112990	Buffalo production
722212	Buffet eating places
337122	Buffets (furniture), wood, manufacturing
333512	Buffing and polishing machines, metalworking, manufacturing
327910	Buffing and polishing wheels, abrasive and nonabrasive, manufacturing
325612	Buffing compounds manufacturing
333991	Buffing machines, handheld power-driven, manufacturing

Code	Description
332813	Buffing metals and metal products for the trade
316110	Buffings, russet, manufacturing
332510	Builder's hardware, metal, manufacturing
233310	Building alterations, industrial, general construction contractors
233320	Building alterations, nonresidential, commercial and institutional buildings, general construction contractors
233220	Building alterations, residential (except single family), general construction contractors
233210	Building alterations, single family, general construction contractors
541310	Building architectural design services
421320	Building blocks (e.g., cinder, concrete) wholesaling
421310	Building board (e.g., fiber, flake, particle) wholesaling
561720	Building cleaning services, interior
561720	Building cleaning services, janitorial
233310	Building components manufacturing plant construction, general construction contractors
233310	Building construction, industrial, general construction contractors
233220	Building construction, residential (except single family), general construction contractors
233210	Building construction, single family, general construction contractors
561790	Building exterior cleaning services (except sand blasting, window cleaning)
235910	Building front metal, construction contractors
541350	Building inspection bureaus
541350	Building inspection services
926150	Building inspections, government
326199	Building materials (e.g., fascia, panels, siding, soffit), plastics, manufacturing
444190	Building materials supply dealers
421390	Building materials, fiberglass (except insulation, roofing, siding), wholesaling

Code	Description
213112	Building oil and gas well foundations on a contract basis
326199	Building panels, corrugated and flat, plastics, manufacturing
322121	Building paper stock manufacturing
421390	Building paper wholesaling
334512	Building services monitoring controls, automatic, manufacturing
925110	Building standards agencies, government
421320	Building stone wholesaling
327121	Building tile, clay, manufacturing
531110	Building, apartment, rental or leasing
213112	Building, erecting, repairing, and dismantling oil and gas field rigs and derricks on a contract basis
531120	Building, nonresidential (except miniwarehouse), rental or leasing
531110	Building, residential, rental or leasing
321991	Buildings, mobile, commercial use, manufacturing
321992	Buildings, prefabricated and portable, wood, manufacturing
332311	Buildings, prefabricated metal, manufacturing
421390	Buildings, prefabricated nonwood, wholesaling
421310	Buildings, prefabricated wood, wholesaling
327999	Built-up mica manufacturing
335110	Bulbs, electric light, complete, manufacturing
311211	Bulgur (flour) manufacturing
422710	Bulk gasoline stations
484220	Bulk liquids trucking, local
484230	Bulk liquids trucking, long-distance
484110	Bulk mail truck transportation, contract, local
484121	Bulk mail truck transportation, contract, long-distance
493190	Bulk petroleum storage
422710	Bulk stations, petroleum
332420	Bulk storage tanks, heavy gauge metal, manufacturing
115210	Bull testing stations

Code	Description
532412	Bulldozer rental or leasing without operator
333120	Bulldozers manufacturing
332992	Bullet jackets and cores (i.e., 30 mm. or less, 1.18 inch or less) manufacturing
321999	Bulletin boards, wood and cork, manufacturing
339113	Bulletproof vests manufacturing
212221	Bullion, gold, produced at the mine
212222	Bullion, silver, produced at the mine
336399	Bumpers and bumperettes assembled, automotive, truck, and bus, manufacturing
333313	Bundling machinery (e.g., box strapping, mail, newspaper) manufacturing
321999	Bungs, wood, manufacturing
339111	Bunsen burners manufacturing
315291	Buntings, infants', cut and sewn from purchased fabric (except apparel contractors)
315212	Buntings, intants', cut and sew apparel contractors
334513	Buoyancy instruments, industrial process-type, manufacturing
321999	Buoys, cork, manufacturing
332313	Buoys, fabricated plate work metal, manufacturing
561621	Burglar alarm monitoring services
561621	Burglar alarm sales combined with installation, maintenance, or monitoring services
334290	Burglar alarm systems and equipment manufacturing
524126	Burglary and theft insurance carriers, direct
339995	Burial caskets and cases manufacturing
421850	Burial caskets wholesaling
315299	Burial garments cut and sewn from purchased fabric (except apparel contractors)
315211	Burial garments, men's and boys', cut and sew apparel contractors
315212	Burial garments, women's, girls' and infants', cut and sew apparel contractors

Code	Description
524128	Burial insurance carriers, direct
339995	Burial vaults (except concrete, stone) manufacturing
327390	Burial vaults, concrete and precast terrazzo, manufacturing
327991	Burial vaults, stone, manufacturing
422990	Burlap wholesaling
711110	Burlesque companies
212325	Burley mining and/or beneficiating
313311	Burling and mending broadwoven fabrics
313312	Burling and mending fabrics (except broadwoven)
335311	Burner ignition transformers manufacturing
421720	Burners, fuel oil and distillate oil, wholesaling
333414	Burners, heating, manufacturing
332811	Burning metals and metal products for the trade
333512	Burnishing machines, metalworking, manufacturing
321999	Burnt wood articles manufacturing
314999	Burnt-out laces manufacturing
112920	Burro production
212399	Burrstones, natural, mining and/or beneficiating
335313	Bus bar structures, switchgear-type, manufacturing
335931	Bus bars, electrical conductors (except switchgear-type), manufacturing
336211	Bus bodies assembling on purchased chassis
336211	Bus bodies manufacturing
541850	Bus card advertising services
485510	Bus charter services (except scenic, sightseeing)
541850	Bus display advertising services
611519	Bus driver training
485210	Bus line operation, intercity
485113	Bus line, local (except mixed mode)
485410	Bus operation, school and employee
532120	Bus rental or leasing

Code	Description
485113	Bus services, urban and suburban (except mixed mode)
488490	Bus terminal operation, independent
561599	Bus ticket offices
485113	Bus transit systems (except mixed mode)
336120	Buses (except trackless trolley) assembling on chassis of own manufacture
421110	Buses wholesaling
487110	Buses, scenic and sightseeing operation
336510	Buses, trackless trolley, manufacturing
333613	Bushings, plain (except internal combustion engine), manufacturing
326199	Bushings, plastics, manufacturing
321999	Bushings, wood, manufacturing
813910	Business associations
611410	Business colleges or schools not offering academic degrees
611310	Business colleges or schools offering baccalaureate or graduate degrees
323112	Business directories flexographic printing without publishing
323111	Business directories gravure printing without publishing
323110	Business directories lithographic (offset) printing without publishing
323119	Business directories printing (except flexographic, gravure, lithographic, screen) without publishing
323113	Business directories screen printing without publishing
511140	Business directory publishers
511140	Business directory publishers and printing combined
511140	Business directory publishing (i.e., establishments known as publishers)
323112	Business forms (except manifold) flexographic printing without publishing
323111	Business forms (except manifold) gravure printing without publishing

Code	Description
323110	Business forms (except manifold) lithographic printing
323119	Business forms (except manifold) printing (except flexographic, gravure, lithographic, screen) without publishing
323113	Business forms (except manifold) screen printing without publishing
323116	Business forms, manifold, printing
421420	Business machines and equipment (except computers) wholesaling
541611	Business management consulting services
561110	Business management services
541720	Business research and development services
611410	Business schools not offering academic degrees
561439	Business service centers (except private mail centers)
561439	Business service centers (except private mail centers) providing range of office support services (except printing)
541611	Business start-up consulting services
325211	Butadiene copolymers containing less than 50 percent butadiene manufacturing
325212	Butadiene copolymers containing more than 50 percent butadiene manufacturing
325199	Butadiene made from alcohol
325110	Butadiene made from refined petroleum or liquid hydrocarbons
325212	Butadiene rubber (i.e., polybutadiene) manufacturing
325110	Butane made from refined petroleum or liquid hydrocarbons
211112	Butane, natural, mining
445210	Butcher shops
332211	Butcher's knives manufacturing
311512	Butter manufacturing
333294	Butter processing machinery manufacturing
422430	Butter wholesaling
311512	Butter, creamery and whey, manufacturing

Code	Description
332911	Butterfly valves, industrial-type, manufacturing
311511	Buttermilk manufacturing
111219	Butternut squash farming, field, bedding plant and seed production
335912	Button cells, primary batteries, manufacturing
333298	Buttonhole and eyelet machinery manufacturing
315211	Buttonhole making apparel contractors, men's and boys'
315212	Buttonhole making apparel contractors, women's, misses', girls', and infants' (except fur)
315212	Buttonhole making, fur goods, women's, girls', and infants', cut and sew apparel contractors
315211	Buttonholing and button covering apparel contractors, men's and boys'
315212	Buttonholing and button covering apparel contractors, women's, misses', and girls'
339993	Buttons (except precious metal, precious stones, semiprecious stones) manufacturing
339911	Buttons, precious metal, precious stones, semiprecious stones, manufacturing
325199	Butyl acetate manufacturing
325212	Butyl rubber manufacturing
324110	Butylene (i.e., butene) made in petroleum refineries
325110	Butylene made from refined petroleum or liquid hydrocarbons
531210	Buyers' agents, real estate, offices
531210	Buying agencies, real estate
531210	Buying real estate for others (i.e., agents, brokers)
332212	C-clamps manufacturing
541512	CAD (computer-aided design) systems integration design services
541512	CAE (computer-aided engineering) systems integration design services
541512	CAM (computer-aided manufacturing) systems integration design services
621512	CAT (computerized axial tomography) scanner centers

Code	Description
334220	CB (citizens band) radios manufacturing
334112	CD-ROM drives manufacturing
334611	CD-ROM, software, mass reproducing
525990	CMOs (collateralized mortgage obligations)
541211	CPAs' (certified public accountants) offices
611699	CPR (cardiac pulmonary resusitation) training and certification
334411	CRT (cathode ray tube) manufacturing
621512	CT-SCAN (computer tomography) centers
334517	CT/CAT (computerized axial tomography) scanners manufacturing
485310	Cab (i.e., taxi) services
336112	Cab and chassis, light trucks and vans, manufacturing
111219	Cabbage farming, field, bedding plant and seed production
233210	Cabin construction
336612	Cabin cruiser
334511	Cabin environment indicators, transmitters, and sensors manufacturing
332510	Cabinet hardware, metal, manufacturing
444190	Cabinet stores, kitchen (except custom), to be installed
235510	Cabinet work on site construction contractors
337214	Cabinets (except wood), office-type, freestanding, manufacturing
337129	Cabinets (i.e., housings), wood (e.g., sewing machines, stereo, television), manufacturing
337110	Cabinets, kitchen (except freestanding), stock or custom wood, manufacturing
421310	Cabinets, kitchen, built in, wholesaling
421210	Cabinets, kitchen, free standing, wholesaling
337124	Cabinets, metal (i.e., bathroom, kitchen) (except freestanding), manufacturing
337124	Cabinets, metal household-type, freestanding, manufacturing
337124	Cabinets, metal, radio and television, manufacturing
337122	Cabinets, wood household-type, freestanding, manufacturing
337211	Cabinets, wood office-type, freestanding, manufacturing
721199	Cabins, housekeeping
513220	Cable TV providers (except networks)
513210	Cable broadcasting networks
485119	Cable car systems (except mixed mode), commuter
487110	Cable car, land, scenic and sightseeing operation
334220	Cable decoders manufacturing
234920	Cable laying
513220	Cable program distribution operators
235310	Cable splicing, electrical, construction contractors
235310	Cable television hookup construction contractors
234920	Cable television line construction
513210	Cable television networks
334220	Cable television transmission and receiving equipment manufacturing
331422	Cable, copper (e.g., armored, bare, insulated), made from purchased copper in wire drawing plants
331422	Cable, copper (e.g., armored, bare, insulated), made in integrated secondary smelting and drawing plants
331222	Cable, iron or steel, insulated or armored, made in wire drawing plants
335929	Cable, nonferrous, insulated, or armored, made from purchased nonferrous wire
332618	Cable, noninsulated wire, made from purchased wire
421510	Cable, wire (except insulated), wholesaling
333111	Cabs for agricultural machinery manufacturing
333120	Cabs for construction machinery manufacturing
333924	Cabs for industrial trucks manufacturing
111339	Cactus fruit farming
541370	Cadastral surveying services
339920	Caddy carts manufacturing
331419	Cadmium refining, primary
337215	Cafeteria fixtures manufacturing
722310	Cafeteria food service contractors (e.g., government office cafeterias, hospital cafeterias, school cafeterias)
337127	Cafeteria furniture manufacturing
337127	Cafeteria tables and benches manufacturing
722212	Cafeterias
325411	Caffeine and derivatives (i.e., basic chemicals) manufacturing
315291	Caftans, infants', cut and sewn from purchased fabric (except apparel contractors)
315211	Caftans, men's and boys', cut and sew apparel contractors
315223	Caftans, men's and boys', cut and sewn from purchased fabric (except apparel contractors)
315212	Caftans, women's, girls', and infants', cut and sew apparel contractors
315231	Caftans, women's, misses' and girls', cut and sewn from purchased fabric (except apparel contractors)
332618	Cages made from purchased wire
235930	Caisson contractors, building construction
234990	Caisson drilling
332420	Caissons, underwater work, manufacturing
311999	Cake frosting manufacturing
311999	Cake frosting mixes manufacturing
311822	Cake mixes made from purchased flour
311340	Cake ornaments, confectionery, manufacturing
311813	Cake, frozen, manufacturing
311812	Cakes, baking (except frozen), made in commercial bakeries
212231	Calamine mining and/or beneficiating

Code	Description
212221	Calaverite mining and/or beneficiating
212312	Calcareous tufa crushed and broken stone mining and/or beneficiating
212311	Calcareous tufa mining or quarrying
325510	Calcimines manufacturing
422950	Calcimines, wholesaling
212392	Calcined phosphate rock mining and/or beneficiating
324199	Calcining petroleum coke from refined petroleum
212399	Calcite mining and/or beneficiating
325188	Calcium carbide, chloride, and hypochlorite manufacturing
325199	Calcium citrate manufacturing
327410	Calcium hydroxide (i.e., hydrated lime) manufacturing
325188	Calcium hypochlorite manufacturing
325188	Calcium inorganic compounds, not specified elsewhere by process, manufacturing
325199	Calcium organic compounds, not specified elsewhere by process, manufacturing
325199	Calcium oxalate manufacturing
327410	Calcium oxide (i.e., quicklime) manufacturing
421420	Calculators and calculating machines wholesaling
333313	Calculators manufacturing
511199	Calendar publishers
511199	Calendar publishers and printing combined
511199	Calendar publishing (i.e., establishments known as publishers)
453998	Calendar shops
323112	Calendars flexographic printing without publishing
323111	Calendars gravure printing without publishing
323110	Calendars lithographic (offset) printing without publishing
323119	Calendars printing (except flexographic, lithographic, gravure, screen) without publishing

Code	Description
323113	Calendars screen printing without publishing
313311	Calendering broadwoven fabrics
333220	Calendering machinery for plastics manufacturing
333292	Calendering machinery for textiles manufacturing
313312	Calendering textile products, apparel, and fabrics (except broadwoven)
112111	Calf (e.g., feeder, stocker, veal) production
315119	Calf high sheer hosiery knitting or knitting and finishing
541380	Calibration and certification testing laboratories or services
332212	Calipers and dividers, machinists' precision tools, manufacturing
336340	Calipers, brake, automotive, truck, and bus, manufacturing
339992	Calliopes (steam organs) manufacturing
532210	Camcorder rental
334310	Camcorders manufacturing
326211	Camelback (i.e., retreading material) manufacturing
333220	Camelback (i.e., retreading materials) machinery manufacturing
316991	Camera carrying bags, all materials, manufacturing
421410	Camera equipment and supplies, photographic, wholesaling
333314	Camera lenses manufacturing
811211	Camera repair shops without retailing new cameras
443130	Camera shops, photographic
711510	Cameramen, independent (freelance)
333315	Cameras (except digital, television, video) manufacturing
334220	Cameras, television, manufacturing
315212	Camisoles, women's and girls', cut and sew apparel contractors
315231	Camisoles, women's, misses' and girls', cut and sewn from purchased fabric (except apparel contractors)
337124	Camp furniture, metal, manufacturing

Code	Description
337125	Camp furniture, reed and rattan, manufacturing
337122	Camp furniture, wood, manufacturing
813940	Campaign organizations, political
441210	Camper dealers, recreational
532120	Camper rental
336214	Camper units, slide-in, for pick-up trucks, manufacturing
721211	Campgrounds
325191	Camphor, natural, manufacturing
325199	Camphor, synthetic, manufacturing
421910	Camping equipment and supplies wholesaling
336214	Camping trailers and chassis manufacturing
421110	Camping trailers wholesaling
721214	Camps (except day, instructional)
713990	Camps (except instructional), day
623990	Camps, boot or disciplinary (except correctional), for delinquent youth
611620	Camps, sports instruction
333515	Cams (i.e., a machine tool accessory) manufacturing
333513	Can forming machines, metalworking, manufacturing
332618	Can keys made from purchased wire
332431	Can lids and ends, metal, manufacturing
332212	Can openers (except electric) manufacturing
335211	Can openers, household-type electric, manufacturing
483211	Canal barge transportation
234990	Canal construction
488310	Canal maintenance services (except dredging)
488310	Canal operation
483212	Canal passenger transportation
221310	Canal, irrigation
333313	Canceling machinery, postal office-type, manufacturing
923120	Cancer detection program administration
622310	Cancer hospitals
541710	Cancer research laboratories or services

Code	Description
311340	Candied fruits and fruit peel manufacturing
713950	Candle pin bowling alleys
713950	Candle pin bowling centers
453998	Candle shops
339999	Candles manufacturing
422990	Candles wholesaling
311320	Candy bars, chocolate (including chocolate covered), made from cacao beans
311340	Candy bars, nonchocolate, manufacturing
311330	Candy stores, chocolate, candy made on premises not for immediate consumption
311340	Candy stores, nonchocolate, candy made on premises, not for immediate consumption
445292	Candy stores, packaged, retailing only
422450	Candy wholesaling
311320	Candy, chocolate, made from cacao beans
111930	Cane farming, sugar, field production
311312	Cane sugar made from purchased raw cane sugar
311311	Cane sugar made in sugarcane mill
422490	Cane sugar, refined, wholesaling
311312	Cane syrup made from purchased raw cane sugar
311311	Cane syrup made in sugarcane mill
339999	Canes (except orthopedic) manufacturing
332999	Canes, metal, manufacturing
332993	Canisters, ammunition, manufacturing
422490	Canned foods (e.g., fish, meat, seafood, soups) wholesaling
311611	Canned meats (except poultry) produced in slaughtering plants
311911	Canned nuts manufacturing
233310	Cannery construction
311711	Cannery, fish
311711	Cannery, shellfish
311421	Canning fruits and vegetables
311421	Canning jams and jellies
333993	Canning machinery manufacturing
311615	Canning poultry (except baby and pet food)
311422	Canning soups (except seafood)
421840	Canning supplies wholesaling
311711	Canning, fish, crustacea, and molluscs
332995	Cannons manufacturing
339112	Cannulae manufacturing
532292	Canoe rental
713990	Canoeing, recreational
311225	Canola (rapeseed) oil, cake and meal, made from purchased oils
311223	Canola (rapeseed) oil, cake and meal, made in crushing mills
111120	Canola farming, field and seed production
332322	Canopies, sheet metal, manufacturing
332431	Cans, aluminum, manufacturing
332431	Cans, metal, manufacturing
332431	Cans, steel, manufacturing
111219	Cantaloupe farming, field, bedding plant and seed production
722213	Canteens, fixed location
722330	Canteens, mobile
321912	Cants, resawed (lumber), manufacturing
314911	Canvas bags manufacturing
339942	Canvas board, artist's, manufacturing
314912	Canvas products (except bags) made from purchased canvas or canvas substitutes
422990	Canvas products wholesaling
316211	Canvas shoes, plastics soled fabric upper, manufacturing
316211	Canvas shoes, rubber soled fabric upper, manufacturing
339942	Canvas, artist's, prepared on frames, manufacturing
313210	Canvases weaving
454390	Canvassers (door-to-door), headquarters for retail sale of merchandise, direct selling
335999	Capacitors (except electronic), fixed and variable, manufacturing
334414	Capacitors, electronic, fixed and variable, manufacturing
421690	Capacitors, electronic, wholesaling
315212	Capes (except fur), women's, girls' and infants', cut and sew apparel contractors
315234	Capes (except fur, waterproof), women's, misses', and girls', cut and sewn from purchased fabric (except apparel contractors)
315292	Capes, fur (except apparel contractors), manufacturing
315212	Capes, fur, women's, girls', and infants', cut and sew apparel contractors
315299	Capes, waterproof (e.g., plastics, rubber, similar materials), cut and sewn from purchased fabric (except apparel contractors)
235810	Capping of water wells construction contractors
333993	Capping, sealing, and lidding packaging machinery manufacturing
325199	Caprolactam manufacturing
315991	Caps (except fur, leather) cut and sewn from purchased fabric (except apparel contractors)
315991	Caps (i.e., apparel accessory) cut and sewn from purchased fabric (except fur, leather, apparel contractors)
315211	Caps (i.e., apparel accessory), men's and boys', cut and sew apparel contractors
315212	Caps (i.e., apparel accessory), women's, girls', and infants', cut and sew apparel contractors
315299	Caps and gowns, academic, cut and sewn from purchased fabric (except apparel contractors)
315211	Caps and gowns, academic, men's and boys', cut and sew apparel contractors
315212	Caps and gowns, academic, women's and girls', cut and sew apparel contractors
335931	Caps and plugs, attachment, electric, manufacturing

Code	Description
332115	Caps and tops, bottle, metal, stamping
336214	Caps for pick-up trucks manufacturing
325998	Caps for toy pistols manufacturing
315191	Caps made in apparel knitting mills
325920	Caps, blasting and detonating, manufacturing
332993	Caps, bomb, manufacturing
315292	Caps, fur (except apparel contractors), manufacturing
316999	Caps, heel and toe, leather, manufacturing
315292	Caps, leather (except apparel contractors), manufacturing
315991	Caps, textiles, straw, fur-felt, and wool-felt, cut and sewn from purchased fabric (except apparel contractors)
315211	Caps, textiles, straw, fur-felt, and wool-felt, men's and boys', cut and sew apparel contractors
315212	Caps, textiles, straw, fur-felt, and wool-felt, women's, girls', and infants', cut and sew apparel contractors
325998	Capsules, gelatin, empty, manufacturing
334290	Car alarm manufacturing
336211	Car bodies, kit, manufacturing
811192	Car detailers
532112	Car leasing
483212	Car lighters (i.e., ferries), inland waters (except on Great Lakes system)
485999	Car pool operation
488999	Car pools, arrangement of
532111	Car rental
532111	Car rental agencies
561599	Car rental reservation services
811111	Car repair shops, general
332999	Car seals, metal, manufacturing
337125	Car seats, infant (except metal), manufacturing
334310	Car stereos manufacturing
421850	Car wash equipment and supplies wholesaling

Code	Description
811192	Car washes
331111	Car wheels, rolled steel, made in steel mills
325188	Carbides (e.g., boron, calcium, silicon, tungsten) manufacturing
332994	Carbines manufacturing
325199	Carbinol manufacturing
325211	Carbohydrate plastics manufacturing
334510	Carbon arc lamp units, electrotherapeutic (except infrared and ultraviolet), manufacturing
325182	Carbon black manufacturing
422690	Carbon black wholesaling
327125	Carbon brick manufacturing
325120	Carbon dioxide manufacturing
325188	Carbon disulfide manufacturing
335991	Carbon electrodes and contacts, electric, manufacturing
325188	Carbon inorganic compounds manufacturing
334290	Carbon monoxide detectors manufacturing
421690	Carbon monoxide detectors, electronic, wholesaling
325199	Carbon organic compounds, not specified elsewhere by process, manufacturing
339944	Carbon paper manufacturing
335991	Carbon specialties for aerospace use (except gaskets) manufacturing
335991	Carbon specialties for electrical use manufacturing
335991	Carbon specialties for mechanical use (except gaskets) manufacturing
325199	Carbon tetrachloride manufacturing
325998	Carbon, activated, manufacturing
312111	Carbonated soda manufacturing
312111	Carbonated soft drinks manufacturing
325188	Carbonic acid manufacturing
333292	Carbonizing equipment for processing wool manufacturing
313312	Carbonizing textile fibers
335991	Carbons, electric, manufacturing
335991	Carbons, lighting, manufacturing
325998	Carburetor cleaners manufacturing

Code	Description
336311	Carburetors, all types, manufacturing
316993	Card cases (except metal) manufacturing
339911	Card cases, precious metal, manufacturing
713290	Card rooms (e.g., poker rooms)
453220	Card shops, greeting
337122	Card table sets (furniture), wood, manufacturing
337124	Card table sets, metal, manufacturing
422130	Cardboard products wholesaling
322130	Cardboard stock manufacturing
322226	Cardboard, laminated or surface coated, made from purchased paperboard
313230	Carded nonwoven fabrics manufacturing
313111	Carded yarn manufacturing
325412	Cardiac preparations manufacturing
333292	Carding machinery for textiles manufacturing
313312	Carding textile fibers
334510	Cardiodynameter manufacturing
334510	Cardiographs manufacturing
621111	Cardiologists' offices (e.g., centers, clinics)
334510	Cardiophone, electric, manufacturing
334510	Cardioscope manufacturing
334510	Cardiotachometer manufacturing
323112	Cards (e.g., business, greeting, playing, postcards, trading) flexographic printing without publishing
323111	Cards (e.g., business, greeting, playing, postcards, trading) gravure printing without publishing
323110	Cards (e.g., business, greeting, playing, postcards, trading) lithographic (offset) printing without publishing
323119	Cards (e.g., business, greeting, playing, postcards, trading) printing (except flexographic, gravure, lithographic, screen) without publishing

Code	Description
323113	Cards (e.g., business, greeting, playing, postcards, trading) screen printing without publishing
322299	Cards, die-cut (except office supply) made from purchased paper or paperboard
322231	Cards, die-cut office supply (e.g., index, library, time recording), made from purchased paper or paperboard
422120	Cards, greeting, wholesaling
*****	Cards, publishing — see specific product
481112	Cargo carriers, air, scheduled
488390	Cargo checkers, marine
488330	Cargo salvaging, marine
336611	Cargo ship building
488390	Cargo surveyors, marine
488490	Cargo surveyors, truck transportation
333319	Carnival and amusement park rides manufacturing
333319	Carnival and amusement park shooting gallery machinery manufacturing
421850	Carnival equipment wholersaling
713990	Carnival ride concession operators (i.e., supplying and servicing in others' facilities)
711190	Carnival traveling shows
212291	Carnotite mining and/or beneficiating
333922	Carousel conveyors (e.g., luggage) manufacturing
333319	Carousels (i.e., merry-go-rounds) manufacturing
332212	Carpenter's handtools, nonelectric (except saws), manufacturing
611513	Carpenters' apprenticeship training
235510	Carpentry (rough and framing) construction contractors
235510	Carpentry (trim and finish) construction contractors
532490	Carpentry equipment rental or leasing

Code	Description
333319	Carpet and floor cleaning equipment, electric commercial-type, manufacturing
335212	Carpet and floor cleaning equipment, household-type electric, manufacturing
532490	Carpet and rug cleaning equipment rental or leasing
313111	Carpet and rug yarn spinning
532299	Carpet and rug, residential, rental
561740	Carpet cleaning on customers' premises
561740	Carpet cleaning plants
561740	Carpet cleaning services
314999	Carpet cutting and binding
235520	Carpet laying or removal construction contractors
313210	Carpet linings (except felt) weaving
313230	Carpet paddings, nonwoven, manufacturing
442210	Carpet stores
333319	Carpet sweepers, mechanical, manufacturing
421220	Carpet wholesaling
314110	Carpets and rugs made from textile materials
321999	Carpets, cork, manufacturing
332311	Carports, prefabricated metal, manufacturing
487110	Carriage, horse-drawn, operation
339932	Carriages, baby, manufacturing
339932	Carriages, doll, manufacturing
334210	Carrier equipment (i.e., analog, digital), telephone, manufacturing
111219	Carrot farming, field, bedding plant and seed production
311991	Carrots, cut, peeled or sliced fresh, manufacturing
722211	Carryout restaurants
336111	Cars, electric, for highway use, assembling on chassis of own manufacture
333131	Cars, mining, manufacturing
541370	Cartographic surveying services
333993	Carton filling machinery manufacturing

Code	Description
322299	Cartons, egg, molded pulp manufacturing
322212	Cartons, folding (except milk), made from purchased paperboard
322215	Cartons, milk, made from purchased paper or paperboard
422130	Cartons, paper and paperboard, wholesaling
711510	Cartoonists, independent
333991	Cartridge (i.e., powder) handheld power-driven tools manufacturing
332992	Cartridge cases for ammunition (i.e., 30 mm.or less, 1.18 inch or less) manufacturing
331421	Cartridge cups, discs, and sheets, copper and copper alloy, made from purchased copper or in integrated secondary smelting and rolling, drawing or extruding plants
422120	Cartridge toner wholesaling
332992	Cartridges (i.e., 30 mm. or less, 1.18 inch or less) manufacturing
339920	Carts, caddy, manufacturing
333924	Carts, grocery, made from purchased wire
333112	Carts, lawn and garden-type, manufacturing
332211	Carving sets manufacturing
333319	Carwashing machinery manufacturing
111219	Casaba melon farming, field, bedding plant and seed production
316110	Case leather manufacturing
325222	Casein fibers and filaments manufacturing
325211	Casein plastics manufacturing
311514	Casein, dry and wet, manufacturing
332321	Casements, metal, manufacturing
316993	Cases, jewelry (except metal), manufacturing
339911	Cases, jewelry, precious metal, manufacturing
316991	Cases, luggage, manufacturing
316991	Cases, musical instrument, manufacturing
321920	Cases, shipping, wood, wirebound, manufacturing

Code	Description
321920	Cases, wood packing, nailed or lock corner, manufacturing
321920	Cases, wood shipping, nailed or lock corner, manufacturing
332439	Cash boxes, light gauge metal, manufacturing
532420	Cash register rental or leasing
333313	Cash registers (i.e., point of sales terminals) manufacturing
421420	Cash registers wholesaling
111335	Cashew farming
211112	Casing-head butane and propane production
326121	Casings, sausage, nonrigid plastics, manufacturing
332313	Casings, scroll, fabricated metal plate work, manufacturing
332322	Casings, sheet metal, manufacturing
233320	Casino construction
721120	Casino hotels
713210	Casinos (except casino hotels)
332510	Casket hardware, metal, manufacturing
339995	Caskets, burial, manufacturing
421850	Caskets, burial, wholesaling
321920	Casks, wood, coopered, manufacturing
111219	Cassava farming, field and seed cassava production
335211	Casseroles, household-type electric, manufacturing
334612	Cassette tapes, pre-recorded audio, mass reproducing
532230	Cassette, prerecorded video, rental
421990	Cassettes, prerecorded audio and video, wholesaling
331511	Cast iron brake shoes, railroad, manufacturing
331511	Cast iron pipe and pipe fittings manufacturing
421510	Cast iron pipe wholesaling
331511	Cast iron railroad car wheels manufacturing
331513	Cast steel railroad car wheels, unfinished, manufacturing
327390	Cast stone, concrete (except structural), manufacturing

Code	Description
327124	Castable refractories, clay, manufacturing
327125	Castable refractories, nonclay, manufacturing
332510	Casters, furniture, manufacturing
332510	Casters, industrial, manufacturing
561310	Casting agencies (i.e., motion picture, theatrical, video)
561310	Casting agencies, motion picture or video
561310	Casting agencies, theatrical
561310	Casting bureaus (e.g., motion picture, theatrical, video)
561310	Casting bureaus, motion picture or video
561310	Casting bureaus, theatrical
331528	Castings (except die-castings), nonferrous metals (except aluminum, copper), unfinished manufacturing
331524	Castings (except die-castings), unfinished, aluminum, manufacturing
331525	Castings (except die-castings), unfinished, copper, manufacturing
331511	Castings, compacted graphite iron, unfinished, manufacturing
331511	Castings, malleable iron, unfinished, manufacturing
331513	Castings, steel (except investment), unfinished, manufacturing
331511	Castings, unfinished iron (e.g., ductile, gray, malleable, semisteel), manufacturing
311223	Castor oil and pomace made in crushing mills
316213	Casual shoes (except athletic, plastic, rubber), men's, manufacturing
316214	Casual shoes (except athletic, rubber, plastic), women's, manufacturing
316219	Casual shoes (except rubber, plastics), children's and infants', manufacturing
524126	Casualty insurance carriers, direct
311111	Cat food manufacturing
325998	Cat litter manufacturing
112990	Cat production

Code	Description
511199	Catalog (i.e., mail order, store merchandise) publishers
511199	Catalog (i.e., mail order, store merchandise) publishers and printing combined
511199	Catalog (i.e., mail order, store merchandise) publishing (i.e., establishments known as publishers)
454110	Catalog (i.e., order taking) offices of mail-order houses
511140	Catalog of collections publishers
511140	Catalog of collections publishers and printing combined
511140	Catalog of collections publishing (i.e., establishments known as publishers)
452990	Catalog showrooms, general merchandise (except catalog mail-order)
323112	Catalogs flexographic printing without publishing
323111	Catalogs gravure printing without publishing
323110	Catalogs lithographic (offset) printing without publishing
323112	Catalogs of collections flexographic printing without publishing
323111	Catalogs of collections gravure printing without publishing
323110	Catalogs of collections lithographic (offset) printing without publishing
323119	Catalogs of collections printing (except flexographic, gravure, lithographic, screen) without publishing
323113	Catalogs of collections screen printing without publishing
323119	Catalogs printing (except flexographic, gravure, lithographic, screen) without publishing
323113	Catalogs screen printing without publishing
336399	Catalytic converters, engine exhaust, automotive, truck, and bus, manufacturing
332995	Catapult guns manufacturing
562998	Catch basin cleaning services
722320	Caterers

Code	Description
722320	Catering services, social
112511	Catfish production, farm raising
325412	Cathartic preparations manufacturing
339112	Catheters manufacturing
334411	Cathode ray tubes (CRT) manufacturing
335999	Cathodic protection equipment manufacturing
212399	Catlinite mining and/or beneficiating
422990	Cats wholesaling
311421	Catsup manufacturing
112111	Cattle conditioning operations
112111	Cattle farming or ranching
333111	Cattle feeding and watering equipment manufacturing
112112	Cattle feedlots (except stockyards for transportation)
311119	Cattle feeds, supplements, concentrates, and premixes, manufacturing
115210	Cattle spraying
422520	Cattle wholesaling
111219	Cauliflower farming, field, bedding plant and seed production
325520	Caulking compounds (except gypsum base) manufacturing
332212	Caulking guns, nonpowered, manufacturing
422690	Caulking materials wholesaling
234120	Causeway construction
325181	Caustic potash manufacturing
325181	Caustic soda (i.e., sodium hydroxide) manufacturing
422690	Caustic soda wholesaling
712190	Caverns (i.e., natural wonder tourist attractions)
337122	Cedar chests manufacturing
325998	Cedar oil manufacturing
235420	Ceiling construction contractors
444190	Ceiling fan stores
335211	Ceiling fans with integral lighting fixture, residential, manufacturing
335211	Ceiling fans, residential, manufacturing

Code	Description
335122	Ceiling lighting fixtures, commercial, industrial, and institutional, manufacturing
335121	Ceiling lighting fixtures, residential, manufacturing
321912	Ceiling lumber, dressed, resawing purchased lumber
321113	Ceiling lumber, made from logs or bolts
235610	Ceiling metal construction contractors
334519	Ceilometers manufacturing
711410	Celebrities' agents or managers
711510	Celebrity spokespersons, independent
111219	Celery farming, field, bedding plant and seed production
212393	Celestite mining and/or beneficiating
325221	Cellophane film or sheet manufacturing
422120	Cellophane tape wholesaling
339992	Cellos and parts manufacturing
513322	Cellular telephone communication carriers
513322	Cellular telephone services
443112	Cellular telephone stores
334220	Cellular telephones manufacturing
421690	Cellular telephones wholesaling
325199	Cellulose acetate (except resins) manufacturing
325211	Cellulose acetate resins manufacturing
325211	Cellulose nitrate resins manufacturing
325211	Cellulose propionate resins manufacturing
325211	Cellulose resins manufacturing
325211	Cellulose xanthate (viscose) manufacturing
325221	Cellulosic fibers and filaments manufacturing
325221	Cellulosic filament yarn manufacturing
326113	Cellulosic plastics film and unlaminated sheet (except packaging) manufacturing

Code	Description
325221	Cellulosic staple fibers manufacturing
327310	Cement (e.g., hydraulic, masonry, portland, pozzolana) manufacturing
327310	Cement clinker manufacturing
333298	Cement kilns manufacturing
234930	Cement plant construction
212312	Cement rock crushed and broken stone mining and/or beneficiating
421320	Cement wholesaling
327420	Cement, Keene's (i.e., tiling plaster), manufacturing
327124	Cement, clay refractory, manufacturing
325520	Cement, rubber, manufacturing
421830	Cement-making machinery wholesaling
213112	Cementing oil and gas well casings on a contract basis
324122	Cements, asphalt roofing, made from purchased asphaltic materials
339114	Cements, dental, manufacturing
812220	Cemetery management services
812220	Cemeteries
812220	Cemetery associations (i.e., operators)
453998	Cemetery memorial dealers (e.g., headstones, markers, vaults)
561730	Cemetery plot care services
333512	Centering machines, metalworking, manufacturing
514120	Centers for documentation (i.e., archives)
624120	Centers, senior citizens'
421730	Central heating equipment, warm-air, wholesaling
325412	Central nervous system stimulant preparations manufacturing
334210	Central office and switching equipment, telephone, manufacturing
333319	Central vacuuming systems, commercial-type, manufacturing
335212	Central vacuuming systems, household-type, manufacturing
327320	Central-mixed concrete manufacturing

Code	Description
551114	Centralized administrative offices
333911	Centrifugal pumps manufacturing
333999	Centrifuges, industrial-type, manufacturing
325411	Cephalosporin, uncompounded, manufacturing
325131	Ceramic colors manufacturing
421320	Ceramic construction materials (except refractory) wholesaling
327999	Ceramic fiber manufacturing
333994	Ceramic kilns and furnaces manufacturing
444190	Ceramic tile stores
327122	Ceramic tiles, floor and wall, manufacturing
611610	Ceramics instruction
311211	Cereal grain flour manufacturing
311211	Cereal grain germ manufacturing
422490	Cereal products wholesaling
541710	Cerebral palsy research laboratories or services
212299	Cerium concentrates mining and/or beneficiating
212299	Cerium ores mining and/or beneficiating
325188	Cerium salts manufacturing
523120	Certificate of deposit (CD) brokers' offices
923110	Certification of schools and teachers
541211	Certified accountants' offices
523930	Certified financial planners, customized, fees paid by client
541211	Certified public accountants' (CPAs) offices
212231	Cerussite mining and/or beneficiating
339113	Cervical collars manufacturing
325188	Cesium and cesium compounds, not specified elsewhere by process, manufacturing
562991	Cesspool cleaning services
325199	Cetyl alcohol manufacturing
335211	Chafing dishes, household-type electric, manufacturing
332999	Chain fittings manufacturing
333923	Chain hoists manufacturing

Code	Description
332323	Chain ladders, metal, manufacturing
332618	Chain link fencing and fence gates made from purchased wire
331222	Chain link fencing, iron or steel, made in wire drawing plants
332618	Chain made from purchased wire
332213	Chain saw blades manufacturing
333991	Chain saws, handheld power-driven, manufacturing
332618	Chain, welded, made from purchased wire
339911	Chains or necklace, precious metal, manufacturing
333613	Chains, power transmission, manufacturing
334519	Chains, surveyor's, manufacturing
421830	Chainsaws wholesaling
337121	Chair and couch springs, assembled, manufacturing
337215	Chair glides manufacturing
337215	Chair seats for furniture manufacturing
337122	Chairs (except upholstered), wood household-type, manufacturing
337214	Chairs (except wood), office-type, manufacturing
337127	Chairs, barber and beauty (i.e., hydraulic), manufacturing
337127	Chairs, barber, beauty shop (i.e., hydraulic), manufacturing
337125	Chairs, cane, wood household-type, manufacturing
339114	Chairs, dentist's, manufacturing
337124	Chairs, metal household-type (except upholstered), manufacturing
337127	Chairs, portable folding, auditorium-type, manufacturing
337127	Chairs, stacking, auditorium-type, manufacturing
337121	Chairs, upholstered household-type (except dining room, kitchen), manufacturing
337211	Chairs, wood office-type, manufacturing
212234	Chalcocite mining and/or beneficiating

Code	Description
212234	Chalcopyrite mining and/or beneficiating
339942	Chalk (e.g., artist's, blackboard, carpenter's, marking, tailor's), manufacturing
212312	Chalk crushed and broken stone mining and/or beneficiating
212312	Chalk, ground or otherwise treated, mining and/or beneficiating
339942	Chalkboards, framed, manufacturing
711130	Chamber musical groups
711130	Chamber orchestras
813910	Chambers of commerce
313210	Chambrays weaving
333512	Chamfering machines, metalworking, manufacturing
316110	Chamois leather manufacturing
422990	Chamois, leather, wholesaling
312130	Champagne method sparkling wine, manufacturing
335122	Chandeliers, commercial, industrial, and institutional electric, manufacturing
335121	Chandeliers, residential, manufacturing
333311	Change making machines manufacturing
325182	Channel black manufacturing
234990	Channel construction
234990	Channel cutoff construction, general construction contractors
332323	Channels, furring metal, manufacturing
325191	Charcoal (except activated) manufacturing
325191	Charcoal briquettes, wood, manufacturing
422990	Charcoal wholesaling
325998	Charcoal, activated, manufacturing
522210	Charge card issuing
813211	Charitable trusts, awarding grants
611699	Charm schools
481212	Charter air freight services
481211	Charter air passenger services
485510	Charter bus services (except scenic, sightseeing)
487210	Charter fishing boat operation

Code	Description
333515	Chasers (i.e., a machine tool accessory) manufacturing
212399	Chasers mining and/or beneficiating
332812	Chasing metals and metal products for the trade
336111	Chassis, automobile, manufacturing
336120	Chassis, heavy truck, with or without cabs, manufacturing
336112	Chassis, light truck and utility, manufacturing
421110	Chassis, motor vehicle, wholesaling
561310	Chauffeur registries
611519	Chauffeur training
315991	Chauffeurs' hats and caps cut and sewn from purchased fabric (except apparel contractors)
315211	Chauffeurs' hats and caps, men's, cut and sew apparel contractors
315212	Chauffeurs' hats and caps, women's, cut and sew apparel contractors
522390	Check cashing services
521110	Check clearing activities of the central bank
522320	Check clearing services (except central banks)
522320	Check clearinghouse services (except central banks)
421420	Check handling machines wholesaling
812990	Check room services
522320	Check validation services
332911	Check valves, industrial-type, manufacturing
333313	Check writing machines manufacturing
316993	Checkbook covers, (except metal), manufacturing
339911	Checkbook covers, precious metal, manufacturing
323116	Checkbooks and refills printing
339932	Checkers and checkerboards manufacturing
611620	Cheerleading instruction, camps, or schools
311513	Cheese (except cottage cheese) manufacturing
311513	Cheese analogs manufacturing
311941	Cheese based salad dressing manufacturing
422450	Cheese confections (e.g., curls, puffs) wholesaling
311919	Cheese curls and puffs manufacturing
333294	Cheese processing machinery manufacturing
311513	Cheese products, imitation or substitute, manufacturing
311513	Cheese spreads manufacturing
422430	Cheese wholesaling
311511	Cheese, cottage, manufacturing
311513	Cheese, imitation or substitute, manufacturing
311513	Cheese, natural (except cottage cheese), manufacturing
313210	Cheesecloths weaving
422690	Chemical additives (e.g., concrete, food, fuel, oil) wholesaling
234930	Chemical complexes or facility construction
541690	Chemical consulting services
541330	Chemical engineering services
313311	Chemical finishing (e.g., fire, mildew, water resistance) broadwoven fabrics
313312	Chemical finishing (e.g., fire, mildew, water resistance) fabrics (except broadwoven and textile products)
422690	Chemical gases wholesaling
421830	Chemical industries machinery and equipment wholesaling
333298	Chemical kilns manufacturing
332710	Chemical milling job shops
333512	Chemical milling machines, metalworking, manufacturing
333298	Chemical processing machinery and equipment manufacturing
541710	Chemical research and development laboratories or services
327112	Chemical stoneware (i.e., pottery products) manufacturing
326191	Chemical toilets, plastics, manufacturing
115112	Chemical treatment of soil for crops
213112	Chemically treating oil and gas wells (e.g., acidizing, bailing, swabbing) on a contract basis
422690	Chemicals (except agriculture) (e.g., automotive, household, industrial, photographic) wholesaling
422910	Chemicals, agricultural, wholesaling
315191	Chemises made in apparel knitting mills
315212	Chemises, women's and girls', cut and sew apparel contractors
315231	Chemises, women's, misses' and girls', cut and sewn from purchased fabric (except apparel contractors)
111339	Cherry farming
113210	Cherry gum, gathering
339932	Chessmen and chessboards manufacturing
325191	Chestnut extract manufacturing
113210	Chestnut gum, gathering
321920	Chests for tools, wood, manufacturing
332999	Chests, fire or burglary resistive, metal, manufacturing
332999	Chests, money, metal, manufacturing
332999	Chests, safe deposit, metal, manufacturing
311340	Chewing gum base manufacturing
333294	Chewing gum machinery manufacturing
311340	Chewing gum manufacturing
422450	Chewing gum wholesaling
312229	Chewing tobacco manufacturing
422940	Chewing tobacco wholesaling
422440	Chicken and chicken products (except packaged frozen) wholesaling
333111	Chicken brooders manufacturing
321920	Chicken coops (i.e., crates), wood, wirebound for shipping poultry, manufacturing
321992	Chicken coops, prefabricated, wood, manufacturing
112310	Chicken egg production
333111	Chicken feeders manufacturing

Code	Description
311119	Chicken feeds, prepared, manufacturing
112340	Chicken hatcheries
332618	Chicken netting made from purchased wire
112320	Chicken production (except egg laying)
311615	Chickens, processing, fresh, frozen, canned, or cooked (except baby and pet food)
311615	Chickens, slaughtering and dressing
422590	Chicks wholesaling
111998	Chicory farming
624410	Child day care centers
624410	Child day care services
624410	Child day care services in provider's own home
624410	Child day care, before or after school, separate from schools
623990	Child group foster homes
624110	Child guidance agencies
624110	Child welfare services
621410	Childbirth preparation classes
622210	Children's hospitals, psychiatric or substance abuse
622310	Children's hospitals, specialty (except psychiatric, substance abuse)
721214	Children's camps (except day, instructional)
422330	Children's clothing wholesaling
511199	Children's coloring book publishers
622110	Children's hospitals, general
316219	Children's shoes (except orthopedic extension, plastics, rubber) manufacturing
315119	Children's socks manufacturing
421920	Children's vehicles (except bicycles) wholesaling
623990	Children's villages
311422	Chili con carne canning
311942	Chili pepper or powder manufacturing
311421	Chili sauce manufacturing
339992	Chimes and parts (musical instruments) manufacturing
335999	Chimes, electric, manufacturing

Code	Description
327390	Chimney caps, concrete, manufacturing
561790	Chimney cleaning services
235410	Chimney construction contractors
561790	Chimney sweep (i.e., cleaning) services
212324	China clay mining and/or beneficiating
337122	China closets, wood, manufacturing
327112	China cooking ware manufacturing
811490	China repair services
327112	China tableware, vitreous, manufacturing
442299	Chinaware stores
421440	Chinaware, commercial, wholesaling
421220	Chinaware, household-type, wholesaling
112930	Chinchilla production
311422	Chinese foods canning
311999	Chinese noodles, fried, manufacturing
111219	Chinese pea farming, bedding plant and seed production
313210	Chintzes weaving
333298	Chip placement machinery manufacturing
322130	Chipboard (i.e., paperboard) stock manufacturing
321219	Chipboard manufacturing
322226	Chipboard, laminated or surface coated, made from purchased paperboard
321113	Chipper mills (except portable)
333112	Chippers (i.e., shredders), lawn and garden-type, manufacturing
333120	Chippers, portable, commercial (e.g., brush, limb, log), manufacturing
333291	Chippers, stationary (e.g., log), manufacturing
422450	Chips (e.g., corn, potato) wholesaling
621310	Chiropractors' offices (e.g., centers, clinics)
332212	Chisels manufacturing
333991	Chissels, handheld power-driven, manufacturing

Code	Description
111219	Chive farming, field, bedding plant and seed production
325199	Chloral manufacturing
325320	Chlordane insecticides manufacturing
325188	Chloride of lime manufacturing
325212	Chlorinated rubber, synthetic, manufacturing
325188	Chlorine compounds, not specified elsewhere by process, manufacturing
325188	Chlorine dioxide manufacturing
325181	Chlorine manufacturing
325199	Chloroacetic acid manufacturing
325192	Chlorobenzene manufacturing
325120	Chlorodifluoromethane manufacturing
325120	Chlorofluorocarbon gases manufacturing
325199	Chloroform manufacturing
325192	Chloronaphthalene manufacturing
325192	Chlorophenol manufacturing
325199	Chloropicrin manufacturing
325212	Chloroprene rubber manufacturing
325212	Chlorosulfonated polyethylenes manufacturing
325188	Chlorosulfonic acid manufacturing
325192	Chlorotoluene manufacturing
311330	Chocolate (coating, instant, liquor, syrups) made from purchased chocolate
311320	Chocolate (e.g., coatings, instant, liquor, syrups) made from cacao beans
422490	Chocolate (except candy) wholesaling
311320	Chocolate bars made from cocoa beans
422450	Chocolate candy wholesaling
311330	Chocolate coatings and syrups made from purchased chocolate
311330	Chocolate covered candy bars made from purchased chocolate
311330	Chocolate covered granola bars made from purchased chocolate
311511	Chocolate drink (milk based) manufacturing

Code	Description
311511	Chocolate milk manufacturing
333294	Chocolate processing machinery manufacturing
311320	Chocolate, confectionery, made from cacao beans
711130	Choirs
334416	Chokes for electronic circuitry manufacturing
325414	Cholera serums manufacturing
325320	Cholinesterse inhibitors used as insecticides manufacturing
311412	Chop suey, frozen, manufacturing
115113	Chopping and silo filling
711510	Choreographers, independent
311412	Chow mein, frozen, manufacturing
311711	Chowders, fish and seafood, canning
311712	Chowders, frozen fish and seafood, manufacturing
621399	Christian Science practitioners' offices (e.g., centers, clinics)
422990	Christmas ornaments wholesaling
453220	Christmas stores
333132	Christmas tree assemblies, oil and gas field-type, manufacturing
111421	Christmas tree growing
335129	Christmas tree lighting sets, electric, manufacturing
339999	Christmas tree ornaments (except electric, glass) manufacturing
327215	Christmas tree ornaments made from purchased glass
327212	Christmas tree ornaments, glass, made in glass making plants
422990	Christmas trees (e.g., artificial, cut) wholesaling
339999	Christmas trees, artificial, manufacturing
454390	Christmas trees, cut, direct selling
334516	Chromatographic instruments, laboratory-type, manufacturing
334513	Chromatographs, industrial process-type, manufacturing
325131	Chrome pigments (e.g., chrome green, chrome orange, chrome yellow) manufacturing
332813	Chrome plating metals and metal products for the trade

Code	Description
325188	Chromic acid manufacturing
212299	Chromite mining and/or beneficiating
325188	Chromium compounds, not specified elsewhere by process, manufacturing
212299	Chromium concentrates beneficiating
212299	Chromium ore mining and/or beneficiating
325188	Chromium oxide manufacturing
331419	Chromium refining, primary
325188	Chromium salts manufacturing
622310	Chronic disease hospitals
334518	Chronographs manufacturing
334518	Chronometers manufacturing
334516	Chronoscopes manufacturing
333512	Chucking machines, automatic, metalworking, manufacturing
333515	Chucks (i.e., a machine tool accessory) manufacturing
337127	Church furniture (except concrete, stone) manufacturing
421490	Church supplies (except plated ware, silverware) wholesaling
233320	Church, synagogue, mosque, temple, and related building construction
813110	Churches
332313	Chutes, fabricated metal plate work, manufacturing
333294	Cider presses manufacturing
311941	Cider vinegar manufacturing
312130	Cider, alcoholic, manufacturing
311941	Cider, nonalcoholic, manufacturing
326199	Cigar and cigarette holders, plastics, manufacturing
321920	Cigar boxes, wood and part wood, manufacturing
316993	Cigar cases (except metal) manufacturing
339911	Cigar cases, precious metal, manufacturing
312229	Cigar manufacturing
453991	Cigar stores
316993	Cigarette cases (except metal) manufacturing

Code	Description
339911	Cigarette cases, precious metal, manufacturing
339999	Cigarette holders manufacturing
339999	Cigarette lighter flints manufacturing
339999	Cigarette lighters (except precious metal) manufacturing
422990	Cigarette lighters wholesaling
333298	Cigarette making machinery manufacturing
322299	Cigarette paper made from purchased paper
322121	Cigarette paper made in paper mills
322299	Cigarette paper, book, made from purchased paper
453991	Cigarette stands, permanent
454390	Cigarette stands, temporary
325221	Cigarette tow, cellulosic fiber, manufacturing
333311	Cigarette vending machines manufacturing
312221	Cigarettes manufacturing
422940	Cigarettes wholesaling
422940	Cigars wholesaling
325411	Cinchona and derivatives (i.e., basic chemicals) manufacturing
327331	Cinder (clinker) block, concrete, manufacturing
233320	Cinema construction
512131	Cinemas
711510	Cinematographers, independent
212299	Cinnabar mining and/or beneficiating
333298	Circuit board making machinery manufacturing
421690	Circuit boards wholesaling
334412	Circuit boards, printed, bare, manufacturing
421610	Circuit breakers wholesaling
335313	Circuit breakers, air, manufacturing
335313	Circuit breakers, power, manufacturing
922110	Circuit courts
334515	Circuit testers manufacturing
421690	Circuits, integrated, wholesaling
313241	Circular (i.e., weft) fabrics knitting
541870	Circular direct distribution services

Code	Description
333292	Circular knitting machinery manufacturing
333991	Circular saws, handheld power-driven, manufacturing
333210	Circular saws, woodworking-type, stationary, manufacturing
514120	Circulating libraries
711190	Circus companies
711190	Circuses
334220	Citizens band (CB) radios manufacturing
325199	Citral manufacturing
325199	Citrates, not specified elsewhere by process, manufacturing
325199	Citric acid manufacturing
325998	Citronella oil manufacturing
325199	Citronellal manufacturing
115112	Citrus grove cultivation services
111320	Citrus groves (except orange)
311119	Citrus pulp, cattle feed, manufacturing
311411	Citrus pulp, frozen, manufacturing
921120	City and town councils
921110	City and town managers' offices
485113	City bus services (except mixed mode)
922110	City or county courts
541320	City planning services
813410	Civic associations
233320	Civic center construction
541330	Civil engineering services
813311	Civil liberties organizations
921190	Civil rights commissions
921190	Civil service commissions
524291	Claims adjusting, insurance
524292	Claims processing services, insurance, third-party
114112	Clam digging
112512	Clam production, farm raising
333515	Clamps (i.e., a machine tool accessory) manufacturing
339112	Clamps, surgical, manufacturing
339992	Clarinets and parts manufacturing
316999	Clasps, shoe (leather), manufacturing
813410	Classic car clubs

Code	Description
711120	Classical dance companies
711130	Classical musical artists, independent
711130	Classical musical groups
212325	Clay (except kaolin, ball) mining and/or beneficiating
327112	Clay and ceramic statuary manufacturing
212325	Clay bleaching
421320	Clay construction materials (except refractory) wholesaling
327124	Clay refractories (e.g., mortar, brick, tile, block) manufacturing
212324	Clay, ball, mining and/or beneficiating
212325	Clay, ceramic and refractory minerals, mining and/or beneficiating
212325	Clay, fire, mining and/or beneficiating
339942	Clay, modeling, manufacturing
212324	Clay, natural, mining and/or beneficiating
333298	Clayworking and tempering machinery manufacturing
812332	Clean room apparel supply services
233310	Clean room construction, general construction contractors
339113	Clean room suits and accessories manufacturing
812320	Cleaners, drycleaning and laundry service (except coin-operated)
335212	Cleaners, household-type electric vacuum, manufacturing
561790	Cleaning (e.g., power sweeping, washing) driveways and parking lots
332813	Cleaning and descaling metals and metal products for the trade
812320	Cleaning and dyeing plants (except rug cleaning plants)
311212	Cleaning and polishing rice
561790	Cleaning building exteriors (except sand blasting, window cleaning)
235990	Cleaning building exteriors construction contractors
561740	Cleaning carpets

Code	Description
422690	Cleaning compounds and preparations wholesaling
335999	Cleaning equipment, ultrasonic (except dental, medical), manufacturing
561720	Cleaning homes
333131	Cleaning machinery, mining-type, manufacturing
561720	Cleaning new building interiors after construction
235990	Cleaning new buildings after construction contractors
561720	Cleaning offices
213112	Cleaning oil and gas field lease tanks on a contract basis
213112	Cleaning out (e.g., bailing out, steam cleaning, swabbing) wells on a contract basis
212113	Cleaning plants, anthracite coal
212111	Cleaning plants, bituminous coal
561740	Cleaning plants, carpet and rug
115210	Cleaning poultry houses
561740	Cleaning rugs
561740	Cleaning services, carpet and rug
561720	Cleaning shopping centers
561790	Cleaning swimming pools
213112	Cleaning wells on a contract basis
213112	Cleaning, repairing, and dismantling oil and gas field lease tanks on a contract basis
321918	Clear and finger joint wood moldings manufacturing
522320	Clearinghouses, bank or check
523999	Clearinghouses, commodity exchange or securities exchange
316219	Cleated athletic shoes manufacturing
332211	Cleavers manufacturing
315299	Clerical vestments cut and sewn from purchased fabric (except apparel contractors)
315191	Clerical vestments made in apparel knitting mills
315211	Clerical vestments, men's and boys, cut and sew apparel contractors
315212	Clerical vestments, women's and girls', cut and sew apparel contractors

Code	Description
316211	Climbing shoes, plastics or plastics soled fabric upper, manufacturing
316211	Climbing shoes, rubber or rubber soled fabric upper, manufacturing
233320	Clinic construction
621111	Clinical pathologists' offices (e.g., centers, clinics)
621330	Clinical psychologists' offices (e.g., centers, clinics)
*****	Clinics, medical — see type
621498	Clinics/centers of health practitioners from more than one industry practicing within the same establishment
621498	Clinics/centers of health practitioners with multi-industry degrees
321999	Clipboards, wood, manufacturing
332212	Clippers for animal use, nonelectric, manufacturing
332211	Clippers, fingernail and toenail, manufacturing
514199	Clipping services, news
332994	Clips, gun (i.e., 30 mm. or less, 1.18 inch or less), manufacturing
332995	Clips, gun (i.e., more than 30 mm., more than 1.18 inch), manufacturing
334518	Clock materials and parts (except crystals) manufacturing
334518	Clock or watch springs, precision, made from purchased wire
334310	Clock radios manufacturing
811490	Clock repair shops without retailing new clocks
448310	Clock shops
334518	Clocks assembling
334518	Clocks assembling from purchased components
421940	Clocks wholesaling
561492	Closed captioning services, real-time (i.e., simultaneous)
512191	Closed captioning services, taped material
513220	Closed circuit television (CCTV)
334220	Closed circuit television equipment manufacturing

Code	Description
525990	Closed-end investment funds (except REITs)
332115	Closures, metal, stamping
422130	Closures, paper and disposable plastics, wholesaling
327910	Cloth (e.g., aluminum oxide, garnet, emery, silicon carbide) coated manufacturing
561990	Cloth cutting, bolting, or winding for the trade
333292	Cloth spreading machinery manufacturing
321999	Cloth winding reels, wood
332618	Cloth, woven wire, made from purchased wire
334512	Clothes dryer controls, including dryness controls, manufacturing
811412	Clothes dryer, household-type, repair and maintenance services without retailing new clothes dryers
321999	Clothes dryers (clothes horses), wood manufacturing
422990	Clothes hangers wholesaling
326199	Clothes hangers, plastics, manufacturing
321999	Clothes poles, wood, manufacturing
326199	Clothespins, plastics, manufacturing
321999	Clothespins, wood, manufacturing
448150	Clothing accessories stores
422330	Clothing accessories, women's, children's, and infants', wholesaling
541490	Clothing design services
532220	Clothing rental (except industrial launderer, linen supply)
811490	Clothing repair shops, alterations only
448130	Clothing stores, children's and infants'
448140	Clothing stores, family
448110	Clothing stores, men's and boys'
453310	Clothing stores, used
448120	Clothing stores, women's and girls'
339931	Clothing, doll, manufacturing
315292	Clothing, fur (except apparel contractors), manufacturing
315211	Clothing, fur, men's and boys', cut and sew apparel contractors

Code	Description
315212	Clothing, fur, women's, girls', and infants', cut and sew apparel contractors
315292	Clothing, leather or sheep-lined (except apparel contractors), manufacturing
315211	Clothing, leather or sheep-lined, men's and boys', cut and sew apparel contractors
315212	Clothing, leather or sheep-lined, women's, girls', and infants', cut and sew apparel contractors
422320	Clothing, men's and boys', wholesaling
315291	Clothing, water resistant, infants', cut and sewn from purchased fabric (except apparel contractors)
315211	Clothing, water resistant, men's and boy's, cut and sew apparel contractors
315228	Clothing, water resistant, not specified elsewhere, men's and boys', cut and sewn from purchased fabric (except apparel contractors)
315239	Clothing, water resistant, not specified elsewhere, women's, misses', and girls', cut and sewn from purchased fabric (except apparel contractors)
315212	Clothing, water resistant, women's, girls' and infants', cut and sew apparel contractors
315291	Clothing, water-repellent, infants', cut and sewn from purchased fabric (except apparel contractors)
315211	Clothing, water-repellent, men's and boys', cut and sew apparel contractors
315228	Clothing, water-repellent, not specified elsewhere, men's and boys', cut and sewn from purchased fabric (except apparel contractors)
315239	Clothing, water-repellent, not specified elsewhere, women's, misses', and girls', cut and sewn from purchased fabric (except apparel contractors)
315212	Clothing, water-repellent, women's, girls', and infants', cut and sew apparel contractors

Code	Description
315299	Clothing, waterproof, cut and sewn from purchased fabric (except apparel contractors)
315211	Clothing, waterproof, men's and boys', cut and sew apparel contractors
315212	Clothing, waterproof, women's, girls', and infants', cut and sew apparel contractors
422330	Clothing, women's, children's, and infants', wholesaling
339994	Cloths (except chemically treated), dusting and polishing, manufacturing
325612	Cloths, dusting and polishing, chemically treated, manufacturing
325998	Clove oil manufacturing
111940	Clover hay farming
111998	Clover seed farming
721310	Clubs, residential
339920	Clubs, sporting goods (e.g., golf, Indian), manufacturing
333613	Clutches and brakes (except electromagnetic industrial controls, motor vehicle) manufacturing
234930	Co-generation plant construction
325413	Coagulation in-vitro diagnostic substances manufacturing
325412	Coagulation in-vivo diagnostic substances manufacturing
333922	Coal and ore conveyors manufacturing
212113	Coal beneficiating plants, anthracite
212111	Coal beneficiating plants, bituminous or lignite (surface or underground)
333131	Coal breakers, cutters, and pulverizers manufacturing
332322	Coal chutes, sheet metal, manufacturing
454319	Coal dealers, direct selling
211111	Coal gasification at mine site
484220	Coal hauling, truck, local
211111	Coal liquefaction at mine site
213113	Coal mining services

Code	Description
213113	Coal mining support services (tunneling, blasting, training, overburden removal)
486990	Coal pipeline transportation
211111	Coal pyrolysis
325192	Coal tar distillates manufacturing
324121	Coal tar paving materials made from purchased coal tar
422690	Coal tar products, primary and intermediate, wholesaling
325211	Coal tar resins manufacturing
421520	Coal wholesaling
212113	Coal, anthracite, mining and/or beneficiating
212111	Coal, bituminous, beneficiating
212112	Coal, bituminous, underground mining or mining and beneficiating
212111	Coal, brown, mining and/or beneficiating
926120	Coast Guard (except academy)
483113	Coastal freight transportation to and from domestic ports
483114	Coastal passenger transportation to and from domestic ports
483113	Coastal shipping of freight to and from domestic ports
812331	Coat (e.g., barber's, beautician's, doctor's, nurse's) supply services
332618	Coat hangers made from purchased wire
315292	Coat linings, fur (except apparel contractors), manufacturing
315211	Coat linings, fur, men's and boys', cut and sew apparel contractors
315212	Coat linings, fur, women's, girls', and infants', cut and sew apparel contractors
448190	Coat stores
315999	Coat trimmings fabric cut and sewn from purchased fabric (except apparel contractors)
315211	Coat trimmings, fabric, men's and boys', cut and sew apparel contractors
315212	Coat trimmings, fabric, women's, girls', and infants', cut and sew apparel contractors

Code	Description
322226	Coated board made from purchased paperboard
322130	Coated board made in paperboard mills
235990	Coating and glazing of concrete surfaces construction contractors
324122	Coating compounds, tar, made from purchased asphaltic materials
332812	Coating metals and metal products for the trade
235990	Coating of concrete structures with plastics, construction contractors
332812	Coating of metal and metal products with plastics for the trade
335110	Coating purchased light bulbs
322222	Coating purchased papers for nonpackaging applications (except photosensitive paper)
322221	Coating purchased papers for packaging applications
311320	Coatings, chocolate, made from cacao beans
315239	Coats (except fur, leather, tailored, waterproof), women's, misses', and girls', cut and sewn from purchased fabric (except apparel contractors)
315228	Coats (except fur, leather, tailored, waterproof, work), men's and boys', cut and sewn from purchased fabric (except apparel contractors)
315292	Coats (including tailored), leather or sheep-lined (except apparel contractors), manufacturing
315212	Coats (including tailored, leather, or sheep-lined), women's, girls', and infants', cut and sew apparel contractors
315292	Coats, artificial leather, cut and sewn from purchased fabric (except apparel contractors)
315211	Coats, artificial leather, men's and boys', cut and sew apparel contractors
315212	Coats, artificial leather, women's, girls', and infants', cut and sew apparel contractors

Code	Description
315292	Coats, fur (except apparel contractors), manufacturing
315211	Coats, fur, men's and boys', cut and sew apparel contractors
315212	Coats, fur, women's, girls', and infants', cut and sew apparel contractors
315291	Coats, infants' (except waterproof), cut and sewn from purchased fabric (except apparel contractors)
315292	Coats, leather, (except apparel contractors)
315211	Coats, leather, men's and boys', cut and sew apparel contractors
315212	Coats, leather, women's, girls', and infants', cut and sew apparel contractors
315211	Coats, men's and boys', cut and sew apparel contractors
315211	Coats, nontailored service apparel (e.g., laboratory, mechanics', medical), men's and boys', cut and sew apparel contractors
315228	Coats, nontailored service apparel (e.g., laboratory, mechanics', medical), men's and boys', cut and sewn from purchased fabric (except apparel contractors)
315212	Coats, nontailored service apparel (e.g., laboratory, medical, mechanics'), women's and girls', cut and sew apparel contractors
315239	Coats, nontailored service apparel (e.g., laboratory, medical, mechanics'), women's, misses', and girls', cut and sewn from purchased fabric (except apparel contractors)
315222	Coats, tailored (except fur, leather), men's and boys', cut and sewn from purchased fabric (except apparel contractors)
315234	Coats, tailored (except fur, leather), women's, misses', and girls', cut and sewn from purchased fabric
315999	Coats, waterproof (e.g., plastics, rubberized fabric, similar materials) rubberizing fabric and manufacturing coats

Code	Description
315211	Coats, waterproof (i.e., plastic, rubberized fabric, similar materials), men's and boy's, cut and sew apparel contractors
315212	Coats, waterproof (i.e., plastics, rubberized fabric, similar materials), women's, girls', and infants', cut and sew apparel contractors
315999	Coats, waterproof, (e.g., plastics, rubberized fabric, similar materials) cut and sewn from purchased fabric (except apparel contractors)
315212	Coats, women's, girls', and infants', cut and sew apparel contractors
331319	Coaxial cable made in aluminum wire drawing plants
421610	Coaxial cable wholesaling
331422	Coaxial cable, copper, made from purchased copper in wire drawing plants
331491	Coaxial cable, nonferrous metals (except aluminum, copper), made from purchased nonferrous metals (except aluminum, copper) in wire drawing plants
335929	Coaxial cable, nonferrous, made from purchased nonferrous wire
334417	Coaxial connectors manufacturing
325188	Cobalt 60 (i.e., radioactive cobalt) manufacturing
325188	Cobalt chloride manufacturing
325188	Cobalt compounds, not specified elsewhere by process, manufacturing
212299	Cobalt concentrates beneficiating
212299	Cobalt ores mining and/or beneficiating
331419	Cobalt refining, primary
325188	Cobalt sulfate manufacturing
325411	Cocaine and derivatives (i.e., basic chemicals) manufacturing
332913	Cocks, drain, plumbing, manufacturing
722410	Cocktail lounges
311999	Cocktail mixes, dry, manufacturing
422820	Cocktails, alcoholic, premixed, wholesaling

Code	Description
311320	Cocoa (e.g., instant, mix, mixed with other ingredients, powder drink, powdered) made from cacao beans
422590	Cocoa beans wholesaling
311320	Cocoa butter made from cocoa beans
311330	Cocoa, powdered drink, prepared, made from purchased chocolate
311330	Cocoa, powdered, made from purchased chocolate
311330	Cocoa, powdered, mixed with other ingredients, made from purchased chocolate
311225	Coconut oil made from purchased oils
311223	Coconut oil made in crushing mills
111339	Coconut tree farming
311999	Coconut, desiccated and shredded, manufacturing
114111	Cod catching
114111	Cod fishing
311711	Cod liver oil extraction, crude, produced in a cannery
311712	Cod liver oil extraction, crude, produced in a fresh and frozen seafood plant
325411	Cod liver oil, medicinal, uncompounded, manufacturing
325411	Codeine and derivatives (i.e., basic chemicals) manufacturing
333993	Coding, dating, and imprinting packaging machinery manufacturing
445299	Coffee and tea (i.e., packaged) stores
722330	Coffee carts, mobile
311920	Coffee concentrates (i.e., instant coffee) manufacturing
311920	Coffee extracts manufacturing
111339	Coffee farming
322299	Coffee filters made from purchased paper
311920	Coffee flavoring and syrups (i.e., made from coffee) manufacturing
333319	Coffee makers and urns, commercial-type, manufacturing

Code	Description
335211	Coffee makers, household-type electric, manufacturing
311920	Coffee roasting
333294	Coffee roasting and grinding machinery (i.e., food manufacturing-type) manufacturing
722213	Coffee shops, on premise brewing
311920	Coffee substitute manufacturing
337122	Coffee tables, wood, manufacturing
422490	Coffee wholesaling
311920	Coffee, blended, manufacturing
312111	Coffee, iced, manufacturing
311920	Coffee, instant and freeze dried, manufacturing
454390	Coffee-break service providers, direct selling
234990	Cofferdam construction
487110	Cog railway, scenic and sightseeing, operation
541720	Cognitive research and development services
333518	Coil winding and cutting machinery, metalworking, manufacturing
332612	Coiled springs (except clock, watch), light gauge, manufacturing
332611	Coiled springs, heavy gauge, manufacturing
335312	Coils for motors and generators manufacturing
336322	Coils, ignition, internal combustion engines, manufacturing
332996	Coils, pipe, made from purchased metal pipe
333313	Coin counting machinery manufacturing
561990	Coin pick-up services, parking meter
316993	Coin purses (except metal) manufacturing
339911	Coin purses, precious metal, manufacturing
421420	Coin sorting machines wholesaling
333313	Coin wrapping machines manufacturing
339999	Coin-operated amusement machines (except jukebox) manufacturing
812310	Coin-operated drycleaners and laundries

Code	Description
713290	Coin-operated gambling device concession operators (i.e., supplying and servicing in others' facilities)
339999	Coin-operated gambling devices manufacturing
421990	Coin-operated game machines wholesaling
334310	Coin-operated jukebox manufacturing
812310	Coin-operated laundry and drycleaning routes (i.e., concession operators)
713990	Coin-operated nongambling amusement device concession operators (i.e., supplying and servicing in others' facilities)
812990	Coin-operated personal service machine (e.g., blood pressure, locker, photographic, scale, shoeshine) concession operators
421440	Coin-operated phonographs and vending machines wholesaling
333311	Coin-operated vending machines manufacturing
339911	Coins menting
421940	Coins wholesaling
221210	Coke oven gas, production and distribution
324199	Coke oven products (e.g., coke, gases, tars) made in coke oven establishments
331111	Coke oven products made in steel mills
421520	Coke wholesaling
324110	Coke, petroleum, made in petroleum refineries
335110	Cold cathode fluorescent lamp tubes manufacturing
332111	Cold forgings made from purchased iron or steel, unfinished
332112	Cold forgings made from purchased nonferrous metals, unfinished
325412	Cold remedies manufacturing
333516	Cold rolling mill machinery, metalworking, manufacturing
331221	Cold rolling steel shapes (e.g., bar, plate, rod, sheet, strip) made from purchased steel
493120	Cold storage locker services

Code	Description
421740	Cold storage machinery wholesaling
233310	Cold storage plant construction
493120	Cold storage warehousing
311991	Cole slaw, fresh, manufacturing
212391	Colemanite mining and/or beneficiating
311612	Collagen sausage casings made from purchased hides
332439	Collapsible tubes (e.g., toothpaste, glue), metal, manufacturing
315191	Collar and cuff sets made in apparel knitting mills
315212	Collar and cuff sets, women's, girls' and infants', cut and sew apparel contractors
315239	Collar and cuff sets, women's, misses' and girls', cut and sewn from purchased fabric (except apparel contractors)
316110	Collar leather, manufacturing
111219	Collard farming, field, bedding plant and seed production
333515	Collars (i.e., a machine tool accessory) manufacturing
316999	Collars and collar pads (i.e., harness) manufacturing
316999	Collars, dog, manufacturing
333613	Collars, shaft for power transmission equipment, manufacturing
525990	Collateralized mortgage obligations (CMOs)
333293	Collating machinery for printing and bookbinding manufacturing
333313	Collating machinery, office-type, manufacturing
453220	Collectible gift shops (e.g., crystal, pewter, porcelain)
812320	Collecting and distributing agents, laundry and drycleaning
561440	Collection agencies
561440	Collection agencies, accounts
221320	Collection, treatment, and disposal of waste through a sewer system
335312	Collector rings for motors and generators manufacturing
453998	Collector's items shops (e.g., autograph, card, coin, stamp)

Code	Description
454110	Collector's items, mail-order houses
611691	College board preparation centers
611691	College entrance exam preparation instruction
611710	College selection services
611310	Colleges (except junior colleges)
611511	Colleges, barber and beauty
611210	Colleges, community
611210	Colleges, junior
333515	Collets (i.e., a machine tool accessory) manufacturing
325620	Colognes manufacturing
422210	Colognes wholesaling
334510	Colonscopes, electromedical, manufacturing
812199	Color consulting services (i.e., personal care services)
325131	Color pigments, inorganic (except bone black, carbon black, lamp black), manufacturing
325132	Color pigments, organic (except animal black, bone black), manufacturing
323122	Color separation services, for the printing trade
334516	Colorimeters, laboratory-type, manufacturing
511199	Coloring book publishing (i.e., establishments known as publishers)
421920	Coloring books wholesaling
316110	Coloring leather
332813	Coloring metals and metal products (except coating) for the trade
339113	Colostomy appliances manufacturing
212299	Columbite mining and/or beneficiating
212299	Columbium ores mining and/or beneficiating
327420	Columns, architectural or ornamental plaster work, manufacturing
332420	Columns, fractionating, manufacturing
321918	Columns, porch, wood, manufacturing

Code	Description
316993	Comb cases (except metal) manufacturing
339911	Comb cases, precious metal, manufacturing
334512	Combination limit and fan controls manufacturing
112990	Combination livestock farming (except dairy, poultry)
334512	Combination oil and hydronic controls manufacturing
333111	Combines (i.e., harvester-threshers) manufacturing
313312	Combing and converting top
333292	Combing machinery for textiles manufacturing
313312	Combing textile fibers
115113	Combining, agricultural
332999	Combs, metal, manufacturing
326199	Combs, plastics, manufacturing
326299	Combs, rubber, manufacturing
334513	Combustion control instruments (except commercial, household furnace-type) manufacturing
541330	Combustion engineering consulting services
562211	Combustors, hazardous waste
562213	Combustors, nonhazardous solid waste
711510	Comedians, independent
711110	Comedy troupes
812990	Comfort station operation
314129	Comforters made from purchased fabrics
511120	Comic book publishers
511120	Comic book publishers and printing combined
511120	Comic book publishing (i.e., establishments known as publishers)
323112	Comic books flexographic printing without publishing
323111	Comic books gravure printing without publishing
323110	Comic books lithographic (offset) printing without publishing
323119	Comic books printing (except flexographic, gravure, lithographic, screen) without publishing

Code	Description
323113	Comic books screen printing without publishing
811310	Commercial and industrial machinery repair and maintenance services
233320	Commercial and institutional building construction management firms
541430	Commercial art services
541430	Commercial artists, independent
311812	Commercial bakeries
522110	Commercial banking
522110	Commercial banks
233320	Commercial building construction
531120	Commercial building rental or leasing
561450	Commercial credit reporting bureaus
541430	Commercial illustration services
541430	Commercial illustrators, independent
335122	Commercial lighting fixtures, electric, manufacturing
523120	Commercial note brokers' offices
523110	Commercial paper dealing (i.e., acting as a principal in dealing securities to investors)
541922	Commercial photography services
531312	Commercial property managing
531210	Commercial real estate agencies
531210	Commercial real estate agents' offices
531312	Commercial real estate property managers' offices
811310	Commercial refrigeration equipment repair and maintenance services
422120	Commercial stationery suppliers wholesaling
334518	Commercial timing mechanisms manufacturing
233320	Commercial warehouse construction, general construction contractors
512110	Commercials, television, production
445110	Commissaries, primarily groceries
522298	Commodity Credit Corporation
523130	Commodity contract trading companies

Code	Description
523140	Commodity contracts brokerages
523140	Commodity contracts brokers' offices
523130	Commodity contracts dealing (i.e., acting as a principal in dealing commodities to investors)
523210	Commodity contracts exchanges
523140	Commodity contracts floor brokers
523130	Commodity contracts floor traders (i.e., acting as a principal in dealing commodities to investors)
523130	Commodity contracts floor trading (i.e., acting as a principal in dealing commodities to investors)
523140	Commodity contracts options brokerages
523130	Commodity contracts options dealing (i.e., acting as a principal in dealing commodities to investors)
523130	Commodity contracts traders (i.e., acting as a principal in dealing commodities to investors)
523140	Commodity futures brokerages
541990	Commodity inspection services
212325	Common clay mining and/or beneficiating
212321	Common sand quarrying and/or beneficiating
212325	Common shale mining and/or beneficiating
923120	Communicable disease program administration
541430	Communication design services, visual
235310	Communication equipment construction contractors
811213	Communication equipment repair and maintenance services
234920	Communication transmission and power line construction management firms
926130	Communications commissions
421690	Communications equipment wholesaling
334220	Communications equipment, mobile and microwave, manufacturing
334210	Communications headgear, telephone, manufacturing
926130	Communications licensing commissions and agencies
335929	Communications wire and cable, nonferrous, made from purchased nonferrous wire
331319	Communications wire or cable made in aluminum wire drawing plants
331422	Communications wire or cable, copper, made from purchased copper in wire drawing plants
331491	Communications wire or cable, nonferrous metals (except aluminum, copper), made from purchased nonferrous metals (except aluminum, copper) in wire drawing plants
311812	Communion wafer manufacturing
813319	Community action advocacy organizations
624190	Community action service agencies
624120	Community centers (except recreational only), adult
624110	Community centers (except recreational only), youth
813219	Community chests
611210	Community colleges
611210	Community colleges offering a wide variety of academic and technical training
925120	Community development agencies, government
813211	Community foundations
621498	Community health centers and clinics, outpatient
923120	Community health programs administration
624210	Community meals, social services
712110	Community museums
924120	Community recreation programs, government
923130	Community social service program administration
711110	Community theaters
335312	Commutators, electric motor, manufacturing
481111	Commuter air carriers, scheduled
485113	Commuter bus operation (except mixed mode)
485112	Commuter rail systems (except mixed mode)
485111	Commuter transit systems, mixed mode (e.g., bus, commuter rail, subway combination)
334310	Compact disc players (e.g., automotive, household-type) manufacturing
421990	Compact discs (CDs), prerecorded, wholesaling
334611	Compact discs (i.e., CD-ROM), software, mass reproducing
334612	Compact discs, prerecorded audio, mass reproducing
334613	Compact discs, recordable or rewritable, blank, manufacturing
335110	Compact fluorescent light bulbs manufacturing
339911	Compacts, precious metal, manufacturing
316993	Compacts, solid leather, manufacturing
112990	Companion animals production (e.g., cats, dogs, parakeets, parrots)
624120	Companion services for disabled persons, the elderly, and persons diagnosed with mental retardation
333314	Comparators, optical, manufacturing
334511	Compasses, gyroscopic and magnetic (except portable), manufacturing
334519	Compasses, portable magnetic-type, manufacturing
541612	Compensation consulting services
541612	Compensation planning services
511140	Compiling mailing lists
311119	Complete feed, livestock, manufacturing
711510	Composers, independent
322214	Composite cans (i.e., foil-fiber and other combinations) manufacturing
562219	Compost dumps
325314	Compost manufacturing
325120	Compressed and liquefied industrial gas manufacturing
332911	Compressed gas cylinder valves manufacturing

Code	Description
422690	Compressed gases (except LP gas) wholesaling
321219	Compression modified wood manufacturing
333220	Compression molding machinery for plastics manufacturing
339991	Compression packings manufacturing
532490	Compressor, air and gas, rental or leasing
421830	Compressors (except air-conditioning, refrigeration) wholesaling
333912	Compressors, air and gas, general purpose-type, manufacturing
421730	Compressors, air-conditioning, wholesaling
336391	Compressors, motor vehicle air-conditioning, manufacturing
421740	Compressors, refrigeration, wholesaling
541710	Computer and related hardware research and development laboratories or services
421430	Computer boards, loaded, wholesaling
421690	Computer boards, unloaded, wholesaling
235310	Computer cable construction contractors
421690	Computer chips wholesaling
541519	Computer disaster recovery services
813410	Computer enthusiasts clubs
811212	Computer equipment repair and maintenance services without retailing new computers
443120	Computer equipment stores
323116	Computer forms (manifold or continuous) printing
337124	Computer furniture, metal household-type, manufacturing
337122	Computer furniture, wood household-type, manufacturing
514210	Computer input preparation services
334119	Computer input/output equipment (except terminals) manufacturing
611420	Computer operator training

Code	Description
422120	Computer paper supplies wholesaling
322231	Computer paper, single layered continuous, die-cut, made from purchased paper
532420	Computer peripheral equipment rental or leasing
421430	Computer peripheral equipment wholesaling
325992	Computer printer toner cartridges manufacturing
421430	Computer printers wholesaling
541511	Computer program or software development, custom
611420	Computer programming schools
541511	Computer programming services, custom
532420	Computer rental or leasing
611519	Computer repair training
334111	Computer servers manufacturing
514210	Computer service bureaus
541511	Computer software analysis and design services, custom
541511	Computer software programming services, custom
511210	Computer software publishers, packaged
511210	Computer software publishing and reproduction
511210	Computer software publishing including design and development, packaged (i.e., establishments known as publishers)
541511	Computer software support services, custom
334613	Computer software tapes and disks, blank, rigid and floppy, manufacturing
611420	Computer software training
454110	Computer software, mail-order houses
421430	Computer software, packaged, wholesaling
443120	Computer stores
541513	Computer systems facilities (i.e., clients' facilities) management and operation services
541512	Computer systems integration analysis and design services

Code	Description
541512	Computer systems integration design consulting services
541512	Computer systems integrator services
334113	Computer terminals manufacturing
514210	Computer time leasing
514210	Computer time rental
514210	Computer time sharing services
621512	Computer tomography (CT-SCAN) centers
611420	Computer training (except repair)
532230	Computer video game rental
541512	Computer-aided design (CAD) systems integration design services
541512	Computer-aided engineering (CAE) systems integration design services
541512	Computer-aided manufacturing (CAM) systems integration design services
334517	Computerized axial tomography (CT/CAT) scanners manufacturing
334512	Computerized environmental control systems for buildings manufacturing
334111	Computers manufacturing
421430	Computers wholesaling
325411	Concentrated medicinal chemicals, uncompounded, manufacturing
311930	Concentrates, drink (except frozen fruit juice), manufacturing
311930	Concentrates, flavoring (except coffee based), manufacturing
311411	Concentrates, frozen fruit juice, manufacturing
421520	Concentrates, metallic, wholesaling
333131	Concentration machinery, mining-type, manufacturing
711130	Concert artists, independent
711320	Concert booking agencies
711310	Concert hall operators
531120	Concert hall, no promotion of events, rental or leasing
711310	Concert managers with facilities
711320	Concert managers without facilities
711310	Concert organizers with facilities
711320	Concert organizers without facilities
711310	Concert promoters with facilities

Code	Description
711320	Concert promoters without facilities
713990	Concession operators, amusement device (except gambling) and ride
722330	Concession stands, mobile
812990	Concierge services
926150	Conciliation and mediation services, government
234110	Concrete (e.g., roads, highways, public sidewalks, streets) construction contractors
325998	Concrete additive preparations (e.g., curing, hardening) manufacturing
422690	Concrete additives wholesaling
327320	Concrete batch plants (including temporary)
235410	Concrete block laying construction contractors
235940	Concrete breaking and cutting construction contractors
421320	Concrete building products wholesaling
235710	Concrete construction contractors (i.e., parking areas, private driveways, sidewalks)
235710	Concrete finishing construction contractors
333120	Concrete finishing machinery manufacturing
235990	Concrete form construction contractors
332322	Concrete forms, sheet metal, manufacturing
327390	Concrete furniture (e.g., benches, tables) manufacturing
333120	Concrete gunning equipment manufacturing
333120	Concrete mixing machinery, portable, manufacturing
421810	Concrete processing equipment wholesaling
235910	Concrete products (e.g., structural precast or prestressed), placement, construction contractors
333298	Concrete products forming machinery manufacturing
327390	Concrete products, precast (except block, brick and pipe), manufacturing

Code	Description
235710	Concrete pumping construction contractors
235910	Concrete reinforcement placement, construction contractors
332312	Concrete reinforcing bars manufacturing
421510	Concrete reinforcing bars wholesaling
332618	Concrete reinforcing mesh made from purchased wire
327390	Concrete tanks manufacturing
327999	Concrete, dry mixture, manufacturing
211112	Condensate, cycle, natural gas production
333294	Condensed and evaporated milk machinery manufacturing
311514	Condensed milk manufacturing
311514	Condensed, evaporated or powdered whey, manufacturing
332410	Condenser boxes, metal, manufacturing
335999	Condensers (except electronic), fixed and variable, manufacturing
334414	Condensers, electronic, manufacturing
421690	Condensers, electronic, wholesaling
332410	Condensers, steam, manufacturing
335312	Condensers, synchronous, electric, manufacturing
421830	Condensing units (except air-conditioning, refrigeration) wholesaling
421730	Condensing units, air-conditioning, wholesaling
421740	Condensing units, refrigeration, wholesaling
326299	Condom manufacturing
813990	Condominium corporations
531312	Condominium managers' offices, commercial
531311	Condominium managers' offices, residential
813990	Condominium owners' associations
561599	Condominium time share exchange services
233220	Condominiums, multifamily, construction

Code	Description
335931	Conductor connectors, solderless connectors, sleeves, or soldering lugs, manufacturing
234920	Conduit construction
327123	Conduit, vitrified clay, manufacturing
331210	Conduit, welded and lock joint, made from purchased iron or steel
335932	Conduits and fittings, electrical, manufacturing
327332	Conduits, concrete, manufacturing
322214	Cones (e.g., winding yarn, string, ribbon, cloth), fiber, made from purchased paperboard
311821	Cones, ice cream, manufacturing
327112	Cones, pyrometric, earthenware, manufacturing
311313	Confectioner's beet sugar manufacturing
311312	Confectioner's powdered sugar made from purchased raw cane sugar
311320	Confectionery chocolate made from cacao beans
333294	Confectionery machinery manufacturing
722213	Confectionery snack shops, made on premises with carryout services
445292	Confectionery stores, packaged, retailing only
422450	Confectionery wholesaling
311340	Confectionery, nonchocolate, manufacturing
531120	Conference center, no promotion of events, rental or leasing
322299	Confetti made from purchased paper
921120	Congress of the United States
336312	Connecting rods, automotive and truck gasoline engine, manufacturing
335931	Connectors and terminals for electrical devices manufacturing
335931	Connectors, electric cord, manufacturing
334417	Connectors, electronic (e.g., coaxial, cylindrical, printed circuit, rack and panel), manufacturing

Code	Description
421690	Connectors, electronic, wholesaling
335313	Connectors, power, manufacturing
335931	Connectors, solderless (wiring devices), manufacturing
335931	Connectors, twist on wire (i.e., nuts), manufacturing
813312	Conservation advocacy organizations
234990	Conservation and development construction
924120	Conservation and reclamation agencies
712190	Conservation areas
611310	Conservatories of music (colleges or universities)
712130	Conservatories, botanical
711510	Conservators, independent
611610	Conservatory of music (except academic)
453310	Consignment shops, used
336350	Constant velocity joints, automotive, truck, and bus, manufacturing
813940	Constituencies' associations, political party
325520	Construction adhesives (except asphalt, gypsum base) manufacturing
813910	Construction associations
541330	Construction engineering services
532412	Construction form rental
522292	Construction lending
532412	Construction machinery and equipment rental or leasing without operator
811310	Construction machinery and equipment repair and maintenance services
421810	Construction machinery and equipment wholesaling
333120	Construction machinery manufacturing
234120	Construction management firms, bridge and tunnel
233320	Construction management firms, commercial and institutional building firms

Code	Description
234110	Construction management firms, highway and street
234930	Construction management firms, industrial nonbuilding
233310	Construction management firms, manufacturing and industrial building
233220	Construction management firms, multifamily
234990	Construction management firms, nonbuilding (except industrial)
234920	Construction management firms, power and communication transmission line
233210	Construction management firms, single family
234910	Construction management firms, water, sewer and pipeline
421610	Construction materials, electrical, wholesaling
322233	Construction paper, school and art, made from purchased paper
322121	Construction paper, school and art, made in paper mills
212321	Construction sand and gravel beneficiating (e.g., grinding, screening, washing)
212321	Construction sand or gravel dredging
333120	Construction-type tractors and attachments manufacturing
928120	Consulates
*****	Consultants — see specific activity
813920	Consultants' associations
531390	Consultants', real estate (except appraisers), offices
541330	Consulting engineers' offices
541330	Consulting engineers' private practices
812990	Consumer buying services
541990	Consumer credit counseling services
561450	Consumer credit reporting bureaus
532210	Consumer electronics rental
811211	Consumer electronics repair and maintenance services without retailing new consumer electronics
421620	Consumer electronics wholesaling

Code	Description
522291	Consumer finance companies (i.e., unsecured cash loans)
922190	Consumer product safety commissions
926110	Consumer protection offices
443112	Consumer-type electronic stores (e.g., radio, television, video camera)
334514	Consumption meters (e.g., gas, water) manufacturing
524128	Contact lens insurance, direct
339115	Contact lenses manufacturing
421460	Contact lenses wholesaling
335931	Contacts, electrical (except carbon and graphite), manufacturing
335991	Contacts, electrical, carbon and graphite, manufacturing
322130	Container board stock manufacturing
336611	Container ship building
484110	Container trucking services, local
484121	Container trucking services, long-distance
327213	Containers for packaging, bottling, and canning, glass, manufacturing
332439	Containers, air cargo, metal, manufacturing
332999	Containers, foil (except bags), manufacturing
421840	Containers, industrial, wholesaling
332439	Containers, light gauge metal (except cans), manufacturing
422130	Containers, paper and disposable plastics, wholesaling
321920	Containers, wood, manufacturing
712110	Contemporary art museums
711120	Contemporary dance companies
623311	Continuing care retirement communities
325412	Contraceptive preparations manufacturing
213112	Contract services for oil and gas fields
*****	Contractors — see specific activity
813910	Contractors' associations
315211	Contractors, men's and boys', cut and sew apparel

Code	Description
315212	Contractors, women's, girls' and infants', cut and sew apparel
325412	Contrast media in-vivo diagnostic substances (e.g., iodine, barium) manufacturing
335314	Control circuit devices, magnet and solid-state, manufacturing
335314	Control circuit relays, industrial, manufacturing
335314	Control equipment, electric, manufacturing
335313	Control panels, electric power distribution, manufacturing
335311	Control transformers manufacturing
332912	Control valves, fluid power, manufacturing
332911	Control valves, industrial-type, manufacturing
921130	Controller's and comptrollers' offices, government
334513	Controllers for process variables (e.g., electric, electronic, mechanical, pneumatic operation) manufacturing
334290	Controlling equipment, street light, manufacturing
335314	Controls and control accessories, industrial, manufacturing
335314	Controls for adjustable speed drives manufacturing
334514	Controls, revolution and timing instruments, manufacturing
623110	Convalescent homes or convalescent hospitals (except psychiatric)
623220	Convalescent homes or hospitals for psychiatric patients
446199	Convalescent supply stores
335221	Convection ovens (including portable), household-type, manufacturing
445120	Convenience food stores
447110	Convenience food with gasoline stations
335931	Convenience outlets, electric, manufacturing
561591	Convention and visitors bureaus
561591	Convention bureaus

Code	Description
531120	Convention center, no promotion of events, rental or leasing
561920	Convention managers
561920	Convention organizers
561920	Convention promoters
561920	Convention services
813110	Convents (except schools)
313311	Converters, broadwoven piece goods
335312	Converters, phase and rotary, electrical equipment, manufacturing
337121	Convertible sofas (except futons) manufacturing
336399	Convertible tops for automotive, truck, and bus, manufacturing
313311	Converting textiles, broadwoven
313312	Converting textiles, narrow woven
316110	Convertors, leather
313312	Convertors, narrow woven piece goods
421830	Conveying equipment (except farm) wholesaling
421820	Conveying equipment, farm, wholesaling
326220	Conveyor belts, rubber, manufacturing
235950	Conveyor system construction contractors
333922	Conveyors, farm-type, manufacturing
311612	Cooked meats made from purchased carcasses
311822	Cookie dough made from purchased flour
722213	Cookie shops, on premise baking and carryout service
311821	Cookies manufacturing
422490	Cookies wholesaling
311821	Cookies, filled, manufacturing
335211	Cooking appliances (except convection, microwave ovens), household-type electric portable, manufacturing
311320	Cooking chocolate made from cacao beans
333319	Cooking equipment (i.e., fryers, microwave ovens, ovens, ranges), commercial-type, manufacturing

Code	Description
421440	Cooking equipment, commercial, wholesaling
421620	Cooking equipment, electric household-type, wholesaling
421720	Cooking equipment, gas, household-type, wholesaling
422490	Cooking oils wholesaling
611519	Cooking schools
331511	Cooking utensils, cast iron, manufacturing
332214	Cooking utensils, fabricated metal, manufacturing
327212	Cooking utensils, glass and glass ceramic, made in glass making plants
421220	Cooking utensils, household-type, wholesaling
327112	Cooking ware (e.g., stoneware, coarse earthenware, pottery), manufacturing
327215	Cooking ware made from purchased glass
327212	Cooking ware made in glass making plants
327112	Cooking ware, china, manufacturing
327112	Cooking ware, fine earthenware, manufacturing
221330	Cooled air distribution
326199	Coolers or ice chests, plastics (except foam), manufacturing
326140	Coolers or ice chests, polystyrene foam, manufacturing
333415	Coolers, refrigeration, manufacturing
333415	Coolers, water, manufacturing
235910	Cooling tower construction contractors
333415	Cooling towers manufacturing
321920	Cooperage manufacturing
321920	Cooperage stock (e.g., heading, hoops, stoves) manufacturing
321920	Cooperage stock mills
421840	Cooperage stock wholesaling
531311	Cooperative apartment managers' offices
233220	Cooperative construction
812331	Cooperative hospital laundries (i.e., linen supply services)

Code	Description
524113	Cooperative life insurance organizations
813990	Cooperative owners' associations
321920	Coopered tubs manufacturing
332212	Coordinate and contour measuring machines, machinists' precision tools, manufacturing
532420	Copier rental or leasing
327123	Coping, wall, clay, manufacturing
327390	Copings, concrete, manufacturing
331525	Copper alloy castings (except die-castings), unfinished, manufacturing
331423	Copper alloys (e.g., brass, bronze) made from purchased metal or scrap
331411	Copper alloys made in primary copper smelting and refining mills
331423	Copper and copper-based shapes (e.g., cake, ingot, slag, wire bar) made from purchased metal or scrap
325131	Copper base pigments manufacturing
212234	Copper beneficiating plants
325188	Copper chloride manufacturing
325612	Copper cleaners manufacturing
325188	Copper compounds, not specified elsewhere by process, manufacturing
331411	Copper concentrate refining
331522	Copper die-casting foundries
331522	Copper die-castings, unfinished, manufacturing
331421	Copper foil made from purchased metal or scrap
332999	Copper foil not made in rolling mills
332112	Copper forgings made from purchased metals, unfinished
331525	Copper foundries (except die-casting)
325188	Copper iodide manufacturing
212234	Copper ore concentrates recovery
212234	Copper ore mine site development for own account
212234	Copper ores mining and/or beneficiating

Code	Description
331423	Copper powder, flakes, and paste made from purchased copper
331421	Copper products (except communication wire, energy wire) made by drawing purchased copper
331421	Copper products (except communication wire, energy wire) made by rolling, drawing, or extruding purchased copper
331421	Copper products (except communication wire, energy wire) made in integrated secondary smelting and extruding mills
331421	Copper products (except communication wire, energy wire) made in integrated secondary smelting mills and drawing plants
331423	Copper secondary smelting and alloying
331423	Copper secondary smelting and refining from purchased metal or scrap
331411	Copper shapes (e.g., bar, billet, ingot, plate, sheet) made in primary copper smelting and refining mills
331411	Copper smelting and refining, primary
235610	Copper smithing contractors, in connection with construction work
325188	Copper sulfate manufacturing
212234	Copper-water precipitates
561439	Copy centers (except combined with printing services)
561439	Copy shops (except combined with printing services)
421420	Copying machines wholesaling
314991	Cord (except tire, wire) manufacturing
335931	Cord connectors, electric, manufacturing
314992	Cord for reinforcing rubber tires, industrial belting, and fuel cells manufacturing
331422	Cord sets, flexible, made from purchased copper in wire drawing plants
331319	Cord sets, flexible, made in aluminum wire drawing plants

Code	Description
331491	Cord sets, flexible, nonferrous metals (except aluminum, copper), made from purchased nonferrous metals (except aluminum, copper) in wire drawing plants
314991	Cordage (except wire) manufacturing
333292	Cordage and rope (except wire) making machines manufacturing
421840	Cordage wholesaling
325920	Cordite explosive materials manufacturing
334210	Cordless telephones (except cellular) manufacturing
313221	Cords and braids, narrow woven, manufacturing
313210	Corduroys weaving
333994	Core baking and mold drying ovens manufacturing
213112	Core cutting in oil and gas wells, on a contract basis
213112	Core drilling, exploration services, oil and gas field
333131	Core drills, underground mining-type, manufacturing
322214	Cores (i.e., all-fiber, nonfiber ends of any material), fiber, made from purchased paperboard
332992	Cores, bullet (i.e., 30 mm. or less, 1.18 inch or less), manufacturing
332997	Cores, sand foundry, manufacturing
321999	Cork products (except gaskets) manufacturing
421840	Cork wholesaling
321999	Corks, bottle, manufacturing
111421	Corms farming
311230	Corn breakfast foods manufacturing
311919	Corn chips and related corn snacks manufacturing
422450	Corn chips and related corn snacks wholesaling
311340	Corn confections manufacturing
321992	Corn cribs, prefabricated, wood, manufacturing
311221	Corn dextrin manufacturing
115114	Corn drying

Code	Description
111150	Corn farming (except sweet corn), field and seed production
311211	Corn flour manufacturing
311221	Corn gluten feed manufacturing
311221	Corn gluten meal manufacturing
333111	Corn heads for combines manufacturing
311211	Corn meal made in flour mills
311221	Corn oil cake and meal manufacturing
311225	Corn oil made from purchased oils
311221	Corn oil mills
311221	Corn oil, crude and refined, made by wet milling corn
333111	Corn pickers and shellers manufacturing
335211	Corn poppers, household-type electric, manufacturing
333294	Corn popping machinery (i.e., food manufacturing-type) manufacturing
333319	Corn popping machines, commercial-type, manufacturing
339113	Corn remover and bunion pad manufacturing
115114	Corn shelling
311221	Corn starch manufacturing
311221	Corn sweeteners (e.g., dextrose, fructose, glucose) made by wet milling corn
311999	Corn syrups made from purchased sweeteners
311213	Corn, malt, manufacturing
339112	Corneal microscopes manufacturing
311612	Corned meats made from purchases carcasses
316999	Corners, luggage, leather, manufacturing
339992	Cornets and parts manufacturing
332322	Cornices, sheet metal, manufacturing
321918	Cornices, wood, manufacturing
112320	Cornish hen production
422490	Cornmeal, edible, wholesaling
212325	Cornwall stone mining and/or beneficiating
923120	Coroners' offices

Code	Description
813211	Corporate foundations, awarding grants
541430	Corporate identification (i.e., logo) design services
541110	Corporate law offices
551114	Corporate offices
115210	Corralling, drovers
332323	Corrals, metal, manufacturing
325998	Correction fluids (i.e., typewriter) manufacturing
922140	Correctional boot camps
561210	Correctional facility operation on a contract or fee basis
922140	Correctional institutions
322211	Corrugated and solid fiber boxes made from purchased paper or paperboard
322211	Corrugated and solid fiberboard pads made from purchased paper or paperboard
322211	Corrugated paper made from purchased paper or paperboard
331221	Corrugating iron or steel in cold rolling mills
315212	Corselets cut and sew apparel contractors
315231	Corselets, women's, misses', and girls', cut and sewn from purchased fabric (except apparel contractors)
315212	Corsets and allied garments (except surgical), women's, cut and sew apparel contractors
315231	Corsets and allied garments (except surgical), women's, misses', and girls', cut and sewn from purchased fabric (except apparel contractors)
339113	Corsets, surgical, manufacturing
325411	Cortisone, uncompounded, manufacturing
212399	Corundum mining and/or beneficiating
316993	Cosmetic bags (except metal) manufacturing
339911	Cosmetic bags, precious metal, manufacturing
325620	Cosmetic creams, lotions, and oils manufacturing

Code	Description
561910	Cosmetic kit assembling and packaging services
446120	Cosmetics stores
422210	Cosmetics wholesaling
812112	Cosmetology salons or shops
611511	Cosmetology schools
541490	Costume design services (except independent theatrical costume designers)
711510	Costume designers, independent theatrical
339914	Costume jewelry manufacturing
448150	Costume jewelry stores
421940	Costume jewelry wholesaling
532220	Costume rental
448190	Costume shops (including theatrical)
315299	Costumes (e.g., lodge, masquerade, theatrical) cut and sewn from purchased fabric (except apparel contractors)
315212	Costumes (e.g., lodge, masquerade, theatrical) women's, girls' and infants', cut and sew apparel contractors
315211	Costumes (e.g., lodge, masquerade, theatrical), men's and boys', cut and sew apparel contractors
337121	Cot springs, assembled, manufacturing
337124	Cots, metal household-type, manufacturing
337122	Cots, wood household-type, manufacturing
311511	Cottage cheese manufacturing
531110	Cottage rental or leasing
721199	Cottages, housekeeping
332722	Cotter pins, metal, manufacturing
422990	Cotton (except raw) wholesaling
339113	Cotton and cotton balls, absorbent, manufacturing
333111	Cotton balers and presses manufacturing
314999	Cotton battings (except nonwoven batting) manufacturing

Code	Description
313111	Cotton cordage spun yarns made from purchased fiber
313210	Cotton fabrics, broadwoven, weaving
313221	Cotton fabrics, narrow woven weaving
111920	Cotton farming, field and seed production
322121	Cotton fiber paper stock manufacturing
115111	Cotton ginning
333111	Cotton ginning machinery manufacturing
333111	Cotton picker and stripper harvesting machinery manufacturing
313111	Cotton spun yarns made from purchased fiber
313113	Cotton thread manufacturing
339113	Cotton tipped applicators manufacturing
115113	Cotton, machine harvesting
422590	Cotton, raw, wholesaling
111920	Cottonseed farming
311225	Cottonseed oil made from purchased oils
311223	Cottonseed oil, cake and meal, made in crushing mills
337121	Couch springs, assembled, manufacturing
337121	Couches, upholstered, manufacturing
311340	Cough drops (except medicated) manufacturing
325412	Cough drops, medicated, manufacturing
325412	Cough medicines manufacturing
334513	Coulometric analyzers, industrial process-type, manufacturing
334516	Coulometric analyzers, laboratory-type, manufacturing
325199	Coumarin manufacturing
325211	Coumarone-indene resins manufacturing
926110	Councils of Economic Advisers
624190	Counseling services

Code	Description
621410	Counseling services, family planning
541110	Counselors' at law offices
541110	Counselors' at law private practices
334519	Count rate meters, nuclear radiation, manufacturing
235990	Counter top construction contractors
334514	Counter type registers manufacturing
337215	Counter units (except refrigerated) manufacturing
333515	Counterbores (i.e., a machine tool accessory), metalworking, manufacturing
332212	Counterbores and countersinking bits, woodworking, manufacturing
334511	Countermeasure sets (e.g., active countermeasures, jamming equipment) manufacturing
334514	Counters (e.g., electrical, electronic, mechanical), totalizing, manufacturing
316999	Counters (i.e., shoe cut stock), leather, manufacturing
333415	Counters and display cases, refrigerated, manufacturing
334514	Counters, revolution, manufacturing
333515	Countersinks (i.e., a machine tool accessory) manufacturing
337215	Countertops (except kitchen and bathroom), wood or plastics laminated on wood, manufacturing
337110	Countertops (i.e., kitchen, bathroom), wood or plastics laminated on wood, manufacturing
326199	Countertops, plastics, manufacturing
327991	Countertops, stone, manufacturing
337110	Countertops, wood, manufacturing
334514	Counting devices manufacturing
713910	Country clubs
711130	Country musical artists, independent
711130	Country musical groups
921120	County commissioners
925120	County development agencies

Code	Description
923110	County supervisors of education (except school boards)
921110	County supervisors' and executives' offices
332919	Couplings, hose, metal (except fluid power), manufacturing
333613	Couplings, mechanical power transmission, manufacturing
332996	Couplings, pipe, made from purchased metal pipe
541870	Coupon direct distribution services
561990	Coupon redemption services (i.e., clearinghouse)
492110	Courier services (i.e., intercity network)
611410	Court reporting schools
561492	Court reporting services
922110	Courts of law, civilian (except American Indian or Alaska Native)
921150	Courts, American Indian or Alaska Native
922110	Courts, civilian (except American Indian or Alaska Native)
928110	Courts, military
922110	Courts, small claims
315211	Coveralls, work, men's and boys', cut and sew apparel contractors
315225	Coveralls, work, men's and boys', cut and sewn from purchased fabric (except apparel contractors)
315212	Coveralls, work, women's, girls', and infants', cut and sew apparel contractors
315239	Coveralls, work, women's, misses', and girls', cut and sewn from purchased fabric (except apparel contractors)
314912	Covers (e.g., boat, swimming pool, truck) made from purchased fabrics
332313	Covers, annealing, fabricated metal plate work, manufacturing
321999	Covers, bottle and demijohn, willow, rattan, and reed, manufacturing
332313	Covers, floating, fabricated metal plate work, manufacturing
111219	Cow pea (except dry) farming, field and seed production
332322	Cowls, sheet metal, manufacturing

Code	Description
111130	Cowpea farming, dry, field and seed production
332618	Crab traps made from purchased wire
114112	Crabbing
333294	Cracker making machinery manufacturing
311821	Crackers (e.g., graham, soda) manufacturing
333518	Cradle assembly machinery (i.e., wire making equipment) manufacturing
337122	Cradles, wood, manufacturing
339932	Craft and hobby kits and sets manufacturing
561920	Craft fair managers
561920	Craft fair organizers
561920	Craft fair promoters
421920	Craft kits wholesaling
451120	Craft supply stores (except needlecraft)
611513	Craft union apprenticeship training programs
111334	Cranberry farming
335314	Crane and hoist controls, including metal mill, manufacturing
532412	Crane rental or leasing without operator
421810	Cranes (except industrial) wholesaling
333120	Cranes, construction-type, manufacturing
333924	Cranes, industrial truck, manufacturing
421830	Cranes, industrial, wholesaling
421810	Cranes, mining, wholesaling
333923	Cranes, overhead traveling, manufacturing
325998	Crankcase additive preparations manufacturing
336312	Crankshaft assemblies, automotive and truck gasoline engine, manufacturing
333512	Crankshaft grinding machines manufacturing
321920	Crates (e.g., berry, butter, fruit, vegetable) made of wood, wirebound, manufacturing

Code	Description
488991	Crating goods for shipping
112512	Crawfish production, farm raising
114112	Crayfish fishing
339942	Crayons manufacturing
311511	Cream manufacturing
325199	Cream of tartar manufacturing
333111	Cream separators, farm-type, manufacturing
333294	Cream separators, industrial, manufacturing
422430	Cream stations wholesaling
422430	Cream wholesaling
311514	Cream, dried and powdered, manufacturing
311512	Creamery butter manufacturing
422430	Creamery products (except canned) wholesaling
422490	Creamery products, canned, wholesaling
313311	Crease resistant finishing of broadwoven fabric
313312	Crease resistant finishing of fabrics (except broadwoven)
561450	Credit agencies
323119	Credit and identification card imprinting, embossing, and encoding
326199	Credit and identification card stock, plastics, manufacturing
524126	Credit and other financial responsibility insurance carriers, direct
561450	Credit bureaus
522210	Credit card banks
522210	Credit card issuing
812990	Credit card notification services (i.e., lost or stolen card reporting)
522320	Credit card processing services
561450	Credit investigation services
524113	Credit life insurance carriers, direct
561450	Credit rating services
541990	Credit repair (i.e., counseling) services, consumer
561450	Credit reporting bureaus
522130	Credit unions
333999	Cremating ovens manufacturing

Code	Description
812220	Crematories (except combined with funeral homes)
111219	Crenshaw melon farming, field, bedding plant and seed production
325192	Creosote made by distillation of coal tar
325191	Creosote made by distillation of wood tar
321114	Creosoting of wood
322299	Crepe paper made from purchased paper
325211	Cresol resins manufacturing
325211	Cresol-furfural resins manufacturing
325192	Cresols made by distillation of coal tar
325192	Cresylic acids made from refined petroleum or natural gas
115115	Crew leaders, farm labor
315119	Crew socks knitting or knitting and finishing
337124	Cribs (i.e., baby beds), metal, manufacturing
337122	Cribs (i.e., baby beds), wood, manufacturing
112990	Cricket production
922120	Criminal investigation offices, government
922190	Criminal justice statistics centers, government
541110	Criminal law offices
111998	Crimson cloves seed farming
624190	Crisis intervention centers
114111	Croaker fishing
313111	Crochet spun yarns (e.g., cotton, manmade fiber, silk, wool) made from purchased fiber
314999	Crochet ware made from purchased materials
335211	Crock pots, household-type electric, manufacturing
327112	Crockery manufacturing
311812	Croissants, baking, made in commercial bakeries
115114	Crop cleaning
333111	Crop driers manufacturing
115112	Crop dusting

Code	Description
524126	Crop insurance carrier, direct
421820	Crop preparation machinery (e.g., cleaning, conditioning, drying) wholesaling
115112	Crop spraying
316999	Crops, riding, manufacturing
339920	Croquet sets manufacturing
713920	Cross country skiing facilities without accommodations
332911	Cross valves, industrial-type, manufacturing
321114	Crossties, treating
311812	Croutons and bread crumbs made in commercial bakeries
421840	Crowns and closures, metal, wholesaling
332115	Crowns, metal (e.g., bottle, can), stamping
327124	Crucibles, fire clay, manufacturing
327125	Crucibles, graphite, magnesite, chrome, silica, or other nonclay materials, manufacturing
311221	Crude corn oil manufacturing
486110	Crude oil pipeline transportation
324110	Crude oil refining
422710	Crude oil terminals
422720	Crude oil wholesaling (except bulk stations, terminals)
211111	Crude petroleum from oil sand
211111	Crude petroleum from oil shale
211111	Crude petroleum production
324110	Crude petroleum refineries
422990	Crude rubber wholesaling
336322	Cruise control mechanisms, electronic, automotive, truck, and bus, manufacturing
483114	Cruise lines (i.e., deep sea passenger transportation to and from domestic ports)
483112	Cruise lines (i.e., deep sea passenger transportation to or from foreign ports)
561599	Cruise ship ticket offices
713210	Cruises, gambling
115310	Cruising timber
311812	Crullers (except frozen) made in commercial bakeries
311813	Crullers, frozen, made in a commercial bakery
421320	Crushed stone wholesaling
333120	Crushing machinery, portable, manufacturing
333131	Crushing machinery, stationary, manufacturing
212111	Crushing plants, bituminous coal
333120	Crushing, pulverizing, and screening machinery, portable, manufacturing
112512	Crustacean production, farm raising
339113	Crutches and walkers manufacturing
421450	Crutches wholesaling
532291	Crutches, invalid, rental
332420	Cryogenic tanks manufacturing
212399	Cryolite mining and/or beneficiating
311340	Crystallized fruits and fruit peel manufacturing
334419	Crystals and crystal assemblies, electronic, manufacturing
335313	Cubicles (i.e., electric switchboard equipment) manufacturing
111219	Cucumber farming (except under cover), field, bedding plant and seed production
111419	Cucumber farming, grown under cover
339993	Cuff links (except precious) manufacturing
339911	Cuff links, precious metal, manufacturing
332999	Cuffs, leg, iron, manufacturing
611519	Culinary arts schools
112310	Cull hen production
212113	Culm bank recovery, anthracite (except on a contract basis)
213113	Culm bank recovery, anthracite, on a contract basis
212111	Culm bank recovery, bituminous coal or lignite (except on a contract basis)
213113	Culm bank recovery, coal, on a contract basis
315212	Culottes, women's, girls' and infants', cut and sew apparel contractors
315239	Culottes, women's, misses', and girls', cut and sewn from purchased fabric (except apparel contractors)
111422	Cultivated florist greens growing
421820	Cultivating machinery and equipment wholesaling
115112	Cultivation services
333111	Cultivators, farm-type, manufacturing
333112	Cultivators, powered, lawn and garden-type, manufacturing
926110	Cultural and arts development support program administration
325414	Culture media manufacturing
326191	Cultured marble plumbing fixtures manufacturing
326199	Cultured marble products (except plumbing fixtures) manufacturing
112512	Cultured pearl production, farm raising
326199	Cultured stone products (except plumbing fixtures) manufacturing
234910	Culvert construction
235710	Culvert construction contractors
327332	Culvert pipe, concrete, manufacturing
332313	Culverts, fabricated metal plate work, manufacturing
332322	Culverts, sheet metal, manufacturing
325110	Cumene made from refined petroleum or liquid hydrocarbons
324110	Cumene made in petroleum refineries
315999	Cummerbunds cut and sewn from purchased fabric (except apparel contractors)
315211	Cummerbunds, men's and boys', cut and sew apparel contractors
332313	Cupolas, fabricated metal plate work, manufacturing
212234	Cuprite mining and/or beneficiating
322299	Cups, molded pulp, manufacturing
422130	Cups, paper and disposable plastics, wholesaling
421220	Cups, plastics (except disposable), wholesaling

Code	Description
326199	Cups, plastics (except foam), manufacturing
326140	Cups, polystyrene foam, manufacturing
235710	Curb construction contractors
327991	Curbing, granite and stone, manufacturing
234110	Curbs and street gutter construction
311513	Curds, cheese, made in a cheese plant, manufacturing
422460	Cured fish wholesaling
311611	Cured hides and skins produced in slaughtering plants
311612	Cured meats (e.g., brined, dried, and salted) made from purchased carcasses
333111	Curers, tobacco, manufacturing
311711	Curing fish and seafood
453220	Curio shops
422990	Curios wholesaling
326299	Curlers, hair, rubber, manufacturing
713990	Curling facilities
335211	Curling irons, household-type electric, manufacturing
111334	Currant farming
333313	Currency counting machinery manufacturing
421420	Currency handling machines wholesaling
335311	Current limiting reactors, electrical, manufacturing
334515	Current measuring equipment manufacturing
335931	Current taps, attachment plug and screw shell types, manufacturing
421610	Current-carrying wiring devices wholesaling
316110	Currying furs
316110	Currying leather
442291	Curtain and drapery stores, packaged
812320	Curtain cleaning services
337920	Curtain or drapery fixtures (e.g., poles, rods, rollers) manufacturing
337920	Curtain rods and fittings manufacturing
321999	Curtain stretchers, wood, manufacturing
235910	Curtain wall construction contractors
332321	Curtain wall, metal, manufacturing
313210	Curtains and draperies made in broadwoven fabric mills
314121	Curtains and draperies, window, made from purchased fabrics
313249	Curtains made in lace mills
313249	Curtains made in warp knitting mills
313241	Curtains made in weft knitting mills
421220	Curtains wholesaling
337121	Cushion springs, assembled, manufacturing
314129	Cushions (except carpet, springs) made from purchased fabrics
326150	Cushions, carpet and rug, urethane and other foam plastics (except polystrene), manufacturing
311520	Custard, frozen, manufacturing
561720	Custodial services
337212	Custom architectural millwork and fixtures, manufacturing on a job shop basis
233310	Custom buildings, industrial, construction
233220	Custom buildings, residential (except single family), general construction contractors
233210	Custom built house construction
325991	Custom compounding (i.e., blending and mixing) of purchased plastics resins
337212	Custom design interiors (i.e., coordinated furniture, architectural woodwork, fixtures), manufacturing
115114	Custom feed mixing and grinding
311119	Custom milling of animal feed
442299	Custom picture frame shops
333513	Custom roll forming machines, metalworking, manufacturing
332114	Custom roll forming metal products
321113	Custom sawmills
311611	Custom slaughtering
315223	Custom tailors, men's and boys' dress shirts, cut and sewn from purchased fabric
315222	Custom tailors, men's and boys' suits, cut and sewn from purchased fabric
315233	Custom tailors, women's, misses' and girls' dresses cut and sewn from purchased fabric (except apparel contractors)
541613	Customer service management consulting services
488510	Customs brokers
921130	Customs bureaus
541614	Customs consulting services
327215	Cut and engraved glassware made from purchased glass
315211	Cut and sew apparel contractors, men's and boys'
315212	Cut and sew apparel contractors, women's, girls', and infants'
111422	Cut flower growing
111422	Cut rose growing
316999	Cut stock for boots and shoes manufacturing
321912	Cut stock manufacturing
327991	Cut stone bases (e.g., desk sets pedestals, lamps, plaques and similar small particles) manufacturing
327991	Cut stone products (e.g., blocks, statuary) manufacturing
333512	Cut-off machines, metalworking, manufacturing
811490	Cutlery (e.g., knives, scissors) sharpening, household-type
421710	Cutlery wholesaling
332211	Cutlery, nonprecious and precious plated metal, manufacturing
339912	Cutlery, precious (except precious plated) metal, manufacturing
335931	Cutouts, switch and fuse, manufacturing
333131	Cutters, coal, manufacturing
332212	Cutters, glass, manufacturing
333515	Cutters, metal milling, manufacturing
113310	Cutting and transporting timber
213112	Cutting cores in oil and gas wells on a contract basis

Code	Description
332212	Cutting dies (e.g., paper, leather, textile) manufacturing
332212	Cutting dies (except metal cutting) manufacturing
333514	Cutting dies, metalworking, manufacturing
315211	Cutting fabric owned by others for men's and boys' apparel
315212	Cutting fabric owned by others for women's, girls', and infants' apparel
339114	Cutting instruments, dental, manufacturing
333512	Cutting machines, metalworking, manufacturing
316110	Cutting of leather
422470	Cutting of purchased carcasses (except boxed meat cut on an assembly-line basis) wholesaling
324191	Cutting oils made from refined petroleum
325998	Cutting oils, synthetic, manufacturing
234990	Cutting right-of-way
113310	Cutting timber
327215	Cutting, engraving, etching, painting or polishing purchased glass
111422	Cuttings farming
325188	Cyanides manufacturing
212325	Cyanite mining and/or beneficiating
211112	Cycle condensate production
325110	Cyclic aromatic hydrocarbons made from refined petroleum or liquid hydrocarbons
324110	Cyclic aromatic hydrocarbons made in petroleum refineries
422690	Cyclic crudes and intermediates wholesaling
325192	Cyclic crudes made by distillation of coal tar
325212	Cyclo rubber, synthetic, manufacturing
325192	Cyclohexane manufacturing
332313	Cyclones, industrial, fabricated metal plate work, manufacturing
325192	Cyclopentane made from refined petroleum or natural gas

Code	Description
325192	Cyclopropane made from refined petroleum or natural gas
325412	Cyclopropane medicinal preparations manufacturing
325191	Cycloterpenes manufacturing
335999	Cyclotrons manufacturing
333512	Cylinder boring machines manufacturing
336312	Cylinder heads, automotive and truck gasoline engine, manufacturing
327332	Cylinder pipe, prestressed concrete, manufacturing
332618	Cylinder wire cloth made from purchased wire
332994	Cylinders and clips, gun (i.e., 30 mm. or less, 1.18 inch or less), manufacturing
332995	Cylinders and clips, gun (i.e., more than 30 mm., more than 1.18 inch), manufacturing
333995	Cylinders, fluid power, manufacturing
336340	Cylinders, master brake (new and rebuilt), manufacturing
332420	Cylinders, pressure, manufacturing
334417	Cylindrical connectors, electronic, manufacturing
332991	Cylindrical roller bearings manufacturing
339992	Cymbals and parts manufacturing
339112	Cystoscopes (except electromedical) manufacturing
334510	Cystoscopes, electromedical, manufacturing
325413	Cytology and histology in-vitro diagnostic substances manufacturing
621511	Cytology health laboratories
621310	DCs' (doctors of chiropractic) offices (e.g., centers, clinics)
621210	DDSs' (doctors of dental surgery) offices (e.g., centers, clinics)
325320	DDT (dichlorodiphenyltrichloroethane) insecticides manufacturing
922120	DEA (Drug Enforcement Administration)

Code	Description
621210	DMDs' (doctors of dental medicine) offices (e.g., centers, clinics)
621112	DOs' (doctors of osteopathy), mental health, offices (e.g., centers, clinics)
621111	DOs' (doctors of osteopathy, except mental health) offices (e.g., centers, clinics)
621391	DPs' (doctors of podiatry) offices (e.g., centers, clinics)
334310	DVD (digital video disc) players manufacturing
112120	Dairy cattle farming
311119	Dairy cattle feeds supplements, concentrates, and premixes, manufacturing
422430	Dairy depots wholesaling
311514	Dairy food canning
112420	Dairy goat farming
112111	Dairy heifer replacement production
541690	Dairy herd consulting services
115210	Dairy herd improvement associations
445299	Dairy product stores
422430	Dairy products (except canned, dried) wholesaling
422490	Dairy products, dried or canned, wholesaling
422430	Dairy products, frozen, wholesaling
112410	Dairy sheep farming
332312	Dam gates, metal plate, manufacturing
234990	Dam, dike, and dock construction
334512	Damper operators (e.g., electric, pneumatic, thermostatic) manufacturing
332322	Dampers, sheet metal, manufacturing
235990	Dampproofing, building, construction contractors
711130	Dance bands
713940	Dance centers, aerobic
711120	Dance companies
711310	Dance festival managers with facilities
711320	Dance festival managers without facilities

Code	Description
711310	Dance festival organizers with facilities
711320	Dance festival organizers without facilities
711310	Dance festival promoters with facilities
711320	Dance festival promoters without facilities
531120	Dance hall rental or leasing
713990	Dance halls
611610	Dance instruction
711120	Dance productions, live theatrical
611610	Dance schools
611610	Dance studios
711120	Dance theaters
621340	Dance therapists' offices (e.g., centers, clinics)
711120	Dance troupes
711510	Dancers, independent
313113	Darning thread (e.g., cotton, manmade fibers, silk, wool) manufacturing
332994	Dart guns manufacturing
339932	Darts and dart games manufacturing
334210	Data communications equipment (e.g., bridges, gateways, routers) manufacturing
514210	Data entry services
334513	Data loggers, industrial process-type, manufacturing
514210	Data processing computer services
541513	Data processing facilities (i.e., clients' facilities) management and operation services
421430	Data processing machines, computer, wholesaling
514210	Data processing services (except payroll services, financial transition processing services)
511140	Database and directory publishers
511140	Database and directory publishers and printing combined
511140	Database and directory publishing (i.e., establishments known as publishers)
511140	Database publishers

Code	Description
511140	Database publishers and printing combined
511140	Database publishing (i.e., establishments known as publishers)
323112	Databases flexographic printing without publishing
323111	Databases gravure printing without publishing
323110	Databases lithographic (offset) printing without publishing
323119	Databases printing (except flexographic, gravure, lithographic, screen) without publishing
323113	Databases screen printing without publishing
111339	Date farming
339943	Date stamps, hand operated, manufacturing
311423	Dates, dried, made in dehydration plant
311340	Dates, sugared and stuffed, manufacturing
334518	Dating devices and machines (except rubber stamps) manufacturing
812990	Dating services
333923	Davits manufacturing
*****	Day camps, instructional — see type of instruction
624120	Day care centers for disabled persons, the elderly, and persons diagnosed with mental retardation
624120	Day care centers, adult
624410	Day care centers, child or infant
624410	Day care services, child or infant
332510	Dead bolts manufacturing
*****	Dealers — see type
561440	Debt collection services
333512	Deburring machines, metalworking, manufacturing
334515	Decade boxes (i.e., capacitance, inductance, resistance) manufacturing
325199	Decahydronaphthalene manufacturing
327112	Decalcomania on china and glass for the trade

Code	Description
339999	Decalcomania work (except on china, glass)
327215	Decorated glassware made from purchased glass
327112	Decorating china (e.g., encrusting gold, silver, other metal on china) for the trade
541410	Decorating consulting services, interior
335129	Decorative area lighting fixtures (except residential) manufacturing
335121	Decorative area lighting fixtures, residential, manufacturing
712110	Decorative art museums
327212	Decorative glassware made in glass making plants
335110	Decorative lamp bulbs manufacturing
315211	Decorative stitching contractors on men's and boys' apparel
315212	Decorative stitching contractors on women's, misses', girls', and infants' apparel
314999	Decorative stitching on textile articles and apparel
321918	Decorative wood moldings (e.g., base, chair rail, crown, shoe) manufacturing
115114	Decorticating flax
483113	Deep sea freight transportation to or from domestic ports
483111	Deep sea freight transportation to or from foreign ports
483114	Deep sea passenger transportation to and from domestic ports
483112	Deep sea passenger transportation to or from foreign ports
333319	Deep-fat fryers, commercial-type, manufacturing
335211	Deep-fat fryers, household-type electric, manufacturing
112990	Deer production
334510	Defibrilators manufacturing
325312	Defluorinated phosphates manufacturing
325998	Defoamers and antifoaming agents manufacturing
325320	Defoliants manufacturing

Code	Description
325998	Degreasing preparations for machinery parts manufacturing
325612	Degreasing preparations, household-type, manufacturing
333415	Dehumidifiers (except portable electric) manufacturing
335211	Dehumidifiers, portable electric, manufacturing
311514	Dehydrated milk manufacturing
311423	Dehydrating fruits and vegetables
311423	Dehydrating potato products (e.g., flakes, granules)
325998	Deicing preparations manufacturing
322110	Deinking plants
322110	Deinking recovered paper
722211	Delicatessen restaurants
333997	Delicatessen scales manufacturing
445210	Delicatessens (except grocery store, restaurants)
445110	Delicatessens primarily retailing a range of grocery items and meats
561440	Delinquent account collection services
623990	Delinquent youth halfway group homes
115114	Delinting cottonseed
332618	Delivery cases made from purchased wire
492210	Delivery service (except as part of intercity carrier network, U.S. Postal Service)
334515	Demand meters, electric, manufacturing
541720	Demographic research and development services
235940	Demolition of buildings or other structures construction contractors
541890	Demonstration services, merchandise
336212	Demountable cargo containers manufacturing
325193	Denatured alcohol manufacturing
313210	Denims weaving
321219	Densified wood manufacturing
333315	Densitometers (except laboratory analytical) manufacturing
334516	Densitometers, laboratory analytical, manufacturing

Code	Description
334513	Density and specific gravity instruments, industrial process-type, manufacturing
621512	Dental X-ray laboratories
339114	Dental alloys for amalgams manufacturing
339114	Dental chairs manufacturing
421450	Dental chairs wholesaling
339114	Dental equipment and instruments manufacturing
421450	Dental equipment and supplies wholesaling
811219	Dental equipment repair and maintenance services
325620	Dental floss manufacturing
339114	Dental glues and cements manufacturing
339114	Dental hand instruments (e.g., forceps) manufacturing
611519	Dental hygienist schools
621399	Dental hygienists' offices (e.g., centers, clinics)
339114	Dental impression materials manufacturing
339114	Dental instrument delivery systems manufacturing
524114	Dental insurance carriers, direct
339116	Dental laboratories
339114	Dental laboratory equipment manufacturing
541710	Dental research and development laboratories or services
611310	Dental schools
621210	Dental surgeons' offices (e.g., centers, clinics)
611519	Dental technician schools
339114	Dental wax manufacturing
325611	Dentifrices manufacturing
422210	Dentifrices wholesaling
813920	Dentists' associations
621210	Dentists' offices (e.g., centers, clinics)
421450	Dentists' professional supplies wholesaling
325620	Denture adhesives manufacturing
325620	Denture cleaners, effervescent, manufacturing

Code	Description
339114	Denture materials manufacturing
339116	Dentures, custom made in dental laboratories
621399	Denturists' offices (e.g., centers, clinics)
561720	Deodorant servicing of rest rooms
325612	Deodorants (except personal) manufacturing
422690	Deodorants (except personal) wholesaling
325620	Deodorants, personal, manufacturing
422210	Deodorants, personal, wholesaling
561720	Deodorizing services
452110	Department stores
812199	Depilatory (i.e., hair removal) salons
325620	Depilatory preparations manufacturing
332813	Depolishing metals and metal products for the trade
524128	Deposit or share insurance carriers, direct
522110	Depository trust companies
339113	Depressors, tongue, manufacturing
332995	Depth charge projectors manufacturing
332993	Depth charges manufacturing
325412	Dermatological preparations manufacturing
621111	Dermatologists' offices (e.g., centers, clinics)
213112	Derrick building, repairing, and dismantling at oil and gas fields on a contract basis
333132	Derricks, oil and gas field-type, manufacturing
325998	Desalination kits manufacturing
327992	Desiccants, activated clay, manufacturing
233320	Designing and erecting combined, commercial, general construction contractors
233310	Designing and erecting combined, industrial, general construction contractors

Code	Description
233220	Designing and erecting combined, residential (except single family housing), general construction contractors
233210	Designing and erecting combined, single family housing, general construction contractors
335211	Desk fans, electric, manufacturing
335122	Desk lamps, commercial, electric, manufacturing
335121	Desk lamps, residential, electric, manufacturing
316999	Desk sets, leather, manufacturing
337214	Desks (except wood), office-type, manufacturing
337122	Desks, wood household-type, manufacturing
337211	Desks, wood office-type, manufacturing
561410	Desktop publishing services
422430	Desserts, dairy, wholesaling
311520	Desserts, frozen (except bakery), manufacturing
311813	Desserts, frozen bakery, manufacturing
811192	Detailing services (i.e., cleaning and polishing), automotive
115112	Detasseling corn
561611	Detective agencies
334519	Detectors, scintillation, manufacturing
922140	Detention centers
325611	Detergents (e.g., dishwashing, industrial, laundry) manufacturing
422690	Detergents wholesaling
331492	Detinning scrap (e.g., cans)
325920	Detonating caps, cord, fuses, and primers manufacturing
325920	Detonators (except ammunition) manufacturing
332993	Detonators, ammunition (i.e., more than 30 mm., more than 1.18 inch), manufacturing
621420	Detoxification centers and clinics (except hospitals), outpatient
622210	Detoxification hospitals
325188	Deuterium oxide (i.e., heavy water) manufacturing

Code	Description
325992	Developers, prepared photographic, manufacturing
336411	Developing and producing prototypes for aircraft
336412	Developing and producing prototypes for aircraft engines and engine parts
336413	Developing and producing prototypes for aircraft parts (except engines) and auxiliary equipment
336414	Developing and producing prototypes for complete guided missiles and space vehicles
336419	Developing and producing prototypes for guided missile and space vehicle components
336415	Developing and producing prototypes for guided missile and space vehicle engines
333315	Developing equipment, film, manufacturing
926110	Development assistance program administration
813311	Developmentally disabled advocacy organizations
235990	Dewatering construction contractors
111334	Dewberry farming
325520	Dextrin glues manufacturing
311221	Dextrin made by wet milling corn
212319	Diabase crushed and broken stone mining and/or beneficiating
212311	Diabase mining or quarrying
325412	Diagnostic biological preparations (except in-vitro) manufacturing
811198	Diagnostic centers without repair, automotive
334510	Diagnostic equipment, MRI (magnetic resonance imaging), manufacturing
334510	Diagnostic equipment, electromedical, manufacturing
421450	Diagnostic equipment, medical, wholesaling
621512	Diagnostic imaging centers (medical)
811219	Diagnostic imaging equipment repair and maintenance services
422210	Diagnostic reagents wholesaling

Code	Description
325413	Diagnostic substances, in-vitro, manufacturing
422210	Diagnostics, in-vitro and in-vivo, wholesaling
332212	Dial indicators, machinists' precision tools, manufacturing
621492	Dialysis centers and clinics
334510	Dialysis equipment, electromedical, manufacturing
325312	Diammonium phosphates manufacturing
332618	Diamond cloths made from purchased wire
339913	Diamond cutting and polishing
333514	Diamond dies, metalworking, manufacturing
327910	Diamond dressing wheels manufacturing
421940	Diamonds (except industrial) wholesaling
212399	Diamonds, industrial, mining and/or beneficiating
421840	Diamonds, industrial, wholesaling
315212	Diaper covers, water resistant and waterproof, cut and sew apparel contractors
315291	Diaper covers, waterproof, infants', cut and sewn from purchased fabric (except apparel contractors)
812331	Diaper supply services
314999	Diapers (except disposable) made from purchased fabrics
422330	Diapers (except paper) wholesaling
322291	Diapers, disposable, made from purchased paper or textile fiber
322121	Diapers, disposable, made in paper mills
422130	Diapers, paper, wholesaling
326299	Diaphragms (i.e., birth control device), rubber, manufacturing
323118	Diaries manufacturing
511199	Diary and time scheduler publishers
212325	Diaspore mining and/or beneficiating
334510	Diathermy apparatus, electromedical, manufacturing
334510	Diathermy units manufacturing
212399	Diatomaceous earth mining and/or beneficitating

Code	Description
327992	Diatomaceous earth processing beyond beneficiation
212399	Diatomite mining and/or beneficiating
325992	Diazo (i.e., whiteprint) paper and cloth, sensitized, manufacturing
325120	Dichlorodifluoromethane manufacturing
325188	Dichromates manufacturing
315212	Dickeys, women's, girls', and infants', cut and sew apparel contractors
315239	Dickeys, women's, misses' and girls', cut and sewn from purchased fabric (except apparel contractors)
333313	Dictating machines manufacturing
421420	Dictating machines wholesaling
561410	Dictation services
323117	Dictionaries printing and binding without publishing
323117	Dictionaries printing without publishing
323121	Dictionary binding without printing
511130	Dictionary publishers
511130	Dictionary publishers and printing combined
511130	Dictionary publishing (i.e., establishments known as publishers)
325211	Dicyandiamine resins manufacturing
333514	Die sets for metal stamping presses manufacturing
333512	Die sinking machines, metalworking, manufacturing
333511	Die-casting dies manufacturing
333513	Die-casting machines, metalworking, manufacturing
331521	Die-castings, aluminum, unfinished, manufacturing
331522	Die-castings, nonferrous metals (except aluminum), unfinished, manufacturing
322299	Die-cut paper products (except for office use) made from purchased paper or paperboard
322231	Die-cut paper products for office use made from purchased paper or paperboard

Code	Description
333994	Dielectric industrial heating equipment manufacturing
333514	Dies and die holders for metal cutting and forming (except threading) manufacturing
333515	Dies and taps (i.e., a machine tool accessory) manufacturing
332212	Dies, cutting (except metal cutting), manufacturing
333514	Dies, metalworking (except threading), manufacturing
333514	Dies, plastics forming, manufacturing
332212	Dies, steel rule (except metal cutting), manufacturing
333514	Dies, steel rule, metal cutting, manufacturing
333618	Diesel and semidiesel engines manufacturing
324110	Diesel fuels manufacturing
812191	Diet centers, non-medical
812191	Diet workshops
311514	Dietary drinks, dairy and nondairy based, manufacturing
325192	Diethylcyclohexane manufacturing
325199	Diethylene glycol manufacturing
621399	Dieticians' offices (e.g., centers, clinics)
813920	Dietitians' associations
336350	Differential and rear axle assemblies, automotive, truck, and bus, manufacturing
334513	Differential pressure instruments, industrial process-type, manufacturing
334516	Differential thermal analysis instruments, laboratory-type, manufacturing
332420	Digesters, industrial-type, manufacturing
325412	Digestive system preparations manufacturing
334119	Digital cameras manufacturing
334111	Digital computers manufacturing
334513	Digital displays of process variables manufacturing
334515	Digital panel meters, electricity measuring, manufacturing

Code	Description
323115	Digital printing (e.g., billboards, other large format graphic materials)
323115	Digital printing (e.g., graphics, high resolution)
333293	Digital printing presses manufacturing
334515	Digital test equipment (e.g., electronic and electrical circuits and equipment testing) manufacturing
334310	Digital video disc players manufacturing
325412	Digitalis medicinal preparations manufacturing
325411	Digitoxin, uncompounded, manufacturing
325211	Diisocyanate resins manufacturing
111219	Dill farming, field and seed production
321113	Dimension lumber, hardwood, made from logs or bolts
321912	Dimension lumber, hardwood, resawing purchased lumber
321113	Dimension lumber, made from logs or bolts
321912	Dimension lumber, resawing purchased lumber
321113	Dimension lumber, softwood, made from logs or bolts
321912	Dimension lumber, softwood, resawing purchased lumber
321912	Dimension stock, hardwood, manufacturing
321912	Dimension stock, softwood, manufacturing
321912	Dimension stock, wood, manufacturing
327991	Dimension stone dressing and manufacturing
327991	Dimension stone for buildings manufacturing
212311	Dimension stone mining or quarrying
325199	Dimethyl divinyl acetylene (di-isopropenyl acetylene) manufacturing
325199	Dimethylhydrazine manufacturing
335931	Dimmer switches, outlet box mounting-type, manufacturing

Code	Description
722110	Diners, full service
337124	Dinette sets, metal household-type, manufacturing
326299	Dinghies, inflatable rubber, manufacturing
336612	Dinghy (except inflatable rubber) manufacturing
337124	Dining room chairs (including upholstered), metal, manufacturing
337125	Dining room chairs (including upholstered), plastics manufacturing
337122	Dining room chairs (including upholstered), wood, manufacturing
337124	Dining room furniture, metal household-type, manufacturing
337122	Dining room furniture, wood household-type, manufacturing
487210	Dinner cruises
711110	Dinner theaters
311412	Dinners, frozen (except seafood-based), manufacturing
311712	Dinners, frozen seafood, manufacturing
422420	Dinners, frozen, wholesaling
326199	Dinnerware, plastics (except polystyrene foam), manufacturing
326140	Dinnerware, polystyrene foam, manufacturing
334515	Diode and transistor testers manufacturing
421690	Diodes wholesaling
334413	Diodes, solid-state (e.g., germanium, silicon), manufacturing
212313	Diorite crushed and broken stone mining and/or beneficiating
212311	Diorite mining or quarrying
325192	Diphenylamine manufacturing
928120	Diplomatic services
311941	Dips (except cheese and sour cream based) manufacturing
325320	Dips (i.e., pesticides), cattle and sheep, manufacturing
311513	Dips, cheese based, manufacturing
311511	Dips, sour cream based, manufacturing
334112	Direct access storage devices manufacturing

Code	Description
513220	Direct broadcast satellite (DBS)
325132	Direct dyes manufacturing
541860	Direct mail advertising services
541860	Direct mail or other direct distribution advertising campaign services
454110	Direct mailers (i.e., selling own merchandise)
331111	Direct reduction of iron ore
454390	Direct selling of merchandise (door-to-door)
513220	Direct-to-home satellite systems
213111	Directional drilling of oil and gas wells on a contract basis
812210	Director services, funeral
323112	Directories flexographic printing without publishing
323111	Directories gravure printing without publishing
323110	Directories lithographic (offset) printing without publishing
323119	Directories printing (except flexographic, gravure, lithographic, screen) without publishing
323113	Directories screen printing without publishing
711510	Directors (i.e., film, motion picture, music, theatrical), independent
711510	Directors, independent motion picture
711510	Directors, independent music
511140	Directory and database publishers
511140	Directory compilers
511140	Directory publishers
511140	Directory publishers and printing combined
511140	Directory publishing (i.e., establishments known as publishers)
541870	Directory, telephone, distribution on a contract basis
524113	Disability insurance carriers, direct
524113	Disability insurance underwriting, direct
624120	Disability support groups
623990	Disabled group homes without nursing care

Code	Description
922190	Disaster preparedness and management offices, government
624230	Disaster relief services
711510	Disc jockeys, independent
623990	Disciplinary camps for delinquent youth
713990	Discotheques (except those serving alcoholic beverages)
812990	Discount buying services
511199	Discount coupon book publishers
511199	Discount coupon book publishers and printing combined
511199	Discount coupon book publishing (i.e., establishments known as publishers)
323112	Discount coupon books flexographic printing without publishing
323111	Discount coupon books gravure printing without publishing
323110	Discount coupon books lithographic (offset) printing without publishing
323119	Discount coupon books printing (except flexographic, gravure, lithographic, screen) without publishing
323113	Discount coupon books screen printing without publishing
452110	Discount department stores
813212	Disease awareness fundraising organizations
115112	Disease control for crops
813212	Disease research (e.g., cancer, heart) fundraising organizations
541940	Disease testing services, veterinary
313249	Dishcloths made in warp knitting mills
313241	Dishcloths made in weft knitting mills
421220	Dishes, household-type (except disposable plastics, paper), wholesaling
422130	Dishes, paper and disposable plastics, wholesaling
327112	Dishes, pottery, manufacturing
339932	Dishes, toy, manufacturing
321999	Dishes, wood, manufacturing
325611	Dishwasher detergents manufacturing

Code	Description
335228	Dishwashers, household-type, manufacturing
421620	Dishwashers, household-type, wholesaling
421440	Dishwashing equipment, commercial-type, wholesaling
333319	Dishwashing machines, commercial-type, manufacturing
335228	Dishwashing machines, household-type, manufacturing
325612	Disinfectants, household-type and industrial, manufacturing
514210	Disk and diskette conversion services
514210	Disk and diskette recertification services
332611	Disk and ring springs, heavy gauge, manufacturing
334112	Disk drives, computer, manufacturing
421430	Disk drives, computer, wholesaling
334613	Diskettes, blank, manufacturing
421690	Diskettes, blank, wholesaling
235950	Dismantling of machinery and other industrial equipment construction contractors
213112	Dismantling of oil well rigs on a contract basis
235940	Dismantling steel oil tanks (except oil field work) construction contractors
333913	Dispensing and measuring pumps (e.g., gasoline, lubricants) manufacturing
325132	Disperse dyes manufacturing
325510	Dispersions, pigment, manufacturing
541850	Display advertising services
421440	Display cases (except refrigerated) wholesaling
337215	Display cases and fixtures (except refrigerated) manufacturing
333415	Display cases, refrigerated, manufacturing
421740	Display cases, refrigerated, wholesaling
321999	Display forms for boots and shoes, all materials, manufacturing

Code	Description
334513	Display instruments, industrial process control-type, manufacturing
541890	Display lettering services
339950	Displays (e.g., counter, floor, point-of-purchase) manufacturing
335912	Disposable flashlight batteries manufacturing
422130	Disposable plastics products (e.g., boxes, cups, cutlery, dishes, sanitary food containers) wholesaling
334511	Distance measuring equipment (DME), aeronautical, manufacturing
325191	Distillates, wood, manufacturing
333994	Distillation ovens, charcoal and coke, manufacturing
422820	Distilled alcoholic beverages wholesaling
325998	Distilled water manufacturing
311213	Distiller's malt manufacturing
312140	Distilleries
421830	Distillery machinery wholesaling
312140	Distilling alcoholic beverages (except brandy)
312130	Distilling brandy
333298	Distilling equipment (except beverage) manufacturing
333294	Distilling equipment, beverage, manufacturing
312140	Distilling potable liquor (except brandy)
334515	Distortion meters and analyzers manufacturing
335313	Distribution boards, electric, manufacturing
335313	Distribution cutouts manufacturing
421610	Distribution equipment, electrical, wholesaling
234910	Distribution line construction, oil and gas fields
221330	Distribution of cooled air
221122	Distribution of electric power
221330	Distribution of heated air
221210	Distribution of manufactured gas
221210	Distribution of natural gas
221330	Distribution of steam heat
335311	Distribution transformers, electric, manufacturing

Code	Description
336322	Distributor cap and rotor for internal combustion engines manufacturing
336322	Distributors for internal combustion engines manufacturing
813910	Distributors' associations
551114	District and regional offices
922130	District attorneys' offices
333120	Ditchers and trenchers, self-propelled, manufacturing
325412	Diuretic preparations manufacturing
332212	Dividers, machinists' precision tools, manufacturing
451110	Diving equipment stores
561990	Diving services on a contract or fee basis
531120	Dock and associated building rental or leasing
488330	Docking and undocking marine vessel services
488310	Docking facility operations
621310	Doctors of chiropractic (DCs) offices (e.g., centers, clinics)
621210	Doctors of dental medicine (DMDs) offices (e.g., centers, clinics)
621210	Doctors of dental surgery (DDSs) offices (e.g., centers, clinics)
621320	Doctors of optometry (ODs) offices (e.g., centers, clinics)
621112	Doctors of osteopathy (DOs), mental health, offices (e.g., centers, clinics)
621111	Doctors of osteopathy (DOs, except mental health) offices (e.g., centers, clinics)
621391	Doctors of podiatry (DPs) offices (e.g., centers, clinics)
621330	Doctors of psychology offices (e.g., centers, clinics)
561439	Document copying services (except combined with printing services)
561439	Document duplicating services (except combined with printing services)
561410	Document preparation services
561410	Document transcription services
325110	Dodecene made from refined petroleum or liquid hydrocarbons

Code	Description
311111	Dog and cat food (e.g., canned, dry, frozen, semimoist), manufacturing
311111	Dog food manufacturing
316999	Dog furnishings (e.g., collars, harnesses, leashes, muzzles), manufacturing
711219	Dog owners, race (i.e., racing dogs)
812910	Dog pounds
112990	Dog production
711212	Dog racetracks
711219	Dog racing kennels
422990	Dogs wholesaling
322299	Doilies, paper, made from purchased paper
339932	Doll carriages and carts manufacturing
339931	Doll clothing manufacturing
452990	Dollar stores
333924	Dollies manufacturing
421920	Dolls wholesaling
339931	Dolls, doll parts, and doll clothing (except wigs) manufacturing
212312	Dolomite crushed and broken stone mining and/or beneficiating
212311	Dolomite mining or quarrying
327410	Dolomite, dead-burned, manufacturing
327410	Dolomitic lime manufacturing
212319	Dolomitic marble crushed and broken stone mining and/or beneficiating
212311	Dolomitic marble mining or quarrying
114111	Dolphin fishing
233320	Dome construction
112920	Donkey production
332321	Door and jamb assemblies, metal, manufacturing
235510	Door and window construction contractors
332321	Door frames and sash, metal, manufacturing
321911	Door frames and sash, wood and covered wood, manufacturing
332322	Door hoods, sheet metal, manufacturing
321911	Door jambs, wood, manufacturing

Code	Description
332510	Door locks manufacturing
332510	Door opening and closing devices (except electrical) manufacturing
335999	Door opening and closing devices, electrical, manufacturing
321918	Door shutters, wood, manufacturing
444190	Door stores
321918	Door trim, wood molding, manufacturing
321911	Door units, prehung, wood and covered wood, manufacturing
541870	Door-to-door distribution of advertising materials (e.g., coupons, flyers, samples)
454390	Door-to-door retailing of merchandise, direct selling
314110	Doormats, all materials (except entirely of rubber or plastics), manufacturing
326199	Doormats, plastics, manufacturing
326299	Doormats, rubber, manufacturing
421310	Doors and door frames wholesaling
326199	Doors and door frames, plastics, manufacturing
321911	Doors, combination screen-storm, wood, manufacturing
332321	Doors, metal, manufacturing
332999	Doors, safe and vault, metal, manufacturing
327215	Doors, unframed glass, made from purchased glass
321911	Doors, wood and covered wood, manufacturing
325510	Dopes, paint, and laquer, manufacturing
336612	Dories building
721310	Dormitories
233320	Dormitory construction
233220	Dormitory construction, general construction contractors
334519	Dosimetry devices manufacturing
333294	Dough mixing machinery (i.e., food manufacturing-type) manufacturing
722110	Doughnut shops, full service
722213	Doughnut shops, on premise baking and carryout service

Code	Description
311812	Doughnuts (except frozen) made in commercial bakeries
311813	Doughnuts, frozen, manufacturing
422420	Doughs, frozen, wholesaling
311211	Doughs, prepared, made in flour mills
311822	Doughs, refrigerated or frozen, made from purchased flour
333210	Dovetailing machines, woodworking-type, manufacturing
332722	Dowel pins, metal, manufacturing
321999	Dowels, wood, manufacturing
315291	Down-filled clothing, infants', cut and sewn from purchased fabric (except apparel contractors)
315211	Down-filled clothing, men's and boys', cut and sew apparel contractors
315228	Down-filled clothing, men's and boys', cut and sewn from purchased fabric (except apparel contractors)
315212	Down-filled clothing, women's, girls' and infants' cut and sew apparel contractors
315239	Down-filled clothing, women's, misses', and girls', cut and sewn from purchased fabric (except apparel contractors)
713920	Downhill skiing facilities without accommodations
235610	Downspout construction contractors
332322	Downspouts, sheet metal, manufacturing
334513	Draft gauges, industrial process-type, manufacturing
334519	Drafting instruments manufacturing
421490	Drafting instruments wholesaling
339942	Drafting materials (except instruments and tables) manufacturing
541340	Drafting services
337127	Drafting tables and boards manufacturing
421490	Drafting tables wholesaling
541340	Draftsmen's offices
711212	Drag strips
333120	Draglines, crawler, manufacturing

Code	Description
325191	Dragon's blood manufacturing
333111	Drags, farm-type equipment, manufacturing
333120	Drags, road construction and road maintenance equipment, manufacturing
212399	Dragstones mining and/or beneficiating
561790	Drain cleaning services
332913	Drain cocks, plumbing, manufacturing
325612	Drain pipe cleaners manufacturing
332999	Drain plugs, magnetic, metal, manufacturing
327123	Drain tile, clay, manufacturing
234990	Drainage project construction
235110	Drainage system installation (e.g., cesspool, septic tank) construction contractors
337110	Drainboards, wood or plastics laminated on wood, manufacturing
213113	Draining or pumping coal mines on a contract basis
213114	Draining or pumping of metal mines on a contract basis
213115	Draining or pumping of nonmetallic mineral mines (except fuels) on a contract basis
611610	Drama schools (except academic)
314121	Draperies made from purchased fabrics or sheet goods
421220	Draperies wholesaling
812320	Drapery cleaning services
339113	Drapes, surgical, disposable, manufacturing
333518	Draw bench machines manufacturing
315192	Drawers, apparel, made in apparel knitting mills
315211	Drawers, men's and boys', cut and sew apparel contractors
315221	Drawers, men's and boys', cut and sewn from purchased fabric (except apparel contractors)
315212	Drawers, women's, girls', and infants', cut and sew apparel contractors

Code	Description
315231	Drawers, women's, misses', and girls', cut and sewn from purchased fabric (except apparel contractors)
325998	Drawing inks manufacturing
331222	Drawing iron or steel wire from purchased iron or steel
331222	Drawing iron or steel wire from purchased iron or steel and fabricating wire products
333292	Drawing machinery for textiles manufacturing
337127	Drawing tables and boards, artist's, manufacturing
332212	Drawknives manufacturing
336611	Dredge building
333120	Dredging machinery manufacturing
234990	Dredging, general construction contractors
315992	Dress and semidress gloves cut and sewn from purchased fabric (except apparel contractors)
315191	Dress and semidress gloves made in apparel knitting mills
315211	Dress and semidress gloves, men's and boys', cut and sew apparel contractors
315212	Dress and semidress gloves, women's, girls', and infants', cut and sew apparel contractors
316219	Dress shoes, children's and infants', manufacturing
316213	Dress shoes, men's, manufacturing
316214	Dress shoes, women's, manufacturing
448190	Dress shops
532220	Dress suit rental
315999	Dress trimmings cut and sewn from purchased fabric (except apparel contractors)
315212	Dress trimmings, women's, girls', and infants', cut and sew apparel contractors
422990	Dressed furs and skins wholesaling
337124	Dressers, metal, manufacturing
337122	Dressers, wood, manufacturing
315191	Dresses made in apparel knitting mills
422330	Dresses wholesaling

Code	Description
315191	Dresses, hand-knit, manufacturing
315291	Dresses, infants', cut and sewn from purchased fabric (except apparel contractors)
315233	Dresses, women's, misses', and girls', cut and sewn from purchased fabric (except apparel contractors)
315212	Dresses, women's, misses', girls', and infants', cut and sew apparel contractors
316110	Dressing (i.e., bleaching, blending, currying, scraping, tanning) furs
315212	Dressing gowns, women's, girls', and infants', cut and sew apparel contractors
315231	Dressing gowns, women's, misses', and girls', cut and sewn from purchased fabric (except apparel contractors)
316110	Dressing hides
311615	Dressing small game
337124	Dressing tables, metal, manufacturing
337122	Dressing tables, wood, manufacturing
421450	Dressings, medical, wholesaling
339113	Dressings, surgical, manufacturing
422490	Dried foods (e.g., fruits, milk, vegetables) wholesaling
311612	Dried meats made from purchased carcasses
212392	Dried phosphate rock mining and/or beneficiating
325510	Driers, paint, and varnish, manufacturing
325992	Driers, photographic chemical, manufacturing
333315	Driers, photographic, manufacturing
334511	Driftmeters, aeronautical, manufacturing
333515	Drill bits, metalworking, manufacturing
332212	Drill bits, woodworking, manufacturing
333512	Drill presses, metalworking, manufacturing
333210	Drill presses, woodworking-type, manufacturing

Code	Description
332999	Drill stands, metal, manufacturing
213112	Drill-stem testing in oil, gas, dry, and service well drilling on a contract basis
235930	Drilled pier construction contractors
235930	Drilled shaft construction contractors
339913	Drilling pearls
336611	Drilling and production platforms, floating, oil and gas, building
213111	Drilling directional oil and gas field wells on a contract basis
333132	Drilling equipment, oil and gas field-type, manufacturing
333131	Drilling equipment, underground mining-type, manufacturing
213111	Drilling for gas on a contract basis
213111	Drilling for oil on a contract basis
213111	Drilling gas and oil field wells on a contract basis
333512	Drilling machines, metalworking, manufacturing
325998	Drilling mud compounds, conditioners, and additives (except bentonites) manufacturing
422690	Drilling muds wholesaling
213111	Drilling oil and gas field service wells on a contract basis
213112	Drilling rat holes and mouse holes at oil and gas fields on a contract basis
333132	Drilling rigs, oil and gas field-type, manufacturing
213113	Drilling services for coal mining on a contract basis
213114	Drilling services for metal mining on a contract basis
213115	Drilling services for nonmetallic mineral (except fuels) mining on a contract basis
213112	Drilling shot holes at oil and gas fields on a contract basis
213112	Drilling site preparation at oil and gas fields on a contract basis
213111	Drilling water intake wells, oil and gas field on a contract basis

Code	Description
235810	Drilling water wells construction contractors
313210	Drills weaving
333131	Drills, core, underground mining-type, manufacturing
339114	Drills, dental, manufacturing
332212	Drills, hand held, nonelectric, manufacturing
333991	Drills, handheld power-driven (except heavy construction and mining type), manufacturing
333131	Drills, rock, underground mining-type, manufacturing
311999	Drink powder mixes (except chocolate, coffee, milk based, tea) manufacturing
311320	Drink powdered mixes, cocoa, made from cacao
311330	Drink powdered mixes, cocoa, made from purchased cocoa
311511	Drink, chocolate milk, manufacturing
332998	Drinking fountains (except mechanically refrigerated), metal, manufacturing
326191	Drinking fountains (except mechanically refrigerated), plastics, manufacturing
333415	Drinking fountains, refrigerated, manufacturing
327111	Drinking fountains, vitreous china, non-refrigerated, manufacturing
722410	Drinking places (i.e., bars, lounges, taverns), alcoholic
312111	Drinks, fruit (except juice), manufacturing
333613	Drive chains, bicycle and motorcycle, manufacturing
336350	Drive shafts and half shafts, automotive, truck, and bus, manufacturing
512132	Drive-in motion picture theaters
722211	Drive-in restaurants
611692	Driver education
611692	Driver training schools (except bus, heavy equipment, truck)
711219	Drivers, harness or race car

Code	Description
333612	Drives, high-speed industrial (except hydrostatic), manufacturing
561790	Driveway cleaning (e.g., power sweeping, washing) services
235710	Driveway construction contractors
713990	Driving ranges, golf
488490	Driving services (e.g., automobile, truck delivery)
332111	Drop forgings made from purchased iron or steel, unfinished
333513	Drop hammers, metal forging and shaping, manufacturing
812320	Drop-off and pick-up sites for laundries and drycleaners
813319	Drug abuse prevention advocacy organizations
623220	Drug addiction rehabilitation facilities (except licensed hospitals), residential
622210	Drug addiction rehabilitation hospitals
624190	Drug addiction self-help organizations
621420	Drug addiction treatment centers and clinics (except hospitals), outpatient
922120	Drug enforcement agencies and offices
422210	Drug proprietaries wholesaling
446110	Drug stores
422210	Druggists' sundries wholesaling
422210	Drugs wholesaling
711130	Drum and bugle corps (i.e., drill teams)
333924	Drum cradles manufacturing
339992	Drums (musical instruments), parts, and accessories manufacturing
332439	Drums, light gauge metal, manufacturing
421840	Drums, new and reconditioned, wholesaling
326199	Drums, plastics (i.e., containers), manufacturing
321920	Drums, plywood, manufacturing
321920	Drums, shipping, wood, wirebound, manufacturing

Code	Description
813319	Drunk driving prevention advocacy organizations
311422	Dry beans canning
422510	Dry beans wholesaling
484230	Dry bulk carrier, truck, long-distance
484220	Dry bulk trucking (except garbage collection, garbage hauling), local
335912	Dry cell primary batteries, single and multiple cell, manufacturing
335912	Dry cells, primary (e.g., AAA, AA, C, D, 9V), manufacturing
233310	Dry cleaning plant construction
325120	Dry ice (i.e., solid carbon dioxide) manufacturing
422690	Dry ice wholesaling
311514	Dry milk manufacturing
333294	Dry milk processing machinery manufacturing
311514	Dry milk products and mixture manufacturing
311514	Dry milk products for animal feed manufacturing
327999	Dry mix concrete manufacturing
311822	Dry mixes made from purchased flour
311823	Dry pasta manufacturing
311823	Dry pasta packaged with other ingredients made in dry pasta plants
335211	Dry shavers (i.e., electric razors) manufacturing
235110	Dry well construction contractors
812320	Drycleaner drop-off and pick-up sites
812320	Drycleaners (except coin-operated)
335224	Drycleaning and laundry machines, household-type, manufacturing
333312	Drycleaning equipment and machinery manufacturing
421850	Drycleaning equipment and supplies wholesaling
812310	Drycleaning machine routes (i.e., concession operators), coin-operated or similar self-service
812320	Drycleaning plants (except rug cleaning plants)
325612	Drycleaning preparations manufacturing

Code	Description
812320	Drycleaning services (except coin-operated)
812310	Drycleaning services, coin-operated or similar self-service
336611	Drydock, floating, building
488390	Drydocks, floating (i.e., routine repair and maintenance of ships and boats)
532210	Dryer, clothes, rental
335224	Dryers, clothes, household-type, gas and electric, manufacturing
421620	Dryers, hair, wholesaling
335224	Dryers, household-type laundry, manufacturing
339111	Dryers, laboratory-type, manufacturing
333312	Dryers, laundry (except household-type), manufacturing
311711	Drying fish and seafood
333298	Drying kilns, lumber, manufacturing
333292	Drying machinery for textiles manufacturing
235420	Drywall construction contractors
421320	Drywall supplies wholesaling
713950	Duck pin bowling alleys
713950	Duck pin bowling centers
112390	Duck production
313210	Ducks weaving
311615	Ducks, processing, fresh, frozen, canned, or cooked
311615	Ducks, slaughtering and dressing
561790	Duct cleaning services
322222	Duct tape made from purchased materials
235610	Duct work, sheet metal, construction contractors
331511	Ductile iron castings, unfinished, manufacturing
331511	Ductile iron foundries
332313	Ducting, fabricated metal plate work, manufacturing
335313	Ducts for electrical switchboard apparatus manufacturing
332322	Ducts, sheet metal, manufacturing
721214	Dude ranches
339920	Dumbbells manufacturing

Code	Description
235950	Dumbwaiter construction contractors
333921	Dumbwaiters manufacturing
212325	Dumortierite mining and/or beneficiating
336212	Dump trailer manufacturing
484220	Dump trucking (e.g., gravel, sand, top soil)
562119	Dump trucking of rubble or brush with collection or disposal
336211	Dump-truck lifting mechanisms manufacturing
333131	Dumpers, mining car, manufacturing
562219	Dumps, compost
562212	Dumps, nonhazardous solid waste (e.g., trash)
315291	Dungarees, infants', cut and sewn from purchased fabric (except apparel contractors)
315211	Dungarees, men's and boys', cut and sew apparel contractors
315224	Dungarees, men's and boys', cut and sewn from purchased fabric (except apparel contractors)
315212	Dungarees, women's girls' and infants', cut and sew apparel contractors
315239	Dungarees, women's, misses', and girls', cut and sewn from pruchased fabric (except apparel contractors)
531110	Duplex houses (i.e., single family) rental or leasing
335931	Duplex receptacles, electrical, manufacturing
233220	Duplexes, double (i.e., one unit above the other) multifamily, construction
233210	Duplexes, single family, construction
325910	Duplicating inks manufacturing
532420	Duplicating machine (e.g., copier) rental or leasing
333512	Duplicating machines (e.g., key cutting), metalworking, manufacturing
311211	Durum flour manufacturing
333411	Dust and fume collecting equipment manufacturing

Code	Description
314999	Dust cloths made from purchased fabrics
235950	Dust collecting equipment construction contractors
421730	Dust collection equipment wholesaling
812332	Dust control textile item (e.g., cloths, mats, mops, rugs, shop towels) supply services
315212	Dusters (i.e., apparel), women's and girls', cut and sew apparel contractors
315231	Dusters (i.e., apparel), women's, misses', and girls', cut and sewn from purchased fabric (except apparel contractors)
333111	Dusters, farm-type, manufacturing
115112	Dusting crops
445310	Duty free liquor shops
531110	Dwelling rental or leasing
332311	Dwellings, prefabricated metal, manufacturing
325998	Dye preparations, clothing, household-type, manufacturing
313311	Dyeing broadwoven fabrics
316110	Dyeing furs
313312	Dyeing gloves, woven or knit, for the trade
316110	Dyeing leather
333292	Dyeing machinery for textiles manufacturing
313312	Dyeing textile products and fabrics (except broadwoven fabrics)
422690	Dyes, industrial, wholesaling
325131	Dyes, inorganic, manufacturing
325191	Dyes, natural, manufacturing
325132	Dyes, synthetic organic, manufacturing
422690	Dyestuffs wholesaling
325920	Dynamite manufacturing
334519	Dynamometers manufacturing
335312	Dynamos, electric (except automotive), manufacturing
335312	Dynamotors manufacturing
335932	EMTs (electrical metallic tube) manufacturing
812199	Ear piercing services

Code	Description
532412	Earth moving equipment rental or leasing without operator
234990	Earth moving not connected with building construction
334220	Earth station communications equipment manufacturing
513390	Earth stations (except satellite telecommunication carriers)
513340	Earth stations for satellite communication carriers
212399	Earth, diatomaceous, mining and/or beneficiating
212325	Earth, fuller's (e.g., all natural bleaching clays), mining and/or beneficiating
327112	Earthenware table and kitchen articles, coarse, manufacturing
327112	Earthenware, commercial and household, semivitreous, manufacturing
311119	Earthworm food and bedding manufacturing
112990	Earthworm hatcheries
339942	Easels, artists', manufacturing
422130	Eating utensils, disposable plastics, wholesaling
332322	Eaves, sheet metal, manufacturing
327112	Ecclesiastical statuary, clay, manufacturing
327420	Ecclesiastical statuary, gypsum, manufacturing
327999	Ecclesiastical statuary, paper mache, manufacturing
327991	Ecclesiastical statuary, stone, manufacturing
332999	Ecclesiastical ware, precious plated metal, manufacturing
541690	Economic consulting services
926110	Economic development agencies, government
928120	Economic development assistance (i.e., international), government
541720	Economic research and development services
332410	Economizers (i.e., power boiler accessory) manufacturing
522298	Edge Act corporations (except international trade financing)

Code	Description
522293	Edge Act corporations (i.e., international trade financing)
332212	Edge tools, woodworking (e.g., augers, bits, countersinks), manufacturing
333315	Editing equipment, motion picture (e.g., rewinders, splicers, titlers, viewers), manufacturing
561410	Editing services
923110	Education offices, nonoperating
923110	Education program administration
923110	Education statistics centers, government
611710	Educational consultants
611710	Educational guidance counseling services
611710	Educational testing evaluation services
611710	Educational testing services
813211	Educational trusts, awarding grants
813920	Educators' associations
114111	Eel fishing
325412	Effervescent salts manufacturing
541614	Efficiency management (i.e., efficiency expert) consulting services
321920	Egg cases, wood, manufacturing
335211	Egg cookers, household-type electric, manufacturing
112340	Egg hatcheries, poultry
311823	Egg noodles, dry, manufacturing
311991	Egg noodles, fresh, manufacturing
112310	Egg production, chicken
112330	Egg production, turkey
311999	Egg substitutes manufacturing
312140	Eggnog, alcoholic, manufacturing
311514	Eggnog, canned, nonalcoholic, manufacturing
311511	Eggnog, fresh, nonalcoholic, manufacturing
311511	Eggnog, nonalcoholic (except canned), manufacturing
111219	Eggplant farming (except under cover), field, bedding plant and seed production
111419	Eggplant farming, grown under cover

Code	Description
422440	Eggs wholesaling
311999	Eggs, processed, manufacturing
334515	Elapsed time meters, electronic, manufacturing
313210	Elastic fabrics, more than 12 inches in width, weaving
313221	Elastic fabrics, narrow woven, manufacturing
339113	Elastic hosiery, orthopedic, manufacturing
325222	Elastomeric fibers and filaments manufacturing
325211	Elastomers (except synthetic rubber) manufacturing
325212	Elastomers, synthetic rubber, manufacturing
332322	Elbows for conductor pipe, hot air ducts, and stovepipe, sheet metal, manufacturing
332919	Elbows, pipe, metal (except made from purchased pipe), manufacturing
921190	Election boards
334512	Electric air cleaner controls, automatic, manufacturing
334513	Electric and electronic controllers, industrial process-type, manufacturing
336111	Electric automobiles for highway use manufacturing
335999	Electric bells manufacturing
335211	Electric blankets manufacturing
421620	Electric blankets wholesaling
335211	Electric comfort heating equipment, portable, manufacturing
335999	Electric fence chargers manufacturing
335311	Electric furnace transformers manufacturing
334512	Electric heat proportioning controls, modulating controls, manufacturing
335110	Electric lamp bulb parts (except glass blanks) manufacturing
335110	Electric lamps (i.e., light bulbs) manufacturing
335110	Electric light bulbs, complete, manufacturing

Code	Description
811310	Electric motor repair and maintenance services, commercial or industrial
421610	Electric motors, wiring supplies, and lighting fixtures wholesaling
339992	Electric musical instruments manufacturing
333618	Electric outboard motors manufacturing
221122	Electric power brokers
221121	Electric power control
221122	Electric power distribution systems
221119	Electric power generation, (except fossil fuel, hydroelectric, nuclear)
221112	Electric power generation, fossil fuel (e.g., coal, oil, gas)
221111	Electric power generation, hydroelectric
221113	Electric power generation, nuclear
221119	Electric power generation, solar
221119	Electric power generation, tidal
221119	Electric power generation, wind
234920	Electric power transmission line and tower construction
221121	Electric power transmission systems
334512	Electric space heater controls, automatic, manufacturing
335211	Electric space heaters, portable, manufacturing
333415	Electric warm air (i.e., forced air) furnaces manufacturing
235310	Electrical construction contractors
541330	Electrical engineering services
811310	Electrical generating and transmission equipment repair and maintenance services
541360	Electrical geophysical surveying services
336322	Electrical ignition cable sets for internal combustion engines manufacturing
335932	Electrical metallic tube (EMTs) manufacturing
561990	Electrical meter reading services, contract
334515	Electrical network analyzers manufacturing

Code	Description
334515	Electrical power measuring equipment manufacturing
235310	Electrical repair construction contractors
811118	Electrical repair shops, automotive
339950	Electrical signs manufacturing
421440	Electrical signs wholesaling
444190	Electrical supply stores
541380	Electrical testing laboratories or services
335211	Electrically heated bed coverings manufacturing
611513	Electricians' apprenticeship training
334515	Electricity and electrical signal measuring instruments manufacturing
334515	Electricity and electrical signal testing equipment manufacturing
334510	Electrocardiographs manufacturing
335999	Electrochemical generators (i.e., fuel cells) manufacturing
333512	Electrochemical milling machines, metalworking, manufacturing
333512	Electrode discharge metal cutting machines manufacturing
333992	Electrode holders, welding, manufacturing
335991	Electrodes for thermal and electrolytic uses, carbon and graphite, manufacturing
334513	Electrodes used in industrial process measurement manufacturing
335110	Electrodes, cold cathode fluorescent lamp, manufacturing
333992	Electrodes, welding, manufacturing
334510	Electroencephalographs manufacturing
334510	Electrogastrograph manufacturing
332912	Electrohydraulic servo valves, fluid power, manufacturing
812199	Electrolysis (i.e., hair removal) salons
325412	Electrolyte in-vivo diagnostic substances manufacturing
334513	Electrolytic conductivity instruments, industrial process-type, manufacturing

Code	Description
334516	Electrolytic conductivity instruments, laboratory-type, manufacturing
333512	Electrolytic metal cutting machines manufacturing
334513	Electromagnetic flowmeters manufacturing
541360	Electromagnetic geophysical surveying services
334514	Electromechanical counters manufacturing
334510	Electromedical diagnostic equipment manufacturing
334510	Electromedical equipment manufacturing
421450	Electromedical equipment wholesaling
334510	Electromedical therapy equipment manufacturing
331112	Electrometallurical ferroalloy manufacturing
334510	Electromyographs manufacturing
333992	Electron beam welding equipment manufacturing
335999	Electron linear accelerators manufacturing
334516	Electron microprobes, laboratory-type, manufacturing
334516	Electron microscopes manufacturing
334516	Electron paramagnetic spin-type apparatus manufacturing
333298	Electron tube machinery manufacturing
334411	Electron tube parts (e.g., bases, getters, guns) (except glass blanks) manufacturing
327215	Electron tube parts, glass blanks, made from purchased glass
327212	Electron tube parts, glass blanks, made in glass making plants
334515	Electron tube test equipment manufacturing
334411	Electron tubes manufacturing
333512	Electron-discharge metal cutting machines manufacturing
235310	Electronic control system construction contractors
514210	Electronic data processing services

Code	Description
511140	Electronic database publishers
511140	Electronic database publishing (i.e., establishments known as publishers)
611519	Electronic equipment repair training
522320	Electronic financial payment services
522320	Electronic funds transfer services
713120	Electronic game arcades
421920	Electronic games wholesaling
334511	Electronic guidance systems and equipment manufacturing
421690	Electronic parts (e.g., condensers, connectors, switches) wholesaling
323122	Electronic prepress services for the printing trade
541710	Electronic research and development laboratories or services
334515	Electronic test equipment for testing electrical characteristics manufacturing
541380	Electronic testing laboratories or services
334514	Electronic totalizing counters manufacturing
339932	Electronic toys and games manufacturing
421690	Electronic tubes (e.g., industrial, receiving, transmitting) wholesaling
334516	Electrophoresis instruments manufacturing
333298	Electroplating machinery and equipment manufacturing
332813	Electroplating metals and formed products for the trade
235210	Electrostatic painting construction contractors
335999	Electrostatic particle accelerators manufacturing
333411	Electrostatic precipitation equipment manufacturing
334510	Electrotherapeutic apparatus manufacturing
335110	Electrotherapeutic lamp bulbs for ultraviolet and infrared radiation manufacturing

Code	Description
334510	Electrotherapy units manufacturing
323122	Electrotype plate preparation services
333293	Electrotyping machinery manufacturing
334516	Elemental analyzers manufacturing
611110	Elementary schools
332323	Elevator guide rails, metal, manufacturing
235950	Elevator installation contractors
421830	Elevators wholesaling
333921	Elevators, passenger and freight, manufacturing
112990	Elk production
325998	Embalming fluids manufacturing
812210	Embalming services
928120	Embassies
313311	Embossing broadwoven fabrics
316110	Embossing leather
323122	Embossing plate preparation services
339943	Embossing stamps manufacturing
313312	Embossing textile products and fabrics (except broadwoven)
313222	Embroideries, Schiffli machine, manufacturing
315211	Embroidering contractors on men's and boys' apparel
315212	Embroidering contractors on women's, misses', girls', and infants' apparel
314999	Embroidering on textile products (except apparel) for the trade
339932	Embroidery kits manufacturing
333292	Embroidery machinery manufacturing
422310	Embroidery products wholesaling
313111	Embroidery spun yarns (e.g., cotton, manmade fiber, silk, wool) made from purchased fiber
313113	Embroidery thread (e.g., cotton, manmade fibers, silk, wool) manufacturing
335122	Emergency lighting (i.e., battery backup) manufacturing
621493	Emergency medical centers and clinics, freestanding

Code	Description
621910	Emergency medical transportation services, air or ground
922190	Emergency planning and management offices, government
624230	Emergency relief services
488410	Emergency road services (i.e., tow service)
624221	Emergency shelters (except for victims of domestic or international disasters or conflicts)
624230	Emergency shelters for victims of domestic or international disasters or conflicts
212399	Emery mining and/or beneficiating
811198	Emissions testing without repair, automotive
541612	Employee assessment consulting services
541612	Employee benefit consulting services
525110	Employee benefit pension plans
525120	Employee benefit plans (except pension)
524292	Employee benefit plans, third-party administrative processing services
485410	Employee bus services
541612	Employee compensation consulting services
561330	Employee leasing services
813930	Employees' associations for improvement of wages and working conditions
561310	Employment agencies
561310	Employment agencies, motion picture or video
561310	Employment agencies, radio or television
561310	Employment agencies, theatrical
561310	Employment placement agencies or services
561310	Employment referral agencies or services
561310	Employment registries
112390	Emu production
325613	Emulsifiers (i.e., surface-active agents) manufacturing
325510	Enamel paints manufacturing

Code	Description
212322	Enamel sand quarrying and/or beneficiating
332214	Enameled metal cutting utensils
332812	Enameling metals and metal products for the trade
333994	Enameling ovens manufacturing
422950	Enamels wholesaling
339114	Enamels, dental, manufacturing
323121	Encyclopedia binding without printing
511130	Encyclopedia publishers
511130	Encyclopedia publishers and printing combined
511130	Encyclopedia publishing (i.e., establishments known as publishers)
323117	Encyclopedias printing and binding without publishing
323117	Encyclopedias printing without publishing
337124	End tables, metal, manufacturing
337122	End tables, wood, manufacturing
111219	Endive farming (except under cover), field, bedding plant and seed production
111419	Endive farming, grown under cover
325411	Endocrine products, uncompounded, manufacturing
422210	Endocrine substances wholesaling
621210	Endodontists' offices (e.g., centers, clinics)
334510	Endoscopic equipment, electromedical (e.g., bronchoscopes, colonoscopes, cystoscopes), manufacturing
325320	Endrin insecticides manufacturing
541690	Energy consulting services
334512	Energy cutoff controls, residential and commercial types, manufacturing
926110	Energy development and conservation agencies, nonoperating
926130	Energy development and conservation programs, government
334515	Energy measuring equipment, electrical, manufacturing
926110	Energy program administration

Code	Description
331319	Energy wire or cable made in aluminum wire drawing plants
331422	Energy wire or cable, copper, made from purchased copper in wire drawing plants
331491	Energy wire or cable, nonferrous metals (except aluminum, copper), made from purchased nonferrous metals (except aluminum, copper) in wire drawing plants
924110	Enforcement of environmental and pollution control regulations
336312	Engine block assemblies, automotive and truck gasoline, manufacturing
325998	Engine degreasers manufacturing
336311	Engine intake and exhaust valves manufacturing
811310	Engine repair (except automotive, small engine)
811111	Engine repair and replacement shops, automotive
811411	Engine repair, small engine
325998	Engine starting fluids manufacturing
421120	Engine testing equipment, motor vehicle, wholesaling
541330	Engineering consulting services
541330	Engineering design services
541710	Engineering research and development laboratories or services
541330	Engineering services
813920	Engineers' associations
421490	Engineers' equipment and supplies wholesaling
541330	Engineers' offices
541330	Engineers' private practices
336412	Engines and engine parts, aircraft (except carburetors, pistons, piston rings, valves), manufacturing
336312	Engines and parts (except diesel), automotive and truck, manufacturing
421860	Engines and parts, aircraft, wholesaling
421120	Engines and parts, automotive, new, wholesaling

Code	Description
421860	Engines and turbines, marine, wholesaling
333618	Engines, diesel and semidiesel, manufacturing
333618	Engines, diesel locomotive, manufacturing
421830	Engines, internal combustion (except aircraft, automotive), wholesaling
333618	Engines, internal combustion (except aircraft, nondiesel automotive), manufacturing
333618	Engines, natural gas, manufacturing
111219	English pea farming (except under cover), field, bedding plant and seed production
111419	English pea farming, grown under cover
332212	Engraver's handtools, nonpowered, manufacturing
339911	Engraving and etching precious (except precious plated) metal jewelry and flatware
339912	Engraving and etching precious metal flatware
421830	Engraving machinery wholesaling
332812	Engraving metals and metal products (except printing plates) for the trade
323122	Engraving printing plate, for the printing trade
333315	Enlargers, photographic, manufacturing
315191	Ensemble dresses made in apparel knitting mills
315212	Ensemble dresses, women's, girls', and infants', cut and sew apparel contractors
315233	Ensemble dresses, women's, misses', and girls', cut and sewn from purchased fabric (except apparel constractors)
711130	Ensembles, musical
926110	Enterprise development program administration
711410	Entertainers' agents or managers
711510	Entertainers, independent

Code	Description
541710	Entomological research and development laboratories or services
115112	Entomological service, agricultural
541690	Entomology consulting services
333291	Envelope making machinery manufacturing
422110	Envelope paper, bulk, wholesaling
333313	Envelope stuffing, sealing, and addressing machinery manufacturing
322232	Envelopes (i.e., mailing, stationery) made from any material
422120	Envelopes wholesaling
813312	Environmental advocacy organizations
541620	Environmental consulting services
235110	Environmental control construction contractors
541330	Environmental engineering services
923120	Environmental health program administration
924110	Environmental protection program administration
562910	Environmental remediation services
541710	Environmental research and development laboratories or services
541380	Environmental testing laboratories or services
325413	Enzyme and isoenzyme in-vitro diagnostic substances manufacturing
325199	Enzyme proteins (i.e., basic synthetic chemicals) (except pharmaceutical use) manufacturing
325411	Enzyme proteins (i.e., basic synthetic chemicals), pharmaceutical use, manufacturing
325132	Eosin dyes manufacturing
325411	Ephedrine and derivatives (i.e., basic chemicals) manufacturing
325211	Epichlorohydrin bisphenol manufacturing
325211	Epichlorohydrin diphenol manufacturing
325212	Epichlorohydrin elastomers manufacturing

Code	Description
325520	Epoxy adhesives manufacturing
325510	Epoxy coatings made from purchased resins
325211	Epoxy resins manufacturing
923130	Equal employment opportunity offices
115210	Equine boarding
522220	Equipment finance leasing
326299	Erasers, rubber or rubber and abrasive combined, manufacturing
213112	Erecting oil and gas field lease tanks on a contract basis
325411	Ergot alkaloids (i.e., basic chemicals) manufacturing
541330	Erosion control engineering services
235950	Escalator installation contractors
333921	Escalators manufacturing
421830	Escalators wholesaling
111219	Escarole farming (except under cover), field, bedding plant and seed production
111419	Escarole farming, grown under cover
812990	Escort services, social
523991	Escrow agencies (except real estate)
531390	Escrow agencies, real estate
325998	Essential oils manufacturing
422690	Essential oils wholesaling
325199	Essential oils, synthetic, manufacturing
541990	Estate assessment (i.e., appraisal) services
541110	Estate law offices
325211	Ester gum manufacturing
325199	Esters, not specified elsewhere by process, manufacturing
812112	Esthetician (i.e., skin care) services
115310	Estimating timber
333295	Etching equipment, semiconductor, manufacturing
332812	Etching metals and metal products (except printing plates) for the trade
325110	Ethane made from refined petroleum or liquid hydrocarbons
211112	Ethane recovered from oil and gas field gases

Code	Description
325193	Ethanol, nonpotable, manufacturing
813410	Ethnic associations
711510	Ethnic dancers, independent
711320	Ethnic festival managers without facilities
711320	Ethnic festival organizers without facilities
711310	Ethnic festival promoters with facilities
711320	Ethnic festival promoters without facilities
325191	Ethyl acetate, natural, manufacturing
325199	Ethyl acetate, synthetic, manufacturing
422820	Ethyl alcohol wholesaling
325193	Ethyl alcohol, nonpotable, manufacturing
312140	Ethyl alcohol, potable, manufacturing
325199	Ethyl butyrate manufacturing
325199	Ethyl cellulose (except resins) manufacturing
325199	Ethyl chloride manufacturing
325199	Ethyl ether manufacturing
325199	Ethyl formate manufacturing
325199	Ethyl nitrite manufacturing
325199	Ethyl perhydrophenanthrene manufacturing
325110	Ethylbenzene made from refined petroleum or liquid hydrocarbons
325211	Ethylcellulose plastics manufacturing
325199	Ethylene glycol ether manufacturing
325199	Ethylene glycol manufacturing
325110	Ethylene made from refined petroleum or liquid hydrocarbons
324110	Ethylene made in petroleum refineries
325199	Ethylene oxide manufacturing
325212	Ethylene-propylene rubber manufacturing
325212	Ethylene-propylene-nonconjugated diene (EPDM) rubber manufacturing
325211	Ethylene-vinyl acetate resins manufacturing
325998	Eucalyptus oil manufacturing

Code	Description
311514	Evaporated milk manufacturing
334519	Evaporation meters manufacturing
333415	Evaporative condensers (i.e., heat transfer equipment) manufacturing
611691	Exam preparation services
421810	Excavating machinery and equipment wholesaling
213112	Excavating mud pits, slush pits, and cellars at oil and gas fields on a contract basis
235930	Excavation construction contractors
333120	Excavators (e.g., power shovels) manufacturing
321999	Excelsior (e.g., pads, wrappers) manufacturing
523999	Exchange clearinghouses, commodities or securities
332410	Exchangers, heat, manufacturing
523210	Exchanges, commodity contracts
523210	Exchanges, securities
335312	Exciter assemblies, motor and generator, manufacturing
531210	Exclusive buyers' agencies
531210	Exclusive buyers' agents, offices of
487210	Excursion boat operation
921140	Executive and legislative office combinations
561110	Executive management services
921110	Executive offices, federal, state, and local (e.g., governor, mayor, president)
541612	Executive placement consulting services
541612	Executive search consulting services
713940	Exercise centers
532292	Exercise equipment rental
451110	Exercise equipment stores
339920	Exercise machines manufacturing
621340	Exercise physiologists' offices (e.g., centers, clinics)
336399	Exhaust and tail pipes, automotive, truck, and bus, manufacturing
333412	Exhaust fans, industrial and commercial-type, manufacturing
811112	Exhaust system repair and replacement shops, automotive

Code	Description
336399	Exhaust systems and parts, automotive, truck, and bus, manufacturing
531120	Exhibition hall, no promotion of events, rental or leasing
624190	Exoffender rehabilitation agencies
624190	Exoffender self-help organizations
316110	Exotic leathers manufacturing
332312	Expansion joints, metal, manufacturing
541710	Experimental farms
213113	Exploration services for coal (except geophysical surveying and mapping) on a contract basis
213114	Exploration services for metal (except geophysical surveying and mapping) on a contract basis
213115	Exploration services for nonmetallic minerals (except geophysical surveying and mapping) on a contract basis
213112	Exploration services for oil and gas (except geophysical surveying and mapping) on a contract basis
422690	Explosives (except ammunition, fireworks) wholesaling
325920	Explosives manufacturing
522293	Export trading companies (i.e., international trade financing)
522293	Export-Import banks
333315	Exposure meters, photographic, manufacturing
622310	Extended care hospitals (except mental, substance abuse)
335999	Extension cords made from purchased insulated wire
321999	Extension ladders, wood, manufacturing
321999	Extension planks, wood, manufacturing
235420	Exterior insulation finishing system construction contractors
321918	Exterior wood shutters manufacturing
325320	Exterminating chemical products (e.g., fungicides, insecticides, pesticides) manufacturing
561710	Exterminating services

Code	Description
421990	Extinguishers, fire, wholesaling
333120	Extractors, piling, manufacturing
311920	Extracts, essences and preparations, coffee, manufacturing
311920	Extracts, essences and preparations, tea, manufacturing
311942	Extracts, food (except coffee, meat), manufacturing
311942	Extracts, malt, manufacturing
325191	Extracts, natural dyeing and tanning, manufacturing
326291	Extruded, molded or lathe-cut rubber goods manufacturing
333220	Extruding machinery for plastics and rubber manufacturing
333292	Extruding machinery for yarn manufacturing
333513	Extruding machines, metalworking, manufacturing
331319	Extrusion billet made by rolling purchased aluminum
331319	Extrusion billet, aluminum, made in integrated secondary smelting and rolling mills
333514	Extrusion dies for use with all materials manufacturing
331319	Extrusion ingot made by rolling purchased aluminum
331319	Extrusion ingot, aluminum, made in integrated secondary smelting and rolling mills
331312	Extrusion ingot, primary aluminium, manufacturing
325412	Eye and ear preparations manufacturing
621991	Eye banks
339112	Eye examining instruments and apparatus manufacturing
325620	Eye make-up (e.g., eye shadow, eyebrow pencil, mascara) manufacturing
622310	Eye, ear, nose, and throat hospitals
316993	Eyeglass cases, all materials, manufacturing
339115	Eyeglass frames (i.e., fronts and temples), ophthalmic, manufacturing
421460	Eyeglasses wholesaling

Code	Description
315211	Eyelet making contractors on men's and boys' apparel
315212	Eyelet making contractors on women's, misses', girls', and infants' apparel
339993	Eyelets, metal, manufacturing
339115	Eyes, glass and plastics, manufacturing
522294	FHLMC (Federal Home Loan Mortgage Corporation)
513112	FM radio stations
522294	FNMA (Federal National Mortgage Association)
313312	Fabric (except broadwoven) finishing
451130	Fabric shops
325612	Fabric softeners manufacturing
332312	Fabricated bar joists manufacturing
332996	Fabricated pipe and pipe fittings made from purchased pipe
332313	Fabricated plate work manufacturing
314991	Fabricated rope products (e.g., nets, slings) made in cordage or twine mills
332312	Fabricated structural metal manufacturing
321213	Fabricated structural wood members (except trusses) manufacturing
313210	Fabrics (except rug, tire fabrics), broadwoven, weaving
314992	Fabrics for reinforcing rubber tires, industrial belting, and fuel cells manufacturing
313311	Fabrics, broadwoven, finishing
313311	Fabrics, broadwoven, mercerizing
313249	Fabrics, knit, made in warp knit fabric mills
313241	Fabrics, knit, made in weft knit fabric mills
313249	Fabrics, lace, made in lace mills
313221	Fabrics, narrow woven, weaving
313230	Fabrics, nonwoven, manufacturing
422310	Fabrics, textile (except burlap, felt), wholesaling
332618	Fabrics, woven wire, made from purchased wire

Code	Description
325620	Face creams (e.g., cleansing, moisturizing) manufacturing
335932	Face plates (i.e., outlet or switch covers) manufacturing
525990	Face-amount certificate funds
812112	Facial salons
422130	Facial tissue wholesaling
322291	Facial tissues made from purchased paper
322121	Facial tissues made in paper mills
561210	Facilities (except computer operation) support services
541513	Facilities (i.e., clients' facilities) management and operation services, computer systems or data processing
541513	Facilities (i.e., clients' facilities) support services, computer systems or data processing
513310	Facilities-based telecommunication carriers (except wireless)
333512	Facing machines, metalworking, manufacturing
334210	Facsimile equipment, standalone, manufacturing
532420	Facsimile machine rental or leasing
811213	Facsimile machine repair and maintenance services
421690	Facsimile machines wholesaling
325992	Facsimile toner cartridges manufacturing
522298	Factoring accounts receivable
233310	Factory construction
711310	Fair managers with facilities, agricultural
711320	Fair managers without facilities, agricultural
711310	Fair organizers with facilities, agricultural
711320	Fair organizers without facilities, agricultural
711310	Fair promoters with facilities, agricultural
711320	Fair promoters without facilities, agricultural
448140	Family clothing stores
621210	Family dentists' offices (e.g., centers, clinics)

Code	Description
713120	Family fun centers
541110	Family law offices
621111	Family physicians' offices (e.g., centers, clinics)
621410	Family planning centers
621410	Family planning counseling services
722110	Family restaurants, full service
722211	Family restaurants, limited service
624190	Family social service agencies
624190	Family welfare services
326220	Fan belts, rubber or plastics, manufacturing
334512	Fan controls, temperature responsive, manufacturing
316110	Fancy leathers manufacturing
335211	Fans (except attic), household-type electric, manufacturing
336322	Fans, electric cooling, automotive, truck, and bus, manufacturing
335211	Fans, household-type kitchen, manufacturing
421620	Fans, household-type, wholesaling
333412	Fans, industrial and commercial-type, manufacturing
421830	Fans, industrial, wholesaling
334514	Fare collection equipment manufacturing
311211	Farina (except breakfast food) made in flour mills
311230	Farina, breakfast cereal, manufacturing
233320	Farm building construction
332311	Farm buildings, prefabricated metal, manufacturing
321992	Farm buildings, prefabricated or portable, wood, manufacturing
813910	Farm bureaus
532490	Farm equipment rental or leasing
813410	Farm granges
115115	Farm labor contractors
811310	Farm machinery and equipment repair and maintenance services
421820	Farm machinery and equipment wholesaling
115116	Farm management services
522292	Farm mortgage lending

Code	Description
493130	Farm product warehousing and storage (except refrigerated)
493120	Farm product warehousing and storage, refrigerated
484220	Farm products hauling, local
484230	Farm products trucking, long-distance
332420	Farm storage tanks, heavy gauge metal, manufacturing
422910	Farm supplies wholesaling
532490	Farm tractor rental or leasing
333111	Farm tractors and attachments manufacturing
333111	Farm wagons manufacturing
333922	Farm-type conveyers manufacturing
813910	Farmers' associations
813910	Farmers' unions
*****	Farming — see type
531190	Farmland rental or leasing
115210	Farriers
112210	Farrow-to-finish operations
541490	Fashion design services
541490	Fashion designer services
722211	Fast food restaurants
421710	Fasteners (e.g., bolts, nuts, rivets, screws) wholesaling
339993	Fasteners (e.g., glove, hook-and-eye, slide, snap) manufacturing
334511	Fathometers manufacturing
334519	Fatigue testing machines, industrial, mechanical, manufacturing
311611	Fats, animal (except poultry, small game), produced in slaughtering plants
311613	Fats, animal, rendering
112112	Fattening cattle
325199	Fatty acid esters and amines manufacturing
325199	Fatty acids (e.g., margaric, oleic, stearic) manufacturing
325199	Fatty alcohols manufacturing
327111	Faucet handles, vitreous china and earthenware, manufacturing
332913	Faucets, plumbing, manufacturing
532420	Fax machine rental or leasing

Code	Description
811213	Fax machine repair and maintenance services
339999	Feather dusters manufacturing
315291	Feather-filled clothing, infants', cut and sewn from purchased fabric (except apparel contractors)
315239	Feather-filled clothing, jackets, and vests, women's, misses', and juniors', cut and sewn from purchased fabric (except apparel contractors)
315211	Feather-filled clothing, men's and boys', cut and sew apparel contractors
315228	Feather-filled clothing, men's and boys', cut and sewn from purchased fabric (except apparel contractors)
315212	Feather-filled clothing, women's, girls', and infants', cut and sew apparel contractors
422590	Feathers wholesaling
339999	Feathers, preparing (i.e., for use in apparel and textile products)
514110	Feature syndicates (i.e., advice columns, comic, news)
522294	Federal Agricultural Mortgage Corporation
926120	Federal Aviation Administration (except air traffic control)
922120	Federal Bureau of Investigation (FBI)
926130	Federal Communications Commission (FCC)
522298	Federal Home Loan Banks (FHLB)
522294	Federal Home Loan Mortgage Corporation (FHLMC)
522294	Federal Intermediate Credit Bank
522292	Federal Land Banks
522294	Federal National Mortgage Association (FNMA)
521110	Federal Reserve Banks or Branches
921130	Federal Reserve Board of Governors
522130	Federal credit unions
922120	Federal police services
522120	Federal savings and loan associations (S&L)
522120	Federal savings banks
813219	Federated charities

Code	Description
813930	Federation of workers, labor organizations
813930	Federations of labor
422910	Feed additives wholesaling
316999	Feed bags for horses manufacturing
314911	Feed bags made from purchased woven or knitted materials
311119	Feed concentrates, animal, manufacturing
311514	Feed grade dry milk products manufacturing
311119	Feed premixes, animal, manufacturing
333111	Feed processing equipment, farm-type, manufacturing
444220	Feed stores (except pet)
453910	Feed stores, pet
311119	Feed supplements, animal (except cat, dog), manufacturing
311111	Feed supplements, dog and cat, manufacturing
112112	Feed yards (except stockyards for transportation), cattle
112111	Feeder calf production
112210	Feeder pig farming
335311	Feeder voltage regulators and boosters (i.e., electrical transformers) manufacturing
421820	Feeders, animal, wholesaling
333131	Feeders, mineral beneficiating-type, manufacturing
112112	Feedlots (except stockyards for transportation), cattle
112210	Feedlots (except stockyards for transportation), hog
112410	Feedlots (except stockyards for transportation), lamb
422910	Feeds (except pet) wholesaling
311111	Feeds, prepared for dog and cat, manufacturing
311119	Feeds, prepared, for animals (except cat, dog) manufacturing
311119	Feeds, specialty (e.g., guinea pig, mice, mink), manufacturing
212325	Feldspar mining and/or beneficiating
327992	Feldspar processing beyond beneficiation

Code	Description
339941	Felt tip markers manufacturing
422990	Felt wholesaling
322121	Felts, asphalt, made in paper mills
313210	Felts, broadwoven, weaving
313230	Felts, nonwoven, manufacturing
235990	Fence construction contractors
331222	Fence gates, posts, and fittings, iron or steel, made in wire drawing plants
331111	Fence posts, iron or steel, made in steel mills
332323	Fences and gates (except wire), metal, manufacturing
421390	Fencing (except wood) wholesaling
332618	Fencing and fence gates made from purchased wire
421390	Fencing and fencing accessories, wire, wholesaling
444190	Fencing dealers
339920	Fencing equipment (sporting goods) manufacturing
321999	Fencing, prefabricated sections, wood, manufacturing
321999	Fencing, wood (except rough pickets, poles, and rails), manufacturing
421310	Fencing, wood, wholesaling
212299	Ferberite ores and concentrates mining and/or beneficiating
333298	Fermentation equipment, chemical, manufacturing
422810	Fermented malt beverages wholesaling
332420	Fermention tanks, heavy gauge metal tanks, manufacturing
212299	Ferralloy ores (except vanadium) (e.g., chromium, columbium, molybdenum, tungsten) mining and/or beneficiating
325188	Ferric chloride manufacturing
325188	Ferric oxide manufacturing
325131	Ferric oxide pigments manufacturing
333319	Ferris wheels manufacturing
331112	Ferroalloys manufacturing
421510	Ferroalloys wholesaling
331112	Ferrochromium manufacturing

Code	Description
325188	Ferrocyanides manufacturing
331112	Ferromanganese manufacturing
331112	Ferromolybdenum manufacturing
331112	Ferrophosphorus manufacturing
331112	Ferrosilicon manufacturing
331112	Ferrotitanium manufacturing
331112	Ferrotungsten manufacturing
332111	Ferrous forgings made from purchased iron or steel, unfinished
421510	Ferrous metals wholesaling
331112	Ferrovanadium manufacturing
483114	Ferry passenger transportation, Great Lakes
336611	Ferryboat building
621410	Fertility clinics
422910	Fertilizer and fertilizer materials wholesaling
115112	Fertilizer application for crops
212393	Fertilizer minerals, natural, mining and/or beneficiating
325314	Fertilizers, mixed, made in plants not manufacturing fertilizer materials
325311	Fertilizers, mixed, made in plants producing nitrogenous fertilizer materials
325312	Fertilizers, mixed, made in plants producing phosphatic fertilizer materials
325311	Fertilizers, natural organic (except compost), manufacturing
325311	Fertilizers, of animal waste origin, manufacturing
325311	Fertilizers, of sewage origin, manufacturing
561730	Fertilizing lawns
333111	Fertilizing machinery, farm-type, manufacturing
111998	Fescue seed farming
711310	Festival managers with facilities
711320	Festival managers without facilities
711310	Festival of arts managers with facilities
711320	Festival of arts managers without facilities
711310	Festival of arts organizers with facilities

Code	Description
711320	Festival of arts organizers without facilities
711310	Festival of arts promoters with facilities
711320	Festival of arts promoters without facilities
711310	Festival organizers with facilities
711320	Festival organizers without facilities
711310	Festival promoters with facilities
711320	Festival promoters without facilities
325412	Fever remedy preparations manufacturing
322214	Fiber cans and drums (i.e., all-fiber, nonfiber ends of any material) made from purchased paperboard
422130	Fiber cans and drums wholesaling
322214	Fiber drums made from purchased paperboard
337125	Fiber furniture (except upholstered), household-type, manufacturing
313221	Fiber glasses, narrow woven, weaving
235310	Fiber optic cable construction contractors
335921	Fiber optic cable manufacturing
334417	Fiber optic connectors manufacturing
322214	Fiber spools, reels, blocks made from purchased paperboard
322214	Fiber tubes made from purchased paperboard
314999	Fiber, textile recovery from textile mill waste and rags
321219	Fiberboard manufacturing
421310	Fiberboard wholesaling
421390	Fiberglass building materials (except insulation, roofing, siding) wholesaling
313210	Fiberglass fabrics weaving
422310	Fiberglass fabrics wholesaling
327993	Fiberglass insulation products manufacturing
325221	Fibers and filaments, cellulosic, manufacturing and texturizing
325222	Fibers and filaments, noncellulosic, manufacturing and texturizing

Code	Description
335991	Fibers, carbon and graphite, manufacturing
327212	Fibers, glass, textile, made in glass making plants
422690	Fibers, manmade, wholesaling
422590	Fibers, vegetable, wholesaling
323121	Fiction book binding without printing
511130	Fiction book publishers
511130	Fiction book publishers and printing combined
511130	Fiction book publishing (i.e., establishments known as publishers)
323117	Fiction books printing and binding without publishing
323117	Fiction books printing without publishing
524126	Fidelity insurance carriers, direct
531390	Fiduciaries', real estate, offices
523991	Fiduciary agencies (except real estate)
332995	Field artillery manufacturing
315211	Field jackets, military, cut and sew apparel contractors
315228	Field jackets, military, men's and boys', cut and sewn from purchased fabric (except apparel contractors)
111421	Field nurseries (i.e., growing of flowers and shrubbery)
334515	Field strength and intensity measuring equipment, electrical, manufacturing
336211	Fifth wheel assemblies manufacturing
111339	Fig farming
711219	Figure skaters, independent
335110	Filaments for electric lamp bulbs manufacturing
111335	Filbert farming
115114	Filbert hulling and shelling
422120	File cards and folders wholesaling
322231	File folders (e.g., accordion, expanding, hanging, manila) made from purchased paper and paperboard
333515	Files (i.e., a machine tool accessory) manufacturing

Code	Description
332212	Files, handheld, manufacturing
337214	Filing cabinets (except wood), office-type, manufacturing
337211	Filing cabinets, wood, office type, manufacturing
333512	Filing machines, metalworking, manufacturing
212399	Fill dirt pits mining and/or beneficiating
325510	Fillers, wood (e.g., dry, liquid, paste), manufacturing
314999	Filling (except nonwoven textile), upholstery, manufacturing
311999	Fillings, cake or pie (except fruits, meat, vegetables), manufacturing
711510	Film actors, independent
514120	Film archives
541380	Film badge testing (i.e., radiation testing) laboratories or services
333315	Film developing equipment manufacturing
421410	Film developing equipment wholesaling
512120	Film distribution agencies
512120	Film distribution, motion picture and video
512131	Film festivals exhibitors
512120	Film libraries, commercial distribution
512199	Film libraries, motion picture or video, stock footage
512191	Film or tape closed captioning
512191	Film or video transfer services
512199	Film processing laboratories, motion picture
711510	Film producers, independent
512110	Film studios producing films
421410	Film, photographic, wholesaling
326113	Film, plastics (except packaging), manufacturing
326112	Film, plastics, packaging, manufacturing
325992	Film, sensitized (e.g., camera, motion picture, X-ray), manufacturing
512110	Films, motion picture production
512110	Films, motion picture production and distribution

Code	Description
422130	Filter papers wholesaling
327112	Filtering media, pottery, manufacturing
336399	Filters (e.g., air, engine oil, fuel) automotive, truck, and bus, manufacturing
333411	Filters, air-conditioner, manufacturing
334419	Filters, electronic component-type, manufacturing
333411	Filters, furnace, manufacturing
333999	Filters, industrial and general line (except internal combustion engine, warm air furnace), manufacturing
322299	Filters, paper, made from purchased paper
221310	Filtration plant, water
212322	Filtration sand quarrying and/or beneficiating
332993	Fin assemblies, mortar, manufacturing
332993	Fin assemblies, torpedo and bomb, manufacturing
522291	Finance companies (i.e., unsecured cash loans)
523140	Financial futures brokerages
523930	Financial investment advice services, customized, fees paid by client
511120	Financial magazine and periodical publishers
511120	Financial magazine and periodical publishers and printing combined
511120	Financial magazine and periodical publishing (i.e., establishments known as publishers)
323112	Financial magazines and periodicals flexographic printing without publishing
323111	Financial magazines and periodicals gravure printing without publishing
323110	Financial magazines and periodicals lithographic (offset) printing without publishing
323119	Financial magazines and periodicals printing (except flexographic, gravure, lithographic, screen) without publishing
323113	Financial magazines and periodicals screen printing without publishing
541611	Financial management consulting (except investment advice) services
523930	Financial planning services, customized, fees paid by client
522320	Financial transactions processing (except central bank)
521110	Financial transactions processing of the central bank
316999	Findings, boot and shoe, manufacturing
339913	Findings, jeweler's, manufacturing
315212	Findings, suit and coat (e.g., coat fromts, pockets), women's, girls', and infants', cut and sew apparel contractors
315999	Findings, suit and coat (e.g., coat fronts, pockets), cut and sewn from purchased fabric (except apparel contractors)
315211	Findings, suit and coat (e.g., coat fronts, pockets), men's and boys', cut and sew apparel contractors
712110	Fine arts museums
611610	Fine arts schools (except academic)
722110	Fine dining restaurants, full service
422110	Fine paper, bulk, wholesaling
114111	Finfish fishing (e.g., flounder, salmon, trout)
112511	Finfish production, farm raising
112511	Finfish, hatcheries
321213	Finger joint lumber manufacturing
561611	Fingerprint services
314110	Finishing (e.g., dyeing) rugs and carpets
325613	Finishing agents, textile and leather, manufacturing
316110	Finishing hides and skins on a contract basis
316110	Finishing leather
333292	Finishing machinery for textile manufacturing
313311	Finishing plants, broadwoven fabric
611110	Finishing schools, secondary
561621	Fire alarm monitoring services
561621	Fire alarm sales combined with installation, maintenance, or monitoring services
922160	Fire and rescue service
212325	Fire clay mining and/or beneficiating
922160	Fire departments (e.g., government, volunteer)
334290	Fire detection and alarm systems manufacturing
334519	Fire detector systems, nonelectric, manufacturing
332321	Fire doors, metal, manufacturing
235990	Fire escape construction contractors
332323	Fire escapes, metal, manufacturing
325998	Fire extinguisher chemical preparations manufacturing
422690	Fire extinguisher preparations wholesaling
421990	Fire extinguishers wholesaling
339999	Fire extinguishers, portable, manufacturing
611519	Fire fighter training schools
561990	Fire fighting services as a commercial activity
314999	Fire hose, textile, made from purchased materials
332911	Fire hydrant valves manufacturing
332911	Fire hydrants, complete, manufacturing
524126	Fire insurance carriers, direct
541380	Fire insurance underwriters' laboratories
922160	Fire investigation service, government
922160	Fire marshals' offices
922160	Fire prevention offices, government
115310	Fire prevention, forest
325998	Fire retardant chemical preparations manufacturing
233320	Fire station construction
421990	Firearms (except sporting) wholesaling
813319	Firearms advocacy organizations
332994	Firearms manufacturing
421910	Firearms, sporting, wholesaling
336611	Fireboat building

Code	Description
327124	Firebrick, clay refractories, manufacturing
315211	Firefighters' dress uniforms, men's, cut and sew apparel contractors
315222	Firefighters' dress uniforms, men's, cut and sewn from purchased fabric (except apparel contractors)
315212	Firefighters' dress uniforms, women's, cut and sew apparel contractors
315234	Firefighters' dress uniforms, women's, cut and sewn from purchased fabric (except apparel contractors)
922160	Firefighting (except forest), volunteer and government
421850	Firefighting equipment and supplies wholesaling
922160	Firefighting services (including volunteer)
339113	Firefighting suits and accessories manufacturing
115310	Firefighting, forest
332999	Fireplace fixtures and equipment manufacturing
333414	Fireplace inserts (i.e., heat directing) manufacturing
335129	Fireplace logs, electric, manufacturing
421720	Fireplaces, gas, wholesaling
235990	Fireproofing buildings construction contractors
321999	Firewood and fuel wood containing fuel binder manufacturing
454319	Firewood dealers, direct selling
421990	Firewood wholesaling
713990	Fireworks display services
325998	Fireworks manufacturing
453998	Fireworks shops (i.e., permanent location)
421920	Fireworks wholesaling
327112	Firing china for the trade
321920	Firkins and kits, wood, coopered, manufacturing
611699	First aid instruction
339113	First aid, snake bite, or burn kits manufacturing
421450	First-aid kits wholesaling

Code	Description
422210	First-aid supplies wholesaling
422460	Fish (except canned, packaged frozen) wholesaling
924120	Fish and game agencies
311711	Fish and marine animal oils produced in a cannery
311712	Fish and marine animal oils produced in a fresh and frozen seafood plant
311711	Fish and seafood chowder canning
924120	Fish and wildlife conservation program administration
311711	Fish egg bait canning
112511	Fish farms, finfish
112512	Fish farms, shellfish
334511	Fish finders (i.e., sonar) manufacturing
311119	Fish food for feeding fish manufacturing
311712	Fish freezing (e.g., blocks, fillets, ready-to-serve products)
325411	Fish liver oils, medicinal, uncompounded, manufacturing
445220	Fish markets
311711	Fish meal produced in a cannery
311712	Fish meal produced in a fresh and frozen seafood plant
332212	Fish wire (i.e., electrical wiring tool) manufacturing
311711	Fish, canned and cured, manufacturing
422490	Fish, canned, wholesaling
311711	Fish, curing, drying, pickling, salting, and smoking
311712	Fish, fresh or frozen, manufacturing
311712	Fish, fresh prepared, manufacturing
422420	Fish, packaged frozen, wholesaling
422990	Fish, tropical, wholesaling
541710	Fisheries research and development laboratories or services
114111	Fisheries, finfish
114112	Fisheries, shellfish
487210	Fishing boat charter operation
336611	Fishing boat, commercial, building
721214	Fishing camps with accommodation facilities
713990	Fishing clubs, recreational

Code	Description
421910	Fishing equipment and supplies (except commercial) wholesaling
213112	Fishing for tools at oil and gas fields on a contract basis
713990	Fishing guide services
332211	Fishing knives manufacturing
314999	Fishing nets made from purchased materials
713990	Fishing piers
114210	Fishing preserves
451110	Fishing supply stores (e.g., bait)
339920	Fishing tackle and equipment (except lines, nets, seines) manufacturing
713940	Fitness centers
421910	Fitness equipment and supplies wholesaling
713940	Fitness salons
713940	Fitness spas without accommodations
326122	Fittings and unions, rigid plastics pipe, manufacturing
421720	Fittings and valves, plumber's, wholesaling
326122	Fittings, rigid plastics pipe, manufacturing
331511	Fittings, soil and pressure pipe, cast iron, manufacturing
713950	Five pin bowling centers
722213	Fixed location refreshment stands
325992	Fixers, prepared photographic, manufacturing
337920	Fixtures (e.g., poles, rods, rollers), curtain and drapery, manufacturing
421610	Fixtures, electric lighting, wholesaling
421440	Fixtures, store (except refrigerated), wholesaling
337215	Fixtures, store display, manufacturing
453998	Flag and banner shops
561990	Flagging (i.e., traffic control) services
332323	Flagpoles, metal, manufacturing
321999	Flagpoles, wood, manufacturing
314999	Flags, textile (e.g., banners, bunting, emblems, pennants), made from purchased fabrics

Code	Description
212311	Flagstone mining or quarrying
327991	Flagstones cutting
321219	Flakeboard manufacturing
331221	Flakes made from purchased iron or steel
331314	Flakes, aluminum, made from purchased aluminum
331111	Flakes, iron or steel, made in steel mills
334516	Flame photometers manufacturing
812332	Flame resistant clothing supply services
334512	Flame safety controls for furnaces and boilers manufacturing
332995	Flame throwers manufacturing
333512	Flange facing machines, metalworking, manufacturing
332991	Flange units, ball or roller bearing, manufacturing
332919	Flanges and flange unions, pipe, metal, manufacturing
315223	Flannel shirts (except work shirts), men's and boys', cut and sewn from purchased fabric (except apparel contractors)
315291	Flannel shirts, infants', cut and sewn from purchased fabric (except apparel contractors)
315211	Flannel shirts, men's and boys', cut and sew apparel contractors
315212	Flannel shirts, women's, girls', and infants', cut and sew apparel contractors
315232	Flannel shirts, women's, misses', and girls', cut and sewn from purchased fabric (except apparel contrctors)
315225	Flannel shirts, work, men's and boys', cut and sewn from purchased fabric (except apparel contractors)
313210	Flannels, broadwoven, weaving
325998	Flares manufacturing
333315	Flash apparatus, photographic, manufacturing
335110	Flash bulbs, photographic, manufacturing
235610	Flashing construction contractors
335912	Flashlight batteries manufacturing
335110	Flashlight bulb manufacturing
335129	Flashlights manufacturing
421610	Flashlights wholesaling
313249	Flat (i.e., warp) fabrics knitting
331221	Flat bright steel strip made in cold rolling mills
327211	Flat glass (e.g., float, plate) manufacturing
421390	Flat glass wholesaling
334119	Flat panel displays (i.e., complete units), computer peripheral equipment, manufacturing
332612	Flat springs (except clock, watch), light gauge, manufacturing
332611	Flat springs, heavy gauge, manufacturing
336212	Flatbed trailers, commercial, manufacturing
484220	Flatbed trucking, local
484230	Flatbed trucking, long-distance
331111	Flats, iron or steel, made in steel mills
321920	Flats, wood, greenhouse, manufacturing
421220	Flatware (except plated, precious) wholesaling
332211	Flatware, nonprecious and precious plated metal, manufacturing
421940	Flatware, precious and plated, wholesaling
311942	Flavor extracts (except coffee) manufacturing
311511	Flavored milk drinks manufacturing
311930	Flavoring concentrates (except coffee based) manufacturing
422490	Flavoring extracts (except for fountain use) wholesaling
325199	Flavoring materials (i.e., basic synthetic chemicals such as coumarin) manufacturing
311930	Flavoring pastes, powders, and syrups for soft drink manufacturing
313111	Flax spun yarns made from purchased fiber
111120	Flaxseed farming, field and seed production
311225	Flaxseed oil made from purchased oils
311223	Flaxseed oil made in crushing mills
531190	Flea market space (except under roof) rental or leasing
531120	Flea market space, under roof, rental or leasing
454390	Flea markets, temporary location, direct selling
453310	Flea markets, used merchandise, permanent
325320	Flea powders or sprays manufacturing
532112	Fleet leasing, passenger vehicle
316110	Fleshers, leather (i.e., flesh side of split leather), manufacturing
334112	Flexible (i.e., floppy) magnetic disk drives manufacturing
332999	Flexible metal hose and tubing manufacturing
322221	Flexible packaging sheet materials (except foil-paper laminates) made by coating or laminating purchased paper
322225	Flexible packaging sheet materials made by laminating purchased foil
334412	Flexible wiring boards, bare, manufacturing
325910	Flexographic inks manufacturing
323122	Flexographic plate preparation services
323112	Flexographic printing (except books, manifold business forms, printing grey goods)
333293	Flexographic printing presses manufacturing
339920	Flies, artificial fishing, manufacturing
334511	Flight and navigation sensors, transmitters, and displays manufacturing
611519	Flight attendant schools
334511	Flight recorders (i.e., black boxes) manufacturing
333319	Flight simulation machinery manufacturing
611512	Flight training schools
212325	Flint clay mining and/or beneficiating
327992	Flint processing beyond beneficiation

Code	Description
339999	Flints, lighter, manufacturing
321113	Flitches (i.e., veneer stock) made in sawmills
334512	Float controls, residential and commercial types, manufacturing
561990	Float decorating services
541490	Float design services
327124	Floaters, glasshouse, clay, manufacturing
713210	Floating casinos (i.e., gambling cruises, riverboat casinos)
332313	Floating covers, fabricated metal plate work, manufacturing
311711	Floating factory ships seafood processing
332812	Flocking metals and metal products for the trade
234990	Flood control project construction
332312	Flood gates, metal plate, manufacturing
335129	Floodlights (i.e., lighting fixtures) manufacturing
321918	Floor baseboards, wood, manufacturing
442210	Floor covering stores (except wood or ceramic tile only)
444190	Floor covering stores, wood or ceramic tile only
421220	Floor coverings wholesaling
326192	Floor coverings, linoleum, manufacturing
326192	Floor coverings, resilient, manufacturing
326192	Floor coverings, rubber, manufacturing
326192	Floor coverings, vinyl, manufacturing
332312	Floor jacks, metal, manufacturing
335121	Floor lamps (i.e., lighting fixtures), residential, manufacturing
235520	Floor laying, finishing, or refinishing construction contractors
421850	Floor maintenance equipment wholesaling
326299	Floor mats (e.g., bath, door), rubber, manufacturing
325612	Floor polishes and waxes manufacturing

Code	Description
332312	Floor posts, adjustable metal, manufacturing
532490	Floor sanding machine rental or leasing
333319	Floor sanding, washing, and polishing machines, commercial-type, manufacturing
335212	Floor scrubbing and shampooing machines, household-type electric, manufacturing
335211	Floor standing fans, household-type electric, manufacturing
327122	Floor tile, ceramic, manufacturing
321214	Floor trusses, wood, manufacturing
335212	Floor waxers and polishers, household-type electric, manufacturing
532490	Floor waxing equipment rental or leasing
332323	Flooring, open steel (i.e., grating), manufacturing
332322	Flooring, sheet metal, manufacturing
321114	Flooring, wood block, treating
321918	Flooring, wood, manufacturing
421310	Flooring, wood, wholesaling
334112	Floppy disk drives manufacturing
561422	Floral wire services (i.e., telemarketing services)
422930	Florist's supplies wholesaling
453110	Florists
327112	Florists' articles, red earthenware, manufacturing
333131	Flotation machinery, mining-type, manufacturing
114111	Flounder fishing
314911	Flour bags made from purchased woven or knitted materials
333294	Flour milling machinery manufacturing
311230	Flour mills, breakfast cereal, manufacturing
311211	Flour mills, cereals grains (except breakfast cereals, rice)
311211	Flour mixes made in flour mills
422490	Flour wholesaling
311822	Flour, blended or self-rising, made from purchased flour

Code	Description
311211	Flour, blended, prepared, or self-rising (except rice), made in flour mills
311213	Flour, malt, manufacturing
311212	Flour, rice, manufacturing
321999	Flour, wood, manufacturing
335314	Flow actuated electrical switches manufacturing
334513	Flow instruments, industrial process-type, manufacturing
327420	Flower boxes, plaster of paris, manufacturing
111421	Flower bulb growing
422910	Flower bulbs wholesaling
111422	Flower growing
327112	Flower pots, red earthenware, manufacturing
111422	Flower seed production
453998	Flower shops, artificial or dried
453110	Flower shops, fresh
561920	Flower show managers
561920	Flower show organizers
561920	Flower show promoters
422930	Flowers wholesaling
339999	Flowers, artificial (except glass, plastics), manufacturing
327123	Flue lining, clay, manufacturing
421320	Flue pipe and linings wholesaling
332322	Flues, stove and furnace, sheet metal, manufacturing
332439	Fluid milk shipping containers, light gauge metal, manufacturing
311511	Fluid milk substitutes processing
333995	Fluid power actuators manufacturing
332912	Fluid power aircraft subassemblies manufacturing
333995	Fluid power cylinders manufacturing
332912	Fluid power hose assemblies manufacturing
333996	Fluid power motors manufacturing
333996	Fluid power pumps manufacturing
332912	Fluid power valves and hose fittings manufacturing
421830	Fluid-power transmission equipment wholesaling

Code	Description
334513	Fluidic devices, circuits, and systems for process control, manufacturing
332313	Flumes, fabricated metal plate work, manufacturing
332322	Flumes, sheet metal, manufacturing
325188	Fluoboric acid manufacturing
335311	Fluorescent ballasts (i.e., transformers) manufacturing
325132	Fluorescent dyes manufacturing
335110	Fluorescent lamp tubes, electric, manufacturing
335122	Fluorescent lighting fixtures, commercial, institutional, and industrial electric, manufacturing
335121	Fluorescent lighting fixtures, residential, manufacturing
335311	Fluorescent lighting transformers manufacturing
325120	Fluorinated hydrocarbon gases manufacturing
325188	Fluorine manufacturing
212393	Fluorite mining and/or beneficiating
325212	Fluoro rubbers manufacturing
325211	Fluoro-polymer resins manufacturing
325212	Fluorocarbon derivative rubbers manufacturing
325222	Fluorocarbon fibers and filaments manufacturing
325120	Fluorocarbon gases manufacturing
325211	Fluorohydrocarbon resins manufacturing
334517	Fluoroscopes manufacturing
334517	Fluoroscopic X-ray apparatus and tubes manufacturing
212393	Fluorspar mining and/or beneficiating
335110	Fluroescent lamp electrodes, cold cathode, manufacturing
332998	Flush tanks, metal, manufacturing
332913	Flush valves, plumbing, manufacturing
339992	Flutes and parts manufacturing
325998	Fluxes (e.g., brazing, galvanizing, soldering, welding) manufacturing
325320	Fly sprays manufacturing

Code	Description
332999	Fly swatters, metal, manufacturing
541870	Flyer direct distribution (except direct mail) services
713990	Flying clubs, recreational
488119	Flying field operators
611512	Flying instruction
335129	Flytraps, electrical, manufacturing
336312	Flywheels and ring gears, automotive and truck gasoline engine, manufacturing
326150	Foam plastics products (except polystrene) manufacturing
326140	Foam polystyrene products manufacturing
422990	Foam rubber wholesaling
422610	Foam, plastics, wholesaling
322223	Foil bags made from purchased foil
332999	Foil containers (except bags) manufacturing
332999	Foil not made in rolling mills
322225	Foil sheet, laminating purchased foil sheets for packaging applications
331315	Foil, aluminum, made by flat rolling purchased aluminum
331315	Foil, aluminum, made in integrated secondary smelting and flat rolling mills
331421	Foil, copper, made from purchased metal or scrap
331491	Foil, gold, made by rolling purchased metals or scrap
331491	Foil, nickel, made by rolling purchased metals or scrap
331491	Foil, silver, made by rolling purchased metals or scrap
422120	Folders, file, wholesaling
561910	Folding and packaging services, textile and apparel
322130	Folding boxboard stock manufacturing
322212	Folding boxes (except corrugated) made from purchased paperboard
322212	Folding paper and paperboard containers (except corrugated) made from purchased paperboard
111422	Foliage growing
711120	Folk dance companies

Code	Description
711510	Folk dancers, independent
445110	Food (i.e., groceries) stores
446191	Food (i.e., health) supplement stores
336999	Food (vendor) carts on wheels manufacturing
624210	Food banks
722330	Food carts, mobile
333294	Food choppers, grinders, mixers, and slicers (i.e., food manufacturing-type) manufacturing
325132	Food coloring, synthetic, manufacturing
311942	Food colorings, natural, manufacturing
722310	Food concession contractors (e.g., convention facilities, entertainment facilities, sporting facilities)
322299	Food containers made from molded pulp
326140	Food containers, polystyrene foam, manufacturing
322215	Food containers, sanitary (except folding), made from purchased paper or paperboard
322212	Food containers, sanitary, folding, made from purchased paperboard
333294	Food dehydrating equipment (except household-type) manufacturing
923130	Food distribution program administration, government
311942	Food extracts (except coffee, meat) manufacturing
926140	Food inspection agencies
811310	Food machinery repair and maintenance services
335211	Food mixers, household-type electric, manufacturing
333993	Food packaging machinery manufacturing
327213	Food packaging, glass, manufacturing
421830	Food processing machinery and equipment wholesaling
233310	Food products manufacturing or packaging plant construction

Code	Description
541710	Food research and development laboratories or services
722310	Food service contractors, airline
722310	Food service contractors, cafeteria
722310	Food service contractors, concession operator (e.g., convention facilities, entertainment facilities, sporting facilities)
421440	Food service equipment (except refrigerated), commercial, wholesaling
923120	Food service health inspections
326111	Food storage bags, plastics film, single wall or multiwall, manufacturing
541380	Food testing laboratories or services
322299	Food trays, molded pulp, manufacturing
333319	Food warming equipment, commercial-type, manufacturing
335228	Food waste disposal units, household-type, manufacturing
311991	Food, prepared, perishable, packaged for individual resale
339113	Foot appliances, orthopedic, manufacturing
621391	Foot specialists' (podiatry) offices (e.g., centers, clinics)
711211	Football clubs, professional or semiprofessional
713990	Football clubs, recreational
339920	Football equipment and supplies (except footwear, uniforms) manufacturing
421910	Football equipment and supplies wholesaling
611620	Football instruction, camps, or schools
711211	Football teams, professional or semiprofessional
316211	Footholds, plastics or plastics soled fabric upper, manufacturing
316211	Footholds, rubber or rubber soled fabric upper, manufacturing
315119	Footies, sheer, knitting or knitting and finishing

Code	Description
451110	Footwear (e.g., bowling, golf, spiked), specialty sports, stores
316211	Footwear (except house slippers), plastics or plastics soled fabric uppers, manufacturing
333298	Footwear making or repairing machinery manufacturing
326199	Footwear parts (e.g., heels, soles), plastics, manufacturing
326299	Footwear parts (e.g., heels, soles, soling strips), rubber, manufacturing
422340	Footwear wholesaling
316219	Footwear, athletic (except rubber or plastics soled with fabric upper), manufacturing
316219	Footwear, children's (except house slippers, orthopedic extension, plastics, rubber), manufacturing
316219	Footwear, children's, leather or vinyl upper with rubber or plastics soles, manufacturing
316213	Footwear, men's (except house slippers, athletic, orthopedic extension, plastics, rubber), manufacturing
316213	Footwear, men's leather or vinyl upper with rubber or plastics soles, manufacturing
316214	Footwear, women's (except house slippers, athletic, orthopedic extension, plastics, rubber) manufacturing
316214	Footwear, women's leather or vinyl upper with rubber or plastics soles, manufacturing
339112	Forceps, surgical, manufacturing
523130	Foreign currency exchange dealing (i.e., acting as a principal in dealing commodities to investors)
523130	Foreign currency exchange services (i.e., selling to the public)
928120	Foreign economic and social development services, government
928120	Foreign government service
611630	Foreign language schools
928120	Foreign missions

Code	Description
541380	Forensic (except medical) laboratories or services
621511	Forensic laboratories, medical
621111	Forensic pathologists' offices (e.g., centers, clinics)
531190	Forest land rental or leasing
115310	Forest management plans preparation
113210	Forest nurseries for reforestation, growing trees
421990	Forest products (except lumber) wholesaling
484230	Forest products trucking, long-distance
532412	Forestry machinery and equipment rental or leasing
811310	Forestry machinery and equipment repair and maintenance services
421810	Forestry machinery and equipment wholesaling
541710	Forestry research and development laboratories or services
115310	Forestry services
333513	Forging machinery and hammers manufacturing
332111	Forgings made from purchased iron or steel, unfinished
331111	Forgings, iron or steel, made in steel mills
811310	Forklift repair and maintenance services
421830	Forklift trucks (except log) wholesaling
333924	Forklifts manufacturing
332212	Forks, handtools (e.g., garden, hay, manure), manufacturing
332211	Forks, table, nonprecious and precious plated metal, manufacturing
331222	Form ties made in wire drawing plants
315211	Formal jackets, men's and boys', cut and sew apparel contractors
315222	Formal jackets, men's and boys', cut and sewn from purchased fabric (except apparel contractors)
532220	Formal wear rental
325199	Formaldehyde manufacturing

Code	Description
325199	Formalin manufacturing
325199	Formic acid manufacturing
333513	Forming machines (except drawing), metalworking, manufacturing
327112	Forms for dipped rubber products, pottery, manufacturing
235990	Forms for poured concrete construction contractors
421420	Forms handling machines wholesaling
332322	Forms, concrete, sheet metal, manufacturing
321999	Forms, display, boot and shoe, all materials, manufacturing
422120	Forms, paper (e.g., business, office, sales), wholesaling
312130	Fortified wines manufacturing
812990	Fortune-telling services
624110	Foster care placement agencies
624110	Foster home placement services
235410	Foundation (e.g., block, brick, stone) construction contractors
235930	Foundation digging (i.e., excavation) construction contractors
235930	Foundation drilling construction contractors
315212	Foundation garments, women's and girls', cut and sew apparel contractors
315231	Foundation garments, women's, misses', and girls', cut and sewn from purchased fabric (except apparel contractors)
325620	Foundations (i.e., make-up) manufacturing
235710	Foundations of buildings, poured concrete, construction contractors
331528	Foundries (except die-casting), nonferrous metals (except aluminum, copper)
331524	Foundries, aluminum (except die-casting)
331525	Foundries, brass, bronze, and copper (except die-casting) manufacturing
331525	Foundries, copper (except die-casting)

Code	Description
331521	Foundries, die-casting, aluminum
331522	Foundries, die-casting, nonferrous metals (except aluminum)
331511	Foundries, iron (i.e., ductile, gray, malleable, semisteel)
331513	Foundries, steel (except investment)
331512	Foundries, steel investment
333511	Foundry casting molds manufacturing
325998	Foundry core oil, wash, and wax manufacturing
332997	Foundry cores manufacturing
811310	Foundry machinery and equipment repair and maintenance services
421830	Foundry machinery and equipment wholesaling
332997	Foundry pattern making
421510	Foundry products wholesaling
212322	Foundry sand quarrying and/or beneficiating
422450	Fountain fruits and syrups wholesaling
335129	Fountain lighting fixtures manufacturing
339941	Fountain pens manufacturing
332999	Fountains (except drinking), metal, manufacturing
332998	Fountains, drinking (except mechanically refrigerated), manufacturing
421720	Fountains, drinking (except refrigerated), wholesaling
421740	Fountains, drinking, refrigerated, wholesaling
327420	Fountains, plaster of paris, manufacturing
333415	Fountains, refrigerated drinking, manufacturing
713920	Four season ski resorts without accommodations
333291	Fourdrinier machinery manufacturing
332618	Fourdrinier wire cloth made from purchased wire
112930	Fox production
335312	Fractional horsepower electric motors manufacturing

Code	Description
333298	Fractionating equipment, chemical, manufacturing
211112	Fractionating natural gas liquids
333319	Frame and body alignment equipment, motor vehicle, manufacturing
332999	Frames and handles, handbag and luggage, metal, manufacturing
421220	Frames and pictures wholesaling
339942	Frames for artist's canvases (i.e., stretchers) manufacturing
333292	Frames for textile making machinery manufacturing
332321	Frames, door and window, metal, manufacturing
321911	Frames, door and window, wood, manufacturing
332999	Frames, metal, lamp shade, manufacturing
332999	Frames, metal, umbrella and parasol, manufacturing
339999	Frames, mirror and picture, all materials, manufacturing
421460	Frames, ophthalmic, wholesaling
533110	Franchise agreements, leasing, selling or licensing, without providing other services
813410	Fraternal associations or lodges, social or civic
524113	Fraternal life insurance organizations
813410	Fraternal lodges
813410	Fraternal organizations
813410	Fraternities (except residential)
721310	Fraternity houses
621493	Freestanding ambulatory surgical centers and clinics
621493	Freestanding emergency medical centers and clinics
311423	Freeze-dried, food processing, fruits and vegetables
335222	Freezers, chest and upright household-type, manufacturing
421620	Freezers, household-type, wholesaling
333415	Freezing equipment, industrial and commercial-type, manufacturing

Code	Description
311712	Freezing fish (e.g., blocks, fillets, ready-to-serve products)
488210	Freight car cleaning services
481112	Freight carriers (except air couriers), air, scheduled
481212	Freight charter services, air
488510	Freight forwarding
482111	Freight railways, line-haul
482112	Freight railways, short-line or beltline
541614	Freight rate auditor services
541614	Freight rate consulting services
483113	Freight shipping on the Great Lakes system (including the St Lawrence Seaway)
541614	Freight traffic consulting services
481212	Freight transportation, air, charter services
481212	Freight transportation, air, nonscheduled
483113	Freight transportation, deep sea, to and from domestic ports
483111	Freight transportation, deep sea, to or from foreign ports
483211	Freight transportation, inland waters (except on Great Lakes system)
311411	French fries, frozen, pre-cooked, manufacturing
311412	French toast, frozen, manufacturing
335312	Frequency converters (i.e., electric generators) manufacturing
334515	Frequency meters (e.g., electrical, electronic, mechanical) manufacturing
334515	Frequency synthesizers manufacturing
235420	Fresco construction contractors
422460	Fresh fish wholesaling
422480	Fresh fruits, vegetables and berries wholesaling
422470	Fresh meats wholesaling
422440	Fresh poultry wholesaling
422460	Fresh seafood wholesaling
339992	Fretted instruments and parts manufacturing
313221	Fringes weaving

Code	Description
325510	Frit manufacturing
114119	Frog fishing
112519	Frog production, farm raising
331111	Frogs, iron or steel, made in steel mills
811118	Front end alignment shops, automotive
421820	Frost protection machinery wholesaling
311999	Frosting, prepared, manufacturing
311411	Frozen ades, drinks and cocktail mixes, manufacturing
311812	Frozen bread and bread-type rolls, made in commercial bakeries
311813	Frozen cake manufacturing
311411	Frozen citrus pulp manufacturing
311520	Frozen custard manufacturing
722213	Frozen custard stands, fixed location
311520	Frozen desserts (except bakery) manufacturing
311412	Frozen dinners (except seafood-based) manufacturing
311822	Frozen doughs made from purchased flour
422460	Frozen fish (except packaged) wholesaling
454390	Frozen food and freezer plan providers, direct selling
326111	Frozen food bags, plastics film, single wall or multiwall, manufacturing
311412	Frozen food entrees (except seafood based), packaged, manufacturing
422420	Frozen foods, packaged (except dairy products), wholesaling
311411	Frozen fruit and vegetable processing
311411	Frozen fruits, fruit juices, and vegetables, manufacturing
311612	Frozen meat pies (i.e., tourtires) made from purchased carcasses
445210	Frozen meat stores
422470	Frozen meats (except packaged) wholesaling
311412	Frozen pizza manufacturing
311412	Frozen pot pies manufacturing

Code	Description
422440	Frozen poultry (except packaged) wholesaling
311412	Frozen rice dishes manufacturing
422460	Frozen seafood (except packaged) wholesaling
311412	Frozen side dishes manufacturing
311412	Frozen soups (except seafood) manufacturing
311412	Frozen waffles manufacturing
111336	Fruit and tree nut combination farming
445230	Fruit and vegetable stands, permanent
311423	Fruit and vegetables, dehydrating, manufacturing
321920	Fruit baskets, veneer and splint, manufacturing
311421	Fruit brining
311421	Fruit butters manufacturing
321920	Fruit crates, wood, wirebound, manufacturing
312111	Fruit drinks (except juice), manufacturing
311942	Fruit extracts (except coffee) manufacturing
111419	Fruit farming, grown under cover
311211	Fruit flour, meal, and powders, manufacturing
333111	Fruit harvesting machines manufacturing
311421	Fruit juice canning
311411	Fruit juice concentrates, frozen, manufacturing
311421	Fruit juices, fresh, manufacturing
445230	Fruit markets
311340	Fruit peel products (e.g., candied, crystallized, glace, glazed) manufacturing
311421	Fruit pickling
311421	Fruit pie fillings, canned
311421	Fruit pie fillings, canning
311520	Fruit pops, frozen, manufacturing
115114	Fruit precooling
115114	Fruit sorting, grading, and packing
445230	Fruit stands, permanent
454390	Fruit stands, temporary

Code	Description
111421	Fruit stock (e.g., plants, seedlings, trees) growing
311930	Fruit syrups, flavoring, manufacturing
115113	Fruit, machine harvesting
115114	Fruit, sun drying
115114	Fruit, vacuum cooling
311340	Fruits (e.g., candied, crystallized, glazed) manufacturing
326199	Fruits and vegetables, artificial, plastics, manufacturing
311423	Fruits dehydrating (except sun drying)
311421	Fruits pickling
339999	Fruits, artificial (except glass, plastics), manufacturing
327215	Fruits, artificial, made from purchased glass
327212	Fruits, artificial, made in glass making plants
311421	Fruits, canned, manufacturing
422490	Fruits, canned, wholesaling
422480	Fruits, fresh, wholesaling
311411	Fruits, frozen, manufacturing
422420	Fruits, frozen, wholesaling
112320	Fryer chicken production
335211	Fryers, household-type electric, manufacturing
311320	Fudge, chocolate, made from cacao beans
311330	Fudge, chocolate, made from purchased chocolate
311340	Fudge, nonchocolate, manufacturing
326299	Fuel bladders, rubber, manufacturing
324199	Fuel briquettes or boulets made from refined petroleum
335999	Fuel cells, electrochemical generators, manufacturing
334413	Fuel cells, solid-state, manufacturing
334519	Fuel densitometers, aircraft engine, manufacturing
336312	Fuel injection systems and parts, automotive and truck gasoline engine, manufacturing

Code	Description
334519	Fuel mixture indicators, aircraft engine, manufacturing
454311	Fuel oil (i.e., heating) dealers, direct selling
422710	Fuel oil bulk stations and terminals
235110	Fuel oil burner construction contractors
422720	Fuel oil truck jobbers
422720	Fuel oil wholesaling (except bulk stations, terminals)
324110	Fuel oils manufacturing
325188	Fuel propellants, solid inorganic, not specified elsewhere by process, manufacturing
325199	Fuel propellants, solid organic, not specified elsewhere by process, manufacturing
336322	Fuel pumps, electric, automotive, truck, and bus, manufacturing
336312	Fuel pumps, mechanical, automotive and truck gasoline engine, manufacturing
334519	Fuel system instruments, aircraft, manufacturing
334519	Fuel totalizers, aircraft engine, manufacturing
421520	Fuel, coal and coke, wholesaling
422720	Fueling aircraft (except on contract basis)
488190	Fueling aircraft on a contract or fee basis
324110	Fuels, jet, manufacturing
321113	Fuelwood made from sawmill waste
722110	Full service restaurants
212325	Fuller's earth mining and/or beneficiating
327992	Fuller's earth processing beyond beneficiating
332313	Fumigating chambers, fabricated metal plate work, manufacturing
115114	Fumigating grain
561710	Fumigating services
334515	Function generators manufacturing
561499	Fundraising campaign organization services on a contract or fee basis
334119	Funds transfer devices manufacturing

Code	Description
525110	Funds, employee benefit pension
525120	Funds, health and welfare
525990	Funds, mutual, closed-end
525910	Funds, mutual, open-ended
525110	Funds, pension
525190	Funds, self-insurance (except employee benefit funds)
812210	Funeral director services
812210	Funeral homes
812210	Funeral homes combined with crematories
524128	Funeral insurance carriers, direct
812210	Funeral parlors
325320	Fungicides manufacturing
315292	Fur accessories and trimmings (except apparel contractors) manufacturing
315211	Fur accessories and trimmings, men's and boys', cut and sew apparel contractors
315212	Fur accessories and trimmings, women's, girls', and infants', cut and sew apparel contractors
315292	Fur apparel (e.g., capes, coats, hats, jackets, neckpieces) (except apparel contractors) manufacturing
315211	Fur apparel (e.g., capes, coats, hats, jackets, neckpieces), men's and boys', cut and sew apparel contractors
315212	Fur apparel (e.g., capes, coats, hats, jackets, neckpieces), women's, girls', and infants', cut and sew apparel contractors
448190	Fur apparel stores
112930	Fur bearing animal production
315292	Fur clothing (except apparel contractors) manufacturing
422330	Fur clothing wholesaling
315211	Fur clothing, men's and boys', cut and sew apparel contractors
315212	Fur clothing, women's, girls', and infants', cut and sew apparel contractors
421930	Fur cuttings and scraps wholesaling
541490	Fur design services

Code	Description
315211	Fur finishers, liners, and buttonhole makers, men's and boys', cut and sew apparel contractors
315212	Fur finishers, liners, and buttonhole makers, women's, girls', and infants', cut and sew apparel contractors
812320	Fur garment cleaning services
811490	Fur garment repair shops without retailing new fur garments
315292	Fur plates and trimmings (except apparel contractors) manufacturing
315211	Fur plates and trimmings, men's and boys', cut and sew apparel contractors
315212	Fur plates and trimmings, women's, girls', and infants', cut and sew apparel contractors
532220	Fur rental
493120	Fur storage warehousing for the trade
316110	Fur stripping
325182	Furnace black manufacturing
332322	Furnace casings, sheet metal, manufacturing
235110	Furnace construction contractors
333411	Furnace filters manufacturing
332322	Furnace flues, sheet metal, manufacturing
234930	Furnace for industrial plant construction
333414	Furnaces (except forced air), heating, manufacturing
333994	Furnaces and ovens, semiconductor wafer, manufacturing
421720	Furnaces, (except forced air), heating, wholesaling
339114	Furnaces, dental laboratory, manufacturing
333414	Furnaces, floor and wall, manufacturing
421830	Furnaces, industrial process, wholesaling
333994	Furnaces, industrial-type, manufacturing
339111	Furnaces, laboratory-type (except dental), manufacturing

Code	Description
333415	Furnaces, warm air (i.e., forced air), manufacturing
421730	Furnaces, warm air (i.e., forced air), wholesaling
333994	Furnances and ovens for drying and redrying, industrial process-type, manufacturing
422320	Furnishings (except shoes), men's and boys', wholesaling
422330	Furnishings (except shoes), women's, girls' and infants', wholesaling
448150	Furnishings stores, men's and boys'
448150	Furnishings stores, women's and girls'
421210	Furniture (except drafting tables, hospital beds, medical furniture) wholesaling
337124	Furniture (except upholstered), metal household-type, manufacturing
337214	Furniture (except wood), office-type, padded, upholstered, or plain, manufacturing
337125	Furniture (except wood, metal, upholstered) indoor and outdoor household-type, manufacturing
532299	Furniture (i.e., residential) rental centers
442110	Furniture and appliance stores (i.e., primarily retailing furniture)
561740	Furniture cleaning on customers' premises
561740	Furniture cleaning services
541420	Furniture design services
321912	Furniture dimension stock, hardwood, unfinished, manufacturing
321912	Furniture dimension stock, softwood, unfinished, manufacturing
321912	Furniture dimension stock, unfinished wood, manufacturing
337215	Furniture frames and parts, metal, manufacturing
337215	Furniture frames, wood, manufacturing
332510	Furniture hardware, metal, manufacturing

Code	Description
321999	Furniture inlays manufacturing
484210	Furniture moving, used
421210	Furniture parts wholesaling
337215	Furniture parts, finished metal, manufacturing
337215	Furniture parts, finished plastics, manufacturing
337215	Furniture parts, finished wood, manufacturing
325612	Furniture polishes and waxes manufacturing
811420	Furniture refinishing shops
811420	Furniture repair shops
811420	Furniture reupholstering shops
332612	Furniture springs, unassembled, made from purchased wire
321912	Furniture squares, unfinished hardwood, manufacturing
442110	Furniture stores (e.g., household, office, outdoor)
453310	Furniture stores, used
327215	Furniture tops, glass (e.g., beveled, cut, polished), made from purchased glass
314999	Furniture trimmings made from purchased fabrics
327991	Furniture, cut stone (i.e., benches, tables, church), manufacturing
337127	Furniture, factory-type (e.g., cabinets, stools, tool stands, work benches), manufacturing
532291	Furniture, home health, rental
339111	Furniture, hospital (e.g., hospital beds, operating room furniture), manufacturing
337121	Furniture, household-type, upholstered on frames of any material, manufacturing
532490	Furniture, institutional (i.e. public building), rental or leasing
337127	Furniture, institutional, manufacturing
339111	Furniture, laboratory-type (e.g., benches, cabinets, stools, tables), manufacturing
532420	Furniture, office, rental or leasing
337211	Furniture, office-type, padded, upholstered, or plain wood, manufacturing

Code	Description
337124	Furniture, outdoor metal household-type (e.g., beach, garden, lawn, porch), manufacturing
337122	Furniture, outdoor wood household-type (e.g., beach, garden, lawn, porch), manufacturing
337127	Furniture, public building (e.g., church, library, school, theater), manufacturing
532299	Furniture, residential, rental or leasing
337127	Furniture, restaurant-type, manufacturing
337122	Furniture, unassembled or knock-down wood household-type, manufacturing
337122	Furniture, unfinished wood household-type, manufacturing
337122	Furniture, wood household-type, not upholstered (except TV and radio housings, and sewing machine cabinets), manufacturing
448190	Furriers
332323	Furring channels, sheet metal, manufacturing
316110	Furs, dressed (e.g., bleached, curried, dyed, scraped, tanned), manufacturing
422990	Furs, dressed, wholesaling
422590	Furs, raw, wholesaling
335313	Fuse clips and blocks, electric, manufacturing
335931	Fuse cutouts, manufacturing
335313	Fuse mountings, electric power, manufacturing
332993	Fuses ammunition (i.e., more than 30 mm., more than 1.18 inch) manufacturing
421610	Fuses, electric, wholesaling
335313	Fuses, electrical, manufacturing
325191	Fustic wood extract manufacturing
337122	Futon frames manufacturing
523140	Futures commodity contracts brokerages
523140	Futures commodity contracts brokers' offices

Code	Description
523130	Futures commodity contracts dealing (i.e., acting as a principal in dealing commodities to investors)
523210	Futures commodity contracts exchanges
335931	GFCI (ground fault circuit interrupters) manufacturing
522294	GNMA (Government National Mortgage Association)
334220	GPS (global positioning system) equipment manufacturing
212319	Gabbro crushed and broken stone mining and/or beneficiating
212311	Gabbro mining or quarrying
316211	Gaitors, plastics or plastics soled fabric upper, manufacturing
316211	Gaitors, rubber or rubber soled fabric upper, manufacturing
212231	Galena mining and/or beneficiating
712110	Galleries, art (except retail)
453920	Galleries, art, retail
713990	Galleries, shooting
316211	Galoshes, plastics or plastics soled fabric upper, manufacturing
316211	Galoshes, rubber, or rubber soled fabric upper, manufacturing
333516	Galvanizing machinery manufacturing
331111	Galvanizing metals and metal formed products made in steel mills
332812	Galvanizing metals and metal products for the trade
334515	Galvanometers (except geophysical) manufacturing
334519	Galvanometers, geophysical, manufacturing
325191	Gambier extract manufacturing
921130	Gambling control boards, nonoperating
713290	Gambling control boards, operating gambling activities
713210	Gambling cruises
713290	Gambling device arcades or parlors, coin-operated
713290	Gambling device concession operators (i.e., supplying and servicing in others' facilities), coin-operated

Code	Description
924120	Game and inland fish agencies
334611	Game cartridge software, mass reproducing
114210	Game preserves, commercial
114210	Game propagation
114210	Game retreats
421430	Game software wholesaling
451120	Game stores (including electronic)
924120	Game wardens
339932	Games (except coin operated), children's and adult, manufacturing
421920	Games (except coin-operated) wholesaling
339999	Games, coin-operated, manufacturing
421990	Games, coin-operated, wholesaling
334611	Games, computer software, mass reproducing
511210	Games, computer software, publishing
334517	Gamma ray irradiation equipment manufacturing
212319	Ganister crushed and broken stone mining and/or beneficiating
235510	Garage door construction contractors
335999	Garage door openers manufacturing
332321	Garage doors, metal, manufacturing
321911	Garage doors, wood, manufacturing
233320	Garage, commercial or institutional, construction contractors
812930	Garages, automobile parking
811198	Garages, do-it-yourself automotive repair
811111	Garages, general automotive repair (except gasoline service stations)
332311	Garages, prefabricated metal, manufacturing
321992	Garages, prefabricated wood, manufacturing
332439	Garbage cans, light gauge metal, manufacturing
562111	Garbage collection services
562213	Garbage disposal combustors or incinerators
562212	Garbage disposal landfills

Code	Description
421440	Garbage disposal unites, commercial-type, wholesaling
333319	Garbage disposal units, commercial-type, manufacturing
335228	Garbage disposal units, household-type, manufacturing
421620	Garbage disposal units, household-type, wholesaling
562212	Garbage dumps
562111	Garbage hauling, local
333994	Garbage incinerators (except precast concrete) manufacturing
327390	Garbage incinerators, precast concrete, manufacturing
562111	Garbage pick-up services
336211	Garbage truck bodies manufacturing
336120	Garbage trucks assembling on chassis of own manufacture
336211	Garbage trucks assembling on purchased chassis
111130	Garbanzo farming, dry, field and seed production
444220	Garden centers
813410	Garden clubs
811411	Garden equipment repair and maintenance services without retailing new garden equipment
327390	Garden furniture, precast concrete, manufacturing
327991	Garden furniture, stone, manufacturing
337122	Garden furniture, wood, manufacturing
326220	Garden hose, rubber or plastics, manufacturing
421820	Garden machinery and equipment wholesaling
333112	Garden machinery and equipment, powered, manufacturing
561730	Garden maintenance services
541320	Garden planning services
327112	Garden pottery manufacturing
444210	Garden power equipment stores
422910	Garden supplies (e.g., fertilizers, pesticides) wholesaling

Code	Description
811411	Garden tool sharpening and repair services
532490	Garden tractor rental or leasing
339999	Garden umbrellas manufacturing
712130	Gardens, zoological or botanical
111219	Garlic farming (except under cover), field, bedding plant and seed production
111419	Garlic farming under cover
811490	Garment alteration and/or repair shops without retailing new garments
812320	Garment cleaning (e.g., fur, leather, suede) services
321999	Garment hangers, wood, manufacturing
316110	Garment leather manufacturing
314911	Garment storage bags manufacturing
315292	Garments, leather or sheep-lined (except apparel contractors), manufacturing
315211	Garments, leather or sheep-lined, men's and boys', cut and sew apparel contractors
315212	Garments, leather or sheep-lined, women's, girls', and infants', cut and sew apparel contractors
313320	Garments, oiling (i.e., waterproofing)
212399	Garnet mining and/or beneficiating
333292	Garnetting machinery for textiles manufacturing
314999	Garnetting of textile waste and rags
315212	Garter belts cut and sew apparel contractors
315231	Garter belts cut and sewn from purchased fabric (except apparel contractors)
315212	Garters, women's, cut and sew apparel contractors
315231	Garters, women's, misses', and girls', cut and sewn from purchased fabric (except apparel contractors)
334513	Gas analyzers, industrial process-type, manufacturing
334516	Gas analyzers, laboratory-type, manufacturing

Code	Description
334513	Gas and liquid analysis instruments, industrial process-type, manufacturing
334512	Gas burner automatic controls (except valves) manufacturing
333414	Gas burners, heating, manufacturing
334513	Gas chromatographic instruments, industrial process-type, manufacturing
334516	Gas chromatographic instruments, laboratory-type, manufacturing
333414	Gas fireplaces manufacturing
421720	Gas fireplaces wholesaling
334513	Gas flow instrumentation, industrial process-type, manufacturing
333999	Gas generating machinery, general purpose-type, manufacturing
421720	Gas hot water heaters wholesaling
334519	Gas leak detectors manufacturing
235990	Gas leakage detection contractors
523999	Gas lease brokers' offices
335129	Gas lighting fixtures manufacturing
421990	Gas lighting fixtures wholesaling
235110	Gas line hookup construction contractors
333298	Gas liquefying machinery manufacturing
234910	Gas main construction
339113	Gas masks manufacturing
561990	Gas meter reading services, contract
421720	Gas ranges wholesaling
333319	Gas ranges, commercial-type, manufacturing
335221	Gas ranges, household-type, manufacturing
333999	Gas separating machinery manufacturing
333414	Gas space heaters manufacturing
332420	Gas storage tanks, heavy gauge metal, manufacturing
336399	Gas tanks assembled, automotive, truck, and bus, manufacturing
333611	Gas turbine generator set units manufacturing
333611	Gas turbines (except aircraft) manufacturing

Code	Description
336412	Gas turbines, aircraft, manufacturing
332911	Gas valves, industrial-type, manufacturing
333992	Gas welding equipment manufacturing
333992	Gas welding rods, coated or cored, manufacturing
213111	Gas well drilling on a contract basis
333132	Gas well machinery and equipment manufacturing
213112	Gas well rig building, repairing, and dismantling on a contract basis
213112	Gas, compressing natural, in the field on a contract basis
221210	Gas, manufactured, production and distribution
221210	Gas, mixed natural and manufactured, production and distribution
211112	Gas, natural liquefied petroleum, extraction
221210	Gas, natural, distribution
211111	Gas, natural, extraction
211112	Gas, natural, liquids, extraction
486210	Gas, natural, pipeline operation
211112	Gas, residue, extraction
333414	Gas-oil burners, combination, manufacturing
422690	Gases, compressed and liquefied (except liquefied petroleum gas), wholesaling
325120	Gases, industrial (i.e., compressed, liquefied, solid), manufacturing
211112	Gases, petroleum, liquefied, extraction
339991	Gasket, packing, and sealing devices manufacturing
339991	Gaskets manufacturing
421840	Gaskets wholesaling
334514	Gasmeters, consumption registering, manufacturing
334514	Gasmeters, large capacity, domestic and industrial, manufacturing
422710	Gasoline bulk stations and terminals
334514	Gasoline dispensing meters (except pumps) manufacturing

Code	Description
336412	Gasoline engine parts (except carburetors, pistons, piston rings, valves), aircraft, manufacturing
336312	Gasoline engine parts (except carburetors, pistons, piston rings, valves), automotive and truck, manufacturing
333618	Gasoline engines (except aircraft, automotive, truck) manufacturing
336412	Gasoline engines, aircraft, manufacturing
336312	Gasoline engines, automotive and truck, manufacturing
324110	Gasoline made in petroleum refineries
421120	Gasoline marketing equipment wholesaling
333913	Gasoline measuring and dispensing pumps manufacturing
486910	Gasoline pipeline transportation
235990	Gasoline pump construction contractors
421120	Gasoline service station equipment wholesaling
447110	Gasoline stations with convenience stores
447190	Gasoline stations without convenience stores
422720	Gasoline wholesaling (except bulk stations, terminals)
447110	Gasoline with convenience stores
211112	Gasoline, natural, production
313312	Gassing yarn (i.e., singeing)
621111	Gastroenterologists' offices (e.g., centers, clinics)
339112	Gastroscopes (except electromedical) manufacturing
334510	Gastroscopes, electromedical, manufacturing
333999	Gate and bridge lifting machinery manufacturing
332911	Gate valves, industrial-type, manufacturing
332323	Gates, holding, sheet metal, manufacturing
332323	Gates, metal (except wire), manufacturing
113210	Gathering of forest products (e.g., barks, gums, needles, seeds)

Code	Description
113210	Gathering, extracting, and selling tree seeds
332212	Gauge blocks, machinists' precision tools, manufacturing
334514	Gauges (e.g., oil pressure, water temperature, speedometer, tachometer), motor vehicle, manufacturing
334513	Gauges (i.e., analog, digital), industrial process-type, manufacturing
334514	Gauges for computing pressure-temperature corrections manufacturing
333314	Gauges, machinist's precision tool, optical, manufacturing
332212	Gauges, machinists' precision tools (except optical), manufacturing
422210	Gauze wholesaling
339113	Gauze, surgical, made from purchased fabric
313210	Gauzes, surgical, made in broadwoven fabric mills
321999	Gavels, wood, manufacturing
333512	Gear cutting and finishing machines, metalworking, manufacturing
332212	Gear pullers, handtools, manufacturing
333513	Gear rolling machines, metalworking, manufacturing
333612	Gearmotors (i.e., power transmission equipment) manufacturing
336350	Gears (e.g., crown, pinion, spider), automotive, truck, and bus, manufacturing
333612	Gears, power transmission (except aircraft, motor vehicle), manufacturing
112390	Geese production
311615	Geese, processing, fresh, frozen, canned, or cooked
311615	Geese, slaughtering and dressing
334519	Geiger counters manufacturing
325998	Gelatin capsules, empty, manufacturing
311999	Gelatin dessert preparations manufacturing

Code	Description
311999	Gelatin for cooking manufacturing
422490	Gelatin, edible, wholesaling
422690	Gelatin, inedible, wholesaling
212399	Gem stone (e.g., amethyst, garnet, agate, ruby, sapphire, jade) mining and/or beneficiating
421940	Gem stones wholesaling
333298	Gemstone processing machinery manufacturing
812990	Genealogical investigation services
921190	General accounting offices, government
811111	General automotive repair shops
112990	General combination animal farming
111998	General combination crop farming (except fruit and nut combinations, oilseed and grain, vegetable)
926110	General economics statistical agencies
484110	General freight trucking, local
484122	General freight trucking, long-distance, less-than-truckload (LTL)
484121	General freight trucking, long-distance, truckload
541611	General management consulting services
622110	General medical and surgical hospitals
421990	General merchandise, durable goods, wholesaling
422990	General merchandise, nondurable goods, wholesaling
921190	General public administration
532310	General rental centers
921190	General services departments, government
452990	General stores
493110	General warehousing and storage
422210	General-line drugs wholesaling
422410	General-line groceries wholesaling
421840	General-line industrial supplies wholesaling
421930	General-line scrap wholesaling
421830	General-purpose industrial machinery and equipment wholesaling

Code	Description
336322	Generating apparatus and parts for internal combustion engines manufacturing
335312	Generating apparatus and parts, electrical (except internal combustion engine and welding), manufacturing
333992	Generating apparatus and parts, welding, electrical, manufacturing
335313	Generator control and metering panels, switchgear-type, manufacturing
532490	Generator rental or leasing
335312	Generator sets, prime mover (except turbine generator sets), manufacturing
333611	Generator sets, turbine (e.g., gas, hydraulic, steam), manufacturing
335311	Generator voltage regulators, electric induction and step-type (except engine electrical equipment), manufacturing
335312	Generators and sets, electric (except internal combustion engine, welding, turbine generator sets), manufacturing
335312	Generators for gas-electric and oil-electric vehicles, manufacturing
336322	Generators for internal combustion engines manufacturing
335312	Generators for storage battery chargers (except internal combustion engine and aircraft), manufacturing
334517	Generators, X-ray, manufacturing
421610	Generators, electrical (except motor vehicle), wholesaling
421120	Generators, motor vehicle electrical, new, wholesaling
421140	Generators, motor vehicle electrical, used, wholesaling
332995	Generators, smoke, manufacturing
621511	Genetic testing laboratories
541710	Genetics research and development laboratories or services
541690	Geochemical consulting services
321992	Geodesic domes, prefabricated, wood, manufacturing
541370	Geodetic surveying services

Code	Description
541370	Geographic information system (GIS) base mapping services
541330	Geological engineering services
213112	Geological exploration (except surveying) for oil and gas on a contract basis
541710	Geological research and development laboratories or services
924120	Geological research program administration
541360	Geological surveying services
541330	Geophysical engineering services
213112	Geophysical exploration (except surveying) for oil and gas on a contract basis
334519	Geophysical instruments manufacturing
541360	Geophysical mapping services
541360	Geophysical surveying services
541370	Geospatial mapping services
541380	Geotechnical testing laboratories or services
235810	Geothermal drilling construction contractors
221330	Geothermal steam production
325199	Geraniol manufacturing
331492	Germanium recovering from scrap and/or alloying purchased metals
331419	Germanium refining, primary
711510	Ghost writers, independent
453220	Gift shops
322222	Gift wrap, laminated foil, made from purchased foil
322222	Gift wrap, laminated, made from purchased paper
422120	Gift wrapping paper wholesaling
561910	Gift wrapping services
212399	Gilsonite mining and/or beneficiating
111219	Ginger root farming (except under cover), field, bedding plant and seed production
111419	Ginger root farming under cover
115111	Ginning cotton
111219	Ginseng farming (except under cover), field, bedding plant and seed production

Code	Description
111419	Ginseng farming under cover
113210	Ginseng gathering
327390	Girders and beams, prestressed concrete, manufacturing
327390	Girders, prestressed concrete, manufacturing
315192	Girdles and other foundation garments made in apparel knitting mills
315212	Girdles, women's, cut and sew apparel contractors
315231	Girdles, women's, misses', and girls', cut and sewn from purchased fabric (except apparel contractors)
813410	Girl guiding organizations
721214	Girls' camps (except day, instructional)
611620	Girls' camps, sports instruction
713990	Girls' day camps (except instructional)
315111	Girls' hosiery, sheer, full length or knee length, knitting and finishing
315119	Girls' socks manufacturing
325411	Glandular derivatives, uncompounded, manufacturing
325412	Glandular medicinal preparations manufacturing
325612	Glass and tile cleaning preparations manufacturing
327215	Glass blanks for electric light bulbs made from purchased glass
327212	Glass blanks for electric light bulbs made in glass making plants
235410	Glass block laying construction contractors
313210	Glass broadwoven fabrics weaving
313221	Glass fabrics, narrow woven weaving
327212	Glass fiber, textile type, made in glass making plants
327212	Glass fiber, unsheathed, made in glass making plants
235920	Glass installation (except automotive) construction contractors
811122	Glass installation, automotive repair
327212	Glass making and blowing by hand

Code	Description
333298	Glass making machinery (e.g., blowing, forming, molding) manufacturing
327213	Glass packaging containers manufacturing
327215	Glass products (except packaging containers) made from purchased glass
327212	Glass products (except packaging containers) made in a glass making plants
212322	Glass sand quarrying and/or beneficiating
421930	Glass scrap wholesaling
811122	Glass shops, automotive
444190	Glass stores
235920	Glass tinting (except automotive) construction contractors
811122	Glass tinting, automotive
235920	Glass work (except automotive) construction contractors
811122	Glass work, automotive
327215	Glass, automotive, made from purchased glass
327212	Glass, automotive, made in glass making plants
421120	Glass, automotive, wholesaling
327211	Glass, plate, made in glass making plants
421390	Glass, plate, wholesaling
333314	Glasses, field or opera, manufacturing
327124	Glasshouse refractories manufacturing
322299	Glassine wrapping paper made from purchased paper
322121	Glassine wrapping paper made in paper mills
327215	Glassware for industrial, scientific, and technical use made from purchased glass
327212	Glassware for industrial, scientific, and technical use made in glass making plants
327215	Glassware for lighting fixtures made from purchased glass
327212	Glassware for lighting fixtures made in glass making plants

Code	Description
442299	Glassware stores
327215	Glassware, art decorative and novelty, made from purchased glass
327212	Glassware, art, decorative, and novelty made in glass making plants
327215	Glassware, cutting and engraving, made from purchased glass
421220	Glassware, household-type, wholesaling
421450	Glassware, medical, wholesaling
325188	Glauber's salt manufacturing
212391	Glauber's salt mining and/or beneficiating
325510	Glaziers' putty manufacturing
235990	Glazing concrete surfaces, construction contractors
235920	Glazing construction contractors
315292	Glazing furs
332812	Glazing metals and metal products for the trade
334511	Glide slope instrumentation manufacturing
487990	Glider excursions
336411	Gliders (i.e., aircraft) manufacturing
334220	Global positioning system (GPS) equipment manufacturing
511199	Globe cover and map publishers
511199	Globe cover and map publishers and printing combined
511199	Globe cover and map publishing (i.e., establishments known as publishers)
323112	Globe covers and maps flexographic printing without publishing
323111	Globe covers and maps gravure printing without publishing
323110	Globe covers and maps lithographic (offset) printing without publishing
323119	Globe covers and maps printing (except flexographic, gravure, lithographic, screen) without publishing
323113	Globe covers and maps screen printing without publishing
332911	Globe valves, industrial-type, manufacturing

Code	Description
339999	Globes, geographical, manufacturing
316110	Glove leather manufacturing
315992	Glove linings (except fur), manufacturing
315292	Glove linings, fur (except apparel contractors), manufacturing
315211	Glove linings, fur, men's and boys', cut and sew apparel contractors
315212	Glove linings, fur, women's, girls', and infants', cut and sew apparel contractors
315992	Gloves and mittens (except athletic), leather, fabric, fur, or combinations, cut and sewn from purchased fabric (except apparel contractors)
315211	Gloves and mittens (except athletic), leather, fabric, fur, or combinations, men's and boys', cut and sew apparel contractors
315212	Gloves and mittens (except athletic), leather, fabric, fur, or combinations, women's, girls', and infants', cut and sew apparel contractors
315992	Gloves and mittens, woven or knit, cut and sewn from purchased fabric (except apparel contractors), manufacturing
315212	Gloves and mittens, woven or knit, women's, girls', and infants', cut and sew apparel contractors
315191	Gloves, knit, made in apparel knitting mills
315211	Gloves, leather (except athletic), men's and boys', cut and sew apparel contractors
315212	Gloves, leather (except athletic), women's, girls', and infants', cut and sew apparel contractors
315992	Gloves, leather (except athletic, cut and sewn apparel contractors), manufacturing
422320	Gloves, men's and boys', wholesaling
326199	Gloves, plastics, manufacturing
339113	Gloves, rubber (e.g., electrician's, examination, household-type, surgeon's), manufacturing

Code	Description
339920	Gloves, sport and athletic (e.g., baseball, boxing, racketball, handball), manufacturing
422330	Gloves, women's, children's, and infants', wholesaling
335110	Glow lamp bulbs manufacturing
339114	Glue, dental, manufacturing
325520	Glues (except dental) manufacturing
422690	Glues wholesaling
311221	Gluten feed, flour, and meal, made by wet milling corn
311221	Gluten manufacturing
325611	Glycerin (i.e., glycerol), natural, manufacturing
325199	Glycerin (i.e., glycerol), synthetic, manufacturing
325411	Glycosides, uncompounded, manufacturing
212313	Gneiss crushed and broken stone mining and/or beneficiating
212311	Gneiss mining or quarrying
112420	Goat farming (e.g., meat, milk, mohair production)
422520	Goats wholesaling
713990	Gocart raceways (i.e., amusement rides)
713990	Gocart tracks (i.e., amusement rides)
336999	Gocarts (except children's) manufacturing
421910	Gocarts wholesaling
339932	Gocarts, children's, manufacturing
339115	Goggles (e.g., industrial, safety, sun, underwater) manufacturing
331491	Gold and gold alloy bar, sheet, strip, and tubing made from purchased metals or scrap
332813	Gold and silver plating metals and metal products for the trade
332999	Gold beating (i.e., foil, leaf)
331419	Gold bullion or dore bar produced at primary metal refineries
332999	Gold foil and leaf not made in rolling mills
331491	Gold foil made by rolling purchased metals or scrap

Code	Description
212221	Gold lode mining and/or beneficiating
212221	Gold ore mine site development for own account
212221	Gold ore mining and/or beneficiating plants
212221	Gold ores, concentrates, bullion, and/or precipitates mining and/or beneficiating
212221	Gold placer mining and/or beneficiating
325910	Gold printing inks manufacturing
331492	Gold recovering from scrap and/or alloying purchased metals
331419	Gold refining, primary
331491	Gold rolling and drawing purchased metals or scrap
323121	Gold stamping books for the trade
813410	Golden age clubs
112511	Goldfish production, farm raising
713910	Golf and country clubs
441229	Golf cart dealers, powered
532292	Golf cart rental
421910	Golf carts (except motorized passenger) wholesaling
336999	Golf carts and similar motorized passenger carriers manufacturing
421860	Golf carts, motorized passenger, wholesaling
336999	Golf carts, powered, manufacturing
234990	Golf course construction
541320	Golf course design services
713910	Golf courses (except miniature, pitch-n-putt)
713990	Golf courses, miniature
713990	Golf courses, pitch-n-putt
713990	Golf driving ranges
421910	Golf equipment and supplies wholesaling
611620	Golf instruction, camps, or schools
713990	Golf practice ranges
451110	Golf pro shops
316219	Golf shoes, men's cleated, manufacturing
316219	Golf shoes, women's cleated, manufacturing

Code	Description
711219	Golfers, independent professional (i.e., participating in sports events)
339920	Golfing equipment (e.g., bags, balls, caddy carts, clubs, tees) manufacturing
335999	Gongs, electric, manufacturing
111334	Gooseberry farming
332212	Gouges, woodworking, manufacturing
445299	Gourmet food stores
522294	Government National Mortgage Association (GNMA)
561210	Government base facilities operation support services
522294	Government-sponsored enterprises providing secondary market financing
336312	Governors for automotive gasoline engines manufacturing
921110	Governors' offices
333618	Governors, diesel engine, manufacturing
333618	Governors, gasoline engine (except automotive), manufacturing
333611	Governors, steam, manufacturing
532220	Gown rental
315299	Gowns (e.g., academic, choir, clerical) cut and sewn from purchased fabric (except apparel contractors)
315211	Gowns (e.g., academic, choir, clerical), men's and boys', cut and sew apparel contractors
315212	Gowns (e.g., academic, choir, clerical), women's, and girls', cut and sew apparel contractors
315212	Gowns, formal, women's and girls', cut and sew apparel contractors
315233	Gowns, formal, women's, misses', and girls', cut and sewn from purchased fabric (except apparel contractors)
315299	Gowns, hospital, surgical and patient, cut and sewn from purchased fabric (except apparel contractors)

Code	Description
315211	Gowns, hospital, surgical and patient, men's and boys', cut and sew apparel contractors
315212	Gowns, hospital, surgical and patient, women's, girls', and infants', cut and sew apparel contractors
315212	Gowns, wedding, women's, cut and sew apparel contractors
315233	Gowns, wedding, women's, misses', and girls', cut and sewn from purchased fabric (except apparel contractors)
333120	Grader attachments manufacturing
333120	Graders, road, manufacturing
234110	Grading construction contractors for highway and street construction
235930	Grading for buildings, construction contractors
333294	Grading, cleaning, and sorting machinery (i.e., food manufacturing-type) manufacturing
333111	Grading, cleaning, and sorting machinery, farm-type, manufacturing
334512	Gradual switches, pneumatic, manufacturing
532220	Graduation cap and gown rental
315299	Graduation caps and gowns cut and sewn from purchased fabric (except apparel contractors)
315211	Graduation caps and gowns, men's and boys', cut and sew apparel contractors
315212	Graduation caps and gowns, women's and girls', cut and sew apparel contractors
311211	Graham flour manufacturing
311821	Graham wafers manufacturing
212399	Grahamite mining and/or beneficiating
312140	Grain alcohol, beverage, manufacturing
325193	Grain alcohol, nonpotable, manufacturing
115114	Grain cleaning
333111	Grain drills manufacturing
115114	Grain drying

Code	Description
233310	Grain elevator construction
422510	Grain elevators wholesaling grain
493130	Grain elevators, storage only
115114	Grain fumigation
115114	Grain grinding (except custom grinding for animal feed)
311119	Grain grinding, custom, for animal feed
484220	Grain hauling, local
484230	Grain hauling, long-distance
488210	Grain leveling and trimming in railroad cars
321999	Grain measures, wood, turned and shaped, manufacturing
333294	Grain milling machinery manufacturing
311211	Grain mills (except animal feed, breakfast cereal, rice)
311119	Grain mills, animal feed
311230	Grain mills, breakfast cereal
311212	Grain mills, rice
333111	Grain stackers manufacturing
422510	Grain wholesaling
311230	Grain, breakfast cereal, manufacturing
312120	Grain, brewers' spent, manufacturing
115113	Grain, machine harvesting
327910	Grains, abrasive, natural and artificial, manufacturing
813410	Granges
235410	Granite (i.e., exterior stonework) construction contractors
212313	Granite beneficiating plants (e.g., grinding or pulverizing)
212313	Granite crushed and broken stone mining and/or beneficiating
212311	Granite mining or quarrying
311320	Granola bars and clusters, chocolate, made from cacao beans
311330	Granola bars and clusters, chocolate, made from purchased chocolate
311340	Granola bars and clusters, nonchocolate, manufacturing
311230	Granola, cereal (except bars and clusters), manufacturing

Code	Description
813211	Grantmaking foundations
311313	Granulated beet sugar manufacturing
311312	Granulated cane sugar made from purchased raw cane sugar
311311	Granulated cane sugar made from sugar cane
333220	Granulator and pelletizer machinery for plastics manufacturing
212319	Granules, slate, mining and/or beneficiating
312130	Grape farming and making wine
111332	Grape farming without making wine
111320	Grapefruit groves
325998	Grapefruit oil manufacturing
311423	Grapes, artificially drying
541430	Graphic art and related design services
541430	Graphic artists, independent
325992	Graphic arts plates, sensitized, manufacturing
611519	Graphic arts schools
541430	Graphic design services
334515	Graphic recording meters, electric, manufacturing
335991	Graphite electrodes and contacts, electric, manufacturing
212399	Graphite mining and/or beneficiating
335991	Graphite specialties for aerospace use (except gaskets) manufacturing
335991	Graphite specialties for electrical use manufacturing
335991	Graphite specialties for mechanical use (except gaskets) manufacturing
327992	Graphite, natural (e.g., ground, pulverized, refined, blended), manufacturing
111940	Grass hay farming
333111	Grass mowing equipment (except lawn and garden) manufacturing
332212	Grass mowing equipment, nonpowered lawn and garden, manufacturing
333112	Grass mowing equipment, powered lawn and garden, manufacturing
111998	Grass seed farming

Code	Description
332323	Gratings (i.e., open steel flooring) manufacturing
333314	Gratings, diffraction, manufacturing
484220	Gravel hauling, local
484230	Gravel hauling, long-distance
212321	Gravel quarrying and/or beneficiating
235710	Gravel walk and driveway construction contractors
541360	Gravity geophysical surveying services
325910	Gravure inks manufacturing
323122	Gravure plate and cylinder preparation services
323111	Gravure printing (except books, manifold business forms, printing grey goods)
333293	Gravure printing presses manufacturing
311422	Gravy canning
311942	Gravy mixes, dry, manufacturing
331511	Gray iron foundries
531190	Grazing land rental or leasing
311613	Grease rendering
339991	Grease seals manufacturing
311225	Grease, inedible, animal and vegetable, refining and blending purchased oils
422990	Greases, inedible animal and vegetable, wholesaling
324191	Greases, petroleum lubricating, made from refined petroleum
325998	Greases, synthetic lubricating, manufacturing
483113	Great Lakes freight transportation
483114	Great Lakes passenger transportation
111219	Green bean farming, field and seed production
111219	Green cowpea farming, field and seed production
111219	Green lima bean farming, field and seed production
111219	Green pea farming, field and seed production
332311	Greenhouses, prefabricated metal, manufacturing

Code	Description
212399	Greensand mining and/or beneficiating
212311	Greenstone mining or quarrying
511191	Greeting card publishers
511191	Greeting card publishers and printing combined
511191	Greeting card publishing (i.e., establishments known as publishers)
453220	Greeting card shops
323112	Greeting cards (e.g., birthday, holiday, sympathy) flexographic printing without publishing
323111	Greeting cards (e.g., birthday, holiday, sympathy) gravure printing without publishing
323110	Greeting cards (e.g., birthday, holiday, sympathy) lithographic (offset) printing without publishing
323119	Greeting cards (e.g., birthday, holiday, sympathy) printing (except flexographic, gravure, lithographic, screen) without publishing
323113	Greeting cards (e.g., birthday, holiday, sympathy) screen printing without publishing
422120	Greeting cards wholesaling
332994	Grenade launchers manufacturing
332993	Grenades, hand or projectile, manufacturing
711212	Greyhound dog racetracks
335211	Griddles and grills, household-type portable electric, manufacturing
332618	Grilles and grillwork made from purchased wire
332323	Grills and grillwork, sheet metal, manufacturing
332323	Grillwork, ornamental metal, manufacturing
333991	Grinders, handheld power-driven, manufacturing
325411	Grinding and milling botanicals (i.e., for medicinal use)
327910	Grinding balls, ceramic, manufacturing
333512	Grinding machines, metalworking, manufacturing
332813	Grinding metal castings for the trade

Code	Description
324191	Grinding oils, petroleum, made from refined petroleum
212399	Grinding pebbles mining and/or beneficiating
212322	Grinding sand quarrying and/or beneficiating
311942	Grinding spices
327910	Grinding wheels manufacturing
212399	Grindstones mining and/or beneficiating
326299	Grips and handles, rubber, manufacturing
311211	Grits and flakes, corn brewer's, manufacturing
212319	Grits crushed and broken stone mining and/or beneficiating
422410	Groceries, general-line, wholesaling
322224	Grocers' bags and sacks made from purchased uncoated paper
326111	Grocery bags, plastics film, single wall or multiwall, manufacturing
333924	Grocery carts made from purchased wire
492210	Grocery delivery services (i.e., independent service from grocery store)
445110	Grocery stores
421840	Grommets wholesaling
326299	Grommets, rubber, manufacturing
812910	Grooming services, animal
335931	Ground clamps (i.e., electric wiring devices) manufacturing
335931	Ground fault circuit interrupters (GFCI) manufacturing
235810	Ground source heat pump construction contractors
322122	Groundwood paper products (e.g., publication and printing paper, tablet stock, wallpaper base) made in newsprint mills
422110	Groundwood paper, bulk, wholesaling
322121	Groundwood paper, coated, laminated, or treated in paper mills
322222	Groundwood paper, coated, made from purchased paper
322121	Groundwood paper, coated, made in paper mills

Code	Description
322122	Groundwood paper, newsprint, made in paper mills
322110	Groundwood pulp manufacturing
624410	Group day care centers, child or infant
623990	Group foster homes for children
623110	Group homes for the disabled with nursing care
623990	Group homes for the disabled without nursing care
623990	Group homes for the hearing impaired
623990	Group homes for the visually impaired
623210	Group homes, mental retardation
621491	Group hospitalization plans providing health care services
524114	Group hospitalization plans without providing health care services
114111	Grouper fishing
235710	Grout constuction contractors
335122	Grow light fixtures (except residential) manufacturing
335121	Grow light fixtures, residential, electric, manufacturing
813910	Growers' associations
212393	Guano mining and/or beneficiating
111998	Guar farming
524127	Guaranteeing titles
561612	Guard dog services
812910	Guard dog training services
561612	Guard services
234110	Guardrail construction
332322	Guardrails, sheet metal highway, manufacturing
332323	Guards, bannisters, and railings, sheet metal, manufacturing
332618	Guards, wire, made from purchased wire
111339	Guavas farming
721199	Guest houses
721214	Guest ranches with accommodation facilities
812910	Guide dog training services
713990	Guide services (i.e., fishing, hunting, tourist)

Code	Description
713990	Guide services, fishing
713990	Guide services, hunting
713990	Guide services, tourist
511199	Guide, street map, publishers
511199	Guide, street map, publishers and printing combined
511199	Guide, street map, publishing (i.e., establishments known as publishers)
336415	Guided missile and space vehicle engine manufacturing
541710	Guided missile and space vehicle engine research and development
336414	Guided missile and space vehicle manufacturing
336419	Guided missile and space vehicle parts (except engines) manufacturing
541710	Guided missile and space vehicle parts (except engines) research and development
421860	Guided missiles and space vehicles wholesaling
336414	Guided missiles, complete, assembling
323112	Guides, street map, flexographic printing without publishing
323111	Guides, street map, gravure printing without publishing
323110	Guides, street map, lithographic (offset) printing without publishing
323119	Guides, street map, printing (except flexographic, gravure, lithographic, screen) without publishing
323113	Guides, street map, screen printing without publishing
339992	Guitars and parts, electric and nonelectric, manufacturing
113210	Gum (i.e., forest product) gathering
325191	Gum and wood chemicals manufacturing
422690	Gum and wood chemicals wholesaling
311340	Gum, chewing, manufacturing
422450	Gum, chewing, wholesaling
322222	Gummed paper products (e.g., labels, sheets, tapes) made from

Code	Description
	purchased paper
422130	Gummed tapes (except cellophane) wholesaling
422120	Gummed tapes, cellophane, wholesaling
332994	Gun barrels (i.e., 30 mm. or less, 1.18 inch or less) manufacturing
332995	Gun barrels (i.e., more than 30 mm., more than 1.18 inch) manufacturing
713990	Gun clubs, recreational
813319	Gun control organizations
334413	Gun effect devices manufacturing
332111	Gun forgings made from purchased iron or steel, unfinished
331111	Gun forgings made in steel mills
332994	Gun magazines (i.e., 30 mm. or less, 1.18 inch or less) manufacturing
332995	Gun magazines (i.e., more than 30 mm., more than 1.18 inch) manufacturing
451110	Gun shops
333314	Gun sighting and fire control equipment and instruments, optical, manufacturing
333314	Gun sights, optical, manufacturing
332612	Gun springs manufacturing
321912	Gun stocks, wood, manufacturing
332510	Gun trigger locks manufacturing
332995	Gun turrets (i.e., more than 30 mm., more than 1.18 inch) manufacturing
325920	Gunpowder manufacturing
421990	Guns (except sporting) wholesaling
332994	Guns (i.e., 30 mm. or less, 1.18 inch or less) manufacturing
332995	Guns (i.e., more than 30 mm., more than 1.18 inch) manufacturing
332994	Guns, BB and pellet, manufacturing
332212	Guns, caulking, nonpowered, manufacturing
421910	Guns, sporting equipment, wholesaling
451110	Gunsmith shops retailing new guns
811490	Gunsmith shops without retailing new guns

Code	Description
235610	Gutter and down spout construction contractors
561790	Gutter cleaning services
332114	Gutters and down spouts sheet metal, custom roll formed, manufacturing
421330	Gutters and down spouts wholesaling
326199	Gutters and down spouts, plastics, manufacturing
234110	Gutters, concrete, street and highway construction
332322	Gutters, sheet metal (except custom roll formed), manufacturing
339920	Gymnasium and playground equipment, manufacturing
713940	Gymnasiums
611620	Gymnastics instruction, camps, or schools
339113	Gynecological supplies and appliances manufacturing
621111	Gynecologists' offices (e.g., centers, clinics)
212399	Gypsite mining and/or beneficiating
327420	Gypsum building products manufacturing
421390	Gypsum building products wholesaling
212399	Gypsum mining and/or beneficiating
327420	Gypsum products (e.g., block, board, plaster, lath, rock, tile) manufacturing
334511	Gyrocompasses manufacturing
334511	Gyrogimbals manufacturing
334511	Gyroscopes manufacturing
311221	HFCS (high fructose corn syrup) manufacturing
325413	HIV test kits manufacturing
621491	HMO (health maintenance organization) medical centers and clinics
334511	HUD (heads-up display) systems, aeronautical, manufacturing
624310	Habilitation job counseling and training, vocational
114111	Haddock fishing

Code	Description
212299	Hafnium mining and/or beneficiating
422310	Hair accessories wholesaling
326299	Hair care products (e.g., combs, curlers), rubber, manufacturing
333111	Hair clippers for animal use, electric, manufacturing
332212	Hair clippers for animal use, nonelectric, manufacturing
335211	Hair clippers for human use, electric, manufacturing
332211	Hair clippers for human use, nonelectric, manufacturing
325620	Hair coloring preparations manufacturing
335211	Hair curlers, household-type electric, manufacturing
332999	Hair curlers, metal, manufacturing
335211	Hair driers, electric (except equipment designed for beauty parlor use), manufacturing
421620	Hair dryers wholesaling
333319	Hair dryers, beauty parlor-type, manufacturing
339999	Hair nets, made from purchased netting
325620	Hair preparations (e.g., conditioners, dyes, rinses, shampoos) manufacturing
422210	Hair preparations (except professional) wholesaling
421850	Hair preparations, professional, wholesaling
812199	Hair removal (i.e., dipilatory, electrolysis) services
812199	Hair replacement services (except by offices of physicians)
325620	Hair sprays manufacturing
812112	Hair stylist salons or shops, unisex or women's
812111	Hair stylist services, men's
812112	Hair stylist services, unisex or women's
812111	Hair stylist shops, men's
812199	Hair weaving services
339994	Hairbrushes manufacturing
422990	Hairbrushes wholesaling
812112	Hairdresser services

Code	Description
812112	Hairdressing salons or shops, unisex or women's
339999	Hairpieces (e.g., toupees, wigs, wiglets) manufacturing
422990	Hairpieces (e.g., toupees, wigs, wiglets) wholesaling
339993	Hairpins (except rubber) manufacturing
326299	Hairpins, rubber, manufacturing
332612	Hairsprings (except clock, watch) manufacturing
114111	Hake fishing
623990	Halfway group homes for delinquents and exoffenders
623220	Halfway houses for patients with mental health illnesses
623220	Halfway houses, substance abuse (e.g., alcoholism, drug addiction)
114111	Halibut fishing
531120	Hall and banquet room, nonresidential, rental or leasing
334413	Hall effect devices manufacturing
531120	Hall, nonresidential, rental or leasing
339912	Hallowware, precious metal, manufacturing
712110	Halls of fame
335110	Halogen light bulbs manufacturing
325192	Halogenated aromatic hydrocarbon derivatives manufacturing
325199	Halogenated hydrocarbon derivatives (except aromatic) manufacturing
311340	Halvah manufacturing
332111	Hammer forgings made from purchased iron or steel, unfinished
332112	Hammer forgings made from purchased nonferrous metals, unfinished
333120	Hammer mill machinery (i.e., rock and ore crushing machines), portable, manufacturing
333131	Hammer mill machinery (i.e., rock and ore crushing machines), stationary, manufacturing
332212	Hammers, handtools, manufacturing
339992	Hammers, piano, manufacturing

Code	Description
321999	Hammers, wood, meat, manufacturing
314999	Hammocks, fabric, manufacturing
337124	Hammocks, metal framed, manufacturing
337122	Hammocks, wood framed, manufacturing
326199	Hampers, laundry, plastics, manufacturing
337125	Hampers, laundry, reed, wicker, rattan, manufacturing
332322	Hampers, laundry, sheet metal, manufacturing
311611	Hams (except poultry) produced in slaughtering plants
311612	Hams, canned, made from purchased carcasses
311615	Hams, poultry, manufacturing
311612	Hams, preserved (except poultry), made from purchased carcasses
327215	Hand blowing purchased glass
333319	Hand dryers, commercial-type, manufacturing
334111	Hand held computers (e.g., PDAs) manufacturing
313249	Hand knitting lace or warp fabric products
812320	Hand laundries
325620	Hand lotions manufacturing
339943	Hand operated stamps (e.g., canceling, postmark, shoe, textile marking), manufacturing
325611	Hand soaps (e.g., hard, liquid, soft) manufacturing
334518	Hand stamps (e.g., date, time), timing mechanism operated, manufacturing
333924	Hand trucks manufacturing
313221	Hand weaving fabric, 12 inches or less (30cm)
313210	Hand weaving fabrics, more than 12 inches (30 cm) in width
316110	Handbag leather manufacturing
448150	Handbag stores
316993	Handbags (except metal), men's, manufacturing
422330	Handbags wholesaling

Code	Description
339911	Handbags, precious metal, manufacturing
316992	Handbags, women's, all materials (except precious metal), manufacturing
713940	Handball club facilities
541870	Handbill direct distribution services
332999	Handcuffs manufacturing
332212	Handheld edge tools (except saws, scissors-type), nonelectric, manufacturing
485991	Handicapped passenger transportation services
611110	Handicapped, schools for, elementary or secondary
611610	Handicrafts instruction
315999	Handkerchiefs (except paper) cut and sewn from purchased fabric
315211	Handkerchiefs (except paper), men's and boys', cut and sew apparel contractors
315212	Handkerchiefs (except paper), women's, girls', and infants', cut and sew apparel contractors
322291	Handkerchiefs, paper, made from purchased paper
321912	Handle blanks, wood, manufacturing
321912	Handle stock, sawed or planed, manufacturing
321999	Handles (e.g., broom, mop, hand tool), wood, manufacturing
422990	Handles (e.g., broom, mop, paint) wholesaling
326199	Handles (e.g., brush, tool, umbrella), plastics, manufacturing
316999	Handles (e.g., luggage, whip), leather, manufacturing
332999	Handles (e.g., parasol, umbrella), metal, manufacturing
327111	Handles, faucet, vitreous china and earthenware, manufacturing
541420	Handtool industrial design services
332212	Handtool metal blades (e.g., putty knives, scrapers, screw drivers) manufacturing
421710	Handtools (except motor vehicle mechanics', machinists' precision) wholesaling

Code	Description
332212	Handtools, machinists' precision, manufacturing
421830	Handtools, machinists' precision, wholesaling
332212	Handtools, motor vehicle mechanics', manufacturing
421120	Handtools, motor vehicle mechanics', wholesaling
333991	Handtools, power-driven, manufacturing
444130	Handtools, power-driven, repair and maintenance services retailing new power-driven handtools
811411	Handtools, power-driven, repair and maintenance services without retailing new power-driven handtools
541990	Handwriting analysis services
541990	Handwriting expert services
336411	Hang gliders manufacturing
233320	Hangar (i.e., aircraft storage buildings) construction
332321	Hangar doors, metal, manufacturing
488119	Hangar rental, aircraft
321999	Hangers, wooden, garment, manufacturing
111422	Hanging basket plant growing
234990	Harbor construction
234990	Harbor dredging construction contractors
488310	Harbor maintenance services (except dredging)
488310	Harbor operation
487210	Harbor sightseeing tours
488330	Harbor tugboat services
213112	Hard banding oil and gas field service on a contract basis
311340	Hard candies manufacturing
212111	Hard coal (except Pennsylvania anthracite) surface mining and/or beneficiating
212113	Hard coal surface mining
212113	Hard coal underground mining
334112	Hard disk drives manufacturing
334613	Hard drive media manufacturing
313210	Hard fiber fabrics, broadwoven, weaving

Code	Description
313111	Hard fiber spun yarns made from purchased fiber
313113	Hard fiber thread manufacturing
313221	Hard fiber, narrow woven, weaving
339113	Hard hats manufacturing
321219	Hardboard manufacturing
332811	Hardening (i.e., heat treating) metals and metal products for the trade
334519	Hardness testing equipment manufacturing
421710	Hardware (except motor vehicle) wholesaling
332618	Hardware cloth, woven wire, made from purchased wire
444130	Hardware stores
421120	Hardware, motor vehicle, wholesaling
326199	Hardware, plastics, manufacturing
335932	Hardware, transmission pole and line, manufacturing
421610	Hardware, transmission pole and line, wholesaling
321912	Hardwood dimension lumber and stock, resawing purchased lumber
325191	Hardwood distillates manufacturing
321211	Hardwood plywood composites manufacturing
321211	Hardwood veneer or plywood manufacturing
339992	Harmonicas manufacturing
334419	Harness assemblies for electronic use manufacturing
711219	Harness drivers
422910	Harness equipment wholesaling
316110	Harness leather manufacturing
332999	Harness parts, metal, manufacturing
711212	Harness racetracks
316999	Harnesses and harness parts, leather, manufacturing
316999	Harnesses, dog, manufacturing
339992	Harps and parts manufacturing
339992	Harpsichords manufacturing
333111	Harrows (e.g., disc, spring, tine) manufacturing

Code	Description
315991	Harvest hats, straw, manufacturing
113210	Harvesting berries or nuts from native and non-cultivated plants
333111	Harvesting machinery and equipment, agriculture, manufacturing
421820	Harvesting machinery and equipment, agriculture, wholesaling
335211	Hassock fans, electric, manufacturing
448150	Hat and cap stores
339999	Hat blocks manufacturing
315991	Hat bodies (e.g., fur-felt, straw, wool-felt) cut and sewn from purchased fabric (except apparel contractors)
315211	Hat bodies (e.g., fur-felt, straw, wool-felt), men's and boys', cut and sew apparel contractors
315212	Hat bodies (e.g., fur-felt, straw, wool-felt), women's, girls', and infants', cut and sew apparel contractors
812320	Hat cleaning services
315999	Hat findings cut and sewn from purchased fabric (except apparel contractors)
315211	Hat findings, men's and boys', cut and sew apparel contractors
315212	Hat findings, women's, girls', and infants', cut and sew apparel contractors
315999	Hat linings and trimmings cut and sewn from purchased fabric (except apparel contractors)
315211	Hat linings and trimmings, men's and boys', cut and sew apparel contractors
315212	Hat linings and trimmings, women's, girls', and infants', cut and sew apparel contractors
112511	Hatcheries, finfish
112340	Hatcheries, poultry
112512	Hatcheries, shellfish
332212	Hatchets manufacturing
315991	Hats (except fur, knitting mill products, leather) cut and sewn from purchased fabric (except apparel contractors)

Code	Description
422320	Hats and caps, men's and boys', wholesaling
422330	Hats and caps, women's, girls' and infants', wholesaling
322299	Hats made from purchased paper
315191	Hats made in apparel knitting mills
315991	Hats, cloth, cut and sewn from purchased fabric (except apparel contractors)
315211	Hats, cloth, men's and boys', cut and sew apparel contractors
315212	Hats, cloth, women's, girls', and infants', cut and sew apparel contractors
315292	Hats, fur (except apparel contractors), manufacturing
315211	Hats, fur, men's and boys', cut and sew apparel contractors
315212	Hats, fur, women's, girls', and infants', cut and sew apparel contractors
315991	Hats, fur-felt, straw, and wool-felt, cut and sewn from purchased fabric (except apparel contractors)
315211	Hats, fur-felt, straw, and wool-felt, men's and boys', cut and sew apparel contractors
315212	Hats, fur-felt, straw, and wool-felt, women's, girls', and infants', cut and sew apparel contractors
315292	Hats, leather (except apparel contractors), manufacturing
315211	Hats, leather, men's and boys', cut and sew apparel contractors
315212	Hats, leather, women's, girls', and infants', cut and sew apparel contractors
315211	Hats, men's and boys', cut and sew apparel contractors
315991	Hats, trimmed, cut and sewn from purchased fabric (except apparel contractors)
315211	Hats, trimmed, men's and boys', cut and sew apparel contractors
315212	Hats, trimmed, women's, girls', and infants', cut and sew apparel contractors
315212	Hats, women's, girls', and infants', cut and sew apparel contractors

Code	Description
333111	Hay balers and presses manufacturing
111940	Hay farming (e.g., alfalfa hay, clover hay, grass hay)
115113	Hay mowing, raking, baling, and chopping
111998	Hay seed farming
422910	Hay wholesaling
311119	Hay, cubed, manufacturing
333111	Haying machines manufacturing
421820	Haying machines wholesaling
562112	Hazardous waste collection services
562211	Hazardous waste disposal facilities
562211	Hazardous waste disposal facilities combined with collection and/or local hauling of hazardous waste
562211	Hazardous waste material disposal facilities
562211	Hazardous waste material treatment facilities
562211	Hazardous waste treatment facilities
562211	Hazardous waste treatment facilities combined with collection and/or local hauling of hazardous waste
111335	Hazelnut farming
551114	Head offices
311212	Head rice manufacturing
624410	Head start programs, separate from schools
315999	Headbands, women's and girls', cut and sewn from purchased fabric (except apparel contractors)
315212	Headbands, women's, girls', and infants', cut and sew apparel contractors
337122	Headboards, wood, manufacturing
321920	Heading, barrel (i.e., cooperage stock), wood, manufacturing
334419	Heads (e.g., recording, read/write), manufacturing
334511	Heads-up display (HUD) systems, aeronautical, manufacturing
446110	Health and beauty aids stores
525120	Health and welfare funds
713940	Health club facilities, physical fitness

Code	Description
422490	Health foods (except fresh fruits, vegetables) wholesaling
422480	Health foods, fresh fruits and vegetables, wholesaling
524114	Health insurance carriers, direct
335110	Health lamp bulbs, infrared and ultraviolet radiation, manufacturing
621491	Health maintenance organization (HMO) medical centers and clinics
233320	Health or athletic club construction
923120	Health planning and development agencies, government
813920	Health professionals' associations
926150	Health professions licensure agencies
923120	Health program administration
541710	Health research and development laboratories or services
813212	Health research fundraising organizations
621999	Health screening services (except by offices of health practitioners)
621111	Health screening services in physicians' offices
721110	Health spas (i.e., physical fitness facilities) with accommodations
713940	Health spas without accommodations, physical fitness
923120	Health statistics centers, government
713940	Health studios, physical fitness
446199	Hearing aid stores
421450	Hearing aids wholesaling
334510	Hearing aids, electronic, manufacturing
621999	Hearing testing services (except by offices of audiologists)
621340	Hearing testing services by offices of audiologists
336211	Hearse bodies manufacturing
532111	Hearse rental
485320	Hearse rental with driver
336111	Hearses assembling on chassis of own manufacture
336211	Hearses assembling on purchased chassis

Code	Description
334510	Heart-lung machine, manufacturing
332410	Heat exchangers manufacturing
235110	Heat pump construction contractors
333415	Heat pumps manufacturing
421730	Heat pumps wholesaling
325992	Heat sensitized (i.e., thermal) paper made from purchased paper
335991	Heat shields, carbon or graphite, manufacturing
332811	Heat treating metals and metal products for the trade
333994	Heat treating ovens, industrial process-type, manufacturing
221330	Heat, steam, distribution
221330	Heated air distribution
335211	Heaters, portable electric space, manufacturing
421620	Heaters, portable electric, wholesaling
333414	Heaters, space (except portable electric), manufacturing
333414	Heaters, swimming pool, manufacturing
335211	Heaters, tape, manufacturing
333415	Heating and air conditioning combination units manufacturing
334512	Heating and cooling system controls, residential and commercial, manufacturing
421720	Heating boilers, steam and hot water, wholesaling
235110	Heating construction contractors
541330	Heating engineering consulting services
333414	Heating equipment, hot water (except hot water heaters), manufacturing
421720	Heating equipment, hot water, wholesaling
421730	Heating equipment, warm air (i.e. forced air), wholesaling
333415	Heating equipment, warm air (i.e., forced air), manufacturing
454311	Heating oil dealers, direct selling
324110	Heating oils made in petroleum refineries
335211	Heating pads, electric, manufacturing

Code	Description
334512	Heating regulators manufacturing
221330	Heating steam (suppliers of heat) providers
335211	Heating units for electric appliances manufacturing
333414	Heating units, baseboard, manufacturing
234990	Heavy construction equipment rental with operator
532412	Heavy construction equipment rental without operator
611519	Heavy equipment operation schools
611519	Heavy equipment repair training
811310	Heavy machinery and equipment repair and maintenance services
336120	Heavy trucks assembling on chassis of own manufacture
336211	Heavy trucks assembling on purchased chassis
325188	Heavy water (i.e., deuterium oxide) manufacturing
332212	Hedge shears and trimmers, nonelectric, manufacturing
333112	Hedge trimmers, powered, manufacturing
316999	Heel caps, leather or metal, manufacturing
316999	Heel lifts, leather, manufacturing
321999	Heels, boot and shoe, finished wood, manufacturing
316999	Heels, boot and shoe, leather, manufacturing
332611	Helical springs, hot wound heavy gauge, manufacturing
332612	Helical springs, light gauge, manufacturing
481212	Helicopter carriers, freight, nonscheduled
481112	Helicopter freight carriers, scheduled
481211	Helicopter passenger carriers (except scenic, sightseeing), nonscheduled
481111	Helicopter passenger carriers, scheduled
487990	Helicopter ride, scenic and sightseeing, operation
336411	Helicopters manufacturing

Code	Description
325120	Helium manufacturing
325120	Helium recovery from natural gas
339113	Helmets (except athletic), safety (e.g., motorized vehicle crash helmets, space helmets), manufacturing
339920	Helmets, athletic (except motorized vehicle crash helmets), manufacturing
561320	Help supply services
212210	Hematite mining and/or beneficiating
325413	Hematology in-vitro diagnostic substances manufacturing
325412	Hematology in-vivo diagnostic substances manufacturing
334516	Hematology instruments manufacturing
325414	Hematology products (except diagnostic substances) manufacturing
325191	Hemlock extract manufacturing
113210	Hemlock gum gathering
621492	Hemodialysis centers and clinics
313111	Hemp bags made from purchased fiber
313111	Hemp ropes made from purchased fiber
313111	Hemp spun yarns made from purchased fiber
315211	Hemstitching apparel contractors on men's and boys' apparel
315212	Hemstitching apparel contractors on women's, girls', and infants' apparel
325110	Heptanes made from refined petroleum or liquid hydrocarbons
325110	Heptenes made from refined petroleum or liquid hydrocarbons
111419	Herb farming, grown under cover
111998	Herb farming, open field
111421	Herbaceous perennial growing
621399	Herbalists' offices (e.g., centers, clinics)
712110	Herbariums
325320	Herbicides manufacturing
711310	Heritage festival managers with facilities

Code	Description
711320	Heritage festival managers without facilities
711310	Heritage festival organizers with facilities
711320	Heritage festival organizers without facilities
711310	Heritage festival promoters with facilities
711320	Heritage festival promoters without facilities
712120	Heritage villages
114111	Herring fishing
325199	Heterocyclic chemicals, not specified elsewhere by process, manufacturing
325199	Hexadecanol manufacturing
325199	Hexamethylenediamine manufacturing
325199	Hexamethylenetetramine manufacturing
325199	Hexanol manufacturing
311611	Hides and skins produced in slaughtering plants
316110	Hides and skins, finishing on a contract basis
422590	Hides wholesaling
316110	Hides, tanning, currying, dressing, and finishing
337122	High chairs, wood, children's, manufacturing
311221	High fructose corn syrup (HFCS) manufacturing
335110	High intensity lamp bulbs manufacturing
331112	High percentage nonferrous alloying elements (i.e., ferroalloys) manufacturing
611110	High schools
611110	High schools offering both academic and technical courses
611110	High schools offering both academic and vocational courses
234110	Highway and street construction management firms
332312	Highway bridge sections, prefabricated metal, manufacturing
234110	Highway construction (except elevated)

Code	Description
234120	Highway construction, elevated
234110	Highway guardrail construction contractors
332322	Highway guardrails, sheet metal, manufacturing
235310	Highway lighting and electrical signal construction contractors
333120	Highway line marking machinery manufacturing
235210	Highway line painting construction contractors
922120	Highway patrols, police
336120	Highway tractors assembled on chassis of own manufacture
336211	Highway tractors assembling on purchased chassis
332510	Hinges, metal, manufacturing
813410	Historical clubs
712120	Historical forts
712110	Historical museums
712120	Historical ships
712120	Historical sites
336399	Hitches, trailer, automotive, truck, and bus, manufacturing
451120	Hobby shops
339932	Hobbyhorses manufacturing
421920	Hobbyists' supplies wholesaling
333515	Hobs (i.e., metal gear cutting tool) manufacturing
711211	Hockey clubs, professional or semiprofessional
713990	Hockey clubs, recreational
339920	Hockey equipment (except apparel) manufacturing
421910	Hockey equipment and supplies wholesaling
611620	Hockey instruction, camps, or schools
339920	Hockey skates manufacturing
711211	Hockey teams, professional or semiprofessional
713990	Hockey teams, recreational
115112	Hoeing
332212	Hoes, garden and mason's handtools, manufacturing
112210	Hog and pig (including breeding, farrowing, nursery, and finishing activities) farming

Code	Description
333111	Hog feeding and watering equipment manufacturing
112210	Hog feedlots (except stockyards for transportation)
422520	Hogs wholesaling
321920	Hogsheads, coopered wood, manufacturing
333923	Hoists (except aircraft loading) manufacturing
421830	Hoists (except automotive) wholesaling
333924	Hoists, aircraft loading, manufacturing
421120	Hoists, automotive, wholesaling
551112	Holding companies (except bank, managing)
551114	Holding companies that manage
551111	Holding companies, bank (except managing)
333313	Holepunchers (except hand operated), office-type, manufacturing
339942	Holepunchers, hand operated, manufacturing
332999	Hollowware, precious plated metal, manufacturing
316999	Holsters, leather, manufacturing
452990	Home and auto supply stores
532310	Home and garden equipment rental centers
235310	Home automation system construction contractors
332115	Home canning lids and rings, metal stamping
621610	Home care of elderly, medical
624120	Home care of elderly, non-medical
444110	Home centers, building materials
624229	Home construction organizations, work (sweat) equity
454390	Home delivery newspaper routes, direct selling
337124	Home entertainment centers, metal, manufacturing
337122	Home entertainment centers, wood, manufacturing
522292	Home equity credit lending
621610	Home health agencies
611519	Home health aid schools

Code	Description
621610	Home health care agencies
532291	Home health furniture and equipment rental
444110	Home improvement centers
233220	Home improvements, residential (except single family), construction
233210	Home improvements, residential single-family, construction
541350	Home inspection services
621610	Home nursing services (except private practices)
621399	Home nursing services, private practice
453998	Home security equipment stores
561920	Home show managers
561920	Home show organizers
561920	Home show promoters
334310	Home stereo systems manufacturing
334310	Home tape recorders and players (e.g., cartridge, cassette, reel) manufacturing
334310	Home theater audio and video equipment manufacturing
333512	Home workshop metal cutting machine tools (except handtools, welding equipment) manufacturing
442299	Homefurnishings stores
421220	Homefurnishings wholesaling
624221	Homeless shelters
624120	Homemaker's service for elderly or disabled persons, non-medical
621399	Homeopaths' offices (e.g., centers, clinics)
813990	Homeowners' associations
813990	Homeowners' associations, condominium
524126	Homeowners' insurance carriers, direct
524128	Homeowners' warranty insurance carriers, direct
623990	Homes for children with health care incidental
623220	Homes for emotionally disturbed adults or children
623110	Homes for the aged with nursing care
623312	Homes for the aged without nursing care

Code	Description
623110	Homes for the elderly with nursing care
623312	Homes for the elderly without nursing care
623990	Homes for unwed mothers
623210	Homes with or without health care, mental retardation
623220	Homes, psychiatric convalescent
311211	Hominy grits (except breakfast food), manufacturing
311230	Hominy grits, prepared as cereal breakfast food, manufacturing
311421	Hominy, canned, manufacturing
333294	Homogenizing machinery, food, manufacturing
311511	Homogenizing milk
212399	Hones mining and/or beneficiating
112910	Honey bee production
311999	Honey processing
422490	Honey wholesaling
111219	Honeydew melon farming, field, bedding plant and seed production
333512	Honing and lapping machines manufacturing
333515	Honing heads (i.e., a machine tool accessory) manufacturing
922140	Honor camps
332313	Hoods, industrial, fabricated metal plate work, manufacturing
332322	Hoods, range (except household-type), sheet metal, manufacturing
335211	Hoods, range, household-type, manufacturing
115210	Hoof trimming
339993	Hook and eye fasteners (i.e., sewing accessories) manufacturing
332722	Hook and eye latches manufacturing
313221	Hook and loop fastener fabric manufacturing
332722	Hooks (i.e., general purpose fasteners), metal, manufacturing
339920	Hooks, fishing, manufacturing
332212	Hooks, handtools (e.g., baling, bush, grass, husking), manufacturing
332722	Hooks, metal screw, manufacturing

Code	Description
331111	Hoops made in steel mills
331111	Hoops, galvanized, made in steel mills
332999	Hoops, metal (except wire), fabricated from purchased metal
321920	Hoops, sawed or split wood for tight or slack cooperage, manufacturing
311942	Hop extract manufacturing
422490	Hop extract wholesaling
111998	Hop farming
333515	Hopper feed devices (i.e., a machine tool accessory) manufacturing
332313	Hoppers, fabricated metal plate work, manufacturing
332439	Hoppers, light gauge metal, manufacturing
422590	Hops wholesaling
334511	Horizon situation instrumentation manufacturing
325413	Hormone in-vitro diagnostic substances manufacturing
325412	Hormone preparations (except in-vitro diagnostics) manufacturing
325411	Hormones and derivatives, uncompounded, manufacturing
112920	Horse (including thoroughbreds) production
332999	Horse bits manufacturing
316999	Horse boots and muzzles manufacturing
711212	Horse racetracks
711219	Horse racing stables
713990	Horse rental services, recreational saddle
711310	Horse show managers with facilities
711320	Horse show managers without facilities
711310	Horse show organizers with facilities
711320	Horse show organizers without facilities
711310	Horse show promoters with facilities
711320	Horse show promoters without facilities
336214	Horse trailers (except fifth-wheel-type) manufacturing
336212	Horse trailers, fifth-wheel-type, manufacturing

Code	Description
487110	Horse-drawn carriage operation
713990	Horseback riding, recreational
311611	Horsemeat produced in slaughtering plants
311111	Horsemeat, processing, for dog and cat food
311421	Horseradish (except sauce) canning
311941	Horseradish, prepared sauce, manufacturing
115210	Horses (except racehorses), boarding
422590	Horses wholesaling
115210	Horses, training (except racehorses)
331222	Horseshoe nails, iron or steel, made in wire drawing plants
115210	Horseshoeing
332111	Horseshoes, ferrous forged, made from purchased iron or steel
541690	Horticultural consulting services
332722	Hose clamps, metal, manufacturing
332912	Hose couplings and fittings, fluid power, manufacturing
332919	Hose couplings, metal (except fluid power), manufacturing
313221	Hose fabrics, tubular, weaving
332999	Hose, flexible metal, manufacturing
421840	Hose, industrial, wholesaling
326220	Hoses, reinforced, made from purchased rubber or plastics manufacturing
326220	Hoses, rubberized fabric, manufacturing
315119	Hosiery (except sheer), women's, girls' and infants', manufacturing
333292	Hosiery machines manufacturing
448190	Hosiery stores
422320	Hosiery, men's and boys', wholesaling
339113	Hosiery, orthopedic support, manufacturing
315111	Hosiery, sheer, women's, misses', and girls' full-length and knee-length, knitting or knitting and finishing
422330	Hosiery, women's and girls', wholesaling
422330	Hosiery, women's, children's, and infants', wholesaling

Code	Description
621610	Hospice care services, in home
623110	Hospices, inpatient care
813920	Hospital administrators' associations
524114	Hospital and medical service plans, direct, without providing health care services
813910	Hospital associations
532291	Hospital bed rental and leasing (i.e. home use)
339111	Hospital beds manufacturing
421450	Hospital beds wholesaling
233320	Hospital construction
421450	Hospital equipment and supplies wholesaling
532291	Hospital equipment rental (i.e. home use)
339111	Hospital furniture (e.g., hospital beds, operating room furniture) manufacturing
532291	Hospital furniture and equipment rental (i.e. home use)
421450	Hospital furniture wholesaling
926150	Hospital licensure agencies
611519	Hospital management schools (except academic)
611310	Hospital management schools offering baccalaureate or graduate degrees
315211	Hospital service apparel, washable, men's and boys', cut and sew apparel contractors
315225	Hospital service apparel, washable, men's and boys', cut and sewn from purchased fabric (except apparel contractors)
315212	Hospital service apparel, washable, women's and girls', cut and sew apparel contractors
315239	Hospital service apparel, washable, women's, misses', and girls', cut and sewn from purchased fabric (except apparel contractors)
611519	Hospitality management schools (except academic)
611310	Hospitality management schools offering baccalaureate or graduate degrees

Code	Description
524114	Hospitalization insurance carriers, direct, without providing health care services
*****	Hospitals — see type
622210	Hospitals for alcoholics
622210	Hospitals, addiction
541940	Hospitals, animal
622110	Hospitals, general medical and surgical
622110	Hospitals, general pediatric
622210	Hospitals, mental (except mental retardation)
623210	Hospitals, mental retardation
622210	Hospitals, psychiatric (except convalescent)
623220	Hospitals, psychiatric convalescent
622210	Hospitals, psychiatric pediatric
622310	Hospitals, specialty (except psychiatric, substance abuse)
622210	Hospitals, substance abuse
721199	Hostels
487990	Hot air balloon ride, scenic and sightseeing, operation
333311	Hot beverage vending machines manufacturing
332812	Hot dip galvanizing metals and metal products for the trade
311612	Hot dogs (except poultry) made from purchased carcasses
311611	Hot dogs (except poultry) produced in slaughtering plants
311615	Hot dogs, poultry, manufacturing
332111	Hot forgings made from purchased iron or steel, unfinished
332112	Hot forgings made from purchased nonferrous metals, unfinished
213112	Hot oil treating of oil field tanks on a contract basis
213112	Hot shot service on a contract basis
333516	Hot strip mill machinery, metalworking, manufacturing
453998	Hot tub stores
421910	Hot tubs wholesaling
321920	Hot tubs, coopered, manufacturing
326191	Hot tubs, plastics or fiberglass, manufacturing

Code	Description
326299	Hot water bottles, rubber, manufacturing
335228	Hot water heaters (including nonelectric), household-type, manufacturing
331111	Hot-rolling iron or steel products in steel mills
333516	Hot-rolling mill machinery, metalworking, manufacturing
331221	Hot-rolling purchased steel
531120	Hotel building, not operating hotel, rental or leasing
531110	Hotel building, residential, rental or leasing
233320	Hotel construction
421440	Hotel equipment and supplies (except furniture) wholesaling
421210	Hotel furniture wholesaling
561110	Hotel management services (except complete operation of client's business)
721110	Hotel management services (i.e., providing management and operating staff to run hotel)
561599	Hotel reservation services
327112	Hotel tableware and kitchen articles, vitreous china, manufacturing
721110	Hotels (except casino hotels)
721110	Hotels with golf courses, tennis courts, and/or other health spa facilities (i.e., resorts)
721120	Hotels, casino
721110	Hotels, membership
721120	Hotels, resort, with casinos
721110	Hotels, resort, without casinos
721120	Hotels, seasonal, with casinos
721110	Hotels, seasonal, without casinos
624190	Hotline centers
333319	Hotplates, commercial-type, manufacturing
335211	Hotplates, household-type electric, manufacturing
235990	House moving construction contractors
235210	House painting construction contractors
111422	House plant growing

Code	Description
812990	House sitting services
316212	House slippers manufacturing
316212	House slippers, plastics or plastics soled fabric upper, manufacturing
316212	House slippers, rubber or rubber soled fabric upper, manufacturing
454390	House-to-house direct selling
532292	Houseboat rental
315191	Housecoats made in apparel knitting mills
315291	Housecoats, infants', cut and sewn from purchased fabric (except apparel contractors)
315212	Housecoats, women's, girls', and infants', cut and sew apparel contractors
315231	Housecoats, women's, misses', and girls', cut and sewn from purchased fabric (except apparel contractors)
315212	Housedresses, women's and girls', cut and sew apparel contractors
315233	Housedresses, women's, misses', and girls', cut and sewn from purchased fabric (except apparel contractors)
443111	Household-type appliance stores
421620	Household-type appliances, electrical, wholesaling
327112	Household-type earthenware, semivitreous, manufacturing
421210	Household-type furniture wholesaling
337121	Household-type furniture, upholstered, manufacturing
337122	Household-type furniture, wood, not upholstered (except TV and radio housings and sewing machine cabinets), manufacturing
325320	Household-type insecticides manufacturing
421620	Household-type laundry equipment (e.g., dryers, washers) wholesaling
327112	Household-type tableware and kitchen articles, vitreous china, manufacturing
334518	Household-type timing mechanisms manufacturing
321999	Household-type woodenware manufacturing

Code	Description
814110	Households, private, employing (e.g., cooks, maids, chauffeurs, gardeners)
814110	Households, private, employing domestic personnel
721199	Housekeeping cabins
721199	Housekeeping cottages
561720	Housekeeping services (i.e., cleaning services)
922140	Houses of correction
531110	Houses rental or leasing
332311	Houses, prefabricated metal, manufacturing
321991	Houses, prefabricated mobile homes, manufacturing
321992	Houses, prefabricated, wood (except mobile homes), manufacturing
233210	Houses, single family attached, construction
233210	Houses, single family detached, construction
233210	Houses, single family semi-detached construction
421220	Housewares (except electric) wholesaling
442299	Housewares stores
421620	Housewares, electric, wholesaling
624229	Housing assistance agencies
531110	Housing authorities operating residential buildings
925110	Housing authorities, nonoperating
233220	Housing construction, multifamily
233210	Housing construction, single family
922120	Housing police, government
925110	Housing programs, planning and development, government
624229	Housing repair organizations, volunteer
336612	Hovercraft building
487210	Hovercraft sightseeing operation
332995	Howitzers manufacturing
321999	Hubs, wood, manufacturing
111334	Huckleberry farming
113210	Huckleberry greens, gathering of
212299	Huebnerite mining and/or beneficiating
115114	Hulling and shelling of nuts

Code	Description
333111	Hulling machinery, farm-type, manufacturing
712110	Human history museums
541612	Human resource consulting services
813311	Human rights advocacy organizations
921190	Human rights commissions, government
813312	Humane societies
541720	Humanities research and development services
421730	Humidifiers and dehumidifiers (except portable) wholesaling
421620	Humidifiers and dehumidifiers, portable, wholesaling
335211	Humidifiers, portable electric, manufacturing
333415	Humidifying equipment (except portable) manufacturing
334512	Humidistats (e.g., duct, skeleton, wall) manufacturing
334512	Humidity controls, air-conditioning type, manufacturing
334519	Humidity instruments (except industrial process and air-conditioning type) manufacturing
334513	Humidity instruments, industrial process-type, manufacturing
212399	Humus, peat, mining and/or beneficiating
721214	Hunting camps with accommodation facilities
713990	Hunting clubs, recreational
315211	Hunting coats and vests, men's and boys', cut and sew apparel contractors
315228	Hunting coats and vests, men's and boys', cut and sewn from purchased fabric (except apparel contractors)
421910	Hunting equipment and supplies wholesaling
713990	Hunting guide services
332211	Hunting knives manufacturing
114210	Hunting preserves
334111	Hybrid computers manufacturing
334413	Hybrid integrated circuits manufacturing
112511	Hybrid striped bass production

Code	Description
327410	Hydrated lime (i.e., calcium hydroxide), manufacturing
332912	Hydraulic aircraft subassemblies manufacturing
333995	Hydraulic cylinders, fluid power, manufacturing
811310	Hydraulic equipment repair and maintenance services
324110	Hydraulic fluids made in petroleum refineries
324191	Hydraulic fluids, petroleum, made from refined petroleum
325998	Hydraulic fluids, synthetic, manufacturing
213112	Hydraulic fracturing wells on a contract basis
332912	Hydraulic hose fittings, fluid power, manufacturing
326220	Hydraulic hoses (without fitting), rubber or plastics, manufacturing
421830	Hydraulic power transmission equipment wholesaling
421830	Hydraulic pumps and parts wholesaling
333996	Hydraulic pumps, fluid power, manufacturing
336340	Hydraulic slave cylinders, automotive, truck, and bus clutch, manufacturing
333611	Hydraulic turbine generator set units manufacturing
333611	Hydraulic turbines manufacturing
332912	Hydraulic valves, fluid power, manufacturing
325188	Hydrazine manufacturing
325188	Hydrochloric acid manufacturing
325188	Hydrocyanic acid manufacturing
234990	Hydroelectric plant construction
325188	Hydrofluoric acid manufacturing
325188	Hydrofluosilicic acid manufacturing
336611	Hydrofoil vessel building and repairing in shipyard
325120	Hydrogen manufacturing
325188	Hydrogen peroxide manufacturing
325188	Hydrogen sulfide manufacturing
311225	Hydrogenating purchased oil
541370	Hydrographic mapping services

Code	Description
541370	Hydrographic surveying services
541690	Hydrology consulting services
334519	Hydrometers (except industrial process-type) manufacturing
334513	Hydrometers, industrial process-type, manufacturing
334512	Hydronic circulator control, automatic, manufacturing
421720	Hydronic heating equipment and supplies wholesaling
333414	Hydronic heating equipment manufacturing
334512	Hydronic limit control manufacturing
334512	Hydronic limit, pressure, and temperature controls, manufacturing
334511	Hydrophones manufacturing
111419	Hydroponic crop farming
325192	Hydroquinone manufacturing
333996	Hydrostatic drives manufacturing
541380	Hydrostatic testing laboratories or services
333996	Hydrostatic transmissions manufacturing
325188	Hydrosulfites manufacturing
339113	Hydrotherapy equipment manufacturing
334519	Hygrometers (except industrial process-type) manufacturing
334513	Hygrometers, industrial process-type, manufacturing
334519	Hygrothermographs manufacturing
621399	Hypnotherapists' offices (e.g., centers, clinics)
325411	Hypnotic drugs, uncompounded, manufacturing
325188	Hypochlorites manufacturing
339112	Hypodermic needles and syringes manufacturing
325188	Hypophosphites manufacturing
321213	I-joists, wood, fabricating
514191	ISP (internet service providers)
339112	IV apparatus manufacturing
312113	Ice (except dry ice) manufacturing
422990	Ice (except dry ice) wholesaling
334512	Ice bank controls manufacturing

Code	Description
335222	Ice boxes, household-type, manufacturing
326199	Ice buckets, plastics (except foam), manufacturing
326140	Ice buckets, polystyrene foam, manufacturing
326150	Ice buckets, urethane or other plastics foam (except polystyrene), manufacturing
332439	Ice chests or coolers, metal, manufacturing
326199	Ice chests or coolers, plastics (except plastics foam) manufacturing
326140	Ice chests or coolers, polystyrene foam, manufacturing
326150	Ice chests or coolers, urethane or other plastics foam (except polystyrene) manufacturing
445299	Ice cream (i.e., packaged) stores
422430	Ice cream and ices wholesaling
311821	Ice cream cones manufacturing
422490	Ice cream cones wholesaling
333294	Ice cream making machinery manufacturing
311520	Ice cream manufacturing
311514	Ice cream mix manufacturing
722213	Ice cream parlors
311520	Ice cream specialties manufacturing
722330	Ice cream truck vendors
333311	Ice cream vending machines manufacturing
422430	Ice cream wholesaling
335211	Ice crushers, household-type electric, manufacturing
333999	Ice crushers, industrial and commercial-type, manufacturing
711211	Ice hockey clubs, professional or semiprofessional
713990	Ice hockey clubs, recreational
334512	Ice maker controls manufacturing
333415	Ice making machinery manufacturing
421740	Ice making machines wholesaling
311520	Ice milk manufacturing
311514	Ice milk mix manufacturing
311520	Ice milk specialties manufacturing

Code	Description
339920	Ice skates manufacturing
711190	Ice skating companies
713940	Ice skating rinks
711190	Ice skating shows
312130	Ice wine
325120	Ice, dry, manufacturing
422690	Ice, dry, wholesaling
312111	Iced coffee manufacturing
312111	Iced tea manufacturing
212399	Iceland spar (i.e., optical grade calcite), mining and/or beneficiating
311520	Ices, flavored sherbets, manufacturing
332999	Identification plates, metal, manufacturing
421410	Identity recorders wholesaling
332993	Igniters, ammunition tracer (i.e., more than 30 mm., more than 1.18 inch), manufacturing
334512	Ignition controls for gas appliances and furnaces, automatic, manufacturing
336322	Ignition points and condensers for internal combustion engines manufacturing
334515	Ignition testing instruments manufacturing
336322	Ignition wiring harness for internal combustion engines manufacturing
335122	Illuminated indoor lighting fixtures (e.g., directional, exit) manufacturing
541430	Illustrators, independent commercial
212299	Ilmenite ores mining and/or beneficiating
327420	Images, small gypsum, manufacturing
327999	Images, small papier-mache, manufacturing
323122	Imagesetting services, prepress
312221	Imitation tobacco cigarettes, manufacturing
335211	Immersion heaters, household-type electric, manufacturing
624230	Immigrant resettlement services

Code	Description
928120	Immigration services
923120	Immunization program administration
621111	Immunologists' offices (e.g., centers, clinics)
334516	Immunology instruments, laboratory, manufacturing
333991	Impact wrenches, handheld power-driven, manufacturing
334515	Impedance measuring equipment manufacturing
334514	Impeller and counter driven flow meters manufacturing
339113	Implants, surgical, manufacturing
213112	Impounding and storing salt water in connection with petroleum production
221310	Impounding reservoirs, irrigation
339114	Impression material, dental, manufacturing
711110	Improvisational theaters
334512	In-built thermostats, filled system and bimetal types, manufacturing
454390	In-home sales of merchandise, direct selling
325413	In-vitro diagnostic substances manufacturing
325412	In-vivo diagnostic substances manufacturing
335110	Incandescent filament lamp bulbs, complete, manufacturing
325998	Incense manufacturing
334512	Incinerator control systems, residential and commercial-type, manufacturing
333994	Incinerators (except precast concrete) manufacturing
562211	Incinerators, hazardous waste, operating
562213	Incinerators, nonhazardous solid waste
327390	Incinerators, precast concrete, manufacturing
235950	Incinerators, small, construction contractors
541213	Income tax compilation services
541213	Income tax return preparation services

Code	Description
333313	Incoming mail handling equipment (e.g., opening, scanning, sorting) manufacturing
339113	Incubators, infant, manufacturing
339111	Incubators, laboratory-type, manufacturing
333111	Incubators, poultry, manufacturing
325998	Indelible inks manufacturing
488190	Independent pilot, air (except owner-operators)
488490	Independent truck driver (except owner-operators)
333515	Indexing, rotary tables (i.e., a machine tool accessory) manufacturing
325998	India inks manufacturing
921190	Indian affairs programs, government
334515	Indicating instruments, electric, manufacturing
334519	Indicator testers, turntable, manufacturing
334513	Indicators, industrial process control-type, manufacturing
325188	Indium chloride manufacturing
624190	Individual and family social services, multi-purpose
523910	Individuals investing in financial contracts on own account
541850	Indoor display advertising services
713120	Indoor play areas
333994	Induction heating equipment, industrial process-type, manufacturing
334416	Inductors, electronic component-type (e.g., chokes, coils, transformers), manufacturing
233310	Industrial and manufacturing building construction contractors
233310	Industrial and manufacturing building construction management firms
813910	Industrial associations
522190	Industrial banks (i.e., known as), depository
522298	Industrial banks (i.e., known as), nondepository

Code	Description
314992	Industrial belting reinforcement, cord and fabric, manufacturing
233310	Industrial building construction, general construction contractors
531120	Industrial building rental or leasing
722310	Industrial caters (i.e., providing food services on a contractural arrangement [except single event base])
422690	Industrial chemicals wholesaling
421840	Industrial containers wholesaling
335314	Industrial controls (e.g., push button, selector, and pilot switches, manufacturing
421610	Industrial controls, electrical, wholesaling
541420	Industrial design consulting services
533110	Industrial design licensing
541420	Industrial design services
926110	Industrial development program administration
541330	Industrial engineering services
811310	Industrial equipment and machinery repair and maintenance services
315211	Industrial garments, men's and boys', cut and sew apparel contractors
315225	Industrial garments, men's and boys', cut and sewn from purchased fabric (except apparel contractors)
315212	Industrial garments, women's and girls', cut and sew apparel contractors
315239	Industrial garments, women's, misses', and girls', cut and sewn from purchased fabric (except apparel contractors)
325120	Industrial gases manufacturing
422690	Industrial gases wholesaling
327212	Industrial glassware and glass products, pressed or blown, made in glass making plants
327215	Industrial glassware made from purchased glass
234930	Industrial incinerator construction contractors
813930	Industrial labor unions

Code	Description
541320	Industrial land use planning services
812332	Industrial launderers
335122	Industrial lighting fixtures, electric, manufacturing
522298	Industrial loan companies, nondepository
336510	Industrial locomotives and parts manufacturing
421830	Industrial machinery and equipment (except electrical) wholesaling
335122	Industrial mercury lighting fixtures, electric, manufacturing
333511	Industrial molds (except steel ingot) manufacturing
331511	Industrial molds, steel ingot, manufacturing
234930	Industrial nonbuilding construction management firms
332997	Industrial pattern manufacturing
234930	Industrial plant appurtenance construction
233310	Industrial plant construction, general construction contractors
334513	Industrial process control instruments manufacturing
325510	Industrial product finishes and coatings (i.e., paint) manufacturing
541710	Industrial research and development laboratories or services
421450	Industrial safety devices (e.g., eye shields, face shields, first-aid kits) wholesaling
325998	Industrial salt manufacturing
422690	Industrial salt wholesaling
212322	Industrial sand beneficiating (e.g., screening, washing)
212322	Industrial sand sandpits and dredging
333997	Industrial scales manufacturing
234930	Industrial structures, construction (except building)
421840	Industrial supplies (except disposable plastics, paper) wholesaling
422130	Industrial supplies, disposable plastics, paper, wholesaling

Code	Description
541380	Industrial testing laboratories or services
621340	Industrial therapists' offices (e.g., centers, clinics)
811310	Industrial truck (e.g., forklifts) repair and maintenance services
532490	Industrial truck rental or leasing
333924	Industrial trucks and tractors manufacturing
421830	Industrial trucks, tractors, or trailers wholesaling
812332	Industrial uniform supply services
421930	Industrial wastes to be reclaimed wholesaling
311611	Inedible products (e.g., hides, skins, pulled wool, wool grease) produced in slaughtering plants
334511	Inertial navigation systems, aeronautical, manufacturing
311422	Infant and junior food canning
311230	Infant cereals, dry, manufacturing
624410	Infant day care centers
624410	Infant day care services
339113	Infant incubators manufacturing
311514	Infants' formulas manufacturing
316219	Infants' shoes (except plastics, rubber), manufacturing
315291	Infants water resistant outerwear cut and sewn from purchased fabric (except apparel contractors)
315291	Infants' apparel cut and sewn from purchased fabric (except apparel contractors)
422330	Infants' clothing wholesaling
315212	Infants' cut and sew apparel contractors
514191	Information access services, on-line
541512	Information management computer systems integration design services
514199	Information search services, on a contract or fee basis
334516	Infrared analytical instruments, laboratory-type, manufacturing
334511	Infrared homing systems, aeronautical, manufacturing
334513	Infrared instruments, industrial process-type, manufacturing
335110	Infrared lamp bulbs manufacturing

Code	Description
335129	Infrared lamp fixtures manufacturing
333994	Infrared ovens, industrial, manufacturing
334413	Infrared sensors, solid-state, manufacturing
621498	Infusion therapy centers and clinics, outpatient
331319	Ingot made by rolling purchased aluminum
331111	Ingot made in steel mills
331319	Ingot, aluminum, made in integrated secondary smelting and rolling mills
331492	Ingot, nonferrous metals (except aluminum, copper), secondary smelting and refining
331312	Ingot, primary aluminium, manufacturing
331419	Ingot, primary, nonferrous metals (except aluminum, copper), manufacturing
421510	Ingots (except precious) wholesaling
421940	Ingots, precious, wholesaling
621399	Inhalation therapists' offices (e.g., centers, clinics)
339112	Inhalation therapy equipment manufacturing
339112	Inhalators, surgical and medical, manufacturing
325998	Inhibitors (e.g., corrosion, oxidation, polymerization) manufacturing
333220	Injection molding machinery for plastics manufacturing
325612	Ink eradicators manufacturing
422120	Ink, writing, wholesaling
339944	Inked ribbons manufacturing
422120	Inked ribbons wholesaling
325910	Inkjet cartridges manufacturing
325910	Inkjet inks manufacturing
325910	Inks, printing, manufacturing
421840	Inks, printing, wholesaling
325998	Inks, writing, manufacturing
316999	Inner soles, leather, manufacturing
326211	Inner tubes manufacturing
337910	Innerspring cushions manufacturing

Code	Description
721191	Inns, bed and breakfast
422690	Inorganic chemicals wholesaling
325131	Inorganic pigments (except bone black, carbon black, lamp black) manufacturing
334119	Input/output equipment, computer (except terminals), manufacturing
115112	Insect control for crops
335129	Insect lamps, electric, manufacturing
332618	Insect screening made from purchased wire
325320	Insecticides manufacturing
333515	Inserts, cutting tool, manufacturing
541350	Inspection bureaus, building
926150	Inspection for labor standards
488490	Inspection or weighing services, truck transportation
488190	Inspection services, aircraft
541350	Inspection services, building or home
235950	Installation of machinery and other industrial equipment construction contractors
213112	Installing production equipment at the oil or gas field on a contract basis
522220	Installment sales financing
311920	Instant coffee manufacturing
311230	Instant hot cereals manufacturing
323114	Instant printing (i.e., quick printing)
311920	Instant tea manufacturing
233320	Institutional and commercial building construction management firms
233320	Institutional building construction
337127	Institutional furniture manufacturing
335122	Institutional lighting fixtures, electric, manufacturing
*****	Instruction — see type of training
512110	Instructional video production
336322	Instrument control panels (i.e., assembling purchased gauges), automotive, truck, and bus, manufacturing

Code	Description
334511	Instrument landing system instrumentation, airborne or airport, manufacturing
333314	Instrument lenses manufacturing
334514	Instrument panels, assembling gauges made in the same establishment
334515	Instrument shunts manufacturing
332612	Instrument springs, precision (except clock, watch), manufacturing
335311	Instrument transformers (except complete instruments) for metering or protective relaying use manufacturing
334519	Instrumentation for reactor controls, auxiliary, manufacturing
421830	Instruments (except electrical) (e.g., controlling, indicating, recording) wholesaling
334513	Instruments for industrial process control manufacturing
334515	Instruments for measuring electrical quantities manufacturing
334511	Instruments, aeronautical, manufacturing
334515	Instruments, electric (i.e., testing electrical characteristics), manufacturing
339112	Instruments, mechanical microsurgical, manufacturing
339992	Instruments, musical, manufacturing
421990	Instruments, musical, wholesaling
421490	Instruments, professional and scientific, wholesaling
331422	Insulated wire or cable made from purchased copper in wire drawing plants
331319	Insulated wire or cable made in aluminum wire drawing plants
421610	Insulated wire or cable wholesaling
331422	Insulated wire or cable, copper, made in integrated secondary smelting and drawing plants
322299	Insulating batts, fills, or blankets made from purchased paper

Code	Description
327993	Insulating batts, fills, or blankets, fiberglass, manufacturing
327124	Insulating firebrick and shapes, clay, manufacturing
327215	Insulating glass, sealed units, made from purchased glass
327211	Insulating glass, sealed units, made in glass making plants
321999	Insulating materials, cork, manufacturing
325998	Insulating oils manufacturing
235990	Insulating pipes and boilers construction contractors
335929	Insulating purchased wire
326150	Insulation and cushioning, foam plastics (except polystrene), manufacturing
326140	Insulation and cushioning, polystyrene foam plastics, manufacturing
321219	Insulation board, cellular fiber or hard pressed wood, manufacturing
235420	Insulation construction contractors
421330	Insulation materials wholesaling
235990	Insulation of pipes and boilers construction contractors
335932	Insulators, electrical (except glass, porcelain), manufacturing
327113	Insulators, electrical porcelain, manufacturing
327215	Insulators, electrical, glass, made from purchased glass
327212	Insulators, electrical, glass, made in glass making plants
421610	Insulators, electrical, wholesaling
325412	Insulin preparations manufacturing
325411	Insulin, uncompounded, manufacturing
524298	Insurance advisory services
524210	Insurance agencies
524210	Insurance brokerages
531120	Insurance building rental or leasing
524113	Insurance carriers, disability, direct
524126	Insurance carriers, fidelity, direct
524114	Insurance carriers, health, direct
524113	Insurance carriers, life, direct
524126	Insurance carriers, property and casualty, direct

Code	Description
524126	Insurance carriers, surety, direct
524127	Insurance carriers, title, direct
524291	Insurance claims adjusting
524291	Insurance claims investigation services
524292	Insurance claims processing services, third party
926150	Insurance commissions, government
524298	Insurance coverage consulting services
524292	Insurance fund, third party administrative services (except claims adjusting only)
524298	Insurance investigation services (except claims investigation)
524298	Insurance loss prevention services
524292	Insurance plan administrative services (except claims adjusting only), third-party
524298	Insurance rate making services
524298	Insurance reporting services
524291	Insurance settlement offices
524298	Insurance underwriters laboratories and standards services
524113	Insurance underwriting, disability, direct
524114	Insurance underwriting, health and medical, direct
524113	Insurance underwriting, life, direct
524126	Insurance underwriting, property and casualty, direct
524127	Insurance underwriting, title, direct
813910	Insurers' associations
323111	Intaglio printing
335312	Integral horsepower electric motors manufacturing
421690	Integrated circuits wholesaling
334413	Integrated microcircuits manufacturing
512220	Integrated record companies (i.e., releasing, promoting, distributing)
512220	Integrated record production and distribution
334515	Integrated-circuit testers manufacturing
334515	Integrating electricity meters manufacturing

Code	Description
334514	Integrating meters, nonelectric, manufacturing
712110	Interactive museums
234910	Interceptor construction
485210	Intercity bus line operation
483113	Intercoastal freight transportation to and from domestic ports
334290	Intercom systems and equipment manufacturing
332410	Intercooler shells manufacturing
483114	Intercostal transportation of passengers to and from domestic ports
333314	Interferometers manufacturing
541410	Interior decorating consultant services
541410	Interior decorating consulting services
541410	Interior design consulting services
541410	Interior design services
541410	Interior designer services
315211	Interlinings (e.g., belt loops, pockets) for suits, coats, and trousers, men's and boys', cut and sew apparel contractors
315212	Interlinings (e.g., belt loops, pockets) for suits, coats, skirts, and dresses, women's, girls' and infants', cut and sew apparel contractors
623210	Intermediate care facilities, mental retardation
921130	Internal Revenue Service
334515	Internal combustion engine analyzers (i.e., testing electrical characteristics) manufacturing
333618	Internal combustion engines (except aircraft, nondiesel automotive, nondiesel truck) manufacturing
421830	Internal combustion engines (except aircraft, nondiesel automotive, nondiesel truck) wholesaling
336412	Internal combustion engines, aircraft, manufacturing
336312	Internal combustion engines, automotive and truck gasoline, manufacturing
928120	International Monetary Fund

Code	Description
522293	International trade financing
514191	Internet access providers
514191	Internet service providers (ISP)
621111	Internists' offices (e.g., centers, clinics)
541940	Internists' offices, veterinary
541930	Interpretation services, language
712190	Interpretive centers, nature
711120	Interpretive dance companies
711510	Interpretive dancers, independent
485210	Interstate bus line operation
485210	Interurban bus line operation
339113	Intra ocular lenses manufacturing
483211	Intracoastal transportation of freight
483212	Intracoastal transportation of passengers
339113	Intrauterine devices manufacturing
325412	Intravenous (IV) solution preparations manufacturing
812990	Introduction services, social
532291	Invalid equipment rental (i.e. home use)
561990	Inventory computing services
541614	Inventory planning and control management consulting services
561990	Inventory taking services
311312	Invert sugar made from purchased raw cane sugar
335312	Inverters, rotating electrical, manufacturing
335999	Inverters, solid-state, manufacturing
561611	Investigation services (except credit), private
561450	Investigation services, credit
561611	Investigators, private
523930	Investment advice consulting services, customized, fees paid by client
523930	Investment advice counseling services, customized, fees paid by client
523930	Investment advisory services, customized, fees paid by client
523110	Investment banking

Code	Description
331524	Investment castings, aluminum, unfinished, manufacturing
331525	Investment castings, copper (except die-castings), unfinished manufacturing
331528	Investment castings, nonferrous metal (except alumninum, copper), unfinished, manufacturing
331512	Investment castings, steel, unfinished, manufacturing
523910	Investment clubs
525990	Investment funds, closed-end
525910	Investment funds, open-ended
325188	Iodides manufacturing
325412	Iodated in-vivo diagnostic substances manufacturing
325188	Iodine, crude or resublimed, manufacturing
334519	Ion chambers manufacturing
325211	Ion exchange resins manufacturing
325211	Ionomer resins manufacturing
325199	Ionone manufacturing
331491	Iridium bar, rod, sheet, strip and tubing made from purchased metals or scrap
212299	Iridium mining and/or beneficiating
331492	Iridium recovering from scrap and/or alloying purchased metals
331419	Iridium refining, primary
421390	Iron and steel architectural shapes wholesaling
325131	Iron based pigments manufacturing
331511	Iron castings, unfinished, manufacturing
325188	Iron compounds, not specified elsewhere by process, manufacturing
332111	Iron forgings made from purchased iron, unfinished
331511	Iron foundries
339113	Iron lungs manufacturing
212210	Iron ore (e.g., hematite, magnetite, siderite, taconite) mining and/or beneficiating
212210	Iron ore agglomerates mining and/or beneficiating

Code	Description
212210	Iron ore beneficiating plants (e.g., agglomeration, sintering)
212210	Iron ore mine site development for own account
331111	Iron ore recovery from open hearth slag
212210	Iron ore, blocked, mining and/or beneficiating
331111	Iron sinter made in steel mills
325188	Iron sulphate manufacturing
235910	Iron work structural, construction contractors
331111	Iron, pig, manufacturing
335224	Ironers and mangles, household-type (except portable irons), manufacturing
332999	Ironing boards, metal, manufacturing
321999	Ironing boards, wood, manufacturing
335211	Irons, household-type electric, manufacturing
334517	Irradiation apparatus and tubes (e.g., industrial, medical diagnostic, medical therapeutic, research, scientific), manufacturing
334517	Irradiation equipment manufacturing
115114	Irradiation of fruits and vegetables
926130	Irrigation districts, nonoperating
421820	Irrigation equipment wholesaling
333111	Irrigation equipment, agriculture, manufacturing
327332	Irrigation pipe, concrete, manufacturing
332322	Irrigation pipe, sheet metal, manufacturing
234990	Irrigation project construction
221310	Irrigation system operation
325110	Isobutane made from refined petroleum or liquid hydrocarbons
211112	Isobutane recovered from oil and gas field gases
325110	Isobutene made from refined petroleum or liquid hydrocarbons
325211	Isobutylene polymer resins manufacturing

Code	Description
325212	Isobutylene-isoprene rubber manufacturing
325212	Isocyanate rubber manufacturing
325192	Isocyanates manufacturing
335311	Isolation transformers manufacturing
211112	Isopentane recovered from oil and gas field gases
325110	Isoprene made from refined petroleum or liquid hydrocarbons
325199	Isopropyl alcohol manufacturing
311422	Italian foods canning
333120	Jack hammers manufacturing
315191	Jackets made in apparel knitting mills
332992	Jackets, bullet (i.e., 30 mm. or less, 1.18 inch or less), manufacturing
315292	Jackets, fur (except apparel contractors), manufacturing
315211	Jackets, fur, men's and boys', cut and sew apparel contractors
315212	Jackets, fur, women's, girls', and infants', cut and sew apparel contractors
332313	Jackets, industrial, fabricated metal plate work, manufacturing
315291	Jackets, infants', cut and sewn from purchased fabric (except apparel contractors)
315292	Jackets, leather (except welders') or sheep-lined (except apparel contractors), manufacturing
315211	Jackets, leather (except welders') or sheep-lined, men's and boys', cut and sew apparel contractors
315212	Jackets, leather (except welders') or sheep-lined, women's, girls', and infants', cut and sew apparel contractors
315211	Jackets, men's and boys', cut and sew apparel contractors
315225	Jackets, nontailored work, men's and boys', cut and sewn from purchased fabric (except apparel contractors)
315239	Jackets, nontailored work, women's, misses', and girls', cut and sewn from purchased fabric (except apparel contractors)

Code	Description
315239	Jackets, nontailored, women's, misses', and girls', cut and sewn from purchased fabric (except apparel contractors)
315228	Jackets, not tailored (except work), men's and boys', cut and sewn from purchased fabric (except apparel contractors)
315211	Jackets, service apparel (e.g., laboratory, medical), men's and boys', cut and sew apparel contractors
315225	Jackets, service apparel (e.g., laboratory, medical), men's and boys', cut and sewn from purchased fabric (except apparel contractors)
315212	Jackets, service apparel (e.g., laboratory, medical), women's and girls', cut and sew apparel contractors
315239	Jackets, service apparel (e.g., laboratory, medical), women's, misses', and girls', cut and sewn from purchased fabric (except apparel contractors)
315291	Jackets, ski, infants', cut and sewn from purchased fabric (except apparel contractors)
315211	Jackets, ski, men's and boys', cut and sew apparel contractors
315228	Jackets, ski, men's and boys', cut and sewn from purchased fabric (except apparel contractors)
315212	Jackets, ski, women's, girls', and infants', cut and sew apparel contractors
315239	Jackets, ski, women's, misses', and girls', cut and sewn from purchased fabric (except apparel contractors)
315222	Jackets, tailored (except fur, leather, sheep-lined), men's and boys', cut and sewn from purchased fabric (except apparelcontractors)
315234	Jackets, tailored (except fur, sheep-lined), women's, misses', and girls', cut and sewn from purchased fabric (except apparelcontractors)
315211	Jackets, tailored, men's and boys', cut and sew apparel contractors

Code	Description
315212	Jackets, tailored, women's, girls', and infants', cut and sew apparel contractors
316999	Jackets, welder's, leather, manufacturing
315212	Jackets, women's, girls', and infants', cut and sew apparel contractors
332212	Jacks (except hydraulic, pneumatic) manufacturing
333999	Jacks, hydraulic and pneumatic, manufacturing
333292	Jacquard card cutting machinery manufacturing
313210	Jacquard woven fabrics weaving
212399	Jade mining and/or beneficiating
611620	Jai alai instruction, camps, or schools
711211	Jai alai teams, professional or semiprofessional
561210	Jail operation on a contract or fee basis
922140	Jails
332321	Jalousies, metal, manufacturing
422690	Janitorial chemicals wholesaling
421850	Janitorial equipment and supplies wholesaling
561720	Janitorial services
561720	Janitorial services, aircraft
332812	Japanning metals and metal products for the trade
316110	Japanning of leather
333994	Japanning ovens manufacturing
325510	Japans manufacturing
327213	Jars for packaging, bottling, and canning, glass, manufacturing
326199	Jars, plastics, manufacturing
711120	Jazz dance companies
711510	Jazz dancers, independent
711130	Jazz musical artists, independent
711130	Jazz musical groups
315211	Jean-cut casual slacks, men's and boys', cut and sew apparel contractors
315224	Jean-cut casual slacks, men's and boys', cut and sewn from purchased fabric (except apparel contractors)

Code	Description
315212	Jean-cut casual slacks, women's, girls', and infants', cut and sew apparel contractors
315239	Jean-cut casual slacks, women's, misses', and girls', cut and sewn from purchased fabric (except apparel contractors)
315291	Jeans, infants', cut and sewn from purchased fabric (except apparel contractors)
315211	Jeans, men's and boys', cut and sew apparel contractors
315239	Jeans, women's, misses', and girls', cut and sewn from purchased fabric (except apparel contractors)
315212	Jeans, women's, misses', girls', and infants', cut and sew apparel contractors
311421	Jellies and jams manufacturing
422490	Jellies and jams wholesaling
311340	Jelly candies manufacturing
315191	Jerseys made in apparel knitting mills
315211	Jerseys, men's and boys', cut and sew apparel contractors
315223	Jerseys, men's and boys', cut and sewn from purchased fabric (except apparel contractors)
315212	Jerseys, women's, girls', and infants', cut and sew apparel contractors
315232	Jerseys, women's, misses', and girls', cut and sewn from purchased fabric (except apparel contractors)
324110	Jet fuels manufacturing
336412	Jet propulsion and internal combustion engines and parts, aircraft, manufacturing
332993	Jet propulsion projectiles (except guided missiles) manufacturing
234990	Jetty construction
339911	Jewel settings and mountings, precious metal, manufacturing
339913	Jeweler's findings and materials manufacturing
332212	Jeweler's handtools, nonelectric, manufacturing
421940	Jewelers' findings wholesaling

Code	Description
422990	Jewelry boxes wholesaling
541490	Jewelry design services
811490	Jewelry repair shops without retailing new jewelry
448150	Jewelry stores, costume
448310	Jewelry stores, precious
421940	Jewelry wholesaling
339914	Jewelry, costume, manufacturing
339911	Jewelry, natural or cultured pearls, manufacturing
339911	Jewelry, precious metal, manufacturing
333514	Jigs (e.g., checking, gauging, inspection) manufacturing
333514	Jigs and fixtures for use with machine tools manufacturing
333991	Jigsaws, handheld power-driven, manufacturing
333210	Jigsaws, woodworking-type, stationary, manufacturing
624310	Job counseling, vocational rehabilitation or habilitation
323119	Job printing (except flexographic, gravure, lithographic, screen)
323112	Job printing, flexographic
323111	Job printing, gravure
323119	Job printing, letterpress
323110	Job printing, lithographic
323110	Job printing, offset
323113	Job printing, screen
336370	Job stampings, automotive, metal, manufacturing
624310	Job training, vocational rehabilitation or habilitation
711219	Jockeys, horse racing
339920	Jogging machines, manufacturing
315191	Jogging suits made in apparel knitting mills
315291	Jogging suits, infants', cut and sewn from purchased fabric (except apparel contractors)
315211	Jogging suits, men's and boys', cut and sew apparel contractors
315228	Jogging suits, men's and boys', cut and sewn from purchased fabric (except apparel contractors)

Code	Description
315212	Jogging suits, women's, girls', and infants', cut and sew apparel contractors
315239	Jogging suits, women's, misses', and girls', cut and sewn from purchased fabric (except apparel contractors)
325520	Joint compounds (except gypsum base) manufacturing
327420	Joint compounds, gypsum based, manufacturing
333210	Jointers, woodworking-type, manufacturing
333613	Joints, swivel (except aircraft, motor vehicle), manufacturing
333613	Joints, universal (except aircraft, motor vehicle), manufacturing
336413	Joints, universal, aircraft, manufacturing
336350	Joints, universal, automotive, truck, and bus, manufacturing
332312	Joists, fabricated bar, manufacturing
332322	Joists, sheet metal, manufacturing
111998	Jojoba farming
711510	Journalists, independent (freelance)
334119	Joystick devices manufacturing
611620	Judo instruction, camps, or schools
326150	Jugs, vacuum, foam plastics (except polystyrene), manufacturing
332439	Jugs, vacuum, light gauge metal, manufacturing
326140	Jugs, vacuum, polystyrene foam plastics, manufacturing
333294	Juice extractors (i.e., food manufacturing-type) manufacturing
335211	Juice extractors, household-type electric, manufacturing
311520	Juice pops, frozen, manufacturing
422490	Juices, canned or fresh, wholesaling
422420	Juices, frozen, wholesaling
311411	Juices, fruit or vegetable concentrates, frozen, manufacturing
311421	Juices, fruit or vegetable, canned manufacturing
311421	Juices, fruit or vegetable, fresh, manufacturing

Code	Description
311411	Juices, fruit or vegetable, frozen, manufacturing
713990	Jukebox concession operators (i.e., supplying and servicing in others' facilities)
334310	Jukeboxes manufacturing
315212	Jumpsuits, women's, girls', and infants', cut and sew apparel contractors
315234	Jumpsuits, women's, misses', and girls', cut and sewn from purchased fabric (except apparel contractors)
335932	Junction boxes, electrical wiring, manufacturing
813910	Junior chambers of commerce
611210	Junior colleges
611210	Junior colleges offering a wide variety of academic and technical training
611110	Junior high schools
313210	Jute bags made in broadwoven mills
422310	Jute piece goods (except burlap) wholesaling
337124	Juvenile furniture (except upholstered), metal manufacturing
337122	Juvenile furniture (except upholstered), wood, manufacturing
337125	Juvenile furniture, rattan and reed, manufacturing
337121	Juvenile furniture, upholstered, manufacturing
623990	Juvenile halfway group homes
511120	Juvenile magazine and periodical publishers
511120	Juvenile magazine and periodical publishers and printing combined
511120	Juvenile magazine and periodical publishing (i.e., establishments known as publishers)
323112	Juvenile magazines and periodicals flexographic printing without publishing
323111	Juvenile magazines and periodicals gravure printing without publishing
323110	Juvenile magazines and periodicals lithographic (offset) printing without publishing

Code	Description
323119	Juvenile magazines and periodicals printing (except flexographic, gravure, lithographic, screen) without publishing
323113	Juvenile magazines and periodicals screen printing without publishing
111219	Kale farming, field, bedding plant and seed production
212324	Kaolin mining and/or beneficiating
327992	Kaolin, processing beyond beneficiation
713990	Kayaking, recreational
327420	Keene's cement manufacturing
321920	Kegs, wood, coopered, manufacturing
311119	Kelp meal and pellets, animal feed manufacturing
334515	Kelvin bridges (i.e., electrical measuring instruments) manufacturing
111998	Kenaf farming
112990	Kennels, breeding and raising stock for sale
711219	Kennels, dog racing
812910	Kennels, pet boarding
212391	Kernite mining and/or beneficiating
211111	Kerogen processing
324110	Kerosene manufacturing
333414	Kerosene space heaters manufacturing
311421	Ketchup manufacturing
325199	Ketone compounds, not specified elsewhere by process, manufacturing
332420	Kettles, heavy gauge metal, manufacturing
332510	Key blanks manufacturing
316993	Key cases (except metal) manufacturing
339911	Key cases, precious metal, manufacturing
333512	Key cutting machines manufacturing
811490	Key duplicating shops
332618	Key rings made from purchased wire
334119	Keyboards, computer peripheral equipment, manufacturing

Code	Description
339992	Keyboards, piano or organ, manufacturing
336322	Keyless entry systems, automotive, truck, and bus, manufacturing
421710	Keys and locks wholesaling
334210	Keysets, telephone, manufacturing
621492	Kidney dialysis centers and clinics
234930	Kiln construction
321999	Kiln drying lumber
327124	Kiln furniture, clay, manufacturing
333994	Kilns (except cement, chemical, wood) manufacturing
333298	Kilns (i.e., cement, chemical, wood) manufacturing
421830	Kilns, industrial, wholesaling
611110	Kindergartens
334519	Kinematic test and measuring equipment manufacturing
561910	Kit assembling and packaging services
336211	Kit car bodies manufacturing
421620	Kitchen appliances, household-type, electric, wholesaling
327112	Kitchen articles, coarse earthenware, manufacturing
444190	Kitchen cabinet (except custom) stores
337110	Kitchen cabinets (except freestanding), stock or custom wood, manufacturing
421310	Kitchen cabinets, built in, wholesaling
337122	Kitchen chairs (e.g., upholstered), wood, manufacturing
337124	Kitchen chairs (including upholstered), metal, manufacturing
337125	Kitchen chairs (including upholstered), plastics manufacturing
332211	Kitchen cutlery, nonprecious and precious plated metal, manufacturing
325612	Kitchen degreasing and cleaning preparations manufacturing
337124	Kitchen furniture, household-type, metal, manufacturing
337124	Kitchen furniture, metal household-type, manufacturing

Code	Description
337122	Kitchen furniture, wood household-type, manufacturing
421440	Kitchen utensils, commercial, wholesaling
332214	Kitchen utensils, fabricated metal (e.g., colanders, garlic presses, ice cream scoops, spatulas), manufacturing
421220	Kitchen utensils, household-type, wholesaling
326199	Kitchen utensils, plastics, manufacturing
442299	Kitchenware stores
327112	Kitchenware, commercial and household-type, vitreous china, manufacturing
327112	Kitchenware, semivitreous earthenware, manufacturing
321999	Kitchenware, wood, manufacturing
339932	Kites manufacturing
111339	Kiwi fruit farming
334411	Klystron tubes manufacturing
314911	Knapsacks (e.g., backpacks, book bags) manufacturing
314911	Knapsacks, made from purchased woven or knitted materials
315211	Knickers, dress, men's and boys', cut and sew apparel contractors
315291	Knickers, infants', cut and sewn from purchased fabric (except apparel contractors)
315228	Knickers, men's and boys', cut and sewn from purchased fabric (except apparel contractors)
315212	Knickers, women's, girls', and infants', cut and sew apparel contractors
315239	Knickers, women's, misses', and girls', cut and sewn from purchased fabric (except apparel contractors)
337122	Knickknack shelves, wood, manufacturing
332211	Knife blades manufacturing
332211	Knife blanks manufacturing
335313	Knife switches, electric power switchgear-type, manufacturing
311812	Knishes (except frozen) made in commercial bakeries

Code	Description
311813	Knishes, frozen, manufacturing
315992	Knit gloves cut and sewn from purchased fabric (except apparel contractors)
315191	Knit gloves made in apparel knitting mills
315211	Knit gloves, men's and boys', cut and sew apparel contractors
315212	Knit gloves, women's, girls', and infants', cut and sew apparel contractors
313113	Knitting and crocheting thread manufacturing
313249	Knitting and finishing lace
313249	Knitting and finishing warp fabric
313241	Knitting and finishing weft fabric
313249	Knitting lace
333292	Knitting machinery manufacturing
313111	Knitting spun yarns (e.g., cotton, manmade fiber, silk, wool) made from purchased fiber
313249	Knitting warp fabric
313241	Knitting weft fabric
332211	Knives (e.g., hunting, pocket, table nonprecious, table precious plated) manufacturing
421710	Knives (except disposable plastics) wholesaling
333515	Knives and bits for metalworking lathes, planers, and shapers manufacturing
333212	Knives and bits for woodworking lathes, planers, and shapers manufacturing
422130	Knives, disposable plastics, wholesaling
335211	Knives, household-type electric carving, manufacturing
339112	Knives, surgical, manufacturing
339992	Knobs, organ, manufacturing
321999	Knobs, wood, manufacturing
333292	Knot tying machinery for textiles manufacturing
333513	Knurling machines, metalworking, manufacturing
322130	Kraft liner board manufacturing
322121	Kraft paper stock manufacturing

Code	Description
212325	Kyanite mining and/or beneficiating
334419	LCD (liquid crystal display) screen units manufacturing
334413	LED (light emitting diode) manufacturing
621399	LPNs' (licensed practical nurses) offices (e.g., centers, clinics)
484122	LTL (less-than-truckload) long-distance freight trucking
321213	LVL (laminated veneer lumber) manufacturing
339942	Label making equipment, handheld, manufacturing
333993	Labeling (i.e., packaging) machinery manufacturing
561910	Labeling services
323110	Labels lithographic (offset) printing on a job-order basis
313221	Labels weaving
422310	Labels, textile, wholesaling
561320	Labor (except farm) contractors (i.e., personnel suppliers)
561320	Labor (except farm) pools
115115	Labor contractors, farm
813930	Labor federations
561330	Labor leasing services
926150	Labor management negotiations boards, government
541612	Labor relations consulting services
926110	Labor statistics agencies
813930	Labor unions (except apprenticeship programs)
*****	Laboratories — see specific type
621512	Laboratories, dental X-ray
233310	Laboratories, manufacturing, construction
621511	Laboratories, medical (except radiological, X-ray)
621512	Laboratories, medical radiological or X-ray
334516	Laboratory analytical instruments (except optical) manufacturing
333314	Laboratory analytical optical instruments (e.g., microscopes) manufacturing
311119	Laboratory animal feed manufacturing

Code	Description
112990	Laboratory animal production (e.g., guinea pigs, mice, rats)
315211	Laboratory coats, men's and boys', cut and sew apparel contractors
315225	Laboratory coats, men's and boys', cut and sewn from purchased fabric (except apparel contractors)
315212	Laboratory coats, women's, cut and sew apparel contractors
315239	Laboratory coats, women's, misses', and girls', cut and sewn from purchased fabric (except apparel contractors)
421490	Laboratory equipment (except dental, medical, ophthalmic) wholesaling
421450	Laboratory equipment, dental and medical, wholesaling
327215	Laboratory glassware (e.g., beakers, test tubes, vials) made from purchased glass
327212	Laboratory glassware (e.g., beakers, test tubes, vials) made in glass making plants
811219	Laboratory instrument repair and maintenance services
512199	Laboratory services, motion picture
334515	Laboratory standards testing instruments (e.g., capacitance, electrical resistance, inductance) manufacturing
541380	Laboratory testing (except medical, veterinary) services
621511	Laboratory testing services, medical (except radiological, X-ray)
621512	Laboratory testing services, medical radiological or X-ray
541940	Laboratory testing services, veterinary
233320	Laboratory, commercial and educational, construction
339111	Laboratory-type centrifuges manufacturing
339111	Laboratory-type distilling apparatus manufacturing
339111	Laboratory-type equipment (e.g., balances, centrifuges, furnaces) manufacturing

Code	Description
339111	Laboratory-type evaporation apparatus manufacturing
339111	Laboratory-type freezers manufacturing
339111	Laboratory-type furniture (e.g., benches, cabinets, stools, tables) (except dental) manufacturing
339111	Laboratory-type sample preparation apparatus manufacturing
333292	Lace and net making machinery manufacturing
316110	Lace leather manufacturing
313249	Lace manufacturing
313249	Lace products (except apparel) made in lace mills
314999	Lace, burnt-out, manufacturing
313221	Laces (e.g. shoe), textile, manufacturing
316999	Laces (e.g., shoe), leather, manufacturing
332812	Lacquering metals and metal products for the trade
333994	Lacquering ovens manufacturing
325510	Lacquers manufacturing
422950	Lacquers wholesaling
325199	Lactic acid manufacturing
311514	Lactose manufacturing
332999	Ladder jacks, metal, manufacturing
321999	Ladder jacks, wood, manufacturing
321912	Ladder rounds or rungs, hardwood, manufacturing
421830	Ladders wholesaling
321999	Ladders, extension, wood, manufacturing
326199	Ladders, fiberglass, manufacturing
332323	Ladders, metal chain, manufacturing
332323	Ladders, permanently installed, metal, manufacturing
332999	Ladders, portable metal, manufacturing
332313	Ladle bails, fabricated metal plate work, manufacturing
332313	Ladles, fabricated metal plate work, manufacturing
312120	Lager brewing

Code	Description
483211	Lake freight transportation (except on Great Lakes system)
483113	Lake freight transportation, Great Lakes
483212	Lake passenger transportation (except on Great Lakes system)
483114	Lake passenger transportation, Great Lakes
325132	Lakes (i.e., organic pigments) manufacturing
311611	Lamb carcasses, half carcasses, primal and sub-primal cuts, produced in slaughtering plants
112410	Lamb feedlots (except stockyards for transportation)
311612	Lamb, primal and sub-primal cuts, made from purchased carcasses
332999	Laminated aluminum foil (except bags, liners) manufacturing
327215	Laminated glass made from purchased glass
327211	Laminated glass made in glass making plants
326130	Laminated plastics plate, rod, and sheet, manufacturing
321213	Laminated structural wood members (except trusses) manufacturing
321213	Laminated veneer lumber (LVL) manufacturing
322225	Laminating foil for flexible packaging applications
332813	Laminating metals and metal formed products without fabricating
322222	Laminating purchased foil sheets for nonpackaging applications
322226	Laminating purchased paperboard
322222	Laminating purchased papers for nonpackaging applications
322221	Laminating purchased papers for packaging applications
313320	Laminating purchased textiles
335311	Lamp ballasts manufacturing
327112	Lamp bases, pottery, manufacturing
325182	Lamp black manufacturing
335110	Lamp bulb parts (except glass blanks), electric, manufacturing

Code	Description
335110	Lamp bulbs and tubes, electric (i.e., fluorescent, incandescent filament, vapor), manufacturing
335110	Lamp bulbs and tubes, health, infrared and ultraviolet radiation, manufacturing
332618	Lamp frames, wire, made from purchased wire
335931	Lamp holders manufacturing
332999	Lamp shade frames, metal, manufacturing
335121	Lamp shades (except glass, plastics), residential, manufacturing
327215	Lamp shades made from purchased glass
327212	Lamp shades made in glass making plants
326199	Lamp shades, plastics, manufacturing
442299	Lamp shops, electric
335931	Lamp sockets and receptacles (i.e., electric wiring devices) manufacturing
421220	Lamps (i.e., lighting fixtures) wholesaling
335122	Lamps (i.e., lighting fixtures), commercial, industrial, and institutional, manufacturing
335121	Lamps (i.e., lighting fixtures), residential, electric, manufacturing
334517	Lamps, X-ray, manufacturing
335129	Lamps, insect, electric fixture, manufacturing
234990	Land clearing
234990	Land drainage construction contractors
234990	Land leveling, irrigation, construction contractors
924120	Land management program administration
421820	Land preparation machinery, agricultural, wholesaling
333120	Land preparation machinery, construction, manufacturing
421810	Land preparation machinery, construction, wholesaling
234990	Land reclamation

Code	Description
925120	Land redevelopment agencies, government
531190	Land rental or leasing
233110	Land subdividers and developers (except cemeteries)
541370	Land surveying services
335312	Land transportation motors and generators manufacturing
541320	Land use design services
541320	Land use planning services
562212	Landfills
332312	Landing mats, aircraft, metal, manufacturing
541320	Landscape architects' offices
541320	Landscape architects' private practices
541320	Landscape architectural services
561730	Landscape care and maintenance services
541320	Landscape consulting services
561730	Landscape contractors (except construction)
541320	Landscape design services
561730	Landscape installation services
541320	Landscape planning services
561730	Landscaping services (except planning)
541930	Language interpretation services
541720	Language research and development services
611630	Language schools
541930	Language services (e.g., interpretation, sign, translation)
541930	Language translation services
335129	Lanterns (e.g., carbide, electric, gas, gasoline, kerosene) manufacturing
339913	Lapidary work manufacturing
334111	Laptop computers manufacturing
311613	Lard made from purchased fat
311611	Lard produced in slaughtering plants
422470	Lard wholesaling
333512	Laser boring, drilling, and cutting machines, metalworking, manufacturing
334413	Laser diodes manufacturing

Code	Description
532230	Laser disc, video, rental
334612	Laser disks, prerecorded video, mass reproducing
334510	Laser equipment, electromedical, manufacturing
334510	Laser systems and equipment, medical, manufacturing
333992	Laser welding equipment manufacturing
316999	Lashes (i.e., whips) manufacturing
321999	Last sole patterns, all materials, manufacturing
212325	Laterite mining and/or beneficiating
326299	Latex foam rubber manufacturing
325510	Latex paint (i.e., water based) manufacturing
325212	Latex rubber, synthetic, manufacturing
332312	Lath, expanded metal, manufacturing
321219	Lath, fiber, manufacturing
327420	Lath, gypsum, manufacturing
321912	Lath, wood, manufacturing
333512	Lathes, metalworking, manufacturing
333210	Lathes, woodworking-type, manufacturing
235420	Lathing construction contractors
321912	Lathmills, wood
316110	Latigo leather manufacturing
812332	Laundered mat and rug supply services
812332	Launderers, industrial
812310	Launderettes
812320	Laundries (except coin-operated, linen supply, uniform supply)
812310	Laundries, coin-operated or similar self-service
812331	Laundries, linen and uniform supply
812310	Laundromats
812320	Laundry and drycleaning agents
314911	Laundry bags made from purchased woven or knitted materials
325612	Laundry bluing manufacturing
812320	Laundry drop-off and pick-up sites

Code	Description
335224	Laundry equipment (e.g., dryers, washers), household-type, manufacturing
333312	Laundry extractors manufacturing
332439	Laundry hampers, light gauge metal, manufacturing
337125	Laundry hampers, rattan, reed, wicker or willow, manufacturing
812310	Laundry machine routes (i.e., concession operators), coin-operated or similar self-service
333312	Laundry machinery and equipment (except household-type) manufacturing
421620	Laundry machinery and equipment, household-type (e.g., dryers, washers), wholesaling
421850	Laundry machinery, equipment, and supplies, commercial, wholesaling
314999	Laundry nets made from purchased materials
333312	Laundry pressing machines (except household-type) manufacturing
812320	Laundry services (except coin-operated, linen supply, uniform supply)
812310	Laundry services, coin-operated or similar self-service
812332	Laundry services, industrial
812331	Laundry services, linen supply
325611	Laundry soap, chips, and powder manufacturing
422690	Laundry soap, chips, and powder, wholesaling
332998	Laundry tubs, metal, manufacturing
326191	Laundry tubs, plastics, manufacturing
325199	Lauric acid esters and amines manufacturing
332998	Lavatories, metal, manufacturing
327111	Lavatories, vitreous china, manufacturing
922190	Law enforcement statistics centers, government
541110	Law firms
541110	Law offices
541110	Law practices
611310	Law schools

Code	Description
333112	Lawn and garden equipment manufacturing
811411	Lawn and garden equipment repair and maintenance services without retailing new lawn and garden equipment
713990	Lawn bowling clubs
561730	Lawn care services (e.g., fertilizing, mowing, seeding, spraying)
422910	Lawn care supplies (e.g., chemicals, fertilizers, pesticides) wholesaling
332212	Lawn edgers, nonpowered, manufacturing
333112	Lawn edgers, powered, manufacturing
561730	Lawn fertilizing services
337125	Lawn furniture (except concrete, metal, stone, wood) manufacturing
337124	Lawn furniture, metal, manufacturing
337122	Lawn furniture, wood, manufacturing
332919	Lawn hose nozzles and lawn sprinklers manufacturing
421820	Lawn maintenance machinery and equipment wholesaling
561730	Lawn maintenance services
811411	Lawn mower repair and maintenance shops without retailing new lawn mowers
421820	Lawn mowers wholesaling
561730	Lawn mowing services
444210	Lawn power equipment stores
561730	Lawn seeding services
561730	Lawn spraying services
444220	Lawn supply stores
532490	Lawnmower rental or leasing
333112	Lawnmowers (except agricultural-type), powered, manufacturing
333111	Lawnmowers, agricultural-type, powered, manufacturing
332212	Lawnmowers, nonpowered, manufacturing
541110	Lawyers' offices
541110	Lawyers' private practices
325412	Laxative preparations manufacturing

Code	Description
112310	Layer-type chicken production
212291	Leaching of uranium, radium, or vanadium ores
335911	Lead acid storage batteries manufacturing
331491	Lead and lead alloy bar, pipe, plate, rod, sheet, strip, and tubing made from purchased metals or scrap
325131	Lead based pigments manufacturing
235990	Lead burning construction contractors
331528	Lead castings (except die-castings), unfinished, manufacturing
331522	Lead die-castings, unfinished, manufacturing
332999	Lead foil not made in rolling mills
212231	Lead ore mine site development for own account
212231	Lead ore mining and/or beneficiating
325188	Lead oxides (except pigments) manufacturing
562910	Lead paint abatement services
562910	Lead paint removal contractors
325131	Lead pigments manufacturing
331492	Lead recovering from scrap and/or alloying purchased metals
331491	Lead rolling, drawing, or extruding purchased metals or scrap
325188	Lead silicate manufacturing
331419	Lead smelting and refining, primary
327992	Lead, black (i.e., natural graphite), ground, refined, or blended, manufacturing
335110	Lead-in wires, electric lamp, made from purchased wire
212231	Lead-zinc ore mining and/or beneficiating
333112	Leaf blowers manufacturing
332212	Leaf skimmers and rakes, nonpowered swimming pool, manufacturing
332611	Leaf springs manufacturing
422590	Leaf tobacco wholesaling
332999	Leaf, metal, manufacturing
334519	Leak detectors, water, manufacturing
813920	Learned societies

Code	Description
611691	Learning centers offering remedial courses
541720	Learning disabilities research and development services
211111	Lease condensate production
213112	Lease tank, erecting, cleaning, and repairing on a contract basis
316999	Leashes, dog, manufacturing
*****	Leasing — see type of property or article being leased
522220	Leasing in combination with sales financing
315292	Leather apparel (e.g., capes, coats, hats, jackets) (except apparel contractors) manufacturing
315211	Leather apparel (e.g., capes, coats, hats, jackets), men's and boys', cut and sew apparel contractors
315212	Leather apparel (e.g., capes, coats, hats, jackets), women's, girls', and infants', cut and sew apparel contractors
316999	Leather belting manufacturing
315292	Leather clothing (except apparel contractors) manufacturing
315212	Leather clothing manufacturing, women's, girls', and infants', cut and sew apparel contractors
315211	Leather clothing, men's and boys', cut and sew apparel contractors
448190	Leather coat stores
316110	Leather coloring, cutting, embossing, and japanning
316110	Leather converters
422990	Leather cut stock (except boot, shoe) wholesaling
316999	Leather cut stock for shoe and boot manufacturing
422340	Leather cut stock for shoe and boot wholesaling
316219	Leather footwear (except house slippers, men's, women's) manufacturing
316213	Leather footwear, men's (except athletic, slippers), manufacturing
316212	Leather footwear, slippers, manufacturing
316214	Leather footwear, women's (except athletic, slippers), manufacturing

Code	Description
812320	Leather garment cleaning services
315211	Leather gloves or mittens (except athletic), men's and boys', cut and sew apparel contractors
315212	Leather gloves or mittens (except athletic), women's, girls', and infants', cut and sew apparel contractors
315992	Leather gloves or mittens (except athletic, cut and sewn apparel contractors) manufacturing
339920	Leather gloves, athletic, manufacturing
422990	Leather goods (except belting, footwear, handbags, gloves, luggage) wholesaling
811430	Leather goods repair shops without retailing new leather goods
448320	Leather goods stores
316993	Leather goods, small personal (e.g., coin purses, eyeglass cases, key cases), manufacturing
316992	Leather handbags and purses manufacturing
316212	Leather house slippers manufacturing
316991	Leather luggage manufacturing
316110	Leather tanning, currying, and finishing
316219	Leather upper athletic footwear manufacturing
316999	Leather welting manufacturing
333298	Leather working machinery manufacturing
313320	Leather, artificial, made from purchased fabric
322226	Leatherboard (i.e., paperboard based) made from purchased paperboard
322130	Leatherboard (i.e., paperboard based) made in paperboard mills
311225	Lecithin made from purchased oils
311223	Lecithin, cottonseed, made in crushing mills
311222	Lecithin, soybean, made in crushing mills
111219	Leek farming, field, bedding plant and seed production
541110	Legal aid services

Code	Description
922130	Legal counsel offices, government
315119	Leggings knitting or knitting and finishing
315291	Leggings, infants', cut and sewn from purchased fabric (except apparel contractors)
316999	Leggings, welder's, leather, manufacturing
315212	Leggings, women's, girls', and infants', cut and sew apparel contractors
315239	Leggings, women's, misses' and girls', cut and sewn from purchased fabric (except apparel contractors)
315239	Leggings, women's, misses', and girls', cut and sewn from purchased fabric (except apparel contractors)
921140	Legislative and executive office combinations
921120	Legislative assemblies
921120	Legislative bodies (e.g., federal, local, and state)
921120	Legislative commissions
111320	Lemon groves
325998	Lemon oil manufacturing
514120	Lending libraries
421460	Lens blanks, ophthalmic, wholesaling
327215	Lens blanks, optical and ophthalmic, made from purchased glass
327212	Lens blanks, optical and ophthalmic, made in glass making plants
326199	Lens blanks, plastics ophthalmic or optical, manufacturing
333314	Lens coating (except ophthalmic)
339115	Lens coating, ophthalmic
333314	Lens grinding (except ophthalmic)
339115	Lens grinding, ophthalmic (except in retail stores)
446130	Lens grinding, ophthalmic, in retail stores
333315	Lens hoods, camera, manufacturing
333314	Lens mounting (except ophthalmic)
339115	Lens mounts, ophthalmic, manufacturing
333314	Lens polishing (except ophthalmic)

Code	Description
339115	Lens polishing, ophthalmic
333314	Lenses (except ophthalmic) manufacturing
339115	Lenses, ophthalmic, manufacturing
111130	Lentil farming, dry, field and seed production
315191	Leotards made in apparel knitting mills
315212	Leotards, women's, girls', and infants', cut and sew apparel contractors
315239	Leotards, women's, misses', and girls', cut and sewn from purchased fabric (except apparel contractors)
212393	Lepidolite mining and/or beneficiating
622310	Leprosy hospitals
*****	Lessors — see specific type of asset or property being rented or leased
333313	Letter folding, stuffing, and sealing machinery manufacturing
333515	Letter pins (e.g., gauging, measuring) manufacturing
561410	Letter writing services
325910	Letterpress inks manufacturing
323122	Letterpress plate preparation services
333293	Letterpress printing presses manufacturing
339950	Letters for signs manufacturing
322231	Letters, die-cut, made from purchased cardboard
111219	Lettuce farming, field, bedding plant and seed production
234990	Levee construction
334513	Level and bulk measuring instruments, industrial process-type, manufacturing
334519	Level gauges, radiation-type, manufacturing
334519	Levels and tapes, surveying, manufacturing
332212	Levels, carpenter's, manufacturing
524126	Liability insurance carriers, direct
514120	Libraries (except motion picture stock footage, motion picture commercial distribution)

Code	Description
512199	Libraries, motion picture stock footage film
512199	Libraries, videotape, stock footage
233320	Library construction
561990	License issuing services (except government), motor vehicle
621399	Licensed practical nurses' (LPNs) offices (e.g., centers, clinics)
926130	Licensing and inspecting of utilities
926150	Licensing and permit issuance for business operations, government
926150	Licensing and permit issuance for professional occupations, government
926120	Licensing of transportation equipment, facilities, and services
311340	Licorice candy manufacturing
332431	Lids and ends, can, metal, manufacturing
332115	Lids, jar, metal, stamping
561611	Lie detection services
334519	Lie detectors manufacturing
611699	Life guard training
524210	Life insurance agencies
524113	Life insurance carriers, direct
339113	Life preservers manufacturing
326199	Life rafts, inflatable plastics, manufacturing
326299	Life rafts, inflatable rubberized fabric, manufacturing
524130	Life reinsurance carriers
541710	Life sciences research and development laboratories or services
561320	Lifeguard supply services
421830	Lift trucks, industrial, wholesaling
316999	Lifts, heel, leather, manufacturing
333298	Light bulb and tube (i.e., electric lamp) machinery manufacturing
335110	Light bulbs manufacturing
421610	Light bulbs wholesaling
335110	Light bulbs, sealed beam automotive, manufacturing
334413	Light emitting diodes (LED) manufacturing
333315	Light meters, photographic, manufacturing

Code	Description
336510	Light rail cars and equipment manufacturing
485119	Light rail systems (except mixed mode), commuter
334511	Light reconnaissance and surveillance systems and equipment manufacturing
334512	Light responsive appliance controls manufacturing
441110	Light utility truck dealers, new only or new and used
441120	Light utility truck dealers, used only
336112	Light utility trucks assembling on chassis of own manufacture
325998	Lighter fluids (e.g., charcoal, cigarette) manufacturing
483211	Lighterage (i.e., freight transportation except vessel supply services)
339999	Lighters, cigar and cigarette (except motor vehicle, precious metal), manufacturing
339911	Lighters, cigar and cigarette, clad with precious metal, manufacturing
422990	Lighters, cigar and cigarette, wholesaling
488310	Lighthouse operation
335991	Lighting carbons manufacturing
421990	Lighting equipment, gas, wholesaling
444190	Lighting fixture stores
335129	Lighting fixtures, airport (e.g., approach, ramp, runway, taxi), manufacturing
335122	Lighting fixtures, commercial electric, manufacturing
421610	Lighting fixtures, electric, wholesaling
335122	Lighting fixtures, industrial electric, manufacturing
335122	Lighting fixtures, institutional electric, manufacturing
335129	Lighting fixtures, nonelectric (e.g., propane, kerosene, carbide), manufacturing
335121	Lighting fixtures, residential electric, manufacturing

Code	Description
561790	Lighting maintenance services (e.g., bulb and fuse replacement and cleaning)
235310	Lighting system construction contractors
711510	Lighting technicians, theatrical, independent
335311	Lighting transformers manufacturing
335311	Lighting transformers, street and airport, manufacturing
335931	Lightning arrestors and coils manufacturing
235990	Lightning conductor construction contractors
335931	Lightning protection equipment manufacturing
325211	Lignin plastics manufacturing
213113	Lignite mining services on a contract basis
212111	Lignite surface mining and/or beneficiating
111130	Lima bean farming, dry, field and seed production
339113	Limbs, artificial, manufacturing
421320	Lime (except agricultural) wholesaling
111320	Lime groves
325998	Lime oil manufacturing
327410	Lime production
212312	Lime rock, ground, mining and/or beneficiating
422910	Lime, agricultural, wholesaling
325320	Lime-sulfur fungicides manufacturing
212312	Limestone (except bituminous) crushed and broken stone mining and/or beneficiating
212312	Limestone beneficiating plants (e.g., grinding or pulverizing)
212311	Limestone mining or quarrying
212319	Limestone, bituminous, mining and/or beneficiating
334512	Limit controls (e.g., air-conditioning, appliance, heating) manufacturing
511199	Limited editions art print publishers
452990	Limited price variety stores

Code	Description
212210	Limonite mining and/or beneficiating
532111	Limousine rental without driver
485320	Limousine services (except shuttle services)
485320	Limousines for hire with driver (except taxis)
325320	Lindane pesticides manufacturing
334512	Line or limit control for electric heat manufacturing
561730	Line slash (i.e., rights of way) maintenance services
335311	Line voltage regulators (i.e., electric transformers) manufacturing
335999	Linear accelerators manufacturing
332991	Linear ball bearings manufacturing
334514	Linear counters manufacturing
325222	Linear esters fibers and filaments manufacturing
332991	Linear roller bearings manufacturing
442299	Linen stores
812331	Linen supply services
421220	Linens (e.g., bath, bed, table) wholesaling
314129	Linens made from purchased materials
327123	Liner brick and plates, vitrified clay, manufacturing
332313	Liners, industrial, fabricated metal plate work, manufacturing
114111	Lingcod fishing
448190	Lingerie stores
422330	Lingerie wholesaling
315212	Lingerie, women's, cut and sew apparel contractors
315231	Lingerie, women's, misses', and girls', cut and sewn from purchased fabric (except apparel contractors)
316110	Lining leather manufacturing
316999	Linings, boot and shoe, leather, manufacturing
314999	Linings, casket, manufacturing
315211	Linings, hat, men's, cut and sew apparel contractors
315999	Linings, hat, men's, cut and sewn from purchased fabric (except apparel contractors)

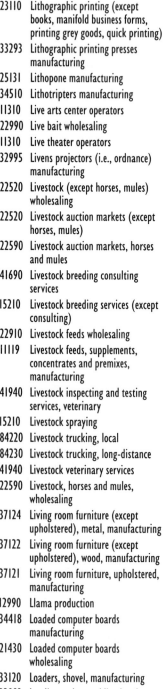

Code	Description
314999	Linings, luggage, manufacturing
332999	Linings, metal safe and vault, manufacturing
332994	Links, ammunition (i.e., 30 mm. or less, 1.18 inch or less), manufacturing
332995	Links, ammunition (i.e., more than 30 mm., more than 1.18 inch), manufacturing
325199	Linoleic acid esters and amines manufacturing
235520	Linoleum construction contractors
326192	Linoleum floor coverings manufacturing
333293	Linotype machines manufacturing
311225	Linseed oil made from purchased oils
311223	Linseed oil, cake and meal, made in crushing mills
327390	Lintels, concrete, manufacturing
325412	Lip balms manufacturing
325620	Lipsticks manufacturing
422690	Liquefied gases (except LP) wholesaling
422710	Liquefied petroleum gas (LPG) bulk stations and terminals
332420	Liquefied petroleum gas (LPG) cylinders manufacturing
454312	Liquefied petroleum gas (LPG) dealers, direct selling
221210	Liquefied petroleum gas (LPG) distribution through mains
324110	Liquefied petroleum gas (LPG) made in refineries
422720	Liquefied petroleum gas (LPG) wholesaling (except bulk stations, terminals)
211112	Liquefied petroleum gases (LPG), natural
325120	Liquid air manufacturing
334513	Liquid analysis instruments, industrial process-type, manufacturing
311313	Liquid beet syrup manufacturing
334516	Liquid chromatographic instruments, laboratory-type, manufacturing

Code	Description
334513	Liquid concentration instruments, industrial process-type, manufacturing
334514	Liquid flow meters manufacturing
211112	Liquid hydrocarbons recovered from oil and gas field gases
334512	Liquid level controls, residential and commercial heating-type, manufacturing
334513	Liquid level instruments, industrial process-type, manufacturing
332420	Liquid oxygen tanks manufacturing
311313	Liquid sugar made from beet sugar
311312	Liquid sugar made from purchased raw cane sugar
311311	Liquid sugar made in sugarcane mill
211112	Liquids, natural gas (e.g., ethane, isobutane, natural gasoline, propane) recovered from oil and gas field gases
445310	Liquor stores, package
311320	Liquor, chocolate, made from cacao beans
311330	Liquor, chocolate, made from purchased chocolate
422820	Liquors wholesaling
312130	Liquors, brandy, distilling and blending
422820	Liquors, distilled, wholesaling
312140	Liquors, distilling and blending (except brandy)
339942	List finders and roledex address files manufacturing
531390	Listing services, real estate
711410	Literary agents
325131	Litharge manufacturing
335912	Lithium batteries, primary, manufacturing
325188	Lithium compounds, not specified elsewhere by process, manufacturing
212393	Lithium mineral mining and/or beneficiating
325910	Lithographic inks manufacturing
323122	Lithographic plate preparation services

Code	Description
323110	Lithographic printing (except books, manifold business forms, printing grey goods, quick printing)
333293	Lithographic printing presses manufacturing
325131	Lithopone manufacturing
334510	Lithotripters manufacturing
711310	Live arts center operators
422990	Live bait wholesaling
711310	Live theater operators
332995	Livens projectors (i.e., ordnance) manufacturing
422520	Livestock (except horses, mules) wholesaling
422520	Livestock auction markets (except horses, mules)
422590	Livestock auction markets, horses and mules
541690	Livestock breeding consulting services
115210	Livestock breeding services (except consulting)
422910	Livestock feeds wholesaling
311119	Livestock feeds, supplements, concentrates and premixes, manufacturing
541940	Livestock inspecting and testing services, veterinary
115210	Livestock spraying
484220	Livestock trucking, local
484230	Livestock trucking, long-distance
541940	Livestock veterinary services
422590	Livestock, horses and mules, wholesaling
337124	Living room furniture (except upholstered), metal, manufacturing
337122	Living room furniture (except upholstered), wood, manufacturing
337121	Living room furniture, upholstered, manufacturing
112990	Llama production
334418	Loaded computer boards manufacturing
421430	Loaded computer boards wholesaling
333120	Loaders, shovel, manufacturing
332993	Loading and assembling bombs

Code	Description
488490	Loading and unloading at truck terminals
488320	Loading and unloading services at ports and harbors
488210	Loading and unloading services at rail terminals
333131	Loading machines, underground mining, manufacturing
334418	Loading printed circuit boards
234990	Loading station construction, mine, general construction contractor
522310	Loan brokerages
522310	Loan brokers' or agents' offices (i.e., independent)
522291	Loan companies (i.e., consumer, personal, small, student)
522292	Loan correspondents (i.e., lending funds with real estate as collaterial)
522390	Loan servicing
541820	Lobbying services
541820	Lobbyists' offices
114112	Lobster fishing
334210	Local area network (LAN) communications equipment (e.g., bridges, gateways, routers) manufacturing
541512	Local area network (LAN) computer systems integration design services
611420	Local area network (LAN) management training
485113	Local bus services (except mixed mode)
492210	Local letter and parcel delivery services (except as part of intercity carrier network, U.S. Postal Service)
492110	Local letter and parcel delivery services as part of intercity courier network
485112	Local passenger rail systems (except mixed mode)
813940	Local political organizations
513310	Local telephone carriers (except wireless)
485111	Local transit systems, mixed mode (e.g., bus, commuter rail, subway combinations)
332722	Lock washers, metal, manufacturing

Code	Description
454390	Locker meat provisioners, direct selling
337215	Lockers (except refrigerated) manufacturing
421440	Lockers (except refrigerated) wholesaling
812990	Lockers, coin operated, rental
333415	Lockers, refrigerated, manufacturing
421740	Lockers, refrigerated, wholesaling
332510	Locks (except coin-operated, time locks) manufacturing
234990	Locks and waterway construction
333311	Locks, coin-operated, manufacturing
421710	Locks, security, wholesaling
421850	Locksmith equipment and supplies wholesaling
561622	Locksmith services
561622	Locksmith services with or without sales of locking devices, safes, and security vaults
561622	Locksmith shops
488210	Locomotive and rail car repair (except factory conversion, factory overhaul, factory rebuilding)
336321	Locomotive and railroad car light fixtures manufacturing
333923	Locomotive cranes manufacturing
333618	Locomotive diesel engines manufacturing
336510	Locomotives manufacturing
336510	Locomotives rebuilding
421860	Locomotives wholesaling
212221	Lode gold mining and/or beneficiating
321992	Log cabins, prefabricated wood, manufacturing
333120	Log debarking machinery, portable, manufacturing
333291	Log debarking machinery, stationary, manufacturing
113310	Log harvesting
484220	Log hauling, local
484230	Log hauling, long-distance
333120	Log splitters, portable, manufacturing

Code	Description
333291	Log splitters, stationary, manufacturing
111334	Loganberry farming
113310	Logging
541330	Logging engineering services
532412	Logging equipment rental or leasing without operator
421810	Logging equipment wholesaling
482112	Logging railroads
336212	Logging trailers manufacturing
213112	Logging wells on a contract basis
334515	Logic circuit testers manufacturing
541614	Logistics management consulting services
333414	Logs, gas fireplace, manufacturing
325191	Logwood extract manufacturing
513310	Long-distance telephone carriers (except wireless)
513330	Long-distance telephone resellers (except satellite)
513340	Long-distance telephone satellite communication carriers
488320	Longshoremen services
333292	Loom bobbins manufacturing
333292	Loom reeds manufacturing
333292	Looms for textiles manufacturing
333292	Loopers for textiles manufacturing
323118	Looseleaf binders and devices manufacturing
422120	Looseleaf binders wholesaling
322233	Looseleaf fillers and paper made from purchased paper
322121	Looseleaf fillers and paper made in paper mills
325620	Lotions (e.g., body, face, hand) manufacturing
713290	Lottery control boards (i.e., operating lotteries)
921130	Lottery control boards, nonoperating
713290	Lottery corporations
713290	Lottery ticket sales agents (except retail stores)
713290	Lottery ticket vendors (except retail stores)
334310	Loudspeakers manufacturing
722410	Lounges, cocktail

Code	Description
315192	Lounging robes and dressing gowns made in apparel knitting mills
315291	Lounging robes and dressing gowns, infants', cut and sewn from purchased fabric (except apparel contractors)
315211	Lounging robes and dressing gowns, men's and boys', cut and sew apparel contractors
315221	Lounging robes and dressing gowns, men's and boys', cut and sewn from purchased fabric (except apparel contractors)
315212	Lounging robes and dressing gowns, women's, girls', and infants', cut and sew apparel contractors
315231	Lounging robes and dressing gowns, women's, misses', and girls', cut and sewn from purchased fabric (except apparel contractors)
333314	Loupes (e.g., jewelers) manufacturing
321911	Louver windows and doors, made from purchased glass with wood frame
332321	Louver windows, metal, manufacturing
332322	Louvers, sheet metal, manufacturing
335121	Low voltage lighting equipment, residential, electric, manufacturing
311340	Lozenges, nonmedicated, candy, manufacturing
422710	Lubricating oils and greases bulk stations and terminals
324110	Lubricating oils and greases made in petroleum refineries
422720	Lubricating oils and greases wholesaling (except bulk stations, terminals)
324191	Lubricating oils and greases, petroleum, made from refined petroleum
325998	Lubricating oils and greases, synthetic, manufacturing
336510	Lubrication systems, locomotive (except pumps), manufacturing
332510	Luggage hardware, metal, manufacturing

Code	Description
314999	Luggage linings manufacturing
336399	Luggage racks, car top, automotive, truck, and bus, manufacturing
811430	Luggage repair shops without retailing new luggage
448320	Luggage stores
421990	Luggage wholesaling
316991	Luggage, all materials, manufacturing
335931	Lugs and connectors, electrical, manufacturing
421610	Lugs and connectors, electrical, wholesaling
421310	Lumber (e.g., dressed, finished, rough) wholesaling
321113	Lumber (i.e., rough, dressed) made from logs or bolts
561990	Lumber grading services
444190	Lumber retailing yards
321113	Lumber stacking or sticking made from logs or bolts
321912	Lumber stacking or sticking, resawing purchased lumber
493190	Lumber storage terminals
321113	Lumber, hardwood dimension, made from logs or bolts
321912	Lumber, hardwood dimension, resawing purchased lumber
321999	Lumber, kiln drying
321213	Lumber, parallel strand, manufacturing
321113	Lumber, softwood dimension, made from logs or bolts
321912	Lumber, softwood dimension, resawing purchased lumber
335122	Luminous panel ceilings, electric, manufacturing
335311	Luminous tube transformers manufacturing
332439	Lunch boxes, light gauge metal, manufacturing
722330	Lunch wagons
311612	Luncheon meat (except poultry) made from purchased carcasses
311611	Luncheon meat (except poultry) produced in slaughtering plants
311615	Luncheon meat, poultry, manufacturing

Code	Description
532111	Luxury automobile rental
485320	Luxury automobiles for hire with driver (except taxis)
325612	Lye, household-type, manufacturing
321219	MDF (medium density fiberboard) manufacturing
621112	MDs' (medical doctors), mental health, offices (e.g., centers, clinics)
621111	MDs' (medical doctors, except mental health) offices (e.g., centers, clinics)
334413	MOS (metal oxide silicon) devices manufacturing
562920	MRF (materials recovery facilities)
621512	MRI (magnetic resonance imaging) centers
334510	MRI (magnetic resonance imaging) medical diagnostic equipment manufacturing
111335	Macadamia farming
422490	Macaroni wholesaling
311823	Macaroni, dry, manufacturing
311991	Macaroni, fresh, manufacturing
332212	Machetes manufacturing
332999	Machine bases, metal, manufacturing
332322	Machine guards, sheet metal, manufacturing
332994	Machine gun belts (i.e., 30 mm. or less, 1.18 inch or less) manufacturing
332995	Machine gun belts (i.e., more than 30 mm., more than 1.18 inch) manufacturing
332994	Machine guns (i.e., 30 mm. or less, 1.18 inch or less) manufacturing
332995	Machine guns (i.e., more than 30 mm., more than 1.18 inch) manufacturing
332722	Machine keys manufacturing
332212	Machine knives (except metal cutting) manufacturing
333515	Machine knives, metal cutting, manufacturing
235950	Machine rigging construction contractors
332710	Machine shops

Code	Description
333515	Machine tool attachments and accessories manufacturing
335311	Machine tool transformers manufacturing
421830	Machine tools and accessories wholesaling
811310	Machine tools repair and maintenance services
333512	Machine tools, metal cutting, manufacturing
333513	Machine tools, metal forming, manufacturing
522220	Machinery finance leasing
421420	Machines, office, wholesaling
332212	Machinist's precision measuring tools (except optical) manufacturing
421830	Machinists' precision measuring tools wholesaling
334511	Machmeters manufacturing
114111	Mackerel fishing
315291	Mackinaws, infants', cut and sewn from purchased fabric (except apparel contractors)
315211	Mackinaws, men's and boys', cut and sew apparel contractors
315228	Mackinaws, men's and boys', cut and sewn from purchased fabric (except apparel contractors)
315212	Mackinaws, women's, girls', and infants', cut and sew apparel contractors
315239	Mackinaws, women's, misses', and girls', cut and sewn from purchased fabric (except apparel contractors)
541840	Magazine advertising representatives (i.e., independent of media owners)
511120	Magazine publishers
511120	Magazine publishers and printing combined
511120	Magazine publishers, publishing only
511120	Magazine publishing (i.e., establishments known as publishers)
337122	Magazine racks, wood, manufacturing
451212	Magazine stands (i.e., permanent)

Code	Description
323112	Magazines and periodicals flexographic printing without publishing
323111	Magazines and periodicals gravure printing without publishing
323110	Magazines and periodicals lithographic (offset) printing without publishing
323119	Magazines and periodicals printing (except flexographic, gravure, lithographic, screen) without publishing
323113	Magazines and periodicals screen printing without publishing
422920	Magazines wholesaling
711190	Magic shows
451120	Magic supply stores
711510	Magicians, independent
327125	Magnesia refractory cement manufacturing
325411	Magnesia, medicinal, uncompounded, manufacturing
212325	Magnesite mining and/or beneficiating
327992	Magnesite, crude (e.g., calcined, dead-burned, ground), manufacturing
331491	Magnesium and magnesium alloy bar, rod, shape, sheet, strip, and tubing made from purchased metals or scrap
325188	Magnesium carbonate manufacturing
331528	Magnesium castings (except die-castings), unfinished, manufacturing
325188	Magnesium chloride manufacturing
325188	Magnesium compounds, not specified elsewhere by process, manufacturing
331522	Magnesium die-castings, unfinished, manufacturing
331491	Magnesium foil made by rolling purchased metals or scrap
332999	Magnesium foil not made in rolling mills
331492	Magnesium recovering from scrap and/or alloying purchased metals
331419	Magnesium refining, primary

Code	Description
331491	Magnesium rolling, drawing, or extruding purchased metals or scrap
331422	Magnet wire, insulated, made from purchased copper in wire drawing plants
331319	Magnet wire, insulated, made in aluminum wire drawing plants
331491	Magnet wire, nonferrous metals (except aluminum, copper), made from purchased nonferrous metals (except aluminum, copper) in wire drawing plants
334613	Magnetic and optical media, blank, manufacturing
334514	Magnetic counters manufacturing
334513	Magnetic flow meters, industrial process-type, manufacturing
333513	Magnetic forming machines, metalworking, manufacturing
541360	Magnetic geophysical surveying services
334119	Magnetic ink recognition devices, computer peripheral equipment, manufacturing
334613	Magnetic recording media for tapes, cassettes, and disks, manufacturing
621512	Magnetic resonance imaging (MRI) centers
334510	Magnetic resonance imaging (MRI) medical diagnostic equipment manufacturing
334516	Magnetic resonance imaging (MRI) type apparatus (except medical diagnostic) manufacturing
334613	Magnetic tapes, cassettes and disks, blank, manufacturing
421690	Magnetic tapes, cassettes, and disks, blank, wholesaling
334112	Magnetic/optical combination storage units for computers manufacturing
334519	Magnetometers manufacturing
334411	Magnetron tubes manufacturing
327113	Magnets, permanent, ceramic or ferrite, manufacturing
332999	Magnets, permanent, metallic, manufacturing

Code	Description
339115	Magnifiers, corrective vision-type, manufacturing
333314	Magnifying glasses (except corrective vision-type) manufacturing
333314	Magnifying instruments, optical, manufacturing
114111	Mahimahi fishing
561310	Maid registries
561720	Maid services (i.e., cleaning services)
337215	Mail carrier cases and tables, wood, manufacturing
332322	Mail chutes, sheet metal, manufacturing
333313	Mail handling machinery, post office-type, manufacturing
561499	Mail presorting services
454110	Mail-order houses
561431	Mailbox rental centers, private
561431	Mailbox rental services combined with one or more other office support services, private
332439	Mailboxes, light gauge metal, manufacturing
322214	Mailing cases and tubes, paper fiber (i.e., all-fiber, nonfiber ends of any material), made from purchased paperboard
532420	Mailing equipment rental or leasing
511140	Mailing list compiling services
511140	Mailing list publishers
421420	Mailing machines wholesaling
334111	Mainframe computers manufacturing
488190	Maintenance and repair services, aircraft (except factory conversion, factory overhaul, factory rebuilding)
561730	Maintenance of plants and shrubs in buildings
488210	Maintenance of rights-of-way and structures, railway
488119	Maintenance services, runway
488310	Maintenance services, waterfront terminal (except dredging)
711211	Major league baseball clubs

Code	Description
812112	Make-up (except permanent) salons
325620	Make-up (i.e., cosmetics) manufacturing
812199	Make-up salons, permanent
523110	Making markets for securities
337125	Malacca furniture (except upholstered), household-type, manufacturing
325320	Malathion insecticides manufacturing
325192	Maleic anhydride manufacturing
531120	Mall property operation (i.e., not operating contained businesses) rental or leasing
331511	Malleable iron foundries
332212	Mallets (e.g., rubber, wood) manufacturing
321999	Mallets, wood, manufacturing
325199	Malonic dinitrile manufacturing
524126	Malpractice insurance carriers, direct
311942	Malt extract and syrups manufacturing
422490	Malt extract wholesaling
311213	Malt flour manufacturing
312120	Malt liquor brewing
311213	Malt manufacturing
333294	Malt milling machinery manufacturing
311213	Malt sprouts manufacturing
422490	Malt wholesaling
311514	Malted milk manufacturing
311213	Malting (germinating and drying grains)
311221	Maltodextrins manufacturing
621512	Mammogram (i.e., breast imaging) centers
422690	Man-made fibers wholesaling
711410	Management agencies for artists, entertainers, and other public figures
611430	Management development training
561110	Management services (except complete operation of client's business)
115116	Management services, farm

Code	Description
711310	Managers of agricultural fairs with facilities
711320	Managers of agricultural fairs without facilities
711310	Managers of arts events with facilities
711320	Managers of arts events without facilities
711310	Managers of festivals with facilities
711320	Managers of festivals without facilities
711310	Managers of live performing arts productions (e.g., concerts) with facilities
711320	Managers of live performing arts productions (e.g., concerts) without facilities
711310	Managers of sports events with facilities
711320	Managers of sports events without facilities
531312	Managers' offices, commercial condominium
531312	Managers' offices, commercial real estate
531312	Managers' offices, nonresidential real estate
531311	Managers' offices, residential condominium
531311	Managers' offices, residential real estate
711410	Managers, authors'
711410	Managers, celebrities'
561920	Managers, convention
711410	Managers, entertainers'
711410	Managers, public figures'
711410	Managers, sports figures'
561920	Managers, trade fair or show
531312	Managing commercial condominiums
531312	Managing commercial real estate
531311	Managing cooperative apartments
523920	Managing investment funds
523920	Managing mutual funds
561110	Managing offices of dentists
561110	Managing offices of physicians and surgeons

Code	Description
561110	Managing offices of professionals (e.g., dentists, physicians, surgeons)
523920	Managing personal investment trusts
531311	Managing residential condominiums
531311	Managing residential real estate
523920	Managing trusts
111320	Mandarin groves
339992	Mandolins manufacturing
333515	Mandrels (i.e., a machine tool accessory) manufacturing
212299	Manganese concentrates beneficiating
325188	Manganese dioxide manufacturing
331112	Manganese metal ferroalloys manufacturing
212299	Manganese ores mining and/or beneficiating
212210	Manganiferous ores valued for iron content, mining and/or beneficiating
212299	Manganiferousares ores (not valued for iron content) mining and/or beneficiating
212299	Manganite mining and/or beneficiating
111339	Mango farming
325191	Mangrove extract manufacturing
234920	Manhole construction contractors
331511	Manhole covers, cast iron, manufacturing
812113	Manicure and pedicure salons
611511	Manicure and pedicure schools
325620	Manicure preparations manufacturing
812113	Manicurist services
323116	Manifold business forms printing
336312	Manifolds (i.e., intake and exhaust), automotive and truck gasoline engine, manufacturing
332996	Manifolds, pipe, made from purchased metal pipe
322231	Manila folders, die-cut, made from purchased paper or paperboard
325221	Manmade cellulosic fibers manufacturing

Code	Description
313221	Manmade fabric, narrow woven, weaving
313210	Manmade fabrics, broadwoven, weaving
313113	Manmade fiber thread manufacturing
325222	Manmade fibers and filaments (except cellulosic) manufacturing
313111	Manmade staple spun yarns made from purchased fiber
541890	Mannequin decorating services
339999	Mannequins manufacturing
421440	Mannequins wholesaling
325920	Mannitol hexanitrate explosive materials manufacturing
334513	Manometers, industrial process-type, manufacturing
561320	Manpower pools
235430	Mantel construction contractors
621399	Manual-arts therapists' offices (e.g., centers, clinics)
421390	Manufactured (i.e., mobile) homes wholesaling
321991	Manufactured (mobile) buildings for commercial use (e.g., banks, offices) manufacturing
321991	Manufactured (mobile) classrooms manufacturing
453930	Manufactured (mobile) home dealers
531190	Manufactured (mobile) home parks
453930	Manufactured (mobile) home parts and accessory dealers
531190	Manufactured (mobile) home sites rental or leasing
321991	Manufactured (mobile) homes manufacturing
221210	Manufactured gas production and distribution
813910	Manufacturers' associations
233310	Manufacturing and industrial building construction management firms
531120	Manufacturing building rental or leasing
532490	Manufacturing machinery and equipment rental or leasing
541614	Manufacturing management consulting services

Code	Description
541614	Manufacturing operations improvement consulting services
511199	Map publishers
511199	Map publishers and printing combined
511199	Map publishing (i.e., establishments known as publishers)
111998	Maple sap concentrating (i.e., producing pure maple syrup in the field)
111998	Maple sap gathering
111998	Maple syrup (i.e., maple sap reducing)
311999	Maple syrup mixing into other products
541370	Mapping (except geophysical) services
541360	Mapping services, geophysical
422920	Maps (except globe, school, wall) wholesaling
323112	Maps flexographic printing without publishing
323111	Maps gravure printing without publishing
323110	Maps lithographic (offset) printing without publishing
323119	Maps printing (except flexographic, gravure, lithographic, screen) without publishing
323113	Maps screen printing without publishing
212319	Marble crushed and broken stone mining and/or beneficiating
212311	Marble mining or quarrying
235430	Marble, granite, and slate work (interior) construction contractors
235410	Marble, granite, and slatework (i.e., exterior) construction contractors
339932	Marbles manufacturing
212393	Marcasite mining and/or beneficiating
325199	Margaric acid manufacturing
311221	Margarine and other corn oils made by wet milling corn
422490	Margarine wholesaling
311225	Margarine-butter blend made from purchased fats and oils

Code	Description
311225	Margarines (including imitation) made from purchased fats and oils
713930	Marinas
928110	Marine Corps
335314	Marine and navy auxiliary controls, manufacturing
488390	Marine cargo checkers and surveyors
488320	Marine cargo handling services
234990	Marine construction
541330	Marine engineering services
333618	Marine engines manufacturing
332510	Marine hardware, metal, manufacturing
332999	Marine horns, compressed air or steam, metal, manufacturing
524126	Marine insurance carriers, direct
712110	Marine museums
611519	Marine navigational schools
325510	Marine paints manufacturing
332410	Marine power boilers manufacturing
334220	Marine radio communications equipment manufacturing
524130	Marine reinsurance carriers
488330	Marine salvaging services
447190	Marine service stations
488510	Marine shipping agency
335911	Marine storage batteries manufacturing
421860	Marine supplies (except pleasure) wholesaling
421910	Marine supplies, pleasure, wholesaling
441222	Marine supply dealers
541990	Marine surveyor (i.e., ship appraiser) services
488330	Marine vessel traffic reporting services
339999	Marionettes (i.e., puppets) manufacturing
339942	Marker boards (i.e., whiteboards) manufacturing
541910	Marketing analysis services
541613	Marketing consulting services
541613	Marketing management consulting services
541910	Marketing research services

Code	Description
339943	Marking devices manufacturing
422120	Marking devices wholesaling
333518	Marking machines, metal, manufacturing
212312	Marl crushed and broken stone mining and/or beneficiating
311421	Marmalade manufacturing
321999	Marquetry, wood, manufacturing
624190	Marriage counseling services (except by offices of mental health practitioners)
922120	Marshals' offices
311340	Marshmallow creme manufacturing
311340	Marshmallows manufacturing
611620	Martial arts instruction, camps, or schools
311340	Marzipan (i.e., candy) manufacturing
335999	Maser (i.e., microwave amplification by stimulated emission of radiation) amplifiers manufacturing
321999	Mashers, wood potato, manufacturing
322222	Masking tape made from purchased paper
332212	Mason's handtools manufacturing
421320	Mason's materials wholesaling
444190	Masonry (e.g., block, brick, stone) dealers
235410	Masonry construction contractors
334516	Mass spectrometers manufacturing
334516	Mass spectroscopy instrumentation manufacturing
234990	Mass transit construction
335211	Massage machines, electric (except designed for beauty and barber shop use), manufacturing
812199	Massage parlors
611519	Massage therapist instruction
512210	Master recording leasing and licensing
422690	Mastics (except construction) wholesaling
321999	Masts, wood, manufacturing
812332	Mat and rug supply services
325998	Matches and match books manufacturing

Code	Description
422990	Matches and match books wholesaling
811310	Materials handling equipment repair and maintenance services
532490	Materials handling machinery and equipment rental or leasing
421830	Materials handling machinery and equipment wholesaling
541614	Materials management consulting services
562920	Materials recovery facilities (MRF)
923120	Maternity and child health program administration
315212	Maternity bras and corsets, women's, cut and sew apparel contractors
315231	Maternity bras and corsets, women's, misses', and girls', cut and sewn from purchased fabric (except apparel contractors)
622310	Maternity hospitals
448120	Maternity shops
541710	Mathematics research and development laboratories or services
332618	Mats and matting made from purchased wire
332212	Mattocks (i.e., handtools) manufacturing
326299	Mattress protectors, rubber, manufacturing
332612	Mattress springs and spring units made from purchased wire
442110	Mattress stores (including waterbeds)
337910	Mattresses (i.e., box spring, innerspring, noninnerspring) manufacturing
337910	Mattresses made from felt, foam rubber, urethane and similar materials
421210	Mattresses wholesaling
326199	Mattresses, air, plastics, manufacturing
326299	Mattresses, air, rubber, manufacturing
311812	Matzo baking made in commercial bakeries

Code	Description
332212	Mauls, metal, manufacturing
321999	Mauls, wood, manufacturing
233320	Mausoleum construction
812220	Mausoleums
311941	Mayonnaise manufacturing
921110	Mayor's offices
624210	Meal delivery programs
311119	Meal, alfalfa, manufacturing
311119	Meal, bone, prepared as feed for animals and fowls, manufacturing
311211	Meal, corn, for human consumption made in flour mills
421830	Measuring and testing equipment (except automotive) wholesaling
333515	Measuring attachments (e.g., sine bars) for machine tool manufacturing
334515	Measuring equipment for electronic and electrical circuits and equipment manufacturing
811219	Measuring instrument repair and maintenance services
334515	Measuring instruments and meters, electric, manufacturing
334513	Measuring instruments, industrial process control-type, manufacturing
332212	Measuring tools, machinist's (except optical), manufacturing
334514	Measuring wheels manufacturing
311613	Meat and bone meal and tankage, produced in rendering plant
311612	Meat canning (except baby, pet food, poultry), made from purchased carcasses
311611	Meat canning (except poultry) produced in slaughtering plants
311422	Meat canning, baby food, manufacturing
311111	Meat canning, dog and cat, pet food, made from purchased carcasses
311615	Meat canning, poultry (except baby and pet food), manufacturing
311612	Meat extracts made from purchased carcasses
333294	Meat grinders, food-type, manufacturing
445210	Meat markets

Code	Description
311615	Meat products (e.g., hot dogs, luncheon meats, sausages) made from a combination of poultry and other meats
311612	Meat products canning (except baby, pet food, poultry) made from purchased carcasses
311111	Meat products, dog and cat, pet food, canning, made from purchased carcasses
311612	Meats (except poultry), cured or smoked, made from purchased carcasses
422470	Meats and meat products (except canned, packaged frozen) wholesaling
311611	Meats fresh, chilled or frozen (except poultry and small game), produced in slaughtering plants
422490	Meats, canned, wholesaling
311611	Meats, cured or smoked, produced in slaughtering plants
422470	Meats, cured or smoked, wholesaling
311612	Meats, fresh or chilled (except poultry and small game), frozen, made from purchased carcasses
422470	Meats, fresh, wholesaling
422470	Meats, frozen (except packaged), wholesaling
422420	Meats, packaged frozen, wholesaling
611513	Mechanic's apprenticeship training
333924	Mechanic's creepers manufacturing
325611	Mechanic's hand soaps and pastes manufacturing
332212	Mechanic's handtools, nonpowered, manufacturing
611519	Mechanic's schools (except apprenticeship)
421120	Mechanic's tools wholesaling
235110	Mechanical construction contractors
541330	Mechanical engineering services
313311	Mechanical finishing of broadwoven fabrics
316110	Mechanical leather manufacturing
334513	Mechanical measuring instruments, industrial process-type, manufacturing

Code	Description
339942	Mechanical pencil refills manufacturing
339941	Mechanical pencils manufacturing
811310	Mechanical power transmission equipment repair and maintenance services
421840	Mechanical power transmission supplies (e.g., gears, pulleys, sprockets) wholesaling
326291	Mechanical rubber goods (i.e., extruded, lathe-cut, molded) manufacturing
421840	Mechanical rubber goods wholesaling
541380	Mechanical testing laboratories or services
333311	Mechanisms for coin-operated machines manufacturing
334518	Mechanisms, clockwork operated device, manufacturing
541840	Media advertising representatives (i.e., independent of media owners)
541830	Media buying agencies
541830	Media buying services
541840	Media representatives (i.e., independent of media owners)
926150	Mediation and conciliation services, government
624190	Mediation, social service, family, agencies
621512	Medical X-ray laboratories
811219	Medical and surgical equipment repair and maintenance services
541430	Medical art services
541430	Medical artists, independent
923130	Medical assistance programs administration, government
531120	Medical building rental or leasing
334510	Medical cleaning equipment, ultrasonic, manufacturing
524298	Medical cost evaluation services
621112	Medical doctors' (MDs), mental health, offices (e.g. centers, clinics)
621111	Medical doctors' (MDs, except mental health) offices (e.g., centers, clinics)
532490	Medical equipment (except home health furniture and equipment) rental or leasing

Code	Description
421450	Medical equipment wholesaling
421450	Medical furniture wholesaling
327215	Medical glassware made from purchased glass
327212	Medical glassware made in glass making plants
421450	Medical glassware wholesaling
541430	Medical illustration services
541430	Medical illustrators, independent
421450	Medical instruments wholesaling
524114	Medical insurance carriers, direct
621511	Medical laboratories (except radiological, X-ray)
621512	Medical laboratories, radiological or X-ray
621511	Medical pathology laboratories
541922	Medical photography services
334517	Medical radiation therapy equipment manufacturing
621512	Medical radiological laboratories
524130	Medical reinsurance carriers
541710	Medical research and development laboratories or services
611310	Medical schools
315211	Medical service apparel, men's and boys', cut and sew apparel contractors
315225	Medical service apparel, men's and boys', cut and sewn from purchased fabric (except apparel contractors)
315212	Medical service apparel, women's, cut and sew apparel contractors
315239	Medical service apparel, women's, misses', and girls', cut and sewn from purchased fabric (except apparel contractors)
524114	Medical service plans without providing health care services
422210	Medical sundries, rubber, wholesaling
421450	Medical supplies wholesaling
611519	Medical technician schools
339112	Medical thermometers manufacturing
334510	Medical ultrasound equipment manufacturing
923130	Medicare and Medicaid administration

Code	Description
325411	Medicinal chemicals, uncompounded, manufacturing
337110	Medicine cabinets (except freestanding), wood household-type, manufacturing
337124	Medicine cabinets, metal household-type, manufacturing
321219	Medium density fiberboard (MDF) manufacturing
212399	Meerschaum mining and/or beneficiating
531120	Meeting hall and room rental or leasing
325211	Melamine resins manufacturing
111219	Melon farming (e.g., cantaloupe, casaba, honeydew, watermelon), field, bedding plant and seed production
111419	Melon farming, grown under cover
313230	Melt blown nonwoven fabrics manufacturing
315291	Melton jackets, infants', cut and sewn from purchased fabric (except apparel contractors)
315211	Melton jackets, men's and boys', cut and sew apparel contractors
315228	Melton jackets, men's and boys', cut and sewn from purchased fabric (except apparel contractors)
315212	Melton jackets, women's, girls', and infants', cut and sew apparel contractors
315239	Melton jackets, women's, misses', and girls', cut and sewn from purchased fabric (except apparel contractors)
813410	Membership associations, civic or social
721110	Membership hotels
812220	Memorial gardens (i.e., burial places)
334418	Memory boards manufacturing
422320	Men's and boys' clothing wholesaling
422320	Men's and boys' furnishings (except shoes) wholesaling
315119	Men's socks knitting or knitting and finishing
114111	Menhaden fishing

Code	Description
623210	Mental retardation intermediate care facilities
622210	Mental (except mental retardation) hospitals
621420	Mental health centers and clinics (except hospitals), outpatient
623220	Mental health facilities, residential
623220	Mental health halfway houses
622210	Mental health hospitals
621112	Mental health physicians' offices (e.g., centers, clinics)
923120	Mental health program administration
623210	Mental retardation facilities (e.g., homes, hospitals, intermediate care facilities), residential
623210	Mental retardation homes
623210	Mental retardation hospitals
561450	Mercantile credit reporting bureaus
313311	Mercerizing broadwoven fabrics
333292	Mercerizing machinery manufacturing
313312	Mercerizing narrow woven textile products and fabrics (except broadwoven)
326111	Merchandise bags, plastics film, single wall or multiwall, manufacturing
421440	Merchandising machines, coin-operated, wholesaling
926120	Merchant Marine (except academy)
813910	Merchants' associations
335912	Mercuric oxide batteries manufacturing
212299	Mercury (quicksilver) mining and/or beneficiating
335999	Mercury arc rectifiers (i.e., electrical apparatus) manufacturing
325188	Mercury chloride manufacturing
325188	Mercury compounds, not specified elsewhere by process, manufacturing
325920	Mercury fulminate explosive materials manufacturing
335110	Mercury halide lamp bulbs manufacturing
212299	Mercury ores mining and/or beneficiating

Code	Description
325188	Mercury oxide manufacturing
332618	Mesh made from purchased wire
331422	Mesh, wire, made from purchased copper in wire drawing plants
331319	Mesh, wire, made in aluminum wire drawing plants
331111	Mesh, wire, made in steel mills
331222	Mesh, wire, made in wire drawing mills
331491	Mesh, wire, nonferrous metals (except aluminum, copper), made from purchased nonferrous metals (except aluminum, copper) in wire drawing plants
561421	Message services, telephone answering
492210	Messenger service
325412	Metabolite in-vivo diagnostic substances manufacturing
332431	Metal cans manufacturing
333298	Metal casting machinery and equipment manufacturing
235610	Metal ceiling construction contractors
333512	Metal cutting machine tools manufacturing
332213	Metal cutting saw blades manufacturing
422690	Metal cyanides wholesaling
333513	Metal deposit forming machines manufacturing
334519	Metal detectors manufacturing
339113	Metal fabric and mesh safety gloves manufacturing
332999	Metal foil containers (except bags) manufacturing
333513	Metal forming machine tools manufacturing
337121	Metal framed furniture, household-type, upholstered, manufacturing
235910	Metal furring contractors
339943	Metal hand stamps manufacturing
333994	Metal melting furnaces, industrial, manufacturing
213114	Metal mining support services (shaft sinking, tunneling, blasting)
336370	Metal motor vehicle body parts stamping

Code	Description
334413	Metal oxide silicon (MOS) devices manufacturing
325612	Metal polishes (i.e., tarnish removers) manufacturing
331314	Metal powder and flake made from purchased aluminum
331423	Metal powder and flake made from purchased copper
331221	Metal powder and flake made from purchased iron or steel
331492	Metal powder and flake nonferrous (except aluminum, copper) made from purchased metal
331111	Metal powder and flake, iron or steel, manufacturing
421510	Metal products (e.g., bars, ingots, plates, rods, shapes, sheets) wholesaling
421930	Metal scrap and waste wholesaling
332116	Metal stampings (except automotive, cans, cooking, closures, crowns), unfinished, manufacturing
421520	Metallic concentrates wholesaling
325131	Metallic pigments, inorganic, manufacturing
325199	Metallic soap manufacturing
313320	Metallizing purchased textiles
541380	Metallurgical testing laboratories or services
421510	Metals sales offices
421510	Metals service centers
421510	Metals, ferrous and nonferrous, wholesaling
421940	Metals, precious, wholesaling
333512	Metalworking lathes manufacturing
532490	Metalworking machinery and equipment rental or leasing
421830	Metalworking machinery and equipment wholesaling
334519	Meteorologic tracking systems manufacturing
811219	Meteorological instrument repair and maintenance services
334519	Meteorological instruments manufacturing
541990	Meteorological services
561990	Meter reading services, contract

Code	Description
334514	Metering devices (except electrical and industrial process control) manufacturing
335313	Metering panels, electric, manufacturing
334514	Meters (except electrical and industrial process control) manufacturing
421830	Meters (except electrical, parking) wholesaling
334515	Meters, electrical (i.e., graphic recording, panelboard, pocket, portable), manufacturing
421610	Meters, electrical, wholesaling
334513	Meters, industrial process control-type, manufacturing
334514	Meters, parking, manufacturing
421850	Meters, parking, wholesaling
334515	Meters, power factor and phase angle, manufacturing
325320	Methoxychlor insecticides manufacturing
325191	Methyl acetone manufacturing
325211	Methyl acrylate resins manufacturing
325199	Methyl alcohol (i.e., methanol), synthetic, manufacturing
325191	Methyl alcohol (methanol), natural, manufacturing
325211	Methyl cellulose resins manufacturing
325199	Methyl chloride manufacturing
325211	Methyl methacrylate resins manufacturing
325199	Methyl perhydrofluorine manufacturing
325199	Methyl salicylate manufacturing
325132	Methyl violet toners manufacturing
325199	Methylamine manufacturing
325199	Methylene chloride manufacturing
311422	Mexican foods canning
311412	Mexican foods, frozen, manufacturing
212399	Mica mining and/or beneficiating
327992	Mica processing beyond beneficiation
327999	Mica products manufacturing

Code	Description
212319	Mica schist crushed and broken stone mining and/or beneficiating
212311	Mica schist mining or quarrying
311119	Micro and macro premixes, livestock, manufacturing
333295	Micro-lithography equipment, semiconductor, manufacturing
334516	Microbiology instruments manufacturing
325413	Microbiology, virology, and serology in-vitro diagnostic substances manufacturing
334111	Microcomputers manufacturing
334413	Microcontroller chip manufacturing
333315	Microfiche equipment (e.g., cameras, projectors, readers) manufacturing
333315	Microfilm equipment (e.g., cameras, projectors, readers) manufacturing
421420	Microfilm equipment and supplies wholesaling
514210	Microfilm recording and imaging services
212299	Microlite mining and/or beneficiating
332212	Micrometers, machinist's precision tools, manufacturing
334310	Microphones manufacturing
334516	Microprobes (e.g., electron, ion, laser, X-ray) manufacturing
334413	Microprocessor chip manufacturing
333314	Microscopes (except electron, proton) manufacturing
334516	Microscopes, electron and proton, manufacturing
334220	Microwave communications equipment manufacturing
334419	Microwave components manufacturing
335221	Microwave ovens (including portable), household-type, manufacturing
333319	Microwave ovens, commercial-type, manufacturing
513330	Microwave telecommunication resellers
334515	Microwave test equipment manufacturing

Code	Description
326199	Microwaveware, plastics, manufacturing
315291	Middies, infants', cut and sewn from purchased fabric (except apparel contractors)
315212	Middies, women's, girls' and infants', cut and sew apparel contractors
315232	Middies, women's, misses', and girls', cut and sewn from purchased fabric (except apparel contractors)
611110	Middle schools
621399	Midwives' offices (e.g., centers, clinics)
721310	Migrant workers' camps
611310	Military academies, college level
611110	Military academies, elementary or secondary
928110	Military bases and camps
315211	Military dress uniforms, men's and boys', cut and sew apparel contractors
315222	Military dress uniforms, men's and boys', cut and sewn from purchased fabric (except apparel contractors)
315234	Military dress uniforms, tailored, women's, misses' and girls', cut and sewn from purchased fabric (except apparel contractors)
315212	Military dress uniforms, women's, cut and sew apparel contractors
332999	Military insignia, metal, manufacturing
314999	Military insignia, textile, manufacturing
712110	Military museums
928110	Military police
928110	Military reserve armories and bases
611310	Military service academies (college)
928110	Military training schools (except academies)
421860	Military vehicles (except trucks) wholesaling
311511	Milk based drinks (except dietary) manufacturing
311514	Milk based drinks, dietary, manufacturing
322130	Milk carton board made in paperboard mills

Code	Description
322226	Milk carton board stock made from purchased paperboard
311511	Milk drink, chocolate, manufacturing
484220	Milk hauling, local
311511	Milk pasteurizing
311511	Milk processing (e.g., bottling, homogenizing, pasteurizing, vitaminizing) manufacturing
333294	Milk processing (except farm-type) machinery manufacturing
112120	Milk production, dairy cattle
311511	Milk substitutes manufacturing
115210	Milk testing for butterfat and milk solids
311511	Milk, acidophilus, manufacturing
422490	Milk, canned or dried, wholesaling
311514	Milk, concentrated, condensed, dried, evaporated, and powdered, manufacturing
311511	Milk, fluid (except canned), manufacturing
422430	Milk, fluid (except canned), wholesaling
311514	Milk, malted, manufacturing
311514	Milk, powdered, manufacturing
311514	Milk, ultra-high temperature, manufacturing
112120	Milking dairy cattle
112420	Milking dairy goat
112410	Milking dairy sheep
421820	Milking machinery and equipment wholesaling
333111	Milking machines manufacturing
311514	Milkshake mixes manufacturing
314999	Mill menders, contract, woven fabrics
316999	Mill strapping for textile mills, leather, manufacturing
421840	Mill supplies wholesaling
315991	Millinery cut and sewn from purchased fabric (except apparel contractors)
422310	Millinery supplies wholesaling
315999	Millinery trimmings cut and sewn from purchased fabric (except apparel contractors)

Code	Description
315211	Millinery trimmings, men's and boys', cut and sew apparel contractors
315212	Millinery trimmings, women's, girls', and infants', cut and sew apparel contractors
422330	Millinery wholesaling
315211	Millinery, men's and boys', cut and sew apparel contractors
315212	Millinery, women's, girls', and infants', cut and sew apparel contractors
333512	Milling machines, metalworking, manufacturing
311212	Milling rice
212399	Millstones mining and/or beneficiating
421310	Millwork wholesaling
337212	Millwork, custom architectural, manufacturing
321114	Millwork, treating
235950	Millwrights
111199	Milo farming, field and seed production
711110	Mime theaters
333922	Mine conveyors manufacturing
213114	Mine development for metal mining on a contract basis
213115	Mine development for nonmetallic minerals mining (except fuels) on a contract basis
234930	Mine loading and discharging station construction
321114	Mine props, treating
562910	Mine reclamation services, integrated (e.g., demolition, hazardous material removal, soil remediation)
213113	Mine shaft sinking services for coal mining on a contract basis
213114	Mine shaft sinking services for metal mining on a contract basis
213115	Mine shaft sinking services for nonmetallic minerals (except fuels) on a contract basis
321114	Mine ties, wood, treated, manufacturing
213113	Mine tunneling services for coal mining on a contract basis

Code	Description
213114	Mine tunneling services for metal mining on a contract basis
213115	Mine tunneling services for nonmetallic minerals (except fuels) on a contract basis
335129	Miner's lamps manufacturing
325131	Mineral colors and pigments manufacturing
311119	Mineral feed supplements (except cat, dog) manufacturing
311111	Mineral feed supplements, dog and cat, manufacturing
212393	Mineral pigments, natural, mining and/or beneficiating
333131	Mineral processing and beneficiating machinery manufacturing
523910	Mineral royalties or leases dealing (i.e., acting as a principal in dealing royalties or leases to investors)
311119	Mineral supplements, animal (except cat, dog), manufacturing
422910	Mineral supplements, animal, wholesaling
311111	Mineral supplements, dog and cat, manufacturing
327993	Mineral wool insulation materials manufacturing
327993	Mineral wool products (e.g., board, insulation, tile) manufacturing
421520	Minerals (except construction materials, petroleum) wholesaling
332993	Mines, ammunition, manufacturing
331111	Mini-mills, steel
713990	Miniature golf courses
337920	Miniblinds manufacturing
334111	Minicomputers manufacturing
926150	Minimum wage program administration
*****	Mining — see type
234930	Mining appurtenance construction contractors
813910	Mining associations
333131	Mining cars manufacturing
541330	Mining engineering services
336510	Mining locomotives and parts manufacturing

Code	Description
421810	Mining machinery and equipment (except petroleum) wholesaling
532412	Mining machinery and equipment rental or leasing
811310	Mining machinery and equipment repair and maintenance services
421830	Mining machinery and equipment, petroleum, wholesaling
531190	Mining property leasing
336112	Minivans assembling on chassis of own manufacture
531130	Miniwarehouse rental or leasing
112930	Mink production
112511	Minnow production, farm raising
711211	Minor league baseball clubs
111998	Mint farming
421220	Mirrors (except automotive) wholesaling
421120	Mirrors, automotive, wholesaling
327215	Mirrors, framed or unframed, made from purchased glass
333314	Mirrors, optical, manufacturing
234990	Missile facility construction
332993	Missile warheads manufacturing
561611	Missing person tracing services
813110	Missions, religious organization
332212	Miter boxes manufacturing
315992	Mittens cut and sewn from purchased fabric (except apparel contractors)
315191	Mittens, knit, made in apparel knitting mills
315992	Mittens, leather (except apparel contractors), manufacturing
315211	Mittens, leather, men's and boys', cut and sew apparel contractors
315212	Mittens, leather, women's, girls', and infants', cut and sew apparel contractors
315211	Mittens, men's and boys', cut and sew apparel contractors
315212	Mittens, women's, girls', and infants', cut and sew apparel contractors
315992	Mittens, woven or knit, cut and sewn from purchased fabric (except apparel contractors)

Code	Description
315211	Mittens, woven or knit, men's and boys', cut and sew apparel contractors
315212	Mittens, woven or knit, women's, girls', and infants', cut and sew apparel contractors
311230	Mix grain breakfast manufacturing
311514	Mix, ice cream, manufacturing
312140	Mixed drinks, alcoholic, manufacturing
111940	Mixed hay farming
485111	Mixed mode transit systems (e.g., bus, commuter rail, subway combinations)
333120	Mixers, concrete, portable, manufacturing
422490	Mixes (e.g., cake, dessert, pie) wholesaling
311211	Mixes, flour (e.g., biscuit, cake, doughnut, pancake) made in flour mills
311822	Mixes, flour (e.g., biscuit, cake, doughnut, pancake), made from purchased flour
325314	Mixing purchased fertilizer materials
531190	Mobile (manufactured) home parks
531190	Mobile (manufactured) home site rental or leasing
531110	Mobile (manufactured) home, on site, rental or leasing
321991	Mobile (manufactured) homes, manufacturing
621512	Mobile X-ray facilities (medical)
621512	Mobile breast imaging centers
811192	Mobile car and truck washes
334220	Mobile communications equipment manufacturing
311119	Mobile feed mill
722330	Mobile food stands
453930	Mobile home dealers, manufactured
321991	Mobile home manufacturing
532120	Mobile home rental (except on site)
235990	Mobile home site setup and tie down construction contractors
484220	Mobile home towing services, local
484230	Mobile home towing services, long-distance

Code	Description
624210	Mobile soup kitchens
333924	Mobile straddle carriers manufacturing
513322	Mobile telephone communication carriers
316219	Moccasins manufacturing
325222	Modacrylic fibers and filaments manufacturing
313111	Modacrylic spun yarns made from purchased fiber
339932	Model kits manufacturing
421920	Model kits wholesaling
339932	Model railroad manufacturing
561310	Model registries
561320	Model supply services
711410	Modeling agents
339942	Modeling clay manufacturing
611519	Modeling schools
711410	Models' agents or managers
339999	Models, anatomical, manufacturing
711510	Models, independent
339932	Models, toy and hobby (e.g., airplane, boat, ship), manufacturing
421690	Modems wholesaling
334210	Modems, carrier equipment, manufacturing
711120	Modern dance companies
337214	Modular furniture systems (except wood frame), office-type, manufacturing
337211	Modular furniture systems, wood frame office-type, manufacturing
233210	Modular house assembly and installation on site, construction
233210	Modular house construction
334518	Modules for clocks and watches manufacturing
112420	Mohair farming
313112	Mohair yarn twisting or winding of purchased yarn
422590	Mohair, raw, wholesaling
334516	Moisture analyzers, laboratory-type, manufacturing
334513	Moisture meters, industrial process-type, manufacturing

Code	Description
311312	Molasses made from purchased raw cane sugar
311313	Molasses made from sugar beets
311311	Molasses made in sugarcane mill
422490	Molasses wholesaling
311312	Molasses, blackstrap, made from purchased raw cane sugar
311311	Molasses, blackstrap, made in sugarcane mill
339991	Molded packings and seals manufacturing
322299	Molded pulp products (e.g., egg cartons, food containers, food trays) manufacturing
421310	Molding (e.g., sheet metal, wood) wholesaling
332321	Molding and trim (except motor vehicle), metal, manufacturing
212322	Molding sand quarrying and/or beneficiating
336370	Moldings and trim, motor vehicle, stamping
321918	Moldings, clear and finger joint wood, manufacturing
321918	Moldings, wood and covered wood, manufacturing
333511	Molds (except steel ingot), industrial, manufacturing
331511	Molds for casting steel ingots manufacturing
333511	Molds for forming materials (e.g., glass, plastics, rubber) manufacturing
333511	Molds for metal casting (except steel ingot) manufacturing
333511	Molds for plastics and rubber working machinery manufacturing
331511	Molds, steel ingot, industrial, manufacturing
112512	Mollusk production, farm raising
212299	Molybdenite mining and/or beneficiating
331491	Molybdenum and molybdenum alloy bar, plate, pipe, rod, sheet, tubing, and wire made from purchased metals or scrap
212299	Molybdenum ores mining and/or beneficiating

Code	Description
331491	Molybdenum rolling, drawing, or extruding purchased metals or scrap
331112	Molybdenum silicon ferroalloys manufacturing
212299	Molybdite mining and/or beneficiating
813110	Monasteries (except schools)
212299	Monazite mining and/or beneficiating
332999	Money chests, metal, manufacturing
525990	Money market mutual funds, closed-end
525910	Money market mutual funds, open-ended
522390	Money order issuance services
334119	Monitors, computer peripheral equipment, manufacturing
325120	Monochlorodifluoromethane manufacturing
334516	Monochrometers, laboratory-type, manufacturing
334413	Monolithic integrated circuits (solid-state) manufacturing
325199	Monomethylparaminophenol sulfate manufacturing
333923	Monorail systems (except passenger-type) manufacturing
485119	Monorail transit systems (except mixed mode), commuter
487110	Monorail, scenic and sightseeing, operation
325199	Monosodium glutamate manufacturing
611110	Montessori schools, elementary or secondary
453998	Monument (i.e., burial marker) dealers
421990	Monuments and grave markers wholesaling
327991	Monuments and tombstone, cut stone (except finishing or lettering to order only), manufacturing
333319	Mop wringers manufacturing
441221	Moped dealers
532292	Moped rental
336991	Mopeds and parts manufacturing
421110	Mopeds wholesaling

Code	Description
339994	Mops, floor and dust, manufacturing
325132	Mordant dyes manufacturing
325613	Mordants manufacturing
325411	Morphine and derivatives (i.e., basic chemicals) manufacturing
522190	Morris Plans (i.e., known as), depository
522298	Morris Plans (i.e., known as), nondepository
333120	Mortar mixers, portable, manufacturing
332993	Mortar shells manufacturing
327125	Mortar, nonclay refractory, manufacturing
332995	Mortars manufacturing
327124	Mortars, clay refractory, manufacturing
522292	Mortgage banking (i.e., nondepository mortgage lending)
522310	Mortgage brokerages
522310	Mortgage brokers' or agents' offices (i.e., independent)
522292	Mortgage companies
524126	Mortgage guaranty insurance carriers, direct
812210	Mortician services
333210	Mortisers, woodworking-type, manufacturing
812210	Mortuaries
235430	Mosaic construction contractors (except fresco)
327122	Mosaic tile, ceramic, manufacturing
813110	Mosques, religious
926130	Mosquito eradication districts
561710	Mosquito eradication services
113210	Moss gathering
531120	Motel building, not operating motel, rental or leasing
233320	Motel construction
561110	Motel management services (except complete operation of client's business)
721110	Motels
325320	Moth repellants manufacturing
421430	Mother boards wholesaling
512110	Motion picture and video production

Code	Description
512110	Motion picture and video production and distribution
512191	Motion picture animation, post-production
512199	Motion picture booking agencies
333315	Motion picture cameras manufacturing
421410	Motion picture cameras, equipment, and supplies wholesaling
541690	Motion picture consulting services
711510	Motion picture directors, independent
512120	Motion picture distribution exclusive of production
532490	Motion picture equipment rental or leasing
512131	Motion picture exhibition
512131	Motion picture exhibitors for airlines
512131	Motion picture exhibitors, itinerant
512120	Motion picture film distributors
512199	Motion picture film laboratories
512120	Motion picture film libraries
514120	Motion picture film libraries, archives
512199	Motion picture film libraries, stock footage
325992	Motion picture film manufacturing
512199	Motion picture film reproduction for theatrical distribution
512199	Motion picture laboratories
512191	Motion picture or video editing services
512191	Motion picture or video post-production services
512191	Motion picture or video titling
711510	Motion picture producers, independent
512110	Motion picture production
512110	Motion picture production and distribution
512191	Motion picture production special effects, post-production
333315	Motion picture projectors manufacturing
512110	Motion picture studios, producing motion pictures

Code	Description
512132	Motion picture theaters, drive-in
512131	Motion picture theaters, indoor
532220	Motion picture wardrobe and costume rental
441221	Motor bike dealers
926120	Motor carrier licensing and inspection offices
485210	Motor coach operation, interurban and rural
335314	Motor control accessories (including overload relays) manufacturing
335314	Motor control centers, manufacturing
335314	Motor controls, electric, manufacturing
421610	Motor controls, electric, wholesaling
721110	Motor courts
484110	Motor freight carrier, general, local
484122	Motor freight carrier, general, long-distance, less-than-truckload (LTL)
484121	Motor freight carrier, general, long-distance, truckload
484210	Motor freight carrier, used household goods
335312	Motor generator sets (except automotive, turbine generator sets) manufacturing
333611	Motor generator sets, turbo generators, manufacturing
441210	Motor home dealers
532120	Motor home rental (except on site)
531190	Motor home rental on site
421110	Motor homes wholesaling
336213	Motor homes, self-contained, assembling on purchased chassis
336120	Motor homes, self-contained, mounted on heavy truck chassis of own manufacture
336112	Motor homes, self-contained, mounted on light duty truck chassis of own manufacture
721110	Motor hotels
721110	Motor inns
721110	Motor lodges
324191	Motor oils, petroleum, made from refined petroleum
325998	Motor oils, synthetic, manufacturing

Code	Description
811310	Motor repair and maintenance services, commercial or industrial
441221	Motor scooters dealers
336991	Motor scooters manufacturing
335314	Motor starters, contractors, and controllers, industrial, manufacturing
561599	Motor travel clubs
333997	Motor truck scales manufacturing
326220	Motor vehicle belts, rubber or plastics, manufacturing
332510	Motor vehicle hardware, metal, manufacturing
326220	Motor vehicle hoses, rubber or plastics, manufacturing
334514	Motor vehicle instruments (e.g., fuel level gauges, oil pressure, speedometers, tachometers, water temperature) manufacturing
421120	Motor vehicle instruments, electric, wholesaling
336360	Motor vehicle interior systems (e.g., headliners, panels, seats, trims) manufacturing
561990	Motor vehicle license issuing services, private franchise
926120	Motor vehicle licensing offices, government
336370	Motor vehicle metal bumper stampings
336370	Motor vehicle metal parts stamping
336370	Motor vehicle metal stampings (e.g., body parts, fenders, hub caps, tops, trim) manufacturing
326199	Motor vehicle moldings and extrusions, plastics, manufacturing
325510	Motor vehicle paints manufacturing
421120	Motor vehicle parts and accessories, new, wholesaling
421140	Motor vehicle parts, used, wholesaling
336360	Motor vehicle seat frames, metal, manufacturing
336360	Motor vehicle seats manufacturing
421130	Motor vehicle tires and tubes wholesaling
326211	Motor vehicle tires manufacturing

Code	Description
488410	Motor vehicle towing services
336360	Motor vehicle trimmings manufacturing
421110	Motor vehicles wholesaling
811490	Motorboat (i.e., inboard and outboard) repair and maintenance services
336612	Motorboat, inboard or outboard, building
441221	Motorcycle dealers
441221	Motorcycle parts and accessories dealers
421120	Motorcycle parts, new, wholesaling
711212	Motorcycle racetracks
711219	Motorcycle racing teams
532292	Motorcycle rental
811490	Motorcycle repair shops without retailing new motorcycles
336991	Motorcycles and parts manufacturing
421110	Motorcycles wholesaling
335312	Motors, electric (except engine starting motors, gearmotors, outboard), manufacturing
421610	Motors, electric, wholesaling
333996	Motors, fluid power, manufacturing
333612	Motors, gear, manufacturing
333618	Motors, outboard, manufacturing
421910	Motors, outboard, wholesaling
336322	Motors, starter, for internal combustion engines, manufacturing
713990	Mountain hiking, recreational
561910	Mounting merchandise on cards
334119	Mouse devices, computer peripheral equipment, manufacturing
213112	Mouse hole and rat hole drilling at oil and gas fields on a contract basis
339992	Mouthpieces for musical instruments manufacturing
325620	Mouthwashes (except medicinal) manufacturing
325412	Mouthwashes, medicated, manufacturing
334518	Movements, watch or clock, manufacturing
512110	Movie production and distribution

Code	Description
512131	Movie theaters (except drive-in)
512132	Movie theaters, drive-in
561730	Mowing services (e.g., highway, lawn, road strip)
325520	Mucilage adhesives manufacturing
213112	Mud service for oil field drilling on a contract basis
811112	Muffler repair and replacement shops
336399	Mufflers and resonators, automotive, truck, and buses manufacturing
315191	Mufflers made in apparel knitting mills
421120	Mufflers, exhaust, wholesaling
315211	Mufflers, men's and boys', cut and sew apparel contractors
315993	Mufflers, men's and boys', cut and sewn from purchased fabric (except apparel contractors)
315999	Mufflers, women's and girls', cut and sewn from purchased fabric (except apparel contractors)
315212	Mufflers, women's, girls', and infants', cut and sew apparel contractors
422910	Mulch wholesaling
333112	Mulchers, lawn and garden-type, manufacturing
112920	Mule production
422590	Mules wholesaling
114111	Mullet fishing
712110	Multidisciplinary museums
233220	Multifamily construction management firms
334515	Multimeters manufacturing
334210	Multiplex equipment, telephone, manufacturing
624190	Multiservice centers, neighborhood
233320	Municipal building construction
212391	Muriate of potash, mining
325412	Muscle relaxant preparations manufacturing
212399	Muscovite mining and/or beneficiating
233320	Museum construction
712110	Museums

Code	Description
111411	Mushroom farming
111411	Mushroom spawn farming
311421	Mushrooms canning
514120	Music archives
711510	Music arrangers, independent
512230	Music book (i.e., bound sheet music) publishers
512230	Music book (i.e., bound sheet music) publishers and printing combined
512230	Music book (i.e., bound sheet music) publishing (i.e., establishments known as publishers)
323117	Music books printing or printing and binding without publishing
339999	Music boxes manufacturing
512230	Music copyright authorizing use
512230	Music copyright buying and licensing
711310	Music festival managers with facilities
711320	Music festival managers without facilities
711310	Music festival organizers with facilities
711320	Music festival organizers without facilities
711310	Music festival promoters with facilities
711320	Music festival promoters without facilities
611610	Music instruction (e.g., guitar, piano)
512230	Music publishers
339992	Music rolls, perforated, manufacturing
611610	Music schools (except academic)
451220	Music stores (e.g., cassette, compact disc, record, tape)
453310	Music stores (e.g., cassette, instrument, record, tape), used
451140	Music stores (i.e., instrument)
621340	Music therapists' offices (e.g., centers, clinics)
512110	Music video production
512110	Music video production and distribution

Code	Description
323112	Music, sheet, flexographic printing without publishing
323111	Music, sheet, gravure printing without publishing
323110	Music, sheet, lithographic (offset) printing without publishing
323119	Music, sheet, printing (except flexographic, gravure, lithographic, screen) without publishing
512230	Music, sheet, publishers and printing combined
512230	Music, sheet, publishing (i.e., establishment known as publishers)
323113	Music, sheet, screen printing without publishing
422990	Music, sheet, wholesaling
711130	Musical artists, independent
711130	Musical groups (except musical theater groups)
339992	Musical instrument accessories (e.g., mouthpieces, reeds, stands, traps) manufacturing
421990	Musical instrument accessories and supplies wholesaling
316991	Musical instrument cases, all materials, manufacturing
532299	Musical instrument rental
811490	Musical instrument repair shops without retailing new musical instruments
339992	Musical instruments (except toy) manufacturing
421990	Musical instruments wholesaling
339932	Musical instruments, toy, manufacturing
711130	Musical productions (except musical theater productions), live
512220	Musical recording, releasing, promoting, and distributing
421990	Musical recordings (e.g., compact discs, records, tapes) wholesaling
711110	Musical theater companies or groups
711110	Musical theater productions, live
711130	Musicians, independent
111219	Muskmelon farming, field, bedding plant and seed production
114112	Mussel fishing

Code	Description
112512	Mussel production, farm raising
111120	Mustard seed farming, field and seed production
311941	Mustard, prepared, manufacturing
523120	Mutual fund agencies (i.e., brokerages)
523120	Mutual fund agents' (i.e., brokers') offices
523920	Mutual fund managing
525990	Mutual funds, closed-end
525910	Mutual funds, open-ended
522120	Mutual savings banks
621511	Mycology health laboratories
325191	Myrobalans extract manufacturing
325411	N-methylpiperazine manufacturing
325212	N-type rubber manufacturing
924110	NOAA (National Oceanic and Atmospheric Administration)
333991	Nail guns, handheld power-driven, manufacturing
333513	Nail heading machines manufacturing
325620	Nail polish remover manufacturing
325620	Nail polishes manufacturing
812113	Nail salons
333991	Nailers and staplers, handheld power-driven, manufacturing
421510	Nails wholesaling
331319	Nails, aluminum, made in wire drawing plants
332618	Nails, brads, and staples made from purchased wire
331222	Nails, iron or steel, made in wire drawing plants
331491	Nails, nonferrous metals (except aluminum, copper), made from purchased nonferrous metals (except aluminum, copper) in wire drawing plants
339950	Name plate blanks manufacturing
332999	Name plate blanks, metal, manufacturing
325998	Napalm manufacturing

Code	Description
325192	Naphtha made by distillation of coal tar
324110	Naphtha made in petroleum refineries
325192	Naphtha, solvent, made by distillation of coal tar
325192	Naphthalene made from refined petroleum or natural gas
325192	Naphthalenesulfonic acid manufacturing
325199	Naphthenic acid soaps manufacturing
325192	Naphthenic acids made from refined petroleum or natural gas
324110	Naphthenic acids made in petroleum refineries
325192	Naphthol, alpha and beta, manufacturing
325192	Naphtholsulfonic acids manufacturing
421220	Napkins (except paper) wholesaling
314129	Napkins made from purchased fabrics
422130	Napkins, paper, wholesaling
322291	Napkins, table, made from purchased paper
322121	Napkins, table, made in paper mills
313311	Napping broadwoven fabrics
333292	Napping machinery for textiles manufacturing
313312	Napping textile products and fabrics (except broadwoven fabrics)
313221	Narrow fabrics weaving
927110	National Aeronautics and Space Administration
522298	National Credit Union Administration (NCUA)
928110	National Guard
926120	National Transportation Safety Board
522110	National commercial banks
712190	National parks
311422	Nationality specialty foods canning
311412	Nationality specialty foods, frozen, manufacturing
212399	Native asphalt mining and/or beneficiating

Code	Description
327310	Natural (i.e., calcined earth) cement manufacturing
212399	Natural abrasives (e.g., emery, grindstones, hones, pumice) (except sand) mining and/or beneficiating
313113	Natural fiber (i.e., hemp, linen, ramie) thread manufacturing
313210	Natural fiber fabrics (i.e., jute, linen, hemp, ramie), broadwoven, weaving
313221	Natural fiber fabrics (i.e., jute, linen, hemp, ramie), narrow woven, weaving
313111	Natural fiber spun yarns (i.e., hemp, jute, ramie, flax) made from purchased fiber
221210	Natural gas brokers
234910	Natural gas compressing station construction
221210	Natural gas distribution systems
333618	Natural gas engines manufacturing
211112	Natural gas liquids (e.g., ethane, isobutane, natural gasoline, propane) recovered from oil and gas field gases
486910	Natural gas liquids pipeline transportation
221210	Natural gas marketers
486210	Natural gas pipeline transportation
211111	Natural gas production
486210	Natural gas transmission (i.e., processing plants to local distribution systems)
211111	Natural gas, offshore production
211112	Natural gasoline recovered from oil and gas field gases
712110	Natural history museums
325199	Natural nonfood coloring, manufacturing
813312	Natural resource preservation organizations
712110	Natural science museums
712190	Natural wonder tourist attractions (e.g., caverns, waterfalls)
312112	Naturally carbonated water, purifying and bottling
712190	Nature centers
712190	Nature parks

Code	Description
712190	Nature preserves
712190	Nature reserves
621399	Naturopaths' offices (e.g., centers, clinics)
334511	Nautical systems and instruments manufacturing
332995	Naval artillery manufacturing
336611	Naval ship building
325191	Naval stores, gum or wood, manufacturing
811219	Navigational instruments (e.g., radar, sonar) repair and maintenance services
421860	Navigational instruments (except electronic) wholesaling
334511	Navigational instruments manufacturing
421690	Navigational instruments, electronic (e.g., radar, sonar), wholesaling
928110	Navy
312120	Near beer brewing
311613	Neatsfoot oil rendering
315292	Neckpieces, fur (except apparel contractors), manufacturing
315211	Neckpieces, fur, men's and boys', cut and sew apparel contractors
315212	Neckpieces, fur, women's, girls', and infants', cut and sew apparel contractors
315191	Neckties made in apparel knitting mills
315211	Neckties, men's and boys', cut and sew apparel contractors
315993	Neckties, men's and boys', cut and sewn from purchased fabric (except apparel contractors)
422320	Neckties, men's and boys', wholesaling
315999	Neckties, women's and girls', cut and sewn from purchased fabric (except apparel contractors)
315212	Neckties, women's, girls', and infants', cut and sew apparel contractors
315191	Neckwear made in a apparel knitting mills
448150	Neckwear stores
315993	Neckwear, men's and boys', cut and sewn from purchased fabric (except apparel contractors)
315211	Neckwear, men's and boys', cut and sew apparel contractors
315212	Neckwear, women's, girls' and infants', cut and sew apparel contractors
111339	Nectarine farming
332991	Needle roller bearings manufacturing
451130	Needlecraft sewing supply stores
339993	Needles (except hypodermic, phonograph, styli) manufacturing
333292	Needles for knitting machinery manufacturing
339112	Needles, hypodermic and suture, manufacturing
334419	Needles, phonograph and styli, manufacturing
422310	Needles, sewing, wholesaling
315211	Needlework art contractors on men's and boys' apparel
315212	Needlework art contractors on women's, girls', and infants' apparel
315192	Negligees made in apparel knitting mills
315212	Negligees, women's, cut and sew apparel contractors
315231	Negligees, women's, misses', and girls', cut and sewn from purchased fabric (except apparel contractors)
813319	Neighborhood development advocacy organizations
325120	Neon manufacturing
339950	Neon signs manufacturing
325212	Neoprene manufacturing
212325	Nepheline syenite mining and/or beneficiating
334516	Nephelometers (except meteorological) manufacturing
334519	Nephoscopes manufacturing
333292	Net and lace making machinery manufacturing
422310	Net goods wholesaling
313210	Nets and nettings, more than 12 inches in width, weaving
313249	Netting made in warp knitting mills
313241	Netting made in weft knitting mills
313249	Netting made on a lace or net machine
326199	Netting, plastics, manufacturing
332618	Netting, woven, made from purchased wire
513111	Network broadcasting service, radio
513111	Network radio broadcasting
541512	Network systems integration design services, computer
513120	Network television broadcasting
513210	Networks, cable television
622310	Neurological hospitals
621111	Neurologists' offices (e.g., centers, clinics)
621111	Neuropathologists' offices (e.g., centers, clinics)
312140	Neutral spirit, beverages (except fruit), manufacturing
422820	Neutral spirits wholesaling
334516	Neutron activation analysis instruments manufacturing
441110	New car dealers
541613	New product development consulting services
321918	Newel posts, wood, manufacturing
451212	News dealers
514110	News picture gathering and distributing services
514110	News reporting services
514110	News service syndicates
514110	News ticker services
511120	Newsletter publishers
511120	Newsletter publishers and printing combined
511120	Newsletter publishing (i.e., establishments known as publishers)
323112	Newsletters flexographic printing without publishing
323111	Newsletters gravure printing without publishing
323110	Newsletters lithographic (offset) printing without publishing
323119	Newsletters printing (except flexographic, gravure, lithographic, screen) without publishing

Code	Description
323113	Newsletters screen printing without publishing
541840	Newspaper advertising representatives (i.e., independent of media owners)
422920	Newspaper agencies wholesaling
511110	Newspaper branch offices
711510	Newspaper columnists, independent (freelance)
514110	Newspaper feature syndicates
333293	Newspaper inserting equipment manufacturing
511110	Newspaper publishers
511110	Newspaper publishers and printing combined
511110	Newspaper publishing (i.e., establishments known as publishers)
323112	Newspapers flexographic printing without publishing
323111	Newspapers gravure printing without publishing
323110	Newspapers lithographic (offset) printing without publishing
323119	Newspapers printing (except flexographic, gravure, lithographic, screen) without publishing
323113	Newspapers screen printing without publishing
422920	Newspapers wholesaling
322122	Newsprint mills
322122	Newsprint paper, manufacturing
422110	Newsprint wholesaling
451212	Newsstands (i.e., permanent)
339941	Nibs (i.e., pen points) manufacturing
331522	Nickel alloy die-castings, unfinished, manufacturing
325188	Nickel ammonium sulfate manufacturing
331491	Nickel and nickel alloy pipe, plate, sheet, strip, and tubing made from purchased metals or scrap
335911	Nickel cadmium storage batteries manufacturing
325188	Nickel carbonate manufacturing
331528	Nickel castings (except die-castings), unfinished, manufacturing

Code	Description
325188	Nickel compounds, not specified elsewhere by process, manufacturing
212234	Nickel concentrates recovery
331522	Nickel die-castings, unfinished, manufacturing
332999	Nickel foil not made in rolling mills
212234	Nickel ore beneficiating plants
212234	Nickel ore mine site development for own account
212234	Nickel ores mining and/or beneficiating
331492	Nickel recovering from scrap and/or alloying purchased metals
331419	Nickel refining, primary
331491	Nickel rolling, drawing, or extruding purchased metals or scrap
325188	Nickel sulfate manufacturing
325411	Nicotine and derivatives (i.e., basic chemicals) manufacturing
325320	Nicotine insecticides manufacturing
713990	Night clubs without alcoholic beverages
722410	Night clubs, alcoholic beverage
337122	Night stands, wood, manufacturing
315192	Nightgowns made in apparel knitting mills
315291	Nightgowns, infants', cut and sewn from purchased fabric (except apparel contractors)
315211	Nightgowns, men's and boys', cut and sew apparel contractors
315221	Nightgowns, men's and boys', cut and sewn from purchased fabric (except apparel contractors)
315212	Nightgowns, women's, girls', and infants', cut and sew apparel contractors
315231	Nightgowns, women's, misses', and girls', cut and sewn from purchased fabric (except apparel contractors)
315192	Nightshirts made in apparel knitting mills
315291	Nightshirts, infants', cut and sewn from purchased fabric (except apparel contractors)
315211	Nightshirts, men's and boys', cut and sew apparel contractors

Code	Description
315221	Nightshirts, men's and boys', cut and sewn from purchased fabric (except apparel contractors)
315212	Nightshirts, women's, girls', and infants', cut and sew apparel contractors
315231	Nightshirts, women's, misses', and girls', cut and sewn from purchased fabric (except contractors)
315192	Nightwear made in apparel knitting mills
315291	Nightwear, infants', cut and sewn from purchased fabric (except apparel contractors)
315211	Nightwear, men's and boys', cut and sew apparel contractors
315221	Nightwear, men's and boys', cut and sewn from purchased fabric (except apparel contractors)
422320	Nightwear, men's and boys', wholesaling
315212	Nightwear, women's, girls', and infants', cut and sew apparel contractors
315231	Nightwear, women's, misses', and girls', cut and sewn from purchased fabric (except apparel contractors)
331419	Niobium refining, primary
326299	Nipples and teething rings, rubber, manufacturing
332996	Nipples, metal, made from purchased pipe
325192	Nitrated hydrocarbon derivatives manufacturing
325311	Nitric acid manufacturing
325212	Nitrile rubber manufacturing
325212	Nitrile-butadiene rubber manufacturing
325212	Nitrile-chloroprene rubbers manufacturing
325192	Nitroaniline manufacturing
325192	Nitrobenzene manufacturing
325211	Nitrocellulose (i.e., pyroxylin) resins manufacturing
325920	Nitrocellulose explosive materials manufacturing
325221	Nitrocellulose fibers manufacturing
325120	Nitrogen manufacturing

Code	Description
325311	Nitrogenous fertilizer materials manufacturing
325314	Nitrogenous fertilizers made by mixing purchased materials
325920	Nitroglycerin explosive materials manufacturing
325192	Nitrophenol manufacturing
325192	Nitrosated hydrocarbon derivatives manufacturing
325132	Nitroso dyes manufacturing
325920	Nitrostarch explosive materials manufacturing
325199	Nitrous ether manufacturing
325120	Nitrous oxide manufacturing
339113	Noise protectors, personal, manufacturing
541380	Non-destructive testing laboratories or services
312120	Nonalcoholic beer brewing
312130	Nonalcoholic wines manufacturing
551112	Nonbank holding companies (except managing)
234990	Nonbuilding structures (except industrial) contractor
234930	Nonbuilding structures, industrial construction
325222	Noncellulosic fibers and filaments manufacturing
325222	Noncellulosic filament yarn manufacturing
325222	Noncellulosic staple fibers and filaments manufacturing
111339	Noncitrus fruit farming
327125	Nonclay refractories (e.g., block, brick, mortar, tile) manufacturing
311514	Nondairy creamers, dry, manufacturing
311511	Nondairy creamers, liquid, manufacturing
325110	Nonene made from refined petroleum or liquid hydrocarbons
311514	Nonfat dry milk manufacturing
331522	Nonferrous (except aluminum) die-casting foundries
331492	Nonferrous alloys (except aluminum, copper) made from purchased nonferrous metals

Code	Description
331492	Nonferrous alloys (except aluminum, copper) made in integrated secondary smelting and alloying plants
331419	Nonferrous metal (except aluminum, copper) shapes made in primary nonferrous metal smelting and refining mills
331491	Nonferrous metal shapes (except aluminum, copper) made by rolling, drawing, or extruding purchased nonferrous metal
331491	Nonferrous metal shapes (except aluminum, copper) made in integrated secondary smelting and extruding mills
331491	Nonferrous metal shapes (except aluminum, copper) made in integrated secondary smelting and rolling mills
331491	Nonferrous metal shapes (except aluminum, copper) made in integrated secondary smelting mills and wire drawing plants
331528	Nonferrous metals (except aluminum, copper) foundries (except die-casting)
331419	Nonferrous metals (except aluminum, copper) made in primary nonferrous metal smelting and refining mills
331492	Nonferrous metals (except aluminum, copper) secondary smelting and refining
331419	Nonferrous metals (except aluminum, copper) smelting and refining, primary
331528	Nonferrous metals (except aluminum, copper) unfinished castings (except die-castings) manufacturing
421510	Nonferrous metals (except precious) wholesaling
331491	Nonferrous wire (except aluminum, copper) made from purchased nonferrous metals (except aluminum, copper) in wire drawing plants
331491	Nonferrous wire (except aluminum, copper) made in integrated secondary smelting mills and wire drawing plants

Code	Description
323121	Nonfiction book binding without printing
511130	Nonfiction book publishers
511130	Nonfiction book publishers and printing combined
511130	Nonfiction book publishing (i.e., establishments known as publishers)
323117	Nonfiction books printing and binding without publishing
323117	Nonfiction books printing without publishing
562219	Nonhazardous waste treatment and disposal facilities (except combustors, incinerators, landfills, sewer systems, sewage treatment facilities)
213115	Nonmetallic minerals mining support services (e.g., blasting, shaft sinking, tunneling) on a contract basis
325412	Nonprescription drug preparations manufacturing
422210	Nonprescription drugs wholesaling
531312	Nonresidential property managing
531120	Nonresidential building (except miniwarehouse) rental or leasing
481212	Nonscheduled air freight transportation
481211	Nonscheduled air passenger transportation
332214	Nonstick metal cooking utensils
337122	Nonupholstered, household-type, custom wood furniture, manufacturing
313230	Nonwoven fabric tapes manufacturing
313230	Nonwoven fabrics manufacturing
313230	Nonwoven felts manufacturing
311999	Noodle mixes made from purchased dry ingredients
311423	Noodle mixes made in dehydration plants
311823	Noodle mixes made in dry pasta plants
311823	Noodles, dry, manufacturing
311991	Noodles, fresh, manufacturing
311999	Noodles, fried, manufacturing

Code	Description
339113	Nose and ear plugs manufacturing
541199	Notary public services
541199	Notary publics' private practices
334111	Notebook computers manufacturing
322233	Notebooks (including mechanically bound by wire, or plastics) made from purchased paper
422120	Notebooks wholesaling
332999	Novelties and specialties, nonprecious metal and precious plated, manufacturing
422990	Novelties wholesaling
316999	Novelties, leather (e.g., cigarette lighter covers, key fobs), manufacturing
339999	Novelties, not specified elsewhere, manufacturing
339911	Novelties, precious metal (except precious plated), manufacturing
321999	Novelties, wood fiber, manufacturing
453220	Novelty shops
315211	Novelty stitching contractors on men's and boys' apparel
315212	Novelty stitching contractors on women's, girls', and infants' apparel
326199	Nozzles, aerosol spray, plastics, manufacturing
332919	Nozzles, fire fighting, manufacturing
332919	Nozzles, lawn hose, manufacturing
332911	Nuclear application valves manufacturing
541690	Nuclear energy consulting services
926130	Nuclear energy inspection and regulation offices
325188	Nuclear fuel scrap reprocessing
325188	Nuclear fuels, inorganic, manufacturing
334519	Nuclear instrument modules manufacturing
334517	Nuclear irradiation equipment manufacturing
325412	Nuclear medicine (e.g., radioactive isotopes) preparations manufacturing

Code	Description
234930	Nuclear reactor containment structure construction
332410	Nuclear reactor steam supply systems manufacturing
332410	Nuclear reactors control rod drive mechanisms manufacturing
332410	Nuclear reactors manufacturing
332313	Nuclear shielding, fabricated metal plate work, manufacturing
332420	Nuclear waste casks, heavy gauge metal, manufacturing
721214	Nudist camps with accommodation facilities
713990	Nudist camps without accommodations
335314	Numerical controls, manufacturing
333512	Numerically controlled metal cutting machine tools manufacturing
812990	Numerology services
621610	Nurse associations, visiting
561310	Nurse registries
611519	Nurse's aides schools
113210	Nurseries for reforestation growing trees
444220	Nursery and garden centers without tree production
337122	Nursery furniture (except upholstered), wood, manufacturing
337124	Nursery furniture, metal, manufacturing
624410	Nursery schools
422930	Nursery stock (except plant bulbs, seeds) wholesaling
111421	Nursery stock growing
111421	Nursery with tree production (except for reforestation)
813920	Nurses' associations
621399	Nurses', licensed practical or registered, offices (e.g., centers, clinics)
621610	Nursing agencies, primarily providing home nursing services
623110	Nursing care facilities
623110	Nursing homes
611519	Nursing schools (except academic)
445292	Nut (i.e., packaged) stores

Code	Description
115114	Nut hulling and shelling
331221	Nut rods, iron or steel, made in cold rolling mills
331111	Nut rods, iron or steel, made in steel mills
333111	Nut shellers, farm-type, manufacturing
446191	Nutrition (i.e., food supplement) stores
621399	Nutritionists' offices (e.g., centers, clinics)
422450	Nuts (e.g., canned, roasted, salted) wholesaling
311320	Nuts, chocolate covered, made from cacao beans
311330	Nuts, chocolate covered, made from purchased chocolate
311340	Nuts, covered (except chocolate covered), manufacturing
311911	Nuts, kernels and seeds, roasting and processing
115113	Nuts, machine harvesting
332722	Nuts, metal, manufacturing
311911	Nuts, salted, roasted, cooked, canned, manufacturing
422590	Nuts, unprocessed or shelled only, wholesaling
325222	Nylon fibers and filaments manufacturing
315111	Nylon hosiery, sheer, women's, misses', and girls' full-length and knee-length, knitting or knitting and finishing
325211	Nylon resins manufacturing
313111	Nylon spun yarns made from purchased fiber
313113	Nylon thread manufacturing
313112	Nylon yarn twisting or winding of purchased yarn
315111	Nylons, sheer, women's, misses', and girls' full-length and knee-length, knitting or knitting and finishing
621320	ODs' (doctors of optometry) offices (e.g., centers, clinics)
321219	OSB (oriented strandboard) manufacturing
325191	Oak extract manufacturing

Code	Description
321999	Oars, wood, manufacturing
111199	Oat farming, field and seed production
311211	Oat flour manufacturing
311230	Oatmeal (i.e., cereal breakfast food) manufacturing
311230	Oats, breakfast cereal, manufacturing
311230	Oats, rolled (i.e., cereal breakfast food), manufacturing
812910	Obedience training services, pet
339992	Oboes manufacturing
713990	Observation towers
622310	Obstetrical hospital
621111	Obstetricians' offices (e.g., centers, clinics)
339992	Ocarinas manufacturing
926150	Occupational safety and health administration
926150	Occupational safety and health standards agencies
813920	Occupational therapists' associations
621340	Occupational therapists' offices (e.g., centers, clinics)
541710	Oceanographic research and development laboratories or services
212393	Ocher mining and/or beneficiating
325131	Ocher pigments manufacturing
339992	Octophones manufacturing
114112	Octopus fishing
332995	Oerlikon guns manufacturing
721310	Off campus dormitories
336999	Off-highway tracked vehicles (except construction, armored military) manufacturing
333120	Off-highway trucks manufacturing
336999	Off-road all terrain vehicles (ATV's), wheeled or tracked, manufacturing
441221	Off-road all-terrain vehicles (ATV), wheeled or tracked, dealers
713290	Off-track betting parlors
624190	Offender self-help organizations
561110	Office administration services
541512	Office automation computer systems integration design services

Code	Description
233320	Office building construction
531120	Office building rental or leasing
561720	Office cleaning services
421420	Office equipment wholesaling
337214	Office furniture (except wood), padded, upholstered, or plain (except wood), manufacturing
532420	Office furniture rental or leasing
442110	Office furniture stores
421210	Office furniture wholesaling
337211	Office furniture, padded, upholstered, or plain wood, manufacturing
561320	Office help supply services
811212	Office machine repair and maintenance services (except communication equipment)
532420	Office machinery and equipment rental or leasing
421420	Office machines wholesaling
561110	Office management services
322121	Office paper (e.g., computer printer, photocopy, plain paper) made in paper mills
322233	Office paper (e.g., computer printer, photocopy, plain paper), cut sheet, made from purchased paper
422120	Office supplies (except furniture, machines) wholesaling
322231	Office supplies, die-cut paper, made from purchased paper or paperboard
561320	Office supply pools
453210	Office supply stores
325910	Offset inks manufacturing
323122	Offset plate preparation services
323110	Offset printing (except books, manifold business forms, printing grey goods)
333293	Offset printing presses manufacturing
211111	Offshore crude petroleum production
211111	Offshore natural gas production
334515	Ohmmeters manufacturing
324110	Oil (i.e., petroleum) refineries
325998	Oil additive preparations manufacturing

Code	Description
324110	Oil additives made in petroleum refineries
422690	Oil additives wholesaling
211111	Oil and gas field development for own account
211111	Oil and gas field exploration for own account
213112	Oil and gas field services (except contract drilling) on a contract basis
333132	Oil and gas field-type drilling machinery and equipment (except offshore floating platforms) manufacturing
336611	Oil and gas offshore floating platforms manufacturing
213111	Oil and gas well drilling services (redrilling, spudding, tailing) on a contract basis
333414	Oil burners, heating, manufacturing
421720	Oil burners, heating, wholesaling
811191	Oil change and lubrication shops, automotive
422690	Oil drilling muds wholesaling
213112	Oil field exploration (except surveying) on a contract basis
532412	Oil field machinery and equipment rental or leasing
336399	Oil filters, automotive, truck, and bus, manufacturing
421120	Oil filters, automotive, wholesaling
422590	Oil kernels wholesaling
523999	Oil lease brokers' offices
211112	Oil line drip, natural gas liquid
333913	Oil measuring and dispensing pumps manufacturing
422590	Oil nuts wholesaling
234930	Oil refinery construction
533110	Oil royalty companies
523910	Oil royalty dealing (i.e., acting as a principal in dealing royalties to investors)
533110	Oil royalty leasing
213112	Oil sampling services on a contract basis
339991	Oil seals manufacturing
211111	Oil shale mining and/or beneficiating

Code	Description
562910	Oil spill cleanup services
332420	Oil storage tanks, heavy gauge metal, manufacturing
532412	Oil well drilling machinery and equipment rental or leasing
213111	Oil well drilling on a contract basis
213112	Oil well logging on a contract basis
421830	Oil well machinery and equipment wholesaling
213112	Oil well rig building, repairing, and dismantling, on a contract basis
421830	Oil well supply houses wholesaling
311613	Oil, animal, rendering
311221	Oil, corn crude and refined, made by wet milling corn
311225	Oil, olive, made from purchased oils
422710	Oil, petroleum, bulk stations and terminals
422720	Oil, petroleum, wholesaling (except bulk stations, terminals)
311225	Oil, vegetable stearin, made from purchased oils
421930	Oil, waste, wholesaling
324199	Oil-based additives made from refined petroleum
333911	Oil-well and oil-field pumps manufacturing
313320	Oilcloth manufacturing
313320	Oiling of purchased textiles and apparel
325998	Oils (e.g., cutting, lubricating), synthetic, manufacturing
325192	Oils made by distillation of coal tar
422490	Oils, cooking and salad, wholesaling
324110	Oils, fuel, manufacturing
422990	Oils, inedible, animal or vegetable, wholesaling
324191	Oils, lubricating petroleum, made from refined petroleum
325998	Oils, lubricating, synthetic, manufacturing
324191	Oils, petroleum lubricating, re-refining used
325613	Oils, soluble (i.e., textile finishing assistants), manufacturing
325411	Oils, vegetable and animal, medicinal, uncompounded, manufacturing

Code	Description
325191	Oils, wood, made by distillation of wood
111191	Oilseed and grain combination farming, field and seed production
422990	Oilseed cake and meal wholesaling
333294	Oilseed crushing and extracting machinery manufacturing
111120	Oilseed farming (except soybean), field and seed production
422590	Oilseeds wholesaling
212399	Oilstones mining and/or beneficiating
111219	Okra farming, field, bedding plant and seed production
623312	Old age homes without nursing care
923130	Old age survivors and disability programs
623312	Old soldiers' homes without nursing care
325222	Olefin fibers and filaments manufacturing
325110	Olefins made from refined petroleum or liquid hydrocarbons
325199	Oleic acid (i.e., red oil) manufacturing
325199	Oleic acid esters manufacturing
325188	Oleum (i.e., fuming sulfuric acid) manufacturing
111339	Olive farming
311225	Olive oil made from purchased oils
311223	Olive oil made in crushing mills
311421	Olives brined
311423	Olives, dried, made in dehydration plant
212325	Olivine, non-gem, mining and/or beneficiating
334511	Omnibearing instrumentation manufacturing
514191	On-line access service providers
233210	On-site mobile home repair construction
233210	On-site modular homes assembly construction
233210	On-site prefabricated homes assembly construction
621111	Oncologists' offices (e.g., centers, clinics)

Code	Description
233210	One family house construction—general construction contractors
812922	One-hour photofinishing services
111219	Onion farming, field, bedding plant and seed production
311421	Onions pickled
212319	Onyx marble crushed and broken stone mining and/or beneficiating
212311	Onyx marble mining or quarrying
512132	Open air motion picture theaters
711110	Opera companies
315991	Opera hats cut and sewn from purchased fabric (except apparel contractors)
315211	Opera hats, men's and boys', cut and sew apparel contractors
315212	Opera hats, women's, girls', and infants', cut and sew apparel contractors
711130	Opera singers, independent
927110	Operating and launching government satellites
339111	Operating room tables manufacturing
511210	Operating systems software, computer, packaged
541614	Operations research consulting services
233320	Operative builders of commercial and institutional buildings
233310	Operative builders of manufacturing and industrial buildings
233220	Operative builders of multifamily housing
233210	Operative builders of single family housing
325411	Ophthalmic agents, uncompounded, manufacturing
421460	Ophthalmic goods (except cameras) wholesaling
339112	Ophthalmic instruments and apparatus (except laser surgical) manufacturing
621111	Ophthalmologists' offices (e.g., centers, clinics)
339112	Ophthalmometers and ophthalmoscopes manufacturing
541910	Opinion research services

Code	Description
325411	Opium and opium derivatives (i.e., basic chemicals) manufacturing
333314	Optical alignment and display instruments (except photographic) manufacturing
334112	Optical disk drives manufacturing
421460	Optical goods (except cameras) wholesaling
446130	Optical goods stores (except offices of optometrists)
212399	Optical grade calcite mining and/or beneficiating
333314	Optical gun sighting and fire control equipment and instruments manufacturing
811219	Optical instrument repair and maintenance services
333298	Optical lens making and grinding machinery manufacturing
334119	Optical readers and scanners manufacturing
514210	Optical scanning services
333314	Optical test and inspection equipment manufacturing
334413	Optoelectronic devices manufacturing
339112	Optometers manufacturing
421460	Optometric equipment and supplies wholesaling
813920	Optometrists' associations
621320	Optometrists' offices (e.g., centers, clinics)
621210	Oral and maxillofacial surgeons' offices (e.g., centers, clinics)
325412	Oral contraceptive preparations manufacturing
621210	Oral pathologists' offices (e.g., centers, clinics)
111310	Orange groves
325998	Orange oil manufacturing
115112	Orchard cultivation services (e.g., bracing, planting, pruning, removal, spraying, surgery)
111998	Orchard grass seed farming
711510	Orchestra conductors, independent
711130	Orchestras
454110	Order taking offices of mail-order houses

Code	Description
421990	Ordnance and accessories wholesaling
421520	Ore concentrates wholesaling
333131	Ore crushing, washing, screening, and loading machinery manufacturing
421520	Ores (e.g., gold, iron, lead, silver, zinc) wholesaling
621991	Organ banks, body
621991	Organ donor centers, body
422690	Organic chemicals wholesaling
325222	Organic fibers and filaments (except cellulosic) manufacturing
325132	Organic pigments, dyes, lakes, and toners manufacturing
541612	Organization development consulting services
928120	Organization for Economic Coperation and Development
928120	Organization of American States
326199	Organizers for closets, drawers, and shelves, plastics, manufacturing
711310	Organizers of agricultural fairs with facilities
711320	Organizers of agricultural fairs without facilities
711310	Organizers of arts events with facilities
711320	Organizers of arts events without facilities
711310	Organizers of festivals with facilities
711320	Organizers of festivals without facilities
711310	Organizers of live performing arts productions (e.g., concerts) with facilities
711320	Organizers of live performing arts productions (e.g., concerts) without facilities
711310	Organizers of sports events with facilities
711320	Organizers of sports events without facilities
325199	Organo-inorganic compound manufacturing
325320	Organo-phosphate based insecticides manufacturing
321219	Oriented strandboard (OSB) manufacturing

Code	Description
327420	Ornamental and architectural plaster work (e.g., columns, mantels, molding) manufacturing
112511	Ornamental fish production, farm raising
421390	Ornamental ironwork wholesaling
235990	Ornamental metalwork construction contractors
332323	Ornamental metalwork manufacturing
111422	Ornamental plant growing
561730	Ornamental tree and shrub services
321918	Ornamental woodwork (e.g., cornices, mantels) manufacturing
339999	Ornaments, Christmas tree (except electric, glass), manufacturing
335129	Ornaments, Christmas tree, electric, manufacturing
327212	Ornaments, Christmas tree, glass, made in glass making plants
327215	Ornaments, Christmas tree, made from purchased glass
623990	Orphanages
325998	Orris oil manufacturing
325192	Orthodichlorobenzene manufacturing
339116	Orthodontic appliance, custom made in dental laboratories
339114	Orthodontic appliances manufacturing
621210	Orthodontists' offices (e.g., centers, clinics)
339113	Orthopedic canes manufacturing
339113	Orthopedic devices manufacturing
421450	Orthopedic equipment and supplies wholesaling
339113	Orthopedic extension shoes manufacturing
339113	Orthopedic hosiery, elastic, manufacturing
622310	Orthopedic hospitals
621111	Orthopedic physicians' offices (e.g., centers, clinics)
327420	Orthopedic plaster, gypsum, manufacturing
316219	Orthopedic shoes (except extension shoes), children's, manufacturing

Code	Description
316213	Orthopedic shoes (except extension shoes), men's, manufacturing
316214	Orthopedic shoes (except extension shoes), women's, manufacturing
448210	Orthopedic shoes stores
621111	Orthopedic surgeons' offices (e.g., centers, clinics)
334515	Oscillators (e.g., instrument type audiofrequency and radiofrequency) manufacturing
334515	Oscilloscopes manufacturing
212299	Osmium mining and/or beneficiating
334516	Osmometers manufacturing
325998	Ossein manufacturing
622110	Osteopathic hospitals
621111	Osteopathic physicians' (except mental health) offices (e.g., centers, clinics)
112390	Ostrich production
621111	Otolaryngologists' offices (e.g., centers, clinics)
334510	Otoscopes, electromedical, manufacturing
337121	Ottomans, upholstered, manufacturing
541850	Out-of-home media (i.e., display) advertising services
441222	Outboard motor dealers
811490	Outboard motor repair shops
333618	Outboard motors manufacturing
421910	Outboard motors wholesaling
713990	Outdoor adventure operations (e.g., white water rafting) without accommodations
721214	Outdoor adventure retreats with accommodation facilities
541850	Outdoor display advertising services
421210	Outdoor furniture wholesaling
451110	Outdoor sporting equipment stores
315191	Outerwear handknitted for the trade
422320	Outerwear, men's and boys', wholesaling
422330	Outerwear, women's, children's, and infants', wholesaling
335932	Outlet boxes, electrical wiring, manufacturing

Code	Description
335931	Outlets (i.e., receptacles), electrical, manufacturing
335931	Outlets, convenience, electric, manufacturing
621420	Outpatient mental health centers and clinics (except hospitals)
621420	Outpatient treatment centers and clinics (except hospitals) for substance abuse (i.e., alcoholism, drug addiction)
621420	Outpatient treatment centers and clinics for alcoholism
621420	Outpatient treatment centers and clinics for drug addiction
541990	Outplacement services
325612	Oven cleaners manufacturing
334512	Oven temperature controls, nonindustrial, manufacturing
811412	Oven, household-type, repair and maintenance services without retailing new ovens
421720	Ovens (except electric), household-type, wholesaling
234930	Ovens construction, industrial
234930	Ovens, baker's, construction
333294	Ovens, bakery, manufacturing
234930	Ovens, coke, construction
333319	Ovens, commercial-type, manufacturing
421440	Ovens, commercial-type, wholesaling
421620	Ovens, electric household-type, wholesaling
335221	Ovens, freestanding household-type, manufacturing
333994	Ovens, industrial process-type, manufacturing
421830	Ovens, industrial, wholesaling
339111	Ovens, laboratory-type, manufacturing
335211	Ovens, portable household-type (except microwave and convection ovens), manufacturing
335221	Ovens, portable household-type convention and microwave, manufacturing
327215	Ovenware made from purchased glass

Code	Description
327212	Ovenware, glass, made in glass making plants
315211	Overall jackets, work, men's and boys', cut and sew apparel contractors
315225	Overall jackets, work, men's and boys', cut and sewn from purchased fabric (except apparel contractors)
315211	Overalls, work, men's and boys', cut and sew apparel contractors
315225	Overalls, work, men's and boys', cut and sewn from purchased fabric (except apparel contractors)
213113	Overburden removal for coal mining on a contract basis
213114	Overburden removal for metal mining on a contract basis
213115	Overburden removal for nonmetallic minerals mining (except fuels) on a contract basis
315211	Overcoats, men's and boys', cut and sew apparel contractors
315222	Overcoats, men's and boys', cut and sewn from purchased fabric (except apparel contractors)
315212	Overcoats, women's, girls', and infants', cut and sew apparel contractors
315234	Overcoats, women's, misses', and girls', cut and sewn from purchased fabric (except apparel contractors)
333922	Overhead conveyors manufacturing
333315	Overhead projectors (except computer peripheral) manufacturing
334119	Overhead projectors, computer peripheral-type, manufacturing
333923	Overhead traveling cranes manufacturing
234120	Overpass construction
316211	Overshoes, plastics or plastics soled fabric upper, manufacturing
316211	Overshoes, rubber, or rubber soled fabric, manufacturing
325199	Oxalates (e.g., ammonium oxalate, ethyl oxalate, sodium oxalate) manufacturing
325199	Oxalic acid manufacturing

Code	Description
339991	Oxial mechanical face seals manufacturing
532291	Oxygen equipment rental (i.e. home use)
325120	Oxygen manufacturing
339112	Oxygen tents manufacturing
114112	Oyster dredging
112512	Oyster production, farm raising
212399	Ozokerite mining and/or beneficiating
333319	Ozone machines for water purification manufacturing
813940	PACs (Political Action Committees)
334210	PBX (private branch exchange) equipment manufacturing
561330	PEO (professional employer organizations)
334510	PET (position emission tomography) scanners manufacturing
326122	PVC pipe manufacturing
621999	Pacemaker monitoring services
334510	Pacemakers manufacturing
326299	Pacifiers, rubber, manufacturing
713990	Pack trains (i.e., trail riding), recreational
445310	Package stores (i.e., liquor)
511210	Packaged computer software publishers
511210	Packaged computer software publishing (i.e., establishments known as publishers)
326112	Packaging film, plastics, single-web or multiweb, manufacturing
115114	Packaging fresh or farm-dried fruits and vegetables
541420	Packaging industrial design services
333993	Packaging machinery manufacturing
421840	Packaging material wholesaling
561910	Packaging services (except packing and crating for transportation)
326150	Packaging, foam plastics (except polystyrene), manufacturing
326199	Packaging, plastics (e.g., blister, bubble), manufacturing
325998	Packer's fluids manufacturing
488991	Packing and preparing goods for shipping

Code	Description
321920	Packing cases, wood, nailed or lock corner, manufacturing
321920	Packing crates, wood, manufacturing
115114	Packing fruits and vegetables
421830	Packing machinery and equipment wholesaling
421840	Packing materials wholesaling
316211	Pacs, plastics or plastics soled fabric upper, manufacturing
316211	Pacs, rubber or rubber soled fabric upper, manufacturing
322232	Padded envelopes manufacturing
314999	Padding and wadding (except nonwoven fabric) manufacturing
422310	Paddings, apparel, wholesaling
321999	Paddles, wood, manufacturing
332510	Padlocks manufacturing
314129	Pads and protectors (e.g., ironing board, mattress, table), textile, made from purchased fabrics or felts
313230	Pads and wadding, nonwoven, manufacturing
322211	Pads, corrugated and solid fiberboard, made from purchased paper or paperboard
322233	Pads, desk, made from purchased paper
321999	Pads, excelsior, wood, manufacturing
322291	Pads, incontinent and bed, manufacturing
332999	Pads, soap impregnated scouring, manufacturing
321999	Pads, table, rattan, reed, and willow, manufacturing
334220	Pagers manufacturing
513321	Paging services
321920	Pails, coopered wood, manufacturing
326199	Pails, plastics, manufacturing
321920	Pails, plywood, manufacturing
321920	Pails, wood, manufacturing
621498	Pain therapy centers and clinics, outpatient
325510	Paint and varnish removers manufacturing

Code	Description
333994	Paint baking and drying ovens manufacturing
339994	Paint rollers manufacturing
422950	Paint rollers wholesaling
811121	Paint shops, automotive
333991	Paint spray guns, handheld pneumatic, manufacturing
333912	Paint sprayers (i.e., compressor and spray gun unit) manufacturing
332999	Paint sticks, metal, manufacturing
326199	Paint sticks, plastics, manufacturing
321999	Paint sticks, wood, manufacturing
444120	Paint stores
325510	Paint thinner and reducer preparations manufacturing
325510	Paintbrush cleaners manufacturing
339994	Paintbrushes manufacturing
422950	Paintbrushes wholesaling
422950	Painter's supplies (except artist's, turpentine) wholesaling
711510	Painters (i.e., artists), independent
332812	Painting metals and metal products for the trade
711510	Painting restorers, independent
235210	Painting, exterior (except roof) and interior, construction contractors
235610	Painting, roof, construction contractors
325510	Paints (except artist's) manufacturing
422950	Paints (except artist's) wholesaling
339942	Paints, artist's, manufacturing
422990	Paints, artist's, wholesaling
325510	Paints, emulsion (i.e., latex paint), manufacturing
325510	Paints, oil and alkyd vehicle, manufacturing
315192	Pajamas made in apparel knitting mills
315291	Pajamas, infants', cut and sewn from purchased fabric (except apparel contractors)
315211	Pajamas, men's and boys', cut and sew apparel contractors
315221	Pajamas, men's and boys', cut and sewn from purchased fabric (except apparel contractors)

Code	Description
315231	Pajamas, women's and girls', cut and sewn from purchased fabric (except apparel contractors)
315212	Pajamas, women's, girls', and infants', cut and sew apparel contractors
339942	Palettes, artist's, manufacturing
212299	Palladium mining and/or beneficiating
321920	Pallet containers, wood or wood and metal combination, manufacturing
333924	Pallet movers manufacturing
333924	Pallet or skid jacks manufacturing
332999	Pallet parts, metal, manufacturing
321920	Pallet parts, wood, manufacturing
532490	Pallet rental or leasing
421830	Pallets and skids wholesaling
322211	Pallets, corrugated and solid fiber, made from purchased paper or paperboard
332999	Pallets, metal, manufacturing
321920	Pallets, wood or wood and metal combination, manufacturing
812990	Palm reading services
311225	Palm-kernel oil made from purchased oils
311223	Palm-kernel oil, cake, and meal made in crushing mills
325199	Palmitic acid esters and amines manufacturing
323121	Pamphlet binding without printing
511130	Pamphlet publishers
511130	Pamphlet publishers and printing combined
511130	Pamphlet publishing (i.e., establishments known as publishers)
323117	Pamphlets printing and binding without publishing
323117	Pamphlets printing without publishing
422920	Pamphlets wholesaling
315991	Panama hats cut and sewn from purchased fabric (except apparel contractors)
315211	Panama hats, men's and boys', cut and sew apparel contractors
315212	Panama hats, women's, girls', and infants', cut and sew apparel contractors
311822	Pancake mixes made from purchased flour
311999	Pancake syrups (except pure maple) manufacturing
311412	Pancakes, frozen, manufacturing
321918	Panel work, wood millwork, manufacturing
334513	Panelboard indicators, recorders, and controllers, receiver industrial process-type, manufacturing
335313	Panelboards, electric power distribution, manufacturing
421610	Panelboards, electric power distribution, wholesaling
235510	Paneling construction contractors
421310	Paneling wholesaling
335313	Panels, generator control and metering, manufacturing
321211	Panels, hardwood plywood, manufacturing
332311	Panels, prefabricated metal building, manufacturing
321992	Panels, prefabricated wood building, manufacturing
321212	Panels, softwood plywood, manufacturing
315192	Panties made in apparel knitting mills
315291	Panties, infants', cut and sewn from purchased fabric (except apparel contractors)
315212	Panties, women's and girls', cut and sew apparel contractors
315231	Panties, women's, misses', and girls', cut and sewn from purchased fabric (except apparel contractors)
315239	Pants outfits (except pantsuits), women's, misses', and girls', cut and sewn from purchased fabric (except apparel contractors)
315212	Pants outfits, women's, girls', and infants', cut and sew apparel contractors
315211	Pants, althletic, men's and boys', cut and sew apparel contractors
315291	Pants, athletic, infants', cut and sewn from purchased fabric (except apparel contractors)
315191	Pants, athletic, made in apparel knitting mills
315228	Pants, athletic, men's and boys' (e.g., gymnastic, ski), cut and sewn from purchased fabric (except apparel contractors)
315212	Pants, athletic, women's, girls', and infants', cut and sew apparel contractors
315239	Pants, athletic, women's, misses', and girls', cut and sewn from purchased fabric (except apparel contractors)
315211	Pants, dress, men's and boys', cut and sew apparel contractors
315224	Pants, dress, men's and boys', cut and sewn from purchased fabric (except apparel contractors)
315291	Pants, infants' waterproof, cut and sewn from purchased fabric (except apparel contractors)
315212	Pants, infants', cut and sew apparel contractors
315291	Pants, infants', cut and sewn from purchased fabric (except apparel contractors)
315292	Pants, leather (except apparel contractors), manufacturing
315211	Pants, leather, men's and boys', cut and sew apparel contractors
315211	Pants, men's and boys', cut and sew apparel contractors
315191	Pants, outerwear, made in apparel knitting mills
315299	Pants, rubber and rubberized fabric, made in the same establishment as the basic material
315291	Pants, sweat, infant's, cut and sewn from purchased fabric (except apparel contractors)
315228	Pants, sweat, men's and boys', cut and sewn from purchased fabric (except apparel contractors)
315212	Pants, sweat, women's, girls', and infants', cut and sew apparel contractors

Code	Description
315239	Pants, sweat, women's, misses', and girls', cut and sewn from purchased fabric (except apparel contractors)
315211	Pants, unisex sweat, cut and sew apparel contractors
315228	Pants, unisex sweat, cut and sewn from purchased fabric (except apparel contractors)
315299	Pants, vulcanized rubber, manufacturing
315299	Pants, waterproof outerwear (except infants'), cut and sewn from purchased fabric (except apparel contractors)
315211	Pants, waterproof outerwear, men's and boys', cut and sew apparel contractors
315212	Pants, waterproof outerwear, women's, girls', and infants', cut and sew apparel contractors
315212	Pants, women's, girls', and infants', cut and sew apparel contractors
315239	Pants, women's, misses', and girls', cut and sewn from purchased fabric (except apparel contractors)
315211	Pants, work (except dungarees, jeans), men's and boys', cut and sew apparel contractors
315225	Pants, work (except dungarees, jeans), men's and boys', cut and sewn from purchased fabric (except apparel contractors)
315291	Pantsuits, infants', cut and sewn from purchased fabric (except apparel contractors)
315212	Pantsuits, women's, girls', and infants', cut and sew apparel contractors
315234	Pantsuits, women's, misses', and girls', cut and sewn from purchased fabric (except apparel contractors)
315212	Panty girdles cut and sew apparel contractors
315231	Panty girdles, women's, misses', and girls', cut and sewn from purchased fabric (except apparel contractors)
315111	Panty hose, women's and girls', knitting or knitting and finishing
111339	Papaya farming

Code	Description
327910	Paper (e.g., aluminum oxide, emery, garnet, silicon carbide), abrasive coated, made from purchased paper
422110	Paper (e.g., fine, printing, writing), bulk, wholesaling
322121	Paper (except newsprint, uncoated groundwood) manufacturing
322121	Paper (except newsprint, uncoated groundwood) products made in paper mills
322121	Paper (except newsprint, uncoated groundwood), coated, laminated or treated, made in paper mills
422130	Paper (except office supplies, printing paper, stationery, writing paper) wholesaling
333291	Paper and paperboard coating and finishing machinery manufacturing
333291	Paper and paperboard converting machinery manufacturing
333291	Paper and paperboard corrugating machinery manufacturing
333291	Paper and paperboard cutting and folding machinery manufacturing
333291	Paper and paperboard die-cutting and stamping machinery manufacturing
421830	Paper and pulp industries manufacturing machinery wholesaling
333291	Paper bag making machinery manufacturing
422130	Paper bags wholesaling
322223	Paper bags, coated, made from purchased paper
322224	Paper bags, uncoated, made from purchased paper
212324	Paper clay mining and/or beneficiating
332618	Paper clips made from purchased wire
331222	Paper clips, iron or steel, made in wire drawing plants
322215	Paper cups made from purchased paper or paperboard
339942	Paper cutters, office-type, manufacturing

Code	Description
322299	Paper dishes (e.g., cups, plates) made from purchased molded pulp
322215	Paper dishes (e.g., cups, plates) made from purchased paper or paperboard
315212	Paper dresses, women's, girls', and infants', cut and sew apparel contractors
315233	Paper dresses, women's, misses', and girls', cut and sewn from purchased fabric (except apparel contractors)
313221	Paper fabric, narrow woven, weaving
313210	Paper fabrics, broadwoven, weaving
235210	Paper hanging or removal construction contractors
332618	Paper machine wire cloth made from purchased wire
333291	Paper making machinery manufacturing
811310	Paper making machinery repair and maintenance services
322121	Paper mills (except newsprint, uncoated groundwood paper mills)
322122	Paper mills, newsprint
322122	Paper mills, uncoated groundwood
322291	Paper napkins and tablecloths made from purchased paper
322299	Paper novelties made from purchased paper
322215	Paper plates made from purchased paper or paperboard
322299	Paper products (except office supply), die-cut, made from purchased paper or paperboard
322231	Paper products, die-cut office supply, made from purchased paper or paperboard
233310	Paper pulp mill construction
332992	Paper shells (i.e., 30 mm. or less, 1.18 inch or less) manufacturing
322121	Paper stock for conversion into paper products (e.g., bag and sack stock, envelope stock, tissue stock, wallpaper stock) manufacturing

Code	Description
322291	Paper towels made from purchased paper
322121	Paper towels made in paper mills
313111	Paper yarn manufacturing
322121	Paper, asphalt, made in paper mills
421390	Paper, building, wholesaling
339944	Paper, carbon, manufacturing
322211	Paper, corrugated, made from purchased paper or paperboard
322122	Paper, newsprint and uncoated groundwood, manufacturing
422120	Paper, office (e.g., carbon, computer, copier, typewriter), wholesaling
325992	Paper, photographic sensitized, manufacturing
421930	Paper, scrap, wholesaling
339944	Paper, stencil, manufacturing
322130	Paperboard (e.g., can/drum stock, container board, corrugating medium, folding carton stock, linerboard, tube) manufacturing
422130	Paperboard and paperboard products (except office supplies) wholesaling
333291	Paperboard box making machinery manufacturing
322130	Paperboard coating, laminating, or treating in paperboard mills
333291	Paperboard making machinery manufacturing
322130	Paperboard mills
322130	Paperboard products (e.g., containers) made in paperboard mills
322226	Paperboard, pasted, lined, laminated, or surface coated, made from purchased paperboard
327999	Papier-mache statuary and related art goods (e.g., urns, vases) manufacturing
713990	Para sailing, recreational
314999	Parachutes manufacturing
213112	Paraffin services, oil and gas field, on a contract basis
324110	Paraffin waxes made in petroleum refineries
325110	Paraffins made from refined petroleum or liquid hydrocarbons
541199	Paralegal services
321213	Parallel strand lumber manufacturing
621399	Paramedics' offices (e.g., centers, clinics)
325132	Pararosaniline dyes manufacturing
621511	Parasitology health laboratories
339999	Parasols manufacturing
325320	Parathion insecticides manufacturing
485991	Paratransit transportation services
561431	Parcel mailing services combined with one or more other office support services, private
561431	Parcel mailing services, private
333997	Parcel post scales manufacturing
316110	Parchment leather manufacturing
922150	Pardon boards and offices
813410	Parent-teachers' associations
624190	Parenting support services
325320	Paris green insecticides manufacturing
234990	Park construction
922120	Park police
332812	Parkerizing metals and metal products for the trade
812930	Parking garages, automobile
561790	Parking lot cleaning (e.g., power sweeping, washing) services
235710	Parking lot construction contractors
812930	Parking lots, automobile
334514	Parking meters manufacturing
561612	Parking security services
488119	Parking services, aircraft
812930	Parking services, valet
233320	Parking structure construction
713110	Parks (e.g., theme, water), amusement
924120	Parks and recreation commission, government
712190	Parks, national
712190	Parks, nature
712130	Parks, wild animal
234110	Parkway construction
611310	Parochial schools, college level
611110	Parochial schools, elementary or secondary
922150	Parole offices
321918	Parquet flooring, hardwood, manufacturing
321918	Parquetry, hardwood, manufacturing
111219	Parsley farming, field, bedding plant and seed production
111219	Parsnip farming, field, bedding plant and seed production
335999	Particle accelerators, high voltage, manufacturing
334516	Particle beam excitation instruments, laboratory-type, manufacturing
334516	Particle size analyzers manufacturing
321219	Particleboard manufacturing
421310	Particleboard wholesaling
337215	Partitions for floor attachment, prefabricated, manufacturing
421440	Partitions wholesaling
322211	Partitions, corrugated and solid fiber, made from purchased paper or paperboard
337215	Partitions, freestanding, prefabricated, manufacturing
332323	Partitions, ornamental metal, manufacturing
441310	Parts and accessories dealers, automotive
421120	Parts, new, motor vehicle, wholesaling
421140	Parts, used, motor vehicle, wholesaling
532299	Party (i.e., banquet) equipment rental
454390	Party plan merchandisers, direct selling
812990	Party planning services
532299	Party rental supply centers
481211	Passenger air transportation, nonscheduled
481111	Passenger air transportation, scheduled

Code	Description
233320	Passenger and freight terminal building construction
333922	Passenger baggage belt loaders (except industrial truck) manufacturing
532112	Passenger car leasing
532111	Passenger car rental
481211	Passenger carriers, air, nonscheduled
481111	Passenger carriers, air, scheduled
485320	Passenger limousine rental with driver (except shuttle service, taxi)
482111	Passenger railways, line-haul
336611	Passenger ship building
483114	Passenger transportation, coastal or Great Lakes
483114	Passenger transportation, deep sea, to and from domestic ports
483112	Passenger transportation, deep sea, to or from foreign ports
483212	Passenger transportation, inland waters (except on Great Lakes system)
532112	Passenger van leasing
532111	Passenger van rental
532111	Passenger van rental agencies
485320	Passenger van rental with driver (except shuttle service, taxi)
532112	Passenger vehicle fleet leasing
111339	Passion fruit farming
928120	Passport issuing services
541921	Passport photography services
311422	Pasta based products canning
333294	Pasta making machinery (i.e., food manufacturing-type) manufacturing
311999	Pasta mixes made from purchased dry ingredients
311823	Pasta, dry, manufacturing
311991	Pasta, fresh, manufacturing
331314	Paste made from purchased aluminum
331423	Paste made from purchased copper
331221	Paste made from purchased iron or steel
331111	Paste, iron or steel, made in steel mills

Code	Description
331492	Paste, nonferrous metals (except aluminum, copper), made from purchased metal
325520	Pastes, adhesive, manufacturing
311421	Pastes, fruit and vegetable, canning
333294	Pasteurizing equipment, food, manufacturing
311511	Pasteurizing milk
311612	Pastrami made from purchased carcasses
311812	Pastries (e.g., Danish, French), fresh, made in commercial bakeries
311813	Pastries (e.g., Danish, French), frozen, manufacturing
311822	Pastries, uncooked, manufacturing
321999	Pastry boards, wood, manufacturing
541199	Patent agent services (i.e., patent filing and searching services)
541110	Patent attorneys' offices
541110	Patent attorneys' private practices
541990	Patent broker services (i.e., patent marketing services)
533110	Patent buying and licensing
533110	Patent leasing
316110	Patent leather manufacturing
325412	Patent medicine preparations manufacturing
621511	Pathological analysis laboratories
621111	Pathologists' (except oral, speech, voice) offices (e.g., centers, clinics)
621111	Pathologists', forensic, offices (e.g., centers, clinics)
621111	Pathologists', neuropathological, offices (e.g., centers, clinics)
621210	Pathologists', oral, offices (e.g., centers, clinics)
621340	Pathologists', speech or voice, offices (e.g., centers, clinics)
621111	Pathologists', surgical, offices (e.g., centers, clinics)
621511	Pathology laboratories, medical
334510	Patient monitoring equipment (e.g., intensive care, coronary care unit) manufacturing
421450	Patient monitoring equipment wholesaling
327331	Patio block, concrete, manufacturing

Code	Description
235710	Patio construction contractors
336611	Patrol boat building
561612	Patrol services, security
541990	Patrolling (i.e., visual inspection) of electric transmission or gas lines
511199	Pattern and plan (e.g., clothing patterns) publishers
511199	Pattern and plan (e.g., clothing patterns) publishers and printing combined
332997	Patterns (except shoe), industrial, manufacturing
421830	Patterns (except shoe), industrial, wholesaling
323112	Patterns and plans (e.g., clothing patterns) flexographic printing without publishing
323111	Patterns and plans (e.g., clothing patterns) gravure printing without publishing
323110	Patterns and plans (e.g., clothing patterns) lithographic (offset) printing without publishing
323119	Patterns and plans (e.g., clothing patterns) printing (except flexographic, gravure, lithographic, screen) without publishing
511199	Patterns and plans (e.g., clothing patterns) publishing (i.e., establishments known as publishers)
323113	Patterns and plans (e.g., clothing patterns) screen printing without publishing
339999	Patterns, shoe, manufacturing
421850	Patterns, shoe, wholesaling
212399	Pavers mining and/or beneficiating
324121	Paving blocks and mixtures made from purchased asphaltic materials
327331	Paving blocks, concrete, manufacturing
327121	Paving brick, clay, manufacturing
234110	Paving construction contractors
333120	Paving machinery manufacturing
522298	Pawnshops
812990	Pay telephone equipment concession operators
513210	Pay television networks

Code	Description
541214	Payroll processing services
111219	Pea (except dry) farming, field and seed production
111130	Pea farming, dry, field and seed production
928120	Peace Corps
813319	Peace advocacy organizations
111339	Peach farming
325132	Peacock blue lake manufacturing
311911	Peanut butter blended with jelly manufacturing
311911	Peanut butter manufacturing
311223	Peanut cake, meal, and oil made in crushing mills
333111	Peanut combines (i.e., diggers, packers, threshers) manufacturing
111992	Peanut farming
311225	Peanut oil made from purchased oils
333294	Peanut roasting machines (i.e., food manufacturing-type) manufacturing
115114	Peanut shelling
115113	Peanut, machine harvesting
111339	Pear farming
339913	Pearl drilling, peeling, or sawing
325131	Pearl essence pigment, synthetic, manufacturing
331511	Pearlitic castings, malleable iron, unfinished, manufacturing
421940	Pearls wholesaling
339914	Pearls, costume, manufacturing
212399	Peat grinding
212399	Peat humus mining and/or beneficiating
212399	Peat mining and/or beneficiating
327999	Peat pots, molded pulp, manufacturing
212321	Pebbles (except grinding) mining and/or beneficiating
212399	Pebbles grinding
111335	Pecan farming
115114	Pecan hulling and shelling
311942	Pectin manufacturing
621111	Pediatricians' (except mental health) offices (e.g., centers, clinics)

Code	Description
621112	Pediatricians', mental health, offices (e.g., centers, clinics)
812113	Pedicure and manicure salons
812113	Pedicurist services
115210	Pedigree (i.e., livestock, pets, poultry) record services
334514	Pedometers manufacturing
813920	Peer review boards
212325	Pegmatite, feldspar, mining and/or beneficiating
316999	Pegs, leather shoe, manufacturing
332994	Pellet guns manufacturing
333131	Pellet mills machinery, mining-type, manufacturing
332992	Pellets, air rifle and pistol, manufacturing
316110	Pelts bleaching, currying, dyeing, scraping, and tanning
422590	Pelts, raw, wholesaling
339112	Pelvimeters manufacturing
339941	Pen refills and cartridges manufacturing
339942	Pencil leads manufacturing
339942	Pencil sharpeners manufacturing
321999	Pencil slats, wood, manufacturing
339942	Pencils (except mechanical) manufacturing
422120	Pencils wholesaling
339941	Pencils, mechanical, manufacturing
335122	Pendant lamps (except residential), electric, manufacturing
335121	Pendant lamps fixtures, residential electric, manufacturing
325613	Penetrants manufacturing
325998	Penetrating fluids, synthetic, manufacturing
325412	Penicillin preparations manufacturing
325411	Penicillin, uncompounded, manufacturing
922140	Penitentiaries
212113	Pennsylvania anthracite mining and/or beneficiating
339941	Pens manufacturing
422120	Pens, writing, wholesaling
523920	Pension fund managing

Code	Description
524292	Pension fund, third party administrative services
525110	Pension funds
525110	Pension plans (e.g., employee benefit, retirement)
332313	Penstocks, fabricated metal plate, manufacturing
325192	Pentachlorophenol manufacturing
325199	Pentaerythritol manufacturing
325110	Pentanes made from refined petroleum or liquid hydrocarbons
325110	Pentanes made from refined petroleum or liquid hydrocarbons
325920	Pentolite explosive materials manufacturing
111219	Pepper (e.g., bell, chili, green, hot, red, sweet) farming
311942	Pepper (i.e., spice) manufacturing
325998	Peppermint oil manufacturing
313210	Percales weaving
114111	Perch fishing
325188	Perchloric acid manufacturing
325199	Perchloroethylene manufacturing
335211	Percolators, household-type electric, manufacturing
332992	Percussion caps (i.e., 30 mm. or less, 1.18 inch or less), ammunition, manufacturing
339992	Percussion musical instruments manufacturing
213112	Perforating oil and gas well casings on a contract basis
711510	Performers (i.e., entertainers), independent
711510	Performing artists, independent
711310	Performing arts center operators
611610	Performing arts schools (except academic)
325199	Perfume materials (i.e., basic synthetic chemicals, such as terpineol) manufacturing
446120	Perfume stores
325620	Perfumes manufacturing
422210	Perfumes wholesaling
511120	Periodical publishers

Code	Description
511120	Periodical publishers and printing combined
511120	Periodical publishing (i.e., establishments known as publishers)
323112	Periodicals flexographic printing without publishing
323111	Periodicals gravure printing without publishing
323110	Periodicals lithographic (offset) printing without publishing
323119	Periodicals printing (except flexographic, gravure, lithographic, screen) without publishing
323113	Periodicals screen printing without publishing
422920	Periodicals wholesaling
621210	Periodontists' offices (e.g., centers, clinics)
334418	Peripheral controller boards manufacturing
421430	Peripheral equipment, computer, wholesaling
333314	Periscopes manufacturing
327992	Perlite aggregates manufacturing
212399	Perlite mining and/or beneficiating
327992	Perlite, expanded, manufacturing
331524	Permanent mold castings, aluminum, unfinished, manufacturing
331525	Permanent mold castings, copper, unfinished, manufacturing
331528	Permanent mold castings, nonferrous metal (except alumninum, copper), unfinished, manufacturing
325620	Permanent wave preparations manufacturing
325188	Peroxides, inorganic, manufacturing
325199	Peroxides, organic, manufacturing
325132	Persian orange lake manufacturing
111339	Persimmon farming
513322	Personal communication services (PCS) (i.e., communication carriers)
334418	Personal computer modems manufacturing
334111	Personal computers manufacturing

Code	Description
522291	Personal credit institutions (i.e., unsecured cash loans)
525920	Personal estates (i.e., managing assets)
522291	Personal finance companies (i.e., unsecured cash loans)
551112	Personal holding companies
525920	Personal investment trusts
523991	Personal investments trust administration
523920	Personal investments trusts, managing
316993	Personal leather goods (e.g., coin purses, eyeglass cases, key cases), small, manufacturing
561612	Personal protection services (except security systems services)
339113	Personal safety devices, not specified elsewhere, manufacturing
422130	Personal sanitary paper products wholesaling
812990	Personal shopping services
525920	Personal trusts
441221	Personal watercraft dealers
336999	Personal watercraft manufacturing
532292	Personal watercraft rental
561320	Personnel (e.g., industrial, office) suppliers
813920	Personnel management associations
541612	Personnel management consulting services
921190	Personnel offices, government
325320	Pest (e.g., ant, rat, roach, rodent) control poison manufacturing
561710	Pest control (except agricultural, forestry) services
926140	Pest control programs, agriculture, government
115112	Pest control services, agricultural
115310	Pest control services, forestry
422690	Pesticides (except agricultural) wholesaling
325320	Pesticides manufacturing
422910	Pesticides, agricultural, wholesaling
812910	Pet boarding services
812220	Pet cemeteries
311119	Pet food (except cat, dog) manufacturing

Code	Description
422490	Pet food wholesaling
311111	Pet food, dog and cat, manufacturing
812910	Pet grooming services
524128	Pet health insurance carriers, direct
541940	Pet hospitals
926150	Pet licensing
453910	Pet shops
812910	Pet sitting services
422990	Pet supplies (except pet food) wholesaling
453910	Pet supply stores
812910	Pet training services
324110	Petrochemical feedstocks made in petroleum refineries
234930	Petrochemical plant construction
324110	Petrochemicals made in petroleum refineries
422710	Petroleum and petroleum products bulk stations and terminals
422720	Petroleum and petroleum products wholesaling (except bulk stations, terminals)
422720	Petroleum brokers
324110	Petroleum coke made in petroleum refineries
324110	Petroleum cracking and reforming
324110	Petroleum distillation
541330	Petroleum engineering services
211112	Petroleum gases, liquefied, recovering from oil and gas field gases
324199	Petroleum jelly made from refined petroleum
324110	Petroleum jelly made in petroleum refineries
324191	Petroleum lubricating oils made from refined petroleum
324110	Petroleum lubricating oils made in petroleum refineries
486110	Petroleum pipelines, crude
486910	Petroleum pipelines, refined
325211	Petroleum polymer resins manufacturing
324110	Petroleum refineries
234930	Petroleum refinery construction
333298	Petroleum refining machinery manufacturing

Code	Description
332420	Petroleum storage tanks, heavy gauge metal, manufacturing
324199	Petroleum waxes made from refined petroleum
211111	Petroleum, crude, production (i.e., extraction)
422990	Pets wholesaling
712130	Petting zoos
337127	Pews, church, manufacturing
339912	Pewter ware manufacturing
233310	Pharmaceutical manufacturing plant construction
325412	Pharmaceutical preparations (e.g., capsules, liniments, ointments, tablets) manufacturing
422210	Pharmaceuticals wholesaling
446110	Pharmacies
813920	Pharmacists' associations
334515	Phase angle meters manufacturing
335312	Phase converters (i.e., electrical equipment) manufacturing
112390	Pheasant production
325192	Phenol manufacturing
325211	Phenol-formaldehyde resins manufacturing
325211	Phenol-furfural resins manufacturing
325211	Phenolic resins manufacturing
325211	Phenoxy resins manufacturing
813211	Philanthropic trusts, awarding grants
212399	Phlogopite mining and/or beneficiating
334510	Phonocardiographs manufacturing
334612	Phonograph records manufacturing
421990	Phonograph records wholesaling
421440	Phonographs, coin-operated, wholesaling
325199	Phosgene manufacturing
212392	Phosphate rock mining and/or beneficiating
325312	Phosphatic fertilizer materials manufacturing
325314	Phosphatic fertilizers made by mixing purchased materials
325132	Phosphomolybdic acid lakes and toners manufacturing

Code	Description
325199	Phosphoric acid esters manufacturing
325312	Phosphoric acid manufacturing
325188	Phosphorus compounds, not specified elsewhere by process, manufacturing
325188	Phosphorus oxychloride manufacturing
325132	Phosphotungstic acid lakes and toners manufacturing
323118	Photo albums and refills manufacturing
422120	Photo albums wholesaling
421410	Photo finishing equipment wholesaling
711510	Photo journalists, independent (freelance)
323122	Photocomposition services, for the printing trade
422120	Photocopy supplies wholesaling
811212	Photocopying machine repair and maintenance services without retailing new photocopy machines
333315	Photocopying machines manufacturing
561439	Photocopying services (except combined with printing services)
325992	Photocopying toner cartridges manufacturing
334413	Photoelectric cells, solid-state (e.g., electronic eye), manufacturing
333293	Photoengraving machinery manufacturing
323122	Photoengraving plate preparation services
812921	Photofinishing labs (except one-hour)
812922	Photofinishing labs, one-hour
812921	Photofinishing services (except one-hour)
812922	Photofinishing services, one-hour
335110	Photoflash and photoflood lamp bulbs and tubes manufacturing
333315	Photoflash equipment manufacturing
541370	Photogrammetric mapping services
322299	Photograph folders, mats, and mounts manufacturing

Code	Description
541922	Photographers specializing in aerial photography
711510	Photographers, independent artistic
325992	Photographic chemicals manufacturing
333315	Photographic equipment (except lenses) manufacturing
421410	Photographic equipment and supplies wholesaling
532210	Photographic equipment rental
811211	Photographic equipment repair shops without retailing new photographic equipment
325992	Photographic film, cloth, paper, and plate, sensitized, manufacturing
333314	Photographic lenses manufacturing
812990	Photographic machine concession operators, coin-operated
443130	Photographic supply stores
326113	Photographic, micrographic, and X-ray plastics, sheet, and film (except sensitized), manufacturing
611610	Photography schools, art
611519	Photography schools, commercial
541922	Photography services, commercial
541921	Photography services, portrait (e.g., still, video)
541922	Photography studios, commercial
541921	Photography studios, portrait
327212	Photomask blanks, glass, made in glass making plants
325992	Photomasks manufacturing
334516	Photometers (except photographic exposure meters) manufacturing
334516	Photonexcitation analyzers manufacturing
325992	Photosensitized paper manufacturing
323122	Phototypesetting services
334413	Photovoltaic devices, solid-state, manufacturing
812990	Phrenology services
325199	Phthalate acid manufacturing
325211	Phthalic alkyd resins manufacturing
325192	Phthalic anhydride manufacturing
325211	Phthalic anhydride resins manufacturing

Code	Description
325132	Phthalocyanine pigments manufacturing
541614	Physical distribution consulting services
621340	Physical equestrian therapeutists' offices (e.g., centers, clinics)
713940	Physical fitness centers
621999	Physical fitness evaluation services (except by offices of health practitioners)
713940	Physical fitness facilities
713940	Physical fitness studios
334519	Physical properties testing and inspection equipment manufacturing
622310	Physical rehabilitation hospitals
541710	Physical science research and development laboratories or services
621340	Physical therapists' offices (e.g., centers, clinics)
621340	Physical therapy offices (e.g., centers, clinics)
621340	Physical-integration practitioners' offices (e.g., centers, clinics)
621111	Physicians' (except mental health) offices (e.g., centers, clinics)
621399	Physicians' assistants' offices (e.g., centers, clinics)
621112	Physicians', mental health, offices (e.g., centers, clinics)
541690	Physics consulting services
541710	Physics research and development laboratories or services
621340	Physiotherapists' offices (e.g., centers, clinics)
339112	Physiotherapy equipment (except electrotherapeutic) manufacturing
325411	Physostigmine and derivatives (i.e., basic chemicals) manufacturing
332510	Piano hardware, metal, manufacturing
339992	Piano parts and materials (except piano hardware) manufacturing
532299	Piano rental
451140	Piano stores
339992	Piccolos and parts manufacturing

Code	Description
336112	Pick-up trucks, light duty, assembling on chassis of own manufacture
333292	Picker machinery for textiles manufacturing
333292	Picker sticks for looms manufacturing
311712	Picking crab meat
333516	Picklers and pickling machinery, metalworking, manufacturing
311421	Pickles manufacturing
311421	Pickling fruits and vegetables
332813	Pickling metals and metal products for the trade
332212	Picks (i.e., handtools) manufacturing
812320	Pickup and drop-off sites for drycleaners and laundries
336214	Pickup canopies, caps, or covers manufacturing
713990	Picnic grounds
326199	Picnic jugs, plastics (except foam), manufacturing
325920	Picric acid explosive materials manufacturing
334511	Pictorial situation instrumentation manufacturing
442299	Picture frame shops, custom
311822	Pie crust shells, uncooked, made from purchased flour
422310	Piece goods (except burlap, felt) wholesaling
451130	Piece goods stores
422990	Piece goods, burlap and felt, wholesaling
234990	Pier construction
531120	Piers and associated building rental or leasing
713110	Piers, amusement
422420	Pies (e.g., fruit, meat, poultry), frozen, wholesaling
311812	Pies, fresh, made in commercial bakeries
311812	Pies, frozen, manufacturing
334419	Piezoelectric crystals manufacturing
334419	Piezoelectric devices manufacturing
112210	Pig farming

Code	Description
331111	Pig iron manufacturing
421510	Pig iron wholesaling
311612	Pig's feet, cooked and pickled, made from purchased carcasses
325132	Pigment, scarlet lake, manufacturing
325132	Pigments (except animal black, bone black), organic, manufacturing
325131	Pigments (except bone black, carbon black, lamp black), inorganic, manufacturing
212393	Pigments, natural, mineral, mining and/or beneficiating
422950	Pigments, paint, wholesaling
114111	Pilchard fishing
313249	Pile fabrics made in warp knitting mills
313241	Pile fabrics made in weft knitting mills
332313	Pile shells, fabricated metal plate, manufacturing
332322	Pile shells, sheet metal, manufacturing
333120	Pile-driving equipment manufacturing
235930	Piling (i.e., bored, cast-in-place, drilled) construction contractors
321114	Pilings, foundation and marine construction, treating
331111	Pilings, iron or steel plain sheet, made in steel mills
321114	Pilings, round wood, cutting and treating
321114	Pilings, wood, treating
332991	Pillow blocks with ball or roller bearings manufacturing
812320	Pillow cleaning services
314129	Pillowcases, bed, made from purchased fabrics
314129	Pillows, bed, made from purchased materials
488490	Pilot car services (i.e., wide load warning services)
488330	Piloting services, water transportation
713120	Pinball arcades

Code	Description
713990	Pinball machine concession operators (i.e., supplying and servicing in others' facilities)
339999	Pinball machines, coin-operated, manufacturing
113210	Pine gum extracting
325191	Pine oil manufacturing
111339	Pineapple farming
325191	Pinene manufacturing
713990	Ping pong parlors
212325	Pinite mining and/or beneficiating
339993	Pins (except precious) manufacturing
339911	Pins and brooches, precious metal, manufacturing
712120	Pioneer villages
331210	Pipe (e.g., heavy riveted, lock joint, seamless, welded) made from purchased iron or steel
332996	Pipe and pipe fittings made from purchased metal pipe
331511	Pipe and pipe fittings, cast iron, manufacturing
333516	Pipe and tube rolling mill machinery, metalworking, manufacturing
332323	Pipe bannisters, metal, manufacturing
326299	Pipe bits and stems, tobacco, hard rubber, manufacturing
339999	Pipe cleaners manufacturing
332996	Pipe couplings made from purchased metal pipe
331511	Pipe couplings, cast iron, manufacturing
333512	Pipe cutting and threading machines, metalworking, manufacturing
332996	Pipe fabricating (i.e., bending, cutting, threading) made from purchased metal pipe
326122	Pipe fittings, rigid plastics, manufacturing
332323	Pipe guards, metal, manufacturing
332999	Pipe hangers and supports, metal, manufacturing
332996	Pipe headers made from purchased metal pipe

Code	Description
331316	Pipe made by extruding purchased aluminum
332323	Pipe railings, metal, manufacturing
325520	Pipe sealing compounds manufacturing
213112	Pipe testing services, oil and gas field, on a contract basis
422940	Pipe tobacco wholesaling
312229	Pipe tobacco, prepared, manufacturing
331316	Pipe, aluminum, made in integrated secondary smelting and extruding mills
327332	Pipe, concrete, manufacturing
331421	Pipe, extruded and drawn, brass, bronze, and copper, made from purchased copper or in integrated secondary smelting and rolling, drawing or extruding plants
332313	Pipe, fabricated metal plate, manufacturing
331111	Pipe, iron or steel, made in steel mills
421510	Pipe, metal, wholesaling
331491	Pipe, nonferrous metals (except aluminum, copper), made from purchased metals or scrap
326122	Pipe, rigid plastics, manufacturing
332322	Pipe, sheet metal, manufacturing
513112	Piped-in music services, radio transmitted
234920	Pipelaying construction contractors
234910	Pipeline (e.g., gas, oil, sewer, water) construction
234910	Pipeline (e.g., gas, oil, water, sewer) construction management
213112	Pipeline construction on oil and gas lease gathering lines to point of distribution on a contract basis
541990	Pipeline inspection (i.e., visual) services
421830	Pipeline machinery and equipment wholesaling
234910	Pipeline rehabilitation construction contractors
488999	Pipeline terminal facilities, independently operated

Code	Description
486990	Pipeline transportation (except crude oil, natural gas, refined petroleum products)
486110	Pipeline transportation, crude oil
486910	Pipeline transportation, gasoline and other refined petroleum products
486210	Pipeline transportation, natural gas
234910	Pipeline wrapping construction contractors
339992	Pipes, organ, manufacturing
339999	Pipes, smoker's, manufacturing
212399	Pipestones mining and/or beneficiating
111335	Pistachio farming
332994	Pistols manufacturing
336311	Pistons and piston rings manufacturing
421830	Pistons, hydraulic and pneumatic, wholesaling
325192	Pitch made by distillation of coal tar
324122	Pitch, roofing, made from purchased asphaltic materials
325191	Pitch, wood, manufacturing
212291	Pitchblende mining and/or beneficiating
334519	Pitometers manufacturing
325411	Pituitary gland derivatives, uncompounded, manufacturing
325412	Pituitary gland preparations manufacturing
722211	Pizza delivery shops
311822	Pizza doughs made from purchased flour
722110	Pizza parlors, full service
722211	Pizza parlors, limited service
422490	Pizzas (except frozen) wholesaling
311991	Pizzas, fresh, manufacturing
311412	Pizzas, frozen, manufacturing
422420	Pizzas, frozen, wholesaling
722110	Pizzerias, full service
722211	Pizzerias, limited-service (e.g., take-out)
314129	Placemats, all materials, made from purchased materials

Code	Description
561310	Placement agencies or services, employment
621991	Placenta banks
212221	Placer gold mining and/or beneficiating
212222	Placer silver mining and/or beneficiating
813110	Places of worship
334417	Planar cable connectors manufacturing
333210	Planers woodworking-type, stationary, manufacturing
333120	Planers, bituminous, manufacturing
333991	Planers, handheld power-driven, manufacturing
333512	Planers, metalworking, manufacturing
332212	Planes, handheld, nonpowered, manufacturing
712110	Planetariums
321912	Planing mills (except millwork)
321918	Planing mills, millwork
321912	Planing purchased lumber
525120	Plans, health and welfare related employee benefit
525110	Plans, pension
561730	Plant and shrub maintenance in buildings
422990	Plant food wholesaling
325311	Plant foods, mixed, made in plants producing nitrogenous fertilizer materials
325312	Plant foods, mixed, made in plants producing phosphatic fertilizer materials
325320	Plant growth regulants manufacturing
561730	Plant maintenance services
111422	Plant, ornamental, growing
111422	Plant, potted flower and foliage, growing
111339	Plantain farming
115112	Planting crops
421820	Planting machinery and equipment, farm-type, wholesaling
333111	Planting machines, farm-type, manufacturing

Code	Description
333513	Plasma jet spray metal forming machines manufacturing
333512	Plasma process metal cutting machines (except welding equipment) manufacturing
333992	Plasma welding equipment manufacturing
621991	Plasmapheresis centers
325414	Plasmas manufacturing
422210	Plasmas, blood, wholesaling
327420	Plaster and plasterboard, gypsum, manufacturing
327420	Plaster of paris manufacturing
327420	Plaster of paris products (e.g., columns, statuary, urns) manufacturing
421320	Plaster wholesaling
327420	Plaster, gypsum, manufacturing
235420	Plastering (i.e., ornamental, plain) construction contractors
212325	Plastic fire clay mining and/or beneficiating
621111	Plastic surgeons' offices (e.g., centers, clinics)
325510	Plastic wood fillers manufacturing
325199	Plasticizers (i.e., basic synthetic chemicals) manufacturing
422610	Plasticizers wholesaling
337125	Plastics (including fiberglass) furniture (except upholstered), household-type, manufacturing
326220	Plastics and rubber belts and hoses (without fittings) manufacturing
325211	Plastics and synthetic resins regenerating, precipitating, and coagulating
422130	Plastics bags wholesaling
422610	Plastics basic shapes wholesaling
313320	Plastics coating of textiles and apparel
326113	Plastics film and unlaminated sheet (except packaging) manufacturing
422990	Plastics foam (except disposable) wholesaling
421840	Plastics foam packing and packaging materials wholesaling
422130	Plastics foam products, disposable (except packaging, packing), wholesaling

Code	Description
315299	Plastics gowns (except infants') cut and sewn from purchased fabric (except apparel contractors)
315291	Plastics gowns, infants', cut and sewn from purchased fabric (except apparel contractors)
315211	Plastics gowns, men's and boys', cut and sew apparel contractors
315212	Plastics gowns, women's, girls', and infants, cut and sew apparel contractors
421830	Plastics industries machinery, equipment, and supplies wholesaling
337110	Plastics laminated over particleboard (e.g., fixture tops) manufacturing
422610	Plastics materials (e.g., film, rod, shape, sheet, tubing) wholesaling
315299	Plastics rainwear cut and sewn from purchased fabric (except apparel contractors)
315211	Plastics rainwear, men's and boys', cut and sewn apparel contractors
315212	Plastics rainwear, women's, girls', and infants', cut and sew apparel contractors
325991	Plastics resins compounding from recycled materials
422610	Plastics resins wholesaling
325991	Plastics resins, custom compounding of purchased
421930	Plastics scrap wholesaling
333220	Plastics working machinery manufacturing
325510	Plastisol coating compounds manufacturing
524126	Plate glass insurance carriers, direct
421390	Plate glass wholesaling
333516	Plate rolling mill machinery, metalworking, manufacturing
332313	Plate work (e.g., bending, cutting, punching, shaping, welding), fabricated metal, manufacturing
331315	Plate, aluminum, made by continuous casting purchased aluminum
331315	Plate, aluminum, made by flat rolling purchased aluminum

Code	Description
331315	Plate, aluminum, made in integrated secondary smelting and continuous casting mills
331315	Plate, aluminum, made in integrated secondary smelting and flat rolling mills
331421	Plate, copper and copper alloy, made from purchased copper or in integrated secondary smelting and rolling, drawing or extruding plants
331111	Plate, iron or steel, made in steel mills
326130	Plate, laminated plastics, manufacturing
331491	Plate, nonferrous metals (except aluminum, copper), made from purchased metals or scrap
332211	Plated metal cutlery manufacturing
421940	Plated metal cutlery or flatware wholesaling
332211	Plated metal flatware manufacturing
332999	Plated ware (e.g., ecclesiastical ware, hollowware, toilet ware) manufacturing
335932	Plates (i.e., outlet or switch covers), face, manufacturing
322299	Plates, molded pulp, manufacturing
326140	Plates, polystyrene foam, manufacturing
332813	Plating metals and metal products for the trade
331491	Platinum and platinum alloy rolling, drawing, or extruding from purchased metals or scrap
331491	Platinum and platinum alloy sheet and tubing made from purchased metals or scrap
332999	Platinum foil and leaf not made in rolling mills
212299	Platinum mining and/or beneficiating
331492	Platinum recovering from scrap and/or alloying purchased metals
331419	Platinum refining, primary
421910	Playground equipment and supplies wholesaling
421920	Playing cards wholesaling

Code	Description
337124	Playpens, children's metal, manufacturing
337122	Playpens, children's wood, manufacturing
315291	Playsuits, infants', cut and sewn from purchased fabric (except apparel contractors)
315212	Playsuits, women's, girls', and infants', cut and sew apparel contractors
315239	Playsuits, women's, misses', and girls', cut and sewn from purchased fabric (except apparel contractors)
711510	Playwrights, independent
532292	Pleasure boat rental
336612	Pleasure boats manufacturing
421910	Pleasure boats wholesaling
315211	Pleating contractors on men's and boys' apparel
315212	Pleating contractors on women's, girls', and infants' apparel
332212	Pliers, handtools, manufacturing
327331	Plinth blocks, precast terrazzo, manufacturing
334119	Plotters, computer, manufacturing
115112	Plowing
333120	Plows, construction (e.g., excavating, grading), manufacturing
421820	Plows, farm, wholesaling
333111	Plows, farm-type, manufacturing
111422	Plug (i.e., floriculture products) growing
332911	Plug valves, industrial-type, manufacturing
213112	Plugging and abandoning wells on a contract basis
335931	Plugs, electric cord, manufacturing
332999	Plugs, magnetic metal drain, manufacturing
321999	Plugs, wood, manufacturing
111339	Plum farming
421720	Plumber's brass goods wholesaling
332212	Plumber's handtools, nonpowered, manufacturing
325520	Plumber's putty manufacturing
611513	Plumbers' apprenticeship training

Code	Description
332919	Plumbing and heating inline valves (e.g., check, cutoffs, stop) manufacturing
421720	Plumbing and heating valves wholesaling
235110	Plumbing construction contractors
532490	Plumbing equipment rental or leasing
421720	Plumbing equipment wholesaling
332913	Plumbing fittings and couplings (e.g., compression fittings, metal elbows, metal unions) manufacturing
332913	Plumbing fixture fittings and trim, all materials, manufacturing
326191	Plumbing fixtures (e.g., shower stalls, toilets, urinals), plastics or fiberglass, manufacturing
421720	Plumbing fixtures wholesaling
332998	Plumbing fixtures, metal, manufacturing
327111	Plumbing fixtures, vitreous china, manufacturing
421720	Plumbing supplies wholesaling
444190	Plumbing supply stores
421310	Plywood wholesaling
321211	Plywood, faced with nonwood materials, hardwood, manufacturing
321212	Plywood, faced with nonwood materials, softwood, manufacturing
321211	Plywood, hardwood faced, manufacturing
321211	Plywood, hardwood, manufacturing
321212	Plywood, softwood faced, manufacturing
321212	Plywood, softwood, manufacturing
332912	Pneumatic aircraft subassemblies manufacturing
334513	Pneumatic controllers, industrial process type, manufacturing
333995	Pneumatic cylinders, fluid power, manufacturing
326220	Pneumatic hose (without fittings), rubber or plastics, manufacturing
332912	Pneumatic hose fittings, fluid power, manufacturing
421830	Pneumatic pumps and parts wholesaling

Code	Description
333996	Pneumatic pumps, fluid power, manufacturing
334512	Pneumatic relays, air-conditioning type, manufacturing
333922	Pneumatic tube conveyors manufacturing
235950	Pneumatic tube system constuction contractors
332912	Pneumatic valves, fluid power, manufacturing
322231	Pocket folders made from purchased paper or paperboard
332211	Pocket knives manufacturing
339911	Pocketbooks, precious metal, manufacturing
339911	Pocketbooks, precious metal, men's, manufacturing
339911	Pocketbooks, precious metal, women's, manufacturing
315211	Pockets (e.g., coat, suit), men's and boys', cut and sew apparel contractors
315212	Pockets (e.g., coat, suit), women's, girls', and infants', cut and sew apparel contractors
621391	Podiatrists' offices (e.g., centers, clinics)
813410	Poetry clubs
711510	Poets, independent
334119	Point of sale terminals manufacturing
421420	Point of sale terminals wholesaling
334119	Pointing devices, computer peripheral equipment, manufacturing
315292	Pointing furs
339114	Points, abrasive dental, manufacturing
334516	Polariscopes manufacturing
334516	Polarizers manufacturing
334516	Polarographic equipment manufacturing
234920	Pole line construction contractors
421610	Pole line hardware wholesaling
327390	Poles, concrete, manufacturing
421510	Poles, metal, wholesaling
321114	Poles, round wood, cutting and treating

Code	Description
321113	Poles, wood, made from from log or bolts
321114	Poles, wood, treating
922120	Police academies
922120	Police and fire departments, combined
315991	Police caps and hats (except protective head gear) cut and sewn from purchased fabric (except apparel contractors)
315211	Police caps and hats (except protective head gear), men's, cut and sew apparel contractors
315212	Police caps and hats (except protective head gear), women's, cut and sew apparel contractors
922120	Police departments (except American Indian or Alaska Native)
315222	Police dress uniforms, men's, cut and sewn from purchased fabric (except apparel contractors)
315234	Police dress uniforms, women's, cut and sewn from purchased fabric (except apparel contractors)
453998	Police supply stores
611519	Police training schools
315211	Police uniforms, men's, cut and sew apparel contractors
315212	Police uniforms, women's, cut and sew apparel contractors
921150	Police, American Indian or Alaska Native tribal
311212	Polished rice manufacturing
333991	Polishers, handheld power-driven, manufacturing
325612	Polishes (e.g., automobile, furniture, metal, shoe) manufacturing
422690	Polishes (e.g., automobile, furniture, metal, shoe, stove) wholesaling
333512	Polishing and buffing machines, metalworking, manufacturing
332813	Polishing metals and metal products for the trade
325612	Polishing preparations manufacturing
327910	Polishing wheels manufacturing

Code	Description
813940	Political action committees (PACs)
813940	Political campaign organizations
711510	Political cartoonists, independent
541820	Political consulting services
541910	Political opinion polling services
813940	Political organizations or clubs
813940	Political parties
115112	Pollinating
114111	Pollock fishing
421830	Pollution control equipment (except air) wholesaling
421730	Pollution control equipment, air, wholesaling
924110	Pollution control program administration
541380	Pollution testing (except automotive emissions testing) services
315191	Polo shirts made in apparel knitting mills
315211	Polo shirts, men's and boys', cut and sew apparel contractors
315223	Polo shirts, men's and boys', cut and sewn from purchased fabric (except apparel contractors)
315212	Polo shirts, women's, girls', and infants', cut and sew apparel contractors
315232	Polo shirts, women's, misses', and girls', cut and sewn from purchased fabric (except apparel contractors)
325211	Polyacrylonitrile resins manufacturing
325211	Polyamide resins manufacturing
325211	Polycarbonate resins manufacturing
325222	Polyester fibers and filaments manufacturing
313112	Polyester filament yarn throwing, twisting, texturizing, or winding of purchased yarn
326113	Polyester film and unlaminated sheet (except packaging) manufacturing
325211	Polyester resins manufacturing
313111	Polyester spun yarns made from purchased fiber
313113	Polyester thread manufacturing

Code	Description
326113	Polyethylene film and unlaminated sheet (except packaging) manufacturing
325211	Polyethylene resins manufacturing
325212	Polyethylene rubber manufacturing
325211	Polyethylene terephathalate (PET) resins manufacturing
325222	Polyethylene terephthalate (PET) fibers and filaments manufacturing
334519	Polygraph machines manufacturing
561611	Polygraph services
325211	Polyhexamethylenediamine adipamide resins manufacturing
325199	Polyhydric alcohol esters and amines manufacturing
325199	Polyhydric alcohols manufacturing
325211	Polyisobutylene resins manufacturing
325212	Polyisobutylene rubber manufacturing
325212	Polyisobutylene-isoprene rubber manufacturing
325211	Polymethacrylate resins manufacturing
325212	Polymethylene rubber manufacturing
325222	Polyolefin fibers and filaments manufacturing
313112	Polypropylene filament yarn throwing, twisting, texturizing, or winding of puchased yarn
326113	Polypropylene film and unlaminated sheet (except packaging) manufacturing
325211	Polypropylene resins manufacturing
313111	Polypropylene spun yarns made from purchased fiber
326140	Polystyrene foam packaging manufacturing
325211	Polystyrene resins manufacturing
325212	Polysulfide rubber manufacturing
325211	Polytetrafluoroethylene resins manufacturing
325510	Polyurethane coatings manufacturing
326150	Polyurethane foam products manufacturing

Code	Description
325211	Polyurethane resins manufacturing
325211	Polyvinyl alcohol resins manufacturing
325211	Polyvinyl chloride (PVC) resins manufacturing
325222	Polyvinyl ester fibers and filaments manufacturing
326113	Polyvinyl film and unlaminated sheet (except packaging) manufacturing
325211	Polyvinyl halide resins manufacturing
325211	Polyvinyl resins manufacturing
325222	Polyvinylidene chloride (i.e., saran) fibers and filaments manufacturing
111339	Pomegranate farming
315299	Ponchos and similar waterproof raincoats (except infants') cut and sewn from purchased fabric (except apparel contractors)
315291	Ponchos and similar waterproof raincoats, infants', cut and sewn from purchased fabric (except apparel contractors)
315211	Ponchos and similar waterproof raincoats, men's and boys', cut and sew apparel contractors
315212	Ponchos and similar waterproof raincoats, women's, girls', and infants', cut and sew apparel contractors
234990	Pond construction
112920	Pony production
713990	Pool halls
713990	Pool parlors
713990	Pool rooms
312111	Pop, soda, manufacturing
311919	Popcorn (except candy covered), popped, manufacturing
311999	Popcorn (except popped) manufacturing
311340	Popcorn balls manufacturing
111150	Popcorn farming, field and seed production
335211	Popcorn poppers, household-type electric, manufacturing
422450	Popcorn wholesaling

Code	Description
311340	Popcorn, candy covered popped, manufacturing
313210	Poplins weaving
621391	Popopediatricians' offices (e.g., centers, clinics)
711130	Popular musical artists, independent
711130	Popular musical groups
532120	Popup camper rental
327113	Porcelain parts, electrical and electronic device, molded, manufacturing
327112	Porcelain, chemical, manufacturing
337122	Porch furniture (except upholstered), wood, manufacturing
337920	Porch shades, wood slat, manufacturing
337124	Porch swings, metal, manufacturing
321918	Porch work (e.g., columns, newels, rails, trellises), wood, manufacturing
114111	Porgy fishing
311422	Pork and beans canning
311611	Pork carcasses, half carcasses, and primal and sub-primal cuts produced in slaughtering plants
311919	Pork rinds manufacturing
311612	Pork, primal and sub-primal cuts, made from purchased carcasses
926120	Port authorities and districts, nonoperating
488310	Port facility operation
332311	Portable buildings, prefabricated metal, manufacturing
321992	Portable buildings, prefabricated wood, manufacturing
332998	Portable chemical toilets, metal, manufacturing
334111	Portable computers manufacturing
335211	Portable cooking appliances (except convection, microwave ovens), household-type electric, manufacturing
335211	Portable electric space heaters manufacturing
335211	Portable hair dryers, electric, manufacturing

Code	Description
335211	Portable humidifiers and dehumidifiers manufacturing
334310	Portable stereo systems manufacturing
334515	Portable test meters manufacturing
562991	Portable toilet pumping (i.e., cleaning) services
562991	Portable toilet renting and/or servicing
326191	Portable toilets, plastics, manufacturing
312120	Porter brewing
812990	Porter services
422810	Porter wholesaling
523920	Portfolio fund managing
541921	Portrait photography services
541921	Portrait photography studios
621512	Position emission tomography (PET) scanner centers
334510	Position emission tomography (PET) scanners manufacturing
334511	Position indicators (e.g., for landing gear, stabilizers), airframe equipment, manufacturing
336312	Positive crankcase ventilation (PCV) valves, engine, manufacturing
334514	Positive displacement meters manufacturing
235510	Post frame construction contractors
332212	Post hole diggers, nonpowered, manufacturing
333120	Post hole diggers, powered, manufacturing
233320	Post office construction
333997	Post office-type scales manufacturing
512191	Post-production facilities, motion picture or video
512191	Post-synchronization sound dubbing
333313	Postage meters manufacturing
421420	Postage meters wholesaling
333311	Postage stamp vending machines manufacturing
491110	Postal delivery services, local, operated by U.S. Postal Service
491110	Postal delivery services, local, operated on a contract basis

Code	Description
337215	Postal service lock boxes manufacturing
491110	Postal services operated by U.S. Postal Service
491110	Postal stations operated by U.S. Postal Service
491110	Postal stations operated on a contract basis
511199	Postcard publishers
511199	Postcard publishers and printing combined
511199	Postcard publishing (i.e., establishments known as publishers)
323112	Postcards flexographic printing without publishing
323111	Postcards gravure printing without publishing
323110	Postcards lithographic (offset) printing without publishing
323119	Postcards printing (except flexographic, gravure, lithographic, screen) without publishing
323113	Postcards screen printing without publishing
422120	Postcards wholesaling
511199	Poster publishers
511199	Poster publishers and printing combined
511199	Poster publishing (i.e., establishments known as publishers)
323112	Posters flexographic printing without publishing
323111	Posters gravure printing without publishing
323110	Posters lithographic (offset) printing without publishing
323119	Posters printing (except flexographic, gravure, lithographic, screen) without publishing
323113	Posters screen printing without publishing
235990	Posthole digging construction contractors
323121	Postpress services (e.g., beveling, bronzing, edging, foil stamping, gilding, tradebinding) on printed materials

Code	Description
327390	Posts, concrete, manufacturing
321114	Posts, round wood, cutting and treating
321114	Posts, wood, treating
311412	Pot pies, frozen, manufacturing
212391	Potash mining and/or beneficiating
325314	Potassic fertilizers made by mixing purchased materials
325188	Potassium aluminum sulfate manufacturing
325188	Potassium bichromate and chromate manufacturing
325199	Potassium bitartrate manufacturing
325188	Potassium bromide manufacturing
212391	Potassium bromide, natural, mining and/or beneficiating
325181	Potassium carbonate manufacturing
325188	Potassium chlorate manufacturing
325188	Potassium chloride manufacturing
212391	Potassium chloride mining and/or beneficiating
212391	Potassium compounds prepared at beneficiating plants
212391	Potassium compounds, natural, mining and/or beneficiating
325188	Potassium cyanide manufacturing
325181	Potassium hydroxide manufacturing
325188	Potassium hypochlorate manufacturing
325188	Potassium inorganic compounds, not specified elsewhere by process, manufacturing
325188	Potassium iodide manufacturing
325188	Potassium nitrate manufacturing
325199	Potassium organic compounds, not specified elsewhere by process, manufacturing
325188	Potassium permanganate manufacturing
325188	Potassium salts manufacturing
212391	Potassium salts, natural, mining and/or beneficiating
325188	Potassium sulfate manufacturing
422450	Potato chips and related snacks wholesaling
311919	Potato chips manufacturing
115114	Potato curing

Code	Description
333111	Potato diggers, harvesters, and planters manufacturing
111211	Potato farming, field and seed potato production
311211	Potato flour manufacturing
332214	Potato mashers manufacturing
311999	Potato mixes made from purchased dry ingredients
311423	Potato products (e.g., flakes, granules) dehydrating
311221	Potato starches manufacturing
311919	Potato sticks manufacturing
311991	Potatoes, peeled or cut, manufacturing
334513	Potentiometric instruments (except X-Y recorders), industrial process-type, manufacturing
334515	Potentiometric instruments (except industrial process-type) manufacturing
339999	Potpourri manufacturing
332420	Pots (e.g., annealing, melting, smelting), heavy gauge metal, manufacturing
332214	Pots and pans, fabricated metal, manufacturing
327124	Pots, glass-house, clay refractory, manufacturing
311612	Potted meats made from purchased carcasses
327112	Pottery products (except plumbing fixtures and porcelain) manufacturing
325314	Potting soil manufacturing
311615	Poultry (e.g., canned, cooked, fresh, frozen) manufacturing
311615	Poultry (e.g., canned, cooked, fresh, frozen) processing
422440	Poultry and poultry products (except canned, packaged frozen) wholesaling
333111	Poultry brooders, feeders, and waterers manufacturing
311615	Poultry canning (except baby, pet food)
115210	Poultry catching services
445210	Poultry dealers

Code	Description
421820	Poultry equipment wholesaling
311119	Poultry feeds, supplements, and concentrates manufacturing
112340	Poultry hatcheries
332618	Poultry netting made from purchased wire
311615	Poultry slaughtering, dressing, and packing
422490	Poultry, canned, wholesaling
422440	Poultry, live and dressed, wholesaling
422420	Poultry, packaged frozen, wholesaling
333991	Powder actuated handheld power tools manufacturing
332812	Powder coating metals and metal products for the trade
325510	Powder coatings manufacturing
331221	Powder made from purchased iron or steel
331314	Powder made from purchased aluminum
331423	Powder made from purchased copper
333513	Powder metal forming presses manufacturing
332117	Powder metallurgy products manufactured on a job or order basis
314999	Powder puffs and mitts manufacturing
331111	Powder, iron or steel, made in steel mills
331492	Powder, nonferrous metals (except aluminum, copper), made from purchased metal
311999	Powdered drink mixes (except chocolate, coffee, tea, milk based) manufacturing
311514	Powdered milk manufacturing
325620	Powders (e.g., baby, body, face, talcum, toilet) manufacturing
311999	Powders, baking, manufacturing
333912	Power (i.e., pressure) washer units manufacturing
234920	Power and communication transmission line construction management services

Code	Description
441222	Power boat dealers
332410	Power boilers manufacturing
335313	Power circuit breakers manufacturing
335313	Power connectors manufacturing
335999	Power converter units (i.e., AC to DC), static, manufacturing
444210	Power equipment stores, outdoor
334515	Power factor meters manufacturing
335313	Power fuses (i.e., 600 volts and over) manufacturing
235950	Power generating equipment construction contractors
221119	Power generation, electric (except fossil fuel, hydroelectric, nonhazardous solid waste, nuclear)
221112	Power generation, fossil fuel (e.g., coal, gas, oil), electric
221111	Power generation, hydroelectric
562213	Power generation, nonhazardous solid waste combustor or incinerator electric
221113	Power generation, nuclear electric
221119	Power generation, solar electric
221119	Power generation, tidal electric
221119	Power generation, wind electric
335312	Power generators manufacturing
421710	Power handtools (e.g., drills, sanders, saws) wholesaling
812320	Power laundries, commercial and family
234920	Power line construction
541990	Power line inspection (i.e., visual) services
334515	Power measuring equipment, electrical, manufacturing
234930	Power plant (except hydroelectric) construction
234990	Power plant, hydroelectric, construction
336330	Power steering hose assemblies manufacturing
336330	Power steering pumps manufacturing
335999	Power supplies, regulated and unregulated, manufacturing
335313	Power switchboards manufacturing

Code	Description
335313	Power switching equipment manufacturing
335311	Power transformers, electric, manufacturing
421610	Power transmission equipment, electrical, wholesaling
421840	Power transmission supplies (e.g., gears, pulleys, sprockets), mechanical, wholesaling
333319	Power washer cleaning equipment manufacturing
532490	Power washer rental or leasing
561790	Power washing building exteriors
336322	Power window and door lock systems, automotive, truck, and bus, manufacturing
333991	Power-driven handtools manufacturing
212399	Pozzolana mining and/or beneficiating
621399	Practical nurses' offices (e.g., centers, clinics), licensed
315299	Prayer shawls cut and sewn from purchased fabric (except apparel contractors)
315191	Prayer shawls made in apparel knitting mills
315211	Prayer shawls, men's and boys', cut and sew apparel contractors
315212	Prayer shawls, women's, girls', and infants', cut and sew apparel contractors
624410	Pre-kindergarten centers (except part of elementary school system)
334612	Pre-recorded magnetic audio tapes and cassettes mass reproducing
327331	Precast concrete block and brick manufacturing
327332	Precast concrete pipe manufacturing
235910	Precast concrete product placement construction contractors
327390	Precast concrete products (except brick, block, pipe) manufacturing
331491	Precious metal bar, rod, sheet, strip, and tubing made from purchased metals or scrap
331492	Precious metals recovering from scrap and/or alloying purchased metals

Code	Description
331419	Precious metals refining, primary
421940	Precious metals wholesaling
212399	Precious stones mining and/or beneficiating
421940	Precious stones wholesaling
811219	Precision equipment calibration
332212	Precision tools, machinist's (except optical), manufacturing
332721	Precision turned products manufacturers (i.e., known as)
334514	Predetermined counters manufacturing
233220	Prefabricated apartment construction
233220	Prefabricated apartment erection
233220	Prefabricated building (except house) erection, residential
444190	Prefabricated building dealers
233310	Prefabricated building erection, industrial
421390	Prefabricated buildings (except wood) wholesaling
332311	Prefabricated buildings, metal, manufacturing
421310	Prefabricated buildings, wood, wholesaling
321992	Prefabricated homes (except mobile homes), wood, manufacturing
332311	Prefabricated homes, metal, manufacturing
233210	Prefabricated house construction
233210	Prefabricated house erection
233320	Prefabricated nonresidential building (except industrial) erection
321992	Prefabricated wood buildings manufacturing
321211	Prefinished hardwood plywood manufacturing
321212	Prefinished softwood plywood manufacturing
621410	Pregnancy counseling centers
325413	Pregnancy test kits manufacturing
233220	Premanufactured housing (except single family) erection
233210	Premanufactured housing erection, single family
334611	Prepackaged software, mass reproducing

Code	Description
213112	Preparation of oil and gas field drilling sites on a contract basis
212113	Preparation plants, anthracite
611110	Preparatory schools, elementary or secondary
311822	Prepared flour mixes made from purchased flour
311211	Prepared flour mixes made in flour mills
422490	Prepared foods (except frozen) wholesaling
422420	Prepared foods, frozen (except dairy products), wholesaling
422430	Prepared foods, frozen dairy, wholesaling
311991	Prepared meals, perishable, packaged for individual resale
311941	Prepared sauces (except gravy, tomato based) manufacturing
488991	Preparing goods for transportation (i.e., crating, packing)
323122	Prepress printing services (e.g., color separation, imagesetting, photocomposition, typesetting)
541350	Prepurchase home inspection services
421990	Prerecorded audio and video tapes and discs wholesaling
512220	Prerecorded audio tapes and compact discs integrated manufacture, release, and distribution
454110	Prerecorded tape, compact disc, and record mail-order houses
624410	Preschool centers
422210	Prescription drugs wholesaling
111421	Preseeded mat farming
311421	Preserves (e.g., imitation) canning
321114	Preserving purchased wood and wood products
313311	Preshrinking broadwoven fabrics
313312	Preshrinking textile products and fabrics (except broadwoven)
921110	President's office, United States
325611	Presoaks manufacturing
333513	Press brakes, metalworking, manufacturing
514199	Press clipping services

Code	Description
332111	Press forgings made from purchased iron or steel, unfinished
332112	Press forgings made from purchased nonferrous metals, unfinished
422130	Pressed and molded pulp goods (e.g., egg cartons, shipping supplies) wholesaling
313230	Pressed felts manufacturing
321999	Pressed logs of sawdust and other wood particles, nonpetroleum binder, manufacturing
333513	Presses (e.g., bending, punching, shearing, stamping), metal forming, manufacturing
333294	Presses (i.e., food manufacturing-type) manufacturing
333210	Presses for making composite woods (e.g., hardboard, medium density fiberboard [MDF], particleboard, plywood) manufacturing
333111	Presses, farm-type, manufacturing
333999	Presses, metal baling, manufacturing
333293	Presses, printing (except textile), manufacturing
321999	Pressing blocks, wood, tailor's, manufacturing
336350	Pressure and clutch plate assemblies, automotive, truck, and bus, manufacturing
334519	Pressure and vacuum indicators, aircraft engine, manufacturing
332911	Pressure control valves (except fluid power), industrial-type, manufacturing
332912	Pressure control valves, fluid power, manufacturing
334512	Pressure controllers, air-conditioning system-type, manufacturing
332214	Pressure cookers, household-type, manufacturing
334513	Pressure gauges (e.g., dial, digital), industrial process-type, manufacturing
334513	Pressure instruments, industrial process-type, manufacturing
327332	Pressure pipe, reinforced concrete, manufacturing

Code	Description
322222	Pressure sensitive paper and tape (except medical) made from purchased materials
334519	Pressure transducers manufacturing
321113	Pressure treated lumber made from logs or bolts and treated
321114	Pressure treated lumber made from purchased lumber
334512	Pressurestats manufacturing
327331	Prestressed concrete blocks or bricks manufacturing
327332	Prestressed concrete pipes manufacturing
327390	Prestressed concrete products (except blocks, bricks, pipes) manufacturing
722213	Pretzel shops, on premise baking and carryout service
422490	Pretzels (except frozen) wholesaling
311919	Pretzels (except soft) manufacturing
422420	Pretzels, frozen, wholesaling
311812	Pretzels, soft, manufacturing
335129	Prewired poles, brackets, and accessories for electric lighting, manufacturing
926150	Price control agencies
111339	Prickly pear farming
331312	Primary aluminum production and manufacturing aluminum alloys
331312	Primary aluminum production and manufacturing aluminum shapes (e.g., bar, ingot, rod, sheet)
335912	Primary batteries manufacturing
334513	Primary elements for process flow measurement (i.e., orifice plates) manufacturing
334512	Primary oil burner controls (e.g., cadmium cells, stack controls) manufacturing
334513	Primary process temperature sensors manufacturing
331312	Primary refining of aluminum
331411	Primary refining of copper
331419	Primary refining of nonferrous metals (except aluminum, copper)
611110	Primary schools
331312	Primary smelting of aluminum

Code	Description
331411	Primary smelting of copper
331419	Primary smelting of nonferrous metals (except aluminum, copper)
335312	Prime mover generator sets (except turbine generator sets) manufacturing
332993	Primers (i.e., more than 30 mm., more than 1.18 inch), ammunition, manufacturing
325510	Primers, paint, manufacturing
323115	Print shops, digital
323119	Print shops, engraving
323112	Print shops, flexographic
323111	Print shops, gravure
323119	Print shops, letterpress
323110	Print shops, lithographic (offset) (except grey goods, manifold business forms, printing books, quick printing)
323114	Print shops, quick
323113	Print shops, screen
334418	Printed circuit assemblies manufacturing
334418	Printed circuit boards loading
421690	Printed circuit boards wholesaling
334412	Printed circuit boards, bare, manufacturing
334419	Printed circuit laminates manufacturing
334119	Printers, computer, manufacturing
421430	Printers, computer, wholesaling
323117	Printing books without publishing
313311	Printing broadwoven fabrics grey goods
313312	Printing fabric grey goods (except broadwoven)
325910	Printing inks manufacturing
421840	Printing inks wholesaling
333292	Printing machinery for textiles manufacturing
323116	Printing manifold business forms
422120	Printing paper (except bulk) wholesaling
422110	Printing paper, bulk, wholesaling
333293	Printing plate engraving machinery manufacturing
323122	Printing plate preparation services

Code	Description
333293	Printing plates, blank (except photosentive), manufacturing
323121	Printing postpress services (e.g., beveling, bronzing, edging, foil stamping) to printed products (e.g., books, cards, paper)
323122	Printing prepress services (e.g., color separation, imagesetting, photocomposition, typesetting)
333293	Printing press rollers manufacturing
333293	Printing presses (except textile) manufacturing
313312	Printing textile products (except apparel)
811310	Printing trade machinery repair and maintenance services
421830	Printing trade machinery, equipment, and supplies wholesaling
323115	Printing, digital (e.g., billboards, other large format graphical materials)
323115	Printing, digital (e.g., graphics, high resolution)
323119	Printing, engraving, on paper products
323112	Printing, flexographic (except books, grey goods, manifold business forms)
323111	Printing, gravure (except books, grey goods, manifold business forms)
323119	Printing, letterpress (except books, grey goods, manifold business forms)
323110	Printing, lithographic (except books, grey goods, manifold business forms, quick printing)
323110	Printing, photo-offset (except books, grey goods, manifold business forms, printing books)
323114	Printing, quick
323113	Printing, screen (except books, manifold business forms, printing grey goods)
233310	Printing/publishing plant construction
333314	Prisms, optical, manufacturing
337127	Prison bed manufacturing

Code	Description
233320	Prison construction
922140	Prison farms
922140	Prisons
522190	Private banks (i.e., unincorporated)
334210	Private branch exchange (PBX) equipment manufacturing
611310	Private colleges (except community or junior college)
561611	Private detective services
525920	Private estates (i.e., administering on behalf of beneficiaries)
814110	Private households employing domestic personnel
814110	Private households with employees
561611	Private investigation services (except credit)
561431	Private mail centers
561431	Private mailbox rental centers
611110	Private schools, elementary or secondary
493190	Private warehousing and storage (except farm products, general merchandise, refrigerated)
493130	Private warehousing and storage, farm products (except refrigerated)
493110	Private warehousing and storage, general merchandise
493120	Private warehousing and storage, refrigerated
451110	Pro shops (e.g., golf, skiing, tennis)
922150	Probation offices
212391	Probertite mining and/or quarrying
334510	Probes, electric medical, manufacturing
339112	Probes, surgical, manufacturing
325411	Procaine and derivatives (i.e., basic chemicals) manufacturing
334513	Process control instruments, industrial, manufacturing
541199	Process server services
541199	Process serving services
311513	Processed cheeses manufacturing
422470	Processed meats (e.g., luncheon, sausage) wholesaling
311612	Processed meats manufacturing
422440	Processed poultry (e.g., luncheon) wholesaling

Code	Description
311615	Processed poultry manufacturing
314999	Processing of textile mill waste and recovering fibers
621111	Proctologists' offices (e.g., centers, clinics)
422910	Produce containers wholesaling
445230	Produce markets
445230	Produce stands, permanent
454390	Produce stands, temporary
422480	Produce, fresh, wholesaling
813910	Producers' associations
711510	Producers, independent
561910	Product sterilization and packaging services
541380	Product testing laboratories or services
524128	Product warranty insurance carriers, direct
334514	Production counters manufacturing
541614	Production planning and control consulting services
541614	Productivity improvement consulting services
813920	Professional associations
711219	Professional athletes, independent (i.e., participating in sports events)
711211	Professional baseball clubs
323121	Professional book binding without printing
511130	Professional book publishers
511130	Professional book publishers and printing combined
511130	Professional book publishing (i.e., establishments known as publishers)
323117	Professional books printing and binding without publishing
323117	Professional books printing without publishing
611430	Professional development training
561330	Professional employer organizations (PEO)
421490	Professional equipment and supplies (except dental, medical, ophthalmic) wholesaling
611691	Professional examination review instructions

Code	Description
711211	Professional football clubs
421490	Professional instruments wholesaling
511120	Professional magazine and periodical publishers
511120	Professional magazine and periodical publishers and printing combined
511120	Professional magazine and periodical publishing (i.e., establishments known as publishers)
323112	Professional magazines and periodicals flexographic printing without publishing
323111	Professional magazines and periodicals gravure printing without publishing
323110	Professional magazines and periodicals lithographic (offset) printing without publishing
323119	Professional magazines and periodicals printing (except flexographic, gravure, lithographic, screen) without publishing
323113	Professional magazines and periodicals screen printing without publishing
813920	Professional membership associations
531120	Professional office building rental or leasing
611310	Professional schools (e.g., business administration, dental, law, medical)
315211	Professional service apparel, washable, men's and boys', cut and sew apparel contractors
315225	Professional service apparel, washable, men's and boys', cut and sewn from purchased fabric (except apparel contractors)
315212	Professional service apparel, washable, women's, cut and sew apparel contractors
315239	Professional service apparel, washable, women's, misses', and girls', cut and sewn from purchased fabric (except apparel contractors)

Code	Description
611620	Professional sports (e.g., golf, skiing, swimming, tennis) instructors (i.e., not participating in sporting events)
711211	Professional sports clubs
711310	Professional sports promoters with facilities
711320	Professional sports promoters without facilities
813920	Professional standards review boards
326130	Profile shapes (e.g., plate, rod, sheet), laminated plastics, manufacturing
326121	Profile shapes (e.g., rod, tube), nonrigid plastics, manufacturing
525990	Profit-sharing funds
512110	Program producing, television
334513	Programmers, process-type, manufacturing
511210	Programming language and compiler software publishers, packaged
541511	Programming services, custom computer
332993	Projectiles (except guided missile), jet propulsion, manufacturing
333315	Projection equipment (e.g., motion picture, slide), photographic, manufacturing
421410	Projection equipment (e.g., motion picture, slide), photographic, wholesaling
532490	Projection equipment rental or leasing, motion picture
333314	Projection lenses manufacturing
333315	Projection screens (i.e., motion picture, overhead, slide) manufacturing
334310	Projection television manufacturing
332995	Projectors (e.g., antisub, depth charge release, grenade, livens, rocket), ordnance, manufacturing
711310	Promoters of agricultural fairs with facilities
711320	Promoters of agricultural fairs without facilities
711310	Promoters of arts events with facilities

Code	Description
711320	Promoters of arts events without facilities
561920	Promoters of conventions with or without facilities
711310	Promoters of festivals with facilities
711320	Promoters of festivals without facilities
711310	Promoters of live performing arts productions (e.g., concerts) with facilities
711320	Promoters of live performing arts productions (e.g., concerts) without facilities
711310	Promoters of sports events with facilities
711320	Promoters of sports events without facilities
561920	Promoters of trade fairs or shows with or without facilities
561410	Proofreading services
111421	Propagation material farming
422710	Propane bulk stations and terminals
324110	Propane gases made in petroleum refineries
211112	Propane recovered from oil and gas field gases
333518	Propeller straightening presses manufacturing
334514	Propeller type meters with registers manufacturing
332999	Propellers, ship and boat, made from purchased metal
524126	Property and casualty insurance carriers, direct
524130	Property and casualty reinsurance carriers
524126	Property damage insurance carriers, direct
531312	Property managers' offices, commercial real estate
531312	Property managers' offices, nonresidential real estate
531311	Property managers' offices, residential real estate
531312	Property managing, commercial real estate
531312	Property managing, nonresidential real estate

Code	Description
531311	Property managing, residential real estate
813990	Property owners' associations
561612	Property protection services (except armored car, security systems)
921130	Property tax assessors' offices
326299	Prophylactics manufacturing
112910	Propolis production, bees
336415	Propulsion units and parts, guided missile and space vehicle, manufacturing
325199	Propylcarbinol manufacturing
324110	Propylene (i.e., propene) made in petroleum refineries
325199	Propylene glycol manufacturing
325110	Propylene made from refined petroleum or liquid hydrocarbons
325211	Propylene resins manufacturing
213113	Prospect and test drilling services for coal mining on contract basis
213114	Prospect and test drilling services for metal mining on contract basis
213115	Prospect and test drilling services for nonmetallic mineral mining (except fuels) on a contract basis
339113	Prosthetic appliances and supplies manufacturing
421450	Prosthetic appliances and supplies wholesaling
446199	Prosthetic stores
621210	Prosthodontists' offices (e.g., centers, clinics)
561612	Protection services (except armored car, security systems), personal or property
812332	Protective apparel supply services
523999	Protective committees, security holders
316211	Protective footwear, plastics or plastics-soled fabric upper, manufacturing
316211	Protective footwear, rubber or rubber-soled fabric upper, manufacturing
561612	Protective guard services
339920	Protectors, sports (e.g., baseball, basketball, hockey), manufacturing

Code	Description
334516	Protein analyzers, laboratory-type, manufacturing
325222	Protein fibers and filaments manufacturing
325211	Protein plastics manufacturing
712190	Provincial parks
334511	Proximity warning (i.e., collision avoidance) equipment manufacturing
111339	Prune farming
332212	Pruners manufacturing
311423	Prunes, dried, made in dehydration plants
115112	Pruning of orchard trees and vines
561730	Pruning services, ornamental tree and shrub
325131	Prussian blue pigments manufacturing
332212	Pry (i.e., crow) bars manufacturing
212299	Psilomelane mining and/or beneficiating
621420	Psychiatric centers and clinics (except hospitals), outpatient
623220	Psychiatric convalescent homes or hospitals
622210	Psychiatric hospitals (except convalescent)
621112	Psychiatrists' offices (e.g., centers, clinics)
812990	Psychic services
621112	Psychoanalysts' (MDs or DOs) offices (e.g., centers, clinics)
621330	Psychoanalysts' (except MDs or DOs) offices (e.g., centers, clinics)
813920	Psychologists' associations
621330	Psychologists' offices (e.g., centers, clinics), clinical
541720	Psychology research and development services
621112	Psychotherapists' (MDs or DOs) offices (e.g., centers, clinics)
621330	Psychotherapists' (except MDs or DOs) offices (e.g., centers, clinics)
541211	Public accountants' (CPAs) offices, certified
541211	Public accountants' (CPAs) private practices, certified

Code	Description
541219	Public accountants' (except CPAs) offices
541219	Public accountants' (except CPAs) private practices
532490	Public address system rental or leasing
811213	Public address system repair and maintenance services
334310	Public address systems and equipment manufacturing
421690	Public address systems and equipment wholesaling
421210	Public building furniture wholesaling
922130	Public defenders' offices
711410	Public figures' agents or managers
923120	Public health program administration, nonoperating
541910	Public opinion polling services
541910	Public opinion research services
921190	Public property management services, government
922130	Public prosecutors' offices
541820	Public relations agencies
541820	Public relations consulting services
541820	Public relations services
813319	Public safety advocacy organizations
922190	Public safety bureaus and statistics centers, government
922190	Public safety statistics centers, government
926130	Public service (except transportation) commissions, nonoperating
813410	Public speaking improvement clubs
611699	Public speaking training
561492	Public stenography services
926120	Public transportation commissions, nonoperating
926130	Public utility (except transportation) commissions, nonoperating
813910	Public utility associations
551112	Public utility holding companies
233320	Public warehouse construction

Code	Description
493190	Public warehousing and storage (except farm products, general merchandise, refrigerated, self storage)
493110	Public warehousing and storage (except self storage), general merchandise
493130	Public warehousing and storage, farm products (except refrigerated)
493120	Public warehousing and storage, refrigerated
*****	Publishers — see specific type
*****	Publishers and printing combined — see specific type of publisher
*****	Publishers or publishing — see specific type
541840	Publishers' advertising representatives (i.e., independent of media owners)
511130	Publishers, book
511130	Publishers, book, combined with printing
511140	Publishers, database
511140	Publishers, directory
511191	Publishers, greeting card
511191	Publishers, greeting card, combined with printing
511120	Publishers, magazine
511120	Publishers, magazine, combined with printing
511199	Publishers, map
512230	Publishers, music
511110	Publishers, newspaper
511110	Publishers, newspaper, combined with printing
511210	Publishers, packaged computer software
511120	Publishers, periodical
511120	Publishers, periodical, combined with printing
511199	Publishers, racing form
511110	Publishing and printing or publishing only, newspaper (i.e., establishments known as publishers)
511191	Publishing, greeting card, (i.e., establishments known as publishers)

Code	Description
311520	Pudding pops, frozen, manufacturing
311999	Puddings, canned dessert, manufacturing
311999	Puddings, dessert, manufacturing
333923	Pulleys (except power transmission), metal, manufacturing
333613	Pulleys, power transmission, manufacturing
321999	Pulleys, wood, manufacturing
213112	Pulling oil and gas field casings, tubes, or rods on a contract basis
621111	Pulmonary specialists' offices (e.g., centers, clinics)
322122	Pulp and newsprint combined manufacturing
322121	Pulp and paper (except groundwood, newsprint) combined manufacturing
322130	Pulp and paperboard combined manufacturing
333291	Pulp making machinery manufacturing
322110	Pulp manufacturing (i.e., chemical, mechanical, or semichemical processes) without making paper
322110	Pulp manufacturing (made from bagasse, linters, rags, straw, wastepaper, or wood) without making paper
322122	Pulp mills and groundwood paper, uncoated and untreated, manufacturing
322110	Pulp mills not making paper or paperboard
322122	Pulp mills producing newsprint paper
322121	Pulp mills producing paper (except groundwood, newsprint)
322130	Pulp mills producing paperboard
322299	Pulp products, molded, manufacturing
333291	Pulp, paper, and paperboard molding machinery manufacturing
212399	Pulpstones, natural, mining and/or beneficiating
113310	Pulpwood logging camps

Code	Description
421990	Pulpwood wholesaling
334515	Pulse (i.e., signal) generators manufacturing
334519	Pulse analyzers, nuclear monitoring, manufacturing
327992	Pumice (except abrasives) processing beyond beneficiation
327910	Pumice and pumicite abrasives manufacturing
212399	Pumice mining and/or beneficiating
212399	Pumicite mining and/or beneficiating
562991	Pumping (i.e., cleaning) cesspools and septic tanks
562991	Pumping (i.e., cleaning) portable toilets
213112	Pumping oil and gas wells on a contract basis
213113	Pumping or draining coal mines on a contract basis
213114	Pumping or draining metal mines on a contract basis
213115	Pumping or draining nonmetallic mineral mines (except fuel) on a contract basis
234910	Pumping station construction
111219	Pumpkin farming, field and seed production
421120	Pumps (e.g., fuel, oil, power steering, water), automotive, wholesaling
336312	Pumps (e.g., fuel, oil, water), mechanical, automotive and truck gasoline engine (except power steering), manufacturing
333911	Pumps (except fluid power), general purpose, manufacturing
316214	Pumps (i.e., dress shoes) manufacturing
421830	Pumps and pumping equipment, industrial-type, wholesaling
333911	Pumps for railroad equipment lubrication systems manufacturing
333996	Pumps, fluid power, manufacturing
333911	Pumps, industrial and commercial-type, general purpose, manufacturing
333913	Pumps, measuring and dispensing (e.g., gasoline), manufacturing

Code	Description
333911	Pumps, oil field or well, manufacturing
333911	Pumps, sump or water, residential-type, manufacturing
313230	Punched felts manufacturing
332212	Punches (except paper), nonpowered handtool, manufacturing
333514	Punches for use with machine tools manufacturing
333513	Punching machines, metalworking, manufacturing
711110	Puppet theaters
339999	Puppets manufacturing
921190	Purchasing and supply agencies, government
522298	Purchasing of accounts receivable
332323	Purlins, metal, manufacturing
316993	Purses (except precious metal), men's, manufacturing
316992	Purses (except precious metal), women's, manufacturing
339911	Purses, precious metal or clad with precious metal, manufacturing
333515	Pushers (i.e., a machine tool accessory) manufacturing
332212	Putty knives manufacturing
421920	Puzzles wholesaling
325320	Pyrethrin insecticides manufacturing
334519	Pyrheliometers manufacturing
212393	Pyrite concentrates mining and/or beneficiating
212393	Pyrite mining and/or beneficiating
325191	Pyroligneous acids manufacturing
212299	Pyrolusite mining and/or beneficiating
327112	Pyrometer tubes manufacturing
334513	Pyrometers, industrial process-type, manufacturing
327112	Pyrometric cones, earthenware, manufacturing
212399	Pyrophyllite mining and/or beneficiating
327992	Pyrophyllite processing beyond beneficiation
332994	Pyrotechnic pistols and projectors manufacturing

Code	Description
325998	Pyrotechnics (e.g., flares, flashlight bombs, signals) manufacturing
325211	Pyroxylin (i.e., nitrocellulose) resins manufacturing
212393	Pyrrhotite mining and/or beneficiating
112390	Quail production
611430	Quality assurance training
541990	Quantity surveyor services
327122	Quarry tiles, clay, manufacturing
333131	Quarrying machinery and equipment manufacturing
421810	Quarrying machinery and equipment wholesaling
316999	Quarters (i.e., shoe cut stock), leather, manufacturing
212399	Quartz crystal, pure, mining and/or beneficiating
334419	Quartz crystals, electronic application, manufacturing
212319	Quartzite crushed and broken stone mining and/or beneficiating
212311	Quartzite dimension stone mining or quarrying
325191	Quebracho extracts manufacturing
112910	Queen bee production
325191	Quercitron extracts manufacturing
323114	Quick printing
811191	Quick-lube shops
327410	Quicklime (i.e., calcium oxide) manufacturing
212299	Quicksilver ores and metal mining and/or beneficiating
314999	Quilting of textiles
314129	Quilts made from purchased materials
111339	Quince farming
325411	Quinine and derivatives (i.e., basic chemicals) manufacturing
523999	Quotation services, securities
523999	Quotation services, stock
334519	RADIAC (radioactivity detection, identification, and computation) equipment manufacturing
525930	REITs (real estate investment trusts)

Code	Description
525990	REMICs (real estate mortgage investment conduits)
522294	REMICs (real estate mortgage investment conduits) issuing, private
621399	RNs' (registered nurses) offices (e.g., centers, clinics)
721211	RV (recreational vehicle) parks
532120	RV (recreational vehicle) rental or leasing
441210	RV dealers
311119	Rabbit food manufacturing
112930	Rabbit production
311615	Rabbits processing (i.e., canned, cooked, fresh, frozen)
311615	Rabbits slaughtering and dressing
711219	Race car drivers
711219	Race car owners (i.e., racing cars)
336999	Race cars manufacturing
711219	Race dog owners (i.e., racing dogs)
711219	Racehorse owners (i.e., racing horses)
711219	Racehorse trainers
711219	Racehorse training
332991	Races, ball or roller bearing, manufacturing
511199	Racetrack program publishers
511199	Racetrack program publishers and printing combined
323112	Racetrack programs flexographic printing without publishing
323111	Racetrack programs gravure printing without publishing
323110	Racetrack programs lithographic (offset) printing without publishing
323119	Racetrack programs printing (except flexographic, gravure, lithographic, screen) without publishing
511199	Racetrack programs publishing (i.e., establishments known as publishers)
323113	Racetrack programs screen printing without publishing
711212	Racetracks (e.g., automobile, dog, horse)
713990	Racetracks, slot car (i.e., amusement devices)

Code	Description
335932	Raceways manufacturing
713990	Raceways, gocart (i.e., amusement rides)
511199	Racing form publishers
511199	Racing form publishers and printing combined
323112	Racing forms flexographic printing without publishing
323111	Racing forms gravure printing without publishing
323110	Racing forms lithographic (offset) printing without publishing
323119	Racing forms printing (except flexographic, gravure, lithographic, screen) without publishing
511199	Racing forms publishing (i.e., establishments known as publishers)
323113	Racing forms screen printing without publishing
711219	Racing stables, horse
711219	Racing teams (e.g., automobile, motorcycle, snowmobile)
334417	Rack and panel connectors manufacturing
336330	Rack and pinion steering assemblies manufacturing
336399	Racks (e.g., bicycle, luggage, ski, tire), automotive, truck, and buses manufacturing
332313	Racks (e.g., trash), fabricated metal plate, manufacturing
332618	Racks, household-type, made from purchased wire
713940	Racquetball club facilities
811219	Radar and sonar equipement repair and maintenance services
334511	Radar detectors manufacturing
421690	Radar equipment wholesaling
513390	Radar station operations
334511	Radar systems and equipment manufacturing
334515	Radar testing instruments, electric, manufacturing
334519	Radiation detection and monitoring instruments manufacturing
541380	Radiation dosimetry (i.e., radiation testing) laboratories or services

Code	Description
812332	Radiation protection garment supply services
339113	Radiation shielding aprons, gloves, and sheeting manufacturing
541380	Radiation testing laboratories or services
325998	Radiator additive preparations manufacturing
326220	Radiator and heater hoses, rubber or plastics, manufacturing
811118	Radiator repair shops, automotive
332322	Radiator shields and enclosures, sheet metal, manufacturing
333414	Radiators (except motor vehicle, portable electric) manufacturing
336399	Radiators and cores manufacturing
421120	Radiators, motor vehicle, wholesaling
335211	Radiators, portable electric, manufacturing
541840	Radio advertising representatives (i.e., independent of media owners)
443112	Radio and television stores
332312	Radio and television tower sections, fabricated structural metal, manufacturing
488330	Radio beacon (i.e., ship navigation) services
513111	Radio broadcasting network services
513111	Radio broadcasting networks
513112	Radio broadcasting stations (e.g., AM, FM, shortwave)
513111	Radio broadcasting syndicates
711510	Radio commentators, independent
541690	Radio consulting services
511120	Radio guide publishers
511120	Radio guide publishers and printing combined
511120	Radio guide publishing (i.e., establishments known as publishers)
323112	Radio guides flexographic printing without publishing
323111	Radio guides gravure printing without publishing
323110	Radio guides lithographic (offset) printing without publishing

Code	Description
323119	Radio guides printing (except flexographic, gravure, lithographic, screen) without publishing
323113	Radio guides screen printing without publishing
334310	Radio headphones manufacturing
326199	Radio housings, plastics, manufacturing
334511	Radio magnetic instrumentation (RMI) manufacturing
513321	Radio paging services communication carriers
421690	Radio parts and accessories (e.g., transitors, tubes) wholesaling
512290	Radio program tape production (except independent producers)
334310	Radio receiving sets manufacturing
811211	Radio repair and maintenance services without retailing new radios
323111	Radio schedule gravure printing without publishing
511120	Radio schedule publishers
511120	Radio schedule publishers and printing combined
511120	Radio schedule publishing (i.e., establishments known as publishers)
323112	Radio schedules flexographic printing without publishing
323110	Radio schedules lithographic (offset) printing without publishing
323119	Radio schedules printing (except flexographic, gravure, lithographic, screen) without publishing
323113	Radio schedules screen printing without publishing
513112	Radio stations (e.g., AM, FM, shortwave)
561410	Radio transcription services
334220	Radio transmitting antennas and ground equipment manufacturing
325188	Radioactive elements manufacturing
541360	Radioactive geophysical surveying services
325412	Radioactive in-vivo diagnostic substances manufacturing

Code	Description
325188	Radioactive isotopes manufacturing
422210	Radioactive pharmaceutical isotopes wholesaling
562112	Radioactive waste collecting and/or local hauling
562211	Radioactive waste collecting and/or local hauling in combination with disposal and/or treatment facilities
562211	Radioactive waste disposal facilities
484230	Radioactive waste hauling, long-distance
562211	Radioactive waste treatment facilities
334519	Radioactivity detection, identification, and computation (RADIAC) equipment manufacturing
334515	Radiofrequency measuring equipment manufacturing
334515	Radiofrequency oscillators manufacturing
541380	Radiographic testing laboratories or services
541380	Radiographing welded joints on pipes and fittings
541380	Radiography inspection services
621512	Radiological laboratories, medical
621512	Radiological laboratory services, medical
621111	Radiologists' offices (e.g., centers, clinics)
421690	Radios (except household-type) wholesaling
421620	Radios, household-type, wholesaling
111219	Radish farming, field and seed production
325188	Radium chloride manufacturing
334517	Radium equipment manufacturing
325188	Radium luminous compounds manufacturing
212291	Radium ores mining and/or beneficiating
235990	Radon remediation construction contractors
541380	Radon testing laboratories or services
326299	Rafts, rubber inflatable, manufacturing
421930	Rags wholesaling

Code	Description
335931	Rail bonds, propulsion and signal circuit electric, manufacturing
331111	Rail joints and fastenings made in steel mills
336510	Rail laying and tamping equipment manufacturing
485112	Rail transportation (except mixed mode), commuter
332323	Railings, metal, manufacturing
321918	Railings, wood stair, manufacturing
923130	Railroad Retirement Board
926120	Railroad and warehouse commissions, nonoperating
333613	Railroad car journal bearings, plain, manufacturing
532411	Railroad car rental and leasing
336510	Railroad cars and car equipment manufacturing
421860	Railroad cars wholesaling
336510	Railroad cars, self-propelled, manufacturing
234990	Railroad construction
331111	Railroad crossings, iron or steel, made in steel mills
421860	Railroad equipment and supplies wholesaling
336510	Railroad locomotives and parts (except diesel engines) manufacturing
339932	Railroad models, hobby and toy, manufacturing
531190	Railroad right of way leasing
336510	Railroad rolling stock manufacturing
336360	Railroad seating manufacturing
334290	Railroad signaling equipment manufacturing
488210	Railroad switching services
488210	Railroad terminals, independent operation
561599	Railroad ticket offices
321114	Railroad ties (i.e., bridge, cross, switch) treating
421990	Railroad ties, wood, wholesaling
333997	Railroad track scales manufacturing
482111	Railroad transportation, line-haul
487110	Railroad transportation, scenic and sightseeing

Code	Description
482112	Railroad transportation, short-line or beltline
487110	Railroad, scenic and sightseeing, operation
482111	Railroads, line-haul
482112	Railroads, short-line or beltline
321999	Rails (except rough), wood fence, manufacturing
421510	Rails and accessories, metal, wholesaling
331319	Rails made by rolling or drawing purchased aluminum
331111	Rails rerolled or renewed in steel mills
331319	Rails, aluminum, made in integrated secondary smelting and drawing plants
331319	Rails, aluminum, made in integrated secondary smelting and rolling mills
331111	Rails, iron or steel, made in steel mills
113310	Rails, rough wood, manufacturing
332312	Railway bridge sections, prefabricated metal, manufacturing
335312	Railway motors and control equipment, electric, manufacturing
234990	Railway roadbed construction
485112	Railway systems (except mixed mode), commuter
488210	Railway terminals, independent operation
482111	Railway transportation, line-haul
487110	Railway transportation, scenic and sightseeing
482112	Railway transportation, short-line or beltline
334519	Rain gauges manufacturing
315211	Raincoats water resistant, men's and boys', cut and sew apparel contractors
313320	Raincoats waterproofing (i.e., oiling)
315299	Raincoats, rubber or rubberized fabric, manufacturing
315291	Raincoats, water resistant, infants', cut and sewn from purchased fabric (except apparel contractors)

Code	Description
315228	Raincoats, water resistant, nontailored, men's and boys', cut and sewn from purchased fabric (except apparel contractors)
315239	Raincoats, water resistant, nontailored, women's, misses', and girls', cut and sewn from purchased fabric (except apparel contractors)
315222	Raincoats, water resistant, tailored, men's and boys', cut and sewn from purchased fabric (except apparel contractors)
315234	Raincoats, water resistant, tailored, women's, misses', and girls', cut and sewn from purchased fabric (except apparel contractors)
315212	Raincoats, water resistant, women's, girls', and infants', cut and sew apparel contractors
315291	Raincoats, water-repellent, infants', cut and sewn from purchased fabric (except apparel contractors)
315211	Raincoats, water-repellent, men's and boys', cut and sew apparel contractors
315228	Raincoats, water-repellent, nontailored, men's and boys', cut and sewn from purchased fabric (except apparel contractors)
315239	Raincoats, water-repellent, nontailored, women's, misses', and girls', cut and sewn from purchased fabric (except apparel contractors)
315222	Raincoats, water-repellent, tailored, men's and boys', cut and sewn from purchased fabric (except apparel contractors)
315234	Raincoats, water-repellent, tailored, women's, misses', and girls', cut and sewn from purchased fabric (except apparel contractors)
315212	Raincoats, water-repellent, women's, girls', and infants', cut and sew apparel contractors
315299	Raincoats, waterproof (except infants'), cut and sewn from purchased fabric (except apparel contractors)
315299	Raincoats, waterproof, infants', cut and sewn from purchased fabric (except apparel contractors)
315211	Raincoats, waterproof, men's and boys', cut and sew apparel contractors
315212	Raincoats, waterproof, women's, girls', and infants', cut and sew apparel contractors
111332	Raisin farming
112990	Raising swans, peacocks, flamingos, or other adornment birds
311423	Raisins made in dehydration plants
333111	Rakes, hay, manufacturing
332212	Rakes, nonpowered handtool, manufacturing
313111	Ramie spun yarns made from purchased fiber
316999	Rands (i.e., shoe cut stock), leather, manufacturing
333315	Range finders, photographic, manufacturing
335211	Range hoods with integral lighting fixtures, household-type, manufacturing
335211	Range hoods, household-type, manufacturing
333319	Ranges, commercial-type, manufacturing
335221	Ranges, household-type cooking, manufacturing
624190	Rape crisis centers
311225	Rapeseed (i.e., canola) oil made from purchased oils
311223	Rapeseed (i.e., canola) oil made in crushing mills
111120	Rapeseed farming, field and seed production
336510	Rapid transit cars and equipment manufacturing
325188	Rare earth compounds, not specified elsewhere by process, manufacturing
212299	Rare earth metal concentrates beneficiating
212299	Rare earth metal ores mining and/or beneficiating
325188	Rare earth salts manufacturing
453310	Rare manuscript stores
111334	Raspberry farming
332212	Rasps, handheld, manufacturing
332212	Ratchets, nonpowered, manufacturing
524298	Rate making services, insurance
334511	Rate-of-climb instrumentation manufacturing
213112	Rathole and mousehole drilling at oil and gas fields on a contract basis
112390	Ratite production
337125	Rattan furniture, household-type, manufacturing
321999	Rattan ware (except furniture) manufacturing
112990	Rattlesnake production
311313	Raw beet sugar manufacturing
422590	Raw farm products (e.g., field beans, grains) wholesaling
316110	Rawhide manufacturing
114111	Ray fishing
325221	Rayon fibers and filaments manufacturing
313111	Rayon spun yarns made from purchased fiber
313113	Rayon thread manufacturing
313112	Rayon yarn throwing, twisting, texturizing, or winding purchased filament
331221	Razor blade strip steel made in cold rolling mills
332211	Razor blades manufacturing
422210	Razor blades wholesaling
316999	Razor strops manufacturing
332211	Razors (except electric) manufacturing
422210	Razors (except electric) wholesaling
335211	Razors, electric, manufacturing
421620	Razors, electric, wholesaling
324191	Re-refining used petroleum lubricating oils
332313	Reactor containment vessels, fabricated metal plate, manufacturing
332410	Reactors, nuclear, manufacturing

Code	Description
333315	Readers, microfilm or microfiche, manufacturing
336211	Ready-mix concrete trucks assembling on purchased chassis
327320	Ready-mixed concrete manufacturing and distributing
531190	Real estate (except building) rental or leasing
531210	Real estate agencies
531210	Real estate agents' offices
531320	Real estate appraisal services
531320	Real estate appraisers' offices
531390	Real estate asset management services (except property management)
813910	Real estate boards
531210	Real estate brokerages
531210	Real estate brokers' offices
531390	Real estate consultants' (except agents, appraisers) offices
522292	Real estate credit lending
531390	Real estate escrow agencies
531390	Real estate escrow agents' offices
531390	Real estate fiduciaries' offices
525930	Real estate investment trusts (REITs)
541110	Real estate law offices
531390	Real estate listing services
525990	Real estate mortgage investment conduits (REMICs)
522294	Real estate mortgage investment conduits (REMICs) issuing, private
531312	Real estate property managers' offices, commercial
531311	Real estate property managers' offices, residential
531130	Real estate rental or leasing of miniwarehouses and self-storage units
531120	Real estate rental or leasing of nonresidential building (except miniwarehouse)
531110	Real estate rental or leasing of residential building
611519	Real estate schools
524127	Real estate title insurance carriers, direct

Code	Description
233110	Real property (i.e., land, except cemetery lots) development or subdivision
561492	Real-time (i.e., simultaneous) closed captioning of live television performances, meetings, conferences, and so forth
333515	Reamers (i.e., a machine tool accessory) manufacturing
333512	Reaming machines, metalworking, manufacturing
235910	Rebar construction contractors
323121	Rebinding books, magazines, or pamphlets
513112	Rebroadcast radio stations
336312	Rebuilding automotive and truck gasoline engines
326212	Rebuilding tires
326212	Recapping tires
422120	Receipt books wholesaling
334220	Receiver-transmitter units (i.e., transceivers) manufacturing
335931	Receptacles (i.e., outlets), electrical, manufacturing
421610	Receptacles, electrical, wholesaling
531120	Reception hall rental or leasing
335122	Recessed lighting housings and trim (except residential), electric, manufacturing
335121	Recessed lighting housings and trim, residential electric, manufacturing
335911	Rechargeable battery packs made from purchased battery cells and housings
335911	Rechargeable nickel cadmium (NICAD) batteries manufacturing
314999	Reclaimed wool processing
326299	Reclaiming rubber from waste or scrap
234990	Reclamation projects construction
337121	Recliners, upholstered, manufacturing
332994	Recoil mechanisms (i.e., 30 mm. or less, 1.18 inch or less), gun, manufacturing
332995	Recoil mechanisms (i.e., more than 30 mm., more than 1.18 inch), gun, manufacturing

Code	Description
332995	Recoilless rifles manufacturing
421840	Reconditioned barrels and drums wholesaling
213111	Reconditioning oil and gas field wells on a contract basis
811310	Reconditioning shipping barrels and drums
321219	Reconstituted wood panels manufacturing
321219	Reconstituted wood sheets and boards manufacturing
312229	Reconstituting tobacco
512210	Record producers (except independent)
711510	Record producers, independent
512210	Record production (except independent record producers) without duplication or distribution
512220	Record releasing, promoting, and distributing combined with mass duplication
451220	Record stores, new
453310	Record stores, used
421620	Recorders (e.g., tape, video), household-type, wholesaling
334513	Recorders, industrial process control-type, manufacturing
334515	Recorders, oscillographic, manufacturing
512290	Recording books on tape or disc (except publishers)
512290	Recording seminars and conferences, audio
512240	Recording studios, sound, operating on a contract or fee basis
711510	Recording technicians, independent
541611	Records management consulting services
314999	Recovered fibers processing
331492	Recovering and refining of nonferrous metals (except aluminum, copper) from scrap
331492	Recovering silver from used photographic film or X-ray plates
621340	Recreational (e.g., art, dance, music) therapists' offices (e.g., centers, clinics)
233320	Recreational building construction

Code	Description
721214	Recreational camps with accommodation facilities (except campgrounds)
713990	Recreational camps without accommodations
713990	Recreational day camps (except instructional)
421910	Recreational equipment and supplies (except vehicles) wholesaling
532292	Recreational goods rental
924120	Recreational programs administration, government
713940	Recreational sports club facilities
713990	Recreational sports clubs (i.e., sports teams) not operating sports facilities
713990	Recreational sports teams and leagues
532120	Recreational trailer rental
441210	Recreational vehicle (RV) dealers
532120	Recreational vehicle (RV) rental or leasing
721211	Recreational vehicle parks
441210	Recreational vehicle parts and accessories stores
421110	Recreational vehicles wholesaling
335999	Rectifiers (except electronic component type, semiconductor) manufacturing
334419	Rectifiers, electronic component-type (except semiconductor), manufacturing
421690	Rectifiers, electronic, wholesaling
334413	Rectifiers, semiconductor, manufacturing
333298	Rectifying equipment, chemical, manufacturing
562111	Recyclable material collection services
562111	Recyclable material hauling, local
484230	Recyclable material hauling, long-distance
421930	Recyclable materials (e.g., glass, metal, paper) wholesaling
325612	Recycling drycleaning fluids
811212	Recycling inkjet cartridges

Code	Description
325998	Recycling services for degreasing solvents (e.g., engine, machinery) manufacturing
325199	Red oil (i.e., oleic acid) manufacturing
925120	Redevelopment land agencies, government
334516	Redox (i.e., oxidation-reduction potential) instruments manufacturing
333612	Reducers, speed, manufacturing
333612	Reduction gears and gear units (except aircraft power transmission equipment, automotive) manufacturing
337125	Reed furniture (except upholstered), household-type, manufacturing
212399	Reed peat mining and/or beneficiating
321999	Reed ware (except furniture) manufacturing
339992	Reeds, musical instrument, manufacturing
339920	Reels, fishing, manufacturing
332999	Reels, metal, manufacturing
326199	Reels, plastics, manufacturing
321999	Reels, plywood, manufacturing
321999	Reels, wood, manufacturing
514120	Reference libraries
561310	Referral agencies or services, employment
624190	Referral services for personal and social problems
486910	Refined petroleum products pipeline transportation
324110	Refineries, petroleum
324110	Refinery gases made in petroleum refineries
421830	Refinery machinery and equipment wholesaling
331312	Refining aluminum, primary
331314	Refining aluminum, secondary
331411	Refining copper, primary
331423	Refining copper, secondary
331419	Refining nonferrous metals and alloys (except aluminum, copper), primary

Code	Description
331492	Refining nonferrous metals and alloys (except aluminum, copper), secondary
335129	Reflectors for lighting equipment, metal, manufacturing
333314	Reflectors, optical, manufacturing
326199	Reflectors, plastics, manufacturing
115310	Reforestation
922140	Reformatories
325991	Reformulating plastics resins from recycled plastics products
334513	Refractometers, industrial process-type, manufacturing
334516	Refractometers, laboratory-type, manufacturing
421840	Refractories (e.g., block, brick, mortar, tile) wholesaling
327124	Refractories (e.g., block, brick, mortar, tile), clay, manufacturing
327125	Refractories (e.g., block, brick, mortar, tile), nonclay, manufacturing
235410	Refractory brick construction contractors
327125	Refractory cement, nonclay, manufacturing
212325	Refractory minerals mining and/or beneficiating
722330	Refreshment stands, mobile
311822	Refrigerated doughs made from purchased flour
333415	Refrigerated lockers manufacturing
484220	Refrigerated products trucking, local
484230	Refrigerated products trucking, long-distance
493120	Refrigerated warehousing
235110	Refrigeration and freezer installation contractors
333415	Refrigeration compressors manufacturing
334512	Refrigeration controls, residential and commercial-type, manufacturing
421740	Refrigeration equipment and supplies, commercial-type, wholesaling

Code	Description
811310	Refrigeration equipment repair and maintenance services, industrial and commercial-type
333415	Refrigeration equipment, industrial and commercial-type, manufacturing
334512	Refrigeration thermostats manufacturing
421740	Refrigeration units, motor vehicle, wholesaling
333415	Refrigeration units, truck-type, manufacturing
334512	Refrigeration/air-conditioning defrost controls manufacturing
532210	Refrigerator rental
811412	Refrigerator, household-type, repair and maintenance services without retailing new refrigerators
335222	Refrigerator/freezer combinations, household-type, manufacturing
335222	Refrigerators (e.g., absorption, mechanical), household-type, manufacturing
421740	Refrigerators (e.g., reach-in, walk-in), commercial-type, wholesaling
421620	Refrigerators, household-type, wholesaling
624230	Refugee settlement services
562212	Refuse collecting and operating solid waste landfills
562111	Refuse collection services
562213	Refuse disposal combustors or incinerators
562212	Refuse disposal landfills
562111	Refuse hauling, local
484230	Refuse hauling, long-distance
315299	Regalia cut and sewn from purchased fabric (except apparel contractors)
315211	Regalia, men's and boys', cut and sew apparel contractors
315212	Regalia, women's, girls', and infants', cut and sew apparel contractors
325221	Regenerated cellulosic fibers manufacturing
925120	Regional planning and development program administration

Code	Description
621399	Registered nurses' (RNs) offices (e.g., centers, clinics)
334514	Registers, linear tallying, manufacturing
332323	Registers, metal air, manufacturing
561310	Registries, employment
335311	Regulating transformers, power system-type, manufacturing
926140	Regulation and inspection of agricultural products
926130	Regulation of utilities
335311	Regulators (i.e., electric transformers), feeder voltage, manufacturing
336322	Regulators, motor vehicle voltage for internal combustion engines manufacturing
335313	Regulators, power, manufacturing
421610	Regulators, voltage (except motor vehicle), wholesaling
624190	Rehabilitation agencies for offenders
622310	Rehabilitation hospitals (except alcoholism, drug addiction)
622210	Rehabilitation hospitals, alcoholism and drug addiction
624310	Rehabilitation job counseling and training, vocational
922150	Rehabilitation services, correctional, government
332618	Reinforcing mesh, concrete, made from purchased wire
524130	Reinsurance carriers
334515	Relays (except electrical, electronic), instrument, manufacturing
421610	Relays wholesaling
335314	Relays, electrical and electronic, manufacturing
624230	Relief services, disaster
624230	Relief services, emergency
323121	Religious book binding without printing
511130	Religious book publishers
511130	Religious book publishers and printing combined
451211	Religious book stores

Code	Description
323117	Religious books printing and binding without publishing
323117	Religious books printing without publishing
511130	Religious books publishing (i.e., establishments known as publishers)
337127	Religious furniture manufacturing
421210	Religious furniture wholesaling
453998	Religious goods (except books) stores
511120	Religious magazine and periodical publishers
511120	Religious magazine and periodical publishers and printing combined
511120	Religious magazine and periodical publishing (i.e., establishments known as publishers)
323112	Religious magazines and periodicals flexographic printing without publishing
323111	Religious magazines and periodicals gravure printing without publishing
323110	Religious magazines and periodicals lithographic (offset) printing without publishing
323119	Religious magazines and periodicals printing (except flexographic, gravure, lithographic, screen) without publishing
323113	Religious magazines and periodicals screen printing without publishing
813110	Religious organizations
421490	Religious supplies wholesaling
311421	Relishes canning
562910	Remediation and clean up of contaminated buildings, mine sites, soil, or ground water
562910	Remediation services, environmental
422310	Remnants, piece goods, wholesaling
233310	Remodeling industrial buildings
233320	Remodeling nonresidential (except industrial) buildings
233220	Remodeling residential (except single family) buildings
233210	Remodeling single family buildings
334290	Remote control units (e.g., garage door, television) manufacturing

Code	Description
541360	Remote sensing geophysical surveying services
213112	Removal of condensate gasoline from field gathering lines on a contract basis
213113	Removal of overburden for coal mining on a contract basis
213114	Removal of overburden for metal mining on a contract basis
213115	Removal of overburden for nonmetallic minerals mining (except fuels) on a contract basis
562920	Removal of recyclable materials from a waste stream
621492	Renal dialysis centers and clinics
311613	Rendering animals (carrion) for feed
311613	Rendering fats
311613	Rendering plants
422990	Rennets wholesaling
233310	Renovating industrial buildings
233320	Renovating nonresidential (except industrial) buildings
233220	Renovating residential (except single family) buildings
233210	Renovating single family buildings
926150	Rent control agencies
532310	Rent-all centers
*****	Rental — see type of article or property being rented
531210	Renting real estate for others (i.e. agents, brokers)
541611	Reorganizational consulting services
522294	Repackaging loans for sale to others (i.e., private conduits)
*****	Repair — see type of article being repaired
323121	Repairing books
233310	Repairing industrial buildings
233320	Repairing nonresidential (except industrial) buildings
233220	Repairing residential (except single family) building
233210	Repairing single family buildings
334210	Repeater and transceiver equipment, carrier line, manufacturing

Code	Description
711110	Repertory companies, theatrical
322231	Report covers made from purchased paper or paperboard
711510	Reporters, independent (freelance)
561491	Repossession services
512199	Reproduction of motion picture films for theatrical distribution
115210	Reproductive flushing services for animals
621410	Reproductive health services centers
561439	Reprographic services
712130	Reptile exhibits, live
321912	Resawing purchased lumber
621910	Rescue services, air
621910	Rescue services, medical
513340	Resellers, satellite telecommunication
513330	Resellers, telecommunication (except satellite)
325411	Reserpines (i.e., basic chemicals) manufacturing
561599	Reservation (e.g., airline, car rental, hotel, restaurant) services
522320	Reserve and liquidity services (except central bank)
234990	Reservoir construction
721310	Residence clubs, organizational
531110	Residential building rental or leasing
561720	Residential cleaning services
721310	Residential clubs
233220	Residential construction (except single family)
233210	Residential construction, single family
623220	Residential group homes for the emotionally disturbed
531110	Residential hotel rental or leasing
531311	Residential property managing
531210	Residential real estate agencies
531210	Residential real estate agents' offices
531210	Residential real estate brokerages
531210	Residential real estate brokers' offices
531311	Residential real estate property managers' offices

Code	Description
531190	Residential trailer parks
211112	Residue gas production
326192	Resilient floor coverings (e.g., sheet, tile) manufacturing
235520	Resilient flooring construction contractors
325211	Resins, plastics (except custom compounding purchased resins), manufacturing
422610	Resins, plastics, wholesaling
422690	Resins, synthetic rubber, wholesaling
334515	Resistance measuring equipment manufacturing
334513	Resistance thermometers and bulbs, industrial process-type, manufacturing
333992	Resistance welding equipment manufacturing
334415	Resistors, electronic, manufacturing
421690	Resistors, electronic, wholesaling
335312	Resolvers manufacturing
334516	Resonance instruments (i.e., laboratory-type) manufacturing
334419	Resonant reed devices, electronic, manufacturing
325192	Resorcinol manufacturing
721120	Resort hotels with casinos
721110	Resort hotels without casinos
334510	Respiratory analysis equipment, electromedical, manufacturing
339113	Respiratory protection mask manufacturing
621399	Respiratory therapists' offices (e.g., centers, clinics)
623110	Rest homes with nursing care
623312	Rest homes without nursing care
561720	Rest room cleaning services
812990	Rest room operation
813910	Restaurant associations
233320	Restaurant construction
421440	Restaurant equipment (except furniture) wholesaling
337127	Restaurant furniture (e.g., carts, chairs, foodwagons, tables) manufacturing
421210	Restaurant furniture wholesaling

Code	Description
561720	Restaurant kitchen cleaning services
492210	Restaurant meals delivery services (i.e., independent delivery services)
722211	Restaurants, carryout
722211	Restaurants, fast food
722110	Restaurants, full service
811420	Restoration and repair of antique furniture
811121	Restoration shops, antique and classic automotive
339113	Restraints, patient, manufacturing
561410	Resume writing services
234110	Resurfacing streets and highways
*****	Retail — see type of dealer, shop, or store
333997	Retail scales (e.g., butcher, delicatessen, produce) manufacturing
813910	Retailers' associations
235710	Retaining wall, concrete, construction contractors
235410	Retaining wall, masonary (i.e., brick, stone), construction contractors
325998	Retarders (e.g., flameproofing agents, mildewproofing agents) manufacturing
339112	Retinoscopes (except electromedical) manufacturing
334510	Retinoscopes, electromedical, manufacturing
813410	Retirement associations, social
623311	Retirement communities, continuing care
623110	Retirement homes with nursing care
623312	Retirement homes without nursing care
531110	Retirement hotel rental or leasing
525110	Retirement pension plans
332420	Retorts, heavy gauge metal, manufacturing
339112	Retractors, medical, manufacturing
326211	Retreading materials, tire, manufacturing
326212	Retreading tires
813110	Retreat houses, religious
115114	Retting flax

Code	Description
811420	Reupholstery shops, furniture
522292	Reverse mortgage lending
234990	Revetment construction
332994	Revolvers manufacturing
235950	Revolving door construction contractors
213111	Reworking oil and gas wells on a contract basis
331419	Rhenium refining, primary
335931	Rheostats (i.e., dimmer switches), current carrying wiring device, manufacturing
334419	Rheostats, electronic, manufacturing
335314	Rheostats, industrial control, manufacturing
212299	Rhodium mining and/or beneficiating
212299	Rhodochrosite mining and/or beneficiating
111219	Rhubarb farming, field and seed production
111419	Rhubarb, grown under cover
339944	Ribbons (e.g., cash register, printer, typewriter), inked, manufacturing
314999	Ribbons made from purchased fabrics
313221	Ribbons made in narrow woven fabric mills
313230	Ribbons made in nonwoven fabric mills
339944	Ribbons, inked, manufacturing
422120	Ribbons, inked, wholesaling
422310	Ribbons, textile, wholesaling
111160	Rice (except wild rice) farming, field and seed production
311212	Rice bran, flour, and meals, manufacturing
311230	Rice breakfast foods manufacturing
311212	Rice cleaning and polishing
115114	Rice drying
311212	Rice flour manufacturing
311213	Rice malt manufacturing
311212	Rice meal manufacturing
311212	Rice milling
311999	Rice mixes (i.e., uncooked and packaged with other ingredients) made from purchased rice and dry ingredients

Code	Description
311423	Rice mixes (i.e., uncooked and packaged with other ingredients) made in dehydration plants
311212	Rice mixes (i.e., uncooked and packaged with other ingredients) made in rice mills
311221	Rice starches manufacturing
311212	Rice, brewer's, manufacturing
311212	Rice, brown, manufacturing
422490	Rice, polished, wholesaling
422510	Rice, unpolished, wholesaling
315211	Riding clothes, men's and boys', cut and sew apparel contractors
315228	Riding clothes, men's and boys', cut and sewn from purchased fabric (except apparel contractors)
315212	Riding clothes, women's and girls', cut and sew apparel contractors
315239	Riding clothes, women's, misses', and girls', cut and sewn from purchased fabric (except apparel contractors)
713990	Riding clubs, recreational
316999	Riding crops manufacturing
611620	Riding instruction academies or schools
713990	Riding stables
713990	Rifle clubs, recreational
332994	Rifles (except recoilless, toy) manufacturing
332994	Rifles, BB and pellet, manufacturing
332994	Rifles, pneumatic, manufacturing
332995	Rifles, recoilless, manufacturing
339932	Rifles, toy, manufacturing
333512	Rifling machines, metalworking, manufacturing
213112	Rig skidding, oil and gas field, on a contract basis
336399	Rims, automotive, truck, and bus wheel, manufacturing
336311	Rings, piston, manufacturing
713940	Rinks, ice or roller skating
212319	Riprap (except granite, limestone) preparation plants
212319	Riprap (except limestone and granite) mining or quarrying
212313	Riprap, granite, mining or quarrying

Code	Description
212313	Riprap, granite, preparation plants
212312	Riprap, limestone, mining or quarrying
212312	Riprap, limestone, preparation plants
483211	River freight transportation
483212	River passenger transportation
713990	River rafting, recreational
713210	Riverboat casinos
333991	Riveting guns, handheld power-driven, manufacturing
333513	Riveting machines, metalworking, manufacturing
332722	Rivets, metal, manufacturing
325320	Roach poisons manufacturing
234110	Road (except elevated) construction
711110	Road companies, theatrical
421810	Road construction and maintenance machinery wholesaling
234120	Road elevated (e.g., bridges) construction
324199	Road oils made from refined petroleum
324110	Road oils made in petroleum refineries
311911	Roasted nuts and seeds manufacturing
112320	Roaster chicken production
335211	Roasters (i.e., cooking appliances), household-type electric, manufacturing
311920	Roasting coffee
333294	Roasting machinery manufacturing
315291	Robes, lounging, infants', cut and sewn from purchased fabric (except apparel contractors)
315192	Robes, lounging, made in apparel knitting mills
315211	Robes, lounging, men's and boys', cut and sew apparel contractors
315221	Robes, lounging, men's and boys', cut and sewn from purchased fabric (except apparel contractors)
315212	Robes, lounging, women's, girls', and infants', cut and sew apparel contractors

Code	Description
315231	Robes, lounging, women's, misses', and girls', cut and sewn from purchased fabric (except apparel contractors)
333120	Rock crushing machinery, portable, manufacturing
333131	Rock crushing machinery, stationary, manufacturing
333132	Rock drill bits, oil and gas field-type, manufacturing
333120	Rock drills, construction and surface mining-type, manufacturing
333131	Rock drills, underground mining-type, manufacturing
711130	Rock musical artists, independent
711130	Rock musical groups
234990	Rock removal, underwater, construction
212393	Rock salt mining and/or beneficiating
336312	Rocker arms and parts, automotive and truck gasoline engine, manufacturing
337122	Rockers (except upholstered), wood, manufacturing
337121	Rockers, upholstered, manufacturing
332313	Rocket casings, fabricated metal work, manufacturing
336412	Rocket engines, aircraft, manufacturing
336415	Rocket engines, guided missile, manufacturing
332995	Rocket launchers manufacturing
336414	Rockets (guided missiles), space and military, complete, manufacturing
332993	Rockets, ammunition (except guided missiles, pyrotechnic), manufacturing
114111	Rockfish fishing
339932	Rocking horses manufacturing
331316	Rod made by extruding purchased aluminum
331319	Rod made by rolling purchased aluminum
333516	Rod rolling mill machinery, metalworking, manufacturing

Code	Description
331316	Rod, aluminum, made in integrated secondary smelting and extruding mills
331319	Rod, aluminum, made in integrated secondary smelting and rolling mills
331421	Rod, copper and copper alloy, made from purchased copper or in integrated secondary smelting and rolling, drawing or extruding plants
326130	Rod, laminated plastics, manufacturing
331491	Rod, nonferrous metals (except aluminum, copper), made from purchased metals or scrap
326121	Rod, nonrigid plastics, manufacturing
325320	Rodent poisons manufacturing
325320	Rodenticides manufacturing
711310	Rodeo managers with facilities
711320	Rodeo managers without facilities
711310	Rodeo organizers with facilities
711320	Rodeo organizers without facilities
711310	Rodeo promoters with facilities
711320	Rodeo promoters without facilities
339920	Rods and rod parts, fishing, manufacturing
326299	Rods, hard rubber, manufacturing
331111	Rods, iron or steel, made in steel mills
421510	Rods, metal (except precious), wholesaling
334519	Rods, surveyor's, manufacturing
332991	Roller bearings manufacturing
711211	Roller hockey clubs, professional or semiprofessional
316110	Roller leather manufacturing
339920	Roller skates manufacturing
713940	Roller skating rinks
333120	Rollers, road construction and maintenance machinery, manufacturing
321999	Rollers, wood, manufacturing
332321	Rolling doors for industrial buildings and warehouses, metal, manufacturing

Code	Description
333516	Rolling mill machinery and equipment, metalworking, manufacturing
333516	Rolling mill roll machines manufacturing
331511	Rolling mill rolls, iron, manufacturing
331513	Rolling mill rolls, steel, manufacturing
321999	Rolling pins, wood, manufacturing
336510	Rolling stock, railroad, rebuilding
311812	Rolls and buns (including frozen) made in commercial bakeries
326299	Rolls and roll coverings, rubber (e.g., industrial, papermill, painters', steelmill) manufacturing
111219	Romaine lettuce farming, field and seed production
315291	Rompers, infants', cut and sewn from purchased fabric (except apparel contractors)
315212	Rompers, women's, girls', and infants', cut and sew apparel contractors
332322	Roof deck, sheet metal, manufacturing
235610	Roof spraying, painting or coating, construction contractors
321214	Roof trusses, wood, manufacturing
326299	Roofing (i.e., single ply rubber membrane) manufacturing
324122	Roofing cements, asphalt, made from purchased asphaltic materials
324122	Roofing coatings made from purchased asphaltic materials
235610	Roofing construction contractors
324122	Roofing felts made from purchased asphaltic materials
444190	Roofing material dealers
421330	Roofing materials (except wood) wholesaling
421310	Roofing materials, wood, wholesaling
327123	Roofing tile, clay, manufacturing
327390	Roofing tile, concrete, manufacturing
332322	Roofing, sheet metal, manufacturing

Code	Description
333415	Room air-conditioners manufacturing
421620	Room air-conditioners wholesaling
337122	Room dividers, wood household-type, manufacturing
333414	Room heaters (except portable electric) manufacturing
335211	Room heaters, portable electric, manufacturing
334512	Room thermostats manufacturing
721310	Rooming and boarding houses
325320	Root removing chemicals manufacturing
311221	Root starches manufacturing
332999	Rope fittings manufacturing
332618	Rope, wire, made from purchased wire
314991	Ropes (except wire rope) manufacturing
421840	Ropes (except wire rope) wholesaling
313111	Ropes, hemp, made from purchased fiber
421510	Ropes, wire (except insulated), wholesaling
339911	Rosaries and other small religious articles, precious metal, manufacturing
212291	Roscoelite (vanadium hydromica) mining and/or beneficiating
111421	Rose bush growing
325211	Rosins (i.e., modified resins) manufacturing
325191	Rosins made by distillation of pine gum or pine wood
422690	Rosins wholesaling
333111	Rotary hoes manufacturing
333111	Rotary tillers, farm-type, manufacturing
334514	Rotary type meters, consumption registering, manufacturing
325320	Rotenone insecticides manufacturing
323111	Rotogravure printing
323122	Rotogravure printing plates and cylinders preparation services
335312	Rotor retainers and housings manufacturing

Code	Description
335312	Rotors (i.e., for motors) manufacturing
325620	Rouge, cosmetic, manufacturing
321920	Round stave baskets (e.g., fruit, vegetable) manufacturing
321912	Rounds or rungs, furniture, hardwood, manufacturing
331111	Rounds, tube, steel, made in steel mills
421990	Roundwood wholesaling
213112	Roustabout mining services, on a contract basis
333991	Routers, handheld power-driven, manufacturing
333292	Roving machinery for textiles manufacturing
233210	Row house single family construction
532292	Rowboat rental
336612	Rowboats manufacturing
713990	Rowing clubs, recreational
112910	Royal jelly production, bees
326220	Rubber and plastics belts and hoses (without fittings) manufacturing
326299	Rubber bands manufacturing
325520	Rubber cements manufacturing
212324	Rubber clay mining and/or beneficiating
326192	Rubber floor coverings manufacturing
326291	Rubber goods, mechanical (i.e., extruded, lathe-cut, molded), manufacturing
421840	Rubber goods, mechanical (i.e., extruded, lathe-cut, molded), wholesaling
422210	Rubber goods, medical, wholesaling
325998	Rubber processing preparations (e.g., accelerators, stabilizers) manufacturing
421930	Rubber scrap and scrap tires wholesaling
339943	Rubber stamps manufacturing
422120	Rubber stamps, wholesaling
313221	Rubber thread and yarns, fabric covered, manufacturing
333220	Rubber working machinery manufacturing

Code	Description
422990	Rubber, crude, wholesaling
325212	Rubber, synthetic, manufacturing
313320	Rubberizing purchased capes
313320	Rubberizing purchased cloaks
313320	Rubberizing purchased clothing
313320	Rubberizing purchased coats
313320	Rubberizing purchased textiles and apparel
212399	Rubbing stones mining and/or beneficiating
562111	Rubbish (i.e., nonhazardous solid waste) hauling, local
562111	Rubbish collection services
562213	Rubbish disposal combustors or incinerators
562212	Rubbish disposal landfills
484220	Rubbish hauling without collection or disposal, truck, local
484230	Rubbish hauling without collection or disposal, truck, long-distance
562119	Rubble hauling, local
562119	Rubble removal services
212399	Ruby mining and/or beneficiating
532299	Rug and carpet rental
561740	Rug cleaning plants
325612	Rug cleaning preparations manufacturing
561740	Rug cleaning services
442210	Rug stores
314110	Rugs and carpets made from textile materials
421220	Rugs wholesaling
321999	Rulers and rules (except slide), wood, manufacturing
332212	Rulers, metal, manufacturing
326199	Rulers, plastics, manufacturing
334519	Rules, slide, manufacturing
624221	Runaway youth shelters
488119	Runway maintenance services
485210	Rural bus services
324191	Rust arresting petroleum compounds made from refined petroleum
325998	Rust preventive preparations manufacturing
325612	Rust removers manufacturing

Code	Description
332812	Rustproofing metals and metal products for the trade
811198	Rustproofing shops, automotive
111219	Rutabaga farming, field and seed production
212299	Ruthenium ore mining and/or beneficiating
212299	Rutile mining and/or beneficiating
111199	Rye farming, field and seed production
311211	Rye flour manufacturing
311213	Rye malt manufacturing
111998	Ryegrass seed farming
325212	S-type rubber manufacturing
522294	SLMA (Student Loan Marketing Association)
114111	Sablefish fishing
325199	Saccharin manufacturing
325620	Sachet, scented, manufacturing
322224	Sacks, multiwall, made from purchased uncoated paper
422130	Sacks, paper, wholesaling
713990	Saddle horse rental services, recreational
325612	Saddle soaps manufacturing
321999	Saddle trees, wood, manufacturing
316110	Saddlery leather manufacturing
332999	Saddlery parts, metal, manufacturing
811430	Saddlery repair shops without retailing new saddlery
451110	Saddlery stores
422910	Saddlery wholesaling
316999	Saddles and parts, leather, manufacturing
332999	Safe deposit boxes and chests, metal, manufacturing
332999	Safe doors and linings, metal, manufacturing
332999	Safes, metal, manufacturing
421420	Safes, security, wholesaling
332911	Safety (i.e., pop-off) valves, industrial-type, manufacturing
316999	Safety belts, leather, manufacturing
541690	Safety consulting services
325920	Safety fuses, blasting, manufacturing

Code	Description
327215	Safety glass (including motor vehicle) made from purchased glass
339993	Safety pins manufacturing
332211	Safety razor blades manufacturing
332211	Safety razors manufacturing
111120	Safflower farming, field and seed production
311225	Safflower oil made from purchased oils
311223	Safflower oil made in crushing mills
441222	Sail boat dealers
339920	Sailboards manufacturing
336612	Sailboat building, not done in shipyards
532292	Sailboat rental
713930	Sailing clubs with marinas
713990	Sailing clubs without marinas
336611	Sailing ships, commercial, manufacturing
314912	Sails made from purchased fabrics
325181	Sal soda (i.e., washing soda) manufacturing
311423	Salad dressing mixes, dry, made in a dehydration plant
311942	Salad dressing mixes, dry, manufacturing
311941	Salad dressings manufacturing
422490	Salad dressings wholesaling
422490	Salad oils wholesaling
311991	Salads, fresh or refrigerated, manufacturing
422120	Sales books wholesaling
323116	Sales books, manifold, printing
522220	Sales financing
541613	Sales management consulting services
325199	Salicylic acid (except medicinal) manufacturing
325411	Salicylic acid, medicinal, uncompounded, manufacturing
212391	Salines (except common salt) mining and/or beneficiating
114111	Salmon fishing
233320	Salon construction
311421	Salsa canning
325998	Salt (except table) manufacturing

Code	Description
311942	Salt substitute manufacturing
213112	Salt water disposal systems, oil and gas field, on a contract basis
212393	Salt, common, mining and/or beneficiating
212393	Salt, rock, mining and/or beneficiating
311942	Salt, table, manufacturing
422490	Salt, table, wholesaling
311612	Salted meats made from purchased carcasses
311821	Saltines manufacturing
422210	Salts, bath, wholesaling
422690	Salts, industrial, wholesaling
334516	Sample analysis instruments (except medical) manufacturing
316991	Sample cases, all materials, manufacturing
334519	Sample changers, nuclear radiation, manufacturing
541870	Sample direct distribution services
323121	Samples and displays mounting
541910	Sampling services, statistical
421320	Sand (except industrial) wholesaling
212321	Sand and gravel quarrying (i.e., construction grade) and/or beneficiating
213112	Sand blasting pipelines on lease, oil and gas field on a contract basis
331524	Sand castings, aluminum, unfinished, manufacturing
331525	Sand castings, copper and copper-base alloy, unfinished, manufacturing
331528	Sand castings, nonferrous metals (except aluminum, copper), unfinished, manufacturing
484220	Sand hauling, local
484230	Sand hauling, long-distance
333120	Sand mixers manufacturing
212322	Sand, blast, quarrying and/or beneficiating
212321	Sand, construction grade, quarrying and/or beneficiating
212322	Sand, industrial (e.g., engine, filtration, glass grinding), quarrying and/or beneficiating

Code	Description
421840	Sand, industrial, wholesaling
316219	Sandals, children's (except rubber, plastics), manufacturing
316213	Sandals, men's footwear (except rubber, plastics), manufacturing
316211	Sandals, plastics or plastics soled fabric upper, manufacturing
316211	Sandals, rubber or rubber soled fabric upper, manufacturing
316214	Sandals, women's footwear (except rubber, plastics), manufacturing
332813	Sandblasting metals and metal products for the trade
235990	Sandblasting of building exteriors construction contractors
333991	Sanders, handheld power-driven, manufacturing
333319	Sanding machines, floor, manufacturing
333210	Sanding machines, woodworking-type, stationary, manufacturing
333291	Sandpaper making machines manufacturing
327910	Sandpaper manufacturing
212319	Sandstone crushed and broken stone mining
212311	Sandstone mining or quarrying
212399	Sandstone, bituminous, mining and/or beneficiating
722211	Sandwich shops, limited service
311612	Sandwich spreads, meat, made from purchased carcasses
311941	Sandwich spreads, salad dressing based, manufacturing
335211	Sandwich toasters and grills, household-type electric, manufacturing
422490	Sandwiches wholesaling
311991	Sandwiches, fresh (i.e., assembled and packaged for wholesale market), manufacturing
322212	Sanitary food container, folding, made from purchased paperboard
422130	Sanitary food containers (e.g., disposable plastics, paper, paperboard) wholesaling
322215	Sanitary food containers (except folding) made from purchased paper or paperboard

Code	Description
562212	Sanitary landfills
322291	Sanitary napkins and tampons made from purchased paper or textile fiber
322121	Sanitary napkins and tampons made in paper mills
322121	Sanitary paper products (except newsprint, uncoated groundwood) made in paper mills
422130	Sanitary paper products wholesaling
322121	Sanitary paper stock manufacturing
322291	Sanitary products made from purchased sanitary paper stock
322121	Sanitary products made in paper mills
332998	Sanitary ware (e.g., bathtubs, lavatories, sinks), metal, manufacturing
421720	Sanitary ware, china or enameled iron, wholesaling
541620	Sanitation consulting services
926130	Sanitation districts, nonoperating
924110	Sanitation engineering agencies, government
212399	Sapphire mining and/or beneficiating
325222	Saran (i.e., polyvinylidene chloride) fibers and filaments manufacturing
332612	Sash balance springs made from purchased wire
332321	Sash, door and window, metal, manufacturing
321911	Sash, door and window, wood and covered wood, manufacturing
316991	Satchels, all materials, manufacturing
334220	Satellite antennas manufacturing
334220	Satellite communications equipment manufacturing
513220	Satellite master antenna television service (SMATV)
513111	Satellite radio networks
513340	Satellite telecommunication carriers
513340	Satellite telecommunication resellers
513390	Satellite telemetry operations on a contract or fee basis

Code	Description
513220	Satellite television distribution systems
513210	Satellite television networks
513390	Satellite tracking stations on a contract or fee basis
325131	Satin white pigments manufacturing
335311	Saturable transformers manufacturing
324122	Saturated felts made from purchased paper
322121	Saturated felts made in paper mills
311423	Sauce mixes, dry, made in dehydration plants
311942	Sauce mixes, dry, manufacturing
311941	Sauces (except tomato based) manufacturing
311941	Sauces for meat (except tomato based) manufacturing
311941	Sauces for seafood (except tomato based) manufacturing
311941	Sauces for vegetable (except tomato based) manufacturing
311421	Sauces, tomato-based, canning
311421	Sauerkraut manufacturing
335211	Sauna heaters, electric, manufacturing
321992	Sauna rooms, prefabricated, wood, manufacturing
812199	Saunas
311612	Sausage and similar cased products made from purchased carcasses
422490	Sausage casings wholesaling
311612	Sausage casings, collagen, made from purchased hides
311611	Sausage casings, natural, produced in slaughtering plant
326121	Sausage casings, plastics, manufacturing
522120	Savings and loan associations (S&L)
524113	Savings bank life insurance carriers, direct
522120	Savings banks
332213	Saw blades, all types, manufacturing
811411	Saw repair and maintenance (except sawmills) without retailing new saws

Code	Description
321113	Sawdust and shavings (i.e., sawmill byproducts) manufacturing
422990	Sawdust wholesaling
321999	Sawdust, regrinding
321113	Sawed lumber made in sawmills
321912	Sawed lumber, resawing purchased lumber
333512	Sawing machines, metalworking, manufacturing
333210	Sawmill equipment manufacturing
532490	Sawmill machinery rental or leasing
421830	Sawmill machinery, equipment, and supplies wholesaling
321113	Sawmills
333210	Saws, bench and table, power-driven, woodworking-type, manufacturing
332213	Saws, hand, nonpowered, manufacturing
333991	Saws, handheld power-driven, manufacturing
339112	Saws, surgical, manufacturing
339992	Saxophones and parts manufacturing
235990	Scaffolding construction contractors
532490	Scaffolding rental or leasing
421810	Scaffolding wholesaling
332323	Scaffolds, metal, manufacturing
334519	Scalers, nuclear radiation, manufacturing
333997	Scales (except laboratory-type) manufacturing
339111	Scales and balances, laboratory-type, manufacturing
339111	Scales, laboratory, manufacturing
114112	Scallop fishing
812199	Scalp treating services
333210	Scarfing machines, woodworking-type, manufacturing
333516	Scarfing units, rolling mill machin--ery, metalworking, manufacturing
333120	Scarifiers, road, manufacturing
325132	Scarlet 2 R lake manufacturing
315191	Scarves made in apparel knitting mills

Code	Description
315211	Scarves, men's and boys', cut and sew apparel contractors
315993	Scarves, men's and boys', cut and sewn from purchased fabric (except apparel contractors)
315212	Scarves, women's, girls', and infants', cut and sew apparel contractors
315999	Scarves, women's, misses', and girls', cut and sewn from purchased fabric (except apparel contractors)
336350	Scattershield, engine, manufacturing
711510	Scenery designers, independent theatrical
532490	Scenery, theatrical, rental or leasing
487990	Scenic and sightseeing excursions, aerial
487110	Scenic and sightseeing excursions, land
487210	Scenic and sightseeing excursions, water
481112	Scheduled air freight carriers
481112	Scheduled air freight transportation
481111	Scheduled air passenger carriers
481111	Scheduled air passenger transportation
212299	Scheelite mining and/or beneficiating
313222	Schiffli machine embroideries manufacturing
333292	Schiffli machinery manufacturing
212319	Schist, mica, crushed and broken stone, mining and/or beneficiating
212311	Schist, mica, mining or quarrying
511120	Scholarly journal publishers
511120	Scholarly journal publishers and printing combined
511120	Scholarly journal publishing (i.e., establishments known as publishers)
323112	Scholarly journals flexographic printing without publishing
323111	Scholarly journals gravure printing without publishing
323110	Scholarly journals lithographic (offset) printing without publishing

Code	Description
323119	Scholarly journals printing (except flexographic, gravure, lithographic, screen) without publishing
323113	Scholarly journals screen printing without publishing
813211	Scholarship trusts (i.e., grantmaking, charitable trust foundations)
511120	Scholastic magazine and periodical publishers
511120	Scholastic magazine and periodical publishers and printing combined
511120	Scholastic magazine and periodical publishing (i.e., establishments known as publishers)
323112	Scholastic magazines and periodicals flexographic printing without publishing
323111	Scholastic magazines and periodicals gravure printing without publishing
323110	Scholastic magazines and periodicals lithographic (offset) printing without publishing
323119	Scholastic magazines and periodicals printing (except flexographic, gravure, lithographic, screen) without publishing
323113	Scholastic magazines and periodicals screen printing without publishing
611110	School boards, elementary and secondary
511130	School book publishers
511130	School book publishers and printing combined
511130	School book publishing (i.e., establishments known as publishers)
323117	School books printing and binding without publishing
323117	School books printing without publishing
233320	School building construction
532120	School bus rental or leasing
485410	School bus services
336211	School buses assembling on purchased chassis
421110	School buses wholesaling

Code	Description
611110	School districts, elementary or secondary
421490	School equipment and supplies (except books, furniture) wholesaling
337127	School furniture manufacturing
421210	School furniture wholesaling
541921	School photography (i.e., portrait photography) services
453210	School supply stores
323121	School text books binding without printing
511130	School textbook publishers
511130	School textbook publishers and printing combined
511130	School textbook publishing (i.e., establishments known as publishers)
323117	School textbooks printing and binding without publishing
323117	School textbooks printing without publishing
611110	Schools for the handicapped, elementary or secondary
611110	Schools for the mentally retarded (except preschool, job training, vocational rehabilitation)
611110	Schools for the physically disabled, elementary or secondary
611512	Schools, aviation
611511	Schools, barber
611511	Schools, beauty
611410	Schools, business, not offering academic degrees
611310	Schools, correspondence, college level
611511	Schools, cosmetology
611610	Schools, drama (except academic)
611110	Schools, elementary
611210	Schools, junior college
611210	Schools, junior college vocational
611630	Schools, language
611310	Schools, medical
611610	Schools, music (except academic)
611310	Schools, professional (colleges or universities)
611110	Schools, secondary

Code	Description
611620	Schools, sports instruction
712110	Science and technology museums
339932	Science kits (e.g., chemistry sets, microscopes, natural science sets), manufacturing
327215	Scientific apparatus glass made from purchased glass
813920	Scientific associations
327215	Scientific glassware made from purchased glass
327212	Scientific glassware, pressed or blown, made in glass making plants
421490	Scientific instruments wholesaling
421490	Scientific laboratory equipment wholesaling
334519	Scintillation detectors manufacturing
335211	Scissors, electric, manufacturing
332211	Scissors, nonelectric, manufacturing
332212	Scoops, metal (except kitchen-type), manufacturing
321999	Scoops, wood, manufacturing
339932	Scooters, children's, manufacturing
339950	Scoreboards manufacturing
212399	Scoria mining and/or beneficiating
313312	Scouring and combing textile fibers
325611	Scouring cleansers (e.g., pastes, powders) manufacturing
332999	Scouring pads, soap impregnated, manufacturing
813410	Scouting organizations
421930	Scrap materials wholesaling
323118	Scrapbooks and refills manufacturing
422120	Scrapbooks wholesaling
333131	Scraper loaders, underground mining-type, manufacturing
333120	Scrapers, construction-type, manufacturing
332321	Screen doors, metal frame, manufacturing
323122	Screen for printing, preparation services
323113	Screen printing (except manifold business forms, printing grey goods, printing books)

Code	Description
323113	Screen printing apparel and textile products (e.g. caps, napkins, placemats, T-shirts, towels)
313311	Screen printing broadwoven fabric grey goods
325910	Screen process inks manufacturing
333999	Screening and sifting machinery for general industrial use manufacturing
333120	Screening machinery, portable, manufacturing
333131	Screening machinery, stationary, manufacturing
212399	Screening peat
212113	Screening plants, anthracite
212111	Screening plants, bituminous coal or lignite
326199	Screening, window, plastics, manufacturing
711510	Screenplay writers, independent
313312	Screenprinting fabric grey goods (except broadwoven) and textile products (except apparel)
334419	Screens for liquid crystal display (LCD) manufacturing
332321	Screens, door and window, metal frame, manufacturing
321911	Screens, door and window, wood framed, manufacturing
333315	Screens, projection (i.e., motion picture, overhead, slide), manufacturing
421310	Screens, window and door, wholesaling
333512	Screw and nut slotting machines, metalworking, manufacturing
333922	Screw conveyors manufacturing
332212	Screw drivers, nonelectric, manufacturing
332722	Screw eyes, metal, manufacturing
333518	Screwdowns and boxes machinery, metal, manufacturing
333991	Screwdrivers and nut drivers, handheld power-driven, manufacturing
333518	Screwdriving machines manufacturing
332212	Screwjacks manufacturing

Code	Description
332722	Screws, metal, manufacturing
711510	Script writers, independent
339920	Scuba diving equipment manufacturing
611620	Scuba instruction, camps, or schools
711510	Sculptors, independent
611610	Sculpture instruction
327420	Sculptures (e.g., gypsum, plaster of paris) manufacturing
327112	Sculptures, architectural, clay, manufacturing
332212	Scythes manufacturing
212399	Scythestones mining and/or beneficiating
114111	Sea bass fishing
114111	Sea herring fishing
713990	Sea kayaking, recreational
111998	Sea plant agriculture
114111	Sea trout fishing
114112	Sea urchin fishing
422460	Seafood (except canned, packaged frozen) wholesaling
311711	Seafood and seafood products canning
311711	Seafood and seafood products curing
311712	Seafood dinners, frozen, manufacturing
445220	Seafood markets
311712	Seafood products, fresh prepared, manufacturing
311712	Seafood products, frozen, manufacturing
422490	Seafood, canned, wholesaling
311712	Seafood, fresh prepared, manufacturing
311712	Seafood, frozen, manufacturing
422420	Seafoods, packaged frozen, wholesaling
339943	Seal presses (e.g., notary), hand operated, manufacturing
422690	Sealants wholesaling
335110	Sealed beam automotive light bulbs manufacturing
325520	Sealing compounds for pipe threads and joints manufacturing
421840	Seals wholesaling

Code	Description
339991	Seals, grease or oil, manufacturing
333992	Seam welding equipment manufacturing
334511	Search and detection systems and instruments manufacturing
514199	Search services, information, on a contract or fee basis
335129	Searchlights, electric and nonelectric, manufacturing
453220	Seasonal and holiday decoration stores
721110	Seasonal hotels
561730	Seasonal property maintenance services (i.e., snow plowing in winter, landscaping during other seasons)
311942	Seasoning salt manufacturing
336360	Seat belts, motor vehicle and aircraft, manufacturing
421120	Seat covers, automotive, wholesaling
321999	Seat covers, rattan, manufacturing
326150	Seat cushions, foam plastics (except polystyrene), manufacturing
316999	Seatbelts, leather, manufacturing
336360	Seats for public conveyances, manufacturing
336360	Seats, railroad, manufacturing
321999	Seats, toilet, wood, manufacturing
488310	Seaway operation
111998	Seaweed farming
114119	Seaweed gathering
311711	Seaweed processing (e.g., dulse)
325199	Sebacic acid esters manufacturing
325199	Sebacic acid manufacturing
611630	Second langauge instruction
453310	Second-hand merchandise stores
522294	Secondary market financing (i.e., buying, pooling, repackaging loans for sale to others)
331492	Secondary refining of nonferrous metals (except aluminum, copper)
611110	Secondary schools offering both academic and technical courses
331492	Secondary smelting of nonferrous metals (except aluminum, copper)
611410	Secretarial schools

Code	Description
561410	Secretarial services
332311	Sections for prefabricated metal buildings manufacturing
321992	Sections, prefabricated wood building, manufacturing
523120	Securities brokerages
523120	Securities brokers' offices
523991	Securities custodians
523110	Securities dealers (i.e., acting as a principal in dealing securities to investors)
523110	Securities dealing (i.e., acting as a principal in dealing securities to investors)
523110	Securities distributing (i.e., acting as a principal in dealing securities to investors)
523210	Securities exchanges
523120	Securities floor brokers
523110	Securities floor traders (i.e., acting as a principal in dealing securities to investors)
523110	Securities flotation companies
523999	Securities holders' protective services
523110	Securities originating (i.e., acting as a principal in dealing securities to investors)
926150	Securities regulation commissions
523110	Securities trading (i.e., acting as a principal in dealing securities to investors)
523999	Securities transfer agencies
523110	Securities underwriting
561621	Security alarm systems sales combined with installation, maintenance, or monitoring services
541690	Security consulting services
561612	Security guard services
561612	Security patrol services
421420	Security safes wholesaling
561621	Security system monitoring services
421610	Security systems wholesaling
325412	Sedative preparations manufacturing
212399	Sedge peat mining and/or beneficiating

Code	Description
333131	Sedimentary mineral machinery manufacturing
314911	Seed bags made from purchased woven or knitted materials
115112	Seed bed preparing
115114	Seed cleaning
322232	Seed packets made from purchased paper
541380	Seed testing laboratories or services
325320	Seed treatment preparations manufacturing
333111	Seeders, farm-type, manufacturing
333112	Seeders, lawn and garden-type, manufacturing
115112	Seeding crops
561730	Seeding lawns
422450	Seeds (e.g., canned, roasted, salted) wholesaling
422910	Seeds (e.g., field, flower, garden) wholesaling
311911	Seeds, snack (e.g., canned, cooked, roasted, salted) manufacturing
541360	Seismic geophysical surveying services
213112	Seismograph exploration (except surveying) for oil and gas on a contract basis
334519	Seismographs manufacturing
334519	Seismometers manufacturing
334519	Seismoscopes manufacturing
212399	Selenite mining and/or beneficiating
331491	Selenium bar, rod, sheet, strip, and tubing made from purchased metals or scrap
325188	Selenium compounds, not specified elsewhere by process, manufacturing
325188	Selenium dioxide manufacturing
331492	Selenium recovering from scrap and/or alloying purchased metals
331419	Selenium refining, primary
624190	Self-help organizations (except for disabled persons, the elderly, persons diagnosed with mental retardation)
624120	Self-help organizations for disabled persons, the elderly, and persons diagnosed with mental retardation

Code	Description
624110	Self-help organizations, youth
525190	Self-insurance funds (except employee benefit funds)
811192	Self-service carwash
812310	Self-service drycleaners and laundries
531130	Self-storage unit rental or leasing
531130	Self-storage warehousing
531210	Selling real estate for others (i.e., agents, brokers)
115210	Semen collection
422590	Semen, bovine, wholesaling
421510	Semi-finished metal products wholesaling
336212	Semi-trailer manufacturing
532120	Semi-trailer rental or leasing
212111	Semianthracite surface mining and/or beneficiating
212112	Semianthracite underground mining or mining and beneficiating
212111	Semibituminous coal surface mining and/or beneficiating
212112	Semibituminous coal underground mining or mining and beneficiating
333295	Semiconductor assembly and packaging machinery manufacturing
335999	Semiconductor battery chargers manufacturing
334413	Semiconductor circuit networks (i.e., solid-state integrated circuits) manufacturing
334413	Semiconductor devices manufacturing
421690	Semiconductor devices wholesaling
334413	Semiconductor dice and wafers manufacturing
335999	Semiconductor high-voltage power supplies manufacturing
333295	Semiconductor making machinery manufacturing
334413	Semiconductor memory chips manufacturing
334515	Semiconductor test equipment manufacturing
333618	Semidiesel engines manufacturing
611110	Seminaries, below university grade

Code	Description
611310	Seminaries, theological, offering baccalaureate or graduate degrees
212399	Semiprecious stones mining and/or beneficiating
711211	Semiprofessional baseball clubs
711211	Semiprofessional football clubs
711211	Semiprofessional sports clubs
331511	Semisteel foundries
311211	Semolina flour manufacturing
624120	Senior citizens activity centers
813311	Senior citizens advocacy organizations
624120	Senior citizens centers
485991	Senior citizens transportation services
623312	Senior citizens' homes without nursing care
325992	Sensitized cloth or paper (e.g., blueprint, photographic) manufacturing
333315	Sensitometers, photographic, manufacturing
334510	Sentinel, cardiac, manufacturing
235110	Septic system construction contractors
562991	Septic tank cleaning services
562991	Septic tank pumping (i.e., cleaning) services
421390	Septic tanks (except concrete) wholesaling
421320	Septic tanks, concrete, wholesaling
332420	Septic tanks, heavy gauge metal, manufacturing
326199	Septic tanks, plastics or fiberglass, manufacturing
334512	Sequencing controls for electric heating equipment manufacturing
335999	Series capacitors (except electronic) manufacturing
212319	Serpentine crushed and broken stone mining and/or beneficiating
212311	Serpentine mining or quarrying
325414	Serums (except diagnostic substances) manufacturing
315211	Service apparel, washable, men's and boys', cut and sew apparel contractors

Code	Description
315225	Service apparel, washable, men's and boys', cut and sewn from purchased fabric (except apparel contractors)
315212	Service apparel, washable, women's, cut and sew apparel contractors
315239	Service apparel, washable, women's, misses' and girls', cut and sewn from purchased fabric (except apparel contractors)
421850	Service establishment equipment and supplies wholesaling
813910	Service industries associations
811310	Service machinery and equipment repair and maintenance services
561720	Service station cleaning and degreasing services
233320	Service station construction
447190	Service stations, gasoline
213111	Service well drilling on a contract basis
213112	Servicing oil and gas wells on a contract basis
337124	Serving carts, metal household-type, manufacturing
337122	Serving carts, wood household-type, manufacturing
335312	Servomotors manufacturing
111120	Sesame farming, field and seed production
711510	Set designers, independent theatrical
541191	Settlement offices, real estate
322213	Setup (i.e., not shipped flat) boxes made from purchased paperboard
322130	Setup boxboard stock manufacturing
234910	Sewage collection and disposal line construction
221320	Sewage disposal plants
333319	Sewage treatment equipment manufacturing
234990	Sewage treatment plant construction
221320	Sewage treatment plants or facilities
562998	Sewer cleaning and rodding services
562998	Sewer cleanout services

Code	Description
234910	Sewer construction
235110	Sewer hookup construction contractors
327123	Sewer pipe and fittings, clay, manufacturing
331511	Sewer pipe, cast iron, manufacturing
327332	Sewer pipe, concrete, manufacturing
221320	Sewer systems
234910	Sewer, water and pipeline construction management firms
422310	Sewing accessories wholesaling
339999	Sewing and mending kits assembling
316993	Sewing cases (except metal) manufacturing
339911	Sewing cases, precious metal, manufacturing
315211	Sewing fabric owned by others for men's and boys' apparel
315212	Sewing fabric owned by others for women's, girls' and infants' apparel
337129	Sewing machine cabinets, wood, manufacturing
443111	Sewing machine stores, household-type
811412	Sewing machine, household-type, repair shops without retailing new sewing machines
333298	Sewing machines (including household-type) manufacturing
421620	Sewing machines, household-type, wholesaling
421830	Sewing machines, industrial, wholesaling
451130	Sewing supply stores
313113	Sewing threads manufacturing
334511	Sextants (except surveying) manufacturing
334519	Sextants, surveying, manufacturing
337920	Shade pulls, window, manufacturing
335121	Shades, lamp (except glass, plastics), residential-type, manufacturing
337920	Shades, window (except outdoor canvas awnings), manufacturing

Code	Description
213113	Shaft sinking for coal mines on a contract basis
213114	Shaft sinking for metal mines on a contract basis
321113	Shakes (i.e., hand split shingles) manufacturing
212325	Shale (except oil shale) mining and/or beneficiating
327992	Shale, expanded, manufacturing
211111	Shale, oil, mining and/or beneficiating
111219	Shallot farming, field and seed production
325620	Shampoos and conditioners, hair, manufacturing
316999	Shanks, shoe, leather, manufacturing
333210	Shapers, woodworking-type, manufacturing
114111	Shark fishing
339994	Shaving brushes manufacturing
333512	Shaving machines, metalworking, manufacturing
325620	Shaving preparations (e.g., creams, gels, lotions, powders) manufacturing
422210	Shaving preparations wholesaling
333513	Shearing machines, metal forming, manufacturing
316110	Shearling (i.e., prepared sheepskin) manufacturing
333991	Shears and nibblers, handheld power-driven, manufacturing
332211	Shears, nonelectric, household-type (e.g., kitchen, barber, tailor) manufacturing
332212	Shears, nonelectric, tool-type (e.g., garden, pruners, tinsnip), manufacturing
333111	Shears, powered, for use on animals, manufacturing
322121	Sheathing paper (except newsprint, uncoated groundwood) made in paper mills
324122	Sheathing, asphalt saturated, made from refined petroleum
333613	Sheaves, mechanical power transmission, manufacturing

Code	Description
115210	Sheep dipping and shearing
112410	Sheep farming (e.g., meat, milk, wool production)
333111	Sheep shears, powered, manufacturing
422520	Sheep wholesaling
326140	Sheet (i.e., board), polystyrene foam insulation, manufacturing
333513	Sheet metal forming machines manufacturing
421330	Sheet metal roofing materials wholesaling
235610	Sheet metal work (except plumbing, heating, air-conditioning) construction contractors
332322	Sheet metal work (except stamped) manufacturing
611513	Sheet metal workers' apprenticeship training
323112	Sheet music flexographic printing without publishing
323111	Sheet music gravure printing without publishing
323110	Sheet music lithographic (offset) printing without publishing
323119	Sheet music printing (except flexographic, gravure, lithographic, screen) without publishing
512230	Sheet music publishers
512230	Sheet music publishers and printing combined
323113	Sheet music screen printing without publishing
451140	Sheet music stores
422990	Sheet music wholesaling
331111	Sheet pilings, plain, iron or steel, made in steel mills
331315	Sheet, aluminum, made by flat rolling purchased aluminum
331315	Sheet, aluminum, made in integrated secondary smelting and flat rolling mills
331421	Sheet, copper and copper alloy, made from purchased copper or in integrated secondary smelting and rolling, drawing or extruding plants

Code	Description
326130	Sheet, laminated plastics (except flexible packaging), manufacturing
326113	Sheet, plastics, unlaminated (except packaging), manufacturing
326299	Sheeting, rubber, manufacturing
314129	Sheets and pillowcases made from purchased fabrics
313210	Sheets and pillowcases made in broadwoven fabric mills
331111	Sheets, steel, made in steel mills
311119	Shell crushing and grinding for animal feed
311119	Shell crushing for feed
332993	Shell loading and assembly plants
212399	Shell mining and/or beneficiating
339999	Shell novelties
331111	Shell slugs, steel, made in steel mills
325510	Shellac manufacturing
422950	Shellac wholesaling
311711	Shellfish and shellfish products canning
311711	Shellfish curing
114112	Shellfish fishing (e.g., clam, crab, oyster, shrimp)
112512	Shellfish hatcheries
311712	Shellfish products, fresh prepared, manufacturing
311712	Shellfish products, frozen, manufacturing
311712	Shellfish, fresh prepared, manufacturing
311712	Shellfish, frozen, manufacturing
332993	Shells, artillery, manufacturing
332992	Shells, small arms (i.e., 30 mm. or less, 1.18 inch or less), manufacturing
624310	Sheltered workshops (i.e., work experience centers)
624221	Shelters (except for victims of domestic or international disasters or conflicts), emergency
624230	Shelters for victims of domestic or international disasters or conflicts, emergency
624221	Shelters, battered women's
624221	Shelters, homeless
624221	Shelters, runaway youth

Code	Description
624221	Shelters, temporary (e.g., battered women's, homeless, runaway youth)
337215	Shelving (except wire) manufacturing
421440	Shelving, commercial, wholesaling
332618	Shelving, wire, made from purchased wire
332812	Sherardizing of metals and metal products for the trade
311520	Sherbets manufacturing
922120	Sheriffs' offices (except court functions only)
922110	Sheriffs' offices, court functions only
332999	Shims, metal, manufacturing
321113	Shingle mills, wood
421330	Shingles (except wood) wholesaling
324122	Shingles made from purchased asphaltic materials
321113	Shingles, wood, sawed or hand split, manufacturing
421310	Shingles, wood, wholesaling
331525	Ship and boat propellers, cast brass, bronze and copper (except die-casting), unfinished, manufacturing
422990	Ship chandler wholesaling
483113	Ship chartering with crew, coastal or Great Lakes freight transportation
483114	Ship chartering with crew, coastal or Great Lakes passenger transportation
483111	Ship chartering with crew, deep sea freight transportation to or from foreign ports
483112	Ship chartering with crew, deep sea passenger transportation to or from foreign ports
483211	Ship chartering with crew, freight transportation, inland waters (except on Great Lakes system)
483212	Ship chartering with crew, passenger transportation, inland waters (except on Great Lakes system)
333923	Ship cranes and derricks manufacturing
561310	Ship crew employment agencies
561310	Ship crew registries
337127	Ship furniture manufacturing
488320	Ship hold cleaning services
235510	Ship joinery construction contractors
235210	Ship painting construction contractors
532411	Ship rental or leasing
336611	Ship repair done in a shipyard
336611	Ship scaling services done at a shipyard
488390	Ship scaling services not done at a shipyard
332312	Ship sections, prefabricated metal, manufacturing
513322	Ship-to-shore broadcasting communication carriers (except satellite)
331422	Shipboard cable made from purchased copper in wire drawing plants
331319	Shipboard cable made in aluminum wire drawing plants
488510	Shipping agents (freight forwarding)
314911	Shipping bags made from purchased woven or knitted materials
332439	Shipping barrels, drums, kegs, and pails, light gauge metal, manufacturing
321920	Shipping cases and drums, wood, wirebound, manufacturing
321920	Shipping cases, wood, nailed or lock corner, manufacturing
813910	Shipping companies' associations
421840	Shipping containers (except disposable plastics, paper) wholesaling
322211	Shipping containers made from purchased paperboard
322211	Shipping containers, corrugated, made from purchased paper or paperboard
321920	Shipping crates, wood, manufacturing
483113	Shipping freight to and from domestic ports (i.e., coastal, deep sea, Great Lakes system)
483111	Shipping freight to or from foreign ports, deep sea
483211	Shipping freight, inland waters (except on Great Lakes system)
326150	Shipping pads and shaped cushioning, foam plastics (except polystyrene), manufacturing
326140	Shipping pads and shaped cushioning, polystyrene foam, manufacturing
421840	Shipping pails, metal, wholesaling
511140	Shipping register publishers
511140	Shipping register publishers and printing combined
511140	Shipping register publishing (i.e., establishments known as publishers)
323112	Shipping registers flexographic printing without publishing
323111	Shipping registers gravure printing without publishing
323110	Shipping registers lithographic (offset) printing without publishing
323119	Shipping registers printing (except flexographic, gravure, lithographic, screen) without publishing
323113	Shipping registers screen printing without publishing
422130	Shipping supplies, paper and disposable plastics, wholesaling
336611	Ships (i.e., not suitable or intended for personal use) manufacturing
421860	Ships wholesaling
336611	Shipyard (i.e., facility capable of building ships)
315223	Shirts, outerwear (except work shirts), men's and boys', cut and sewn from purchased fabric (except apparel contractors)
315225	Shirts, outerwear work, men's and boys', cut and sewn from purchased fabric (except apparel contractors)
315291	Shirts, outerwear, infants', cut and sewn from purchased fabric (except apparel contractors)
315191	Shirts, outerwear, made in apparel knitting mills
315211	Shirts, outerwear, men's and boys', cut and sew apparel contractors

Code	Description
315223	Shirts, outerwear, unisex (i.e., sized without regard to gender), cut and sewn from purchased fabric (except apparel contractors)
315212	Shirts, outerwear, women's, girls', and infants', cut and sew apparel contractors
315232	Shirts, outerwear, women's, misses', and girls', cut and sewn from purchased fabric (except apparel contractors)
315291	Shirts, underwear, infants', cut and sewn from purchased fabric (except apparel contractors)
315192	Shirts, underwear, made in apparel knitting mills
315211	Shirts, underwear, men's and boys', cut and sew apparel contractors
315221	Shirts, underwear, men's and boys', cut and sewn from purchased fabric (except apparel contractors)
315212	Shirts, underwear, women's, girls', and infants', cut and sew apparel contractors
315231	Shirts, underwear, women's, misses', and girls', cut and sewn from purchased fabric (except apparel contractors)
111411	Shitake mushroom farming
111419	Shitake mushroom farming, grown under cover
336330	Shock absorbers, automotive, truck, and bus, manufacturing
448210	Shoe (except bowling, golf, spiked) stores
326299	Shoe and boot parts (e.g., heels, soles, soling strips), rubber, manufacturing
322212	Shoe boxes, folding, made from purchased paperboard
322213	Shoe boxes, setup, made from purchased paperboard
541490	Shoe design services
321999	Shoe display forms, all materials, manufacturing
316991	Shoe kits (i.e., cases), all materials, manufacturing
333298	Shoe making and repairing machinery manufacturing
421830	Shoe manufacturing and repairing machinery wholesaling
326199	Shoe parts (e.g., heels, soles), plastics, manufacturing
335211	Shoe polishers, household-type electric, manufacturing
325612	Shoe polishes and cleaners manufacturing
421850	Shoe repair materials wholesaling
811430	Shoe repair shops without retailing new shoes
316999	Shoe soles, leather, manufacturing
448210	Shoe stores, orthopedic
451110	Shoe stores, specialty sports footwear (e.g., bowling, golf, spiked)
321999	Shoe stretchers manufacturing
321999	Shoe trees manufacturing
422340	Shoes wholesaling
316219	Shoes, athletic (except rubber or plastics soled with fabric upper), manufacturing
316219	Shoes, ballet, manufacturing
316219	Shoes, children's and infant's (except house slippers, orthopedic extension, plastics, rubber), manufacturing
316219	Shoes, cleated or spiked, all materials, manufacturing
316213	Shoes, men's (except house slippers, athletic, rubber, extension shoes), manufacturing
339113	Shoes, orthopedic extension, manufacturing
316211	Shoes, plastics or plastics soled fabric upper (except cleated athletic shoes), manufacturing
316211	Shoes, rubber or rubber soled fabric upper (except cleated athletic), manufacturing
316219	Shoes, theatrical, manufacturing
316214	Shoes, women's (except house slippers, athletic, orthopedic extension, plastic, rubber), manufacturing
316219	Shoes, wooden, manufacturing
812990	Shoeshine parlors
812990	Shoeshine services
321920	Shook, box, manufacturing
713990	Shooting clubs, recreational
713990	Shooting galleries
713990	Shooting ranges
233320	Shop construction
421120	Shop equipment, service station, wholesaling
422130	Shopping bags, paper and plastics, wholesaling
531120	Shopping center (i.e., not operating contained businesses) rental or leasing
233320	Shopping center or mall construction
812990	Shopping services, personal
*****	Shops — see type
235990	Shoring and underpinning construction contractors
111421	Short rotation woody tree growing (i.e., growing and harvesting cycle ten years or less)
482112	Short-line railroads
522298	Short-term inventory credit lending
311223	Shortening (except soybean) made in crushing mills
311222	Shortening , soybean, made in crushing mills
311225	Shortening made from purchased fats and oils
422490	Shortening, vegetable, wholesaling
315291	Shorts, outerwear, infants', cut and sewn from purchased fabric (except apparel contractors)
315191	Shorts, outerwear, made in apparel knitting mills
315211	Shorts, outerwear, men's and boys', cut and sew apparel contractors
315228	Shorts, outerwear, men's and boys', cut and sewn from purchased fabric (except apparel contractors)
315212	Shorts, outerwear, women's, girls', and infants', cut and sew apparel contractors
315239	Shorts, outerwear, women's, misses', and girls', cut and sewn from purchased fabric (except apparel contractors)

Code	Description
315192	Shorts, underwear, made in apparel knitting mills
315211	Shorts, underwear, men's and boys', cut and sew apparel contractors
315221	Shorts, underwear, men's and boys', cut and sewn from purchased fabric (except apparel contractors)
213112	Shot hole drilling, oil and gas field, on a contract basis
332813	Shot peening metal and metal products for the trade
332992	Shot, BB, manufacturing
332992	Shot, lead, manufacturing
332992	Shot, pellet, manufacturing
332992	Shot, steel, manufacturing
235710	Shotcrete construction contractors
332992	Shotgun shells manufacturing
332994	Shotguns manufacturing
333120	Shovel loaders manufacturing
332212	Shovels, handheld, manufacturing
333120	Shovels, power, manufacturing
337215	Showcases (except refrigerated) manufacturing
421440	Showcases (except refrigerated) wholesaling
333415	Showcases, refrigerated, manufacturing
314129	Shower and bath curtains, all materials, made from purchased fabric or sheet goods
332913	Shower heads, plumbing, manufacturing
332998	Shower receptors, metal, manufacturing
332999	Shower rods, metal, manufacturing
316211	Shower sandals or slippers, rubber, manufacturing
332998	Shower stalls, metal, manufacturing
326191	Shower stalls, plastics or fiberglass, manufacturing
115210	Showing of cattle, hogs, sheep, goats, and poultry
333111	Shredders, farm-type, manufacturing
212399	Shredding peat mining and/or beneficiating
114112	Shrimp fishing

Code	Description
112512	Shrimp production, farm raising
813110	Shrines, religious
561910	Shrink wrapping services
313311	Shrinking broadwoven fabrics
313312	Shrinking textile products and fabrics (except broadwoven)
561730	Shrub services (e.g., bracing, planting, pruning, removal, spraying, surgery, trimming)
111421	Shrubbery farming
311712	Shucking and packing fresh shellfish
488490	Shunting of trailers in truck terminals
488210	Shunting trailers in rail terminals
334515	Shunts, instrument, manufacturing
332321	Shutters, door and window, metal, manufacturing
321918	Shutters, door and window, wood and covered wood, manufacturing
326199	Shutters, plastics, manufacturing
321918	Shutters, wood, manufacturing
485999	Shuttle services (except employee bus)
333292	Shuttles for textile weaving machinery manufacturing
446199	Sick room supply stores
332212	Sickles manufacturing
212210	Siderite mining and/or beneficiating
234110	Sidewalk construction, public
235710	Sidewalk, private, construction contractors
421330	Siding (except wood) wholesaling
235610	Siding construction contractors
444190	Siding dealers
324122	Siding made from purchased asphaltic materials
321113	Siding mills, wood
321113	Siding, dressed lumber, manufacturing
326199	Siding, plastics, manufacturing
332322	Siding, sheet metal, manufacturing
421310	Siding, wood, wholesaling
212393	Sienna mining and/or beneficiating
325131	Sienna pigment manufacturing
333294	Sieves and screening equipment (i.e., food manufacturing-type) manufacturing

Code	Description
333298	Sieves and screening equipment, chemical preparation-type, manufacturing
333999	Sieves and screening equipment, general purpose-type, manufacturing
333131	Sieves and screening mineral beneficiating equipment manufacturing
332618	Sieves manufacturing
333294	Sifting machine (i.e., food manufacturing-type) manufacturing
333314	Sights, telescopic, manufacturing
487210	Sightseeing boat operation
487110	Sightseeing bus operation
487110	Sightseeing operation, human-drawn vehicle
235990	Sign contractors, installation (on buildings)
234110	Sign erection (i.e., highway, street) contractors
611630	Sign language instruction
611630	Sign language schools
541930	Sign language services
541890	Sign lettering and painting services
331422	Signal and control cable made from purchased copper in wire drawing plants
331319	Signal and control cable made in aluminum wire drawing plants
334515	Signal generators and averagers manufacturing
421610	Signal systems and devices wholesaling
335311	Signaling transformers, electric, manufacturing
334290	Signals (e.g., highway, pedestrian, railway, traffic) manufacturing
421990	Signs (except electrical) wholesaling
339950	Signs and signboards (except paper, paperboard) manufacturing
421440	Signs, electrical, wholesaling
325188	Silica gel manufacturing
212322	Silica mining and/or beneficiating
212322	Silica sand quarrying and/or beneficiating

Code	Description
325188	Silica, amorphous, manufacturing
325188	Silicofluorides manufacturing
331112	Silicomanganese ferroalloys manufacturing
327910	Silicon carbide abrasives manufacturing
334413	Silicon wafers, chemically doped, manufacturing
327992	Silicon, ultra high purity, manufacturing
325199	Silicone (except resins) manufacturing
325211	Silicone resins manufacturing
325212	Silicone rubber manufacturing
313210	Silk fabrics, broadwoven, weaving
541430	Silk screen design services
333292	Silk screens for textile fabrics manufacturing
313111	Silk spun yarns made from purchased fiber
313113	Silk thread manufacturing
313112	Silk throwing, spooling, twisting, or winding of puchased yarn
422590	Silk, raw, wholesaling
212325	Sillimanite mining and/or beneficiating
327390	Sills, concrete, manufacturing
233320	Silo construction
321918	Silo staves, wood, manufacturing
321912	Silo stock, wood, manufacturing
327390	Silos, prefabricated concrete, manufacturing
332311	Silos, prefabricated metal, manufacturing
331491	Silver and silver alloy bar, rod, sheet, strip, and tubing made from purchased metals or scrap
332999	Silver beating (i.e., foil, leaf)
325188	Silver bromide manufacturing
331419	Silver bullion or dore bar produced at primary metal refineries
325188	Silver chloride manufacturing
325188	Silver compounds, not specified elsewhere by process, manufacturing
332999	Silver foil and leaf not made in rolling mills

Code	Description
331491	Silver foil made by rolling purchased metals or scrap
325188	Silver nitrate manufacturing
212222	Silver ores mining and/or beneficiating
325612	Silver polishes manufacturing
331492	Silver recovering from scrap and/or alloying purchased metals
331492	Silver recovering from used photographic film or X-ray plates
331419	Silver refining, primary
331491	Silver rolling, drawing, or extruding purchased metals or scrap
532299	Silverware rental
421940	Silverware, precious and plated, wholesaling
333515	Sine bars (i.e., a machine tool accessory) manufacturing
711130	Singers, independent
813410	Singing societies
812990	Singing telegram services
233210	Single family construction management firms
531110	Single family house rental or leasing
621512	Single photon emission computerized tomography (SPECT) centers
213113	Sinking shafts for coal mining on a contract basis
213114	Sinking shafts for metal mining on a contract basis
332998	Sinks, metal, manufacturing
326191	Sinks, plastics, manufacturing
327111	Sinks, vitreous china, manufacturing
212210	Sintered iron ore produced at the mine
212392	Sintered phosphate rock mining and/or beneficiating
334290	Sirens (e.g., air raid, industrial, marine, vehicle) manufacturing
541611	Site location consulting services
541620	Site remediation consulting services
562910	Site remediation services
541611	Site selection consulting services
812990	Sitting services, house
812910	Sitting services, pet

Code	Description
313311	Sizing of broadwoven fabrics
313312	Sizing of fabric (except broadwoven)
339920	Skateboards manufacturing
339920	Skates and parts, ice and roller, manufacturing
713990	Skeet shooting facilities
331111	Skelp, iron or steel, made in steel mills
711510	Sketch artists, independent
321999	Skewers, wood, manufacturing
541320	Ski area design services
541320	Ski area planning services
532292	Ski equipment rental
713920	Ski lift and tow operators
721110	Ski lodges and resorts with accommodations
315191	Ski pants made in apparel knitting mills
315291	Ski pants, infants', cut and sewn from purchased fabric (except apparel contractors)
315211	Ski pants, men's and boys', cut and sew apparel contractors
315228	Ski pants, men's and boys', cut and sewn from purchased fabric (except apparel contractors)
315212	Ski pants, women's, girls', and infants', cut and sew apparel contractors
315239	Ski pants, women's, misses', and girls', cut and sewn from purchased fabric (except apparel contractors)
713920	Ski resorts without accommodations
315191	Ski suits made in apparel knitting mills
315291	Ski suits, infants', cut and sewn from purchased fabric (except apparel contractors)
315211	Ski suits, men's and boys', cut and sew apparel contractors
315228	Ski suits, men's and boys', cut and sewn from purchased fabric (except apparel contractors)
315212	Ski suits, women's, girls', and infants', cut and sew apparel contractors

Code	Description
315239	Ski suits, women's, misses', and girls', cut and sewn from purchased fabric (except apparel contractors)
234990	Ski tow construction
532490	Skid rental or leasing
213112	Skidding of rigs, oil and gas field, on a contract basis
321920	Skids and pallets, wood or wood and metal combination, manufacturing
332999	Skids, metal, manufacturing
711219	Skiers, independent (i.e., participating in sports events)
421910	Skiing equipment and supplies wholesaling
713920	Skiing facilities, cross country, without accommodations
713920	Skiing facilities, downhill, without accommodations
611620	Skiing instruction, camps, or schools
623110	Skilled nursing facilities
561910	Skin blister packaging services
611620	Skin diving instruction, camps, or schools
339112	Skin grafting equipment manufacturing
422990	Skins, dressed, wholesaling
422590	Skins, raw, wholesaling
316110	Skins, tanning, currying and finishing
561611	Skip tracing services
316110	Skirting leather manufacturing
315234	Skirts (except tennis skirts), women's, misses', and girls', cut and sewn from purchased fabric (except apparel contractors)
315191	Skirts made in apparel knitting mills
315291	Skirts, infants', cut and sewn from purchased fabric (except apparel contractors)
315239	Skirts, tennis, women's, misses', and girls', cut and sewn from purchased fabric (except apparel contractors)
315212	Skirts, women's, misses', girls', and infants', cut and sew apparel contractors

Code	Description
339920	Skis and skiing equipment (except apparel) manufacturing
316110	Skivers, leather, manufacturing
611620	Sky diving instruction, camps, or schools
235610	Skylight construction contractors
332322	Skylights, sheet metal, manufacturing
331419	Slab, nonferrous metals (except aluminum, copper), primary
331312	Slab, primary aluminum, manufacturing
331111	Slab, steel, made in steel mills
315191	Slacks made in apparel knitting mills
315291	Slacks, infants', cut and sewn from purchased fabric (except apparel contractors)
315291	Slacks, jean-cut casual, infants', cut and sewn from purchased fabric (except apparel contractors)
315191	Slacks, jean-cut casual, made in apparel knitting mills
315211	Slacks, jean-cut casual, men's and boys', cut and sew apparel contractors
315224	Slacks, jean-cut casual, men's and boys', cut and sewn from purchased fabric (except apparel contractors)
315212	Slacks, jean-cut casual, women's, girls', and infants', cut and sew apparel contractors
315239	Slacks, jean-cut casual, women's, misses', and girls', cut and sewn from purchased fabric (except apparel contractors)
315211	Slacks, men's and boys', cut and sew apparel contractors
315224	Slacks, men's and boys', cut and sewn from purchased fabric (except apparel contractors)
315212	Slacks, women's, girls', and infants', cut and sew apparel contractors
315239	Slacks, women's, misses', and girls', cut and sewn from purchased fabric (except apparel contractors)
333120	Slag mixers, portable, manufacturing

Code	Description
235410	Slate (i.e., exterior) construction contractors
212319	Slate crushed and broken stone mining and/or beneficiating
212311	Slate mining or quarrying
327991	Slate products manufacturing
311611	Slaughtering, custom
311991	Slaw, cole, fresh, manufacturing
332212	Sledgehammers manufacturing
339932	Sleds, children's, manufacturing
621498	Sleep disorder centers and clinics, outpatient
337215	Sleeper mechanisms, convertible bed, manufacturing
314999	Sleeping bags manufacturing
316999	Sleeves, welder's, leather, manufacturing
333294	Slicing machinery (i.e., food manufacturing-type) manufacturing
339993	Slide fasteners (i.e., zippers) manufacturing
332618	Slings, lifting, made from purchased wire
212324	Slip clay mining and/or beneficiating
335312	Slip rings for motors and generators manufacturing
421220	Slipcovers wholesaling
314129	Slipcovers, all materials, made from purchased materials
316212	Slipper socks made from purchased socks
315119	Slipper socks made in sock mills
422340	Slippers wholesaling
316219	Slippers, ballet, manufacturing
316212	Slippers, house, manufacturing
315192	Slips made in apparel knitting mills
315212	Slips, women's and girls', cut and sew apparel contractors
315231	Slips, women's, misses', and girls', cut and sewn from purchased fabric (except apparel contractors)
713990	Slot car racetracks (i.e., amusement devices)
713290	Slot machine concession operators (i.e., supplying and servicing in others' facilities)

Code	Description
713290	Slot machine parlors
339999	Slot machines manufacturing
333512	Slotting machines, metalworking, manufacturing
562212	Sludge disposal sites
333999	Sludge tables manufacturing
327331	Slumped brick manufacturing
486990	Slurry pipeline transportation
213112	Slush pits and cellars, excavation of, on a contract basis
541940	Small animal veterinary services
332992	Small arms ammunition (i.e., 30 mm. or less, 1.18 inch or less) manufacturing
926110	Small business development agencies
811411	Small engine repair and maintenance shops
311615	Small game, processing, fresh, frozen, canned or cooked
311615	Small game, slaughtering, dressing and packing
522291	Small loan companies (i.e., unsecured cash loans)
331492	Smelting and refining of nonferrous metals (except aluminum, copper), secondary
421830	Smelting machinery and equipment wholesaling
331492	Smelting nonferrous metals (except aluminum, copper), secondary
331419	Smelting of nonferrous metals (except aluminum, copper), primary
333994	Smelting ovens manufacturing
332420	Smelting pots and retorts manufacturing
212231	Smithsonite mining and/or beneficiating
334290	Smoke detectors manufacturing
421620	Smoke detectors, household-type, wholesaling
332995	Smoke generators manufacturing
311612	Smoked meats made from purchased carcasses
422990	Smokers' supplies wholesaling
453991	Smokers' supply stores

Code	Description
332313	Smokestacks, fabricated metal boiler plate, manufacturing
621999	Smoking cessation programs
312229	Smoking tobacco (e.g., cigarette, pipe) manufacturing
333311	Snack and confection vending machines manufacturing
722213	Snack bars (e.g., cookies, popcorn, pretzels), fixed location
722330	Snack stands, mobile
111219	Snap bean farming (i.e., bush and pole), field and seed production
335931	Snap switches (i.e., electric wiring devices) manufacturing
114111	Snapper fishing
488490	Snow clearing, highways and bridges, road transportation
321912	Snow fence lath manufacturing
321999	Snow fence, sections or rolls, manufacturing
333415	Snow making machinery manufacturing
111219	Snow pea farming, field and seed production
333120	Snow plow attachments (except lawn, garden-type) manufacturing
333112	Snow plow attachments, lawn and garden-type, manufacturing
561790	Snow plowing driveways and parking lots (i.e., not combined with any other service)
561730	Snow plowing services combined with landscaping services (i.e., seasonal property maintenance services)
421810	Snow plows wholesaling
488490	Snow removal, highway
532292	Snow ski equipment rental
421810	Snowblowers (except household-type) wholesaling
333112	Snowblowers and throwers, residential-type, manufacturing
421820	Snowblowers, household-type, wholesaling
441229	Snowmobile dealers
711212	Snowmobile racetracks
711219	Snowmobile racing teams

Code	Description
336999	Snowmobiles and parts manufacturing
421110	Snowmobiles wholesaling
713990	Snowmobiling, recreational
339920	Snowshoes manufacturing
315191	Snowsuits made in apparel knitting mills
315291	Snowsuits, infants', cut and sewn from purchased fabric (except apparel contractors)
315211	Snowsuits, men's and boys', cut and sew apparel contractors
315228	Snowsuits, men's and boys', cut and sewn from purchased fabric (except apparel contractors)
315212	Snowsuits, women's, girls', and infants', cut and sew apparel contractors
315239	Snowsuits, women's, misses', and girls', cut and sewn from purchased fabric (except apparel contractors)
312229	Snuff manufacturing
422940	Snuff wholesaling
327111	Soap dishes, vitreous china and earthenware, manufacturing
332999	Soap dispensers, metal, manufacturing
325611	Soaps (e.g., bar, chip, powder) manufacturing
212399	Soapstone mining and/or beneficiating
711211	Soccer clubs, professional or semiprofessional
713990	Soccer clubs, recreational
611620	Soccer instruction, camps, or schools
711211	Soccer teams, professional or semiprofessional
923130	Social Security Administration, federal
923130	Social assistance cost-sharing, government
813319	Social change advocacy organizations
813410	Social clubs
812990	Social escort services
813410	Social organizations, civic and fraternal

Code	Description
541720	Social science research and development services
813319	Social service advocacy organizations
624190	Social service agencies, family
624190	Social service centers, multipurpose
422120	Social stationery wholesaling
813920	Social workers' associations
621330	Social workers' offices (e.g., centers, clinics)
541720	Sociological research and development services
541720	Sociology research and development services
332212	Sockets and socket sets manufacturing
335931	Sockets, electric, manufacturing
315119	Socks knitting or knitting and finishing
315119	Socks, men's and boy's, manufacturing
316212	Socks, slipper, made from purchased socks
315119	Socks, slipper, made in sock mills
111421	Sod farming
333111	Sod harvesting machines manufacturing
561730	Sod laying services
325181	Soda ash manufacturing
212391	Soda ash mining and/or beneficiating
212391	Soda ash, natural, mining and/or beneficiating
327213	Soda bottles, glass, manufacturing
312111	Soda carbonated, manufacturing
311821	Soda crackers manufacturing
333415	Soda fountain cooling and dispensing equipment manufacturing
421440	Soda fountain fixtures (except refrigerated) wholesaling
311930	Soda fountain syrups manufacturing
312111	Soda pop manufacturing
325199	Sodium acetate manufacturing
325199	Sodium alginate manufacturing
325188	Sodium aluminate manufacturing

Code	Description
325188	Sodium aluminum sulfate manufacturing
325188	Sodium antimoniate manufacturing
325320	Sodium arsenite insecticides manufacturing
325188	Sodium arsenite manufacturing
325199	Sodium benzoate manufacturing
325181	Sodium bicarbonate manufacturing
325188	Sodium bichromate and chromate manufacturing
325188	Sodium borate manufacturing
212391	Sodium borates, natural, mining and/or beneficiating
325188	Sodium borohydride manufacturing
325188	Sodium bromide manufacturing
325181	Sodium carbonate (i.e., soda ash) manufacturing
212391	Sodium carbonates, natural, mining and/or beneficiating
325188	Sodium chlorate manufacturing
325412	Sodium chloride pharmaceutical preparations manufacturing
212393	Sodium chloride, rock salt, mining and/or beneficiating
212391	Sodium compounds prepared at beneficiating plants
212391	Sodium compounds, natural (except common salt), mining and/or beneficiating
325188	Sodium cyanide manufacturing
325199	Sodium glutamate manufacturing
325188	Sodium hydrosulfite manufacturing
325181	Sodium hydroxide (i.e., caustic soda) manufacturing
325188	Sodium hypochlorite manufacturing
325188	Sodium inorganic compounds, not specified elsewhere by process, manufacturing
325188	Sodium molybdate manufacturing
325199	Sodium organic compounds, not specified elsewhere by process, manufacturing
325199	Sodium pentachlorophenate manufacturing
325188	Sodium perborate manufacturing
325188	Sodium peroxide manufacturing
325188	Sodium phosphate manufacturing

Code	Description
325188	Sodium polyphosphate manufacturing
325412	Sodium salicylate preparations manufacturing
325188	Sodium silicate (i.e., water glass) manufacturing
325188	Sodium silicofluoride manufacturing
325188	Sodium stannate manufacturing
325188	Sodium sulfate manufacturing
212391	Sodium sulfate, natural, mining and/or beneficiating
325199	Sodium sulfoxalate formaldehyde manufacturing
325188	Sodium tetraborate manufacturing
325188	Sodium thiosulfate manufacturing
325188	Sodium tungstate manufacturing
325188	Sodium uranate manufacturing
335110	Sodium vapor lamp bulbs manufacturing
337121	Sofa beds and chair beds, upholstered, manufacturing
337121	Sofas, convertible (except futons), manufacturing
337121	Sofas, upholstered, manufacturing
722213	Soft drink beverage bars, nonalcoholic, fixed location
332431	Soft drink cans manufacturing
311930	Soft drink concentrates (i.e., syrup) manufacturing
445299	Soft drink stores, bottled
333311	Soft drink vending machines manufacturing
312111	Soft drinks manufacturing
422490	Soft drinks wholesaling
311812	Soft pretzels made in a commercial bakery
325613	Softeners, leather or textile, manufacturing
541511	Software analysis and design services, custom computer
611420	Software application training
511210	Software computer, packaged, publishers
541519	Software installation services, computer
541511	Software programming services, custom computer

Code	Description
511210	Software publishers
511210	Software publishers, packaged
443120	Software stores, computer
421430	Software, computer, packaged, wholesaling
334611	Software, packaged, mass reproducing
321912	Softwood dimension lumber and stock, resawing purchased lumber
325191	Softwood distillates manufacturing
321212	Softwood plywood composites, manufacturing
321212	Softwood veneer or plywood, manufacturing
234990	Soil compacting service
924120	Soil conservation services, government
331511	Soil pipe, cast iron, manufacturing
562910	Soil remediation services
325998	Soil testing kits manufacturing
541380	Soil testing laboratories or services
334413	Solar cells manufacturing
421690	Solar cells wholesaling
926130	Solar energy regulation
333414	Solar energy heating equipment manufacturing
235110	Solar heating construction contractors
421720	Solar heating panels and equipment wholesaling
333414	Solar heating systems manufacturing
335122	Solar lighting fixtures (except residential), electric, manufacturing
335121	Solar lighting fixtures, residential, electric, manufacturing
421330	Solar reflective film wholesaling
334519	Solarimeters manufacturing
331491	Solder wire, nonferrous metals (except aluminum, copper), made from purchased metals or scrap
333992	Soldering equipment (except hand held) manufacturing
332212	Soldering guns and irons, handheld (including electric), manufacturing
332212	Soldering iron tips and tiplets manufacturing

Code	Description
335931	Solderless connectors (electric wiring devices) manufacturing
316110	Sole leather manufacturing
335314	Solenoid switches, industrial, manufacturing
332911	Solenoid valves (except fluid power), industrial-type, manufacturing
332912	Solenoid valves, fluid power, manufacturing
334419	Solenoids for electronic applications manufacturing
316999	Soles, boot and shoe, leather, manufacturing
541110	Solicitors' offices
922130	Solicitors' offices, government
541110	Solicitors' private practices
325188	Solid fuel propellants, inorganic, not specified elsewhere by process, manufacturing
562213	Solid waste combustors or incinerators, nonhazardous
562212	Solid waste landfills combined with collection and/or local hauling of nonhazardous waste materials
562212	Solid waste landfills, nonhazardous
711130	Soloists, independent musical
325132	Solvent dyes manufacturing
324110	Solvents made in petroleum refineries
334511	Sonabuoys manufacturing
421690	Sonar equipment wholesaling
334511	Sonar fish finders manufacturing
334511	Sonar systems and equipment manufacturing
512230	Song publishers
512230	Song publishers and printing combined
512230	Song publishing (i.e., establishment known as publishers)
711510	Song writers, independent
325612	Soot removing chemicals manufacturing
325199	Sorbitol manufacturing
111199	Sorghum farming, field and seed production
311211	Sorghum flour manufacturing

Code	Description
111998	Sorghum sudan seed farming
311999	Sorghum syrup manufacturing
813410	Sororities (except residential)
721310	Sorority houses
115114	Sorting, grading, cleaning, and packing of fruits and vegetables
532490	Sound and lighting equipment rental or leasing
234990	Sound barrier construction, highways
512191	Sound dubbing services, motion picture
235310	Sound equipment construction contractors
421330	Sound insulation wholesaling
235420	Sound proofing construction contractors
512240	Sound recording studios (except integrated record companies)
512220	Sound recording, integrated production, reproduction, release, and distribution
512220	Sound recording, releasing, promoting, and distributing
332431	Soup cans manufacturing
624210	Soup kitchens
311423	Soup mixes made in a dehydration plant
311999	Soup mixes, dry, made from purchased dry ingredients
422490	Soups (except frozen) wholesaling
311422	Soups (except seafood) canning
311711	Soups, fish and seafood, canning
311412	Soups, frozen (except seafood), manufacturing
311712	Soups, frozen fish and shellfish, manufacturing
422420	Soups, frozen, wholesaling
311511	Sour cream manufacturing
311511	Sour cream substitutes manufacturing
453220	Souvenir shops
311941	Soy sauce manufacturing
311222	Soybean cakes and meal manufacturing
311225	Soybean cooking oil made from purchased oils

Code	Description
111110	Soybean farming, field and seed production
325222	Soybean fibers and filaments manufacturing
311222	Soybean flour and grits manufacturing
311222	Soybean millfeed made in oil mills
311222	Soybean oil mills
311222	Soybean oil, cake, and meal, made in crushing mills
311222	Soybean oil, crude, manufacturing
311222	Soybean oil, deodorized, made in oil mills
311222	Soybean oil, refined, made in crushing mills
325211	Soybean plastics manufacturing
311222	Soybean protein concentrates manufacturing
311222	Soybean protein isolates made in crushing mills
422510	Soybeans wholesaling
336419	Space capsules manufacturing
927110	Space flight operations, government
333414	Space heaters (except portable electric) manufacturing
927110	Space research and development
334220	Space satellites, communications, manufacturing
332313	Space simulation chambers, fabricated metal plate work, manufacturing
339113	Space suits manufacturing
481212	Space transportation, freight, nonscheduled
334511	Space vehicle guidance systems and equipment manufacturing
336414	Space vehicles, complete, manufacturing
332212	Spades and shovels, handheld, manufacturing
311422	Spaghetti canning
311421	Spaghetti sauce canning
111219	Spaghetti squash farming, field, bedding plant and seed production
422490	Spaghetti wholesaling
311823	Spaghetti, dry, manufacturing
313210	Spandex broadwoven fabrics

Code	Description
325222	Spandex fiber, filaments, and yarn manufacturing
113210	Spanish moss gathering
212399	Spar, iceland, mining and/or beneficiating
327113	Spark plug insulators, porcelain, manufacturing
334515	Spark plug testing instruments, electric, manufacturing
336322	Spark plugs for internal combustion engines manufacturing
312130	Sparkling wine manufacturing
321999	Spars, wood, manufacturing
713940	Spas without accommodations, fitness
316999	Spats, leather, manufacturing
326299	Spatulas, rubber, manufacturing
337129	Speaker cabinets (i.e., housings), wood, manufacturing
813410	Speaker clubs
334310	Speaker systems manufacturing
711410	Speakers' bureaus
711510	Speakers, independent
325998	Spearmint oil manufacturing
711510	Special effect technicians, independent
512191	Special effects for motion picture production, post-production
485991	Special needs passenger transportation services
336211	Special purpose highway vehicle (e.g., firefighting vehicles) assembling on purchased chassis
336211	Special purpose highway vehicle (e.g., firefighting vehicles) bodies manufacturing
336120	Special purpose highway vehicles (e.g., firefighting vehicles) assembling on heavy chassis of own manufacture
421830	Special purpose industrial machinery and equipment wholesaling
525990	Special purpose vehicles
445299	Specialty food stores
316110	Specialty leathers manufacturing
513210	Specialty television (e.g., music, sports, news) cable networks

Code	Description
335311	Specialty transformers, electric, manufacturing
422210	Specialty-line pharmaceuticals wholesaling
334516	Specific ion measuring instruments, laboratory-type, manufacturing
235990	Spectator seating construction contractors
334516	Spectrofluorometers manufacturing
334516	Spectrographs manufacturing
334516	Spectrometers (e.g., electron diffraction, mass, NMR, Raman) manufacturing
334519	Spectrometers (e.g., liquid scintillation, nuclear) manufacturing
334516	Spectrophotometers (e.g., atomic absorption, atomic emission, flame, fluorescence, infrared, raman, visible) manufacturing
334515	Spectrum analyzers manufacturing
339112	Speculums manufacturing
541930	Speech (i.e., language) interpretation services
621340	Speech clinicians' offices (e.g., centers, clinics)
621340	Speech defect clinics
621340	Speech pathologists' offices (e.g., centers, clinics)
621340	Speech therapists' offices (e.g., centers, clinics)
333612	Speed changers (i.e., power transmission equipment) manufacturing
611699	Speed reading instruction
333612	Speed reducers (i.e., power transmission equipment) manufacturing
441310	Speed shops
334511	Speed, pitch, and roll navigational instruments and systems manufacturing
711212	Speedways
621991	Sperm banks, human
113210	Sphagnum moss gathering
212231	Sphalerite mining and/or beneficiating
339112	Sphygmomanometers manufacturing

Code	Description
111998	Spice farming
111419	Spice farming, grown under cover
311942	Spice grinding and blending
311942	Spice mixtures manufacturing
445299	Spice stores
311942	Spices and spice mix manufacturing
422490	Spices wholesaling
331112	Spiegeleisen ferroalloys manufacturing
332913	Spigots, plumbing fixture fitting, manufacturing
321999	Spigots, wood, manufacturing
331111	Spike rods made in steel mills
332618	Spikes made from purchased wire
331222	Spikes, iron or steel, made in wire drawing plants
421510	Spikes, metal, wholesaling
111219	Spinach farming, field, bedding plant and seed production
333292	Spindles for textile machinery manufacturing
313111	Spinning carpet and rug yarn from purchased fiber
333292	Spinning machinery for textiles manufacturing
333513	Spinning machines, metalworking, manufacturing
332116	Spinning unfinished metal products
313111	Spinning yarn from purchased fiber
332618	Spiral cloth made from purchased wire
312140	Spirits, distilled (except brandy), manufacturing
422820	Spirits, distilled, wholesaling
333513	Spline rolling machines, metalworking, manufacturing
321920	Splint baskets for fruits and vegetables, manufacturing
339113	Splints manufacturing
316110	Splits, leather, manufacturing
212393	Spodumene mining and/or beneficiating
321999	Spokes, wood, manufacturing
114119	Sponge gathering
331111	Sponge iron
422990	Sponges wholesaling

Code	Description
332999	Sponges, metal scouring, manufacturing
326199	Sponges, plastics, manufacturing
326299	Sponges, rubber, manufacturing
313311	Sponging broadwoven fabrics
313312	Sponging textile products and fabrics (except broadwoven)
313112	Spooling of yarn
313112	Spooling of yarns for the trade
321999	Spools (except for textile machinery), wood, manufacturing
333292	Spools for textile machinery manufacturing
332211	Spoons, table, nonprecious and precious plated metal, manufacturing
315222	Sport coats (except fur, leather), men's and boys', cut and sewn from purchased fabric (except apparel contractors)
315292	Sport coats, fur (except apparel contractors), manufacturing
315211	Sport coats, fur, men's and boys', cut and sew apparel contractors
315292	Sport coats, leather (including artificial and tailored) (except apparel contractors), manufacturing
315211	Sport coats, leather (including artificial and tailored), men's and boys', cut and sew apparel contractors
315211	Sport coats, men's and boys', cut and sew apparel contractors
315211	Sport shirts, men's and boys', cut and sew apparel contractors
315223	Sport shirts, men's and boys', cut and sewn from purchased fabric (except apparel contractors)
532112	Sport utility vehicle leasing
532111	Sport utility vehicle rental
336112	Sport utility vehicles assembling on chassis of own manufacture
421110	Sport utility vehicles wholesaling
811490	Sporting equipment repair and maintenance without retailing new sports equipment
421910	Sporting firearms and ammunition wholesaling

Code	Description
339920	Sporting goods (except ammunition, clothing, footwear, small arms) manufacturing
421910	Sporting goods and supplies wholesaling
532292	Sporting goods rental
451110	Sporting goods stores
453310	Sporting goods stores, used
711310	Sports arena operators
611620	Sports camps (e.g., baseball, basketball, football), instructional
315228	Sports clothing (except team uniforms), men's and boys', cut and sewn from purchased fabric (except apparel contractors)
315239	Sports clothing (except team uniforms), women's, misses', and girls', cut and sewn from purchased fabric (except apparel contractors)
315191	Sports clothing made in apparel knitting mills
315211	Sports clothing, men's and boys', cut and sew apparel contractors
315299	Sports clothing, team uniforms, cut and sewn from purchased fabric (except apparel contractors)
315212	Sports clothing, women's and girls', cut and sew apparel contractors
713940	Sports club facilities, physical fitness
713990	Sports clubs (i.e., sports teams) not operating sports facilities, recreational
711211	Sports clubs, professional or semiprofessional
421910	Sports equipment and supplies wholesaling
532292	Sports equipment rental
711310	Sports event managers with facilities
711320	Sports event managers without facilities
711310	Sports event organizers with facilities
711320	Sports event organizers without facilities

Code	Description
711310	Sports event promoters with facilities
711320	Sports event promoters without facilities
711410	Sports figures' agents or managers
451110	Sports gear stores (e.g., outdoors, scuba, skiing)
712110	Sports halls of fame
611620	Sports instruction, camps, or schools
611620	Sports instructors, independent (i.e., not participating in sporting events)
711219	Sports professionals, independent (i.e., participating in sports events)
315191	Sports shirts made in apparel knitting mills
711310	Sports stadium operators
713990	Sports teams and leagues, recreational or youth
711211	Sports teams, professional or semiprofessional
621340	Sports therapists' offices (e.g., centers, clinics)
561599	Sports ticket offices
711219	Sports trainers, independent
422320	Sportswear, men's and boys', wholesaling
325612	Spot removers (except laundry presoaks) manufacturing
333992	Spot welding equipment manufacturing
335129	Spotlights (except vehicular) manufacturing
336321	Spotlights, vehicular, manufacturing
332322	Spouts, sheet metal, manufacturing
422950	Spray painting equipment (except industrial-type) wholesaling
421830	Spray painting equipment, industrial-type, wholesaling
333111	Sprayers and dusters, farm-type, manufacturing
421820	Sprayers, farm, wholesaling
333912	Sprayers, manual pump, general purpose-type, manufacturing
115112	Spraying crops
561730	Spraying lawns

Code	Description
333111	Spreaders, farm-type, manufacturing
421820	Spreaders, fertilizer, wholesaling
333112	Spreaders, lawn and garden-type, manufacturing
115112	Spreading lime for crops
311513	Spreads, cheese, manufacturing
332722	Spring pins, metal, manufacturing
332722	Spring washers, metal, manufacturing
312112	Spring waters, purifying and bottling
333513	Spring winding and forming machines, metalworking, manufacturing
332612	Springs and spring units for seats made from purchased wire
337910	Springs, assembled bed and box, made from purchased spring
334518	Springs, clock and watch, made from purchased wire
332611	Springs, heavy gauge, manufacturing
332612	Springs, light gauge (except clock, watch), made from purchased wire
332612	Springs, precision (except clock, watch), manufacturing
421510	Springs, steel, wholesaling
235110	Sprinkler system construction contractors
333999	Sprinkler systems, automatic fire, manufacturing
421850	Sprinkler systems, fire, wholesaling
421820	Sprinklers, agricultural, wholesaling
332919	Sprinklers, lawn, manufacturing
333613	Sprockets, power transmission equipment, manufacturing
113210	Spruce gum gathering
213111	Spudding in oil and gas wells on a contract basis
313230	Spunbonded fabrics manufacturing
332212	Squares, carpenters', metal, manufacturing
713940	Squash club facilities
339920	Squash equipment (except apparel) manufacturing
111219	Squash farming, field, bedding plant and seed production

Code	Description
114112	Squid fishing
332999	Stabilizing bars, cargo, metal, manufacturing
711219	Stables, horse racing
713990	Stables, riding
333924	Stackers, industrial, truck-type, manufacturing
421830	Stackers, industrial, wholesaling
333924	Stackers, portable (except farm), manufacturing
233320	Stadium and arena construction
711310	Stadium operators
337127	Stadium seating manufacturing
531120	Stadium, no promotion of events, rental or leasing
561330	Staff leasing services
335129	Stage lighting equipment manufacturing
327211	Stained glass and stained glass products made in glass making plants
327215	Stained glass products made from purchased glass
331513	Stainless steel castings (except investment), unfinished, manufacturing
331111	Stainless steel made in steel mills
325510	Stains (except biological) manufacturing
422950	Stains wholesaling
325132	Stains, biological, manufacturing
332323	Stair railings, metal, manufacturing
321918	Stair railings, wood, manufacturing
332323	Stair treads, metal, manufacturing
326299	Stair treads, rubber, manufacturing
332323	Staircases, metal, manufacturing
332323	Stairs, metal, manufacturing
333921	Stairways, moving, manufacturing
321918	Stairwork (e.g., newel posts, railings, staircases, stairs), wood, manufacturing
321999	Stakes, surveyor's, wood, manufacturing
333111	Stalk choppers (i.e., shredders) manufacturing
332323	Stalls, metal, manufacturing
325998	Stamp pad ink manufacturing

Code	Description
339943	Stamp pads manufacturing
339911	Stamping coins
339943	Stamping devices, hand operated, manufacturing
333513	Stamping machines, metalworking, manufacturing
336370	Stamping metal motor vehicle body parts
336370	Stamping metal motor vehicle moldings and trims
332116	Stampings (except automotive, cans, cooking, closures, crowns), metal, unfinished, manufacturing
713210	Stand alone casinos (except slot machine parlors)
334515	Standards and calibration equipment for electrical measuring manufacturing
813920	Standards review committees, professional
926150	Standards, setting and management, agencies, government
334515	Standing wave ratio measuring equipment manufacturing
337215	Stands (except wire), merchandise display, manufacturing
711510	Standup comedians, independent
325188	Stannic and stannous chloride manufacturing
339942	Staple removers manufacturing
333991	Staplers and nailers, handheld power-driven, manufacturing
339942	Staplers manufacturing
332618	Staples made from purchased wire
421710	Staples wholesaling
331222	Staples, iron or steel, made in wire drawing plants
325520	Starch glues manufacturing
311221	Starches (except laundry) manufacturing
325612	Starches, laundry, manufacturing
112310	Started pullet production
336322	Starter and starter parts for internal combustion engines manufacturing
928120	State Department
522110	State commercial banks

Code	Description
522130	State credit unions
923110	State education departments
561310	State operated employment job services offices
922120	State police
522120	State savings banks
921130	State tax commissions
334413	Static converters, integrated circuits, manufacturing
334512	Static pressure regulators manufacturing
332410	Stationary power boilers manufacturing
327112	Stationery articles, pottery, manufacturing
323110	Stationery lithographic (offset) printing on a job-order basis
322233	Stationery made from purchased paper
453210	Stationery stores
422120	Stationery supplies wholesaling
335312	Stators for motors manufacturing
327420	Statuary (e.g., gypsum, plaster of paris) manufacturing
422990	Statuary (except religious) wholesaling
327112	Statuary, clay and ceramic, manufacturing
327991	Statuary, marble, manufacturing
327999	Statuary, vases, and urns, papier-mache, manufacturing
212399	Staurolite mining and/or beneficiating
321920	Staves, barrel, sawed or split, manufacturing
316999	Stays, shoe, leather, manufacturing
722110	Steak houses, full service
722211	Steak houses, limited service
812199	Steam baths
561790	Steam cleaning building exteriors
213112	Steam cleaning oil and gas wells on a contract basis
332410	Steam condensers manufacturing
333319	Steam cookers, commercial-type, manufacturing
335211	Steam cookers, household-type, manufacturing

Code	Description
611513	Steam fitters' apprenticeship training
235110	Steam fitting construction contractors
332919	Steam fittings, metal, manufacturing
221330	Steam heat distribution
333414	Steam heating equipment manufacturing
221330	Steam heating systems (i.e., suppliers of heat)
334512	Steam pressure controls, residential and commercial heating-type, manufacturing
221330	Steam production and distribution
333999	Steam separating machinery manufacturing
221330	Steam supply systems, including geothermal
333319	Steam tables manufacturing
487110	Steam train excursions
332911	Steam traps, industrial-type, manufacturing
333611	Steam turbine generator set units manufacturing
333611	Steam turbines manufacturing
532411	Steamship rental or leasing
325199	Stearic acid esters manufacturing
325199	Stearic acid manufacturing
325199	Stearic acid salts manufacturing
311613	Stearin, animal, rendering
212399	Steatite mining and/or beneficiating
327113	Steatite porcelain insulators manufacturing
331111	Steel balls made in steel mills
332431	Steel cans manufacturing
331513	Steel castings (except investment), unfinished, manufacturing
332111	Steel forgings made from purchased steel, unfinished
331513	Steel foundries (except investment)
235510	Steel framing construction contractors
331512	Steel investment castings, unfinished, manufacturing
331512	Steel investment foundries
332312	Steel joists manufacturing

Code	Description
331111	Steel manufacturing
331111	Steel mill products (e.g., bar, plate, rod, sheet, structural shapes) manufacturing
331111	Steel mills
332312	Steel railroad car racks manufacturing
327910	Steel shot abrasives manufacturing
421510	Steel wholesaling
332999	Steel wool manufacturing
421510	Steel wool wholesaling
235910	Steel work structural, construction contractors
235990	Steeplejacks
311221	Steepwater concentrate manufacturing
336330	Steering boxes, manual and power assist, manufacturing
336330	Steering columns, automotive, truck, and bus, manufacturing
336330	Steering wheels, automotive, truck, and bus, manufacturing
327215	Stemware made from purchased glass
327212	Stemware, glass, made in glass making plants
325910	Stencil inks manufacturing
339944	Stencil paper manufacturing
339943	Stencils for painting and marking (e.g., cardboard, metal) manufacturing
561410	Stenographic services (except court or stenographic reporting)
333313	Stenography machinery manufacturing
561492	Stenography services, public
561492	Stenotype recording services
332999	Stepladders, metal, manufacturing
321999	Stepladders, wood, manufacturing
337129	Stereo cabinets (i.e., housings), wood, manufacturing
532210	Stereo equipment rental
811211	Stereo equipment repair shops without retailing new stereo equipment
421620	Stereo equipment wholesaling
443112	Stereo stores (except automotive)

Code	Description
441310	Stereo stores, automotive
325212	Stereorubber manufacturing
339114	Sterilizers, dental, manufacturing
339113	Sterilizers, hospital and surgical, manufacturing
339111	Sterilizers, laboratory-type (except dental), manufacturing
332313	Sterilizing chambers, fabricated metal plate work, manufacturing
325411	Steriods, uncompounded, manufacturing
339112	Stethoscopes manufacturing
488320	Stevedoring services
339920	Sticks, sports (e.g., hockey, lacrosse), manufacturing
325132	Stilbene dyes manufacturing
324110	Still gases made in petroleum refineries
332420	Stills, heavy gauge metal, manufacturing
333293	Stitchers and trimmers book binding equipment manufacturing
315211	Stitching, decorative and novelty, contractors on men's and boys' apparel
315212	Stitching, decorative and novelty, contractors on women's, girls', and infants' apparel
314999	Stitching, decorative and novelty, on textile articles and apparel
523120	Stock brokerages
523120	Stock brokers' offices
711212	Stock car racetracks
711219	Stock car racing teams
711110	Stock companies, theatrical
523210	Stock exchanges
512199	Stock footage film libraries
512290	Stock music and other audio services
523120	Stock options brokerages
523110	Stock options dealing (i.e., acting as a principal in dealing securities to investors)
523210	Stock or commodity options exchanges
514199	Stock photo agencies
523999	Stock quotation services

Code	Description
523999	Stock transfer agencies
321912	Stock, chair, unfinished hardwood, manufacturing
112111	Stocker calf production
315111	Stockings (except socks), sheer, manufacturing
315111	Stockings, sheer, women's, misses', and girls', full-length and knee-length, knitting or knitting and finishing
488999	Stockyards (i.e., not for fattening or selling livestock), transportation
212319	Stone (except limestone and granite) beneficiating plants (e.g., grinding)
212311	Stone (except limestone and granite) mining or quarrying
333131	Stone beneficiating machinery manufacturing
332213	Stone cutting saw blades manufacturing
235410	Stone setting construction contractors
313311	Stone washing broadwoven fabrics
313312	Stone washing textile products, apparel, and fabrics (except broadwoven)
333298	Stone working machinery manufacturing
421320	Stone, building or crushed, wholesaling
212319	Stone, crushed and broken (except granite or limestone), mining and/or beneficiating
332212	Stonecutters' handtools, nonpowered, manufacturing
212399	Stones, abrasive (e.g., emery, grindstones, hones, pumice), mining and/or beneficiating
421940	Stones, precious and semiprecious, wholesaling
327999	Stones, synthetic, for gem stones and industrial use, manufacturing
327112	Stoneware (i.e., pottery products) manufacturing
212325	Stoneware clay mining and/or beneficiating
235410	Stonework construction contractors

Code	Description
337124	Stools, metal household-type (except upholstered), manufacturing
337122	Stools, wood household-type (except upholstered), manufacturing
621999	Stop smoking clinics
332911	Stop valves, industrial-type, manufacturing
332913	Stopcock drains, plumbing, manufacturing
321999	Stoppers, cork, manufacturing
326299	Stoppers, rubber, manufacturing
421610	Storage batteries (except automotive) wholesaling
335911	Storage batteries manufacturing
335312	Storage battery chargers (except internal combustion engine-type) manufacturing
421390	Storage bins wholesaling
334112	Storage devices, computer, manufacturing
486210	Storage of natural gas
332420	Storage tanks, heavy gauge metal, manufacturing
235910	Storage tanks, metal, construction contractors
421510	Storage tanks, metal, wholesaling
233320	Store construction
541850	Store display advertising services
337215	Store display fixtures manufacturing
421440	Store equipment (except furniture) wholesaling
235510	Store fixture construction contractors (i.e., built-in, on site)
421440	Store fixtures (except refrigerated) wholesaling
235910	Store front metal, installation, construction contractors
421210	Store furniture wholesaling
*****	Stores — see type
562998	Storm basin cleanout services
332321	Storm doors and windows, metal, manufacturing
321911	Storm doors and windows, wood framed, manufacturing
711510	Storytellers, independent
312120	Stout brewing
332322	Stove boards, sheet metal, manufacturing
327123	Stove lining, clay, manufacturing
332322	Stove pipes and flues, sheet metal, manufacturing
811412	Stove, household-type, repair and maintenance services without retailing new stoves
335221	Stoves, ceramic disk element, household-type, manufacturing
333319	Stoves, commercial-type, manufacturing
421720	Stoves, cooking and heating (except electric), household-type, wholesaling
335221	Stoves, household-type cooking, manufacturing
333924	Straddle carriers, mobile, manufacturing
332211	Straight razors manufacturing
332911	Straightway (i.e., Y-type) valves, industrial-type, manufacturing
333999	Strainers, pipeline, manufacturing
321219	Strandboard, oriented, manufacturing
332618	Stranded wire, uninsulated, made from purchased wire
316110	Strap leather manufacturing
332999	Strappings, metal, manufacturing
316999	Straps (except watch), leather, manufacturing
316993	Straps, watch (except metal), manufacturing
339911	Straps, watch, precious metal, manufacturing
541611	Strategic planning consulting services
213112	Stratigraphic drilling, oil and gas field exploration on a contract basis
321999	Straw baskets manufacturing
315991	Straw hats manufacturing
422910	Straw wholesaling
111333	Strawberry farming
234110	Street and highway construction management firms
488490	Street cleaning service
234110	Street construction
335129	Street lighting fixtures (except traffic signals) manufacturing
234110	Street maintenance or repair
511199	Street map guide publishers
234110	Street paving
485119	Street railway systems (except mixed mode), commuter
421810	Street sweeping and cleaning equipment wholesaling
454390	Street vendors (except food)
722330	Street vendors, food
234990	Streetcar line construction
336510	Streetcars and car equipment, urban transit, manufacturing
713940	Strength development centers
336211	Stretch limousines assembling on purchased chassis
321999	Stretchers, curtain, wood, manufacturing
339113	Stretchers, medical, manufacturing
333513	Stretching machines, metalworking, manufacturing
111219	String bean farming, field and seed production
314991	Strings manufacturing
339992	Strings, musical instrument, manufacturing
212113	Strip mining, anthracite, on own account
212111	Strip mining, bituminous coal or lignite, on own account
212111	Strip mining, lignite, on own account
331421	Strip, copper and copper alloy, made from purchased copper or in integrated secondary smelting and rolling, drawing or extruding plants
331111	Strip, galvanized iron or steel, made in steel mills
331111	Strip, iron or steel, made in steel mills
331491	Strip, nonferrous metals (except aluminum, copper), made from purchased metals or scrap
211111	Stripper well production
213113	Stripping overburden services for coal mining on a contract basis

Code	Description
213114	Stripping overburden services for metal mining on a contract basis
213115	Stripping overburden services for nonmetallic minerals mining (except fuels) on a contract basis
334515	Stroboscopes manufacturing
335110	Strobotrons manufacturing
339932	Strollers, baby, manufacturing
212393	Strontianite mining and/or beneficiating
325188	Strontium carbonate manufacturing
325188	Strontium compounds, not specified elsewhere by process, manufacturing
212393	Strontium mineral mining and/or beneficiating
325188	Strontium nitrate manufacturing
421510	Structural assemblies, metal, wholesaling
421390	Structural assemblies, prefabricated (except wood), wholesaling
421310	Structural assemblies, prefabricated wood, wholesaling
421320	Structural clay tile (except refractory) wholesaling
327121	Structural clay tile manufacturing
321114	Structural lumber and timber, treating
321213	Structural members, glue laminated or pre-engineered wood, manufacturing
333516	Structural rolling mill machinery, metalworking, manufacturing
331319	Structural shapes made by rolling purchased aluminum
331319	Structural shapes, aluminum, made in integrated secondary smelting and rolling mills
331111	Structural shapes, iron or steel, made in steel mills
235910	Structural steel construction contractors
332312	Structural steel, fabricated, manufacturing
339932	Structural toy sets manufacturing
321213	Structural wood members (except trusses), fabricated, manufacturing

Code	Description
336330	Struts, automotive, truck, and bus, manufacturing
325411	Strychnine and derivatives (i.e., basic chemicals) manufacturing
327999	Stucco and stucco products manufacturing
235420	Stucco construction contractors
321113	Stud mills
115210	Stud services
522294	Student Loan Marketing Association (SLMA)
813410	Student clubs
611710	Student exchange programs
522291	Student loan companies
813410	Students' associations
813410	Students' unions
233320	Studio construction
334220	Studio equipment, radio and television broadcasting, manufacturing
541430	Studios, commercial art
321912	Studs, resawing purchased lumber
332322	Studs, sheet metal, manufacturing
921120	Study commissions, legislative
339931	Stuffed toys (including animals) manufacturing
333294	Stuffer, sausage machinery, manufacturing
113310	Stump removing in the field
325920	Styphnic acid explosive materials manufacturing
325110	Styrene made from refined petroleum or liquid hydrocarbons
324110	Styrene made in petroleum refineries
325211	Styrene resins manufacturing
325211	Styrene-acrylonitrile resins manufacturing
325212	Styrene-butadiene rubber containing less than 50 percent styrene manufacturing
325212	Styrene-chloroprene rubber manufacturing
325212	Styrene-isoprene rubber manufacturing
212111	Subbituminous coal surface mining and/or beneficiating

Code	Description
212112	Subbituminous coal underground mining or mining and beneficiating
332994	Submachine guns manufacturing
336611	Submarine building
333514	Subpresses, machine tool, manufacturing
334210	Subscriber loop equipment, telephone, manufacturing
513210	Subscription television networks
551114	Subsidiary management offices
623220	Substance abuse (i.e., alcoholism, drug addiction) halfway houses
623220	Substance abuse facilities, residential
813319	Substance abuse prevention advocacy organizations
621420	Substance abuse treatment centers and clinics (except hospitals), outpatient
335311	Substation transformers, electric power distribution, manufacturing
512191	Subtitling of motion picture film or video
485113	Suburban bus line services (except mixed mode)
485112	Suburban commuter rail systems (except mixed mode)
485111	Suburban transit systems, mixed mode (e.g., bus, commuter rail, subway combinations)
541850	Subway card display advertising services
336510	Subway cars manufacturing
421860	Subway cars wholesaling
234990	Subway construction
485119	Subway systems (except mixed mode), commuter
339112	Suction therapy apparatus manufacturing
812320	Suede garment cleaning services
313311	Sueding broadwoven fabrics
313312	Sueding textile products and fabrics (except broadwoven)
111991	Sugar beet farming
115113	Sugar beets, machine harvesting
311221	Sugar made by wet milling corn
333294	Sugar refining machinery manufacturing

Code	Description
325998	Sugar substitutes (i.e., synthetic sweeteners blended with other ingredients) made from purchased synthetic sweeteners
325199	Sugar substitutes (i.e., synthetic sweeteners blended with other ingredients) made in synthetic sweetener establishments
311312	Sugar, cane, made from purchased raw cane sugar
311311	Sugar, clarified, granulated, and raw, made in sugarcane mill
311312	Sugar, confectionery, made from purchased raw cane sugar
311313	Sugar, confectionery, made from sugar beets
311311	Sugar, confectionery, made in sugarcane mill
311312	Sugar, granulated, made from purchased raw cane sugar
311313	Sugar, granulated, made from sugar beets
311311	Sugar, granulated, made in sugarcane mill
311312	Sugar, invert, made from purchased raw cane sugar
311313	Sugar, invert, made from sugar beets
311311	Sugar, invert, made in sugarcane mill
311313	Sugar, liquid, made from sugar beets
311311	Sugar, raw, made in sugarcane mill
422590	Sugar, raw, wholesaling
311312	Sugar, refined, made from purchased raw cane sugar
422490	Sugar, refined, wholesaling
111930	Sugarcane farming, field production
311311	Sugarcane mills
311311	Sugarcane refining
115113	Sugarcane, machine harvesting
624190	Suicide crisis centers
532220	Suit rental
315999	Suit trimmings cut and sewn from purchased fabric (except apparel contractors)
315211	Suit trimmings, men's and boys', cut and sew apparel contractors

Code	Description
332510	Suitcase hardware, metal, manufacturing
316991	Suitcases, all materials, manufacturing
315211	Suits (i.e., nontailored, tailored, work), men's and boys', cut and sew apparel contractors
315212	Suits (i.e., nontailored, tailored, work), women's, misses', girls', and infants', cut and sew apparel contractors
315191	Suits made in apparel knitting mills
339113	Suits, firefighting, manufacturing
315291	Suits, infants' (e.g., warm-up, jogging, snowsuits), cut and sewn from purchased fabric (except apparel contractors)
422320	Suits, men's and boys', wholesaling
315239	Suits, nontailored (e.g., jogging, snow suit, warm-up), women's, misses', and girls', cut and sewn from purchased fabric (except apparel contractors)
315228	Suits, nontailored (e.g., jogging, snow, ski, warm-up), men's and boys', cut and sewn from purchased fabric (except apparel contractors)
339113	Suits, space, manufacturing
315222	Suits, tailored, men's and boys', cut and sewn from purchased fabric (except apparel contractors)
315234	Suits, tailored, women's, misses', and girls', cut and sewn from purchased fabric (except apparel contractors)
325411	Sulfa drugs, uncompounded, manufacturing
212391	Sulfate, sodium, mining and/or beneficiating
325188	Sulfides and sulfites manufacturing
325188	Sulfocyanides manufacturing
325411	Sulfonamides, uncompounded, manufacturing
325188	Sulfur and sulfur compounds, not specified elsewhere by process, manufacturing
325188	Sulfur chloride manufacturing
325188	Sulfur dioxide manufacturing

Code	Description
325188	Sulfur hexafluoride gas manufacturing
325320	Sulfur insecticides manufacturing
212393	Sulfur mining and/or beneficiating
211112	Sulfur recovered from natural gas
325188	Sulfur recovering or refining (except from sour natural gas)
212393	Sulfur, native, mining and/or beneficiating
325188	Sulfuric acid manufacturing
422690	Sulfuric acid wholesaling
325192	Sulphonated derivatives manufacturing
311423	Sulphured fruit and vegetables manufacturing
325191	Sumac extract manufacturing
721214	Summer camps (except day instructional)
713990	Summer day camps (except instructional)
721110	Summer resort hotels
711110	Summer theaters
235110	Sump pump construction contractors
333911	Sump pumps, residential-type, manufacturing
115114	Sun drying of dates, prunes, raisins, and olives
115114	Sun drying of fruits and vegetables
115114	Sun drying of tomatoes
812199	Sun tanning salons
111120	Sunflower farming, field and seed production
311223	Sunflower seed oil, cake and meal, made in crushing mills
446130	Sunglass stores
339115	Sunglasses and goggles manufacturing
421460	Sunglasses wholesaling
336399	Sunroofs and parts, automotive, truck, and bus, manufacturing
325620	Sunscreen lotions and oils manufacturing
315291	Sunsuits, infants', cut and sewn from purchased fabric (except apparel contractors)

Code	Description
325620	Suntan lotions and oils manufacturing
331111	Superalloys, iron or steel, manufacturing
331492	Superalloys, nonferrous based, made from purchased metals or scrap
445110	Supermarkets
325312	Superphosphates manufacturing
452910	Superstores (i.e., food and general merchandise)
921190	Supply agencies, government
332913	Supply line assemblies, plumbing (i.e., flexible hose with fittings), manufacturing
624190	Support group services
339113	Supports, orthopedic (e.g., abdominal, ankle, arch, kneecap), manufacturing
325412	Suppositories manufacturing
524126	Surety insurance carriers, direct
325613	Surface active agents manufacturing
422690	Surface active agents wholesaling
334516	Surface area analyzers manufacturing
334512	Surface burner controls, temperature, manufacturing
322226	Surface coating purchased paperboard
333120	Surface mining machinery (except drilling) manufacturing
333295	Surface mount machinery for making printed circuit boards manufacturing
339920	Surfboards manufacturing
335999	Surge suppressors manufacturing
621111	Surgeons' (except dental) offices (e.g., centers, clinics)
541940	Surgeons' offices, veterinary
621210	Surgeons', dental, offices (e.g., centers, clinics)
115112	Surgery on trees and vines
541940	Surgery services, veterinary
421450	Surgical appliances wholesaling
339112	Surgical clamps manufacturing
339113	Surgical dressings manufacturing

Code	Description
339113	Surgical implants manufacturing
811219	Surgical instrument repair and maintenance services
421450	Surgical instruments and apparatus wholesaling
339112	Surgical knife blades and handles manufacturing
621111	Surgical pathologists' offices (e.g., centers, clinics)
339112	Surgical stapling devices manufacturing
339113	Surgical supplies (except medical instruments) manufacturing
421450	Surgical supplies wholesaling
334510	Surgical support systems (e.g., heart-lung machines) (except iron lungs) manufacturing
421450	Surgical towels wholesaling
311711	Surimi canning
311712	Surimi, fresh and frozen, manufacturing
213112	Surveying (except seismographic) oil or gas wells on a contract basis
541370	Surveying and mapping services (except geophysical)
421490	Surveying equipment and supplies wholesaling
811219	Surveying instrument repair and maintenance services
334519	Surveying instruments manufacturing
541360	Surveying services, geophysical
321999	Surveyor's stakes, wood, manufacturing
611699	Survival training instruction
315999	Suspenders cut and sewn from purchased fabric (except apparel contractors)
315211	Suspenders, men's and boys', cut and sew apparel contractors
315212	Suspenders, women's, girls', and infants', cut and sew apparel contractors
811118	Suspension repair shops, automotive
339113	Sutures, surgical, manufacturing
213112	Swabbing oil or gas wells on a contract basis

Code	Description
333513	Swaging machines, metalworking, manufacturing
487210	Swamp buggy operation
323121	Swatches and samples, mounting for the trade
332999	Swatters, fly metal, manufacturing
315299	Sweat bands cut and sewn from purchased fabric (except apparel contractors)
315191	Sweat bands made in apparel knitting mills
315211	Sweat bands, men's and boys', cut and sew apparel contractors
315212	Sweat bands, women's, girls', and infants', cut and sew apparel contractors
315191	Sweat pants made in apparel knitting mills
315291	Sweat pants, infants', cut and sewn from purchased fabric (except apparel contractors)
315228	Sweat pants, men's, boys', and unisex (i.e., sized without regard to gender), cut and sewn from purchased fabric (except apparel contractors)
315211	Sweat pants, men's, boys', and unisex, cut and sew apparel contractors
315212	Sweat pants, women's, girls', and infants', cut and sew apparel contractors
315239	Sweat pants, women's, misses', and girls', cut and sewn from purchased fabric (except apparel contractors)
315191	Sweat suits made in apparel knitting mills
315291	Sweat suits, infants', cut and sewn from purchased fabric (except apparel contractors)
315211	Sweat suits, men's and boys', cut and sew apparel contractors
315228	Sweat suits, men's and boys', cut and sewn from purchased fabric (except apparel contractors)
315212	Sweat suits, women's, girls', and infants', cut and sew apparel contractors

Code	Description
315239	Sweat suits, women's, misses', and girls', cut and sewn from purchased fabric (except apparel contractors)
316110	Sweatband leather manufacturing
315191	Sweater jackets made in apparel knitting mills
315291	Sweater jackets, infants', cut and sewn from purchased fabric (except apparel contractors)
315211	Sweater jackets, men's and boys', cut and sew apparel contractors
315228	Sweater jackets, men's and boys', cut and sewn from purchased fabric (except apparel contractors)
315212	Sweater jackets, women's, girls', and infants', cut and sew apparel contractors
315239	Sweater jackets, women's, misses', and girls', cut and sewn from purchased fabric (except apparel contractors)
315191	Sweater vests made in apparel knitting mills
315291	Sweater vests, infants', cut and sewn from purchased fabric (except apparel contractors)
315211	Sweater vests, men's and boys', cut and sew apparel contractors
315228	Sweater vests, men's and boys', cut and sewn from purchased fabric (except apparel contractors)
315212	Sweater vests, women's, girls', and infants', cut and sew apparel contractors
315239	Sweater vests, women's, misses', and girls', cut and sewn from purchased fabric (except apparel contractors)
315191	Sweaters made in apparel knitting mills
315291	Sweaters, infants', cut and sewn from purchased fabric (except apparel contractors)
315211	Sweaters, men's and boys', cut and sew apparel contractors
315228	Sweaters, men's and boys', cut and sewn from purchased fabric (except apparel contractors)
315212	Sweaters, women's, and girls', and infants', cut and sew apparel contractors

Code	Description
315239	Sweaters, women's, misses', and girls', cut and sewn from purchased fabric (except apparel contractors)
315191	Sweatshirts made in apparel knitting mills
315291	Sweatshirts, infants', cut and sewn from purchased fabric (except apparel contractors)
315211	Sweatshirts, men's and boys', cut and sew apparel contractors
315223	Sweatshirts, men's and boys', cut and sewn from purchased fabric (except apparel contractors)
315223	Sweatshirts, outerwear, unisex (sized without regard to gender), cut and sewn from purchased fabric (except apparel contractors)
315212	Sweatshirts, women's, girls', and infants', cut and sew apparel contractors
315232	Sweatshirts, women's, misses', and girls', cut and sewn from purchased fabric (except apparel contractors)
334515	Sweep generators manufacturing
334515	Sweep oscillators manufacturing
335212	Sweepers, household-type electric vacuum, manufacturing
325612	Sweeping compounds, absorbent, manufacturing
111219	Sweet corn farming, field and seed production
111219	Sweet pepper farming, field, bedding plant and seed production
115114	Sweet potato curing
111219	Sweet potato farming, field and seed potato production
311812	Sweet yeast goods (except frozen) manufacturing
311813	Sweet yeast goods, frozen, manufacturing
311999	Sweetening syrups (except pure maple) manufacturing
611620	Swimming instruction
325998	Swimming pool chemical preparations manufacturing
561790	Swimming pool cleaning and maintenance services
235990	Swimming pool construction contractors

Code	Description
326199	Swimming pool covers and liners, plastics, manufacturing
333319	Swimming pool filter systems manufacturing
333414	Swimming pool heaters manufacturing
335129	Swimming pool lighting fixtures manufacturing
453998	Swimming pool supply stores
713940	Swimming pools
421910	Swimming pools and equipment wholesaling
339920	Swimming pools, above ground, manufacturing
315191	Swimsuits made in apparel knitting mills
315291	Swimsuits, infants', cut and sewn from purchased fabric (except apparel contractors)
315211	Swimsuits, men's and boys', cut and sew apparel contractors
315228	Swimsuits, men's and boys', cut and sewn from purchased fabric (except apparel contractors)
315212	Swimsuits, women's, girls', and infants', cut and sew apparel contractors
315239	Swimsuits, women's, misses', and girls', cut and sewn from purchased fabric (except apparel contractors)
448190	Swimwear stores
422320	Swimwear, men's and boys', wholesaling
422330	Swimwear, women's, children's, and infants', wholesaling
311119	Swine feed, complete, manufacturing
311119	Swine feed, supplements, concentrates, and premixes, manufacturing
422520	Swine wholesaling
335932	Switch boxes, electrical wiring, manufacturing
335931	Switch cutouts manufacturing
335313	Switchboards and parts, power, manufacturing
421610	Switchboards, electrical distribution, wholesaling

Code	Description
335931	Switches for electrical wiring (e.g., pressure, pushbotton, snap, tumbler) manufacturing
334419	Switches for electronic applications manufacturing
335313	Switches, electric power (except pushbotton, snap, solenoid, tumbler), manufacturing
421610	Switches, electrical, wholesaling
421690	Switches, electronic, wholesaling
335931	Switches, outlet box mounting-type, manufacturing
334512	Switches, pneumatic positioning remote, manufacturing
334512	Switches, thermostatic, manufacturing
335313	Switchgear and switchgear accessories, manufacturing
335313	Switching equipment, power, manufacturing
334210	Switching equipment, telephone, manufacturing
488210	Switching services, railroad
114111	Swordfish fishing
332211	Swords, nonprecious and precious plated metal, manufacturing
212313	Syenite (except nepheline) crushed and broken stone mining and/or beneficiating
212311	Syenite (except nepheline) mining or quarrying
212325	Syenite, nepheline, mining and/or beneficiating
212221	Sylvanite mining and/or beneficiating
711130	Symphony orchestras
813110	Synagogues
335312	Synchronous condensers and timing motors, electric, manufacturing
335312	Synchronous motors manufacturing
334515	Synchroscopes manufacturing
514110	Syndicates, news
339992	Synthesizers, music, manufacturing
311340	Synthetic chocolate manufacturing
325212	Synthetic rubber (i.e., vulcanizable elastomers) manufacturing
422690	Synthetic rubber wholesaling

Code	Description
327999	Synthetic stones, for gem stones and industrial use, manufacturing
325199	Synthetic sweeteners (i.e., sweetening agents) manufacturing
339112	Syringes, hypodermic, manufacturing
422490	Syrup (except fountain) wholesaling
311313	Syrup made from sugar beets
311930	Syrup, beverage, manufacturing
311312	Syrup, cane, made from purchased raw cane sugar
311311	Syrup, cane, made in sugarcane mill
311320	Syrup, chocolate, made from cacao beans
311330	Syrup, chocolate, made from purchased chocolate
311999	Syrup, corn (except wet milled), manufacturing
311221	Syrup, corn, made by wet milling
311930	Syrup, flavoring (except coffee based), manufacturing
311920	Syrup, flavoring, coffee based, manufacturing
422450	Syrup, fountain, wholesaling
111998	Syrup, pure maple (i.e., maple syrup reducing)
311999	Syrup, sweetening (except pure maple), manufacturing
311999	Syrup, table, artificially flavored, manufacturing
541512	Systems integration design consulting services, computer
541512	Systems integration design services, computer
448190	T-shirt shops, custom printed
315291	T-shirts, outerwear, infants', cut and sewn from purchased fabric (except apparel contractors)
315191	T-shirts, outerwear, made in apparel knitting mills
315223	T-shirts, outerwear, men's and boys', cut and sewn from purchased fabric (except apparel contractors)
315211	T-shirts, outerwear, men's, boys' and unisex, cut and sew apparel contractors

Code	Description
315223	T-shirts, outerwear, unisex (i.e., sized without regard to gender), cut and sewn from purchased fabric (except apparel contractors)
315212	T-shirts, outerwear, women's, girls', and infants', cut and sew apparel contractors
315232	T-shirts, outerwear, women's, misses', and girls', cut and sewn from purchased fabric (except apparel contractors)
315291	T-shirts, underwear, infants', cut and sewn from purchased fabric (except apparel contractors)
315192	T-shirts, underwear, made in apparel knitting mills
315211	T-shirts, underwear, men's and boys', cut and sew apparel contractors
315221	T-shirts, underwear, men's and boys', cut and sewn from purchased fabric (except apparel contractors)
315231	T-shirts, underwear, women's, misses', and girls', cut and sewn from purchased fabric (except apparel contractors)
315212	T-shirts, underwear, women's, misses', girls', and infants', cut and sew apparel contractors
334519	T-squares (drafting) manufacturing
334510	TENS (transcutaneous electrical nerve stimulator) manufacturing
325920	TNT (trinitrotoluene) manufacturing
334310	TV (television) sets manufacturing
443112	TV (television) stores
532490	TV broadcasting and studio equipment rental or leasing
337124	TV stands and similar stands for consumer electronics, metal, manufacturing
337125	TV stands and similar stands for consumer electronics, plastics, manufacturing
337122	TV stands and similar stands for consumer electronics, wood, manufacturing
532299	Table and banquet accessory rental

Code	Description
327112	Table articles, coarse earthenware, manufacturing
327112	Table articles, earthenware, manufacturing
327112	Table articles, fine earthenware (i.e., whiteware), manufacturing
327112	Table articles, vitreous china, manufacturing
332211	Table cutlery, nonprecious and precious plated metal, manufacturing
339912	Table cutlery, precious metal, manufacturing
335121	Table lamps (i.e., lighting fixtures) manufacturing
812331	Table linen supply services
311225	Table oil made from purchased oils
311221	Table oil, corn, made by wet milling
311942	Table salt manufacturing
327991	Table tops, marble, manufacturing
337110	Table tops, wood, manufacturing
112310	Table-egg chicken production
314129	Tablecloths (except paper) made from purchased materials
313249	Tablecloths made in a lace mills
313249	Tablecloths made in a warp knitting mills
313210	Tablecloths made in broadwoven fabric mills
313241	Tablecloths made in weft knitting mills
322291	Tablecloths, paper, made from purchased paper
337214	Tables (except wood), office-type, manufacturing
337124	Tables, metal household-type, manufacturing
337122	Tables, wood household-type, manufacturing
337211	Tables, wood, office-type, manufacturing
322233	Tablets (e.g., memo, note, writing) made from purchased paper
322121	Tablets (e.g., memo, note, writing) made in paper mills
332999	Tablets, metal, manufacturing
421220	Tableware (except disposable, plated, precious) wholesaling

Code	Description
327215	Tableware made from purchased glass
327212	Tableware made in glass making plants
532299	Tableware rental
422130	Tableware, disposable, wholesaling
421940	Tableware, precious and plated, wholesaling
327112	Tableware, vitreous china, manufacturing
334515	Tachometer generators manufacturing
451110	Tack shops
321999	Tackle blocks, wood, manufacturing
451110	Tackle shops (i.e., fishing)
339920	Tackle, fishing (except line, nets, seines), manufacturing
421710	Tacks wholesaling
331222	Tacks, iron or steel, made in wire drawing plants
332618	Tacks, metal, made from purchased wire
212210	Taconite concentrates or agglomerates beneficiating
212210	Taconite ores mining and/or beneficiating
334511	Taffrail logs manufacturing
213111	Tailing in oil and gas field wells on a contract basis
811490	Tailor shops, alterations only
332211	Tailor's scissors, nonelectric, manufacturing
315211	Tailored dress and sport coats, men's and boys', cut and sew apparel contractors
315222	Tailored dress and sport coats, men's and boys', cut and sewn from purchased fabric (except apparel contractors)
421850	Tailors' supplies wholesaling
722211	Take out eating places
212399	Talc mining and/or beneficiating
327992	Talc processing beyond beneficiation
325620	Talcum powders manufacturing
711410	Talent agencies
711410	Talent agents
541214	Talent payment services

Code	Description
325191	Tall oil (except skimmings) manufacturing
311611	Tallow produced in a slaughtering plant
311613	Tallow produced in rendering plant
334514	Tally counters manufacturing
334514	Tallying meters (except clocks, electrical instruments, watches) manufacturing
333120	Tampers, powered, manufacturing
332995	Tampions guns manufacturing
111320	Tangelo groves
111320	Tangerine groves
332995	Tank artillery manufacturing
336211	Tank bodies for trucks manufacturing
562998	Tank cleaning and disposal services, commercial or industrial
562991	Tank cleaning services, septic
315291	Tank tops, infants', cut and sewn from purchased fabric (except apparel contractors)
315211	Tank tops, men's and boys', cut and sew apparel contractors
315191	Tank tops, outerwear, made in apparel knitting mills
315223	Tank tops, outerwear, men's and boys', cut and sewn from purchased fabric (except apparel contractors)
315232	Tank tops, outerwear, women's, misses', and girls', cut and sewn from purchased fabric (except apparel contractors)
315192	Tank tops, underwear, made in apparel knitting mills
315221	Tank tops, underwear, men's and boys', cut and sewn from purchased fabric (except apparel contractors)
315231	Tank tops, underwear, women's, misses', and girls', cut and sewn from purchased fabric (except apparel contractors)
315212	Tank tops, women's, girls', and infants', cut and sew apparel contractors
336212	Tank trailer, liquid and dry bulk, manufacturing

Code	Description
334514	Tank truck meters manufacturing
336211	Tank trucks (e.g., fuel oil, milk, water) assembling on purchased chassis
532411	Tanker rental or leasing
484220	Tanker trucking (e.g., chemical, juice, milk, petroleum), local
484230	Tanker trucking (e.g., chemical, juice, milk, petroleum), long-distance
327390	Tanks, concrete, manufacturing
327111	Tanks, flush, vitreous china, manufacturing
332420	Tanks, heavy gauge metal, manufacturing
336992	Tanks, military (including factory rebuilding), manufacturing
333315	Tanks, photographic developing, fixing, and washing, manufacturing
421510	Tanks, storage metal, wholesaling
326199	Tanks, storage, plastics or fiberglass, manufacturing
321920	Tanks, wood, coopered, manufacturing
316110	Tannery leather manufacturing
333298	Tannery machinery manufacturing
325191	Tannic acid (i.e., tannins) manufacturing
325188	Tanning agents, inorganic, manufacturing
325199	Tanning agents, synthetic organic, manufacturing
316110	Tanning and currying furs
325191	Tanning extracts and materials, natural, manufacturing
812199	Tanning salons
212299	Tantalite mining and/or beneficiating
212299	Tantalum ores mining and/or beneficiating
331419	Tantalum refining, primary
711120	Tap dance companies
339942	Tape dispensers manufacturing
512120	Tape distribution for television
332212	Tape measures, metal, manufacturing
334310	Tape players and recorders, household-type, manufacturing

Code	Description
421620	Tape players and recorders, household-type, wholesaling
532210	Tape recorder rental
561990	Tape slitting (e.g., cutting plastic or leather into widths) for the trade
334112	Tape storage units (e.g., drive backups), computer peripheral equipment, manufacturing
512191	Tape transfer service
332991	Tapered roller bearings manufacturing
322231	Tapes (e.g., adding machine, calculator, cash register) made from purchased paper
322222	Tapes (e.g., cellophane, masking, pressure sensitive), gummed, made from purchased paper or other materials
313221	Tapes weaving
421690	Tapes, blank, audio and video, wholesaling
422120	Tapes, cellophane, wholesaling
334613	Tapes, magnetic recording (i.e., audio, data, video), blank, manufacturing
339113	Tapes, medical adhesive, manufacturing
421450	Tapes, medical and surgical, wholesaling
313230	Tapes, nonwoven fabric, manufacturing
421990	Tapes, prerecorded, audio or video, wholesaling
334519	Tapes, surveyor's, manufacturing
422310	Tapes, textile, wholesaling
313320	Tapes, varnished and coated (except magnetic), made from purchased fabric
235420	Taping and finishing drywall construction contractors
311221	Tapioca manufacturing
333512	Tapping machines, metalworking, manufacturing
333515	Taps and dies (i.e., a machine tool accessory) manufacturing
335931	Taps, current, attachment plug and screw shell types, manufacturing
316999	Taps, shoe, leather, manufacturing

Code	Description
325211	Tar acid resins manufacturing
324121	Tar and asphalt paving mixtures made from purchased asphaltic materials
325191	Tar and tar oils made by distillation of wood
325192	Tar made by distillation of coal tar
324110	Tar made in petroleum refineries
324122	Tar paper made from purchased asphaltic materials and paper
324122	Tar paper, building and roofing, made from purchased paper
322121	Tar paper, building and roofing, made in paper mills
324122	Tar roofing cements and coatings made from purchased asphaltic materials
211111	Tar sands mining
336411	Target drones, aircraft, manufacturing
336413	Targets, trailer type, aircraft, manufacturing
541614	Tariff rate consulting services
541614	Tariff rate information services
111219	Taro farming, field and seed production
314912	Tarpaulins made from purchased fabrics
421330	Tarred felts wholesaling
311941	Tartar sauce manufacturing
325199	Tartaric acid manufacturing
325199	Tartrates, not specified elsewhere by process, manufacturing
812199	Tattoo parlors
722410	Taverns (i.e., drinking places)
561440	Tax collection services on a contract or fee basis
541110	Tax law attorneys' offices
541110	Tax law attorneys' private practices
523910	Tax liens dealing (i.e., acting as a principal in dealing tax liens to investors)
541213	Tax return preparation services
921130	Taxation departments
541850	Taxicab card advertising services
485310	Taxicab dispatch services
485310	Taxicab fleet operators

Code	Description
485310	Taxicab organizations
485310	Taxicab owner-operators
485310	Taxicab services
421110	Taxicabs wholesaling
711510	Taxidermists, independent
421850	Taxidermy supplies wholesaling
334514	Taximeters manufacturing
813319	Taxpayers' advocacy organizations
311920	Tea (except herbal) manufacturing
445299	Tea and coffee (i.e., packaged) stores
311920	Tea blending
111998	Tea farming
327212	Tea kettles, glass and glass ceramic, made in glass making plants
422490	Tea wholesaling
311920	Tea, herbal, manufacturing
312111	Tea, iced, manufacturing
311920	Tea, instant, manufacturing
113210	Teaberries gathering
923110	Teacher certification bureaus
561310	Teacher registries
333319	Teaching machines (e.g., flight simulators) manufacturing
421490	Teaching machines (except computers), electronic, wholesaling
332214	Teakettles and coffee pots, fabricated metal (except electric, glass), manufacturing
335211	Teakettles, electric, manufacturing
327212	Teakettles, glass and glass ceramic, manufacturing
315299	Team athletic uniforms cut and sewn from purchased fabric (except apparel contractors)
315211	Team athletic uniforms, men's and boys', cut and sew apparel contractors
315212	Team athletic uniforms, women's and girls', cut and sew apparel contractors
325199	Tear gas manufacturing
313311	Teaseling broadwoven fabrics
313312	Teaseling fabrics (except broadwoven)
325412	Technetium medicinal preparations manufacturing

Code	Description
327212	Technical glassware and glass products, pressed or blown, made in glass making plants
327215	Technical glassware made from purchased glass
511120	Technical magazine and periodical publishers
511120	Technical magazine and periodical publishers and printing combined
511120	Technical magazine and periodical publishing (i.e., establishments known as publishers)
323112	Technical magazines and periodicals flexographic printing without publishing
323111	Technical magazines and periodicals gravure printing without publishing
323110	Technical magazines and periodicals lithographic (offset) printing without publishing
323119	Technical magazines and periodicals printing (except flexographic, gravure, lithographic, screen) without publishing
323113	Technical magazines and periodicals screen printing without publishing
511130	Technical manual and paperback book publishers
511130	Technical manual and paperback book publishers and printing combined
323121	Technical manual paper (books) binding without printing
511130	Technical manual publishers
511130	Technical manual publishing (i.e., establishments known as publishers)
323117	Technical manuals and papers (books) printing and binding without publishing
323117	Technical manuals and papers (books) printing without publishing
711510	Technical writers, independent
315212	Teddies, women's, cut and sew apparel contractors
315231	Teddies, women's, misses', and girls', cut and sewn from purchased fabric (except apparel contractors)
624110	Teen outreach services

Code	Description
339114	Teeth (except customized) manufacturing
339116	Teeth, custom made in dental laboratories
421450	Teeth, dental, wholesaling
513322	Telecommunications carriers, cellular telephone
513310	Telecommunications carriers, wired
532490	Telecommunications equipment rental or leasing
234920	Telecommunications line (e.g., telephone, telegraph) construction
541618	Telecommunications management consulting services
513310	Telecommunications networks, wired
513330	Telecommunications resellers
235310	Telecommunications wiring installation contractors
513310	Telegram services
812990	Telegram services, singing
421690	Telegraph equipment wholesaling
561422	Telemarketing bureaus
561422	Telemarketing services on a contract or fee basis
334513	Telemetering instruments, industrial process-type, manufacturing
513390	Telemetry and tracking system operations on a contract or fee basis
334416	Telephone and telegraph transformers, electronic component-type, manufacturing
334210	Telephone answering machines manufacturing
421620	Telephone answering machines wholesaling
561421	Telephone answering services
337215	Telephone booths manufacturing
561422	Telephone call centers
334210	Telephone carrier line equipment manufacturing
334210	Telephone carrier switching equipment manufacturing
513310	Telephone carriers, facilities-based (except wireless)
513340	Telephone communications carriers, satellite

Code	Description
513322	Telephone communications carriers, wireless (except satellite)
513330	Telephone communications resellers (except satellite)
624190	Telephone counseling services
323112	Telephone directories flexographic printing without publishing
323111	Telephone directories gravure printing without publishing
323110	Telephone directories lithographic (offset) printing without publishing
323119	Telephone directories printing (except flexographic, gravure, lithographic, screen) without publishing
323113	Telephone directories screen printing without publishing
541870	Telephone directory distribution services, door-to-door
511140	Telephone directory publishers
511140	Telephone directory publishers and printing combined
511140	Telephone directory publishing (i.e., establishments known as publishers)
811213	Telephone equipment repair and maintenance services without retailing new telephone equipment
421690	Telephone equipment wholesaling
234920	Telephone line construction
561422	Telephone solicitation services on a contract or fee basis
443112	Telephone stores (including cellular)
514199	Telephone-based recorded information services
334210	Telephones (except cellular telephone) manufacturing
421690	Telephones wholesaling
334220	Telephones, cellular, manufacturing
334210	Telephones, coin operated, manufacturing
334113	Teleprinters (i.e., computer terminals) manufacturing
512191	Teleproduction services
333314	Telescopes manufacturing
334310	Television (TV) sets manufacturing

Code	Description
541840	Television advertising representatives (i.e., independent of media owners)
443112	Television and radio stores
513120	Television broadcasting networks
513120	Television broadcasting stations
337129	Television cabinets (i.e., housings), wood, manufacturing
421410	Television cameras wholesaling
512110	Television commercial production
561310	Television employment agencies
511120	Television guide publishers
511120	Television guide publishers and printing combined
511120	Television guide publishing (i.e., establishments known as publishers)
323112	Television guides flexographic printing without publishing
323111	Television guides gravure printing without publishing
323110	Television guides lithographic (offset) printing without publishing
323119	Television guides printing (except flexographic, gravure, lithographic, screen) without publishing
323113	Television guides screen printing without publishing
326199	Television housings, plastics, manufacturing
513220	Television operations multichannel multipoint distribution services (MMDS)
513220	Television operations, closed circuit
513220	Television operations, multipoint distribution system
454110	Television order, home shopping
334411	Television picture tubes manufacturing
711510	Television producers, independent
532210	Television rental
811211	Television repair services without retailing new televisions
421620	Television sets wholesaling
512110	Television show production
512120	Television show syndicators
513210	Television subscription services

Code	Description
332312	Television tower sections, fabricated structural metal, manufacturing
334220	Television transmitting antennas and ground equipment manufacturing
234920	Television transmitting tower construction
334220	Television, closed-circuit equipment, manufacturing
212221	Telluride (gold) mining and/or beneficiating
331419	Tellurium refining, primary
813319	Temperance organizations
334512	Temperature controls, automatic, residential and commercial-types, manufacturing
334513	Temperature instruments, industrial process-type (except glass and bimetal thermometers), manufacturing
334512	Temperature sensors for motor windings manufacturing
327215	Tempered glass made from purchased glass
332811	Tempering metals and metal products for the trade
334519	Templates, drafting, manufacturing
339115	Temples and fronts (i.e., eyeglass frames), ophthalmic, manufacturing
813110	Temples, religious
561320	Temporary employment services
561320	Temporary help services
624221	Temporary housing for families of medical patients
624221	Temporary shelters (e.g., battered women's, homeless, runaway youth)
561320	Temporary staffing services
713950	Ten pin bowling alleys
713950	Ten pin bowling centers
813319	Tenants' advocacy associations
813990	Tenants' associations (except advocacy)
813319	Tenants' associations, advocacy
713940	Tennis club facilities
234990	Tennis court construction
713940	Tennis courts

Code	Description
421910	Tennis equipment and supplies wholesaling
339920	Tennis goods (e.g., balls, frames, rackets) manufacturing
611620	Tennis instruction, camps, or schools
711219	Tennis professionals, independent (i.e., participating in sports events)
315191	Tennis shirts made in apparel knitting mills
315291	Tennis shirts, infants', cut and sewn from purchased fabric (except apparel contractors)
315211	Tennis shirts, men's and boys', cut and sew apparel contractors
315223	Tennis shirts, men's and boys', cut and sewn from purchased fabric (except apparel contractors)
315212	Tennis shirts, women's, girls', and infants', cut and sew apparel contractors
315239	Tennis shirts, women's, misses', and girls', cut and sewn from purchased fabric (except apparel contractors)
315191	Tennis skirts made in apparel knitting mills
315212	Tennis skirts, women's and girls', cut and sew apparel contractors
315239	Tennis skirts, women's, misses', and girls', cut and sewn from purchased fabric (except apparel contractors)
334519	Tensile strength testing equipment manufacturing
321999	Tent poles, wood, manufacturing
336214	Tent trailers (hard top and soft top) manufacturing
532292	Tent, camping, rental
532299	Tent, party, rental
314912	Tents made from purchased fabrics
335931	Terminals and connectors for electrical devices manufacturing
334113	Terminals, computer, manufacturing
422710	Terminals, petroleum
561710	Termite control services
325320	Termite poisons manufacturing
331111	Terneplate made in steel mills
421510	Terneplate wholesaling

Code	Description
331111	Ternes, iron or steel, long or short, made in steel mills
325199	Terpineol manufacturing
114119	Terrapin fishing
235430	Terrazzo construction contractors
327390	Terrazzo products, precast (except brick, block and pipe), manufacturing
313210	Terry broadwoven fabrics weaving
325199	Tert-butylated bis (p-phenoxyphenyl) ether fluid manufacturing
611710	Test development and evaluation services, educational
213114	Test drilling for metal mining on a contract basis
213115	Test drilling for nonmetallic minerals mining (except fuel) on a contract basis
334515	Test equipment for electronic and electrical circuits and equipment manufacturing
334515	Test sets, ignition harness, manufacturing
525920	Testamentary trusts
334519	Testers for checking hydraulic controls on aircraft manufacturing
421830	Testing and measuring equipment, electrical (except automotive), wholesaling
334519	Testing equipment (e.g., abrasion, shearing strength, tensile strength, torsion) manufacturing
541380	Testing laboratories (except medical, veterinary)
621511	Testing laboratories, medical
541940	Testing laboratories, veterinary
541940	Testing services for veterinarians
488190	Testing services, aircraft
611710	Testing services, educational
333993	Testing, weighing, inspecting, packaging machinery manufacturing
325199	Tetrachloroethylene manufacturing
325411	Tetracycline, uncompounded, manufacturing
325199	Tetraethyl lead manufacturing
325920	Tetryl explosive materials manufacturing

Code	Description
314911	Textile bags made from purchased woven or knitted materials
422990	Textile bags wholesaling
313210	Textile broadwoven fabrics mills
561990	Textile cutting services
541490	Textile design services
325613	Textile finishing assistants manufacturing
333292	Textile finishing machinery (e.g., bleaching, dyeing, mercerizing, printing) manufacturing
314999	Textile fire hose made from purchased material
561910	Textile folding and packaging services
327212	Textile glass fibers made in glass making plants
327112	Textile guides, porcelain, manufacturing
316999	Textile leathers (e.g., apron picker leather, mill strapping) manufacturing
421830	Textile machinery and equipment wholesaling
532490	Textile machinery rental or leasing
811310	Textile machinery repair and maintenance services
333292	Textile making machinery (except sewing machines) manufacturing
233310	Textile mill construction
313210	Textile mills, broadwoven fabrics
313221	Textile mills, narrow woven fabric
313221	Textile narrow woven fabric mills
325910	Textile printing inks manufacturing
333292	Textile printing machinery manufacturing
313210	Textile products (except apparel) made in broadwoven fabric mills
313249	Textile products (except apparel) made in lace mills
313221	Textile products (except apparel) made in narrow woven fabric mills
313249	Textile products (except apparel) made in warp knitting mills
313241	Textile products (except apparel) made in weft knitting mills
313312	Textile products finishing

Code	Description
325613	Textile scouring agents manufacturing
421930	Textile waste wholesaling
313320	Textile waterproofing
422310	Textiles (except burlap, felt) wholesaling
325221	Texturizing cellulosic yarn made in the same establishment
333292	Texturizing machinery for textiles manufacturing
325222	Texturizing noncellulosic yarn made in the same establishment
313112	Texturizing purchased yarn
212299	Thallium mining and/or beneficiating
711110	Theater companies (except dance)
711110	Theater companies (except dance), amateur
711120	Theater companies, dance
421410	Theater equipment (except seats) wholesaling
711310	Theater festival managers with facilities
711320	Theater festival managers without facilities
711310	Theater festival organizers with facilities
711320	Theater festival organizers without facilities
711310	Theater festival promoters with facilities
711320	Theater festival promoters without facilities
711310	Theater operators
611610	Theater schools
337127	Theater seating manufacturing
421210	Theater seats wholesaling
531120	Theater, property operation, rental or leasing
711120	Theaters, dance
711110	Theaters, dinner
711110	Theaters, live theatrical production (except dance)
512131	Theaters, motion picture (except drive-in)
512132	Theaters, motion picture, drive-in
512131	Theaters, motion picture, indoor

Code	Description
711110	Theaters, musical
512132	Theaters, outdoor motion picture
711320	Theatrical booking agencies (except motion picture)
315299	Theatrical costumes cut and sewn from purchased fabric (except apparel contractors)
315211	Theatrical costumes, men's and boys', cut and sew apparel contractors
315212	Theatrical costumes, women's, girls', and infants', cut and sew apparel contractors
711120	Theatrical dance productions, live
561310	Theatrical employment agencies
532490	Theatrical equipment (except costumes) rental or leasing
711310	Theatrical production managers with facilities
711320	Theatrical production managers without facilities
711310	Theatrical production organizers with facilities
711320	Theatrical production organizers without facilities
711310	Theatrical production promoters with facilities
711320	Theatrical production promoters without facilities
711110	Theatrical repertory companies
711110	Theatrical road companies
339999	Theatrical scenery manufacturing
711110	Theatrical stock companies
711410	Theatrical talent agents
561599	Theatrical ticket offices
532220	Theatrical wardrobe and costume rental
713110	Theme parks, amusement
325411	Theobromine and derivatives (i.e., basic chemicals) manufacturing
333314	Theodolites manufacturing
334519	Theodolites, surveying, manufacturing
611310	Theological seminaries offering baccalaureate or graduate degrees
334517	Therapeutic X-ray apparatus and tubes (e.g., medical, industrial, research) manufacturing

Code	Description
*****	Therapists' offices — see type
421450	Therapy equipment wholesaling
334516	Thermal analysis instruments, laboratory-type, manufacturing
334516	Thermal conductivity instruments and sensors manufacturing
334513	Thermal conductivity instruments, industrial process-type, manufacturing
326140	Thermal insulation, polystyrene foam, manufacturing
541380	Thermal testing laboratories or services
334415	Thermistors (except industrial process-type) manufacturing
334513	Thermistors, industrial process-type, manufacturing
334519	Thermocouples (except industrial process, aircraft type, glass vacuum) manufacturing
334512	Thermocouples, glass vacuum, manufacturing
334513	Thermocouples, industrial process-type, manufacturing
335999	Thermoelectric generators manufacturing
333993	Thermoform, blister, and skin packaging machinery manufacturing
333220	Thermoforming machinery for plastics manufacturing
334516	Thermogravimetric analyzers manufacturing
334519	Thermometer, liquid-in-glass and bimetal types (except medical), manufacturing
421450	Thermometers wholesaling
334513	Thermometers, filled system industrial process-type, manufacturing
339112	Thermometers, medical, manufacturing
325211	Thermoplastic resins and plastics materials manufacturing
325211	Thermosetting plastics resins manufacturing
325212	Thermosetting vulcanizable elastomers manufacturing

Code	Description
332911	Thermostatic traps, industrial-type, manufacturing
334512	Thermostats (e.g., air-conditioning, appliance, comfort heating, refrigeration) manufacturing
336399	Thermostats, automotive, truck, and bus, manufacturing
334519	Thickness gauging instruments, ultrasonic, manufacturing
332999	Thimbles for wire rope manufacturing
334413	Thin film integrated circuits manufacturing
333295	Thin layer deposition equipment, semiconductor, manufacturing
115112	Thinning of crops, mechanical and chemical
325188	Thiocyanate manufacturing
325199	Thioglycolic acid manufacturing
325212	Thiol rubber manufacturing
212299	Thorite mining and/or beneficiating
212299	Thorium ores mining and/or beneficiating
711212	Thoroughbred racetracks
422310	Thread (except industrial) wholesaling
333515	Thread cutting dies (i.e., a machine tool accessory) manufacturing
313312	Thread finishing
333292	Thread making machinery manufacturing
313113	Thread mills
333513	Thread rolling machines, metalworking, manufacturing
313113	Thread, all fibers, manufacturing
421840	Thread, industrial, wholesaling
326299	Thread, rubber (except fabric covered), manufacturing
333512	Threading machines, metalworking, manufacturing
115113	Threshing service
453310	Thrift shops, used merchandise
333298	Through-hole machinery, printed circuit board loading, manufacturing
325221	Throwing cellulosic yarn made in the same establishment

Code	Description
325222	Throwing noncellulosic yarn made in the same establishment
313112	Throwing purchased yarn
334519	Thrust power indicators, aircraft engine, manufacturing
332991	Thrust roller bearings manufacturing
334413	Thyristors manufacturing
325412	Thyroid preparations manufacturing
325320	Tick powders or sprays manufacturing
561599	Ticket (e.g., airline, bus, cruise ship, sports, theatrical) offices
561599	Ticket (e.g., airline, bus, cruise ship, sports, theatrical) sales offices
561599	Ticket (e.g., amusement, sports, theatrical) agencies
561599	Ticket (e.g., amusement, sports, theatrical) sales agencies
561599	Ticket agencies, amusement
561599	Ticket agencies, sports
561599	Ticket agencies, theatrical
561599	Ticket offices for foreign cruise ship companies
331111	Tie plates, iron or steel, made in steel mills
448150	Tie shops
331222	Tie wires made in wire drawing plants
315191	Ties made in apparel knitting mills
327390	Ties, concrete, railroad, manufacturing
315993	Ties, men's and boys' hand sewn (except apparel contractors), manufacturing
315211	Ties, men's and boys' hand sewn, cut and sew apparel contractors
321113	Ties, railroad, made from logs or bolts
321114	Ties, wood railroad bridge, cross, and switch, treating
321113	Ties, wood, made from logs or bolts
421990	Ties, wood, wholesaling
315119	Tights knitting or knitting and finishing
112511	Tilapia production

Code	Description
325520	Tile adhesives manufacturing
235430	Tile construction contractors
333298	Tile making machinery (except kilns) manufacturing
444190	Tile stores, ceramic
327122	Tile, ceramic wall and floor, manufacturing
327124	Tile, clay refractory, manufacturing
327121	Tile, clay, structural, manufacturing
321999	Tile, cork, manufacturing
327123	Tile, roofing and drain, clay, manufacturing
327123	Tile, sewer, clay, manufacturing
421320	Tile, structural clay (except refractory), wholesaling
114111	Tilefish fishing
333994	Tilemaking kilns manufacturing
326192	Tiles, floor (i.e., linoleum, rubber, vinyl), manufacturing
421820	Tillers, farm, wholesaling
333112	Tillers, lawn and garden-type, manufacturing
421990	Timber and timber products (except lumber) wholesaling
113310	Timber piling
113310	Timber pole cutting
234990	Timber removal, underwater
113110	Timber tracts operations
115310	Timber valuation
321114	Timber, structural, treating
321113	Timbers, made from logs or bolts
321213	Timbers, structural, glue laminated or pre-engineered wood, manufacturing
334518	Time clocks and time recording devices manufacturing
334513	Time cycle and program controllers, industrial process-type, manufacturing
334518	Time locks manufacturing
323118	Time planners/organizers and refills manufacturing
334512	Time program controls, air-conditioning systems, manufacturing
421420	Time recording machines wholesaling

Code	Description
561599	Time share exchange services, condominium
334518	Time stamps containing clock mechanisms manufacturing
335313	Time switches, electrical switchgear apparatus, manufacturing
334518	Timers for industrial use, clockwork mechanism, manufacturing
326220	Timing belt, rubber or plastics, manufacturing
335314	Timing devices, mechanical and solid-state (except clockwork), manufacturing
336312	Timing gears and chains, automotive and truck gasoline engine, manufacturing
334518	Timing mechanisms, clockwork, manufacturing
335312	Timing motors, synchronous, electric, manufacturing
331491	Tin and tin alloy bar, pipe, rod, sheet, strip, and tubing made from purchased metals or scrap
331419	Tin base alloys made in primary tin smelting and refining mills
325188	Tin chloride manufacturing
325188	Tin compounds, not specified elsewhere by process, manufacturing
332999	Tin foil not made in rolling mills
212299	Tin metal concentrates beneficiating
212299	Tin metal ores mining and/or beneficiating
325188	Tin oxide manufacturing
332431	Tin plate cans manufacturing
421510	Tin plate wholesaling
331492	Tin recovering from scrap and/or alloying purchased metals
331419	Tin refining, primary
331491	Tin rolling, drawing, or extruding purchased metals or scrap
325188	Tin salts manufacturing
235610	Tin smithing contractors, in connection with construction work
331111	Tin-free steel made in steel mills
325412	Tincture of iodine preparations manufacturing
332212	Tinner's snips manufacturing

Code	Description
331111	Tinplate made in steel mills
339999	Tinsel manufacturing
325998	Tint and dye preparations, household-type (except hair), manufacturing
325620	Tints, dyes, and rinses, hair, manufacturing
234930	Tipple construction
212111	Tipple operation, bituminous coal mining and/or beneficiating
316999	Tips, shoe, leather, manufacturing
421130	Tire and tube repair materials wholesaling
332618	Tire chains made from purchased wire
314992	Tire cord and fabric, all materials, manufacturing
336360	Tire covers made from purchased fabric
441320	Tire dealers, automotive
325998	Tire inflators, aerosol, manufacturing
333220	Tire making machinery manufacturing
333319	Tire mounting machines, motor vehicle, manufacturing
333220	Tire recapping machinery manufacturing
421830	Tire recapping machinery wholesaling
326211	Tire repair materials manufacturing
811198	Tire repair shops (except retreading), automotive
326212	Tire retreading, recapping or rebuilding
333220	Tire shredding machinery manufacturing
421130	Tire tubes, motor vehicle, wholesaling
326211	Tires (e.g., pneumatic, semi-pneumatic, solid rubber) manufacturing
421130	Tires, motor vehicle, wholesaling
326199	Tires, plastics, manufacturing
421930	Tires, scrap, wholesaling
421130	Tires, used (except scrap), wholesaling

Code	Description
111421	Tissue culture farming
322121	Tissue paper stock manufacturing
422130	Tissue paper, toilet and facial, wholesaling
327113	Titania porcelain insulators manufacturing
212299	Titaniferous-magnetite ores, valued chiefly for titanium content, mining and/or beneficiating
331491	Titanium and titanium alloy bar, billet, rod, sheet, strip, and tubing made from purchased metals or scrap
325131	Titanium based pigments manufacturing
331528	Titanium castings (except die-castings), unfinished, manufacturing
212299	Titanium concentrates beneficiating
331522	Titanium die-castings, unfinished, manufacturing
325188	Titanium dioxide manufacturing
332112	Titanium forgings made from purchased metals, unfinished
212299	Titanium ores mining and/or beneficiating
331419	Titanium refining, primary
331491	Titanium rolling, drawing, or extruding purchased metals or scrap
541191	Title abstract companies, real estate
541191	Title companies, real estate
524127	Title insurance carriers, real estate, direct
541191	Title search companies, real estate
512191	Titling of motion picture film or video
334516	Titrimeters manufacturing
335211	Toaster ovens, household-type electric, manufacturing
421620	Toasters, electric, wholesaling
335211	Toasters, household-type electric, manufacturing
422940	Tobacco (except leaf) wholesaling
422590	Tobacco auction markets
111910	Tobacco farming, field and seed production

Code	Description
115114	Tobacco grading
333111	Tobacco harvester machines manufacturing
321920	Tobacco hogshead stock, manufacturing
321920	Tobacco hogsheads, manufacturing
312210	Tobacco leaf processing and aging
339999	Tobacco pipes manufacturing
316993	Tobacco pouches (except metal) manufacturing
339911	Tobacco pouches, precious metal, manufacturing
333298	Tobacco processing machinery (except farm-type) manufacturing
312229	Tobacco products (e.g., chewing, smoking, snuff) manufacturing
422940	Tobacco products wholesaling
312229	Tobacco products, imitation (except cigarettes) manufacturing
312229	Tobacco sheeting services
312210	Tobacco stemming and redrying
453991	Tobacco stores
422590	Tobacco, leaf, wholesaling
339920	Toboggans manufacturing
316999	Toe caps, leather, manufacturing
311340	Toffee manufacturing
311991	Tofu (i.e., bean curd) (except frozen desserts) manufacturing
311520	Tofu frozen desserts manufacturing
332722	Toggle bolts, metal, manufacturing
325612	Toilet bowl cleaners manufacturing
332998	Toilet fixtures manufacturing
326191	Toilet fixtures, plastics, manufacturing
327111	Toilet fixtures, vitreous china, manufacturing
316993	Toilet kits and cases (except metal) manufacturing
339911	Toilet kits and cases, precious metal, manufacturing
322291	Toilet paper made from purchased paper
322121	Toilet paper made in paper mills
325620	Toilet preparations (e.g., cosmetics, deodorants, perfumes) manufacturing
422210	Toilet preparations wholesaling

Code	Description
562991	Toilet renting and/or servicing, portable
321999	Toilet seats, wood, manufacturing
422210	Toilet soaps wholesaling
422130	Toilet tissue wholesaling
332999	Toilet ware, precious plated metal, manufacturing
325620	Toilet water manufacturing
422210	Toiletries wholesaling
334210	Toll switching equipment, telephone, manufacturing
325110	Toluene made from refined petroleum or liquid hydrocarbons
324110	Toluene made in petroleum refineries
325192	Toluidines manufacturing
111219	Tomato farming (except under cover), field, bedding plant and seed production
111419	Tomato farming, grown under cover
333111	Tomato harvesting machines manufacturing
325992	Toner cartridges manufacturing
325992	Toner cartridges rebuilding
422120	Toner cartridges wholesaling
325132	Toners (except electrostatic, photographic) manufacturing
325992	Toners, electrostatic and photographic, manufacturing
339113	Tongue depressors manufacturing
316999	Tongues, boot and shoe, leather, manufacturing
339112	Tonometers, medical, manufacturing
332439	Tool boxes, light gauge metal, manufacturing
321920	Tool chests, wood, manufacturing
321999	Tool handles, wood, turned and shaped, manufacturing
541420	Tool industrial design services
337127	Tool stands, factory, manufacturing
331111	Tool steel made in steel mills
444130	Tool stores, power and hand (except outdoor)
333515	Toolholders (i.e., a machine tool accessory) manufacturing

Code	Description
333515	Tools and accessories for machine tools manufacturing
421120	Tools and equipment, motor vehicle, wholesaling
339114	Tools, dentist's, manufacturing
421710	Tools, hand (except motor vehicle, machinists' precision tools), wholesaling
332212	Tools, hand, metal blade (e.g., putty knives, scrapers, screw drivers)
333991	Tools, handheld power-driven, manufacturing
332212	Tools, handheld, nonpowered (except kitchen-type), manufacturing
421830	Tools, machinists' precision, wholesaling
332212	Tools, woodworking edge (e.g., augers, bits, countersinks), manufacturing
339994	Toothbrushes (except electric) manufacturing
422210	Toothbrushes (except electric) wholesaling
335211	Toothbrushes, electric, manufacturing
421620	Toothbrushes, electric, wholesaling
325611	Toothpastes, gels, and tooth powders manufacturing
321999	Toothpicks, wood, manufacturing
316999	Top lifts, boot and shoe, leather, manufacturing
484220	Top soil hauling, local
212325	Topaz, non-gem, mining and/or beneficiating
315211	Topcoats, men's and boys', cut and sew apparel contractors
315222	Topcoats, men's and boys', cut and sewn from purchased fabric (except apparel contractors)
541370	Topographic mapping services
541370	Topographic surveying services
422490	Toppings (except fountain) wholesaling

Code	Description
336399	Tops, convertible automotive, manufacturing
332995	Torpedo tubes manufacturing
332993	Torpedoes manufacturing
336350	Torque converters, automotive, truck, and bus, manufacturing
335312	Torque motors, electric, manufacturing
332611	Torsion bar manufacturing
334519	Torsion testing equipment manufacturing
311919	Tortilla chips manufacturing
311830	Tortillas manufacturing
334514	Totalizing fluid meters manufacturing
334514	Totalizing meters (except aircraft), consumption registering, manufacturing
339999	Toupees manufacturing
422990	Toupees wholesaling
487110	Tour bus, scenic and sightseeing, operation
561520	Tour operators (i.e., arranging and assembling tours)
561591	Tourism bureaus
926110	Tourism development offices, government
713990	Tourist guide services
721199	Tourist homes
561591	Tourist information bureaus
721110	Tourist lodges
336413	Tow targets, aircraft, manufacturing
488410	Tow truck services
336211	Tow trucks (including tilt and load) assembling on purchased chassis
336611	Towboat building and repairing
532411	Towboat rental or leasing
812331	Towel (except shop, wiping) supply services
327111	Towel bar holders, vitreous china and earthenware, manufacturing

Code	Description
812332	Towel supply services, shop or wiping
325620	Towelettes, premoistened, manufacturing
313210	Towels and washcloths made in broadwoven fabric mills
313249	Towels and washcloths made in warp knitting mills
313241	Towels and washcloths made in weft knitting mills
421220	Towels and washcloths wholesaling
314129	Towels or washcloths made from purchased fabrics
421840	Towels, industrial, wholesaling
322291	Towels, paper, made from purchased paper
322121	Towels, paper, made in paper mills
421450	Towels, surgical, wholesaling
234920	Tower construction, radio and television transmitting/receiving
336399	Towing bars and systems manufacturing
483211	Towing service, inland waters (except on Great Lakes system)
488410	Towing services, motor vehicle
233210	Town house construction
531110	Town house rental or leasing
233220	Town house-type apartment construction
541320	Town planners' offices
541320	Town planning services
562910	Toxic material abatement services
562910	Toxic material removal contractors
621511	Toxicology health laboratories
325414	Toxoids (e.g., diphtheria, tetanus) manufacturing
339932	Toy furniture and household-type equipment manufacturing
451120	Toy stores
339932	Toys (except dolls, stuffed toys) manufacturing
421920	Toys (including electronic) wholesaling
339931	Toys, doll, manufacturing

Code	Description
339931	Toys, stuffed, manufacturing
333515	Tracer and tapering machine tool attachments manufacturing
332993	Tracer igniters, ammunition (i.e., more than 30 mm., more than 1.18 inch), manufacturing
339920	Track and field athletic equipment (except apparel, footwear) manufacturing
335121	Track lighting fixtures and equipment, residential, electric, manufacturing
484220	Tracked vehicle freight transportation, local
484230	Tracked vehicle freight transportation, long-distance
487110	Tracked vehicle sightseeing operation
339113	Traction apparatus manufacturing
811310	Tractor, farm or construction equipment repair and maintenance services
532490	Tractor, farm, rental or leasing
532490	Tractor, garden, rental or leasing
333120	Tractors and attachments, construction-type, manufacturing
333111	Tractors and attachments, farm-type, manufacturing
333112	Tractors and attachments, lawn and garden-type, manufacturing
333120	Tractors, crawler, manufacturing
421820	Tractors, farm and garden, wholesaling
421110	Tractors, highway, wholesaling
333924	Tractors, industrial, manufacturing
421830	Tractors, industrial, wholesaling
811411	Tractors, lawn and garden repair and maintenance services without retailing new lawn and garden tractors
336120	Tractors, truck for highway use, assembled on chassis of own manufacture
813910	Trade associations
522293	Trade banks (i.e., international trade financing)
323121	Trade binding services

Code	Description
926110	Trade commissions, government
926110	Trade development program administration
561920	Trade fair managers
561920	Trade fair organizers
561920	Trade fair promoters
511120	Trade journal publishers
511120	Trade journal publishers and printing combined
511120	Trade journal publishing (i.e., establishments known as publishers)
323112	Trade journals flexographic printing without publishing
323111	Trade journals gravure printing without publishing
323110	Trade journals lithographic (offset) printing without publishing
323119	Trade journals printing (except flexographic, gravure, lithographic, screen) without publishing
323113	Trade journals screen printing without publishing
511120	Trade magazine and periodical publishers
511120	Trade magazine and periodical publishers and printing combined
511120	Trade magazine and periodical publishing (i.e., establishments known as publishers)
323112	Trade magazines and periodicals flexographic printing without publishing
323111	Trade magazines and periodicals gravure printing without publishing
323110	Trade magazines and periodicals lithographic (offset) printing without publishing
323119	Trade magazines and periodicals printing (except flexographic, gravure, lithographic, screen) without publishing
323113	Trade magazines and periodicals screen printing without publishing
561920	Trade show managers
561920	Trade show organizers
561920	Trade show promoters

Code	Description
611513	Trade union apprenticeship training programs
813930	Trade unions (except apprenticeship programs)
813930	Trade unions, locals
533110	Trademark licensing
523130	Trading companies, commodity contracts
452990	Trading posts, general merchandise
523110	Trading securities (i.e., acting as a principal in dealing securities to investors)
561990	Trading stamp promotion and sale to stores
561990	Trading stamp redemption services
334290	Traffic advisory and signalling systems manufacturing
922110	Traffic courts
541330	Traffic engineering consulting services
235210	Traffic lane painting construction contractors
514110	Traffic reporting services
334290	Traffic signals manufacturing
234990	Trail building
721214	Trail riding camps with accommodation facilities
713990	Trail riding, recreational
234990	Trailer camp construction
336399	Trailer hitches, motor vehicle, manufacturing
531190	Trailer park or court, residential
421120	Trailer parts, new, wholesaling
532120	Trailer rental or leasing
336214	Trailers for transporting horses (except fifth-wheel-type) manufacturing
336214	Trailers, camping, manufacturing
336212	Trailers, fifth-wheel type, for transporting horses, manufacturing
421830	Trailers, industrial, wholesaling
421110	Trailers, motor vehicle, wholesaling
115210	Training horses (except racehorses)
315212	Training pants (i.e., underwear), infants', cut and sew apparel contractors

Code	Description
315291	Training pants (i.e., underwear), infants', cut and sewn from purchased fabric (except apparel contractors)
711219	Training race dogs
711219	Training racehorses
339932	Trains and equipment, toy, electric or mechanical, manufacturing
713990	Trampoline facilities, recreational
485119	Tramway systems (except mixed mode), commuter
487990	Tramway, aerial, scenic and sightseeing operation
325412	Tranquilizer preparations manufacturing
336350	Transaxles, automotive, truck, and bus, manufacturing
334220	Transceivers (i.e., transmitter-receiver units) manufacturing
561410	Transcription services
334510	Transcutaneous electrical nerve stimulators (TENS) manufacturing
334419	Transducers (except pressure) manufacturing
334519	Transducers, pressure, manufacturing
484110	Transfer (trucking) services, general freight, local
523999	Transfer agencies, securities
421610	Transformers (except electronic) wholesaling
335311	Transformers, electric power, manufacturing
334416	Transformers, electronic component-types, manufacturing
421690	Transformers, electronic, wholesaling
335311	Transformers, ignition, for use on domestic fuel burners, manufacturing
335311	Transformers, reactor, manufacturing
335311	Transformers, separate solid-state arc-welding, manufacturing
335912	Transistor radio batteries manufacturing

Code	Description
334413	Transistors manufacturing
421690	Transistors wholesaling
541850	Transit advertising services
922120	Transit police
926120	Transit systems and authorities, nonoperating
485111	Transit systems, mixed mode (e.g., bus, commuter rail, subway combinations)
327320	Transit-mixed concrete manufacturing
624229	Transitional housing agencies
334519	Transits, surveying, manufacturing
541930	Translation services, language
234920	Transmission and distribution line construction
335311	Transmission and distribution voltage regulators manufacturing
316999	Transmission belting, leather, manufacturing
326220	Transmission belts, rubber, manufacturing
336399	Transmission coolers manufacturing
421610	Transmission equipment, electrical, wholesaling
324191	Transmission fluids, petroleum, made from refined petroleum
325998	Transmission fluids, synthetic, manufacturing
221121	Transmission of electric power
486210	Transmission of natural gas via pipeline (i.e., processing plants to local distribution systems)
335932	Transmission pole and line hardware manufacturing
811113	Transmission repair shops, automotive
332312	Transmission tower sections, fabricated structural metal, manufacturing
336350	Transmissions and parts, automotive, truck, and bus, manufacturing
421690	Transmitters wholesaling
334513	Transmitters, industrial process control-type, manufacturing
333111	Transplanters, farm-type, manufacturing

Code	Description
115112	Transplanting services
*****	Transportation — see mode
481212	Transportation by spacecraft, freight
926120	Transportation departments, nonoperating
421860	Transportation equipment and supplies (except marine pleasure craft, motor vehicles) wholesaling
336360	Transportation equipment seating manufacturing
541614	Transportation management consulting services
926120	Transportation regulatory agencies
926120	Transportation safety programs, government
483111	Transporting freight to or from foreign ports, deep sea
483112	Transporting passengers to or from foreign ports, deep sea
212319	Trap rock crushed and broken stone mining and/or beneficiating
212311	Trap rock mining or quarrying
332618	Traps, animal and fish, made from purchased wire
332913	Traps, water, manufacturing
421910	Trapshooting equipment and supplies wholesaling
713990	Trapshooting facilities, recreational
333319	Trash and garbage compactors, commercial-type, manufacturing
335228	Trash and garbage compactors, household-type, manufacturing
326111	Trash bags, plastics film, single wall or multiwall, manufacturing
562111	Trash collection services
326199	Trash containers, plastics, manufacturing
562213	Trash disposal combustors or incinerators
562212	Trash disposal landfills
562111	Trash hauling, local
484230	Trash hauling, long-distance
332313	Trash racks, fabricated metal plate work, manufacturing
621493	Trauma centers (except hospitals), freestanding

Code	Description
561510	Travel agencies
511130	Travel guide book publishers
511130	Travel guide book publishers and printing combined
511130	Travel guide book publishing (i.e., establishments known as publishers)
323117	Travel guide books printing and binding without publishing
323117	Travel guide books printing without publishing
561520	Travel tour operators
721211	Travel trailer campsites
441210	Travel trailer dealers
421110	Travel trailers (e.g., tent trailers) wholesaling
336214	Travel trailers, recreational, manufacturing
624190	Travelers' aid centers
522390	Travelers' check issuance services
316991	Traveling bags, all materials, manufacturing
711190	Traveling shows, carnival
334411	Traveling wave tubes manufacturing
212312	Travertine crushed and broken stone mining and/or beneficiating
212311	Travertine mining or quarrying
337127	Tray trucks, restaurant, manufacturing
321920	Trays, carrier, wood, manufacturing
322299	Trays, food, molded pulp, manufacturing
333315	Trays, photographic printing and processing, manufacturing
332618	Trays, wire, made from purchased wire
321999	Trays, wood, wicker, and bagasse, manufacturing
326211	Tread rubber (i.e., camelback) manufacturing
332323	Treads, metal stair, manufacturing
921130	Treasurers offices', government
321114	Treating purchased wood and wood products
321114	Treating wood products with creosote or other preservatives
113310	Tree chipping in the field

Code	Description
111421	Tree crop farming (except forestry), short rotation growing and harvesting cycle
111335	Tree nut farming
311225	Tree nut oils (e.g., tung, walnut) made from purchased oils
311223	Tree nut oils (e.g., tung, walnut) made in crushing mill
561730	Tree pruning services
561730	Tree removal services
113210	Tree seed extracting
113210	Tree seed gathering
113210	Tree seed growing for reforestation
561730	Tree services (e.g., bracing, planting, pruning, removal, spraying, surgery, trimming)
333111	Tree shakers (e.g., citrus, nut, soft fruit) manufacturing
561730	Tree surgery services
561730	Tree trimming services
339999	Trees and plants, artificial, manufacturing
422930	Trees wholesaling
321918	Trellises, wood, manufacturing
234990	Trenching
333120	Trenching machines manufacturing
234120	Trestle construction
321114	Trestle parts, wood, treating
325221	Triacetate fibers and yarns manufacturing
921150	Tribal chief's or chairman's office, American Indian or Alaska Native
921150	Tribal councils, American Indian or Alaska Native
921150	Tribal courts, American Indian or Alaska Native
325199	Trichloroethylene manufacturing
325199	Trichlorophenoxyacetic acid manufacturing
325199	Tricresyl phosphate manufacturing
339932	Tricycles (except metal) manufacturing
336991	Tricycles, metal, adult and children's, manufacturing
325199	Tridecyl alcohol manufacturing
332321	Trim and molding (except motor vehicle), metal, manufacturing

Code	Description
332321	Trim, metal, manufacturing
321918	Trim, wood and covered wood, manufacturing
333112	Trimmers, hedge, electric, manufacturing
332212	Trimmers, hedge, nonelectric, manufacturing
333112	Trimmers, string, lawn and garden-type, manufacturing
315292	Trimmings, fur (except apparel contractors), manufacturing
315211	Trimmings, fur, men's and boys', cut and sew apparel contractors
315212	Trimmings, fur, women's, girls', and infants', cut and sew apparel contractos
316999	Trimmings, shoe, leather, manufacturing
325920	Trinitrotoluene (TNT) manufacturing
325199	Triphenyl phosphate manufacturing
333315	Tripods, camera and projector, manufacturing
212399	Tripoli mining and/or beneficiating
339112	Trocars manufacturing
485119	Trolley systems (except mixed mode), commuter
487110	Trolley, scenic and sightseeing, operation
339992	Trombones and parts manufacturing
212391	Trona mining and/or beneficiating
421940	Trophies wholesaling
332999	Trophies, nonprecious and precious plated metal, manufacturing
339912	Trophies, precious (except precious plated) metal, manufacturing
453998	Trophy (including awards and plaques) shops
321999	Trophy bases, wood, manufacturing
112511	Tropical fish production, farm raising
422990	Tropical fish wholesaling
561730	Tropical plant maintenance services
335129	Trouble lights manufacturing
332322	Troughs, elevator, sheet metal, manufacturing

Code	Description
332313	Troughs, industrial, fabricated metal plate work, manufacturing
335211	Trouser pressers, household-type electric, manufacturing
315191	Trousers made in apparel knitting mills
315211	Trousers, men's and boys', cut and sew apparel contractors
315224	Trousers, men's and boys', cut and sewn from purchased fabric (except apparel contractors)
114111	Trout fishing
112511	Trout production, farm raising
332212	Trowels manufacturing
532120	Truck (except industrial) rental or leasing
233310	Truck and automobile assembly plant construction
811192	Truck and bus washes
336211	Truck bodies and cabs manufacturing
336211	Truck bodies assembling on purchased chassis
336214	Truck campers (i.e., slide-in campers) manufacturing
441310	Truck cap stores
611519	Truck driving schools
111219	Truck farming, field, bedding plant and seed production
522220	Truck finance leasing
421120	Truck parts, new, wholesaling
811310	Truck refrigeration repair and maintenance services
811111	Truck repair shops, general
447190	Truck stops
532120	Truck tractor rental or leasing
336120	Truck tractors for highway use, assembling on chassis of own manufacture
336211	Truck tractors for highway use, assembling on purchased chassis
421110	Truck tractors, road, wholesaling
811121	Truck trailer body shops
421110	Truck trailers wholesaling
488490	Truck weighing station operation
532490	Truck, industrial, rental or leasing

Code	Description
327320	Truck-mixed concrete manufacturing
488490	Trucking terminals, independently operated
484210	Trucking used household, office, or institutional furniture and equipment
484110	Trucking, general freight, local
484122	Trucking, general freight, long-distance, less-than-truckload (LTL)
484121	Trucking, general freight, long-distance, truckload
484220	Trucking, specialized freight (except used goods), local
484230	Trucking, specialized freight (except used goods), long-distance
336120	Trucks, heavy, assembling on chassis of own manufacture
333924	Trucks, industrial, manufacturing
421830	Trucks, industrial, wholesaling
336112	Trucks, light duty, assembling on chassis of own manufacture
333120	Trucks, off-highway, manufacturing
421110	Trucks, road, wholesaling
111419	Truffles farming, grown under cover
339992	Trumpets and parts manufacturing
316991	Trunks (i.e., luggage), all materials, manufacturing
332313	Truss plates, metal, manufacturing
321214	Trusses, glue laminated or pre-engineered wood, manufacturing
321214	Trusses, wood roof or floor, manufacturing
321214	Trusses, wood, glue laminated or metal connected, manufacturing
523991	Trust administration, personal investment
523991	Trust companies, nondepository
813211	Trusts, charitable, awarding grants
813211	Trusts, educational, awarding grants
813211	Trusts, religious, awarding grants
325612	Tub and tile cleaning preparations manufacturing
331210	Tube (e.g., heavy riveted, lock joint, seamless, welded) made from purchased iron or steel
332912	Tube and hose fittings, fluid power, manufacturing

Code	Description
331316	Tube blooms made by extruding purchased aluminum
331316	Tube blooms, aluminum, made in integrated secondary smelting and extruding mills
331316	Tube made by drawing or extruding purchased aluminum
333516	Tube rolling mill machinery, metalworking, manufacturing
331111	Tube rounds, iron or steel, made in steel mills
331316	Tube, aluminum, made in integrated secondary smelting and drawing plants
331316	Tube, aluminum, made in integrated secondary smelting and extruding mills
331111	Tube, iron or steel, made in steel mills
326121	Tube, nonrigid plastics, manufacturing
331315	Tube, welded, aluminum, made by flat rolling purchased aluminum
331315	Tube, welded, aluminum, made in integrated secondary smelting and flat rolling mills
325414	Tuberculin (i.e., tuberculo-protein derived) manufacturing
622310	Tuberculosis and other respiratory illness hospitals
332996	Tubes made from purchased metal pipe
334517	Tubes, X-ray, manufacturing
334411	Tubes, cathode ray, manufacturing
334411	Tubes, electron, manufacturing
421690	Tubes, electronic (e.g., industrial, receiving, transmitting), wholesaling
334411	Tubes, klystron, manufacturing
331421	Tubing, copper and copper alloy, made from purchased copper or in integrated secondary smelting and rolling, drawing or extruding plants
332999	Tubing, flexible metal, manufacturing
331210	Tubing, mechanical and hypodermic sizes, cold-drawn stainless steel, made from purchased steel

Code	Description
421510	Tubing, metal, wholesaling
331491	Tubing, nonferrous metals (except aluminum, copper), made from purchased metals or scrap
326299	Tubing, rubber (except extruded, molded, lathe-cut), manufacturing
331111	Tubing, seamless steel, made in steel mills
331111	Tubing, wrought iron or steel, made in steel mills
332998	Tubs, laundry and bath, metal, manufacturing
235410	Tuck pointing construction contractors
212312	Tufa, calcareous, crushed and broken stone, mining and/or beneficiating
212311	Tufa, calcareous, mining or quarrying
333292	Tufting machinery for textiles manufacturing
336611	Tugboat building
532411	Tugboat rental or leasing
488330	Tugboat services, harbor operation
326199	Tumblers, plastics, manufacturing
332813	Tumbling (i.e., cleaning and polishing) metal and metal products for the trade
114111	Tuna fishing
811118	Tune-up shops, automotive
325188	Tungstates (e.g., ammonium tungstate, sodium tungstate) manufacturing
331491	Tungsten bar, rod, sheet, strip, and tubing made by rolling, drawing, or extruding purchased metals or scrap
331492	Tungsten carbide powder made by metallurgical process
325188	Tungsten compounds, not specified elsewhere by process, manufacturing
212299	Tungsten concentrates beneficiating
212299	Tungsten ores mining and/or beneficiating
811490	Tuning and repair of musical instruments
339992	Tuning forks manufacturing

Code	Description
234120	Tunnel and bridge construction management firms
234120	Tunnel construction
332313	Tunnel lining, fabricated metal plate work, manufacturing
213113	Tunneling services for coal mining on a contract basis
332313	Tunnels, wind, fabricated metal plate work, manufacturing
334513	Turbidity instruments, industrial process-type, manufacturing
334516	Turbidometers, laboratory-type, manufacturing
334513	Turbine flow meters, industrial process-type, manufacturing
333611	Turbine generator set units manufacturing
334514	Turbine meters, consumption registering, manufacturing
333611	Turbines (except aircraft) manufacturing
421830	Turbines (except transportation) wholesaling
421860	Turbines, transportation, wholesaling
561730	Turf (except artificial) installation services
422440	Turkey and turkey products (except packaged frozen) wholesaling
112330	Turkey egg production
311119	Turkey feeds, prepared, manufacturing
112340	Turkey hatcheries
112330	Turkey production
325613	Turkey red oil manufacturing
311615	Turkeys, processing, fresh, frozen, canned, or cooked
311615	Turkeys, slaughtering and dressing
812199	Turkish bathhouses
812199	Turkish baths
332722	Turnbuckles manufacturing
333512	Turning machines (i.e., lathes), metalworking, manufacturing
321912	Turnings, furniture, unfinished wood, manufacturing
111219	Turnip farming, field, bedding plant and seed production

Code	Description
325191	Turpentine made by distillation of pine gum or pine wood
422690	Turpentine wholesaling
212399	Turquoise mining and/or beneficiating
333512	Turret lathes, metalworking, manufacturing
332995	Turrets, gun, manufacturing
114119	Turtle fishing
112519	Turtle production, farm raising
611691	Tutoring, academic
532220	Tuxedo rental
315211	Tuxedos cut and sew apparel contractors
315222	Tuxedos cut and sewn from purchased fabric (except apparel contractors)
313210	Twills weaving
421840	Twine wholesaling
314991	Twines manufacturing
421830	Twist drills wholesaling
513321	Two-way paging communication carriers
323122	Typesetting (i.e., computer controlled, hand, machine)
333293	Typesetting machinery manufacturing
422120	Typewriter paper wholesaling
811212	Typewriter repair and maintenance services
339944	Typewriter ribbons manufacturing
333313	Typewriters manufacturing
421420	Typewriters wholesaling
561410	Typing services
212291	Tyuyamunite mining and/or beneficiating
531130	U-lock storage
922130	U. S. attorneys' offices
311514	UHT (ultra high temperature) milk manufacturing
335999	UPS (uninterruptible power supplies) manufacturing
339992	Ukuleles and parts manufacturing
212391	Ulexite mining and/or beneficiating
336411	Ultra light aircraft manufacturing
325131	Ultramarine pigments manufacturing

Code	Description
333512	Ultrasonic boring, drilling, and cutting machines, metalworking, manufacturing
335999	Ultrasonic cleaning equipment (except dental, medical) manufacturing
339114	Ultrasonic dental equipment manufacturing
335999	Ultrasonic generators sold separately for inclusion in tools and equipment manufacturing
339113	Ultrasonic medical cleaning equipment manufacturing
334510	Ultrasonic medical equipment manufacturing
333513	Ultrasonic metal forming machines manufacturing
334510	Ultrasonic scanning devices, medical, manufacturing
334519	Ultrasonic testing equipment (except medical) manufacturing
333992	Ultrasonic welding equipment manufacturing
621512	Ultrasound imaging centers
335110	Ultraviolet lamp bulbs manufacturing
335129	Ultraviolet lamp fixtures manufacturing
334516	Ultraviolet-type analytical instruments manufacturing
325131	Umber manufacturing
212393	Umber mining and/or beneficiating
339999	Umbrellas manufacturing
422320	Umbrellas, men's and boys', wholesaling
322122	Uncoated groundwood paper mills
811198	Undercoating shops, automotive
333131	Underground mining machinery manufacturing
235940	Underground tank removal construction contractors
234120	Underpass construction contractors
812210	Undertaker services
421850	Undertakers' equipment and supplies wholesaling
335129	Underwater lighting fixtures manufacturing

Code	Description
334511	Underwater navigational systems manufacturing
234990	Underwater rock removal
315192	Underwear made in apparel knitting mills
315192	Underwear shirts made in apparel knitting mills
315291	Underwear shirts, infants', cut and sewn from purchased fabric (except apparel contractors)
315211	Underwear shirts, men's and boys', cut and sew apparel contractors
315221	Underwear shirts, men's and boys', cut and sewn from purchased fabric (except apparel contractors)
315212	Underwear shirts, women's, girls', and infants', cut and sew apparel contractors
315231	Underwear shirts, women's, misses', and girls', cut and sewn from purchased fabric (except apparel contractors)
315192	Underwear shorts made in apparel knitting mills
315291	Underwear shorts, infants', cut and sewn from purchased fabric (except apparel contractors)
315211	Underwear shorts, men's and boys', cut and sew apparel contractors
315221	Underwear shorts, men's and boys', cut and sewn from purchased fabric (except apparel contractors)
315212	Underwear shorts, women's, girls', and infants', cut and sew apparel contractors
315231	Underwear shorts, women's, misses', and girls', cut and sewn from purchased fabric (except apparel contractors)
315291	Underwear, infants', cut and sewn from purchased fabric (except apparel contractors)
315211	Underwear, men's and boys', cut and sew apparel contractors
315221	Underwear, men's and boys', cut and sewn from purchased fabric (except apparel contractors)
422320	Underwear, men's and boys', wholesaling
422330	Underwear, women's, children's, and infants', wholesaling
315231	Underwear, women's, misses', and girls', cut and sewn from purchased fabric (except apparel contractors)
315212	Underwear, women's, misses', girls', and infants', cut and sew apparel contractors
923130	Unemployment insurance program administration
812331	Uniform (except industrial) supply services
315991	Uniform hats and caps cut and sewn from purchased fabric (except apparel contractors)
315211	Uniform hats and caps, men's and boys', cut and sew apparel contractors
315212	Uniform hats and caps, women's, and girls', cut and sew apparel contractors
315232	Uniform shirts (except team athletic), women's, misses', and girls', cut and sewn from purchased fabric (except apparel contractors)
315223	Uniform shirts (except team athletic, work), men's and boys', cut and sewn from purchased fabric (except apparel contractors)
315211	Uniform shirts, men's and boys', cut and sew apparel contractors
315299	Uniform shirts, team athletic, cut and sewn from purchased fabric (except apparel contractors)
315212	Uniform shirts, women's and girls', cut and sew apparel contractors
315225	Uniform shirts, work, men's and boys', cut and sewn from purchased fabric (except apparel contractors)
448190	Uniform stores (except athletic)
451110	Uniform stores, athletic
812332	Uniform supply services, industrial
315299	Uniforms, band, cut and sewn from purchased fabric (except apparel contractors)
315211	Uniforms, band, men's and boys', cut and sew apparel contractors
315212	Uniforms, band, women's, girls', and infants', cut and sew apparel contractors
315211	Uniforms, dress (e.g., fire fighter, military, police), men's, cut and sew apparel contractors
315222	Uniforms, dress (e.g., fire fighter, military, police), men's, cut and sewn from purchased fabric (except apparel contractors)
315212	Uniforms, dress (e.g., military, police, fire fighter), women's, cut and sew apparel contractors
315234	Uniforms, dress, tailored (e.g., fire fighter, military, police), women's, misses', and girls', cut and sewn from purchased fabric (except apparel contractors)
315228	Uniforms, nontailored (except work), men's and boys', cut and sewn from purchased fabric (except apparel contractors)
315225	Uniforms, nontailored work, men's, cut and sewn from purchased fabric (except apparel contractors)
315191	Uniforms, nontailored, made in apparel knitting mills
315211	Uniforms, nontailored, men's and boys', cut and sew apparel contractors
315212	Uniforms, nontailored, women's and girls', cut and sew apparel contractors
315239	Uniforms, nontailored, women's, misses', and girls', cut and sewn from purchased fabric (except team athletic, apparel contractors)
315299	Uniforms, team athletic, cut and sewn from purchased fabric (except apparel contractors)
315211	Uniforms, team athletic, men's and boys', cut and sew apparel contractors
315212	Uniforms, team athletic, women's and girls', cut and sew apparel contractors
335999	Uninterruptible power supplies (UPS) manufacturing
525120	Union health and welfare funds
525110	Union pension funds

Code	Description
315192	Union suits made in apparel knitting mills
315291	Union suits, infants', cut and sewn from purchased fabric (except apparel contractors)
315211	Union suits, men's and boys', cut and sew apparel contractors
315221	Union suits, men's and boys', cut and sewn from purchased fabric (except apparel contractors)
315212	Union suits, women's, girls', and infants', cut and sew apparel contractors
315231	Union suits, women's, misses', and girls', cut and sewn from purchased fabric (except apparel contractors)
813930	Unions (except apprenticeship programs), labor
332919	Unions, pipe, metal (except made from purchased pipe), manufacturing
448140	Unisex clothing stores
422330	Unisex clothing wholesaling
812112	Unisex hair stylist shops
333414	Unit heaters (except portable electric) manufacturing
335211	Unit heaters, portable electric, manufacturing
525990	Unit investment trust funds
323116	Unit set forms (e.g., manifold credit card slips) printing
928120	United Nations
813219	United fund councils
813219	United funds for colleges
333613	Universal joints (except aircraft, motor vehicle) manufacturing
336413	Universal joints, aircraft, manufacturing
336350	Universal joints, automotive, truck, and bus, manufacturing
611310	Universities
813410	University clubs
511130	University press publishers
923110	University regents or boards, government
311812	Unleavened bread made in commercial bakeries

Code	Description
337121	Upholstered furniture, household-type, custom, manufacturing
337121	Upholstered furniture, household-type, on frames of any material, manufacturing
421850	Upholsterers' equipment and supplies (except fabrics) wholesaling
314999	Upholstering filling (except nonwoven fabric) manufacturing
811420	Upholstery (except motor vehicle) repair services
561740	Upholstery cleaning on customers' premises
561740	Upholstery cleaning services
316110	Upholstery leather manufacturing
451130	Upholstery materials stores
811121	Upholstery shops, automotive
332612	Upholstery springs and spring units made from purchased wire
316110	Upper leather manufacturing
316999	Uppers (i.e., shoe cut stock), leather, manufacturing
332111	Upset forgings made from purchased iron or steel, unfinished
332112	Upset forgings made from purchased nonferrous metals, unfinished
333513	Upsetters (i.e., forging machines) manufacturing
212291	Uraninite (pitchblende) mining and/or beneficiating
325188	Uranium compounds, not specified elsewhere by process, manufacturing
212291	Uranium ores mining and/or beneficiating
325188	Uranium oxide manufacturing
331419	Uranium refining, primary
325188	Uranium, enriched, manufacturing
212291	Uranium-radium-vanadium ore mine site development for own account
212291	Uranium-radium-vanadium ores mining and/or beneficiating
485113	Urban bus line services (except mixed mode)

Code	Description
485112	Urban commuter rail systems (except mixed mode)
541320	Urban planners' offices
925120	Urban planning commissions, government
541320	Urban planning services
485111	Urban transit systems, mixed mode (e.g., bus, commuter rail, subway combinations)
325311	Urea manufacturing
325211	Urea resins manufacturing
325211	Urea-formaldehyde resins manufacturing
326150	Urethane foam products manufacturing
325212	Urethane rubber manufacturing
621493	Urgent medical care centers and clinics (except hospitals), freestanding
332998	Urinals, metal, manufacturing
326191	Urinals, plastics, manufacturing
327111	Urinals, vitreous china, manufacturing
621511	Urinalysis laboratories
327420	Urns (e.g., gypsum, plaster of paris) manufacturing
335211	Urns, household-type electric, manufacturing
621111	Urologists' offices (e.g., centers, clinics)
441229	Used aircraft dealers
441310	Used automotive parts stores
441320	Used automotive tire dealers
453310	Used bicycle (except motorized) shops
441222	Used boat dealers
441120	Used car dealers
421110	Used cars wholesaling
484210	Used household and office goods moving
453930	Used manufactured (mobile) home dealers
453310	Used merchandise stores
441221	Used motorcycle dealers
421140	Used parts, motor vehicle, wholesaling

Code	Description
441210	Used recreational vehicle (RV) dealers
441320	Used tire dealers
421130	Used tires, motor vehicle, wholesaling
441229	Used utility trailer dealers
541618	Utilities management consulting services
332311	Utility buildings, prefabricated metal, manufacturing
326199	Utility containers (e.g., baskets, bins, boxes, buckets, dishpans, pails), plastics (except foam), manufacturing
511210	Utility software, computer, packaged
441229	Utility trailer dealers
532120	Utility trailer rental or leasing
336214	Utility trailers manufacturing
421110	Utility trailers wholesaling
326220	V-belts, rubber or plastics, manufacturing
334310	VCR (video cassette recorder) manufacturing
531190	Vacant lot rental or leasing
531190	Vacation and recreation land rental or leasing
721214	Vacation camps (except campgrounds, day instructional)
115210	Vaccinating livestock (except by veterinarians)
541940	Vaccination services, veterinary
325414	Vaccines (i.e., bacterial, virus) manufacturing
422210	Vaccines wholesaling
332439	Vacuum bottles and jugs manufacturing
336340	Vacuum brake booster, automotive, truck, and bus, manufacturing
326220	Vacuum cleaner belts, rubber or plastics, manufacturing
443111	Vacuum cleaner stores, household-type
335212	Vacuum cleaners (e.g., canister, handheld, upright) household-type electric, manufacturing
335212	Vacuum cleaners and sweepers, household-type electric, manufacturing

Code	Description
421620	Vacuum cleaners, household-type, wholesaling
333319	Vacuum cleaners, industrial and commercial-type, manufacturing
235950	Vacuum cleaning systems, built-in, construction contractors
333912	Vacuum pumps (except laboratory) manufacturing
339111	Vacuum pumps, laboratory-type, manufacturing
335314	Vacuum relays manufacturing
332420	Vacuum tanks, heavy gauge metal, manufacturing
327215	Vacuum tube blanks, glass, made from purchased glass
327212	Vacuum tube blanks, glass, made in glass making plants
334411	Vacuum tubes manufacturing
488119	Vacuuming of airport runways
333112	Vacuums, yard, manufacturing
812930	Valet parking services
316991	Valises, all materials, manufacturing
325191	Valonia extract manufacturing
333512	Valve grinding machines, metalworking, manufacturing
421840	Valves (except hydraulic, plumbing, pneumatic) wholesaling
332911	Valves for nuclear applications manufacturing
332911	Valves for water works and municipal water systems manufacturing
336311	Valves, engine, intake and exhaust, manufacturing
332912	Valves, hydraulic and pneumatic, fluid power, manufacturing
421830	Valves, hydraulic and pneumatic, wholesaling
332911	Valves, industrial-type (e.g., check, gate, globe, relief, safety), manufacturing
332919	Valves, inline plumbing and heating (e.g., cutoffs, stop), manufacturing
421720	Valves, plumbing and heating, wholesaling
316999	Vamps, leather, manufacturing

Code	Description
532120	Van (except passenger) rental or leasing without driver
532112	Van (passenger) leasing
532111	Van (passenger) rental
336213	Van and minivan conversions on purchased chassis
811121	Van conversion shops (except on assembly line or factory basis)
484210	Van lines, moving and storage services
212291	Vanadium ores mining and/or beneficiating
325199	Vanillin, synthetic, manufacturing
337110	Vanities (except freestanding), stock or custom wood, manufacturing
337122	Vanities, freestanding, wood, manufacturing
337124	Vanities, metal household-type, manufacturing
316993	Vanity cases, leather, manufacturing
337110	Vanity tops, wood or plastics laminated on wood, manufacturing
485999	Vanpool operation
488999	Vanpools, arrangement of
336112	Vans, commercial and passenger light duty, assembling on chassis of own manufacture
334512	Vapor heating controls manufacturing
335110	Vapor lamps, electric, manufacturing
333999	Vapor separating machinery manufacturing
335211	Vaporizers, household-type electric, manufacturing
334513	Variable control instruments, industrial process-type, manufacturing
311612	Variety meats, edible organs, made from purchased meats
311611	Variety meats, edible organs, made in slaughtering plants
452990	Variety stores
334415	Varistors manufacturing
325510	Varnishes manufacturing
422950	Varnishes wholesaling
332812	Varnishing metals and metal products for the trade

Code	Description
313320	Varnishing purchased textiles and apparel
327420	Vases (e.g., gypsum, plaster of paris) manufacturing
327215	Vases, glass, made from purchased glass
327212	Vases, glass, made in glass making plants
327112	Vases, pottery (e.g., china, earthenware, stoneware), manufacturing
325132	Vat dyes, synthetic, manufacturing
332420	Vats, heavy gauge metal, manufacturing
332439	Vats, light gauge metal, manufacturing
711110	Vaudeville companies
332999	Vault doors and linings, metal, manufacturing
332999	Vaults (except burial), metal, manufacturing
339995	Vaults (except concrete) manufacturing
112111	Veal calf production
311611	Veal carcasses, half carcasses, primal and sub-primal cuts, produced in slaughtering plants
311612	Veal, primal and sub-primal cuts, made from purchased carcasses
325411	Vegetable alkaloids (i.e., basic chemicals) (e.g., caffeine, codeine, morphine, nicotine), manufacturing
111211	Vegetable and melon farming, potato dominant crop, field and seed production
111219	Vegetable and melon farming, vegetable (except potato) and melon dominant crops, field, bedding plants and seed production
111211	Vegetable and potato farming, potato dominant crop, field and seed potato production
111219	Vegetable and potato farming, vegetable (except potato) dominant crops, field, bedding plants and seed production
321920	Vegetable baskets, veneer and splint, manufacturing
311421	Vegetable brining

Code	Description
422990	Vegetable cake and meal wholesaling
311421	Vegetable canning
321920	Vegetable crates, wood, wirebound, manufacturing
422910	Vegetable dusts and sprays wholesaling
111419	Vegetable farming, grown under cover
311211	Vegetable flour manufacturing
311211	Vegetable flour, meal, and powders, made in flour mills
311411	Vegetable juice concentrates, frozen, manufacturing
311421	Vegetable juices canning
311421	Vegetable juices, fresh, manufacturing
445230	Vegetable markets
333294	Vegetable oil processing machinery manufacturing
311223	Vegetable oils (except soybean) made in crushing mills
311225	Vegetable oils made from purchased oils
115114	Vegetable precooling
115114	Vegetable sorting, grading, and packing
311221	Vegetable starches manufacturing
115114	Vegetable sun drying
115114	Vegetable vacuum cooling
311423	Vegetables dehydrating
311421	Vegetables pickling
422490	Vegetables, canned, wholesaling
311991	Vegetables, cut or peeled, fresh, manufacturing
422480	Vegetables, fresh, wholesaling
311411	Vegetables, frozen, manufacturing
422420	Vegetables, frozen, wholesaling
115113	Vegetables, machine harvesting
333997	Vehicle scales manufacturing
321912	Vehicle stock, hardwood, manufacturing
336991	Vehicle, children's, metal manufacturing
339932	Vehicles, children's (except bicycles and metal tricycles), manufacturing

Code	Description
421920	Vehicles, children's (except bicycles), wholesaling
421110	Vehicles, recreational, wholesaling
336321	Vehicular lighting fixtures manufacturing
316110	Vellum leather manufacturing
313210	Velvets, manmade fiber and silk, weaving
454210	Vending machine merchandisers, sale of products
333311	Vending machines manufacturing
421440	Vending machines wholesaling
333210	Veneer and plywood forming machinery manufacturing
321920	Veneer baskets, for fruits and vegetables, manufacturing
321211	Veneer mills, hardwood
321212	Veneer mills, softwood
321999	Veneer work, inlaid, manufacturing
811490	Venetian blind repair and maintenance shops without retailing new venetian blinds
321918	Venetian blind slats, wood, manufacturing
337920	Venetian blinds manufacturing
235110	Ventilating construction contractors
421730	Ventilating equipment and supplies (except household-type fans) wholesaling
333412	Ventilating fans, industrial and commercial-type, manufacturing
335211	Ventilating kitchen fans, household-type electric, manufacturing
335211	Ventilation and exhaust fans (except attic fans), household-type, manufacturing
561790	Ventilation duct cleaning services
332322	Ventilators, sheet metal, manufacturing
523910	Venture capital companies
212319	Verde' antique crushed and broken stone mining and/or beneficiating
212311	Verde' antique mining or quarrying
212399	Vermiculite mining and/or beneficiating
327992	Vermiculite, exfoliated, manufacturing

Code	Description
325412	Vermifuge preparations manufacturing
325131	Vermilion pigments manufacturing
312130	Vermouth manufacturing
337920	Vertical blinds manufacturing
488390	Vessel supply services
332420	Vessels, heavy gauge metal, manufacturing
315299	Vestments, academic and clerical, cut and sewn from purchased fabric (except apparel contractors)
315211	Vestments, academic and clerical, men's and boys', cut and sew apparel contractors
315212	Vestments, academic and clerical, women's and girls', cut and sew apparel contractors
315292	Vests, leather, fur, or sheep-lined (except apparel contractors), manufacturing
315211	Vests, leather, fur, or sheep-lined, men's and boys', cut and sew apparel contractors
315212	Vests, leather, fur, or sheep-lined, women's, girls', and infants', cut and sew apparel contractors
315211	Vests, men's and boys', cut and sew apparel contractors
315228	Vests, nontailored, men's and boys', cut and sewn from purchased fabric (except apparel contractors)
315239	Vests, nontailored, women's, misses', and girls', cut and sewn from purchased fabric (except apparel contractors)
315222	Vests, tailored, men's and boys', cut and sewn from purchased fabric (except apparel contractors)
315234	Vests, tailored, women's, misses', and girls', cut and sewn from purchased fabric
315212	Vests, women's, girls', and infants', cut and sew apparel contractors
813410	Veterans' membership organizations
923140	Veterans' affairs offices
923140	Veterans' benefits program administration, government
813311	Veterans' rights organizations

Code	Description
421490	Veterinarians' equipment and supplies wholesaling
339112	Veterinarians' instruments and apparatus manufacturing
422210	Veterinarians' medicines wholesaling
541940	Veterinarians' offices
541940	Veterinarians' practices
541940	Veterinary clinics
325412	Veterinary medicinal preparations manufacturing
541710	Veterinary research and development laboratories or services
541940	Veterinary services
541940	Veterinary services, livestock
541940	Veterinary services, pets and other animal specialties
541940	Veterinary testing laboratories
234120	Viaduct construction
523910	Viatical settlement companies
339992	Vibraphones manufacturing
334519	Vibration meters, analyzers, and calibrators, manufacturing
541380	Vibration testing laboratories or services
333120	Vibrators, concrete, manufacturing
421410	Video cameras (except household-type) wholesaling
334310	Video cameras, household-type, manufacturing
421620	Video cameras, household-type, wholesaling
811211	Video cassette recorder (VCR) repair services without retailing new video cassette recorders
532210	Video cassette recorder rental
334310	Video cassette recorders (VCR) manufacturing
334613	Video cassettes, blank, manufacturing
334612	Video cassettes, pre-recorded, mass reproducing
512191	Video conversion services (i.e., between formats)
532210	Video disc player rental
532230	Video disc rental for home electronic equipment (e.g., VCR)

Code	Description
713290	Video gambling device concession operators (i.e., supplying and servicing in others' facilities)
713120	Video game arcades (except gambling)
339932	Video game machines (except coin-operated) manufacturing
532230	Video game rental
713290	Video gaming device concession operators (i.e., supplying and servicing in others' facilities)
541921	Video photography services, portrait
512191	Video post-production services
512110	Video production
512110	Video production and distribution
512120	Video productions, distributing
532210	Video recorder rental
334612	Video tape or disk mass reproducing
532210	Video tape player rental
532230	Video tape rental for home electronic equipment (e.g., VCR)
532230	Video tape rental stores
451220	Video tape stores
334613	Video tapes, blank, manufacturing
421690	Video tapes, blank, wholesaling
421990	Video tapes, prerecorded, wholesaling
541921	Video taping services, special events (e.g., birthdays, weddings)
512199	Videotape libraries, stock footage
311941	Vinegar manufacturing
115112	Vineyard cultivation services
325199	Vinyl acetate (except resins) manufacturing
325211	Vinyl acetate resins manufacturing
326113	Vinyl and vinyl copolymer film and unlaminated sheet (except packaging) manufacturing
325211	Vinyl chloride resins manufacturing
313320	Vinyl coated fabrics manufacturing
325222	Vinyl fibers and filaments manufacturing
326192	Vinyl floor coverings manufacturing
235520	Vinyl flooring construction contractors
325211	Vinyl resins manufacturing
421330	Vinyl siding wholesaling

Code	Description
316219	Vinyl upper athletic footwear manufacturing
325222	Vinylidene chloride fiber and filament manufacturing
325211	Vinylidene resins manufacturing
339992	Violas and parts manufacturing
339992	Violins and parts manufacturing
325413	Viral in-vitro diagnostic test substances manufacturing
325414	Virus vaccines manufacturing
325221	Viscose fibers, bands, strips, and yarn manufacturing
334519	Viscosimeters (except industrial process type) manufacturing
334513	Viscosity instruments, industrial process-type, manufacturing
332212	Vises (except machine tool attachments) manufacturing
621610	Visiting nurse associations
561591	Visitors bureaus
325412	Vitamin preparations manufacturing
446191	Vitamin stores
422210	Vitamins wholesaling
325411	Vitamins, uncompounded, manufacturing
711130	Vocalists, independent
611513	Vocational apprenticeship training
624310	Vocational habilitation job counseling
624310	Vocational habilitation job training facilities (except schools)
624310	Vocational rehabilitation agencies
624310	Vocational rehabilitation job counseling
624310	Vocational rehabilitation job training facilities (except schools)
624310	Vocational rehabilitation or habilitation services (e.g., job counseling, job training, work experience)
561421	Voice mailbox services
621340	Voice pathologists' offices (e.g., centers, clinics)
212399	Volcanic ash mining and/or beneficiating
212319	Volcanic rock crushed and broken stone mining and/or beneficiating

Code	Description
212311	Volcanic rock, mining or quarrying
335311	Voltage regulating transformers, electric power, manufacturing
421610	Voltage regulators (except motor vehicle) wholesaling
336322	Voltage regulators for internal combustion engines manufacturing
334413	Voltage regulators, integrated circuits, manufacturing
335311	Voltage regulators, transmission and distribution, manufacturing
334515	Voltmeters manufacturing
813212	Voluntary health organizations
624229	Volunteer housing repair organizations
333313	Voting machines manufacturing
421850	Voting machines wholesaling
322214	Vulcanized fiber products made from purchased paperboard
325212	Vulcanized oils manufacturing
333220	Vulcanizing machinery manufacturing
541511	WEB (i.e., internet) page design services, custom
332992	Wads, ammunition, manufacturing
333295	Wafer processing equipment, semiconductor, manufacturing
321219	Waferboard manufacturing
334413	Wafers (semiconductor devices) manufacturing
335211	Waffle irons, household-type electric, manufacturing
311412	Waffles, frozen, manufacturing
926150	Wage control agencies, government
339932	Wagons, children's (e.g., coaster, express, and play), manufacturing
333111	Wagons, farm-type, manufacturing
333112	Wagons, lawn and garden-type, manufacturing
321918	Wainscots, wood, manufacturing
561421	Wakeup call services
621111	Walk-in physicians' offices (e.g., centers, clinics)
532291	Walker, invalid, rental
339932	Walkers, baby (vehicles), manufacturing
333921	Walkways, moving, manufacturing

Code	Description
334518	Wall clocks manufacturing
235210	Wall covering or removal construction contractors
422950	Wall coverings (e.g., fabric, plastic) wholesaling
335122	Wall lamps (i.e., lighting fixtures), commericial, institutional, and industrial electric, manufacturing
335121	Wall lamps (i.e., lighting fixtures), residential electric, manufacturing
327122	Wall tile, ceramic, manufacturing
421310	Wallboard wholesaling
327420	Wallboard, gypsum, manufacturing
316993	Wallets (except metal) manufacturing
339911	Wallets, precious metal, manufacturing
444120	Wallpaper and wall coverings stores
325612	Wallpaper cleaners manufacturing
322222	Wallpaper made from purchased papers or other materials
422950	Wallpaper wholesaling
111335	Walnut farming
115114	Walnut hulling and shelling
712110	War museums
316991	Wardrobe bags (i.e., luggage) manufacturing
532220	Wardrobe rental
337124	Wardrobes, metal household-type, manufacturing
337122	Wardrobes, wood household-type, manufacturing
452910	Warehouse clubs (i.e., food and general merchandise)
332311	Warehouses, prefabricated metal, manufacturing
493190	Warehousing (except farm products, general merchandise, refrigerated)
493110	Warehousing (including foreign trade zones), general merchandise
493110	Warehousing and storage, general merchandise
813910	Warehousing associations
493130	Warehousing, farm products (except refrigerated)
493120	Warehousing, refrigerated

Code	Description
531130	Warehousing, self storage
334511	Warfare countermeasures equipment manufacturing
421730	Warm air heating equipment wholesaling
335211	Warming trays, electric, manufacturing
315191	Warmup suits made in apparel knitting mills
315291	Warmup suits, infants', cut and sewn from purchased fabric (except apparel contractors)
315211	Warmup suits, men's and boys', cut and sew apparel contractors
315228	Warmup suits, men's and boys', cut and sewn from purchased fabric (except apparel contractors)
315212	Warmup suits, women's, girls', and infants', cut and sew apparel contractors
315239	Warmup suits, women's, misses', and girls', cut and sewn from purchased fabric (except apparel contractors)
313249	Warp fabrics knitting
333292	Warping machinery manufacturing
524128	Warranty insurance carriers (e.g., appliance, automobile, homeowners, product), direct
315211	Washable service apparel (e.g., barbers', hospital, professional), men's and boys', cut and sew apparel contractors
315225	Washable service apparel (e.g., barbers', hospital, professional), men's and boys', cut and sewn from purchased fabric (except apparel contractors)
315212	Washable service apparel, women's and girls', cut and sew apparel contractors
315239	Washable service apparel, women's, misses', and girls', cut and sewn from purchased fabric (except apparel contractors)
321999	Washboards, wood and part wood, manufacturing
532210	Washer, clothes, rental
212113	Washeries, anthracite

Code	Description
212111	Washeries, bituminous coal or lignite
333131	Washers, aggregate and sand, stationary, manufacturing
332722	Washers, metal, manufacturing
234930	Washery, mining, construction
811412	Washing machine, household-type, repair and maintenance services without retailing new washing machine
335224	Washing machines, household-type, manufacturing
333312	Washing machines, laundry (except household-type), manufacturing
561720	Washroom sanitation services
562213	Waste (except sewage) treatment facilities, nonhazardous
562119	Waste (except solid and hazardous) collection services
562119	Waste (except solid and hazardous) hauling, local
562112	Waste collection services, hazardous
562111	Waste collection services, nonhazardous solid
221320	Waste collection, treatment, and disposal through a sewer system
562213	Waste disposal combustors or incinerators, nonhazardous solid
562211	Waste disposal facilities, hazardous
562212	Waste disposal landfills, nonhazardous solid
234990	Waste disposal plant construction
484220	Waste hauling, hazardous, local
484230	Waste hauling, hazardous, long-distance
562112	Waste hauling, local, hazardous
562111	Waste hauling, local, nonhazardous solid
484220	Waste hauling, nonhazardous, local
484230	Waste hauling, nonhazardous, long-distance
924110	Waste management program administration
421930	Waste materials wholesaling
562920	Waste recovery facilities
562112	Waste transfer stations, hazardous
562111	Waste transfer stations, nonhazardous solid

Code	Description
562211	Waste treatment facilities, hazardous
562211	Waste treatment plants, hazardous
322214	Wastebaskets, fiber made from purchased paperboard
316993	Watch bands (except metal) manufacturing
339914	Watch bands, metal (except precious), manufacturing
339911	Watch bands, precious metal, manufacturing
335912	Watch batteries manufacturing
327215	Watch crystals made from purchased glass
326199	Watch crystals, plastics, manufacturing
334518	Watch jewels manufacturing
811490	Watch repair shops without retailing new watches
448310	Watch shops
334518	Watchcase manufacturing
334518	Watches and parts (except crystals) manufacturing
421940	Watches and parts wholesaling
333415	Water (i.e., drinking) coolers, mechanical, manufacturing
325412	Water (i.e., drinking) decontamination or purification tablets manufacturing
337124	Water bed frames, metal, manufacturing
337122	Water bed frames, wood, manufacturing
337910	Water bed mattresses manufacturing
327111	Water closet bowls, vitreous china, manufacturing
332998	Water closets, metal, manufacturing
339942	Water colors, artist's, manufacturing
561990	Water conditioning services
924110	Water control and quality program administration
421740	Water coolers, mechanical, wholesaling
221310	Water distribution (except irrigation)

Code	Description
221310	Water distribution for irrigation
221310	Water filtration plant operation
334512	Water heater controls manufacturing
811412	Water heater repair and maintenance services without retailing new water heaters
333319	Water heaters (except boilers), commercial-type, manufacturing
421720	Water heaters (except electric) wholesaling
335228	Water heaters (including nonelectric), household-type, manufacturing
421620	Water heaters, electric, wholesaling
326220	Water hoses, rubber or plastics, manufacturing
213111	Water intake well drilling, oil and gas field on a contract basis
334519	Water leak detectors manufacturing
234910	Water main and line construction
713110	Water parks, amusement
331511	Water pipe, cast iron, manufacturing
234990	Water power project construction
335211	Water pulsating devices, household-type electric, manufacturing
235110	Water pump construction contractors
333319	Water purification equipment manufacturing
334513	Water quality monitoring and control systems manufacturing
325510	Water repellant coatings for wood, concrete and masonry manufacturing
315228	Water resistant jackets and windbreakers, nontailored, men's and boys', cut and sewn from purchased fabric (except apparel contractors)
315239	Water resistant jackets and wind-breakers, not tailored, women's, misses' and girls', cut and sewn from purchased fabric (except apparel contractors)
315228	Water resistant outerwear (except overcoats), men's and boys', cut and sewn from purchased fabric (except apparel contractors)

Code	Description
315239	Water resistant outerwear (except overcoats), women's, misses', and girls', cut and sewn from purchased fabric (except apparel contractors)
315291	Water resistant outerwear infants', cut and sewn from purchased fabric (except apparel contractors)
315212	Water resistant outerwear, women's, girls', and infants', cut and sew apparel contractors
315222	Water resistant overcoats, men's and boys', cut and sewn from purchased fabric (except apparel contractors)
315234	Water resistant overcoats, women's, misses', and girls', cut and sewn from purchased fabric (except apparel contractors)
315211	Water resistant, men's and boys', cut and sew apparel contractors
316211	Water shoes, plastics or plastics soled fabric upper, manufacturing
316211	Water shoes, rubber or rubber soled fabric upper, manufacturing
532292	Water ski rental
454390	Water softener service providers, direct selling
421720	Water softening and conditioning equipment wholesaling
422690	Water softening compounds wholesaling
333319	Water softening equipment manufacturing
561990	Water softening services
445299	Water stores, bottled
221310	Water supply systems
235110	Water system balancing and testing construction contractors
332420	Water tanks, heavy gauge metal, manufacturing
483212	Water taxi services
332913	Water traps manufacturing
221310	Water treatment and distribution
333319	Water treatment equipment manufacturing
421830	Water treatment equipment, industrial, wholesaling
421850	Water treatment equipment, municipal, wholesaling

Code	Description
234990	Water treatment plant construction
221310	Water treatment plants
333611	Water turbines manufacturing
235810	Water well drilling (except oil or gas field water intake) construction contractors
333132	Water well drilling machinery manufacturing
312111	Water, artificially carbonated, manufacturing
422490	Water, bottled (except water treating), wholesaling
325998	Water, distilled, manufacturing
312111	Water, flavored, manufacturing
312112	Water, naturally carbonated, purifying and bottling
234910	Water, sewer, and pipeline construction management firms
315228	Water-repellent outerwear (except overcoats), men's and boys', cut and sewn from purchased fabric (except apparel contractors)
315239	Water-repellent outerwear (except overcoats), women's, misses', and girls', cut and sewn from purchased fabric (except apparel contractors)
315291	Water-repellent outerwear, infants', cut and sewn from purchased fabric (except apparel contractors)
315211	Water-repellent outerwear, men's and boys', cut and sew apparel contractors
315212	Water-repellent outerwear, women's, girls', and infants', cut and sew apparel contractors
315222	Water-repellent overcoats, men's and boys', cut and sewn from purchased fabric (except apparel contractors)
315234	Water-repellent overcoats, women's, misses', and girls', cut and sewn from purchased fabric (except apparel contractors)
712190	Waterfalls (i.e., natural wonder tourist attractions)
488310	Waterfront terminal operation (e.g., docks, piers, wharves)
326199	Watering cans, plastics, manufacturing

Code	Description
325611	Waterless hand soaps manufacturing
111219	Watermelon farming, field, bedding plant and seed production
334514	Watermeters, consumption registering, manufacturing
315999	Waterproof outerwear cut and sewn from purchased fabric (except apparel contractors)
315211	Waterproof outerwear, men's and boys', cut and sew apparel contractors
315999	Waterproof outerwear, rubberizing fabric and manufacturing outerwear
315212	Waterproof outerwear, women's, girls', and infants', cut and sew apparel contractors
313320	Waterproofing apparel, fabrics and textile products (e.g., oiling, rubberizing, waxing, varnishing)
235990	Waterproofing construction contractors
713990	Waterslides (i.e., amusement rides)
234990	Waterway construction
332911	Waterworks and municipal water system valves manufacturing
334515	Watt-hour and demand meters, combined, manufacturing
334515	Watt-hour and time switch meters, combined, manufacturing
334515	Watt-hour meters, electric, manufacturing
325191	Wattle extract manufacturing
334515	Wattmeters manufacturing
713940	Wave pools
334515	Waveform measuring and/or analyzing equipment manufacturing
339999	Wax figures (i.e., mannequins) manufacturing
712110	Wax museums
325612	Wax removers manufacturing
322222	Waxed paper for nonpackaging applications made from purchased paper
322221	Waxed paper for packaging applications made from purchased paper

Code	Description
422130	Waxed paper wholesaling
422690	Waxes (except petroleum) wholesaling
324199	Waxes, petroleum, made from refined petroleum
324110	Waxes, petroleum, made in petroleum refineries
325612	Waxes, polishing (e.g., floor, furniture), manufacturing
313320	Waxing purchased textiles and apparel
115114	Waxing, fruits or vegetables
112210	Weaning pig operations
336992	Weapons, self-propelled, manufacturing
541990	Weather forecasting services
924120	Weather research program administration
321918	Weather strip, wood, manufacturing
421330	Weather stripping wholesaling
334519	Weather tracking equipment manufacturing
333999	Weather vanes manufacturing
331422	Weatherproof wire or cable made from purchased copper in wire drawing plants
331319	Weatherproof wire or cable made in aluminum wire drawing plants
332321	Weatherstrip, metal, manufacturing
314999	Weatherstripping made from purchased textiles
313221	Weaving and finishing narrow fabrics
313210	Weaving and finishing of broadwoven fabrics (except rugs, tire fabric)
313210	Weaving broadwoven fabrics (except rugs, tire fabrics)
313210	Weaving broadwoven felts
313221	Weaving fabric less than 12 inches (30cm)
313210	Weaving fabrics more than 12 inches (30cm) in width
333292	Weaving machinery manufacturing
313221	Weaving narrow fabrics
314110	Weaving rugs, carpets, and mats
313221	Webbing weaving

Code	Description
321999	Webbing, cane, reed, and rattan, manufacturing
812990	Wedding chapels (except churches)
315212	Wedding dresses, women's, cut and sew apparel contractors
315233	Wedding dresses, women's, misses', and girls', cut and sewn from purchased fabric (except apparel contractors)
541921	Wedding photography services
812990	Wedding planning services
561730	Weed control and fertilizing services (except crop)
115112	Weed control services for crops
926140	Weed control, agriculture, government
333111	Weeding machines, farm-type, manufacturing
313241	Weft fabrics knitting
811219	Weighing equipment (e.g., balance, scales) repair and maintenance services
812191	Weight loss centers, non-medical
812191	Weight reducing centers, non-medical
713940	Weight training centers
541890	Welcoming services (i.e., advertising services)
331222	Welded iron or steel wire fabric made in wire drawing plants
339113	Welder's hoods manufacturing
316999	Welders' aprons, leather, manufacturing
316999	Welders' jackets, leggings, and sleeves, leather, manufacturing
333992	Welding equipment manufacturing
532412	Welding equipment rental or leasing
422690	Welding gases wholesaling
421830	Welding machinery and equipment wholesaling
333514	Welding positioners (i.e., jigs) manufacturing
811310	Welding repair services (e.g., automotive, general)
331491	Welding rod, uncoated, nonferrous metals (except aluminum, copper), made from purchased metals or scrap

Code	Description
421840	Welding supplies (except welding gases) wholesaling
333992	Welding wire or rods (i.e., coated, cored) manufacturing
235990	Welding, on site, construction contractors
332313	Weldments manufacturing
923130	Welfare administration, nonoperating
923130	Welfare programs administration
624190	Welfare service centers, multi-program
213112	Well casing running, cutting and pulling, oil and gas field on a contract basis
331210	Well casings (e.g., heavy riveted, lock joint, welded, wrought) made from purchased iron or steel
331111	Well casings, iron or steel, made in steel mills
213111	Well drilling (i.e., oil, gas, water intake wells) on a contract basis
532412	Well drilling machinery and equipment rental or leasing
333132	Well logging equipment manufacturing
213112	Well logging, oil and gas field, on a contract basis
213112	Well plugging, oil and gas field, on a contract basis
213112	Well pumping, oil and gas field, on a contract basis
213112	Well servicing, oil and gas field, on a contract basis
213112	Well surveying, oil and gas field, on a contract basis
332322	Wells, light, sheet metal, manufacturing
316110	Welting leather manufacturing
448140	Western wear stores
316110	Wet blues manufacturing
313230	Wet laid nonwoven fabrics manufacturing
322130	Wet machine board mills
311221	Wet milling corn and other vegetables
339920	Wet suits manufacturing
325613	Wetting agents manufacturing

Code	Description
487210	Whale watching excursions
234990	Wharf construction
488310	Wharf operation
311211	Wheat bran manufacturing
311230	Wheat breakfast cereal manufacturing
111140	Wheat farming, field and seed production
311211	Wheat flour manufacturing
311211	Wheat germ manufacturing
311213	Wheat malt manufacturing
334515	Wheatstone bridges (i.e., electrical measuring instruments) manufacturing
811118	Wheel alignment shops, automotive
532291	Wheel chair rental
334511	Wheel position indicators and transmitters, aircraft, manufacturing
332212	Wheel pullers, handtools, manufacturing
333924	Wheelbarrows manufacturing
339113	Wheelchairs manufacturing
421450	Wheelchairs wholesaling
336399	Wheels (i.e., rims), automotive, truck, and bus, manufacturing
327910	Wheels, abrasive, manufacturing
331111	Wheels, car and locomotive, iron or steel, made in steel mills
421120	Wheels, motor vehicle, new, wholesaling
327910	Wheels, polishing and grinding, manufacturing
336330	Wheels, steering, automotive, truck, and bus, manufacturing
327910	Whetstones manufacturing
212399	Whetstones mining and/or beneficiating
311512	Whey butter manufacturing
311514	Whey, condensed, dried, evaporated, and powdered, manufacturing
311513	Whey, raw, liquid, manufacturing
311511	Whipped topping (except dry mix, frozen) manufacturing
311514	Whipped topping, dry mix, manufacturing

Code	Description
311412	Whipped topping, frozen, manufacturing
335211	Whippers, household-type electric, manufacturing
311511	Whipping cream manufacturing
316999	Whips, horse, manufacturing
316999	Whipstocks manufacturing
339113	Whirlpool baths (i.e., hydrotherapy equipment) manufacturing
421450	Whirlpool baths wholesaling
493190	Whiskey warehousing
325131	White extender pigments (e.g., barytes, blanc fixe, whiting) manufacturing
331528	White metal castings (except die-castings), unfinished, manufacturing
713990	White water rafting, recreational
235210	Whitewashing construction contractors
212312	Whiting crushed and broken stone, mining and/or beneficiating
114111	Whiting fishing
325131	Whiting manufacturing
334519	Whole body counters, nuclear, manufacturing
*****	Wholesale — see type of product
561520	Wholesale tour operators
813910	Wholesalers' associations
337125	Wicker furniture (except upholstered), household-type, manufacturing
313221	Wicks manufacturing
334210	Wide area network communications equipment (e.g., bridges, gateways, routers) manufacturing
448150	Wig and hairpiece stores
422990	Wigs wholesaling
339999	Wigs, wiglets, toupees, hair pieces, manufacturing
712130	Wild animal parks
111199	Wild rice farming, field and seed production
721214	Wilderness camps
711510	Wildlife artists, independent
924120	Wildlife conservation agencies
813312	Wildlife preservation organizations

Code	Description
712190	Wildlife sanctuaries
212231	Willemite mining and/or beneficiating
337125	Willow furniture (except upholstered), household-type, manufacturing
321999	Willow ware (except furniture) manufacturing
333923	Winches manufacturing
421830	Winches wholesaling
924120	Wind and water erosion control agencies, government
334519	Wind direction indicators manufacturing
926130	Wind generated electrical power regulation
333611	Wind powered turbine generator sets manufacturing
333611	Wind turbines (i.e., windmill) manufacturing
315291	Windbreakers, infants', cut and sewn from purchased fabric (except apparel contractors)
315211	Windbreakers, men's and boys', cut and sew apparel contractors
315228	Windbreakers, men's and boys', cut and sewn from purchased fabric (except apparel contractors)
315212	Windbreakers, women's, girls', and infants', cut and sew apparel contractors
315239	Windbreakers, women's, misses', and girls', cut and sewn from purchased fabric (except apparel contractors)
333292	Winding machinery for textiles manufacturing
313112	Winding purchased yarn
313112	Winding, spooling, beaming and rewinding of purchased yarn
333611	Windmills, electric power, generation-type, manufacturing
333111	Windmills, farm-type, manufacturing
235510	Window and door construction contractors
325612	Window cleaning preparations manufacturing
561720	Window cleaning services
541890	Window dressing or trimming services, store
332321	Window frames and sash, metal, manufacturing
321911	Window frames and sash, wood and covered wood, manufacturing
332618	Window screening, woven, made from purchased wire
332321	Window screens, metal frame, manufacturing
321911	Window screens, wood framed, manufacturing
235990	Window shade installation construction contractors
811490	Window shade repair and maintenance shops
337920	Window shade rollers and fittings manufacturing
337920	Window shades (except awnings) manufacturing
421220	Window shades and blinds wholesaling
444190	Window stores
811122	Window tinting, automotive
442291	Window treatment stores
321918	Window trim, wood and covered wood moldings, manufacturing
321911	Window units, wood and covered wood, manufacturing
421310	Windows and window frames wholesaling
326199	Windows and window frames, plastics, manufacturing
321911	Windows, louver, wood, manufacturing
332321	Windows, metal, manufacturing
321911	Windows, wood and covered wood, manufacturing
336322	Windshield washer pumps, automotive, truck, and bus, manufacturing
336399	Windshield wiper blades and refills manufacturing
336322	Windshield wiper systems, automotive, truck, and bus, manufacturing
326199	Windshields, plastics, manufacturing
312130	Wine coolers manufacturing
422820	Wine coolers, alcoholic, wholesaling
445310	Wine shops, packaged
312130	Wineries
312130	Wines manufacturing
422820	Wines wholesaling
312130	Wines, cooking, manufacturing
325998	Wintergreen oil manufacturing
336399	Wipers, windshield, automotive, truck, and bus, manufacturing
313230	Wipes, nonwoven fabric, manufacturing
421840	Wiping cloths wholesaling
421510	Wire (except insulated) wholesaling
421510	Wire and cable (except electrical) wholesaling
333298	Wire and cable insulating machinery manufacturing
331222	Wire cages, iron or steel, made in wire drawing plants
331222	Wire carts (e.g., grocery, household, industrial), iron or steel, made in wire drawing plants
331422	Wire cloth made from purchased copper in wire drawing plants
331319	Wire cloth made in aluminum wire drawing plants
331422	Wire cloth, copper, made in integrated secondary smelting and drawing plants
331222	Wire cloth, iron or steel, made in wire drawing plants
331491	Wire cloth, nonferrous metals (except aluminum, copper), made from purchased metals or scrap
331222	Wire garment hangers, iron or steel, made in wire drawing plants
514110	Wire photo services
331111	Wire products, iron or steel, made in steel mills
331222	Wire products, iron or steel, made in wire drawing plants
421510	Wire rope (except insulated) wholesaling
333923	Wire rope hoists manufacturing

Code	Description
421510	Wire screening wholesaling
331319	Wire screening, aluminum, made in integrated secondary smelting and drawing plants
331491	Wire screening, nonferrous metals (except aluminum, copper), made from purchased nonferrous metals (except aluminum, copper) in wire drawing plants
561422	Wire services (i.e., telemarketing services), floral
514110	Wire services, news
331319	Wire, armored, made in aluminum wire drawing plants
331319	Wire, bare, made in aluminum wire drawing plants
331422	Wire, copper (except mechanical) (e.g., armored, bare, insulated), made from purchased copper in wire drawing plants
331422	Wire, copper (except mechanical) (e.g., armored, bare, insulated), made in integrated secondary smelting and drawing plants
331221	Wire, flat, rolled strip, made in cold rolling mills
331319	Wire, insulated, made in aluminum wire drawing plants
421610	Wire, insulated, wholesaling
331222	Wire, iron or steel (e.g., armored, bare, insulated), made in wire drawing plants
331421	Wire, mechanical, copper and copper alloy, made from purchased copper or in integrated secondary smelting and rolling, drawing or extruding plants
331491	Wire, nonferrous metals (except aluminum, copper), made from purchased nonferrous metals (except aluminum, copper) in wire drawing plants
331491	Wire, nonferrous metals (except aluminum, copper), made in integrated secondary smelting mills and wire drawing plants
513330	Wired telecommunication resellers
333518	Wiredrawing and fabricating machinery and equipment (except dies) manufacturing

Code	Description
333514	Wiredrawing and straightening dies manufacturing
513322	Wireless data communication carriers (except satellite)
513330	Wireless telecommunication resellers (except satellite)
513322	Wireless telephone communications carriers (except satellite)
213112	Wireline services, oil and gas field, on a contract basis
336322	Wiring harness and ignition sets for internal combustion engines manufacturing
421610	Wiring supplies wholesaling
325191	Witch hazel extract manufacturing
212299	Wolframite mining and/or beneficiating
212399	Wollastonite mining and/or beneficiating
422330	Women's and children's clothing accessories wholesaling
813410	Women's auxiliaries
923130	Women's bureaus
422330	Women's clothing wholesaling
813410	Women's clubs
624221	Women's shelters, battered
321213	Wood I-joists manufacturing
325191	Wood alcohol, natural, manufacturing
325199	Wood alcohol, synthetic, manufacturing
422990	Wood carvings wholesaling
113310	Wood chipping in the field
321113	Wood chips made in sawmills
332213	Wood cutting saw blades manufacturing
325191	Wood distillates manufacturing
321911	Wood door frames and sash manufacturing
333298	Wood drying kilns manufacturing
321114	Wood fence (i.e., pickets, poling, rails), treating
421310	Wood fencing wholesaling
325510	Wood fillers manufacturing
235520	Wood flooring construction contractors
321918	Wood flooring manufacturing

Code	Description
421310	Wood flooring wholesaling
321999	Wood flour manufacturing
337121	Wood framed furniture, upholstered, household-type, manufacturing
321999	Wood heel blocks manufacturing
321999	Wood heels, finished, manufacturing
321918	Wood moldings (e.g., pre-finished, unfinished), clear and finger joint, manufacturing
325191	Wood oils manufacturing
421990	Wood products (e.g., chips, posts, shavings, ties) wholesaling
321114	Wood products, creosoting purchased wood products
322110	Wood pulp manufacturing
422990	Wood pulp wholesaling
421310	Wood shingles wholesaling
321918	Wood shutters manufacturing
421310	Wood siding wholesaling
333414	Wood stoves manufacturing
422690	Wood treating preparations wholesaling
333210	Wood verneer laminating and gluing machines manufacturing
321911	Wood window frames and sash manufacturing
321999	Wood wool (excelsior) manufacturing
442299	Wood-burning stove stores
321999	Woodenware, kitchen and household, manufacturing
532412	Woodworking machinery and equipment rental or leasing
421830	Woodworking machinery wholesaling
333210	Woodworking machines (except handheld) manufacturing
333292	Wool and worsted finishing machinery manufacturing
313210	Wool fabrics, broadwoven, weaving
313221	Wool fabrics, narrow woven, weaving
313111	Wool spun yarn made from purchased fiber
313312	Wool tops and noils manufacturing

Code	Description
422590	Wool tops and noils wholesaling
314999	Wool waste processing
313112	Wool yarn, twisting or winding of purchased yarn
422590	Wool, raw, wholesaling
311941	Worcestershire sauce manufacturing
333313	Word processing equipment, dedicated, manufacturing
561410	Word processing services
624229	Work (sweat) equity home construction organizations
337127	Work benches manufacturing
812332	Work clothing and uniform supply services, industrial
422320	Work clothing, men's and boys', wholesaling
315211	Work coats and jackets, men's and boys', cut and sew apparel contractors
315225	Work coats and jackets, men's and boys', cut and sewn from purchased fabric (except apparel contractors)
624310	Work experience centers (i.e., sheltered workshops)
315191	Work gloves and mittens, knit, made in apparel knitting mills
315992	Work gloves, leather (except apparel contractors), manufacturing
315211	Work gloves, leather, men's and boys', cut and sew apparel contractors
315212	Work gloves, leather, women's and girls', cut and sew apparel contractors
315225	Work pants (except dungarees, jeans), men's and boys', cut and sewn from purchased fabric (except apparel contractors)
315211	Work pants, men's and boys', cut and sew apparel contractors
315211	Work shirts, men's and boys', cut and sew apparel contractors
315225	Work shirts, men's and boys', cut and sewn from purchased fabric (except apparel contractors)
316213	Work shoes, men's (except rubber or plastics protective footwear), manufacturing

Code	Description
721310	Workers' camps
525190	Workers' compensation insurance funds
923130	Workers' compensation program administration
721310	Workers' dormitories
213111	Workover of oil and gas wells on a contract basis
624310	Workshops for persons with disabilities
334111	Workstations, computer, manufacturing
928120	World Bank
813319	World peace and understanding advocacy organizations
112990	Worm production
422990	Worms wholesaling
313210	Worsted fabrics weaving
321999	Wrappers, excelsior, manufacturing
333993	Wrapping (i.e., packaging) machinery manufacturing
422130	Wrapping paper (except giftwrap) wholesaling
339999	Wreaths, artificial, manufacturing
488410	Wrecker services (i.e., towing services), motor vehicle
235940	Wrecking, buildings or other structures, construction contractors
332212	Wrenches, handtools, nonpowered, manufacturing
333991	Wrenches, impact, handheld power-driven, manufacturing
711219	Wrestlers, independent professional
711310	Wrestling event managers with facilities
711320	Wrestling event managers without facilities
711310	Wrestling event organizers with facilities
711320	Wrestling event organizers without facilities
711310	Wrestling event promoters with facilities
711320	Wrestling event promoters without facilities
711510	Writers of advertising copy, independent

Code	Description
711510	Writers, independent (freelance)
813410	Writing clubs
325998	Writing inks manufacturing
422120	Writing paper (except bulk) wholesaling
322233	Writing paper and envelopes, boxed sets, made from purchased paper
322121	Writing paper made in paper mills
322233	Writing paper, cut sheet, made from purchased paper
337124	Wrought iron furniture (except upholstered), household-type, manufacturing
332996	Wrought iron or steel pipe and tubing made from purchased metal pipe
331111	Wrought iron or steel pipe and tubing made in steel mills
212299	Wulfenite mining and/or beneficiating
212399	Wurtzilite mining and/or beneficiating
334515	X-Y recorders (i.e., plotters (except computer peripheral equipment)) manufacturing
335110	X-mas tree light bulbs manufacturing
334517	X-ray apparatus and tubes (e.g., control, industrial, medical, research) manufacturing
325992	X-ray film and plates, sensitized, manufacturing
334517	X-ray generators manufacturing
541380	X-ray inspection services
334517	X-ray irradiation equipment manufacturing
621512	X-ray laboratories, medical or dental
421450	X-ray machines and parts, medical and dental, wholesaling
334517	X-ray tubes manufacturing
325320	Xanthone insecticides manufacturing
325110	Xylene made from refined petroleum or liquid hydrocarbons
324110	Xylene made in petroleum refineries
339992	Xylophones and parts manufacturing

Code	Description
713930	Yacht basins
336612	Yacht building, not done in shipyards
713930	Yacht clubs with marinas
713990	Yacht clubs without marinas
532292	Yacht rental without crew
336611	Yachts built in shipyards
111219	Yam farming, field and seed production
335121	Yard Lights, residential electric, manufacturing
422310	Yard goods, textile (except burlap, felt), wholesaling
332212	Yardsticks, metal, manufacturing
321999	Yardsticks, wood, manufacturing
313111	Yarn spinning mills
313111	Yarn spun from purchased fiber
333292	Yarn texturizing machines manufacturing
313112	Yarn throwing, twisting, and winding of purchased yarn
313111	Yarn, carpet and rug, spun from purchased fiber
325221	Yarn, cellulosic filament, manufacturing
325221	Yarn, cellulosic filament, manufacturing and texturizing
327212	Yarn, fiberglass, made in glass making plants
325222	Yarn, noncellulosic fiber and filament, manufacturing
325222	Yarn, noncellulosic fiber and filament, manufacturing and texturizing
422990	Yarns wholesaling
511199	Yearbook publishers
511199	Yearbook publishers and printing combined
511199	Yearbook publishing (i.e., establishments known as publishers)
323112	Yearbooks flexographic printing without publishing
323111	Yearbooks gravure printing without publishing

Code	Description
323110	Yearbooks lithographic (offset) printing without publishing
323119	Yearbooks printing (except flexographic, gravure, lithographic, screen) without publishing
323113	Yearbooks screen printing without publishing
311999	Yeast manufacturing
422490	Yeast wholesaling
611699	Yoga instruction, camps, or schools
311511	Yogurt (except frozen) manufacturing
311514	Yogurt mix manufacturing
422430	Yogurt wholesaling
311520	Yogurt, frozen, manufacturing
111334	Youngberry farming
624110	Youth centers (except recreational only)
813410	Youth civic clubs
813410	Youth clubs (except recreational only)
813410	Youth farming organizations
624110	Youth guidance organizations
721199	Youth hostels
813410	Youth scouting organizations
624110	Youth self-help organizations
813410	Youth social clubs
713990	Youth sports leagues or teams
325222	Zein fibers and filaments manufacturing
325188	Zinc ammonium chloride manufacturing
331491	Zinc and zinc alloy bar, plate, pipe, rod, sheet, tubing, and wire made from purchased metals or scrap
325131	Zinc based pigments manufacturing
335912	Zinc carbon batteries manufacturing
331528	Zinc castings (except die-castings), unfinished, manufacturing
325188	Zinc chloride manufacturing
325188	Zinc compounds, not specified elsewhere by process, manufacturing
331522	Zinc die-castings, unfinished, manufacturing

Code	Description
331492	Zinc dust reclaiming
332999	Zinc foil and leaf not made in rolling mills
325188	Zinc hydrosulfite (i.e., zinc dithionite) manufacturing
212231	Zinc ore mine site development for own account
212231	Zinc ores mining and/or beneficiating
325188	Zinc oxide (except pigments) manufacturing
325412	Zinc oxide medicinal preparations manufacturing
331492	Zinc recovering from scrap and/or alloying purchased metals
331419	Zinc refining, primary
331491	Zinc rolling, drawing, or extruding purchased metals or scrap
325188	Zinc sulfide manufacturing
212231	Zinc-blende (sphalerite) mining and/or beneficiating
212231	Zincite mining and/or beneficiating
333298	Zipper making machinery manufacturing
313221	Zipper tape weaving
339993	Zippers (i.e., slide fasteners) manufacturing
422310	Zippers wholesaling
331491	Zirconium and zirconium alloy bar, rod, billet, sheet, strip, and tubing made from purchased metals or scrap
212299	Zirconium concentrates beneficiating
212299	Zirconium ores mining and/or beneficiating
331419	Zirconium refining, primary
331491	Zirconium rolling, drawing, or extruding purchased metals or scrap
339992	Zithers and parts manufacturing
925120	Zoning boards and commissions
712130	Zoological gardens
712130	Zoos
111219	Zucchini farming, field, bedding plant and seed production